BT

W9-BVK-329

DATE DUE

JUN 2 1 1984	JAN 0 3 1994		
AUG 2 1984			
AUG 2 7 1984	NOV 1 6 1998		
AUG 2 2 1985	JUN 1 4 1999		
OCT 3 1 1985	MAY 2 1 2002		
SEP 8 1986	JUL 2 2 2002		
OCT 2 0 1987	APR 0 6 2004		
NOV 1 0 1987	APR 2 6 2004		
NOV 2 5 1989			
MAY 1 4 1990			
DEC 1 0 1991			
JUN 0 2 1992			

Also by Kenneth Silverman

A Cultural History of the American Revolution

The Life and Times of

COTTON MATHER

Kenneth Silverman

1817

HARPER & ROW, PUBLISHERS, New York

Cambridge, Philadelphia, San Francisco, London
Mexico City, São Paulo, Sydney

285.8

Grateful acknowledgment is made for permission to reprint:

Excerpt from *The Collected Essays and Occasional Writings of Katherine Anne Porter* by Katherine Anne Porter. Copyright © 1970 by Katherine Anne Porter. Reprinted by permission of Delacorte Press/Seymour Lawrence and Joan Daves.

Excerpt from *Main Currents in American Thought, Volume One: 1620–1800* by Vernon L. Parrington. Copyright 1927 by Harcourt Brace Jovanovich, Inc., renewed 1955 by Vernon L. Parrington, Jr., Louise P. Tucker, Elizabeth P. Thomas. Reprinted by permission of the publisher.

Excerpt from *The European Witch-Craze of the Sixteenth and Seventeenth Centuries and Other Essays* by H. R. Trevor-Roper. (Harper Torchbook edition, 1969). Reprinted by permission of Harper & Row, Publishers, Inc.

FIRST EDITION

Designer: Sidney Feinberg

Library of Congress Cataloging in Publication Data
Silverman, Kenneth.
    The life and times of Cotton Mather.
    Includes bibliographical references and index.
    1. Mather, Cotton, 1663–1728. 2. Massachusetts—
History—Colonial period, ca. 1600–1775. 3. Puritans—
Massachusetts—Biography. I. Title.
F67.M43S57 1984   285.8'32 0924 [B]   83-48385
ISBN 0-06-015231-1

---

84 85 86 87 88 10 9 8 7 6 5 4 3 2 1

For my teacher and friend, Lewis Leary
And for my brother, Alex

Contents

V. COTTON MATHER
(1724–1728)

Illustrations follow page 306

Acknowledgments

MANY persons and institutions made this book possible by preserving, transmitting, and interpreting Cotton Mather's life and works for three centuries. Most of them must necessarily but unjustly go unnamed, yet to be able to acknowledge some publicly is a rich and complex pleasure. First, my thanks to the following for allowing me to use and to quote from manuscripts in their collections: the American Antiquarian Society, Worcester, Mass.; the Bodleian Library, Oxford, England; Department of Rare Books and Manuscripts, Boston Public Library, by courtesy of the Trustees of the Boston Public Library; Department of Manuscripts, the British Library, London; the Brown University Library, Providence, R.I.; the Francis A. Countway Library, Harvard Medical School, Boston; the Houghton Library, Harvard University, Cambridge, Mass., by permission of the Houghton Library; the Historical Society of Pennsylvania, Philadelphia; the Henry E. Huntington Library, San Marino, Calif.; the Massachusetts Historical Society, Boston; the National Library of Scotland, Edinburgh, with permission of the Trustees of the National Library of Scotland; Rare Books and Manuscripts Division, the New York Public Library (Astor, Lenox, and Tilden Foundations), New York City; the Royal Society, London; Mather Collection (#38-632), the Tracy W. McGregor Library, University of Virginia Library, Charlottesville; the Yale University Library, New Haven, Conn.

For various favors I also feel grateful to Alfred Owen Aldridge, Patricia Bonomi, Ursula Brumm, Everett Emerson, Mason I. Lowance, Patricia Thompson, Louis Tucker, James W. Tuttleton, and Aileen Ward. Christopher Jedrey found me a room in Lowell House at Harvard University when the inns were full, and Kathryn M. Carey guided me through the

Boston court records. Marcus A. McCorison and his superb staff at the American Antiquarian Society were, as always, lavish in both help and hospitality, especially Jo-Anne Beales, Bill Joyce, and Georgia Bumgardner. I am also obliged to my colleagues Josephine Hendin, for her encouraging comments on the work-in-progress, and Robert Raymo, for his expert advice on Mather's Latin. Michael G. Hall of the University of Texas very generously gave much time to a detailed reading of the manuscript. His unmatched knowledge of Increase Mather and of seventeenth-century New England political life spared me many errors.

Sometimes in the course of writing the book I have had in mind the rudderless ship where Whitman's captain chalks in large letters on a board, "*Be of good cheer, we will not desert you.*" For their large hearts I thank my friends Sacvan Bercovitch, Guen Chabrier, Tom and Gina Davis, Daniel Fuchs, Eugene Goldberg, Flora Kaplan, John Kuehl, Peter Shaw, and Jack Zipes. My final acknowledgments I hardly know whether to call debts or boasts, for I owe most to a beautiful young scholar and to a young man of rare integrity who happen also to be my children, Willa Zahava Silverman and Ethan Leigh Silverman.

K.S.

New York City
5 February 1983

... the *silent Saint* shall now *speak aloud* unto us: Even in *holding his Peace* he shall now *speak aloud* unto us: A *Dumb Man* shall now *speak* unto us. It shall be done, I will not say, *Miraculously,* but I hope, it will be done *Remarkably,* and very *Profitably.* The very *silence* will have in it a *Voice* to be greatly hearken'd to. And if I declare to you, That my Design is, to strike my Hearers *Dumb,* it will be a *Kindness* for them.

—*Silentiarius* (1721)

THE LIFE AND TIMES OF COTTON MATHER

I

COTTONUS MATHERUS
(1663–1686)

⟨~∘⟩

He was perhaps the *principal Ornament* of this Country, and the *greatest Scholar* that was ever bred in it.

But besides his universal *Learning;* his exalted *Piety* and extensive *Charity,* his entertaining *Wit,* and singular *Goodness of Temper* recommended him to all, that were Judges of real and distinguishing Merit.

—*New-England Weekly Journal,* February 19, 1728

If young Mr. Mather publishes his father's Life I should be glad to see his memory honored with an Elogium wherein his Merits are touched with delicacy, so as to make them shine but not glare. That great Man was worthy of the utmost labors of the Muse. . . .

—ISAAC WATTS to Mather Byles, January 23, 1729

His Son . . . can have therefore no Occasion to invent any Additions to his Dear Father's History . . . indeed, if He had Published all that his Written Memorials would have enabled him, or that himself and others have been Witnesses of, He had not only swell'd the Volume to too large a size for the present Age to bear, and thereby hurt its Usefulness; but he must have also given such a full Account of this extraordinary Person as would have exceeded the Belief of those who were Strangers to him. The very bare Narration would have rather looked like the celebrated Life of *CYRUS,* and be disputed by Posterity whether it were design'd and drawn for a mixt Romance, or a real History.

—THOMAS PRINCE, Preface to Samuel Mather's *The Life of the Very Reverend and Learned Cotton Mather, D.D. & F.R.S.* (1729)

The man who is possessed of a power to act the tyrant when he thinks proper, let him become possessed of it as he may, is at least an USURPER of power that *cannot* belong to him in any free state—Power is intoxicating: There have been few men, if any, who when possessed of an *unrestrained* power, have not made a very bad use of it—They have generally exercised *such* a power to the terror both of the good and the evil, and of the good more than the evil. . . .

—"COTTON MATHER" (pen name of Samuel Adams), *Boston Gazette,* November 25, 1771

Ah pity the wretches that lived in those days,
(Ye modern admirers of novels and plays)
When nothing was suffered but musty, dull rules,
And nonsense from Mather and stuff from the schools!

—PHILIP FRENEAU, "Sketches from American
History" (1781)

When I was a boy, I met with a book entitled "Essays to do Good," which I think was written by your father. It had been so little regarded by a former possessor, that several leaves of it were torn out; but the remainder gave me such a turn of thinking, as to have an influence on my conduct through life; for I have always set a greater value on the character of a *doer of good,* than on any other kind of reputation; and if I have been, as you seem to think, a useful citizen, the public owes the advantage of it to that book.

—BENJAMIN FRANKLIN to Samuel Mather,
May 12, 1784

1

Quantum Nomen! Quanta Nomina!

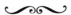

ESTEEM, prestige, position, and respect belonged to Cotton Mather by birth, for his flesh and name united two of the most honored families in early New England, the Cottons and the Mathers.

Both his grandfathers were Moses-like figures, leaders and lawgivers during the great exodus of English Puritans from England to America. Richard Mather, his paternal grandfather, had studied at Oxford University and, like other Puritan ministers, was harassed for flouting the practices of the Church of England. When he admitted to an official of a church court that in his fifteen years of preaching he had never worn a surplice, he was told, *"It had been better for him, that he had gotten Seven Bastards."* Suspended from his pulpit, he migrated to Massachusetts in disguise and settled at Dorchester, where he preached for nearly thirty-four years. In addition to acting as a Harvard Overseer and working at the conversion of the Indians, he drafted the famous Cambridge Platform of 1648, by which the New England Puritans codified and published to the world their distinctive form of church government—known, because of its emphasis on the autonomy of individual congregations, as Congregationalism.

Cotton Mather's maternal grandfather, John Cotton, was also a renowned English minister, as well as a graduate of Cambridge University and the author of nearly three thousand pages of published sermons. When John Winthrop's historic fleet of four ships sailed to Massachusetts Bay in 1630, the vanguard of the Puritan hegira, it was John Cotton who preached the farewell sermon. He reminded the emigrants that after Jeroboam set up golden calves for worship, godly Israelites abandoned his kingdom and moved to Jerusalem. Thus, he implied, Scripture warranted the Puritans' own flight from idolatrous England to the New World, where they might have "liberty of the Ordinances"—liberty to observe the religious forms and ceremonies prescribed by God in the New Testament, purged of such merely human additions as the wearing of elaborate clerical vestments, the hearing of confession and praying to saints, the hierarchy of bishops and cardinals. Two years later Cotton was summoned to an ecclesiastical court to answer for his religious views. He went into hiding, and at the age of forty-eight emigrated. His congregation in England followed him to America, where he became the minister of the First Church of Boston.

The moral and political authority of Cotton Mather's grandfathers lived on in the next generation. Two of John Cotton's sons, and four of Richard Mather's, graduated from Harvard College and entered the ministry. The devotion of the two families to the Puritans' Christian Israel in America meant that eight of Cotton Mather's closest male relatives were ministers: both his famous grandfathers, five of his six uncles—and of course his father, Increase Mather.

*

Except for uncertain health, Increase Mather demonstrated even in youth that the eminence of Richard Mather would not diminish in him, but expand. Born in Dorchester on June 21, 1639, he learned Latin and Greek grammar from his father, and entered Harvard at the age of twelve. But his concerned parents withdrew him a while for private instruction, fearing the effect of the college diet, he said, on "my weak natural constitution of Body." At the age of fifteen he was first smitten by what became a lifelong ailment, "a sore disease, which was apprehended to be the stone, but I suppose it was a spice of the strangury [slow painful emission of urine]"—classic afflictions of the sedentary scholar. Terror of dying coupled with the death of his mother in 1655 produced an extremity of anguish in his soul, resulting in an experience of religious conversion followed by a considerable period of inward peace. On his eighteenth birthday he preached his first sermon; soon after he preached in Dorchester, from Richard Mather's own pulpit.

Increase improved his education and preparation for the ministry by spending the next four years abroad. His eldest brother, a minister in Dublin, encouraged him to come to Ireland. Increase wished to do so, and prevailed on his father for permission. Stricken after about a month abroad with measles and a month later with smallpox, he however recovered and took a Master's degree at Trinity College. His commencement exercises so pleased the scholars that they "did publicly *Hum* me; a vanity which I never saw practised before nor since; nor to any one but myself." For the next three years he preached in England and Guernsey. During this time he felt a troubled, prophetic intimation of impending change. The impression came with such strength that while preaching in the city of Gloucester, young as he was, he publicly prophesied that faithful witnesses of Christ must expect new suffering. Several weeks later, monarchy was restored in England after a decade of Puritan rule, bringing with it new demands for conformity to the ceremonies of the Church of England. Increase himself, as he recalled with gratification, was "persecuted out of two places . . . before I was 22 years of age." Hoping to find at least temporary shelter and greatly desiring to see his father again, he returned in September 1661 to New England. At the first sight of Richard Mather he wept abundantly—"I think the only time that I ever wept for Joy." His love was returned, for when Increase once again preached at his father's church in Dorchester, Richard Mather could hardly pronounce the blessing for his own tears.

Returned from England, Increase settled into public and domestic life. He found himself with invitations to preach from no fewer than twelve congregations. Often self-deprecating and with no very high opinion of humanity, he considered his popularity a result of his years abroad, which made him seem a stranger in Massachusetts, "and people are apt to run after strangers though they have little in them of real worth." He chose to settle where he believed he would be most serviceable for Christ and His people, in the Boston North Church. On March 6, 1662, he married Maria Cotton, the daughter of the great John Cotton, now dead. The families had been drawn together in 1656 when Richard Mather, widower, married Cotton's widow. As Increase described his marriage to his step-sister, he was "brought into acquaintance with her by means of my Fathers having married her mother."

*

The first eight years of their marriage, Increase Mather and Maria Cotton lived in the house where Maria had been born. It had been built on the slope of an eighty-foot hill known as Cotton's Hill—one of the three peaks of Trimountain, a high ridge on whose central peak a beacon was set to notify the surrounding country of danger. This ridge dominated a nearly islanded peninsula, almost completely surrounded by water but attached to the mainland by a skinny neck, so low that the spring tide sometimes washed its road. Below this ridge lay Boston.

Although settled only about thirty years, Boston was the largest town in North America, containing in 1663 about three thousand inhabitants. Most of the houses seem to have been small (not twenty of them, by a 1673 report, had ten rooms), built of wood, and set close together as in London. Many were built near the shoreline, with wharves extending into the harbor. Cobblestones paved some streets, but most were dirt, roamed by stray horses and swine. The outstanding building was the multipurpose Town House, the center of New England's civic and business life, containing the various courts of the colony and the town's free library, but serving as well for town meetings and an armory. Set at the main intersection of Boston and surrounded by many shops, it was a two-story structure with a projecting first floor upheld by ten-foot-high pillars, the spaces between which served as an open-air exchange for merchants and shipmasters.

The Mathers' house, perhaps a fifteen-minute walk from the Town House, stood on about an acre and a half of land, with fences, a garden, and fruit trees. Sir Henry Vane, an early governor of Massachusetts, had lived there and to the original building had annexed a second one. In this "double house" on a steep hill overlooking Boston, the couple's first child was born at a quarter past ten in the morning, February 12, 1663. Always mindful of the prestigious past, Increase named the child Cotton in honor of Maria's father, "the most Eminent Man of God that ever *New-England* saw."

Virtually nothing is known about Cotton Mather's early relation to his mother. Indeed very little is known about his first years as a whole, although much can be inferred from the hopes and anxieties of his father. Increase made a formidable parent: loving, encouraging, and principled, but also high-strung, morose, and mysterious. "Strong affections," as he remarked, "bring strong afflictions," and during Cotton's frequent childhood illnesses, the father's intense love for his son caused him equally intense anxiety. In October 1664 he recorded in his diary, "Fears of Cotton's death because so ill." A month later he wrote, "This day Cotton taken very ill of vomiting and purging. I troubled because loved him so strongly." The next June the child suffered "extreme pains," leaving Increase crying to God to spare his life. During a new illness with high fever two months later, Cotton, now two and a half years old and able to speak, said: "Father, Ton [i.e., Cotton] would go see God." The child's pious wish to die "went to my heart," Increase wrote, "lest Lord should take him away by death."

These and Increase's several other bouts of acute distress over Cotton's health arose not only from the child's actual illnesses and from the high infant mortality rate in New England, but also from a huge invest- ment of hope. Very early in his son's life he felt an inner supernatural conviction that Cotton had been specially chosen: "if ever Father had a particular Faith for a child, then I had so for that child, of whom I could with Assurance say, God has blessed him, yea, and He shall be blessed." And Cotton early bore out his father's certainty. By his own later account of his childhood, he learned to write before going to school and began to pray just as he began to speak, not repeating standard forms of prayers but inventing prayers for himself. In encouraging such hopeful signs, In- crease likely observed at home the parental practices he often urged on his congregation: to spend much time educating their children's minds and hearts; pray much for their conversion; explain to them sadly their corruption by nature; and charge them, with the greatest solemnity, "to know and serve the God of their Fathers."

While such nurture demanded much time and close personal supervi- sion, Increase was also often remote and forbidding. A deeply private man, he wrote on the title page of his diary some verses describing his melancholy yearning for solitude:

> Give me a Call
> To dwell
> Where no foot hath
> A Path
> There will I spend
> And End
> My wearied years
> In tears

Increase's love of withdrawal and his often-expressed dislike of visitors were in part vocational, a relish for prayer and reading that fitted him for the ministry, in keeping with the Hebraic and Puritan view of study as a form of worship. He said once that he "loved to be in no place on the Earth, so much as in my Study." Usually there by about seven in the morning, he sometimes stayed until after midnight, appearing only for meals or to supervise religious instruction and devotion in his family. He seldom spent fewer than sixteen hours a day in his study. "He lov'd this *Study*," a contemporary wrote, "to a kind of excess, and in a manner *liv'd* in it from his Youth to a great Old Age."

Yet Increase Mather's love of privacy was personal as well. He carried the lonely austerity of his study into public life, being, as his son emphasized later, "HEART SERIOUS." While displaying the neatness, carriage, and conduct of a gentleman, his behavior was grave: *"His very Countenance carried the Force of a Sermon with it."* Contemptuous of loquacity and ornament, in both his preaching and his social life, he spoke little and plainly. This was no "Starch'd *Appearance,* and a *Tartuff* cover," his son later believed, but rather that, having a true fear of God, he guarded his heart. Some of his reserve in personal relationships he tried to foster in his children, teaching them to maintain a moderate disposition, suspect others, and suppress resentment. For instance, the "Rules of Behavior" drawn up by Cotton's brother Nathanael (born when Cotton was six) include such wary injunctions as: "Believe not all you hear, and speak not all you believe"; "Never impart that to a Friend, which may Impower him to be your Enemy"; "If you have an *Injury* done you, you do your Adversary too much Honour to take notice of it; and think too meanly of your self to Revenge it."

On larger, impersonal issues, however, Increase's solitariness assumed a militant aspect. The conviction of serving a sacred cause made many Puritans blunt, but Increase was unusual in the frequency and boldness of his displays of crotchety dissent. Indifferent to current opinion and defiant of majorities and authorities of every sort, he heeded his conscience. When he took his M.A. at Trinity College he refused to wear the customary ceremonial hood and cap. When the Restoration was proclaimed he refused to toast the new king's health, explaining he would "pray for the Kings health but drink for my own." When the celebrated aged minister Michael Wigglesworth was about to remarry—having in view a woman who was unbaptized, not yet twenty years old, and his serving maid—Increase told him tartly: "if there were an eminency of the fear of God discernible in your Damosel, notwithstanding her obscurity upon other accounts, there would be less of scandal in proceedings. But I do not hear any one but yourself speak much concerning that matter." Fearless as well, he acted as part of an underground, during Cotton's youth, hiding the regicides Goffe and Whalley from crown officials pursuing them in New England.

But Increase's inwardness went far beyond love of study, personal reserve, or feisty outspokenness. It was also a realm of mystical experience and of depressive longings for annihilation. Like others he believed that singular devotion to contemplation and prayer produced a heightened susceptibility to psychical events, *"Presagious Impressions."* Once he felt his soul strangely moved with thoughts of heaven; three days later he learned that "at *That very Time,*" a hundred miles away, his brother

Eleazer had died. Another time while praying in his study he found his heart exceedingly melted, "and me thought, I saw God before my eyes." The experience was so strong that he feared falling into a trance. Often he received strange intimations that he would shortly die; they sometimes arrived with guilty feelings of inadequacy in his ministry. On one such occasion, for instance, he recorded feeling "ashamed to think how little I have done for God and for Jesus Christ, and how short I have fallen of the obligations the Lord has brought me under." God, he sensed, "may now justly put an end to my days, and take me out of the world because I am (and ever have been) an unprofitable servant." These hints of mortality he often revealed in his published writings and sermons, and he often spoke from his pulpit, a contemporary said, "in the most solemn and affecting manner, of his *Desires to depart.*"

Whatever Increase's congregation made of his frequent announce-ments of his imminent death, his son can have taken them only as dread-ful threats of abandonment. They already echo in Cotton's remarkable comment to him, at the age of two and a half, "Father, Ton would go see God." However loving and attentive, this was a father not easily pleased, whose attention was not guaranteed, and whose concern often seemed to lie elsewhere than here and now.

*

The years of Cotton's infancy and early childhood were for Increase Mather a period of turbulent dissatisfaction, for the church and place in which he settled left him feeling painfully unfulfilled. The North (or Second) Church had been formed in 1650, the first sermon there having been preached by his brother Samuel. The congregation had invited In-crease to settle with them soon after his return from England, but he held out for two years, "finding a great averseness in my spirit to comply there-with." His aversion had several sources. Although he preached to the congregation regularly on a salaried basis, ordination meant a lifelong holy commitment to them. Distance probably also counted, for the church lay in the other, north end of Boston, perhaps a mile from his south-end home on Cotton's Hill. Many ministers in Increase's genera-tion, too, were beginning to fall out with their congregations over such matters as salary and admissions policy. Above all, he was aware of his family's distinction and, having sampled the richness of cosmopolitan life abroad, he greatly hoped to return to England, if liberty toward Dissent-ers was granted.

The brethren of the church held a day of prayer asking God to incline

Increase to accept their call. The same day he felt a strong impression on his mind to do so, and relented. But he stipulated conditions: that if persecuted, insufficiently paid, in poor health, or called to greater service, he be free to move elsewhere or return to England—threats of abandonment in a different form. Obviously he accepted the invitation with intense repugnance, for the prospect of his ordination touched off a severe religious crisis. On four separate days between April 10 and 19, 1664, a month before his ordination, he recorded feeling "Dead in receiving sacrament," his heart "lifeless." Agonies of religious doubt made him listless and sleepless, fearful of being unable to preach, "Grieved, grieved, grieved, with temptations to Atheism." How long this crisis lasted is uncertain, but his son later wrote that "Furious and Boisterous *Temptations* unto *Atheism*" embittered "the more *Early Years* of his Ministry." In this mood he was ordained at the North Church on May 27, 1664, his father, Richard Mather, assisting in the ceremony.

Immediately Increase regretted his decision. He learned that some members of his church opposed offering him a substantial maintenance, and that a motion had even come before the legislature to ask the church to forbear ordaining him altogether. These "unworthy dealings" made him feel, just a month after his ordination, that he would rather suffer under prelacy in England than stay in Boston and "suffer under them that looked upon as godly *[sic]*." As he settled into his ministry, other members of the church criticized him for grousing over his pay, threatening to leave, or acting dictatorially, so that he found himself not only feeling unappreciated but also unable to study or to sleep, and owing money to his butcher. For three years he complained about his wretched situation in his diaries, his grievances alternating with anguished exclamations of religious doubt:

> Many thoughts of heart whether to continue in Boston. Strong inclinations to move to Connecticut.
> ... much troubled and disturbed in my spirit to think how little encouragement and how much disrespect I have met with in Boston.
> Melancholy and inclination to leave Boston because of the miserable uncertain maintenance. . . .
> Heart full of sad thoughts.

His resentment of his inadequate salary was allayed when some wealthy persons joined his church and contributed extra money for his support. Later in life he grew more affectionate toward his flock, but he never wholly overcame or stopped speaking of his desire to return to England, "to follow my studies and increase learning, and where I might have suitable encouragement in outward respects."

What must have been a discontented household mood during Cotton Mather's first few years was aggravated by the inevitable bickering of a young couple, however pious, learning to live together. Not much is known about Maria Cotton, two years younger than Increase. Both her husband and her son later praised her affection, godliness, and self-sacrificing nature. Increase described her as a woman of a "very loving tender disposition" who strove never to displease him: "Her honor for me was too great. For She has said to many, that She thought I was the best Husband, and the best man in the whole world." Given his solitary temperament and vocation, he also saw her as an ideal wife: "I kept close to my Study, and committed the management of the affairs of the Family to her." Cotton clearly felt loved by her and later praised her as a pattern of piety: a woman who read over the Bible perhaps twice a year, performed private devotions perhaps six times a day, kept whole days of fasting and prayer, and was humble, modest in attire, and charitable to the poor.

But these eulogies came forty years later. Increase's diaries for the earliest years of his marriage offer few glimpses of Maria, and they all reveal less sugar than vinegar. Hardly three months after Cotton's birth, he found his wife also dissatisfied with him. When he asked her "in a loving way" to explain just how he had misconducted himself, she said she "expected no good either for soul or body" from him, for he "was never like to have any." Some people, she assured him, considered it "a 1000 pities" that she had married him; if she wanted, she "might have had better." Next month Increase recorded that Maria felt ill-requited in her esteem for him: "you set down my bad and I set down your good," she said. And she added a dash of venom: "if my bad ones be no more than your good ones they not very many." Another ambiguous entry suggests that Maria was distressed by Increase's complaints about Boston, and by living with her new husband and infant son in her father's house (and perhaps with her mother): "This morning my wife desired me with tears to leave her fathers house, wishing that I would rather leave Boston than live here, because her mother had spoken to her &c."

In the fall of 1669, when Cotton was six, Increase succumbed to serious emotional difficulties. They may have been precipitated by the death, that April, of his father. Now blind in one eye, Richard Mather became ill at Increase's house with a violent fit of the stone and was taken home to Dorchester to die a week later. That fall, Increase himself experienced extreme pain in his left side and a violent fever that "brought me to the

gates of death." These subsided but gave way to "Hypochondriacal affection," that is, melancholy or depression. The depression shut Increase in
for the winter, incapacitating him for preaching until March 1670, and
then "very weak in body." Around the spring of 1671 he began suffering
attacks of "Ephialtes," severe nightmares later described by his son as
"little short of Mortal." His considerable medical reading taught him that
victims of Ephialtes were vulnerable to apoplexy, epilepsy, or mania. He
became persuaded (or, as he put it later, Satan took advantage of his
melancholy to persuade him, "though there was no ground for it") that
his own fate would be mania.

The possibility of going insane filled Increase with "inexpressible
sorrows and fears." For several weeks he lodged at Lynn to drink from its
noted spring, on the widespread theory that "melancholy Hypochondriacal vapors" originated in the spleen and might be remedied by mineral
waters. But the nightmares returned almost every night, depriving him of
rest and leading him to fear that his faith in God to relieve him would
prove a delusion. Despite periods of revival and sound sleep, the nightmares persisted through the summer and fall, waking him before day,
convincing him that "my Ephialtes would issue in a Mania." Pouring out
his heart, he begged God either to answer his prayers for survival or to
deny them. This prolonged bout of Ephialtes seems to have passed in the
fall of 1671, but he suffered terrifying nightmares recurrently throughout
the rest of his life.

During this period, probably in 1671, the family moved into a new
house, in the other, north, end of Boston. What occasioned the move is
unknown; perhaps Increase's emotional state or Maria's unhappiness over
residing in her father's house, or simple convenience. The new house
was only a short walk from the North Church, to whom it belonged, and
the family was growing. By about the time of the move, Cotton was one of
five Mather children, a new infant having arrived every two years: Maria
(March 1665), Elizabeth (January 1667), Nathanael (July 1669), and Sarah (November 1671)—for each of whom Increase prayed each day and
night by name, except when ill and unable to pray at all.

Cotton later called the North End "the Island of *North-Boston.*" It was
in fact a genuine island, roughly the shape of a reversed **P**. The stem of
the **P** was separated from the South End of Boston by a canal, spanned by
two drawbridges. Larger bodies of water surrounded the bowl of the **P**:
the Mill Pond (which worked a grist mill and a saw mill), the Charles
River, and Boston Harbor. This was a compact, brisk shipbuilding and
commercial area with many wharves and coffee houses, described by a

visitor in 1663 as "the most elegant and populous part of the town." In addition to the many merchants and shipbuilders who wished to live near their warehouses and wharves, the street traffic thickened with travelers to or from Charlestown, Cambridge, or the north, who needed to use the Charlestown ferry. The most conspicuous features of the neighborhood were the Mill Creek, in which butchers cast entrails and garbage, and windmill hill (later Copp's Hill), rising about fifty feet from the sea, the burial ground of the North Church. Increase's life and his family's centered in the part of the End known as Clark's Square, an important social district near which lived many families of wealth and consequence. Here, only a street or so from the wharves extending into Boston Harbor, stood the North Church, apparently built, like the two other Boston meeting-houses, of clapboards and shingles, its bell ringing out at nine each night and five each morning.

By moving near his flock Increase did not improve his relation to them. In debt and oppressed by "outward wants and Family straits," he began compiling a fresh list of resentments, praying to Christ either to move his people to give him a comfortable living or to "remove me to another people who will take care of me." The indifference of some members of his congregation to his welfare again stirred angry, sorrowful fantasies of departure and death. Only his absence would make him appreciated: "When I am gone, my poor people will believe that the grief which I sustained by their neglects of me and mine, was unprofitable for them." Worse, Increase's pinching circumstances hindered his studies and his ministry. He could be content to be poor, he wrote at the end of 1672, as long as he could serve God undistractedly: "but to be in debt to the dishonor of the Gospel, is a wounding killing thought to me; yea so grievous as that if it be not remedied in a little Time it will bring me with sorrow to my grave."

*

From the time of the family's move, just before or after 1671, come the first substantial details of Cotton Mather's life. Some survive in forms that invite omission and distortion, accounts written long after the events by family members with didactic, apologetic, or self-justifying motives. Even so, they make clear part of what it meant to grow up a Cotton and a Mather, and the son of Increase Mather.

Not surprisingly, Cotton's piety was precocious. Before he was able to take notes in church while listening to his father and other preachers, he would come home from the service and write out what he remembered.

He read Scripture ardently, for a time nothing less than fifteen chapters a day, divided into morning, noon, and night exercises. Presumably emulating his father's paternal and ministerial pedagogy, with a touch of his own ingenuity, he composed prayers for his school friends and "Obliged them to *Pray.*" He also "Rebuked my Play-mates, for their Wicked *Words* and *Ways.*" As a result, he learned at the age of seven or eight that part of the meaning of being a Mather was to undergo ingratitude. For his play-mates did not always take his concern for their souls kindly: "Sometimes I Suffered from them, the persecution of not only *Scoffs,*" he recalled, "but *Blows* also, for my Rebukes." Increase responded to this like someone whose father had been persecuted for not wearing a surplice and who had himself been harassed out of two places before the age of twenty-two. He seemed "very *Glad,* Yea, almost *Proud,* of my Affronts; and I then wondered at it, tho' afterwards, I better understood his Heavenly Principle."

In study and learning Cotton was equally precocious and equally a Mather. For his formal schooling he attended the public school in the South End run by the gifted poet Benjamin Tompson and then by the legendary Ezekiel Cheever, the first great schoolmaster in America. A teacher in Boston for thirty-eight years, Cheever combined in his teaching Christian piety and classical learning. A sort of "*Christian Terence,*" as Cotton later described him, he not only labored to improve his sdents' Latin prose style but also prayed with them daily, catechized them weekly, and dressed plainly to set them an example of Puritan tradition. Cheever praised Cotton's diligence, but how much of his classical learning Cotton got from Cheever and how much from his father or on his own is unclear. Cotton's constitution being "Tender and Weakly," and the school being in the other end of Boston, the anxious Increase kept him home during the winter. Cotton spent the time reading church history and developing his budding facility and love for language. Able even earlier to write out what he remembered of sermons and to create prayers, by around the age of eleven he had read in Cato, Tully, Ovid, and Virgil, gone through a great part of the New Testament in Greek, "read considerably" in Homer, and begun Hebrew grammar. He now spoke Latin "so readily" that he could not only write notes of sermons as the preacher spoke in church, but even write them in Latin while the preacher spoke in English.

By 1674 Cotton had mastered the entrance requirements for Harvard College and was admitted, he wrote later, "upon a Strict Examination of the President and Fellows." No account of his examination remains, but the college laws required for admission a working knowledge of Latin and Greek, and signs of academic promise:

> When any Scholar is able to read and understand Tully Virgil or any such ordinary Classical Authors, and can readily make and speak or write true Latin in prose and hath Skill in making verse, and is Competently grounded in the Greek Language; so as to be able to Construe and Grammatically to resolve ordinary Greek, as in the Greek Testament, Isocrates, and the minor poets, or such like, having withal meet Testimony of his towardliness, he shall be capable of his admission into the College.

Increase Mather entered Harvard at the age of twelve; his son entered at the age of eleven and a half—the youngest student admitted to the college in its history.

Cotton's brilliant entrance, however, was flawed. He had developed a stammer. For a Mather, of course, such a handicap was all but ruinous. The firstborn son of a rising minister, the grandson of two famous ministers, and the nephew of five other ministers, there was no question but that he would be raised for the ministry himself. Yet the stammer, he wrote later, made such a career " a Thing as much despaired of, as anything in the World." Increase saw what his son's impediment meant for the tasks of preaching and public prayer, and worried "lest the Hesitancy in his speech should make him uncapable of improvement in the work of the ministry, whereunto I had designed him." On October 7, 1674, he fasted and prayed in concern over Cotton's stammer, calling him and Maria into his study, where they prayed together, and with "many Tears bewailed our sinfullness, and begged of God mercy in this particular." He resolved to trust in God and let Him do what He saw good, whether He chose to remove the impediment or not.

Just when and why Cotton Mather's stammer manifested itself is uncertain. However speculative, the question deserves brief discussion because feelings about his speech guided or colored many of his later activities, sometime subtly. Increase first mentions the stammer in his diary of October 1674, a few months into Cotton's freshman year at Harvard. Only portions of this diary have survived, however, and the diaries for the preceding six years, which may have contained entries concerning Cotton's stammer, are missing. Thus the affliction may have developed well before 1674. In fact stuttering, to use the current term, can begin even before the third year; most stutterers, eighty-five to ninety percent, begin stuttering before the age of eight. The notion of an onset to stuttering is itself misleading, since nearly all children have some natural disfluency of speech. A child "begins" stuttering when its disfluency first strikes a parent as abnormal, or when some provocations abruptly intensify it. The likelihood that Cotton's speech problems began several years before the age of eleven is strengthened by a later remark of his son Samuel. An *"uncommon Impediment in his Speech,"* he wrote about his father, appeared "from his Cradle."

In explaining the causes of stuttering, modern speech pathologists differ, some emphasizing the organic, others the psychological. Cotton's several childhood ailments may have contributed, since many stutterers seem to have had rheumatic fever and scarlet fever. But even most authorities who emphasize physiology grant importance to psychological influences. As the son of a father to whom great affections meant great afflictions, who spent sixteen hours daily in his study and welcomed his son's chastisement by the ungodly, Cotton Mather fits a widely accepted model of stutterers as "sensitive" children of overanxious and perfectionist parents who set lofty standards of achievement and conduct. That Increase Mather was a man who garnered invitations to preach from a dozen different congregations cannot have helped; extra pressure is created when a child's parents or siblings are endowed with particularly effective speech that is an object of family pride. Even if exceptionally good speech has never been demanded of some minister's or lawyer's or teacher's son, one authority writes, it is "reasonably sure that he inflicted on himself all of the consequences of such demands merely in the natural process of competing with his father."

Whether Cotton Mather's stutter began in early childhood or close to puberty, and whatever its causes, it exposed him to ridicule and made him highly self-conscious and highly sensitive to criticism of what he said. "I know one, who had been very much a *Stammerer,*" he wrote late in his life, " and no words can tell, how much his Infirmity did Encumber and Embitter the first years of his Pilgrimage." Speaking impersonally but evidently from distressing personal experience, he described the stutterer's tension and embarrassment in speech situations, "when he feels God continually *Binding* of him; and when Every *Business* and Every *Company,* wherewith he is concerned, puts him in *Pain,* how to get thro' the *Speaking Part* which he has before him." Even more painfully, people of no goodness or breeding subject him to *"Inhumane Derision,"* so that he feels unfit for, and perhaps averse to, the delights of human society. The "one" he knew, Mather wrote, poured out to Christ "Thousands of *Supplications* for a *Free Speech.*"

Christ was not the only Comforter, for the closeness of Puritan social and family ties meant that Cotton need not struggle with his humiliation alone. Besides praying at home with his concerned parents, he received a visit in his chamber at Harvard (probably after freshman year) from Elijah Corlet, an aged, famous schoolmaster and a sympathetic person. Corlet told him: "*My Friend,* I now Visit you for nothing, but only to Talk with you about the *Infirmity* in your *Speech,* and offer you my Advice about it; Because I suppose tis a Thing that greatly Trouble [*sic*] you." Observing that no one ever stuttered when singing psalms (many stutterers can sing fluently), he advised Cotton to speak very deliberately, with a "a *Drawling* that shall be little short of *Singing.*" He illustrated the method by reciting the first verse in Homer and prolonging every syllable. The drawling, he suggested, was at least preferable to stuttering, and would give him time to command his thoughts and to substitute a pronounceable word for one that he anticipated might be blocked. And by using the method for a while he would soon become habituated to speaking correctly, and by degrees grow able to speak at a normal pace, "Tho' my Advice is," he concluded, "Beware of *Speaking too fast,* as Long as you Live."

*

Other problems than his stutter faced Cotton Mather at Harvard. At the time of his admission, physical, demographic, and administrative problems had put the school in the sorriest state in its history. Because Harvard was the training ground for the New England ministry, its sinking condition long remained a matter of deep public concern. Set on a large plain, the physical college consisted essentially of the President's house, a small brick Indian school, and the College Hall, making a compact unit around the college yard. But the Indian college was little used and was maintained as a printing house. The College Hall, a two-story wood building enclosing most of the college facilities (library, recitation hall, dormitory, and study), was collapsing, and by 1677 became uninhabitable. A large new brick hall was under construction at public expense, but probably no students moved in until the spring of 1678, just months before Cotton's graduation.

No ampler facilities were in a sense needed, because the number of college-age boys in the families that had founded and used the school had dwindled, threatening its very existence. When Cotton attended, Harvard enrolled perhaps no more than twenty students all together; his own class had only four. Administration was erratic. Between 1672 and 1685 no fewer than thirteen official attempts were made to retain a president, resulting in a succession of short-term administrations. When Cotton entered, the president was Leonard Hoar, a Harvard graduate himself (1650), recently returned to Boston after taking a medical degree in England. A man with lively scientific interests and a friend of the English chemist Robert Boyle, he hoped to raise funds toward building an arboreum, a chemical laboratory, and an "ergasterium for mechanic fancies," and by these means to effect Harvard's "resuscitation from its ruins."

But in the depleted state of the college neither President Hoar nor Cotton Mather prospered. Cotton's student life under Hoar seems to have begun auspiciously. The president assigned him for his first declamation a topic that acknowledged his family's achievement and his own promise: "Telemacho *veniet, vivat modo, fortior AEtas*"—that the son of Ulysses might one day be even braver than his father. But at the moment Cotton Mather was an eleven-year-old boy and probably already a stutterer, among students whose ages ranged from about fifteen to eighteen. After only a month or two at college he returned home. He had received, Increase wrote, "some discouragement . . . by reason that some of the scholars threatened him, &c., as apprehending that he had told me of their miscarriages." Unfortunately the nature of the discouragement, the threats, and the miscarriages is entirely unknown. But Cotton may have stayed home the rest of his freshman year, studying with his father and on his own.

President Hoar fared even worse. The General Court (Massachusetts' bicameral legislature) held an extraordinary session in October 1674 to deal with the college's "languishing and decaying condition." Because of the paucity of students, it dismissed all of the school's salaried officers, and ruled that if by the next Court the college was in the same condition Hoar would be dismissed. Next month all but three students left. In March Hoar resigned his presidency and by the winter he was dead. Increase, prone to attribute death to ingratitude, believed Hoar was "brought into a consumption by the grief he sustained through afflictions when President of the college." By the time Cotton returned for his sophomore year the college had a new president, the minister of Cambridge, Urian Oakes.

The change in administration apparently did not ease Cotton's difficult situation at Harvard. His discomfort may even have grown, because a few days before Hoar resigned, Increase Mather accepted an appointment by the college Overseers as a nonresident Fellow of the college, and then became active in its affairs, not always helpfully. When he learned that students were saying he desired the presidency, he rode to Cambridge to complain to President Oakes, who assured him everyone knew he could have the presidency if he desired it and prayed him for the good of the college to bear with the students' "Jealousy." Increase made equally plain his anger over his son's treatment at the school. Less than a month into Cotton's sophomore year, Increase was troubled to learn that he had been "abused" by some students. Like the "discouragement" Cotton received as a freshman, the nature of this "abuse" is unknown—perhaps hazing and fagging, or some taunt for his stutter. But it was presumably what goaded Increase into riding to Cambridge to speak with Oakes and one of the Fellows about withdrawing his son again. Understandably, given the Mather name and the few students, they resisted. Increase did at least remove Cotton from under the instruction of his current tutor, and may have again kept him home a while. In September he also threatened to resign his position as Fellow because he too, he said, "had been so abused," and because the Corporation had dealt with him grievously in summoning students to ask them "who told tales to me"—which may have figured in Cotton's abuse. Deeply protective toward the young, however strict, he also complained to the Overseers about the general practice of hazing freshmen.

The demoralized atmosphere at the college during Cotton's sophomore year was deepened by a violent event, which his father claimed to have foreseen. Early in 1674 Increase felt persistent intimations that God would strike New England by sword. Believing that when God intended heavy judgments He often forewarned some servant, he preached two sermons on Ezekiel 7:7: The day of Trouble is near. The summer of 1675 fulfilled his prophecy. King Philip's War erupted, almost wholly destroying more than a dozen towns, and leaving many Indians from several tribes slaughtered, sold into slavery, or dead of exposure in what for them was a virtual war of annihilation. By one estimate almost every person in Boston lost a relation or near friend; the debt incurred by Massachusetts seems to have exceeded the value of the whole personal property of its inhabitants.

While Cotton was enrolled at the college in the winter and spring of 1675–76, towns such as Medfield, Groton, and Rehoboth suffered bloody and fiery raids. The fighting came within twenty miles of Boston; ongoing construction of the new College Hall was suspended. Cotton witnessed his father's many prayers to God for victory, and believed them efficacious. Increase set apart a special day to beseech God to cut off the Indian leader, King Philip, by a providential stroke. In "less than a Week, after This," Cotton recalled, *"the Thing was Accomplished."* Philip was shot and quartered, Boston receiving his hands, Plymouth his head. Cotton later recalled how with his own hands he detached Philip's jaw from his skull.

The war hardly ended when Cotton, now nearly fourteen, understood himself to have witnessed the accomplishment of another of his father's prophecies. Increase had become "strongly possessed" with fears that Boston would be punished by a judgment of fire. On November 19, 1676, he again preached his congregation a warning sermon. But he found them unmoved. When he went home he paced his study, weeping, saying, *"O Lord God, I have told this people in thy Name that thou art about to cut off dwellings, but they will not believe me."* Maria did not trust his prophetic sense either. He feared their house would burn, and urged her to move from it with him and the children. Unawed and unpersuaded, she considered his forebodings "only a phansy in my head."

Increase frequently suffered from insomnia, but the fact that he was awake at about five o'clock in the morning on November 27 he attributed to Providence: "God (and I believe his Angels) did so influence that I could not sleep that morning," he wrote. Smelling something, he rose and looked out the window. Then, "some began to cry fire."

Cotton Mather saw his family's house burn down, in a conflagration that also destroyed his father's meetinghouse and threatened to consume Boston. Breaking out in a building opposite the Mathers' house from a carelessly set candle, the fire headed on wind toward the Mathers' living quarters. Increase's immediate thought was to get the children out of the house. Next he tried to save his many manuscripts and his more than a thousand books, whose loss "would more afflict me," he said, "than to be deprived of all other outward effects." He went to his much loved study and—apparently with the house aflame—gave his most valuable manuscripts to Cotton to carry off. Then he began throwing books down the stairs as fast as he could. Before he managed to clear the study people called to him that if he stayed longer he would be killed.

Increase lost by fire about eighty books, his father's letters, a trunk of his mother's writings, the winter provision in the cellar, the clothing in the garret, and some English money and gold that were filched, seemingly while his goods lay in the street. But he rescued the beds, bedding, linens, most of the chairs, and—the "great mercy"—a thousand books and most of his manuscripts. Luckily for history these included a work he then had in his library, the manuscript of William Bradford's *History of Plymouth Plantation.* By one account the fire devoured about forty-five dwellings, the North Church, and several warehouses, leaving seventy or eighty families homeless. Except for a heavy downpour of rain it would probably have destroyed the whole North End and endangered Charlestown also, for fireflakes drifted over the river and fell there on houses and barns.

After the fire the Mathers stayed a few days with John Richards, a prominent member of the North Church, then moved for a while to another house. For six months Increase preached at the other Boston meetinghouses, until his church was rebuilt. In October 1677 he bought some land near the North Church, which probably became the site of what he called "the house which was built for me" (presumably by his congregation). Still standing in the nineteenth century, it was then described as a two-story building with dormer windows, complemented by a large garden and orchard.

*

No record remains of Cotton's childhood thoughts and feelings about King Philip's War, or the burning of his home, or his abuse by fellow students. But in later life he could study and work productively amid heavy personal burdens, and even as he reached puberty, his powers of concentration were great. Despite his trials he seems to have breezed through the required junior and senior curriculum at Harvard. Although the college trained ministers, it was not a divinity school, but rather aimed at educating both religious and civic leaders. Its 1650 charter declared that the school intended to educate young men "in all manner of good literature, arts, and sciences." While the first two years of study emphasized Greek, Hebrew, and logic, the third introduced ethics, and the fourth included metaphysics, mathematics, rhetoric, oratory and theology.

Cotton later wrote that before the age of fourteen he composed Hebrew exercises and "*Ran* thro' the other Sciences, that *Academical Studies* ordinarily fall upon"—apparently meaning that he completed most of the curriculum by the middle of his junior year. By then he had also composed systems of logic and physics that were used by other students; had advanced in arithmetic (never his strong subject, he admitted) "as far as was Ordinary"; and had learned "the Use of the *Globes*" (and drawn a map of New England that was sent to his uncle Nathaniel, a minister in Dublin). By following Elijah Corlet's advice to speak very deliberately he gained at least enough fluency to enable him to make the required declamations. Already a prodigious reader, he had also "read over" hundreds of books. Several of the first books he owned as a student have survived, such as Wilhelm Schickard's *Horologium Hebraeum* (1639; a Hebrew grammar) and Archibald Simson's *Hieroglyphica Animalium Terrestrium* (1622; on natural history). Passed from father to son, they bear Increase Mather's name as the previous owner and donor, and beneath that the inscription "Cottonus Matherus, 1674."

Cotton usually took for his student declamations some article of natural philosophy, that is, of science. Significantly for his later life, he was attending a school that sanctioned and taught the Copernican view of the universe, and that owned a three-and-a-half-foot telescope. His stutter played into his scientific interests, for at some time during his college years the impediment led him almost to despair of becoming a minister, and to apply himself to becoming a physician. As an unsought result, he began imagining he had "almost every *Distemper* that I read of, in my studies." To cure his fancied maladies he sometimes administered medicines to himself, not only needlessly but also hurtfully.

Cotton came down with a real malady as well. And as happened to his father when he was afflicted with urological ailments in adolescence, this illness, or another close to it in time, brought on a religious crisis. At about the age of fourteen he fell into "great Symptoms of an *Hectic*" (extreme emaciation), severe enough to make him think, "*I am going apace to the Gates of the Grave, I am deprived of the Residue of my Years.*" Even before he became ill, his "diverse Miscarriages" had made him suspect he had never truly been moved by God's Spirit, that he was but a "*Refined Hypocrite.*" With the onset of his illness, and of fear that he would die, his suspicions became gnawing. He trembled to think, he recalled later, that after his high hopes for himself and the commendation of others, he would turn out to be a "*Castaway.*" His life at Harvard may have aggravated his self-doubt. His first extant letter, likely written in his senior year, speaks not only of his "deceitful heart" but also of "residing in a place of much temptation" where he is "debarred the special opportunities of seeking and seeing the face of God, which have once been enjoyed." Apparently he meant that being at Cambridge he could not regularly hear his father preach, although during his last two years he very often returned to Boston for Increase's Sunday sermon, and occasionally for his Thursday lecture.

For whatever reasons, Cotton labored under a sense of his vileness and unacceptableness to God. He confided his worries to Increase, who told him there was no repentant sinner whom Christ would not freely accept. His father's assurances quickened his spirit. While praying and thinking of being reconciled to God he felt "Strange, and Strong, and

Sweet Intimations" that Christ had accepted him. Once while praying he experienced what seemed a genuine influx of divine grace: "I sensibly felt an unaccountable *Cloud* and *Load* go off my Spirit," he recalled, "and from that Minute I was as much altered, by a New *Light*, and *Life,* and *Ease* arriving to me, as the Sunrise does change the World, from the Condition of *Midnight*."

During his last two years at Harvard Cotton also began to expand and refine his religious life in general. In 1676 he started taking detailed notes on sermons he heard, and the next year began serving as an amanuensis for his father, transcribing important documents into his church records. Around the same age he began to observe entire days of private prayer and fasting, and seems to have seriously begun the Puritan devotional art of meditation, trying to devise a logical daily method and even writing a discourse on the practice. Now or perhaps in his first year after graduation, he also joined a society of pious young men who met the evening following every Sabbath to pray, sing psalms, and propose devout questions. At these meetings he made some *"Probationary Essays"* toward the ministry, presumably attempting to preach impromptu sermons.

*

At the Commencement Day exercises for the class of 1678, President Urian Oakes regaled the audience with a copious Latin oration, in which he remarked that Cotton Mather, at the age of fifteen, already showed signs that he would emulate and honor his father, his two prestigious grandfathers, and his five uncles. Part of his oration he addressed, in his wittily florid style, to the new baccalaureate himself, to "COTTONUS MATHERUS."

"*Quantum Nomen!*" Oakes said, What a Name! Or rather, he corrected himself, "*quanta Nomina!*" What Names! He would say nothing of the boy's reverend father, in the audience, since he did not wish to praise him to his face. But if this youth, he continued in Latin, brought back in himself the piety, learning, ingenuity, judgment, prudence, and gravity of his reverend forebears he could be said to have done his part well. And President Oakes believed that would happen:

> . . .*nec despero futurum, ut in hoc Juvene*
> COTTONUS *atq;* MATHERUS *tam re quam*
> *Nomine coalescant et reviviscant,—*

"I do not despair that in this youth COTTON and MATHER shall in fact as in name coalesce and revive."

2

The Solemnest Work in the World

THE MINISTRY, for which Cotton Mather had been designed since birth, was both the main public role in Puritan culture and a transcendent, sacred calling. *"To preach the unsearchable Riches of Christ,"* Cotton knew, to nurture in others that miraculous transformation of being signifying their salvation, was "the Solemnest Work in the World," and for five years he prepared himself with exhausting dedication.

In his sixteenth year Cotton was admitted by rite to the North Church and began preaching informally to neighbors. He inaugurated his formal career by acknowledging his dual Cotton and Mather descent. He preached his first public sermon, on August 22, 1680, at his grandfather Richard Mather's church in Dorchester; the next Sabbath he preached for his father in Boston; and the Sabbath after that he preached in the Boston church once led by his grandfather John Cotton. His early efforts won praise and notice. The brethren of Increase's church voted in September to have Cotton assist his father in preaching, as a ministerial candidate, once every two weeks or oftener. Flattering letters reached him and his father from ministers and church members in Ireland, the West Indies, and both Englands, praising him as a "hopefull sprout," observing his "extraordinary pregnancy," comparing him to young Timothy. One woman told Increase in 1681 that she had come into a Boston shop to buy spectacles when his son, whom she had never seen before, walked in. It surprised her to "so fix my eyes upon one I did not know," yet the boy seemed so grave and becoming that "I could not forbear asking him if he were not a Mather." Cotton was aware of it himself. *"Lord,"* he prayed, *"I know Thou will signalize me, as thou hast my Father, my Grandfathers, and my Uncles before me. Hallelujah."*

But that Cotton would be signalized was not so certain. For a day or two before preaching his first public sermons he felt "horribly *Buffeted* and *Unhinged*," his efforts even to pray for deliverance hobbled by mental confusion. By crying earnestly to Christ he managed to perform the service comfortably, but at around the same time he was shaken, like his father, by Ephialtes or nightmares, which sometime "handled me so Severely" that he expected to become apoplectic, or to die. These too he alleviated by prayer, and by eating no meat and taking an herbal remedy made of peony. But there were other fears also, including, several times during his candidacy, the threat of his father's imminent death. Spitting blood and thought to be consumptive, Increase became so ill in 1680 that between mid-April and early September he could not administer communion, and had to baptize his daughter Hannah not in church but at home. Nor was Increase ever ill quietly. Dissatisfied with his ministry and feeling that his destiny lay in England, he often used his illness to repay the ungrateful, warning them that his soul was about to take flight. All New England prayed for him when he became ill in 1681; another illness in 1683 sent rumors throughout Boston and surrounding towns that he was dying or dead.

Cotton feared being left alone by Increase, partly because Puritan culture stressed entire dependence on one's father for a model of behavior. Ideal children, he remarked in a later sermon, "are not mere *Pictures,* which may have something of the figure and feature in them, but they are Children that will *talk* and *walk* just like their father." Thus when Increase fell ill, Cotton importuned that he "may not therewith be taken from us; but still be continued as our Watchman, many days." When Increase recovered, he often thanked God for "a *Father,* given me from the Dead." Often he prayed for the "Life and Health of my dear *Father,* whom I may reckon among the richest of my Enjoyments."

Increase's grave illnesses cannot have eased the burblingly confused state of love, envy, rivalry, and dependence in which Cotton prepared to join his father in the ministry of the North Church. In addition, Puritan culture prescribed that parents' love should be returned more largely. Preaching to some young people in 1683, Cotton urged: "You should endeavor to *requite* your parents, for whom, I profess to you, you can *never do enough.*" Feeling that he too could never do enough for his father, he frequently served as Increase's amanuensis, copying over his sermons and tracts, and transcribing some of the manuscript of his celebrated *Remarkable Providences.* By such means he no doubt wished to honor and repay the father who had counseled him and prayed fervently for his health and salvation. But to display loyalty and admiration might also secure Increase's uncertain devotion to him, perhaps magically insure his continued life. Voluminously he wrote down his father's words as Increase preached in church, his notes on his father's sermons from the beginning of 1683 to February 1684 filling around two hundred pages. The nature of some of his favors to Increase, too, suggests a desire to demonstrate to him his own disinterest in competition. For instance, he gave his father several gifts. At the age of eighteen he bought Increase a Spanish Indian servant. Two years later he and some acquaintances offered to pay for the publication in London of some of Increase's discourses. He also owned a watch with a "Variety of Motions," of which Increase was "desirous." Although very fond of the watch himself, he presented it to his father, thinking, *"I owe him a great deal more than this."*

Cotton was correct in believing he could *"never do enough"* for his father; although throughout his son's candidacy Increase often prayed for the preservation of his life and the success of his service to God, he opposed Cotton's joining him in the ministry of the North Church. The brethren appointed the young man as a probationary preacher to them in 1680, but he was not ordained for another five years. In that period the church voted seven times for his continuance with them and, with growing annoyance, for his permanent settlement. Their frequently expressed desire to have Cotton as a colleague with his father partly arose from the scarcity of New England–trained ministers, corresponding to the drop in enrollment at Harvard, and probably also from their apprehension of being left without a minister by Increase's death. But they desired Cotton also because he proved himself an effective preacher, as appears in the language of their votes, which "earnestly desire" his continuance, and praise "the ministerial gifts wherewith the Lord hath graciously endowed" him.

How intently the North Church sought Cotton became particularly clear in the fall of 1681, when the Harvard administration voted to make Increase president of the college. However dissatisfied with his congregation in relatively urban Boston, Increase disdained rustic Cambridge, and interpreted the vote as a slight. Exactly twenty years before he had preached his first sermons in Boston, he grumbled, "and now I am voted out of the Town." He did preside over the 1681 commencement, at which he handed Cotton his M.A. degree. But he told the Overseers he could not accept the presidency without the consent of his church. They opposed the appointment not only because they wished to keep Increase as their minister but also, they explained, because they hoped Cotton might be "settled among us with his father," and that for them to release Increase was "a likely way to be deprived of them both."

Yet Increase did not want the North Church to have them both. He antagonized his flock, many of whom, he noticed, "seemed to be troubled" at his opposition to Cotton's settlement. Indeed the family's pride in dynastic succession makes Increase's resistance puzzling. Considering that he felt mistreated by his congregation, he may have been galled by their enthusiasm for his son; or he may have feared Cotton's rivalry and possible dissent. Perhaps he simply wished to avoid any suspicion of nepotism. He may even have been speaking for Cotton, who may have felt unready for ordination at this time. That seems unlikely, but it jibes with the explanation later given by Cotton's son Samuel. Cotton declined ordination by the church, Samuel wrote, "*partly* because they were not in extreme *Want*, having his *Father* with them, who was hearty and strong [as Increase certainly was not], and partly from a *modest* Opinion, and low Apprehension of himself and his Talents." Perhaps it was true both that Increase opposed Cotton's ordination and that Cotton feared it. Whatever the case, Increase told his flock that he did not wish to share his pulpit with his son. When one of his illnesses led him to advise the brethren to seek his replacement, they unanimously elected Cotton. But Increase explained that he was "very backward in consenting to their desires because of my Relation to him."

Cotton also received many invitations in 1681 and 1682 from the church at New Haven. Citizens and public officials of the town wrote to Increase to say that having heard so much and so well of his son they would count it "a great favor from God, if we may enjoy his ministry among us." They recognized, however, that Cotton had become popular at the North Church, and told Increase that "your son is so dear and precious to your society that it will be a breaking thing to part with him." These warm and persistent invitations proved awkward for Cotton. He told the New Haven church that his removal from Boston would turn the flock against his father, "if after so many Importunate *Votes* of theirs, for my Settlement here, he had any way permitted my Removal from them." In at least one sense, and probably more, his reply was disingenuous. Having been taught to "walk and talk" like his father, he no more wanted to preach in rustic New Haven than his father to dwell in Cambridge. By birth and disposition he had been designed, and now designed himself, for larger service, for the North Church in Boston, "as *Great* a Place, as any in these Parts of the World."

Yet Increase seems to have advised his son to accept the second-rate offer from New Haven. Later in life Cotton wrote that his father "(I thought) Encouraged me, to Accept an Invitation to a *Small* and *Mean Congregation.*" Whether the church involved was at New Haven or somewhere else, and whether the uneasy parenthesis indicates skepticism or continued resentment, Cotton considered the offer beneath him and found his father's advice that he accept it deflating. The "Humiliations," he later wrote, of "Leading an obscure Life among the poor Husbandmen, assaulted my Mind with sore Discouragements."

*

Cotton spent much of the five years of his candidacy in battering, tireless self-examination. To accept ordination he must be sure he was no longer a creature driven unawares by sin, but one to whom God had granted the grace to perceive, and thus the desire to live for, God's goodness. And anguishingly he recognized, as all Puritans did, that to dispel unloving and rebellious feelings in himself—his portion of the universal legacy of original sin—was beyond his doing. No more than the blind can force themselves to see could he overcome his sinful nature by Scripture reading, self-persuasion, or any act of his will. To purge himself required the supernatural work of God's Holy Spirit on his heart, transforming his entire way of feeling about the world. "O undertake for me, Deliver me," he cried, "*My Diseases are so complicated, that I am not able so much as distinctly to mention them unto thee; much less can I remedy them.*"

To discern whether such a deliverance had taken place in him was the wracking, everyday work of Cotton's entire candidacy, especially from the age of eighteen when, he wrote, his "Mind was Exceedingly taken up, with the great Action, of, *A Closing with the Lord Jesus Christ.*" He strove now not to understand faith, repentance, and holiness, but rather to experience them. His method for attaining this "*Impressive*" knowledge began with trying to identify and rebuke his sins, then seeking pardon for them. The two-step process might last days, weeks, or months, and might falter in doubt and have to be repeated. Prostrate on his study floor he bewailed his listlessness, sloth, lukewarmness, and many other sins, especially lust and pride. He identified with an aging minister who had been found guilty of adultery, and feared that "I, who am a *young Man,* in my single Estate, should be left by God, unto some Fall, whereby His Blessed Name would suffer." Apparently guilt-ridden over masturbation performed or considered, he confessed to God the loathsome defilement of his soul: "*Lord, Wherewithal shall a young man cleanse his way?* . . . . . . I have certainly been one of the filthiest Creatures upon Earth." To halt the "irregularities which my Thoughts within me have hurried me into," he resolved to practice extraordinary austerities and to emulate Saint Augustine in perpetual celibacy.

Cotton also felt embittered and confused over his "cursed *Pride*, the Sin of *young Ministers.*" He wished to become what he understood his father to have been, the father whose fellow graduates publicly "hummed" him, " a Young Man every where Admired, and Applauded, and Accepted, and Flock'd after." Yet he recognized that his ambitious desire to become a famous preacher like Increase dishonored his sacred obligation to use his ministry to glorify not himself but God alone. Often he recorded his pleasure in preaching in a populous place, "the *Metropolis* of the whole English *America,*" and of garnering a great and growing reputation. But he just as often warned himself against his "abominably proud Fishing for popular Applause." In 1681 he spent a special day of humiliation to castigate his pride, indicting himself for desiring greater renown than his age or ability merited, and for congratulating himself when answering questions readily or preaching well. "*Proud Thoughts,*" he lamented, "fly-blow my best Performances!"

The stains on his soul tormented Cotton, producing anguished cries of his unworthiness for salvation. Summoning his sins into his mind in the hope of cracking his hard heart, he cursed himself for a "poor, broken, sorry despicable Vessel," a "rotten Stump." He was "feeble and worthless," "miserably defective," "crabbed, foolish, despicable," "*unsavoury Salt,* fit for nothing but the Dunghill." How could such a thing love God, much less lead others to love Him? His disfigurement made him worthy not of the ministry, but rather "worthy of *Death, Death, Death* forever."

But having identified and bewailed his sins Cotton prayed God to fill his soul with love, and as he hoped, his long bouts of self-condemnation and humiliation gave rise to an assured sense that God had forgiven him. One such cleansing epiphany occurred after much secret prayer in September 1681, when he felt that his heart no longer relished lust and pride: "*Oh! I feel! I feel! I feel! I love the Lord Jesus Christ; I love Him dearly, I love Him greatly, yea, I love Him above all.*" Another such moment arrived in August 1683, when he spent about two weeks preaching with his father in rural Lynn. While enjoying the solitude of the fields he felt "strong and strange *Assurances*" not only that God had pardoned him, but also that He designed to make him His instrument, "*not only to bless me, but also to make me a Blessing.*"

This certainty, however, Cotton found hard to sustain. Time and again, he soon worried whether it was illusory, then doubted the genuineness of his repentance, until his sureness dissolved into fresh doubts, leaving him where he began. Returning from Sabbath worship in March 1681, for instance, he felt an assurance that left him saying, "*I believe that I am a chosen Vessel, and that the Lord will pour mercy unto me . . . It will be so!*" But six days later his belief collapsed into "Discouraging Fears, that I should not be able to go thro' the work." His inability to believe in the reality of his conversion gave rise to self-accusations of heart-deadness and formality, of mimicking the conversion process without experiencing it: "I am but a very *Parrot* in Religion!" The inauthenticity of even his keenest epiphanies left him with a sense of desertion and rejection by God: "Oh! how hath He *broken my Heart,* and ground it . . . into Powder, before Him! How is the inflexible *Stone* turn'd into pliable *Flesh!*"

However brokenhearted, Cotton also knew that God's abandonment of him, like all forms of affliction, was intended to draw him closer to Himself. By raising then crushing his conviction, God meant to produce in him more perfect understanding of his sinful nature, preparatory to a genuine experience of conversion and a more able ministry. So he trusted: "I believe, that when the Lord has *broken* me, and fitted me for further Mercy, and laid me low before Him, He will *raise* me up, in bestowing of great *Comfort* on me and employing me in great *Service* for Him." For being broken the only remedy was to repeat the process of identifying and bewailing his sins in the hope of pardon, even should the pardon prove transient and illusory. Alternately rejoicing and despairing of his conversion throughout his candidacy, he was repeatedly forced to recommence the work of closing with Christ, and to "anew go over all the Sorrowful and Heart-breaking Hours."

Cycles of assurance and doubt were common, even formulaic, among Puritans. But Cotton saw himself as trying to serve God more strenuously than others, and as suffering more than others by His abandonment. God had favored him with two quickened faculties, which "(however *vile* I am) I cannot but acknowledge." First, God had given him "*A tender Heart,*" a sensitivity that made him unable to "live quietly under the smaller neglects of God, which the Generality of Christians give way unto." Second, "*an active Mind,*" an ingenuity that made him uneasy except when doing something to promote God's Kingdom. Now and throughout his life he believed deeply in a hierarchy of the pious, and aspired to join the elite. "My Heart is insatiably *pressing,*" he wrote at around the age of nineteen, "after the *High Attainments* of Religion."

Such high attainments differed greatly from what Cotton later called the "Low, Dull, Slothful Measures, of the *Common* and *Barren* Christianity." The distinction lay in vigorous constancy and imaginativeness. To press after high attainments of religion meant living in heaven while on earth, and Cotton resolved in 1685 "to be continually abounding in the Thoughts of God. Nor would I be one waking quarter of an Hour without them." Not only the abundance of devotion counted but also the manner. He wished, he wrote later, to use "my Wit, as well as my Grace" and to lend his devotions "a certain charming *Elegancy,* and Sacred *Curiosity.*" He strove to invent ever new, ever more ingenious and striking methods of praising God. Indeed, ingenuity or "curiosity" would become one of his distinctive values, a measure for him of all accomplishment. Devoting one's life to God involved for him a play of imagination that made it akin to art.

Some means of living in heaven while on earth Cotton performed daily or almost daily, often laying down schedules of devotion for himself. Secret prayer (private prayer, as opposed to public prayer in church or family prayer at home) he considered "the straight way to the City of God," a daily duty. He later recommended that it be practiced in a locked or barred room to prevent disturbance and permit intimate confession of secret sin, begging the Lord's mercy while lying prostrate on the floor, mouth in the dust. Occasionally he devoted entire days to secret prayer, and in 1683 even drew up an elaborate routine for them, in fourteen numbered steps. He began the day by expressing to God his belief that the Lord rewarded those who sought Him diligently. Then, in order, he read chapters of Scripture, meditated on his vileness, sang hymns, proposed profitable questions to himself, supplicated God for pardon of sin, sang another hymn, meditated, prayed again, sang a psalm—and so on until he ended the day by "renouncing all Apprehension of *Merit,* in my own Duties, and relying upon the Lord Jesus Christ alone, for Acceptance and Salvation." Twice a week or more, as mentioned earlier, he also recorded sermons in his voluminous notebooks, often adding his own resolves upon hearing them. Almost daily he also recorded his prayers, meditations, and religious experiences in a diary, with occasional comment on his domestic circumstances, or about social and political events. These diaries, the lengthiest surviving of any American Puritan, begin in 1681 and end in February 1725, although he probably began them earlier and kept them until his death: eighteen years have unfortunately been lost.

As if he had cast God Himself in the image of Increase Mather, for whom he could *"never do enough,"* Cotton invented literally thousands of other means of demonstrating his devoutness. Taking pleasure in the *"Variety* of *Contrivance"* that flooded from him he decided to spend at least a tithe of his income on pious purposes; to precede every act with the thought *"let me now do this* (or, *I will do this) for God"*; to preface the recording of every act in his dairy with a statement that he did it for God's glory; to ask each morning, and review each evening, questions designed to strengthen grace in him; to sing hymns every morning and night, of his own composing; to make his rising thoughts concern some passage of Scripture, disposing him to fear God all day; to write letters to people needing help; to penalize himself if he omitted any religious exercise he had prescribed, or failed to annex a pious thought to each sentence of his prayers, or on the Sabbath spoke any word incongruous with the day—and to donate the self-imposed fines to the poor. He even set apart a special day on which to invent "Contrivances" on the question, What may I do for God? The answers, he said, issued in "Thousands of *Resolves."* He drew others into his contrivances as well. He often prayed and fasted with groups of religious young men, and from the age of seventeen he undertook the tuition of several scholars, some older than himself, in Hebrew, discoursing with them individually in his study about their salvation. When two people unexpectedly visited him during a day-long fast in 1685 he invited them to join his devotions, which included preaching them three sermons, each about an hour long.

Not even this was enough. Cotton wished to have God in his thoughts every waking moment. To attain that high end he practiced a "spiritual *Alchemy."* This meant ceaselessly creating brief petitions and supplications—"Ejaculatory Prayers"—and sending them to Heaven in an all-day stream of spontaneous praying. He often based the "ejaculation" on some present thing or person, viewing the entire world as a preacher: "The *Meanest Objects* in the House, or in the Street, have afforded me Thousands of Lessons, which I have immediately Sent up to Heaven." Transmuting his moment-to-moment sensory experience into a glorification of God, he could form prayers not only before acts of worship or while hearing sermons or singing psalms, but also while traveling in the road, eating dinner, walking down the street, or just sitting in his study. Although he chose to "not be so *pharisaical* as to show it," when encountering a tall man he might pray, *"Lord,* give that Man, *High Attainments* in Christianity"; seeing a black person he asked, *"Lord, wash* that poor Soul *white* in the *Blood* of thy Son"; feeling unnoticed by someone (a reveal-ing category) he said, "*Lord,* help that Man, to take a *due Notice* of the Lord Jesus Christ." As the wit of these ejaculations suggests, his motives in distilling thousands of brief prayers from mundane experience were both devotional and aesthetic, aimed at glorifying God but also at "the pleasing of my Fancy."

As Cotton noted in his diaries several times during his candidacy, he was not always able to complete the devotional tasks he prescribed for himself. Yet he found the prescribing a goad to the performance, and a help in producing the "heavenly *Way of Living*" he sought. And it was enough. He feared that by his "macerating Exercises" he had wasted his strength, wounded his body, and thereby broken the sixth command-ment. The "Excesses of my Devotions" atop his occasional, intense re-gimes of secret fasting and prayer sometime did damage his health. In January 1684 they brought splenetic maladies and the possibility of con-sumption, threatening his life, he believed. Wondering whether he had made his duties into murders and injured the very service he intended to glorify, he asked God to pardon and pity him for the sake of Jesus Christ.

*

"Give my Stammering Tongue leave to say; Oh! That we *knew the Day of our Visitation.*" Thus Cotton urged immediate repentance upon the audience of his first recorded sermon, preached when he was sixteen. As his self-conscious candor indicates, Elijah Corlet's advice to him had not wholly succeeded, Modern speech therapists would not recommend Cor-let's method of speaking very deliberately, for the effort to scan approach-ing speech situations produces a strained vigilance, and the avoidance of hard-to-pronounce words invites bizarre substitutions or odd circumven-tions, not curing the inability but masking or avoiding it. Just the same, Cotton managed to control the impediment effectively enough so that by the time he gave his first formal sermons, in 1680, Increase observed gratefully that despite his "natural Infirmity" he delivered himself in preaching and prayer "without any considerable Hesitancy."

During the first three years of Cotton's candidacy the severity of his stutter fluctuated. Shortly after his eighteenth birthday he recorded that his preaching was free of it; but a year later it "threatened such a Return upon me as to render me unserviceable." While following Corlet's ad-vice, he spent on the matter "many Thousands of solicitous Thoughts," and sought help by prayer. Some solace he found in the fact that the speech difficulties of Moses had continued even after he began his ministry:

> Oh! Thou that *madest Man's Mouth*, didst Thou not make the Mouth of the Stammering *Moses* to speak? Didst thou not open the Lips of *Jeremiah*, when he pleaded, *I cannot speak?* Did not my Lord Jesus cure a man that had *an Impediment in his Speech?* Oh! Lord, Oh! Lord, I am sensible, that one Touch, one Word of thine will relieve my Infirmity. Oh! touch my Tongue: Say, *Ephphatha* and my mouth will be opened!

On his knees in prayer he often received strong persuasions that the Lord's Ephphatha—"Be Opened"—would be spoken, promising *"greater Supplies of Speech in store for me, than I ever yet received."* But he never fully conquered the impediment, and when it remitted he feared its return.

Cotton tried as well to understand the cause and significance of his stutter. Like any other affliction, it represented God's chastisement for sin: "by my early Wickedness and Filthiness, I have provoked Thee," he wrote at around nineteen, "to take away from me one of the greatest Conveniencies, enjoyed by thy reasonable Creatures." In fact, God had scourged him far more mildly than the depth of his depravity deserved: "tho' thy *Rod* has been very heavy in this regard upon me.... Lord, I deserve, not only a *Stammering, Slowness,* but also a total *Dumbness* in my Speech." But as Cotton and other Puritans also understood affliction, God's rod descended in loving concern. The purpose of his stutter was to lead him to examine himself, become conscious of his sin, and renounce it. God bound his tongue not to make him despair, but to make him eminently holy, "yea, to make me more happy than other men."

In seeking the iniquitous causes of his stutter, Cotton fastened on two related sins: pride and anger. He understood that his desire for fame corrupted his obligation to use his tongue selflessly to serve God. His stutter, then, was the ignominious mark of his "ambitious Affectation of Praeheminencies." Determining to use his tongue as God's, not as his own, he chastised its sins and declared in August 1683 that he "asked for a *Tongue* only to serve Him, and bespeak the Loves and Lives of my Neighbours for Him." In return for improvements in his speech he vowed not to reach after improvements too high for him. The same year he drew up "RULES OF SPEECH" in which he resolved not only to speak very deliberately, but also to consecrate his speech to God, to rarely come into company without seeking useful discourse, and to pray daily, *"Lord, let my Mouth show forth thy Praise."*

In fact, Cotton was probably correct in viewing his stutter as a punishment for his pride, only he applied the rod himself. The impediment may well have arisen in an attempt to block ambitious thoughts, dangerously charged with the thrill of showing up a father who had been invited to preach by a dozen different congregations. He was also probably correct in associating his stutter with anger. "*Stammerers* are often of too *Choleric* a Disposition*," he wrote in later life, "and *Sooner Angry* than they should be; whereas they of all People, should always maintain the *Meekness of Wisdom.*" The possibility that certain kinds of anger might themselves be linked to pride he set before himself at the age of nineteen, when he took notes on a sermon preached by his father. Increase observed that seemingly causeless anger is really caused: "pride is the spring whence causeless Anger does usually proceed." Cotton recorded in his notebook his father's view that to give vent to unprovoked anger by intemperate language reveals an unmanly spirit, while meekness is excellent and like to God, who is slow to anger. Judging from the "Rules of Behavior" composed by Cotton's brother Nathanael, Increase inculcated similar lessons at home, and they were borne in on Cotton again as he resolved to read books that might teach him "the Government of the Tongue." Out of one English work he copied at length injunctions against retorting when one is disparaged or defamed: "beware of a Transport of *Anger;* that you speak not harshly or unadvisedly against him; or too passionately for thyself"; "Watch against all bitter, and over-passionate Speeches against *malignant Opposers* of the Truth." While it remained Cotton's duty as a minister and a Puritan openly to denounce ungodliness, he repeatedly cautioned himself to speak ill of no one except for good reason and right purpose, and to be circumspect in his speech.

Cotton seems to have brought his stutter under satisfactory control a few months short of his twenty-first birthday, when he thanked God for the "miraculous Freedom of my *Speech.*" Yet it recurred in later life, and his speaking seems to have become permanently marked by Corlet's advice: his son Samuel wrote that his father always spoke with "much *Deliberation.*" There were other lasting effects of his long attempt to master the impediment, as he attempted to overcome its underlying anger and pride by demanding of himself the opposite behavior. However ambitious, he must appear selfless. However angry, he must appear mild, a conciliator. However much a stutterer, he must entrance large audiences. This wish to spellbind asserts itself in an utterly un-Puritan image which crops up several times in Cotton's early writing, that of a theater. Once, when concerned about the small size of his audience, he cautioned himself, as if he were on stage, that the eye of God "shall be *Theatre* enough." Similarly, in a letter written around 1682, he apologized for his brevity by saying he "comes just like Cato on the stage . . . only to go off again." His desire to captivate seems equally apparent in his determination to lend his devotional exercises "a certain charming *Elegancy,* and Sacred Curiosity," as if to entertain God Himself. In fact the youthful stutterer would become the most noted conversationalist of his time, much admired and sought after by contemporaries for his erudite and beguiling wit.

Meanwhile, Cotton had become highly sensitive to others' reception of what he said. When his speech was ignored he managed both to acknowledge and to deny his limitations by first denigrating and then congratulating himself, in a way that left him feeling at once big and small. Throughout a dinner he attended, for instance, he sat silently, creating ejaculatory prayers by "spiritual alchemy" in his mind. His youth, he felt, excluded him from conversation with his elders; and the other tabletalk, he decided next, was "too trivial to be Worthy of my Attention." Once, finding his congregation thinner than usual, he countered his discouragement first by considering his unworthiness, then by adding that many ministers more excellent than himself "would count themselves happy, if they might preach quietly to a Company one quarter so big." Or he sometime soothed his hurt pride by glorying in defeat. In the voting to choose a preacher for the annual artillery sermon in 1686 he received few votes, even though he was closely connected to a captain in the militia, and was passed over. Out of this he made a show of gladly welcoming rejection, establishing his superiority by putting those who did not choose him to speak beneath his notice. "I took some Satisfaction, I hope," he wrote, "in being overlooked, as to that Choice."

Cotton's deliberateness and self-idealization in managing his speech extended to his writing as well. Even his childhood and adolescent script is neat, precise, in fact visually interesting; some is printlike, as if a substitute for publication. His fine handwriting made him serviceable throughout his middle and late teens as an amanuensis for many important church and government documents, most notably for writing up the decisions of the unprecedented Reform Synod which gathered in Boston in 1679–80 to discuss pressing social and moral reforms. Twenty eminent ministers of New England signed Cotton's lengthy document, the list headed by the signature of the legendary preacher to the Indians, John Eliot. From the viewpoint of Cotton's fears about his speech, the beautiful clarity of the hand, the borderlike margins, bold capitals, and other carefully wrought devices all declare that surely this could not be the work of a stutterer.

And beginning in youth, Cotton probably handwrote as much as any human being ever has. The sermon notebooks alone which he kept between the ages of thirteen and thirty-two, with about two hundred and fifty words per page, contain roughly seven thousand pages. Far lengthier than the surviving sermon notebooks of any other American Puritan, they summarize in detail around a thousand sermons by leading New England ministers, about many of which little or nothing would otherwise be known. They not only suggest unusual patience, stamina, and concentration, but also seem to flaunt an ability to produce unlimited numbers of words with superb clarity, on a page if not by tongue. Later in life Cotton would achieve such astonishing feats of language as the ability, he said, to "write very good Spanish" by studying it only "a few leisure Minutes in the Evening of every Day, in about a Fortnight, or three weeks Time"— claiming in effect to have learned a language he also published in after studying it about three hours. Later he also observed that stutterers' pride in being able to speak a few words clearly makes them perversely loquacious, so that "there is nothing more frequent, than for *Stammerers* to speak Ten times more than they need to." Indeed by displaying his copious mastery of engaging language in every form, the youthful stutterer would become one of the most prolific writers in American history.

Some connection between Cotton's written and spoken language was noticed later by his friend Thomas Prince, who compared his prose with his speech and described both as "very *emphatical.*" A connection seems clear enough in Cotton's first published work, his *Poem Dedicated to . . . Urian Oakes* (1682), a funeral elegy on the recently deceased president of Harvard. Having chosen to appear in print, at the age of nineteen, in a classic New England form, he began the poem by cataloguing the New England elegists who preceded him, starting with his grandfather John Cotton. Like his comparable *Elegy on . . . Nathanael Collins* (1685, memorializing a Harvard-trained minister), the poem offers a summary of the minister's virtues and assesses the meaning of his death to family, friends, and community.

However traditional, Cotton's first poems record his highly personal transference to writing of habits and attitudes connected with his difficulties in speaking. He presents himself as a mute: "I the *dumb* son of *Croesus.*" But as if in denial of his speechlessness, both poems are unusually long for American Puritan elegies, amounting together to thirty-seven pages of verse: "My *Love,*" he explains, "is Talkative." Despite the solemn elegiac occasions, too, he labors to entertain and impress by language, placing Collins's relatives on a "*Stage*" to comment on the "*Tragedy.*" Exhibitions of cleverness choke or divert the forward flow of mourning verse—exclamations, rhetorical questions, italics, curious lore, classical references, esoteric allusions, half-page stacks of footnotes, and many puns. Cotton writes of his halting verse, "I strive to *run,* but then I want my *feet*"; the argument over how many angels can dance on the point of a needle, he says, is perhaps a "*needless Point.*" Wittily he compares Oakes's death to the loss of a tooth, and measures the depth of Collins's sermons by remarking that "*Elephants/* Might take content" in them. Both these rhapsodically insincere and pretentiously ornamental poems bespeak someone concerned less with what he is saying than with sounding copious and charming.

Cotton's stutter may echo more directly in the strange awkwardness of the elegies. Their gawky unmelodiousness suggests what he later described as the "broken and blundering" speech of stutterers, and seems not so much unmusical as pathological:

> Some *Elogyes* compose to try their Wits;
>   The Gout, (r) the *Feavour,* // yea & *Injustice,* (s)
> *Folly* (t) and *Poverty* (u) have in the Fits
>   Of Ranting Writers had a *comeliness.*

> My *Theme,* my *Humour* is not such an one:
>   Who to prove *Cicero* not eloquent,
> Pen'd Books (x) who *truth* & *worth* for *guards* disown
>   Such only count *Collins not excellent.*

Whether the inept clumsiness of Cotton's verse derived from his speech difficulties, he had no gift at all for rhyming or for verse rhythm, although he would attempt to write poetry throughout life. Increase sent copies of his son's first published work to several persons, one of whom replied bluntly that however hopeful Cotton's prospects as a minister, "in my thoughts he will never win the laurel for his poesy."

*

Cotton's affections and social sense were strong, his interests broad, his appetite for learning large, and while trying to live in heaven he also enjoyed earth. By the time of his family's move to the North End of Boston from Cotton's Hill he was one of five children; by 1684 he was one of ten, a new brother or sister having arrived about every two years: Samuel

(August 1674), Abigail (April 1677), Hannah (May 1680), Catherine (September 1682), and Jerusha (April 1684). Around the age of seventeen he undertook to engage his sisters Maria, Elizabeth, and Sarah in the service of Christ, calling them successively into his study and explaining in pathetical terms their obligation to give themselves to Christ.

Cotton says virtually nothing about the other Mather children in his diaries. But his closest relation seems to have been with his brother Nathanael, six and a half years his junior, to whom he presented a volume of manuscript sermons preached by their grandfather John Cotton. The gift was appropriate, for the extraordinarily pious Nathanael prayed constantly, tackled rabbinic learning and philological problems of Scripture, and wrestled soul-searchingly with the problem of his conversion. Cotton tutored Nathanael as well, but found that he was "forced often to chide him *to* his Recreations, but never that I remember *for* them." An unrelenting student, Nathanael was admitted to Harvard at the age of twelve, and four years later was suffering pains in his joints. Like his father he also experienced spells of depression, and sometime fashioned himself *"Deodatus Melancholicus."* Increase also designed him for the ministry, but he felt unworthy and directionless, considered the prospect awesome, and wrote that "the Thoughts of it have almost amazed me so that I am much Perplexed in my Studies." Judging from his later biography of Nathanael, Cotton felt a little awed by his brother's grave piety and talent for learning but critical of his disregard for his health.

Among his numerous relatives Cotton most often visited his mother's brother, the minister John Cotton of Plymouth. A rather fat man with a "Handsome Ruddy yet grave Countenance," he could cite chapter and verse for almost any words of Scripture quoted to him. Although regarded as a "living Index to the Bible," something in him was quirky and unreliable. He had had the unhappiness, in 1664, to be excommunicated from the church of his own father, the famous John Cotton, for "lascivious unclean practises with three women." Perhaps because of this clouded reputation, Increase often took a high-handed, suspicious tone with him, as if John Cotton were seeking some advantage.

But the many surviving letters of John and his "comely fat" wife Joanna reveal a loving and good-natured couple, whose warmth extended to and was returned by Cotton. His uncle saluted him as "Endeared Cousen," while Cotton dubbed his aunt Joanna his "Plymouth-mother." He stayed with the Cottons in the summer of 1678, just after graduating from Harvard, studying industriously but delighting in the pleasant air. Because smallpox was then visiting Boston he considered his removal to

Plymouth "some special providence," although he feared, his uncle wrote, "going into the jaws of infection." When he did return to Boston, he, his brother Nathanael, and his sister Sarah all became mildly infected, his sister Maria more seriously. During another Plymouth sojourn he became a party to an obscure but farcical-sounding lawsuit, in which John Cotton brought a complaint against a man who allegedly had sold a watch belonging to him. The man denied having the watch, but Cotton Mather testified in court that he himself had delivered it to the man.

From Boston Cotton often wrote to his uncle, sending family news and political intelligence in a respectful but rather showy tone:

Honored Sir,
        You know I suppose how if a few of the eldest are *vocales,* then the rest either *semi-vocales* or mutes. Behold! how I make a virtue of necessity. Time and business have formerly forbad me to do that which at present it but just [as much?], *ut canis* [*ad nilum?*].

This, the opening of Cotton's first surviving letter, written when he was about fourteen, inaugurates a monumental correspondence he would cultivate throughout life.

Within his family Cotton also found precedent and encouragement for his keen scientific interests, already evident in his Harvard declamations and his flirtation with a career in medicine. His grandfather John Cotton, although steeped in medieval notions of physical reality, had considered it a divinely imposed duty to "study the nature and course, and use of all Gods works." His brother Nathanael read natural philosophy and the works of Francis Bacon, wrote up some experiments, investigated the "abstruse parts" of mathematics and astronomy, and expressed an allegiance to "the Mechanical Hypothesis of the Honorable Robert Boyle"— an atomistic view of the universe as composed of identical elementary particles. Increase Mather, after the spectacular appearance of Halley's comet in 1680, undertook a course of reading in the latest European astronomical studies, from which he emerged (or which perhaps confirmed him in being) a champion of observation and mathematical reasoning and an opponent of the abstract logic of Aristotle. Increase observed stars through the Harvard telescope, but found it irksome to travel to Cambridge and proposed in 1682 that a telescope and other scientific instruments be placed in the Town House. Although his *Kometographia* (1683) persists in treating comets as portents of coming events, it also recognizes that comets move like planets, cites the work of Johann Kepler, and dabbles in astronomical mathematics.

The Cotton and Mather families were hardly alone in their scientific interests. Many Puritans experimented with and encouraged science, and in Cotton's youth the Copernican system, the materialist philosophy of Descartes, and other revolutionary ideas that transformed the picture of the universe were beginning to take hold in New England. In 1683 was founded a Boston Philosophical Society, a step toward creating what became a Boston scientific community. Indirectly the group grew from the Royal Society of London, which tried to promote the new science in America and had corresponded with science-minded New Englanders since at least the mid-seventeenth century. But the specific proposal for a local scientific society came from Increase Mather, who hoped, he said, to lay "the foundation for that which will be for future edification." The Society first met in the spring of 1683, then fortnightly until 1688. No records of its meetings remain, if any were kept, so its membership and proceedings are largely unknown; but many persons in and near Boston had active scientific interests and may have participated. Cotton clearly became involved in the Society, for at least one meeting took place at his home, and he was befriended by one of the members, Dr. William Avery.

Cotton later described the Society's purpose as "Improvements in *Philosophy* and Additions to the Stores of *Natural History*." Evidently the members collected observations on novel natural phenomena in America, perhaps planning to compile a natural history of New England. Some such project may explain the obscure petition to the General Court in 1684, signed by Cotton, his father, and Dr. Avery, requesting an eight-mile tract of land "to make Some Essays towards the promoting of Learning together with and by the Improvement of Land among us." The Society also corresponded with at least one European scientist, Wolferdus Sanguerdius of Leiden, to whom it sent astronomical observations, and drawings of a parhelion and of a double rainbow which he published in his *Philosophia Naturalis* (2d ed. Leiden, 1685).

Although far older than Cotton, Dr. Avery enjoyed the young man's friendship. "I have longed more to have Commerce with your self," he wrote him in 1683, "than with most men that I know tho it be but in a little paper well blotted." One of the first physicians in America, Avery owned scientific apparatus and invented medical instruments himself. A contemporary described him as a "great inquirer," skilled in "chemical physick" generally and particularly in the work of the iatrochemist Jean Baptiste Van Helmont, a figure who would later become important to Cotton also. Avery described to Cotton his work on digestion, advised him on purchasing recent works on chemistry, and employed him as an amanuensis for some correspondence with the great English chemist Robert Boyle. Like many English scientists, Boyle was intrigued by the New World as a potential source of new and unusual material for investigation, and he asked Avery for observations about the air of New England, and expressed interest in its minerals. A letter from Avery to Boyle in August 1683 discusses at length chemicals and vessels to be used in various experiments. Cotton transcribed the letter for the elderly Avery, and may have written part of it himself, since some of the language sounds much like his own.

Cotton also took time during his candidacy to correspond with a Hartford minister about the change in polarity of a compass, and to observe Halley's comet through the Harvard telescope. He owned a microscope, too, and obviously found pleasure in viewing the "little *eels*," of which he could see "*incredible hundreds playing about in one drop of water.*" His first published work having been a poem, his second was a "mathematical Composure," *The Boston Ephemeris* (1683). Together with the dates of court sessions and elections, and a section on biblical chronology, this almanac contains the times and dates of eclipses, and a technical description of Halley's comet. It also includes an essay to encourage scripture knowledge "because," Cotton wrote, "if we design only to edifie the *Students* of *Astronomy* among us, Alas! there is scarce *One* of a *City* and two of a *Tribe* to be addressed." But in fact his observations through telescope and microscope were acts of devotion themselves, giving new grounds for praising the Almighty by enhancing his sense of the perfect design of things. "*Every Wheel* in this *huge clock*," he preached in his twentieth year, "moves just according to the *Rule* which the *All-wise Artist* [ga]ve it at the first."

*

The beginning of the end of Cotton's much delayed ordination came in July 1684, when he had preached at the North Church for four years. In that time, the brethren said, they had "more than once expressed their desire of his being settled," and with some irritation they now voted again that he "without further delays be ordained." Increase did not so much consent as give way. Ill once again, he had urged his flock to secure a second "Teaching officer." He accepted their choice of his son for the reason, he said, that they "could not agree in calling any other."

But Increase still did not consider Cotton an appropriate colleague for himself. A month or so later, after another illness, he preached a peculiar sermon, comparing his recovery to that of Hezekiah, the Old Testament

king of Judah, who had fought against death although mortally ill. Hezekiah probably resisted death, Increase said, because he "had no son to
succeed him, so that if God had taken him away, there must have been
great Trouble in the Kingdom." He thus implied that he himself had
struggled against his illness because his church had no successor to him,
although the brethren's insistent votes for Cotton suggest they would
have had no trouble choosing one. Cotton's ordination was postponed
seven months more—and after another vote for it in April 1685, was nearly postponed again. This time the reason given for the delay was the
shocking news that the king, as we shall see, was about to reorganize the
government of New England. That, Cotton wrote, as if doubting the explanation himself, was how it had been "represented unto me."

   Cotton's ordination was set, at last, for Wednesday, May 13, 1685. As
the date approached he made fresh vows, promising the Lord to be a
faithful pastor, contented with his condition and unresentful of slights.
With his ordination only two weeks away, however, his "closing" with
Christ remained incomplete. Woeful sights of his sinfulness alternated
still with convictions that he was cleansed. Receiving assurances on May 4
that all controversy between God and his soul had ended, he wrote up
and signed a covenant, engaging to renounce worldly vanities and to have
Him as his chief Good. But like his many earlier assurances this one also
waned. Days before his ordination he again felt confused and melancholy, doubtful of his fitness for the weighty work, apprehensive that
God's supporting presence might be denied him, altogether "Buffeted,
and mortified and macerated with Strong *Temptations,* and broken to
pieces."

   On the morning of his ordination, Cotton's assurances returned glow-
ingly. He was in his study, praying on his knees and meditating on what
the ministry entailed, when he experienced, in tears, an "astonishing
Irradiation from Heaven," a guarantee that he would in his ministry enjoy
a mighty presence of the Lord Jesus Christ. The exaltation, the "rapturous
Touches and *Prospects,*" became nearly unbearable: "I was forced most
unwillingly to shake them off; they would have been too hard for me, and
I would not have others take notice of any Effects thereby left upon me."

   In this state of controlled rapture, his soul "inexpressibly irradiated
from on High," Cotton entered the North Church. Here he beheld "one
of the vastest Congregations that has ever been seen in these parts of the
World." Exactly how many attended is unknown, but the church had
three tiers of galleries, and a good congregation meant fifteen hundred to
two thousand persons, one-third to nearly one-half the population of Bos-

ton. Many ministers and other dignitaries from churches in Boston and neighboring towns took part, as did the governor of Massachusetts and the revered, aged John Eliot.

Cotton began the daylong ritual by offering public prayers for about an hour and a quarter. Then to demonstrate, as the candidate customarily did, that he understood the work for which he was about to be separated, he preached for an hour and three-quarters. Nothing indicates that his stutter hampered him, but by the text he chose, John 21:17, he invoked his troubled "closing" and the frequent postponements. When the resurrected Jesus asked his disciple Peter whether he loved Him, Peter replied that he did; but as if doubting him, Christ repeated the question two more times: "Peter was grieved because he said unto him the third time, Lovest thou me? And he said unto him, Lord, thou knowest all things; thou knowest that I love thee. Jesus saith unto him, Feed my sheep."

Having spoken three hours in the morning, Cotton sat silent in the afternoon as Increase preached. He wrote down his father's words in his sermon notebook and, underlining certain statements, filled eleven pages. Increase took for his subject the nature of the ministry, emphasizing its solemnity and high demands. Occasionally referring directly to "My son Cotton Mather," he said that the ministry was a "Work." It was a work, first, in the sense of a difficult labor, requiring wearisome preaching, meditation, and study. It was also an awful work, for the minister in watching over souls does the Lord's work. Nor is everyone qualified for this work. Among the earliest Christians there were "extraordinary Ministers" called directly from Heaven, qualified for the ministry by being divinely endowed with miraculous gifts. But the age of miracles having ended, the qualifications now were ministerial, not miraculous: large knowledge, an ability to interpret Scripture, a desire to glorify God, and, most important, the experience of conversion, a calling from the Holy Ghost. Ministers, Increase concluded, must "addict themselves to the Ministry," must be spiritual in discourse and conversation, spiritual in preaching, indeed spiritually minded—for which Scripture compares them to angels.

Cotton's ordination as a minister followed. Such ceremonies well conducted could be moving and instructive, leaving, Cotton wrote later, "*Floods of Tears* in the affected Spectators, and lasting *Impressions of Piety* upon them." The custom in the New England churches was for the moderator to ask the visiting elders and messengers of neighboring churches whether they objected to the ordination; none objecting, the moderator then asked whether they knew of anything in the candidate's doctrine or morals that might forbid his ordination; nothing being named, the brethren were asked to signify with raised hands that they abided by their choice of the minister.

Now Increase Mather and the ministers John Allen and Samuel Willard lay their hands on Cotton's head. In this position Increase charged his son to feed dutifully the flock of God over which the Holy Ghost had appointed him shepherd, to give himself to meditation, reading, exhortation, and doctrine, and to make himself exemplary by his own purity, charity, and faith. If his son kept this charge, Increase said,

> . . . the Lord of Hosts will give you a Place among His Holy Angels that stand by, and are Witnesses of this Days-Solemnity, and of your being thus solemnly apart to the special Service of God, and of Jesus Christ; And if you do thus, when the Lord Jesus shall appear, you shall appear with Him in glory. He, who is the chief Shepherd will then give unto you a Crown of Glory which shall never fade away.

After this dramatic "Imposition of Hands," a minister chosen to represent the elders and messengers of the churches customarily gave the new minister his right hand in token of fellowship in God's service, as James, Peter, and John to Paul and Barnabas.

The minister chosen to step forth was John Eliot. Now past eighty, he had lived in New England since it was an unchristian wilderness, for more than fifty years. Giving Cotton the "Right Hand of Fellowship" as the latest continuator of a sacred succession, he said to him: "*Brother, Art thou a Lover of the Lord Jesus Christ? Then, I pray Feed his Lambs.*" The solemnity and tradition of the event, Cotton wrote afterward in his diary, produced a "greater Number of moved Hearts and weeping Eyes, than perhaps have been at any Time here seen together."

Elevated into partnership with his father in a prestigious church, and to the honorable place designed for him in the line of Cottons and Mathers, Cotton felt small and weak. Some time after his ordination, he took the notes he had written on his father's sermon and, using a different pen, interlined his private responses to them. Where his father had said "Solomon my son is young and tender," he wrote, "The like here." Where Increase told the congregation, "I have been at the gates of the Grave," Cotton commented, "more than once within these four or five years." Increase may again have been ill at the time of Cotton's ordination, for he took the occasion to announce once more that his death might be near. He did so indirectly, referring in his sermon to the story in Numbers 20:26 of Aaron and his son Eleazar. The reference was not lost upon

Samuel Sewall, who noted in his diary that Increase had thereby intimated "he knew not but that God might now call him out of the World."
Increase may have done no more than mention Aaron and Eleazar; to
have applied the larger episode in which they figured to himself and his
son, could be interpreted only as a gesture of bitter reproach. For Aaron
the priest did not simply transmit his ministry to his son. Rather, an angry
God stripped him of his priestly garments and put them upon Eleazar;
immediately after his son replaced him, Aaron died. Whether or not Cotton interpreted Increase's reference to mean that his father considered
himself demoted and mortally threatened by his ordination, he at least
wrote in his notebook that *"When the priests garments were put upon
Eleazar, then Aarons death was near."*

With this fearful prospect, and with how much guilt can only be con-
jectured, Cotton also recorded a resolve to find some method of extraordinary prayerfulness for his father's life. Increase himself told the congregation that if his son were left alone he would need their prayers. And
Cotton concluded the afterthoughts in his notebook with a brief prayer of
his own: "O mighty Redeemer by whose Spirit I am call'd unto the work
of the Ministry in this time and place, Help Help a frail creature to discharge all the Duties of it."

*

Within about a year after his ordination Cotton had been initiated into
most of the duties of the New England ministry. On June 28, 1685, he for
the first time administered communion; in July he for the first time gave
the "Country-Lecture"; beginning in October he participated in a formal
excommunication, taking testimony of witnesses who had seen a member
of the congregation, Ruth Fuller, holding on to the gate before her house,
drunk; toward the end of the year he began catechizing visits, stopping by
the houses of his flock each afternoon to catechize their young, seldom
departing without "many *Tears* of Devotion dropt by all sorts of Persons"
in the family, work he found rewarding but also fatiguing. As an ordained
Boston minister he was also made an Overseer of Harvard, sometime in
1685. The same year, the Overseers unanimously devolved the care of the
college on Increase, asking him to act as president until the establishment of a permanent administration. Still refusing to reside in Cambridge, he acted as "Rector," commuting between the North End and the
Harvard Yard by ferry and horse.

Cotton preached extensively. Over two days in January 1686, he gave
five sermons, and he filled pulpits in Watertown, Charlestown, Dorches-

ter, and other places around Boston. One particular sermon called on his fullest abilities, brought him wide notice, and became the occasion, he said, "of my being *shown unto Israel.*" In March 1686, a man named James Morgan, about thirty years old, was found guilty of murder and sentenced to be hanged. Condemned criminals were usually brought to church to be made the living objects of an exemplary sermon. Morgan himself asked Cotton to preach his execution sermon, as this genre became known, so that on March 7, Cotton found himself preaching at the North Church before a "vast Concourse of People." He addressed simultaneously the congregation and the criminal, who sat in the auditorium, probably chained, holding a Bible. Using Morgan as a frightening example of the results of brothels, swearing, and other prevalent vices, he exhorted him to look toward Christ:

> When the numerous crowd of *Spectators* are, three or four days hence, throng'd about the place where you shall then *breathe your last* before them all, then do you with the heart-piercing *groans of a deadly wounded man* beseech of your *Fellow-sinners* that they would *Turn now every one from the evil of his way.*

Cotton was not mistaken in predicting a large crowd, for on the morning of Morgan's hanging—the first execution in Boston in nearly seven years—Increase Mather preached to a gathering estimated, amazingly, at five thousand persons. Amidst this huge crush in the North Church a "crazed woman," as Samuel Sewall described her, either screamed that the gallery was falling, or else beat another woman, whose flight from her was mistaken for a rush to safety from a falling gallery. Either way, people fled the church in panic, and the governor moved the proceedings to the South Church. There Cotton took notes as his father preached on the nature of murder, praying at the same time that he might be as helpful as possible to "the poor man."

Morgan perhaps sensed compassion in Cotton or felt some bond with his youth, for he requested his company on the public march to the hanging. As they walked together to the gallows, about a mile outside Boston, they were followed by thousands of people. Some had traveled fifty miles to be present. En route, by Cotton's account, Morgan repeatedly thanked him for his help, and reviled himself for lying, drinking, breaking the Sabbath, and keeping evil company. Before a "huge Multitude" gathered at the place of execution, near which was a coffin, Cotton prayed with Morgan. Although he constantly pressed on his flock the need for immediate repentance, he believed that no repentance could come too late to make salvation possible, and he told Morgan to pray in his final moment on earth, that they might meet on Judgment Day at the right hand of Jesus. Morgan climbed the ladder to the noose. Cotton said to him, "*Farewell* poor heart, *Fare thee well.*"

Cotton's concern for Morgan's body and soul did not keep him from realizing that his role in the execution had brought him new prominence. His performance was so affecting, he recorded, that people throughout the country "very greedily desired the Publication," and the event produced his first published sermon, *The Call of the Gospel* (1686). It particularly pleased him that the sermon appeared together with the execution sermons by his father and by the Rev. Joshua Moodey, placing him, "a *sorry Youth,* in conjunction with *two* of the venerablest Men in the Land." As he noted proudly too, these sermons "sold exceedingly," calling for a second edition the next year, to which the publisher added a nine-page transcript of his conversation with Morgan on the death march. Having stepped impressively before the public, the same fall he was chosen for the first time to deliver the traditional "Artillery Sermon," marking the day for selecting leaders of the militia. In themselves such sermons were "things of considerable Observation." But Cotton took special pride in having been chosen to preach in Cambridge, to the artillery company of Middlesex County, while as a Bostonian he resided in Essex County. Never before had the Middlesex militia chosen for their Artillery Day preacher a minister from another county, "and this was my poor self." The event produced his second published sermon, *Military Duties* (1687).

While pleased by his early success Cotton was learning, however, that to be "shown unto Israel" meant also to be exposed unto Israel. Some found his florid language not entertaining but affected. Increase may have intended to warn him against verbal display when, in his sermon on Cotton's ordination, he told of an "Elaborate young Man" to whom someone said, "I wanted the Spirit of God in your sermon." To others, Cotton seemed unmistakably "elaborate." One minister congratulated Increase on his son's wealth of evangelical knowledge but added, "I only wish he delivered truths in your style, in that plainness of expression which the Gospel teach." Samuel Sewall too remarked that an otherwise excellent sermon by Cotton was found distasteful or "somewhat disgusted" for such expressions as "sweet-scented hands of Christ, Lord High Treasurer of AEthiopia, Ribband of Humility."

If Cotton's plush language hid from others his grave doubts about his ability, he was himself undeceived. Nearly a year after his ordination he again cautioned himself to watch his tongue lest he be punished by stuttering, and to use a "deliberate, considerable, profitable speech." Acutely conscious of being twenty-four years old in a role where venerableness was esteemed, he saw himself as "a young *person,* and a younger *pastor.*" His sense of his youthfulness also curbed any desire to outperform his father, toward whom he continued to act with respectful submission. When an address to the General Court was proposed, shortly before his ordination, he felt that "*Little* can be done by so *little* a person, as I am, in this matter," and he decided simply to "confer with my *Father,* as a sorry *Remembrancer.*" Increase fed this sense of subordinate littleness by his reluctance, even after Cotton's ordination, to acknowledge him as a colleague. When their execution sermons on James Morgan were published together in a single volume, Increase referred in the Preface, less enthusiastically than fatalistically, to "*my Son (whom the Lord Jesus has fixed in the same Church to which I am related).*"

Especially, Cotton feared that by his inexperience he might do something to bring the ministry into disrepute: "O Lord, " he prayed, "of all the Plagues in the World, I beseech Thee, do not suffer this to come upon me." A year after his ordination he took part in a church council at Malden which voted to temporarily suspend Thomas Cheever, a minister accused among other things of uttering obscenities at a Salem tavern. Sitting in a formal council and officially condemning the son of his old schoolmaster, Ezekiel Cheever, he felt not like one of the judges, but like the young offender: "having seen a poor *young Minister* terribly stigmatized for his Misdemeanours, by a Council, whereof I was myself a Member, I thought; *What if God should single me out now to be so publickly loaded with Shame for Sin?*"

Cotton completed his entry into the ministry, in mid-1686, by marrying. He chose very carefully, often seeking divine guidance, for a minister's wife was not only his companion but must also be a model of wifely, motherly, and neighborly behavior to the community. At the same time, bachelor ministers were much sought after, and its paternal authority lent the Puritan ministry a distinct erotic appeal, so that he found himself soon after ordination with "many Invitations" to marry. He seems to have considered several eligible women, promising that if God directed him to one who would honor his calling he would twice a year, every year, join her in keeping a private day of Thanksgiving to Him. Ministers in New England being, as Increase often complained, underpaid, he also prayed to be afforded through marriage a comfortable and well-provided home, "without the Distresses and the Temptations, which *Poverty* does expose unto."

Around his birthday in February 1686, Cotton began courting Abigail Phillips of Charlestown, the daughter of "worthy, pious, and credible Parents." Her father, Colonel John Phillips, a justice of the peace prominent in military affairs, owned houses and pastureland in and near Charlestown, plus an interest in a mill. Cotton pursued Abigail piously but vigorously. For three months he let scarce a week pass without spending a day of prayer for his success, and he fashioned his addresses to Abigail after Christ's methods of engaging souls. To remind himself that his courtship must serve the same purpose as all his other activities, to glorify God,he entered in his diary an anecdote concerning Rabbi Gamaliel, the teacher of Saint Paul, who, refusing to lay by the yoke of God's Kingdom a single hour, said over the scriptural passages in his phylacteries on his wedding night. What made the reminder necessary was perhaps that during his courtship, perhaps because of it, he felt the sting of disbelief, a weakening of faith, in fact the beginnings of a severe religious crisis. "O that the wonderful, Amazing, Everlasting Love of God to me," he cried in March, "might cause me to love Him again, with a Love as strong as Death."

Despite mounting spiritual turmoil, Cotton married Abigail Phillips on May 4, 1686. He was three months past twenty-three, she one month under sixteen. He found some renewal of spiritual strength on the morning of his wedding day, which he spent in secret prayer in Boston. Once again he experienced an assurance of Christ's love for him, and became tearfully certain that "in my *married Estate,* He had reserves of rich and great Blessings for me." Arriving in Charlestown with time to spare, he took his Bible into a garden and read the account in John 2 of the marriage in Cana, turning each verse into one pious thought and one supplication to God.

The wedding, Cotton decided, was an event—attended by many ministers and other prominent persons, celebrated with "Splendid Entertainments" at Abigail's house, withal marked by "many Circumstances of Respect and Honour, above most that have ever been in these parts of the World." After living a while with Colonel Phillips in Charlestown the couple moved to Boston around the early fall, to a house Increase had temporarily inhabited after the great fire of 1676 consumed his own. Here, as a very young college student, Cotton had many hundreds of times beseeched the Lord. "I could not but observe the Providence of God," he remarked, "in ordering my *Comforts* now, in those very Rooms, where I had many years before, sought Him with my *Prayers*."

From the first, Cotton felt happy in his marriage to Abigail and thanked God for granting him "a *Meet Help*, an extremely desireable Companion for my *Joys* and *Griefs*." As he had hoped, he was materially prosperous too, having received a good portion "*in*, as well as *with*, my Consort." He went from room to room of his house, deliberately gazing on the "Parcels of the *Estate*, whereof I am now become the owner"; rather, he reconsidered as he mentally gave back the parcels to God, the steward. The novel sexual license of marriage seems to have troubled him some, for he prayed to be freed from the "Slavery" of a "Lust seeming to assault me with a commission." But the household of course remained deeply devout. To aid Abigail in her so-far unconverted state, he offered conference and example, and prayed with her daily. The couple also invited neighbors for an hour of prayer and psalmody on Sabbath evenings, but their pious hospitality proved too inviting, bringing "such an unexpected Resort unto my House, that there was ordinarily near an hundred People at a Time, (and more than one Room could hold)."

Yet as happened to Increase just after his ordination, Cotton following his marriage underwent a tormenting assault of religious doubt, lasting about eight months. Only weeks after the wedding he found his soul "daily Enflamed" by the "fiery Darts" of atheism. The Christ he so often beseeched prostrate in the dust for his father's life and an unfettered tongue seemed now a dubious being: "O," he prayed, "That the foolish prejudices which my unbelief is ready to entertain against Jesus Christ, may be all removed." After his innumerable pious contrivances and ingenious devotions, his alchemizing street signs and flowers into prayers, he doubted the reality of Spirit: "O That my firm Belief of Invisible things may be as a shield unto me, defending me from those Temptations." The very soul whose sins of lust and pride he had striven in brokenhearted cycles of assurance and doubt to purge, might not exist: "O That I might beyond all Doubt or Darkness, be effectually convinced of the Immortality of my own soul." Indeed, he had arrived at the place appointed for him since birth, but as an unfamiliar being, disloyally changed: "O That I may not in any wise Lose that kindness to the Truths and ways of God, which I have had in my younger years."

A year before his marriage Cotton had visited his friend Thomas Shepard, a minister in Charlestown about four and a half years younger than himself. Ill, Shepard had said to him as they parted, "*Sir, I beg the Lord Jesus to be with you unto the End of the World!*" The next night Shepard died.

II

MR. COTTON MATHER
(1687–1703)

~•~

In the rear of the procession rode a figure on horseback, so darkly conspicuous, so sternly triumphant, that my hearers mistook him for the visible presence of the fiend himself; but it was only his good friend, Cotton Mather, proud of his well-won dignity, as the representative of all the hateful features of his time; the one blood-thirsty man, in whom were concentrated those vices of spirit and errors of opinion that sufficed to madden the whole surrounding multitude.

—NATHANIEL HAWTHORNE, "Alice Doane's Appeal"
(1834)

"It is difficult, my children," observed Grandfather, "to make you understand such a character as Cotton Mather's, in whom there was so much good, and yet so many failings and frailties."

—NATHANIEL HAWTHORNE, *Grandfather's Chair*
(1841)

Was Cotton Mather honestly credulous? Ever ready to dupe himself, he limited his credulity only by the probable credulity of others. He changes, or omits to repeat, his statements, without acknowledging error, and with a clear intention of conveying false impressions. He is an example how far selfishness, under the form of vanity and ambition, can blind the higher faculties, stupefy the judgment, and dupe consciousness itself. His self-righteousness was complete, till he was resisted.

—GEORGE BANCROFT, *History of the United States*
(12th ed., 1846)

... those who know only the eccentricities of Cotton Mather know little about him. Those who suppose they comprehend him, because they are familiar with the current anecdotes about him, or imagine that he could be fairly sketched by a few strong touches, could not be under a greater misapprehension. The truth is, few characters are less intelligible; few harder to describe; few are so many-sided; few have so little uniformity; few have so great a variety of qualities, in such strange admixture; few show such supposed inconsistencies; few present themselves in such ever-shifting positions and hues, such kaleidoscopic changes and combinations; few exhibit such surprising contrasts, such an apparent jumble of great and small, sharp and flat, wise and simple, saintly and ordinary. To group all these elements together, to arrange and blend them into any thing like a complete and satisfactory portrait, would be a task that requires more penetration and skill than have ever yet been exercised upon his biography. . . .

—CHANDLER ROBBINS, *A History of the Second Church* (1852)

. . . though, in my previous night-readings, Cotton Mather had but amused me, upon this particular night he terrified me. A thousand times I had laughed at such stories. Old wives' fables, I thought, however entertaining. But now, how different. They began to put on the aspect of reality. Now, for the first time it struck me that this was no romantic Mrs. Radcliffe who had written the *Magnalia,* but a practical, hard-working, earnest, upright man, a learned doctor, too, as well as a good Christian and orthodox clergyman. What possible motive could such a man have to deceive? His style had all the plainness and unpoetic boldness of truth. In the most straightforward way, he laid before me detailed accounts of New England witchcraft, each important item corroborated by respectable townsfolk, and, of not a few of the most surprising, he himself had been eye-witness. Cotton Mather testified whereof he had seen. But, is it possible? I asked myself.

—HERMAN MELVILLE, "The Apple-Tree Table" (1856)

3

The Glorious Revolution

OVER THE NEXT fifteen years, three convulsive events shook the political, social, and religious life of New England. Of Cotton Mather's reaction to the first event, the Glorious Revolution of 1689, little is known, because his diaries between 1687 and 1692 are missing. That is doubly unfortunate because for most of the time his father was in London, leaving him in Boston alone. Although this biography otherwise narrates his life from inside, as he witnessed it himself, the present chapter perforce treats it largely as seen by others.

Yet in reacting to the upheavals of the time, Cotton Mather shared with many other New Englanders a single interpretive framework. He and they explained events according to a long-lived public sense of vulnerability. As a persecuted minority in England, Puritans had grown used to expecting attack. Their settlement in America, however, did not ease their apprehensions. Instead, it demonstrated that their entire community was unstable and precarious, that troublesome and vast change could come at any time, and they lived under severe strain of invasion and disintegration.

*

The mentality of invasion arose from threats both external and internal. However the first settlers hoped to leave behind the corruptions and violence of Europe, they remained part of an international community. Holland, at war with England in the 1670s, made no distinction between mother country and colony, and seized vessels wherever New England traded; a day of public fasting was kept in 1673 to implore divine protection against Dutch attack. Invasion by a more potent and nearer enemy to

England, France, was a chronic threat, and Christian Israel had much to fear as well from its Indian neighbors, who raided often and bloodily. If not the Puritans' life and property, then their religious solidarity was menaced by incursions of other sects. Quakers—in the Puritan view, open heretics—first intruded on Boston in 1656 and kept returning despite severe punishments: for the first intrusion, loss of an ear; for the second, loss of the second ear; for the third, a hot iron through the tongue; for repeated intrusions, death: in the early 1660s three incorrigible Quakers were hanged. Baptists opened a church at Charlestown in 1665 and, although banished from the colony, managed to stay. And never far off was the prospect of a still more disruptive settlement in New England of Episcopal churches and an American bishop, backed by the crown.

The elements in New England were harsh and invasive also, protection minimal. An earthquake struck in and around Boston in 1663, transmitting six or more shocks over three days that moved objects on shelves and drove people in fright from their rocking houses. As a busy port Boston also awaited sudden calamities of the sea. The churches constantly invoked prayers for congregants then upon the waves; there were frequent reports of lost ships, and many widows. A combustible heap of contiguous houses, Boston lived under the constant threat of fire, too. Three years after the blaze that destroyed Increase Mather's house and church, a major fire destroyed eighty homes and seventy warehouses with a loss of £150,000, a toll proportionate to that suffered by London in the Great Fire of 1666. The very air threatened the community, bringing egg-sized hail, lightning to split houses, drought to blast wheat, and lethal measles, scarlet fever, and smallpox. As many as three of every ten infants in Boston died, compared with one in sixty in present America. The smallpox epidemic that struck just after Cotton Mather's graduation killed an estimated eight hundred persons; the coffins passed each other in the street.

The Puritans' habit of interpreting such events as judgments of God expanded their feeling of vulnerability. When houses rocked in 1663 it was thought, said one contemporary, that "these *Earthquakes* might portend the shaking the Foundations of our Churches, and of our Civil State." In the brilliant appearance of Halley's comet Increase Mather saw a portent of worse ahead:

> I am persuaded, that the floods of great water are coming. I am persuaded that God is about to open the windows of heaven, and to pour down the Cataracts of his Wrath, ere this Generation (wherein *Atheism* and *Profane-*

ness are come to such a prodigious height) I say, ere this Generation is passed away.

The idea that New England's plague of fire, war, disease, and drought represented divine punishment for its internal rot became more vehemently proclaimed the more the rot spread. And the 1680s, many felt, climaxed an insidious religious and social deterioration that had been evident for at least twenty years (see the note in Documentation). Writing in the eighteenth century, the minister Thomas Prince observed that a decay of piety occurred in New England a little after 1660, "And this increased to 1670, when it grew very visible and threatening, and was generally complained of and bewailed bitterly by the Pious among them; And yet much more to 1680, when but few of the first Generation remained." Sermons preached throughout New England bemoaned this decay and articulated the fear of the godly that, as one wrote, "New England hath seen its best days."

Among the chief signs that the moldering foundations of church and state might soon be overturned was the failure of many young persons to experience grace, that inward supernatural cleansing of perception which signified salvation. According to the original Congregational theory, only the gracious—the Saints—were entitled to full church membership, that is to taking the Lord's Supper and having their children baptized. The failure of many of the new generation to experience grace meant that fewer persons took communion and far fewer were being baptized. To deal with declining church membership, seventy church representatives met in March 1662 at the Boston First Church to discuss the question "Who are the subjects of baptism?" Their answer modified the original theory, extending baptism to the children of godly persons who were not full church members, that is, who had not experienced grace but had been baptized themselves and who professed an intellectual faith and submitted to church discipline. This famous Halfway Covenant carried at the Synod by better than seven votes to one, but resulted in a flood of controversial pamphlets and bitter divisions in many churches. Indeed, Increase Mather had refused to vote with the majority, although it included Richard Mather, his eminent father. From his deathbed Richard asked his son no longer to oppose the Halfway Covenant, but under Increase the North Church still stubbornly refused to baptize children of the unregenerate. At issue was simply whether to adhere to original Congregational theory and see church membership dwindle, or open the church to the ungracious and, in the minds of some, betray the Fathers.

Christian Israel felt equally threatened by the social expression of this decay, a transformation of manners and morals that weakened the Puritans' strict sexual code and their devotion to family life. In 1672, a county court convicted a woman named Alice Thomas "of great suspicion to keep a brothel-house." This was apparently the first brothel in Boston, although from 1670 to 1680 the Suffolk County Court sat on eleven more cases of prostitution. Other signs of a growing sexual excess were more violent, exotic, or unfeeling. Samuel Sewall mentions a Haverhill man who raped Goodwife Nash of Amesbury in a pasture; a boy executed for committing bestiality with a mare in broad daylight in an open yard; and, in 1685, the discovery in the stall of a tobacco shop of an abandoned infant pinned in a cloth: "So far as I can hear," Sewall remarks, "this is the first Child that ever was in such a manner exposed in Boston." By the 1680s ministers had also to vie for attention with French and English dancing masters, such as the Francis Stepney who held mixed dances on lecture days and reportedly boasted that "by one Play he could teach more Divinity than Mr. [Samuel] Willard or the Old Testament." Taverns proliferated, and drunkenness, many alleged, was rampant; in April 1680 the selectmen approved licenses to sell beer, wine, cider or all three to more than thirty different persons. Others complained of widespread contention and a spirit of calumny, as if, Urian Oakes said in 1673, "there were some Lying Office set up in New England." The deep, underlying social change to which all these complaints and incidents point may have contributed to an increase in suicide, against which several ministers preached. In 1677, one diarist recorded within six months that a Plymouth woman who had nineteen children killed herself while pregnant with the twentieth; a man named John Tomlin, of Boston, hanged himself "under discontent"; an old man in Boston cut his throat; and another Boston woman "in trouble of mind" starved herself to death.

The courts and churches struggled to repel this social blight, but it only spread. The courts passed new laws ordering constables to present to the selectmen the names of idlers, allowing county courts to fine women who disported naked breasts and arms, considering as riotous single persons who rode out of town to drink and revel, empowering grand juries to bring to trial men who wore long hair, their own or wigs. The ministry took the part of the Old Testament Jeremiah, and joined in denouncing the degenerate younger generation, none more vigorously than Increase Mather. "Where was there," he asked in one of his many jeremiads, "ever a place so like unto New Jerusalem as New-England hath been?"—"hath been," however, for this was the New England, Increase said, of the unconverted, not zealous for God "but luke warm and wofully indifferent in the matters of Religion." The great Reform Synod of 1679–80 that gathered in Boston compiled a list of the "provoking Evils" of the land: pride in apparel, sleeping at sermons, neglect of church fellowship, Sabbath-breaking, lack of family prayer, naked breasts, mixed dances, unlawful gaming, lying, swearing, talebearing, litigiousness, drunkenness, overcharging. In these cankers, the Synod declared, was engrossed "this perishing people."

But however alarming it found the threat of war, elemental disaster, or inner decay, the mentality of invasion doted longest and most apprehensively on the undeclared intentions of the mother country. At the time of Cotton Mather's birth all New England waited anxiously to learn the disposition of the new monarchy, restored after more than a decade of Puritan rule in England. The new king, Charles II, sent a letter in June 1662, expressing satisfaction in the loyalty of the people of Massachusetts and promising to confirm and preserve their charter. But these gracious reassurances came with some demands. The king expected that liberty of conscience would be extended to Episcopalians. Congregational church membership, too, would no longer be required for voting privileges, but all landholders "orthodox in religion, (though of different persuasions concerning church government)" would be allowed to vote for civil and military officials. To be sure that Massachusetts complied, the king dispatched four observers, who arrived in July 1664. Ominously they came with about four hundred troops aboard two ships of war—the first vessels of the Royal Navy ever to enter Boston Harbor.

The royal commissioners were instructed to do more than observe. They also carried secret instructions to try to persuade the Massachusetts government to seek a "supplement" to the original charter of 1629. As Puritans understood this charter, it set forth and legitimated the purposes that had impelled the first immigrants to cross the Atlantic and found what John Winthrop called a City upon a Hill. To give up the charter was not only to deny their beginnings, however, but also to jeopardize their future. The charter, granted by Charles I, created a joint-stock trading company out of which the government of Massachusetts had evolved. Although the charter was little more than a commercial license for the Massachusetts Bay Company, the Puritans' view of their migration as a mission made the charter in their eyes sacred. It became, Michael G. Hall says, "illogically but in fact, a constitution as precious to the Boston Puritans in 1660 as the United States Constitution was to become for its citizens after 1789." Under the terms of the charter the Puritans had managed to live and to think of themselves as a small independent church-state, a purified American Israel separated from a corrupt Old World. The policy of the new king, however, was to make Massachusetts think of itself again—as did the other North American colonies—as a colony, existing to benefit the mother country.

The move against the charter was aimed particularly at empowering the king to appoint the governor of Massachusetts himself. The charter had granted the Massachusetts Bay Company the right, as a trading company, to choose its own officers; as the Bay Company became the Commonwealth of Massachusetts, the governor of the Company became in effect an elected political leader. Now to deny Massachusetts the right of electing its governor was to snap the tie between church and state on which the continuance of Christian Israel depended. In Puritan theory, church and state, Moses and Aaron, were coordinate authorities, strengthening each other jointly to enforce the moral law. The Cambridge Platform of 1648 assigned civil authority the duty of restraining and punishing idolatry, blasphemy, and heresy, and of coercing schismatical or corrupt individual congregations. Beyond that, government was charged with declaring days of public fasting and humiliation, passing laws against drunkenness or Sabbath-breaking, encouraging the college and schools, and supporting the ministry. Since a revocation of the charter almost certainly involved appointing a non-Puritan governor, it meant weakening the church and altering the Puritan character of the state.

In their own behavior the royal commissioners afforded a preview of what might be expected from a non-Puritan government in Massachusetts. They sent reports to London depicting New Englanders (with considerable accuracy) as rustic and antimonarchical, and warning that Harvard might continue to provide "schismatics to the Church" and "rebels to the King." They also set up as a court of appeals to review sentences already passed by the Massachusetts court. One was the case of John Porter, about thirty years old. This unruly man had been sentenced for saying, among other things, that he "cared not a turd" for Judge Hathorne. He also set fire to his father's woodpile, beat the man's servants, chopped down his fence, threatened to burn his house and kill his cattle, and called him a "liar, and simple Ape, shittabed." On top of that Porter tried to stab one of his own brothers, and cursed his mother as a "Rambeggur, Gamar Shithouse, Gamar Pisshouse," placing her as "the rankest sow in the town." For this oversized contempt of traditional filiopiety, the Massachusetts courts sent Porter to the Boston jail. He escaped, however, and presented himself before three of the commissioners, who granted him protection until his appeal could be heard.

Domestic and international political problems distracted the king's attention from New England until 1676. Then Edward Randolph, a leading advocate of strict royal control over Massachusetts, was sent on the first of his five portentous missions to America. He wrote home that the colony's losses and heavy expenses during King Philip's War made it ripe for a change in government. Yet the status of Massachusetts remained undecided for another decade. While Cotton Mather reached puberty, graduated from Harvard, and trained for his ministry, Randolph arrived and departed, composing censorious accounts of the Puritans' antimonarchical sentiments. Rumors often spread through New England that the charter was about to be revoked and a royal governor appointed. Massachusetts authorities fended off or made small concessions to demands from London, and reminded the king in petitions that for the liberty of living as they lived, "our fathers, and some of us with them, left their native land, with all their pleasant and desirable things."

In the public debate over how to deal with the long-threatening loss of autonomy, some urged submission, others compromise, others defiance. Perhaps the boldest spokesman for preserving the charter and its sacred privileges was Increase Mather. When the Rev. Samuel Willard denounced as madness a suggestion for resisting to the end, Increase told him that had Willard's grandfather heard him, "He would have Boxed his Ears." At a town meeting in January 1684, Increase spoke passionately to the question of whether, as he put it, to make "a full submission and entire Resignation of our charter and the privileges of it to the Kings pleasure." He answered that to submit was to "sin against God." Recalling the risky response of the biblical Naboth, when King Ahab demanded his vineyards—"God forbid, that I should give away the Inheritance of my Fathers"—he said he hoped "there is not one Freeman in Boston that will dare to be guilty of so great a sin." By one account he even excited his audience to defend the charter by arms. The meeting voted unanimously to resist the king's recent offer to "regulate" the charter for the mutual good of New England and the crown.

That New England's existence was precarious, Increase of course understood with special, visionary clarity. Foremost among the Jeremiahs recalling the rising generation to their Fathers' ways, he had publicly prophesied such other threats as King Philip's War, the smallpox epidemic that struck several of his children, and the fire that destroyed his home. A few weeks after his speech he spent a day of prayer and fasting in his beloved study. Once more emerging from it prophetically moved, confident that God had heard his pleas, he called out: *"God will deliver New England! God will deliver New England! God will deliver New England."*

*

On Friday morning, May 14, 1686—ten days after Cotton Mather's marriage—Edward Randolph arrived in Boston from England for the fifth time in a decade, bearing the revocation of the Massachusetts charter and the king's commission for a new government.

The following Monday at the Town House the commission was shown to the General Court, in a room filled with spectators. Some judges urged a protest, but Samuel Sewall spoke against it: "the foundations being destroyed," he asked, "what can the Righteous do." The possibility of some form of resistance was discussed at small private meetings over the next few days, but laid aside. A week later the General Court met for the last time. The Rev. Samuel Nowell prayed God to pardon the magistrates and deputies for capitulating, then thanked the Lord for the mercies He had shown to Massachusetts in the fifty-six years it had existed. Those assembled sang verses from Habakkuk. With "Many Tears Shed in Prayer and at Parting," Sewall recorded, the marshal-general declared the court adjourned until October. But it was a gesture. The charter of the Governor and Company of Massachusetts Bay had been nullified, together with all the rights and privileges founded on it. Massachusetts, formerly a City on a Hill, was now an English colony.

Until the arrival of the new governor later in the year, Massachusetts was ruled by a council, under a native of Massachusetts, Joseph Dudley. He understood his regime to be provisional and more or less preserved established laws and customs. Edward Randolph, however, immediately challenged the concept of a Puritan state. The Lords of Trade and Plantation in London had been advised for several years to create an outpost of the Church of England in Massachusetts, if only to offset the authority of the Puritan clergy. Randolph, now a councillor in the new government, had brought with him to Boston an Anglican clergyman named Robert Ratcliffe; ten days after arriving he suggested that Ratcliffe be allowed to establish a ministry in one of the three Boston meetinghouses. That was resisted, but Ratcliffe was allowed to preach in a room of the Town House. The event, on Sunday, June 6, attracted a large audience, perhaps because of its novelty, although at least one listener also found Ratcliffe's preaching "Extraordinary; he being as well an Orator as a Preacher." For the first time in New England's history a minister had worn a surplice and had publicly read the liturgy from the Anglican Book of Common Prayer.

The full meaning to Massachusetts of the loss of its charter appeared with the arrival of the new governor on December 20, 1686. Edmund Andros was sent to rule over the Dominion of New England, an enlarged, newly unified territory that incorporated Massachusetts Bay, Plymouth, New Hampshire, Maine, and the Narragansett country; by 1688 it would include Rhode Island, Connecticut, New York, and the Jerseys as well. Bostonians scrutinized his arrival for clues to his intentions, but came away uncertain. Ominously he debarked, Sewall noticed, in a "Scarlet Coat Laced." Ominously too, when oaths were administered in the Town House he kept his hat on. To the ministers present he spoke about the need of Church of England worshipers for one of the Boston meeting-houses, and suggested it could be used by two congregations. The Boston ministers met next day to consider his suggestion and agreed they could not consent; Increase Mather and Samuel Willard delivered their answer "in great plainness," Sewall said. But instead of confronting them, Andros apparently hedged. "He seems to say," as Sewall reported his response, "will not impose."

Andros's seeming appeasement hardly lasted through the New Year. He decided that members of the Church of England needed a place of worship and, with Good Friday approaching, he sent Randolph to get the keys to the South Church. Sewall and some others waited on him and showed him a deed proving the land and house belonged to them and said "that we can't consent to part with it to such use." According to Increase Mather, Andros then threatened to seize all the meetinghouses in the country. On Good Friday the sexton of the South Church was "prevailed upon," in Sewall's phrase, to ring the church bell and open the door. For the first time a Puritan meetinghouse in New England was used for Anglican services. Thereafter the services were held jointly in the South Church with Congregational services. The arrangement pro-duced friction: Andros and other Anglican churchgoers were supposed to clear the meetinghouse by half past one; on one Sabbath they did not finish until after two, filling the street outside with Puritans "gazing and moving to and fro because had not entrance into the House"—a "sad Sight," Sewall found it. At the same time plans moved forward to build a separate Church of England chapel in Boston.

The new government affected not only the churches. It also abolished the Assembly (the lower house of the legislature), limited town meetings to one a year, and required juries to admit more non-Congregationalist jurors. Trade, which thrived on evasions of the Navigation Acts, was curtailed by the now strict enforcement of them. Andros also demanded the right to oversee the accounts of the college—to Puritans the nursery of the ministry, to the king's representative a seedbed of Congregational sedition. He sent the Anglican minister Ratcliffe to sit conspicuously in the pulpit during the 1687 commencement, with Increase Mather presiding. He gave the most injurious offense, however, by repatenting land titles, on the ground that they had been voided by the revocation of the charter. Land titles granted by the former government of Massachusetts, rather than by the crown, were invalid. When a sheriff was sent to dispossess a family inhabiting Deer Island in Boston Harbor and to take possession of the place in the king's name, two selectmen protested on behalf of the town of Boston. Andros's attorneys told them "there was no town of Boston, nor was there any town in the country." Those whose forefathers Christ had led as a chosen people into the wilderness now must petition for royal patents to land they already owned, and pay a fee for the repatenting service.

A possible means of protest arose around May 1687. Increase's prophetic assurance had been to some extent validated; on the same day that he cried "*God will deliver New England*"—as he observed—King Charles II died. Although Charles's successor, James, was a Catholic, the new king issued a Proclamation of Indulgence declaring liberty of conscience to both Roman Catholics and Dissenters, news of which came to Boston in May. Some ministers apparently took the Proclamation as a sign of James's sympathy to Dissenters, and saw in it the possibility of appealing to him directly, bypassing Andros. Increase proposed that the ministers send an address thanking James for the Proclamation. When the address came off "very seasonably" in London, he proposed a second address, not from the ministers only but from the churches. Andros, enraged, forbade holding a day of thanksgiving for the address, and threatened to set troops by the church doors to prevent it. But the message of thanks went ahead, with the added proposal that someone from Boston present it in London. When several persons advised Increase himself to bear the address he spent a day of prayer, asking God to declare His will in the matter through the brethren of the North Church. Next day he "mentioned the thing to the church," which unanimously consented to his mission.

Barely two weeks later, on December 24, Increase Mather was arrested. He was charged with having defamed Edward Randolph, but he and others considered the charge simply an effort to keep him in Boston.

Much mutual animosity had arisen between the two men, but the charge stemmed from some treasonable letters, allegedly written by Increase. One very lengthy letter, read to the king and Council and in part published in London, intimated that Randolph had set the great Boston fire of 1676 (which broke out the day after one of his arrivals) and charged the English people, including the king, with "whoring after their own lusts." Increase protested that "not so much as one line of it was ever written by me," and laid the forgery to Randolph, "a child of the Devil." The court that heard the case, on January 31, cleared Increase and required Randolph to pay the costs of the suit. Exultant, Increase preached a powerful sermon on Rom. 8:31, telling his congregation that "When God is for a Man, they that are Against him shall do him good; whether they will or no."

Increase now openly publicized his departure for England, while Andros tried again to hold him in Boston. On March 18 Increase delivered a farewell sermon, reminding his congregation that Christ's love for the Saints is indestructible and everlasting—as, implicitly, was his for them—and that although he had often rebuked his flock, Christ too may be wrathful over sin, "But a Father Loves in his Anger." Andros brought a new court action on the same charge of defamation, and on March 27 sent an officer to arrest Increase again. But the officer was denied entry to the house, even though Increase was unaware of his purpose. As Increase later reported the episode, he happened that morning to take some "working physic," which "caused me to refuse to speak with the officer altho I knew nothing of his design." Not until rumors circulated that he had been arrested did he realize that Andros was again seeking to detain him. Then he stayed home several days with the doors shut.

About ten o'clock on the night of March 30, Increase commended his family to God and left his house, disguised in a wig and white cloak. A man named Thurton, whom Randolph had appointed to spy on Increase and prevent his slipping away, saw him leave the house. But according to Increase, Thurton told him that he lost heart and felt powerless to lay hands on him. Increase spent the night in Charlestown, at the house of his son's father-in-law, Col. Phillips. With Randolph's men searching for him, however, he fled to Rumney Marsh.

About eleven o'clock on the night of April 3, some of Increase's friends and his sons Cotton and Samuel came to Rumney Marsh and escorted him to a ketch, which brought him to a ship bound for England, away from Randolph, Andros, and the others "whose names," Increase wrote, "will stink in New England to the worlds end." He took with him young Samuel, leaving Cotton behind and, for the first time, without him.

*

Because Cotton Mather's diaries from 1687 through 1691 are missing, virtually nothing is known of his reaction to these events. Luckily, a fragment of his 1688 diary remains, recording his feelings during and just after Increase's disguised flight. Increase had often warned of his departure, of course, and since childhood Cotton Mather had prayed earnestly for his health. With his father now departing in fact, and in dangerous circumstances, he responded with extreme anxiety.

While Increase was hiding in Charlestown, Cotton Mather prayed and sang psalms that applied to his situation, and "kept wrestling with God, for his Preservation." He held a daylong fast after his father's removal to the ketch, loathfully confessing his unworthiness for mercy but nevertheless asking it, "especially such a Mercy, as the Enjoyment of such a Father, as mine." News brought to him the same day of fresh perils menacing his father's escape produced such distress that he threw himself on his study floor and, mouth in the dust, begged for his father's deliverance. When his father-in-law, Col. Phillips, arrived at night to announce that a single wind had sped Increase forward and retarded his pursuers, and that Increase was now safely aboard ship, he believed the Lord had heard his prayers.

Cotton Mather's anxiety was not only for his father's safety but also for his own survival. Increase's mission put him in sole charge of a flock which had for years been denied his ordination, and thrust him to the front of grave political affairs. Even while absorbed in praying for his father's safety it occurred to him that "my Father had now left me, alone, in a great *Place* and in a great *Work.*" Above all he feared disgracing his ministry. The possibility that, deprived of his father's guidance, he might dishonor God, "was to me, the dreadfullest Thought in the World." He prayed for assistance, and felt an assurance that God would be with him. Yet like many earlier assurances this one faltered. Days or perhaps weeks after Increase left, he dreamed that, being left alone, he was put upon preaching a sermon for which he had no time to prepare. But as usually also happened, fresh confidence followed doubt. Forced in his dream to the "Extremity" of improvising a sermon, he chose the text "I will never leave thee, nor forsake thee." Parts of the dreamed sermon were so vivid that he remembered them after waking and used them in preaching the next Sabbath.

Other fragmentary evidence shows that however alarmed by the consequences of his father's political role, Cotton Mather was not wholly unprepared for them either. Moves against the charter, begun at the time of his birth, persisted through his teens and the period of his candidacy. At the age of seventeen, six years before Andros arrived, he took notes as John Eliot preached that the civil and religious liberties secured by the Fathers and enjoyed by their descendants might have to be defended: "shall we betray our Liberties . . . Let us do as our fathers have done—Die in the possession of these things." Intermittently over the next few years he recorded new threats with dismay, expressing scorn for Edward Randolph as a man "born to do mischief," reporting to his uncle John Cotton the royal attempts in New Hampshire to offer Anglican communion and baptism, praying mightily for "Deliverance for this poor Country." When the Catholic King James was proclaimed in Boston by military display, he withdrew for a day of private humiliation to lament the danger to Protestantism of his accession. He realized, too, that the troubled times might demand his public and active engagement. As news circulated in the summer of 1685 that Massachusetts was about to have a new governor, he underlined in his sermon notebook a statement by his father concerning times of persecution: *"The Ministers of God must then stand in the fore-front of the battle, and be the first that shall be shot down."*

Exactly how soon Cotton Mather came to stand on the front line is unknown, but it was no longer than five months after his father's departure. The occasion was the birth of a son to King James by his second wife. Previously, James's successor was his oldest daughter Mary, a Protestant married to the Protestant William of Orange. But the infant prince now took precedence, and would be reared as a Catholic. On September 1, Andros sent an order to Cotton Mather, beginning, "In his Majesty's name, you are hereby required. . . ." Andros demanded that he publicly read in the North Church a proclamation for a day of thanksgiving to honor the royal birth—the inception, that is, of a possible Catholic ruler of New England—and there "stir up your hearers to the solemn work of the day, as is required by the same." Andros made clear, also, that this was an order: "and hereof you are not to fail."

Andros had cause to impress on Cotton Mather his superior authority, but may not have known it fully. For one, Increase was relaying to his son in letters, now unfortunately lost, news of his successes at court. By June he had had two audiences with the king, in the second of which James asked him whether Andros had performed satisfactorily; he replied by naming all of the governor's violations of New England's rights. He spoke with James again in July and, very encouragingly, again in October, when the king told him that "property, liberty, and our College should all be confirmed to us." Andros had another reason for showing his authority, although he may have been unaware of it also. At some time or other, Cotton Mather somehow obtained and copied passages of letters from Randolph that made plain his animus toward New England. In the letters, sent to the Earl of Rochester and others in the English hierarchy, he described New Englanders as a "perverse people" amenable only to force, and said he considered it no crime "being the occasion of subverting their old Arbitrary government."

One month into the new year, 1689, a warrant was sent out to arrest Cotton Mather and hold him for trial. Details of the case are again missing, but he was accused of having been, in Randolph's words, "the abettor, if not the author, of a scandalous libel." This obviously contrived charge involved a work published in Cambridge more than two years earlier, *A Brief Discourse Concerning the unlawfulness of Common Prayer Worship.* The pamphlet appeared anonymously and was quite certainly written by Increase; Cotton, however, probably edited it and supervised its printing. The author of the *Brief Discourse,* identified only as a minister, attacked the Common Prayer Book and such Anglican practices as the use of a ring in marriage, making a sign of the cross in baptism, and kneeling at communion. These he condemned as superstitious and *"in a great measure Popish and Heathenish."* According to one supporter of Andros, the thrust of the work was to insinuate "unto the Common People, that the Governor and all of the Church of *England* were Papists and Idolators, and to stir them up to Faction and Rebellion."

The Mathers' longtime friend Wait Winthrop, a member of the Council, managed to squash the order of arrest, although Cotton Mather became the target of new threats shortly after his birthday in February. The court now charged him with breaching the Act of Uniformity and began, he said, "tearing me to pieces, with their horrible *Talons.*" Under a "Storm of *Persecution* from the Church of England," he offered himself as an example of willing self-sacrifice for Christ. Amidst his troubles he preached to a congregation of nearly two thousand persons on the same text his father had used after being cleared of defaming Randolph—If God be for us, who can be against us—attempting to convey, he said, "a glorious Triumph, over Enemies and Sufferings."

The new threat of arrest apparently hovered over Cotton Mather for two months, until lifted by an event in England. The birth of James's son, and consequent prospect of a Catholic king, had induced William of Orange to land in England with a Dutch army, hoping to overthrow James and regain the throne for Protestantism. Rumors of his landing circulated in Boston early in the year, but dependable news seems to have come the first week in April 1689, when John Winslow (grandson of the Plymouth founder) returned from the West Indies with a copy of a document proclaiming William as king. When Andros learned of this inflammatory arrival he demanded Winslow's papers; Winslow refused, and was jailed for bringing into the country a treasonous libel. Andros issued his own proclamation, requiring the people and officers to be in a state of readiness should the usurper send forces to New England.

What remains of Cotton Mather's reaction to news of the Glorious Revolution in England are notes for a powerfully suggestive sermon he preached on April 14, entitled "The Mystery of Providence." He spoke on the cryptic prophetical text Ezekiel 1:16: "The fashion of the wheels and their work was like unto a chrysolite: and they four had one form, and their fashion, and their work was as one wheel in another wheel." He justified the Revolution by interpreting the wheels as the state of human affairs, intricately moved by God's providence "for the Best Issue and event that can be, His own glory." Perhaps more personally, he preached that those chosen by God are sometime brought low, but then "the wheel turns again, upon the Foes of God." His surviving notes leave unclear, however, whether he tried to rouse his congregation to rise against Andros. "Men do Gods Business," he told them, "when they go on their own Errands"—rather ambiguous counsel which might be construed as advising either rebellion or quietism.

Four days later, on April 18, Cotton Mather apparently was to be arrested. The same day, Boston took arms against Andros's government. Mather left no account of his direct part in the revolt, but Randolph later repeatedly accused him of being one of the "chief designers." Randolph claimed that although the uprising was defended as "the act of all the people," it was actually plotted by some prominent church members, some older magistrates, and six ministers: the Baptist minister Milborne, and the Congregationalist ministers Moodey, Morton, Allen, Willard, and "young Mather." (Mather was now twenty-six, while the average age of the other Congregationalist ministers Randolph mentions was nearly sixty.) Randolph even charged that on the night of April 17, Mather held a meeting of armed men at his house.

Whatever Cotton Mather's part in fomenting the revolt, on the morning of April 18 the captain of the frigate *Rose,* a warship guarding Boston Harbor, was seized, to prevent the ship's either firing on or sailing from

Boston. (Andros planned to escape on the ship to France, it was rumored, leaving the city open to French attack.) News of the captain's detainment, a contemporary said, ran "like Lightning" through Boston, inspiring "the most unanimous Resolution." Drums beat a call to arms, small groups rounded up supporters of Andros, and by midafternoon more than a thousand armed colonists swarmed in from Charlestown.

Cotton Mather spent much of the day in the Council chamber of the Town House, the pillared two-story civic center at the heart of the South End. There the Boston ministers and other prominent citizens formed a revolutionary council, including the octogenarian Simon Bradstreet, who had been governor before the charter was revoked. Around noon a statement was read from the gallery to a crowd assembled in the street below, entitled a "Declaration of the Gentlemen, Merchants, and Inhabitants of Boston and the Country Adjacent." Contemporary sources differ on whether this statement was prepared a few days before the uprising or in the heat of it. Mather's part in composing and delivering it is also highly arguable. Some later writers have ascribed it to him but no evidence whatsoever exists that he wrote it; the style sometimes sounds like his, sometimes not. The author or authors of the Declaration would be worth knowing, for he or they composed a deeply innovative political document. The Declaration marks a secular drift in New England political thought from the theological and providential treatment of affairs to constitutional and legal ones, and from a communal conception of the rights belonging to God's Chosen People to a conception of the rights of Englishmen. It also launches a New England revolutionary tradition that would culminate in 1776.

All that can confidently be said is that Cotton Mather enthusiastically approved of the Declaration. Its pacific sentiments appealed to his wish, in defiance of his underlying anger, to act the part of the meek conciliator. He also feared and disapproved rash action that might be both bloody and politically damaging to a New England already too well-known abroad for its alleged disorderliness. Especially, as a "Gentleman" himself, he scorned an armed rural mob. He and the other gentlemen hoped to contain the revolt, avoid bloodshed, and safeguard the political prisoners while awaiting instructions from England. As Mather later summed up their thinking, the gentlemen agreed that although New England had as compelling grounds for a revolution as Old England, yet they would if possible extinguish any popular attempt at an *"Insurrection,"* awaiting orders from London. But "if the Country people, by any unrestrainable Violences" pushed toward revolution, then to prevent bloodshed by an "ungoverned *Mobile*" they would appear with and present the Declaration.

As later printed, the *Declaration of the Gentlemen* (1689) consists of twelve brief articles. They treat the Andros administration as part of a larger effort to extinguish Protestantism in the name of Rome, and rehearse familiar grievances against the Dominion government: jail for refusing to swear on the Bible, revocation of land titles, Joseph Dudley's infamous statement in Council that New Englanders "were all *Slaves* and the only difference between them and *Slaves* is their not being bought and sold," and so on. While the gentlemen offer these grievances as justification for the seizure of government officials, they painstakingly explain that they intended only to secure the officials for the fate decided upon at home, "for what Justice, Orders from his Highness with the *Parliament* shall direct." New Englanders, the document makes plain in every way, are not revolutionaries, but orderly, loyal subjects of the king.

Whether Cotton Mather wrote the Declaration or not, he probably delivered it from the gallery of the Town House. He went there, according to his son Samuel, when it became clear to the provisional council that the people had become "driving and furious," and he "reasoned down the Passions of the Populace." Had he "lisped" a syllable against those who had tried to jail him, Samuel said, perhaps "the People would by a sudden *Council of War* have try'd, judg'd and hang'd all those ill Men, who would have treated him otherwise."

Cotton Mather seems to have been at the Town House also when, apparently later in the day, Andros himself was brought from the fort on Fort Hill. When the governor demanded to know the reason for the uprising, he was told, by one account, that Bostonians would have his government and that he was now a prisoner. When asked to give orders for the surrender of the fort, he replied he would sooner die. Mather was certainly present when Randolph was brought in, for Randolph later recorded that he found Mather there "writing orders" along with four other ministers. Because Andros refused to command the fort to surrender, it was decided to have Randolph deliver the command in Andros's name. Someone clapped a pistol to Randolph's head and threatened to shoot him if he refused. He was forced to go, and the garrison at the fort surrendered. When Randolph's captors demanded that he deliver the same false message at Castle William, in the harbor, he did so, but those at the Castle held out for a day before capitulating.

By then apparently thousands on foot and horse had poured into Boston from the countryside, in "rage and heat," by one account, insisting that Andros be chained and imprisoned in the fort, as he was. Randolph and the interim governor Joseph Dudley were detained, together with as many as fifty other sympathizers and supporters. By nightfall the Dominion of New England had ceased to exist, and Boston again lay under Puritan rule, ending a revolt that was managed, Mather said emphatically later, "without the least *Bloodshed* or *Plunder,* and with as much *Order* as ever attended any *Tumult,* it may be, in the World."

*

Having filled his father's place at the front line during the revolt, Cotton Mather stayed there in the unsettled period afterward, especially in his role as peacemaker. The toppling of King James following the revocation of the charter left Massachusetts' form of government uncertain. Some New Englanders called for independence of the mother country, others for a military government; but most desired to return to the charter government that had existed before Andros. In the confusion, public affairs were conducted by the Town House group that styled itself a Council for Safety of the People and Conservation of Peace, most of whose members doubted the wisdom and legality of returning to the charter. Beset by demands for resumption, however, the council tried to resolve the issue by calling a convention of town representatives. The convention voted to reinstate the pre-Andros government, but because several towns had not submitted their views and others had failed to instruct their delegates, a second, larger convention was gathered. It began meeting in Boston on May 22, the time when for over fifty years, except under Andros, Massachusetts Puritans had held their annual election.

Cotton Mather preached to the convention the next day. The occasion was doubly momentous. Not only was Massachusetts to decide its form of government, but to give this annual election sermon was also one of the highest civic honors afforded the clergy. At twenty-six, Mather was by far the youngest minister to do so in the history of colonial Massachusetts. Conscious of addressing "as much of New England in this great congregation as can well be reach'd by the voice of one address," he acknowledged his youth: "For my own part, I confess my self but a *Child,* and among the meanest, the smallest of your *children* too." His feeling of inadequacy was probably compounded by uncertainty, for despite popular determination to reinstate the charter, he seems to have felt that it had been legally annulled, and to have grasped that the question must ultimately be decided by Parliament. He thus did not recommend a form of government to the convention himself, but rather described the spirit in which the debate should be conducted. The convention, as had been feared, opened in heated division and contention. This contention Mather depicted as itself the most dangerous of the many provoking evils for which God had been punishing New England by fire, drought, and civil strife. Passionately imploring each man to stop considering his scheme of government best and accept the other man's as next best, he pleaded for peace:

> He that Considers the Feverish *Paroxysms* which this Land is now raging in, through mere Misunderstandings about the *Means* leading to the *End* wherein we are generally agreed, and how ready we are to treat one another with fiery Animosities, had need cry, *Peace, Peace!* . . . I am old enough to cry *Peace!* and in the Name of God I do it. *Peace!* my dear Country-men; Let there be *Peace* in all our *Studies, Peace* in all our *Actions,* and *Peace* notwithstanding all our Differences.

Many who heard the sermon, his son Samuel wrote later, "fell into Tears and the whole Body of the People present immediately united in the *Methods of Peace* Mr. MATHER proposed unto them." Even so, Mather was probably not pleased by the outcome. Next day at least forty-two of the fifty-one towns represented voted to maintain the "rights and privileges" of Massachusetts by returning to the old charter, and reappointed the aged Simon Bradstreet as governor.

Whatever his doubts about the wisdom of the vote, Cotton Mather remained politically conspicuous under this restored but temporary government. From his pulpit he continued to justify the revolt against the "*Arbitrary disposals* of four or five Men, that beyond all measure hated us." He drafted a document proclaiming a day of Thanksgiving for the "Restoration of our Lately Invaded Liberties," and probably also had a hand in writing two addresses felicitating William and Mary on the success of the Revolution in England. He must also have helped produce *The Present State of New-English Affairs* (1689), a broadside containing a letter to him from his father. Here Increase described his interview with the new king in July, at which William "*kindly*" accepted the revolt in Boston and said, hedgingly, that New Englanders "*Should have their Ancient Rights and Privileges Restored and Confirmed unto them*"—if it were in his power.

Cotton Mather remained a prominent political figure also in the eyes of Andros's former underlings and supporters, some of whom referred to Mather privately as "the young Pope." Joseph Dudley, a native New Englander whose service under Andros made him much reviled, wrote to Mather twice in June 1689 from jail, seeking his influence in "rolling away the stone from the mouth of this Sepulchre, where I am buried alive." Randolph, in jail himself, wrote to London complaining that "young Mr. Mather" and "others of the gang" continued to promote anti-monarchical principles, "and will oppose all commands from their Majesties which will not serve their interest (by them called the interest of Jesus Christ)." Other supporters of Andros accused Mather of stirring up hostility toward Church of England members in Boston. King's Chapel, the Anglican church for which subscriptions were raised under Andros, had opened for worship in June, just after the revolt. Its minister, Samuel Myles, charged Mather with fomenting acts of desecration against the building: "Young Mr. Mather informs the people that the reason of all our Calamities is permitting of the high place [i.e., the Church of England] among us, to this purpose hath he spoken in public several times of late." The new chapel, he said, was already "battered and shattered," its windows no sooner mended than broken again.

In July the king sent an order recalling Andros, Randolph, Dudley, and the others seized in the revolt to England, there to answer any complaints against them. Their removal did nothing to improve political affairs in Boston, for the temporary government under Simon Bradstreet proved unstable and ineffectual, a continuing source of contention. Letters from Boston in the summer after the revolt abound in such comments as "All is confusion here" or "Every man is a Governor." Compounding the confusion, King William declared war on France in the summer of 1689, after only three months of his reign. The war spilled over into the colonies, opening seventy years of European warfare in America and exposing New England to a new invasion, this time, Mather wrote, from "whole Armies of Indians and Gallic Blood Hounds." Mather was dining at Samuel Sewall's house in February 1690 when Governor Bradstreet brought confirmation of news of the destruction of Schenectady by the French and Indians, with the massacre of sixty persons, and reports of pregnant women ripped up and of children having their brains dashed out or freezing to death during a march to Albany. In mid-March came news of a French-Indian attack on Salmon Falls, killing or capturing eighty persons and burning all the houses.

To eliminate France from America became for Protestant New England not only a victory over Catholicism and a dream of safety, but also a means of showing loyalty to William and gaining his favor for a new charter. Cotton Mather actively supported the Bradstreet government's decision to launch expeditions against Canada, regarded by many, he said, as "the seminary of our troubles from the Indians." On March 20, 1690, he delivered a rousing speech to the General Court recommending the Canada expedition as "a great Service to be done for their Majesties: K. WILLIAM, and Q. MARY, whom God grant long to Reign." His language illustrates the underlying significance to him and others of the revolt of 1689: once stubbornly independent, Massachusetts was becoming an enthusiastic member of the English Empire.

The expedition was led by a member of the North Church, Sir William Phips. In May he took Port Royal and forced the inhabitants to swear allegiance to the English crown. His success emboldened more ambitious moves against Montreal and Quebec. These failed dismally. A large new fleet under Phips, thirty-two vessels with about two thousand men, sailed in early August, a month after alarming rumors of a French landing at Cape Cod, and near the end of a smallpox epidemic that took some 320 lives. Everything went wrong: smallpox erupted, commanders disagreed, supplies ran out, tempestuous weather mauled the ships. Phips estimated that by disease and casualty he lost two hundred men, but other estimates run as high as a thousand. The troops who survived returned to Boston unpaid and mutinous, and complaining of neglect, of men found dead in holes before they were missed, some having their eyes and cheeks eaten by cats. The treasury of Massachusetts, moreover, squandered fifty thousand pounds. To pay for the war the government levied heavy taxes. The disastrous expedition left Massachusetts at the end of 1690 feeling more vulnerable than ever, burdened by an unstable government, a depleted treasury, an exultant enemy on its borders, mourning in many homes, and the sense of a miserable defeat.

In this edgy atmosphere, dissatisfaction with Bradstreet's shaky interim government greatly increased. Despite his many calls for peace, Cotton Mather may have covertly contributed to the unrest, for he was accused of being the author of *Publick Occurrences,* sometimes called the first American newspaper. On its appearance in September, Bradstreet and the Council instantly ordered the paper suppressed, on the grounds that it was unlicensed, contained doubtful reports of events, and criticized the government. One specific objection seems to have been a report of the Canada expedition to the effect that the Mohawk Indians allied with the English failed to supply the canoes they had promised and lied about providing additional forces. The government, the paper suggested, had "too much confided" in these "miserable Savages."

Cotton Mather found that people believed he wrote the paper. The

government, aware that his name was being "tossed about it," issued a
severe proclamation, whose first line "thunders against *some,*" Mather
said (interpreting "some" as himself), "that had published that scandalous thing." Yet he admitted agreeing with the criticism of the Mohawks
and said he considered the newspaper "noble, useful, and laudable." In
fact, his denial, as he gave it to his uncle John Cotton, sounds slippery:
"the publisher had not one line of it from me, only as accidentally meeting him in the high-way, on his request, I showed him how to contract
and express the report of the expedition." Whether or not he wrote the
paper, he took the accusation as an expression of ingratitude toward himself, "who have deserved so very ill of the country," and it awakened fears
of tarnishing his ministry: "a few such tricks will render me uncapable of
serving either God or man in New England."

*

The gap in Cotton Mather's diaries during this tumultuous time makes
for a surprising contrast. Where his diaries break off in 1687 they depict a
newly married young minister hungry for applause but agitated by religious doubt, worried about his father's health, cautious about his speech,
and disturbed by morbid nightmares. But when he appears again in the
accounts of others after his father's flight to England, he is a "young
Pope," threatened with jail for seditious libels, "writing orders" on a
revolutionary council, calming angry mobs.

Although this contrast, we shall see, is less drastic than it seems, these
years did bring Cotton Mather several maturative experiences beside the
political ones. Early in 1688, his and Abigail's five-month-old child, "perhaps One of the Comeliest Infants that have been seen in the world,"
died of "Convulsions." Committed to the idea that a minister must be an
example to his flock, he preached the same afternoon on the nature of
affliction, offering his hearers "such considerations as I would this day
quiet my own tempestuous, rebellious heart with," namely that affliction
is meant to induce us to seek the reasons for His chastisement. Yet he had
looked often on the infant's "Lovely Features and Actions," and he acknowledged that "few outward, earthly anguishes are equal to these. The
dying of a Child is like the tearing of a limb from us."

In October 1689, Cotton Mather also journeyed to Salem to attend his
dying nineteen-year-old brother Nathanael. Endowed with the Mathers'
prophetic streak, Nathanael had had a strange presage of early death, and
since at least early fall had been seriously ill, apparently with a malignant

tumor on his hip. A relentless scholar, he studied, in his own description, until "*He thought his Bones would all fall asunder.*" An incision had been made on his hip, which Cotton believed gave good hope of recovery; but Nathanael's continual sedentary studies, he said, had produced "*putrid Juices*" in his blood, which the incision circulated, giving rise to a fever which ended his life. Cotton admired his brother's learning, but saw in him a reprehensible contempt for his health. He disapproved of Nathanael's being less a pattern to young students than a caution, "for it may be truly written on his Grave, *Study kill'd him.*" Taking this "humble Self loathing Young-Man" as both a model of piety and a warning against self-abuse, within two weeks after Nathanael's death he had compiled a biography of him, *Early Piety Exemplified,* which he sent to his father for publication in London, the first of his works to be published abroad.

Never able to "*do enough,*" Cotton Mather recognized a similar tendency to self-abuse in himself. Indeed, while embroiled in decisive political affairs and tending a large flock he did much else. He drafted documents for others, sat on church councils, joined an association of ministers in Cambridge, became in 1690 a Fellow of Harvard College, and partook in a pamphlet war against some Quakers (one of whom dubbed him "*The College-Boy of New-England*"). He also bought a new house and land, where he would live nearly the next thirty years, for the substantial sum of two hundred pounds. He had scarcely moved in before he invited to stay with him and Abigail a tormented young girl whom he tried by fervent prayer to depossess of devils (see the next chapter). Between 1689 and 1691 he also published some twenty-two titles, not to mention an extremely ambitious series of twenty connected sermons on typology which he composed and preached between August 1688 and November the following year. Increase felt that people were unreasonable in giving Cotton more work than his "weak" constitution could manage and that he was but "too apt to comply with their desires." Thus aware of his son's desire to please, he feared that his prolonged stay abroad might shorten Cotton's life. Twice from London he wrote to John Richards, probably the most prominent member of the North Church, imploring him: "do not Let him kill Himself. He will do it, if you do not hinder him." In fact the strain and overwork told. Partly by "excessive Toil" in his ministry, Cotton wrote in April 1692, "My *Health,* has been lamentably broken for diverse Years."

Much of this may suggest new boldness and authority in Cotton Mather during his father's absence. Yet when writing to Increase in May 1690, he seems hardly the same person who, two months earlier, had exhorted the government to attack Canada:

> But have you indeed come to resolutions of seeing New England no more? . . . I am sorry for myself, who am left alone in the midst of more cares, fears, anxieties, than, I believe, any one person in these territories, and who have just now been within a few minutes of death by a very dangerous fever, the relics whereof are yet upon me.

This whining manipulation of his father's concern for his health was apparently the reply to a prior letter from Increase, in which he raised before his son the dread prospect of his permanent settlement in England, because of criticism at home of his labors for the charter and inadequate payment. Identifying himself in his reply with "This distressed, enfeebled, ruined country," Cotton petitioned Increase to return on behalf of all New England, pleading that the country (himself included) had resolved not only to repay "our debts, which our affairs in your hands have made," but also such a requital "of all your pains for us, as would have been proper when you should have arrived here." Having learned Increase's lessons well, he closed with a veiled death threat:

> I confess that I write with a most ill-boding jealousy that I shall never see you again in this evil world; and it overwhelms me into tears which cannot be dried up, unless by this consideration, That you will shortly find among the spirits of just men made perfect, Your son. . . .

Cotton Mather's missing diaries in this period leave his inner life hidden. Yet this anxious, exploitative letter suggests that much of the difference between "the young Pope" and the uncertain young minister was that between others' view of Cotton Mather and his view of himself. While temporarily assuming his father's place in public affairs, he remained inwardly deferential and unconfident, and yearned for Increase to return.

While awaiting his father, Cotton Mather was nearly forced to flee to England himself. Rumors spread that the king would appoint as the new governor Sir Edmund Andros or Colonel Charles Kirk. The possible resurrection of Andros was frightening; he and his crew, Increase remarked later, would have "revenged themselves on and murdered the best men in New England." But the possible advent of "That Monster *Kirk*," as Cotton Mather called him, was horrendous. To Kirk were attributed such atrocities as having hanged ninety wounded men and having executed thirty more by tens during an officers' dinner, upon successive toasts to the king, the queen, and Lord Jeffreys. When these rumors reached Boston, seemingly in the fall of 1691, they set off other rumors that Increase Mather had sent for his family, or that Cotton had been bound over in jail awaiting the new governor's vengeful pleasure. In fact Cotton awaited certain news, having decided that if Andros was returned, he and half a dozen important persons would flee to England.

The rumors came to nothing, for on Saturday evening, May 14, 1692, Increase Mather returned from London aboard the frigate *Nonesuch,* bringing with him his young son Samuel and the new governor, Sir William Phips, the former leader of the disastrous Canada campaign. Eight companies of troops escorted Phips to his house, then brought Increase to his. Cotton's pleasure and relief in his father's return was very likely dampened by illness, justifying his father's concern for his health. Just two weeks earlier he felt so overcome by "Vapour" and "an aguish Indisposition" that he could see "nothing but a *speedy Death* approaching." Ill or not, he wrote on the evening of his father's return: "*Oh! what shall I render to the Lord, for all his Benefits!*"

Increase's four years abroad had not made him less disgruntled, or less awesome to his son. Perhaps with both himself and Cotton in mind, only three months after his return he was again warning his congregation that the "faithful ministers of God are no less subject to death than other men," and that "Prophets may be killed by laying too great burdens on them." Dissatisfied anew with Boston, he began within a year having prophetic inklings of his return to England and prayed for encouraging signs, although now reluctant to leave because of the dangerous voyage and the anguish of departing again from his family, "and most of all the thoughts of leaving my son Cotton." Eight days after Increase's return, Cotton recorded in his notebook "My dear Fathers first Sermon, after his Arrival." In a blotchy, uncharacteristically infirm hand that suggests illness he took twenty-five pages of notes—the lengthiest entry among the hundreds of sermons he set down. And instead of entering the sermon serially with those of other ministers he had recorded during the year, he placed it in the middle of the notebook, numbering the page as "1," as if beginning a new year, a new existence. For eighteen months following he recorded virtually his father's sermons alone. A thirty-year-old man who had led a political revolt, he sat in church time after time writing down his father's words, taking over three hundred pages of notes on Increase's sermons.

If the Mathers had not changed, the governor had. Sir William Phips's speech upon landing, presumably in the candlelit Town House, made an auspicious contrast to the arrival of the scarlet-coated Andros. By one account he said that God had sent him to New England to serve his country, and that "all the privileges and laws and liberties as was practical [i.e., practiced] in the days of Old should be as they were before." Auspiciously too, as he was reading aloud his commission as governor he noticed that the sun was setting, marking the beginning of the Sabbath; he stopped reading, explaining that "he would not Infringe upon the lords day." It greatly pleased Cotton Mather also to have as governor a man "whom I baptised . . . and one of my own Flock, and one of my dearest Friends." (Phips had grown up in a frontier community lacking a settled minister, and had been baptized by Cotton Mather in adulthood.) That Increase and the other agents had been allowed to nominate several members of the governor's Council also promised renewed cooperation between the government and the clergy, Moses and Aaron: "instead, of my being made a Sacrifice to wicked *Rulers,* all the *Councellors* of the Province, are of my own Father's Nomination; and my *Father-in-Law,* with several *related* unto me, and several *Brethren* of my own church, are among them."

Cotton Mather also considered the new charter obtained by his father better than the former one. In fact, although Increase lacked diplomatic experience or training, his vigorous persistence had prevailed against court intrigues, wrangling, and betrayals to win what he considered a favorable charter for Massachusetts. In April 1691, he had presented New England's case personally before Queen Mary, stressing the country's willingness to enlarge the crown's dominion in America and its need for a settled government; the same month, in the king's bedchamber, he asked William "that they may be restored to their ancient privileges." On November 4, 1691, he formally accepted the new charter in the name of New England, in the king's presence. The best political minds he could consult, he said later, counselled him to "*Take your NEW CHARTER and be Thankful for it!*"

Encouragement to accept the charter was needed, for it differed from the old charter in undeniably essential ways. King William did not completely abandon the stricter colonial policy inaugurated by his predecessor, Charles II, at the Restoration. Although he allowed the Massachusetts agents to nominate Phips, the new charter empowered the sovereign to appoint a governor, lieutenant governor, and secretary. The appointed governor was given large powers himself, including a veto over acts of the General Court, and his consent was necessary for the appointment of all other officers nominated by the Court. The charter also granted liberty of conscience to all Christians except Catholics and eliminated religious discrimination by tying suffrage to property. Even though the new governor belonged to the North Church, the irreducible meaning of the new charter was that Massachusetts was not a Wilderness Zion but a royal possession.

Opposition to the charter Increase accepted was widespread, including a faction that unrealistically insisted on nothing less than a restoration of the old charter. Increase preached many sermons justifying what he had done, scorning the ingratitude of New Englanders toward their public servants: "A Government has been settled among us. And, what an ungrateful generation of Men may think of it, I know not; but I am sure, Five years ago, such Favours, would have been of high Account with us." Cotton, defending at once the charter and his father, preached on June 9 before Phips and the new General Court, praising the charter for securing to the country "all *Christian Liberties,* and all *English Liberties."* He said nothing, however, about what had once been considered the distinctive liberties of New England, which now scarcely existed.

Cotton also wrote and circulated in manuscript, around 1692, four Aesopian beast fables, works even more un-Puritan than his gaudy early elegies but indicative of his love for entertaining tales and his unmistakable gift for narrative. One fable describes such favorable features of the new charter as its confirmation of earlier land titles and its provision for the election of the governor's Council by the lower house of the Assembly. Jupiter (King William) granted:

> that the birds might be everlastingly confirmed in their titles to their nests and fields. He offered that not so much as a twig should be plucked from any tree the birds would roost upon, without their own consent. He offered that the birds might constantly make their own laws, and annually choose their own rulers. . . . He offered that it should be made impossible for any to disturb the birds in singing of their songs to the praise of their Maker, for which they had sought liberty in the wilderness.

Despite this benignly pastoral vision of freedom and security under the new charter, in another fable Cotton presented Increase as Mercury at Jupiter's court, laboring to rebuild the sheeps' fold but finding it "necessary to comply with such directions as Jupiter . . . had given for the new shaping of the folds; otherwise he saw the poor sheep had been left without any folds at all." However Cotton wished to justify his father's energetic and unselfish work, there was no denying that Increase had accomplished not what he wanted but as much as he could.

The charter's full implications for Christian Israel would appear later.

For now, New England had another problem, unrelated but bedazzling. Increase Mather spoke of it in the first sermon he preached after his return, when he found the jails filled with accused witches. Recently invaded by Andros and Randolph, fire and smallpox, Quakers and Anglicans, French and Indians, New England amazedly faced a new invasion: "There is," as Cotton set down his father's dark words, "a power of Devils in our Air that are seeking to hurt us."

4

Letters of Thanks from Hell

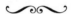

i

To COTTON MATHER and others, the enchantments that befell Salem Village early in 1692 seemed to repeat some earlier bizarre events in Boston.
Three and a half years before, soon after his father's flight to London,
Mather had visited the young daughter of a Boston mason named John
Goodwin. When he tried to pray with the girl she turned deaf and could
not hear again until the prayer ended. She and three more of Goodwin's
six children had become subjects of widespread comment and amazement. Scores of spectators saw their necks twist almost around or gazed
on such tortures as Mather described:

> One while their Tongues would be drawn down their Throats; another-
> while they would be pull'd out upon their Chins, to a prodigious length.
> They would have their Mouths opened unto such a Wideness, that their
> Jaws went out of joint; and anon they would clap together with a Force
> like that of a strong Spring-Lock. The same would happen to their Shoul-
> der-Blades, and their Elbows, and Hand-wrists, and several of their joints.
> They would at times ly in a benummed condition; and be drawn together
> as those that are ty'd Neck and Heels; and presently be stretched out, yea,
> drawn Backwards, to such a degree that it was fear'd the very skin of their
> Bellies would have crack'd.

These afflictions had begun after Goodwin's eldest daughter questioned
a laundress who was suspected of stealing family linens. The washerwom-
an's mother in turn "bestow'd very bad Language" on the Goodwin girl,
who was immediately taken with fits, which soon after seized three other
Goodwin children as well.

83

Thus Goody Glover, "an ignorant and a scandalous old Woman," as Mather described her, was tried for bewitching the Goodwin children. An Irish Catholic, she understood English but could speak only Gaelic, and conveyed her meaning through an interpreter. Small images were exhibited that had been found in her house, "Puppets, or Babies," Mather said, "made of Rags, and stuff'd with Goat's hair." She acknowledged that to torment objects of her malice she stroked the images with her finger, wetted with spittle. When she handled an image in court, one of the Goodwin children fell into fits. The judges asked whether she had assistants: "looking very pertly in the Air," Mather reported, she replied she had, and then confessed, "that she had One, who was her Prince." The court appointed five or six physicians to examine her and advise on her sanity. They found her sane, and she was sentenced to death.

As Glover lay in jail awaiting execution, Cotton Mather visited her twice. Driven by both curiosity and duty, he hoped to learn about the invisible world, to satisfy himself that her confession was credible, and to persuade her to repent her witchcraft. He asked many questions; after long silence, speaking through an interpreter, she said she wished to answer "but *they* would not give her leave." When he asked, "*They!* Who is that *They?*" she said "They" were her saints or spirits (the same Gaelic word, he noted, served for both). She never denied practicing witchcraft, but revealed little more to him than that she had attended meetings with five others, including "her Prince." He exhorted her to break her covenant with Hell and give herself to Christ. He asked a reasonable thing, she said, but she could not do it, nor without her spirits' permission could she desire or consent to his prayers. He prayed with her anyway, for which she thanked him with many good words. But he no sooner left, he recorded later, "than she took a stone, a long and slender stone, and with her Finger and Spittle fell to tormenting it."

Glover warned that because others cooperated in the witchcraft her execution would not relieve the Goodwin children. After her hanging their torments multiplied. They barked like dogs, purred like cats, fluttered like geese, "carried with an incredible Swiftness thro the Air, having but just their Toes now and then upon the ground, and their Arms waved like the Wings of a Bird." As though mad they climbed high fences. One of the boys groaned of being roasted on a spit run through his mouth and out his foot, shrieked that knives cut him, had his head invisibly nailed to the floor, "that it was as much as a strong man could do to pull it up." Although many observed these seizures, including several ministers, Mather was kept away by other business. Yet he wished to ease the tortured children, and hoped to gather eyewitness evidence to confute skeptics. He took the eldest Goodwin child, Martha, about thirteen years old, into the three-story home he had recently bought for himself and Abigail. The first few days she behaved normally, indeed seemed pious and industrious. But on the morning of November 20 she cried, "Ah, *They* have found me out!"

At once Martha Goodwin's fits resumed, only now in Cotton Mather's house. She would choke on a ball the size of a small egg; when she tried to bite a roasted apple her arms stiffened; she flew and dove, reeled and spewed as if drunk. They, she announced, were scheming a fall or blow or other harm to Abigail. Two phenomena fascinated Mather especially, the first involving an invisible chain. They would chain Martha and haul her from her seat toward the fire. When he stomped the hearth she screamed, protesting that he jarred the chain and hurt her back. He managed—as he would not be allowed to forget—to defend her from the chain: "Once I did with my own hand," he wrote, "knock it off, as it began to be fastened about her." They also brought Martha a horse, upon which she sprang and, settling in a riding posture, sometimes ambled, sometimes trotted, sometimes galloped furiously. "In these motions we could not perceive that she was stirred by the stress of her feet, upon the ground; for often she touch't it not." Once she rode up the stairs through the open door of his study, where she dismounted and exclaimed, "They are gone; they are gone! They say, that they cannot,—God won't let 'em come here!" Self-possessed again she sat in the study reading Scripture and pious books much of the afternoon. But when she returned downstairs "the Daemons were in a quarter of a minute as bad upon her as before, and her Horse was Waiting for her." Mather tried to return her to his study, but she became "twisted and writhen," weighed three times as much as before, was pulled from his hands and shoved on him, and he at last dragged her up the stairs only with help and by "incredible Forcing" while she screamed, "They say I must not go in!" As soon as she entered she stood up and said, in an altered tone, "now I am well."

However amazed by the workings of the invisible world, Mather remained alertly curious and made some wary experiments. He realized he might easily "be too bold, and go too far"; but he also saw an opportunity to propose and solve many "Problems which the pneumatic Discipline is concerned in." He tested the devils' telepathic abilities, although inconclusively. That devils can read thoughts was indicated when he called Martha by name, having in mind some religious expedient for her relief. Her neck went limp, as if broken, and he could not revive her until he "laid aside my purpose of speaking what I thought." A different experiment, however, indicated that devils had no telepathic power. When the Goodwin children were being undressed, the body part involved became so contorted there was "no coming at it." To see what would happen if one thing were thought but another thing said, an instruction was given to untie the child's neckcloth, followed by the untying of the child's shoe. Yet what became "strangely inaccessible" was not the shoe but the neckcloth. The conflicting results led Mather to speculate that some devils could read thoughts, others not, and that "Perhaps all Devils are not alike sagacious." He particularly wanted to determine Martha's ability to read religious books. Although such book tests were used as evidence of witchcraft or possession, he regarded them as a "fanciful Business" that devils might use as an ingenious trap. Just the same the book tests worked. When Martha tried to read the Bible her eyes became "strangely twisted and blinded." She could read from Quaker or Catholic books, but the sight of John Cotton's *Milk for Babes* convulsed her. And when she opened Increase Mather's *Mystery of Christ* she was "immediately struck backwards as dead upon the floor."

Even more than Cotton Mather hoped to learn about the invisible world he hoped to depossess Martha and the other "Haunted Children" by fervent and repeated prayer. But devotional exercises held for her relief were the worst of all the provocations that could be given her. When prayers were begun, "the Devils would still throw her on the Floor, at the feet of him that prayed." To drown out the prayers she whistled, sang, and made odd noises, beating and kicking whoever prayed although her fist and foot always recoiled a few hairs breadths from him, as if rebounding against a wall. As prayer continued she lay for dead, "her Belly swelled like a Drum, and sometimes with croaking Noises in it." Nevertheless, and despite several seeming cures followed by relapses, the prayers of Mather and the other Boston ministers ultimately restored the Goodwin children. John Goodwin, regretting that his daughter had been to Mather "but a troublesome guest," publicly thanked him, grateful that "his bowels so yearned towards us in this sad condition."

Mather's experience with Martha Goodwin had important results in his life. The five or six weeks she spent in his home brought him first-hand experience of evil spirits, and he resolved "after this, never to use but just one grain of patience with any man that shall go to impose upon me a Denial of Devils, or of Witches." In January 1691, too, Martha was herself admitted to membership in his church. He also produced his first important book-length publication, *Memorable Providences, Relating to*

Witchcrafts and Possessions (1689). He clearly intended to write an important book on an important witchcraft case, comparable to works by outstanding English ministers and demonologists. He succeeded, for his bout with invisible horses and chains inspired him to some of his most absorbing narrative writing and his cleverest organization, the brief sections and lively pace overcoming the repetitiousness of the events. The work appeared in a second edition in London in 1691 and a third edition in Edinburgh in 1697, and was often remembered later as it merged into a broad stream of tales of the supernatural. The London edition contained a recommendation by the prestigious Richard Baxter, who rejoiced, Mather learned, to leave behind someone "likely to prove so great a Master Builder in the Lords Work."

The book had another important effect also. About eighteen months after it appeared, some other young girls became topics of comment and amazement as they too succumbed to convulsive fits. According to the minister John Hale, they were "in all things afflicted as bad as John Goodwin's children at Boston, in the year 1689. So that he that will read Mr. Mather's Book of *Memorable Providences,* page 3 etc., may Read part of what these Children, and afterward sundry grown persons suffered by the hand of Satan, at Salem Village, and parts adjacent."

*

The linking of Cotton Mather with the Salem witchcraft trials began in his own time and persists to the present. In the popular imagining of the American past the man and the event are nearly synonymous. Yet the exact connection between the two remains obscure. Two questions are involved: did Mather excite accusations of witchcraft at Salem? and did he promote the trial and sentencing of the witches? For the first, John Hale's remark suggests that at least some contemporaries viewed the eruption at Salem as Mather had taught them to see cases of witchcraft. At one peak of the trials, in June 1692, a man named Brodbent wrote from Boston that "young Mather spoke pretty true when he preached a sermon about two years ago that the old landlord Satan would Arrest the Country out of their hands." Robert Calef, Mather's angriest and most dogged critic, charged that by being "the most active and forward of any minister in the country" in the Goodwin case, and by printing his account of it, Mather "conduced much to the kindling of those flames" at Salem that "threatened the destruction of this country."

Even ignoring Calef's debatable accuracy as a historian and his personal antagonism to Mather, there remains no doubt that in the eighteen months or so between the Goodwin case and the Salem outbreaks, Mather kept calling public attention to the existence of devils and witches. In a last-minute "Notandum" added to *Memorable Providences* sometime after June 1689, he informed readers that since he had completed his history another "very wonderful Attempt" had been made on a different family in Boston, "(probably by Witchcraft)," and he speculated that God may have permitted it in order to expose more witches. His preaching can be charted to show that he continually reminded his congregation of a hostile invisible world. In 1690 he described how Quakers at their meetings are "taken with a strange *Quaking,* which look'd so like a *Diabolical Possession."* The same year he told a youth group that while he was preparing one of his works, "the *Devil* from the mouth of a possessed person, in the Audience of several standers-by, threatened me with much *Disgrace* for what I was about." Again in 1690, upon a new burst of fighting with the French and Indians, he preached that "The *Devils* are stark mad, that the *House of the Lord our God,* is come into these Remote Corners of the World; and they fume, they fret prodigiously." In 1691, warning against the public discontent that prevailed after the revolt, he asked, "How many doleful Wretches, have been decoy'd into *Witchcraft* it self, by the opportunities which their *Discontent* has given the *Devil,* to visit 'em and seduce 'em?" More examples from Mather's published and unpublished writings of 1690–92 could be cited. But these alone suggest that given the size of his congregation and the frequency of his preaching, he did much to keep alive in Massachusetts a sense of the malice of the invisible world.

Yet in preaching about devils in New England, Cotton Mather was not the first, and far from alone. Later history associates him with it because he published many of his sermons while other American Puritan ministers did not, although they held and preached similar ideas. The Charlestown minister Charles Morton, and three Boston ministers including Samuel Willard, wrote and endorsed a Preface to Mather's *Memorable Providences,* attesting that they had been "Eye and Ear-Witnesses" to many of the "most considerable things" in the Goodwin case as Mather described them. Morton, in one of his own sermons in 1688, told his congregation that in such disasters as droughts, God "improves Evil Angels as His Instruments and Executioners." Willard preached an entire series of sermons on devils in 1692. Increase Mather preached two such lengthy series, in 1683 and 1685.

More important, if obvious, belief in devils was not unique to Cotton Mather nor to New England Puritanism, but worldwide and ancient. According to a national Gallup poll taken in 1980, thirty-four percent of American adults believe in the devil as a personal being who directs evil forces. The possessed children in Boston and Salem represent only late, transatlantic instances of a vastly larger recurrence of witchcraft cases in Europe in the seventeenth century. In Bavaria, for example, a judge claimed the death of 274 witches in 1629; in Bonn, three- and four-year-old children were accused of having devils for lovers; at Bamberg a witch house and torture chamber were built and six hundred witches are said to have been burnt in ten years. Witchcraft cases were chronic in seventeenth-century America also, not only in New England but likewise in New York, Pennsylvania, and Virginia. Colonial courts tried more than eighty such cases from 1647 to 1691, resulting in twenty executions and many more fines, banishments, and whippings. Dozens of other episodes circulated by conversation and gossip. Their number clearly increased in New England during the 1680s, around the time of the Goodwin affair. Various sources tell of the devil appearing in 1684 to a Cambridge man, making a noise like a bird; of a 1683 case in Maine with ringing frying pans, mysterious arm bites, and floorboards buckled by invisible feet; of a fifty-year-old church deacon from Hadley who in 1684 suffered pinpricks and glossolalia, one of whose breasts was rendered like a woman's, and whose genitals were wounded or burned—and many more.

It must also be stressed that if the Salem possessions resembled those of the Goodwin children, both were in many features stereotypical. They conformed to a pattern classic in European outbreaks of witchcraft since at least the early sixteenth century. Almost invariably, the accuser and accused knew each other intimately, often as neighbors. The accuser had suffered some strange illness, accident, or other personal misfortune for which no natural explanation was apparent. He or she was aware, however, of having offended a neighbor, usually by having failed to discharge some hitherto customary social obligation, and accused the neighbor of having produced the illness or accident in revenge. The victims' symptoms were also stereotypical and monotonous—convulsions, speech difficulties, the sticking with or throwing up of pins and nails, appearances of cats, hogs, or other animals. On both sides of the Atlantic, finally, cases of witchcraft were distinctly community events. Whatever the behavior of ministers and magistrates, the responsibilty for prosecution and hanging ultimately rested on neighborhood people, who snooped on, accused, and gave evidence against each other. In their occasion, symptoms, and resolution, both the Goodwin affair and the Salem affair typify witchcraft cases throughout Europe and America throughout the seventeenth century. The enormous likelihood is that the girls at Salem would have become possessed, and their alleged tormentors would have been tried and hanged, had Cotton Mather never existed.

To us, the Goodwin children seem not possessed but turbulently rebellious. From the secular viewpoint of modern psychoanalysis and anthropology, their antics merely ventilated severely repressed desires and disapproved behavior. Similar demonic possessions of course still occur frequently in many cultures, preventing psychotic breaks with reality by affording underlying conflicts expression in a culturally shared idiom of spiritual beings which relates them to the people's larger religious life. Instead of driving the burdened person to an isolating private reality, the idiom of demonic possession allows inaccessible experiences to be made public and intelligible. Cotton Mather was unwittingly correct in equating diabolism with discontent, for much of the Goodwin children's behavior represented hostility toward Puritan standards. Through their fits they acted out with impunity the worst fears of those ministers who denounced the rising generation for wanting to explore sex, taunt their parents, and deride the ministry. "They" wanted Martha Goodwin "to keep Christmas with them!" so at Christmas Martha and her sister "were by the Daemons made very drunk." In Puritan New England, demonic possession was a culturally comprehensible and permissible assault on Puritan ideals, a jeremiad against the Jeremiad.

When read in the awareness of a society that demanded utter submission from the young, Cotton Mather's account of the Goodwin children becomes a tale of sassy adolescents who loathed washing their hands, going to bed, or doing their chores:

> If any useful thing were to be done to them, or by them, they would have all sorts of Troubles fall upon them. . . . at whiles, they would be so managed in their Beds, that no Bed-clothes could for an hour or two be laid upon them; nor could they go to wash their Hands, without having them clasp't so oddly together, there was no doing of it. . . . Whatever Work they were bid to do, they would be so snap't in the member which was to do it, that they with grief still desisted from it. If one ordered them to Rub a clean Table, they were able to do it without any disturbance; if to rub a dirty Table, presently they would with many Torments be made uncapable.

Puritan religious life also angered the children. When John Goodwin spoke to one of his sons about going to church, Mather wrote, "the Boy would be cast into such Tortures and Postures, that he would sooner Die than go out of doors." When Martha treated Mather with a "Sauciness that I had not been used to," when she knocked at his study door saying someone wished to see him although no one was there, when she called to him impertinently and threw small things at him, Mather rightly intuited that her tormentors designed "to disturb me in what I was about." These were no ethereal tormentors, however, but the restless spirit inside Martha and her generation, who would in his lifetime cease whistling and kicking and begin satirizing the ministry in essays, poems, and mock sermons. Martha Goodwin's heir in Boston, stripped of the grotesque legitimating guise of demonic possession, was the archetypal rebellious adolescent Benjamin Franklin.

Mather and his contemporaries of course located the source of Martha's behavior elsewhere, in an ever present, ever malicious world of invisible devils. Like others, Mather often wrote and preached about them, drawing his ideas from Scripture, patristic writings, demonological treatises, and notes on his father's sermons, but often adding his own speculations. Devils are the moving force in witchcraft, as Mather defined it: "the Doing of *Strange* (and for the most part *Ill*) Things by the help of *evil Spirits, Covenanting* with (and usually *Representing* of) the woful Children of Men." For him and most others the essence of witchcraft was this diabolic covenant, a parody of Christian practice, wherein witches promise to serve devils and devils promise to aid witches. The witch has no innate magical power, but can act only by virtue of the confederacy; not the witch but the devil produces the supernatural events in witchcraft.

Mather held the traditional Christian view that devils are fallen angels: "A *Devil* was once an *Angel,* but Sin has brought him to be a *Fallen* Angel; an Angel full of Enmity to God and man." Devils represent an entire order of creation, like human beings or animals, and can think and go about. They are confined as punishment to the several miles of dark air above the earth, where they mingle with the tormented souls of millions upon millions of the damned, excommunicated from the company of good angels, who dwell in heaven near God's throne. The fact that some men have been saved while they are damned fills the evil angels with tormented malice toward mankind, against whom they act with pitiless cruelty. Their number far exceeds the numbers of humanity, about whom they "*swarm* like the Frogs of *Egypt* in every chamber of our houses." Since the myriads of devils are united in one enmity, however, we speak as if there were one devil, "as we say, The Turk, or the Spaniard." One or many, they welcome an opportunity to do mischief in the world: "These are they by whom Witches do exert their Devillish and malignant Rage upon their Neighbours."

In their physical natures, devils as Mather conceived them were "a *spiritual* and a *rational* Substance." The definition may seem self-contradictory, but by "spiritual" Mather did not mean immaterial. Rather, like the Cambridge Platonists Joseph Glanvill and Henry More, he meant something between current popular conceptions of matter and spirit: the finest imaginable materiality, light and invisible, capable of being detached from or infused into more solid substances. To Mather, "spirit" also connoted vigor, and especially when he speaks of devils as spirits he intends not some limp fog but the acrid quickness of "spirits" of ammonia. Devils are vivacious agents who "dart" or "buzz" blasphemous thoughts into the mind, always in motion to undo men's souls, filling the air like midsummer flies.

Mather's view of the devil as "a *spiritual* and a *rational* Substance" intensified his desire to witness and publicize cases of witchcraft. To many persons of his time, the philosophical assumptions used to disprove a belief in witches threatened to deny the reality of Spirit itself. Disbelief in witchcraft joined declining manners, radical political theories, and the new science in becoming linked with forms of atheism. A logic that ran No Witches, No Spirit, No God, guides Thomas Browne's remark that those who deny witches "do not only deny them, but Spirits; and are obliquely and upon consequence a sort not of Infidels, but Atheists." As Mather himself told his congregation, "Since there are Witches and Devils, we may conclude that there are also Immortal Souls." He and others often identified doubts about Spirit with the ancient sect of the Sadducees, who in the time of Christ denied the resurrection of the dead and the existence of angels. Sadducism in the late seventeenth century became a code word for atheistical tendencies, and in the 1680s the target of a burgeoning literature in England. Mather's *Memorable Providences* belongs with such works as Nathaniel Crouch's *The Kingdom of Darkness: or The History of Daemons, Specters, Witches . . . obviating the common Objections and Allegations of the Sadduces [sic] and Atheists of the Age* (1688)—one of many works that assert the reality of supernatural phenomena as an indirect way of defending Christianity itself. Mather even reasons in *Memorable Providences* that God allowed devils to torment the Goodwin children expressly to give modern atheism the lie: "The Devils themselves are by Compulsion come to confute the Atheism and Sadducism, and to reprove the Madness of ungodly men."

Mather also longed to receive such "Letters of Thanks from Hell" because he sometimes doubted the reality of Spirit himself. Like every Puritan he found that during his conversion and his later growth in grace, the devil darted blasphemous thoughts into his mind. He had resolved at the age of eighteen to strive for a sharper sense of the *"Reality of Invisibles"* and had prayed during the religious crisis at the time of his marriage to be preserved from atheistic tendencies in himself: "O that my firm Belief of Invisible things may be as a shield unto me, defending me from those Temptations which, O Lord, Thou knowest, I find to be fiery darts." His intense curiosity about the Goodwin children was driven in part by a need to allay his own doubts. His dealings with them savor of *folie à deux,* as he played out his longing for evidence of Spirit while they played out their hostility to it. Once he tried to get Martha to own that she desired God's mercies and men's prayers, and to signify her desire by raising her hand. She refused, so he raised her hand himself and said, "Child, if you desire those things, let your hand fall, when I take mine away."

Mather's determined defense of spirit may seem to imply that he rejected the growingly materialistic view of nature in the late seventeenth century. Scientists of his time tried to dissociate the concept of matter from occult ideas with which it had been invested, so as to consider its purely physical properties. Ultimately the more precise formulation of celestial mechanics and the other triumphs of the scientific revolution did create skepticism about witchcraft, and discredited Spirit. But the effect was not immediate. In its early stages the experimental philosophy even dignified belief in the supernatural because, having seen many old ideas about nature upset by new discoveries, it held that no belief should be rejected out of hand and it regarded dismissive unbelief as a form of dogmatism. Also, the new science never completely discarded the older science it evolved from; even advanced thinking in the period was shot through with Pythagorean mysticism, cosmological fantasy, and Neoplatonist vitalism. Many scientists, being Christians as well, tried to harmonize older pneumatological views with new scientific theories. The chemist Robert Boyle wrote *Some Physico-theological Considerations about the Possibility of the Resurrection* (1675), discussing the Resurrection in terms of chemical transformations; Joseph Glanvill was both a preeminent demonologist and a member of the Royal Society, which he urged to investigate apparitions and demons.

In the style of the leading Christian scientists of his time, Cotton Mather dealt with pneumatological questions in both religious and scientific terms. Preaching about thunder in 1694, for instance, he proposed that thunder is produced according to "the Common Laws of Matter and Motion," perhaps by clouds clashing until their vapors take fire from contact. He also presented (and favored) the alternative chemical view that thunder results from decomposing vegetable matter on earth, which wafts to the atmosphere explosive "vapours of *Niter* and *Sulphur.*" But neither account, he explained, denies diabolic agency: "it is a Scriptural and a Rational Assertion, That in the Thunder there is oftentimes by the Permission of God, the Agency of the Devil. The Devil is the prince of the *Air,* and when God gives him leave, he has a vast Power in the *Air,* and *Armies* that can make Thunders." God makes the mechanical or chemical laws, but may allow good or evil angels to mobilize them, although their influence is but the influence of instruments, "Instruments directed, ordered, limited by him, who is the *God of Thunders.*" Mather used the same scientific-pneumatological thinking to explain how devils can use natural causes of disease to spread plagues, or why women more often become possessed than men (owing to the physiology of menstruation). He found nothing in new scientific ideas contrary to his belief in Spirit. At the height of the Salem crisis he wrote *Winter-Meditations* (1693), which discusses the formation of fossils and gives thanks that "we are Born in an Age of *Light.*" For Mather devils and telescopes both proved the existence of God and confuted Sadducism.

　　Cotton Mather's concern for Martha Goodwin was rewarded by reassuring proof of an invisible world. But he also learned or became confirmed in methods of dealing with devils, which he would bring to the new cases at Salem. Like all Puritans he regarded holy water, crosses, and the entire Catholic rite of exorcism as gross superstition. He equally opposed the widespread efforts to relieve victims of witchcraft by popular magic. To conjure with bottles, horseshoes, and spells, he said, was "to *oppose Witchcraft* it *self* with Witchcraft." Such magic might even tempt the devil to intervene: "for ought I know, the frequent and constant Practice of certain *Magical Ceremonies* may have Invested many Persons with all the Diabolical ministry of Witches, who have not been well aware of what they have been adoing." Abjuring exorcism and magic, he followed Mark 9:29: "This kind can come forth by nothing, but by prayer and fasting." In Reformed tradition, the most powerful, and the only acceptable, method of depossession was prayer. In liberating Martha Goodwin Mather fought her devils with "no other weapons but Prayers and Tears, unto Him that has the Chaining of them."

　　The Goodwin case also confirmed Mather in certain ideas about detecting witches. For one, it persuaded him to abhor irresponsible accusations of witchcraft, such as apparently flourished in Boston: "An Ill-look, or a cross word will make a Witch with many people, who may on more ground be counted so themselves. There has been a fearful deal of Injury done in this way in this Town, to the Good-name of the most credible persons in it." In his jail visits to Goody Glover and his work with Martha he solemnly kept to himself the names of any other persons they implicated. In the "Discourse on Witchcraft" he preached during the case he also solemnly cautioned his congregation against taking reports of apparitions as evidence of witchcraft: "Suppose that a Person *bewitched* should pretend to see the Apparition of *such* or *such* an one, yet this may be no infallible Argument of their being Naughty people. It seems possible that the Devils may so traduce the most *Innocent,* the most praise-worthy."

The surest test for witchcraft, Mather believed, was credible confession. Here he followed the eminent English theologian and jurist William Perkins, who argued that "*Among the sufficient means of Conviction, the first is, the free and voluntary Confession of the Crime, made by the party suspected and accused, after Examination.*" Goody Glover had herself demonstrated her hellish trade by handling her images in court, and her confession had stood up to the exactest scrutiny of her sanity by several physicians. Such confessions could not be disregarded without eliminating all judgment of human affairs and making a conviction for any crime whatsoever impossible: "all the *Murders,* yea, and all the *Bargains* in the World must be mere *Imaginations* if such *Confessions* are of no Account."

*

The new invasion from the invisible world began around February 1692, in Salem Village (now Danvers), Massachusetts. As described in *A Modest Inquiry* (1702), the classic account by the Rev. John Hale:

> . . . Mr. Samuel Paris, Pastor of the Church in Salem-Village, had a Daughter of Nine, and a Niece of about Eleven years of Age, sadly Afflicted of they knew not what Distempers; and he made his application to Physicians, yet still they grew worse; And at length one Physician gave his opinion, that they were under an Evil Hand. This the Neighbours quickly took up, and concluded they were bewitched.

Choked, convulsed, pinched, and rendered speechless by invisible agents, the girls were as badly afflicted as the Goodwin children had been, Hale said, yet "there was more in these Sufferings, than in those at Boston, by pins invisibly stuck into their flesh, pricking with Irons."

Despite the prayers of ministers at Salem and nearby towns the afflictions continued. Other young girls complained of being similarly molested, and identified three women or their shapes as the tormentors: a West Indian slave, Tituba; a bedridden old woman, "Gammer"Osborne; and a pauper who begged for food around the Village, Sarah Good. On February 29, warrants went out for their arrest on suspicion of witchcraft.

Pretrial examinations were held in Salem Village. Cotton Mather's old teacher, Ezekiel Cheever, recorded the examination of Sarah Good, on March 1, as conducted by the local officials. Good's examination has special importance because of her prominence in the subsequent trials, but also typifies the nature of the other examinations, and a part of it can stand for them all:

Q. Sarah Good, what evil spirit have you familiarity with?
A. None.
Q. Have you made no contract with the devil?
Good answered no.
Q. Why do you hurt these children?
A. I do not hurt them. I scorn it.
Q. Who do you employ, then, to do it?
A. I employ nobody.
Q. What creature do you employ then?
A. No creature. But I am falsely accused.
Q. Why did you go away muttering from Mr. Parris's house?
A. I did not mutter, but I thanked him for what he gave my child.
Q. Have you made no contract with the devil?
A. No.

H [Judge Hathorne] desired the children, all of them, to look upon her and see if this were the person that had hurt them, and so they all did look upon her and said this was one of the persons that did torment them. Presently they were all tormented.

Q. Sarah Good, do you not see now what you have done? Why do you not tell us the truth? Why do you thus torment these poor Children?
A. I do not torment them.
Q. Who do you employ then?
A. I employ nobody. I scorn it.

Witnesses brought in against Good, including the other accused witches, offered plentiful evidence of her diabolic behavior. Tituba testified that Good had "a thing all over hairy," that she saw Good's name in the devil's book, and that she and Good rode together on a pole, holding each other. A man testified that Good appeared to him when he was in bed, bringing an "unusual light"; she sat on his foot, but when he kicked at her she and the light vanished. William Good, Sarah's husband, testified that the night before his wife's examination he saw below her right shoulder, and had never seen before, "a wart or tit." Good's own daughter Dorcas testified that her mother had three birds which afflicted the children and other persons.

A jury found Good and Tituba guilty of witchcraft. They were remanded on May 25 to the Boston jail and apparently chained. Good was then either pregnant or had recently given birth, for during her imprisonment she is known to have been nursing an infant, which died in the jail. Meanwhile, the number of afflicted and accused persons had jumped. By the third week in March the afflicted were not three but ten, including an old woman and four married women. More examinations were conducted in the thronged meetinghouse, where the cries of the enlarged group of the afflicted, one witness said, produced "an hideous scrietch and noise." Those examined included Sarah Good's daughter Dorcas. Only four or five years old, she had testified against her mother but was now accused of witchcraft herself. She was made to look upon the afflicted girls, who tormentedly complained of being bitten, and produced the marks of a set of small teeth. The court remanded Dorcas Good also to the Boston jail, where she would remain, chained, for about another eight months.

By April 11, the swelling numbers of afflicted and accused, and the growing uproar in the face of the Bradstreet government's uncertainty about what to do, meant that new examinations had to be moved from Salem Village to Salem town. They were held not only before local officials but before the deputy governor, six magistrates, and a large audience that included several ministers, who saw and heard the afflicted spasmodically swoon, cry, and scream when the accused looked upon them. How many persons were in jail by May 14, when at last the new governor, Sir William Phips, arrived with Increase Mather, is uncertain. Phips wrote that he found the prisons "full of people" and the number of complaints increasing daily. Having to deal not only with them, but also with the fighting against the allied French and Indians to the east, he decided to bring those who had been examined and jailed to trial. Before leaving for the east himself he appointed a seven-man commission of oyer and terminer, including Samuel Sewall, Wait Winthrop, John Richards, and, to head the court, William Stoughton—four very close friends of the Mathers.

As these events unfolded, Cotton Mather was seriously ill, his health "lamentably broken," as he wrote, in part by "excessive Toil." At some time he suggested that the afflicted girls be separated and scattered, and offered to take in six of them himself, as he had taken in Martha Goodwin, to "see whether without more bitter methods, *Prayer* with *Fasting*

would not put an End unto these heavy Trials." His offer was not accepted, however, and his continued poor health kept him from accompanying
John Richards to Salem for the court sessions, as Richards had requested:
"the least excess of travel, or diet, or anything that may discompose me,"
he explained, "would at this time threaten perhaps my life itself, as my
friends advise me."

However ill, Cotton Mather had pondered the happenings at Salem
much and carefully, reflecting on his experience with Martha Goodwin.
On the day the accused witches jailed in Boston were ordered returned to
Salem for trial, May 31, he wrote Richards a long letter (five printed pages
in modern editions), summarizing his views on the earlier examinations
and offering firm, considered advice on the impending trials, where Richards would sit as a judge. The views he offered he probably kept throughout his life: first, that there are witches capable of enormous crimes, who
should be executed; second, that witches who commit lesser crimes
should be punished in a lesser way; third, that the identification and
conviction of *all* witches demands the most extreme caution—although
this last point, we shall see, he sometimes presented with disturbing
qualifications.

Much as he cautioned his congregation at the time of the Goodwin
case, Cotton Mather now particularly warned Richards about the use of
so-called spectral evidence: testimony that mischief had been done by a
specter or apparition of the accused. Such testimony had already been
offered during the examinations at Salem, the Indian Tituba, for instance,
testifying that Sarah Good afflicted the children "in her own shape." Such
evidence was admissible in English witchcraft trials for a century before
Salem, and as late as 1712, and was enthusiastically endorsed by the chief
judge of the new court, William Stoughton. Yet Mather adamantly opposed using spectral evidence as proof of witchcraft. He reiterated to
Richards that devils have sometime represented the shapes of innocent
and even very virtuous persons, that spectral evidence lends itself to the
accusation of people who have acted maliciously but not diabolically,
and that the devil's chief means of creating havoc in society might be to
cause the condemnation of the innocent:

> . . . if upon the bare supposal of a poor creature's being represented by a
> specter, too great a progress be made by the authority in ruining a poor
> neighbor so represented, it may be that a door may be thereby opened for
> the devils to obtain from the courts in the invisible world a license to
> proceed unto most hideous desolations upon the repute and repose of
> such as have yet been kept from the great transgression.

Mather felt that for advancing these cautions some might consider him a "witch advocate" himself—that is, a defender of witches. Nevertheless he urged Richards that persons accused by spectral evidence should not be reckoned "witches to be immediately exterminated," but that such evidence should be used only as a "presumption" that might justify a search for further evidence against them.

Such further evidence might consist of information an alleged witch could not have obtained without diabolical assistance, or of puppets used to torment victims, or of teats and similar body marks used for the devil's "cursed succages." But Mather cautioned that such evidence was also inconclusive. It should be taken rather as an intimation of guilt, leading to conviction only when found "in concurrence with other things." The most reliable evidence of witchcraft, he told Richards—again as in the Goodwin case—was credible confession. He emphasized "credible," forbidding the use of torture and dismissing confessions resulting from a "delirious brain, or a discontented heart."

On the ultimate question of punishment, Cotton Mather believed that unmistakably identified witches who had acted destructively in a spirit of intense malice should be executed. Just the same, he was deeply schooled in lessons of restraint and meekness, and except when meeting a direct military threat, as from the French or Indians, he abhorred violence. Only recently, in a sermon before the General Assembly, he had accused the Fathers themselves of overzealousness in sending Quakers to the gallows. He urged Richards to consider whether it was necessary to hang or burn "every wretched creature that shall be hooked into some degree of witchcraft." He recognized that the Mosaic law commanded "Thou shalt not suffer a witch to live." But he explained that devils easily convert "poor mortals" to witchcraft, particularly the forlorn or distempered—as he feared many had become, owing to the unsettled state of the country. Since devils easily lure the distressed into witchcraft he proposed lesser punishments for lesser witches, such as making a public renunciation of the devil.

*

By the standards Cotton Mather set forth to John Richards, the new court on which Richards sat was reckless and severe. Meeting for the first time in Salem on June 2 under Lieutenant Governor William Stoughton, it heard testimony against Bridget Bishop, the thrice-married owner of an unlicensed tavern, whose patrons drank late into the night and played shuffleboard. The testimony included spectral evidence by John Londer of Salem, aged thirty-two, that awakening in the dead of night he "did clearly see said Bridget Bishop, or her likeness, sitting upon my stomach." Two workmen testified that in Bishop's cellar they found puppets made of hog bristles and rags, stuck with headless pins. The court found Bishop guilty of witchcraft, and on June 10 she was led up a rocky elevation on the western side of Salem town and hanged—the first of the accused witches to be executed.

Bishop's execution alarmed many ministers, Cotton Mather among them. He drew up a statement entitled *The Return of Several Ministers* (1692), which was presented to Governor Phips and his Council around June 15. In behalf of the group of twelve ministers he expressed dissatisfaction with the court's incautious treatment of evidence, and argued that presumptions on which accused witches might be jailed, much less convictions on which they might be hanged, "ought certainly to be more considerable, than barely the Accused Persons being Represented by a *Spectre* unto the Afflicted." He also criticized two other features of the trials. Regarding evidentiary tests in which the accused witches were made to touch or look at the afflicted, he and the other ministers said they could not "esteem Alterations made in the Sufferers, by a *Look* or *Touch* of the Accused to be an Infallible Evidence of Guilt; but frequently Liable to be abused by the Devils Legerdemains." Regarding the crowded, noisy courtroom, he also cautioned the judges to admit "as little as is possible of such Noise, Company, and Openness, as may too hastily expose them that are Examined."

Had this document—and Cotton Mather's feelings—ended here, Mather might never have become a villain to history. But the document concludes with a flabbergasting "Nevertheless." Its final clause, as if discarding the preceding attack on the court's methods, urges the Phips government to push on the trials:

> Nevertheless, We cannot but humbly Recommend unto the Government, the speedy and vigorous Prosecution of such as have rendered themselves obnoxious, according to the Direction given in the Laws of God, and the wholesome Statutes of the English Nation, for the Detection of Witchcrafts.

The obscure, semiliterate Bostonian Robert Calef, soon to become Mather's antagonist, remarked that although the *Return of Several Ministers* appeared anonymously, its nature plainly identified the author as Mather. For the document, he said, was "perfectly ambidexter, giving as great or greater encouragement to proceed in those dark methods, than cautions against them." Mather himself seems to have recognized the startling inconsistency, for in later reprinting the document he omitted the final, blatantly contradictory clause.

Calef's very astute comment points to complexly intertwined features of Cotton Mather's personality and situation that would frustrate him throughout the Salem trials. What in part betrayed him into offering "ambidexter" advice were feelings of deference, loyalty, and youthful subordination to the judges. These often break through his earlier letter to John Richards, which speaks of "your honorable hands" or "your most worthy hands" while offering "my poor thoughts" and "my little skill." In fact, the judges were not only older, prominent men but also longtime family friends. Richards was not only a wealthy merchant, captain of the militia, selectman, and treasurer of Harvard, but also a property owner in the Mathers' neighborhood and a member of their church for nearly thirty years, as long as Increase was its minister. When Cotton Mather became an assistant to his father in 1680, Richards was the largest contributor to his salary; when Cotton married Abigail Phillips, Richards performed the ceremony; whenever some important church matter pended, Cotton consulted Richards, whose approval he deemed essential to gaining the brethren's consent. Cotton's ties to the other new judges were similarly close. Wait Winthrop, who had squashed an order to arrest him during the Andros administration, he ranked "among the Best of my Friends"; Adam Winthrop and John Foster were important members of his church; Samuel Sewall often went to hear him preach and admired his sermons, and they frequently dined together and corresponded.

And, in particular, Cotton Mather recognized "a real friend to New-England" in William Stoughton, the chief justice of the trials and the most vigorous prosecutor. This never married man, by whose signature on a warrant of execution witches were taken from jail and hanged, was intimate with both Mathers. Before entering the magistracy he had preached together with Increase; when Cotton was sixteen he inscribed to him a gift copy of Theophilus Gale's *The Court of the Gentiles* (1672); he attended Cotton's ordination as a representative of the Dorchester church; he was one of the judges before whom Edward Randolph lost his suit against Increase for defamation; and it was through Increase's influence that, when Phips became governor, Stoughton received a commission as lieutenant governor. In writing to and about the Salem court, Cotton Mather was addressing not only judges whom he felt were abusing evidence, but simultaneously neighbors, old friends, members of his church, persons to whom he owed favors and "for whom," he wrote, "no man living has a greater veneration."

Cotton Mather's relation with these judges was doubly compromised, however, for they also embodied the new government his father had all but created. Richards, Sewall, Foster, and the two Winthrops were members of the Council; Stoughton was lieutenant governor; and the man who appointed them, Sir William Phips, was "one of my own Flock, and one of my dearest Friends." To oppose the court meant opposing a government for whose existence a revolt had been waged, and to open again the breach, only recently healed, between ministry and magistracy, Aaron and Moses. Among the blessings of the new charter, Cotton had argued, was to have "our *Judges as at the First* . . . and that no *Judges,* or *Counsellors,* or *Justices* can ever hereafter be Arbitrarily Imposed upon us." Moreover, in the murmuring between the revolt and the arrival of Phips, and the more recent disquiet over the charter, Mather had spoken and labored strenuously and publicly to still jealousies, contentions, and factions by pleading that the new government be respected. On almost the same day he wrote to John Richards urging caution at the trials, he lamented in a sermon to the General Assembly how "every *Public Servant* must carry two *Handkerchiefs* about him, one to wipe off *Sweat,* of Travail, another to wipe off the *Spit* of Reproach." And he insisted that "'tis of inexpressible importance, that *Public Servants* be not abused for what they do." Whatever his own views on identifying and trying witches, he was not about to pillory public officials for theirs. An inveterate peacemaker, a leader of the revolt, and Increase Mather's son, he felt obliged to defend the new government, which meant he must also "wipe off the *Spit* of Reproach" from the court that was its first creation.

The "ambidexterity" of Cotton Mather's position had a less personal source as well. He genuinely believed that "most of the *Judges*" acted prudently and patiently, under "*Agony* of Soul" themselves. His respect for their honest efforts only complicated his conflict: "tho' I could not allow the *Principles,* that some of the Judges had espoused," he wrote, "yet I could not but speak honourably of *their* Persons, on all Occasions." His belief that the judges had acted prudently caused people to revile him, he said, "as if I had been the Doer of all the hard Things, that were done, in the Prosecution of the *Witchcraft.*" The charge was particularly unjust in the sense that he was himself deeply uncertain about the meaning of the events at Salem, an uncertainty compounded by chronic self-doubt, by his view of the devil as a uniquely subtle adversary, and by his longing for proofs of the invisible world to allay his own atheistical thoughts and to combat Sadducism. Salem was, he admitted, a "thorny affair," and to determine guilt in this "work of darkness" was itself a matter "much in the dark."

Indeed, Cotton Mather was not firmly convinced that the Salem girls had been bewitched. Just before the trials began, he told Richards, in extremely circumspect language, that the girls' afflictions might be due to possessions initiated not by witches but by devils themselves: "the devils may (tho' not often, yet sometimes) make most bloody invasions upon our exterior concerns, without any witchcrafts." A revised passage in his diary suggests that for a long while he remained uncertain whether the girls' symptoms came from devils invading their bodies or tortures inflicted from outside, whether they represented, that is, possession or witchcraft. Originally he wrote that houses at Salem were "filled with the horrid Cries of Persons possessed by evil Spirits"; at some time he deleted the word "possessed" and substituted the word "tormented." Even here he remained uncertain, for in explaining the revision he added that "There seem'd"—still a qualification—"an execrable *Witchcraft,* in the Foundation of this wonderful Affliction." Other possibilities occurred to him also. He speculated to Richards that the Salem outbreak might represent neither witchcraft nor incidental possession, but the approaching millennium, since Scripture foretold that at the time of the Second Coming Christ would dispossess the devils of their aerial abode to make a New Heaven. Agitated signs of his uncertainty fill his early letter to Richards—"I suppose," "I believe," "I do suspect," "Perhaps," "'tis probable," "I am ready to think," "'tis worth considering." Indeed, hardly a statement by him in this early period of the Salem outbreak is free from doubts, and from qualifications and reservations within and atop them.

In sum, the situation created by Salem called on Cotton Mather for answers he did not have, and he found it unmanageable. Any action might be wrong, no action was very certain. Emotionally and intellectually zigzagging every way betwixt disapproval of the trial methods, reverence for the judges, desire to defend the new government, longing for signs of the invisible world, uncertainty over the meaning of events, fear of speaking rashly, and lack of self-assurance, he on the one hand continued to urge caution on the judges, and on the other continued to defend their rash judgments, meanwhile continually hoping they would turn out to be right.

*

The court turned out, however, to be energetic. By one contemporary account, perhaps exaggerated, ten days after the hanging of Bridget Bishop more than seven hundred persons stood accused of witchcraft and over a hundred accused witches lay in prison. On June 28, Stoughton's court met for the second time, and in one day tried five accused witches. They included one of the original three accused witches, Sarah Good, who had been in the Boston jail for a month.

Despite the cautions of Mather and the other ministers against spectral evidence, Governor Phips wrote, Stoughton "persisted vigorously in the same method, to the great dissatisfaction and disturbance of the people." Much of the evidence presented at Good's trial was spectral, but it was overwhelming. Among others, Sarah Bibber, aged thirty-six, testified that one night she found Good's "apparition . . . standing by my bedside, and she pulled aside the curtain and turned down the sheet and looked upon my child 4 years old and presently upon it, the child was struck into a great fit that my husband and I could hardly hold it." Johanna Childen testified that the apparitions of Good and her infant appeared to her, and the infant's apparition accused Good of murdering it; Susannah Sheldon, aged about eighteen, testified that Good's apparition "most violently pulled down my head behind a Chest and tied my hands together with a whale band and almost Choked me to death." Others connected Good with mysterious and strange deaths of cows or the transportation of a broom into an apple tree, and much more. The court condemned Good and the four other accused women to death, and they were hanged at Salem on July 19. Before her execution Good reportedly said to the assistant minister of the Salem town church, Nicholas Noyes, "I am no more a Witch than you are a Wizard, and if you take away my Life, God will give you Blood to drink."

Considering Cotton Mather's adamant warnings about convicting suspected witches on spectral evidence and rushing them to the gallows, he might be expected to find the five hangings shocking. Instead, he found the judges' sentences "miraculously" confirmed. Hardly were the five hanged, he wrote, "impudently demanding of God a miraculous vindication of their innocency," when God produced evidence of their guilt. It arrived in the form that he, and William Perkins behind him, considered most reliable, as "credible confession." "Immediately upon" the hangings, five persons from the town of Andover made "a most ample, surprising, amazing confession" of witchcraft, and declared the five newly executed to have been of their company.

The confession of the Andover witches is among the least-known incidents of the Salem witchcraft trials, but for Cotton Mather it was a turning point. Sometime in the early summer of 1692, an Andover man named Joseph Ballard sent to Salem for some of the possessed girls, hoping they could identify the specters afflicting his wife, who was ill and later died of a fever. Others in Andover enlisted the girls for similar purposes. The girls acted in the Andover sickrooms as they had in the Salem court: they fell into fits and named the persons whose specters they saw tormenting the sick. Fifty persons in Andover were soon accused of witchcraft and thirty to forty sent to prison. Children, parents, grandparents, husbands and wives, accused and implicated each other. They were probably motivated by fear. Many who confessed reasoned that so far only witches who had refused to confess had been hanged. Six Andover women later drew up a statement explaining that they had confessed because "there was no other way to save our lives." According to an accused Salem witch, John Proctor, a statement implicating the Salem witches was drawn from two of the Andover witches by torture. He wrote from the Salem prison to "Mr. Mather" (probably Increase, but possibly Cotton) and four other Boston ministers, that his own son and two of the confessing Andover witches had been tied "Neck and Heels till the Blood was ready to come out of their Noses."

Cotton Mather may have attended some of the trials of the Andover witches himself, for he wrote, seemingly in August, that he had "lately seen; Even poor Children of several Ages, even from seven to twenty, more or less, *Confessing* their Familiarity with Devils." The confessing witches divulged much information about the workings of the invisible world. They denied from firsthand experience that devils could take the shape of innocent persons without their consent. Cautions against the admission of spectral evidence were discarded at the Andover trials. The local minister, Francis Dane, surmised that the reason family members turned on each other was that "the Conceit of Spectre Evidence as an infallible mark did too far prevail with us."

Virtually all the confessed Andover witches offered the same account of the devil's operation. The devil, they unanimously agreed, was a small black man. He got them to undo their allegiance to the Congregational church by renouncing their baptism, and had them seal their covenant with him by signing his book. Sixteen-year-old Richard Carrier, for instance, was one of many confessed witches who described the devil as a black man with a "high Crowned hat" who promised to reward his service with new clothes and a horse: "he told me also that he was Christ, and I must believe him, and I think I did So, I Set my hand to his book it was a little Red book I wrought with a Stick and made a red Colour with it and I promised to Serve him." The confessed witches all also described the devil's methods of rebaptizing people and of giving communion, offering only minor variations on whether his book was red or made of birchbark, and whether he dipped heads to baptize or flung initiates bodily in the water.

But the most spectacular revelations concerned a diabolic conspiracy. Witch after witch testified to riding poles to meetings where as many as five hundred witches plotted New England's ruin. Here too the evidence was overwhelming. When Mary Lacey, Jr., was asked why the devil wished to hurt the people of Salem, she replied, "the Devil would set up his Kingdom there and we should have happy days." William Barker, Sr., testified that at a meeting of about a hundred witches in Salem Village he learned that "Satans design was to set up his own worship, abolish all the churches in the land." Susannah Post testified that she had attended a witch meeting of two hundred, where she heard there were five hundred witches in the country. Mary Toothaker said that at a Salem Village witch meeting "they did talk of 305 witches in the country. She saith their discourse was about the pulling down the Kingdom of Christ and setting up the Kingdom of satan." Many of the confessed Andover witches who had attended these large meetings, moreover, identified the two ring-leaders of the conspiracy—a woman named Martha Carrier and a former minister named George Burroughs.

To Cotton Mather the Andover confessions not only tended to confirm the justice of the new court but also suggested that the Salem witchcraft horribly and drastically differed from the Goodwin case, representing not the possession of some young energumens but war from the invisible world aimed at destroying Christian Israel. This conspiratorial view of witchcraft outbreaks was common among European ecclesiastics. Indeed the notion of a diabolic plot against Christianity can be traced to antiquity, in fantasies of the existence within society of another small and secret society threatening its existence. Like cases of individual possession, such fantasies disburden repressed material, in this instance unacknowledged hostility to Christianity. Whether or not the Andover witches were projecting their covert animus against Congregationalism, their confessions struck deep and resoundingly into New England's mentality of invasion. Their talk of a plot to throw down all the churches in the land was entirely familiar, only it attributed to diabolic agency what had recently been laid to Andros and Randolph, and what for years had been decried as the inevitable result of exposed bosoms, dancing masters, and public drunkenness.

Cotton Mather himself was led to conclude that a diabolic plot was afoot to destroy New England: "more than One Twenty have Confessed that they have Signed unto a Book, which the Devil show'd them, and Engaged in his Hellish Design of Bewitching and Ruining our Land." Knowing the devil to be a wily adversary, skilled at sophistry, parody, and inversion, he had some doubt about the credibility of the Andover confessions. But the sheer number of them, and the support they gave to each other and to other evidence from Salem, persuaded him that they must in essentials be true. Satan may have woven delusions into some circumstances of the confessions, he allowed, "but one would think, all the Rules of Understanding Humane Affairs are at an end, if after so many most Voluntary Harmonious Confessions, made by Intelligent Persons of all Ages, in sundry Towns, at several Times, we must not believe the main strokes wherein those Confessions all agree."

On August 4, Mather made known to his congregation his changed understanding of the outbreak at Salem. It was a portentous day. The North Church was holding a special fast, as examinations of the Andover witches proceeded amidst continuing confessions. New trials of six more witches were scheduled at Salem the day after. And in the morning came news of a tremendous earthquake in Jamaica that reportedly killed over two thousand persons, sent the sea flowing across the island in a few minutes, and sank the iniquitous town of Port Royal. Appropriately, Mather chose the text Revelation 12:12: "Woe to the Inhabitants of the Earth, and of the Sea; for the Devil is come down unto you, having great Wrath; because he knoweth, that he hath but a short time."

Like other Puritan ministers, Cotton Mather usually did not preach at length on biblical prophecy. Its obscurities invited reckless predictions of the place and time of the Second Coming that often discredited its study, so that the subject was usually confined to discourse among the learned. Yet he had speculated in his early letter to Richards that Salem might be a harbinger of the end of time, and now from his pulpit he recalled the notion that the span allotted from the first Sabbath at the creation of the world to the founding of the New Jerusalem was twenty-three hundred years, of which at the time of Christ's resurrection seventeen or eighteen hundred years remained. The present, then, was near the time Revelation signified as the "*Evening* of the World," when the "*Evening Wolves* will be much abroad." Then people shall hear often about "*Apparitions* of the Devil, and about poor people strangely Bewitched." Then the devil, knowing Christ's Kingdom was at hand, would offer baptism and communion and make other despairing efforts to erect his own kingdom, "with a most Apish Imitation." Then, with the devil clapped up prisoner in or near the bowels of the earth, there would come repeated earthquakes, "and this perhaps by the energy of the Devil in the *Earth*," such earthquakes as had been reported this morning, whereby Jamaica "was at once pull'd into the Jaws of the Gaping and Groaning Earth."

Knowing his time was near, the devil fretted especially, Mather told his congregation, over New England. There the Puritans had claimed "a corner of the World, where he had reign'd without any controul for many Ages." Mather here referred to a popular notion, elaborated as early as 1634 by the English divine Joseph Mede, that before the coming of Christ the devil led the Indians to the New World as his own Chosen People, hoping to put at least some part of mankind beyond the reach of the gospel. Many persons thus viewed America at the time of its settlement as uniquely the land of the devil, an image reinforced and enhanced by the Indians' well-known practice of ceremonial magic. When a band of Puritans built evangelical churches and brought the gospel to the devil's domain, Mather continued, New England became to him a "vexing *Eyesore*," and he essayed by every means to "undermine his Plantation, and force us out of our Country." Indian powwows "used all their Sorceries to molest the first Planters"; fires often "laid the chief Treasure of the whole Province in ashes"; Andros and others schemed "to deprive us of those *English Liberties*, in the encouragement whereof these Territories have been settled." The outbreak at Salem was the latest of the roiled devil's frantic attempts to invade and reclaim New England. At the hellish meetings revealed by the Andover witches, "these Monsters have associated themselves to do no less a thing than, *To destroy the Kingdom of our Lord Jesus Christ, in these parts of the World.*"

Mather's sermon indicates that however convinced he had become of the existence of a diabolic conspiracy, he remained bewildered over the question of how infallibly to detect and prosecute the other conspirators, for his remarks on the matter were again perfectly ambidexter. He assured his congregation that the judges had used spectral evidence only as a basis for further inquiry, but that God had providentially strengthened it by supplying other evidence, so that "some of the *Witch Gang* have been fairly Executed." Speaking as if fully convinced himself that the spectral shapes were those of guilty persons, he told his congregation that all of the witches "have their *Spectres*, or Devils, commission'd by them, and representing of them," and he summarized at length the testimony of the Andover witches:

In the Prosecution of these Witchcrafts, among a thousand other unaccountable things, the *Spectres* have an odd faculty of clothing the most substantial and corporeal Instruments of Torture, with Invisibility. . . . These wicked *Spectres* have proceeded so far, as to steal several quantities of Money from diverse people, part of which Money has, before sufficient Spectators, been dropt out of the Air into the hands of the Sufferers, while the *Spectres* have been urging them to subscribe their *Covenant with Death*.

Mather's dozens of sober, unqualified references to "Spectres" torturing, filching, or molesting, however, confusingly give way to assertions of doubt concerning the justice of accusations and convictions based on spectral evidence. He warned that in this obscure affair the devil might be trying to shame New England with "perhaps a finer Thread, than was ever yet practised upon the World," and beside his assurances that those executed had been indeed guilty, he expressed continuing bafflement; "The whole business is become hereupon so *Snarled,* and the determination of the Question one way or another, so *dismal,* that our Honourable Judges have a Room for *Jehoshaphat's* Exclamation, *We know not what to do!*"

The judges who met the next day, August 5, could have taken Mather's sermon as either encouragement or warning. In either case they sentenced to death six accused witches, five of whom were hanged on August 19: John Proctor, George Jacobs, Sr., and John Willard of Salem Village; George Burroughs of Maine; and Martha Carrier of Andover. Another condemned witch, Proctor's wife, Elizabeth, was pardoned because pregnant.

For the first time, Cotton Mather attended the executions. Until now, he seems to have avoided any direct contact with the judicial proceedings. He did preach to some accused witches imprisoned in Boston, and he may have attended some of the examinations at Andover; his diary mentions, too, that his compassion for the judges' difficulty was increased "by my Journeys to *Salem*"—presumably only to speak with them, since he attended none of the trials. His presence at the hangings on August 19 is the only documented instance of his personal participation in the proceedings.

The two surviving accounts of Cotton Mather's appearance both make it seem that he tried to justify the hangings, but both accounts are open to interpretation. In the first, Samuel Sewall, who attended also, recorded that before a "very great number" of spectators, George Burroughs prayed and made a speech protesting his innocence, which moved "unthinking persons" present to speak "hardly" about his sentence. All those about to be hanged also protested their innocence, Sewall said, but "Mr. Mather says they all died by a Righteous Sentence." In the second account, by Robert Calef, Burroughs spoke so solemnly and seriously from the gallows ladder as to win "the Admiration of all present." His fervent prayers, concluding with the Lord's Prayer, moved many to tears, "so that it seemed to some, that the Spectators would hinder the Execution." But as soon as Burroughs was turned off, Calef continued, "Mr. Cotton Mather, being mounted upon a Horse, addressed himself to the People, partly to declare, that he was no ordained Minister, and partly to possess the People of his guilt; saying, That the Devil has often been transformed into an Angel of Light; and this did somewhat appease the People, and the Executions went on."

Both these accounts, from which Mather's reputation has permanently suffered, have been questioned. Sewall refers only to "Mr. Mather," leaving it open whether he means Cotton or Increase; Calef disliked Cotton Mather, is often misleading, and wrote after the event. Yet it seems likely that the accounts refer to Cotton Mather and are essentially accurate. That Increase would have defended Burroughs' hanging is improbable because, even though he attended Burroughs' trial earlier in the month, he objected even more strenuously than did his son to the trial methods, and had interviewed several Andover witches in prison, where he heard them retract their confessions. Calef's account, secondly, squares with Cotton Mather's consistent defense of the judges. Just two days before the hangings Cotton wrote a rather incoherent letter to one judge, John Foster, ending, "I entreat you that whatever you do, you strengthen the hands of our honorable judges in the great work before them." Moreover, Cotton despised murmuring countryish mobs, such as he tried to pacify during the revolt of 1689. In political terms the spectators at the hangings were to him essentially the same mob, a threat to the stability of New England's fragile government. The one unconvincing note in Calef's account is that to assure the crowd of Burroughs' guilt, Mather told them the devil often appears as an angel of light—meaning that Burroughs might be a witch even though he had ostensibly been a minister. Whenever Mather invoked this idea he applied it to specters, never to persons. When he spoke of the devil taking an innocent shape he always meant it as a warning against condemning someone on the basis of spectral evidence. To have invoked the same idea to condemn someone presumed guilty implies a vicious perversion of justice out of keeping with Mather's personality.

Although the accounts do remain open for interpretation, the strongest argument for crediting them is that Cotton Mather's new understanding of the conspiracy against New England made the hangings for him unique. Two of those executed, Burroughs and Martha Carrier, were identified by the Andover witches as the very heads of the diabolic plot. Burroughs' trial produced testimony that, as the "chief of all the persons accused for witchcraft," he sounded the trumpet to call other witches together. Martha Carrier's own children, as well as other witches, testified that "the Devil had promised her, she should be *Queen of Heb.*" Mather himself called Burroughs the "Ringleader" and Martha Carrier a "rampant Hag." For him, the persons being executed included the veritable King and Queen of American Hell.

*

With apparently hundreds of witches accused or jailed, reports of torture, and new trials scheduled for early September, the hard words spoken at the Salem gallows spread. Public opposition to the trials had been evident for months. In late June, the Baptist minister William Milborne, a leader in the revolt against Andros, was arrested for circulating a petition to the General Assembly asking them to weigh the validity of spectral evidence. The accusations, moreover, had reached notable persons, including the eminent Boston minister Samuel Willard, several members of Governor Phips's Council, and Phips's own wife. Some of the original afflicted girls had accused the prominent shipmaster John Alden, a founder of the South Church and son of the Plymouth settlers John and Priscilla Alden; he was jailed in Boston for fifteen weeks before escaping to Duxbury. It was even said that the accused included Cotton Mather's mother, Maria, although he denounced the story as a lie fabricated by a Quaker.

Accustomed to putting down rebelliousness in himself, Cotton Mather saw in the mounting opposition to the trials a need to defend the new government more vigorously both at home and abroad. Four days before new trials were to begin, he offered to assist William Stoughton in "the weighty and worthy undertakings wherein almighty God has employed your Honor as His instrument for the extinguishing"—the word seems lethal—"of as wonderful a piece of devilism as has been seen in the world." He sent for Stoughton's approval part of a work-in-progress in which he sought, "even with something of designed contrivance," to end contention and restore peace, to "flatten that fury which we now so much turn upon one another." Aware of New England's reputation in London for disorder, he asked Stoughton's permission to include a digest of the trials, to vindicate the country as well as the judges and juries. Unwilling to misrepresent current dissatisfaction with the trial methods, however, he told Stoughton gingerly that he would submit for his correction any places where he had "let fall, as once or twice, the jealousies among us, of innocent people being accused." Anticipating criticism of the book, he hoped not only for Stoughton's permission but also for his protection, and ended with a blushing request for his endorsement:

> For me to beg that either Your Honor singly, or the judges jointly, would in a line or two signify unto the world that my labors have your approbation. . . . This were an arrogance whereupon I dare not presume. Although a favor of that kind bestowed upon me would somewhat lay before the world an intimation of that holy, pious, fatherly frame of spirit, with which you are herein concerned for us, yet, I say, I dare not aspire so far as to ask it.

This manipulative tactic of getting-by-renouncing, probably derived from his relation to his father, he would use increasingly to extort favors from austere or influential persons on whom he felt dependent.

While Cotton Mather wrote on in defense of the trials, the death sentences multiplied. New trials began in Salem on September 9; the court condemned nine persons. One of them, eighty-year-old Giles Corey, refused to plead his indictment; on September 19, heavy stones were laid on him in a field until he was crushed to death. According to Robert Calef, Corey's tongue came out of his mouth and "the Sheriff with his Cane forced it in again, when he was dying."

The next day, Cotton Mather wrote to the clerk at Salem, Stephen Sewall, saying he was beset by objections against the proceedings but willing to "expose myself unto the utmost for the Defense of my Friends with you." He asked Sewall to send narratives of a half-dozen or more trials to include in his book. However willing to expose himself, he also understood the risk in defending an increasingly unpopular cause. Wanting the court to share the risk with him, he asked that the trial account come in some quasi-official form, such as a letter to him. His request was strengthened, he told Sewall, by Governor Phips himself having "laid his positive commands upon me to desire this favor of you"—perhaps, he seems to hint, because of spectral accusations against his wife. Phips's intervention suggests that he in some degree oversaw the writing of Mather's book, and may even have coaxed him into producing it. Or Phips may have wished to take over the direction of the work from Stoughton, of whose conduct he now wholly disapproved. In any case, two days after writing to Sewall, Mather met with him and Stoughton in Boston to discuss publication of the book.

The same day, September 22, the trials at Salem neared a crisis with the hanging of eight of the nine witches condemned earlier in the month: Mary Easty, Alice Parker, Ann Pudeator, Margaret Scott, Wilmott Reed, Samuel Wardwell, Mary Parker, and Martha (the wife of Giles) Corey. A week after this, the most numerous of the Salem executions, Governor Phips returned from Pemaquid, Maine, where he had visited the scene of combat against the French and Indians. Throughout the examination and trials, the fighting in the east had heightened the frenzied atmosphere by producing apprehensive rumors of expected raids on Massachusetts. On his return, Phips found general dissatisfaction with the court and a widespread belief that some of those executed had been innocent.

Advice came to Phips, perhaps at his request, from a group of ministers, in the form of a short treatise written by Increase Mather and now or later subscribed by the others, published afterward as *Cases of Conscience Concerning Evil Spirits Personating Men* (1693). ("Cases of Conscience" refers to works of casuistry, that is, resolutions of moral dilemmas by skilled theologians.) In a postscript added for publication, Increase praised the judges as "wise and good Men" acting "with all Fidelity according to their Light." But their light he saw as darkness, what the ministers in their Preface impugn contemptuously as "*something vulgarly called* Spectre Evidence, *and a certain sort of* Ordeal *or trial by the sight and touch.*" No less than his son, Increase believed unquestioningly in the invisible world. In *Cases of Conscience* he speaks solemnly of "bewitched Water" that rubbed on the eyes affords supernormal vision. But unlike his son, he desired not to put down a diabolic conspiracy— which the treatise fails to mention—but to prevent innocent persons from disgrace or hanging. It became his vocation, he wrote, "to be very tender in Cases of Blood, and to imitate our Lord and Master, *Who came not to destroy the Lives of Men, but to save them.*" Refuting the court methods on scriptural, philosophical, and commonsense grounds, he made his meaning personal and unmistakable: "This then I declare and testify, that to take away the Life of any one, merely because a *Spectre* or Devil, in a bewitched or possessed Person does accuse them, will bring the Guilt of innocent Blood on the Land." To show their concurrence with Increase's views, fourteen ministers signed their names to his work—perhaps all the leading ministers in and near Boston, except one.

The one was Cotton Mather, who took this occasion to publicly dissent from his father for the first time. He declined the subscription, he said, "with all the modesty I could use" and explained to his colleagues that his own book, now in press, had his father's approval and would "sufficiently declare my opinion." But his certainty of a diabolic plot and his scorn for popular unrest gave him larger reasons as well, which he confided to his uncle John Cotton. For one, he feared that by concentrating on the weakness of spectral evidence, his father's treatise might serve to halt the trials but divert attention from the conspiracy which made them necessary: "our witch-advocates" would be able to "cavil and nibble" learnedly at the proceedings against one or another witch, "while things as they lay in bulk, with their whole dependences, were not exposed; but also everlastingly stifle any further proceedings of justice." He also feared that the treatise might, unwittingly, turn public wrath against and thus endanger the judges, "who would (tho' beyond the intention of the worthy author and subscribers) find themselves brought unto the bar before the rashest *Mobile.*" Finally he hoped to uphold the authority and stability of the new government and to contain the growing quarrel between it and the ministry. As usually happened, his efforts to bring peace increased contention. He found that his refusal to subscribe gained him "raging asperity" and filled the country with a "great slander"—*"That I run against my own father and all the ministers in the country,* merely because I run between them when they are like mad men running against one another."

Around mid-October, just as popular and ministerial clamor against the trials was bringing them to a halt, Cotton Mather's *Wonders of the Invisible World* (1692) appeared in print, defending them. He made no secret of having written the book under wrenching stress: "None, but *the Father, who sees in secret,*" he said, "knows the Heart-breaking Exercises, wherewith I have composed what is now going to be exposed." Describing himself as "One of the least among the Children of *New-England,*" he opened with a nervously self-justifying "Author's Defence" that gives an agonized explanation of his motives:

> . . . there may be few that love the Writer of this Book; but give me leave to boast so far, there is not one among all this Body of People, whom this *Mather* would not study to serve as well as to love. With such a *Spirit of Love,* is the Book now before us written: I appeal to all *this World;* and if *this* World will deny me the Right of acknowledging so much, I appeal to the *other,* that it is *not written with an Evil Spirit.*

Mather's distress may account for the book's formlessness. It is a jumble of sermons and parts of sermons, snippets from English works, letters, attestations, "Matchless CURIOSITIES," heaped without beginning, middle, or end around a digest of five of the Salem trials. Mather made no attempt to conceal the vicissitudes of composition. Having apparently garnered his material while impatiently awaiting trial transcripts from the Salem clerk, he made the reader wait with him, promising in the text to present the trial accounts next, and failing to. After the first hundred pages he writes, "I shall no longer detain my Reader from his expected Entertainment, in a brief account of the Trials." But what follows is another stall, a narrative of some English witchcraft trials in the 1680s.

Although the book remains a mélange, Mather supplied an opening statement of design. His main purpose, he said, was to extract fruitful improvements from the "amazing Dispensations now upon us." These appear as exhortations to reform the provoking causes of God's Controversy with New England. The "subordinate Ends"—to which he devoted by far the bulk of the book—were three. First, to expose the diabolic conspiracy: "I have indeed set myself to countermine the whole PLOT of the Devil, against *New-England,* in every branch of it, as far as one of my *darkness,* can comprehend such a *Work of Darkness.*" This purpose he realized by giving more than a third of the book to an expanded version of the apocalyptic sermon he had preached following the Andover confessions. Insensitive or indifferent to redundancy, he here repeated much of what he said in a previous section titled "Enchantments Encountered." Mather's second "subordinate" end was dual: to contribute to the ongoing work of such noted English pneumatologists as Richard Baxter, and to reassure the mother country that New England was orderly. In one, reserving for a moment the other, he succeeded, for *Wonders* was advertised in large type in the *London Gazette,* reviewed and summarized at length in the *London Compleat Library,* and published quickly in three English editions.

Mather's final "subordinate" end, however, outreached him, that of clarifying his views, "taking off the false Reports, and hard Censures about my Opinion in these Matters." The book clarifies much less than it screens. The assemblage of redundant fragments and the repeated stalls make everything seem the prologue to a prologue, creating an effect of endless jerky beginnings, obscured by tedious verbosity and an insuperable difficulty in getting to the point. A simultaneous saying and unsaying, the book resembles a gigantic stammer. Cries of conspiracy alternate with appeals for calm, and these with doubts that Satan might spread havoc by using genuine witches to implicate the blameless. Mather seems to leave unquestionable that in the five cases he treats at length, real and malicious witches were executed. To vindicate the methods of the court he shows that the evidence against the accused, in the sheer numbers who testified for the prosecution, was conclusive. To reassure readers in London that the court followed established precedent, he prints prominent English legal opinions on detecting and convicting witches, and summarizes important English witchcraft trials.

Yet even this defense, straightforward in itself, seems in context half-hearted and forced, for Mather hedged it around with hints of coercion, warning winks at the reader, tipoffs to his discomfort. Although he had asked Stoughton's permission to publish an account of the trials, he presents the account as if written on command. One of his several prologues confesses that he has no prejudice against the persons convicted, "But having received a Command so to do, I can do no other than shortly relate the chief *Matters of Fact,* which occur'd in the Trials." With a similar plaint of duress, his account of Burroughs' trial begins: "the Government requiring some Account of his Trial to be inserted in this Book, it becomes me with all Obedience to submit unto the Order." And his digest of the trials concludes, "Having thus far done the Service imposed upon me. . . ."

These insistent disclosures of unwillingness make the whole book seem a sort of bluff. The likelihood is that sometime between conceiving and publishing the work, Cotton Mather became disenchanted by Stoughton, whose tenacious trust in spectral evidence was under attack even from Richard Baxter in England. In the book he clearly tried to disengage himself from Stoughton. For instance, instead of the "line or two" of approbation he had requested, Stoughton provided a page-and-a-half panegyric to Mather as his defender, beginning:

> Such is your Design, most plainly expressed throughout the whole; such your Zeal for God, your Enmity to Satan and his Kingdom, your Faithfulness and Compassion to this poor People; such the Vigour, but yet great Temper of your Spirit; such your Instruction and Counsel, your *Care of Truth,* your Wisdom and Dexterity . . . that all Good Men must needs desire the making of this your Discourse public to the World . . . [italics reversed.]

Mather included this self-interested endorsement, but placed it just before his embarrassed statement of purpose, which begins: "I LIVE by *Neighbours* that force me to produce these undeserved Lines." In his

"Author's Defence" too he carefully distinguished his own parts of the book from the trial digests composed, he implied, at Stoughton's behest: "For the Dogmatical part of my Discourse, I want no Defence; for the Historical part of it, I have a very Great One; the Lieutenant-Governour of *New-England* having perused it, has done me the Honour of giving me a Shield, under the Umbrage whereof I now dare to walk abroad." But his actual uneasiness under Stoughton's self-serving protection he confided to his diary: "The Shield given by the Lieut. Governour, of the Province, under which, That Book is walk'd abroad, is enough, and, I confess, too much."

Cotton Mather's book appearing just as, to almost everyone's relief, the trials were halting, the result was predictable. *Wonders of the Invisible World* became, and remains, as Mather called it, "that reviled Book." Inopportunely also, his father's *Cases of Conscience* appeared in print just after *Wonders,* and many "besotted People" believed that Increase had written in deliberate opposition to it. In a postscript to *Cases of Conscience,* Increase asserted that he had approved his son's work before it was printed, and that "nothing but my Relation to him, hindred me, from recommending it unto the world"—his explanation also of his failure to support his son's ordination with him. Yet father and son always tried to present a united front when they disagreed, as here they undeniably did. The drift of *Wonders of the Invisible World* is that devils have broke loose in New England, of *Cases of Conscience* that at Salem innocent people are being killed. Having refused to drink one king's health, and having spoken with two other kings and a queen in their own quarters, Increase did not find a William Stoughton awesome, unlike his deferential son, whose crime, morally, lay not in promoting the trials but in doing nothing to stop them.

But Cotton Mather had again been hauled in every direction. Finally wary of Stoughton but still certain that real witches had been hanged, he was also at odds with his father, hopeful of making a place for himself among noted pneumatologists, and apparently under conflicting pressures from the governor and lieutenant governor, while remaining, as before, apprehensive of the devil's subtlety, cautious about contributing to public discontent, hopeful of combatting Saducees, fatally anxious to please, and simply baffled. A passage of his manuscript autobiography which seems to have belonged to his original diary for 1692 speaks of his "Fear, Lest under my Extraordinary *Trials* from the *Invisible World,* I have at any time gratified the *Hidden Desires* of *Evil Angels,* or Entertained any Disposition to see broken the Good, Wise, Right *Order* wherein *Humane Affairs* are fixed by the Lord."

Cotton Mather did receive some praise for *Wonders of the Invisible World,* and later in the year he entered in his diary some approving, vindicating comments by others. Yet he remained unhappy over what he had done, and wrote in the margin the hesitant, ambidexter consolation: "(Upon the severest Examination, and the solemnest Supplication, I still think, that for the main, I have, *written Right.*)"

*

About ten days after the publication of Cotton Mather's book, on October 26, a bill was sent to the Assembly calling for a fast day and a convocation of ministers to determine what to do next in the trials. Because of the "season and manner" of presenting the bill, Samuel Sewall wrote, the Salem court considered itself dismissed. The court was due to end anyway, since it had been established before the legislature could meet under the new charter to arrange a system of courts, and it became defunct when the legislature established a superior court for the whole province. A further session of the Salem court had been scheduled, however, and on October 28 Stoughton went to discuss its fate with Phips and the Council. They met him, Sewall said, with "great silence," and next day Phips declared that Stoughton's court "must fall." Phips estimated that at least fifty accused witches were still in prison, some of whom he released on bail. Because some judges now conceded that the trials had been too violent and agreed to adopt a different method of evidence, Phips permitted the scheduling of a new court in Salem—the last—just after the new year.

Despite the suspension of the trials and his reservations about *Wonders of the Invisible World,* Cotton Mather hoped to "do yet more, in a direct *opposition* unto the Devil." Late in the year he wrote to John Richards, now not as a judge but as a leading member of his church, asking his support in making an important change in church policy. He told Richards that the information given by the Andover witches about the devil's parodic rites of baptism and communion had "increased my uneasiness, under that sin of omission wherein I reckon myself to live." The "sin" was the failure of the North Church to conform to the requirements for baptism proposed by the Halfway Covenant Synod of 1662. To recall: the Synod met to deal, among other things, with the decline in membership threatening the existence of the New England churches. It voted to alter the original Congregational ideal, by which only the children of parents who had experienced regenerating grace were to be baptized and admitted to the church. Instead it recommended that the children of persons who were Virtuous Christians but had not received grace could also be baptized and admitted, declaring their desire to attain a state of grace.

Increase Mather had strenuously opposed the compromise, and until the time of the Salem trials the North Church admitted only children of the regenerate.

Because of Increase's opposition, the North Church evidently contained a large number of unbaptized adolescents and adults. And the claims on such people by legions of devils, Cotton told Richards, made the problem of their baptism urgent. He had been forced to turn away "scores of godly people" who sought baptism, because of antagonism to halfway membership by two people, of whom Richards was one. He did not ask Richards to support the new policy, but only to continue as a member of the North Church if it were adopted. Those who offered themselves for baptism, he assured him, would be examined rigorously. They would have to be "instructed and orthodox" in Christianity, bring testimony signed by more than one full church member that they were of a "virtuous conversation," and declare their "study to prepare themselves further for the table of the Lord." Richards presumably agreed, as Increase Mather must have also, for on January 15, 1693, Cotton entered in the church records the admission of Mary Sunderland and the baptism of her son John, "the first, so Admitted" under the Halfway Covenant proposed thirty years earlier. Baptisms in the church quickly doubled, from 54 in 1692 to 104 in 1693. Although it pleased Mather that his church had peaceably resolved a long-vexing issue, the resolution also gave him more work, and he noted that "my Charge of such as now submitted themselves unto my *ecclesiastical Watch,* was exceedingly increased."

About three years earlier, it should be added, Cotton Mather had decisively addressed the related issue of grace. Disappointingly to those who had invented the tradition-breaking compromise of 1662, many children of the unregenerate who were baptized under the Halfway Covenant also failed to experience grace and were denied communion, thus kept from full church membership and voting privileges. To help bring such persons to the Lord's Table, Mather published in 1690 his extremely important *Companion for Communicants,* copies of which were distributed at the North Church on May 25, the day when John and Martha Goodwin, parents of the depossessed children, were admitted to full membership. This work marks the beginning of an evangelistic sacramental piety in New England intended to bring more worshipers to communion, thus to fill the churches again with Visible Saints, a movement climaxed by the Great Awakening of the 1730s.

The crux of Mather's *Companion* is the test he provided by which worshipers might decide whether they can rightfully approach the Lord's Table. The issue contained hazards on either side: to stay away from communion while in a state of grace and to take communion lacking a state of grace were alike sinful. Mather's test is answerably elusive, as are those of other ministers in the period who tried to relax requirements for admission so as to fill the thinning churches while preserving an illusion of maintaining the Fathers' pristine requirement that only Saints could take communion. "We are to *Examine* our selves," Mather wrote, "and if upon the *Examination* we do not find full cause to pronounce ourselves *Unregenerate*, we are to come, tho' we have many *Fears*, whether we be indeed *Regenerate* or no." The principle that worshipers may take communion if certain they are not *un*regenerate did prove effective in filling out the communion table of the North Church. One church member, Joseph Green, took to heart Mather's rule that, as he put it, "if a person could not conclude themselves to be unconverted they ought to approach," and found that Mather's *Companion* "so moved me to come to the Lords table that I began to think of closing wholly with Jesus Christ." However practical, Mather's principle of "Probable" regeneration had little in common with the endless wrestling, doubts, and devotions he had undergone in his youthful closure with Christ, or with the exacting admissions standards of the earlier New England churches.

The acceptance of the Halfway Covenant by the North Church coincided with the ending of the Salem trials. The new court appointed by Phips met in Salem in January 1693, and using a different method of treating spectral evidence, acquitted forty-nine of the fifty-two persons under trial. The king's Attorney General advised Phips that the remaining three should also be cleared. Stoughton, however, signed a warrant for their execution. Openly at odds with Stoughton now, Phips sent a reprieve, which so enraged Stoughton that he refused to sit longer on the bench. By February 21, Phips felt confident enough that the witchcraft crisis was over to write home that the elimination of spectral evidence had "dissipated the black cloud that threatened this Province with destruction."

Now Cotton Mather's face-to-face engagement with the invisible world could begin.

ii

On November 29, with the Salem trials suspended, Cotton Mather took several people to keep a day of prayer with a seventeen-year-old energumen named Mercy Short. An orphan, she had been redeemed from Indians in the east, who had killed her father, mother, brother, and sister, and carried her captive to Canada. In the summer of 1692 she was sent on an errand to the Boston prison, where the convicted Sarah Good, awaiting execution, asked her for a little tobacco. Mercy threw a handful of shavings at her, saying, "That's Tobacco good enough for you." Good cursed her, producing fits that disappeared and recurred for several months. Mercy seems to have been taken in by a family in Mather's neighborhood, in the "Haunted Chamber" of whose house groups of five to fifty persons came to fast, pray, or simply observe her possession. When Mather arrived on November 29 she lay insensible, but when he began preaching on Mark 9:29—"And he said unto them, This kind can come forth by nothing, but by prayer and fasting"—she sprang at him and tore a page out of his Bible.

With the trials ending, Mather felt reluctant to publicize the case. Although he wrote and apparently circulated an account of it, entitled "A Brand Pluck'd out of the Burning," he did not publish the manuscript, for Mercy Short provided much information that confirmed the necessity and justice of the trials. She gave fresh evidence against Sarah Good and Martha Carrier, corroborating evidence that French and Indians attended witch meetings to "concert the methods of ruining New England," news that the devil planned to burn all Boston, and vindication of the judges' use of spectral evidence. Even in his manuscript Mather forbore comment on Mercy Short: "such is the froward, flouting sidred [cidered, i.e., soured], and proud Humour, whereunto the people are now Enchanted, no man in his Wits would fully expose his Thoughts unto them, till the charms which enrage the people are a little better Dissipated."

Yet Mercy Short's possession had several unique features that Mather could not ignore. Her devils, like those of the Goodwin children and the Salem girls, pinched and scorched her, and showed their contempt for the ministry by stopping her mouth and ears during prayer, attacking her with special violence when she attended Mather's church. But Mercy Short was not merely afflicted: she seemed borne to Hell itself. The devils cut off her sight and hearing from the visible world and routed them into direct communion with the Powers of Darkness, her open but unreceptive eyes visualizing only "the Hellish Harpies that were now fluttering about her." Cast into Outer Darkness she argued tremendously with her tormentors: "Oh You horrid Wretch! You make my very Heart cold within me. It is an Hell to me, to hear You speak so! Are you *God?* No, be gone, you Devil! Don't pester me any more with such horrid Blasphemies!" In Mercy Short, haunted by evil angels and tortured by cruciating fires,

Mather beheld the very state of the damned itself. In other ways too Mercy brought him and the other spectators close up to the invisible world. Once when invisible flames flashed on her the room smelled of brimstone; when devils stuck pins in her, "those we took out, with Wonderment"; when a hot iron plunged down her throat, "we saw the Skin fetch'd off her Tongue and Lips."

These and many other drawings-near to the realm of spirit led Mather to further pneumatological speculations, for instance that long fasts were "strangely Agreeable" to persons who "have something more than Ordinary to do with the Invisible World." His most far-reaching speculation concerned the presence in Mercy's room of "a Substance that seem'd like a Cat, or Dog," experienced by several onlookers as invisible but palpable. In trying to explain this quasi-material presence he invoked a concept that would, we shall see, fascinate him all his life: the view that spirit contains "an Innate Power by which it can attract suitable matter out of all Things for a Covering or Body, of a proportionable Form and Nature to itself." He had already used this concept in *Wonders of the Invisible World* to expand the traditional understanding of witchcraft as a diabolic covenant: "*Witchcraft* seems to be the Skill of Applying the *Plastic Spirit* of the World, unto some unlawful purposes, by means of a Confederacy with *Evil Spirits.*"

The notion of a plastic spirit—essentially an old idea new-named, similar to classical ideas of a vegetative soul—had the allegiance of nearly every important thinker in England at the time. In effect the last hold on the supernatural, it appealed to those who, like Mather, recognized the new mechanistic picture of nature but clung to Christian belief. Plastic spirit was a DNA-like program for matter, an immaterial agent pervading the universe, creating and upholding animated substances as a sort of surrogate of God, whom it at once involved in and disengaged from running the universe. Instead of overseeing the creation and growth of every leaf or ant, God imbued the universe with the plastic spirit, a vital force acting for ends God assigned it, but not conscious of so acting. Mather recognized that the concept in effect explained one unknown by another and could be attacked. Yet it was something to go on, and as an intermediary between the visible and invisible worlds it offered a satisfyingly materialistic explanation of the means by which devils could take material shapes.

Just as important, Mercy Short brought Mather information that the devils had laid designs against him. She revealed that at one of their meetings the witches used a Catholic book of devotion, written in

French, fetched from his own study. When he examined the book he found to his surprise a leaf of it doubled over. A night or two later he left the book on a table in his study, careful to see that every page lay flat, yet next morning he found three pages unaccountably folded. A commonplace of demonology held that the devil most plagues the best men. The rebukes of his playmates had taught Mather as much in childhood, but since the time of the Goodwin case he had come to feel with increasing certainty that the devils had chosen him as a special victim of their wrath. Even before he said so himself, he heard it remarked during the Salem outbreak that the assault of evil angels was "intended by *Hell,* as a particular Defiance, unto *my* poor Endeavours, to bring the Souls of men unto Heaven." He had spent a day virtually every week during the summer of the trials in a private fast, asking God for both a good issue from the amazements of Salem and for his own preservation "from the Malice and Power of the *evil Angels.*" In August, after the wildly spreading Andover accusations, he twice raised to one of the judges, John Foster, the possibility of God permitting "such a terrible calamity to befall myself as that a specter in my shape should so molest my neighbourhood as that they can have no quiet."

On March 28, 1693, the devils assaulted Cotton Mather lethally. Between four and five in the morning, Abigail gave birth to the couple's first son, whom they named Increase. The infant looked comely and hearty but its bowels were obstructed, preventing the elimination of feces. Unnamed correctives were made but the infant languished "in its Agonies" until the night of April 1, when it died. An autopsy disclosed that, in Mather's words, the "lower End of the *Rectum Intestinum,* instead of being *Musculous,* as it should have been, was *Membranous,* and altogether closed up." The imperforate anus, he felt, gave "great Reason to suspect a *Witchcraft.*" A few weeks before her delivery, Abigail had been accosted by "an horrible *Spectre,* in our Porch, which Fright caused her Bowels to turn within her."

Mather may have expected some tragedy to befall him, for the specters which tormented Mercy Short boasted of having frightened Abigail, "in hopes, they said, of doing Mischief unto her *Infant* at least, if not unto the *Mother.*" But to Mather the most remarkable and portentous feature of Mercy Short's case concerned her deliverance. In addition to the evil angels buzzing about her she was attended by another spirit. It never became visible, or more audible than a whisper; rather it communicated "chiefly by an Impulse, most powerfully and sensibly making Impressions upon her Mind." Mather compared it to the spirit New Foundlanders call "White-Hat," which before a dangerous storm appeared on shore crying "Hale up!"

Mercy's "Wonderful Spirit" told her how to answer the devils' temptations and assured her she would triumph. It induced her to leaf through a Bible randomly and alight at the most pertinent possible place, and told her that on Thursday evening, March 16, between nine and ten o'clock, she would be delivered. Mather, present that evening, reported that the specters tried all night to torture her, but could not; she was "Hedged by some unseen Defence." When at last, in the name of Christ, she bid the devils be gone, "they flew away Immediately, striking another young Woman down for Dead upon the Floor as they went along." Her troublers never returned. In January 1694, she was admitted to the North Church in full communion, not only depossessed, that is, but having experienced grace.

Such good angels as assisted Mercy Short, Mather noted, had made themselves known during some important European witchcraft cases as well. During the notorious outbreak at Mohra, Sweden, bewitched children talked of being forbidden to carry out the devil's commands by a "White Angel." Good angels lingered in the background at Salem also, where one of the afflicted girls testified to seeing "a man in white, with whom she went into a Glorious Place . . . where was no Light of the Sun, much less of Candles, yet was full of Light and Brightness, with a great Multitude in White Glittering Robes."

Mather began longing for communion with good angels himself. Around two and a half months after the depossession of Mercy Short, he kept a fast day whose special purpose was to petition for angelic favors. He asked God "please to grant unto me, the Enjoyment of those *Angelical* Kindnesses and Benefits, which use to be done by *His Order,* for His *Chosen Servants.*" Wary of slipping into an antinomian disregard for Scripture, sermons, and other means provided by God for human worship and understanding, he cautiously asked for only the angelical assistances mentioned in Scripture as belonging to the elect, although in some heightened form, "in a Manner and Measure, more *Transcendent,* than what the great *Corruptions* in the generality of *Good Men,* permitted them to be made Partakers of." He also promised that if granted any direct angelical communication he would not forsake the written Word, but on the contrary would contemplate it more reverently than before. And he would be discreet, concealing "with all *prudent Secrecy,* the *Extraordinary Things,* which I may perceive done for me by the *Angels,* who love *Secrecy* in their Administrations." Having prayed and resolved, he wrote in his diary: "I do now believe, that some *great Things* are to be done for me, by the *Angels* of God."

Mather's prayers for communication with angels were highly unusual for a Puritan. Reformed tradition of course maintained that angels existed, and he often spoke of their nature and function to his congregation. Like evil angels, good angels, as he described them, are "Spiritual and Rational Substances," forming a mighty host, *"Ten thousand times Ten Thousand."* In heaven they throng around the throne of Christ, serving as ministers to His pleasure, having in custody the souls of departed Saints, who with quiet expectation await the restoration of their bodies. When they fly to earth they perform many of the same tasks as evil angels, but in reverse, curing diseases evil angels may spread, guarding the faithful some evil angels molest. As regents of the Prince of the kings of the earth, they mobilize decisive political events: "When Monarchs fall, and Nations and Empires have Amazing Changes brought upon them, the Angels of God accomplish it." Especially they love to visit places of secret prayer, as on the other side it tortures devils to be there. So earth, like heaven, teems with good angels, invisible but ever present.

While Mather's views on good angels were entirely traditional, his hope for close communion with them was not. Since the time of Christ, according to the general Reformed position, good angels, but not evil angels, had ceased to appear. Increase Mather himself argued strenuously that although the angelic ministry continues, "it is an unwarrantable and a very dangerous thing, for men to wish, that they might see, and that they might converse with Angels." Indeed Richard Baxter considered the non-appearance of angels a boon, for such appearances invite idolatry, fear, and error: angels "act according to their spiritual nature, without deceit; and they serve us without any terrible appearances . . . whereas if they appeared to us in visible shapes, we might easily be affrighted, confounded, and left in doubt, whether they were good angels indeed or not." The problem of distinguishing movements of good spirits from those of evil spirits—St. Paul's *diakrisis pneumatōn* or spiritual discernment—particularly argued against the desire for angelic communion. Converse with angels, Baxter warned, was very probably "converse with Devils that are Transformed into seeming Angels of Light."

However it risked mistaking diabolical imposture for angelic visitation, Mather's hope of receiving "great Things" from the good angels was quickly realized. One Sabbath about a month after his special day of prayer, he went to preach on an island in Boston Harbor, to some troops from a warship returned from the West Indies. Enroute to the island aboard Governor Phips's barge he became "vehemently *sick*." His companions insisted that he return to Boston, and as soon as he came home he recovered. It turned out that his sudden illness may have rescued him from death. The troops he nearly visited were stricken with yellow fever, which became epidemic in Boston: "had I gone, and Conversed among So Infectious a Company," he wrote, "it would probably have Cost me my Life, as it proved Mortal unto very many others of my Neighbours." He felt he knew, too, how to interpret his deliverance: "I believe, 't was a *Good Angel*, which there struck me *sick*."

Mather made another surprising journey the first week in September, to Salem. He hoped to collect material there for an ambitious new book, *Magnalia Christi Americana*, and to help preserve the trial record, so that the "complete History" of the recent witchcraft might not be lost. For the sake of public peace he had kept largely to himself confirming evidence of the justice of the trials, which now was reinforced. While in Salem he spoke with a woman named Carver, who had been strangely visited by "some *shining Spirits*, which were *good Angels*, in her opinion of them." He kept secret some things she intimated, but recorded in his diary her assurance that a new storm of witchcraft would break out, for the purpose of chastising the "Iniquity that was used in the wilful Smothering and Covering of *the Last*." Many who had fiercely opposed the discovery of the Salem witches, she said, would at last be convinced. Once again the evil angels assaulted Mather. He had taken with him three sermons to preach in Salem but they were "*stolen*," under circumstances "that I am somewhat satisfied, The Spectres, or Agents in the *invisible World*, were the *Robbers*."

As if in fulfillment of Mrs. Carver's prophecy, when Mather returned to Boston he found that a pious young woman in his congregation, Margaret Rule, had become "horribly arrested by *evil Spirits*." Her specters boasted of having stolen his sermon notes but confessed they could not suppress them. (The notes were returned to him on October 5, although in eighteen separate quarters of sheets found scattered about the streets of Lynn.) Margaret Rule's afflictions lasted more than five weeks, during which Mather assisted her and prayed for her deliverance as a sister of his flock. Among other things her tormentors tried to get her to sign a thick red book (narrow but about a cubet long), and "before a very Numerous Company of Spectators" once levitated her to the ceiling. Another time spectators thought they saw something stir on her pillow; a man set his hand there and, to his horror, believed he felt, but could not see, "a living Creature, not altogether unlike a Rat."

In its other manifestations, Margaret Rule's affliction resembled Mercy Short's, including the appearance to her of "a wonderful *Spirit,* in White and bright Raiment, with a *Face unseen.*" Comfortingly it stood by her bedside, counselling her to keep faith in God and resist the temptations of the evil angels. The spirit also bid her consider Mather her father, and obey him, "for he said, the Lord had given her to me." Mather's several pneumatological experiments had convinced him that an expulsion of demons could not be achieved until the holding of a third fast; when Rule's miseries had lasted more than five weeks, the white spirit notified her that Mather had now kept a third fast, and said: "be of good cheer you shall speedily be delivered." The evil angels as they approached her now found themselves forced to recoil, unable to stick pins in their puppets. Rule could see their "Black Master" strike and kick them, "like an Overseer of so many Negro's" until tiring of their useless attempts they said furiously, "Well you shant be the last," and flew from the room.

It was probably during the possession of Margaret Rule—between roughly September 10 and the end of October, 1693—that there occurred to Cotton Mather *"Res Mirabilis Et Memoranda,"* a strange and memorable thing. He recorded it in Latin, on a separate page of his diary, probably because of his earlier promise to respect the angels' love of secrecy. But he probably also wished to conceal the account from others. For this experience—although it far surpassed in intensity his many castings-out of demons, and although after long seeking it at last introduced him to the invisible world himself—this experience contained the greatest possibility of self-deception.

Mather wrote: *Post Fusas, maximis cum Ardoribus, Iejuniisque* Preces—After outpourings of prayer, with the utmost fervor and fasting—*apparuit* ANGELUS, *qui* Vultum *habuit solis instar Meridiani* Micantem—there appeared an Angel, whose face shone like the noonday sun—*Caetera* Humanum, *at prorsus* imberbem: Caput *magnifica* Tiarâ *obvolutum;*—He was completely beardless, but in other respects human, his head encircled by a splendid tiara;—*In* Humeris, Alas:—On his shoulders were wings:—*Vestes deinceps Candidas et Splendidas;* Togam *nempe* Talarem: *et* Zonam *circà Lumbos, orientalium cingalis non absimilem.*—His garments were white and shining; his robe reached to his ankles; and about his loins was a belt not unlike the girdles of the peoples of the East.

The angel that appeared to Mather explained that he had been sent by Christ to answer *cujusdam Juvenis precibus*—the prayers of a certain youth—and to bear back his reply. Many things the angel told him Mather thought it improper to transcribe. But among other things not to be forgotten the angel prophesied the great work he would do for the church *in* Revolutionibus *jam Appropinquantibus*—in the revolutions now at hand. He declared that the destiny of this youth was best expressed in the words of the prophet Ezekiel. Mather wrote down the texts of Ezekiel 31: 3, 4, 5, 7, and 9 as spoken to him by the angel, a prophecy of fruitfulness, power, and fame:

> *Behold, he was a Cedar in Lebanon, with fair branches, and with a Shadowing Shroud, and of an High Stature, and his Top was among the Thick Boughs. The waters made him great, the Deep Set him up on High with her Rivers running about his plants. His Height was Exalted above all the Trees of the Field, and his Boughs were multiplied, and his Branches became Long, because of the multitude of waters, when he shot forth.*
>
> *Thus was he fair in his greatness, in the Length of his Branches, for his Root was by the Great Waters. Nor was any Tree in the Garden of God like unto him, in his Beauty. I have made him fair by the multitude of his Branches, so that all the Trees of Eden, that were in the garden of God, envied him.*

Interpreting the text for him as it applied to his future, the angel explained that the lengthening of the tree's branches referred to *de* Libris *ab hoc Juvene componendis et non tantum in* America, *sed etiam in* Europa, *publicandis*—the books to be composed and published by this youth, not only in America, but also in Europe.

The appearance of the figure whose shoulders were wings left Mather feeling both astonished and perplexed. Domine Jesu!, he wrote, *Quid sibi vult haec Res tam Extraordinaria?* Lord Jesus! What is the meaning of this marvel? *Servum Tuum Indignissimum,* a most unworthy servant, he prayed to be delivered and defended from the wiles of the devil.

*

However extraordinary, Cotton Mather's angelic visitation seems comprehensible, even inevitable. It climaxed years of ever closer contact with the invisible world, beginning with the two-and-a-half-year-old's wish to "go see God," through his adolescent closure with Christ, his grappling with Martha Goodwin's invisible chains, the diabolic death of his malformed infant. The visitation may have been more immediately induced by Mather's preceding period of fervent prayer and fasting, since extreme sensory deprivation, as in persons locked in a room or adrift at sea, can produce hallucinations. Mather himself remarked on a connection between fasting and supernormal experience in Mercy Short's case, and he later wrote guardedly that he knew *"Certain Measures"* which might produce "Amazing Acquaintance with the Angelical Assistances."

As a Puritan, also, Cotton Mather was born into a society that daily felt the nearness of the invisible world and wove magical and supernatural notions into the very texture of his thinking, beginning in childhood. His particular childhood may have specially shaped him for a visitation, for adult beliefs in ghosts, spirits, and other supernatural beings sometime begin in childhood fantasizing about absent parents, such a parent as Increase often threatened to be and often was. It seems significant that the time of his visitation, the fall of 1693, coincided with an again renewed prospect of Increase's return to England as an agent for Massachusetts, at the suggestion of Governor Phips. When Increase prayed about the matter, he himself received extraordinary suggestions that he must go abroad, suggestions he considered "either divine or Angelical." As these impressions lasted, he started a course of reading on angels, and around March began preaching an impressive series of sermons on angelology, lasting into February 1694, on which Cotton took twenty-three pages of notes. While angels were intimating to Increase Mather that he should leave Boston, an angel appeared to his son predicting that his lengthening branches would reach Europe.

Like the demons who denounced ministers through the mouths of teen-aged energumens, the figure whose shoulders were wings spoke Cotton Mather's own thoughts. Among other things, the angel gave expression to the "ambitious Affectation of Praeheminencies" that had troubled him since youth, the much censored longing for applause and fame which the childlike view he maintained of himself helped restrain. Mather's need to demonstrate copious productivity appears as early as his youthful stammer, of course, and all of his writings teem with images of size. The angel merely articulated these while omitting the guilty reproofs that otherwise accompanied them, forecasting that a "certain youth" would enjoy some enormous potency: he would be set on high, his height exalted above all the trees of the field, his branches become long because of the multitude of waters when he shot forth. Explaining Ezekiel's prediction of the "*greatness, in the Length of his Branches,*" as referring to the books Mather would publish not only in America but also in Europe, the angel in effect promised him a transatlantic penis.

Mather's need at this time for reassurance against his feelings of littleness may have been due not only to the renewed prospect of his father's return to England but also to mounting criticism of his activities. Already under attack for his behavior during the trials and for his "reviled Book," he drew added criticism for his recent labors to depossess Mercy Short and Margaret Rule and for his continued preaching about devils. He deserved it, too, because now he acted on his own, without government coercion or the pressure of confused loyalty, having come to believe that he had conspired in obstructing justice. He had always warned against releasing the names of persons identified by the afflicted as their spectral tormentors. But he now also believed that some specters, identified by persons who had become afflicted since the trials ended, represented genuine witches. And he worried that his extreme caution had led him "to Sin in what I have done, such have been the Cowardice and Fearfulness whereunto my regard unto the dissatisfactions of other People has precipitated me." Thus he continued to withhold names while feeling "able to Convict some such Witches as ought to Die."

As Mather usually did when his judgment and his inclination conflicted, he adopted an inflammatory compromise. Although he accused no one by name, for eighteen months after the trials ended he kept alluding in his sermons to "the matchless *Enchantments* and *Possessions,* that have abounded in our Neighborhood" and kept warning that "the DEVIL, is more desirous to Regain poor *New England,* than any one *American* Spot of Ground." His remarks evidently provoked outrage, for he speaks in various places of the "cursed *Reproaches*" of "this unworthy, ungodly, ungrateful People" or of the "hard representations wherewith some Ill Men have given my conduct." The hostility toward him confounded his belief that he continued to act with enormous restraint for the sake of public peace, doing far less to expose witches than he could or should. It plainly touched on old, sore feelings of ingratitude, which the angelic visitation, and its promise of future honor and potency, may have allayed. "The very *Angels* of God," he told his congregation, "they take notice how we do acquit ourselves under any of our *Trials.* It is no matter whether *our Neighbours* do see our virtuous Carriage or no; *Gods Angels,* they see it."

Mather's most vigorous and persistent accuser was the otherwise obscure Robert Calef, probably a merchant, clothier, or dyer with whom Mather had some earlier acquaintance. However socially inconspicuous, it was Calef who had correctly observed in Mather the dangerous ambidexter habit of "carrying both fire to increase, and water, to quench, the conflagration." Calef saw the Salem trials as an unmitigated horror, a "tremendous judgment of God upon this country," the trial methods such "that most would have chosen to have fallen into the hands of the barbarous enemy, rather than . . . into the hands of their brethren in church fellowship." And now, as Calef saw this sequel to the Salem trials, now after the greatest blemish to religion that ever befell New England, after the governor with the crown's approval had stopped the executions, after it began being acknowledged that a mistake had been made, now Cotton Mather was sitting beside Margaret Rule surrounded by spectators, inquiring "Who is it that Afflicts you?"

On September 13—near the probable time of Mather's angelic encounter—Calef visited Rule's house, drawn by curiosity "and so much the rather because it was reported Mr. M_____ would be there that Night." He found the energumen lying still and speaking little, attended by thirty or forty people, including both Mathers. Shocked by what followed, he wrote out the same night an account highly discrediting to Cotton, who tries to get Rule to name her specters publicly, asks her leading questions, and lewdly feels her body:

> . . . they being sat, the Father on a Stool, and the Son upon the Bedside by her, the Son began to question her, Margaret Rule, how do you do? then a pause without any answer. *Question.* What, do there a great many Witches sit upon you? *Answer.* Yes. *Q.* Do you not know that there is a hard Master? Then she was in a Fit; He laid his hand upon her Face and Nose, but, as he said, without perceiving Breath; then he brush'd her on the Face with his Glove, and rubb'd her Stomach (her breast not covered with the Bedclothes) and bid others do so too. . . . *Q.* Who is it that Afflicts you? *A.* I know not, there is a great many of them (about this time the Father question'd if she knew the Spectres? An attendant said, if she did she would not tell; the Son proceeded) *Q.* You have seen the Black-man, hant you? *A.* No. *Reply;* I hope you never shall. *Q.* You have had a Book offered you, hant you? *A.* No. *Q.* The brushing of you gives you ease, don't it? *A.* Yes. She turned her self and a little Groan'd. *Q.* Now the Witches Scratch you and Pinch you, and Bite you, don't they? *A.* Yes. Then he put his hand upon her Breast and Belly, *viz.* on the Clothes over her, and felt a Living thing, as he said, which moved the Father also to feel, and some others; *Q.* Don't you feel the Live thing in the Bed? *A.* No. . . .

Calef secured two persons willing to verify his account, which he showed to several of his and of Mather's friends.

This "lying *Libel,*" as Mather called it, presented him doing exactly what he strove mightily not to do, disparaged him for discharging the solemn obligations of his ministry, and produced "*Paroxysms* in the Town." According to Calef, Mather made the episode "Pulpit news," called him "one of the worst of Liars," and threatened to have him arrested for slander. Mather's indignation must in this instance have been partly justified. Calef's memory cannot have served him well enough to write up at home, hours later, what poses as a verbatim transcript of the dialogue between Rule and the Mathers, occupying nearly two closely printed pages. Just the same, Mather seems to have been uncertain how to respond. Calef was brought before a justice of the peace on a warrant issued by Increase and Cotton Mather, to answer at the next court for "Scandalous Libels." But when Calef appeared no one appeared against him, and he was dismissed. Why Mather dropped the suit is unclear. Always wary of his tendency to blurt out resentment, he perhaps came to feel that he had overreacted in bringing the suit: "I did at first," he confided in his diary, "it may be too much resent the Injuries of that Libel."

Instead Mather indignantly attacked Calef's account in a lengthy letter to him on January 15, 1694. Calef's "pretended Narrative," he said, presented nothing about him or his father either truly or fairly. Where Calef portrayed them as coaxing new accusations from Rule, they on the contrary always charged her to "rather Die than tell the Names of any whom she might Imagine that she knew." Where Calef attributed to them such leading questions as "how many Witches sit upon you?" they on the contrary never used and deliberately avoided such questions. Especially, where Calef said that Cotton Mather "rub'd Rule's stomach, her Breast not being covered," spectators could confirm the charge to be "a gross (if not a doubled) Lie," a lie contrived to besmirch him. You "cannot but know," he told Calef, "how much this Representation hath contributed, to make People believe a Smutty thing of me."

Calef, however, retracted nothing. Replying to Mather's letter three days later, he reiterated his accusations but denied having said that Rule's breast was uncovered. Mather in paraphrasing his account, Calef said, omitted "those material words 'with the Bed-Clothes'"—an unfair retort, since Calef's account clearly implies that Rule was partly naked. The suggestion of prurience, he added, was created by Mather himself, in publicly discoursing about the event at dinner at the home of Governor Phips. Chiefly Calef indicted Mather for evading the potentially explosive social implications of the episode, "as if I were giving Characters, Reflections, and Libels, etc. concerning your self and Relations."

Mather and Calef continued their dispute through an exchange of lengthy letters and documents lasting into 1696, debating in detail many more pneumatological issues than can be discussed here. The entire epistolary duel evinces class antagonism: Mather the Harvard-educated ministerial son of a prestigious family writing to a semi-literate clothier with a condescension that makes evident his suppressed contempt, Calef writing with a cuttingly exaggerated respect occasionally breaking into open denunciation that makes equally plain his irritation with Mather's assumption of superiority. Although Calef's expression of his ideas is often elliptical and murky, it conveys, sometime eloquently, his conviction that at Salem innocent people had been legally murdered, and that by continuing to cast out alleged demons and to promulgate his pneumatology, Mather was brewing new Salems.

On his side of the debate, Calef hammered with impassioned insistence at a fundamental point which he pressed Mather, and other Boston ministers, to answer. Shifting his focus from spectral evidence to an issue prominent in earlier witchcraft literature—that of God's permission of witchcraft—he accused the judges of attributing to human beings, and punishing them for, powers belonging only to devils or to God. The judges acted on the principle that a witch can commission the devil to afflict mortals; but for Calef "only the Almighty that sets bounds to his rage . . . can commission him to hurt and destroy." With Mather more particularly in mind, he also challenged the notion that devils can invisibilize matter. His letters to Mather are pervaded by scorn for his credulousness and gleeful taunts for his memorable statement that with his own hands he had knocked off Martha Goodwin's invisible chains. Over and over with grinding sarcasm, Calef proposed to Mather that the methods used to defeat supposed witches savored of witchcraft themselves, such as "knocking off invisible chains."

Calef kept needling Mather to deal with his "Fundamentals," but Mather ignored him until February 1695, when he sent a thirty-two page treatise on witchcraft. Written as an epistle to someone else, as if he disdained addressing Calef directly, it was his last substantial work on the seven-year-long invasion of spirits. He devoted about a third of the treatise to elaborating a "preliminary *Position*": that by their fall, the evil angels did not lose all their angelical powers. He offered both scriptural and *"experimental"* proofs—"the *pinches* that I have seen given to them; the *Blisters* that I have seen Rais'd on them"—and concluded by explaining manifestations of the invisible world, more assuredly than before, in terms of the plastic spirit:

> That there is a *Plastic Spirit* permeating of the World, which very powerfully operates upon the more corporeal parts of it: and . . . the *Angels,* both good and bad, are on the account of their *Natures,* the most Able of all creatures, to Apply that *Spirit* unto very many and mighty purposes.

He devoted another third or more of the treatise to such miscellaneous questions as the form of witch-covenants, and most of the rest to the question of God's justice in permitting diabolic attacks on mankind.

But to Calef's fundamental question, whose importance he acknowledged, Mather allowed about one page of obfuscation, evasion, and contradiction. Indeed, Calef's question exposed a serious confusion in Mather's understanding of the invisible world. If, as Mather remarked himself,
"The *Devils* can do *no Evil,* without a special permission from our Great
God," how could mortal witches "Commissionate" them? In his sketchy
answer, Mather agreed with Calef that God limits the devils' power and
must permit them to act. But he suggested, in characteristically elastic
language, that "It seems possible that the *Devils* having a sufficient and
antecedent Permission to do mischiefs may yet Hook in cursed *Witches* to
consent with them." As Calef later pointed out to Mather, if the devils
"Hook in" the witches then the witches do not commission them. Mather
also proposed that if witchcraft is the *"Skill of Applying the plastic Spirit
of the World unto unlawful Purposes,"* then the witches' consent as much
contributes to the effects wrought by the devils as the longings of a pregnant woman, by means of the plastic spirit also, contribute to shaping the
fetus. Here Mather simply forgot or disregarded his own earlier definition, quoted in the last paragraph, which assigns the power of using the
plastic spirit not to witches but to devils. Finally, Mather speculated that
God "seems to have made a *Grant* unto those Destroying Spirits, that
when they are with such and such wicked *Ceremonies* called for, they
shall make a mischievous Descent." This very slippery statement of what
God "seems to" have done glides by the real question of whether, having
made their descent, the devils also carry out the witches' desires. In this
feeble, final show of answering Calef, Mather managed to be no more
lucid or persuasive than in *Wonders of the Invisible World.*

Mather loaned his treatise to Calef with the condition that he return it
in two weeks and promise not to copy it. After reading it, Calef replied
that he did not wonder at Mather's stipulations, considering its "crude
matter and impertinent absurdities." Before returning the manuscript he
covered the margins, in most cases justly, with about a hundred jeering
annotations for Mather's perusal. He accused Mather of begging the question by bare assertions, of evading it by lengthy discussion of the power of
fallen angels, and of confusing it by introducing the occult concept of
plastic spirit. In outraged marginalia he spat out his horror over the Salem
hangings and slashed Mather for his credulous innocence: "You have
told the world that already in your several books . . . Plastic Spirit, whats
that. Sure some inkhorn term. . . . An easy trick for any Salem hocus to
perform . . . turning men to cats and dogs riding a pole through the air,

and the rest of such ridiculous and brutish stuff . . . . is this worse than knocking off invisible chains with the hand. . . ."

*

The good angels who appeared to Mercy Short, Margaret Rule, and Mrs. Carver of Salem made their largest descent on Boston in the fall of 1694, about a year after Cotton Mather's own visitation. This epilogue to the Salem trials is very little known, mainly because Mather's diaries for 1694 and 1695 are missing, and the events survive only in fragmentary and sometimes considerably later accounts. But by August 1694, the number of reported visitations, it seems, prompted the Cambridge Association of ministers to propose for discussion the topic, "Whether angelical visits by visible appearance to the people of God in these days are wholly ceased; or, if not ceased, what are the marks whereby we may distinguish them from diabolical?"

The counterdescent of good angels apparently coincided with, and perhaps inspired, a religious revival in the North Church. On a single day in September 1694, Cotton Mather entered in the church records thirteen admissions to full membership (that is, thirteen recent experiences of grace)—exceeding the number of admissions to the church for most entire *years.* (In all of 1695, only eight persons were admitted.) "In the Air," Increase observed the same month, "Angels have been descending and there making melody to the Lord." The angelic music seems to have rung loudest in October, when there occurred in the North End, Cotton wrote later, "a strange Descent of *Shining Spirits,* that had upon them great marks of their being such *Angels* as they Declared themselves to be." The angels told the persons they visited that Increase Mather need not perplex himself about going to England, for God would bring to pass what would be most for His Glory, "*And the Angels of* GOD *will attend him, wheresoever His Providence may dispose of him.*"

Both Mathers regarded these visitations warily, alert to diabolic imposture. In one case a spiritually troubled woman in the North Church applied to Cotton for advice. While in his study she fell into a lifeless trance, eyes transfixed. When she revived she pointed to a place in the room where, she said, she had seen a "a most Glorious Appearance of An Angel in a Shining Apparel." Fearing a trick of the devil, Mather told her to be very cautious. But at a private religious meeting of young women she again became entranced and was told, she said, "Our Friend Mather is Apt to doubt we are good Angels, but tell him for to Convince him that we are these things, for he'll be here in half an hour, that he's now

Studying Such a Sermon on Such a Text." When Mather arrived he revealed that he had indeed been thinking of a sermon on that text. Ultimately the angels told the woman, however, that because their appearance puzzled Increase Mather, "we will because we loath to grieve him, never visit you any more."

A second young woman in the North Church heard a voice offering her religious counsel. Cotton Mather at first suspected a *"loose Imagination,"* but again learned that the *"Invisible Whisperer"* disclosed to her secrets which he knew to be true and she did not. Yet two features of her story disturbed him. She balked at visiting him as her pastor, and when she did visit she developed a strange inability to relate her experiences, suggesting that she was "under the Enchantments of a *Spirit* who was lothe, I should examine too narrowly his *Devices.*" Also, the spirit revealed to her some hidden miscarriages of others and commanded her to speak with them about their iniquities. Mather knew these persons to be innocent and foresaw that her accusations would endanger neighborhood peace. On balance he concluded the woman's voices "had no Angelical Aspect" and he required her to discountenance the unseen speaker and be afraid of hearing from him. When the spirit returned next she told it: *"I desire no more to hear from you; Mr.* Mather says *you are a Devil, and I am afraid you are. If you are an Angel of the Lord, give me a Proof of it."* The spirit did not answer, and never returned, persuading Mather that his skepticism had aborted a *"Begun Witchcraft* of the most *explicit* sort."

However cautious about his own and other visitations, Mather never doubted that his life had been "wondrously Signalized, by the Sensible Ministry of those *Angels.*" Loath to be guilty of ungratefully neglecting the angels, as did "the Generality of the Faithful," he kept a day of secret thanksgiving, probably late in 1694, to offer extraordinary praises to God for them and obtain "a more Notable Share of their Influence, than had ever yet been granted me." In the morning, aside from singing many hymns relating to angels, he contemplated with the aid of Scripture the existence, properties, and relations of the good angels, and the honor owing to them. In the afternoon he searched his diaries for entries concerning divine mercies which might have been subordinately executed through the operation of angels.

Reinterpreting decisive moments in his life in view of his recent understanding of angelic agency, Mather listed fourteen particular mercies. Among them were the wise parental governance afforded him in childhood, which "had a *Bias* very often given to it, by the *Angels* of God"; his childhood preservation from dangers, "by the *Angels* Looking after me";

the kind conduct of his tutors, "which doubtless the *Angels* influenced"; his preservation from epidemical illnesses, "by an Hedge of *Angels* about me." His call to the ministry in so remarkable a place as Boston, too, was "full of *Angels.*" He found many more angelically guided mercies in his later life also, which he similarly avowed from his study floor with rapturous Hallelujahs. In the surprising opening of his "Door of *Utterance,*" in the "astonishing *Impulse*" that often impinged on his mind when speaking and writing, in his marriage, family, and household provision, here too "I were Blinder than a Stone, if I should not see *Angels* my Providers."

Nor, ever mindful of repaying gifts, did Cotton Mather fail to consider what returns he should make to God for these angelic benefits. A proper return, he decided, was to become angelical himself, like the angels continually to behold and to admire God's glories, continually to study the mysteries of redemption and the approach of the millennium, continually to aid the churches of Christ, continually post on God's errands. Indeed he closed his special day of thanksgiving with something itself "a Little *Angelical,*" making a list of poor people in his flock and resolving with some care to have their necessities relieved against the approaching winter.

5

The Parter's Portion

SIR WILLIAM PHIPS was not John Winthrop. The first royal governor under
the new charter, he had been baptized in adulthood by Cotton Mather
and was a member of his congregation; Mather looked for close association with him. But Phips had spent his life adventurously at sea, and
whatever he imbibed of the piety of the North Church did not extinguish
in him the temperament of a corsair.

Six months into his governorship, Phips brawled on Scarlett's Wharf
with a man named Richard Short. Phips was uncommonly tall, as Mather
described him, "and *Thick* as well as *Tall,* and *Strong* as well as *Thick.*"
Short, at the time Phips called him a liar, was lame in one hand and had
been ill in bed for a week. When Short denied being a liar, Phips struck
him with his cane, and when Short fell over a gun, Phips kept striking
him until his head was fractured. Phips exploded again when he came
across a customs collector named Brenton unloading seized goods. According to one witness, Phips began caning Brenton and pushing him
around the wharf, calling him villain, demanding that he return the goods
immediately or "he would beat him until he broke his Bones."

The governor treated members of his own government hardly more
subtly. When the Speaker of the Assembly opposed him he declared the
man "no more Speaker." The Speaker protested, but Phips stopped him,
saying, "I have declared you to be no more Speaker, and so I do not allow
you to speak." Having governed less than three years Phips was ordered
home in 1694 to answer complaints against him, including some £20,000
in damages. On November 17, Mather and others accompanied him
aboard his yacht as he departed. About three months later he died in

London, and the affairs of Massachusetts again passed to a temporary ruler, the lieutenant governor and former chief justice of the Salem court, William Stoughton.

The unreliability of the government under the new charter was borne in on Mather again by the arrival in May 1699 of the second crown-appointed governor, the Irish peer Lord Bellomont. Except for Andros, he was the first person to govern Massachusetts as neither a native nor an immigrant. Being also the first who was a nobleman, he received a lavish welcome—military guard, toasts, drums beating, trumpets sounding, fireworks, colors displayed, ordnance booming, "such a vast Concourse of people," one Bostonian said, "as my poor eyes never saw the like before." Five days later the ministers, hoping for the governor's favor, waited on him as a body. Cotton Mather prepared an address, which Increase handed to Bellomont; but the governor, Cotton wrote proudly, "immediately gave it back into my Hand; asking me to read it unto him," as he did, requesting Bellomont's goodwill toward the churches and toward languishing Harvard.

Cotton Mather's hope for renewed influence in government proved doubly short-lived, first because Bellomont quickly came to regard him as given "to preach moderation, and not to practice it," then because as governor of both New England and New York Bellomont spent only fourteen months of his three-year reign in Boston. In his absence, the government again devolved on Stoughton. Stoughton himself died in 1701, however, and after fifteen years of bobbing and flux the government of Massachusetts passed, again temporarily, to the Council.

The succession of brief and sometime exotic governments showed that in one of its concerns the old mentality of invasion had not been unrealistic, for the loss of the charter and the accession of William and Mary were transforming the meaning of New England. As the imposition of royal government began being defined in practical political terms, local politics were reshaped along English lines, and Massachusetts adjusted itself to the tone and demands of the mother country. Mather was keenly aware that an exclusivist Christian Israel could no longer exist, and he tried strenuously to adapt the New England churches to these drastically changed circumstances. Despite his cries about the devil reclaiming a uniquely sanctified New England for his own, in the decade following the trials he continually proclaimed that New Englanders were not a special purified remnant but were, above all, loyal colonial Englishmen. "It is no Little Blessing of God, that we are a part of the *English*

Nation," he told the General Assembly in 1700. "Our Dependence on, and Relation to, that brave *Nation,* that man deserves not the Name of an *English man,* who despises it."

In this spirit of reunion, Mather also proclaimed New England Congregationalism restored to the Church of England, and sought a rapprochement with other English Protestants, particularly Presbyterians. The two sects had long been divided by their view of a national church. Presbyterians viewed local congregations as part of the Church of England, responsible to church courts; Congregationalists insisted on the independence of local churches, joined only by informal fellowship and advice. But upon William's accession, leaders of the two groups met in London, with the active participation of Increase Mather, and tried to effect a union. They produced in 1691 a document that demonstrated their agreement on basic articles of faith and abolished the distinction between them: *Heads of Agreement Assented to by the United Ministers In and About London: Formerly called Presbyterian and Congregational.* Cotton Mather joined in giving up the identity of Congregationalism, whose name had been conferred by his own grandfather John Cotton. The Nonconformist churches, he wrote in 1700, "have needlessly been sometimes Distinguished into *Presbyterian* and *Congregational,* but are now, I hope, losing the Distinction, in that more *Christian* Name of *United Brethren.*"

Mather moved even further from Congregational exclusivism in response to King William's Toleration Act of 1689. The Act profoundly affected English Nonconformists, for in legally recognizing their right to worship it left them without a cause to fight, sapped their zeal, and sped their decline. In abolishing religious persecution, the Act in effect also made New England Puritanism unnecessary, for it removed what had impelled the first settlers to flee old England. The Toleration Act emboldened in Mather a latent ecumenism. Not long after his father's return from England he had run "the Hazard of much Reproach" by preaching to the General Assembly against civil punishment for conscientious religious dissent, making him, he believed, "the only *Minister* Living in the Land, that have testified against the *Suppression* of *Heresy,* by *Persecution.*"

To show himself a true Englishman, respectful of English law, Mather would now no more regard Episcopalians as a danger to New England, any more than Episcopalians after the Toleration Act would regard Nonconformists as a threat to them. Indeed he took pleasure in observing that the New England churches welcomed Episcopalians and others to transient communion: "we have with delight seen godly Congregationals and

Presbyterians, and Episcopalians, and Antipaedobaptists [i.e., Baptists], all members in the same churches; and sitting together without offence about their Lesser Differences, at the same Holy Table." Beginning around 1692 he began urging Congregationalists not to "*Monopolize* all Godliness to our own *Little Party*," since Christians who keep differing modes of worship can still be in a state of salvation: "every *Difference in Religion,* does not make a *Different Religion.* And if we think our own *Understandings* to be a *Standard* for all the Rest of Mankind, we do certainly, *Think of our selves above what we ought.*"

While opening Christian Israel to non-Congregationalists and reaching beyond it for union with English Presbyterians, Mather also forwarded important innovations in the relation of the Congregational churches to each other. For one, he tried to promote interchurch councils and synods. His desire to strengthen the churches through cooperation was influenced by Presbyterian practice and probably by the new charter, which weakened the churches in depriving them of dependable government support. In recommending various unions of churches he ventured on dangerous ground, however, for Congregationalism stressed the autonomy of individual churches and viewed overseeing bodies as a move toward episcopacy and even papacy. Largely because Increase Mather feared a drift in that direction, it was said, no church synod was held in New England for forty years.

Yet in an unpublished essay on the utility of synods, written around 1699, Cotton Mather professed his "Abhorrence of unaccountable *Independency*" in churches and depicted the congregations of New England as "bound up" with each other in the "Same Common Interests of Christianity." He recommended that each church respect the advice of prominent ministers, pledge to maintain intimate association with other churches, and freely account for its practices to any church inquiring after them. He also recommended the calling of church councils to consult on inflammatory disputes in individual churches. If the council when called failed to reclaim an erring church, it could declare the church unfit for communion with other churches and deprive it of the legal privileges they enjoyed—for instance, forbidding members of the wayward church to take communion at other churches. In fact, such councils and assemblies were multiplying at the turn of the century, and Mather attended several himself in Salem, Marlborough, and other places.

In the same spirit of innovation, Mather also promoted clerical associations. Congregationalists had long mistrusted these also: several New England ministers who gathered fortnightly at one of their homes, Governor John Winthrop recorded in 1633, met with objections and stirred fear that they might become a presbytery. On the other hand, many ministers among Cotton Mather's generation saw in clerical associations a means of reaffirming the importance and independence of their office. In 1690 twenty-two ministers meeting in Charlestown had founded a Cambridge Association of Ministers, modeled after similar groups in England. With Cotton Mather often acting as secretary they met at Harvard every six weeks to discuss religious topics and hear cases from individual churches or persons. Drawing material from their records, Cotton published *Thirty Important Cases* (1699), in the Preface to which he noted that such meetings had been approved by the United Ministers in England, "formerly called *Presbyterian* and *Congregational*," and encouraged ministers elsewhere to hold regular meetings on the Cambridge model. While recognizing that no more than occasional meetings could be expected, he saw no danger, he said, of "overwhelming the *Rights* of *Particular Churches* by *Classical* Combinations."

Mather also wished clerical groups to test ministerial candidates, to prevent the ordination of the unqualified or fraudulent. Two cases illustrate the need. The first Mather recounted in a delightful narrative, *A Warning to the Flocks* (1700), which tells the adventures of a preacher named Samuel May, who arrived with his wife from England in 1699. May's "Ragged, Wretched, Forlorn Circumstances" at first moved Mather's compassion. Mather found him work preaching to private religious meetings, and soon May had a large following. Soon also, Mather found him unable to name a single minister in London. Mather's suspicions mounted when he received from May a short note containing eighteen misspellings. He declared May "a BARBER" and prayed that he would be exposed. The chance came when he heard May preach at a private meeting and identified his sermon as a plagiarism. May not only denied it but also induced his followers to requite Mather's defamation of him by throwing into his house "insolent, bitter, bloody *Libels*." After May at last "went off with a Stink" to England, several Boston women deposed that if a young woman became affected by his ministry he spent hours counseling her to lie with him, "which he said, was *no Sin*, for *David* and *Solomon* did as much." They need not fear becoming pregnant by him, he added, "*for none ever were so!*" May's alleged wife turned out to be his mistress, and the impostor himself turned out to be Samuel Axel, a Hampshire brickmaker. The case notified churches, Mather said, to beware of hiring "*New Preachers*, of whose Endowments and Principles, they have not had a Reasonable Attestation."

A more dolorous case occurred in Mather's own family. His uncle John Cotton—the son of the great John Cotton, and his dearest relative since childhood—was charged in 1697 with what Samuel Sewall called "Notorious Breaches of the Seventh Commandment" or what a Plymouth shipbuilder described as "attempting to be too Familiar with one of his Church Members Wife." A council of neighboring churches recommended that the Plymouth church dismiss him, as it did. Although greatly distressed over the "terrible and amazing Circumstances, of my poor Uncle," Cotton Mather considered the recommendation just. A few months after the dismissal he apparently sent the Cotton family, as he often did, one of his recent publications. But it arrived with an anonymous letter, John Cotton lamented, with "no superscription to it, no inscription no subscription . . . neither is there a word who sent the Book." The snub hurt the more because he had damaged his standing with the church council by defending Mather, although one of the council members "very much" despised him. (Desolate and confused, John Cotton managed to secure a ministry in South Carolina. En route he visited his nephew in Boston and "very peremptorily," Cotton Mather said, denied "the most, and the worst" of the charges against him, but in less than a year he was dead, of an epidemic of yellow fever in Charleston that killed nearly two hundred people.)

In or out of his family such cases worried Mather, and in hopes of ensuring a learned and ethical clergy he published *Proposals for the Preservation of Religion in the Churches, by a Due Trial of Them that Stand Candidates for the Ministry* (1702). Here he recommended giving groups of ordained ministers a part in the process of candidacy and ordination, otherwise the concern of individual churches. He proposed that every ministerial candidate be examined by and preach before such a group, and obtain from four or five already ordained ministers testimonials to his knowledge of learned languages, skill in preaching, theological learning, soundness of principle, and ability to refute error. Although concurred in by nearly thirty ministers, Mather's proposals were not adopted. In fact they lay well outside the spirit of primitive New England Congregationalism, amounting to a crypto-Presbyterianism by which more or less formal panels of ministers might if not license ministerial candidates, at least police them.

In calling for more frequent church councils and for clerical associations, Mather departed from Congregational principles in the name, of course, of preserving Congregational orthodoxy. The inconsistency is uncomfortable but understandable. It becomes perplexing, however, if one adds that while calling for a Congregational-Presbyterian merger and for hospitality to all Protestant sects, Mather at the very same time continued to act the part of a Jeremiah, bemoaning and chastising the decline from the religion of the Fathers, for example in *Things for a Distress'd People to Think Upon* (1696):

> *New England* once abounded with *Hero's* worthy to have their Lives written, as Copies for future Ages to write after; But, *These are Ancient Things!* A *Public Spirit* in all that sustained any *Public Office,* and a fervent *Inclination* to Do Good, join'd with an Incomparable *Ability* to do it, once ran through *New England;* But, *These are Ancient Things!* . . . There seems to be a shameful *Shrink,* in all sorts of men among us, from that *Greatness,* and *Goodness,* which adorned our Ancestors: We grow *Little* every way; *Little* in our Civil Matters, *Little* in our Military Matters, *Little* in our Ecclesiastical Matters; we dwindle away, to *Nothing.* . . .

In fact, during the same years that he forwarded ecumenism and toleration, Mather published more works than ever before on the urgent need for reformation, aimed at restoring (if it ever existed) a special, spiritually minded Puritan community of praying families, children who did not play at the rear of the meetinghouse on Sabbaths, boys and girls who shunned mixed dances, cheerfully obedient servants catechized by caring masters, and sailors who sang psalms instead of bawdy songs.

Mather did not concede, or perhaps could not see, the conflict between his simultaneous calls for openness and exclusiveness. But the discrepancy has led modern historians to offer directly contradictory interpretations of his views in these years. Richard Lovelace, for instance, argues that Mather "put himself on record in favor of toleration in his earliest published sermons" and that he "seems to have been considerably in the vanguard of the conservative leadership of the colony." Contrarily, Robert Middlekauff writes that Mather's endorsements of toleration in the early 1690s were "undoubtedly insincere" and that he in fact "confined the guarantees of toleration as tightly as possible."

If not insincere, Mather's several innovations may at least have been politic. The demonstration of New England's loyalty to the empire was an old game. Mather's many expressions of loyalty to the crown often came in the presence of crown officials such as Lord Bellomont, and several of his ecumenical writings were published in England, perhaps to show New England's appreciation for William's policy of toleration. Mather had other compelling reasons for urging a reconciliation with England, including strong ecumenical tendencies that had long existed within Puritanism (Richard Baxter was a pioneer ecumenist), the hope of regaining a voice in English affairs, the need for allies in the raging struggle against Catholic Europe and the looming war against rationalism, and his prophetic sense, as we shall see, of impending revolutions that would unite all of Christianity.

It is more likely, however, that Mather's insincerity (or political trimming) lay in the other direction, that his simultaneous calls for liberalism and orthodoxy deferred not to English Protestantism but to Boston Puritanism. His policy on admission to communion was more liberal than his father's, and he may have been genuinely attracted to ecumenism and church union but maintained a show of greater orthodoxy than he felt out of respect to his father's ideals. However that may be, he undoubtedly in many ways enjoyed the more various and cosmopolitan world in part created by the new charter. While he deeply respected the Wilderness Zion of the Fathers, his yearnings for bigness and fame, his lively sympathy with new fashions and ideas, and his identification with the more aristocratic and urbane sections of society did not relish the sense of living in some isolated city on a hill. Something of unashamed worldliness appears in his attitude toward the wearing of large perriwigs, which became fashionable in New England around 1690, as they had in England thirty years earlier. The English Puritan William Prynne denounced those who "purchase the hairy excrements of some other person," for to him and most other Puritans wigs smacked of effeminacy, pride, and affectation, suggesting Stuart courtiers, theatrical costumes, and old men trying to look young. Yet in his one surviving portrait Cotton Mather wears a profuse perriwig, nearly shoulder length. Samuel Sewall considered wigs a profane abomination and was surprised when in 1691 he understood Mather to be defending them in a sermon as "an innocent fashion, taken up and used by the best of men." "I expected not," Sewall said, "to hear a vindication of Perriwigs in Boston Pulpit by Mr. Mather."

Sewall's surprise, in what it registers about Cotton Mather, does not differ from the contrary interpretations of Mather's ideas offered by modern historians, nor from Robert Calef's earlier perception that Mather brought both fire to increase and water to quench the conflagration. In fact, hardly a trait of Mather's maturing personality is more striking than his preoccupation with seeming irreconcilables and his view of himself as a peacemaker between warring factions—originating, it seems clear, in his unsuccessful youthful attempt to settle conflicts in himself, of which an earlier expression was his stammer. The discrepancy now between his twin attraction to the metropolitan world of London and the world of his grandfathers indeed seems a continuation of the earlier conflict between the pride and ambition he recognized in himself, and his dutiful wish to use his ministry in God's service alone.

Whether trying to calm contending political factions after the revolt or running between Moses and Aaron during the Salem trials, Cotton Mather's conciliatory efforts often brought him enmity from both sides, what he called the "*Parter's Portion.*" He suspected, as he wrote in *Blessed Unions* (1692), that his current calls for toleration of rival religious claims and his attempt to close the gaps between different Protestant sects would get him the "*Parter's Portion*" also. That happened, his dole arriving through what he saw as a new invasion of the New England churches.

*

In another dozen years, Lydia Lee George would become the chief delight of Cotton Mather's life, and his greatest torment. But in 1701 she was the young wife of a prosperous organizer of a new Boston church, concerned that she had spent too much time and thought on her apparel and indulged the vanity of vying with others. Reassuringly her twenty-eight-year-old pastor, Benjamin Colman, counseled that her dress suited her birth, rank, age, and education. He criticized those who equate religion with plainness and "morosely judge all that wear more buttons, than they allow themselves." Since she had been brought up to dress richly, and her wealthy husband approved it, he said, "it is not offensive nor grievous to sober Christians: It is not good to indulge scruples too much, for they will grow upon you apace to your great discomfort."

This genial advice typified the young minister, who was known for his courtly tenderness toward women, and for powdering his hair. Those who knew Benjamin Colman invariably depicted him as pious but polished—a tall, spare figure neatly dressed, with a fair complexion and kindly mien, notable for his "Politeness and Elegance in Conversation" and his "inimitably soft and tuneful" voice—in short, a ministerial man of fashion. He had begun life less genteelly. Born in Boston and a member of the North Church, he had his early schooling from Mather's schoolmaster, Ezekiel Cheever, graduated from Harvard in 1692, preached a while at Medford, and added an M.A. in 1695. Shortly after, he went to England where, like many later Americans, he underwent a sea change. French privateers seized his ship, put him in the hold, and imprisoned him in France. Set free, he reached England with a few shillings in his pocket, of which a spark in Portsmouth bilked him. Finally settled in London, he preached there and in other English cities, attended the conference at which Increase Mather worked for the union of Congregationalists and Presbyterians, and wrote a poem on his flirtation with the daughter of the Massachusetts agent, Sir Henry Ashurst, comparing her to a candle and himself to a fly.

A Presbyterian board appointed Colman minister at Bath—a choice situation because of the resort there of the gentry. In his two years at Bath he met many fashionable families, including that of the poet "Philomela" (Elizabeth Singer), a "Heavenly maid," as he called her. "Music, poetry, and painting were her three beauties and delights." Upon visiting the family's home he versified the paradisal beauty of its grounds, viewing them as an eligible bachelor:

> Such Eden's streams, and banks, and tow'ring groves;
> Such Eve herself, and such her muse and loves.
> Only there wants an Adam on the green,
> Or else all Paradise might here be seen.

Such an Adam Elizabeth's family seem to have desired Colman to become. But he responded instead to a call that came in the summer of 1699 from the organizers of the new Boston church, inviting him to be their pastor. Apparently suspecting that opposition to their church might prevent his ordination in Boston, they advised him to be ordained by a board in London. Their advice defied Congregationalist principles, by which a minister could be ordained only by a particular church. But like some other ministers in his generation, Colman saw his identity as a minister less in terms of native tradition than in terms of English modes of religious life. When he returned to Boston in November 1699, he had been ordained, though still a member of the North Church, by the London Presbytery, in the Presbyterian manner.

The organizers of the new church were a group of Boston merchants, several of whom had subscribed in 1689 toward building a Church of England chapel. Led by the wealthy Thomas Brattle, the church later became known as the Brattle Street Church. The organizers claimed that a new church was needed because the older meetinghouse lacked enough "convenient seats." In fact, their new building—in the South End, about two streets from the Town House—was meaningfully innovative. Instead of the central turret distinctive to earlier New England meetinghouses, it had a full tower and spire at one end, like the churches of England. The building stood out from the other Boston churches in more than architecture, for the organizers also desired to make what they said were needed changes in worship.

In December, shortly after Colman's return, the organizers published a three-page *Manifesto* setting forth their principles. Calling in their defense upon the recent spirit of ecumenism, they said they intended only the true and pure worship of God as revealed in Scripture but conformable to the "Churches of the UNITED BRETHREN in *London,* and throughout all *England.*" Only in a few particulars, they said, did they "see cause to depart from what is ordinarily Professed and Practised by the Churches of CHRIST here in *New-England.*" The particulars included the reading of Scripture by the minister without explication; the omission of a public relation of converting experience as a requirement for entry to communion; and the extension of the power of choosing a minister beyond communicants to every baptized adult person. (In psalm singing the church also very soon abandoned the custom of "lining-out," that is, of alternately reading and singing psalms line by line—an important step toward the development of musical literacy in New England.) A contemporary later described the Brattle church as "midway between the Church of England and Dissenters." That seems correct, for the new church tried to retain its Congregational roots but inclined to benignity rather than zeal, sought contact with moderate Anglicans, and identified the church more with the entire congregation than with the core of Saints.

In fact the Brattle church was a somewhat advanced version of the vision of transatlantic and intersectarian harmony Cotton Mather had been popularizing for the last half-dozen years. Mather's response, however, was not welcoming but wrathful. He denounced the new church as the work of "Head-strong" men whose *Manifesto,* coming in the wake of Andros and the evil angels, attempted once again to "utterly subvert our Churches." In seeing "another *Day of Temptation* begun upon the Town and Land," he resembled the man to whom promiscuous means someone having one more affair than himself. He damned as dangerous innovations ideas only slightly left of innovations he had introduced himself. Having relaxed admissions requirements in his own church, he scorned the new church's still more lax failure to require a relation of conversion experience. While speaking proudly of sharing the communion table with Presbyterians, Baptists, and moderate Anglicans, he had no desire to create them out of Congregationalists, as Colman had in effect been in accepting Presbyterian ordination. Chiefly he seems to have objected to the Brattle group's rejection of church covenants—explicit public agreements by groups of Saints to worship together—not so much for its democratizing tendency as for making the operation of the church secretive and unneighborly. Ministers who would be faithful to Christ, he believed, would have to appear on the front lines again, and no little part must "unavoidably fall to my Share."

As a first maneuver, Mather sent the *"Innovators"* a long monitory letter. Although "most lovingly penn'd," he said, it only raised their "impetuous Lusts, to carry on the *Apostasy*." Colman, while not yet formally dismissed from the Mathers' church, was installed as minister of the new church on December 12. On December 24 the Brattle church worshiped for the first time in its new meetinghouse and apparently drew, as it did afterward, a large crowd; Sewall remarked that his own congregation was "pretty much thin'd by it." The Brattle organizers had requested Colman to ask the other Boston ministers, as a token of fellowship, to join them in a day of fasting. Perhaps thinking it futile to resist Colman's influence, and perhaps serving his sense of himself as a peacemaker, Mather drew up a letter to Colman on December 28, signed also by his father and by the Boston minister James Allen, offering to preach and pray with the Brattle congregation provided they lay aside their *Manifesto* and simply declared their adherence to the *Heads of Agreement* of the United Brethren. Otherwise they could not join in fellowship, "Lest we partake in the guilt of those great Irregularities whereby you have given just cause of offence." The Brattle group's response has not survived but must have been unfavorable, since a week later Mather denounced them afresh in his diary as "ignorant, arrogant, obstinate, and full of Malice and Slander, and they fill the Land with *Lies,* in the Misrepresentation whereof, I am a very singular Sufferer."

With Sewall and some others acting as intermediaries between the Mathers and the Brattle church—"Was some heat," Sewall said, "but grew calmer"—a compromise was reached whereby the church agreed to announce its adherence to the *Heads of Agreement* and to follow Congregational practice in making a public declaration of church covenant. A "wonderful Joy fill'd the Hearts of our good People, far and near," Mather wrote, "that we had obtained thus much from them." On January 28 he formally dismissed Colman from the North Church and three days later he and his father joined the young minister in a public fast at the Brattle church. Increase, who did not easily put bygones to rest, preached on the doctrine that we must follow peace—so far as it consists with holiness. Cotton, Sewall recorded, prayed "excellently and pathetically for Mr. Colman and his Flock. Twas a close dark day."

But the darkness had only begun. While negotiating with the Brattle church, the Mathers had prepared for press a lengthy blast at it. Cotton speaks of the book as a joint effort, but it seems to have been very largely

Increase's work. After devising a compromise with the church, Cotton wrote, "we laid aside what was in the Press; resolving in a more comfortable, and I hope, effectual Way, to endeavour the Establishment of our Churches." But Increase decided to publish the book anyway, perhaps because the Brattle Street innovations seemed more dangerous to him than they seemed to his son. Although Increase had already preached and prayed at the new church, his book attacking it appeared in March, entitled *The Order of the Gospel* (1700). In 144 pages he argued against seventeen distinct principles of the Brattle church, defending the right of churches to demand written or oral evidence of regenerating experience before admitting a member to communion, questioning the ordination of ministers without the approbation of neighboring churches, and concluding that to espouse Brattle principles was to "give away *the whole Congregational cause* at once, and a great part of the *Presbyterian Discipline* also."

By coincidence, Increase's arguments against the Brattle church anticipated the announcement a few months later of some new but related innovations which gave the controversy redoubled intensity. This time the apostate was not a youth but a nearly sixty-year-old member of Increase's generation, the Northampton minister Solomon Stoddard, whose *Doctrine of Instituted Churches* appeared in London in the spring or early summer. Stoddard was, and remains, a highly controversial figure in the development of New England, whom some historians have seen as an early voice of democracy. His book gave comprehensive expression to views he had been promoting in western Massachusetts for twenty years, particularly that communion should not be limited to those who had experienced grace. In this he probably intended no more than to halt the widely lamented decline, where other attempts at reform had failed. But to open the communion table to all church members was to discard the most fundamental ideas of Puritan theology and church government, the distinctive Congregational understanding of the church as an elite group of Saints. Some saw Stoddard's views as the fatal outcome of the undermining doctrine of halfway membership promulgated since 1662, and Increase Mather had attacked Stoddard as early as 1677 for advancing notions certain to "corrupt Churches and ruin all in a little time."

Now, atop the opening of the Brattle church, Stoddard argued in print the even more extreme idea that communion might itself lead to Sainthood, might be "a means also to work saving Regeneration." Some eminent Presbyterians had advocated this view earlier, but to most Congregationalists it conjured up a communion table surrounded by thieves, drunkards, and adulterers hoping to drink and eat their salvation. To his very radical proposal, Stoddard added an astonishing concept of the church. He would conceive a congregation not as a coterie of Saints but as merely a group of people assembled by God in the same place. Since a church was only a neighborhood phenomenon it deserved no independent ecclesiastical power. Stoddard forthrightly advocated Presbyterianizing the churches, subjecting them to collective governance under synods composed of representatives from various churches. Even more broadly he questioned the whole vision of a supposed primitive Congregational church of uniquely pure principles. Many mistakes in church government, he said, had been made by people who "have a Veneration for antiquity and adopt the sayings of Ancient Fathers for Canonical."

Having seen vast changes in the political and social life of his childhood, Cotton Mather now began to witness the transformation of its religious life as well. Although dismayed by the appeal of Stoddard's "wretched *Novelties*" to a "carnal, giddy, rising Generation," he noted sorrowfully that hardly any but himself and his father dared "appear with any Strength of Argument, or Fortitude, in Defence of our invaded *Churches.*" Undaunted himself, when Stoddard visited Boston in the summer to assert his views before an assembly of ministers, he stood up and spoke at length against "a *Book* of a reverend Person, here present." In choosing the *"Parter's Portion"* he found himself having somehow to denounce Stoddard's and Colman's Presbyterian ideas plausibly while continuing to celebrate the Congregationalist-Presbyterian union. He attempted this feat by identifying them as Presbyterians-*manquê,* observing that "the Gentlemen in the Design against our Churches, will needs be call'd *Presbyterians:* but they very unjustly arrogate that Name. . . . Our Controversy with them indeed is, because they will not be *Presbyterians.*" He warned that of the continual attempts to unhinge the New England churches, none was more daring and explicit than Stoddard's. In creating national synods Stoddard would divest individual churches of their power of self-reform, and give over their governance to synods whose decrees would be impotent in New England, lacking "a *civil Magistrate,* that will make them *cut.*" Wishing to abolish conversion as a requirement for communion, Stoddard would have "those that *know themselves* ungodly Wretches come to the *dreadful Mysteries.*" The devil's initial plot against New Englanders, now far advanced, was to extinguish their godliness: "The *next plot* of Satan, is to confound our Holy *Church-Order,* and make us, with our own Hands pull down our House."

Caught in the odd logic of his situation, Mather turned his dispute

with Stoddard and Colman into a bizarre quarrel over which Congregationalists were the true Presbyterians. He prepared a Boston edition of
the work of a well-known English Presbyterian, John Quick's *Young Mans
Claim unto the Sacrament of the Lords-Supper.* In doing so he hoped to
show the close similarity between true Presbyterianism and orthodox
New England Congregationalism, to vouch for which he added to the
work signed attestations by such Puritan elder statesmen as John Higginson. At the same time he also tried to show how Stoddard and Colman
exploited the name Presbyterian to cloak their *"Disorderly Undertakings"* and, while nominally Congregationalists, "would not have Things
to be as the Eminent *Planters,* and General *Synods,* of our Churches have
left them unto us." He prefaced Quick's work with a fifty-nine-page essay,
signed by him and his father but seemingly written by himself, entitled
"A Defense of Evangelical Churches." While he felt "Tenderness" for
Stoddard he characterized him caustically as an "Ingenious and Contem-
plative Gentleman, in his Retirements" and condemned "the *Presbyterianism* that runs down *Connecticut* River." Lunging also at Colman and
other "Raw youths . . . under the name of *Presbyterians,*" he labeled both
men *"Presbyterian Formalists,"* as opposed to the true or *"Reforming
Presbyterians."* Stoddard's call for national synods of clergymen—as opposed to his own call for clerical associations—he attacked as a move
toward episcopacy and thence to papacy. Stoddard's wish to open communion to the knowingly unregenerate—as opposed to his own (liberal)
view that a "probable hope" of grace qualifies for admission—he called a
"Popish Fancy," rejected by Presbyterians and even Episcopalians as undoing the very form and matter of the churches. Those most eminent for
holiness, he concluded, had failed to stand up against the *"New model-
lers* of our Churches," leaving him and his father to do so though they
"bring all the raging Obloquy imaginable upon us."

Raging obloquy, however, was hardly Benjamin Colman's style, which
inclined rather to well-bred reasonableness, with a reserve of saucy wit.
In mid-December appeared a delayed reply to Increase's *Order of the
Gospel,* a pamphlet entitled *The Gospel Order Revived.* Published anonymously, it was taken as the work of Colman and some others sympathetic
to the Brattle church, whose principles it defends on scriptural, logical,
and historical grounds against Increase's charges. Through these patient
arguments, however, runs a vein of rather sneeringly sly personal attack.
The writers refer to Increase repeatedly, with accumulating irony, as the
"Reverend Author." Where Increase objected to what he called *"Dumb
Reading"*—the Brattle practice of reading Scripture without explica-

tion—they snip at the "complicated . . . Malignity in the Phrase" and at
Increase's immodesty in thinking "any one of his Sermons or short Comments, can edify more than the reading of twenty Chapters." Sometimes
thus needlingly and sometimes brusquely, they accuse Increase of mis-
representing the authorities he cites, treating as the practice of all the
New England churches what are simply his own views, and crying up
Presbyterian principles in London but denouncing them in Boston,
where his own interest is touched. Particularly they deride his overzealousness in storming over niggling issues and wailing "*Oh Apostacy! Apostacy!*" In scoffing at Increase's emotionalism, Colman and the others in
effect repudiated the whole theory of decline. They note that a generation ago the change in baptismal policy was decried as a woeful declen-
sion, but the present generation feel "the happy effects of it, and rising
up at the Reformers names, do call them blessed." Declaring themselves
not apostates but simply "less Rigid than others of the Reverend Authors
severity," the writers end by vowing not to answer any further charges,
however noisy.

The publication of *The Gospel Order Revived* created new issues between the Mathers and the innovators, calling attention to the Mathers'
political influence in Boston. The pamphlet had been published in New
York, as Stoddard's *Doctrine of Instituted Churches* had been published
in London. The Brattle group charged that the Mathers' control of the
Boston press was responsible for the New York imprint, and a six-month
delay in publication, Boston printers being "so much under the awe" of
Increase Mather that the printer Bartholomew Green refused to issue the
work. Green denied the charge in a ten-page pamphlet, to which Cotton
Mather supplied an anonymous endorsement. Green said he neither refused to print the pamphlet nor was told anything by Increase to discourage its printing. When members of the Brattle church brought him the
manuscript, he explained, he agreed to print it; but when they insisted
that it be published anonymously he asked them first to secure the governor's approval, at which they went away angrily. Two of those who
brought the manuscript to Green, however, attested that they asked him if
he would print it with the permission of Cotton Mather; Green readily
said he would, and they told him "it was a shame so Worthy a Minister as
Mr. *Stoddard* must send as far as *England* to have his Book printed, when
young Mr. *Mather* had the Press at his pleasure."

The publication of *The Gospel Order Revived* exposed a far deeper
issue as well. Although Increase refused to answer Colman, considering it
beneath his dignity to notice, he said, "the impotent *Allatrations* of so

little a thing as that *Youth* is," Cotton retaliated against the "Young *Pseu-do-presbyterian*" in a twenty-four-page pamphlet entitled *A Collection, of Some of the Many Offensive Matters, Contained in . . . The Order of the Gospel Revived* (1701). To damn the Brattle group in their own words he simply listed the "vile Things" in their pamphlet, "barely to *Recite* which is enough to *refute* them." But in his controversy with the new church he had come to detect a more profound threat to New England than any dispute over ordination or church membership—a growing temper of disrespect. Colman and the others did not so much oppose the Gospel Order as "Elegantly *Scoff*" at it. The inner meaning of the Brattle church, he now saw, was that New England having just repulsed devils was being invaded by satirists.

The two were of course the same, for those who tweaked Increase Mather as the "Reverend Author" crying "*Oh Apostacy!*" embodied spirits akin to those who prodded the Goodwin children to howl and stomp at the ministers who prayed for them. The organizers of the new church, Cotton wrote, "have not only *departed from* the Religion of their Fathers but are become *Mockers* of it." Slightly exaggerating the actual language of their pamphlet, he denounced Colman and the others for their "*Squib*" on "*The Old Men and Women, that are for the Good Old Way,*" their treating public relations of conversion experiences as "*Talkative Brethren Standing up to Relate Experiences.*" "*Mocking is Catching,*" he warned, and having often preached against disrespect for elders, he foresaw that the children of New England might learn from the innovators to deride "the most Serious things that are done in our Churches, and carry on the *Mocking Humour.*" Nothing in the Brattle church seemed to him more dangerous than its airiness toward authority and tradition: "There is no one thing, which does more threaten or disgrace *New-England,* than want of due Respect unto *Superiors;* even that Abomination, *In thee they set Light by Fathers.*"

All of the issues dividing the Mathers and the new church were summed up deliciously in some anonymous verses written on a copy of *The Gospel Order Revived* and handed around Plymouth. "Blackman," in the first stanza, is Colman; the second stanza puns on the names of the ministers Bradstreet, Woodbridge, and Stone—taken by some to be the authors of the pamphlet; "Relations," in the third stanza, refers to public relations of conversion experiences; in the last stanza, "Mico" is John Mico, a wealthy founder of the new church. The writer depicted the Mathers defending the religion of the Fathers against Brattle Street's romanizing tendency and gentility:

A Simple Poem on the Authors and Designs of This Book.

> Begging Manifesto proves but a great Pesto.
> > Blackman is Synodalian.
> Pray stay there and stop, lest next hap & hop
> Ben't Peters chair Italian.
>
> The old strait Gate is now out of Date,
> The street it must be broad;
> And the Bridge must be wood, tho not half so good
> As firm Stone in the Road.
>
> Relations are Rattle with Brattle & Brattle;
> Lord Brother mayn't command:
> But Mather and Mather had rather & rather
> The good old way should stand
>
> Saints Cotton & Hooker, o look down, & look here
> Where's Platform, Way, & the Keys?
> O Torey what story of Brattle Church Twattle
> To have things as they please
>
> Our merchants cum Mico do stand Sacro Vico;
> Our Churches turn Genteel:
> Parsons grow trim and trigg with wealth wine & wigg
> And their crowns are covered with meal.

More revealing than the content of the poem is its bantering treatment of both the innovators and the Fathers, both Blackman and Saint Hooker. The lighthearted tone confirms Cotton Mather's insight that the Brattle Street controversy foretold the erosion not only of the Gospel Order but more deeply of Puritan gravity, of the particular sensibility of New England, of not just the Fathers' principles but of their spirit.

Despite the uproar over the "great Pesto," within a year or so Mather's enmity toward Colman gave way to what became lifelong cooperation with him, and slightly tense respect. The circumstance that resolved their quarrel is one of several important details lacking in what information about the controversy remains, another being Colman's part in writing *The Gospel Order Revived*. Their reconciliation probably involved no dramatic event or change of principle, for Mather's behavior toward Colman resulted as much from personal feelings as from religious ideals. As we shall see, in Mather's later life his stifled feelings of competition with Colman and envy of his popularity erupted. They may have existed from the first, for throughout the controversy his bitterest attacks on Colman, ten years his junior, dwell on youthful brashness, intimating resentment over Colman's indulging expansive qualities he shared but harnessed.

Indeed Colman and Mather may have been drawn together by simple affinity, for they were in many ways alike—learned, courteous, pious, conciliatory, and fancying themselves among the better sort. Raised in Mather's church, Colman greatly respected the founders of New England. But acknowledging himself to be "something of a *Presbyterian* under our Congregational Form," he felt no disloyalty in adjusting the founders' vision to changed times. Mather, adding constant professions of reverence for the Fathers, did the same. In preaching a new toleration, calling for councils and associations, and offering an attenuated test for communion, he surely fostered a climate of innovation where ideas like Colman's and Stoddard's could thrive, and conspired in creating what he condemned. Rather guilty acknowledgment of siding more with the innovators than he made known appears in his keeping his quite Presbyterian essay on the utility of synods unpublished. At a convention of ministers in Boston in 1705, however, he openly joined Colman in recommending standing councils of ministers to determine church affairs in a geographical area—a real move toward Presbyterianism. Increase Mather did not endorse the proposal, and later publicly declared his opposition to it.

If Cotton Mather restrained his views out of respect for his father it was ironic, for the New England Increase held up against the innovators, the primitive Congregationalism of the Gospel Order, was a New England whose destruction many people accused him of having negotiated. Cotton's defense of his father's acceptance of the charter rightly placed him in some minds among the innovators himself, while his attack on Colman and Stoddard made him seem conservative to others—The Parter's Portion. But his quarrel with the Brattle church was less over their innovations than over their flaunting them. Without a show of loyalty to the Fathers and an appearance of historical continuity, he feared, all authority and all forms of social order would collapse.

*

Because of its public nature, Mather's quarrel with Colman and Stoddard is the most conspicuous event in his life in the decade following the Salem trials. Yet it stands out only as a boulder in a stream, for other deep concerns flowed around and beyond it. The next chapter describes how for years following his visitation by the angel, Mather experienced exhilarating but finally disillusioning psychical phenomena. In the same period he also conceived two magisterial works, including the book for which he remains best known, his history of New England, *Magnalia Christi Americana*.

Mather proposed the work to himself in the early summer of 1693 and in July received formal encouragement from the Cambridge Association of Ministers, which offered him all necessary assistance for the "exact forming" of it and requested a monthly progress report. The dying off of first-generation American Puritans, however, had long made the need for such a history a subject of public discourse. Increase Mather considered it "one of New England's Sins that no better course hath been taken that the memory of the great things the Lord hath done for us be transmitted to posterity." Several people encouraged Increase to undertake the work himself. In writing *Magnalia,* Cotton answered a call that had sounded for nearly twenty-five years and had seemed likely to be answered by his father. A simultaneous call had gone out since the 1670s for a related history of God's providences toward New England, proposals for which were drawn up by a group of church elders in 1681. In March 1694, Increase in conjunction with the Harvard Fellows and some other ministers issued renewed proposals for compiling such a history, asking ministers around the country to submit credibly attested accounts of deliverances of the distressed, judgments against the wicked, fulfillments of scriptural prophecies, "*Apparitions, Possessions, Inchantments,* and all Extraordinary Things wherein the Existence and Agency of the *Invisible World,* is more sensibly demonstrated." Cotton Mather filled this call also by including as Book VI of *Magnalia* a history of memorable divine providences in New England.

Mather having begun writing the book toward the end of 1693, it was prematurely announced for publication in London as early as 1697. But he did not ship the heavy manuscript until June 1700, near the height of his quarrel with Colman. While working on *Magnalia* and trying to arrange its publication, he published parts of it as independent short works, no fewer than seventeen of which he reprinted virtually verbatim in the book. For two years after sending the manuscript he lived in repeatedly thwarted hope of seeing the book in print. One ship from London after another brought him no news at all or reports of ceaseless clogs, delays, and possible failure—the London booksellers were "cold" toward the project, subscriptions were "uncertain," everything stood in "extreme Hazard of Miscarrying." Sometimes resigned, sometimes painfully disappointed, Mather now consented to "so humbling a Trial, as the Loss of my Church-History," now fretted over the waste of "the vast Pains I have taken in composing it." Even the news of its imminent publication, as it came to Mather in a letter from the London Presbyterian minister John Quick, was discouraging. Quick told him that because the presswork had been given to the London printer Thomas Parkhurst, truncations could be expected, and interpolations, and textual errors, and type and paper that would "afflict" him. That had been Quick's own experience with Parkhurst, who "horribly maimed and wounded" one of Quick's works, sending it into the world as his when, he told Mather, "Sir, it's no more mine, than if you should chop off my hands, arms, and legs, and [binding?] pieces of wood to those parts, you should say, this is whole Mr. Quick."

As published in London in 1702, *Magnalia Christi Americana* did contain perhaps three hundred typographical errors. Just the same it was unmistakably a grandly imagined and formidable work: about eight hundred folio pages of double columns, divided in seven substantial books— history of the settlement of New England; lives of the governors; lives of the leading ministers (the longest book); history of Harvard College, with the lives of eminent graduates; account of the New England manner of worship; "Remarkables of Divine Providence"; and a history of the invasion of the New England churches by heretics, Andros, devils, Indians, and others. Mather gathered this information industriously and from many sources: surviving diaries, letters, and other papers; his father's correspondence; the manuscript histories of New England by William Hubbard and William Bradford; personal acquaintance with surviving members of the earlier generations, the sermon notebooks in which he had taken down their words firsthand, informants who had known them. The minister Samuel Stone seems to have loaned him the "Chronological Decads" he composed, fastened by rings so they could be hung up away from rodents. It amounted to less information than Mather desired, and he complains several times in *Magnalia* of having to scant a subject because people failed to send him adequate material. But of course he never felt he had given enough, and despite his apologies the enduring importance of his book partly lies in its sheer amassment of precious information about the early history of New England—about leaders in church and state, Puritan relations with the Indians, the development of Harvard, the 1689 revolt, the expeditions against Canada, the Salem trials. He also included many significant documents (for instance, relating to the Halfway Covenant), and verses (usually elegies) by such leading Puritan poets as Benjamin Tompson, so that *Magnalia* also contains a documentary history of early New England and a small anthology of early American Poetry.

What unifies this seven-vault archive of fact, reminiscence, document,

verse, and legend is Mather's ever present narrative voice—learned, facetious, emphatic, at once intimate and grand, distinctively showmanlike, as
if history were some banquet and he the master of ceremonies. His geniality again suggests the conciliator, and indeed the vast, miscellaneous
materials take shape under two not very harmonious intentions. First he
conceived the work as a contribution to his ceaseless call throughout the
1690s for reform, as a way, he wrote, "of keeping *Alive,* as far as this poor
Essay may contribute thereunto, the Interests of *Dying Religion* in our
Churches." To do so, as Sacvan Bercovitch, the most profound interpreter
of his works, remarks, he lifted New England history into the realm of
heroic action. Beginning with the epical opening, modeled on the opening of the *Aeneid,* he created an archaic-seeming World of the Fathers.
Before the appearance of his life of John Eliot in 1691, only two biographies of New England ministers had been published: of his grandfather
John Cotton (by John Norton) and of his grandfather Richard Mather (by
Increase Mather). But *Magnalia* contains, depending on how one defines
the term, about fifty biographies of eminent New Englanders, ranging
from a few pages to nearly book length, plus perhaps dozens of brief
biographical sketches. The subjects of this Puritan pantheon are mostly
dead or aged members of the earlier generations, called to life as embodi-
ments of standards from which the present generation has fallen away.
The book's most pervasive image is probably resurrection: to halt the
"visible *shrink* in all Orders of Men among us, from that *Greatness,* and
that *Goodness,* which was in the *first Grain,*" Mather decided, "I'll show
them, the *Graves* of their *dead Fathers.*" The lives accordingly take exemplary patterns, illustrating the behavior of ideal Saints, ministers, and
magistrates. Yet Mather's unfailing zest for the curious also provides indi-
vidualizing scraps of memorable conversation, and such enlivening vi-
gnettes of personal conduct as Thomas Hooker closing his eyes with his
own hand just before dying.

Typical of Mather's revival of the heroic past is his fine biography of
John Eliot, the first Puritan preacher to the Indians, whom he had known
and revered since a child. Having come to Boston in the first wave of
emigration and died in 1690 at the age of eighty-six, Eliot appears in
Mather's ideal portrait as a *summa* of New England Congregationalist
ideals—a model father, a great Bible student and Sabbath keeper, a comforter of the poor and distressed, a skilled spiritualizer of earthly objects,
and a prophet, a majestic man who walked all day in the light of God's
countenance and grew more heavenly and savory toward his end. As
Mather describes him, Eliot preached without froth, carrying Christ with

him wherever he went, so that "like *Mary's* opened Box of *Ointment,* he fill'd the whole Room with the Perfumes of the *Graces* in his Lips." As an evangelist he personally catechized blacks, whose brutal treatment he deplored, and brought the Indians no diluted Christianity but pure Scripture worship, the creed of primitive believers. Above all he was a man although pleasant and affable yet uniquely mortified, "so nailed unto the *Cross* of the Lord Jesus Christ, that the Grandeurs of this World were unto him just what they would be to a *dying Man.*" He ate but one plain dish for supper, never drank wine, spoke with *"boiling Zeal"* against men who wore their hair with "Luxurious, Delicate, Feminine Prolixity," and dressed himself utterly without adornment, his loins, like John the Baptist's, circled with a leather girdle. When he saw a minister looking self-satisfied he told him, *"Study Mortification Brother, Study Mortification!"*

Eliot's wonderful rebuke, however, speaks from a world which the new charter had forever doomed to silence. While Mather resurrected the vanishing first generation as a model for the degenerate present he did not share its zeal for separation and did not cherish the tribal myth of a Chosen People that once gave New England meaning. He also intended the book specifically for an English audience, anxious again to exhibit New England's affection for the mother country, aware, and not distressed, that New England's place in history was that of one outpost in a taut new transatlantic imperial network. *Magnalia* accordingly looks back at the World of the Fathers across the Glorious Revolution, the Act of Toleration, and other dramatic events that made its heroism seem not so much epically nation-building as superfluous.

Virtually the whole book qualifies the Virgilian opening sentence: "I WRITE the *Wonders* of the CHRISTIAN RELIGION, flying from the Depravations of *Europe,* to the *American Strand.*" What drove Christianity to America, Mather shows repeatedly, were not the "Depravations of *Europe*" but, far less cosmically, a knot of high-Church romanists acting in an aberrant moment of English history. His "General Introduction" defines his subject as the history of "PROTESTANTS that highly honoured and affected *The Church of* ENGLAND, and humbly Petition to be a *Part* of it." The theme of flight from English persecution becomes a matter less for tribal mythologizing than for apology:

> Good men in the Church of *England,* I hope, will not be offended at it, if the *Unreasonable Impositions,* and Intolerable Persecutions, of certain Little-Soul'd *Ceremony-Mongers,* which drove these worthy Men out of their Native Country, into the horrid Thickets of *America,* be in their *Lives* complained and resented. For, distinguishing between a *Romanizing*

Faction in the Church of England, and the *True* Protestant Reforming *Church of* England . . . the First Planters of *New England,* at their first coming over, did in a Public and a Printed Address, call the Church of *England,* their *Dear Mother.* . . . Nor did they think, that it was their *Mother* who turned them out of Doors, but some of their angry *Brethren,* abusing the Name of their *Mother,* who so harshly treated them.

Many individual biographies similarly emphasize the forefathers' allegiance to England. Mather records John Higginson telling emigrants about to leave in 1629 for America, "*We will not say as the Separatists were wont to say at their leaving of* England, Farewel, *Babylon!* Farewel *Rome!* But *we will say,* Farewel Dear *England!* Farewel the Church of God in *England* and all the Christian Friends there!" The world of the Fathers recreated in *Magnalia* is populated not only by doctrinal purists but also by loyal Englishmen pining for home. Although the book has justly been described as a monument of New England orthodoxy, the greatest of the Jeremiads, it disharmoniously embodies another form at which New England had also become adept, the petition to the throne.

Indeed Mather recreates even the world of doctrinal purity in the light of his current vision of toleration and reunion. He depicts New Englanders as model ecumenists who "dare make no Difference between a *Presbyterian,* a *Congregational,* an *Episcopalian,* and an *Anti paedo-baptist,* where their *Visible Piety,* makes it probable, that the Lord Jesus Christ has received them." In the course of *Magnalia* he frequently promotes the Congregationalist-Presbyterian union, significantly including in Book Five, among such essential Congregational documents as *The Cambridge Platform,* the London *Heads of Agreement,* declaring it the best exposition of existing Congregationalism and placing it in the very mainstream of New England Puritanism. He remarks that he expects to be criticized for what he has done not only by the High Church party in England and the degenerate young at home, but in effect by the Fathers themselves, by "some among us, who very strictly profess the *Congregational Church-Discipline,* but at the same time they have an unhappy Narrowness of Soul, by which they confine their value and Kindness too much unto their own Party; and unto those my *Church History* will be offensive."

Although Mather set out on one hand to halt the "visible *shrink*" from the Fathers' grandeur, the Puritans of *Magnalia* exist as a Chosen People in only a sorely diminished sense. The Fathers' role in history, he speculates, may have been to serve as a model to Protestant churches elsewhere in the impending worldwide Reformation (see the next chapter), illustrating the qualifications needed in those attempting the reformation and the solutions for problems that might obstruct it. To play this illustrative role may have been why Christ brought His servants to America, that "He might there, *To* them first, and then *By* them, give a *Specimen* of many Good Things, which He would have His Churches elsewhere aspire and arise unto." But in the reformed, panchristian world it might inspire, New England itself would not survive as New Jerusalem; indeed it might have no place. "*This* being done," Mather speculates, "He knows not whether there be not *All done,* that *New-England* was planted for; and whether the Plantation may not, soon after this, *Come to Nothing.*"

Perhaps no feature of the book more dramatically reveals Mather's drift from the Fathers than his devoting the longest section of "The Great Works of Christ in America"—eighty pages in the most recent edition of *Magnalia*—to Sir William Phips. Before becoming governor and caning people on Scarlett's Wharf, Phips made his mark in the world as a rowdy treasure hunter commanding a debauched crew: "for swearing and cursing," one sailor said, "I bless God I never heard the like before in all the ships as ever I have sailed in." Phips did not hold himself aloof. A decade before becoming governor he made a ten-week stay in Boston with his crew, some of whom began brawling in a tavern. When constables ordered the crew members to return to ship, Phips defied them. They promised to tell Governor Bradstreet but he said "he did not care a t___d for the governour for he had more power than he had," and when brought to trial and rebuked by Bradstreet he threw his orders at him.

Yet Mather gave this choleric adventurer star billing in his gallery of *Ecclesiarum Clypei*—Shields of the Churches. His reasons for doing so are largely obvious. At the time Increase Mather was allowed to nominate Phips as the first governor under the new charter, he represented for better or worse the future of New England. As a member of the North Church, we have seen, he also represented the Mathers' hope of renewed access to government circles. While Mather did not conceal from his readers Phips's hot temper, he emphasized his piety and his concern for New England. Eligible for important posts at home, he preferred to live among the people of God in Massachusetts, invariably desiring their good, sharing the motto of the Emperor Hadrian, "NOT FOR MY SELF, BUT FOR MY PEOPLE."

Mather had a less obvious reason for featuring Phips as well: he relished his derring-do. Phips's dashing assaults and squeaky escapes inspired his capacity for imaginative identification with his subjects and gave scope to his considerable gift for narrative. As a result, his biography of Phips often reads like something less from Foxe's *Book of Martyrs* than from *Les Trois Mousquetaires.* Mather retails, for instance, Phips's repulse of an attempted mutiny:

> One day while [Phips's] Frigot lay *Careening,* at a desolate *Spanish* Island, by the side of a Rock, from whence they had laid a Bridge to the Shore, the Men, whereof he had about an *Hundred,* went all, but about Eight or Ten, to divert themselves, as they pretended, in the *Woods:* Where they all entered into an *Agreement,* which they Sign'd in a Ring, That about seven a Clock that Evening they would seize the Captain, and those Eight or Ten, which they knew to be True unto him, and leave them to perish on this Island, and so be gone away unto the *South Sea* to *seek their Fortune.* Will the Reader now imagine, that Captain *Phips* having Advice of this Plot but about an Hour and half before it was to be put in Execution, yet within *Two Hours* brought all these Rogues down upon their Knees to beg for their Lives? But so it was!

The mutinous knaves, Mather continues, fetched the ship's carpenter to the woods and asked him to join them. He begged for time to think it over and was returned to the ship, with a spy to keep watch over him. Pretending to be seized by a fit of cholic, he ran to Phips's cabin for a dram. Instead he told Phips of the plot. Phips gathered his seven or eight remaining crew, including his gunner, and

> demanded of them, whether they would stand by him in the Extremity, which he informed them was now come upon him; whereto they reply'd, *They would stand by him, if he could save them;* and he Answer'd, *By the help of God he did not fear it.* All their Provisions had been carried Ashore to a Tent, made for that Purpose there; about which they had placed several Great Guns to defend it, in case of any *Assault* from the *Spaniards,* that might happen to come that way. Wherefore Captain *Phips,* immediately ordered those Guns to be silently Drawn'd and Turn'd; and so pulling up the Bridge, he charged his Great Guns aboard, and brought them to Bear on every side of the Tent. But this time the *Army of Rebels* comes out of the Woods; but as they drew near to the Tent of Provisions, they saw such a change of Circumstances, that they cried out, *We are Betray'd!* And they were soon confirm'd in it, when they heard the Captain with a stern Fury call to them, *Stand off, ye Wretches, at your Peril!*

The mutineers fell on their knees to beg Phips's pardon, but he seized their weapons, took them aboard, then got rid of them in Jamaica.

Although *Magnalia* places Phips as a successor in the honored gubernatorial line of William Bradford and John Winthrop, he seems an exemplar not of the Governor but of the Self-Made Man. "Reader, enquire no further who was his *Father?*" Mather writes. "Thou shalt anon see, that he

was, as the *Italians* express it, *A Son to his own Labours!*" As the story of
the son of a gunsmith in a frontier village on the Kennebec River who
"rose from so *little*," the life of Phips falls between such Puritan spiritual
biographies as that of John Eliot, and the *Autobiography* of Benjamin
Franklin. In Phips the Fathers' piety can be seen overlaid with "Enterpriz-
ing *Genius*," the Puritan Saint has shaded off into the "*Knight of Honesty;*
for it was *Honesty* with *Industry* that raised him." To the several differences between Mather's viewpoint and that of the world he resurrects, the
life of Phips adds another, which Mather equally celebrates—the growth
of business enterprise in America.

Like John Eliot, Phips enjoyed prophetic foresight, but what it assured
him of was material success. When he was eighteen his friends urged him
to settle permanently in Maine, but he had, Mather writes, "an Unaccountable *Impulse* upon his Mind, persuading him, as he would privately
hint unto some of them, *That he was Born to greater Matters.*" Instead he
bound himself apprentice to a ship's carpenter, which trade he followed a
while in Boston, where for the first time he learned to read and write. He
also married the widow of a "well-bred Merchant." He confided to her
his belief that "the Providence of God" would ultimately make him the
"Owner of a *Fair Brick-House* in the *Green-Lane* of *North-Boston.*"
Phips's assurances, like John Eliot's, came true, not after fervent prayer
but after six years hunting sunken Spanish galleons. Mather describes
with zestful wonder how in January 1687 Phips reached a wreck in Porto
Plata, Hispaniola, and after diving three months brought up thirty-four
tons of treasure. This fantastic horde included copper guns, silver candlesticks and stirrups, gold chains and cups, and more than 37,000 pounds
troy in silver pieces-of-eight. The find was reported in newsletters and
pamphlets, communicated to the kings of Europe, and made the talk of
London. As his share Phips received more than £11,000, some of which
he invested in Boston real estate, plus part of the spoils. His wife received
a gold cup worth nearly £1000. In consideration of his services to the
crown he was knighted. The turning point in Mather's account of Phips's
fabulous strike is the remarkable cry of this Shield of the Churches, after a
diver disclosed to him a lump of silver at last dredged from the deep:
"*Thanks be to God! We are made.*"

The disparate voices of Phips's "*Thanks be to God! We are made*" and
Eliot's "*Study Mortification Brother, Study Mortification!*" together or-
chestrate *Magnalia Christi Americana* and define a historical moment.
Mather's attempt to make them both bespeak "The *Wonders* of the

CHRISTIAN RELIGION" dramatizes the survival in fact and memory of the first generation's mortified living, reverence toward ministers, and relation of conversion experiences into the new epoch of commercial enterprise, imperial expansion, and perriwigs. They survived tenuously, of course: mortification was not the style of young ministers like Benjamin Colman, and Phips was the last governor for at least twenty years who could be included without deliberate mockery among the Shields of the Churches. That Mather could comfortably celebrate both Eliot's leather girdle and Phips's golden cups testifies also to how much he remained drawn to both heaven-mindedness and worldly ambition. It seems likely that he welcomed the new atmosphere of toleration and reunion exactly because it legitimized his suppressed urbanity. In his life of Eliot, he first tells how the saintly evangelist hated men's wearing long hair, then remarks indulgently, "Doubtless, it may be lawful for us to accommodate the *length* of our *Hair* unto the modest *Customs* which vary in the *Churches of God.*"

For all its ideological weight, *Magnalia* is a deeply literary work. Whether bringing to life the mortified piety of the Fathers or defending long hair and the *Heads of Agreement,* Mather was above all bidding for international attention as an American writer. Mixing the largest political and eschatological events with "Entertainments for the Curious," the book abounds in such vivid narratives as the captivity of Hannah Duston and the depossession of the Goodwin children, in wonder stories of ghosts and strange premonitions of death. With his appetite for believe-it-or-nots, Mather could not resist appending to his life of the minister Thomas Thacher a long account of a deaf and dumb member of Thacher's church who learned to convey her understanding of the doctrine of the Trinity in sign language. Mather's literary ambitions also declare themselves with stentorian gorgeousness in his "Massy" style—the copious matter, the intricately witty, graceful, or dense openings (the first sentence of the life of Phips runs 254 words), the formal invention, the trilingual puns and quotations and universal allusions. The style itself reveals much about New England at the turn of the century, rendering the first generation's heaven-mindedness in a language that reaches for cosmopolitan elegance but attains provincial grandioseness. If the epic ambitions of *Magnalia,* its attempt to put America on the cultural map, recall such later American works as *Moby-Dick* (to which it has been compared), its effort to rejoin provincial America to the mainstream of English culture recalls rather *The Wasteland.* Genuinely Anglo-American in outlook, the book projects a New England which is ultimately an en-larged version of Cotton Mather himself, a pious citizen of "The Metropo-lis of the whole English America."

For all its aspiring bulk, *Magnalia* is dwarfed beside the leviathan Mather "set upon" at about the same time, "*another,* and a *greater*" book on which he would labor the rest of his life. In this gigantic "Biblia Americana" he intended nothing less than to interpret all of Scripture in the light of "all the Learning in the World." The dazing scope of the work was probably inspired by the angel's prophecy of the books he would publish to exalt his height above all the other trees of the field. Its con-tent, however, derived from his opinion that none of what he called the "*professed Commentaries*" on Scripture had yet afforded "a thousandth Part of so much *Illustration* unto it, as might be given."

In several ways the project uniquely suited Mather's temperament and talents. It satisfied his vaulting ambition, his taste for combining piety and elegance, and his continuing need to allay feelings of smallness and show extraordinary fecundity in producing language. It also put to use his ability to read with unusual speed, which several persons who knew him observed:

> In two or three Minutes turning thro' a Volume, he cou'd easily tell whether it wou'd make Additions to the Store of his Ideas. If it cou'd not, He quickly laid it by: If otherwise, he read it, passing over all those Parts which contained the things he had known before, perusing those Parts only that represented something *Novel,* which he Pencil'd as he went along . . . and all this with wonderful Celerity.

Swift and wide reading was essential, for he hoped to create, in contrast to the "*professed Commentaries,*" something at once entertaining, mod-ern, and comprehensive. He would gather in one work more scriptural glosses from the "*scattered Books* of learned Men, than in any of the *ordinary Commentators.*" He would also search out strikingly pungent or fresh illustrations, "more entertaining for the *Rarity* and *Novelty* of them, than any that have been hitherto seen together." Since he and many oth-ers considered their age one of abundant new insight into the meaning of biblical texts, he would include as well all the "*Improvements,* which the *later Ages* have made in the Sciences." Approaching Scripture from every conceivable angle—scientific, patristic, classical, chronological, philo-logical, theological, typological, historical, geographical—he would as-semble "in *one Heap,* Thousands of those *remarkable Discoveries of the deep Thing[s] of the Spirit of God,* whereof *one,* or *two,* or a few sometimes, have been, with good Success, accounted *Materials* enough to advance one into *Authorism.*" He does not exaggerate: for the Mississippian flood of handwriting he disgorged in composing the work he might have published two hundred separate titles.

Mather began the trunk-sized manuscript in the late summer of 1693. He secured six huge folio volumes and divided them according to books of the Old and New Testaments. Then he laboriously entered glosses on various texts, in double columns and in catechistical form ("Q. Some Remark, I pray you, upon that great word, HALLELUJAH?"). He did not work serially through separate books of the Bible but on the entire Bible at once, filing glosses here and there in his folios as he came across them in his reading. Nearly every page of the manuscript thus shows several distinct stages of his handwriting over thirty years or more. He also began, but at some time gave up, separate double-columned auxiliary notebooks to list his authorities for each chapter of every book in Scripture, intending an eight-hundred page index of his sources. Originally he planned to write one gloss each morning, believing that in seven years—a godlike number—he would have a set of "learned, charming and curious *Notes* on His Word, far beyond any that hath yet seen the Light." Praying often for divine aid in coming upon apt illustrations, he found by 1697 that he already had "an huge Number of *golden Keys,* to open the *Pandects* of Heaven, and some Thousands of charming and singular Notes." In 1702 he included in the Preface to *Magnalia* a sort of progress report on his work to the learned world.

Later chapters will follow Mather's woeful frustrations with "Biblia Americana." But one earlier-written section deserves notice here because its date makes it evident that although the political turmoil of the late 1680s ended the Boston Philosophical Society (the fledgling scientific group founded by Increase), Mather's scientific interests remained strong. His treatise-length illustration on the first chapter of Genesis occupies over fifty-one double-columned folio pages, written over a decade or more. A portion of it dated 1702 represents his summary of Edmund Dickinson's *Physica Vetus et Vera,* published the same year. In a manner typical of all of "Biblia Americana" he follows Dickinson's ideas closely but clothes them "very much in my own Expressions," trying to show that current atomistic ("corpuscularian") conceptions of matter not only agree with the biblical account of creation but in fact offer one of the chief proofs of God.

"Let it not surprize you now, if, I tell you," Mather writes, "That the *Mosaic philosophy,* was no other than the *Corpuscularian.*" Following

Dickinson, he interprets the "Water" mentioned at the opening of Genesis as in fact referring to atoms, on the ground that in Moses' time the word ordinarily meant an immense multitude. Then he gives a wholly atomistic account of creation, beginning with the first day:

> In the Beginning was universal Matter by God first created of nothing; a wondrous congeries of all sorts of particles, unform'd, and unmov'd; and Every where separated from one another with Empty Spaces. This Universal Matter was put into Motion, by the Spirit of God, and not Left unto a fortuitous Motion and Concourse. Thus was there given unto Matter, that Force which we call Nature; for Nature is nothing but that Motion which the Spirit of God has imprinted upon Matter, and which He perpetually governs with his infinite Wisdom.

In forwarding Dickinson's view of Genesis, Mather was following a somewhat conservative train of scientific thought. The corpuscularian philosophy, devised and named by Robert Boyle, was widespread in England before the end of the century, but soon outmoded by Newtonian ideas—some of which Mather entered into later-written portions of his illustration on the same text. But although conceived in the spirit of Descartes and Boyle rather than of Newton, this early portion of "Biblia Americana" looks forward to Mather's becoming probably the most influential spokesman in New England for a rationalized, scientized Christianity.

In many sermons of the time and in two notable published works—Winter-Meditations (1693) and Christianus per Ignem (1702)—Mather also popularized for American audiences the language, discoveries, and habits of thought of the new science. The same capacity for wonder that he invested in his accounts of devils, Indian captivities, or treasure hunts he here devoted to such current matters of scientific study as fossils, volcanoes, and the formation of snow, and to rapt descriptions of the miracles unveiled by microscope and telescope, from the "exquisite workmanship" in the eye of a frog to the "Innumerable Millions" of stars—"How Regular to the Hundredth part of a Minute, are they in their Motions?" Such discoveries of modern science, he told his readers and listeners, "Declare the Glory of God, and show forth His Handy work," and invite our meditation on the deity revealed in the creation.

6

Particular Faiths

UNTIL MAY 1702, Abigail Mather is a shadowy figure in Cotton Mather's diaries, disembodied but clearly loved, "My dear Consort." But in May, ill, she miscarried of a son after a four or five months' pregnancy. Mather observed that it was the very week of their sixteenth anniversary, and at the time of their marriage Abigail herself had been just sixteen. He told his father: "*I seem to feel in my Mind, the Bodings of a dark Cloud hanging over my Family.*" Lapsing into a serious illness that puzzled the ablest physicians, Abigail became the central figure of her husband's diary as, with a few illusory remissions, she lay dying over the next seven months.

Cotton Mather's bodings both heralded grave doubt about his prophetic powers and climaxed nearly a decade of heightened psychic awareness, an agitated inner drama played out privately against his public conflict with Colman and Stoddard and the other events of the 1690s. In the years following his angelic visitation he spent much time fasting, often melted to tears by his psychical intimations, exalted but also unnerved by his nearness to the invisible world. Whether the angel itself returned is uncertain, owing to his caution in speaking of the event and to the loss of his diaries for 1694 and 1695. If no angels became visible they at least came close. Praying on the evening of his birthday in 1697 he found that "the *good Angels* of the Holy Spirit, were so near unto me, in my rapturous Praises of my Lord-Redeemer, that the Prae-Libations of Heaven which I enjoy'd . . . are *not fit here to be uttered.*" Another time he received a promise that an angel would appear to him in the future. He recorded the message in Latin, as he had done before, so that if Abigail looked at his diary she could not read it. In June 1698, it was infused (*infusum*) into him that a heavenly angel of my dearest Savior—*quod Coelestis quidam charissimi mei Salvatoris Angelus*—would at some time before his death when it seemed good to God show himself to me visible—*mihi se visibiliter exhibuerit*. The angel would appear in order to reveal certain matters *de Ecclesia, et Rebus novissimis*—concerning the church and the Last Things.

Such revelations would be of the keenest interest to Mather, for he prized the study of Last Things, of eschatology. His millennial expectations had been aroused by the Revolution of 1689, the invasion of devils, and his own angel, who prophesied the great works he would do "in the revolutions that are now in hand." A belief that the millennium might be near had also quickened his calls for reform and his enthusiasm for such signs of the extension of Protestantism as the Act of Toleration. The long series of European conflicts that began soon after the accession of King William, often pitting Protestant against Catholic interests, brought Mather many prophetic intimations of the collapse of infidelism and papacy and the establishment of God's true Kingdom. Several times he received "a strong Persuasion, that some very *overturning Dispensations* of Heaven, will quickly befall the *French* Empire," or felt a "marvellous Impression upon my Spirit" about a great religious revival in England, Scotland, and Ireland. He often prayed fervently for the fulfillment of these intimations, believing that secret prayer does "an incredible deal, towards Jogging the *High Wheels of Providence,* and Shaking of Churches, and Empires." Suspecting that the Lord might be preparing to take possession of the Spanish Indies he published a catechism of basic Protestant beliefs in Spanish (*La Fe del Christiano,* 1699, seemingly the only work in Spanish produced in seventeenth-century America), and also addressed an open letter "To the JEWISH Nation," bidding them desist from "your Damnable *Rebellion* against the CHRIST of GOD!" His prayers and publications were rewarded, he noted in 1698, with "astonishing Answers," such as the revival of Protestantism in the principality of Orange, "in the Bowels of *France.*" He thanked Christ for having "informed, inclined, and assisted . . . a vile Sinner, in a Corner of *America,* to foresee, and put on that Work of His."

Like many others, Mather read such events in the light of the prophetic books, especially Daniel in the Old Testament and Revelation in the New. He tried to fit them to the obscure imagery of vials, seals, beasts, woes, and candlesticks in which the scriptural prophets were understood to have laid out the approach of the millennium and of the Second Coming of Christ. Many viewed the revival of Protestant persecution in France upon revocation of the Edict of Nantes, for instance, as the realization of the Slaying of Witnesses described by Revelation. Mather fully appreciated the weakness of human learning in penetrating the dark language of the prophetic books, and the likelihood of interpretive error. He always approached them cautiously, and although he encouraged his congregation to read them he regarded eschatology as a subject for the elite: "*Apocalyptical Studies* are fittest for those Raised Souls," he wrote, "whose *Heart-Strings* are made of a Little *Finer Clay* than other mens."

At this time Mather's eschatological views followed those of his father and of the learned Joseph Mede of Christ's College, Cambridge. He set them forth in a ninety-one-page manuscript which he completed in 1703 but did not publish, entitled "Problema Theologicum." Here he drew a sort of schedule for the Second Coming, whose harbingers would be, among other events, the collapse of the papacy, the ceasing of Turkish hostilities against Europe, and the enlargement of the church by the conversion of the Jews. Increase Mather mentioned the same preconditions in his many sermons on the subject in the same years, but added the appearance of such awful works of God as famines, eclipses, pestilences, and huge earthquakes. Cotton's eschatology put less emphasis on natural upheavals, although in an almanac published in 1699 he too observed that the course of nature had recently been "every where most Wonderfully Altered"—plagues raging, the sun beginning to darken (according to astronomers), the seasons not as they used to be, "*Earthquakes* prodigiously multiplied," all suggesting "Further and Greater CHANGES upon the World." Mather shared these eschatological intimations with his congregation, filling his sermons of the period with prophecies of "a REVOLUTION *and a* REFORMATION *at the very Door.*"

Together with hints of the impending fulfillment of Daniel and Revelation, Mather received other strange intimations and providential favors, sometime less cosmic than comic. Several times when on journeys he found that threatened storms would be delayed until he returned home. Once, traveling to Salem and Ipswich, his road became swarmed, to everyone's alarm, by a "strange Descent of Hundreds of Bears"—"but I met none of them." When suffering heartburn he found it "darted into my Mind" to apply "*Philip Paris*'s Plaister" to his chest, which he did and was cured. His acts of self-sacrifice were mysteriously repaid. Lacking money to buy a new cloak although he needed one, he recalled Christ stripped of His garments and assured himself he would never want proper clothing: "Immediately after these Thoughts," a woman in his congregation surprised him with a present of a handsome and costly cloak. Again, after leaving some pious books or pamphlets behind during a pastoral visit, as he usually did, he reflected that no other minister in New England would put himself to such expense, and perhaps he should not do so either. Feeling a mental "Impulse" that something would happen to encourage his practice, he gave way to a "sudden inclination" to step in the house of a certain widow. She had come into part of the library of the famous Charles Chauncey, and pressed him to accept some forty books—not only an encouragement to continue distributing free religious works but also a help, he added, in filling his "Biblia Americana."

If the caliber of Cotton Mather's psychical experiences did not quite match his father's supposed ability to predict wars and other major events accurately, they did cause surprise. Once he felt God incline him to mention in public prayers the name of a church member held in captivity; the same afternoon that very person arrived home safe, "whereof much Notice was taken by the people of God in the Place." It seemed to him also that his intimations had their price, and that his moments of communion with heaven were often followed by some illness, public dispute, or other vexation. In one such case, he received what he considered intimations about the time and manner of his death. While he was preaching the next day, a chimney on his house caught fire, threatening his and his neighbors' homes. The large congregation ran from the church to quench the blaze, "and I was thus mark'd out for Talk all over."

With these many unsettling paranormal experiences seems to have come a return of Mather's youthful speech difficulties. How or whether the two were related—indeed, whether the difficulties did recur—is again uncertain because Mather's 1694 and 1695 diaries are missing. After the gap, however, his 1696 diary suddenly contains much new concern about fluency. On a day of secret prayer in March he asked Christ for "a more free, and fit, and useful *Speech.*" Lying prostrate on his study floor in May he received a vivid assurance, as if "spoken from Heaven," that speech would be supplied him, "and a greater *Freedom* of it . . . than ever I yet enjoyed." In October, for the first time in years, he set down rules for the governance of his tongue, reminiscent of the measures he once laid on himself to control his stammer: to let fall from his tongue only thoughts that glorified Christ, to avoid loquacity but on the contrary to "affect much *Deliberation.*" Whatever the origin of these renewed speech difficulties—if that is what the entries represent—they seem to have recurred over several years, for again in August 1699 he particularly thanked God "that I should be a great *Stammerer,* and yet be made not only a Preacher of the Gospel, but also my *Utterance* in preaching be not the least *Ornament* of it."

*

One sort of psychical experience came to Mather more often than any other, and more troublingly: the Particular Faith. He meant by the term "a little degree of the *Spirit of Prophecy*" granted by God to the devotional elite for abounding in secret prayer—some divinely sent intimation, perhaps conveyed through the invisible ministry of good angels, that a particular prayer would be answered. He seems to distinguish the Particular Faith from other forms of prayerful assurance by its quasi-hallucinatory definiteness. It is a vivid persuasion that one shall "Receive this *Particular Mercy* from the Lord: And this persuasion is not a mere Notion, and Fancy, but a *Special Impression from Heaven.*" The impression comes with a "certain powerful, Heart melting, Heavenly *Afflatus,*" quite as if an angel had spoken directly. Being entirely sensory, its actuality defies description: "*How do I know this Operation from a counterfeit?* My Answer is, That no words of mine can answer the Question; I *know* it, as I know the *Fire* to be the *Fire;* I *feel* it, but no words of mine can express, how it *feels.*"

Most of Mather's Particular Faiths concerned subjects of his secret prayers, often his own family, especially his children. Prayer was needed, given Boston's susceptibility to high infant mortality, fatal accident, and epidemic disease. By early 1696, when Mather was thirty-three, he and Abigail had had six children, of whom four were already dead, all but one in infancy. His firstborn child, Abigail, had died in 1687, aged five months; the most recent to die, in February 1696,was his infant daughter Mehetabel, probably smothered accidentally in its swaddling clothes by its nurse. Understandably his other children became the subject of fervent prayer, and then of Particular Faiths. In January 1699, his daughter Hannah ("Nancy"), about a year old, fell into the fire, so badly burning the right side of her face and her right hand and arm that her life seemed threatened. The fire that burned her, Mather wrote, only fired the zeal of his prayers for her, which God raised to a "Degree of a *Particular Faith* in her behalf." Nancy lived, but the following year she became ill of a pain in her bowels, which grew extreme. Again Mather found himself "Irradiated from Heaven with a *Particular Faith,* for some Help to be sent from Heaven unto the dying Child." Nancy began vomiting, however, and one of the physicians concluded she would certainly die. Astonishingly, on a

Sabbath, she began "running and laughing the whole Forenoon, about the House," and survived.

Only two months later, Mather's newborn son Samuel was taken with convulsions. Since Samuel's birth Mather had often tried to get his "Heart Raised, unto a *Particular Faith* for that Child," assuring him that God would accept Samuel, his only son, for the ministry. His failure to receive such a Particular Faith, however, made him continually apprehensive that the child, though hearty, would die in infancy. After Samuel survived more than a hundred convulsive fits, as Mather put it, "an odd thing" happened. Coming out of a fit about midnight, Samuel "most unaccountably fell a Laughing, yea, into a very great *Laughter,* and this held for diverse Minutes." The spectators were amazed, "indeed were so amazed, that they could hardly keep from Swooning." After its laughter the infant had no more fits until about ten o' clock in the morning, when it was seized with another fit and died.

Mather's longing for Particular Faiths regarding his children was most fervent on behalf of the son whose development, we shall see, would preoccupyingly both cheer and darken much of his later life—Increase, Jr., born to him and Abigail on July 9, 1699. In several ways Increase, Jr.'s, birth seemed portentous. Years before, Mather wrote, "A Son had been foretold unto me, in an Extraordinary Way." He always felt acute empathy, close to fear, with women's labor pains, and as signs of Abigail's approaching travail grew on her he set aside the day for prayer and fasting in his study. Abigail did not give birth, however, and to be fit for church services the next day, a Sabbath, he commended her to God and retired. At around one in the morning he awoke, feeling a "Concern upon my Spirit." He returned to his study, threw himself on his knees, and implored God's mercy on Abigail in her distress. At about a quarter to two, while he was pleading with God, "the People ran to my Study-door with Tidings, *that a Son was born unto me.*" As he continued praising God, on his knees, he received wonderful advice from heaven. The boy, he was told, would become a minister to continue the tradition of Cottons and Mathers, already three generations long, "a Servant of my Lord Jesus Christ throughout eternal Ages."

The Christ-like birth announcement makes clear how much hope Mather invested in the boy—the first of his male children to survive— from the beginning. This was a "Son given to me in answer to many Prayers among the People of God, and a Son of much Observation and Expectation." The day of the birth he entered in his church records, in large letters, his baptism of "My INCREASE." He decided on the name in honor of his father, as he had done before in naming the infant which died of an imperforate anus. (Increase, Sr., commented that he preferred a different name, but his neighbors "would not be satisfied except his Name were Increase.") To mark the baptism Cotton preached a sermon on the duty of parents to bring their children to Christ, especially since their children derived through them the misery of original sin. In hope of creating a son of unceasing heaven-mindedness, he began writing for him an exemplary, book-length autobiography, on which he worked over the next three years, relating his own spiritual development from childhood to the time of Increase, Jr.'s, birth. Entitled "Paterna," it consists largely of his methods of private devotion and his search for new ways of praising God, depicting his inner life as a continuous hum of praise.

Increase, Jr., became the subject of Particular Faiths as Cotton learned his father's lesson that strong affections bring strong afflictions. In his eighth month, the child was also taken with dangerous convulsions. Mather fasted two entire days, praying for his son's life yet resigning him to God. In one of his fits Increase somehow sucked in a pin through the silver nipple of his bottle and almost choked to death. Mather continued his prayers, awaiting a sign; once "a strange Thing was from Heaven said unto me: my Son shall yet live." But for at least another month Increase's convulsions returned, ceased, and then returned again, as Mather now feared the death of "My little and lovely and only Son" and then heard it told him from heaven that the child would live. In late April Increase's convulsions grew extreme and seemed incurable. Still Mather received assurances from heaven that his son would recover—"The good Angel of the Lord has told me so!"

Increase, Jr., did survive, confirming his father's Particular Faiths. But at the same time Mather received a surprising disappointment, in this case involving his father, and the older Increase's decade-long struggle over the Harvard presidency. The complex details of the episode—which drew in several governors and governmental bodies, the Harvard Corporation, and many influential persons—belong more to the biography of Increase Mather than of Cotton. They became subjects of Cotton Mather's Particular Faiths as they affected his father's desire, as acting president or "Rector" of Harvard, to obtain a charter for the college in England.

Under the Phips government, Harvard had been declared a corporation, with power to receive gifts and grant degrees; but this charter was disallowed in England, largely because it failed to provide for royal visitation and royal oversight of the college. Two further charters were drawn up in Boston and also disallowed. Supporters of Increase Mather urged that he be returned to England to seek a college charter. But they met opposition from a party headed by Elisha Cooke—a Boston physician and the town assessor—who adamantly held out for the old Massachusetts charter and reviled Increase for having negotiated the new one. Increase's own desire to take up the new agency went beyond the college. Uncomfortable in Boston since his education abroad, he wished to be sent to England because he was a peevish man of sophisticated intellect and worldly experience who felt cramped and unappreciated in provincial circumstances. Also, his discontent swelled on accusations that he had betrayed the country, and the prospect of leaving it became more tempting with the Act of Toleration, granting new liberty in England to Dissenters like himself. As he said in one of his continuing threats of desertion, his congregation well knew "that I have had a strong bent of spirit to spend (and to end) the remainder of my few days in England."

For years after Increase returned from his original charter agency, moreover, the belief that he would return to England had come to him, often and repeatedly, as a Particular Faith—for him also, a cherished phenomenon of devotional life. Cotton, having made a team with his father in almost every other aspect of their ministry, now joined him in experiencing Particular Faiths concerning his agency. They came for the first time in June 1699, as the General Court again considered the settlement of the college. He had prayed over the matter many times, without having his mind lifted to a Particular Faith one way or the other. But this day he for the first time experienced it: "it was in a powerful Manner assured me from Heaven, that my Father shall one Day be carried into *England* . . . and that the *Particular Faith* which had introduced it, shall be at last made a matter of wonderful Glory and Service unto the Lord." Probably spurred by his Particular Faith, he drew up an address on July 7, signed by some other ministers, asking the governor and General Assembly to consider sending an agent abroad for Harvard. The Assembly again took up the question of a college charter on the 18th, which Cotton reserved for a day of fasting and prayer. About noon, as he was crying to heaven to arrange his father's voyage, and while the Assembly was voting or debating, there came to him an unutterable assurance from heaven that his father would be carried into England, "and that at this very Time there was occurring that which would one Day accomplish it."

This time Mather's Particular Faith was answered by "a most unintelligible Dispensation." At just noon, as he received his assurance, the bill for the college was not being enacted by the Assembly but vetoed by Governor Bellomont. Bellomont apparently tried to get the Assembly to reconsider the matter, but the members had sat for many weeks and were anxious to return home, as many had done already; they refused to take further action until their next session. The confused outcome—occurring, Mather believed, even as he was receiving a contrary Particular Faith in his study—left him troubled. "Lord," he called, "preserve my Faith, and assist me to wait with an holy and humble Patience, for the Issue of these mysterious Things!" The issue was nearly a year in arriving, however, and meantime his father also, he recorded, became discouraged "about the accomplishment of the *Particular Faith,* which had seemed so often infused from Heaven into our Minds." On the last day of 1699 he once more lay the matter before God in his study, at noon. He failed to have a Particular Faith, however, until, as he ended his petitions, his mind "suddenly felt a strange and a strong Operation from Heaven upon it," causing him to say aloud: "*The Lord will do it, The Lord Will do it, my Father shall be carried into* England."

The test of this Particular Faith came the following June. During the Mathers' controversy with the Brattle church, the question of a college charter again arose in the Assembly, in such circumstances that if it failed it was unlikely to be revived again. Cotton's conviction having been several times aroused then defeated, he found himself "in extreme Distress of Spirit." His distress also grew, he recognized, from his knack for landing in uncomfortably conflicted situations. "My *Flesh,*" he observed, would be "on all Accounts imaginable against my Father's Removal from me"; but "my Faith" having been "so supernaturally raised for it, the Thoughts of that's being wholly disappointed, were insupportable." He cast himself on his study floor, pleading that he had always believed a Particular Faith to be a work of heaven on the minds of the devout, telling God that if his belief proved wrong he would be thrown into confusion. His distressed plaints failed to rouse him—"my Heart had the Coldness of a Stone"—until he suddenly felt the inexpressible afflatus: "if an *Angel* from Heaven had spoken it articulately to me, the Communication would not have been more powerful and perceptible." It was "told" him that God "had not permitted us to be deceived in our *Particular Faith.*" Assured that God delighted in him and his father as faithful servants, he called out in tears, "*He will do it, He will do it!*"

But it, Mather added lugubriously, "All came to nothing!" Governor Bellomont, who had favored Increase's agency, deserted it, and instead was allowed to present the case for the charter in England himself: "all Expectation of a Voyage for my Father into *England* on any such Occasion," Mather wrote, "is utterly at an End." The end, although real, was hard to accept. "*Wait!*" he advised himself. "*Wait!*"

But by the next month there was less than ever to wait for, as the General Assembly began ousting Increase from the Harvard presidency altogether. The Council had several times voted a requirement that the president reside in Cambridge, and had repeatedly pressed Increase to move there. He had sidestepped their resolves by threatening to resign, and by offering such objections as his unwillingness to give up preaching to fifteen hundred souls in Boston "only to expound to 40 or 50 children few of them capable of edification by such exercises." Although during his sixteen years as president Increase had resided in Cambridge only six months, he had been able by staying in Boston to consult often with the governor and legislature, and had helped reshape Harvard's policies and halt its slide. At the same time, his abhorrence of Cambridge became an effective weapon for Elisha Cooke, who together with some supporters of the Brattle church tried to oust him from Harvard by forcing him to live there. In July, the General Assembly voted that the president must reside in Cambridge, and appointed a committee to tell Increase it was expected that he repair to and reside at Cambridge as soon as possible.

Perhaps because there no longer seemed a hope of his going to England, and because friends advised him that if he resisted he would be widely reproached and would die with infamy, Increase hastened disconsolately to Cambridge, the place, Cotton said, "which of all under Heaven, was most abominable to him." Cotton felt as he had when his father escaped to England, "left alone, in the Care of a vast Congregation," concerned lest he fail to perform his duties adequately. His worry underestimated his father's disgust with Cambridge, for in three months Increase was back in Boston, having preached only once in the College Hall. He held out until the following March, when the House approved a new order providing that if he refused the presidency the governance of the college should go to the Rev. Samuel Willard. Increase moved to Cambridge again. On his father's birthday, June 21, Cotton found "to my Astonishment" a new hope of Increase's charter agency to England, "which had such a Sentence of Death upon it, about a year ago." He recorded experiencing no Particular Faith about it, however, and it too came to nothing. Increase, after living in Cambridge another three months, asked the General Court to choose a new president and delivered a farewell sermon to the scholars, telling them to expect for their service to Christ not honor but "rather to be *Despised and Rejected of Men;* rather to have all manner of *Indignities* heaped upon you."

Both Mathers felt the effects of Cooke's success in maneuvering Increase into resigning the presidency. Added to the uncertain dependability of the government and the popularity of the Brattle church, it meant to them a serious loss of influence. Cotton later viewed the episode as having ended his father's public life. Increase, stricken with gout and feeling himself aging, not only gave up hopes of returning to England; something gone of his old sour vitality, he also became, he said, "desirous to die where I am." He speculated, too, that the angels who transmit Particular Faiths might actually be ignorant of "some" future events. They might cause motions in men's spirits not according to what will certainly happen but according to what might come to pass "in probability."

*

Abigail Mather had already been ill when in May 1702 she miscarried of a son. The illness worsened, so that not even the most capable physicians, Mather wrote, knew "what to judge of or what to do for." She seems to have had breast cancer, later probably complicated by an infectious disease. Mather says little of her in his diaries until this illness, but in choosing her he had sought a wife who would honor the ministry and be a model to the community. From the beginning of their marriage he had resolved to help her toward her conversion by example, conference, and joint prayer, and his efforts succeeded in the fall of 1689, when she was admitted to the North Church as a full member. He praised not only her piety, however, but also her "obliging Deportment" to him, her discretion in ordering their affairs, "and the Lovely *Off-Spring* I have received by her." Later he would add that she also had a "melancholy Temper," her spirit having been broken by her father's second marriage, "bringing home a Mother-in-law, tho' he did well in it."

A week after Abigail's miscarriage Mather fasted and prayed for her in his study, hoping for an irradiation from heaven concerning her recovery. Instead, deprived of "the agreeable Charms of her *Person*," he found his mind buffeted by sexual longings, "*impure Thoughts*, which exceedingly abased me before the Lord." He set apart another day of fasting and prayer, this time with Abigail in her room. And this time, thankfully, he felt "the blessed Breezes of a *Particular Faith*, blowing from Heaven upon my mind." The breezes returned when he prayed alone in his study that afternoon, and encouraged him to assure Abigail that she would live longer.

Yet the very next day Abigail seemed to have in fact died. A physician was summoned from church. Although Abigail revived, Mather was called to her room the next night because she again seemed to be dying. About one or two in the morning he held a vigil in his study, and assurances

came to him that God intended to restore her, and came again the next
morning with hope, joy, and wonder when he prayed with her. That day,
indeed, a "critical Salivation" began in Abigail. The salivation was auspicious, for it reduced her fever. But it did not stop, it became profuse and
continued for a week and left her drained. Mather observed another day
of prayer and fasting on June 24, and his Particular Faith was astonishingly renewed despite the extremity of Abigail's condition: "God, and His
good Angel, has assured me from Heaven, that tho' my Consort be in such
dying Circumstances, yet she shall not die, but live." But next Friday, she
grew still worse, "if it could be," and her progressive deterioration, in
defiance of his heavenly promises, was unmistakable, leaving no likelihood of anything after all but her death. For Mather the likelihood was
dreadful enough, "But Lord!" he wrote, "how aggravated a Calamity must
be her Death, if such a Sting, as the Disappointment of my *Particular
Faith,* must be added unto it!"

Instead of dying, Abigail continued languishing through midsummer.
Mather knew well enough the Puritan lesson of weaned affections, that
we must love this life as children who although they cling to their mother's breast must give it up inevitably. Yet while he freely gave his wife up
to the Lord, he admitted, "I could not *give her over.*" If God spared her
he would do much in return—study new methods of family prayer, use
his ordeal to glorify Christ, try to be more exemplarily chaste and holy
than ever. Part of one night he spent calling on God from his bedroom
floor, "with so little of Garment on as to render my lying there painful to
my tender Bones." Once he allowed himself a respite of bitterness: "I am
kept up all Night, that I may see her die, and therewith see the terrible
Death of my Prayer and Faith." But again prophetic certainty returned
and, on the evening of August 23, with visionary intensity. As he sat in his
study it was said to him, "*Go into your great Chamber and I will speak
with you!*" He did so, confessing from the floor his loathsome worthiness
to be thunderstruck into dust and ashes, until the inexpressible afflatus
came, leaving on his agitated soul a sweet, calm, and sanctifying impression that caused him to say:

> *My Father* loves me, and will fill me with His *Love,* and will bring me to
> Everlasting *Life. My Father* will never permit anything to befall me, but
> what shall be for *His Interest. . . .* The Condition of my Dear *Consort, my
> Father* will give me to see His Wonderful Favour in it.

At the end of August, after fourteen weeks of pain and continued salivation, and now with feverish scurvy as well, Abigail took such a bad turn

that she terrified him "with extreme Apprehensions of her Dissolution."

The weeks—as Mather began tallying the ordeal—of September passed amid the same wearing counterpoint of assurances from heaven and alarms from the sickroom. News arrived of the death in London of Abigail's second brother, a young merchant, "her Darling." Ill himself, he had gone abroad in hopes of a curative sea voyage, but after he left, Mather wrote, Abigail said with a "more than ordinary Passion and Agony, *that she desired, God would never let her live to hear of the Death of that young man!*" When the news of his death arrived, Mather and the rest of the family put on mourning costume but by "prudent Management" kept Abigail uninformed. He tried meanwhile to keep up his many other activities—writing, preaching at other towns and before the recently arrived new governor, Joseph Dudley, awaiting with great consternation the long-delayed publication of his *Magnalia.*

Mather pondered, too, this latest engagement with the invisible world. Perhaps, he considered, God had designed by these trials a special exercise of his prayer and faith. Or perhaps he had interpreted too casually the meaning of the Holy Ghost and His angel in the Particular Faiths they had given him. It might be that God, in demonstrating His being loathe to deny anything Mather importunately asked, intended not to prevent Abigail's death but only to delay it until she and he were better prepared. Or when God says *"that He has heard me,"* He might intend something other than Abigail's recovery, a future blessing he could not possibly anticipate, but in which the Particular Faith would be accomplished.

By October, after more than twenty weeks' languishing, Abigail fell into the symptoms of a "hopeless *Consumption*" and was now "wasted." Yet the end of the month seemed to bring one ground for hope and one for thanksgiving. Abigail had a prophetic dream, perhaps a visitation. A "grave Person" appeared to her—in her sleep, she supposed ("in her sleep, no doubt," Mather wrote years later)—accompanying a woman in such wretched circumstances that Abigail praised God for making her own condition less so. The grave person told her that the intolerable pain in her breast could be eased by applying to it warm wool cut from a living sheep, and that her continued salivation would be stemmed if she strengthened her glands by drinking gum mastic and gum isinglass dissolved in a tankard of spring water. She told the dream to her main physician, who encouraged trying it. To Mather's great surprise she revived quickly. Twice she managed to get up from her sickroom and visit him in his study, where they gave thanks together to God. A week later, on Thursday, October 29, at last arrived from England a copy of *Magnalia*

Christi Americana. For a change Mather set apart the next day for thanksgiving, praising God for "His watchful and gracious Providence over that Work, and for the Harvest of so many Prayers, and Cares, and Tears, and Resignations, as I had employ'd upon it."

Pleased with seeing his large book in print, Mather learned, the same day, that Abigail's namesake, their eight-year-old daughter "Nibby," had smallpox. The deadly disease had arrived in Boston in June, for the first time in thirteen years. The town selectmen had tried to contain it, moving an infected family, isolating an infected black person, quarantining some infected seamen, but in its sweep through Boston, twice-envenomed by a simultaneous epidemic of scarlet fever, it would kill more than three hundred persons. "God prepare me, God prepare me," Mather cried, "for what is coming upon me!"

Within a month Mather's house became a hospital, where to attend Abigail and now his children also, he ultimately used "near one hundred Watchers." Soon the maid became "horribly full" of pocks and distracted; five-year-old Nancy succumbed; three-year-old Increase, Jr., was smitten "pretty full and blind, and sore; tho' not so bad as his Sister." Although it was a large house, Mather decided that no room was better suited to caring for his sick children than his study—a "large, yet a warm chamber" filled with books, from which his "little Folks" called him to pray with them scarcely less than ten or a dozen times a day, as he did.

Always busy, Mather became doubly so. He also prayed with his sick neighbors, large numbers of whom he visited. Finding it impossible to visit them all, but considering it his duty to counsel them in the epidemic, he had three men distribute to the many stricken families in his neighborhood copies of his *Wholesome Words; or, A Visit of Advice to Families visited with Sickness* (1702?), which he had published at his own expense. While Abigail and the children lay ill, he also continued preaching elaborate sermons from his pulpit. "Our afflictions," he told his congregation in November, "must not prevent, no, they must promote, and provoke our glorifying of God." He interpreted the epidemic as he did all untoward events. That his study happened to serve ideally for the children's sickroom he saw as God's humiliation for not serving Him as he should have done in his study, "which provokes Him to chase me out of it." With the same reasoning he urged the afflicted to examine their condition, to see whether "perhaps the Spotted Faces of the *Sick* in the Family, are such as our Heavenly Father has been *Spitting* upon: Shall *He Spit in our Faces, and shall we not be Ashamed?*" In facing death too, he counseled, the family's duty was to exhibit, as a token of faith, the profoundest resignation: "Whatever Flower in our Garden be Cropt, tho' it be our *Isaac,* yet Resign it, and let it be said of us, Gen. XXII. 12. *Now I know that thou Fearest God, because thou hast not witheld* any thing from Him!"

Whatever Mather's fears for his children, still "the most exquisite of my Trials," he wrote, "was the Condition of my lovely Consort." Abigail had decayed for six months and her condition was hopeless. Obviously aware that her enfeeblement had taxed those around her, she once said, *"I shall make you all weary!"* Seemingly aware of her husband's pride in his capacity to give inexhaustibly, she added, *"I don't mean you,* Mr. Mather!" He felt unsure how to glorify God to her amid the enclosing distress and confusion, yet set himself to doing so "after my sorry Manner"—praying with her, catechizing her, discoursing on heaven, preparing her for death, which came on December 1. "At last, the black Day," Mather wrote. "I had never yet seen such a black Day, in all the Time of my Pilgrimage. The *Desire of my Eyes* is this Day to be taken from me."

Abigail lingered in pain the whole morning. Presumably because of his grief, Mather was later unable to recall his conversations with her. He did remember asking her to tell him what fault she had observed in his behavior that she would advise him to correct; she replied, to his wonder, that she knew of none, but that his behavior had helped bring her nearer to God. As she began dying Mather wished to signify his acquiescence, as he counseled others to do, thereby to glorify God. It occurred to him to kneel by her bedside and take her hand, "a dear Hand, the dearest in the World." Then he showed his Savior his utter resignation to His will: "I gently put her out of my Hands, and laid away a most lovely Hand, resolving that I would never touch it any more!" It was, he said, "the hardest and perhaps the bravest Action, that ever I did." To acknowledge his resignation, Abigail, who had called for him continually, ceased to call for him during the two hours she remained alive. Immediately after her death he prayed with her weeping father and the other mourners in her room.

Mather took pride in the many who honored Abigail, the next Friday, at her funeral: "Indeed, I do not know of a Gentlewoman, who has died in this Land, these many years, more generally esteemed and lamented." Her five infants and young children by Mather who had died before her had been buried with common grave stones, but now some members of the North Church built a costly tomb to contain Abigail's and the children's remains together. At the funeral Mather gave each person who had attended her a copy of one of his works, containing a twelve-line poem,

pasted in on a paper, that began, "Go then, My DOVE, but now no longer *mine;* / Leave *Earth,* and now in *heavenly Glory* shine." Two days later he preached her funeral sermon. Taking for his text the death of the prophet Ezekiel's wife—Son of Man, Behold I take away the Desire of thine Eyes with a Stroke—he presented himself as a sad commentary upon it: "Your Eyes do behold," he said, "what it is, for the God of Heaven, to take away from a Son of Man, the Desire of His Eyes with a Stroke."

While stressing such customary pulpit themes as the need for self-examination under affliction, Mather did not conceal his own mood of sorrowful deprivation. He composed for the occasion perhaps the loveliest of his several paeans to married love, in the tradition of Anne Bradstreet's intimately domestic but scriptural poems to her husband. Some relatives, he remarked to his congregation, do not like each other. But the consorts in a loving marriage know a special joy at once erotic, spiritual, and natural. They can never see each other enough, for the sight of the beloved is the very condition of their happiness:

> The God of Love sometimes does dispose them whom He has made Consorts in the Conjugal Relation, greatly to Love and prize one another. The Consorts are to each other the Desire of their Eyes, and they so love each other that they Love to be as much as may be in the Sight of each other. . . . They live together Like Abraham and Sarah; Like Isaac and Rebeckah; Like Jacob and Rachel. They Live together in such Love that they could freely Die for one another; and when either of them does Die, it gives a thousand Deaths to the Survivor. . . . He loves her and her Love, and rejoices in his loving Hind, and his pleasant Roe. He had rather lose all his possessions, than suffer the loss of one whom God has thus Enriched him withal. He can scarce Relish any thing in his House, if his Eyes have not her also before him.

If the passage suggests the strength of Mather's attachment to Abigail, the unusually many blots and strikeouts in the surviving manuscript betray his strain in recalling it. He wrote the sermon, he said, under "the most grievous Desolations of his *Mind,* as well as of his *House,* that ever were upon him."

As the year ended, Mather reviewed the events of the last eight months to see what mercies they contained to balance his heavy loss. For one, his children had almost been consumed in the "*Fiery Furnace* of the *Small pox,*" but had all emerged alive; he had made many pastoral visits to "venomous, contagious loathsome Chambers," and had been preserved as well. Abigail's death could itself be considered a mercy, he decided, for it spared her painful knowledge of reverses in her family.

Given her melancholy temper, she would have suffered greatly to learn of the death abroad of her second brother, as she nearly did. Oddly, Mather thought, a letter addressed to her from London containing an account of his death arrived at the house about three hours after she died. There was more bad news to oppress her also. Her youngest brother had recently been captured by the French, and her sottish eldest brother was disgracing his family and hastening to his ruin. All this had been concealed from Abigail during her illness but would, Mather believed, "without a Miracle, have brought such a Disorder of Mind upon her, as would have rendered my Condition insupportable."

Mather's concern for "my Condition" perhaps sounds selfishly uncomprehending, icy. But he recognized and admitted that he himself felt relieved by Abigail's death. Her illness, on display before helpless physicians, attendants, and children, had been long and dehumanizing, six months of wasting fevers, incapacitating feebleness, severe breast pains, and bedridden hallucinations. So at last after her death Mather acknowledged, with weariedly grim realism, "all the Fatigues, which her long Illness obliged me to go through, and with all possible Tenderness." Had she gone on as she was, "my Health would infallibly have been destroy'd, if she had recovered a little more, and so far that I should have run the venture of sleeping with her, My feeble Constitution, would undoubtedly have run into a Consumption. And my Children would also have suffered miserably in their Education."

Still, it was a sore death, more trying by far, Mather felt, than the earlier deaths of his children. He had resignedly "laid away a most lovely Hand." Perhaps Abigail's extreme weakness, or the children's education, and his own vulnerable health made her death a mercy; but, he added, "my extravagant Fondness for her, would upon any Terms have detained her here." Until recently, he realized in January, he had rarely cried except when thinking of salvation, and then in joy. "But now, scarce a Day passes me without a Flood of Tears, and my Eyes even decay with weeping."

To the extent that Mather could escape his grief over Abigail's death he only ran into what locked him back in it, the *"Miscarriage of a Particular Faith!"* Abigail had died despite repeated assurances from heaven that she would live. "Truly, nothing has ever yet befallen me, that has come so near to it." He had many thoughts on this "astonishing Sting." He believed that in her misery Abigail had prayed, at cross-purposes from him, for her release, which in the court of heaven had overruled the effect of all his own prayers and hopes for her recovery. Or perhaps as God does nothing without purpose, He may defeat Particular Faiths as a warning against pride. Mather observed that the phrase "Son of Man," stressing human limitation, is used nearly a hundred times about Ezekiel, even though the prophet was admitted to familiarity with angels. God may have taken Ezekiel's wife to remind him that despite his angelic converse he was mortal: "The Angels of God, would have this brave man see That he was but a Son of Man," and they supplied "Enough in that one point, I take away the Desire of thine Eyes with a Stroke, to convince him of his being so."

Or, Mather speculated, God may have confounded him so that he could be serviceable in cautioning others about self-deceit. He conveyed this message in a sermon he preached two weeks after Abigail's death, on the doctrine, "*Tho' Faith be no Folly, yet Faith may be mixed with Folly.*" When we pray for some worldly thing, he told his congregation, God sometime favors us with "so much of a *Particular Faith,* as to say, *the Lord hath heard the Voice of my Weeping.*" But our strong desire for the thing may lead us to interpret the Particular Faith too literally, as if meaning that "*the Thing must be done in just such or such a manner.*" All that is meant in a Particular Faith, he cautioned, is that something will be done toward the blessing we desire which will demonstrate God's willingness to gratify us.

Yet Mather's puzzling over God's purpose in raising then frustrating his hopes produced no answer. He contented himself with thinking that God might allow him in the future to understand the working of a Particular Faith. And meanwhile he would be wary: "I have met with enough, to awaken in me a more exquisite Caution, than ever I had in my Life, concerning it."

*

Only two months after Abigail's death, a young gentlewoman wrote several letters to Mather, then visited him at his house. He had just turned forty, she was twenty-three, and she proposed that he marry her. She confessed to him that, his widowerhood having allowed her more liberty to think of him, she found him irresistible, "charmed with my Person, to such a Degree, that she could not but break in upon me, with her most importunate Requests, that I would make her mine." She assured him that what impelled her was the more than ordinary value she placed on his ministry, and that her highest consideration in wanting to be his wife was her eternal salvation.

Mather never names this young gentlewoman, so forward for her salvation, but she was almost certainly Katharine Maccarty, the daughter of a

Boston landholder and shopowner who had helped found King's Chapel. Mather thought Kate attractive and suitable, "a young Gentlewoman of incomparable Accomplishments . . . . one of rare Wit and Sense; and of a comely Aspect; and extremely Winning in her Conversation." Yet he tried to discourage her, portraying his life to her as a regimen of prayers, fasts, and "macerating Devotions and Reservations." But Kate told him she desired nothing so much as to share his macerations; his macerated way of living was exactly what "animated" her, she said. Considering her youth, and that she had been a "very airy Person," Mather was not entirely convinced. Yet he remained drawn to her and flattered by her attention, and suggested they take time to see if the question could be resolved. For himself he would pray and fast, and wait and see: "What Snares may be laying for me, I know not."

As Mather pondered this "odd Matter" he saw clearly that his wishes and his ministry conflicted. In himself he found "a mighty Tenderness for a person so very amiable." Breeding required that she be treated with honor and respect; religion required that instead of rashly rejecting her he continue the relationship so as to make her Christ's. But he foresaw violent opposition to the match, worried about the example he might set to young people in his flock, and feared making a bad mistake. His confusion sent him to his study floor often, calling for God's assistances until after midnight, and so wracked and wasted him that in mid-February he wrote Kate to "vehemently beg, as for my Life" that she end her pursuit. But to give up seeing her was not so easy: "such was my flexible Tenderness, as to be conquered by the Importunities of several, to allow some further Interviews." He determined to make these interviews revolve around her conversion, drawing from the "witty Gentlewoman" her tearful consent to the articles of the covenant of grace.

Gossip about the piquant affair tightened Mather's agitation. His "Relatives" (probably his father) believed he overvalued Kate, took the situation with extreme distaste, and treated him strangely and harshly. As the "ingenious Child" continued pressing him, news went around Boston that he was courting her. With most people Kate had a bad name, he discovered, partly because of "the Disadvantages of the Company which has continually resorted unto her unhappy Father's House." People also blamed him for his earliness in courting. The noise made him suspect a design of Satan to destroy his ministry—"Is it because I have done much against that Enemy?"—a possibility which as always left him overwrought: "There is Danger of my dying suddenly, with smothered Griefs and Fears." By mid-March, after long deliberation, he saw unquestionably

that marriage with Kate would damage his name and vocation. He resigned himself once again to laying aside a lovely hand, a person who
"for many charming Accomplishments, has not many Equals in the *English America.*" In thus giving himself to Christ, howbeit in novel form,
he discerned "no unhappy Symptom, I hope, of Regeneration in my
Soul."

Sign of grace or no, Mather's decision only sharpened his distress. The
stubborn appeal of Kate's physical attractiveness and social charms evidently aroused severe guilt and anger. A highly sexual man, Mather became tempted, he wrote with indefinite frankness, to *"Impurities"* and,
worse, sometime to blasphemy, atheism, "and the Abandonment of all
Religion, as a mere Delusion; and sometimes, to self-Destruction itself."
His imagination began giving shape to a new trouble: Kate might retaliate
for being rejected. Apparently he had not let her down lightly, for he
speaks of the "coarse, tho' just, Usage that she has had from me." These
might provoke her to a "thousand Inventions" to scandalize a town
where new lies about him and the broken courtship were being invented
daily anyway. Despite his disappointment in Particular Faiths he sought
relief from his misery by pleading the question to heaven. On April 13 he
decided to spend no less than three successive days fasting and praying in
his study, something he believed had never been done before by anyone.
The extraordinary devotions produced "Extraordinary Things . . . that
cannot be related. I will only say, the Angels of Heaven are at work for
me." He set aside other days of fasting and prayer of similar fervency,
whose rapture exhausted his spirit, "made me faint and sick; they were
insupportable; I was forced, even to withdraw from them, lest I should
have swoon'd away."

Mather's heavenly messages had to contend, however, with Kate's
mother, Elizabeth—a woman, he thought her at first, "of an extraordinary
Character for her Piety." While he was out of town on a trip to Salem, she
and her daughter both wrote to and visited his father, and some of his
neighbors, to renew their suit. By now he was bent on hearing nothing
more of it, whatever the risk of revenge. But Elizabeth wrote to him herself; if her letter is any clue to her daughter's personality, Mather's jitteri-
ness is understandable, for although semiliterate, its pious flattery is
crafty, winning, and exquisitely manipulative. Elizabeth blessed him and
God for the little conversation the minister had granted her daughter
because it concerned, she knew, "that noble Design of bringing her nearer
to the Lord-Redeemer." Her daughter's interest in Mather was wholly
soteriological: "I am sure, Heaven knows, that was her whole Design, in

Addressing your worthy person." Her daughter thought, she said, that heaven might have ordered for the everlasting good of her soul "a Relation to so Heavenly a man (which she always thought more Like an Angel than a man)."

Susceptible to flattery but not to idolatrous armbending, Mather seems to have sent back a stiff warning that the Maccartys' hounding him was both unwanted and dangerous to his strained health. His letter is lost but its content reverberates in the reply Elizabeth wrote on June 7, which she delayed sending, she said, knowing it was his day for administering the Lord's Supper and concerned lest anything in it "might in the least discompose you at such a time." She had never, she said, received "any of the like unkind Letter from any person." Her own letter is poorly preserved and difficult to read, but seems to imply that Mather had sent other no-nonsense letters as well, which she sat on her couch afraid to open, crying to God that "this holy man means thus to distress me." In one letter he apparently spoke of his dying by excessive perturbation, so that she drenched "the paper throwly with my tears," hoping God would not suffer "such a star of the first magnitude to be removed from us, by which a great part of the world will be darkened." Mather's show of resentment and nervous strain seems to have convinced Elizabeth to retreat, for she assured him her greatest grief would be to be shut out of his and his father's prayers. In closing she presented Kate's thanks for a book Mather had given or sent her, presumably by him. Her daughter was reading his works, she added, "with the greatest Delight imaginable."

Mather felt that the Maccartys, in affirming that he had treated them honorably and righteously, had fully vindicated his behavior. Yet more than ever impertinent stories spread through Boston that made him contemptible, tales that he was actively wooing Kate, insinuations that he had gone too far in the suit to abandon it decently. The falsehoods and notoriety atop months of frazzling temptation and resistance swelled his anger: "these things do exceedingly unhinge me; and cause me sometimes to *speak unadvisedly with my Lips.* Tis well, if they do not perfectly kill me."

Unexpectedly Mather found relief just two houses from his own. His neighbor Mrs. Elizabeth Hubbard, widowed four years and nearing thirty years of age, offered the sobriety and respectability Kate lacked. She was "a Gentlewoman of Piety and Probity, and a most unspotted Reputation; a Gentlewoman of good Wit and Sense, and Discretion at ordering an Household; a Gentlewoman of incomparable Sweetness in her Temper, and Humor; a Gentlewoman honourably descended and related; and a very comely person." Yet Mather had reservations, among them that Elizabeth had a son, about the age of Increase, Jr. He reasoned that he had often urged Abigail to take some fatherless child into their family, feed and clothe it that God might bless his own children: "Why then should I think much to educate the Son of a Gentlewoman from whom I expect so much service to mine?" Visiting Elizabeth's house the first time on July 14, he found himself entertained if not exactly like an angel, yet with "more than ordinary Civility, Affection, and Veneration." His reservations also faded some, as Elizabeth turned out to be "an abundantly more agreeable Person, than ever I imagined," a reparation for his grief in Abigail's death, his disappointment in Particular Faiths, the resignations of the last fifteen months.

The lingering possibility that Kate might demand revenge for her "defeated Love" had kept Mather uneasy, and now came to life. Enraged, she threatened to be a thorn in his side, to contrive every possible way "to vex me, affront me, disgrace me, in my Attempting a Return to the married State with another Gentlewoman." Now able to see unconfusedly that she was a person perhaps of rare wit but of little grace, he did not try to mollify her. Instead he carried the matter to Christ, who this time answered; Kate wrote to him promising not to execute "those Disquietments, which in her Passion she had threatened." Astonished at this work of heaven, he offered God a sacrifice of love and praise.

His engagement, it also amazed Mather to think, created satisfaction in town and country alike. He too felt satisfied, and eager. Having lived celibate more than a year, it pleased him to think of "arriving speedily to the Enjoyment of a most lovely Creature," although in connection with this prospect a strong fancy troubled him, smacking of guilt, that before he could be married he would die. Rather, on the evening of August 18, he was married. He spent the entire day in his study in thanksgiving, tendering particular thanks to God for "my astonishing Preservations, from undoing myself, my Ministry, and my Family, under the amazing Temptations, which in the Time of my Widowhood, I have met withal." By God's help he had not made some scandalous, unredeemable mistake.

But he had come close; Kate had had her attractions. With his genius for compromise, he offered thanks too, if not exactly fervent ones, that God had provided "the most agreeable Consort (all things considered) that all *America* could have afforded me."

III

THE REVEREND COTTON MATHER
D.D. & F.R.S. (1703–1713)

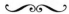

> Cotton Mather came galloping down
> All the way to Newbury town,
> With eyes agog and ears set wide,
> And his marvellous inkhorn at his side;
> Stirring the while in the shallow pool
> Of his brains for the lore he learned at school,
> To garnish the story, with here a streak
> Of Latin, and there another of Greek:
> And the tales he heard and the notes he took,
> Behold! are they not in his Wonder-Book?
>
> —JOHN GREENLEAF WHITTIER, "The Double-Headed
> Snake of Newbury" (1859)

A field near the graveyard. GILES COREY lying dead, with a great stone on his breast. . . .

MATHER

> O sight most horrible! In a land like this,
> Spangled with Churches Evangelical,
> Inwrapped in our salvations, must we seek
> In mouldering statute-books of English Courts
> Some old forgotten Law, to do such deeds?
> Those who lie buried in the Potter's Field
> Will rise again, as surely as ourselves
> That sleep in honored graves with epitaphs;
> And this poor man, whom we have made a victim,
> Hereafter will be counted as a martyr!
>
> —HENRY WADSWORTH LONGFELLOW, *Giles Corey of the
> Salem Farms* (1868)

The tendency of the stately old families of New England to constitutional melancholy has been well set forth by Dr. Cotton Mather, that delightful old New

England grandmother, whose nursery tales of its infancy and childhood may well be pondered by those who would fully understand its far-reaching maturity. As I have before remarked, I have high ideas of the wisdom of grandmothers, and therefore do our beloved gossip, Dr. Cotton Mather, the greatest possible compliment in granting him the title.

—HARRIET BEECHER STOWE, *Oldtown Folks* (1869)

In 1721, this disease [smallpox], after a respite of nineteen years, again appeared as an epidemic. In that year it was that Cotton Mather, browsing, as was his wont, on all the printed fodder that came within reach of his ever-grinding mandibles, came upon an account of inoculation as practised in Turkey, contained in the "Philosophical Transactions." He spoke of it to several physicians, who paid little heed to his story; for they knew his medical whims, and had probably been bored, as we say now-a-days, many of them, with listening to his "Angel of Bethesda," and satiated with his speculations on the *Nishmath Chajim*.

The Reverend Mather,—I use a mode of expression he often employed when speaking of his honored brethren,—the Reverend Mather was right this time, and the irreverent doctors who laughed at him were wrong. . . .

—OLIVER WENDELL HOLMES, "The Medical Profession in Massachusetts" (1869)

7

Joseph Dudley

As THE NEW century opened, Cotton Mather was newly remarried, nearing forty, and about to replace his father as the most prominent minister in America. Increase's declining role in public life was partly owing to his ouster from the Harvard presidency and his decision to abide in New England, but also to his advancing age and failing health. In 1704, aged sixty-five, he had fits of what he understood to be apoplexy. He also suffered kidney pains and began urinating blood and stones. Over the next half-dozen years he recorded having insomnia, cholic, and pains in his jaw and teeth, and took to wearing fur gloves for the gout in his hands. To treat his losses of memory he administered to himself sixty drops of oil of lavender and a mouthful of gingerbread. Extremely fearful that his mind would fail, he hoped to die soon: "If I die quickly some few will lament my death. Whereas if I live a while longer I shall be useless. It is a great mercy for a minister not to outlive his work."

Increase conspired in his decline by his inveterate view of himself as moribund, now to a degree justified by objective conditions of his health. His announcements of his imminent death multiplied: "It is but a very little Time that I have now to be in the World," he told his congregation in 1703, "I am wasting continually." "*I must shortly put off this my Tabernacle,*" he told his readers in 1705. "The Time of my Departure hence, drawing on apace," he prefaced another work in 1711. In 1704 he considered choosing his successor, a partner to his son. Not anyone would be suitable for their large congregation, and he found the younger candidates not as loyal to the Cambridge Platform as he wished, and grown accustomed, lazily he thought, to reading all their sermons. He believed the most suitable choice was Cotton's younger brother Samuel, now in his mid-twenties and preaching in England. But Samuel was disinclined, and Increase decided to promote his candidacy no further, leaving the matter of his successor open.

Ironically, Increase's waning effectiveness and the troubled events of the next decade brought Cotton Mather not only greater prominence but also lessened influence in Boston. Cotton's pain over the discrepancy may be more complexly appreciated by sketching, before the narrative resumes, the more intimate side of the ministry he had established twenty or so years after his ordination—not its shifting involvement in public affairs, but something of its little-changing daily color and routine.

The congregation Mather served remained probably the largest in New England, containing about fifteen hundred people. Of these about four hundred were admitted to the Lord's Supper. He preached, that is, to a largely unregenerated audience, hoping to supervise their conversion, although in the more than forty years of his ministry the new admissions to communion amounted to only 574 women and 342 men. The congregation included such prosperous and notable persons as John Richards and Samuel Scarlett; a large number of maritime people (perhaps a quarter of his flock); a large number of widows (about a sixth of the communicants); many children; and numerous blacks. At least after 1711, he and his father received identical salaries of £3 per week, raised from weekly contributions at the church that averaged around £10, the remainder buying wood, bellropes, or casks of communion wine, or paying the numerous guest preachers, who received £1. Increments over the succeeding years brought Cotton's salary to £4 by 1725. These meager salaries were filled out by free repairs and firewood for their homes and gifts of money customarily left them in the wills of wealthy congregants, or occasionally donated by the church itself or by wealthy and pious friends who belonged to other churches.

Mather approached his ministry with thoughtful devotion and exceeding care. He strove to preach "as excellent and well studied Sermons as ever I can and contrive all my public Exercises in the most edifying manner that I am able." He undoubtedly succeeded; much other evidence confirms his several comments that when he preached outside Boston people flocked to hear him, and that in his own church he attracted very large audiences: "Few Ministers in the World, preach unto the like; it would be beyond the Strength of a mortal Man, to preach unto much bigger." Preaching once on Sunday, and often a second time at the so-called Thursday Lecture (a practice introduced to New England by his grandfather John Cotton), he produced seventy or so formal sermons a year, neatly handwritten in small booklets. In his earlier, and perhaps also his later, ministry he composed part of the sermon kneeling at his chair in a prayerful position, writing on a *"Table-Book"* of slate open before him—carefully weighing the meaning of his texts in their original languages, consulting scriptural commentaries, and praying much. In preparing each sermon, he reckoned, he usually spent seven hours.

Differing considerations dictated Mather's choice of sermon subjects. Occasionally he preached on a text "assigned" him in a dream or took his cue from a local event. Once as a thunderstorm broke outside his church he began preaching extemporaneously on thunder and later published the sermon. Other times he addressed his sermon to a particular public occasion—an execution, a funeral, Election Day—or to a specific group in his congregation, to sailors or children or merchants or women, by this means making his pulpit a forum for commenting on the life of the town. Sometimes he preached a series of connected sermons on the same text. His ministry required him to return again and again to such crucial points as conversion, prayer, and affliction, both to remind older congregants and instruct new ones who had not heard his message before. His ingenious aesthetic sense enjoyed the challenge of varying the presentation while repeating the substance. He noted in the Preface to one published sermon that he had published many sermons on youthful piety, using "a *Variety of Tunes,* for the Engaging of *Young* Minds. . . . And yet the *Tunes* are not *All Spent;* Early Piety is here Set unto a *New* one." The otherwise bewildering fact that much of his published writing repeats the same ideas is partly explained by his practical need to keep driving home the same essential ideas over forty years while varying the "tune" to keep the same congregation interested.

Mather devoted equally energetic care to delivering his sermons, which usually ran an hour and a half or an hour and three-quarters, about average for New England sermons. When he began his ministry his uncle Nathaniel urged him to follow other ministers in the family in preaching without notes. Yet sermon notes came into general use in Mather's lifetime and, as his many surviving manuscript sermons indicate, he often wrote out in full the major portion of his sermon—the lengthy exposition of doctrine—with brief notes for the concluding application, to encourage a freer, semi-improvised delivery for the ending. Just the same, he distinguished between the *"Neat using* of *Notes,* and the *dull Reading* of them," and advised other ministers to use notes only for reference:

> Let your *Notes* be little other than a *Quiver*, on which you may cast your
> Eye now and then, to see what *Arrow* is to be next fetch'd from thence;
> and then, with your Eye as much as may be on them whom you speak to,
> Let it be shot away, with a *Vivacity* becoming *One in Earnest.*

As this comment suggests, he endeavored to leave his congregation both
instructed and stirred. To begin preaching in a heightened spiritual state,
he urged ministers to "go directly from your Knees in your *Study* to the
Pulpit." Beginning neither too fast nor too loud, he tried to make his
sentences short enough to be intelligible to the listeners and transcriba-
ble by those who wrote as he preached, speaking deliberately and emphasizing key words. He followed conventional Puritan theory in also
urging ministers to conclude vigorously, to abandon exposition and argument and in parting strike by lively questions, appeals, and expostula-
tions for the worshiper's own conscience, "that flaming *Preacher* in the
Bosom of the Hearer." Pouring similar fervor into the public prayers he
offered before and after sermons, he once became so enraptured that he
prayed aloud before his congregation the better part of two hours, his
soul "soaring and flaming towards Heaven." He apologized for the unusual length, in the sermon that followed.

However demanding, preaching comprised only part of Mather's ministry. He also faithfully kept the church records, made pastoral visits, baptized and catechized children, married couples (fifty-two of them in
1709), appeared at funerals, wrote letters of recommendation, and promoted private religious societies, of which he was connected at one time
to more than twenty. Many hours he spent comforting the afflicted and
dying; by the age of thirty-four, he estimated, he had beheld the death
agonies of others hundreds, perhaps thousands of times. As a member of
the clerical fraternity he also preached at ordinations and sat on church
councils, still occasionally writing up their decisions. But in fact he performed as a minister all the time, his congregants ever in mind, ever
aware of serving them as a model. He prayed for them in his study and
tried to say something serviceable when passing them on the street.
Once, in addition to other devotions of the day, he prayed for each of the
full communicants of his church distinctly and by name—nearly four
hundred of them.

Some at least of Mather's efforts were rewarded, for many people
loved and honored him for his ministry. They often commented in their
diaries or to others on his soul-saving power and warmth, appreciatively

left him small bequests in their wills, or wrote to him commending his "Compassionate Regard for the Good of Souls" and asking for his help. A distressed man named Edward Goddard, for instance, wrote him a touching letter concerning his son, a ministerial candidate who had been doing poorly at Harvard. The boy had been suffering head and stomach pains so that his father had to remove him from school. Goddard seemingly sensed that his son's problems were as much emotional as physical, for he told Mather that the boy felt depressed by his intellectual limitations and had a habit of "looking at things as Almost Insuperable to make them really so." He prayed Mather's advice and assistance in finding some method to release his son's abilities by making him feel less discouraged. Nor is there reason to doubt the several stories Mather tells himself of deathbed thanks for his ministry, such as the expiring person who cried to him: *"Oh! Dear Sir, you are the Man! You are the Man, that have brought me home unto God! It is by your Means, that the Lord has brought me home to Himself. I must love you dearly; I shall do so, to my last Breath."*

But no aspect of his ministry brought Mather greater prominence than the prodigious number of his publications. He quite outdid the angel's prophecy in 1693 that a certain youth would compose and publish many books in America and Europe, for from then through his quarrel with Colman he published around 90 works, and from 1702 to 1713 no fewer than 135 more, for the rest of his life averaging each year 10 published works. Ultimately he would publish some 388 separate titles. Viewed in comparison with the output of other New England ministers the total seems even more incredible, for publication was seldom more than a small part of a minister's work and most ministers eschewed it altogether. Of the over five hundred ministers born in New England before 1703, 66 percent never published anything, 11 percent published only a single work, only 5 percent published ten or more. Mather not only published far more than any other New England minister; he probably published more than all the New England ministers before his time combined. The titles range greatly in nature and length from a batch of funeral sermons on women (containing paeans to New England womanhood), to a long affectionate elegy on his old schoolmaster, Ezekiel Cheever (notable for the relative smoothness of its rhyme and meter), to the magisterial *Magnalia.* Intermittently he seems to have tried to pace or stamp some design on this deluge, for instance by deliberately publishing one title a month, or by roughly alphabetizing his titles over two years, producing in 1710, for instance, *Bonifacius, Christianity Demonstrated, Dust and Ashes, Eliz-*

abeth in her Holy Retirement, and so on.

One reason Mather published so much is that he often left one of his brief works behind on pastoral visits, with the caution: *"Remember, that I am speaking to you, all the while you have this Book before you!"* These household tokens of his ministry, he felt, enabled him to preach to his flock every day. He sometime published a new work only because the impression of an earlier work on the same topic had run out, a practice which again helps explain the large amount of repetition among his works, for he must have exhausted printings of his works quickly. In a day of pastoral visits he usually gave away half a dozen copies, and he estimated that he gave away at least six hundred copies of his works annually. In the first decade of the new century he also tried to expand greatly the distribution of his inexpensive religious books and pamphlets outside Boston, "sprinkling the *Salt* of Religion," as he said, "about the World." Thus he had a bundle of one thousand copies of his *Family-Religion, Excited and Assisted* (1705) sent for distribution to prayerless families in "every Town in all these Colonies, and to some other Places," and had his *Sailours Companion* (1709)—reproving smutty talk, masturbation, and sodomy—lodged in every sizable ship sailing out of New England. Concerned that his own behavior might fail to exemplify his widely disseminated advice, he reminded himself to read over his own works on Sabbath evenings, "lest my own Books, do not at last prove my own Condemnation." Considering that many of his other publications were bought briskly—*Good Fetch'd Out of Evil* (1706), a collection of captivity narratives, sold a thousand copies in a week—it is imaginable that numerous people overseas, many people in the colonies, most people in New England, and nearly everyone in Boston owned some of his works. By 1710 he may well have become the best-known man in America.

The sheer number of Mather's works, however awesome, misrepresents in several ways the nature and actual scope of his writing. He wrote many thousands of pages which were not published in his lifetime, and they include such ambitious works as the dozen connected, lengthy sermons he preached between March 1701 and April 1703, on the first two chapters of Ephesians (texts he considered of "a peculiar Excellency"), covering such basic Christian doctrines as original sin, providence, predestination, and communion—enough for a sizable volume of theology. Between 1700 and about 1723 he also cultivated a series of commonplace books or "Quotidiana," about six hundred pages of which remain. Valuable as a guide to his very wide reading, the books contain choice passages in English, French, Latin, and Greek about geography, science, demonology, Martin Luther, religious customs among the Jews, as well as maxims, comments on prose style, and rather surprising quotations from Dryden, Waller, and Cowley, and references to the Louvre and to Holbein. As before he also kept detailed diaries, wrote (sporadically now) after the preacher in church, and swelled his mammoth ongoing "Biblia Americana."

Mather also maintained a voluminous correspondence. There is no knowing how many letters he wrote, for many have been lost, but by a single ship to England in 1712 he sent more than thirty letters. His six hundred or so surviving letters make the largest extant correspondence of any American Puritan, but represent only the remains of what may have been more than five thousand letters, sent literally around the world. Through his European correspondence he tried to keep informed on religious and intellectual developments abroad, but also to extend his reputation and influence and to show the Old World what an American could do. He wrote to Germany, Holland, India, France, the West Indies, Scotland, and often to England, where his correspondents included such luminaries as Daniel Defoe and Isaac Watts, and perhaps Joseph Addison and Sir Isaac Newton. At home he kept in touch with other ministers and with friends far and near, such as John Winthrop, Jr., in Connecticut and even Samuel Sewall at the other end of Boston, with whom he often exchanged by mail ideas about scriptural prophecy, bits of verse, translations. To some friends he sent very lengthy news letters, commenting for pages on recent European events as reported in America's first genuine newspaper, *The Boston News-Letter,* begun in 1704. Conscious of often addressing, he said, "the politer sort of Persons," he read attentively the letters of other learned men, gathered into a commonplace book for his own use some of their "taking Flowers" of rhetoric, and worked many of his letters into polished, bantering literary epistles. And he seems to have made a preliminary draft of nearly every letter he sent.

Mather alternately gloried in and condemned his vast verbal fecundity, still troubled in middle age by "that particular Lust, my Pride . . . affectations of Grandeur, and Inclinations to be thought Somebody." Writing in the 1690s, he at one time thanked God for "publishing more of my Composures than any Man's, that ever was in *America,*" and at another time blamed himself for publishing too much: "I *do* confess, That I have written too many *Books,* for one of my small Attainments." Recurrently he discovered that other people, too, were "prejudiced against me for printing so many Books," including his own father. In print Increase often condemned the publishing of many books as a "*Vanity* which the

Earth Groans under"; less indirectly, in his Preface to one of Cotton's own works he chided those who neglect the Bible "and go to the *endless Writings of Men.*"

The intensity of Mather's conflict over his writing may be judged from the evident abundance in his works of unconscious strategies for resolving it, stammerlike devices that at once express and cancel. In trying to make peace between his ambition and his guilt, he often simultaneously concealed and revealed his authorship. To give one of many examples: he published his *Decennium Luctuosum* (1699) anonymously, and in some introductory remarks asked the reader's indulgence for not revealing the author's name: "All the *Favor* he desires of you, is, That you would *not Enquire after him;* or ask, *who he is?* but that, as he is at best, but an *Obscure* Person, he may continue in yet more *Obscurity.*" In short space he repeated this request three times, asking that the book be read like the writing on Belshazzar's wall, "where the Hand only was to be seen, and not who's it was"; reporting the existence of an academy of "*Innominati*" at Parma, into which "the Author of this *History,* would be glad of an Admission"; citing a Ludovicus Nihili ("*Lewis* of *Nothingham*") and repeating that "the Author will count himself not a little favoured, if he may pass for one of no more Account, than a, *No body.*" As if the facetiously learned style of these requests for anonymity were not enough to identify the work as his, Mather managed to litter the book with clues to his authorship. The "*Nameless Writer*" includes a dialogue between a Quaker and a Puritan identified as "Friend M.," reveals himself to be a Harvard graduate, refers to the *Life of Phips* and *Wonders of the Invisible World,* and compares his father to a famous rabbi who had an also famous rabbi for a son. The book ends by announcing publication of a new work "by Mr. *Cotton Mather.*"

In a variant of this ambidexter tactic, Mather several times published in the character of an anonymous friend of Cotton Mather's, for instance reprinting one brief piece as the work of "Mr. Mather the Younger, as I have been inform'd." A charming instance of Mather's ability to preen himself even in hiding appears in his diary for 1700. He wrote down a quatrain, presumably sent him by an admirer, interpreting his name as greater than the sum of its Cotton and Mather parts:

> For *Grace* and *Act* and an Illustrious *Fame*
> Who would not look from such an *Ominous Name,*
> Where *Two Great Names* their Sanctuary take,
> And in a *Third* combined, a *Greater* make!

Through these four lines of tribute he ran a threadlike line of ink, striking them out in a way that presents no obstacle to their being read. Beneath the (un)obliterated verses he wrote an explanation, in whose parenthesis his conflict only surfaces again in fresh form: "Too gross Flattery for me to Transcribe; (tho' the Poetry be good.)"

Most revealingly of all, Mather often presented himself as being asked, begged, or virtually forced to produce a work. His *Small Offers* (1689), for example, begins with a statement that he is publishing the work unwillingly, on command of his patron:

> It is indeed a piece of *Self-Denial* that your Commands have obliged me unto; for whatever others may think of *Appearing in Print,* my own Opinion of it is, that unless a man be extremely unacquainted both with himself, and with the world, he will be rather *Afraid* or *Asham'd* of it, than *Taken* with it.

This denial of responsibility for his own writings seems mirrored in many facets of Mather's career and of the style and form of his works. As an amanuensis for others, a dedicated recorder of others' sermons, an anthologist of others' choice comments, a practitioner of a "massy " style woven of allusions to others and quotations from others, he often produced with great labor works at once his own and not his own, the extreme case being of course his "Biblia Americana," a gigantic collection of the works and words of others, at once toweringly self-aggrandizing and utterly self-effacing, distinctively by Cotton Mather and not by him at all.

Whatever his misgivings about the extent of his writings, Mather felt none about the busyness of his larger ministry, and took sly pleasure in identifying himself with the Spanish bishop named Fructuosus—Be Fruitful. To get through his "vast Variety of Employments" he arose at seven or eight in the morning (and, constantly accusing himself of sloth, constantly resolved to rise earlier), and usually retired around eleven at night or later, taking an agreeable book with him to read until he fell asleep. A general picture of his activities, leaving aside his also-busy family life, appears at the end of his diary for 1711. Every day of the year, he wrote, he had spent something on pious uses and had recorded some deed for someone's benefit; nearly every day he had written illustrations for "Biblia Americana," many more than a thousand for the year. During the year he had also preached many sermons to private societies in addition to his public sermons, published nearly as many works as there are months (and prepared others yet unpublished), made "many hundreds" of visits, managed "scores of Correspondences," performed "number-less" devotional exercises, and read over "many scores" of books. It was a year, he added, in which "I have been a most unprofitable servant."

Unlike his father, Mather accepted his heavy load with uncomplaining zest, at least in this period of his life. Indeed, although the two men continued working as a ministerial team, their personalities had come to differ distinctly. Both were deeply devout, studious, sensitive to criticism, inwardly taut; but while Increase remained disgruntled, private, laconic, melancholy, Cotton, although moody himself, was very often sociable, ornamental, jocose, amiable. The difference stamps their handwriting—Increase's brambled to the point of illegibility, Cotton's gracefully lucid, meant to be read—and appears perhaps most winningly in a facet of Cotton Mather's personality now beyond reach. Everyone who knew and liked him commented on his ability to extemporize, to convert his vast learning and tenacious memory entertainingly into inventive and fanciful conversation. The "Abundance within his *lips* overflow'd," Benjamin Col-man wrote. "Here he excell'd, here he shone; being exceeding communi-cative, and bringing out of his *Treasury* things new and old, without measure." Atop Mather's inner conflicts and unceasing activity, the strain it must have cost the youthful stammerer to become the best-remembered conversationalist of his time can only be guessed, and was successfully masked. His protégé Thomas Prince later remarked that anyone who knew Mather casually might suppose from his erudition that he spent all his life studying, but on becoming aware of his constant instruction of others would decide he spent all his time in conversation, and on know-ing him more intimately and learning of his numberless labors would conclude he had no time for study or talk but must spend his whole life in action. Yet while giving out the energy of three lives, Prince wrote, "He never seemed to be in a *Hurry*. . . . He would always entertain us with Ease and Pleasure, even in his Studying Hours, as long as we pleas'd, or cou'd venture to hinder Him."

✳

The political influence otherwise owing to Mather for his prominence was denied him by the arrival of a new governor. Under the administra-tion of Joseph Dudley he became more estranged from the government than at any other time since the reign of Sir Edmund Andros fifteen years earlier.

Both Mathers had been friendly with Dudley long before he became governor, and were related to him through marriage. His family's renown in New England's political history, indeed, was only slightly less than theirs in its ecclesiastical history. Dudley's father, Thomas (seventy years his senior), was the second governor of Massachusetts; his sister Anne married another governor of Massachusetts, Simon Bradstreet, and became famous as the poet Anne Bradstreet. Joseph Dudley himself, born in Roxbury in 1647, had been graduated from Harvard and trained for the ministry. Increase Mather, whom he regarded as a spiritual adviser, at one time recommended that his congregation call Dudley as his assistant in the North Church. But Dudley entered politics, became a representative to the General Court from Roxbury, and was invested with several important public trusts.

With the appointment of Governor Andros, Dudley lost the respect not only of the Mathers but also of most of New England. Under Andros he willingly became censor of the colony press and chief justice of the Superior Court. To him was attributed the infamous remark, delivered from the bench, "that the people in New England were all slaves, and that the only difference between them and slaves was their not being bought and sold." How the son of a former governor of Massachusetts might come to consider his countrymen all slaves was perhaps explained by Dudley's colleague, Edward Randolph, who accused him of misappropriating funds, and wrote that he would "cringe and bow to anything; he hath his fortune to make in the world."

Particularly because of his judicial role in enforcing laws passed under Andros, Dudley was scorned by many as a traitor to Massachusetts. When Andros was overthrown he became, by one account, "in a peculiar manner the object of the people's displeasure," and was jailed in Boston. To help get himself released, we have seen, he called on Cotton Mather's "steady friendship and respect," and sent him a lengthy letter from jail justifying his past. He claimed that he had worked to preserve the original charter, refuted charges that he had become tainted with popery, denied he had taken bribes, and insisted he privately had argued with Andros against repatenting lands. What if anything Mather did toward Dudley's release is unknown; popular enmity with Dudley left little to do. While imprisoned, Dudley fell ill and the Council allowed him to return to Roxbury under a guard; the same night, two to three hundred Bostonians broke open his house and, it was said, "led him back to gaol like a dog." When he was at last returned to England he was confronted with a list of charges prepared by a committee of colonists accusing him of 119 illegal acts.

Dudley's political career seemed finished. But he greatly desired to return to office in New England, and clearly understood that he might turn the growth of royal authority in the colonies to his advantage. And he abounded in one indispensable quality of a politician, resilience. When Sir William Phips was recalled to England, Dudley succeeded in having him arrested in an action for twenty thousand pounds. To his disappoint- ment, however, upon Phips's death the government of Massachusetts passed not to him but to the Earl of Bellomont. Instead Dudley was made deputy governor of the Isle of Wight; he also obtained a commission, after which he was known as Colonel Dudley. Returning to England as a member of Parliament, he used his position to satisfy his intellectual curiosity and cultivated taste, and to gain a place in English society. He became friendly with Sir Richard Steele and with John Chamberlayne, gentleman-in-waiting to Prince George and a member of the Royal Soci- ety, to which Dudley submitted two scientific papers, one about the cir- culation of juices in fruit trees. He also seems to have made a fourth in a string quartet with what he called a "gang of halfpenny viol-players." He wished to be regarded as an English gentleman, had indeed become an Englishman. Yet he remained also a pious and affectionate husband and father, and missed his family, who remained in Roxbury. He often wrote longingly to his wife, "My Dearest Soul," describing his life in England as an "exile" and asking that God "in his Mercy restore me to my family and country."

Dudley began determinedly pushing his return to New England in the summer of 1701, apparently upon the death of the perennial acting gover- nor, William Stoughton. Dudley enlisted support in London by advertis- ing himself as a loyal servant of the king, who designed as governor to foster the Church of England, enforce the Acts of Trade, and keep New England "in a strict dependance upon the Crown and Government of England." He neatly parried criticism against him, the most slashing and persistent of which came from the Massachusetts agent in London, Sir Henry Ashurst. Ashurst made opposition to Dudley virtually a crusade, "standing at the sluice alone," he said, "and fencing against friends and enemies in the cause." Ashurst reiterated in conversation and letters his passionately certain belief that if Dudley became governor, New England would be ruined. "You must, gentlemen, look about you," he wrote to Boston, "I think your all is in danger." Dudley charged Ashurst with spreading a smear that he had promised the Bishop of London that, if he became governor, he would immediately make every man in New Eng- land conform to the Church of England. To counter such charges Dudley got several London Presbyterian ministers to sign and send to Increase

Mather a letter approving him as prudent and sober, respected by the present government, and loyal to his birth, a man whose "family Estate and Interest is in your Country."

Dudley also sought support for his governorship from New England itself, especially from the Mathers. That took skill, for it had been said in Boston that "both the Mr Mathers Intend to deal with him for his wickedness." Ashurst, moreover, had warned Cotton Mather that Dudley's "soul is as black as his hat and would ruin both you and I if in his power." Undeterred, Dudley began corresponding with Cotton Mather early in 1701. Mather seems to have ignored his first few letters but Dudley wrote a particularly well-calculated letter in May, chiding his silence and deftly working the carrot and the stick. Ingratiatingly, he suggested that he had personally mellowed and wanted peace, reminded Mather that he was a New Englander by birth and education, and assured him that his long exile abroad had given him "a New Value of my Country and the Religion and Virtue that dwells in it." Threateningly, he reported that the House of Lords was debating a new bill to repeal the Massachusetts charter and that many pretenders to the government of New England had come forward, many of whom might feel far less affection for the country than himself.

Mather of course had no little gift for transmitting crossed signals, and he sent Dudley an exceedingly wary reply. To Dudley's chiding his initial silence, he responded in an excessively polite tone which could be taken as flattery should Dudley succeed in becoming governor or as contempt should he fail: "I have obtained for myself a most agreeable pleasure in the rebuke which I have incurred from you. For what can be more pleasant than to be rebuked, when the rebuke itself is the greatest expression of kindness and service, only to chastise me and fall the more sensibly upon me." Fudging masterfully, Mather said that "the tribes of New England are now generally conspiring in their wishes to see Your Honour brought back in the highest capacity of usefulness unto them,"—leaving Dudley to decide whether "generally conspiring in their wishes" meant "wish" and whether "highest capacity of usefulness" meant the governorship, and in effect telling him he was both wanted and not wanted. Just the same, having suffered under Andros and Bellomont and having had before him the prospect of the murderous Kirke, Mather acknowledged Dudley's basic argument that unless he were appointed a worse governor might be. He told Dudley that he and his father had often declared that if Dudley were returned he would serve the mutual interest of the crown and of New England "beyond what could be expected from any other person."

Like his defense of the Salem judges, Mather's endorsement of Dudley, however it insinuated his displeasure, remained an endorsement. Apart from its pragmatic recognition of the realities of imperial politics, it probably reflected his and his father's hope that Dudley's avowals of personal change were sincere, and their sense that his return was probable, so his goodwill worth cultivating. They also had a common enemy with Dudley in Elisha Cooke, who as an adamant supporter of the old charter opposed Increase Mather and Dudley both. The Mathers' support for Dudley incensed the still battling Sir Henry Ashurst. He described to Increase his audience before the king and Council, himself on one side, the hated Dudley on the other. The king had been unwilling to appoint Dudley, Ashurst said, believing the people disliked him; but Dudley produced and read a letter from Cotton Mather (perhaps the one discussed above), as evidence that all the ministers in the land, and the whole Assembly, were "impatient for his coming." By one account, Ashurst accused Cotton Mather of betrayal, claiming he once described Dudley to him as "the cause of the Evil that has come upon this Country" and now calls him "the fittest person to be our Governour." When Ashurst demanded to know the reason for Mather's conversion, according to this account, Mather pronounced him a "madman" and denied having written anything against Dudley in seven years.

However recent or tactical, Mather's conversion was premature, as Dudley's arrival in Boston intimated. Memories of Dudley's conduct under Andros made a cordial welcome uncertain; some people said publicly they would oppose his landing. Still, convoyed by two armed vessels, Dudley reached Scarlett's Wharf on June 11, 1702, saluted by cannons from ships in port, Castle William in the harbor, and forts in town. Samuel Sewall, always adept at reading character out of attire, noticed disapprovingly that he arrived wearing "a very large Wig." Dudley was accompanied, too, by an elderly minister, George Keith, who he explained had been sent to America by the Bishop of London. After being congratulated in the name of the Council, Dudley was escorted by a large entourage of troops and prominent gentlemen from waterside to the Court chamber in the Town House, where before the court, the ministers, and as many others as could crowd in, his commission as governor was read. Then Increase Mather, Sewall recorded, "crav'd a Blessing" and Cotton Mather "Return'd Thanks." Dudley in taking his oath laid his hand on and kissed the Bible, contrary to Puritan custom. When he addressed the representatives in the chamber he made no apology for his career under Andros, nor did he try to conciliate the men who had imprisoned him in 1689. He departed for Roxbury in a coach drawn, Sewall added, by six horses "richly harnessed."

Five days later Cotton Mather was afforded another spectacle, this of his own gullibility. When Dudley visited him on June 16, he advised the new governor to adopt a bipartisan policy amid the various squabbling local factions. Ever the peacemaker, he offered his opinion that Dudley would be wise to treat the different parties—"if in our case, I may use so Coarse a Word as Parties"—evenhandedly, including himself and his father. In this connection he mentioned Nathaniel Byfield, a longtime member of the Executive Council, and Byfield's father-in-law, John Leverett, the Speaker of the House. Dudley should act, he recommended, so that no one could say "*you take all your Measures from the two Mr. Mathers*" or by the same token that "*you go by no Measures in your Conduct, but Mr.* Byfield's, *and* Mr. Leverett's." He gave this advice, he explained, not from prejudice against the two men but as a service to Dudley, considering that in their attitude toward the new government the people already stood divided. The value Dudley attached to Mather's advice became known to him quickly. "The Wretch," he groaned, "went unto those Men, and told them, that I had advised him, to be no ways advised by them: and inflamed them into an implacable Rage against me."

*

Dudley proved divisive, and largely unpopular, from the day he landed. Far from heeding Mather's bipartisan advice, he granted office only to his own supporters, and favored a narrow group composed of Anglicans, overseas merchants dependent on their British connections, and religious liberals such as Brattle, Leverett, and Colman.

From the beginning and repeatedly over the next few years, Dudley clashed with the House of Representatives. He fought them over his salary, over some pressing issues of defense, and over their choices for Speaker and for members of the governor's Council. His instructions from Queen Anne requiring him to see that the Council was "well affected" to the crown, he tried to purge it of diehard defenders of the old charter, men presumably tainted by antimonarchical sentiment. He vetoed five councillors chosen by the House in the 1703 elections, all supporters of the old charter, including Elisha Cooke. Cooke and another of the five were elected again the following year, and again Dudley vetoed the choice, and vetoed Cooke again a third time in 1706. Loftily he explained to the House that in choosing councillors they had passed over men of ability and station who were disposed to serve the crown, for others less qualified and in some cases of "little or mean estate." Cooke in fact was allied to the best families in Massachusetts and had a greater estate than Dudley; but in England he had zealously prosecuted complaints against Dudley and Andros. To some, the real irritant between Dudley and the House seemed to be the unhealable wounds of 1689. One contemporary wrote in 1703 that Dudley "hath given several instances of his remembering the old quarrel, and they [the House] resolve on their parts never to forget it; so that it is generally believed he will never gain any point from them."

Dudley offended others by his favor to the Church of England. Mather's ecumenical vision of Episcopalians joining Congregationalists at communion never included High Churchmen, whom he counted as virtual papists. But Dudley's governorship paralleled the reign of Queen Anne, whose tone—by contrast with that of the deceased Calvinistic King William—was High Church. George Keith, the Quaker-turned-Anglican minister who had accompanied Dudley, published soon after his arrival in Boston a sermon listing six rules which would bring Dissenters into the Church of England. The Church of England chapel, surviving but seemingly quiescent since the time of Andros, flourished under Dudley. The governor headed a petition in 1703 to the Archbishop of Canterbury asking assistance in erecting a new building; a decade later the congregation numbered about eight hundred persons and the chapel had been doubled in size by the addition.

Dudley's patronage encouraged others to extend the Church's influence in New England. The ministers of King's Chapel set about trying to open other Church of England chapels in neighboring towns, and the Anglican Society for the Propagation of the Gospel relayed to Dudley in 1705 the idea of enticing Harvard students to take holy orders in England and work for the SPG. Members of King's Chapel repaid Dudley for his support by countering complaints against his administration that reached London. In 1706 they addressed the Lord Bishop of London (a member of the queen's Privy Council) testifying to the success of his leadership and promising that his continuance in government would be "most Acceptable to all her Majesty's Good Subjects, Merchants and Planters, that have their Dependance on the Government of England as well as the Church here."

Quid pro quo was not only the reward for Dudley's support of the Church but clearly also one of the motives. For all his polish, warmth, and other attractive personal qualities, Dudley had his fortune to make in the world, as Edward Randolph said, and his politics could be whorish. Much of his favor to the Church amounted to obeisance to people of possible influence. George Keith returned to England after only about a year in Boston, complaining that Dudley after inviting him along on the crossing took not the least notice of him from the day he left England. Dudley's support for the chapel seems to have been ideological and personal as well as political, part of his dedication to the imperial ideal of an English colonial administrator, of a piece with his profuse wig and large outlays for food, his wish to marry his children into prominent families, his permitting public celebrations of coronation day or the queen's birthday even when they fell on the Sabbath. "Let us," he told the Council, "be English-men."

At first the Mathers treated Dudley characteristically, Increase direct, Cotton ambiguously indirect. Increase, dismayed that Dudley nominated "very ungodly men to be in place of power," bluntly and publicly told him that he believed the governor still brooded over his earlier imprisonment in Boston and still sought revenge. He dedicated to Dudley a sermon on *The Excellency of a Publick Spirit* (1702), in which he asked leave "to speak freely to you," and advised him to put memories of his jailing behind: "In some Remarkables you have been like *Joseph.* Let me pray you to imitate *Joseph,* not only in Seeking the good of those under your Government, as He did; but in a perfect forgetting whatever may have seemed grievous unto you." He also warned Dudley away from the "wicked men that solicited to have our *former Charter* taken from us," and, calling attention to his alleged Anglicanism, reminded him that people still spoke of his honored father, the former governor, as "*one that loved the true Christian Religion, and the pure Worship of God.*" When opposition to Dudley later mounted, Increase told him to his face that in his position "I would sooner go 3000 miles than continue to be a governour." Increase also took on George Keith in a pamphlet war and, with Cotton, preached and prayed publicly against attempts to open other Anglican churches outside Boston.

By contrast, Cotton Mather approached Dudley sounding complex harmonies of respect for his family, scorn for his untrustworthiness, gratitude for his treatment of the old-charter faction and, above all, recognition of his power and its usefulness to the ministry. In the sermon he preached to the General Assembly two weeks after Dudley's arrival he neither reproached the governor nor flattered him; with Dudley present, and the occasion demanding a panegyric, he described an ideally good man without mentioning him. In emphasizing that a good man governs his resentments and forgives his enemies, however, he drew a pattern of vengefulness to which Dudley could fit himself if he chose:

> There are men of an implacable and inveterate *Malice;* If once they apprehend that another man has, it may be, stood in the way of their little Interests, they will pursue that man, with an immortal *Malice* and *Venom;* They will never be Reconciled unto one, whom they imagine to have some way or other Lessen'd them; No, but watch all occasions to vent their Spite against him, though they should go contrary even to themselves in doing it.

Actually the Mathers' and others' fear of Dudley's vengefulness was probably misjudged, and in Cotton's case probably intensified by projection. The nineteenth-century historian John Gorham Palfrey was closer to the truth in seeing Dudley as an adroit politician who had "schooled himself to humiliations," and understood too well the conditions of success to seek to satisfy his pride at the expense of his effectiveness.

Mather and Dudley managed to acknowledge both their mutual dislike and their mutual recognition of each other's usefulness by keeping their contacts politely tart. The flavor can be sampled in two letters Dudley sent Mather around 1706. Mather evidently gave him part of "Biblia Americana," hoping Dudley might use his influence abroad to have the work published. In reply Dudley sent an amiable and pious letter pervaded by mocking self-assurance, at once respectful and cutting. In telling Mather that he profited greatly from men of learning, for instance, he rebuked his halfhearted support: "if such men knew the value I have for their Conversation and the benefit I have by it, They would give it me more." In return for the perusal of "Biblia Americana" he offered, outrageously, corrections of its biblical learning, explaining that "If I should not offer at these two or three [trifles?], you would not believe I had read it." In language rivaling in fuzziness Mather's own pseudo-assurances to him, he described the mountainously rising "Biblia" as "an Elaborate work, which I should be glad to see made public"—leaving Mather to decide whether "elaborate" meant "good," whether "I should be glad" meant "I will help," and whether "made public" meant "published."

While playing now-you-see-it-now-you-don't with Dudley personally and publicly, privately Mather dubbed him "a *fop* in *boots*" and worked to overthrow him. Efforts to remove Dudley began virtually as he stepped ashore; a month after his arrival, rumors circulated of a plot to assassinate him. New Englanders complained continually to London of the governor's hot temper, violations of the charter, packing of courts, attempts to secure offices for his son. Sir Henry Ashurst, having tirelessly fought Dudley's appointment, just as tirelessly spent money and sought allies to remove him.

Mather's main choice to replace Dudley was Sir Charles Hobby—a choice no less pragmatic than his initial endorsement of Dudley, since Hobby's morals were considered loose and he belonged to the Church of England. But Mather believed that Hobby treated Nonconformists respectfully and seems to have felt he might wean him to Congregationalism. In November 1703, he sent a florid letter to the parliamentary leader Lord Nottingham, recommending Hobby as governor because "the gentleman who is our present governor has rendered himself so universally unacceptable that there is a likelihood of his removal." As governor, Mather urged, Hobby would not cut himself off from other branches of government, as Dudley had done, by so "trampling on them, as to render them intractable." His efforts to promote Hobby, however, were tempered by fears of enraging Dudley. When in 1704 he saw a possibility for getting Hobby the governorship by piling up complaints against Dudley in London, he advised Hobby against making the complaints lest they "unhinge" Dudley. Mather's hopes for Hobby were thus aroused and then thwarted repeatedly. In January 1706 he looked forward to Hobby's appointment by May, but May brought news that just when Hobby was to receive his commission Dudley's official life became "wondrously revived" by the arrival of five thousand pounds of Portuguese gold, "with advantageous representations."

This hint of bribery foreshadows Mather's eventual break with Dudley, which resulted in part from the governor's conduct of Queen Anne's War. Dudley's appointment coincided with the outbreak of over a decade of fighting between England and the combined French and Indians in America—one theater in a far larger struggle between the France of Louis XIV and a coalition of England, Austria, Prussia, and several minor states. For Bostonians the war meant French privateers capturing vessels almost in sight of the town and recurrent frightening rumors of a massive French invasion of New England. The war also brought Indian attacks on outlying towns and villages, such as the 1704 nightime raid on Deerfield, when fifty French soldiers and two-hundred Indians killed fifty of the three-hundred inhabitants and carried off more than a hundred, including the Rev. John Williams and his wife, Eunice, Cotton Mather's cousin, who remained with her captors and married into the tribe. It meant, too, a further threat to the loosening moral atmosphere by the presence in Boston of English and American sailors, increased numbers of poor, the depletion of the Massachusetts treasury at the rate of about thirty thousand pounds a year, and the making of many private fortunes through wartime commerce.

Mather preached and published much on the attendant social and economic problems. In *The Souldier Told What He Shall Do* (1707) and *Frontiers Well-Defended* (1707) he animadverted against prostitution, gambling, and other "VICES OF THE CAMP" and provided an anti-Catholic catechism for use in frontier communities who might be exposed to French papists. Some of Mather's beliefs could only encourage economic individualism, for instance that social distinctions were ordained by Providence and that wealth might be used for pious ends. Yet in his preaching he always tried to Christianize the marketplace, and now he fervently denounced cutthroat or questionable business practices. In such wartime sermons as *Lex Mercatoria. Or, the Just Rules of Commerce Declared* (1705) he blasted as "detestable *Hobbianism*" the "General *Scramble*" of unbridled economic exploitation, of men reverting as if in a state of nature to "*Sharks,* that are all for themselves, and that would gladly make *Minims and Morsels* of all mankind beside themselves."

That Dudley's handling of the war gave his enemies a noisy issue against him was ironic, for the need of wartime unity reduced factional struggle in Boston, and whatever his other limitations, Dudley made an effective wartime governor. Patriotically dedicated to eliminating the menace of France, and much experienced in Indian affairs, he tried vigorously to raise troops, introduced the use of snowshoes (enabling scouting parties to operate in winter), and strengthened fortifications in Boston Harbor, a labor involving hundreds of tradesmen, artisans, soldiers, and slaves in digging trenches and building a blockhouse and powderhouse.

Nevertheless, in the early summer of 1706, some men employed by Dudley to effect a prisoner exchange with the French were said to have been trading with them, including Dudley's friend Captain Samuel Vetch. Allegations of this illegal trade with a despised enemy, Mather wrote, "raised a mighty Flame among the People." Those accused were stiffly fined by the General Court, despite doubts over whether the crime, committed if at all in Nova Scotia, came under the jurisdiction of a Massachusetts court. More fateful, Dudley himself was accused of allowing and perhaps profiting from the trade. In June 1707, twenty New Englanders, headed by the respected Salem merchant Nathaniel Higginson, petitioned the queen to remove Dudley from office for having "countenanced a private trade and correspondence with the French of Canada and the Indians in their interest, and furnished them with ammunitions and provisions."

Mather and Sir William Ashurst seem now to have joined in a major attack on Dudley, a forty-six-page pamphlet entitled *A Memorial of the Present Deplorable State of New-England . . . by the Male-Administration of their Present Governour* (1707). Probably written and compiled by Mather and published in London by Ashurst, the work appeared anonymously and under a Boston imprint. Despite his pleas to Dudley to forget the past, Mather began by rehearsing charges of twenty years ago, that under Andros Dudley had given offices to cronies, silenced opponents by threatening to seize their estates, called New Englanders slaves. Then Mather brought a plethora of new charges against Dudley, supported by many letters and affidavits: that Dudley sold public offices; extorted letters of support for his administration; accepted bribes to grant tavern licenses; raised three times as much money to prosecute the war as was needed; hushed up the discovery of bullets, bought in Massachusetts, found concealed among peas in a French ship; and, most damaging, that he "countenanced" the sale of gunshot and other supplies to the French and Indians by his son William and his friend Vetch, under cover of redeeming captives. One letter Mather included drew on the old mentality of invasion, making Dudley seem not just corrupt but sinister. The writer gave his belief that Dudley was deliberately leading on the French and Indians to destroy all they could, thereby to put New England "to such vast Charges, as will Ruin the whole Government, by Killing some and Impoverishing the rest." The *Memorial's* many charges and attestations in effect build a case against Dudley for high treason.

Copies of Mather's pamphlet and of the petition to the queen did not reach Boston until late October or November, by which time Dudley had become the target of new charges. He had proposed to the General Court in March an expedition against Port Royal, in French Acadia. Mather, entirely sharing Dudley's hatred of the Sun King's France, enthusiastically approved the assault, which was accompanied, he wrote, by "as great an army of prayers to Heaven as we had employed on any occasion." Dudley mustered fifteen transports and eight sloops, defended by guard ships. The large fleet anchored off Port Royal near the end of May, but found itself barricaded by thick woods and marshes from the fort, whose strength had been underestimated. Instead of besieging the fort the expedition turned aside and attacked nearby French settlements, burning houses, drowning corn, destroying cattle and sheep. The utter failure to attempt the fort produced uproar in Boston. Officers returning from the expedition were met at Scarlett's Wharf by several women, who gave them large wooden swords, calling to each other, "Is your piss-pot charg'd, neighbor? So-ho, souse the cowards. Salute Port Royal." A drove of jeering children and servants followed the soldiers to the Town House, and by afternoon hundreds of boys with wooden swords and daggers or old gunstocks were marching through town crying "Port Royal! Port Royal!" to drumbeat. The debacle inspired new rumors about Dudley, this time that he had tried to restrain the expedition, hoping to preserve the fort for more lucratively treacherous trade with the French.

The new accusations put Dudley in no mood to act the forgiving Joseph when copies of the anonymous *Memorial* and of the petition reached Boston. Whether he attributed the pamphlet to Mather is unknown, but enraged in any case, he sent off for publication a counter-pamphlet in his defense. He also demanded a vote from the Council clearing him of charges in the petition. Here his determination and his canniness at infighting triumphed. Samuel Sewall, a member of the Council, asked that the question of the petition be delayed until after the Sabbath, but Dudley wanted action. He ordered the Council secretary to draw up a vote, which was rushed through and sent to the House for confirmation. The House delayed, however, until Dudley himself assured it that the Council had unanimously voted to vindicate him—which "gall'd me," Sewall wrote, "yet I knew not how to contradict him before the Houses." According to Sewall, Dudley read before a House conference extracts of "many" letters by Cotton Mather—letters dated later than the *Memorial* but "giving him a high character." The House too cleared Dudley by voting that the charge against him of trading or allowing a trade with the French and Indians was a "scandalous and wicked accusation." To clinch Dudley's case, one subscriber to the petition to the queen, being brought before the Council, said he knew nothing of the truth of the charges, had signed "under provocation," and was sorry for what he had done.

Dudley's remarkable comeback left Mather sputtering in private. "Everything," he wrote, "is betrayed." The governor's official vindication he saw as a case of the best lacking all conviction and the worst being full of passionate intensity: indecisive opposition and delays in the House, "voting, and unvoting, in the same day, and at last the squirrels perpetually running into the mouth open for them," attempts to "blanch Ethiopians and blacken honest men," the "castration of all common honesty." Dudley's vindication, he told a correspondent, represented a debasement of civic morality: "Bribery, a crime capital among the Pagans, is already a peccadillo among us." If the climate of Dudley's administration continued, there would soon be "not so much as a shadow of justice left in the country."

The justness of Mather's indignation is debatable. Dudley's scrupulous biographer, Everett Kimball, argues that the accusations against him rested on doubtful rumor and malicious suspicion, and that the House probably voted his innocence because they had no evidence of his complicity. Yet Samuel Sewall came to believe that Dudley at least knew of illegal trading and, resentful as well of Dudley's steamrollering, he publicly withdrew his vote of vindication on the Council. Suspicions of bribery, also, hung continually over Dudley, who undoubtedly understood well-placed money. Once when someone remarked in Council that no man in England was made a captain without giving the Duke or Duchess of Marlborough five hundred guineas, Dudley observed that "there had not been any admitted these thousand years but in a way like that." Hints of securing places for friends and squeezing money from New England also appear in letters to Dudley from others during his governorship. His friend at the Royal Society, John Chamberlayne, for instance, suggested to him that "a little provender from New England will make my horses look plumper and slicker . . . and your land Sr., I hear, is famous both for oats and hay!" Dudley, he said, "is so great an husbandman and knows so well how to cultivate the most barren and ungratefull grounds, that next harvest you will not only have a crop sufficient to supply your own occasions, but even to export to the most remote and distant regions."

Dudley did send Chamberlayne what may have been some "provender"—gifts of precious and costly walnut, for making into cabinets. At the least, Dudley's long experience in colonial administration made him aware of the perquisites a governor might enjoy, and his genuine devotion to the crown entailed a sense of station that required concern for his and his family's comfort.

*

In the added uproar of one further fracas, Mather's wary restraint toward Dudley at last cracked. He and his father both realized that Dudley's connections could be helpful in securing from London a permanent charter for Harvard, without which the school could not give the doctorate degree, and the legitimacy of its B.A. and M.A. was questionable. The hope of obtaining a charter was very likely one of his strongest motives for avoiding a break with the governor. But on October 28, a few days before the Council met to vindicate Dudley, the Harvard Fellows chose as their new president Dudley's own candidate, John Leverett. The choice virtually ended Mather's influence at the college. It had declined anyway because the temporary president, Samuel Willard, was Dudley's brother-in-law, and because since his father's ouster he had absented himself from meetings of the Harvard Corporation and was regarded as having abdicated his place, which the Corporation filled.

But the man Dudley supported as president and helped elect was in Mather's mind close to the worst possible choice. John Leverett was the grandson of a governor of Massachusetts, and at one time or other had occupied nearly every important public office short of the governorship. But as he was also a lawyer by profession and, at the least, an Anglican sympathizer, Mather considered him unqualified and potentially dangerous. It was preposterous, he said, "to make a Lawyer, and one who never affected the study of Divinity, a president for a College of Divines," and given Leverett's religious leanings, it would be less hypocritical for the college to be "directly Voted in the hands of the Bishop of London." He saw Leverett's election as an overt effort "to betray the College, and to destroy all the Churches of New England."

In behalf of Leverett's credentials it could be said that he had studied law rather for public service than personal profit, had served as a Harvard tutor for a dozen years, and that although never ordained he read divinity and could preach. As for his menace to the Congregational identity of Harvard, Leverett himself dismissed the charge as a scare, an attempt to "put every body into Terrour that I have led the voyaging Israelites back to Egypt." Some recent scholars have agreed, seeing Leverett as at most a religious liberal on the model of Benjamin Colman or as a complex man not very different from Mather himself in remaining doctrinally orthodox but magnifying Reason and moving toward the idea of a benevolent deity.

Yet Mather's view of Leverett as basically an Anglican was shared by many contemporaries, including Leverett's supporters. The Massachusetts agent Henry Newman had been a pupil at Harvard under Leverett, and wrote approvingly that while Increase Mather as president thundered against all who went over to the Church of England, tutors Leverett and Brattle dared to recommend the reading of Anglican writers and "made more Proselytes to the Church of England than any two men ever did that liv'd in America." As president, Leverett stayed closely in touch with the Anglican Society for the Propagation of the Gospel, which hoped to recruit potential Anglican ministers from New England youths at Harvard. Sir Henry Ashurst, a benefactor of Harvard, became unwilling to support the New England schools because under Leverett, he said, Harvard was "bringing up a strange generation," and because Dudley was using the president to "defeat the religious designs of founders and benefactors." Mather's vision of a Harvard supervised by the Bishop of London was exaggerated but not irrational.

In one of the several deft political maneuvers of his administration, Dudley while pushing through his own vindication by the House also forwarded Leverett to the presidency. Probably at Dudley's instigation, thirty-nine ministers signed an address recalling that it was under Leverett as their tutor that most of the "now Rising Ministry in New England were happily Educated," and affirming that no one else would be so acceptable to them as president. With two exceptions, however, all the ministers who signed came from towns outside Boston. Mather scoffed at this "Sham-recommendation" as having been concocted in the "most fallacious and fraudulent manner, that ever was heard of." It misrepresented the Corporation's choice of Leverett as unanimous when in fact only seven or eight members voted for him, he said, and Dudley's "Tools" used lying insinuations to collect the signatures.

However Dudley obtained the testimonial, he presented it to the Council on November 11, amidst his own struggle for vindication, and on January 14 met with the Council again, in the College library, to install Leverett as president. Taking Leverett by the hand, Dudley led him into the College Hall, where he ceremonially transferred to him the College seal, keys, and records. With a "Noble Fire" lighted and before an audience including Colman, Sewall, and ministers from six neighboring towns, the erudite governor delivered a Latin address, observing that Leverett's appointment had been approved by the ministry, hoping that an again flourishing Harvard would benefit New England, and promising that the new president could depend on the government for patronage and counsel.

For Mather, who of course did not attend, the ceremony could have seemed only a grisly parody of his hoped-for cooperation between Moses and Aaron. Coming atop Dudley's resilient recovery from accusations of treason, it ended Mather's six-year dalliance with the governor and unfettered his much guarded tongue. Both Mathers joined the attack. A week after Leverett's inauguration, Increase sent Dudley a long letter charging him, among other things, with the failure of the College to obtain a charter. This time Cotton outdid his father in frankness. The same day he sent Dudley a letter over twice as long, some seven full pages in modern printed editions. Coming from him, this essay-length malediction was unprecedented, for in his writings and from his pulpit he had always preached obedience to rulers. Indeed, except under Andros, probably no other minister in the history of New England spoke as vehemently against a governor as Mather did now. Aware of this himself, he began by explaining that he had always offered his earlier reproaches in "the language of the tribe of Napthali," pastorally counseling Dudley rather than reviling him. But he had learned the futility of applying to him "modes of addressing used among persons of the most polite education." Now he felt compelled to speak in a manner befitting rather "an ignorant mob."

It was his own letter, read to King William, Mather began, which helped deliver Dudley the governorship—a letter sent in the belief that Dudley repented his "wicked and horrid things," a letter sent despite the "venoms" Dudley streamed against him following the 1689 revolt, a letter that earned him nothing but "extreme displeasure in the country." And it was his duty to tell Dudley wherein he had not pleased the Lord: "Sir, your snare has been that thing, the hatred whereof is most expressly required of the ruler, namely *covetousness.*" The many ways in which Dudley's administration declared his "disposition to make haste to be rich" he would now specify. There was, he said, bribery, in which Dudley's son joined; there was, many believed, his countenancing "unlawful trade with the enemies"; there was the sham vindication by a House which voted several times over to "generally declare that they could not clear you from that unlawful trade."

And there was, more recently, the fort at Port Royal—an easy capture but that Dudley "absolutely *forbad*" it, "preemptorily *forbad*" it. But here the history of Dudley's covetousness grew "too black" to be pursued, darkened into treason:

> The expedition baffled. The fort never so much as demanded. The forces retreating from the place as if they were afraid of its being surrendered. . . . And all possible care taken that after all, *nobody shall be to blame!* I dare not, I cannot meddle with these mysteries. . . . All I say is, the country is ruined, and the premises declare whose conduct very much of the ruin is owing to.

And there was also, Mather did not forget, the governor's abuse of him. Dudley intercepted and distributed his correspondence, told lies about him in public, affronted people for no other reason than their living in his part of town. By his covetous deceit, plotting, and manipulation the governor had brought himself on ill terms with heaven and for the sake of his soul must reconcile himself with the Divine Majesty before the coming Judgment, when the Lord would demand to know how far he had aimed in his government at serving Him. In concluding, Mather called up his former ambidexter politeness with Dudley, but raised to a key of gracious bitchiness: "if the troubles you brought on yourself should procure your abdication and recess unto a more private condition, and your present parasites forsake you, as you may be sure they will, I should think it my duty to do you all the good offices imaginable."

Taken aback by Mather's bluntness, Dudley did not reach for spiteful, or any other, courteousness. "Yours of the 20th instant I received," he began his reply, "and the contents, both as to the matter and manner, astonish me to the last degree." In astonishment he was not alone, for Mather's letter created commotion and expectation. Samuel Sewall, to whom Mather lent a copy, waited with concern to see "what the issue of this plain home-dealing will be!"; Dudley's supporter Ebenezer Pemberton, the minister of the South Church, said that if he were governor he would "humble" Mather "though it cost him his head." Dudley tried to do that, reminding Mather of the Christian forbearance appropriate in a minister and the respect due a governor:

I must think you have extremely forgot your own station, as well as my character; otherwise it had been impossible to have made such an open breach upon all the laws of decency, honour, justice, and christianity, as you have done in treating me with an air of superiority and contempt, which would have been greatly culpable towards a christian of the lowest order, and is insufferably rude towards one whom divine Providence has honoured with the character of your Governour.

As Mather had invoked for Dudley the ghost of Andros, Dudley brought back some specters himself. He said the Mathers based their charges against him on town gossip, that they intended "to withdraw the Queen's liege people from that duty and subjection which the laws of our holy religion do enjoin," and that they had concealed their animosity toward him for twenty years, awaiting a time when "you thought you could serve yourselves by exposing me"—the old case against the Mathers as credulous, antimonarchical, and self-interested. And authoritarian: their rage at him, Dudley said, betrayed their selfish insistence on having their own way—"the college must be disposed against the opinion of all the ministers in New England, except yourselves, or the Governour torn in pieces." While offering to satisfy their complaints if they visited him in a respectful spirit, the governor also laid down the law: "In the mean time, I expect you as subjects to the Queen, as christians, as messengers of the gospel of peace, to lay aside all methods that tend to blow up sedition."

Dudley's stiff personal rebuke to Mather was followed by the governor's public ridicule of him. Sometime later in the year appeared Dudley's earlier-written *Modest Inquiry into the Grounds and Occasions of a Late Pamphlet* (1707), published in London in response to the *Memorial* probably put together by Mather and Ashurst. Dudley countered vigorously the various affidavits they brought against him, for instance retorting that the Boston-made bullets found in the French peas amounted to enough smallshot "to shoot a few sea Fowl." At the same time he caustically derided Mather's "*Hereditary Rancour,*" his boasts about his large number of publications, and his opposition to all government, "even though it were *Angelical.*" To show up Mather's "seeming Sanctity" he also dragged into print Kate Maccarty, the young woman who had courted Mather five years earlier, before his remarriage to Elizabeth Hubbard Clark. In Dudley's version of the affair—offered as factual but seemingly an old joke refurbished—Mather frequently called on a local "Gentlewoman of *Gayety.*" Because his visits offended some of his congregation he promised to avoid her, but his "*Vicious* Inclinations" sapped his good intentions. The intrigue went on, Kate and Cotton mutually swearing that "NEITHER OF THEM SHOULD CONFESS THEIR SEEING EACH OTHER." Their clandestine visits, however, again became public news, and this time Mather was accused by his own father, a scene Dudley undertook to reproduce. Cotton, "after two or three HEMS to recover himself," said to Increase: "INDEED, FATHER, IF I SHOULD SAY I DID SEE HER, I SHOULD TELL A GREAT LIE."

Later generations can savor the ironic rightness of this canard—Mather existing in the American imagination as a sort of un–George Washington—but Mather's own reaction is unknown. Some time during the year appeared a forty-eight-page fusillade entitled *The Deplorable State of New-England.* The pamphlet more amply documents earlier charges against Dudley, and implicates Leverett in reducing the charges against the convicted traders; but the range of the barrage also takes in the Council and many of the New England clergy for supporting them both. Mather was suspected of having a hand in writing the pamphlet, earning him the "Malice" not only of Dudley, he said, but of his Council and of the clergy as well. While the other North End ministers sat "feasting with our wicked Governor" in September 1709, he was excluded because, he felt, of his "provoking Plainness and Freedom, in telling this *Ahab* of his wickedness." Banished from the table of the governor, he took his reproofs to the pulpit. A scriptural anecdote he related to his congregation was understood by Samuel Sewall to mean that "not the prophet, but the K[ing] was hurt by his Estrangement." As Sewall also understood, Dudley responded with conspicuous absence: "Dr. Cotton Mather Preaches from those words, That which is Crooked cannot be made Straight. . . . Governor not at Lecture."

*

For Mather, the cost of his exchanges with Dudley was increasing isolation. This itself may explain why many others were now emboldened to attack Mather as well. Their freedom with him, unimaginable thirty years earlier, also sprang from the vast change of mores in his lifetime, occurring too organically to be traced step by step but palpable to members of his generation. In 1688 it was "They" who wanted Martha Goodwin to keep Christmas with them and got her "very drunk"; by 1711, boys and girls in the North Church, without becoming energumens, openly celebrated Christmas with a frolic, a reveling feast, and a ball.

Pranks had often been played on Mather; in 1703 someone threw at his gate a picture of a hanged man with his name over it. But in his growing prominence, in the increasingly permissive social atmosphere, and now with his public chastisement by the government, he became frequently the butt of scurrilous letters, defamatory broadsides, derisive gossip, and even physical threats. To mention only a few in 1711 and 1712: he learned, for instance, that some "Finished Rake" was making it a point in his travels to "load me with his lying Calumnies, wherever he has come." A ship captain, a stranger to him, imagined himself the subject of some reproofs Mather delivered from his pulpit and came to his house drunk about nine at night with a drawn cutlass, swearing he would be "content to lie a year in Hell, if he might have the Satisfaction of killing me." Several times "knots of riotous Young Men" gathered under his window at night to sing "profane and filthy Songs," on one occasion attacking people with clubs taken from his woodpile.

Abuse issued from abroad also. Some Quakers printed in London in 1710 a broadside entitled *A Just Reprehension of Cotton Mather,* accusing him of "*Scribling* against the said People, tho' *Covertly,* as if *ashamed* of his *Work.*" John Winthrop came across a "sort of farce or comedy" about him and his father, "pretended to have been acted at the play-house in

London," where it was apparently written and printed. To Mather the most enduringly hurtful of these stabs, by far, came in the historian John Oldmixon's two-volume *The British Empire in America* (London, 1708). In mocking *Magnalia Christi Americana* as resembling a schoolboy's exercise, Oldmixon unknowingly turned his knife in a still livid ulcer, the place Mather probably remained most sensitive, his use of language:

> The *History of New-England* written by *Cotton Mather,* a Man of Fame in his Country, as appears by the barbarous Rhimes before it in Praise of the Author, is a sufficient Proof, that a Man may have read hundreds of Latin Authors, and be qualify'd to construe them, may have spent his Youth in a .College, and be bred up in Letters, yet have neither Judgment to know how to make a Discourse perspicuous, nor Eloquence to express his Sentiments so that they may please and persuade. . . .

No other work of history ever published, Oldmixon continued,

> is so confus'd in the Form, so trivial in the Matter, and so faulty in the Expression, so cramm'd with Puns, Anagrams, Acrosticks, Miracles and Prodigies, that it rather resembles School Boys Exercises Forty Years ago, and *Romish* Legends, than the Collections of an Historian bred up in a Protestant Academy.

Throughout his life Mather alluded to these remarks in letters and published works, reviling with the sarcasm of smothered fury "the malicious and satanic pen of one *Oldnixson* (some such name)," whose own history, he added, has "far more lies than pages in it."

Mather of course had many admirers also, and his isolation in Boston was to some degree offset by prestigious recognition abroad—compliments about *Magnalia* from the Anglican Lord Mayor of London, unexpected letters and gifts from Sir Richard Blackmore and other eminent persons he had not met. Most comfortingly of all, in May 1710, the University of Glasgow awarded him a Doctor of Divinity degree, representing the highest scholastic honor attainable. Mather considered this a distinction to be greatly cherished, the "apex and summit of academic dignities." Besides, he esteemed the Church of Scotland for its notably pure worship and outstandingly able ministry, "a Set of Burning and Shining Lights . . . no where to be Equalled on the Face of the Earth." As the first American recipient, moreover, he took special pride in being shown such proofs of international respect as no person in America had won before him, and as news of the award spread he received many letters of congratulation.

Inwardly Mather always sought acclaim, but how deeply in this difficult time he craved it appears in his response, which was both guilty and
effusive. It was "proposed and advised" to him, he said—as if rationaliz-
ing one of his too numerous publications—to wear a ring in token of his
honorary doctorate. Inscribed on the ring were a tree and a quotation
from Psalms 1:3. ("And he shall be like a tree planted by the rivers of the
water"), the whole encircled by the words *GLASCUA RIGAVIT*—Glasgow
waters, or irrigates. To convince himself that he might wear the ring without pridefulness, he drafted more than a page of possible justifications,
for instance that the sight of it would continually prompt him to cry, "*O
make me a very fruitful Tree, and help me to bring forth seasonable Fruit
continually!*" Apparently still unconvinced, several weeks after making a
case for himself he added that if prideful thoughts arose he would quash
them by considering his humiliating circumstances, "and alas, I have
enough of these!"

But however guilty Mather felt, he felt far more grateful. His reply to
the University of Glasgow—a learned, gracious letter promising to prove
himself worthy—was published in Boston as a pamphlet of twelve pages.
Thus began his voluminous, years-long correspondence with members of
the University and of the Church of Scotland. The depth of his appreciation can be gauged by the obligatory character of his earlier letters. He
wrote in August 1713, for instance, that "I have not much material to add
unto my Last, which I wrote three or four Months ago." The reason he
wrote when he had little to say, he explained, was to "just Let you see,
that we can't forget you"—as if the esteem accorded him had to be repaid
every other day. Later, however, Mather settled into an unusually rich
correspondence with divines and academicians in Scotland, sending long
discussions of biblical prophecy or detailed news of missionary work, and
receiving lengthy admiring letters in return. The learned Scottish minister and ecclesiastical historian Robert Wodrow relished his own exchanges of letters with Mather as "one of the greatest satisfactions kind
Providence has allowed me." The correspondence not only demonstrates
Mather's eminence abroad but also marks the beginning of a century-long
and mutually fruitful communion between Scottish and American intellectuals—men drawn together by their sense of shared problems in living
in cultural provinces of the British empire.

However honored abroad, Mather could do little right in Boston at
this time. Detractors jumped on his degree. A man named John Banister
published verses on what he called Mather's "Diploma," hailing him not

as a distinguished fellow citizen but as a verbose megalomaniac:

On C. Mr's. Diploma

> The mad enthusiast, thirsting after fame,
> By endless volum'ns thought to raise a name.
> With undigested trash he throngs the Press;
> Thus striving to be greater, he's the less.

In Banister's account, the degree was not awarded to Mather but whee-
dled by him, to restore his crushed pride after the publisher of *Magnalia*,
Thomas Parkhurst, fed up with Mather's outmoded theology and history,
refused to publish "Biblia Americana": "Parkhurst says, *Satis fecisti*,/ My
belly's full of your Magnalia Christi." Thwarted, and envious of the doctorate his father "stole" from Harvard, Mather longed for a doctorate himself, but was repulsed by President John Leverett (the "Keeper" below);
rather than go unhonored, he decided to beg a degree abroad:

> Daz'd with the stol'n title of his Sire,
> To be a Doctor he is all on fire;
> Would after him, the Sacrilege commit
> But that the Keeper's, care doth him affright.
> To Britain's Northern Clime in haste he sends,
> And begs an Independent boon from Presbyterian friends;
> Rather than be without, he'd beg it of the Fiends.
> Facetious George brought him this Libertie
> To write C. Mather first, and then D.D.

The writer and publisher of these verses were brought before Judge Samuel Sewall, who fined them and bound them over to the Sessions Court.
Mather's enemies John Leverett and Ebenezer Pemberton visited Sewall
to protest his action. Leverett reminded him that in their letters the Mathers had treated Governor Dudley "barbarously," and the animated Pemberton began "capering with his feet," Sewall reported, and exclaimed
that if the Mathers ordered it Sewall would shoot him through. The libel
case came before a grand jury, to whom Mather seems to have sent a
message in Banister's defence, but the outcome is unknown.

The question of the respect due Mather for his honorary degree stayed
alive another year, because the Harvard Corporation voted to cite the
degree next to his name in a forthcoming cumulative catalogue of Harvard graduates. Hugely grateful for this recognition also, Mather sent the
Corporation a long florid Latin letter making clear that he prized their
acknowledgment, but characteristically assuring them that, despite his

recognition from Glasgow, Harvard retained its own: "once alumnus, always a son most observant and most obedient." President Leverett, forced to decide whether to insert the title beside Mather's name, asked Dudley about some "dutifull Letters" that, he heard, Mather had recently written the governor; but Dudley was "pleased to assure him" he had received no letters from Mather "since the undutiful One" of 1708. When Leverett learned, however, that Dudley told Pemberton he would not have the title omitted on his account, Leverett "Upon the whole of All Considerations" ordered a "D.D." printed beside Mather's name.

The addition did nothing to restore Mather's influence at Harvard, any more than Dudley's tacit consent restored his place at the governor's table. Since the 1689 revolt, Mather had grown accustomed to having a say in the political affairs of New England; a decade later, the sphere of his influence had shrunk to the North Church. And in the spring of 1712 this began slipping from him also. To deal with some crowding in his church, resulting from a growth in the population of the North End, he apparently allowed the building of some pews, contrary to earlier practice in New England meetinghouses, where people sat on benches. Some members of the North Church—perhaps objecting to the idea of pews, or wanting pews for themselves, or simply feeling crowded—resented the new seating arrangements and, Mather wrote, "made me the object of many Calumnies." There began to be talk of leaving his ministry, D.D. or no, and building a new church. Wary of doing something intemperate that might make things worse, he decided not to oppose the move. But the prospect of losing part of his congregation stunned him, and in the privacy of his diary he excoriated these "Uncivil, Uncourteous, Unthankful, Unhelpful, Disobliging People."

Within a year a fourteen-man committee of the North Church had asked and received permission from the brethren to form a new church. Anticipating that many others might follow this nucleus out, Increase told the swarmers that if they set their meetinghouse at a healthy distance from his own, he would "do all for them that a Father could do for his children." They erected the New North Church about three streets away, provoking him to predict that "a blasting from God will be upon them first or last." How many persons left the Mathers' ministry is unknown, but they made a visible emptiness. To Cotton the congregation seemed in "very diminutive Circumstances," even approaching "something of a Dissolution." He worried not only about the possible design of Satan to destroy the North Church but also about the intensity of his aging father's grief, and cautioned himself to stay calm. As a gesture of amity he preached to the swarmers, on whom his "courteous and candid way" made such an impression that they volunteered to publish the sermon although, he added with suppressed spite, "I were hardly six minutes preparing it"—compared to his normal seven hours.

Publicly forbearing, Mather raged in his diaries against the "Proud Crew, that must have Pews for their despicable Families." Behind scenes he tried to frustrate them. The new congregation desired for its pastor John Barnard, himself a member of the North Church. According to Barnard, the Mathers feared that his selection would entice prominent members of their church to desert them and flock to him. Cotton Mather told him candidly, he wrote: "Mr. Barnard, do you think we could easily bear to have the best men in our house leave us. . . . No, sir, we cannot part with such men as these." Increase Mather, he said, styled him a "*manifesto man*" because of his friendship with Benjamin Colman and blocked his election by persuading five members of the fourteen-man committee not to vote for him. The new minister, John Webb, was chosen by a minority of the committee.

At Webb's ordination in the nearby New North Church, Increase and Cotton Mather nevertheless assisted in the ceremonial laying on of hands, and Cotton Mather offered the ceremonial hand of fellowship—for them a humbling occasion at which Governor Joseph Dudley, not humblingly for him, lent his dignifying presence to the strayed sheep.

8

Bonifacius

"THE MINISTER's *Tongue*," said Cotton Mather, "is the chief Instrument of his profession.... How extremely difficult is it, for a man that speaks much and often so to govern his Tongue, as to speak nothing amiss." His own tongue had always given him trouble, of course, not only by stuttering. Once after a rumor reached him that Samuel Sewall had criticized his father before the Council, he denounced Sewall so loudly in a Boston bookshop that people could hear him in the street. And now as the many humiliations, snubs, and desertions of Dudley's administration weighed heavily on his fragile self-esteem, they severely tested his impulse, when he felt unappreciated, to snarl. Always defiantly struggling to master his temptation to speak rashly, he now made the governance of the tongue a major topic of his ministry and diaries, while his isolation in Boston emphasized perhaps the most distinctive features of his personality and redirected some of his energies for a decade.

With unrelenting, sometimes ferocious, sternness, Mather admonished himself not to let fly when excluded from the governor's table, or faced with a depleted congregation, or versified as a drone. Impatient with his weakness in suffering slights, he constantly scolded his inability to "preserve that Sedate, and Serene, and Comfortable Frame of Mind which belongs to the *Peace* of God," constantly fretted that "I am too ready to express my Resentment," constantly resolved to "Keep a mighty Guard on my Language, that I may not Speak unadvisedly with my Lips." Preoccupied with his own self-control, he became more condemnatory than ever of angry reviling and gossip in others. For men, even good men, to speak evil of one another was the "special Vice" of Boston, he believed, and he lashed his townspeople with the same hard reproaches he

227

laid on himself: "On your Knees," he commanded in one sermon, "Abhor your selves, Condemn your selves, for the Sin of your *Unruly Tongue.*" And again: "beware of *Rash Words* in your *passion. . . . Cursed is the Anger,* for it is raging, it is Hellish." Hellish it would, yet again, be punished in Hell: "O *Tongues,* that *are set on Fire of Hell. . . .* The *Owners* of such *Tongues . . .* must one Day *gnaw their Tongues* for Anguish, and Cry out, '*Oh! For a drop of Water to cool my Tongue!*'"

In whole works devoted to the problem of temperate speech, such as *Golden Curb for the Mouth* (1707; rpt. 1709), Mather counseled two methods of treating insult. First, conformity to Christ in mortification—becoming invulnerable by becoming nothing: "Be always really, heartily, inwardly *loathing your self;* really esteem others *Wiser* and *Better* than your self; really shun *Honours,* be averse to them, afraid of them; never be uneasy at being *over-looked* by other Men." Second, unrelaxing self-control: "Upon the first *advice* of any *Abuse* offered unto you, resolve . . . *I will keep my Mouth with a Bridle, while I have before me what the unbridled Mouth of Wickedness has uttered of me.*" When abusive letters arrived he received them emotionlessly, adding them to the large tied bundle on which he had written "*Libels: Father, forgive them!*" As in following Elisha Corlet's "Method of Deliberation" he once paused before every syllable, he now scrutinized every word. "I so took heed against Sinning with my Tongue," he noted approvingly in 1712, "that I did not Utter One Word all the Day, (though I Spoke on many occasions,) but what, I think, I may say, I did well to utter it."

In his mighty effort to wall in his outraged sense of rejection, Mather also hit upon one strategy that altered his life and in part determined his particular place in American history. He decided to deal with malice and betrayal by Doing Good. The design of Doing Good, of course, was hardly a novelty in Christianity or in Mather's career. His early notebooks record several sermons on the theme by Boston ministers, including his father; he preached on it himself during his earliest ministry, telling his congregation in one youthful sermon that "We all came into the World upon a very important *Errand,* which *Errand* is, To *Do* and to *get* Good." Indeed, the question "*What Good may I do?*" had been, he recalled in his autobiography, the subject of his daily thoughts "ever since I was a Lad."

Yet Mather's acts of Good beginning around 1710 differed from these earlier preachings and resolves in being specifically prompted by feelings of isolation and disregard. He made it a practice Tuesday mornings of each week, for instance, to single out his personal enemies, "as many of them, as I can know of," and to consider "*what good may I do unto them?*" He applied this method of substituting good for evil to his own thoughts and fantasies as well, promising himself that whenever he perceived the upwelling of some ill thought he would "extinguish it, and contradict it, with forming a good Thought, that shall be directly contrary unto it." Somewhat later he came to see Doing Good as God's reward to well-intentioned men enfeebled by rage. A good man, he wrote,

> if he should happen to be of an *Ill Temper,* the *Grace* of GOD in him overcomes and mortifies this *Ill Temper;* 'Tis a *Burden* to him; and he takes a *Revenge* upon it, by multiplying Acts of *Goodness,* that shall repair the *Errors* into which Base Passions have betray'd him.

This description of an inherently good man betrayed by strong inclinations of which he disapproves, not only conveys the way Mather had come to see himself but also comes near summarizing the man he was.

With incitements to his ill temper multiplying, Mather's effort to contain it became virtually a way of life. He returned to the straining generosity of his adolescence, when because one could "*never do enough*" for one's father he transcribed Increase's manuscripts and gave him a cherished watch, or poured forth novel devotions to God with boundless ingenuity. Now again he would be fertile and inventive, but in Doing Good. "Oh! may we be men always devising of Good!," he exhorted his congregation in 1709, "May our Devices of Services wherein we shall do good be Exquisite, be Numberless! May we be full of that wisdom which will find out well devised Inventions, to do good in the world."

How fully Mather now dedicated himself to this "virtuous *Epicurism in Usefulness*" is registered dramatically in the changed form of his diaries. Previously he had kept a separate daily record of attempts to Do Good, from which he annually culled the most important and transferred them to his diary at the end of the year. But now he resolved that each day of his life he would ask the question, "*What shall I render to the Lord,*" and he would enter the answer in his diary as a "GOOD DEVISED," abbreviated as "G.D." Beginning in 1711, he overhauled the entire format of his diaries, making the heart of each day's entry a "G.D.," some particular, intended act of Good. A five-day sample will illustrate the whole:

> 2. [Second day of the week, in February 1711] G.D. Unto the Sacrifices of the Lord's-Day Evening in my Family, I would often add this; take a Book of Piety, and make each of the capable Children read some short pungent Passage in the hearing of all. . . .
> 3. G.D. I have a little Nephew, for whom I have not hitherto done all

that I have to do, towards his Conversion and Salvation. . . . I will send for
him; and bestow on him the little Book of the *Religion of the Morning*. . . .

    4. G.D. By a vessel now going for *Carolina,* and thence for *Scotland,* I
would send some Instruments of Piety. . . .

    5. G.D. One of our *Societies for the Suppression of Disorders,* have
thro' I know not what Feebleness, disbanded. I would, by the means of an
active Person or two, try to revive it. . . .

    6. G.D. An aged and pious Man, fallen into great Penury. . . . I will
procure needful Garments for him. . . .

Although Mather continued to memorialize his prayers and fasts, for at
least the next several years he wrote far less than before about his inner
spiritual struggles and far more about his services in the world. "The
grand Intention of my Life is," he declared conclusively in 1713, "*to Do
Good.*"

    Mather's numberless acts of Good did not escape contamination from
the contrary feelings of envy and resentment from which they often arose,
a subject to which the end of this chapter will return. Just the same, he
was a deeply charitable man, whose keen sympathy for others' distress
pervades his many earlier, empathetic accounts of persons captured by
Indians, vexed by evil angels, or hounded by ecclesiastical authorities.
Outcast himself during Dudley's administration, he grew more and more
to identify with other outcasts. "I see no Person miserable," he wrote in
1705, "but my Heart is very sensibly touched with their Miseries, I would,
if I could, with all my Heart, help them in their Miseries." The growth in
the numbers of poor during Dudley's reign, largely as a result of the long
war effort, inspired him also to keep a "Catalogue of the Poor," to visit
imprisoned debtors, send money to indigent persons in neighboring
towns, provide books for impoverished ministerial candidates or clothing
for a poor Indian and his wife. His humane concern was well enough
known so that when the Boston selectmen ordered a town meeting in
1710 to take up the question of poor relief, they specifically desired his
presence. His whole life substantiates his later statement to his son that
his ability to write in seven languages, his pleasure in feasting on "the
Sweets of all the *Sciences,*" his enjoyment of history ancient and modern—none of this afforded him as much delight "as it does, to Relieve the
Distresses of any one Poor, Mean, and *Miserable Neighbour.*"

    Mather's program for Doing Good gained confidence and direction
from his reading of the German Pietists, one of the most pervasive spiritual and intellectual influences on his adult life. Their names begin appearing in his diaries in late 1709, as he also begins mentioning "the *Devices*

of Good which I form and write in the Morning." He shared the Pietists' concern that the Reformation of the sixteenth century had reformed doctrine without reforming society. To complete this partial Reformation the Pietists hoped to abolish slavery, refine social justice, ameliorate the condition of the poor, and curb exploitative business practices in the emerging commercial state. Mather admired much else in German Pietism as well: its emphasis on pastoral work and involvement in community life, its far-flung missionary work, perhaps especially its ecumenical attempt to reduce dogma to essentials. Elements of these of course existed in Mather's religion already, and there had been much earlier interchange between German Pietists and English Puritans.

Some more personal sources of Mather's attraction to the Pietists at this time are implied in his admiration for John Arndt, often considered the founder of Pietism. The true Christian described in his *True Christianity* (*De Vero Christianismo,* London, 1708)—a work Mather praised for bringing "Millions of Souls into the Life of GOD"— was someone Mather wished and felt compelled to become, combining profound ethical concern with self-denying Christ-mysticism. For Arndt, true faith fructifies into good works organically, by its inward impulse and nature. In language Mather well understood, the Preface to the English edition of *True Christianity* describes good works as *"fruits of the Spirit, rivers of living water;* because they are brought forth by a believer as *freely* as a good tree yields its fruits, and a plentiful fountain its water. The true christian is constantly employed about doing good, and laying out what he has received." Mather understood equally well Arndt's complementary stress on benign deadness to the world, "heroic meekness." Having tasted true love, Arndt wrote, the true Christian is gentle, courteous, and patient, "not apt to conceive any bitterness, much less to utter it by cursing and railing speeches, which even unman a man; but to imitate Christ Jesus, who did not cry out, or so much as open his mouth against the wrath of his crucifiers, but spake from the cross mere benediction and life."

One other side of Pietism that deeply appealed to Mather was the spiritual entrepreneurship of its organizer, "the incomparable Dr. Franckius." Just Mather's age, August Hermann Francke served for thirty-six years as both a minister and a professor of Greek and Oriental languages at the University of Halle, the most famous theological center in Europe in its time. With something of Mather's own zealous ingenuity, Francke erected at Halle an exemplary educational-philanthropic community, devoted not to transmitting information but to creating ideal Christian adults—persons who would be pious, well-mannered, honorable in business, and sensitive to human needs. Mather found the size, boldness, and success of Francke's enterprise dazzling, and initiated a fifteen-year correspondence with him in Germany. Around March 1711, he sent Francke a long adulatory Latin letter declaring that Francke's piety had crossed the Atlantic and "inflamed the same piety in American churches." As proof he enclosed some of his own sermons which he said reflected Francke's ideals, plus a donation for Francke's school and an appeal for his friendship. Francke responded, magnificently, with a Latin letter seventy pages long—a further demonstration to Mather that he was better appreciated abroad than at home.

Mather publicized Francke's remarkable institution in his own *Nuncia Bona* (1715), largely based on Francke's own account of it to him. Seeing in Francke much of himself, he depicted the German as erudite and pious, but above all a man of "peerless *Industry,*" the inventor and overseer of more vast projects in thirty years than a succession of equally capable men could have completed in a century and a half. Emphasizing the numbers and the scale, he described with wonder the components of Francke's benevolent utopia: the sixteen-hundred-scholar German school; the Latin, Greek, and Hebrew school where "Vast numbers" of poor children received free tuition; the Tynaecium for young gentlewomen and the Cherotrophea for poor widows; the printing presses that dispatched pious books as far off as Siberia and in a few years issued more editions of the Bible—some in modern Slavonic and other lesser tongues—"than in the whole Period of the Time, from the *Reformation* until *Now,*" and never before so cheaply; especially the five-hundred-student *Orphano-Tropheum* or orphan house, with its huge auditorium and dining room, and its *Officina Pharmaceutica,* where "the noblest Remedies upon Earth are known"—and many and much more. In sum, Mather depicted Francke as a seminal force in modern Christianity: "The Vast Number of Souls brought Home to God and made Instances of *Serious Piety!*—the Vast Number of *Instruments* qualified here to do good abroad in the World! More than all *Europe* will soon feel, yea, has already felt the precious Effects of the *Franckian* Education."

The impact of Arndt's self-abnegating charity and of Francke's imaginative enterprise marks several other works by Mather at this time, such as *The Heavenly Conversation* (1710; an essay in "AMERICAN PIETISM") and *Orphanotrophium* (1711), but especially *Bonifacius* (1710), one of his major writings and a representative product of American culture. First published in Boston as a book of just over two hundred pages, it was quoted by the Pietists themselves and, remaining popular into the nineteenth century, appeared in more than fifteen later editions. Although Franckean ideas are here tempered by Mather's elitism and indignation, the work exudes enthusiasm for the vast opportunities of Doing Good. The world, Mather notes with Franckean zest, now contains by some computations more than seven hundred million people—"an ample field among all these, to *do good* upon!" These large numbers need three essential kinds of good:

> There needs abundance to be done, that the great GOD and His CHRIST may be more known and served in the world. . . . There needs abundance to be done, that the *evil manners* of the world, by which men are *drowned in perdition,* may be reformed. . . . There needs abundance to be done, that the *miseries* of the world may have *remedies* and *abatements* provided for them; and that miserable people may be relieved and comforted.

The Good Mather intends, that is, consists of spreading the Reformation, correcting provoking evils, and relieving those in need.

Mather offered his suggestions for doing these three sorts of Good in chapters addressed to individual social groups, such as ministers, physicians, and rich men. To spread Christ and reform manners, for instance, he recommended that ministers distribute books of piety, that the wealthy devote a tithe of their income to pious purposes, and that neighbors exhort prayerless families among them. But he more prominently emphasized relieving the poor and miserable: he advised, for instance, that the wealthy provide scholarships for orphans and that lawyers undertake *pro bono* work to help the poor and needy. His concern in the book often extends beyond such immediate objects of relief to the long-range welfare of humanity, in terms already touched by Enlightenment ideals of progress. In addressing physicians, for instance, he urged them not to rest content with the present state of medicine but rather to read and think much, so as "to *find out,* and *give out,* something very considerable for the *good of mankind.*" Presciently, he also suggested that physical ills may be related to emotional distress, and advised physicians to treat the patient's "*interior state*" as well as body. Citing the Italian physician Georgi Baglivi, he recommended that physicians experiment with "*the art of curing by consolation,*" using artful conversation to discover "what matter of anxiety, there may have been upon the mind of his *patient,*" and then using "all the ways he can devise to take it off." Mather concluded with a "CATALOGUE OF DESIRABLES" that specifies such large-scale

Franckean Goods to be performed as christianizing heathen places like Malabar and building charity schools.

Among the several facets of its importance, *Bonifacius* is a revealing biographical document. It records a period in Mather's life when he diverted his attention from the supernatural to the civic, from New England to the world, from regeneration to progress. The traits and events that led him in these directions were many: disappointment in his Particular Faiths, admiration for the Pietists, sympathy for the poor and ill, kinship with Enlightenment ideas, encroaching middle age—and isolation in Boston. For Mather in part took up Pietist ideas to outflank Joseph Dudley. *Magnalia,* written only a dozen years earlier, views the history of New England as being embodied in and transmitted through three groups of men: governors, ministers, and presidents of Harvard. But now the governor was a "wretch," the ministers sat feasting at his table, and the Harvard president was an Anglican lawyer. No longer appealing solely to them, *Bonifacius* enlists lesser social authorities and people of prestige—heads of household, men of wealth, minor officialdom—to whom Mather would in effect now entrust the continuance of New England history. For the advance of the larger Reformation the book looks outside New England altogether, reposing its hopes for the future of Protestantism not in a Puritan City on a Hill which might be its vanguard, nor even in an alliance of all English Protestants, but in a worldwide Pietistic evangelical movement.

In recognizing the need to enlist the voluntary support of others in philanthropic enterprises, Mather also hit on a method destined long to characterize movements for social betterment in America. Many commentators have recognized in *Bonifacius* the nascent spirit of Benjamin Franklin, contributor to the Philadelphia hospital, promoter of subscription libraries, organizer of discussion groups for mechanics, founder of the Union Fire Company, devotee of civic improvement. Four years old when *Bonifacius* appeared, Franklin himself later wrote that it produced "such a turn of thinking, as to have an influence on my conduct through life; for I have always set a greater value on the character of a *doer of good,* than on any other kind of reputation; and if I have been . . . a useful citizen, the Public owes the advantage of it to that book."

Franklin's remark should not be read backward to mean that Mather himself had drifted into secularism or felt content to be a "useful citizen." Both he and the Pietists maintained a delicate synthesis of engagement with the prevailing culture and mortification to life. He insisted at the opening of *Bonifacius* that only the regenerate could Do Good, for only those who had experienced grace could know what Good is, which largely meant advancing the Reformation. Franklin emulated Mather's ingenuity in contriving projects for Doing Good, but he lacked Mather's fervor for private mystical conversion and worldwide evangelical reformation, and he conceived goodness as making life more comfortable. When Mather begins sounding like Franklin in *Bonifacius,* it is not because he has abandoned inward piety but because he has moved away in thought from New England, as Franklin later did in person. Missing from *Bonifacius* is what the charter took away and Governor Dudley put beyond reach, the unhesitating cooperation of government in satisfying important needs and impulses of Congregational piety. The same absence helped create the more variegated and permissive Boston that could nurture Benjamin Franklin, a figure hard to imagine under the government of John Winthrop.

Because Mather often used Doing Good to countermand his anger, the benevolent directives of *Bonifacius* are perversely but inevitably encompassed by resentment. Quoting an unnamed writer, possibly himself, Mather remarks: "There is not any revenge more heroic, than that which torments envy by doing of good." The chapter-length Preface and Conclusion that bracket the book similarly twist Arndt's "heroic meekness," born in mystical identification with Christ, into Matherean "magnanimous *courage,*" born in anticipation of abuse. The Preface hammers at the masochistic precept that "a man of *good merit,* is a kind of *public enemy,*" and sets forth the dismal rewards of Doing Good in paragraphs successively headlined "MISCONSTRUCTION," "DISCOURAGEMENTS," "INGRATITUDE," "ENVY," and "DERISION." Mather's warnings echo not the incomparable Francke but the smutty serenaders stealing clubs from his woodpile, Joseph Dudley guffawing over Kate Maccarty—"INDEED, FATHER, IF I SHOULD SAY I DID SEE HER, I SHOULD TELL A GREAT LIE"—and, behind them, jeers about his knocking off invisible chains, the humiliations of the stammerer, cuffs to the pious child who rebuked his playmates:

> *Essays to do good* shall be derided, with all the *art* and *wit,* that [the devil] can inspire in his *Janizaries.* . . . Exquisite *profaneness* and *buffoonery* shall try their skill to laugh people out of them. The men who abound in them shall be exposed on the *stage; libels,* and *lampoons,* and *satires,* the most poignant that ever were invented, shall be darted at them; and *pamphlets* full of lying stories, be scattered, with a design to make them *ridiculous.*

Gloating for pages about the "hopes of disaffected men, to see you *come to nothing*," Mather fixed in *Bonifacius* the myth of himself that would rule much of his later life, an elaborated version of his earlier inability to *"do enough"*: Do Good, Be Spurned, Do More Good.

Besides its value for Mather in managing his rage, Doing Good also reduced his guilt over his ambitiousness. The two, he had always understood, were most intimately related, his anger swelling whenever in his hunger for applause he was served with scorn. Although he published *Bonifacius* anonymously, he confessed to unashamed pride in it: "'Tis a vanity in writers, to compliment the readers, with a, 'Sorry 'tis no better.' Instead of *that,* I freely tell my readers: I have written what is not unworthy of their perusal. If I did not think so, truly, I would not publish it." The statement makes a notable and surprising contrast to his many earlier stratagems for subtly denying-claiming authorship; similar statements appear in several of his other works in this period, on whose title pages he boldly identified himself as "Cotton Mather, D.D." Clearly what changed his view of his writing was the feeling that Doing Good provided a plausible rationale for his ambition. "I will venture to say," he wrote in *Bonifacius,* "the book is full of *reasonable* and *serviceable* things; and it would be well for us, if such things were hearkened to; and I have *done well* to offer them."

Brazened by Doing Good, Mather also included in *Bonifacius* an advertisement, more than four pages long, for "Biblia Americana." He defended the self-endorsement by invoking his newfound rationale: "To bestow the censure of *pride* and *vanity,* on the proposing of such a work for publication, would be therewith to reproach all attempts in such a way to serve the public." Not only did he intend Doing Good, but also, he added frankly, he had labored on the book fifteen years, and "It is a *lawful* and a *modest* thing, for a man to desire, that so much of a short life, as has been spent in such a preparation, should not be *spent in vain.*" That the gigantic effort might be wasted, it should be added, had already shown itself a grim possibility. During an illness four years earlier, in 1706, he had put a climactic spurt of effort into the work, fearing he might die before he could complete it. The intense application only worsened his health, but enabled him by May of that year to thank God for having "so happily finished my great Work"—which he had not. In the fall he sent to England an advertisement for the book entitled "An American Offer to serve the Great Interests of Learning and Religion in Europe." But this seems never to have been published, or at least not to have won subscribers. He kept adding illustrations, and included the new advertisement in *Bonifacius* in hopes of moving "some generous minds, to forward an undertaking so confessedly worthy to be prosecuted."

Mather's advertisement states that two folio volumes are now ready for publication, designed for "all impartial Christians, of whatever denomination or subdivision in Christianity." To such readers he promises a stupendous feast. Among its themselves-gorging main courses, as described in the advertisement, are his arrangement of Scripture in the order of events, "which exhibition alone, will do the service of a valuable commentary"; the amendment and refinement of existing translations; the rescue from misinterpretation of the laws of Israel, with a history of the city of Jerusalem from the days of Melchisedec to the present; the reconciling of apparent contradictions in Scripture; the linking of Old Testament types with their New Testament antitypes; and an "elaborate and entertaining" history of the Jewish people in every place from the birth of Christ to the present.

Among his other choice offerings, Mather also promises to have applied recent works of travelers to explaining biblical geography, including the location of Paradise and the peoples of the whole earth; recent historical knowledge to clarifying scriptural texts concerning ancient idolatry, agriculture, architecture, and warfare; talmudic and other Jewish writings to demonstrating the truth of Christianity; the most recent scientific knowledge to understanding the Creation, the Flood, and the Conflagration, as well as the plants, animals, diseases, astronomical events, and powers of the invisible world mentioned in Scripture; and all of history to illustrating the fulfillment of biblical prophecy. Having also heavily seasoned the work with characteristic and intriguing lore about Indians, angels, medicine, classical poetry, and much else, he promises the treats of "many thousands of curious notes, found scattered and shining, in the writings both of the *ancients* and the *moderns,* laid here together in a grateful amassment."

After advertising "Biblia Americana" through *Bonifacius,* however, Mather continued collecting material. In the year 1711 alone he gathered more than a thousand illustrations, adding them to those which in the completed work range from a brief paragraph to thirty or forty double-columned large folio pages. Fattening apace, the omnivorous work was on its way to becoming one of the *"Libri Elephantini,"* as he called books that require *"twelve hundred and sixty oxhides for a covering."*

*

Nammatchekodtantamooonganunnonash. Christianizing the Indians of New England—in whose language this transliterated word, Mather scoffed, means "lusts"—was for him a major goal of the broader attempt to spread the Reformation, thus a major component of Doing Good. "The Greatest Service that can be done to Mankind," he wrote, "is to introduce *Pure Christianity* every where." His wish to forward this service among the Indians in his region took new energy from his admiration of Pietist missions in far-off places like India, and from increased efforts of other religious groups which made those of Dissenters seem halfhearted: "The *Mahometans* out-do us; The *Quakers* out-do us; The *Socinians* out-do us; The *Papists* make us Ashamed. . . . They will bear the Loathsome and Irksome Wigwams of the Indians in an howling Wilderness, if they may but *Win* over the Savages to their Superstitions."

But in fact some progress, from Mather's viewpoint, had been made in converting local Indians to New England Protestantism. In a five-page "Appendix" to *Bonifacius* he described the current state of missionary efforts in Massachusetts. War over the last fifty years had desolated at a stroke "whole nations" of New England Indians, greatly reducing their number. The Indians to the east were being deluded by the Catholic French, who taught them that Christ "was a *Frenchman,* and that the *English* murdered Him." On the other hand, most of the Indians currently under English influence had to some degree been christianized. By Mather's count, Martha's Vineyard had ten Christian congregations, Nantucket at least three; the mainland had between twenty and thirty, with about three thousand Indians under Christian instruction by ten English preachers and twenty to thirty Indian teachers. Worship in the Indians' churches, moreover, clung more closely to the religion of the first settlers than in some present Congregational churches—marked by pertinent prayers, orthodox sermons, and particularly pleasing psalmody, "with a melody outdoing many of the English." The present aims of the missionary work, Mather concluded, should be to preserve the Christianity already developed among the Indians, progress in anglicizing them, and rid them of the drunkenness which threatened their christianization. But in practice, he concluded, these aims are "encumbered with difficulties, beyond what can be by most men in the bare *theory* imagined."

In converting the Indians of New England, Mather and others hoped not only to spread the Reformation, but also to pacify a fierce and proud enemy. On this point—having passed his entire life close by recurrent and murderous Indian fighting, in which he lost a relative—he discarded his role of peacemaker. While he embraced Christian Indians as brethren in Christ he damned infidel Indians as "Ravenous howling *Wolves,*" at once brutal, infantile, and diabolic. He exhorted some troops in 1689 to literally exterminate them: *"Turn not back* till they are *consumed: Wound* them that they shall not be *able to Arise;* Tho' they *Cry;* Let there be none to *Save them;* But *Beat* them small as the *Dust before the Wind,* and *Cast them out,* as the *Dirt in the Streets."* He also ridiculed unconverted Indians as bestially ignorant: having never seen a ship until the arrival of Europeans, although they dwelt amidst superlative ship timber; using stone implements, in an iron-rich country; their habitations a few poles stuck in the earth, their medicine a heated cave for sweats. Mocking the Indians' sesquipedalian-sounding language, he proposed calling the bloodiest of them by one of their own *"Indian* Long-winded words," and devised the macaronic name *"Bombardo-gladio-funhast-flammi-loquentes."* Because he also considered Indians "lazy drones" and "impudent liars" lacking in all family government, he also feared their effect on white neighbors and captives, some of whom showed a propensity to join Indian society.

More than that, unconverted Indians were to Mather, and to many others, children of the devil. Early travelers to America had observed again and again that the Indians' religion consisted in worshiping the devil as God. Mather often speaks of Indian powwows raising devils in the shape of bears, or practicing "Diabolical *Charms"* to keep English dogs from attacking them, or fashioning arrowhead-shaped pieces of leather to be taken up by some demon and conveyed into the bodies of persons to be afflicted. Many believed that as the devil was "God's ape" and as, in Joseph Mede's view, America was uniquely the land of the devil, so the Indians were a satanic parody of the Puritans, the Chosen People of the devil as the Israelites, and then the Puritans, were the Chosen People of God. The Rev. John Higginson speculated to Mather that Indians who settled around Mexico were conducted there by the devil "very strangely Emulating what the Blessed God gave to *Israel* in the Wilderness." Mather even considered the possibility that the Salem outbreak might in part have arisen from the black arts of Indian sagamores, well known to be "horrid *Sorcerers,* and hellish *Conjurers,* and such as conversed with *Daemons."*

In hopes of redeeming and quelling the natives of New England Mather threw himself into the missionary work, as into everything else, energetically. In 1698 he had been appointed a commissioner of the oldest Protestant missionary organization, the New England Company, founded by act of Parliament in 1649 to convert the New England Indians to Christianity. The Company invested funds and from the interest sent money to the commissioners, who included Increase Mather and Samuel Sewall. The commissioners then disbursed salaries to itinerant missionaries, and funds to Indian preachers and to settlers who provided allied charitable and educational services. Mather attended the commissioners' meetings, held at their homes or at the Town House, and became the New England Company's chief informant on the missionary work, sending them such tokens of progress as a poem in Latin and Greek by a "pregnant Indian youth" and long epistolary reports. These were greatly appreciated and commended in London (in further contrast to his reception at home), where his chief correspondent was Sir William Ashurst (Sir Henry's younger brother), a former Lord Mayor of London who was governor of the company from 1696 to 1720.

Mather's involvement in the Company intensified just as his own *Bonifacius* was published and just as a complex and much debated problem for the Company also came to the fore again. This was whether to convert the Indians in their own tongues or to anglicize them first and pursue their conversion in English. The question also bore on the huge project of reprinting John Eliot's famous Indian Bible. Written in a transliterated version of the Natick dialect, and first published in 1663, two hundred leatherbound copies were immediately circulated for the Indians' use. In 1708, the New England Company undertook to reissue Eliot's Bible, but its strange-looking words and its length made the presswork painfully vexing, slow, and expensive. In July 1709, a fire in Samuel Sewall's bedroom also destroyed the printing paper. Mather seems to have doubted the usefulness of the project but hesitated to publicize his opinions, perhaps because of his respect for Eliot. Samuel Sewall was probably speaking for Mather when he relayed to Sir William Ashurst in 1710 the objections of some commissioners: that Indian teachers complain of the absence of Indian terms for Christian concepts; that different tribes have different dialects; that many Indians find Eliot's written approximations of their speech unintelligible. Moreover, Sewall said, if the Indians retained their language they would retain with it "a Tincture of other Savage Inclinations, which do but ill suit, either with the Honor, or with the design of Christianity," whereas the expense of reprinting Eliot's Bible might go far toward teaching the Indians English. Writing to Ashurst himself, Mather observed that most commissioners opposed the reprinting but that to anglicize the Indians "is much more easy to be talked of than to be accomplished." In any event he urged that the presswork could be done more cheaply in London than in Boston, where he estimated it would take more than seven years. But no London printers knew the language, and in fact the reprint was doomed never to appear.

Mather also personally attended several communities of christianized Indians. In July 1712, he and other commissioners visited the languishing settlement at Natick, reduced, largely by long years of war, to scarce thirty families. The commissioners hoped to restore the population by inducing neighboring Indians to move in with them. Mather preached at the Indian meetinghouse (in a pulpit without Bible, cushion, or hourglass), talked with the Indians about their political affairs, heard an Indian minister perform religious exercises in an Indian language, and received "handsome Returns of Thanks." Desiring to bring the Indians into compact, English-style communities, he greatly approved the purchase by the Company in 1713 of Martha's Vineyard, in an effort to consolidate local christianized Indians. His manner with such Indians was paternalistic, but wholly without the hollering vengefulness he directed at pagan Indians. He told some Indians who were being settled at Gay Head, for instance, that "tho' we would have you own your dependence on the good and great protectors you have in London, who have bought this land for your benefit, yet we shall use all the care of kind fathers to make your condition comfortable." While oblivious to the cost, in human agony, of the Indians' depletion and resettlement, Mather recognized that the first Puritans had settled on Indian territory, and wished the Indians' rights to their little remaining land be respected. Thus he urged that "the *Reliques* of the *Aboriginal Natives* here, upon whose Land we were Entered, might have an Everlasting and Unalienable Claim unto some Little Scraps of a Vast Country, once entirely Possessed by their Ancestors."

Mather and the commissioners hoped not to christianize the Indians of New England but, more accurately, to Puritanize them. They accordingly distrusted the Anglican missionary efforts of the rival Society for the Propagation of the Gospel in Foreign Parts. Chartered in 1701 and composed of prominent prelates and politicans, the SPG had been organized by the Bishop of London to study the Church of England's status in the colonies. Mutual abhorrence of the work of Jesuit missionaries to some degree enforced cooperation between the SPG and the New England Company. Indeed, Ashurst laid before some bishops in the Society Mather's *Letter; About the Present State of Christianity among the Christianized Indians* (1705), as proof that "our ministers (tho' not Episcopal) are Capable of Doing Good." The bishops were impressed by Mather's description of the purity of Congregational worship in some Indian churches, so much so that the Archbishop of Canterbury himself ordered the pamphlet to be presented at a meeting of the SPG. The Society became curious about the New England Company's methods, asked to inspect its charter, and requested from Ashurst an account of its funding operations, assuring him they had "no sinister Ends in this Inquiry."

Mather generally approved this ecumenical cooperation with the SPG. But still apprehensive about the possible establishment of an American episcopate, he also deplored the presence of High Churchmen in the Society, and suspected SPG missionaries of trying to convert not Indians but Congregationalists. A rather ambidexter letter by him in 1706, seemingly intended for the SPG, was withheld from the Society because of what his English correspondent called its "hard Expressions." He began by praising the "worthy Persons, who compose the Society," but added his hope that they would shun High Churchmen—"highflyers," as he barbedly called them, "who may be crept in." He also criticized the Society for sending missionaries to towns that had been well instructed in Christianity for generations, on the pretext of gospelizing a few scandalous families. The missionaries were trying, he suggested, to subvert "the most instructed Christians in the World," persons "not yet so illuminated" as to demand Episcopal ordination and Church of England ceremonies. If they kept trying to undermine Congregationalist strongholds, he said, the "noble Society for the Propagation of Religion in America, will greatly wound Religion, and their own Reputation also." His distrust of the SPG grew steadily, so that by 1716 he was referring to it as the "Society for the Molestation of the Gospel in foreign Parts."

Mather received no salary as a commissioner, but the Company in 1709 awarded him £25 in consideration of his "great Services in promoting the work of Converting the Indians by his writings and other ways." Mather did increase his value to the Company by publishing virtually a title a year relating to Indian affairs. These include *An Epistle to the Christian Indians* (1700; Indian title, *Wussukwhonk En Christianeue asuh peantamwae Indianog*), offering in Indian and English a compressed description of the whole of Congregational theology and church government; *A Monitory, and Hortatory Letter, To those English, who debauch the Indians* (1700), denouncing the sale of strong drink to the Indians, which makes them unemployable, destructive, and sotted beyond christianizing; *Hatchets to Hew Down the Tree of Sin* (1705), containing an English-Indian digest of Massachusetts laws against buggery, incest, and other crimes; and *Another Tongue brought in* (1707), providing a quadrilingual catechism in Iroquois, Latin, English, and Dutch for use by traders in beaver skins among the Iroquois, to counter Catholic missionary efforts among them.

Writing from a nonmissionary viewpoint, Mather also published many accounts of Indian fighting and captivity. They include one of his most vividly written works, *Decennium Luctuosum* (1699), recounting the decade of Indian warfare between 1688 and 1698. As history the book is notable for its many comments on historical theory and on the style and veracity of other historians, and for its indefatigably gathered and carefully sifted information. Yet Mather compared it to *The Iliad,* for in exultantly describing the destruction of the "Rapacious *Wolves*" he saw himself as genuinely an epical writer, narrating the heroic origins of an emergent civilization, occupying in early America something of Homer's position in ancient Greece. Intent as always on holding as well as informing his readers, he managed by many formal inventions and witty transitions to accommodate his digressive and fanciful imagination, so as to include every last bloody butchery or hair-raising escape, and many "charming and useful Entertainments." To an unusual degree among his works the book abounds in alliteration, foreshadowing, metaphor, and other purely literary devices, in a style at once erudite, pious, and racy. For instance, in telling how the celebrated Hannah Dustan of Haverhill rose in the dead of night and, with a nurse and a young boy, hatcheted her Indian captors to death, skinning ten scalps, he effectively used syntax and sentence rhythm to convey staggering:

> they struck such Home Blows, upon the Heads of their *Sleeping Oppressors,* that e're they could any of them Struggle into any Effectual Resistance, *at the Feet of* those poor Prisoners, *they bowed, they fell, they lay down; at their feet they bowed, they fell; where they bowed, there they fell down Dead.*

Mather also reproduced much amusing dialogue, most delectably a remark made to him by a Quaker, who rudely accused him of doing all the talking: *"Thou art a Monster, all Mouth, and no Ears."*

*

A final, outstandingly personal and consequential plan for Doing Good Mather proposed in his diary in July 1711: "There is one good Interest, which I have never yet served, and yet I am capable of doing some small Service for it." Having always believed that Christ and God were glorified in the progress of human knowledge resulting from the study of nature, he now decided to make a "valuable Collection of many Curiosities, which this Country has afforded; and present it unto the Royal Society." In thus promoting still another good cause, he sent to Lon-

don in batches of four to a dozen over the next twelve years, some eighty-
two scientific dispatches.

Founded around 1660, the Royal Society took as one of its main purposes the accurate collection, classification, and interpretation of scientific data. It kept an enormous correspondence with *virtuosi* all over the
world (of whom only a small number were elected Fellows), carried
without charge by ships of the East India and other English trading companies, and in packets of the Secretary of State. In relation to himself,
Mather regarded the Society's work with mingled hope of joining a superior world aloof from the mundane bickering and ignorance of common
humanity, desire to Do Good, revenge toward his enemies in Boston, and
admiration for new learning:

> how worthy it [the Society's undertaking] is to be pursued by gentlemen
> who would *show themselves men;* how useful it has already been to man-
> kind, and capable of being yet more applied unto the *best of purposes;* a
> tendency it has to refine and sweeten the minds of men, and reconcile
> them unto *just regards* for *true merits* in one another; with an extirpation
> of that noxious clamor-wort, the *party-spirit;* and, finally, how generously
> the more polite literators of the world go on in it, with a decent contempt
> on the banters of the *brutish among the people.* . . .

His communications to the Society, entitled "Curiosa Americana," ani-
matedly project this Matherean mixture of snobbery, altruism, resentment, and inquisitiveness.

In addition to being scientific communications, the Curiosa are literary letters, written, Mather said, with "my most exquisite Contrivance,"
and containing some of his most polished and shapely prose. They radi-
ate with greater liveliness than perhaps any of his other works the personality that many contemporaries found gracious and entertaining. On one
letter he sketched diagrams of the planetary motions, doodling into the
the sun half-moon eyes and a large smile. His delight in writing to the
ostensibly more receptive world outside Boston registers also in the play-
ful tone of the letters, particularly their elaborately turned salutations and
closings, which pun on the subject of the dispatch. For instance, a later
letter on "Uncommon Dentition"—about a Harvard student whose gums
presented not teeth but a *"White, Sharp, continued Edge"*—ends with
the flourish: "nothing, that ever my *Teeth* ever had under the Mastication
can be so grateful to me, as the Instructive Things, which you can and
will give me to feed upon. I beseech you, Let there be therein a *Continual Feast* allow'd unto, Sir. . . ." Aware of his self-delighted difficulty in
settling down to the subject, he asked one correspondent at the Society to

abide his "little excursions" as "one of those natural weaknesses which all men of breeding indulge in one another."

The weakness was as much cultural, however, as personal. Mather's evident discomfort in addressing sophisticated, cosmopolitan men, members of the Commonwealth of Learning to which he aspired but felt inadequate, arose from a sense of living, as he wrote, "in an infant country entirely destitute of philosophers." For all his exuberance he freely and frequently acknowledged how the New World lagged behind the Old in knowledge, and often seems to say that he is only telling the English virtuosi what they already know: "These Things are so much better known to you," he writes in a letter on rainbows, "that I can make no Apology for the *Little Touch* I now give upon them, Except it should be this; I was willing to have you think, that your *American* Friends also are not utterly unacquainted with them." The Curiosa exude the provincial strangulation of the country fop, of someone self-consciously addressing the learned world without being certain what it is.

In terms of the Society's own interests, Mather's justification for addressing it at all was the hope of communicating "all New and Rare Occurrences of Nature, in these parts of the World." The Curiosa, that is, contain an embryonic element of nationalism. Mather often reminds the Society that his subjects are *American* curiosities: a black snake that fell from the sky, in Lynn; a tree limb found seventeen feet underground, in Springfield; a huge balancing rock that teeters during storms, in Gloucester. Far more descriptive than explanatory, the letters make no larger claim than to add to the Society's worldwide collection of natural history some remarkable specimens from America, to be deciphered by virtuosi abroad and by them fitted into larger schemes of natural philosophy. In choosing the humble informant's role, Mather for a change realistically assessed his abilities and limitations, contributing useful data to major European scientific debates that lay beyond his competence and also his access. Just the same, probably no other colonial American writer was as aware of physically inhabiting the New World as Mather, and as preoccupied with seeing how it differed from the Old World. Feeling both challenged to report the uniqueness of his country and pained by the relative crudeness of its intellectual life, he wrote invariably as "your American Friend"—a condition of which he was at once proud and embarrassed.

Mather collected his scientific lore widely. Some came from his own observation, such as the egg grown inside another egg which he had held in his own hand (an example of "monstrous impregnation"). Several of his own earlier writings supplied other curiosa, beginning with a collection of natural oddities he had made in Latin as a youth. He also took materials from his father's *Illustrious Providences,* revealingly. For minus the lightened style, Mather's Curiosa closely resemble the remarkable providences he and his father had always collected. Providences display the wonders of God in history, declaring His judgments and will; Curiosa display the wonders of God in nature, declaring His workmanship and the operation of natural law. Mather also used his father's method of soliciting well-attested information about natural rarities from ministers and other credible persons throughout New England, for instance asking physicians for accounts of unusual cures in their practices. Once he sent the Boston physician John Perkins to investigate reports of a prodigious intestinal worm; Perkins found, even after souvenir-mongers had taken pieces away, 118 feet remaining.

Mather's favorite source was probably John Winthrop of Connecticut (1681-1747), "a Friend, who is better to me than a Brother." His affection for this younger man sprang from his veneration toward the three previous generations of prominent Winthrops, beginning with the John Winthrop who led the great migration of 1630 to New England. The next two generations combined public service and scientific curiosity to become, Mather wrote, "a Family sent into the world on purpose to help and heal its Maladies." The library of the second John Winthrop (1606–1676)—the first governor of Connecticut—contained the poems of John Donne and a huge collection of alchemical works; he was also the first colonial Fellow of the Royal Society, in fact a charter member of the Society itself. The third generation of Winthrops was represented by Wait-Still Winthrop (1642–1717), Chief Justice of Massachusetts and, Mather called him, a "Master of Medicines." These he gave free to multitudes of poor people, including a remedy composed of nitre and antimony, invented by his father, called Rubila. Mather's friend John Winthrop was Wait-Still's son. Together with their joint sense of prominent family descent and mutual scientific interest, they commiserated on a feeling of being more refined and intelligent than their neighbors, and mistreated by them.

Mather frequently praised the younger Winthrop as a Christian philosopher and gentleman, but felt that he failed to live up to his possibilities and heritage. Winthrop's correspondence does leave an impression of self-pampering shallowness: one letter speaks of his distaste for shopping in Boston—"Everything very ordinary . . . . slimsy gaudy things"—but of finding at one store an attractive camblet, "the genteelest thing I had seen anywhere." Genteel camblet or no, Mather often asked Winthrop to use his "philosophical Genius and Gentlemanly Leisure" to provide material for him to send to the Royal Society, such as a description of the color, horns, and other features of the moose, and an account of a remarkably violent storm that buried sheep under sixteen-foot-high snowbanks. With Mather's request for material on the water-dove he had limited success; as he told Mather, he was going to send a water-dove itself but a cat got into his study and tore it to pieces.

Mather's letters to the Royal Society encompass virtually all the sciences of his time, including astronomy, botany, zoology, geology, and meteorology. Given his intention in youth of becoming a physician, his confessed weakness in mathematics, and his delighted fascination with the flocks of pigeons around Boston, it is not surprising that the largest number deal with medicine, the fewest with mathematical sciences, and perhaps the best-humored with ornithology. Occasionally he enclosed scientific specimens, in one instance six or seven dried plants which he had been unable to find listed in any European herbal, and presumed to name. Another time he sent as a specimen of a fossil a thickly encrusted piece-of-eight given him by Sir William Phips from his fabulous underwater horde; it had hung in Mather's library nearly thirty years. To make plain what these communications, written between 1712 and 1724, reveal about Mather's role in the development of American science, would require a separate book-length study relating them to the state of European scientific knowledge at the time. Instead, reserving a few general comments for later discussion of his last Curiosa, his first series of Curiosa shall be summarized in tabular form below as representative of the whole, followed by brief analysis of the lengthy manuscript he sent the Society in 1715.

The first series of Curiosa, just over a hundred manuscript pages, consists of thirteen letters written over two weeks in November 1712, and addressed to Dr. John Woodward and to Richard Waller. Woodward, the Society's Provincial Secretary, was an eminent geologist whose still celebrated *Essay Toward a Natural History of the Earth* (1695) called attention to the existence of strata in the earth's crust; Waller, Secretary of the Society for more than twenty-five years, was a businessman who wrote on physiology, zoology, and linguistics. Each letter essentially treats a single subject, but with frequent asides. Mather also addressed a lengthy plea through Woodward to "Ingenious and opulent men" to publish his "Biblia Americana," from which he also drew the first of his Curiosa:

1. On Giants, discussing the remains of an alleged giant unearthed

near Albany, New York, in 1705, one of whose teeth and some of whose bones Mather says he had the satisfaction of handling, including a presumed thigh bone seventeen feet long.

2. Local Flora, some used for cures, including an Indian cure for syphillis.

3. Ornithology, with a finely accurate description of a hummingbird, and the speculation that some birds may migrate to small planetary bodies surrounding the earth but too small to be observed by present telescopes.

4. Strange Antipathies, and the Force of Imagination, with cases of "Husbands who *breed* for their Wives" and of a New Englander who had a stone at the root of his tongue yet urinated in intolerable pain as if it had been in his bladder.

5. Monstrous Births, in Latin.

6. Cures Appearing in Dreams (including the warm-wool cure dreamed by Mather's deceased wife Abigail), with the suggestion that such dreams may be the work of good angels, although possibly of evil angels doing good for evil ends.

7. Tiny Wounds That Have Proved Mortal And Extremely Grievous Wounds That Have Not, including the story of a dropsiacal New England woman who vomited pieces of skin, and whose autopsy disclosed that she had "*no Bowels* at all" and "not so much as a bit of a Bladder."

8. Indian Methods of Keeping Time.

9. Rainbows, with three diagrams, citations of Descartes, Halley, and Newton, and remarks on rainbows as prognostics.

10. Apparitions, including a case Mather reports several times elsewhere concerning a man named Joseph Beacon, to whom appeared the specter of his recently murdered brother, revealing to him the murderer's identity.

11. Rattlesnakes.

12. Thunder and Earthquakes, with description of a large rock in Taunton containing allegedly prehistoric inscriptions in "unaccountable Characters."

13. Demography (essentially), speculating on the population of the world before the Flood and describing cases of extraordinary childbearing and longevity, including a woman who had thirty-nine children and a Rhode Islander aged 110 who had been married to his wife—herself more than 100—for more than eighty years, with the "further odd Circumstance of their Friendship, that they constantly Eat upon one Trencher at the Table."

Even these capsule summaries may seem to confirm the standard charge against Mather of credulity. But in what strikes a modern reader as fantastic in them, his Curiosa differ little from other contributions to the Royal

Society, which received his letters, we shall see, with enthusiasm. Besides, his Curiosa equally represent the observations and beliefs of his many informants, and obviously were generally held. Boston newspapers often printed reports about, for instance, a "Merman or Sea Monster" sighted at Brest, or a pond in Rhode Island from which at one time were taken 700,000 bass, "by a moderate Computation." Indeed, several freak events reported by Mather are rather simply explained and still occasionally occur. His communication to the Society on "A Woolen Snow," concerning the fall of quantities of wool from the sky, is no more unaccountable than the hundred and fifty fish that dropped to earth from the heavens in Australia in 1974, presumably sucked up from the sea by a waterspout created by high oceanic winds.

After sending a second series of Curiosa, in ten letters, in 1714, Mather sent the following year the manuscript of a work entitled "The Christian Virtuoso," asking that it be deposited in the Society's archives if it did not find a publisher. The work appeared in over three hundred pages in 1721 as *The Christian Philosopher*—the first general book on science to be written in America. It differs fundamentally from his "Curiosa Americana," aiming not to describe striking natural phenomena in America but to summarize significant findings of European scientists, including recent ideas about gravity and about the speed of light. With rapturous admiration for new scientific learning—"*Ideas,* like the *Sands on the Seashore,* for the vast *variety* of them!"—Mather quotes the work of such eminent figures as Flamsteed, Leeuwenhoek, Huygens, and, repeatedly, "The incomparable Sir *Isaac Newton.*" He meant literally his statement that *The Christian Philosopher* represents "A Collection of the Best Discoveries in Nature," for like "Biblia Americana" the book is an amassment of illustrations and quotations. The "very little" of his own in the work, he points out, amounts to a few curiosa and some pious "improvements" that draw from observations on comets or volcanos the proper religious significance. Indeed an important part of his purpose was to show others the spirit in which he had pursued his own "Enquiries into the Wonders of the Universe, so it is both an Instruction and a Pattern to a serious Mind." He tried to demonstrate, that is, how a Christian might come to terms with the new science itself.

Like most virtuosi in the Royal Society, Mather believed that the investigation of nature could lead only to the good of man and the greater glory of God. The two writers on whom he drew most frequently in *The Christian Philosopher* were John Ray and William Derham, the authors respectively of *The Wisdom of God Manifested in the Works of the Cre-*

ation (London, 1691) and *Physico-Theology, or a Demonstration of the Being and Attributes of God from His Works of Creation* (London, 1713). For Ray, Derham, and other so-called physico-theologians, recent scientific disclosures of the vastness of the stars or the complexity of the human body but proved the existence of divine purpose in the cosmos. Following them, Mather in *The Christian Philosopher* also delineated a minutely purposive universe, where lice exist to deter people from slovenliness, and teething is deferred to protect the nipples of wetnurses:

> How surprisingly is the *Head* and the *Neck* of the *Swine* adapted for his rooting in the *Earth!* How the Neck, Nose, Eyes and Ears of the *Mole,* adapted in the nicest manner to its way of subterraneous living! The strong Snout of the *Swine,* such that he may sufficiently thrust it into the Ground, where his Living lies, without hurting his Eyes; and of so sagacious a Scent, that we employ them to hunt for us and even his *wallowing in the Mire,* is a wise Contrivance for the Suffocation of troublesome Insects!

Imagining a Creator supercopious in benevolent ingenuity, Mather moved almost effortlessly in his thinking between theological and scientific modes of explanation.

But the very piety evident in such thinking—widespread among Christian scientists of the eighteenth century—obscured its dangerous implications, and unwittingly led Mather close to irreligion. Although the physico-theological disclosure of an intricately contrived universe was meant to provide a rational foundation for Christianity, it tended in practice to displace Christianity. In trying to prove God's existence from natural phenomena, and in using new standards of proof and debate, it quietly relegated essential Christian ideas to the background, especially losing sight of the Son. Mather shared unawares in some of this subversive shift in emphasis. The Creator he depicts in *The Christian Philosopher* no longer seems the wrathful Jehovah of the jeremiads, but rather the smiling Deity of liberal eighteenth-century Protestantism, ordering things so, that "whatever is natural is delightful, and has a tendency to Good." Only half-a-dozen pages from the end of the book, moreover, does Mather introduce a section on the Savior, by saying "the CHRIST of God must not be forgotten"—as He almost is. Indeed the clockwork universe described in *The Christian Philosopher* seems an altogether improbable setting for the great drama of Redemption:

> The Great God has contrived a mighty *Engine,* of an Extent that cannot be measured, and there is in it a Contrivance of wondrous *Motions* that can-

not be *numbered.* He is infinitely gratified with the View of this *Engine* in all its *Motions,* infinitely grateful to Him so glorious a Spectacle!

Such a predictable universe seems inconsistent with inflows of supernatural grace, much less with ghosts who reveal murderers, evil angels who foment earthquakes, and other unscheduled wonders of the invisible world.

Mather shrank, however, from fully accepting a mechanical universe. He did so at the expense of some raggedness in his thinking but in the name of his own experience. Having witnessed the invisible world himself, he announced in *The Christian Philosopher,* his belief in it was unshakable: "I do here in the first place most religiously affirm, that even my *Senses* have been convinced of such a World, by as clear, plain, full *Proofs* as ever any Man's have had of what is most obvious in the *sensible World.*" Nor was Mather prepared to give up arguing the existence of God from the potency of witches, to argue it solely from the snouts of swine. After praising the power of the mind and the inventions of the age, he ended his book by remarking that the enginelike wonders of the visible creation dwindle "compared to those that are out of sight, those that are found among the *Angels that excel in Powers.*" He made room for pneumatological phenomena in a mechanical universe by emphasizing the limitations of reason and uncertainties in the science of his time. He viewed human reason, especially in humanity's fallen state, as a blunted instrument, incapable of penetrating all of *"covered Nature"*—"Every Thing puzzles us. Even the Nature, yea, the *Extent* of an *Atom,* does to this Day, puzzle all the Philosophers in the World." Such puzzles left aspects of the universe open to nonmechanical interpretation.

One measure of Mather's resistance to a wholly mechanistic view of nature is his treatment of comets, one of several spectacular celestial and atmospheric phenomena viewed by his father, and many others, as omens. In earlier life he had had little difficulty conceiving such events as operating under natural law, but through the agency of angels or devils. More recent scientific notions evidently made it less easy for him to think so. In *The Christian Philosopher* he cited Newton's speculation that vapors from comets may fall into the earth's atmosphere by gravity and nourish vegetation. "If this be so," Mather reasoned, "the Appearance of *Comets* is not so dreadful a thing, as the *Cometomantia,* generally prevailing, has represented it." The "If" is significant, for the element of doubt allowed him to cite opposing opinions that comets may be ministers of divine justice or habitations of animals in a state of punishment, and to propose that some celestial spectacles might be prognostics, others not.

Mather also considered mechanical principles inadequate to explain large areas of biology. In pondering vital phenomena involving the pursuit of goals he continued to entertain the ancient idea of a plastic spirit—a spiritual power or life force akin to the soul, working within matter to produce the configurations of various beings. He found such vitalistic, as opposed to mechanistic, thinking necessary to understand phenomena like the regrowth of plants from parts of their stems. In a 1716 curiosa concerning generation, for instance, he speculated on the possibility of regrowing amputated limbs. In conceiving generation he accepted the contemporary theory of "animalcules," suggested by microscopic study of sperm cells: living things exist infolded as tiny seeds, invisible to the eye but containing "the whole *Bodies* of the *Animals,* even to all their *Nerves* and *Fibres*"; generation is the augmentation of the original tiny parts within the seed. He speculated that the plastic spirit which animates and directs this augmentation might be able to renew an augmented part which had been lost or removed. As always, he recognized that the notion of plastic spirit was occult; but in this case he found mechanical hypotheses equally so: "I was trying for a more mechanical Account of this matter, without flying to the *Plastic Vertue;* which if I call *unintelligible,* I must confess my Mechanism to be so too." Although drawn to the mechanical view of nature and in awe of the scientists who composed it, he thus never surrendered his belief in Spirit. "The more progress we make in *Experimental philosophy,*" he wrote later, "the oftener we shall find ourselves driven to something so much beyond *mechanical principles.*"

In conceiving of matter as energy, modern physics to a degree vindicates Mather's clinging to a vitalistic universe. Doing so, however, prevented him from fully appreciating the science of his time. His communications to the Royal Society also disclose two more of his serious limitations as a scientist. For one, he had little interest in the experimental method—that is, in the active questioning of nature under conditions defined by the experimenter—as opposed to bare observation of the phenomena nature presents. Such experiment was of the essence of the new science, distinguishing it from Aristotelianism and scholasticism. His limited mathematical knowledge also barred him from any real understanding of the advance in the exact mathematical description of nature that was one of the great achievements of science in the period. To judge Mather by such standards may however be unfair. Science was never for him an autonomous activity, but always a handmaid to religion. He fully recognized his inferiority to the great virtuosi of Europe, and always spoke of his scientific work, except in medicine, with modesty.

Leaving aside Mather's single greatest scientific accomplishment, which still lay ahead, he figures most importantly in the history of American science as a disseminator and popularizer of new scientific knowledge. From his pulpit he promoted the Copernican view of a heliocentric system and, invisible chains to the contrary, he took a rationalistic delight in exploding such popular superstitions as the theory of spontaneous generation and the cure of scrofula by the touch of a seventh son. Some more specific scientific contributions can be credited to him as well. Beginning in *Bonifacius* and continuing through "Curiosa Americana" and his later medical works, he gave pioneering attention, unappreciated at the time, to psychogenic causes of illness. His Curiosa also contain what seems to be the earliest known account of plant hybridization, confirming the then newly announced doctrine that flowering plants reproduce sexually—the basis for the Linnaean system of classifying plants. He also noted for what seems to have been the first time, the fact of dominance, later important in Mendel's theory of heredity. His profound curiosity about generation, we shall see, would lead him to major contributions to the treatment of smallpox. Finally, the observations on natural phenomena which he sent to London represented a wholly new level of performance by a colonial contributor to the Royal Society. Through the network of the Society's correspondence and publication, he not only gained a reputation in many parts of Europe for his own scientific work, but also advertised to the Old World the growing scientific community in the New.

The Royal Society rewarded Mather's efforts to Do Good. Secretary Waller reported to him in July 1713 that his first series of Curiosa "very well pleased and Entertained" the members, and that his future communications would be "extremely acceptable." Waller and Dr. Woodward also prepared some more detailed notes on their or the members' reactions, calling his account of the largeness of American wild turkeys and eagles "remarkable," and praising as seemingly new his description of the juice in the rattlesnake's gallbladder—withal indicating that the Curiosa received respectful and thoughtful attention. In his need at this time for encouragement, Mather had hinted that he would be pleased to see his work acknowledged in the Society's published *Transactions,* begun in 1665 and regularly received by the Fellows. An eight-page extract from the first series was published in the April–June 1714 *Transactions,* apparently making Mather the first New Englander since Governor John Winthrop of Connecticut to be published in that prestigious journal, which circulated throughout the world.

Seeking recognition even more blatantly, Mather upon sending his first series decided also to send a "Modest Intimation" that he would enjoy becoming a member of the Royal Society himself. The hint took the ambidexter form of an inverted confession, to Waller, of his unworthiness: "I cannot presume so much upon my own merits as to dream of being thought worthy to be admitted a member of that more than illustrious Society." He had in fact already been voted into the Society; in October 1713, he received news that at the next election "I shall be made, A FELLOW OF THE ROYAL SOCIETY." Giddy with delight in the distinction, he replied to Waller that he had resolved to send contributions annually to the Society for the rest of his life. Hereafter he often printed the designation "F.R.S." on the title pages of his works, together with his "D.D." from Glasgow. Although membership in the Society signified serious interest in science rather than technical or professional competence, the honor was genuine, for he had become only the eighth colonial elected to one of the most illustrious scientific bodies in the world.

In the "F.R.S." beside his name, Mather saw a signally surprising favor of heaven, "One that will much encourage me, and fortify me, in my Essays to do Good." It also gained him one advantage he sought from these essays. It heightened, he wrote, "the superior Circumstances, wherein my gracious Lord places me above the Contempt of envious Men." It exalted him above the other trees of the field, especially above the Governor Dudleys, the rasping serenaders, the swarmers who wanted pews for their despicable families, putting him, so he supposed, beyond their reach.

*

Despite Mather's strenuous attempts at this time to guard his wrath, it often slipped irresistibly by his watchfulness. Sometime it passed in the guise of a provocativeness which incensed his contemporaries more than any other feature of his personality. For all his geniality, many who knew him sensed in his behavior, as modern readers cannot but sense in many of his writings, something awry, a disturbing discrepancy between act and intent. This unsynchronized quality in Mather—an aggravated version of the ambidexterity earlier noticed by Robert Calef—was of course the product of his enormous strain in returning benignity for abuse, of the fact that his goodwill and good cheer were often deliberately reversed expressions of hurt pride, anger, and discouragement. This underside often seeped through—as the buoyant essays to Do Good of *Bonifacius* come encased in scornful warnings against "INGRATITUDE" and "DERISION"—tainting his behavior and his writing with a pervasive and provocative ambivalence.

The defining moods and gestures of Matherese—to give this ambivalence a name—are belligerent courtesy, self-flattering modesty, fretful calm, denigrating compliments, unacceptable offers. Mather came more and more to use such gallingly provocative tactics on his contemporaries, helping to explain why they often acted toward him with what he considered base ingratitude. A Scots minister named John Squire, for instance, visited New England around 1715, but refused to take communion with New England churches, and in Mather's view acted with unbecoming levity and arrogance. Squire's disrespect riled Mather the more because of his pride in his D.D. from Glasgow, and his much publicized veneration for the Church of Scotland. Although infuriated, he decided to Do some Good, and invited Squire to lodge with him, at no cost. As added inducements he promised Squire that the accommodations would be inferior to few in Boston and the library superior to any. A brotherly offer, until his final inducement, where his contempt broke through: "To which this easy Circumstance will be added; that all the while you stay, you shall not hear those Things, which we take to be your Weaknesses, uneasily insisted on." Squire was not disarmed by such palpable combinations of hospitality and condemnation: "your Civilities," he told Mather, "Savour the worse to me that they are cast so frequently in my teeth."

Squire was not alone in finding Mather's private language of self-control jolting. Modern readers still react with puzzled annoyance to the obtuseness of Matherese, the spectacle it affords of a vengeful egotist nakedly transparent, and all unknowingly, through his contrarily expressed forgiveness and charity. Benjamin Colman detected his practice of simultaneously saying and unsaying, and admonished him for it. After Mather apparently wrote to him expanding fulsomely on the subject of charity, Colman replied that he was glad for Mather's enthusiasm on this subject but cautioned him that he would not be perfect in charity himself until he displayed "as much Care not to provoke Wrath, as power afterward to despise, or triumph over, it." Colman's acute remark suggests that Matherese served more than simply Mather's anger. For Mather also felt intensely guilty about his anger: in "my Hatred and Malice towards other Men," he wrote, "I have been a Degree of a Murderer." Thus in provoking others to condemn and revile him, he evidently also sought to thrash his own hated murderousness. More than any other characteristic of

Mather's, it is this impossibly provocative fusion of the conciliator and the troublemaker, of his goodwill and his rage, that has always made him seem at once splendid and contemptible.

When not surfacing through his benevolence, Mather's anger sometimes simply took a different route around his guardedness. He had always exhorted and denounced the rising generation, but his many sermons to the young around 1710 seem to translate into dire warnings to them the pent-up hurt he felt toward Dudley, Leverett, and others. To cite only two brief instances, from sermons published in 1710 and 1712, of this redirected rage:

> [The minister] is above the reach of Hurt from your Malignity. You do but add unto his *Crown,* as often as you Express your Disaffection to him. Do, Go on to make him the Object of your Venom; Throw all the Dirt of a *Street* upon him, if you please; Do, *Go on still in your Trespasses.* You will *Wound* your selves, and none but your selves Wretches. . . .
>
> Silly Children, the Minister of God is above all your Silly Attempts. You can't hurt *him.* If the Wrath of God, had not left you bereft of your Wits, you would feel, that you hurt but *your selves.* Your Venomous *Arrows* are all Shot against a *Rock.* They'll prevail nothing against an *Iron Pillar,* and a *Brasen Wall!*

Astonishingly, on virtually the same days that Mather could subject the children in his congregation to these sniggering anathemas he could compose genteel Curiosa to the Royal Society, praising the works of human reason. More astonishing and also distressing, he could in this period at one moment praise Francke for his beneficence to poor children, and at another threaten children in his own flock, uncharacteristically, with punitive incineration:

> There are *Children,* whose Doom will be to be *Burnt to Death,* in the *Day of the Lord that shall burn like an Oven.* There are *Children,* whom God will send into *Everlasting Fire with the Devil and his Angels.* And what *Children?* Why, *Wicked* Children; The *Children* that make themselves the *Children of the Devil.* . . . Go into the *Burying-Place,* CHILDREN; you will there see *Graves* as Short as your selves. Yea, you may be at *Play* one Hour; *Dead, Dead* the Next. Little do you dream, CHILDREN, How near you may be to an *Evil Time;* Any more than the *Fish* which you sometimes Catch, are aware of their *Evil Time!*

In discharging his stifled anger at powerless objects, Mather called attention to the side of himself that was both chaotic and, in the popular mind, longest remembered.

Mather's tantrums and provocations are redeemed, if at all, by two consistent features of his personality. First, his concern for human misery, however at times enmeshed with baser feelings, was genuine, and issued in innumerable acts of kindness. Also, since adolescence he had been himself anguishedly aware of his envy and rage. With countless self-condemnings and resolves he struggled to subdue these traits in himself, of which he sternly disapproved but which nearly always mastered him. It was his destiny, his tragedy, often to end up lamenting: "I can't Sufficiently preserve that Sedate, and Serene, and Comfortable Frame of Mind which belongs unto the *Peace of God*."

Mather's exasperating difficulty in composing himself had a further unfortunate result. He fought off his sense of rejection, we have seen, by multiplying his efforts to please and by seeking recognition outside Boston. Such comfort as he gained was bound to be imperfect and transient, for his feeling of insufficiency was ingrained, and his offerings to London or Glasgow brought with them the same personality that often antagonized his neighbors. His attempts to attain elsewhere the acceptance denied him in Boston extended a vicious cycle—Do Good, Be Spurned, Do More Good, Be More Spurned—and won him a heavy burden of further disappointment.

Some of this result can be seen by looking a little beyond the period of Mather's quarrel with Governor Dudley, to about 1715. His spat with the Scots minister John Squire already suggests how the consolation he felt in being welcomed by luminaries in the Church of Scotland throve on the distance separating him from them. Facing another visiting Scotsman in Boston, young [Patrick?] Erskine, he found himself again repulsed. Evidently hoping to demonstrate yet again his gratitude for the D.D., he invited the youth to visit him as often as possible, made him "as handsome a treat at my table as I could," and tried artfully to drop improving admonitions on him. These may have been no more artful than those he offered Squire, for Erskine, he complained, proved "unaccountably shy" of visiting him. Worse, Erskine married without consulting him and, as Mather put it, "the plot was carried on with such privacy" that he knew nothing of it for some time after it succeeded. Still worse, Erskine and his wife had their marriage performed by Benjamin Colman and joined his Brattle church.

Mather's stepped-up promotion of "Biblia Americana" abroad also begot fresh resentment. His five-page notice in *Bonifacius* apparently having failed to attract subscribers, he advertised the work again in England in 1716, this time in a sixteen-page pamphlet entitled *A New Offer To the*

Lovers of Religion and Learning. By now the ever burgeoning work had grown, by Mather's reckoning, to more than three times the size of *Magnalia Christi Americana*. The new advertisement contained a specific subscription plan: interested persons would send in their names affixed to a promise to take off a two-volume set, at a price set by the bookseller with the advice of three unexceptionable London ministers.

Yet English readers proved no hungrier for Mather's *New Offer* than young Erskine for his invitations. Baffled and hurt by the rejection, and more usually the silence, he wrote one letter after another, trying to account for the neglect of him. The English, he bitterly told one London correspondent, count New Englanders "what we really are, of too little use or worth for them to converse withal." The London booksellers, he told another correspondent, showed no interest because "*In one word, they are booksellers.*" Particularly he blamed the London Dissenting ministers, to whom he had often applied for help in publishing the work. They "do not seem to overvalue literature," he snipped, "Nor do they seem to think that it is much for their interest or honor to have any of their number do things of much consideration in the commonwealth of learning"—just what he expected, he told still another correspondent, "from men of their Narrow Spirits." Forsaken by those who should have appreciated him most, he issued an extraordinary spiteful warning to some Dissenting ministers in London that if they "cast it off," the work might be published under the auspices of "eminent Persons" in the Church of England.

The *New Offer* having failed in Scotland also, Mather tried to soothe himself by thinking that were the work not in English his admirers among the German Pietists would publish it. But from his London go-between with the Pietists, Anthony William Boehm, he got only the discouraging advice to copy out the whole of "Biblia Americana" (which might have taken years) and to lodge the transcript with an eminent London divine, for viewing by persons who might consider subsidizing its publication. Boehm also brusquely criticized the *New Offer,* pointing out to Mather that he had advised subscribers to send in their names—but had failed to tell them where or to whom!

Mather was wholly unable to accept the explanation given him by literally dozens of persons, that "Biblia Americana" was a valuable work but prohibitively costly to publish. In his mind, those who failed to confirm his worth were not simply shying from a project that could have cost little less than the reprinting of Eliot's Indian Bible but were, as many others had done, affronting a great and unselfish man. Snubbed in London, he responded as he often did in Boston, by grandiose self-promotion offered with accusative sarcasm: "I do not Expect," he told one London bookseller, "that my own having, near two hundred and forty times, entertain'd my Friends with publishing by the way of the press, Treatises and composures on various Arguments, and in various (Living as well as dead) Languages, will obtain for me with some, the Favour of being thought capable of any valuable performance." To elicit guilt and let off steam he made this harumphing enumeration of his many works amidst his many other employments a sort of set piece, the numbers of works growing with each new cajoling letter he sent. Since the age of seventeen, he told Sir William Ashurst, he had had

> lying upon him, the ponderous Employments of the Evangelical Services, which the greatest Church in these Colonies has expected from him, and . . . he has in this while undergone the Humiliations of publishing more than Two hundred and fifty Books, of several Dimensions, on various Arguments, in Diverse Languages; yet . . . there is performed in the *Biblia Americana,* more than all that is promised in the Advertisement.

If only a few "persons of Quality" overseas favored the work, Mather felt certain, "Vast Subscriptions would soon be sent in." But they did not; the subscriptions never came. In October 1716, he wrote in his diary that the publication of "Biblia Americana" was "to be despaired of."

Mather's service to the New England Company also proved often thankless. He complained to the directors in London about the inadequacy of their remittances, which forced the commissioners to pay from their own pockets toward the salaries of ministers and schoolteachers employed in the field. President Leverett of Harvard provided a further annoyance: Dudley appointed him a magistrate to the Indians without the commissioners' concurrence and demanded that he be paid from Company funds. Finding the other commissioners sluggish as well, Mather several times offered to resign, but was kept going by the Company's gratitude for his work. When they awarded him £25 he wrote to London saying he considered himself repaid in the pleasure of serving them and wished to decline the gift, but accepted it as affording him "opportunities for continual and considerable expense of Time and Thought; and purse too (tho' that an Article not worth mentioning)"—which, translated (parentheses in Matherese often revealing-concealing the gist), means he disdained the money but needed it because the Company was forcing him to spend his own funds on its behalf. In Matherese again he begged the Company in 1712 to dismiss him because of his many other obligations, managing in the course of confessing his ineptitude to reveal himself to be invaluable:

> The uttermost that I can pretend unto, is, To give my constant Attendance at the Meetings; and a small Assistance to the Shaping of our Projections; and write Letters upon occasion to the Indian preachers and churches; or perhaps give Directions to the Instruments employ'd by your Commissioners; and receive and pursue Addresses to the Commissioners from such as please now and then, to make use of me in so befriending of them.

As always now, appreciation cooled him off and inspired higher flights of Doing Good: "The Corporation in *London,* having refused to dismiss me, (as I desired,) . . . I would more than ever set myself to serve them."

New frustrations came to Mather even from his election to the Royal Society. His first series of Curiosa, a hundred pages of manuscript, appeared in the *Transactions* as an eight-page summary. Whether the shrinkage disappointed him is unknown, but his Scots correspondent Robert Wodrow read the summary abroad and wrote him sympathetically, "It is my loss and that of many others, that we have not the full copies of your valuable letters, referred to in that short abstract." Nor do we know if Mather winced over the abstract writer's account in the *Transactions* of "Biblia Americana," which reported that Mather had described a large work in manuscript, "but does not name the Author." (Like his failure to tell readers of the *New Offer* where to send their subscriptions, the slip suggests self-sabotaging guilt over the towering ambition of the work.) Mather may not even have received a copy of the summary, for he complained to John Winthrop that "Our friends of the Royal Society do strangely neglect us (or packets miscarry). I hear of many things of mine published; but I never saw them."

Mather also discovered that his name was somehow omitted from the catalogue of the Society's Fellows. Of course he did not howl over this latest bit of ill-fated disregard, but rather made known his hurt to the Society in a promise of greater service. He would annually treat it to so many communications, he wrote to London, "that if every member of that illustrious body whose name stands in the catalogue (an honor not yet obtained for mine) will do but half as much, the stores in your collection will soon become considerable."

9

Of 15, Dead, 9

AT THE TIME of Governor Dudley's arrival, Mather had married Elizabeth Hubbard Clark, a young widow twelve years younger than himself. Her father was the Boston physician Dr. John Clark, whose father had been a physician also; on her mother's side she may have been related to an English noble family, the Saltonstalls. She had been briefly married to a Boston mariner named Richard Hubbard, with whom she had a son around 1699. Later accounts describe her as a woman of "singular *good-Humour* and incomparable Sweetness of Temper," having a "very handsome engaging *Countenance.*"

Elizabeth may have grown up in the Anglican church, for her father is known to have attended the first Church of England meeting held in New England, in 1686, under the Rev. Robert Ratcliffe. At some time, however, she heard the Mathers preach, and it was their preaching, according to Cotton, that turned her to Christ; three years after their marriage she was admitted to communion in the North Church. Indeed until her illness and death in 1713 left him more painfully isolated than ever, he entered in his diary little else about her than his efforts to assist her spiritual development and make her an asset to his ministry. He emphasized to her three points on which ministers' wives had made their names precious to posterity: constancy and fervency in their devotions; ingenuity and labor in instructing their families in piety; and compassion toward the miserable in their neighborhood. Thus he looked out for suitable books of piety for her, recommending that she attempt to draw from them matter for her private devotions, and urged her to take notes after the preacher during sermons, as he did, both for her own advantage and as an example to others. He resolved to say something instructive to her whenever she came to his study, or he to her in their room, or when she brought him his "short Breakfast" and sat with him as he drank it. He also encouraged her to visit their neighbors frequently and contrive some act whereby she might say when she left, "Some Good has been done, where she was."

Mather and Elizabeth lived in the house he had inhabited for most of his first marriage, a few streets from his father's house and from the North Church. Apparently a substantial, three-story building on a plot 38' by 120', it expressed his belief that God allowed humanity a middle estate— neither so much nor so little comfort as to make people unmindful of their souls. No very exact picture of the house can be reconstructed, but it had a fence, a gate, a well, and a yard, and was sizable enough for Mather to hold large meetings in. The house also had a garden, which he tried fashioning into a "Sort of an earthly Paradise," using its trees and herbs as subjects of his devotions in the time he spent there. Among the known appurtenances inside were a stove, a *"Repeating Clock, and a very curious One,"* and "agreeable mottos" which he resolved to post in every room. Aside from a parlor apparently reserved for receiving visitors, the center of the house for Mather was his large study, containing a "very *easy Chair."* Above the door in capital letters he posted, as a warning to tedious visitors or interrupting friends, the motto "BE SHORT"—although, his son Samuel added, "let him be ever so busy when a Friend came to see him, he threw all by."

The center of this center, something Mather had greatly desired and valued since youth, was his cherished library. At the time he married Elizabeth he owned between two and three thousand books. They stood in "Boxes," presumably stacked against the walls of his study—not only a predictably large number of religious and theological works in several languages, but also many volumes of history, classical literature, and Neoplatonic philosophy, and important scientific works by Boyle, Descartes, Gassendi and others, a testimony to his prodigious learning and curiosity. The earliest surviving volume from his collection may be Conrad Lycosthenes' *Apophthegmata* (Geneva, 1668), which he owned at the age of ten. From at least that time his library grew both gradually and through such accessive leaps as his purchase at the age of nineteen of ninety-six books from the Harvard library (offered for sale as duplicates), and his acquisition in 1709 of a group of six hundred sermons. Many books passed down in the family, and many volumes bear inscriptions of several generations of Mathers. He kept his collection current by often sending to London for recent books and journals and by managing to inspect new arrivals in America: "Seldom any *new Book* of Consequence finds the way from beyond-Sea, to these parts of *America,* but I bestow the Perusal upon it." Living near his father, who also read and acquired books voraciously, he had easy access to his father's library, so that Increase's collection "which was not much Less than Mine, was also in a manner *Mine.*"

How many books Mather accumulated in his lifetime is uncertain, but by the end of his life he probably owned the largest library in America. In 1686, when Mather was twenty-three, the English bookseller John Dunton visited him and judged his collection even at that time one of the finest private libraries he had ever seen: "as the Famous Bodleian Library at Oxford, is the Glory of that University, if not of all Europe," Dunton wrote, "so I may say, That Mr. Mather's Library is the Glory of New-England, if not of all America. I am sure it was the best sight that I had in Boston." Mather's son Samuel is said to have put the total collection—probably including the library of Increase Mather—at seven or eight thousand volumes, plus a very large holding of manuscripts passed down in the family through five generations.

Entering middle age in these years, Mather found himself the head of a large household. Both his parents were aging and ailing, Increase, we have seen, suffering various ills and fearful of diminishing mental power. Cotton rarely mentions his mother, Maria Mather, although she too had various serious ailments, being at one time so lamed by rheumatism that she could not stand for more than six weeks, and was growing infirm and feeble. As she turned seventy, in 1711, he gave thought to helping prepare her for appearing before God, and resolved to discourse with her "as prudently and as takingly as I can, on that illustrious Point." He had also brought to his marriage with Elizabeth the four children surviving of the nine he had had with his first wife—Katharine, Abigail ("Nibby"), Hannah ("Nancy"), and Increase, Jr. By 1711 he and Elizabeth had had four children more: Elizabeth (b. 13 July 1704), Samuel (b. 30 October 1706), Nathanael (b. 16 May 1709), and Jerusha (b. April 1711). Nathanael, apparently named for Mather's dead brother, however survived only six months. Elizabeth presumably also brought to the house her son by her first marriage, although Mather never mentions him. Nevertheless, as he neared fifty, Mather was perforce more a parent than ever before, the father of five daughters and two sons ranging in age from Katharine, now about twenty-two, to the newborn Jerusha, the other children being seventeen, fourteen, twelve, seven, and five years old.

Mather's household also had numerous long- and short-term servants and slaves—male and female, white, Indian, and black. He often publicly denounced what seemed to him illegal and brutal aspects of the growing colonial slave trade. In 1723, after several Boston blacks committed a series of arsons and even threatened to burn down the town, he asked Bostonians to consider whether blacks are "always treated according to the Rules of Humanity?. . . . . . Are they treated as those, that are of one Blood with us, and those that have Immortal Souls in them, and are not mere Beasts of Burden?" Unlike Samuel Sewall, however, Mather was in no sense an abolitionist, and he generally thought blacks superstitious and stupid. In his view, Christian law allowed slavery but "wonderfully Dulcifies, and Mollifies, and Moderates the Circumstances of it." He appealed rather for humane treatment of slaves, and especially for their christianizing, in the face of prevailing views that conversion would make slaves discontented or might even entitle them to liberty, Christians in theory being forbidden to keep other Christians as slaves. Mather attacked these views in *The Negro Christianized* (1706), where he reminded slaveowners that "They are *Men,* and not *Beasts,* that you have bought," and urged that far from becoming restive, christianized slaves would serve their masters more patiently and faithfully. Mather did much else toward christianizing black slaves: trying to promote the work by act of Parliament in England; publishing for householders a streamlined, three-question catechism to instruct their "poor Stupid Abject *Negro's*"; paying from his own pocket the weekly wages of a schoolmistress to teach blacks to read; and resolving to entertain the religious society of blacks of the North Church piously at his house.

In 1706 some members of his congregation spent forty or fifty pounds to buy him a young black man "of a promising Aspect and Temper." Seeing the acquisition as a "mighty Smile of Heaven upon my Family," he named the slave Onesimus, after the runaway slave in the New Testament who was converted and became virtually a son to Paul. Since for Mather and other Puritans, servants were to be treated as family members—as persons, that is, for whose salvation the householder was obliged to be deeply concerned—he labored with a combination of piety and contempt for Onesimus' conversion. Consistent with his belief that blacks did not differ from the rest of humanity in their capacity for salvation, he found Onesimus governed best by "the Principles of Reason, agreeably offered unto him," encouraged him to read and write every day, and allowed him to marry. (Whether Onesimus' wife joined the Mather household is unclear; the couple had a son, who died, however, in 1714.) He also permitted Onesimus to work outside the house and gain an independent income, charging him to keep the rules of honesty and to devote part of his income to pious purposes. For all that, Mather did not differ from most other Puritans in regarding blacks as alien and untrustworthy. He kept a "strict Eye" on Onesimus' company and activities, including "some Actions of a thievish Aspect."

Amidst his multitudinous duties and services, and despite his many upsets, Mather enacted his domestic role with great thoughtfulness and affection. He viewed parental love and responsibility as, next to devotion to God, the supreme human fact: "*Nature* knows not a greater Passion. . . . *To all men Living, their Children are as dear as their very Lives.*" He conceived child nurture as a joint venture among parents, ministers, and schoolmasters, aimed at making children gentlemanly and ladylike Christians—pious, literate, and well-mannered. In his many published works on the subject he advised that Scripture learning should begin as soon as children come out of swaddling clothes and can learn anything; later they should be made to read Scripture every day, form prayers out of what they read, and repeat sermons. When children reach a suitable age, parents should pray and weep with them, making them "*Witnesses* of the *Agonies,* with which you Address the Throne of Grace on their Behalf. *They'll never forget it!*" Mather also wished children to attain secular learning and to come to think that "to learn all the brave Things in the world, is the bravest Thing in the world." To this end he urged that they be taught to spell and read well and to keep neat writing books, entering into them profitable thoughts. To inculcate benignity in them, parents should set them doing kind services for other children and caution them to return good for evil.

To induce children to act upon such principles of reason and honor, Mather believed, parents must beget in them a high opinion of the parents' love for them. And to earn such affectionate respect from their children, parents must avoid harshness. Although Mather discounted the child's own will and counted a parent's word absolute law, he deplored all severity in child rearing: "The *slavish* way of *Education,* carried on with raving and kicking and scourging (in *Schools* as well as *Families,*) tis abominable; and a dreadful Judgment of God upon the World." He allowed for blows only in cases of very extreme misbehavior, and then not in fury or passion. As a general principle of discipline, he recommended that parents so combine pleasure and instruction that being deprived of instruction is punishment enough.

Mather conscientiously applied these principles to raising his own children, on whom he lavished attention. Except for his preaching and pastoral visits, he spent his day at home, shuttling between his family and his study, into which he often called the children to converse or to pray.

Each morning at nine (and again each evening) the family gathered for catechizing, praying, Scripture reading, and psalm singing, the children who were at school in the neighborhood coming home to take part in the devotions. He seems also to have required the children to write daily in their blank books, at a stated hour during which he gave them materials "both devotionary and scientifical." He outfitted each child with a one-shelf library taken from his own collection, adding some book to their stock each week, especially works by himself and his father. Privately he prayed constantly for their conversion and physical well-being, and tried each night to take an account of how they had spent their time during the day.

True to his own views on discipline, Mather sought to grace his instruction of his children with the same ingenuity and facetiousness for which contemporaries valued his conversation. He tried in his table talk to "Entertain" their minds and polish their manners by discoursing on novel and useful subjects. Before rising he would every day relate a story that might be helpful to "the *Olive Plants about the Table.*" Whenever coming upon one of them by-the-way he let fall some memorable and instructive sentence, a practice requiring, he found, "some Study, and Labour, and Contrivance. But who can tell, what may be the Effect of a *continual Dropping?*" Combining teaching and amusement, he similarly filled time with them on the road in his "Chariot," offered inventively pious reminders when they were at sports or games, "which the Circumstances of their play may lead them to think upon," and improved such other family activities as baking, gardening, or laying in provisions (*"Lord,"* he exclaimed when brewing, *"let us find in a glorious Christ, a provision for our thirsty Souls"*). When he gave the children money or some other gift he tendered as well some maxim which if they practiced, he told them, would be worth more to them than "the Little Thing which I now bestow."

As Mather proposed, the agreeableness of his instruction also proved useful in discipline. He tried to make his children feel privileged in being taught by him, so that the sorest punishment they could feel was "To be chased for a while out of *my Presence*"—a somewhat manipulative use of his children's dependence on his approval, reminiscent of his own childhood relation to his own withdrawn father, who spent sixteen hours a day in his study. Mather's many aggravations at this time seem to have made some difficulty for him in preventing angry outbursts against his children, and he occasionally reminded himself that upon any occasion of discipline he must "with all possible Decency govern my Passion.

My Anger shall not break out, into any froward, peevish, indecent Expressions. I will only let them see, that I don't like what I take notice of." But generally Mather was a notably mild and amiable parent. His success in reproducing his own affectionate domestic values in his children is illustrated by an episode in 1711 in which little Samuel mistreated his sister Elizabeth. Mather gave Lizzy a piece of fruit, but gave none to Sammy to punish him for "being so cross to her." The father no sooner turned his back, he discovered, "but the good-condition'd Creature fell into Tears, at this Punishment of her little Brother, and gave to him a Part of what I had bestowed upon her."

In attending to his children's material needs Mather was less successful. His wish to provide for them in case he died was quickened by uncertain health—a lingering morning cough and recurrent head and jaw pains that sometimes restricted his ministerial work, the headaches forcing him one morning to "lie down like a Stag in a Net." He treated these with various remedies and by riding horseback a few miles out of town—a practice he constantly recommended to others. Yet he realized he could leave little behind for his children's upkeep. His salary furnished no more than their subsistence and education and, unlike his father, he grumbled little over insufficient pay and cared little about financial matters. He could only hope that God would reward his service by providing for his children if he died. But the largeness of his family, and probably also the wider economic straits of Dudley's administration, sometimes left him and his children pressed. He noted in 1709 that having fallen into some wants, "I had not Clothes fit to be worn. . . . And one or two of my Children are no better accommodated." It was only in answer to prayers that in 1711 Increase, Jr., came by clothing for the winter. Nor were the hard times eased by Mather's insistence, whatever his own circumstances, on Doing Good: "Tho' I can get no better Clothes than Rags for myself," he wrote, "yet the Lord honours me, by making me the happy Instrument of clothing other people. The Poor have numberless Reliefs, out of my Purse, and by my Means from others, and the Naked are clothed."

In preparing his children for adult social life, Mather trained his daughters to be gentlewomen, his sons to be ministers. He resolved to have the girls cook at least one new thing a week, but he also had them write daily and read in one of the sciences, and he taught them shorthand and Hebrew. His pious but affable eldest daughter, Katharine ("Katy"), a "*Lamb* inexpressibly dear . . . a *Constellation* of every thing that could Endear a Daughter," became not only able with the needle and knowledgeable about the table, but also dextrous with her pen and in wax sculpturing, highly accomplished in Hebrew, and skillful in both instrumental and vocal music. To enable her to Do Good, Mather also determined on having her obtain knowledge of medicine. Proud that he had provided for her "so polite an education," he prayed to God to see her well married.

Mather's two sons, however, were turning out to have sharply differing personalities. His and Elizabeth's son Samuel early showed a bent for the Mather family's several generations of learning. By the age of six, in 1712, Sammy could read so well that Mather decided to supply him continually with Latin and English distichs to be learned by heart, with rewards for learning them. His son by his first marriage, Increase, Jr., also gave early signs of realizing the advice Mather had received from heaven that the boy would be "a Servant of my Lord Jesus Christ throughout eternal Ages." In addition to Creasy's formal schooling, Mather wrote out verses for him to memorize, hoping to improve him at once in goodness and reading, and sent him as well each day for instruction to the older Increase, the boy's grandfather. By about 1712, when he was thirteen, Creasy had grown so proficient in classical languages that Mather considered holding their "daily discourse" entirely in Latin, and planned to have Creasy turn the Greek of Posselius into Latin verse. To foster Creasy's conversion, Mather wrote down for him "certain Questions of the last Importance," and obliged him to write answers. He also rewarded the boy with money for transcribing works that might inform his mind and manners, and tried to have school themes assigned him that would promote goodness and virtue. Often he called Creasy into his study to sit with him as he read aloud various "Documents of Piety, and of Discretion," including parts of "Paterna," the autobiography he had begun writing for Creasy at his birth.

But Creasy somehow failed to feel the allure of the Mather past and of the Lord's service. Mather suspected that the boy ignored secret prayer and, calling him into his study, made him promise to desist from a prayerless life. Worried also that bad company was corrupting Creasy, he warned him to shun "vicious and wicked Lads" and urged him to spend Sabbath evenings with serious youths, reading pious works. As his own son began exhibiting the evils of the rising generation which he had often denounced from his pulpit, he prayed repeatedly to God to grant Creasy His converting influences, and often moaned into his diary: "I am full, full of Distress, concerning my little Son *Increase*. . . . . . My poor

Son *Increase!* Oh! the Distress of Mind, with which I must let fall my daily Admonitions upon him."

When Creasy reached thirteen, the time for his admission to Harvard, he failed to follow his father, grandfather, and five uncles into the school. Instead, after long deliberation, Mather decided to steer him toward the business world, and redirected Creasy's education toward secular life. Like his father, the boy had an elegant handwriting that might have suited him to work as an accountant or scribe, and he now concentrated on perfecting his writing and ciphering. Believing that Creasy had an aptitude for mathematical studies, Mather encouraged him to master geometry, trigonometry, and navigation. And to give the boy a polish that might serve him in business life, he also had Creasy trained in fencing and music. Just the same, he keenly wished him to appreciate the life of the mind, and tried to "ply him with all possible Methods for a most liberal Education in other Points [than business]; that he may be a man very useful in the World." When Creasy was fourteen, in mid-1713, Mather began seeking a businessman to whom he could be apprenticed, and by the fall seems to have located a religious merchant family to take him in.

*

The winter of 1713 brought the worst epidemic of measles in colonial American history. The disease first appeared near Newport, Rhode Island, in the summer, broke out at Harvard College in September, and by October arrived in Boston, where, Mather estimated later, it infected thousands of people and killed 160 in two months. To gird his neighbors for what might be coming, he decided to devote his public sermons and prayers to the subject of affliction. Fearing as well that his own household might share deeply in the common calamity, he undertook to make more numerous expressions of piety at home, to prepare his children for death, and to send up many supplicatory prayers himself, "that so the Wrath of Heaven may inflict no sad Thing on my Family."

In about two weeks Mather's entire family had been smitten, beginning with Creasy. Having survived choking on a pin during infancy and smallpox contracted during the epidemic of 1702, the boy fortunately recovered quickly, and Mather obliged him to write up special resolutions for his future conduct. But Creasy was no sooner well than Nibby, who had gotten smallpox in the same epidemic, lay "very sick" of measles, followed by "dear *Katy*" (although in "somewhat more favorable Circumstances"), and then by Mather's wife, Elizabeth, who had very recently given birth. Within only a few days his daughters Nancy, Lizzy, and Jerusha—aged seven, nine, and two—also took the disease, and Sammy, aged seven, as well as the Mathers' maidservant. "Help Lord," Mather wrote, "and look mercifully on my poor, sad, sinful Family, for the Sake of the Great Sacrifice!"

As such threats to the public welfare always did, the epidemic quickened Mather's desire to Do Good, and he proposed fighting it not only by prayer but also by his considerable medical knowledge. Certain that proper care might save many lives that would likely be lost through mismanagement, he considered printing a pamphlet of advice and lodging it among sick families, and inserting brief directions for treating measles in the newspaper. He clearly hoped, however, to avoid antagonizing local physicians by presuming on their expertise, and consulted beforehand with some doctors, who seem to have declined joining him in publishing the pamphlet but approved of his doing so himself. Even so, when the two-page work appeared later in the year, as the measles spread into the countryside, he specified that he intended his instructions for people unable to afford physicians, or beyond their reach. But at whatever risk of criticism from the medical profession, he hoped to distribute it widely to save lives: "Tho' doubtless my Action may expose me to some Invectives, yet my Conformity to my dear Saviour, in what He did for the sick, will be my inexpressible Consolation."

One historian of medicine has called Mather's *Letter About a Good Management under the Distemper of the Measles* (1713) "particularly because of its originality, one of the very few classics of early American medicine." Abandoning his habitual attempt to charm, Mather wrote his instructions "in the plainest manner that is possible," so that any nurse could administer them. After observing that in Europe measles usually proved a light malady, but in these parts of America "*Grievous* to most, *Mortal* to many," he described the symptoms of each stage of the disease, beginning with headache, eye pains, and dry cough, and reaching a turning point about three days after the eruption of red specks, often with such frightening but usually transient symptoms as vomiting and fainting. In mild cases he recommended allowing patients to maintain their routine until the specks appear, then to stay warm and at home, feeding sparingly on bland food. In more serious cases patients should lie warm in bed, consulting a physician if high fever persists. Aside from suggesting such remedies as teas or hot honey, the brunt of Mather's *Letter* is its reiterated caution against overtreatment, which may only worsen the disease: "*Don't kill 'em!* That is to say, With mischievous Kindness. Indeed, if we stopt here, and said no more, this were enough to save more *Lives,* than our *Wars* have destroyed." Mather's main, and important, advice was in effect to let nature take its course.

Elizabeth was the first in his family to die. Since first learning of the outbreak of the disease in Rhode Island, he had felt a "strong Distress on my Mind" that it would be calamitous to his family, and had related his premonition to friends "often, often." He was particularly apprehensive for Elizabeth because of her advanced pregnancy, as the disease often proved fatal to women who were with child. She gave birth on October 30, very easily, but somewhat prematurely—the result, Mather concluded, of her "too diligent an Attendance on her sick Family." Mather baptized the twins on November 1, naming the girl Martha, after Elizabeth's mother, and the boy Eleazer, after the biblical Martha's brother, a "priestly Name" identical with Lazarus.

Three days after the baptism Mather saw that symptoms of measles had begun appearing on Elizabeth. A few days after that she was in a "dangerous Condition," unable to rest, raising fears that she might die or become distracted. He apparently did not pray for Particular Faiths, as he had during his first wife's long illness a decade earlier. Several times in the interval he had been strongly tempted to regard powerful mental impressions as Particular Faiths from heaven, but "having been *once* buffeted in that Experience, I durst hardly any more countenance it." Despite Elizabeth's long sleeplessness, her mind had remained lucid, and he prayed with her many times, tried to offer consoling discourses, and readied her for death. It comforted her, he thought, to see that his children by his first marriage were as fond of her as her own.

On November 8, with his children lying ill and much sickness in the neighborhood, Mather preached at the North Church on the text John 18:11, The Cup which my Father has given me, shall not I drink it? Not without overtones of older, displaced bitterness he depicted Christ's submission to suffering: a man exposed to contempt for his ministry, jeered at, defiled by spit, yet patient under affliction, a pattern for all afflicted believers, "When the *Cup* appointed for you, is imposed on you, *Now* take it," he admonished his congregation. "Perhaps, 'tis the *Cup* of a *Funeral.* That which was the *Desire of thine Eyes,* and the Delight, and the Darling of thy Family, must have its *Funeral.* . . . Take it." The same day he observed, at home, "surprising Symptoms of Death" on Elizabeth, who had lain sleepless whole days and nights.

Whatever Mather's own council of patient submission, the prospect of Elizabeth's death was not easy. The marriage, despite his initial uncertainties about it, had worked out well, and he had found Elizabeth a woman of conspicuous piety, virtuous deportment, and benign temper, beloved by many. "To part with so desirable, so agreeable a Companion, a Dove from such a Nest of young ones too! Oh! the sad Cup, which my Father has appointed me!" He had prayed and cried to God often that this particular cup would pass from him, but somehow without being able to produce in himself the appropriate spiritual state. Now he saw the meaning of his deadness of heart: "My Supplications have all along had, a most unaccountable Death and Damp upon them!" Elizabeth died on the afternoon of November 9, ten days after giving birth. In the room with her body Mather again tried to persuade himself into a state of resignation in which to suffer without complaint the will of God in taking "my dear, dear, dear Friend."

The next to die, on November 14, was Mather's maidservant, as he learned on arising that morning. She had been stricken about two weeks earlier, together with his children, but her measles passed into a "malignant Fever." He found some compensation for her death in the fact that she had come to his family a "wild, vain, airy Girl" but had grown disposed to serious religion, awakened to fervent secret prayer, and at last brought into covenant and baptized, "and my poor Instructions, were the means that God blessed for such happy Purposes." With her death he resolved to intensify his own repentance for any miscarriages in his behavior toward his servants.

The twins Eleazer and Martha died next. Elizabeth's easy delivery had encouraged Mather to hope that he had been mistaken in his earlier premonition of family disaster. But only two weeks after the twins' birth, and a day after the passing of his maidservant, he found both newborns "languishing in the Arms of Death." Eleazer died first, at about midnight three days later, Martha two days after that.

The need to anticipate and bear up under the death of children had been a prominent theme of Mather's ministry. He had often reminded his congregation that at least half the children of men die before the age of twenty, and that "In the *Deaths* of your Children, Endured with a due Submission, to the *Father of Spirits,* you offer up some of your Fattest *Sacrifices.*" His own power of quietly sacrificing his most choice was called upon, for although most of his other children seem to have recovered by the time of the twins' death, his daughter Jerusha, about two and a half years old, still lay dangerously ill with a high fever. She had been named for his youngest sister, who had died in childbed of her first child at the age of twenty-six—a woman of promising intellectual ability and a "considerable Mistress" of her pen, of whom he had been greatly fond.

With the loss of Elizabeth and the twins, not to mention the deaths of five other young children during his first marriage, the "dying Circumstances" of "dear pretty Jerusha" were to Mather nearly insupportable: "I begg'd, I begg'd, that such a bitter Cup, as the Death of that lovely child, might pass from me." On the night of November 21, Jerusha asked him to pray with her, as he did with distress but without protest to God, having earlier in the day attended the funeral of his twins. She lay speechless many hours, he recorded, but finally her speech returned a little to her and she said the minute that she died *"That she would go to Jesus Christ."*

Next day, with Jerusha lying dead in the house, Mather preached to his congregation as one who had seen five deaths in his family in less than two weeks and was tomorrow, he said, "to attend the Funeral of a Child which was Two years and seven months old." His calamities had become a matter of town talk, and he was aware that the "Eyes of the People are much upon me." Eager to have at least "the Happiness to do the more Good for every Evil that befalls me," he had something to offer his listeners: although he had fervently hoped for Jerusha's recovery, he had once again found—*"Nevertheless!"*—that the God who created and loved him had strengthened him to acknowledge that love by submissive acquiescence. Thus he stood in his pulpit as a model of "ONE who *Lives* in the midst of *Deaths*," and took as his doctrine *"Dying Daily,"* whose several meanings he elucidated. To die daily means to keep a lively sense that we daily progress toward death, that every day may be our dying day; means to die to the world, mortifying ourselves so as to regard the world as a *"Despicable* Thing." In dying daily we draw out the bitterness from death itself. Determined to make his cross bear still more fruit, "tho' the cross be but a dry sort of a tree," he preached another sermon three days after Jerusha's funeral, on the doctrine that A Good Man is a Strong Man. But this day, a day, he said, "which truly may be called, a *Night,* rather than a *Day,*" he confessed with some weariness to his own need for strength. "The Poor Man, who Preaches these Things," he told his congregation, "is far from asserting his own *Claim* to all this Character; and his *Want* of it, is the bitterest *Cup* in his *Adversity.* All that he can say, is, That when you, O dear People of God, are Pressing after this Character, he hopes, you will Pray for *him,* that he may share with you, in so great a Consolation."

In December, with his household recovered, Mather began dedicating himself to new or more active exercises of devotion. He felt that the events of the last month—"a *Month* which *devoured* my Family"—obliged him to renew his practice of setting apart whole days of prayer and fasting. The unfamiliar quiet in the house owing to the removal of small children from it also allowed new exertions for his surviving children, none now under seven years old. He would labor for Creasy's conversion, and furnish each living child with a "Closet of Remedies" by which they might relieve the miserable. For himself, he prayed for divine aid in behaving with discretion and purity in his single state. Some "silly People" had already brought him " a foolish Message from a Gentlewoman," but he felt he must spend the rest of his life in widowerhood.

As Mather digested and began to ruminate on his loss, he doted particularly on the meaning of Sacrifice. Since God had lately so much called him to such a work, he desired to develop a special skill and will for it. He proposed an exercise to himself: he would look on all his enjoyments, very often look on the dearest and most valuable of them, and in looking conceive to himself a sacrificing thought. "*O my dear Saviour,*" he would think, "*If thou shalt be most glorified, by my having this taken from me, I resign it, I forego it, I am content and willing to be without it.*" Accustoming himself to Sacrifice would earn him a true share in the royal Priesthood. By accustoming himself to sacrifice, too, he would be "prepared for *all Events.*" At some moment he wrote out on the back cover of one of his notebooks the names of all the children he had fathered, drawing a line to separate the offspring he had had by his first and second wives, both now dead.

> Abigail
> Katharin[e]
> Mary
> Increase
> Abigail
> Mehetabel
> Hannah
> Increase
> Samuel
> _____
> Elizabeth
> Samuel
> Nathanael
> Jerusha
> Eleazer
> Martha

Beside the list he wrote down the dreadful tally:

> Of 15,
> Dead, 9
> Living, 6

As was his custom, Mather closed his diary for the year 1713 on February 11, 1714, the day before his birthday, noting that "The fifty first Year of my Age is terminated."

Mather's fifty-second year began badly. On April 4, his mother, Maria Mather, died at the age of seventy-two. He and his father preached and published complementary sermons on her death. Increase dedicated his sermon to his children, telling them they had lost a "Tender Mother" and compulsorily reminding them they "will very shortly be *Fatherless* as well as Motherless," yet composing a loving tribute to his companion of fifty-two years, a woman, he said, who "did me good and not evil all the days of her life." Cotton, in his sermon, drew for his congregation the character of an ideal mother, one with a strong natural inclination to comfort her children, pray for them in distress, teach them their catechism, groan to heaven over their spiritual estate. When such a mother sees a son now a man, and a worthy and useful and noted man, then her affection to such a son will be "very Passionate, very Rapturous, very Marvellous, nothing will be equal to the Transport of it." Then he explained that in making his ideal portrait of a mother he had had, of course, "somebody *sitting* before me for it."

Of course, too, Mather cautioned his flock that while sorrow for a mother's death is allowable, God has better comforts for His children than has the most affectionate mother in the world, God extends to His children more than maternal consolation, takes mothers away to bring His children to more entire dependence on Him alone, teaches His children not to expect comfort from the children of men, in whom there can be no comfort.

IV

SILENCE DOGOOD
(1714-1724)

⤳⤳

"Mather. *What* a force. . . ."

—VALÉRY LARBAUD, quoted in William Carlos
Williams, *In the American Grain* (1925)

The diary of Cotton Mather is a treasure-trove to the abnormal psychologist. The
thing would be inconceivable if the record were not in print. What a crooked and
diseased mind lay back of those eyes that were forever spying out occasions to
magnify self! He grovels in proud self-abasement. He distorts the most obvious
reality. His mind is clogged with the strangest miscellany of truth and marvel. He
labors to acquire the possessions of a scholar, but he listens to old wives' tales with
greedy avidity. In all his mental processes the solidest fact falls into fantastic perspective.

—VERNON LOUIS PARRINGTON, *The Colonial Mind
1620–1800* (1927)

His character was now definitely formed, his mind at fourteen had reached the limit
of its growth: all else afterward was mere expansion in the sense of things observed
and memorized, a collected mass of information, but the actual capacity of his mind
was measured finally at adolescence. He was a typical wonder-child.

—KATHERINE ANNE PORTER, "Affectation of
Praehiminincies (A.D. 1663–1675)" (1934)

. . . a witches' chowder
(All my eye and Cotton Mather!)

—ROBERT FROST, "Clear and Colder" (1936)

Read (if you can) the writings of the great doctors of seventeenth-century Calvin-
ism, the heirs of Calvin and Beza, Buchanan and Knox. Their masters may have been
grim, but there is a certain heroic quality about their grimness, a literary power
about their writing, an intellectual force in their minds. The successors are also
grim, but they are grim and mean. Perkins and 'Smectymnuus' in England, Rivetus
and Voëtius in Holland, Baillie and Rutherford in Scotland, Desmarets and Jurieu in
France, Francis Turrettini in Switzerland, Cotton Mather in America—what a gallery

of intolerant bigots, narrow-minded martinets, timid conservative defenders of re-
pellent dogmas, instant assailants of every new or liberal idea, inquisitors and witch-
burners!

—H. R. TREVOR-ROPER, *The European Witch-Craze*
. . . and Other Essays (1969)

. . . twisted with subtlety, like the dark, learned, well-connected Cotton Mather. The
supreme bookman: Mather wrote 450 books, all printed. It seems a slander that he
could have done so much harm when all his nights and days were spent writing and
looking up brilliant quotations.

Mather, the Salem witch-hanger, was a professional man of letters employed to
moralize and subdue. His truer self was a power-crazed mind bent on destroying
darkness with darkness, applying his cruel, high-minded obsessed intellect to the
extermination of witch and neurotic. His soft bookish hands are indelibly stained
with blood—a black image to set against our white busts of Washington and Lincoln. Perhaps in his cross-examinations of the harmless and foolish, Cotton Mather
oddly exposed a deep, symbolic, incongruous intelligence that nearly made him
immortal.

—ROBERT LOWELL, "New England—and Further"
(1977)

10

Lydia Lee George

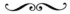

AT THE TIME of Cotton Mather's birth, his family home on Cotton's Hill overlooked an islanded peninsula on the edge of a wilderness, inhabited by about three thousand Puritans. But now, some fifty years later, Boston had about twelve thousand diverse inhabitants, and its handsome houses, public amusements, and tempting shops made it in many minds a city.

To be sure, Boston remained in ways a vulnerable place—occasionally rattled by earthquakes (one tremor shifted wall stones at Cambridge in 1705), swept by epidemic diseases, imperiled by fire. In October 1711, a drunken oakum picker accidentally ignited rubbish in the backyard of an old South End tenement, touching off the most destructive fire in the history of the colonies. Unextinguished for seven hours and visible twenty leagues at sea, the conflagration consumed whole streets of houses—including the treasured First Church and the Town House—and lay the central district of Boston in ashes. A growing and heterogeneous populace met such disasters with thoughts less of invasion, however, than of expansion. Members of the First Church erected a new and much finer meetinghouse—in brick, seventy-two feet long, its three stories surmounted by a bell tower that dominated the center of Boston. A new Town House went up, enclosing the courts and the government meeting rooms; also made of brick and more imposing than the old Town House, it quickly became Boston's showplace.

Indeed a half century after Cotton Mather's birth, Boston everywhere manifested physical growth and urbanization. Of the town's three thousand houses, about a third were now brick or stone, often distinguished by fine masonry, in part to resist fire, a hazard also reduced by a fire department of twenty men and six engines. Streets had been widened, extended, and given official names, and until it proved too expensive were effectively cleaned by carts and horses hauling off dirt and refuse at town expense. By 1720 the town had the finest highway system in the colonies, superior to that of most English cities, and a sewer system that provided the best drainage of any town in America or England.

Despite the restraining effects of war, too, Boston had become the main entrepôt in the colonies for European goods. Through it, New Hampshire lumber, Connecticut grain, and New York furs passed to Europe, England, and the West Indies, to be exchanged for wines, salt, and other foreign commodities. Boston also led all other towns in shipbuilding. Ship masts in the harbor, said one observer in 1719, "make a kind of Wood of Trees like that which we see upon the River of Thames." In 1716 a lighthouse was completed at the entrance in the harbor to facilitate navigation. A new fortification, Fort William, was built in the harbor, mounted with about a hundred pieces of ordnance. The crowded shoreline, dense with wharves, gained a spectacular addition in 1714, together with the rebuilding of the South End, by the completion of the extraordinary Long Wharf. Built the width of King Street, the wharf extended this main street of Boston into the bay for nearly a third of a mile, providing a pier at which even very large ships could unload without the help of lighters. Debarked at the Long Wharf, a visitor could proceed directly up King Street about eight hundred feet to the new Town House, at the heart of Boston.

To walk that gently arching path was to have an alluring, Fifth Avenue view of the town's vigorous commercial life. A stroller might begin by inspecting the cornucopia of goods sold from warehouses built on the Long Wharf itself—rigging and casks of nails, cider and wine, women's muffs and necklaces, gunpowder and indigo, "choice Pictures, fit for any Gentleman's Dining Room or Stair-case"—then proceed up King Street, a busy commercial thoroughfare, past the shops of the London jeweler James Boyer, or of Andrew Faneuil offering silks and French salt, or Philip Hedman vending fine black cloth and *"New fashion Looking-Glasses,"* stopping perhaps at Selby's or Hall's Coffee House along the way, or detouring to the signs of the Bunch of Grapes, the Baker's Arms, or the "Black Boy a Grinding," until arriving at the central Town House, surrounded by a thriving merchant exchange and the Exchange Tavern, there to browse at still other retail shops selling cloth or books or prints or toys.

Social life kept pace with commercial. In their houses, furniture, tables, and dress, it was said, Bostonians lived as splendidly and showily as the most considerable tradespeople in London. Between 1700 and 1711 sixteen new booksellers opened; by 1720 the town had five busy printing presses and three newspapers. New elementary schools had been established, and under President Leverett once tottering Harvard had revived. The fifteen or twenty undergraduates of fifty years ago had multiplied by 1719 to one hundred and twenty; by the next year many of them were housed in Massachusetts Hall, a brick building a hundred feet long and forty wide. Around town at various times, one might take lessons in dancing, treble violin, and spinet from George Brownell; see "Moving Pictures" featuring animated mills and ships; attend a horse race run in Cambridge for a £20 purse; or on the Bowling Green watch a man named John Coleson baiting a bear.

Urban pleasures also brought urban problems. With its several bawdy houses, rampant public drunkenness, and increasing numbers of poor, Boston experienced much petty crime, and with that an uncustomary locking of doors and a growing constabulary. In 1711 an act was passed for suppressing robberies and assaults, punishing muggers by branding in the forehead and six months' imprisonment, with death for a second conviction. Civic violence was aggravated by Boston's ever larger number of slaves, who were sold all over town, including near the churches. Scarce a house in Boston except the very poor, it was reported, lacked black servants, and every issue of the *News-Letter* carried ads for "A Negro Man Aged about 16 years, to be Sold," "A Negro Child to be given for the Rearing," "A Negro Girl aged about Eight years, to be Sold." The slave population was not only large but also resentful, prone to theft, rape, murder, and arson. In the summer of 1723, after a few blacks had been publicly whipped for setting fires, it was rumored that blacks planned to burn down Boston itself.

Here a John Eliot in his apostolic leather girdle could only have seemed, for better or worse, preposterous, while, as one English visitor wrote in 1719, "A Gentleman from *London* would almost think himself at home in *Boston*." This Boston of wharves laden with muffs and prints, of pilastered brick houses—and of exhibitions of bearbaiting—made a fit setting for Cotton Mather's marriage to Lydia Lee George.

*

In some ways, Lydia seemed to Mather such a woman as he had not dared marry when, a dozen years earlier, he resigned young Kate Maccarty. Among many appealing elements of her past and personality, she was the daughter of the Rev. Samuel Lee, no longer a well-known figure, but one of the most intelligent and forceful men in the history of early New England: "hardly ever a more *Universally Learned* Person," Mather remarked, "trod the *American Strand.*" Educated at Oxford and appointed by Cromwell to the ministry of an Independent church near London, he emigrated in 1686 to New England, settling as a minister in Bristol, Rhode Island, where his inheritance from his very wealthy father enabled him to erect a fine house.

Although Lee returned to England after the Glorious Revolution of 1689, his few years' stay in New England impressed. From America he sent home naturalistic accounts of the Indians, of rattlesnakes, and of American diseases and epidemics. Several of his sermons were published in Boston and rank among the very best American Puritan sermons by their originality, verbal artistry, and deep acquaintance with natural science. The sale of his library in Boston in 1693 occasioned the first printed sale catalogue of books in New England: about one thousand titles in sixteen double-columned pages, including "*Newtons* Astronomy." To Lydia and his three other daughters he left a rich estate of £1300 each, plus his many manuscripts on chemistry, medicine, and other subjects. Inevitably Lee's interests and accomplishments brought him in touch with the Mathers. His daughter Anne was a member of their church, and in one letter he speaks of Increase as his "*highly honoured friend*" and mentions sending two books to "your good son." Cotton took extensive notes on nine sermons preached by Lee, and wrote a Preface to Lee's *Great Day of Judgment* (1692). He also extracted much material from Lee's published and manuscript writings for "Biblia Americana," with admiring acknowledgments of their authorship.

This heritage of intellectual distinction and family wealth already recommended Lydia to Mather. But her previous marriage added the extra attraction of civic prominence and probably even greater wealth. Her deceased husband, the merchant John George, had been a leader in the growth of Boston. A town selectman in 1701 and 1713, George was placed on a committee of thirty-one chosen in 1708 to formulate a scheme for the better government of Boston; five years later he and some associates proposed to the General Court the erection of the lighthouse at the entrance to the harbor. He was also one of the original proprietors of the Long Wharf, perhaps the greatest civic project undertaken in colonial Boston. Earlier he had owned a warehouse on the Boston dock, where he sold among other wares gunpowder, grindstones, and anchors, in partnership with a man named Nathan Howell, who was also his son-in-law and co- or part-owner with him of at least three sloops. With the building of the Long Wharf, George moved his warehouse there, dispensing maritime supplies from the great wharf itself. His sizable business dealings involved him in sizable litigation: the court cases involving him occupy nearly a page and a half in the index to the Judicial Court files.

Well-to-do and socially visible, the Georges were liberal in their religion. John George was one of the original subscribers toward building a Church of England chapel in Boston in 1689, and later one of the original undertakers of Colman's Brattle church, to which he and his wife, and their son-in-law Nathan Howell, belonged. Colman's close advisory relation with Lydia is revealing of her worldliness. Not long after the founding of the church, as noted earlier, Lydia asked his advice about her manner of dress, confessing she spent too much thought on it and indulged the "vanity of Vying with others." Colman however reassured her that her dress was suitable to her plentiful estate, high birth, and prominent station: "You have been educated in the wearing rich apparel; Mr. George chooses you should continue it, it is not offensive nor grievous to sober Christians." This education cannot have been slowed by George's death in November, 1714, at the age of forty-nine. Making Lydia sole executrix of his will, he left her a great estate that included their pew in the Brattle church, a black servant and an Indian woman, and two-thirds the value of his household goods, of his part of the Long Wharf, of his warehouse, and of the stocks and profits of his partnership with Nathan Howell.

Mather waited scarcely a month after George's death before visiting this rich and distinguished widow, accompanied by his children. As Lydia's pastor, Benjamin Colman told Increase Mather that some people placed "inconvenient constructions" on the visit, presumably because of the recency of George's death. Cotton, who had grown if not warm toward Colman at least affably correct, explained that he had intended writing to Lydia instead, and was aware at the very time of the visit that "I did imprudently." His misgivings arose not only from the timing, but also, as he told Colman, from his "unrecommendable circumstances." For one thing, his financial situation was the reverse of Lydia's. During his quarrel with Dudley over the allegedly illicit trade with the French, he had been compelled to rebuke one of the traders, John Phillips, the brother of his deceased wife Abigail. In doing so he enraged his father-in-law, who, it was hinted to him, had cut him and his children from his will.

Even more than he felt unpresentable, Mather felt weary. His years of public quarreling and of isolation in Boston, the harrowing deaths in his family only a year ago, had left him worthy to be called, he said, "*Medio-*

morto, that is, Half-dead." He told Colman that although people kept suggesting that he marry, and although he was sometimes foolishly tempted, he had grown used to a mortified life and at last always came to his senses:

> It is, I confess, too natural for us foolish old men, when we have a whimsy from every quarter buzzed into our ears, to think a little, *what there may be in it.* I have, no doubt, foolishly enough been ready to fall into this weakness. But as yet my old age has not got so far but that I presently recollect, I presently am sensible of the *delusion,* presently bring all to rights, as a dying man ought to do.

Despite the sensible tone, Mather's assurances to Colman that he was too impoverished and worn out to consider marriage seem to have been in part motivated by a different concern: that Colman would resent his suit as an effort to lure Lydia from his ministry, conceivably from his affections. For Mather added in a postscript that he had told Lydia in person and in writing that Colman's "conversation would be so profitable and so comfortable there would never be the least need of any other." And he hoped, he said, "I need not ask you to continue in affording as much of it as is possible to one so very worthy of it." This curious hope sounds like jealousy expressed in Matherese. However that may be, Mather assured Colman that he had resolved to visit Lydia no more, affording neighbors no reason to suspect him "of any designs not proper for me."

But actually Mather was smitten by Lydia George, and felt not "*Mediomorto*" but rejuvenated. For a while he continued his suit eagerly but from a distance. In February or March 1715, he sought help from Mrs. Gurdon Saltonstall, the wife of the governor of Connecticut. Buoyant, he told her he had "struck for a very valuable fish" but must dangle an unknown number of months, like the whaler who knows to "let the fish run for a considerable and convenient while." While he sat it out he asked Mrs. Saltonstall to write in his favor to Lydia, promising that the best people in the country approved her entertaining his suit.

In the same confidently ebullient mood Mather sent Lydia herself a long letter of courtship. Mixing affection, formality, and banter, it was nicely composed to disclose the depth of his feeling without making her feel rushed. He addressed her as "Madam," as in recognition of her social rank and accomplishments she seems generally to have been called. Respectful also of her intelligence, clearly an important ingredient in her appeal to him, he began by offering, earnestly but good-humoredly, a sort of syllogism from whose premises her "good skill at making inferences" might draw the correct conclusions about him. If, he said, he were a person who spent his life doing good to people of all sorts, who loved his neighbors, and who prayed for those who abused him, then it could be "reasonably inferred" that someone who might come in the nearest possible relation to him would be "loved by him as much as can be wished by her." Admiring Lydia's "wisdom," he said, and feeling honored to be sometime admitted to her tea table, he wished to take no step of which she would disapprove, nor press for any public appearance she might judge unseasonable. But in the privacy of his letter he wished her to know that his regard for her qualities, and his desire to devote himself to her, were enormous:

> ... he begs your leave that it may not be thought too soon for him to tell you, that your bright accomplishments, your shining piety, your polite education, your superiour capacity, and the most refined sense, and incomparable sweetness of temper, together with a constellation of all the perfections that he can desire to see related unto him, have made a vast impression upon him.

Ready to strike now, he also made it plain that he considered Lydia a record catch:

> If ever he should be so inexpressibly happy as to enjoy you, he could not but receive you as a wondrous gift of God unto him; a token that the unworthiest of men had yet obtained favor of the Lord. Such an idea he has conceived of you, that everything you shall be or say or do, will forever please him; and the pleasing of you will be his continual study and rapture.

In his desire to marry Lydia, he added, he had the general approbation of the public, especially the "more praying people," and he concluded by asking permission to say to her personally the same things he had written to her.

Lydia did grant Mather at least one interview alone with her, around March 21, 1715—in order, she said, that he might fully know her mind. This she did not bother to disclose in syllogisms. Regarding his suit, she said she desired to "hear no more of it," and that he would "speak and think no more of it." During their several hours of conversation she told him nothing else he wanted to hear, either. She suggested that other available persons would be more "agreeable" than herself, in whom people's prayers for him were more likely to be answered. Had he mentioned nothing of marriage, his visits, as a minister, would have been a consolation and satisfaction. But she forbid him to write her any more letters, and insisted on his making it known that, as to their rumored courtship, "there is nothing in it."

While hearing out this flat rejection, Mather tried to be, he said, "as calm, and as pertinent, and as obliging, as my dull Wits" allowed. He proposed that instead of saying "there is nothing in it," he would tell people that his suit was a matter which "Madam is not at present disposed to hear of." Lydia made the obvious but discouraging reply: people would say, "why does she entertain him? if she have no purpose hereafter to allow of his Intentions?" No, she was firm on it, she wanted him to discontinue. He said at last that, as a testimony of his esteem for her, he would entirely sacrifice his satisfaction to hers. She answered, "*Say, and Hold.*"

Rejection always unstabilized Mather, but Lydia's made him writhe. He blamed himself for having blunderingly antagonized her: "I have hitherto done just nothing that is Right. And it is a killing thing to me, to think, that I have been led into Steps, that have been so very offensive, and have occasion'd so much Trouble, to a person for whom I must always have so great a veneration." A relative of Lydia's suggested that he try to see her one more time, but he feared reviving the gossip which had helped alienate Lydia from him. The prospect of receiving further "wounds from an Hand, I so much admire" also worried him: "My tender Spirit and Health will suffer so much, and I shall be so unhinged for my Employments." And would persistence help? Lydia had made known unambiguously, bluntly, dismally, what she wanted: "that I would come no more." Brooding on her charge to him—"*Say, and Hold*"—he reaffirmed his decision to respect her wishes, and to stay away, "tho, the Earth could not afford me a greater pleasure, than her most agreeable Conversation."

But only for a while. For by this time Mather was deeply, romantically in love with Lydia. Although his first two wives, Abigail Phillips and Elizabeth Clark, make phantom figures in his diaries, little mentioned until their deaths, it is clear that in marrying them he sought irreproachably pious women whom he might bring to Christ and who would honor the ministry. But Lydia appealed to his restrained or disguised sensuality, worldliness, and ambition. His diaries speak little of wishing to aid her salvation and much of her endearments and station, little of his prayers but much of his fondness. Unable now to stay away, he decided to interpret Lydia's prohibitions against his visits as temporary, and reached out to her through her relative Thomas Craighead, an Irish minister and physician recently arrived in New England. He asked Craighead to assure Lydia that he would honor his resolutions to "keep out of sight" until

Colman directed him to appear, although formed merely "to gratify her; whom I can undergo anything to oblige, even while I have never yet received one favorable word or Look from her." Delay he would, but he could not desist. He also asked Craighead to tell Lydia that despite her protests, "I can by no means lay aside those vast Respects but must renew my Endeavors one Day, to make her yet more sensible of them."

In the spring Mather managed to penetrate Lydia's fear of gossip and, perhaps, her reservations about him. His courtship may have been spurred by the remarriage in May of his seventy-six-year-old father—"The marvellous old man," he noted two years earlier, "continues to do notable things"—who married Ann Lake Cotton, the fifty-two-year-old widow of his nephew. By what means Cotton Mather forwarded his own suit is unknown; the surviving evidence consists of several undated drafts of letters and notes, apparently written in April and May, indicating both progress and delight. One scrap reads: "I was never got so far in it, as I now with unspeakable Joy find myself. And now, my Lovely Creature, Do you go study my Lesson; and get beyond me." The draft of another letter, playfully addressed to "my *Mabel*," again hints at Lydia's attachment to Colman, and Mather's view of him as a rival for her attention; it reassures her that "The only Damage you are Like to suffer by me, is, that I am Like to take you from the ministry of so true a *Chrysostom*," and promises to repair the damage by procuring "your Enjoyment of as much of him, as I can help you to." Although the scraps also contain routine admonitions that Lydia not set her love for him above love for God, they generally read less like communications from the minister of the North Church than like *billets-doux:* "My—(Inexpressible!) I am afraid you been't well, because my head has ached pretty much this afternoon. The pain of my heart will be much greater than that of my head if it be really so"—signed, "one who loves you inexpressibly."

On June 24, Lydia Lee George and Cotton Mather put their signatures to a prenuptial contract. Many colonies permitted such agreements, by which women might preserve their property rights after marriage; Increase Mather and his new wife had legally bound themselves to have no say in each other's estates. The contract between the wealthy Lydia and the penurious Cotton, however, protected Lydia alone. Her desire for such an agreement can be variously interpreted: fear of being exploited as a rich widow; distrust of Mather's financial sense; the desire to be in control. Whatever its impetus, the contract stipulated that because Lydia was "vested in her own right with some Considerable Estate," it was not unreasonable that she retain power to manage it "according to her own

mind and Will." Mather agreed to give her sole and complete management of the property she owned and its income, to:

> Impower and employ as she shall think fit All the Lands Tenements mon-
> ey goods Chatells or other Estate whatsoever which of right is belonging
> appertaining or payable unto her, and to take Receive and dispose of her
> own use all the Issues profits benefits and Incomes thence to be made. . . .

More specifically, Lydia's control over her estate was understood to exist
"without any Let hindrance or denial of the sd Cotton Mather." Mather
bound himself to the agreement under a huge penalty of two thousand
pounds.

Ten days later, on July 5, Mather and Lydia were married, by Increase
Mather. Cotton spent the following night in private devotions, making
"New Espousals to HIM," thanking God for affording him such a consort.
On the Sabbath he preached at the Brattle church—once the site of his
sorest anger, now of his greatest joy—"which I am robbing of an invaluable treasure and beauty." He chose a text from I Sam., concerning "the
dark Hours of a *sorrowful Spirit*" who poured out petitions to God in his
darkness and was answered.

It seemed that way. "Perhaps the married State," Mather wrote a
month after the wedding, "never Exhibited an Example of a Greater Harmony, than what is between me, and the admirable Companion, which
Heaven has bestowed upon me." His pleasure with Lydia ended the long
period of cheerless mortification and angry gloom brought on by his
quarrels with Governor Dudley, his fears of an Anglican Harvard, satiric
verses on his "Diploma," the losses of his children and of Elizabeth, a
six-year rut of endless misconstructions transformed into Goods Devised,
endless celebrations of the "*Heavenly Skill* of *Sacrificing.*" Now reaping
instead, his life renewed, he filled his letters and diaries for the next
eighteen months with superlative praises for the "best of women in the
American World," the "greatest of all my Temporal Blessings," the "Collection of a Thousand Lovelinesses!"

No portrait of Lydia has come down, but Mather found her, among her
other attractions, beautiful. Doting on her charming physical presence,
he again and again was forced to remind himself that her "Beauty lies in
her having so much of His Image upon her," to caution himself that "in
the midst of the Admirations wherewith I Look upon her, I must presently
think, She is nothing but what God makes her to be." Argue himself as he
would, delight in Lydia's creatureliness tinged even their mutual devotions with carnality. When they often prayed together in his study with

tears and moans, he found himself inspired: "The Company of my Excellent Consort with me, had its Influence, to make the Services of the Day go on with the more Soaring Devotions. I took her with me into my Library; where we together poured out our Souls, and our prayers, and our Tears before the Lord; and also blessed Him for one another."

Whatever subtle sensuality lay in such soaring devotions together, Mather of course took seriously the challenge of refining Lydia's religious life. He wished, he said, to help her toward "those Attainments in the *royal Priesthood,* wherein the Life of my own Spirit lies." To this end he resolved to convey to her the main thoughts in his reading of the Pietist John Arndt, and to encourage her visits to the poor in the neighborhood. His success is uncertain, for no record exists of her being admitted to the North Church, and she evidently missed Colman's ministry; an unaddressed letter by Mather, quite certainly to Colman, remarks that Lydia "Laments it as the principal Calamity of our End of the Town, that she sees you so seldom." Just the same, Mather found to his delight that her refinements of education, birth, and station were matched by superior spiritual capacities: "oh! how happy am I," he wrote, "in the Conversion of so fine a Soul, and one so capable of rising and soaring to the higher Flights of Piety!" Lydia could do nothing wrong.

Mather's removal to a handsome new house sharpened his feeling of unaccustomed pleasure and good fortune. The house had been rented for him by his congregation before his marriage, late in January 1715; he probably proposed their doing so, perhaps to make his prospects seem more appealing to Lydia. Although the congregation rented the house only "until some further provision be made for him," he apparently lived there the rest of his life, the church supplying his rent and repairs. Confusions in the surviving records make it difficult to locate the house certainly, but it seems to have stood on Ship Street in the North End, close beside the wharves and harbor.

Mather now lived in what seems to have been an unusually fine wooden building, much more ample and comfortable than his first two homes, befitting Lydia's rank. Three and perhaps four stories high, it contained both a little and great parlor, a great chamber, and several garrets and cellars, with adjoining yards, gardens, and pastureland. The size may be estimated from Mather's having convened a church council in his "spacious Hall," and gathered a local "Society of Pious Children" in his "capacious Library, which is three Stories above my Study." In the garden he strolled and meditated, enjoying the springtime arrival of the "glories of Nature." He walked too among the vessels wharved just below the house, talking to the seafaring people and giving them books of piety. Whether to manage this large house Lydia brought with her the servants willed her by her deceased husband is unknown; Mather took along his servant Onesimus, but Onesimus began to prove "wicked, and grows useless, Froward, Immorigerous [rebellious]." Around 1716 Mather allowed him to purchase his release, by putting up money toward buying a black youth to serve in his stead—probably the "little Boy" Mather acquired in November 1716, whom he named Obadiah. Onesimus continued to help around the house, however, and in addition to Obadiah and very likely other servants, domestic chores were shared for a while by a Spanish Indian girl.

Altogether, in his new habitation Mather felt as happy as he believed the world could make him, and he often exclaimed cheerfully over the welcome, surprising reversal of his fortunes: "A most wonderful Prosperity! A valuable Consort! A Comfortable Dwelling! A kind Neighbourhood! . . . Blessings without Number."

*

To Mather's great content and gratification, Lydia quickly formed an affectionate relationship with his six surviving children. He found them willing to obey her directions and follow her example, taking "unspeakable Delight, in the Incomparable Mother, which God had bestow'd upon them." Once when Lydia left on a trip, Mather described for her in a letter the lamentations "among all your Children, when that word Mother not come home, was heard among us . . . . We are not sensible that the sun shines into any Room in the House, nor that our Chocolate has any Sugar in it." (As a chirpy token of his own lovelorn condition "while the best Creature I ever saw is out of my sight," he began growing a beard.) His daughter Abigail may not have moved with him into the new house, for a month after her father's marriage she herself married an attorney named Daniel Willard. (A year later the couple presented Mather his first grandchild, a girl.) Lydia also had a daughter, Katharin, who had been married to John George's partner Nathan Howell. After his death she married the young merchant Samuel Sewall, the judge's nephew; the couple may have lived a while with the Mathers.

Samuel, about eight and a half years old at the time of Mather's remarriage, showed a dismaying appetite for diversion. Mather often pondered what to do to raise his mind "above the debasing Meannesses of Play," and among other things composed and had him turn into Latin some sentences about the right uses of play. To nourish the boy's conversion he also considered having him keep sermon notebooks, as he had done, and offered Sammy his library foɪ holding religious exercises with a "Society of sober and pious Lads." Like his father too, Sammy retained in his personality something sportive, but by the age of twelve or thirteen had begun exhibiting his father's learning, literary tastes, and piety as well. Able by then to converse with Mather in Latin, he kept a commonplace book of "Quotidiana," the entries indicating a bent at once scientific, literary, and filiopietistic—material from Grew's *Cosmologia Sacra* (1701) and from Bayle on comets, but also excerpts from Boileau on style, verse quotations from Dryden and Pope, and illustrations from "Biblia Americana." By the summer of 1719 the "very promising little Spark," as Mather delightedly thought him, was ready for entrance to Harvard.

Sammy's admission forced Mather to palliate his bitter relation to John Leverett, still the college president. He wrote to Leverett in July 1719, recommending Sammy's qualities and asking Leverett's care for him as president, tutor, and surrogate father. Sammy, he said, was of a "capacity good enough . . . is of a temper singularly sweet and sociable, is of unspotted morals, not without a tincture and a tendency of the more vital piety, has the manly prudence and reserve in which his years are somewhat anticipated." With that he left Sammy to Leverett's "wise, and kind, and paternal tuition"—as he brought himself to describe the man he still considered unworthy of the presidency, and privately detested. With his habitually elaborate paternal care, he also wrote out for Sammy an essay-length set of "Directions for a SON going to the College," advising him to read Scripture daily, peruse books of piety (including *Magnalia Christi Americana,* especially for the "lives of the excellent persons in it"), and fix his mind on the fact that the chief end of his life was to serve God. For Sammy's success in his studies, Mather advised above all that he shun "profane and vicious persons, as you would the pestilence."

One dark intrusion on Mather's new happiness came from his daughter Katharine. Not only had he always owned a special fondness for daughters: "The Tenderness of one for the dearest *Lamb* in the World," he wrote, "could not be represented in a more lively Expression of it than this; *It was unto him as a Daughter.*" But he had also given special care to politely educating and cultivating this "*Lamb* inexpressibly dear to him," so that Katy could make waxworks, play musical instruments and sing, compose pious verses, and read Latin and Hebrew fluently. A remarkable example of youthful piety also, and very much a child of Cotton Mather, without being crabbed or morose she delighted in religious retirements, experienced conversion, and wrote on one occasion, "I take an unspeakable pleasure in all manner of *Beneficence*. If I can see *Opportunities* to *Do Good,* I need no *Arguments* to move me to it." Seemingly a sweet and brave girl she apparently got along well with her new step-mother, whom she would not call "mother-in-law" because Lydia acted toward her like a real mother.

But about a year and a half after Mather's marriage, Katharine became the tenth of his fifteen children to die. Like her siblings she had been infected during the 1713 measles epidemic; she survived, but to a residue of the infection was attributed her falling ill in April 1716, the beginning of an eight-month decline that ended with her death in December, of what was described as consumption. As Mather again set before himself the sacrifice he must be prepared to make, he traced her deterioration in his diary, punctuating the otherwise blissful account of his new marriage with cries of "Ah! My dying Daughter! My dear dying Daughter!" As Katy lingered, wasted by consumption and given up by the physicians, he tried to treat her by a root grown in Lebanon, Connecticut, and sent him by his friend John Winthrop; known as Culvers Root, it was to be dried, pulverized, and mixed with honey into hazelnut-sized pills. But by November Katharine could not attend family prayers, and Mather prayed with her daily in her room. In December she expressed doubts about her acceptability to Christ; he told her that her trial of faith was from Satan, who knew she was to go where he could not, and that "she should see herself called into a *Marvellous Light.*" He spent much time near the end sitting with her, trying "to strengthen her in her Agonies." She died on a Sabbath at three in the morning and was mourned, despite the snow and cold, at a large funeral. That she might outlive her death by doing good after it, Mather published *Victorina* (1717), a sermon on the pleasures of true piety, containing an account of her life.

Katharine's death did not diminish Mather's satisfaction in his marriage. He was pleased, too, by signs of maturity in his often errant son, Increase, Jr. Alone of Mather's children, sixteen-year-old Creasy was not at home for his father's wedding, being then in England. Mather had agreed to pay the boy's passage aboard a ship commanded by the son of the merchant John Frizzell, there to travel as a passenger but to perform and learn the duties of a sailor. Although resigned to Creasy's having chosen a life of action rather than of study, he seems to have had reservations about Creasy's entering the maritime trades, but thought it harmful to disregard the boy's actual abilities: "I have been perhaps too willing to indulge and follow the genius of a child in the choice of a business for him," he confided to Sir William Ashurst, "as knowing that if that be not very much consulted, a child will never prove considerable." As he sometimes did in other circumstances, he wrote out a letter to Frizzell, for Creasy to send and sign as if by himself. "'Tis too well known," he had Creasy explain, "that my inclination is more for business than for learning. And being inclined unto the business of the sea, my friends have a prospect of my arriving sooner to some figure on that element than on the long wharf or the dock." In the letter he had Creasy tell Frizzell that having perfected himself in the theory of navigation, he must take to sea to learn the practice. Though a novice, he hoped he would not have to "enter at the cook-room-door." Yet he promised to obey orders and apply himself to every shipboard duty of which his superiors judged him capable. He also requested a fortnight's leave, upon arriving in London, to visit his uncle Samuel in Witney.

The visit turned into a stay of several months. Samuel, about ten years younger than Cotton, was the minister of a Congregational church in Witney, near Oxford. He invited Creasy to remain with him in the belief that Increase Mather—so long and so often planning or foreseeing a return to England—was at last actually about to return, to deliver an address from the Massachusetts ministers to the new king. (The North Church voted unanimously against Increase's mission, however: "I am now like to die in New England," Increase lamented, "whereas two months ago I was like to die in England.") Samuel found Creasy troublesome. The boy arrived in Witney with debts he had somehow incurred, only ten shillings in his pocket, and but one shirt, "so bare in every respect," Samuel said, "that I was perfectly ashamed." Samuel had credit extended to Creasy at a local store so he could buy clothing, and wrote to Cotton asking him to send a remittance for his son, to be managed by someone else. "I perceive," he told his brother, "he is infected with the disease which is the blemish of the Family viz. to spend inconsiderately and take no thought about providing against future unavoidable occasions. If I can I will cure him."

But curing Creasy was not simple. His mother—Mather's first wife, Abigail—had died when he was only three, and his father's remarriage rapidly produced several other children by a stepmother. Something in Creasy had stayed restless and turbulent. Samuel found that when he took the boy on a visit to tempting London, he had to "keep a pretty strict eye over him"; he decided to keep him at Witney, lest he return to his father "with a worse Character than he had when he came." Mather wrote to Creasy sometime in the fall to reinforce his brother's admonitions, instructing him to heed Samuel's lessons and urging him to make "all the Vices of Dishonesty, Debauchery, and False-speaking . . . abominable to you."

Mather's disappointment in Creasy's erratic behavior was tempered, however, by recognition and respectful love of his spiritedness and lack of malice. Thus he was wracked to learn in April that Creasy had been stricken with rheumatism and had lost the use of his limbs: "Oh! The Anguish with which I am to cry unto God, that He would yet be gracious to this poor Child, and make him a new Creature, and an useful Man, and return him to me! Oh! the Resignation to which I am called on this Occasion!"

For once, Mather was spared very protracted anguish about his children. The letter from Samuel informing him of Creasy's illness was apparently long delayed, for only a month after he received it, Creasy himself returned from abroad. He returned not only, it seems, hale, but to Mather's relief also greatly changed, "much polished, much improved, better than ever disposed. . . . I am astonished at the Favors of the prayer-hearing Lord. O my Father, my Father, how good a thing it is to trust in thy fatherly Care!" To Mather's further delight, Creasy stepped immediately on his return into a "luciferous, agreeable, and honorable" business. Its exact nature is unknown, but Mather speaks of Creasy's being fixed in "the Business of the Store-house," with an expectation of being taken into a partnership.

*

By the time Mather courted Lydia George, his violent exchange of denunciatory letters and pamphlets with Joseph Dudley lay some seven years behind, and his relation to the governor had regained something of its initial tone of barbed courtesy based on recognition of mutual usefulness. Many different considerations probably drew Mather back into Dudley's orbit. For one, Dudley had proved his staying power. Although Sir Henry Ashurst had continued in London his crusade to have Dudley removed, he found the governor a person "of such insinuation . . . that only Satan himself hath greater," and he accomplished nothing. Mather seems to have resigned himself to cooperating with Dudley to salvage what vestige of political influence remained to him. Although his relation to John Leverett's Harvard was also a "very Imperfect Sort of Thing," he served with Dudley in 1712 as part of a commission to manage a large bequest to the college. Mather cannot have found such cooperation agreeable, but it was practical. The bequest had become a matter of legal contention in England, and without the authority of Dudley and the Mathers to administer it might conceivably have been lost. Compared with Dudley's stormy first half-dozen years as governor, too, the later half-dozen were quiet; the Treaty of Utrecht in 1713 for a while ended England's warfare against France, and brought the English North American colonies an extended period of peace for the first time since 1688.

Dudley also gave Mather less reason to fear his support for the Church of England, which demonstrated itself to be nominal. Although the governor signed a petition in 1713 from the Boston Anglican chapel, endorsing a scheme to establish bishops in America, the minister of the chapel complained that Dudley in fact belonged to a Congregational church in Roxbury, where he lived, and had not taken communion at the chapel for years. Mather was conscious, in addition, of Dudley's advancing age: laid up with gout in 1715, the governor had to be carried to the Town House in a sedan chair, and borne in it up most of the stairs. Finally, amidst the new generation that had grown up since the abrogation of the old charter, Dudley cut a less anomalous and threatening figure. Time had made it less inconceivable that the government should rest in one who saw New England not as Christian Israel but as crown territory.

Nothing so nearly reconciled Mather to Dudley, however, as the death of Queen Anne in August 1714, which brought new attempts to remove the governor. The event triggered the same reaction that had first won Dudley the governorship, namely fears that if he were not appointed someone worse might be. About two months after the queen's death, Mather wrote to William Ashurst in London, saying that "of late Months" he had lived in "Good Correspondence" with Dudley, and shared the general opinion that Massachusetts would be happier in him than in some who might be "*Strangers to us; or not of our Nation.*" The reasoning was well founded, for early in 1715 the new king, George I, appointed as governor Col. Elizeus Burgess, a man who had been tried for the murders of two men, one of whom he killed in a duel, the other, an actor, at a tavern. Yet Mather's reasoning also proved unnecessary, for Burgess resigned his office and never crossed the Atlantic. For a while, Lt. Gov. William Tailer acted as governor, until the arrival, in October 1716, of Samuel Shute.

Mather was glad for the political changes initiated by the new king, coinciding with the happy first years of his marriage. He rated George's accession a "great thing," replacing the High Church climate of Anne's reign by a monarch "so little in the French interests." The new governor pleased him even more, for Samuel Shute had a distinguished military record in fighting the French and, more important to Mather, belonged to a prominent family of English Dissenters. His grandfather was the famous Presbyterian minister Joseph Caryl, author of a twelve-volume commentary on the Book of Job; his brother, Lord Barrington, led the Dissenting interest in Parliament. In Mather's mind, Shute augured a government if not on the model of John Winthrop exactly, then of William Phips, one that while serving the crown would also hearken to Boston's Congregationalist ministers. After more than fifteen years of political impotence, he saw hope of regaining his place at the governor's table.

Shute no sooner arrived in Boston than Mather decided to "improve my Acquaintance, which I am like to have with him, for all the good Purposes imaginable." He preached before the new governor on October 11, and not long after sent him a rather obsequious letter complimenting his "wisdom and goodness," his "generous concern" for the public, and the "charms of Your Excellency's Speech." While everyone would be zealous to serve Shute, he said, the governor would "never have a more hearty Servant" than himself. Faithful to his promise, he lent Shute all his support, sometimes at the cost of personal compromise. Like Dudley, Shute seems to have been wary of offending any large religious group in Boston. Thus although he apparently joined a Congregational church in 1717, the following year he headed subscriptions for a new gallery at King's Chapel, where he attended Sabbath worship. Far from damning Shute, Mather praised him for showing no "Partiality for Little Parties in Religion." He also urged that the governor's salary of £1000 be increased.

For his efforts, Mather at first enjoyed with Shute the most cordial relationship he had had with any governor since Phips. Indeed he became virtually Shute's friend, often writing to him flatteringly, advising him on public appointments, sending publications, and receiving from him "singular Testimonies of Regard." At least once Shute invited him to send a servant to his cellar to take away a gift of wine, which Mather promised to do, adding unctuously: "Your Wine is good; but the Kind Aspect of your Excellency with it, upon him to whom you send it, sublimes it into Nectar." Inclined to evaluate others in extremes of best and worst, Mather believed that even had the people of Massachusetts retained their right to elect their own governor, they would have chosen Shute: "under the Best of Governours," he wrote in 1718, "our People enjoy all the Tranquillity which can in this present Evil World be looked for."

The change of administrations also brought to prominence a protégé of Mather's, the highly capable, and satirical, Jeremiah Dummer. Born into the affluent Boston merchant class in 1681, he took a B.A. and M.A. at Harvard, then visited Europe and did graduate work in Holland, where he published several works. He returned to New England to preach, but decided to leave the ministry and also declined a professorship of philology at Harvard. Instead he went into business and returned to London, where he played cards and watched "the great female beauties" at the House of Lords ("I tho't I could have gaz'd at them for ever"). As the growing regularization of New England's ties with the mother country brought awareness of the need for constant representation at Whitehall, he was appointed agent for Massachusetts, a role he considered "a very great honour." Later he was appointed agent for Connecticut and New Hampshire as well. His access in London to such persons as Addison, Steele, and Newton gave him a voice in the appointment of colonial officials, and in delaying measures in Parliament directed against the colonies. Resourceful and effective, Dummer could have become, it was later remarked in New England, prime minister.

Dummer greatly admired Mather and felt "bless'd," he said, to have such a "Dear and Worthy Friend." He looked up to Mather as the pattern of a "useful conversation" in life, although a lofty one: "I follow halting after his footsteps tho' far behind and at a great distance." Mather's company and person not only inspired Dummer but also amused him. He enjoyed their trips to Salem—Mather, he noted, "thinks wherever he comes, that he's up to the knees in Pigs"—and shared Mather's quarters there, later sending from London some verses by Waller to be hung in a frame in their bedchamber. Mather on his side recognized Dummer's diplomatic skill and influence, dedicated to him an important but now lost work called "Religio Generosi," and used him as a go-between with London publishers. He also found Dummer exasperating, a potential Creasy who however overcame his worst propensities. He attacked in print, and urged Dummer to retract, his unorthodox views on the Sabbath. Orthodox or not, Dummer may have been the one person who could criticize Mather's writing without enraging him. Their correspondence is enlivened by much tongue-in-cheek byplay about the number of Mather's publications, which Dummer several times told him frankly was damaging to him. This Mather took with half-amused indulgence laced with subtle hurt, in one instance sending Dummer a recent work with the apology that he did not ordinarily "nauseate you, with any of my published Composures." Somewhat acid, but lively and admiring, Dummer was the sort of man Mather could not resist.

Dummer's value to Mather, and to New England, became particularly evident in the founding of Yale College. Mather's own part in creating Yale has often been interpreted as an expression of his scorn for John Leverett, and toward Harvard under his presidency. But nothing in Mather's work for Yale suggests a motive beyond desiring to see a Congregational college in Connecticut, where he had such good friends as Governor Saltonstall and John Winthrop, and had long been concerned for the christianizing of the Mohegan Indians. It is true that Mather's name was mentioned for the rectorship of the new college, although it so appears only in private correspondence, and he may not have known of it. It is also true that at the time of his involvement with Yale, he complains in his diaries of the "Venom and Malice which the disaffected Rulers of our College, treat me withal!" But for all his disgruntlement he never cut himself off from Harvard affairs entirely (in 1714 he served once again as an Overseer), and it seems unlikely that he would have risked antagonizing Leverett at a time when Sammy was just entering Harvard under his tutelage. Besides, Colman and others also worked to promote Yale without feeling disenchanted about Harvard, and in their recruitment the two schools were too distant from each other to be competitors.

Yale College began taking shape in 1716, when the trustees of a small collegiate school at Saybrook voted to move to New Haven. The costs of raising and furnishing new buildings were great, but a benefactor was available in the person of Elihu Yale, a London diamond merchant who had been born in Boston of New Haven stock. As a young man Yale had emigrated to Madras, India, where he made a fortune. Becoming president of the East India Company, he had lived protected by several hundred guards, carried on an ostrich-fan-shaded palanquin. Yale intended bestowing a charity on some college at Oxford; but Jeremiah Dummer pointed out to the Saybrook Collegiate School that Yale was, after all, a Connecticut man by birth, and his bounty would be more suitably bestowed at home. Dummer himself solicited a gift of books for the school from Yale, part of a library of perhaps a thousand volumes which he begged or otherwise obtained from people in London: Steele sent complete sets of the *Tatler* and *Spectator*, Newton took down from his own shelves copies of his *Opticks* and his *Principia*.

Mather wrote to Yale soliciting his aid for the new school. As a member of the Church of England, Yale had doubts about supporting an "Academy of Dissenters," as he called it, the school being clearly intended to serve Congregational interests. Tactfully Mather appealed to him as a New Englander, and depicted the religious life of New England as based on "Catholic and generous principles of Christianity, and . . .

beyond the Narrow Spirit of a party." He stressed to Yale that the God who gives power to get wealth makes the wealthy no more than trustees of it, and mentioned a particular method of Doing Good:

> The Colony of *Connecticut*, having for some years had a College at *Saybrook*, without a collegiate way of living for it, have lately begun to erect a large Edifice for it in the Town of *New-Haven*. The charge of that expensive Building is not yet all paid; Nor are there yet any Funds, of Revenues, for Salaries to the Professors and Instructors of the Society.

Then he proposed to Yale that for his beneficence he might have a monument that would be "much better than an *Egyptian pyramid*": the school forming at New Haven, he suggested, "might wear the Name of, YALE-COLLEGE." About five months later there arrived in Boston Yale's gift of three bales of goods to be sold for the school's benefit, plus a large box of books and a full-length portrait of the king by Kneller—the largest gift the school had ever received from a private person, worth about £800.

Mather was greatly pleased that he had been able to help the new college, but somewhat uneasy over having in effect christened it. He apologized to Governor Saltonstall for his "inexcusable presumption" in making himself "so far the God-father of the Beloved Infant, as to propose a Name for it." He did so, he explained, because he had been told that Yale might exceed his previous generosity if the school were named after him, and he asked Saltonstall to comply with his proposal. At the commencement of September 10, 1718, the trustees met in their new building in New Haven and formally gave the college Yale's name. They also wrote to Mather, effusively thanking him for his "noble and charitable regard to our infant Nursery"—regard, we shall see, that would turn to shocked regret.

*

A simultaneous and far-reaching development in Mather's religious life shared in the harmony of his new marriage and his contentment with the new government. For twenty-five years, since the attempted union between English Presbyterians and Congregationalists, he had entertained the hope of unifying the Protestant churches. The failure of the United Brethren did not end his ecumenical enthusiasm, which now revived as an articulated vision of a pan-Christian union that would disregard variations of polity and worship and rest on a few distilled Gospel principles of vital piety. His efforts place him in the mainstream of religious revivalism reaching through the Great Awakening of the eighteenth century to such modern expressions of ecumenism as the World Council of Churches.

Around 1715 Mather exuberantly began detailing and publicizing what he called a "RELIGION OF THE EVERLASTING MAXIMS." Its first expression was *The Stone Cut out of the Mountain* (Latin title, *Lapis e Monte Excisus*; 1716), a "little Thing," he called it, "which is of greater Expectation with me, than anything that I have ever yet been concerned in." How much he expected of the work appears in his trying to have it translated into several languages, and in his hope of sending copies of it to eminent members of Parliament and to Hindus in Malabar, as well as to England, Scotland, Holland, Switzerland, France, Germany, and India. Although the diminutive work is but an octavo pamphlet of thirteen pages in English, with thirteen pages of facing Latin translation, its brevity was an achievement, the result, Mather said, "of more than a Little contemplation. St. Barnaby's Day would not be long enough to recite all the views which the author had in the composing of it." As he also observed, Luther's essays demonstrated that, if distributed far and at the right time, "Little Engines of Piety" might accomplish wonders.

In *Lapis*, Mather reduced religion to fourteen unshakable maxims on which Christians throughout the world of whatever sect, except Catholics, would agree. He made it unnecessary to list them here, for over the next year or so, as he continued vigorously to preach and promote this "Universal Religion," he reduced the number of maxims to three. These he summarized in *Malachi* (1717): belief in the Trinity, utter reliance on Christ for salvation, and love of neighbor out of respect for Christ. "*Real* and *Vital* PIETY"—the basis of Christian union—thus consists simply of "*Fearing* of God, and in *Prizing* of His CHRIST, and in *Doing of Good* unto Men." Mather conspicuously omitted matters of church organization or discipline, which he devalued to "*Lower* and *Lesser* points of Religion," subject to great diversity. No longer writing as someone committed to the Congregational ideal of church government, that is, he trumpeted a religion that could have existed had the Cambridge Platform never been drafted:

> Sirs; They are not External *Rites* and *Forms*, that will distinguish, *The People of* GOD. The *Kingdom of GOD comes not* with the *Observation* of such things as those. No; 'Tis a People found with various *Rites*, and in various *Forms. Hear this, All ye People; Give Ear, all ye Inhabitants of the World.* The PEOPLE of GOD, are All that cordially embrace our *Everlasting* MAXIMS of PIETY, and *Live unto GOD* upon them, in whatever *Subdivision* of *Christianity,* they are to be met withal.

This was a religion not for the Christian Israel of the Fathers but, as Mather said, for "millions of people in the world."

Mather's Universal Religion brought him equally far from the pneumatological realm of energumens and ringleted angels. He considered his Maxims of Piety a *"Reasonable Religion,"* suitable for rationalistic, cosmopolitan persons who valued such social by-products of vital piety as fair dealing, the suppression of ill will, and helping others. Quoting Francke, he emphasized that these benevolent effects are superior to supernatural exhilaration and prophetic ability:

> To have such a *Discerning* of our selves and our Interests, as these MAXIMS would help us to, is a more *Glorious* Thing, than to have a sight so refin'd, as to *Discern Spirits*. To have our *Evil Tempers* mended and cured by these MAXIMS, is a more *Glorious* Thing than to cast out *Evil Spirits*. To behave our selves *Wisely* as these MAXIMS teach us, from a *Foresight* of our *Eternal Judgment*, is a more *Glorious* Thing than to *Foresee* and *Foretel* Futurities.

In all but renouncing a thirst for the invisible world, Mather also came close to reducing the supernatural experience of grace itself to rational understanding. Noting that the many discourses concerning tests for grace sometimes leave the candidate for conversion in "as much *obscurity* and *perplexity* as before," he proposed assent to his three everlasting maxims as a *"Short* and a *Sure"* test for grace. Assent to them means that "Thou art most certainly *passed from Death to Life.* And the Experience of such Things as these, is preferable to all the *Joys of Impulse,* whereof some Enjoy the Raptures; tho' those also may be *Better than Life."* Minimizing the two essential features of Congregationalism, its view of the church and its mystical piety, Mather's Universal Religion aimed rather at quenching the fires of religious controversy, creating harmony in society, allowing scope to reason, and doing good to others out of fear of God and love to Christ.

Mather's ecumenism increasingly convinced him, also, of the need to indulge religious differences. His many calls for toleration make him seem more a figure of the Enlightenment than of the seventeenth-century, closer to Thomas Jefferson than to John Cotton: "PERSECUTION, That *Prince of Devils* which fills the World with *Desolations. . . .* 'Tis an *Hellish Monster* which all Mankind ought with an *United Cry* to chase from off the Face of the Earth!" Mather went far himself in practicing this toleration. In a published letter to Francis De la Pillonniere, a professed Arminian who had converted to Protestantism from Catholicism, he admitted that as a Calvinist he must differ with him, yet proposed that in being animated by the same "Maxims of Piety," Arminians and Calvinists could together help create a second, "reformed Reformation," a "NEW PEOPLE of the good Men in the *several Parties.*" In an even bolder display of the Universal Religion Mather preached in 1718 at the ordination of Elisha Callender, a Baptist minister. He apologized to Callender's congregation if, as Baptists, they had received unbrotherly treatment in the past from fellow Bostonians, and he proclaimed: "*Liberty of Conscience* is the Native Right of Mankind."

Many different features of his life and time drew Mather, popularly imagined as the quintessential Puritan bigot, into the vanguard of religious toleration. An ecumenical movement, to recall, had existed within at least a sector of English Puritanism since the Elizabethan period, and was particularly marked in Richard Baxter. It intertwined with the ecumenism of the German Pietists, who praised Mather's *Lapis* for emphasizing "Substantials" rather than "Circumstantials." Although Francke produced the greatest ecumenical and missionary network since the Reformation (joining Germany, Holland, England, America, France, Italy, Switzerland, Poland, Russia, South Africa, India, and the Scandinavian countries), the immediate German Pietist influence on Mather's own ecumenism was likely Philipp Jakob Spener, who reduced the whole of Christianity simply to a confession of sin and a profession of faith in Christ.

Mather's career in Boston under Andros, Dudley, and now Shute enforced his ecumenical notions by making it impossible for him to conceive New England any longer as the redeemer of the English nation. To put the case a different way, his ecumenism celebrated the world created by the new charter. Where he once railed at the innovative Brattle church as a satanic invasion, he now proclaimed the growing cosmopolitanism of Boston as a model for a second Reformation. In fact the variety of worship in the town was increasing in proportion to the increase in the number of churches; as Mather noted in 1717, the place had become something of a sectarian melting pot, containing ten places of worship, of which seven were "Churches of the UNITED BRETHREN" divided only by differences in circumstantials. The feuding in Boston which had accompanied this transformation also fed Mather's ecumenism for, consciously at least, he came to abominate public quarrels. His ecumenism was a large-scale expression of his deep-rooted and complex desire for reconciliations of all kinds.

At various times, it needs special emphasis, Mather's religious liberalism expanded or contracted, for his disposition to embrace other sects changed with changing political, social, and personal events. Around 1715 it was also quickened by again-aroused millennial expectations, such as he had felt before in the 1690s. Eschatology and ecumenism were intimately related, for the millennium would not arrive before the achievement of Christian unity. The Universal Religion of *Lapis* and *Malachi* was both Mather's response to signs of evolving unity which he perceived and his attempt to foster them. Virtually all commentators on prophecy insisted that the exact date of the Second Coming could not be known; but 1716, the year in which Mather published *Lapis*, had become something of an exception. It was the year chosen by the most learned scholar of prophecy in the English church, Joseph Mede, as the time for Christ's return. Newton's associate, William Whiston, had also made very detailed computations and had announced in his *Essay on the Revelation of Saint John* (1706) that 1716 would see the fall of Catholicism—that is, of Antichrist. Mather respected these predictions, and had declared as early as *Bonifacius* (1710) that "M.DCC.XVI is a-coming." Again he watched for such other harbingers of the millennium as the fall of the Turkish empire, the conversion of the Jews, and great earthquakes or similar remarkable providences. He interpreted the death in 1715 of the "French *Moloch*" Louis XIV—"the Greatest *Adversary* of . . . *Christianity*, that ever was in the World!"—as a certain preliminary to the Second Coming, a shaking of the ground toward that "Stupendous *Earthquake*" that would "issue in wondrous *Glory to the God of Heaven*." Taking the adoption of the Universal Religion as itself the "greatest Sign that some of us can see of the Kingdom of God approaching," he closed his *Lapis* by making it known that "The *Great Trumpet* is now to be Blown."

One other ambitious religious undertaking by Mather at nearly this time deserves mention here, although its consequences emerged only after the early years of his marriage. His lifelong enthusiasm for psalm singing earned him a place in the history of American music. He valued psalmody because, like most Puritans, he considered it a form of prayer, but his special delight in it perhaps stemmed from his early speech problems, as many stutterers can sing without difficulty. He collected many illustrations on ancient Hebrew music into "Biblia Americana," urged singing as a daily act of devotion, and regularly sang with his family at household prayers, and by himself, especially during his many fasts, vigils, and illnesses. He also composed "Vast Numbers" of hymns, a few of which he transcribed in his diary or included in other works. Apparently he wrote and published an entire book of hymns, *Songs of the Redeemed* (1697), although no copy is known to have survived.

In 1718 Mather published an ingenious 464-page psalter, with commentary, entitled *Psalterium Americanum*. His innovative, fourfold aim he explained in a seven-page set of proposals for printing the elaborate work by subscription. He considered no current version of Psalms satisfactory because all of them sacrificed exactness to "the *Clink* of the *Rhime*." To preserve the meaning he decided to follow some "famous pieces of Poetry, which this Refining Age has been treated withal," and to produce a translation in what he called, with his habitual insensitivity to poetry, blank verse. He apparently understood by blank verse simply unrimed verse, for the translations are in unrimed iambic tetrameter and trimeter. In striving for a highly literal version, Mather had two further purposes in mind. Following a long line of Reformed thought he viewed Psalms as "the most *Prophetical Book* in the World," a forecast in Old Testament types of the religion of the New Testament. To render the Hebrew exactly was to delineate darkly the coming of Christ, and he included in *Psalterium* a very large number of glosses (mostly taken from "Biblia Americana"), interpreting the Old Testament texts as prophecies of the Redeemer. By translating literally he also hoped to undermine a recent and increasingly popular fashion in psalmody, the deliberate departures from Hebrew being made by his correspondent and "very dear Friend" Isaac Watts, whose *Psalms of David Imitated in the Language of the New Testament* (1719) later dominated colonial Protestantism. As the title suggests, Watts attempted not to translate the Psalms but to rewrite or imitate them in Christian terms, ending the divorce in Protestant worship between preaching and singing, by which churchgoers heard about Christ but sang about David. Although Mather delighted in Watts's "excellent composures" and reprinted many of them, he frowned on having a psalter "without any Air of the Old Testament in it," its typological references to Christ being shed along with the "*Jewish Dress*." By contrast with Watts's christianized psalms, Mather's *Psalterium* transforms the Old Testament songs into a millennial saga of the coming of Christ and the conversion of the Jews, providing "*The Gospel according to* DAVID."

Mather had a musical reform in mind as well. By making his translations in "blank verse" he proposed simplifying Congregational psalmody by reducing the number of metrical patterns to be sung. (Probably to make a larger repertoire of tunes possible if desired, however, he made use of a clever typographical device, employed earlier by Richard Baxter, by which singers might elect to pronounce or omit extra bracketed syllables.) Some such reform was needed for, like many other Protestant leaders in England and America, Mather believed that over the last few generations psalmody had steadily deteriorated. In 1717 he found some members of his own family "so indifferent at Singing" that he often had to omit it from evening family worship. By 1720 many other New England ministers were complaining about the carelessness in singing and the lack of a musical standard.

To improve public singing, several churches attempted to teach their congregants to read music, sparking the angriest and longest-argued aesthetic debate in early America. In the "more polite city of Boston," Mather wrote later, note reading met with general acceptance; but "in the country, where they have more of the *rustic*, some numbers of older and angry people bore zealous testimonies against these wicked innovations, and this bringing in of popery." Some members of a congregation near Boston were so "set upon their old *howling*" that they declared for the Church of England. Contention grew so intense as to require the calling of several church councils to compose differences. What made the issue divisive was in part that the skill of reading notes could be used in singing not only the sacred but also the profane; one handwritten singing book from Westboro, Massachusetts, in 1721 contains not only devotional tunes but also "Love Triumphant" and "The Beaux Delight." The introduction of musical literacy and skill also very often pitted young against old, gifted against bumbling, town against country. Those who defended regular singing, as note reading was called, made their case in about a dozen sermons, instructional works, and pamphlets published in New England from 1720 to 1727, arguing on scriptural and other grounds for trained performance.

Often sympathetic to the young and to new ideas, especially in this period, Mather actively allied himself with the proponents of regular singing. He preached in March 1721 to a society of persons learning to sing, before a full house, where the singing, Samuel Sewall found, was "extraordinarily Excellent, such as has hardly been heard before in Boston." He also contributed to the debate a pamphlet entitled *The Accomplished Singer* (1721), in essence a lengthened reworking of the Introduction to his *Psalterium*. Here he deplored the degeneration of psalmody into "*Odd Noise*," and urged the young especially to learn to read music. Christians, he said, should "Serve our GOD with our *Best*, and *Regular Singing* must needs be *Better* than the confused Noise of a Wilderness."

In arguing for the development of musical literacy in New England, Mather sided with the future health of the arts in America. In 1721 his nephew and disciple, Thomas Walter, published in Boston *The Grounds and Rules of Musick Explained,* one of the first two American books of music instruction. Within the next half century the fateful controversy over regular singing led to the creation in New England of singing schools, then of singing masters to conduct them, and at last of native tunesmiths to compose music for them. Ultimately one recipient of Mather's multifarious energies was the Boston singing master and tunesmith William Billings, whose 1770 collection, *The New-England Psalm Singer,* was the first volume of American-composed music.

neteenth-century photograph
Increase Mather's house.
*Boston Public Library, Print
Department.*)

neteenth-century drawing of
e North Church. (*Boston Pub-
Library, Print Department.*)

Old North Church.
In North Square Boston.

Samuel Sewall (1652–1730), the Mathers' close friend, by John Smibert (1688–1751). (*Museum of Fine Arts, Boston.*)

Governor Joseph Dudley (1647–1720), artist unknown. (*Massachusetts Historical Society, Boston.*)

Map of Boston in 1722, by Captain John Bonner (ca. 1643–1726). (*Massachusetts Historical Society, Boston.*)

THE
New-England Courant.

From MONDAY January 29. to MONDAY February 5. 1722

Aliud eſt maledicere, aliud accuſare. Cic.

JUDICIOUS Author obſerves, That there is nothing in which Men more deceive themſelves than in what the World call Zeal. There are ſo many Paſſions which hide themſelves under it, and ſo many Miſchiefs ariſing from it, that ſome have gone ſo far as to ſay, it would have been for the Benefit of Mankind, if it had never been reckoned in the Catalogue of Virtues. The fatal Effects of Zeal among our Selves, has almoſt perſwaded me to be of this Opinion. A furious pretended Zeal, which only regards Matters of Opinion, has been improv'd againſt my ſelf with a Deſign to deſtroy my Reputation and Intereſt amongſt thoſe who are Strangers to my Perſon: And that this Deſign might be the better carried on, ſome Perſons have been ſo *undutiful* to the Reverend Dr. *Increaſe Mather*, as to perſwade him to prefix his Name to an Advertiſement In the laſt Weeks *News-Letter* and *Gazette*, wherein the mildeſt Appellation I meet with, is that of a wicked and curſed Libeller. This Charge I now lye under from the oldeſt Miniſter in the Country, and in order to clear my ſelf I ſhall firſt give an Account of the firſt Cauſe of the Difference between us.

The Week before the *Courant* of *Jan.* 1. came out, a Grandſon of Dr. *Increaſe Mather* brought me the following Account of the Succeſs of Inoculation in *London*,

A Paſſage in the London Mercury, Sept. 16.

'Great Numbers of Perſons in the City and the Suburbs 'are under the Inoculation of the Small Pox. Among the 'reſt, the eldeſt Son of a noble Duke in Hanover Square, 'had the Small Pox inoculated upon him.

This he ſaid his Grandfather deſir'd me to inſert in my next, and affirm'd that he had tranſcrib'd it himſelf, and that it was Word for Word with the Account in the *London Mercury*. About Noon on the Day that the *Courant* came out, I ſaw the Four firſt Pages of the *London Mercury* of *Sept.* 16. and found nothing in them, but that *the eldeſt Son of a noble Duke in Hanover Square, had the Small Pox inoculated upon* him *INCOGNITO.* Here our young Spark was detected in a downrig t Falſhood, and loſt his Credit with *Couranto*; and I had great Reaſon too to believe that the firſt Part of the above Paragraph was not in the other Half-Sheet of the *Mercury*, becauſe both Paſſages related to Inoculation, and might (no doubt) have been as well inſerted together. The next Week I inſerted a Letter in the *Courant*, which aſſerted, that the former Parr of the Paſſage, viz. *Great Numbers of*

proving it. Whether he remembers it or no, his Grandſon *Biles*, by his Order, deſir'd me to ſet him down as a Cuſtomer ſome Time ago; but upon the Appearance of a Letter in the *Courant*, wherein a certain Clergyman was touch'd upon, he dropt it as a Subſcriber, but ſent his Grandſon al moſt every Week for a conſiderable Time to buy them by which Method he paid more for the Paper and was more a Supporter of it, than if his Name had been continu'd in the Liſt. At length, being weary with ſending, he became a Subſcriber again, and expreſſ'd no Diſlike of the Paper till after Mr. *Muſgrave* had publiſh'd his Grandſon's Letter in the *Gazette* of *Jan.* 15. So that he neither had and paid me for one Paper after that which he ſo much diſlikes. The Truth of this I am ready to declare upon Oath, againſt the Teſtimony of all the Men in the Country. And that he has been a Subſcriber, and conſequently a Supporter of the Paper, the following Letter under his own Hand, will ſufficiently prove.

Mr *Franklin*,

'I Had Thoughts of taking your *Courant* (upon Tryal) for 'a Quarter of a Year; but I ſhall not now. In one of 'your Courants you have ſaid that *if the Miniſters of God* 'are *for a Thing, it is a Sign it is from the Devil,* and have 'dealt very falſly about the *London Mercury*. For theſe and 'other Reaſons, I ſhall NO MORE be concerned with you.

Your well wiſhing, but grieved Friend,
I. Mather.

In the next Place he ſays, *In one of his vile Courants,* he *inſinuates, that if the Miniſters of God do approve of a Thing,* its *a ſign it is of the Devil, which is a horrid Thing to be related.*

The Words in the *Courant* are in a Dialogue (by an unknown Hand) between a Clergyman and Layman, and are exactly as follows,

Cl. But I find, all the Rakes in Town are againſt Inoculation, and that induces me to believe it is a right Way.

Laym. Moſt of the Miniſters are for it, and that induces me to think it is from the D——l; for he often makes uſe of good Men as Inſtruments to obtrude his Deluſions on the World.

The Doctor muſt know, that Satan once ſtood up againſt Iſrael, and provoked *DAVID* to number the People. *Joab*, his wicked General, was not ſo eaſily provok'd to this Evil: The King's Word was abominable to *him*. This is Doctrine which I have often heard from the Pulpit, and if I am condemn'd for publiſhing it, I may venture to ſay (in the Words of the Doctor's Grandſon, that I have Company *of which I need not be aſhamed.*

Again, *And altho' in one of the* Courants it *is declared, that the* London Mercury Sept. 16. 1921. *affirms,* That Great Numbers of Perſons in the City and Suburbs are under the Inoculation of the Small Pox; *in his next* Courant he *aſſerts,* That it was ſome buſy Inoculator, that impoſed on the Publick in ſaying to.

Benjamin Colman (1673–1747),
minister of the Brattle church, en-
graved from a painting by John
Smibert (1688–1751). (*American
Antiquarian Society, Worcester,
Mass.*)

The Reverend Benjamin Colman DD

Suffolk, ſſ. GEORGE, by the Grace of GOD of Great Britain, France and Ireland, KING, Defender of the Faith, &c.

To the Sheriff of Our County of *Suffolk* his Under-Sheriff or Deputy, Greeting.

WE Command you that you Summon *Doctor Cotton Mather of Boston in the County of Suffolk Clerk & Lidia his Wife as she is Execx of the Last will & Testamt of John George late of Boston afores? Mercht decd & also ye? Cotton Mather as admr to ye Estate of Nathan Howell late of Boston afores? Merchant deced* (if *they* may be found in your Precinct) to Appear before Our Juſtices of Our Inferiour Court of Common Pleas to be Holden at *Boſton*, within and for Our said County of *Suffolk*, on the Firſt *Tueſday* of *April* next: Then and there in Our said Court to Anſwer to *Mary Mico of Boston afores? Relict of George? Sole Admin? to the Estate of her late husband John Mico of Boston afores? Mercht. decd, In a plea of the Case, for that the Defts qualifyed as afores? neglect and refuse to pay to the plntiff qualifyed as afores? the Sum of One hundred fifty Seven pounds ..teen Shillings and four pence money remaining due from Estate of the d? George & Howell to ballance the annexed Accompt.*

Summons to Cotton and Lydia Mather, concerning a debt of £157 14s.
(*Supreme Judicial Court, Boston.*)

Richard Mather (1596–1669), Cotton Mather's paternal grandfather, by John Foster (1648–1681). (*American Antiquarian Society, Worcester, Mass.*)

Increase Mather (1639–1723), Cotton Mather's father, attributed to Jan van der Spriett (d. 1693). (*Massachusetts Historical Society, Boston.*)

Cotton Mather (1663–1728), engraved by Peter Pelham (1697–1751). (*American Antiquarian Society, Worcester, Mass.*)

Samuel Mather (1706–1785), Cotton Mather's son and successor, by John Greenwood (1727–1792). (*American Antiquarian Society, Worcester, Mass.*)

John Dolbeare

FAIR DEALING
between Debtor *and* Creditor.

A very brief ESSAY
UPON
The CAUTION to be used,
about **coming** in to

DEBT,

And **getting** out of it.
Offered at BOSTON-Lecture;

5. d. XI. m. 17$\frac{15}{16}$.

By Cotton Mather, D.D. & F.R.S.

Stultus est Debitor, qui gaudens Pecunias acci-
pit, et Tempus quo reddere debeat, non attendit.
Gregor. in Moral.

BOSTON:
Printed by B. Green, for Samuel Gerrish,
at his Shop over against the North side of
the Town-House. 1716.

Typical title page of a work by Cotton Mather, with his "D.D. & F.R.S."
(*American Antiquarian Society, Worcester, Mass.*)

11

Tria Carcinomata

MATHER's newfound happiness was brief. By the spring of 1717, a year after Creasy's return from England, he was once again sputtering over the boy's unruliness, devoting whole days of supplication to ask an end of Creasy's "Course of Impiety." He had little belief in the proverbial minister's son, indeed considered it a "Popish and Cursed LIE, that the Children of *Ministers* do usually miscarry more than *Others*." Yet he was beginning to admit the possibility that Creasy would in fact miscarry, that from his miraculous rescue in England he would drown again past saving.

"Suppose," Mather asked himself, "that a Child of my singular Love and Hope, should fall into Sin, and be after wondrous Means of Recovery, yet so abandoned of God, and so ensnared in Vice, that there may [be] terrible Cause to fear lest he prove a Cast-away." How in such circumstances, Mather wondered, should he act? He must be sure not to confuse his grief with his shame. He must separate his pain over Creasy's abandonment to sin, from his vexation at "missing the Reputation and Satisfaction which a Child of more honourable Behaviour might bring unto me." Preparing himself, distressed, he took the boy into his library, prayed with him, pleaded with him. By making Creasy "see and feel my Agonies for him," he did induce him to express repentance. "Methinks," he wrote cautiously, "I hear the glorious One saying to me, *Concerning thy Son I have heard thee*!"

But by November Mather heard, or felt, something else as well, a "strong Impression on my Mind, that some very trying and grievous Thing is near unto me." Such impressions had often misled him, of course, but not this one. Two days later a "thing" came to pass, not just trying and grievous, but shocking. Mather was informed or, rather, "astonished with

307

an Information," that a prostitute had named Creasy as the man who got
her pregnant. A "Harlot big with a Bastard," as he put it, "accuses my
poor Son *Creasy*, and lays her Belly to him." People whose judgment he
trusted believed Creasy innocent, but Mather felt no less bewildered and
humiliated: "Oh! Dreadful Case! Oh, Sorrow beyond any that I have met
withal! what shall I do now for the foolish Youth! what for my afflicted
and abased Family?"

However shaken, Mather acted with uncustomary aplomb. Illegiti-
macy was a common problem in early New England, and hardly a session
of the Boston court failed to hear a bastardy case, usually assigning the
onus and responsibility to the woman. Only two months after the charge
against Creasy, for instance, a Boston court ordered a "Putative Father" to
pay three shillings a week for as long as the court declared, while it
imposed a fine of £3 and ten stripes at the public whipping post on his
lover, a woman wonderfully named "Elinor Redhead." Mather seems to
have managed to prevent Creasy's case from coming to court by keeping
Creasy "confined and retired with me, until the Storm shall be blown
over." With Creasy sequestered in his house, Mather plied him with directions for spending his time, assigned him sermons to read, prayed with
him and Lydia in the study, meanwhile warning himself to stay calm under his provocations.

But despite Mather's concern and continuous prayers for him, Creasy,
"My poor Son," was intractable. Only two weeks after the disclosure, the
boy "made a worse Exhibition of himself unto me . . . than I ever yet met
withal." Mather's failure to produce some lasting reform in Creasy made
him feel more helpless than ever: "O my God, what shall I do? what shall
I do?" Although his affection for Creasy was great, so now was his disappointment. Probably at around this time, in late 1717, he started writing a
continuation of "Paterna," the exemplary autobiography he had begun
writing for Creasy at the time of his birth. He addressed this second part,
however, to Sammy. He also revised the first part to make it seem that it
too had been written not for Creasy but for his more promising younger
son, who might more usefully see in his father's life a model of constant
devotion and unceasing heaven-mindedness.

Powerless to reclaim Creasy, Mather now also looked on helplessly as
his blissful marriage turned riotous. Nothing of the turmoil appears in his
diary for 1718, which scarcely mentions Lydia. Instead, Mather recorded
the domestic events of 1718 in a separate notebook, where he explained
why he omitted them from his diaries. There he wrote: "The Consort, in
whom I flattered myself with the View and Hopes of an uncommon En-

joyment, has dismally confirmed it unto me, that our *Idols* must prove our *Sorrows.*"

Whatever her other attractions, Lydia hardly matched Mather's picture of an ideal Puritan wife. This person, as he depicted her in his popular conduct book, *Ornaments for the Daughters of Zion* (Cambridge, 1692), regarded her husband as a divinely appointed guide, whom she always addressed with respect, whose moments of rage she always strove to mollify with meekness, whose will she so obligingly obeyed that "If her *Abraham* give order, *Make Ready quickly three Measures of Meal* or the like, 'tis as *quickly* done." The wellborn, wealthy, and worldly Lydia, however, was no one to measure Mather's meal quickly. She was instead highly independent-minded, as well as vain, jealous, manipulative, and perhaps psychopathic. Her father, the brilliant Rev. Samuel Lee, had expected his daughters to marry into the best and most honorable families. But one of them conducted a very public quarrel with her husband; another married a Rhode Islander "supposed to be rich but deceived her"; another clandestinely married Lee's own servant, Harry. And Lydia married Cotton Mather. And Cotton Mather had heard Lee observe in one of his sermons that the Emperor Augustus called his three daughters *Tria Carcinomata*—three cancers.

Early in their marriage, Lydia had sometime exposed her "proud Passions" to Mather, but he had overcome them, he said, with mildness and patience. In 1718, however, she exploded in "prodigious Paroxysms." Scarcely able to deal with her, he found it "a Year of such Distresses with me, as I have never seen in my Life before." It was not merely that Lydia reviled him. It was that her revilings came and went. When her paroxysms exhausted themselves she once more treated him lovingly, indeed with a "Fondness, that it may be, few Wives in the World have arriv'd unto." Yet the paroxysms always returned, and as they returned they grew more frequent. At last she so outrageously insulted him that Mather believed she might be mad, "which may be somewhat Hereditary," or even possessed. Whether genetic or diabolical in origin, Lydia's outbursts revived one of his worst fears. Throughout 1718 he lived in "a continual Anguish of Expectation, that my poor Wife, by exposing her Madness, would bring a Ruin on my Ministry."

Among the objects of Lydia's "Venom" were Mather's diaries, which she seems to have inspected. Fear of her paroxysms led him to record "not one disrespectful Word of this proud Woman." To allay her suspicions about what his diaries contained he prepared a "true Account, given at the Desire of my Consort, under my hand." This weirdly pathetic document consists of seven pages of extracts from his diaries since the time of their marriage, all related to Lydia and all demonstrating that his private ruminations about her were approving and affectionate—an anthology of diary references to Lydia as his "Lovely Consort," his "Discreet Consort," his "Excellent, Religious, and Ingenious Consort," his "dear, amiable, valuable Consort." He concluded the extracts with a signed statement avowing that if his diaries for 1718 mentioned any "*uncommon Distresses*," these were to be understood as referring to some of the children, "and nothing to be misapplied unto her."

Fear of what Lydia might be capable of doing also led Mather to hide his diaries. But in her "indecent Romaging" Lydia found them, and kept them. He would, she said, "never see them any more." In the hope of getting her to give the diaries back he offered to blot out whatever she disliked. She refused. Seemingly bent on tormenting him, she offered instead the hope that she might return his diaries for the last four or five years "some time or other."

Lydia turned her wrath at Mather against his children as well. Early in their marriage he had thanked God in his diary for bestowing "an excellent Mother" on them; now he went back to this passage and added, in the margin, "*Ah! quam deceptus!*" Although pained by the "dreadful Distresses which a furious and froward Stepmother brings upon my Family," he felt obliged to encourage the "several abused Children" to obey Lydia. He called them into his study and pressed them to regard "the sad Things that are come upon them" as, like all affliction, a loud argument for turning to God. The children's problems were compounded by an economic crisis in 1719, so severe that Mather saw the possibility of a revolution. Lydia apparently refused to help out from her own estate, for the scarcities and soaring prices forced Mather to cut back on household expenses, including those of the children. Sammy was perhaps affected most, for Mather was unable to continue paying for his college education, raising the possibility that this "son of uncommon Hopes" might have to discontinue his preparation for the ministry. As if providentially, there arrived at Harvard a bequest from an English Baptist named Thomas Hollis, from the interest of which, at the suggestion of Increase Mather, a scholarship was provided for Sammy. Hollis consented, expressing regret that the grandson of Increase Mather should come under the character of the "poor in this World."

Increase himself added to his son's trials when, around the spring of 1719, his health took a sudden bad turn. Now eighty-one years old, Increase had been in uncertain health the past two years anyway, suffering gout, losses of memory, and stomach trouble. To these were added renewed nightmares that became so severe he feared his breath might stop. The brethren of the North Church kept a day of prayer for a successor to him. Feeling "Broken with Age," he filled his diary with crotchety protests of "Time lost by Impertinent visitors," complaints that his sermons "stick in the birth." In June 1719, fearful that when dying he would be unable to speak—as his father, Richard Mather, had been—he drew up his will. Cotton seems to have spent much time with him despite his own difficulties, wanting his father to be "wholly out of the Pain; which my Absence always gives him."

Mather dealt with his accumulating burdens in ways both old and new. His love for Lydia, or at least the experience of having loved her, lingered and craved some object. In March 1718, he made a virtually unique entry in his diary in Greek, presumably so Lydia could not read it. It speaks of his need to mourn bitterly his "former pollutions" and of his belief that God does not require him "utterly to lay aside my fondness for my lovely Consort," suggesting that he resorted to masturbation or that despite their wrangling he maintained sexual relations with her. Apparently, however, his thoughts wandered to other women, for he also wrote, in Greek, "I must abhor the least tho't of regard unto any other Person but this dearly beloved of my soul." More familiar, his troubles brought renewed demands for self-mortification and for governing his tongue, such as he had enforced on himself at the height of his estrangement from Governor Dudley. After barely three years of satisfaction and pleasure, he again saw himself as a Christ-like victim, and found secret pleasure in thinking of "the Gratification which is done unto Him, in the sad Things which tear me to Pieces before him." Again he mightily inculcated on himself the need to "suppress all Ebullitions of sinful Wrath and Rage; all wrathful and raging Expressions, and unadvised Speeches." Again dead to the world, he decided not to have his portrait painted, although he had sat for some drafts of it, and felt tempted to destroy his diaries himself and to keep them no more.

Mather's distress also awakened an older form of coping. For the first time in twenty-five years, it seems, he began communing with angels. "I am tried unto the uttermost, in my domestic Circumstances," he wrote at the end of January 1719, "But my dear SAVIOUR . . . admits me to such Communion with Himself as makes me a glorious Compensation." His diaries leave it uncertain whether angels appeared to him as palpably as they did in 1693; the descriptions consist mostly of rapt exclamations and statements of the incommunicability of the experiences: "unutterable!

unutterable! unutterable! . . . . . . wonderful! wonderful! Astonishing!" In March 1718, he devoted a day of fasting and prayer to angels that dazzled him by its glory: "the Flights, which I thus took among the holy ANGELS. I find my Pen unable to write the Things, and the Terms, to which my Soul mounted up as with the Wings of an Eagle." He interpreted his several amazing enjoyments during the year as God's requital for his woes, "a rich Compensation, for all the Sorrows, which are appointed for me."

*

On March 9, 1719, Mather began needing richer compensation than ever before. That day a deputy sheriff came to his house and, with Mather away, read a summons to Lydia. It directed them to appear in court to answer a claim of £157 made by Mary Mico, the widow of a Boston merchant, for supplies she had sold to Lydia's deceased former husband, John George, and his also deceased business partner and son-in-law Nathan Howell.

This ominous summons was the outcome of a seemingly benign event. In June 1716, one year after his marriage, Mather had agreed to administer the goods, rights, and credits of the estate of Nathan Howell, who had been married to Lydia's daughter. The exact value of the estate is unknown, but may be gauged from an inventory taken after perhaps £4000 in debts had been cleared. It shows a very large estate worth over £7609, consisting of warehoused goods, buildings, land, and ships, and of nearly £5000 in uncollected debts. The inventory also shows debts owing from the estate in the amount of £4157.

In taking on the administration of this estate, Mather had perforce also taken on some of the unsettled affairs of the defunct Howell-George partnership, and of the deceased John George himself, for whom Howell had been acting as an administrator. And in addition to discharging the complex accounts of what had been a large mercantile firm, he to some extent had also assumed responsibility for looking after Howell's two young children, George and Nathan, who in 1716 were about three and a half and two years old. Their father, also, had not left the world tidily. Howell, as Mather remembered him, had been a "sorry, sordid, froward and exceedingly wicked Fellow," and a spendthrift as well: "Had he lived, he had soon brought a Noble to Nine-pence."

Mather undertook this large load out of love for Lydia. He was "conquered," he explained, "by the Importunity of those unto whom it was impossible for him to deny any thing," and he hoped that what money remained after settling the estate might enable Lydia to do some "special Service for God and His Kingdom." He also felt that the payment of debts due a great number of creditors would be a justice pleasing to heaven, and he wished to do a kindness to the widow and the two young orphans, unfortunate sons of a "wretched Father." For all that, he accepted the administration knowing, as he often freely confessed, that he had no talent for business, and had made keeping out of debt "a great Point of Religion with me." Having often preached on the dangers of debt, only six months before assuming the administration he had cautioned his congregation against the risks of suretyship. Quoting Solomon's saying that *"He that is Surety for a Stranger shall be sore Broken for it"* (Prov. 11:15), he had warned that although it is a breach of charity never to stand surety, doing so demands exquisite caution: *"Think over and over again; Am I Safe? Does God call me into any Sponsorial Hazard? Do not the Circumstances of my Family forbid my coming into them? Shall I not by'nd by Repent most bitterly, and even tear my Hair for the Vexation of my coming under these Encumbrances?"* In speaking of hair-tearing vexations, Mather was more than usually prophetic.

Mather explained later that he had always protested against meddling in the administration himself, but instead, with the consent and advice of the relatives concerned, had turned it over to attorneys. At first he hired Pelatiah Whittemore and Daniel Willard, the husband of his daughter Abigail. Notices were placed in the *News-Letter* beginning in January 1717, calling on those who owed money to the estates of George and Howell to pay their debts through Willard and Whittemore, "that so the Trouble which will otherwise necessarily follow, may be prevented." The trouble, however, was not prevented, and what followed was unlikely to make Mather or his ministry popular.

Forever bent on Doing Good, and having pleaded often from his pulpit for creditors not to beleaguer debtors, Mather found himself now a large creditor, again and again hauling debtors into court. His first taste of being a financial shark seems to have come on December 14, 1716, when on his behalf as administrator of the Howell estate, a writ of attachment was issued against a Plymouth mariner named Michael Packanet, who owed the estate £9 15s. The judicial procedure began with the issuance of this writ against the defendant, who was summoned to appear later for a hearing of the case at the Court of Common Pleas. Packanet had no goods to attach so he was put into the Plymouth jail. In January, Mather took to court Nathaniel Oliver, a merchant, and Timothy Thornton, a shipwright, who owed the estate some £6000. They also were ordered to jail unless they paid the debt, part of which they managed to return as the case continued into the spring.

For Mather this was merely an initiation into years of lawsuits. In 1717 alone he pressed no fewer than twelve suits on behalf of the estate, mostly involving small sums owed by people of even smaller means. For instance, on March 3, a writ was issued against Nicholas Davison, a Newbury mariner who owed the Howell estate nearly £7. A sheriff went to his house and, unable to find him, attached two chairs and left a summons. The same day a writ went out against a Plymouth yeoman named Eliezer Dunham, who owed £4 2s 1d; the sheriff handed him a summons and attached a trunk. On March 18 a writ was issued for Benjamin James, a Marblehead fisherman who owed £5 18s for shrouds and twine. When the last two cases were heard at the Court of Common Pleas on April 2, Mather reached some unspecified agreement with Dunham, but the writ against James was dismissed as not having been served. The court heard the case against Davison on July 2, and ordered payment to Mather, plus damages and court costs.

These cases can stand as representative of the many others in which at Mather's instigation the sheriff confronted some fisherman or shipwright or blacksmith, attaching his tables or trunks or chairs for the sums he owed for cordage, cod line, or dock nails. Some cases were more complicated. At least two involved residents of Maine, one of whom both owed money to John George and had sold land to Nathan Howell and then committed acts of trespass upon it. At least one case, for £9 15s 3d, resulted in a jury trial, which found against Mather and charged him for court costs as administrator of the estate.

Other of Mather's suits did not succeed either, usually, it seems, because the debtors were impoverished mariners unable to pay. And by the end of 1717, although he had acted as administrator for eighteen months, many more debts remained outstanding. Feeling he must "hasten the Settlement of Affairs," he transferred the attorneyship from Whittemore and Willard to Samuel Sewall, the judge's nephew. Sewall ran a notice in the *News-Letter* calling on debtors to pay, so the estate could satisfy its creditors. For Nathan Howell had left creditors as well, plenty of them. By about 1719 Mather's attorneys had with "vast Fatigue, and much projection and contrivance" paid out nearly £4000, much of it in small sums, owed by the estate.

The sheriff who appeared with a summons at Mather's house on March 9, 1719, seems to have come with the first suit not by the estate, but against it. Mary Mico, the widow of a Boston merchant, charged John

George and Nathan Howell with owing some £157 for canvas, oakum, cable, and other supplies. She sued for the money, naming Lydia as executor of the estate of John George, and Mather as administrator of the estate of Nathan Howell. Unfortunately, because Mather's diaries for 1719 and 1720 have not survived, his reaction to receiving the summons is unknown. It may be estimated, however, from the sermon he delivered two days later, on Acts 19:36.: *Ye ought to do nothing Rashly.*

The manuscript probably contains more crossouts and blots than that of any other sermon Mather wrote, implying that he composed it in the very state the sermon condemns. Apoplectically he warned his congregation to beware of every form of rashness, many of which he had committed himself, especially including the undertaking of sureties:

> O *Citizen of Zion*, Engage nothing but wh[at] thou *mayst* Engage, and what thou *should*[st] perform, nothing but what is within thy *Compass*, and will not be against thy *Comfort*. . . . And there is one sort of *Rash Engagements*, which you must shun above the rest, if you would keep out of Sore Entanglements. You shall be informed what they are; prov XI. 15. *He that is Surety for a Stranger shall* [smart] *for it*. . . .

As if regarding the summons from the perspective of his betrayed passion for Lydia and his frustrated concern for Creasy, disappointments that should have schooled him in distrust, he also condemned rash marriages and rash hopes for children:

> Be sure we admit and Cherish *Rash Expectations*, when we hope to find that in *Creatures*, which they will not afford unto us. . . . Alas, how prone are we to Look for more from *Creatures*, than they will yield unto us. . . . Tis often so, that we Likewise *Expect* this and that great Consolation from such or such a particular Creature. We have a *Child* perhaps whereof we say, *This Same shall* comfort us! Anon we find so much *Vanity*, and so much *Vexation*, attending the *Creature*, that we see, *Twas Rashly done to look for Grapes from Thorns*. . . .

Badly rasped by reaching for such grapes himself, Mather concluded that human comfort is concerned in not acting from passion.

Aside from venting his angry self-reproach in public, Mather seems to have drawn up for the court hearing, in July, a document entitled "The Answer of the Administrator upon the Estate of *Nathan Howel* [sic] deceased, unto the Citation served upon him." In it he explained that much had been paid to creditors from the estate already, including a considerable part of the debt to Mico. In the process, one of the attorneys (possibly Whittemore) was "suspected of some disallowable proceedings," both attorneys had been let go, and a new, single attorney chosen. He petitioned for a postponement of the hearing until the next court session, "Long before which Time, he hopes, Everything will be done unto the just Satisfaction, not only of Mrs. *Mico* but also of the other creditors." Whether he ever presented this document is unknown, but in July the court ordered payment to the widow Mico, plus damages and court costs. After the judgment was rendered, Cotton and Lydia both appeared in court and entered into recognizance with sureties to appeal their case at the next Superior Court.

Mather began trying desperately to disentangle himself from the administration. At the end of the year he wrote to Samuel Sewall, presumably believing that as the probate judge who had granted him the administration, Sewall could release him from it. The situation was awkward for Sewall, and complicated. On the one hand, Mather was his lifelong close friend. But Sewall's nephew (confusingly also named Samuel Sewall) had married Lydia's daughter, the former wife of the deceased Nathan Howell, and the couple were now at odds with Mather over the administration. The younger Sewall had at first agreed to act as an attorney in the business himself, but had then withdrawn; or rather his wife Katharin had forbidden him to act—harboring, Mather believed, "ill intentions to plague" him, although he had married the couple himself. The younger Sewall, as the stepfather of the two Howell children, was also pressuring Mather to hasten settlement of the estate.

Judge Sewall did not reply to Mather for two months, when he apologized for his long delay and sympathized with Mather's wish to "obtain freedom from this perplexing Administration." He suggested that Mather prepare an inventory of what had been received by and paid from the estate, and of the money owing the attorneys—quickly, Sewall said, "for your sake, and for the Orphans, and my own." Although the inventory was prepared it did nothing toward releasing Mather from his administration. Sewall, either because he lacked authority to help Mather, or because of the involvement of his nephew, failed to act.

With his passion for respectability, his sense of himself as a model to his children and the community, his solemn pride in his ministry, for Mather to find himself on the wrong side of the law proved fearsomely unnerving. His liability for huge unpaid debts; the writs, the sheriffs, the courts and their threats of force; the possible, and freezingly ignominious, shadow of debtors' prison—all aroused in him a near-shattering anxiety. On the night of April 13, sometime after nine o'clock, Judge Sewall received an anonymous letter, purporting to be from a friend of Mather's, with a request to burn the letter after reading.

The author—who may well have been Mather himself, although the letter is not in his hand—drew an alarming picture of Mather's condition. Overwhelmed by the administration of the estate, he was sinking under such "heavy and many troubles" that unless help came speedily "we shall quickly lose him." So dispirited he could speak to no one and talk of nothing, he lived in a state of dread: "every one that knocks at his door surprizes him, that his heart dies within him, as he sayes, fearing there is an Arrest to be serv'd on him, or some body to dun him for a Debt." Worse, the younger Sewall has led him to think that he contemplates prosecuting him for maladministration. The writer implored Sewall not to be swayed by his nephew or his nephew's wife, but despite their interference to help rid Mather of the administration. Otherwise, he said, the result would be "the Death, or . . . some thing worse than that soon coming on that distressed tho' worthy Gentleman."

This letter also contains the one surviving clue to Lydia's apparent failure to relieve Mather by covering the debts herself. Their marriage contract, of course, forbad him any access to her wealth, under a penalty of £2000, and she may simply have wished to torment him. Or she may have run out of funds herself, although since the contract mentions that she had come into a "Considerable Estate" this seems unlikely. Sewall's anonymous correspondent, however, noted that Mather's "Terrible wife" would "have a great Estate whether there be one or no," suggesting that Lydia did not credit the inventory Mather had prepared, but believed that her deceased former husband had left funds sufficient to satisfy creditors. For whatever reason, Mather was forced to pay off the debts of the estate himself.

The seriousness of Mather's situation was deepened by the simultaneous economic crisis in Boston which had forced him to find scholarship money for Sammy. People were unable to get work, the value of bills of credit had fallen and, by one account, a "great Part of the Town can hardly get Bread to satisfie Nature." The lack of a medium of exchange forced many to labor for goods, then faced them with selling off long-held homes at half-value as creditors called in debts and demanded money. A vast number of lawsuits resulted, allowing lawyers and other court officers, it was claimed, to "grow Rich on the Ruins of their Neighbours." The April 1720 court session in one county alone issued more than a thousand writs.

Mather depicted his superlative share in this general plight in an undated "Statement" which he characterized as "*One Small Instance of the Hardships, which the Dealings of the people in the Country run into.*" After describing how he had indiscreetly allowed his name to stand as the administrator of an estate, he told of his many problems in discharging a debt of £50 owing, with interest, to someone in Hartford. The debt had been paid, but the man's attorney now demanded an additional £20 to cover the debt and interest "at the Extravagant price whereto silver is risen at this day." Mather asked the Hartford creditor to forgo this surcharge, considering the financial difficulty which the depreciation of bills of credit had brought upon everyone. He explained that he had profited nothing from handling the estate, but on the contrary had put up "*between Three and Four hundred*" pounds of his own to answer creditors, leaving him an "Empty Pocket" and nothing else in the world "but a Few Books, and a little Houshold stuff and plate, that I could call my own." Despite Mather's entreaties and the intercession of prominent people in Hartford, the creditor insisted. Indeed through his lawyer—"counting me too mean a person to receive a line from him"—he threatened Mather with either paying the twenty pounds or going to jail. Mather did pay, and from his own funds. Overcoming evil with good he refused to name the person who had thus "*extorted* from a poor Minister," but instead concluded with his hope "to meet with him in *Paradise,* who would have laid me in *Prison.*"

Certain that Sewall's nephew and Lydia's daughter, his own stepchild, wished to harm him, Mather was by the fall fixed in believing that his deliverance lay only in getting Judge Sewall to release him from the administration. In October he wrote to Paul Dudley, the son of his former foe, Joseph Dudley. "No words can express the anguish," he said, "with which this petition comes to you." Sewall, he said, had often promised to free him from the administration, and he asked Dudley to visit the judge and be resolute in making him act: "see him do what he must for my relief, even . . . before you stir out of the room." Whether Dudley went to see Sewall is unknown, but Mather's demanding request again failed. Sewall refused to act.

Apparently despairing of Sewall's help, Mather in early November petitioned a higher authority, the governor's Council. In his defense he drew up a set of "Reasons why the Administrator on the Estate of *Nathan Howel* [*sic*] deceased should be Released from the Bonds of Administration Humbly Offered." First, he told the Council, in letting himself be "unhappily drawn into" the business he had acted indiscreetly, harmed his ministry, and received from those who benefited from his work only "unaccountable Ingratitude." Second, he had shown himself, he admitted, to be altogether unqualified: "Were he, *Non compos mentis*, This would be thought enough to Release him; Now if there has not been enough either to *Declare* him so, or to *Render* him so; yet there is enough to represent him as Incompetent." Third, the administration having been carried on with entire fidelity, thousands of pounds in debts had been paid, large sums had been collected, and the "Trouble which remains, is very little in comparison of that which has been already waded through." Mostly, however, Mather pleaded the misery to which his rash act of compassion had reduced him: "the Sufferings of the present Administrator are so Insupportable, and he is in such peculiar circumstances, that he cannot but press for a Release from his Bonds, with an Importunity, which he hopes will move the Compassion of them who can deliver him."

Auspiciously, this time Mather had the support of the younger Sewall and his wife Katharin, who also petitioned the Council to discharge Mather and reimburse him for his expenses. Their motives were not entirely selfless, for at the same time Sewall's wife petitioned for an adjustment of a personal debt connected with the estate. Nevertheless, the Council allowed Mather £200 out of the estate for his trouble and expense in the administration, and agreed to dismiss him—"in case any proper person will undertake the same."

But no proper person did so. The new year found Mather still in charge of the estate, with large new demands being made against it. The beating in his private life apparently lamed his ministry, for when preaching on his birthday, February 12, he found that "my *locks are cut*. I performed so pitifully." What impaired his performance may have been a return of his stutter, for he added, without further explanation, "This last bout has been the most shocking that I have had this twenty years." He had been invited to preach the lecture the same week, "But I can't—I can't," and he asked another minister to substitute for him. He also wrote abroad in April to the New England Company, "so discouraged by some occurrences," he said, as to ask again to be dismissed from his work as an Indian commissioner.

Mather needed no more discouragement, but Creasy provided some. "My Miserable, miserable, miserable Son *Increase!*," he moaned on April 4. "The Wretch has brought himself under public Trouble and Infamy by bearing a Part in a Night-Riot, with some detestable Rakes in the Town. Oh! What shall I do?" While struggling to extricate himself from the administration he fumed anew over Creasy, determined that until his son showed signs of repentance he would, this time, "chase him out of my Sight; forbid him to see me." He seems to have sent Creasy for a while to Increase Mather, who also denounced the boy for having acted to "the dishonor of God and of his friends and Relations." With Creasy out of sight, Mather decided to write him a "tremendous Letter," setting his crime before his eyes and, after so much coddling, threatening that until the boy genuinely repented he would "never own him or do for him, or look on him."

As always, Mather's storming left unmoved his fixed love for Creasy. Much in his son's personality mirrored his own more amiable self, and he cherished Creasy's many virtues—"a singular sweetness of temper (which, alas, has been a snare unto him), a ripe wit, a sharp sense, the ornaments of a gentlemanly education." While offering prayers at a baptism on April 23, he found himself thinking of Creasy and, in tears, he asked God why He called the children of men: "Was it, that they might be given up to Blindness and Hardness, and Madness? Was it that they might have the Distempers of their Souls lie uncured, when one gracious Word of thine can cure them?" The answer was of course no; he would yet believe, yet see God perform wonders for his children. "Ah, poor *Increase*," he wrote. "Tho' I spake against him, yet I earnestly remember him, and my Bowels are troubled for him."

Seeking some help in reforming Creasy, Mather introduced the boy to the young minister Thomas Foxcroft. That Creasy himself desired Foxcroft's acquaintance he saw as a hopeful sign that his son might yet learn serious piety, adherence to business, and horror of evil company. He wrote to Foxcroft hoping he would allow Creasy some improving visits, promising that "when you see him, you will certainly love him."

*

Weighed down by Lydia's paroxysms, Creasy's escapades, and his creditors' demands, Mather simultaneously began paying for his friendly support of Governor Shute. The new administration created discord, and all of the governor's enemies became his.

Opposition to Shute solidified over the economic crisis in Massachusetts, although it first gathered around a related issue, the founding of a public bank. As Mather explained the issue, which originated in Dudley's administration, for several years much of the business of Massachusetts had been conducted in government bills of credit. As the province by raising taxes managed to pay off its large debt, incurred during long years of war, these bills were being retired to the public treasury and destroyed, depleting the circulating medium. Businessmen complained that the number of bills in circulation was "no more than *a sprat in a whale's belly*," and far too few for the country's commerce. To provide a medium of trade, a group of men proposed forming a private bank which would issue its own bills. This plan met with violent opposition, however, and as an alternative the Dudley government proposed issuing and lending out more bills of credit like the earlier ones. Mather had supported the private bank scheme, perhaps because its sponsors were political antagonists of Dudley. He did so without conviction, however, acknowledging both his own naiveté in finance and the sincerity of those who claimed that the government's scheme would better serve the public interest.

The change of administrations put Mather on the wrong side of the bank issue. Those who favored the private bank, once political antagonists of Dudley, now became political antagonists of Shute, who opposed the issuance of more paper bills altogether. Never more than lukewarm in his support for the private bank, Mather came around to Shute's position and was accused of having changed his views, although he insisted that "*cujus contrarium.* I have never done so, to any one man in the world." He might have escaped serious public attack except that the private bank became the nexus of wider political arguments, and those who favored it aligned themselves against Shute over many other issues as well. Preeminent in this opposition, and both supporters of the private bank, were Oliver Noyes, a wealthy real estate speculator and founder of the Brattle church; and Elisha Cooke, Jr., son of the Elisha Cooke who for years had unforgivingly denounced Increase Mather's acceptance of the new charter. The elder Cooke had died in 1715, leaving the son probably the wealthiest man in the colony. The younger Cooke also inherited his father's political following, and assembled something like a political machine in Boston, which elected to the House representatives hostile to Shute. By 1719 they found much to be hostile about. For in the economic crisis that developed, not only did money disappear from circulation, but also the value of bills of credit depreciated, trade in general declined, and inflation became severe. The crisis, we have seen, worsened Mather's own difficulties in discharging the debts of the estate, and also produced many pamphlets, much talk of reviving the private bank scheme, and bitter divisions in towns, churches, and even families.

Amid this plethora of other trials, Mather exerted himself to support Shute, on whom much of the blame was laid. On March 12, 1719, only three days after a sheriff first appeared at his door summoning him to court, he preached a sermon before the General Assembly, recommending Shute's policies. As the grand expedient for relieving the economic crisis he urged not the issuance of more paper bills, which Shute opposed, but public frugality—an argument that had long been used against the private bank, and which in effect blamed the people, not the government, for the crisis. He also urged total loyalty to Shute as expressive of loyalty to the crown. For in opposition to Shute he foresaw the possibility in Boston of "*Raging Waves of the Sea* . . . Mutinous, and Seditious, and Rebellious Actions." To oppose Shute, he implied, was to reawaken suspicions in London about the loyalty of New Englanders, and perhaps to risk loss of the present charter. Shute and his allies pressed to have the sermon printed at government expense, although Mather's vision of social convulsion made Samuel Sewall fear that the printing might itself invite Parliament to revoke the charter. Shute tried to have the matter voted on, but met stiff resistance and broke off the debate; the sermon apparently was printed at government expense.

Mather had been warned from London by Jeremiah Dummer that moves might be made there to remove Shute. In a further show of support, Mather wrote abroad to Shute's brother, Lord Barrington, praising the governor as "generally and passionately beloved." He intended this long, highly laudatory letter privately, no doubt to enlist Barrington's help; but it somehow made its way into an English newspaper in May 1719 and was reprinted in Boston, bringing down on him the "fury and outrage" of Noyes, Cooke, and their party of "venomous malcontents." Aggravatingly, Shute seemed to take no notice of the assault; in fact Mather was told that people in the government derided him behind his back—a thing, he said, "I must believe with discretion." Discretion never having been one of his strengths, least of all when he was besieged, he spread a report that Cooke, alleged to be a heavy drinker, had been drunk for several days. The story was challenged, forcing him to draw up a written retraction for Cooke to use in absolving himself. But having retracted he continued referring to Shute's enemies in his correspondence as a "party of Tipplers."

Opposition to Shute and contention in Boston came to a head in the spring of 1720. By then many people in financial distress saw Cooke as their spokesman against the government, while Cooke had become not only Shute's political adversary but also personally repugnant to him, among other reasons because of a report that in company, and too punch-drunk to stand or walk, he had implicitly called Shute a "Blockhead." In May, the House chose Cooke for its Speaker. Shute negatived the choice

on the ground that Cooke had ill-treated the king's governor, and directed the House to choose a different speaker. Shute also negatived the
choice of two councillors, Nathaniel Byfield and John Clark, who had
been staunch supporters of Cooke. The governor's negative enraged the
House and begot a heated debate on questions of privilege, and of
whether a governor had power to overturn a House decision. Shute reminded the representatives that Governor Dudley had also disallowed a
Speaker, and had been confirmed in his right to do so in London (as
Shute was later). He advised the members to choose another Speaker,
and to reserve their asserted right until the matter could be laid before
the king. The House refused, in reply to which Shute dissolved the session.

Apprehensive that such political chaos might endanger the charter,
Mather seems to have doubted the wisdom of Shute's negative on Cooke.
But he just as strongly considered Shute well disposed to New England, a
mild man pricked to act intemperately by Cooke's truculence. Indeed
Shute's behavior bears out the impression of him given later by Thomas
Hutchinson, that he was a man of integrity but a lover of ease and lacking
artfulness, anxious to avoid controversy but without skill in doing so. To
defend Shute, but also in the larger hope of quieting the building uproar,
Mather, it seems quite certain, produced an anonymously published pamphlet entitled *News from Robinson Cruso's Island* ([1720]). Even granting
his ingrained ability to continue working amidst defeat and disappointment, his ability to do so now seems remarkable, for the tumult over
Cooke occurred little more than a month after the anonymous letter to
Sewall depicting his state of dread as he awaited arrest. In whatever state,
he told of Robinson Crusoe coming to Boston, here called the island of
"*Insania*," just when some "rash Men willing to see the Country all in
Confusion" insisted on having Cooke, the ideal choice for Speaker had
the intent been to spite the governor. Crusoe delivers a speech chastising
Cooke's supporters for bringing chaos on the country and forcing the
good-tempered Shute to act dictatorially, simply for the pleasure of ill-
treating him. He warns that they are again risking the charter, betraying
the country under "*the Hypocritical disguise of contending for your Privileges.*"

Although the House called on Shute to punish the "authors" of the
pamphlet for libeling some of its members, suspicions that Mather was
the single author were apparently rife. In July appeared a rebuttal, *Reflections upon Reflections: Or, More News from Robinson Cruso's Island*
(1720). Obviously with Mather in mind, the author attributed the earlier

pamphlet to "one, whose *Scribendi Cacoethes* [itch for scribbling] has made him famous on both sides the *Atlantick*" and whose brain "is over-charged with so great a variety of News, that the Country feels themselves on many accounts the *worse for him*." He dismissed Mather's suggestion that in choosing Cooke the House had led a "good Spirited" governor to act harshly, insisting that the choice of a Speaker was one of Massachusetts' valued political rights. Mather's "Learned Jargon," he said, was aimed at frightening New England out of its privileges and rendering "our selves obnoxious to the Curse of succeeding Generations."

Mather, probably hoping to disconnect his name from the Crusoe pamphlet, drew up a three-page tract entitled "A Few Remarks . . . on the Choice of A *Speaker*," where he announced:

> To prevent such mistakes as people have run away withal, about the Authors of the Late Account of *Cruso's* Island, (and some other things,) it must be known that the publisher of that and of these Remarks, is no native of *Boston*.

This Matherese avowal of course leaves open the possibility that even though Mather was not the "publisher" of the pamphlet, he was the author. He did not publish "A Few Remarks," perhaps because it qualifies his support for Shute, representing more candidly his view that the governor had acted unwisely. This time he disguised himself not as Crusoe but, cleverly, as an anonymous member of the House who is opposed to negativing Cooke and desires to preserve the House's privileges. But this member distinguishes between the House at large and the "Shortsighted and Hot-headed Party" within it who champion Cooke fanatically, a party who "being disappointed of a private Bank, and of a Governor, whom they Expected, have all along mal-treated our present Governor, hoping to tire out his gracious patience and goodness with Bad Usages." Since Shute had laid the matter before the king, he urged the representatives to waive the controversy and go on with public affairs, warning that if Cooke's party were allowed to further embroil things, the crown would take notice of the "*ungovernable Spirit*" in Massachusetts and reconsider the charter.

Mather was also accused of persuading Shute to negative Dr. John Clark, one of the newly elected councillors. The charge discomforted Mather the more because Clark was the brother of his deceased wife Elizabeth and, as a physician, had attended her during her final illness. The Clarks, also, were now caring for Mather's daughter Liza, his dead wife's namesake and their niece. She may have been driven from Mather's house by Lydia's turn against his children, but in any case she seemed to him the "lively image" of Elizabeth, a living reminder of a happier past and of a "never-to-be-forgotten mother." Clark, believing his former brother-in-law had advised Shute against him, had publicly expressed aversion toward Mather, so Mather instead wrote to Clark's wife. He swore "as before the Glorious Lord" that he had been in no way "directly or indirectly accessory or instrumental to this negative," but on the contrary had advised Shute against it. All he had ever done, he said, had been to express his unhappiness over the misunderstanding between Shute and Clark; those who gave these innocent remarks a defamatory appearance did so to sow discord. Thanking the Clarks for their goodness to Liza, he lamented that his character lay "much at the mercy of lying and loathsome talebearers."

A new session of the House was scheduled for July. Seemingly on the chance that it might stubbornly again choose Cooke for Speaker, Mather prepared, apparently for Shute's use, a memorandum entitled "In case, the Representatives make Choice of E.C. for their Speaker." Here he disclosed to the governor his real view and suggested that, if pressed by the House, Shute should accept Cooke's nomination. He also offered Shute a face-saving but plausible rationale. Shute could claim that although the recalcitrance of the House might well be answered by prorogation, everyone knew that his chief desire "forever is, the prosperity and Tranquillity of the people." Aware of the need to resolve urgent public problems, he would therefore "suspend those Expressions which he might justly give ... until His Majesty's pleasure be further known." Mather's coaching was unnecessary, for in its new session the House, after three votes in which Cooke led the field, chose as Speaker a representative from Salem. They also reduced Shute's salary, however, and told him plainly that "whoever was of advice to his excellency" had not consulted the king's interest or the public good.

At this point Mather might reasonably have ended his covert campaign against Shute's foes. Instead, some unnamed scurrilities against him goaded him to act with, he confessed, "perhaps too quick and Keen" resentment. Writing to several correspondents around August, he mocked Cooke and his allies as "*idiots* and *fuddlecaps* and *men that love and make a lie*," and called them "*American* (worse than *African*) monsters." His letter or letters somehow got to Cooke, who with two or three representatives, Mather said, made him "sufficiently sensible of the Resentments which they have upon it; and they want not for will or skill, to do it further unto the last Extremity." He seems upon Shute's request to have apologized for the epithets, but he continued to tell others that they were deserved. In December someone in Cooke's party published still another pamphlet, *New News from Robinson Cruso's Island* (1720), attacking Mather for slandering people privately, for caricaturing New Englanders as "*worse than the Savage Monsters of Africa*," and for stirring up old fears about the charter. The writer advised him not to meddle in state affairs, of which he knew nothing, and offered a caricature himself: Mather as Pope, "the great DON-DAGO, the *Primate wou'd be* of our Island." As Mather admitted to his friend John Winthrop, "I own myself not a match for them."

In this Mather was several ways correct. Not only was he ignorant of finance and engulfed in domestic problems, but the private bank issue and the negative on Cooke brought with them a dramatic change in political perspective. The pamphleteers spoke for a new, increasingly powerful segment of society that could consider social issues without reference to the original Puritan vision of a covenanted people, to whom the resolution of New England's problems was not moral but financial and political. They became, as Perry Miller remarked, "the first authors in New England to argue a case with hardly so much as a genuflection in the direction of religion." The language of their politics was not that of provoking evils and public fasts, but that of privilege, depreciation, and the balance of trade.

Neither upbringing nor inclination qualified Mather to discourse in this language, much less to handle its accompanying infighting and chicanery. Yet as he undertook to defend Shute he was himself drawn into the game. The charges that he self-servingly changed his views on the bank or betrayed his brother-in-law or gossiped about Cooke's tippling are only instances of repeated accusations of underhandedness and smear tactics. In 1717, a middle-aged Harvard graduate named Joseph Parsons charged him with communicating to the New South Church, to which Parsons had been proposed for the ministry, a private letter that, he said, "*utterly ruined*" him there. Mather dismissed the charge as false, but the following year he was similarly accused of having communicated to a man named Rogers a letter addressed to him from a man named Emerson, in which Emerson had used "Invectives" against Rogers. Mather flatly denied that Emerson had sent him such a letter, much less had he confided it to Rogers. Whether Mather acted treacherously in these cases is unknown, but in similar cases much condemning evidence has survived. To give only two examples, around 1720 he wrote to the merchant John Frizzell. to whom he had written before in Creasy's name. Now he fabricated an anonymous letter (like the one Samuel Sewall received describing Mather's dread), asking Frizzell to help subsidize publication of one of his works. Frizzell had been a member of his congregation, and Mather knew him well. Yet in the letter Mather introduced himself as "one that never spoke to my remembrance one word to you in all my Life." To appreciate the letter's utter deceitfulness, it must be stressed that the document is entirely in Mather's hand and that he wrote it himself:

> I have the honour of some acquaintance with Dr. Mather, the younger, a person whom you as well as I have a high value for. Among his other favors, he communicated unto me a composure of his entitled *The Work of the Day*. . . . The composure, if I have any judgment, is a most illustrious and uncommon performance: 'tis filled with rich and rare thoughts, and among the entertainments which eminent men have given us, I have not seen the thing that equals it. Let me peruse it never so often, every paragraph still appeared new to me, and I still discovered new treasures and beauties in it.

Mather went on to urge the wealthy Frizzell to help bring "this noble work of the Doctor's into the world," signing himself "Your unknown friend and servant."

The other case exposes Mather offering one opinion to a person's face and another behind his back. In the summer of 1720, the Harvard Overseers considered granting an honorary M.A. degree to Daniel Neal, a London Congregational minister who had written a two-volume *History of New-England* (London, 1720). Neal sent a copy to Mather, who returned a buttery reply. New Englanders, he said, should be grateful "that any men of worth should count such a poor, despised, maligned country as ours worthy of their cognizance." But he added that New England was never famous for gratitude to its benefactors, and warned Neal not to be surprised if his "well-penned History" failed to receive "just consideration of your merits." In actuality, Mather was enraged. Neal had given an unflattering picture of the New England ministry, and had commented of the *Magnalia* that had the author *"put his Materials a little closer together, and disposed them in another Method, his Work would have been more acceptable to this Part of the World."* Although Mather told Neal that "some of our best men are considering of the most proper way to testify their . . . thankful reception of what you have done for us," these were not remarks for which he would gladly see Harvard award an honorary M.A.

The day before a college committee concerned with awarding the degree was to meet, Mather wrote to two unnamed persons, asking them to convey his views to "your honorable President." The phrase itself was two-faced, for when writing "under the darkest concealment" to Shute, he referred to Leverett rather as "the (pretended) President." He admitted that in public he spoke "with all due tenderness of Mr. Neil's [sic] performance," and in fact believed he deserved some acknowledgment; but he would reveal to them thoughts which the "law of goodness will release me from uttering unto others." Concerning criticism against his *Magnalia* he was, naturally, indifferent—both to "the invectives which that poor work has undergone, and," certainly, to "the compliments (very excessive ones) which I have received from eminent persons in more than three nations upon it." But in fact Neal's history, he said, was only his own *Magnalia* annalized and denuded into a "dry political story." Neal treated Harvard as if no one educated there could write modern English; Neal took his story of the Salem witchcraft trials from "such a senseless, lying, malicious wretch as Calef"; and Neal, to "pass by a thousand other things," was simply a "very weak and shallow man." (The letter did not prevent the Overseers from awarding Neal the degree.)

In the past, Mather's resentments had found subtler outlets than overt lying, talebearing, and duplicity. This moral deterioration in Mather seems the result both of his exhausting personal problems and of his compliance with changed standards of political life in Massachusetts, whose earlier tribal solidarity was becoming fragmented by party interests, and whose members, as Mather wrote, were becoming "all generally Alienated from one another, broken into Factions, and Sacrificing all to *Cursed Animosities.*" Politically and emotionally out of his depth, Mather was now simply unable to manage his rage becomingly. When his foe Oliver Noyes, a popular leader in the House, died in March 1721, of apoplexy, he exulted. "Methinks," wrote the minister of the North Church, "I see a wonderful Token for good in this Matter; And I go on with humble Supplications to the Lord."

*

Mather's ministry dealt him two final aggravations. The first was the revival of the Arian heresy in England, climaxed by the divisive Salters' Hall controversy of 1719. Arianism arose during the earliest period of Christianity from the attempt to reconcile the unity of the godhead with the distinction of personality in the Trinity. Arius, writing in the fourth century, distinguished the Father from the Son, endowing Christ with free will and a capacity for change, implicitly making Him neither divine nor eternal. As an institution Arianism formed the religion of the eastern half of the Roman Empire until late in the fourth century; as a doctrine, it figured in later Christian disputes as well. It had a revival among rationalistic theologians in eighteenth-century England, and was linked to Newtonianism, as Newton's passionate belief in One Creator similarly relegated Christ to an inferior role. Mather had preached and written against Arianism sporadically. In 1702, for instance, he argued that the doctrine of the Trinity was known only through revelation and could not be comprehended by reason, and treated rationalistic Arians as "Fools, that will believe nothing, except they can put their Hands into the Sides of it."

That Arianism might become genuinely troublesome began to strike Mather in 1711, as the doctrine began winning adherents through the writings of the rationalist William Whiston. Trained for the ministry and ordained, Whiston yet pioneered the offering of public lectures on science, and in 1703 had succeeded Newton as professor of mathematics at Cambridge. He had also come to find the doctrine of the Trinity unacceptable, announced his view in 1708, and was eventually deprived of his professorship. Mather admired Whiston as both a talented mathematician and a prolific writer on theology, had a correspondence with him (which has not survived), and often cited his scientific writings in "Biblia Americana." But Whiston's attempts to promote the Arian diminishment of Christ alarmed him. "My learned Friend *Whiston*," he wrote in 1711, "is likely to raise a prodigious Dust in the world, by reviving the *Arian* Opinions." He feared the dust raised not only in the world but also in himself, for his own strong rationalistic bent had long made him susceptible to weakenings of belief. "I am likely," he added, " to have my own Mind shock'd with more than ordinary Temptations on this Occasion." Indeed the next year he began reeling from doubts about the Trinity, his mind "hideously assaulted and harassed" by temptations to Arianism. By importuning God, however, he managed to receive a "Sweet Satisfaction . . . in His Truth, concerning Three Eternal Persons in His infinite Godhead."

Mather wrote several anti-Arian tracts over the next few years. But although thankful that Arianism had not crossed the water and contaminated New England, he looked perturbedly on its steady advance abroad, helped along by the other outstanding English Arian, Dr. Samuel Clarke, an English divine and disciple of Newton, whose *Scripture Doctrine of the Trinity* (1712) declared the Father alone supreme. By 1717 it had become evident to Mather that Arianism had slowly made its way not only into the Church of England but among the young Dissenting ministers also. A sharp turning point came in February and March 1719, when a

group of English Nonconformists—Presbyterians, Baptists, and Congregationalists—met in Salters' Hall in London. They were called to advise on
how to treat three Dissenting ministers in the west of England who were
suspected of Arianism. In the course of deciding, a suggestion was made
that the Assembly should itself declare adherence to orthodox Trinitarian
views, as laid down in the first of the Thirty-nine Articles and in the fifth
and sixth questions of the the Westminster Catechism. Failure to subscribe to such a declaration could easily be interpreted as a sign of holding Arian views. Yet the proposal split the assembly: sixty-three ministers
agreed to subscribe, fifty-three refused, on the ground that they would
not make human (that is, nonscriptural) creeds a test of soundness of
faith. Sixty ministers who wished to subscribe set up an assembly of their
own.

Mather learned of the Salters' Hall dispute just as he began litigating
the first suits against the Howell estate. However preoccupied, he was
thunderstruck. News of apparently broad inroads of Arianism, and of a
serious split among the English Dissenters, seemed to him "the most
grievous tidings that ever came over the Atlantic unto us." Blaming Whiston and Clarke as "the two grand satanic tools of this mischief," he dispatched a rush of letters pouring out dismay over the great "Schism arisen
among our United Brethren" and over the ministers who refused to subscribe. Isaac Watts assured him that the subscribing ministers themselves
believed that only a very few London Dissenters had become Arians, and
that the nonsubscribing ministers refused not because they were Arians
but because the subscription was "begun in a disorderly manner breaking
in upon other business and with much anger," and because they feared
such a subscription might be used as a religious test to exclude persons
from the ministry or from communion. Mather was apparently unconvinced, perhaps because he always suspected Watts's own religious leanings. Indeed Watts, a liberal and at times perplexed Calvinist who later
moved towards Unitarianism, admitted to Mather that he believed people
could be saved by conceiving Christ as omnipotent, omniscient, and al-
sufficient "and yet not equal with God the Father."

Mather regarded the nonsubscribers' refusal to endorse a nonscriptural statement of creed as an effort to use the ideal of Christian union to
promulgate Arianism. The Salters' Hall controversy thus exposed the ecumenical Universal Religion he had been fostering as another of his conflictedly conciliatory attempts to resolve the irreconcilable. His vision of
reasonable men of different sects united by a few maxims of vital piety
had of course been an imperfect thing. It excluded Catholics because of

their doomed role in Protestant eschatology, and Mather never meant it to encourage Congregationalists to give up their sectarian identity. His toleration, as Richard Lovelace remarks, was "most successful when it was directed toward those who did not have the drawback of being his neighbors." Mather wished to continue forwarding his "Syncretism of Piety" and to oppose religious persecution, yet to bar Arians from the Christian union for denying Eternal power and godhead to Christ, transforming the Savior into a mortal idol. He sent a barrage of letters to Dissenters abroad trying to make clear the difference between toleration and acceptance of heresy, indulgence and communion, forbearance and fellowship.

Mather also set forth his views publicly in *Some American Sentiments on the Great Controversy of the Time*, a formal epistle addressed to four London ministers and dated July 1, 1720, the same time as his defense of Shute over the negativing of Cooke. That sensitive episode, together with the recent attack on his style by Daniel Neal and the continued "unaccountable contempt" of London Dissenters toward publishing "Biblia Americana," may explain his beginning, in Matherese, with a defiant *mea culpa:*

> We should not be insensible, (having been very publicly inform'd of it) *That the Style and Manner of the* New-England *Writers does not equal that of the Europeans:* Nor should *he* who now writes, and who among them is the *least of the Ministers, and the lowest in Merit,* be without a very humble Sense of his Inability in point of *Sense,* as well as of *Style,* to offer any thing worthy of Consideration among the *Europeans.*

Having thus, as often before, defended himself against abuse in advance of receiving it, Mather attempted to square the ideal of Christian union with the exclusion of Arians from it. At the moment, he said, two truths demand realization: first, that no one is to be forced by civil penalties to a religious belief contrary to conscience; second, that all who truly live to God are united by certain maxims of piety entitling them to communion with each other. But these truths must be served cautiously, or Christianity be subverted. Concerning "the *plausible* Cry now so much in vogue, of *Nothing to be subscribed but the Express Words of Scripture,*" he observed that every heretic, even a papist, would so subscribe, and gain license to perpetrate damnable heresies under cover of orthodoxy. A meaningful union of Christian sects must include an express belief in the Trinity as a basis for communion and salvation, requiring not merely profession of belief in Scripture, but renunciation of Arianism. Otherwise many may claim communion with the pan-Christian church yet "continue under the Power of those *Heresies,* which are inconsistent with the *Life of* GOD in the Soul." Such claims, he suspected, signified "a strong and a deep *Conspiracy* in our very sinful Nation, to dethrone the Eternal SON of GOD."

Mather's professions of religious liberalism had led him into a compromised position two decades earlier, when he first endorsed the Presbyterian-Congregational union in London, then blasted the creation of the Brattle church at home. As happened then too, others now accused him of contradicting himself. They reproved his stand on Salters' Hall, he said, for "not consisting well with my zealous profession for a union on the terms of piety," a charge he thought "to be pitied rather than answered." One of his critics, the Baptist Thomas Hollis (whose bequest to Harvard was providing a scholarship to Sammy), pointed out that in demonstrating his Universal Religion, Mather had not long ago preached, surprisingly and generously, at the ordination of Thomas Callender, a Baptist minister. In his much publicized sermon Mather had denounced intolerance, yet he now called the nonsubscribers at Salters' Hall heretics. Mather must have received a misleading account of the controversy, Hollis suggested, or he would not impute damning sins to "his Brethren who Love the Lord Jesus. . . . so contrary to the Catholic charity he expressed" in his sermon. Invoking an old ghost, Hollis also complained that in alluding to a "plot" against Christianity, Mather was fomenting discord while those in England were seeking harmony. The charge that Mather overreacted to the events at Salters' Hall was probably just. Benjamin Colman wrote of a similar subscription crisis at an Irish assembly somewhat later, that he did not approve of those who declined the subscription, "yet I am far from imputing Arianism to them. I am herein water to Dr. Mathers Heat."

At the same time, Mather was setting up his ministry for serious damage. This second aggravation began in 1720 with the Rev. Peter Thacher of Weymouth. As Benjamin Colman related the precipitating events, Thacher had grown melancholy and in ill health at Weymouth, so he asked his church to dismiss him to go elsewhere. The relation between a minister and his flock being to many New Englanders, Colman remarked, "like that between husband and wife," the church refused. Yet Thacher insisted, got support from neighboring ministers, and the church released him. In Boston, Thacher was invited to preach as the colleague of the Rev. John Webb at the New North—the church that had been formed by the swarmers who had abandoned the Mathers' church.

Almost all the Boston ministers disapproved Thacher's conduct in securing his dismission from Weymouth, except the Mathers. They perhaps admired his acknowledged learning, piety, and ministerial gifts, for they are said to have advised and assisted him about his move from Weymouth, and they invited him to preach for several months with them. But Thacher encountered resistance within the New North itself. Forty or fifty congregants vehemently opposed his settlement with them, arguing that a minister ought to stay where God had appointed him, and deeming it unethical for a larger and wealthier congregation to deprive a smaller one. They felt strongly enough about Thacher's ordination to warn that if it proceeded they would swarm from the New North and form still another new congregation.

Shaken by the prospect of a third Congregational meetinghouse rising in the North End, Mather and his father "turned Cat in pan," as a contemporary put it, and became Thacher's "utter Enemies," helping him "into a Snare and there leave[ing] him." Having at first advised and assisted him, they now worked to obstruct his settlement at the New North, lest his opponents there band together as a new church, another rival to their own. They joined Colman and some other Boston ministers in arguing that a pastor should not be removed from his flock except for very weighty reasons, such as did not appear in Thacher's case, nor without a church council, which had not been called. They also urged the dissidents in the New North not to build another meetinghouse.

Despite this resistance from Mather and the others, Thacher's admirers in the New North pushed for and obtained his installation, which was a fiasco. The Mathers, by one account, persuaded other ministers not to attend the ceremony; apparently only two participated, one of whom was Thacher's uncle. Thacher and his uncle came to the church out a back gate and through alleys to escape interception by a hostile crowd determined to block the installation. When the crowd realized they had slipped by, it stomped into the gallery and, standing instead of sitting, protested the ceremony so noisily that no prayers could be conducted. In the din, a minister called for and received the consent of the brethren and of Thacher to what passed for his installation: "no Bear Garden certainly was ever like it," one contemporary said, "such Treatment and Language had they, that hardly was ever given to the vilest of men."

The end result of this row reached Mather on April 30, 1721, little more than two weeks after Creasy's "night-Riot," calling him "unto an uncommon Trial," he said, "wherein it will be found, whether I am Dead unto Creatures." Thacher's opponents in the New North had decided to withdraw and build the New Brick Church, popularly and appropriately referred to as the "*Revenge* Church of Christ." As Mather had feared, too, in order to fill their house the "enraged, violent, boisterous Men" who built the New Brick persuaded a "mighty Number" of his own flock to join them. He thus found his congregation abandoning him a second time, seduced by "the Religion of Pues which with a proud, vain, formal People seems to be now the chief Religion of the Town." Acknowledging that this new, very large, and nearby church was the finest in New England, while his own was in "crazy condition," he drafted a set of subscriptions toward building a new meetinghouse for his congregation. It grieved him too that his father took much to heart the swarming of these "foolish People from Him in His Age."

How many left Mather's ministry is unknown, but must have been substantial. "Tis incredible," he wrote on May 1, "what Numbers are swarming off." Just the same, in the customary show of fellowship he was asked several days later to preach the first sermon in the new church. In it he praised the New Brick as the most "*Beautiful House*" in the land, and at the end of the sermon he spoke directly to the many before him who had left his ministry. Although Increase, who was present, was apparently too ill to preach, he could not have surpassed his son in deploying pastoral concern for the salvation of the swarmers' souls as the vehicle for conveying squirming contempt for their treachery. Cotton offered the Judases Christ-like absolution for having crucified him and his father:

> When our dear SAVIOUR was within a Few Minutes of His Death, we read, *Many of them*, who attended on His Ministry, *Went away and walked no more with Him*. A very *Great Withdraw* from our Ministry many may think it will be a *Trouble* to us; and if we were not used unto *higher Sentiments*, than the People who offer it, it might be so. But we have *Learned CHRIST* better than that. I do assure you, *My Friends*, I hope you will find it more of a *Triumph* than of a *Trouble* to us.

Fusing his father's long-suffering manner with Matherese, he suggested that the building of the new church was timely, for he and Increase were about to die:

> 'Tis a Circumstance, that carries a Strong and a Strange *Consolation* in it; That our Claim to the *Royal Priesthood* is just finishing in this Addition to the many *Sacrifices*, which our Lives have been fill'd withal. That we have now done with a *World*, that has nothing in it worth Staying for; That we are just Entering into the *Joy of our Lord*, and are within a Few Weeks of seeing the *Best Hour* that ever we saw. . . .

Reminding the swarmed members how diligently he and Increase had labored for their salvation, he ended with lovingly regretful insinuations that little of it seemed to have done any good. Of this bravura kiss of death he observed in his diary: "with high Strains of Sacrificing, I give all the People to see, how easily and cheerfully we endure their Departure from us."

Suddenly, just two weeks later, Mather's multiplying defeats in his church, his family, and the government were for the moment swept from his mind, replaced by a public catastrophe. Unaware that it also held for him a personal triumph, he recorded on May 26: "The grievous Calamity of the *Small-Pox* has now entered the Town. The Practice of conveying and suffering the *Small-pox* by *Inoculation*, has never been used in *America*, nor indeed in our Nation. But how many Lives might be saved by it, if it were practised?"

12

The Paths of the Destroyer

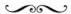

THE SMALLPOX epidemic that struck Boston in April 1721 lasted a full year and infected half the city, yet it was not unexpected. Smallpox seemed to break out at regular intervals, the last epidemic having come in 1702–3. Because of the isolation of Massachusetts, the great infectious diseases there tended to be epidemic rather than endemic. Smallpox, measles, or diphtheria might arrive devastatingly, then disappear for years; when enough nonimmune people accumulated, it came again.

Mather himself observed that beginning in 1630 smallpox arrived in Boston precisely every twelve years. Betweentimes some vessel would bring the disease, but it would not spread. Yet in the twelfth year "no precaution would keep it off"; it would become "so raging, so reaching" as to afflict even fetuses, who were "born full of it upon them." Somehow for the seventh epidemic, predictable by Mather's computations in 1714, the pattern did not hold. He speculated that the irregularity was owing to the measles epidemic of 1713 that killed three of his children and his wife, the "compassion of Heaven" refusing to add smallpox "unto what we suffered the year before." Both Mathers later took credit for having warned prophetically against the near approach of the disease. About six months before the outbreak Increase preached a sermon predicting some heavy judgment on Boston; a month or two later Cotton was stirred by a heavenly afflatus to deliver a lecture on Trouble Near, in which he too foretold "the speedy Approach of the destroying Angel."

Civic authorities seem to have been no less aware than the ministry that an epidemic might come soon. A law passed in February 1718 required ships carrying infectious diseases to anchor near Spectacle Island in the harbor, so that the infected persons and cargo that might transmit infection could be removed to the island's public hospital. The law was tested in October 1720, when a sloop arrived from the Canary Islands bearing smallpox. Several persons were put ashore at the island's "Pest house," then allowed to continue to Boston in fresh clothing after being declared healthy. The captain of the ship, however, apparently died, and the selectmen ordered that no one who had attended him in his illness might enter Boston until judged to be uncontaminated.

It was the *Seahorse,* a ship from Salt Tortuga owned by John Frizzell, that brought the lethal epidemic of 1721. On April 15 the Council debated whether to grant the ship entry to Boston. Although the *Seahorse* seems to have stayed in the harbor, on May 8 the selectmen reported that a black man from the ship was in Boston, and stricken. They voted to have Dr. John Clark (Mather's former father-in-law) board the ship and report on its condition. A second black man, a servant in Boston (whether connected with the ship is uncertain), had also taken the disease, and to isolate him the selectmen appointed two "prudent persons" to seal off the house in which he lay, allowing no one to leave or enter without their permission. Four days later, apparently after Dr. Clark made his report, the selectmen noted that two or three other men aboard the *Seahorse* also had smallpox, and voted to ask Governor Shute to call a council, to advise about sending the ship to Spectacle Island.

The next week a group composed of justices, selectmen, Overseers of the Poor, and constables searched Boston houses. They reported finding no house contaminated but the one sequestering the black servant, who they said had almost recovered. This report, like the many later official announcements, may have been designed less to inform the public than to prevent panic, for the selectmen voted just the same to clean the streets and lanes, impressing carts to carry off dirt and requiring twenty-six free male blacks and mulattos to work six days at the task. By the last week in May there were not one or two or three infected persons, but eight, one of them in Bennett Street, at the North End.

Mather feared for his children and himself, smallpox being probably the most infectious of all diseases. His friend Dr. Zabdiel Boylston graphically described some of its hideous effects:

Purple Spots, the bloody and parchment Pox, Hemorahages of Blood at the Mouth, Nose, Fundament, and Privities; Ravings and Deliriums; Convulsions, and other Fits; violent inflamations and Swellings in the Eyes and Throat; so that they cannot see, or scarcely breathe, or swallow any thing, to keep them from starving. Some looking as black as the Stock, others as white as a Sheet; in some, the Pock runs into Blisters, and the

Skin stripping off, leaves the Flesh raw. . . . Some have been fill'd with loathsome Ulcers; others have had deep, and fistulous Ulcers in their Bodies, or in their Limbs or Joints, with Rottenness of the Ligaments and Bones: Some who live are Cripples, others Idiots, and many blind all their Days. . . .

To such rank ravaging two of Mather's surviving children, Elizabeth and Sammy, were vulnerable, having been born since the last epidemic. They were both terrified of catching the disease. Mather called to heaven for guidance about whether to send them out of town, and for help in submitting "if these dear Children must lose their Lives." Because he would inevitably be called into the rooms of the sick, he felt his own life must also become threatened as the epidemic inevitably spread. Concerned also for the general public, he asked ministers to hold days of fasting and prayer, adapted his own sermons and prayers to the calamity, and called for aid to the "Miserables neglected and perishing in Sickness."

Mather's charitable and zealous concern for the sufferers led him to a more important resolution also. He decided to propose to the Boston physicians that they try a new method of preventing the disease. For years, beginning with his boyhood interest in medicine, his life had moved him toward this resolution. In adolescence, when acting as an amanuensis for the physician William Avery, he had communicated to Robert Boyle in London some of Avery's theories about smallpox. During the previous smallpox epidemic in 1702–3 he had pressed Boston physicians to use the more moderate methods of managing the disease favored by the famous physician Sydenham. More recently, in 1716, he had addressed to the Royal Society an essay on "Curiosities of the smallpox" in the course of which he urged Dr. John Woodward to help bring inoculation into experiment and fashion in England. "For my own part," he added, "if I should live to see the smallpox again enter into our city, I would immediately procure a consult of our physicians, to introduce a practise which may be of so very happy a tendency."

Mather now did that. He drew up an address, dated June 6, 1721, which was circulated in manuscript among local physicians, describing a *"Wonderful Practice"* lately come into use in some parts of the world. In fact, inoculation had been performed as folk medicine for centuries in Africa, India, China, and even in parts of Europe. Late in the seventeenth century, accounts of the Asiatic practice began arriving in England, and began to be studied and recommended after the operation had become popular in Turkey early in the eighteenth century. The first recorded inoculation in England had been performed only two months before

Mather's address, in April 1721, smallpox having struck London almost simultaneously with the epidemic in Boston, and probably also introduced by ships from the West Indies.

Mather based the method he recommended to the Boston physicians on two accounts published earlier in the *Transactions* of the Royal Society. The first, in 1714, had been sent from Constantinople by a physician named Emanuel Timonius, and appeared in the issue that carried the summary of Mather's *Curiosa;* the second, in 1716, had come from a Venetian named Jacob Pylarinus, who had observed the practice in Smyrna. The accounts seem to have been discussed in the Boston intellectual community after their appearance, and Mather received some confirmation of the success of inoculation from people in his neighborhood who had recently come from Constantinople. But Mather had learned about inoculation "many months" before the appearance of Timonius' account. His black servant Onesimus had described to him the use of inoculation among his people, the Guramantese, and had shown him a scar on his arm left by it. Onesimus' description, Mather told the Royal Society, was "the same that afterwards I found related unto you by your Timonius."

In his letter to the Boston physicians Mather briefly described the practice related to him by Onesimus (and afterward confirmed to him by other Africans), then in greater detail summarized the published accounts of Timonius and Pylarinus. To the Africans, Mather said, a merciful God brought an "*Infallible Preservative,*" which he tried to describe in Onesimus' own words: "People take Juice of *Small-Pox*; and cutty-skin, and putt in a Drop; then by'nd by a little *sicky, sicky*; then very few little things like *Small-Pox*; and no body die of it; and no body have *Small-Pox* any more." Mather's use of dialect here mattered, for now and later the opponents of inoculation made much of the social class and intellectual credentials of those testifying to its effectiveness. Keenly aware that Onesimus' folkish narrative would not be persuasive enough, Mather added the fuller description of "Superiour Persons in the *Levant.*"

As Mather summarized the account of Dr. Timonius, inoculation had been used in the Levant for about forty years, and having overcome irrational prejudices against it had over the last eight years proved successful on thousands of persons: not one of those inoculated died of the disease. At Constantinople the inoculation is ideally performed at the beginning of winter or spring, using as healthy a young person as can be found who is stricken with smallpox. Twelve or thirteen days into the illness, some of the youth's larger pustules are pricked with a needle, the matter being pressed out into a washed vessel and carried without delay to the inoculee in a stopped bottle, kept warm in the bosom of the messenger. The inoculation is performed in a warm room. First, several small cuts are made with a needle or lancet in the patient's arm muscles. Then on each cut is placed a drop of the matter, or "variole," which is mixed well with the flowing blood. The wound is covered by a concave object, such as a walnut shell, and bound so that the arm is not rubbed by garments. Usually, according to Timonius, ten or twenty pustules break out on the inoculee, who stays at home, keeping warm and on a light diet. The incision runs with pus several days, but in a short time the pocks dry and fall off, rarely pitting.

The method Pylarinus observed, Mather continued, differed only slightly, originating in Smyrna also as folk medicine among the "Mean, Coarse, Rude Sort of People." Pylarinus described the procedure used by a "notable *Inoculatrix*" who advised performing the inoculation only in winter. Instead of incisions she made pinpricks with a gold or iron needle in the forehead, chin, cheeks, wrists, and insteps (unnecessarily many, Pylarinus felt). The wounds often became sore and sometime produced abscesses in some "Emunctory" (a body organ that drains off useless secretions). But, like Timonius, Pylarinus affirmed that ill consequences had been rare. For himself, Mather told the physicians, he felt "very confident no Person would miscarry in it, but what *would most certainly* have miscarried upon taking the Contagion in the *Common Way.*"

How many physicians read Mather's address is unknown, as is the number of physicians then operating in Boston, but only one of them immediately responded, Dr. Zabdiel Boylston. Born in Brookline, he had been trained in medicine by his father, and ran an apothecary shop where he sold surgical instruments and a wide variety of drugs "both Galenical, and Chymical" as well as painters' colors and nostrums for growing hair. His wares do not inspire confidence, but they are deceptive. Before the smallpox epidemic he had performed some virtuoso feats of surgery. Especially interested in lithotomy, in 1707 he successfully removed an egg-sized stone from a thirteen-year-old boy whose life had been given up. In 1718, in the presence of several ministers and other spectators, he did a mastectomy on Mrs. Edward Winslow, whose life was also despaired of because of the bleeding, growth, and stench of a cancer on her left breast. Her husband waited two years to be sure the cancer did not return, then published personal testimonials to Boylston's skill in two Boston newspapers, observing that several doctors had labored unsuccessfully to relieve her "dreadful" cancer until Boylston "cut her whole Breast off" and dressed the surgery "in the space of five Minutes by the Watch of one then present," wholly curing her. Eventually becoming the first American-born physician to be celebrated in England, Boylston later lectured at the Royal College of Physicians and was received with exceptional honor at the Royal Society.

Boylston approved of Mather's versions of the Levant accounts, and believed that in giving them to the physicians Mather had acted out of compassion. Mather wrote to him on June 24, praising the "very much good which a gracious God employs you and honours you to do in a miserable world," and suggesting that if after serious deliberation Boylston thought it advisable to try the inoculation, "it may save many lives that we set a great value on." Two days later, Boylston inoculated a thirty-six-year-old black servant, a two-and-a-half-year-old black child, and his own six-year-old son Thomas. The adult became free of symptoms in two or three days, but Boylston believed he had had the pox before. The children began having complaints by the sixth day, became somewhat hot and sleepy on the seventh, showed about a hundred "kind and favourable" pocks by the ninth—and after that soon were well.

The news of Boylston's experiments and of Mather's encouragements to them scared most Bostonians. Civic authorities had made futile efforts to contain the epidemic and allay public dread, appointing more guards, moving the grammar school to the Town House after three cases broke out in School Street, publishing bromidic progress reports that understated the size and seriousness of the epidemic. ("It is a thousand pities," Boylston later remarked, "our Select-Men made so slight and trifling a Representation of the Small-Pox, that had always prov'd so fatal in *New-England*.") Many people feared that inoculation would not halt the inexorably spreading disease but spread it further. The fear was not unjustified, because if used indiscriminately inoculation could in some circumstances spread the disease and, as then practiced, could have painful and revolting side effects. A reliable account of a successful inoculation later in the year reported that the patient wished he had not been inoculated; after the eruptions began, his pupils dilated, his incisions ran, and about eighty pustules appeared on his face, others on his scrotum.

Mather found himself and Boylston becoming objects of panicky abuse: "They rave, they rail, they blaspheme; they talk not only like Idiots but also like *Franticks*." He was of course no stranger to vilification. And feeling he had acted neither self-interestedly nor conflictedly, he enjoyed despite the abuse an "unspeakable Consolation," he said, in having instructed the physicians in a method of "infallibly" saving lives. Equally confident, Boylston placed an ad in the Boston *Gazette* affirming that his three experiments had validated the accounts of Timonius and Pylarinus: their success showed that no one need fear receiving many pustules from the inoculation, being scarred in the face, or ever taking the disease again. He also served notice that in a few weeks he planned to perform further inoculations. Before doing so, however, he publicly invited the other Boston physicians to visit his patients and judge his success.

With Mather certain of his cause, and Boylston determined to proceed, the selectmen took testimony on July 21 from a Dr. Lawrence Dalhonde—a *"French* Fellow of a very vicious Character," as Mather called him, who had witnessed disastrous inoculations in Europe. He testified that in Italy twenty-five years ago he had seen thirteen soldiers inoculated, of whom three were unaffected, six made a difficult recovery but developed tumors and gangrene, and four died; in Spain an inoculated soldier became frenzied, and his autopsy disclosed infected lymph glands and ulcerated lungs. The Boston physicians found Dalhonde's testimony so convincing that instead of accepting Boylston's invitation they signed a statement asserting that inoculation tends to infuse the blood with "malignant Filth," spreads infection, kills many, and would likely have the "most dangerous Consequence" in Boston.

Three days after Dalhonde's interview, a pseudonymous correspondent to the *News-Letter* amplified the attack on Boylston. Mather, he said, out of a "Pious and Charitable design of doing good," had recommended inoculation to the local physicians, who all declined except a "certain *Cutter for the Stone.*" Reckless and inept, and lacking an academic degree, Boylston tried inoculation at his home in Dock Square, the most public trading place in Boston, and during the stifling heat of summer, although the Levant relations advised attempting it only in winter and spring, with the result that his own inoculated child took a violent fever and barely escaped with his life. The writer also hinted that Boylston's acts could be construed as felonious, a *"Propagating of Infection and Criminal."*

These charges of incompetence provoked a sharp exchange between Boylston's defenders and detractors. Benjamin Colman, for one, thought the letter grossly partial in rebuking Boylston but pardoning Mather, who "push'd on the Attempt and openly rejoic'd in it," Colman said, adding that he believed both men had hoped to do good. In the next week's *Gazette*, he joined Cotton and Increase Mather and three other ministers in expressing distress over the lampooning of Boylston as a *"Cutter for the Stone."* By his dexterity as a surgeon, they said, Boylston had honored the country and shown compassion for many miserable people; although lacking a degree he had studied hard and observed much, and practiced long and with great success. The ministers' endorsement was answered the next week by a writer who dismissed them as "*Six Gentlemen of Piety and Learning, profoundly ignorant of the Matter.*" In recommending the "Practice of the Greek old Women," he said, they pretended to expertise on "one of the most intricate practical Cases in Physick." In defending Boylston they fancied him "some *Romantick Character*, something beyond that of candid *Sydenham*," begarlanding him with "all the fulsome common Place of *Quack Advertisements.*" In fact many readers, he said, took their endorsement for humor.

This flurry opened what became a nearly year-long war of pamphlets and letters-to-the-editor, in which the successive attacks, counterattacks, and counter-counterattacks grew ever more bitter and personal. Meanwhile the disease was becoming epidemic. On July 29 the selectmen again assessed the town and discovered 168 persons infected—a probably undervalued count, as the reassuring tone of their report suggests: "and but Eighteen by GOD's Goodness are Dead, and Several of them lost by Carelessness and not by the Distemper." Public apprehension surged with the news that parts of the Mediterranean and France were being visited with bubonic plague, which could be brought to New England atop the smallpox. One newspaper writer implied that inoculation might make people more vulnerable to plague and even breed it, because plague boils break out in emunctories, the very places where the Levant accounts said that abscesses sometime appear after inoculation. As Boston newspapers told grisly stories of the streets of Marseilles strewn with dead cats and of slaves carting off corpses, Governor Shute issued a proclamation on August 4, requiring every vessel arriving from France or the Mediterranean to undergo a forty-day quarantine before unloading.

Despite the thickening air of menace and a reprimand from the selectmen and justices, who forbad any further inoculations, Boylston inoculated seven other persons in July, and seventeen in August, of whom one died. Mather, undaunted also, prepared a short essay on the treatment of smallpox containing a notable medical point. The cause of smallpox was at the time wholly unknown. But in discussing inoculation Mather speculated that the disease might be an "*Animalculated Business*"—that is, that it might originate in tiny organisms, a suspicion which has been confirmed, he said, by viewing the pustules under a microscope. He does not make clear whether he or someone else in Boston raised or confirmed this possibility. If he came himself to the belief that smallpox was caused by a pathogenic organism, he must be credited with having stumbled unaided on the momentous germ theory of disease.

Opposition to Mather's and Boylston's further efforts now produced a permanent forum and a formidable spokesman. On August 7, 1721, appeared the first issue of *The New-England Courant*, a newspaper published by James Franklin (who had printed in 1719 Mather's *Vigilius*, a sermon on drowsy devotions), soon to be joined by his younger brother Benjamin. Its chief aim, one contributor wrote, was "to oppose the *doubtful* and *dangerous* Practice of *inoculating* the *Small Pox*," and for nearly ten months the *Courant* inveighed relentlessly against the inoculators' character, credentials, and beliefs. But the paper also set itself satirically against the college, the magistrates, the wealthy, and much of the Massachusetts establishment. More clearly than any other features of New England's life, its lively verse and prose about cuckoldry and bachelordom,
· its serialization of Fielding's *Jonathan Wild*, its assaults on efforts to date the Second Coming, its tone of tongue-in-cheek irreverence, giving authority to once-marginal social tendencies gathering throughout Mather's lifetime, sounded the funeral knell of the Puritan Fathers. The paper also now gave a public voice to Mather's and Boylston's main antagonist, Dr. William Douglass, whose presence in the debate highlighted the amateurism of Mather and Boylston both. A Scotsman educated at Edinburgh, Paris, and Leyden (where he studied with Boerhaave), Douglass was the one physician in Boston with an academic degree in medicine. Indeed it was he who apparently loaned Mather—a "credulous vain preacher," Douglass called him—the accounts by Timonius and Pylarinus which Mather knew, "that he might have something to send home to the Royal Society who had long neglected his communications as he complained."

Douglass first sprang on the inoculators in two anonymous pieces in the *Courant* in August. In the first, a grim satire, he told of reading at the same time a defense of inoculation and also news of an intended expedition against the eastern Indians. The two blending in his mind produced a brainstorm: fight the Indians by inoculation. He would arm some inoculators with lancets and nutshells, supply pus and "Negro Yaws" for ammunition, and award a £5 bounty for each Indian killed by inoculation, and double that for each Indian who "survives, conveys and spreads the Infection among his *Tribe*." More soberly and frontally, in his second essay he rejected inoculation as a desperate remedy more suitable for plague, dangerous in itself and useless in preventing smallpox from occurring in the common way. He also accused the inoculators of playing down the severity of the reaction, which he said included violent fevers and ulcers in the groin and other glandulous parts, with swelling and loss of the use of limbs, as in cases of venereal disease. In the spirit of the selectmen, he also claimed that the number of burials since the arrival of smallpox was no greater than the number during the same period in other years. The real danger in the epidemic, he warned, was social chaos, which might destroy commerce and frighten others out of sending provisions to Boston.

What made Douglass worth hearing was not simply his professional training but also his essential seriousness. No Neanderthal or fool, he observed the epidemic with inquisitive scientific interest, recording "intricate incidents" in hope of learning the "mazes" of smallpox. Nor did he doubt the potential value in inoculation. Rather, as a knowledgeable physician, he deplored the present methods of performing it, pointing out correctly that inoculated persons might communicate the disease if not kept in isolation until the infection ran its course; the disease might more certainly be escaped, he said, by merely moving to the country. He also thought the inoculators people with little knowledge and rash impulses, and believed the practice must be tested by other than "*Greek old Women, Madmen and Fools.*" As this crack suggests, Douglass gained added confidence in his views from his haughtiness, his medical degree and foreign birth making him feel superior to others in Boston and act toward them patronizingly. He was also somewhat avaricious. Many physicians opposed inoculation, Benjamin Colman said later, "because it would have saved the Town Thousands of pounds that is now in their pockets," and Douglass cared about making money from the many smallpox victims he treated during the epidemic. Explaining afterward to a correspondent why he had not had time to write up his medical observations, he said he found it "more natural to begin by reducing my smallpox accounts into bills and notes for the improvement of my purse." However motivated, Douglass on his own and through the *Courant* helped organize Boston against the inoculation.

*

The tense, charnal atmosphere ate at Mather's patience and energy. Day after day throughout the summer, he fulminated in his diary against the "false Reports, and blasphemous Speeches, and murderous Wishes." The situation also called to his demonology, in which such massive onslaughts against mankind as epidemics and such obstructions to human progress as attempts to impede scientific knowledge, were characteristic works of evil angels. Believing that only their unwelcome presence could explain the rage against inoculation, he saw Boston benighted by the

"Power of Darkness," "Satanic Fury" again astir, the place become "a dismal Picture and Emblem of *Hell; Fire* with *Darkness* filling of it." Only their presence could explain the "crying Wickedness of this Town, (A Town at this time strangely possessed with the Devil,) and the vile Abuse which I do myself particularly suffer from it, for nothing but my instructing our base Physicians, how to save many precious Lives." Repeatedly he applied for "uncommon Assistance" from above so that he would not act frowardly, "or fall into any of the common Iniquities, of Lying, and Railing and Malice."

Very tryingly, Mather found the festering epidemic no restraint on his wife, his errant son, or his creditors. In July Lydia took into the household a young woman related to her (her niece, it seems certain), whom Mather regarded as negligent in piety and a usurper: "my own Children must be turned and kept out of Doors, and their Place be taken by a Stranger so unacceptable to me." Creasy apparently had been sent away again for improvement, but Mather found him still impenitent, and by September seemingly again in debt: "A vile Sloth, accompanied with the Power of Satan still reigning over him, ruins him, destroys him." He decided to ask the boy to live with him once more "that I may have him under my Eye continually." Once he returned, Mather gave him reading to transcribe and extract for his commonplace books, and as ever prayed for the conversion of "my miserable Son *Increase.*"

Smallpox or no, creditors to the Howell estate dunned Mather vigorously. Shortly before the epidemic, in April, he and Lydia had defaulted on a claim against both the Howell and George estates by the wealthy Boston merchant Andrew Faneuil, for nearly £120, a large amount that Faneuil had long demanded. Apparently now wholly out of funds to pay Faneuil, and still unable to win his release from the administration, Mather petitioned the court for permission to sell part of Howell's warehouse on the Long Wharf, which was granted. Although he managed thus to satisfy Faneuil's claim, he was unable to sell other property to settle other claims, seemingly because the court's decision applied only to Faneuil. And each sale had to be approved by Lydia's daughter and her husband, relatives who he believed had "laid a deep Design, assisted with crafty and cruel Adversaries, if they can, to ruin me." Having profited nothing from the estate, but being owed much by it, he was by July in "considerable *Poverty,*" owning not "a Foot of Land in all the World. My Salary is not enough to support me comfortably, I meet with many Wants and Straits: in my Diet, much; in my Habit, more." The little estate he had had been sold, and the money gone to pay debts; if he put something aside for his necessities, it disappeared. He began forwarding new dunning letters to his attorneys, promising creditors he would spur their efforts to satisfy the claims.

But having borne the deaths of ten of his children already, Mather worried most that smallpox might visit his family. His first concern was for the two frightened adolescents born after the last epidemic—Elizabeth, about to turn seventeen, and Sammy, nearly fifteen. Sammy came home from the college in June, as the disease spread in the North End, and was afraid to return to Cambridge; Liza lived even "in greater Fears than he." Mather wished to have them inoculated. But he also wished to avoid further exciting the town: the "cursed Clamour of a People strangely and fiercely possessed of the Devil, will probably prevent my saving the Lives of my two Children, from the Small-pox in the Way of Transplantation." He importuned heaven for their safety, and to quicken Liza's flights to Christ gave her a book relating the death of a young Frenchwoman. Sammy, however, begged to have himself inoculated. Mather reasoned on one side that if he denied Sammy and the boy took the disease he would have to answer for it; on the other that if he agreed and the inoculation miscarried "my Condition would be insupportable." But other circumstances argued for inoculating him: ten "remarkable Experiments" had been successfully performed in the North End; Sammy's Harvard roommate and best friend had died of smallpox; Increase Mather advised that the inoculation be performed but kept secret. Deciding that "I could not answer it unto God, if I neglected it," Mather uncertainly consented.

A few days after the inoculation Sammy became "pretty full" of pocks and his fever had risen beyond expectation. Mather thought his condition "very hazardous." He believed both that Sammy had been infected before the inoculation, and that the procedure had been imperfectly performed, Sammy receiving only one incision, and that "so small as to be hardly worthy the Name of one." Again the possibility of the death of one of his children confronted him, this time the death of "so hopeful a son." He set apart August 25 as a day of prayer for Sammy, begging that he might live and fulfill his ministry. Girding himself, however, he contrasted the meaning to him of his family with the meaning of an "infinitely more desirable Christ," who would abundantly satisfy him "in the Withdraw of these and all Creatures from me." While praying in his study on August 30, mentally offering Sammy as a sacrifice to God, he decided to open his Bible at random; if the place he chanced on did not provide appropriate matter for meditation, he would turn to and meditate on the story of Jesus' miraculous cure of the son of a nobleman. To his surprise, the

Bible opened at that very place, offering to his eye the line: Go thy Way, thy Son liveth. The same evening Sammy's fever rose to a distressing degree. Apparently delirious, Sammy made a fervid request, "under an Impression of such Violence upon him, as if it came from some superior Original." He asked impassionedly to have a vein opened in him, with the result that his condition eased utterly and he smoothly recovered.

Unexpectedly, however, two of Mather's children born before the last epidemic and presumed immune had also become stricken—conceivably, but improbably, by some other disease. They were his daughter Hannah, about twenty-five years old, and his twenty-seven-year-old daughter Abigail, the wife of his attorney, Daniel Willard, and now in late pregnancy, near to giving birth. Hannah had remained unmarried, perhaps because as a child she had fallen into a fire, so seriously burning the right side of her face and her right hand and arm that her life was feared for; her face may have remained badly scarred. On September 3 the physicians announced that "poor *Nancy*, dear *Nancy*" had not many hours to live. Praying with her often to prepare her, Mather felt a "strange Light" on his mind that she would recover, a persuasion encouraged when for a few minutes she regained her senses and speech and told him that she too had received some inner assurances. Although Nancy did recover, Abigail, "Nibby"—a good and kindly woman, Mather thought her—also lay in "dying Circumstances," and in this condition gave birth to a daughter. Named "Resigned," the infant was to be baptized on September 24; but that day she died, apparently while Mather was conducting services in church, with the baptismal water standing ready. Mather had little time to grieve, for the next days occupied him with strengthening Nibby in her own death struggle. Ironically, Nibby's mother and namesake had died (of breast cancer) during the previous smallpox epidemic, her eight months of suffering initiating with a miscarriage. Nibby, fearing for the state of her soul and longing for deliverance, died a hard death between ten and eleven on the evening of September 26—the eleventh of Mather's fifteen children to die.

Now nearly sixty years old, Mather had discovered the proper, and for him the logical, response to hard deaths, not meekness so much, or submission, but, better, silence. The day before Nibby's burial he preached a sermon later published as *Silentiarius* (1721), a title rich in personal history. Having given much energetic discipline to mastering his unruly speech, or much ingenuity to denying its quirks by gorgeous fluency, he now took for his doctrine the concept that "Our GOD is never more *Praised* than by our *silence*." Righteousness demands, he said, the recognition that whatever sad things befall us, and whatever good things, representing God's will they must be received in noiseless uncomplaint. Recognition that *"The Lord is in thy Adversity"* demands, he repeated over and again, the *"Holy silence* wherewith we are to Glorify Him." Unspeakingly we must let our feelings grow as cold as may be and bear our sad things with mortified muteness, "the *Holy silence* of those who are *Crucified unto the World."* A man hanging on a cross "has *little to say,* unto any thing that *this World* has to offer unto him," is in his silence free among the dead. For himself too, he told his congregation, he would try to hold his peace: "IT becomes *me* to do so, who have this Day, a DAUGHTER (together with *her* New-born *Daughter,*) waiting to be *Buried out of my Sight,* whom others as well as I, could not but always with much Affection *Look* upon."

*

A canvass of the town at the end of September, perhaps again understated, counted 2757 persons infected since the beginning of the epidemic, of whom 203 had died. Fear of contamination had also in effect embargoed Boston, so that with winter at hand, grain, butter, and firewood were not coming into town and sold at inflated prices. To deal with the crisis, public officials provided a ferry to Boston from the harbor for wood-vending sloopmen who feared entering the town, ordered Indian hostages suspected of being diseased moved from the Cambridge prison to Castle Island, and distributed funds from the public treasury to relieve the many otherwise able people financially reduced by the epidemic. Considering inoculation little less dangerous than the epidemic itself, a town meeting voted in November to require the immediate removal of any in town found inoculated, and the selectmen voted to require any person coming to Boston from another town seeking inoculation to be sent to the Spectacle Island hospital.

Mather and Boylston, however, persisted in administering and justifying inoculation. Boylston inoculated 31 persons in September, 18 more in October, and 103 in November, as the epidemic began reaching its worst intensity in Boston. With some 322 persons in the North Church stricken in mid-October, Mather daily visited "loathsome" sickrooms and himself fell ill of a fever brought on, he believed, "by the Poisons of infected Chambers." Although wondering "Is my Hour come?" (and adding, "Tis welcome"), he joined Boylston at the end of October in publishing a defense of inoculation in the *Gazette,* partly to repudiate false rumors,— for instance, that those inoculated stank. In their view, inoculation had

succeeded beyond even their hopes. They claimed that only one inoculee, a Mrs. Dixwell, had died, and everyone who knew the case believed
her death was not caused by inoculation. A few inoculees had erupted in
more pustules than the Levant accounts mentioned, but they had undergone little sickness; most inoculees had had few pustules, and had experienced "in a manner, *Nothing*." Some who were dying of smallpox or
had seen its terrors, Mather and Boylston concluded, had begged their
friends to become inoculated.

Someone tried to kill Mather about two weeks later. One person who
came to Boston seeking inoculation was Mather's nephew Thomas Walter, the minister at Roxbury—a supporter of the method and a leader in
the regular singing movement. A few months earlier, an anti-inoculator
had attacked Walter in print as an "*obscene* and *fuddling Merry-Andrew*,"
depicting him and another debauched spark with some punch on a bed,
together with "two Sisters of not the best Reputation in the World." Mather
put the young minister up in his own "Lodging-Room," where, inoculated, Walter lay on November 14. Toward three o'clock in the morning,
somebody threw into the room a "fired Granado." Had the ball landed on
Walter's head, Mather said, its weight alone would have killed him. But
the grenade was also loaded, the upper part with powder, the lower with
a mix of powder and turpentine "and what else I know not." Had it
exploded, Mather believed, it would probably have killed anyone in the
room, and certainly have set fire to the room itself and soon destroyed the
house. But the grenade, in passing through the window, struck the iron in
the middle of the casement, so that when the grenade hit the floor the
"fired Wild-fire" in the fuse shook out. When the grenade was examined
there was found, tied around it with a string, the message: "COTTON
MATHER, *You Dog, Dam you; I'l inoculate you with this, with a Pox to
you*."

The attempted assassination was much talked of in Boston and, thankful, Mather marked his "miraculous" deliverance by preaching on the
text, This night there stood by me the Angel of the God whose I am, and
whom I serve. Yet while he felt providentially rescued, the episode also
confirmed with frightening lifelikeness his ancient conviction that no
gifts suffice to win love, that, like Christ, those who Do Good are
spurned. His execution had been sought, he wrote, for "such a Crime as
this. I have communicated a never-failing and a most allowable Method,
of preventing Death." As the bomb had not only terrorized Mather's family but also endangered neighboring houses, Governor Shute, upon a
request by the House, made a proclamation at the college on November

16, directing the sheriffs, constables, and other officers to identify the would-be assassin, calling on other citizens to help, and promising to give a reward of £50 plus a pardon to any accomplice who came forward and confessed.

Not everyone, Mather discovered, was eager to help. Some applauded the bomb throwing and promised, he said, "that tho' the first Blow miscarried, there will quickly come another, that shall do the Business more effectually." Intent as always on returning good for evil, he prayed for the welfare of the "unknown Person, who sought my Death by the fired Granado," and now found in himself a new, unfamiliar sort of thankfulness. Although he lived daily expecting another attempt to kill him, he became filled with joy at the prospect of his approaching martyrdom. Indeed, if he caught himself asking to be spared, his mouth became strangely stopped, his heart strangely cold; but when he thought of "suffering Death for saving the Lives of dying People," he became ravished by a "Joy unspeakable and full of Glory." Experiencing the divine consolations that sometimes irradiated the minds of martyrs, which previously he knew only in his reading, he began to fear doing anything for his safety, even to long for the hour of his assassination.

Insidiously the smallpox spread outside Boston to Newport, New London, Plymouth, Salem, Ipswich, Sandwich, Roxbury, and many other New England towns. Mather and Boylston promoted the new method there also: in all about 135 inoculations were performed outside Boston, it was estimated, nearly a hundred of them by Boylston. In early December, Mather gave copies of a description of the method, perhaps in manuscript, to physicians and others "in several Parts of the Countrey." As these towns tried to stave off the disease with quarantines and fasts, the inoculations produced pamphlet controversies similar to Boston's, and other like results. Mather learned that a minister at Marblehead, for wanting to be inoculated, was "likely to be murdered by an abominable People, that will not let him save his Life."

Mather also addressed himself to the simultaneous, although worse, smallpox epidemic in populous London, and its attendant controversy. As earlier noted, inoculation in London began in April 1721, with the daughter of Lady Mary Wortley Montagu. Mather seems not to have been aware of this when, in May, he proposed the method to the Boston physicians. Reports of the Boston inoculations were printed in London newspapers, just as Boston newspapers ran accounts of the London inoculations, the English inoculators citing Mather, the English anti-inoculators citing Douglass. In November Mather wrote the first of three communications on smallpox which he sent to the Royal Society. It gives a full historical narrative of the Boston crisis from May to November, followed by a step-by-step description of the Boston method, which was quickly published in the Society's *Transactions*. Here Mather offered several revisions of the Levant accounts, which he said had understated the number of pocks that erupt on the inoculees; the Boston inoculations usually brought not ten or twenty, but in some persons hundreds of them and in others very few. While experimenting, Mather indicated, Boylston introduced some changes in the Levant method, dressing the incisions with warmed cabbage leaves instead of a concave object, and taking the variole from an inoculee instead of from a smallpox victim. In an important updated communication to the Royal Society a few months later, announcing the successful inoculation in America of, now, almost three hundred persons, Mather added several curiosa observed in Boston, such as the seeming immunity to the disease of persons who had been smitten first by plague, and the failure of pigeons to hatch during the epidemic. Boston experience also taught that in some seemingly hopeless cases, cure has been achieved by blistering the patient's wrists, ankles, or both, allowing the discharge to run until the danger is over.

Whether the accounts from Boston helped to turn English public opinion for or against the inoculation has been debated. Whether it helped or hurt, Mather's second communication was quoted extensively in, and the full text appended to, the second edition of *Mr. Maitland's Account of Inoculating the Small Pox Vindicated* (London, 1722). Dr. Charles Maitland, an eminent physician who had practiced inoculation in Turkey, had himself earlier provided support for the Boston inoculators. In August 1721, he successfully inoculated seven prisoners in Newgate (upon condition of their receiving the king's pardon) before about twenty-five physicians, surgeons, and apothecaries, news of which appeared in Boston newspapers. Maitland's lead and the example of Lady Mary Wortley Montagu did win some favor for inoculation in London. How much Mather's own communications contributed is speculative. The two facts may not be related, but five days after Mather's second communication was presented at the Royal Society, the British royal princesses submitted themselves to inoculation.

*

By about mid-December Boston had become so generally infected as to make further inoculations useless. As the epidemic peaked, the focus of controversy surrounding it shifted from the safety of inoculation to the office to enforce their ignorance often carried an undercurrent of class antagonism, as appears in two pamphlets by a man named John Williams. An acquaintance of the Mrs. Dixwell who was widely alleged to have died of inoculation, he seems to have run a "tobacco-cellar" where he dispensed tobacco, drugs, and free medical advice. Mather flicked him off as a "sorry *Tobacconist;* who could hardly spell a Word of *English,* (even the word *English,* from his acute Pen was *Engleche*)." But here Mather missed, and in a degree confirmed, Williams's point. For in trying to show that neither Scripture nor medical theory justified inoculation, Williams flaunted rather than hid his rudimentary knowledge and garbled reasoning. Most ministers, he wrote, are "of a contrary Party to the Bulk of the People, with respect to the public Affairs here in this Town," and he paraded illustratively as an illiterate mechanic, one of the commons whom the ministers disdain as a vulgar mob and consider stupid for lacking a Harvard degree. Tracing the history of ministerial error in New England back through inoculation and the banking crisis, he began with the Salem witchcraft trials, "when so many innocent Persons lost their Lives." Many other anti-inoculators made the same taunting connection. Douglass observed that all countries have been subject to infatuation, which in New England seems to have concentrated in some of the ministry, as shown by "The *Persecution of the Quakers* about the Year 1658, the *hanging of those suspected of Witchcraft,* about the Year 1691. . . . and *Inoculation,* or *Self-procuring the Small Pox,* in the Year 1721."

Pro-inoculation allies of the ministry returned these shafts point by point. Typical of many counterthrusts is a sixteen-page pamphlet entitled *Vindication of the Ministers of Boston* (1722), published "By Some of their PEOPLE." (Mather seems to have supplied material for this pamphlet, and may have written parts of it.) Alert to the *Courant* writers' "saucy" tactic of preaching Providence and Scripture to the ministers, they thought it "very strange and ridiculous, to see the Satyrists play the Divine." The Boston ministers, they said, were neither meddlesome in politics nor ignorant of medicine; rather they desired the good of the community, and their ranks perhaps contained men "such as the best PHYSICIANS in the Land, need not be ashamed to *advice* withal." Among such men they particularly praised "the *Learned* Dr. COTTON MATHER, *Fellow of the Royal Society,*" who scorns to "draw his GENEROUS PEN for his own *Vindication,* against the many foolish PAMPHLETS that are pointed at him; and who changes not his *Temper* for all their invidious Calumnies."

Mather needed vindicating, for those who rose up at the ministry usually marked him out as the chief ministerial spokesman for inoculation, and the most authoritarian and ignorant. The many charges of deceit made against him during his defense of Governor Shute clung and were now repeated, ranging in seriousness from the *Courant's* hits at his "Equivocations, mental Reservations, and Jesuitical Evasions" to Douglass's charges of blatant lying. At the time of the first inoculations, in May, Mather and his supporters had justified the experiments on the ground that Mather first cautiously sought the counsel of the Boston physicians, and gave them the accounts from the Levant and from his servant Onesimus. In the first months of 1722, however, Douglass reviewed these earlier events and claimed that Mather had set Boylston experimenting before the physicians had a chance to meet and that, when consulted, the physicians condemned the practice. He also charged that Mather did not send him a copy of his letter to the physicians, excluding him from the consultations. Mather's reason, he implied, was that he owned the issue of the *Transactions* which contained the original, Latin, account by Pylarinus, enabling him to see what, to win support, Mather had omitted, mistranslated, and falsified. Douglass said that Mather translated as "ill consequences," for instance, a Latin word meaning "mortal," suggesting in his translation that inoculation might have side effects where the Latin of Pylarinus indicated it might be mortal. Mather challenged Douglass to produce the volume so the accuracy of his rendering could be judged. Douglass refused, with the unpersuasive excuse that concern for the lives of his neighbors obliged him to keep the account out of circulation.

Mather's detractors often struck for his jugular, declaring their hilarity over his many publications. One after another chuckled publicly over his "innate Itch of Writing," derided his want of "Grammar Learning," mirthfully quoted him against himself, requoted Oldmixon on *Magnalia* ("so confus'd in the Form, so trivial in the Matter, and so faulty in the Expression"), flouted without naming those who "have so great an Opinion of their own Works, although there is no Beauty nor comeliness in them," took off his literary posturing: "*I am a Man of Letters . . . but all the illiterate Scribblers of the Town* (the Leather Apron Men) *are* proud and vain Fellows." Douglass aimed for an equally vulnerable place, ridiculing "Curiosa Americana" as "trivial credulous Stories"—for instance Mather's "Fancy" that pigeons in New England roosted in "some undiscover'd Satellite" of the earth—advising that instead of writing on inoculation Mather "write some Observations on a *Physical Account of a Phantom* he does not comprehend." Many others gibed at Mather's D.D. and F.R.S., for instance explaining that the University of Glasgow had "gratify'd his

Vanity" with a D.D. out of respect for New England, or that he won homage by coyly showing himself receptive to it, having, the *Courant* said, "kept an open Breast to receive *Honours of all Sorts*." One pamphleteer, cheekily addressing himself to "the Very Reverend and Learned Dr. COTTON MATHER" (otherwise "C.M. D.D. and F.R.S."), travestied Mather's self-puffery and annoyingly advertised sonship: "*The young Gentleman* has been above Forty Years a celebrated Preacher, and has been so acknowledged by *Foreign Universities,* as no *American* ever was before him, and justly merits the Honour of being a Member of the ROYAL SOCIETY: He has a GREAT NAME in distant Lands; and *foreign Countries* have a great *Veneration* for him."

Mather's membership in the Royal Society, an important item in the squabble over his qualifications, itself came under suspicion. Doubts about it were first raised by John Checkley, an apothecary and self-proclaimed virtuoso who had studied at Oxford. Although born in Boston of old Puritan stock, Checkley was an Anglican, and he accused the New England churches of praying to the devil. He had also seen a printed list of Fellows of the Society and noticed, as Mather had noticed earlier, that it did not include Mather's name. Just before the epidemic, he wrote to the astronomer Edmund Halley at the Society, asking him to send proof, if any existed, of Mather's membership. It would be, he said, "an Act of Charity to a disturbed, persecuted . . . Son of our holy Mother Church of England," and would help him defend himself against "these Sons of Strife, Schism, and Sedition." As the inoculations began, Checkley became associated with Douglass and the anti-inoculators of the *Courant.*

Amidst the winter campaign against the ministry, and before the truth of the matter could be determined, the anti-inoculators publicly questioned the authenticity of Mather's F.R.S. In January the *Courant,* while alleging that a supposed account of successful inoculations from London had been invented by Boston inoculators, said the account was no more to be found in a certain London newspaper "than COTTON MATHER D.D. is to be found in the List of the *Royal Society*." Douglass recommended in a pamphlet that Harvard might disown Mather, "as it seems the *Royal Society* have already done, by omitting his Name in their yearly Lists." Mather wrote to Dr. Woodward asking him to confirm his election, but for some reason received no reply; indeed it took him two full years to establish his membership. When Checkley's letter was read before the Society, in June 1721, an official explained that the membership lists excluded the names of Fellows who had not been inducted in person. Dr. Waller explained to Mather that the lists were not official rosters; rather, they were used in voting at yearly elections, and consequently they omitted the names of Fellows who could not attend the elections. To silence charges of impersonation against Mather, the Society decided to investigate the case thoroughly. But their goodwill only disclosed a real discrepancy. Somehow the minutes of the Society's meetings failed to show that any vote had ever been taken on Mather's candidacy.

Mather wrote to the Society in May 1723, saying he relied on its justice to clear him, but would instantly comply should the Fellows intend him to "lay aside my pretensions to be at all related unto that illustrious body." At the time he wrote he seems to have been unaware that, the previous month, Dr. Woodward had explained to the Society that Mather had been nominated for membership a decade ago; the nomination was to have been voted upon, but somehow the ballot was never taken. After Woodward laid out the situation, the Society voted and elected Mather a Fellow. There is no question, however, but that Mather's correspondents in the Society believed, and had led him to believe, that he had been elected a Fellow in 1713.

This onslaught of diatribe and insinuation against Mather angered his sons. Creasy, despite his own running battle with his father, exposed himself to danger, Mather recorded, "by a violent and passionate Resentment of an Indignity, which a wicked Fellow offered unto me," although no details of this incident survive. Sammy, having prospered from inoculation himself, defended his father truculently in the *Gazette*. There he charged James Franklin and his *Courant* with trying "to Vilify and Abuse the best Men we have," and threatened that "there is a Number of us who resolve, that if this wickedness be not stop'd, we will pluck up our Courage, and see what we can do in our way to stop it." Sammy's article appeared anonymously but was quickly identified as his, bringing down on him a half-dozen separate blasts. He was dubbed an "Ill-bred School-Boy," a "young scribbling Collegian," a "*Chip of the old Block* (by Direction)." One Couranteer quoted a line from his father's *Magnalia*—"Bloody fishing at *Oyster* River; and Sad work at *Groton*"—and observed that Sammy's readers would feel "*There is bloody Fishing* for Nonsense *at* Cambridge, *and sad Work at the* College." Another condemned Sammy's "poysonous and more than Humane Malice" as a lasting reproach to Harvard, but concluded: "It seems the *venomous Itch of Scribbling* is Hereditary; a Disease transmitted from the *Father to the Son*."

Although well practiced in receiving comeuppance, Mather had never before been so publicly, relentlessly, and ferociously clawed. Considering his many other nerve-fraying trials at the time and his quick temper, he acted with remarkable and uncustomary restraint. Privately he railed in his diary against the "prodigious Nonsense, and Folly, and Baseness ever now and then expressed by the People," and probably supplied some material for pamphlets and articles by his defenders. Once he also stopped James Franklin, the publisher of the *Courant,* in the street and with an "Air of great Displeasure," according to Franklin, warned him that *"many Curses"* awaited those who made it their business to traduce ministers: *"The Lord will smite thro' the Loins of them that rise up against the Levites. I would have you consider of it, I have no more to say to you."* Otherwise Mather this time obeyed his own injunctions to beware of speaking intemperately and of spreading false reports. But the silence he imposed on himself in the insulting hullaballoo left him depressed: "By a dark and a faint Cloud striking over my Mind," he wrote on December 31, "I begin to feel some Hazards, lest my Troubles, whereof I have a greater Share than any Minister in the Country, grow too hard for me, and unfit me and unhinge me for my Services."

In this defeated mood, Mather addressed a meeting of ministers on January 16 and implied that he was considering moving his ministry from Boston. By daily pursuing his desire to Do Good, he said, he had "entirely ruined myself as to this World, and rendered it really too hot a Place for me to continue in." He and his conduct had become subjects of the "most false Representations imaginable," which he might easily have confuted but chose to bear in silence. As a result, except among a few of his "little Remnant of a Flock," his serviceableness had become crippled. "I must employ my Faculties," he told the ministers, "in projections to do good in more distant Places"; he had "there"—without saying where—"a Prospect of some Things, whereof I shall know more hereafter." Promising to cooperate with other ministers in their own designs, he announced the cessation of his: *"I have done! I have done! I have done* treating you with any more of my Proposals."

Mather's announcement of his withdrawal from public affairs, and perhaps from Boston itself, failed to convince the anti-inoculators. Even after his address, they repeatedly lambasted him for reviling the town in daily speech ("Who is it that in common Conversation makes no Bones of calling the Town a MOB?") and for claiming that the *Courant* was run by a Hell-Fire Club, referring to the notorious London clubs whose members blasphemously styled themselves God the Son or St. John the Baptist, and under such names toasted the devil. Douglass accused Mather of being the author of a scurrilous pamphlet, published around February, entitled *A Friendly Debate; or, A Dialogue Between Academicus; And Sawny &*

Mundungus, Two Eminent Physicians (1722). It does seem probable that Mather collaborated in writing this rather nasty skit, in which the pro-inoculation character Academicus defends Mather as a "Celebrated Preacher" well-read in medicine, the sense and style of whose writing "charm all Competent Judges." In addition to praising Mather, the skit ridicules Douglass as a malicious liar and the tobacconist Williams as an illiterate, turning upon them the same caricatures that had earlier been applied to Mather. Here it is Douglass who pompously swaggers, denouncing the other Boston physicians as *"Illiterate Numskulls . . . while, I traffic to the Metropolis of Literature, and receive ample Communications from the very learned* A.S.F.R.S. & M.D." Academicus even darkly hints that Douglass and his supporters conspired in the attempted assassination of Mather. Williams appears as the moronic Mundungus (a slap at the allegedly cheap quality of his tobacco), who believes that the best place to write a treatise on inoculation is a tobacco cellar; or, in his wretched spelling, that the best place to *"rigte tretes on Inokelacion is a Thobacko ciller."* The pamphlet offers as an appendix a dictionary of the *"Mundungian Language,"* and proposes designating Williams Professor of Mundungian at Harvard.

By the time this skit saw print, the epidemic was dramatically waning, nearly revealing its toll. The selectmen ascertained in February that some 5889 persons had been infected, of whom 844 had died. By early spring the surrounding controversy had degenerated into almost entirely *ad hominem* screeching. In its issue of March 19–26, 1722, the *Courant* compared Mather to a *"peevish Mongrel"* and to *"Dunghill Cocks"* and called him, among other things, a *"Baboon."* Whatever the nadir of catcalling, the most resonant and auspicious epithet appeared in the April 2 *Courant,* which published the first of a series of satirical essays by James Franklin's sixteen-year-old brother, Benjamin. At an even younger age he had published and written two ballads (no copies of which survive), but these essays mark his literary debut and offer in the bud the adult Franklin's inimitably sly boldness. He created for his pseudonymous narrator a homely widow at whose house lodges the minister of the town, by whose assistance she promises to beautify her writings with "a Sentence or two in the learned Languages, which will not only be fashionable, and pleasing to those who do not understand it, but will likewise be very ornamental." By nature the widow is a person of "extensive Charity, and a great Forgiver of *private* Injuries." But she is likewise endowed with "a natural Inclination to observe and reprove the Faults of others, at which I have an excellent Faculty." She is called Silence Dogood.

In that devastatingly felicitous name, Franklin summed up what Mather had become in the minds of many Bostonians, a biddyish seriocomic martyr eternally vaunting his tiresome benevolence and meekness. Although Silence Dogood did not join the *Courant's* war on the inoculators, her satires of Harvard and of New England funeral elegies also sum up the effects on Puritan Boston of a half-century of religious bickering, political melees, economic crises, crown politics, and urban growth—the outspokenness of the rambunctious young, the new spirit of amusement, the diminished force of custom, the declining authority of the ministry.

*

The selectmen found isolated smallpox cases in the spring, including two in April; one of these, a collarmaker, was buried late at night to avoid the possibility of infecting people who had recently returned to Boston, having fled town to escape the epidemic. But by mid-May, about a year after its outbreak, the epidemic was all but over. Ads in the *Courant* called to gentlemen wishing to "Recreate themselves with a Game of *Billiards*." About a hundred regular singers in the New Brick Church performed three-part singing from the gallery, a decisive innovation, in effect a concert of sacred music by trained singers separated from the congregation.

Ironically for Mather, just as the epidemic ended it meshed with his ongoing troubles over the Howell estate. Out of funds himself, we have seen, he had tried to satisfy creditors by selling off part of Howell's property on the Long Wharf, although these sales had first to be approved by the court and by Lydia's daughter, Katharin, and her husband Samuel Sewall, people who "intend my Hurt." In January he had been able to give part of George's warehouse to a creditor to pay off more than £250 owing from the estate. In May he again petitioned the court to sell some property, but Sewall and his wife, along with their two children George and Nathan Howell (and Lydia and her troublesome niece), were now at the hospital or pest house on Spectacle Island, where the selectmen had removed them on May 15. (By a different account, they were driven there by a "mobbish Crew" in Boston.) The Sewalls and two other people had become subjects of Boylston's six final inoculations, on May 11 and 12. A visitor found them supplied with nurses and necessaries, the two children, aged eight and ten, playing about without complaint, but Katharin's menstrual schedule thrown off by the inoculation, and the incisions on her and her husband running badly. Under inoculation, Sewall addressed the court clerks from Spectacle Island, saying he had been informed that

Mather had petitioned to sell some of Howell's real estate; if the court found it true that the "Bad Debts" made the estate insufficient to satisfy creditors, he said he had no objection to disposing of the property.

These final inoculations apparently stirred rumors and apprehensions in country towns that "great Numbers" in Boston were again infected, and brought some final salvos against Mather and Boylston. Boylston was brought before a town meeting, where he solemnly promised to inoculate no one else without permission from town authorities. Recalling that Mather had continued his pneumatological experiments even after the witchcraft trials ended, the *Courant* scowled that although inoculation seemed to have exited in January it had returned, "like the Infatuation Thirty Years ago, after several had fallen Victims to the mistaken Notions of Dr. M_____r and other learned Clerks concerning Witchcraft."

Impaled by the *Courant* as a pontifical bogeyman of the superstitious past, Mather had in fact spoken on behalf of the future. Inoculation was the first major achievement in preventive medicine. Credit for introducing it can be given to no single person, but Mather and Boylston made the first large-scale test of the practice, a critical event in its eventual adoption in Europe and America, and in the history of immunology. Although Douglass continued to doubt the safety of the method, with the epidemic over he conceded confidentially to Cadwallader Colden in New York that smallpox "seems to be somewhat more favourably received by inoculation than received in the natural way." Here if nowhere else Mather had been, unambidextrously, on the right side.

To say that Mather's behavior seems in retrospect heroic leaves open the question of his motives at the time. Did he blunder ahead on skimpy evidence and knowledge, as the anti-inoculators charged, propelled by arrogance about his ministerial rank, vanity about his accomplishments, pride in his family name, and contempt for the mob? Was he driven, as Perry Miller believed, by neurosis? On the contrary, Mather's every comment about smallpox in his published and unpublished works bespeaks long and much pondering of the disease, intelligent trust in Boylston's gifts, strenuous self-control in a furnace of abuse, and transcending these a desire that his neighbors live, not die. True, he was not a trained physician. But none of the English colonies had licensing authority, medical schools, or general hospitals, and many ministers practiced medicine. Indeed a professional physician such as Douglass would likely have done less than Mather, whose zealous efforts during the epidemic required as much moral enthusiasm as medical understanding, and whose science and religion nourished each other.

Of course Mather could not escape being what he was, and his daily conversation and behavior during the crisis may often have carried provocatively Matherean fire and water. By the same token, part of Mather remained genuinely nurturing and generous. Toward those who risked inoculation he felt a paternal intimacy: "being all of them indeed my *Patients,*" he wrote, "I would consider them as my *Relatives.*" As the disease reached unstoppably into several parts of Europe at the end of the year, he also considered sending an account of the Boston experiments to Holland: "Who can tell, but Hundreds of Thousands of Lives, may be saved by this Communication." Moreover, he consistently gave the real credit for inoculation to Boylston: "*this* is the gentleman," he wrote later. "When the rest of our doctors did rather the part of butchers or tools for the destroyer to our perishing people, and with envious and horrid insinuations infuriated the world against him, this worthy man had the courage and conscience to enter upon the practise." Boylston, Mather said generously, and "he alone, with the blessing of Heaven, saved the lives of I think several hundreds; yea, at one time he saved a whole town from a fearful desolation."

A year after the epidemic Mather sent the Royal Society a seventeen-page essay on smallpox. In its final blast at Mather, the *Courant* had gloated to think that he was sending further accounts to England, for the Royal Society, they observed, had for its secretary the eminent Dr. James Jurin, a "Man of solid Judgment" who took pride in detecting "whimsical groundless Conceits, credulous Relations, and false or trivial Reasonings." Again the *Courant* was wrong, for the Fellows devoted to Mather's essay, and his other communications, three consecutive meetings. Their interest was evidently intensified by the decimating continuance of smallpox in London, where by one count more than two thousand persons died of the disease in 1722, and more than three thousand in 1723. In his essay Mather refuted a host of religious and seemingly commonsense objections to inoculation. Written in retrospect, his arguments are better organized and more assured than in his earlier writings on the subject, based now on "*Constant Experience*"—a pounding refrain in the essay—and offered with conclusive firsthand experience of the success of inoculation "upon both *Male* and *Female,* both *Old* and *Young,* both *strong and weak; Whites* and *Blacks;* on *Tawnies,* on Women in *childbed* . . . on Women *with child,* at all Seasons." He also rehearsed for the Society his personal role in the epidemic, his initial appeal to the Boston physicians, the dubious satisfaction they and Douglass and Williams might derive from "seeing above a Thousand of their Neighbours within a few months killed before their eyes," the rage against himself of people who "actually *seek* the *Death* of the Friends, that only show them how to save their Lives."

But the gist of Mather's message to the Society was in his impassioned beseeching tone, a plea for the adoption of the method in England and elsewhere. In his final paragraphs he hypothetically interrogated those who vehemently opposed inoculation. Had they "no dread at all," he would ask them, "of being accessory to the *Innumerable Deaths,* which may be, in part, owing to their boisterous Opposition." Was it not bold presumption in them, he would ask, to make that a sin which God the Judge of all commanded as a duty? Was it not criminal ingratitude to the God of health to treat with neglect and contempt a method of sparing lives from so great a death, and to multiply abuses on those who thankfully and obediently embraced His blessing? He answered his questions himself, hardly sounding like a Silence Dogood:

> *We,* that cry with a loud voice to them, *Do yourselves no Harm,* and show them, How to keep themselves from *the paths of the Destroyer,* are conscious of nothing, but of a *pity for Mankind* under the *Rebukes of God;* A concern to see the *madness of the people;* A desire to have our neighbours *do well;* and a solicitude for a *Better State of the World.* And all the Obloquies, and Outrage we suffer, for our Charity, We shall entertain as *Persecutions* for A *Good Cause,* which will not want its Recompences.

13

Crackling of Thorns Under a Pot

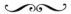

THE TWO YEARS that followed the smallpox epidemic were the most har-rowing of Mather's life. The departures from him, each more comfortless than the one before, began in the fall of 1722. On September 25, fasts were held at the Old North and the other New England churches, to evoke an effusion of God's spirit on the rising generation. Such fasts were of course frequent, but for Mather the occasion and aftermath of this one were specially ominous. Indeed giving both the morning and the after-noon sermons, he preached all day, on the text Matt. 9:18, *My Daughter is even now dead*. For once this was not literally his daughter nor literally a death, although it brought little less distress.

Together with its ominous occasion, soon to be explained, the fast marked the last appearance in his pulpit of Increase Mather. Now eighty-five years old and ailing, he had been treated gently or ignored by the anti-inoculators even though he too had sponsored the new method. In the wake of the epidemic he felt so debilitated by age that he had no hopes of preaching another sermon. His gouty right hand had become "*Paralitical*" and shook so that he was unable to pen a long discourse. On September 4 he wrote an attestation for his son's *Coelestinus* (1723) in which he announced that he was every hour looking and longing for heaven. Such announcements were also frequent, of course, but as he performed during the fast-day ceremonies three weeks later, one congre-gant observed that he prayed "so low that I could hardly hear a word; was spent." Two days after the fast he fainted, suffering what his son believed was apoplexy. He revived in a few minutes, but "it so enfeebled him," Cotton wrote, "that he never went abroad any more."

Other losses beset Mather as Increase lay dying. Unexpectedly he lost a different father on December 27, when Governor Shute boarded the *Seahorse*—the ship that had brought in smallpox—and suddenly left for England, having notified no one of his departure. Shute had become "tired and soured," Mather wrote, by opposition from a "little and wretched" but politically powerful clique, old-line frustrated supporters of the private bank who misled the House into producing votes "which any Governor must count intolerable." These votes included one to cut his annual salary by £200, but he had wrangled constantly with the House, increasingly so around 1722. Mather had counted on his cordial relation with Shute to restore his political effectiveness. Considering the accusations Shute might make against New England, perhaps again endangering the charter, he not only regretted Shute's departure but also expected "miserable changes, and very heavy chains, to be hastened upon us."

Mather quickly gained the displeasure of the interim government, under acting governor William Dummer (the brother of Jeremiah Dummer). In February 1722, near the end of the epidemic, he had preached on the text They shall go out of one Fire, and another Fire shall devour them (Ezek. 15:7). Upon Shute's departure, Mather claimed that this reference to "another Fire" ten months earlier had been a prophecy of the near dissolution of the government and of new threats against the charter by Shute's complaints in London. The *Courant* made sport of his claim and spoofed his breastbeating ("behold a more *Cruciating* fire is devouring us! Ah sinful people of *New-England*"). In reply to the paper's continuing attack on the ministry, Mather began publishing in the *Boston News-Letter* a nine-part series of articles on "The State of Religion," a lengthy miscellany of pieces with extracts from his own *Advice, To the Churches of the Faithful* (1702). Either thoughtlessly or deliberately, he included extracts from this earlier work that criticized the "iniquities" of two English monarchs and that upbraided the Church of England for harboring "a Set of men, who call themselves *Protestants,* and yet Assert and Attempt an Ecclesiastical Coalescence with a *Foreign Jurisdiction.*" Outdated aspersions on former English rulers and on the English church were unlikely at this sensitive time to please authorities in London to whom Shute was addressing complaints about New England's loyalty. For his carelessness or misjudgment, Mather found the new government viewing him as "a publisher of dangerous libels," forbidding him to continue his series, and directing him to "look upon it as a piece of proper modesty, to be as little as possible in their presence."

Losing money also, Mather remained never-endingly dunned for large sums he could not pay, and in this, as in little else, now being copied by Creasy. One suit came from the Cambridge minister Nathaniel Appleton, for £264; another from Joseph Baxter of Medfield, for £318. In both cases Mather and Lydia defaulted by not appearing in court, and were ordered to pay the debts. But he seems to have successfully appealed the judgments because of irregularities in the writs, and he retaliated by later suing Baxter for £161 owing to the Howell-George estate, the sheriff attaching Baxter's house and land to the value of £200. Creasy, at last walking and talking just like his father, was bound over in March 1723 for £3 he owed to a Boston tailor named Foxley Sanderson, ordered to "not depart without license" but to answer the charge in court. As his father often did, he failed to appear, and the court ordered payment plus damages. In June Creasy was sued twice, once for £8 owing to a Boston widow and again for the same amount on a promissory note nearly two years old to Increase Gatchel, a dancing master and vendor of "Choice good Italian Fiddle-Strings." Creasy's debt to Gatchel provides at least a peep at what dismayed Mather about the boy's company. When some young men were denied admission to Gatchel's Hanover Street dancing school, they shattered all of his windows and threatened to kill him.

In these circumstances Mather awaited the loss of his father. Increase lingered helplessly, sometime judged unable to live out the week. To return now to the occasion of the September fast, Mather and many others attributed Increase's moribund state to his grief over the figurative death of the figurative daughter. The "daughter" was a minister named Timothy Cutler, who two weeks before the fast had closed his public prayers with the words "*and let all the people say, amen.*" Had Cutler been an Anglican preaching at King's Chapel his choice of words would have gone unnoticed. But he had been born in Charlestown and educated at Harvard, and was rector of Yale College; and he had publicly closed the Yale commencement by thus reciting the words of the Episcopal form of prayer. This was the death. It was as if the president of the United States at the Tomb of the Unknown Soldier on the Fourth of July had sung the *Internationale.*

Mather was aghast at the "treacherous Rector," not only as a founder of Yale but also as a minister. For the day after the infamous commencement Cutler had declared, as Samuel Sewall put it tersely, that "there was no Minister in New England." Cutler, one Yale tutor, and five neighboring Congregational ministers met with the college trustees in the Yale library. Each speaking for himself said he had come to consider his Congregational ordination invalid, and to believe that only ordination according to the Church of England practice might entitle him to administer the ordinances. Three of the defectors were ultimately dissuaded, but the trustees excused Cutler from the rectorship and he left for England to be reordained as an Anglican. One exultant Anglican contemporary, comparing Cutler's rebellion to the overthrow of Governor Andros in 1689, called it the "glorious revolution of the ecclesiastics of this country." To the Mathers it represented not merely the climax of long-mounting anti-ministerial sentiment, but also a direct threat. Cutler's passage abroad was paid by a group of Bostonians who wished him to serve as minister to a new Anglican church which they hoped to erect in Boston, a companion to the chapel that had been built under Andros. As King's Chapel stood in the South End, they proposed placing the new Anglican church in the North End—a perhaps five-minute walk from the Mathers' church.

The tumult brought Mather an offer of the rectorship of Yale. The invitation must have been tempting for, a contemporary noted, the "Contumelies and unworthy treatment he has met with in Boston would facilitate his parting with it." But probably his father's grave illness, his continuing litigation, his liking for Boston as the metropolis of America, and the reluctance of his church to release him decided him against it. While Boston newspapers reported Cutler's spectacular departure, however, he received letters from several Connecticut ministers lamenting that Yale, though newly founded, should "groan out Ichabod." The ministers confided their fear that Cutler's declaration might encourage Anglican proselytizing in Connecticut and that many students "leavened" by him might assume his principles. They sought Mather's advice on checking these threats and on handling the issue of apostolic succession. In denying the validity of their ordination, the defectors had alleged, and probably would allege again, that in the past some ministers in Connecticut had been invalidly ordained by laymen; these ministers had acted in later ordinations, presumably rendering them invalid also. The grim situation, they told Mather, demanded a stand: "we must put on our armour and fight, or else let the good old cause, for which our fathers came into this land, sink and be deserted."

Mather and the other Boston ministers had no intention of watching "the good old cause" sink. To the defenses of Boston Congregationalism which now, one Anglican said, "glutted" every town in Connecticut, Mather contributed three anonymous works. When promoting his Maxims of Universal Piety he had not envisioned an apostate like Cutler, much less his apostasy coinciding with the death of Increase Mather, and what that meant to the survival of the world of the Fathers. In his rejoinders

Mather dropped the gladsome ecumenical language of the Universal Religion, already toned-down to exclude Arians, and took up the old bludgeoning idiom of the covenanted people. Cutler and the others, he said, were "Degenerate Offspring" of their infinitely better fathers, treacherous "Sons of *New England*" who would "assist the *Common Enemy*," papistical "*Cudweeds*" who cast indignity on the "Leaders of the Flock that followed our Saviour Into this Wilderness." Especially had they betrayed their fathers, and were collaborating with Rome, in fussing over lay ordination, "that vile, senseless, wretched whimsey of an uninterrupted succession." No longer calling on Congregationalists to join godly Episcopalians at communion, he now emphasized that the New England churches had been "Planted on the very Design of withdrawing from the *Episcopal Impositions.*" While he recommended patiently affording the defectors time to rethink their views, he said he saw no reason why, as they had disowned their ordination, their flocks might not disown them.

Increase reacted to these events, Mather wrote, with "too extreme a concern of his Mind." But atop his mental distress, which included delirium and bouts of forgetfulness, Increase also suffered exhausting bodily infirmities. A torturous hiccup sometime seized him for a week or two without stop, then intermitted, but returned with such violence as to corrode his diaphragm. He was also wracked by stones, which had first afflicted him at the time of his conversion, when he was fifteen. Cotton had probably witnessed the sore effects as a child, when a violent fit of stone struck his grandfather Richard Mather at Increase's house in 1699, the prelude to his death a week later. Cotton worried that he might die of the ailment himself. Increase's pain from the stone was excruciating beyond the power of fortitude to manage. Once Samuel Sewall stopped at Increase's house and heard him cry out, "Pity me! Pity me!"

Helpless to pluck out the unremitting scalding in Increase's body, Cotton tried to comfort his father spiritually. Increase was troubled by the state of his soul, and "in the Minutes of the Darkness wherein he lay thus *feeble and sore broken*," Cotton wrote, "he sometimes let fall expressions of some *Fear* lest he might after all be Deceived in his *Hope* of the *Future Blessedness.*" Yet he resisted his own doubts, often calling to Christ, promising to mention His righteousness and His alone. On February 19 he told Cotton, joyfully, "*I now see, that I was deceived, when I fear'd Lest I might be deceived.*" Scarce allowing Cotton to leave his room without some prayer, he also had his grandsons transcribe the account he had made in adolescence, seventy years earlier, of his conversion, and he read the relation consolingly. Whether these grandsons included Creasy is unknown, but Samuel Sewall thought it must have been "pleasant" to Increase to live to have Sammy, in the summer of 1723, graduated from Harvard.

Appropriately, Increase's final three days on earth began with a premonition. Coming out of a "Dark Minute," as Cotton recounted it, he said: "*It is now Revealed from Heaven to me, That I shall quickly, quickly, quickly be fetch'd away to Heaven, and that I shall Die in the Arms of my Son.*" After this he kept calling for Cotton, who did what he could to strengthen him. Near noon on Friday, August 23, with Increase visibly near death, Cotton said to him: "*Sir, The Messenger is now come to tell you; This Day thou shalt be in Paradise. Do you Believe it, Sir, and Rejoice in the Views and Hopes of it?*" Increase said "*I do! I do! I do!*" and died in his arms. The Westfield poet-minister Edward Taylor wrote that "Cutler's Cutlary gave th'killing Stob." But the autopsy performed on Increase's body revealed a polyp on his bladder and six large gravelly stones, some over an inch around. Only one of them, an observer said, "would have been Enough to have tortured a Giant to Death."

Mather had always seen his father as a celebrity, and felt proud of the honors accorded Increase at his funeral, "a Greater *Funeral,*" he wrote, "than had ever been seen for any *Divine,* in *these* (and some Travellers at it, said, *in any other*) parts of the World." Increase had earned the homage, too: through his charter agency he had irrevocably transformed the life of New England, whose purity he had labored to maintain from his conspicuous pulpit for sixty years. The pallbearers thus included acting governor Dummer, John Leverett as president of Harvard, his old friend Samuel Sewall, and Benjamin Colman, aided by twelve "under bearers" from the North Church. Before the pall walked 160 students from Harvard; behind came a "vast number of Followers," in Sewall's description, including fifty ministers—a good part of the entire ministry of New England. As an also vast number of spectators looked on from the streets of Boston, the procession bore the coffin around the North Church, past Increase's house, up Hull Street, to Copp's Hill, the cemetery of the North Church. There Increase was buried in the Mather family tomb near his first wife, Maria Cotton.

Increase had drawn up a will four years earlier. His soul, he wrote, had been given to God in Christ more than sixty years ago; his goods, except his library, amounted to little. "It has been thought that I have bags by me," he explained, "which is a great mistake. I have not twenty pounds in silver, or in Bills." He specified that his black servant Spaniard should not be sold, but given his liberty and "esteemed a Free Negro." His widow apparently received nothing, their prenuptial contract providing that neither should figure in the other's estate. To his son Samuel, preaching in England, he left only a fourth of his library, noting that Samuel had honored his father's name but that more had been spent on Samuel's education than on the other children's, and that Samuel had gained a large estate through marriage. Another fourth of his library he gave to his "Fatherless grandson" Mather Byles, the son of his daughter Elizabeth, requesting that Cotton see to the young orphan's education; that the boy would not add to his son's financial burdens, he left him all his clothing except a chamblet cloak. To his grandson Sammy he left his three folio volumes of Piscator's *Commentary;* to Creasy, his other grandson and namesake, he left nothing.

What little money and few goods remained Increase gave to Cotton. This included his pendulum watch, pendulum clock, silver tankard, and chamblet cloak, as well as all his manuscripts and half his library, desiring that the latter not be sold. Had he any great estate, he added, he would have given the greater part to Cotton. For Cotton was, he said, "a great comfort to me from his childhood having been a very dutiful son and a singular blessing both to his Father's Family and flock."

Considering that Increase had at last fulfilled his lifelong threat of abandonment, that he had reinforced through long and daily contact his unusually potent role as his son's model, critic, confidant, and rival, and that the two men had been for more than forty sometimes momentous years close colleagues, links in a dynasty, Mather's feelings about his father's death must have surged at him from every side, a swirl of competing pains. Most unfortunately, however, Mather's diaries for the period are missing, his extant letters scarcely mention the event, and what remains of his reaction is anticlimactic and uninformative. The lost documents may conceivably have recorded his sorrow. Or Mather may have been steeled against his father's death by repetition, Increase having in effect been dying all his life. He may also have been distracted by his many other problems and keeping his vow of silence. Or his feelings may have been too deeply delicate to submit for public scrutiny, or raced so fast as to outrun expression. For whatever reasons, his surviving remarks about his father's death are surprisingly indirect and dispassionate.

Two days after Increase's death, as pulpits throughout New England filled with mourning sermons, Mather again entered the North Church. There, thirty-eight years earlier, he had heard his father preach his ordination sermon and had felt Increase's hand laid upon him, symbolically passing on the ministerial succession. What he delivered, however, was a formal sermon on the character of a Good Man, one who prays much, contrives good, and spreads truth—a routine sermon he might have preached on the death of any other minister. He did offer an adulatory sketch of Increase's life, and toward the end he did comment that "this House is this Day become a *Bochim;* and we are a Congregation of *Weepers*." But he made no attempt to stand forth as an example of resignation. And he well knew that his rather tidy and low-keyed sermon could not be taken for a tribute to his father: "in this very great Auditory," he acknowledged, "there will not be One that will approve of my Performance. They will all to a Man complain, *That I have spoke too Little.*" He promised to make amends by writing his father's biography, but the intention hardly seems to justify or account for the sermon's unexpected impersonality. The 239-page biography he published the next year does give a colorfully full and historically valuable account of Increase's life (on which this biography has often drawn), and makes clear Mather's near worshipful sense of his father's greatness, and his indignation over (and identification with) his father's ill treatment by others. Yet despite its title, *Parentator* is not a life of his father but, as he refers to Increase, of "Mr. *Mather*," a famous but misappreciated New England minister. The biography says virtually nothing of their personal bond.

Mather may have disclosed some of his feelings, indirectly, in the wholly detached sermon he preached three weeks after Increase's death, on the suggestive text God, our Father (Phil. 4:20, the same text on which Increase had preached after the death of his own father, Richard Mather). Addressing himself to all those who have lost fathers, he explored the doctrine of Adoption, by which God makes all believers His children. The intended audience and the subject themselves intimate a renewal of childlike feelings of helplessness in Mather, and need for a substitute father. He did not mention Increase, but something of the inner strain of denial perhaps shows in his opening remark that the doctrine defies expression by the "stammering Tongue of a sinful and shallow mortal." Read in this way, many of Mather's seemingly impersonal comments convey resisted feelings of vulnerability and diminishment following Increase's death, and residual resentment over his failings as a parent. As if he felt somehow safer when Increase was alive, he instructed those who found themselves fatherless to think, "I have a Father, that will provide for me, protect me, advise me, uphold me, take my part against my Enemies." His sense of capability always needing to be authenticated by the approval of Increase (and others), he also wrote as if his father's death had left hollow the meaning of his being a minister, a doctor of divinity, a

Fellow of the Royal Society: "perhaps the biggest and bravest of them appears but an Empty Title; well, But This thy Title: A Child of God! O Glorious Title! Nothing, Nothing in this World can equal it." If Mather felt littler in his father's absence, however, part of him also remembered that Increase could be present but unavailable and nearly unpleasable. In consoling other orphans for the loss of their earthly fathers, he reminded them that the Everlasting Father still lives, "A Father who give[s] me infinitely better than ever any earthly Father did. . . . A Father infinitely fuller of pity."

What few other clues to Mather's state of mind can be dug from his other works of the period point to longings for substitute, supernatural guardianship and for contact beyond the grave. In the angelological tract *Coelestinus* (1723), written during Increase's last illness, he observed that "one such significant *Friend,* as a *Good Angel* concerned for us, will signify more than . . . if all the *Friends* in the World refuse to be any further concerned for us." He seems also to have hoped for, but greatly feared, converse with Increase's ghost. Several people in his neighborhood, he said, had been visited by spirits of the dead and he may himself have been visited by the spirit of his brother Nathanael. He did not regard communications with the dead as unlawful, nor to be confused with necromancy, since the departed elect are the "Nobler Members of the *Family,* which we in a *Lower State* belong unto. And they may be thus convers'd withal." Thus in the published version of the sermon he preached immediately after Increase's death, he depicted Increase replying to a series of questions from "the *Courts of the Lord,*" that is, from heaven. Yet in some other works of this time he warned that visitations by spirits of the dead can be even more disturbing than angelic visitations. Seeing angels, he remarked in *The Lord-High-Admiral* (1723), puts people "in Frightful *Sweats;* Their *Hair* stands; their *Blood* runs cold; They are almost scared out of their *Wits.* . . . 'Tis rather more so, when the *Ghosts* of the *Dead* visit us, and show themselves unto us."

Whatever else Increase's death meant to Mather, his daily existence as he neared his sixtieth year, his way of life, would never again be the same. On December 18 his father's successor, and soon perhaps his own also, was installed at the North Church—Joshua Gee. Raised under the Mathers' ministry, Gee was respected as a learned man of powerful intellect, but also considered indolent; no Increase Mather, he never developed his potential. The carefully conducted installation was widely taken as reasserting the validity of Congregational ordination against Cutler and the other apostates. One spectator wrote that "if I had been wavering about the validity of our ordination before, I should have been then fixed and established by the solemnity and religious devotion visible in all parties at the sacred action." Cotton Mather delivered the charge, Colman and other ministers imposed hands.

On January 19, Mather entered blotchily into his assiduously kept and usually neat church records the baptism of a man named James Cox. It was the first baptism administered by Gee, "And indeed," Cotton wrote, "the First, that has been administered, by any Hand, but that of *Mather* (Father and Son,) in the old North Church, for more than half an hundred years together."

*

Other vexations and crises left Mather little time to mourn. Within about six weeks after Increase's death, the "miserable apostate" returned from England, where he had been awarded the degree of S.T.D. by both Oxford and Cambridge universities and had been ordained a priest. One Bostonian reported that when news came that Cutler had been made "Doc Devinity," three Boston Anglicans were "so zealous to tell doc mather that they called him out of bed to acquaint him with it."

Shortly after arriving, Cutler preached at King's Chapel, railing against Congregational ordination and, by one account, sparing not to "Belch it out That we have no Ministers but two or Three." On December 29 he presided over the first large meeting held in the new Church of England chapel in the North End. This formidable new building, following on the erection of Queen Anne's Chapel at Newbury in 1713 and St. Michael's at Marblehead in 1714, made visible how substantially the Church of England had penetrated once purely Congregational territory. About seventy feet long and built of brick, many of its features inspired by Wren's churches in London, the chapel was originally thirty-five feet high, exclusive of the wooden spire that was added later, from which were hung the lanterns that set off Paul Revere's ride. It was not merely the outstanding church building in the North End, but the first great Georgian church in America.

Mather usually shrugged off the activities of Anglican ministers in New England. When any arrived, he either made a show of welcoming them under the Universal Maxims of Piety, scorned New Englanders who flocked to them as "ignorant, vicious, contemptible people," or dismissed them as debauched rakes. His nonchalance could be justified by such recent cases as that of James McSparran, a Scots Presbyterian who had been invited to settle as pastor in Bristol, Rhode Island. Mather urged against his settlement because of some alleged misconduct, and wrote abroad to inquire after his credentials. McSparran offered to go abroad himself to secure proof but, like Cutler, returned with Anglican ordination, and started a Church of England parish in Rhode Island. In 1721 a woman named Frances Davis testified under oath that McSparran had stayed at her parents' house and lured her to his bedroom. She said "he would have me sit on the Bed, but I said I would not, but he put his Hand round my Waste, and shoved me along, and set me down on the Bed, and then sat by Me, and pulled me down on the Bed." This "grievous wolf," as Mather called him, also tried to take off her petticoat and to feel her belly but succeeded only in clutching her leg as high as her knee. McSparran knew, the woman testified, that she resented his behavior, and told her "that if I came to Naraganset I should not come Home a Maid again." In light of such cases Mather disdained protesting the presence of Anglican ministers, reasoning that protest would induce the English Diocesan to send over abler ministers, while those already in America "have generally been such Ignorant wretches, and such debauched and finished villains, that, like the rattlesnakes in our country, they carry with them what warns and arms our people against being poisoned with them."

The mediocre success of the new chapel in the North End at first bore out Mather's strategy of allowing Church of England ministers to condemn themselves. Cutler himself estimated his listeners at about four hundred; Mather ordinarily preached to four times that number. Mather gloated over a report to him from a woman who had attended Cutler's church that "it was amazing to see, how few there, and what a sort of shabby people they were." Cutler also quarreled bitterly with his South End Anglican colleague, the lecturer at King's Chapel, the Rev. Henry Harris, who suspected that Cutler's conversion was insincere and chiefly inspired by "the prospect of a new Church in this Town." Cutler in turn blasted him as "in Lying and Villainy . . . a perfect over match for any dissenter."

But Mather soon discovered that Anglican infighting and the size of the Queen's Chapel congregation were no measures of Cutler's zeal. With something of the convert's combativeness, Cutler renounced his beginnings (Cambridge he described as a "Snotty Town of the Same Name" as English Cambridge) and saw himself as the vanguard of a thorough anglicanizing of New England. Believing it would "never be well" until Harvard became "an Episcopal College," he prosecuted a claim to be admitted by right, as a "teaching elder" of Boston, to a place on the

Harvard Board of Overseers. The Overseers rejected the claim, which however created a sensation. He proseletyzed outside Boston too,—for instance, conducting Church of England services in Scituate.

Mather later felt some of the apostate's "killing Stob" himself when, in a real show of force, Cutler managed to prevent the calling of a Congregational church synod. In May 1725, Mather addressed a memorial to the General Court, in behalf of a convention of ministers. The ministers, he wrote, had observed a "great and Visible Decay of Piety" in New England, had recalled their ancestors' use of synods to "recover And Establish the Faith and order of the Gospel," and now wished to convene representatives of the several churches to consider the evils that had provoked the "Judgments of Heaven." No general synod had been held in New England for more than forty-five years, since before the loss of the charter, and behind Mather's airing of the musty covenantal idiom of the Fathers, Anglicans correctly sensed insecurity. The calling of the synod was partly meant as a display of undying tribal solidarity, to squelch enthusiasm for the further spread of the Church of England. The outspoken Anglican John Checkley, who had first questioned Mather's membership in the Royal Society, wrote that the synod was intended to halt the building of new Anglican churches, and might end in creating "something like the solemn League and Covenant, to prejudice the rising Generation against the Church."

The Council approved Mather's memorial, and sent it to the House for concurrence. But Cutler and Samuel Myles (rector of King's Chapel) addressed a vigorous counter memorial to the House and Council. Basically they charged that in calling for a synod, Mather's memorial undertook to speak for all New England, and thus treated the Church of England as if it did not exist. They also argued that because by royal authority the American colonies were annexed to the Diocese of London, it would be undutiful to the king and inconsistent with the rights of the Bishop of London to call the synod before knowing the king's pleasure. Both the Council and the House rejected this memorial as containing "indecent reflections" and "groundless insinuations." Unabashed, Cutler and Myles then complained directly to the Bishop of London, who brought the matter before the Lords Justices. Opinion in London was that, if called, the synod would reach decisions hostile to the English church, and would encourage English Dissenters to propose a synod as well, putting them in competition with the established church. The attorney general and solicitor general decided the issue on legal grounds, giving it as their opinion that synods cannot lawfully be called without royal license, and that the ministers' application through Mather to the provincial legislature was a contempt of the king. The synod never met.

Mather professed to consider Anglican fears of the proposed synod "Unaccountable!" But surely he found nothing obscure in this plain demonstration of the loosening Congregational grasp on New England's religious life, any more than in the addition soon after to Cutler's fine new church, so near his own, of a large green curtain trimmed with scarlet and white lace, and an altarpiece painted with cherubs and festoons.

While looking for Cutler to shame himself, Mather also eyed warily the complaints being made in London by the angered Governor Shute, which might risk the charter. Jeremiah Dummer wrote home that some Lords of the Regency, after hearing Shute's case against the House, declared that Massachusetts was again "dancing to the Old tune" of sedition, and under any government but Shute's mild one would be judged guilty of treason. Mather and Colman, probably to cool Shute off, tried to enlist the Boston ministers around November 1723 in composing an address to him, but it seems that the greater number of them proved unwilling.

In Boston Mather's support of Shute gained him "the utmost rage of the satanic party," he said, including "attempts made upon my very life," details of which are unknown. But at the same time he had lost favor with Shute himself. The governor's unannounced departure to make representations against Massachusetts in London had apparently left Mather uncertain whether to offer public prayers for his voyage; as the *Courant* pointed out, to pray for Shute's voyage amounted to praying for the destruction of Massachusetts. Mather thus learned that Shute had struck him from "the list of his Friends" because of a "mis-report" to him "of my being at a loss how to mention his voyage in our public prayers, immediately upon his very sudden withdraw from us." Shute probably was not pleased either by an earlier "misreport" that Mather had called his brother, Lord Barrington, an Arian (which Mather denied, saying, "I never spoke it, never wrote it, never thought it"). Obviously hoping he retained enough of Shute's esteem to persuade him not to hazard the charter, he wrote to the governor himself in early December, with somewhat timorous formality—the tone, compared with the bonhomie of his earlier letters to Shute, itself registering estrangement. He told the governor: "I cannot wish to Your Excellency the infelicity of ever being the instrument, or so much as the occasion, of bringing any hardships upon a people (be the faults of a small party among them what they will!) whose ancestors deserved and purchased all the liberties their charters have engaged unto them."

Mather's fidelity to Shute produced a new scandal, and friction between Mather and Jeremiah Dummer. The House, wanting to defend itself in London against Shute's complaints, appointed Elisha Cooke, Jr., a
special agent to appear at court to explain its side of the quarrel. Cooke
was of course Shute's personal and political enemy, the man he had negatived as Speaker. The choice also displeased Dummer, the regular Massachusetts agent, who disliked Cooke and his colleagues. Cooke's supporters in Boston, presumably, now undertook to discredit Dummer and
Mather. Around March 1724, Mather discovered that his study had been
"knavishly and c—kishly riffled," he said, and six pounds of money stolen ("enough to bear the expense of several tankards"). Also stolen was a
letter to Mather from Dummer, criticizing Cooke, who was now his co-
agent. Somehow the letter turned up in Cooke's hands. Copies of it were
spread around Boston, with malicious comments, and with insinuations
that Mather had himself released the letter and betrayed Dummer.

Mather denied this angrily. "I would much sooner have died," he
said, "than have been guilty of so vile an Action, as to betray a Friend, and
to his Enemies what he writes unto me." Dummer seems to have distrusted his denial, however thumping. He wrote him a rather Matherean
letter, of unqualified exoneration followed by qualification. He was sure,
Dummer said, that the letter came to Cooke "not with your privity"; but
he added, "A little thing can't efface the remembrance of the many happy
hours I have formerly pass'd in your Company. I say this in case you had
inadvertantly given out my letter." As Mather put it, Dummer "rejected
me as well as my Apologies" and looked on him as a "Sinner."

Mather may well have been innocent, for around the same time the
study of his friend Samuel Penhallow was also rifled, and a letter to him
from Mather was also shown around. Sometime later, too, Dummer had
Cooke to dinner at his London apartment and asked him how he came by
the letter, but Cooke refused to say. When Dummer added that he had
since written only one other letter to Mather, Cooke replied with a sneer
that he had that letter too at home. The espionage anyway proved unnecessary, for Cooke's agency failed. Shute successfully defended himself on
points of law in official hearings, and the House was forced to accept an
"explanatory charter" declaring the governor's power to negative the
choice of Speaker. Having won his fight against the House, Shute, despite
recurrent rumors to the contrary, never returned to New England.

As he had done when similarly under fire during Dudley's administration and the smallpox epidemic, Mather resolved once again to withdraw
as far as he could from political affairs. He had become disillusioned with

Shute and Lord Barrington, his two former friends, "the Two Gentleman-Brothers (I wish I could say, on all accounts, Gentlemen,) whose odd usages of me, have made me to be . . . Ashamed of my Hope, concerning them." On April 4, shortly after the exposure of Dummer's letter, he turned down a dinner invitation from the acting governor, explaining that the government's having silenced his pen a year earlier, and his public notoriety, had forced him to retire "from the old Familiarities of the Table, as well as other Freedoms, which I once been used unto." He secluded himself not from imagined slights, he emphasized, but because of dejection born in real difficulty. His withdrawal "may be smiled at as Vapour; yet this Vapour will appear to be Reason unto one under the power of it; having at the same time a thousand other more heavy Loads upon him."

The load now included such nervewracking demands against the estate that he feared for his health and sanity. The harassments during his seven-year ordeal with the administration had been "beyond all expression miserable." But the current demands against him, for sums he really did not owe, seemed large enough to ruin him. And there seemed no possibility of avoiding the ruin. He felt bitterly deserted as well: "The Friends who might be capable of helping me, keep at a Distance from me, and appear to do little for me. The Relatives on whose Account, I have brought all this Distress upon myself, treat me like Monsters of Ingratitude." Even God seemed to have turned from him, stirring worrisome thoughts of atheism: "My continual Cries to God, all this while, seem to have no Answer, but a Growth of my Confusions . . . . . . And from the strange Dispensations that I meet withal, sometimes hideous Temptations to Infidelity are shot in upon me." The only prospect of a way out, he believed, lay in wiping himself out, "selling all my Goods to pay the Debts, and breaking up my Family." He called out to the Redeemer, "I sink, I sink; Oh! Reach out thy Hand, and save me!"

Worst of all, Mather's predicament had a revelatory effect. Like some precipitant giving body to invisible crystals in a solution, it gave shape to what had imperceptibly constituted his life, bringing before his view the hidden but all suffusing pattern of his existence. He was a man whose lot it was, he could now see, to have been denied his very self. He was a man whose unique fortune it was to be taken precisely for what he was not. To find himself near ruin for paying the debts of people who despised him was not incidental to his life but of its pervasive substance, a life that had been somehow turned inside out, where reality and appearance were perversely transposed. How much had he done for sailors, in sermons, in prayers, in books, in projections?

AND YET, there is not a Man in the world, so Reviled, so slandered, so cursed, among the *Sailors.*

How much had he done for the salvation and comfort of blacks?

AND YET, some, on purpose to affront me, call their *Negro's,* by the Name of *Cotton Mather,* that so they may with some Shadow of Truth, assert Crimes as committed by one of that Name, which the Hearers take to be *me.*

How much had he done for the profit and honor of the female sex, especially in publishing biographies of holy women?

AND YET, Where is the Man, whom the *female Sex* have spit more of their Venom at? I have cause to Question, whether there are twice Ten in the Town, but what have at some time or other spoken basely of me.

Had he not kept a catalogue of all his relatives, and each week devised some good for one or another of them?

AND YET, Where is the Man, who has been tormented with such monstrous *Relatives?* Job said, *I am a Brother to Dragons.*

Had he not written many books to advance piety and promote the Kingdom of God, more than three hundred and thirty of them?

AND YET, I have had more *Books* written against me; more Pamphlets to traduce me, and reproach me, and bely me, than any man that I know in the World.

For pages in his diary Mather extended this ranting catechism of bewildering misperceptions of his being, and bewilderingly mean rewards for his services. He had comforted his parents "AND YET" received the contrary of comfort from his children; had made "Applications without Number" for the country's interest "AND YET" been loaded with calumny and aversion; had labored for the reputation of Harvard "AND YET" it showed him more contempt than if he were "the greatest *Blockhead* that ever came from it"; had done more to vindicate the reputation of Scotland than perhaps any other Englishman "AND YET" no Englishman had been so defamed by Scots tongues and pens; had hardly ever, for fifty years, neglected to say something useful in company "AND YET" his company was as little sought as that of any minister he knew.

Near the end of his list of "Dark Dispensations" Mather returned in his diary to the most oppressive and urgent of them, the one that might ruin him:

XIII. *What has a gracious Lord given me to do,* in *Alms,* and in Disbursements on *pious Uses?* For whole Years together, *not one Day* has passed me, in which I have not been able to say, that I have done something that Way.

AND YET, tho' I am strangely provided for, yet I am a very *poor Man.* I have not a Foot of Land upon Earth. Except a *Library* and a little *Household Stuff,* I have nothing upon Earth. And this also I am now offering unto my Creditors, to satisfy for Debts, whereof I never did myself owe a Farthing. My very *Library,* the Darling of my little Enjoyments, is demanded from me. . . .

To perfect the mind-fuddling sting of these brutal paradoxes, Mather observed, even his constant preaching about affliction as God's chastisement for sin had been inverted and turned against him. People pointed at him as by far the most afflicted minister in all New England—and inferred he must consequently be the greatest sinner, "and are pretty Arbitrary in their Conjectures on my punished Miscarriages." In searching for consolation he told himself that Christ had taken possession of him, and that he had been granted a strong persuasion of a future state, to which would be postponed his receipt of "the whole Harvest of my mean Studies to glorify God."

About two weeks after Mather poured out this long entry came the moment he had dreaded all his life. The exact circumstances are unknown, but to him they seemed final. "I must either be lodg'd in the Prison," he wrote on April 2, "or forc'd into a private Withdraw." From the earliest days of his ministry he had taken notice of sorry examples of men, including his own uncle John Cotton, who through lust, avarice, or other personal weakness had disgraced their sacred vocation, and he had prayed often to be spared such a fate, the more fervently because of his honored family. But it seemed evident to him now that he had not been spared, or that others had dragged him down, and that his role as a minister was ended. Preparing to take the virtually unthinkable step, "a step which much more than all New England will ring of," he had decided to find by God's direction and by hard study the most important and affecting things to say in taking "my Farewel of the Flock withal."

The same evening, however, Mather received a "marvellous Appearance of GOD my SAVIOUR!" When feeling doomed he had often thought acrimoniously of the friends who might have eased his situation but had failed to come forward, "like Persons in a Maze and a doze." That evening, however, four leading members of his congregation, "men full of Prudence and Goodness," visited him. Awakened to the extremity of his situation, they kindly rebuked his anxiety, and promised they would immediately undertake to extricate him, "and that without any further Thought of mine."

*

But there was Lydia . . . and Creasy. On April 7, five days after Mather was visited by concerned members of his flock, he wrote in his diary: *Misera mea Conjux in Paroxysmos illos vere Satanicos, a quibus per Annos quosdam fuerit plerumque Liberata (Vel ego Saltem Liberatus) iam rursus delapsa*—My poor wife has now again lapsed into those truly Satanic paroxysms from which for some years she had been for the most part free (or at least I was free).

Exactly what set Lydia off is uncertain, but for months the household atmosphere must have been explosively irritable. A proud woman, she cannot have been pleased by Mather's financial condition, which apparently reduced him to accepting doles; in March he had thanked his landlord for "obliging presents for the support of my family." Nor can she have enjoyed the notoriety. Feeling criminal, he seems to have declined invitations to preach at other churches, and in turning down a dinner invitation he explained that his "well-known circumstances of prosecution to *restore what I took* not away, rendered it a disgrace unto such a table, as well as unto any pulpit, for me to make my appearance there." The presence in the house of Lydia's niece cannot have made its mood less touchy, for Mather thought her contemptible, "a monstrous Liar and a very mischievous Person, and a sower of Discord, and a Monster of Ingratitude." Lydia had already given signs of her discontent, venting an "unreasonable and implacable Aversion" toward Hannah, the daughter who had been severely burned during infancy, "My dear, dear *Nancy;* a Child of so many Afflictions all her Days"; Mather weighed finding another home for Nancy to board in. The immediate cause of Lydia's renewed outbursts on April 7, however, may have been a fresh suit brought against Mather. During the April court session, an executor of the estate of the Boston merchant Joseph Buckley sued Mather and his former attorney (and son-in-law) Daniel Willard for debts contracted in 1717, of £444. It was probably the largest single suit Mather ever faced. He again did not appear in court to answer and was ordered to pay £209 plus court costs.

Lydia's new paroxysms came with volcanic violence, and Mather found them unbearable. Lydia began spewing, he wrote, *absurdissimis ac sordidissimis mutitur Stomachationibus*—the most absurd and obscene outbursts of splenetic anger, blowing her top. Believing that her "*Insan-*

iae" had been ordained by Christ to arouse his prayers and test his patience, he lay his troubles before God. Creasy was away again at sea, but Lydia's "horrid, froward, malicious Disposition" now also began raging over Sammy too. He prayed not only for patience but also for protection.

Virtually week by week, as happened five years earlier, Lydia's assaults alternated with wooings, but of an ardor, erotic in Mather's description of it, on the same order as her reviling. Thus two weeks after Lydia's initial paroxysms he wrote, in Latin, that not only was everything at home again calm and cheerful, but also that *fere Extatico erga me Amore, condita*— Lydia behaved with an almost frenzied show of love toward him. Only Mather's account of these episodes survives, leaving it unclear whether Lydia suffered from a clinically severe emotional disturbance or was only fed up with Mather's behavior. At his best he could act needlingly, at his worst impossibly. And his letters and diaries for the period groan with a dull self-disgust, self-deprecating remarks about his uselessness, dejected plaints that his ministry is finished. Whether he behaved at home in this black mood is unknown. But in his description of them, Lydia's ravings sometimes seem no more than extreme versions of conduct he had often received from, and often provoked in, others. Indeed his chronicle of Lydia's emotional rhythms seems loosely geared to times when a fresh lawsuit was pressed or an older one resolved.

Whatever the case, Mather found Lydia's metamorphoses unaccountable: *tam inexplicabilis est conjugis meae ad Extrema se Vertentis incertissima mutabilitas!*—how inexplicable is the unpredictable changeableness of my wife directing herself *ad extrema*. Two weeks after the house had become calm and peaceful he was again writing, *Familia mea per furentis uxoris insaniam rursus misere distracta ac turbata*—My household is again wretchedly torn asunder, and thrown into disorder through the madness of my raging wife. But, the following week, serenity again and ardor: *mea conjux in mei non tantum Amorem flagrantissimum, sed at Admirationem rapta!*—Lydia was enraptured not only with the most flagrant love for him but also with the most extreme admiration. On the downside of these swings Mather prayed for the safety of himself and his children; on the upswings he resolved to be patient, and tried to help Lydia by strewing their conversation with holy thoughts. Her ardor during her recoveries guiltily excited him. While trying to maintain her calm and to restore their marriage with soothing displays of love, he warned himself not to let his mollifying grow too intense, presumably sexual: "O! Let all possible Purity accompany it, and let me watch against all such inordinate Affection, as may grieve the holy Spirit of GOD!"

A historically fascinating, if not very revealing, glimpse of Mather's condition at this time is provided by Benjamin Franklin. Now twenty years old, the recent creator of Silence Dogood returned to Boston from his first trip to Philadelphia in late April or early May, visited Mather in his library, and later recounted their leavetaking in his *Autobiography*. Mather showed him a shortcut out of the house, through a narrow passage crossed by an overhead beam:

> We were all talking as I withdrew, he accompanying me behind, and I turning partly towards him, when he said hastily, "*Stoop, stoop!*" I did not understand him till I felt my head hit against the beam. He was a man that never missed any occasion of giving instruction, and upon this he said to me: "*You are young, and you have the world before you;* STOOP *as you go through it, and you will miss many hard thumps.*"

Franklin remarked that he often thought of Mather's useful advice when he saw misfortune brought on people by their "carrying their heads too high." Mather had begun looking up himself, however. By early June, not long after Franklin's visit, he believed he saw some relief ahead: "I am not without very great Hopes, that the Designs of Satan to discompose my Family and prejudice my Ministry, are gloriously and eternally defeated."

But with July came new demands on the estate for more than four hundred pounds. "I feel the Iron . . . entering into my Soul," Mather wrote, wearing down. "I cry to my SAVIOUR, as *Peter* just ready to sink in the Waves." He managed to pay one debt, of over two hundred pounds, when members of his congregation again privately gathered money for him, which he accepted with desperate relief, "even fainting with a Sense of Gratitude." To show his profound thanks he published at his own expense a sermon on being temporally poor but spiritually rich in Christ, copies of which he gave his benefactors, writing in their names himself. He had often privately denounced many in his flock as foolish and worldly. But now he wrote an apologetic, self-pitying Preface to the work, bemoaning his unworthiness to serve people so "*fill'd with knowledge and full of Goodness*"; they had been to him, he professed, "what might have been more equally look'd for, if I *had been,* what I *should have been,*" and he promised to act again as their pattern. The promise soured four days after he wrote the Preface, however, when he was apparently presented with a new claim on the estate, also for more than two hundred pounds. He could meet the debt only if the creditor agreed to take his library, "which tho' so very dear to me above all temporal Possessions, I offer to Depredation." Once more, however, a few members of his congregation gave him the necessary money.

Inundated with new demands, Mather also found a change in Lydia's outbursts. They were becoming daily and more dangerous. On the last day of June, although he unfortunately provides no details, she fled from church and attempted violence on him and his household (*summas mihi meisque tentat Injurias*). In July she acted so tempestuously that he believed it necessary to banish her perfidious niece and to send ill-treated Nancy away. Otherwise wholly at a loss what to do, he turned to Christ with fearful eyes, he said, swollen with tears, praying that if the Redeemer did not snatch him from the water, *pereo, obruor, Actum est*—I perish, I am overwhelmed, it is finished. On July 31, Lydia's raging mood once more receded. Composed again, *meque summis cum Amoris Ardoribus amplexata*—she embraced her husband with the greatest heats of love.

The next five weeks heaped on Mather a new outrage, Lydia's departure . . . and then another departure, climactic and undoing. The outrage arose from the death in May of John Leverett, who had gone to bed well but in the morning, a Sabbath, was found dead. Leverett's death left open the presidency of the college, for which Mather was an obvious although now tarnished candidate. Mather had always detested Leverett, but with Sammy attending Harvard as a scholarship student had treated him cordially and requested his "wise, and kind, and paternal tuition." With Leverett gone, Mather referred to him as an *"Infamous Drone."* He did not conceal his opinion of Leverett's administration when undertaking an inquiry at the behest of the Overseers in August 1723. The date matters, for Sammy had graduated a month earlier, leaving Mather no longer dependent on "that unhappy Man, who sustained the Place of President." Leverett being no longer useful to him, he called stridently for an investigation of the state of the college on eleven counts, including whether it had not undergone a "notorious decay" of "solid learning"; whether Latin had not been discountenanced; whether the books most read by students were not "plays, novels, empty and vicious pieces of poetry"; whether the theological recitations were not cursory, the tutors uncaring, and the education in general designed to promote principles destructive of New England's religious, political, and social ideals. The Overseers investigated Leverett's administration but upheld it against Mather's indictments.

With Leverett's death Mather believed himself to be a desired successor. The stain of his many lawsuits and his now public quarrels with Lydia would seem a liability in the office, but he was told, he said, that his presidency was "most generally wished for." Benjamin Colman, himself a leading candidate for the presidency, doubted Mather's prospects. "Were the Doctors spirit of Government," he remarked, "esteemed equal to his

Literature we should go into no other name but his." But Mather's "spirit of Government" had never been estimable, and he himself suspected that his chances were dim. Choosing to stay home from the July commencement—that "insipid, ill-contrived, anniversary Solemnity"—he restricted his hopes to praying that the presidency "not be foolishly thrown away."

But Mather learned that it had indeed, by his standards, been thrown away, and rather in his face. The presidency was offered to the Rev. Joseph Sewall, the thirty-six-year-old son of Judge Samuel Sewall. With still another Sewall uprisen to torment him, Mather wrote on August 12: "I am now informed, that yesterday the six Men, who call themselves the Corporation of the College met, and Contrary to the epidemical Expectation of the Country [i.e. that he would be selected], chose a modest young Man, of whose Piety (and little else) every one gives a laudable Character." As he often did when defeated, he turned affliction into advantage, and saw in this drubbing "unspeakable cause to admire the Compassion of Heaven." The dismissal of him was a saving joy. Actually he had dreaded "what the Generality of sober People expected and desired; the Care of the College, to be committed unto me." Actually he had always foreknown that the presidency would have earned him not prestige but sorrow: "I had a dismal Apprehension of the Distresses, which a call to *Cambridge* would bring upon me." Actually he was thankful that he had been redeemed by having been rebuffed: "the Slight and Spite of my six Friends, has produced for me an eternal Deliverance." But not even by the gratifying logic of Matherese could he hide his wrath from himself, and his tirade of self-content wound down into the recognition that he had spoken "with a little too much Alacrity." He called on God to "Help me to a wise Behaviour!"

This subsurface seething may have agitated Mather's mood the next night, August 13, and perhaps detonated Lydia's full fury. She became finally utterly disgusted and may have had some sort of breakdown, "a prodigious Return of her Pangs upon her," Mather called it, "that seemed little short of a proper Satanical Possession." His remarks on Joseph Sewall make it evident that he felt rancorous himself; yet by his understanding nothing more happened between them during the day than that he somehow, unaccountably, managed to displease her. "What was pretended as the Introduction to the present, was, that forsooth, for a Day to two, my Looks and Words were not so very kind as they had been. A mere Fancy and Whimsey!" That Mather had behaved distantly seems not unlikely, but Lydia now had no patience for being told that her feelings of rejection were imaginary: "the bare telling her so, threw her into . . .

Violences, wherein she charged me with Crimes, which obliged me to rebuke her lying Tongue, with Terms I have not been used unto." The battle seems to have raged all day, through "a thousand unrepeatable Invectives."

At midnight Mather got out of bed and retired to his study to pour out his soul to God. But Lydia would not let him escape. She arose also and, in a "horrid Rage," said she would never stay with him or live with him. In the dead of night, collecting her niece and maid, she left the house. As she had gone to lodge with a neighbor, Mather feared the scandal she might enflame by telling "numberless Lies, which a Tongue set on Fire of Hell, would make no Conscience of." He spent the rest of the night keeping a vigil with Sammy and Nancy in his library, praying and singing psalms until nearly morning, when he at last went to bed and found some rest.

Mather kept busy over the following days, yet amidst preaching on contentedness with one's condition or deciding how to handle a troublesome minister at Harwich, he brooded on the Harvard presidency and Lydia's departure. His rejection by the Corporation, as he began to assess it a bit more realistically than before, was a mixed dispensation. He would have found the work of the presidency fatiguing and troublesome ("I could never have lived a Year to an End!"). But he could no longer deny that the office might have brought him many opportunities to nourish the New England churches. Perhaps God had reserved him for other, different opportunities to do good. Mostly he worried about how his own abhorred vanity might be affected by the choice of Joseph Sewall, the "preferring of a Child before me, as my Superiour in Erudition, or in a Capacity and Vivacity to manage the Government of an Academy, or in Piety and Gravity." Although the Corporation had snubbed him for his inferior, he felt it would be "a Crime in me to be disturbed at the choice," and he prayed for help in tolerating the insult without becoming incensed and impetuous.

Mather found it even harder to comprehend Lydia's leaving him. It seemed incredible to him that the woman in whom he had invested his fullest capacity to love could value his bountiful affection not at all. Her departure stood forth as the crowning instance of his queerly inverted destiny, an "AND YET" unmatchable in its perverse betrayal. "She, whom I have perpetually studied in the most exquisite Ways, to serve, and please, and gratify, and have even undone myself to oblige her, not only does by her unaccountable Humours . . . wherein she expresses the greatest Hatred and Contempt for me, prove the most heavy Scourge to me, that ever I met withal, but also takes, various Methods, all she can to ruin my Esteem in the World, and the Success of my Ministry." The blame, he believed, was entirely hers, for he had given her no reason to mistreat him. Her behavior said as much, for her "lucid Intervals" were always "filled with Expressions of the most enamoured Fondness for me." Feeling spent and hopeless, he resolved to pray formally seven times a day (once more than usual), hoping God might grant him "comfortable Circumstances relating to the Death, which is approaching to me." Returned to celibacy after Lydia's flight, he also asked divine aid in conquering what he always knew had been excessive, and now also recognized as unworthy, desire for her: "my Consort's leaving of my Bed . . . affords me Occasions of particular Supplications, that the Holiness and Purity whereto I am so singularly called of GOD, may have its perfect Work, and that I may no longer so foolishly dote as I have done, upon a Person who treats me with such a matchless Ingratitude, and Malignity."

Two days after writing this, on the morning of August 20, as he was projecting new services for God, Mather received overwhelmingly crushing news: "my Son *Increase,* is lost, is dead is gone." He staggered under the dreadful news: "Ah! My Son *Increase!* My Son! My Son! My Head is Waters, and my Eyes are a Fountain of Tears! I am overwhelmed!"

At the time that he became the twelfth of Mather's children to die, Creasy was about twenty-five years old. Despite the young man's many failings, Mather had always cherished him, perhaps more than any of his other children. Certainly he took greater pride in Sammy, in whom, he had written, "a gracious GOD wonderfully makes up to me, what I miss of Comfort in his miserable Brother." As Creasy had not, Sammy had undergone conversion and had been admitted to the North Church; as Creasy had not, Sammy had graduated from Harvard; as Creasy particularly had not, Sammy was following his father, grandfather, and great-grandfathers into the ministry. Yet Creasy had also been his first son to survive infancy and at the time of his birth Mather had received heavenly advice that the child would be "a Servant of my Lord Jesus Christ throughout eternal Ages." When not irate with Creasy, he saw him as Sammy later described him, a boy "*well beloved* by all who knew him, for his *Superiour good Nature* and *Manners,* his *elegant Wit* and *ready Expressions.*" If Sammy perpetuated his father's learning and piety, in Creasy were much of his father's facetiousness, gentlemanly charm, and unenacted rebelliousness.

Creasy, Mather was informed, had been aboard a ship bound from Barbados to St. Peter's, Newfoundland. The ship had been out five months without arriving, and the passengers including Creasy were believed to have perished in the sea. Why Creasy undertook another voyage is unknown—on business, perhaps, or in some connection with the lawsuits against him in the spring. Mather, as a preacher to a seafaring congregation, well knew that such voyages could be perilous, and regularly preached to his flock on death by water. "*Drowning,*" he wrote in one sermon, "is one of those *Accidents,* than which there is none more frequent; Thus is *the Lamp of Young men put out*! It is *at once* plung'd into the Water, and in less than three minutes perhaps it is *put out.*" How often in New England had been heard "concerning our Sons," he wrote, the words "*The Young Men are Dead.*" Mather's acquaintance with the dangers of the sea may explain why, for a month and a half before he received news of Creasy's fate, he had been having presentiments of some misfortune overtaking Creasy, which he recorded cryptically in his diary. On July 1 he had written: "Oh! what Advice from Heaven, is come to me this Day, about my poor Son *Increase!* Yea, how many Times have I been of late overwhelmed with Afflations, which tell me, that—" at which the entry breaks off. Four weeks later he recorded, again cryptically, "My Son *Increase!* my Son, my Son!"

But no afflations prepared or consoled Mather for the killing news that arrived on August 20. Added to the appalling threats of jail, the demeaning denial to him of the Harvard presidency, and Lydia's withering indifference to his love, it made a weight he felt he could withstand only with God's help: "O my God, I am oppressed; undertake for me." At the time of his drowning Creasy was unconverted, too, and Mather feared for his soul. Before leaving on his voyage, Creasy had written out and left on Mather's table an "Instrument of a Soul repenting and returning to GOD," lamenting his rejection of Christ and promising to choose only godly companions and to follow his business industriously. Mather prayed that this last-minute repentance might win Creasy his salvation: "If the Papers which he left in my Hands, were sincere and his Heart wrote with his pen, all is well! Would not my GOD have me to hope so?" Yet he had his doubts; Creasy's drowning itself suggested that God had refused him. Taking the manuscript autobiography he had begun for Creasy (but in pique rededicated to Sammy), he at some time wrote in after the account of Creasy's birth: "tho' this were a Son of Great *Hopes,* and One Son who Thousands and Thousands of *Prayers,* were Employ'd for him; Yet after all, a Sovereign GOD would not Accept of him. He was Buried in the *Atlantic* Ocean."

Three days after Mather learned about Creasy, and probably in response to the news, Lydia returned home. She returned, too, chastened and conciliatory: "my poor Wife, returning to a right Mind, came to me in my Study, entreating that there might be an eternal Oblivion of every thing that has been out of Joint, and an eternal Harmony in our future Conversation." Toward making this new start he and Lydia promised to pray oftener together than ever before, and joined in raising prayers to God, their arousing devotions being followed on Lydia's part, Mather added, by "Tokens of the greatest Inamoration." However wretched and confused she had made him by her paroxysms and her flight, he continued fixedly to love her. Through the late fall he increased his efforts to please her, especially resolving to see things her way, to improve "in Compassion to her with regard unto the Things which threaten her Comfort."

However fulsome Lydia's "Inamoration" it could not distract Mather from his bursting anguish. Nor entirely could his faith. He deeply wished to glorify God by silent acquiescence in His judgments. He even praised his Savior for enabling him to bear all the sacrifices He called him to, including the "continual Dropping which I suffer in my Family." Yet as if ambidextrously sounding out Governor Dudley or some other mortal tormentor who returned hurt for good, his praise was embittered: "I freely submit and consent unto it, that the Glorious Lord should continue the Sorrows of it upon me all the few remaining Days of my Pilgrimage, and never give me any release until I die."

Indeed what Mather's obedient resignation tried to submerge kept churning up. The Servant of Christ throughout eternal ages who had fathered a bastard and owed money to a dancing master was buried in the Atlantic Ocean. It kept returning to him: "that heavy, heavy, heavy, and amazing Heap of Distresses, which I have in the Death of my Son *Increase, my Son, my Son!*" He sought as always to make his dry cross yield fruits of righteousness. He lay plans to awaken the young to turn to God. He decided to do something toward catechizing the girls in his congregation. Yet almost daily he numbly reverted in his diary, with little further remark, to what had happened to him. "The Death of my Son *Increase,*" he wrote one day; then, on others, "Ah my Son! my Son! . . . . . . The Death of my poor son INCREASE . . . . . . the Death of my Son."

To screw his anguish tightly to the bottom, Mather remained under personal attack, even from those close to him. Constantly, indeed, each one of his troubles had driven more deeply into him the woe from another, each new difficulty with the Howell estate rendering Lydia's paroxysms the more painful, his grief over Creasy swelling his disappointment in being passed over for Joseph Sewall. Now, despite the "heavy Calami-

ties upon me," some denounced his ministry, taking "all possible Pains
... to fix a vile Character on me among the People of God," depicting
him as "a Person from whose Hands the Bread of Life is by no means to
be received." Yet under the shadow of whatever notoriety he noticed that
when he once more mounted his pulpit on August 30, to offer himself as
an example of forbearance under affliction, unusually many young people came to hear him, from several parts of Boston, including some who
had earlier swarmed from his ministry. Preaching on early piety, a favorite
theme, he told them that "upon Computation" more than half the children born die before the age of seventeen. That the young should cry for
the safety of their own souls and live as if they were about to die, were
lessons born in dumb departedness, "the *Loud Voice* from the Mouths of
Some, who have gone down to the *Place of Silence!—The Young Persons,*
who have been *in the Morning like the Flowers of the Field,* but have been
cut down before the Evening."

Within the week after he preached this sermon, Mather twice received
news that was astonishing. The first arrived on September 5. "We are
surprised with very probable Advice," Mather wrote, "that my poor Son
Increase is yet living." The ship on which Creasy had been voyaging had
lost all its masts, but after a "long, long, sad Passage" it had landed in
Newfoundland. After his dismal fears, tempting him to atheism, that God
had chosen not to requite his acts of good, the news was doubly joyous:
"O the astonishing Dispensations of Heaven! must it always be so, that I
must see a Sentence of Death upon good Things; and then will the GOD
of Patience and of Consolation, give me to see some Comfort in them!"
Spared, Creasy might yet be converted, although after his many disappointments Mather still felt cautious about reforming him. "If it be so,
Oh! may the Distresses of the poor Prodigal bring him home to GOD. Oh!
may I yet see strange Answers and Effects of the Prayers that have been
employ'd for him!"

There was need in fact for caution about "my Son that was dead and is
alive." The second astonishing news arrived two days later, when Mather
learned that the God of Patience and of Consolation had not chosen to
requite him. "'T was another Vessel," he wrote. The previous report had
been misleading. It had concerned a different ship: "the good News of
poor *Creasy's* being rescued and revived from Death, is all come to nothing." Creasy, it was now certain, was dead. "*Lord,*" Mather called once
more, "*Thou hast lifted me up, and cast me down.* Oh! Let there not be
thy *Indignation* and *Wrath,* in what is done unto me!"

*

Two months later, in November, the cruel plot of Creasy's fate was played out again for Mather with different actors. Joseph Sewall having declined the Harvard presidency, the office was again open, and the Corporation passed over Mather a second time. The rebuke touched on old resentment toward Benjamin Colman, a member of the Corporation, going back to the opening of the Brattle church, unhealed by twenty years of friendship, and likely compounded by Lydia's ties to Colman's ministry.

On November 6, Mather dispatched a vicious letter blaming Colman personally for having denied him the presidency. In surpassing Matherese, he first thanked Colman for considering him qualified on account of his "Biblia Americana"—"for I know you can't on any other account"—then offered his concurrence in Colman's defeat of his hopes: "I do with the greatest acquiescence and gratitude approve the declaration of your sentiments to all the country, that I am on other accounts utterly disqualified. Yea, for erudition too, as well as capacity and activity for management." What evidence remains of Colman's part in choosing the president makes Mather's high dudgeon seem irrational; at most Colman may have reported to others the view of the Corporation (of which he was only one member) that while they respected Mather's learning they doubted his ability to govern Harvard because of his temper. But Mather could see the situation only as another "AND YET," and he concluded with hearty thanks for being spurned: "I do with all possible sincerity thank you for the inexpressible ease you have given to, Sir. . . ."

On November 18 the Corporation chose for president Colman himself. "I rejoice, I rejoice, I feel a secret Joy in it," Mather wrote in his diary, "that I am thus conformed unto Him who was despised and rejected of Men." The Corporation of the "miserable College" having again treated him with their customary malignity, he felt he could easily "throw Confusion upon the Men, who would make me low in the Eyes of all the Country," but instead he looked to God for help in bearing his condition with "Prudence, and Patience, and Silence." In fact, Colman had been away from academic studies for thirty years and saw in the presidency a financial loss to himself. He declined the post, which went to the Rev. Benjamin Wadsworth, for whose encouragement the House voted £1000 of public funds toward building a handsome presidential residence.

For all the many strains in their long acquaintance, Mather genuinely liked Colman, and the following year praised in print Colman's *"pious, and acute, and cogent Pen."* His nasty letter was probably a by-product of his distraught state. For as December drew on there remained the "dreadful Sacrifice," the thing he returned to, "the grievous Calamity befalling me in the Death of my poor Son *Increase*." As he seems to have done after his father's departure, he seems after Creasy's death also to have thought of his ghost returning. In a sermon on the death of a seventeen-year-old girl he remarked that we know little of the condition of departed souls, of what vehicles they use, "and how much of what they had in *this World;* they carry away out of the *Shipwreck* with them."

As the event receded what stood out for Mather was the demand to draw from it services to God, so that "the Child, who did so little Good, but much ill, in all the Days of his Life, may do some good at his Death." One result was *The Words of Understanding* (1724), a set of savagely mournful sermons that betray his unwillingness, despite all his calls for resignation, to subdue his will. Introducing the book as the work of Creasy's *"Afflicted* FATHER, *upon his Extinction in the* Atlantic *Ocean,"* he in one place used the sudden premature deaths of "lovely *Young People"* to emphasize the need for early piety, and imagined for himself and his readers Creasy's drowning:

> Perhaps, by perishing in the *Water,* on which they were *doing Business,* they have been extinguished!—And by being Lost, none can say how, or when, or where, *at Sea,* their *Light put out in obscure Darkness.* . . . TO see a *sparkling Youth* pass through a curious and polite Cultivation; Brilliant, with a ready Wit, a singular sweetness of Temper, and many Circumstances inviting us to look for *something* from him;—And,—*All at once extinguished.*

The entire work resounds with muffled rage at past tormentors, at Shute, at Harvard, at his father, at spouses who although not so criminal as adulterers yet "carry it so Basely, so Bitterly, so Frowardly, to their *Mates,* that they deserve to have the *Doves of the Valleys pluck out their Eyes.*" Identifying himself and Creasy with Christ as doomed Sons, Mather also summed up what he had learned from life, that man is born for troubles without number or evasion:

> When we are wading thro' some grievous and some tedious Trouble, we are prone to flatter our selves, *Well, this is the last! If I were once got well out of this Trouble, all would be well.* 'Tis a great mistake. There will soon come *another Trouble* in the room of that which is gone. Men are *Fools,* if they think, their *mirth* can last any longer, than *Sparks,* or than the *Crackling of thorns under a Pot.* . . .

Late in December, Mather's cruciating fire crackled once more. Sammy had begun preaching, and now hoped to improve his training—by sailing the Atlantic to London. In part Mather wished to keep Sammy at home simply because he valued the young man's conversation and cultivation as his greatest relief. But it might also happen to Sammy. *"Lord,"* Mather wrote, *"what Sacrifices dost thou call me to! My Son, my only Son, Samuel, whom I have at home with me."* Sammy was passionately set upon the voyage, and Mather believed a refusal might lead him to "grievous Temptations." Besides, clearly becoming a Mather himself, Sammy had been experiencing a "strange Persuasion" that he would prosper in England. Full of distress all over again and fatalistic, Mather threw himself on God's will: *"I sacrifice him, O my GOD and SAVIOUR, I sacrifice him to thy Holy Pleasure!"*

As had not happened often to Mather, this proved a prayer-hearing God. Mather allowed Sammy to make the voyage. But God, he found, disposed him to persuade Sammy not to make it by way of the West Indies, rather aboard a ship bound more directly to London. Somehow the ship's departure was aborted, however. And in January, after this defeat of his intentions, Sammy gave up the idea of sailing abroad altogether. Unspurned for once by reality, Mather had been allowed to fortify himself against loss without having to bear it. "I have . . . had an Opportunity to make a Sacrifice of my only Son; and yet," he wrote thankfully, "without the actual Accomplishment thereof, to receive him again as from the Dead."

V

COTTON MATHER

(1724–1728)

An Inventory of the Estate of Dr Cotton Mather late Deced taken by us the Subscribers July 23d 1728 as it was shew'd to us by his widow Mrs. Lydia Mather & the Children

12 Flag Chairs 24/ 8 Leather Chairs 2 of 'em high backt 24/	£ 2. 8.
17 Low Turkey work Chairs some defective @6/	5. 2.
10 Turkey work Chairs 5 broke	2.
2 Broken Cane Chairs 10/ & a Cane Couch 44/ 14 Cane Chairs	
@14/£9.16.	12.10.
1 Feather Bed No. 1. 65 at 2/3	7. 6. 3.
1 Ditto 2. 47 2/6	5.17. 6.
1 Do. 3. 57 2/4	6.13.
3 Bolsters & 5 Pillows 44 2/3 £5 4d 3 Old Ruggs 10/	5.10.1½.
1 Old Quilt and 2 Blanketts 30/ 4 Old Bedsteads 50/	4.
2 Old Oval Tables and a broken Stone Table	1. 6.
2 Old Chest of Draws Table & dressing box	3.
A Japan Looking Glass 50/ 2 Ditto black frames £4	6.10.
1 pr. Old China Curtains & Vallens lased, bedstead & Curtain Rods .	5.
1 pr. of Red Curtains Motheaten	1.
4 pr. brass Andirons 2 pr. of Iron Dogs, other broken Dogs	4.
1 pr. brass fire Shovel & Tongs, and an old warming pan	1. 1.
114 Pewter Viz. 18 Dishes, a pasty-plate, pye plate, cheese plate	
broken pewter	11. 8.
1½ doz. Pewter Plates 34/ Knives & forks 10/	2. 4.
2 brass Skillets, 1 Saucepan, 2 Candlesticks skimer, frying pan trennel	
spit	2.
1 brass Kettle 33 £4. 19/ One Copper 35 £7	11.19.
17 Iron 8/ Belmettle Mortar 15/	1. 3.
1 Old Standing Candlestick 10/ a Cross cut Saw 30/ Lumber 20/ . .	3.
1 Bed & Bolster 75 @ 2/6	9. 7. 6.
147 oz. of Silver Plate @ 16/6 Viz. One Tankard, 2 Servers, 1 pair	
Candlesticks Snuffers & Standish, & Tea Pott Several Broken	
Spoons, one Spout Cup, 1 Sugar dish, 2 Porringers	121. 5. 6.
	235.10. 10.
500 Acres of wast Land Scituate in the County of Hampshire as appears	
to us by Deed Cost	36.

                              John Barnard
                              John Goldthwait
                              Graffton Feveryear
Suffolks: By the Honble. Samuel Sewall Esq Judge of Pro:&c

Nathaniel Goodwin Adminr: presented the foregoing and made Oath that it contains a true and perfect Inventory of the Estate of the Rev. Dr. Cotton Mather aforesaid deceased so far as hath come to his knowledge and that if more hereafter appear he will Cause it to be added. The subscribing apprizers were at the same time sworn as the Law Directs.
Boston August 5th 1728.
                                                        Samuel Sewall
Exam per *John Boydell Reg*

14

As Merry as One Bound for Heaven

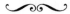

A COUGH, a "grievous Breast-beater," accompanied by fever and a suffocating asthma, confined Mather to his house for about five weeks at the end of 1724 and early in 1725. His diaries after this "winter of much feebleness," if he kept any, are missing. Information about his daily round during the last three years of his life is therefore scant, but his correspondence and the remarks of others indicate that he remained in fairly good health through most of 1725 and 1726, then in the spring of 1727 underwent the first of three increasingly serious bouts of illness.

Seemingly drained by his illness in 1724–25, and by Creasy's death and the double loss of the Harvard presidency, Mather again withdrew from government affairs. Jeremiah Dummer applauded his "noble Resolution" to quit politics and "Solace your self in your Study and the business of your Divine Profession." Mather might well have retired from New England's political life, for although turbulent throughout his lifetime it had become relatively quiet. The Indian war ended with a peace treaty in December 1725, and while Samuel Shute remained in England, William Dummer administered the government without serious conflict. Mather's private life, as far as is known, had eased as well. In October 1724, Joseph Tallcott of Hartford brought an action against the Howell estate and was awarded £71 plus costs of the suit. But this may well have been the final demand against the estate; no further suits appear in the court records. Nor apparently did Lydia's return home after Creasy's death produce new domestic warfare. Here the lack of Mather's diaries is specially tantalizing, but the surviving bits of evidence about his marriage suggest reconciliation, however arrived at.

Sixty-two years old in 1725, Mather was, by his own standards and those of the time, an old man. In *A Good Old Age* (1726) he observed that scarce three persons in a hundred live to seventy, and he commended the work to those "whose Arrival to, or near, SIXTY, ranks them among, The AGED." He had not expected to live so long. Once he had fancied that he would die when he had written 365 works. But when he looked at his catalogue in 1726 he found he had written more than 369—not to mention the "much more bulky and weighty and wealthy" works that remained unpublished—so that "I know not the death of my death."

Despite Mather's filiopietism, his view of old age was unsentimental. He cited approvingly the Oriental maxim "that *old age is to be reckoned no part of life.*" In "Biblia Americana" he drew an ugly picture of the stage: the mercurial spirit of youth exhausted, the mouth disabled for singing, teeth unable to chew, stomach squeamish, arms trembling, thighs shrunk, the aged person grown headachy, gray, deaf, fearful of stumbling—*"Clouds* of Ignorance, prejudice, and mistake, then impair the *understanding;* the *Memory* becomes feeble and faithless; the *Imagination* grows conceited . . . *Suspicious* of Evil, but *Lothe to Believe any Good.*" The condition, Mather felt, was however lamentable also incurable, thus futile and graceless to protest. To those liable to such follies of old age as hoarding, trying to act young, or refusing to retire, his advice was severe: "Good Sir, Be so Wise, as to *Disappear* of your own Accord as soon and as far as you lawfully may."

Some of these, and other, effects of age now wore on Mather himself. Grateful for having escaped the stone, he offered special thanks on his sixty-first birthday for arriving at "this great Age, free from the grievous Diseases, which carry Horror with them." On the other hand, he had begun wearing spectacles, perhaps the ones Thomas Hollis had taken from his own nose and sent him in friendship. In his enthusiasm for material progress and for alleviating human misery, he regarded spectacles as a wonderful invention. "We that are *Old People,*" he wrote, "are marvelously Blessed of GOD, by the *Use of Glasses,* which preserves the power of *Reading* with us. Inexcusable has been the Ingratitude of Mankind, shamefully to bury in Oblivion the Name of the *Benefactor* that was the *First Inventor of Spectacles;* when there stand on Record so many Execrable *Oppressors* and *Murderers* of Mankind, under the Name of *Conquerors.*" Nostalgia set in also. In 1724 Mather published his first public sermon, which he had preached to a religious society when just sixteen years old. Several times he wrote to friends with whom he had not corresponded in years, inquiring whether one or another mutual acquaintance "be yet sojourning in this Land of the Dying."

But above all, old age meant to Mather uniquely a time for productivity, Fructuosus. His recovery from the long illness at the end of 1724 brought a swell of initiative: "The very little Time that remains of my Pilgrimage thro' this evil World, must be carried on with new Measures. No Time is to be lost. I must be at Work for my Glorious Lord continually and assiduously, and more than ever." Making one final attempt to "*do enough,*" he expended in his final years a torrential energy, reading and writing, his son Samuel said, "as if he had but newly taken a *Pen* or *Book* into his Hand."

Except his withdrawal from political life, scarcely one of Mather's many interests failed of embodiment in some publication or activity in the final three or four years of his life. He continued adding illustrations to his never-to-be-published "Biblia Americana." As a Protestant statesman, always watchful for the fate of international Protestantism, he was shocked by new edicts against French Protestants and by a similar revival of persecutions in Poland, Hungary, and Germany, prompting him to call attention to the Protestants languishing overseas in dungeons or executed, in such works as *Une Grande Voix du Ciel a la France* (1725) and *Suspiria Vinctorum* (1726). Still also alarmed about Arianism, he continued writing to England denouncing its spread. Most of his colleagues in the German Pietist movement had died, but he received accounts from Pietist missionaries in the East Indies, and the expectation of answers from him. His correspondence remained demandingly huge: letters, as always, from Scotland, even longer and more frequent than before; from sympathizers or those in distress, people of no repute who sought his counsel from afar; from his old and dear friend John Winthrop, whom he pressed to move to Boston from New London, Winthrop himself now being hauled to court over the administration of an estate.

Mather also continued serving as a commissioner for the New England Company, and continued to find the "Languid Aspect" of the work discouraging. Yet he believed Christianity had become fairly widespread among the Indians, and rated the success of their conversion "one of New England's peculiar glories." To promote further progress, he urged reinstituting the practice of appointing "*A visitor of all the Indian villages,*" who would return from his visits with suggestions to the commissioners for redress and reform. Until the last year or two of his life he strove to get others' accounts of missionary work printed, although his own last lengthy writing on the subject was a discourse delivered before the commissioners at Samuel Sewall's house, published in 1721 as *India Christiana*—notable for its speculations on how the Indians came to America, a

subject of popular controversy well into the eighteenth century. (He inclined to the view that the Indians were Asiatic in origin, and that Asia
and America had once been contiguous.) He also published a *Proposal
for an Evangelical Treasury* (1725), urging that a fund for missionary
endeavors be collected from donations in the churches.

In his final years Mather turned over the keeping of the North Church
records to Joshua Gee, but otherwise he does not seem to have restricted
his ministerial duties. The astonishing thirty-nine titles he published between 1725 and 1727 include works on every major theme of his ministry:
baptism (*Baptismal Piety*), marriage (*Mystical Marriage*), grace (*Signa-
tus*), dishonest gain (*The Balance of the Sanctuary*), charity (*Some Seasonable Advice unto the Poor*), catechizing (*Instructor*). Mather's age
and celebrity now ranked him as the foremost minister in New England,
and his name routinely headed lists of signatories to ministerial petitions
and addresses. He still personally presided over many church councils,
sometime writing up the council decisions himself. For the last times
now, he preached and published sermons on such traditional occasions
as a royal accession (*Christian Loyalty,* 1727) and, for more than the tenth
time, capital executions. Having no reason to be fond of pirates (they
immediately forced their captives, he heard, "*To curse Dr. M_____*"),
he preached in July 1726 on the execution of the villainous William Fly,
who with several crew members had taken over a ship after throwing the
captain and mate overboard, and set out pirating. His undiminished narrative ability appears in his compelling relation of the pirates' capture
and of the obdurate Fly being led to the gallows—cursing, blaspheming,
but holding a nosegay, settling the noose on his own neck (with an aside
to the hangman that he did not know his trade), smiling until at the
entrance to Boston Harbor his corpse dangled from chains.

On one grimly customary event Mather was called to preach, mercifully, for the last time. On August 7, 1726, midway through his sixty-third
year, his twenty-two-year-old daughter Elizabeth died. She had survived
the 1721 smallpox epidemic although non-immune, and in 1724, about a
month before the news of Creasy's death, Mather had performed her marriage to a shipmaster named Edward Cooper. Now for the last time he
dramatized the need for early piety to young members of his congregation by using as an example the death of his own child, "a *Young Person,*
of a Polite Education, in the Fresh Bloom of *Youth* . . . just Entering into
the World, in Comfortable Circumstances." As for himself, the "Poor Old
Sacrificer," Elizabeth had been one of his three remaining children. He
had been called on, he explained, for "the *Thirteenth* (and not the

Least!) Sacrifice of this One Sort, *the Amputation and Resignation of a Desirable Offspring.*" Of fifteen, only Sammy and Nancy were left.

*

Mather earnestly wished to leave some personal legacy to the New England churches and ministry, and did so in two of his most important and lengthiest late works. Although the apostate Cutler continued challenging the Congregational establishment, Mather looked hopefully on the rising generation of ministers who were about to replace his father and himself, "*Excellent Young Men,*" he thought them, "who Study and Resolve their Duty, and are the *Rain-bows* of our Churches." He was not mistaken, for they included one of the most profound thinkers in American history, the grandson of his old rival Solomon Stoddard, young Jonathan Edwards, who was ordained pastor at Northampton early in 1727. Among this new generation Mather felt closest to Thomas Prince, an older member although twenty-five years his junior. In 1718 he had encouraged Prince's settlement at the Old South church, apparently unfazed that Prince had recently returned from England wearing, Samuel Sewall as usual noticed, a wig and russet coat. By 1726 Prince had come to be, Mather wrote, "as Cordial and Constant a Friend unto me, as any I have in the world." In his last few years he put Prince to many tasks, asking him to enlist subscribers to his works, to teach and care for his orphaned nephew Mather Byles, to get material for his communications to the Royal Society, and to read and comment on his manuscripts.

Mather's successors also included Samuel, whose carefully nurtured career now was blossoming. Sammy's earliest sermons, preached when he was seventeen, won "uncommon acceptance," Mather wrote, and he was praised for "an early piety, for a manly discretion, for some erudition, and none of the worst tempers." When attending the Yale commencement in 1724, while not yet eighteen, he was awarded an honorary M.A. degree (probably in gratitude to his father). Sammy's swift success greatly pleased Mather, but also made him wary. Lest the boy become prideful he resolved to inculcate in him "the profoundest Humility, that he may express a due Gratitude unto the glorious Lord who so remarkably smiles upon him; and a Conduct so full of Wisdom, that he may not make them ashamed who have promoted him, and that he may not fail the just Expectation of the World concerning him." However cautious, Mather felt by the fall of 1724 that Sammy had advanced far enough to be shown unto Israel, as after many delays he had been a half-century before. On October 25, still short of eighteen, Sammy preached on a text recommended to him by Mather, He is my Father's God and I will exalt Him (Exod. 15: 2). He spoke now from the place where two generations of Mathers had garnered much of whatever respect they could claim in the world, the North Church—"in the Pulpit," Mather wrote, "where his Father and Grandfather before him, have served our Glorious Lord."

Mather viewed Sammy and the other young ministers as the hopes of the New England churches, and in a spirit at once of apostolic continuity, professional friendship, and paternal care he reached out to them as "My YOUNGER BRETHREN in the Evangelical MINISTRY." As a legacy to these young colleagues he prepared several works on the ministry, whose substance is comprehended in his book-length manual for ministers, *Manuductio ad Ministerium* (1726). Addressing himself to *"My Son"*—a hypothetical ministerial candidate, but suggesting some surrogate for Creasy—he here summarized his long professional experience. The tone of the book, except at the beginning and end, is urbane and convivial, and thus emblematic of the ideal of the ministry it promulgates, an ideal derived from humanist scholarship and Reformed doctrine but also from Pietist activism and personal practice.

Mather equated the function of the minister with the chief end of life itself, namely the service of God. But he defined this service broadly to include "Whatever contributes unto the *Welfare* of *Mankind,* and such a *Relief* of their Miseries, as may give the Children of Men better *Opportunities* to *Glorify* Him." He envisioned ministers such as he had striven to become himself, not only thunderous preachers winning souls to Christ from their pulpits, but also humane, liberal, and erudite gentlemen sensible of the large human good to be achieved by scientific advancement, capable of moving people to pious ends by entertaining conversation, and aware that true piety is not limited to one sect. The training he proposed thus consists not only of Scripture reading and fervent private devotions, but also of acquiring a high gloss of civility, the "Pursuit of that *Learning,* and those *Ingenuous* and *Mollifying Arts,* which may distinguish you from the more *Uncultivated* Part of Mankind." As a guide to behavior in society he recommended "Wise Observation of what you see passes in the Conversation of Politer People." He also recommended the active study of science, and acquaintance with (but not absorption in) poetry and music, including, for ministers so disposed, the refreshment of learning to play well on some musical instrument.

Mather equally emphasized urbane polish in theological study and preaching, to make the minister "a *Skilful Artist* for the Work of your GOD." Nearly as much a writer as a preacher himself, he not surprisingly paid much attention in his manual to the writing of sermons and to literary style. Resentful to the end of his life over criticisms of his prose, he also gave space to defending his "Massy *Way of Writing*," however fallen out of taste and derided by a "Lazy, Ignorant, Conceited Set of Authors." "The Writer pretends not unto *Reading*," as he explained his stylistic practice, "yet he could not have writ as he does if he had not *Read* very much in his Time; and his Composures are not only a *Cloth of Gold*, but also stuck with as many *Jewels*, as the Gown of a Russian Embassador." Such a style would come back in use when a better taste returned, he predicted, and meanwhile he asked for the same indulgence in style as in modalities of religion. "Every Man will have his own *Style*, which will distinguish him as much as his *Gate*," and people ought to "handsomely *indulge* one another in this, as *Gentlemen* do in other Matters." Still irate after twenty years over Oldmixon's twitting, he cursed for one last time that writer's *English Empire in America* as "the most foolish and faithless Performance in this Kind, that ever Mankind was abused withal."

Mather did not forget other abusers either. In addressing his "sons" he also imparted to them the less palatable experience he had gained from Calef onward, so that for all its amiable liberality *Manuductio*, like *Bonifacius*, begins and ends in gall. The twenty-page Latin Preface reeks of his rejection for the Harvard presidency and of compensatory triumph in his honorary D.D. years earlier, spitefully dedicating the work to studious youths in academies, "Principally in that of Glasgow; Next, to those in New England." "I know how meanly I am furnished," Mather told them, "and all New-England know it, and deem me utterly incapable of addressing Persons of Academical Education; and they rightly judge as I do." The personal recommendations in the equally rancid concluding section range from simple cynicism:

> One must not *Spend all he hath;* nor *Do all he can;* nor *Tell all he knows;* nor *Believe all he hears.*

to a sort of ecclesiastical Machiavellianism:

> [Influential persons] will soon fall out with you, if you don't keep Touch with them, in all their Designs; and when you cease to be their *Tool,* they will most *Forgetfully* and *Ungratefully* abandon you.

to near paranoia:

> Let them that have abused you, *know nothing* that you *know any thing* of the matter. For such is the *Baseness* of many People, that (measuring *you* by themselves) they will *hate* you, because you *know* that they have *hurt*

you; and they will persist in their *Hatred,* which they must Justify, because they imagine, that you *can't Forgive them.*

Growing however old, Mather thus composed his legacy to the future ministers of New England in spunkiest Matherean counterpoint, My Sons You Are the Hopes of Our Flocks piped against They Don't Have Cotton Mather to Kick Around Any More.

To the churches, as distinct from the ministry, Mather bequeathed a book-length account of their principles and practices, *Ratio Disciplinae* (1726). The work had a rocky history, for Mather originally wrote it in 1701, but its publication and later revision were several times delayed. In 1726, greatly revised, it was again ready for publication, but this time two-thirds of the manuscript blew away, it seemed irretrievably; some of the pages, however, were picked up by strangers, others found in a garden, others in a woodpile. That was fortunate, because *Ratio Disciplinae* contains much of what is known specifically today about New England's manner of worship—the gathering of a church, marriage and ordination ceremonies, administration of baptism and communion, and much else. Mather believed the work would "prove one of the usefullest things that ever were offered unto the churches," a substitute for an updated platform of church discipline, such as might have been written by the proposed church synod of 1725, which the government had refused to convene. He also intended the book for readers abroad, to show "unto the Churches in the *other Hemisphere,* the Relation of what is practised in these Regions of *America."* *Ratio* belongs with such early American classics as Crèvecoeur's *Letters from an American Farmer* (1782) in demonstrating to Europeans basic differences between the New World and the Old.

Mather devoted most of the book to straightforward descriptions of specific church practices, inviting consultation rather than summary here. This historically valuable information also serves to illustrate, however, an ambidexter point. On one hand Mather repeatedly emphasizes that the New England churches are Congregational (thus uniquely close to the form of the primitive church), and demonstrates their orthodoxy by citing matching practices recommended by the church Fathers and by continental Reformers. But he equally emphasizes that the New England churches are not fractiously individualistic, and demonstrates their spirit of tolerant cooperation by stressing their use of church councils and the variety that prevails among them in the practice of circumstantials. The churches have made Franckean Piety the only basis for admission: "A Charitable Consideration of nothing but PIETY in admitting to Evangelical Privileges, is a Glory that the Churches of *New-England,* would lay claim unto." Thus although Congregational, the New England churches have from the beginning renounced the idea of independency: "Every *particular Church* is to consider it self as a part of the *Catholic,* and owes a Duty to the *whole Visible Church* of our Lord in the World."

Of course Mather had long tried unsteadily to maintain this equilibrium between seeing New England as a pristine Wilderness Zion and as but one outpost of international Protestantism, tilting one way or another according to the deeds of government in Boston and London, his own treatment at home and abroad, activities of the Church of England, among other things. But *Ratio Disciplinae* indicates that at the end of his life he believed that the founders' ideal had failed. A person "must not be called, A *Calumniator,*" he writes, who frankly informs Europeans "That they will not find *New-England* a New Jerusalem." Most New Englanders are sober and well acquainted with religion, but worldliness and apostasy are growing. As to the country's looked-for role as a beacon in the coming worldwide reformation, "some of their *Seers* have not been without melancholy Apprehensions, lest *New England* have now done the most that it was intended for." These words—unchanged from Mather's first drafting of the work in 1701—suggest that he and his father had seen too much of life in New England to believe that it could ever be perfect or exemplary there, and that to them the City upon a Hill remained in the realm of what-might-have-been.

On balance, what Mather lost in exclusivism he gained in liberality. At the end of his life he returned to his ecumenism, and extended it to include Quakers, whom he had always regarded as not less subversive of Christianity than Catholics. In his remarkable *Vital Christianity* (1725)— significantly, published in Philadelphia—he declared that he "*unspeakably* abhors *and* laments *the abominable* Persecution *which you have suffered in former Days.*" Now viewing virtually all Christians as one, he owned a unity with Quakers in sharing a "Christ within" (construed as taking Christ for a pattern of holiness), and on this principle he embraced Quakers as fellow Christians, "our beloved *Friends.*"

*

Age did not dampen Mather's enthusiasm for science. Partly because of his constant encouragement of scientific study he could now look out on a much enlarged Boston scientific community. Several Bostonians were sending specimens and observations to the Royal Society, and the *Boston News-Letter* invited local scientific contributions so that it might some degree serve for the "*Philosophical Transactions* of *New England.*" Continuing his encouragement, Mather took up Dr. Jurin's suggestion that he interest his friends in meteorology, and presented a Boston tradesman named Grafton Feveryear with a barometer—evidently the first used for meteorological observation by New Englanders, the results of which were forwarded to the Society in 1727. As always he particularly fostered the young, especially Sammy's contemporary Isaac Greenwood, a Harvard graduate and member of his church whom, like several other young men in his last years, he decided to treat "as a sort of a Son." Bearing a letter of recommendation to the Royal Society from Mather, Greenwood went to London, where he spoke with Newton and became an assistant to Dr. Jean Théophile Desaguliers, curator of experiments at the Society and inventor of the planetarium. He brought back with him to Boston apparatus for scientific demonstrations and, in January 1727, launched a series of sixteen public lectures on science, the first of their kind in New England. The same year the Harvard Corporation appointed him to a new professorship of mathematics and natural philosophy, making Mather's protégé probably the first American to earn his living by science.

Mather was disappointed, however, in his own relation to the Royal Society during his final years. He continued sending communications, but often complained privately about the Society's failure to publish more of them or to send copies of what it had published already. Sometimes the Society replied tardily or not at all, which he feared meant either indifference or lost mail. The second fear was not fanciful, for his entire series of Curiosa for 1720—twelve letters on the whale, the Mississippi River, the quadrature of the circle, and other subjects—seems to have disappeared after being delivered to Isaac Newton as president of the Society. Despite concern over his packets miscarrying, and some resentment, he sent seven letters in 1723 and a final collection of ten letters in 1724, none of which was published, however, in the *Transactions.*

In sending his 1724 series, Mather explained that the reason he did not send Curiosa as often as he wished was partly that he had been writing, and had now completed, a large new medical work he might soon try to publish in New England. His preoccupation is understandable, for except his defense of inoculation, *The Angel of Bethesda* is his single most important achievement in science—the only comprehensive American medical work of the entire colonial period, filling in its modern edition some 322 large pages. Mather first mentions it in the "catalogue of desirables" that concludes *Bonifacius* (1710), so that the book may well have been the off-and-on labor of fourteen years. His threefold purpose was religious, medical, and in a broad sense scientific. He wished to supply for those in ill health, ingenious pious "improvements" of their condition. ("Let thy Odious *Breath*," he advised victims of scurvy, "cause thee to think, *in Speaking, how much has my Throat been like an Open Sepulchre!*") He also wanted to offer general and specific rules for preserving health: temperate diet, no tobacco, wholesome exercise, refreshment by toast and tea (which he relished himself and specially recommended to ministers after preaching). But mostly he tried to provide a popular pharmacopeia or colonial Dr. Spock, a "*Family-physician*" by whose scores of remedies families might "Save *Life,* and *Health,* and *Money.*" Accordingly the work emits a warm charity, sympathy for human suffering, and particular care for the poor.

Mather classified his remedies according to diseases as they were identified in his time, ranging from smallpox to stinking feet ("Be not slovenly, wear Socks, often shifting 'em"). He treated as illnesses conditions that would now be viewed as symptoms, such as headaches, and presented as single diseases such conglomerates as "fevers"—confusions of a sort which lingered in medical thought into the nineteenth century. Eclectic in medical theory as elsewhere, he borrowed from the published medical works of competing schools: the Galenical school of botanical remedies as well as the school of chemical remedies, even to a less extent from the occult school. The book quotes more than two hundred and fifty medical writers, and repeats several remedies verbatim from Robert Boyle's *Medicinal Experiments* (London, 1688), a collection in part intended to supply cheap prescriptions for poor people in America. Mather did not simply list prescriptions, however. Instead he related them in a perky conversational style invigorated by questions, interjections, and sallies of erudition, dividing the work into sixty-six sections called, with his usual formal wit, Capsulas.

Some of Mather's remedies remain of value, such as the use of citrus juice to treat scurvy. But many others must strike modern readers as weird: a wolfskin girdle for epilepsy; a needle first thrust into a centipede for treating toothache; a dead hand applied to wens and tumors "till the Patient feel the *Damp* sensibly Strike into him"; a clyster made of fresh butter in which have been fried the parings of stone-horse hooves. Many of these are folk remedies, and Mather so represented them, noting that "some have said" they work without vouching for their efficacy himself. But some of his other, equally weird remedies are based on contemporary medical theory. One large group, including many remedies taken from

Boyle, derive from a theory of repellency, by which it was believed that some illnesses could be expelled by repulsive substances, including vermin, pig dung, and human excrement. Discreetly apologizing that "Tis hardly *Good Manners* to write so much about it," Mather yet offered cow's urine as a remedy for asthma, "powdered *Mouse-dung*" when other means fail to relieve ischury, and boy's urine as a gargle for sore throat ("Some fancy, a Mixture from diverse Lads").

The Angel of Bethesda also contains Mather's maturest reflections on several medical ideas he had long contemplated. He devoted the longest Capsula to the symptoms and treatment of smallpox. The Capsula entitled "Ephphatha. or, Some Advice to Stammerers"—another backward glance of his last years—represents the first treatise on stuttering written in America. The seventh Capsula, "*Conjecturalies*. or, Some Touches upon, A *New Theory* of many *Diseases*," expands his earlier speculations on the germ theory of disease. Mather now proposed that the "Invisible *Velites*" or their eggs might "insinuate themselves by the *Air*" and infiltrate bodily juices; being numerous and perhaps of different sorts, they might be responsible not only for smallpox but also for such such other varying diseases as syphillis, consumption, measles, and agricultural blight. Also merging and refining his earlier brief writings on psychogenic illnesses, he tried to show that many diseases arise from or are exacerbated by distress. He treated specific emotional and mental ills as well, to some of which he may have become sensitized by his father and Lydia, including nightmares, melancholia, and insanity. He urged understanding treatment of disturbed persons: "*We that are Strong must bear the Infirmities of the Weak;* and with a patient, prudent, Manly Generosity, pity them, and Humor them like *Children,* and give none but *Good Looks* and *good Words* unto them. . . . Tis not *They* that Speak; Tis their *Distemper!*" How many of these conjectures and conclusions Mather arrived at himself is arguable. He derived many of his comments on the germ theory, for instance, from Benjamin Marten's *A New Theory of Consumption* (London, 1720). Whatever their originality, however, Mather's remarks at least speak for his humane open-mindedness, and his prescient ability to select from contemporary science ideas of lasting importance.

In the most imaginative Capsula of *The Angel of Bethesda,* Mather consolidated several of these ideas in the single master concept of a "*Nishmath-Chajim.* The Probable SEAT of all Diseases, and a General CURE for them." The Nishmath-Chajim is his fullest elaboration, after years of pondering the notion, of the plastic spirit, an attempt to harmonize his scientific and religious ideas, his understanding of matter and of spirit, his natural philosophy and pneumatology, his vitalistic and mechanistic views of the universe—Mather's own unified field theory. In conceiving the Nishmath-Chajim he drew particularly on the notion of an Archeus propounded by the devout Swiss physician Jean Baptiste van Helmont, whose works he had known since youth. As defined in Van Helmont's huge folio *Oriatrike or, Physick Refined* (London, 1662), the Archeus is the inner "air" in every material object which determines its development, a soullike entity responsible for all change and coming-into-being in the thing, the governor of generation, the "chief Workman, containing the fruitfulness of generations and Seeds, as it were the internal efficient cause." Mather's Nishmath-Chajim is the body's Archeus, its own unique plastic spirit, a set of biological signals directing its activities without its volition. It is that by which the body "knows" to digest, "the *Spirit,* whose *Way we know not, for shaping the Bones,* and other Parts, *in the Womb of her that is with Child.*" Neither pure matter nor pure spirit, it may be "of a *Middle Nature,* between the *Rational Soul* and the *Corporeal Mass,*" a superfine matter whose particles, cohering by some unknown principle, may be finer than those of light. Most important, it may be through the Nishmath-Chajim that body and soul interact: "It wonderfully receives also *Impressions* from *Both* of them. And perhaps it is the *Vital Tie* between them."

Mather saw this vitalistic Nishmath-Chajim as the possible link between a diverse host of unexplained natural and pneumatological phenomena—muscular motion, digestion, psychogenic illness, nidification (the instinct in birds to build nests), and the waxing of the human body from the original infolded animalcule, as well as witchcraft, ghosts, and teleportation. Because the Nishmath-Chajim connects body and soul, and is affected by mental tranquillity, Mather following Helmont urged attending it in the treatment of disease: the physician who can find a way to "Brighten, and Strengthen, and Comfort, the *Nishmath-Chajim,* will be the most Successful Physician in the World." Having never wholly abandoned his pneumatology (he thought recently that Satan "obtained a permission" to scatter the pages of his *Ratio Disciplinae*) he believed that a fuller understanding of the Nishmath-Chajim might explain "Indisputable and Indubitable Occurrences of *Witchcrafts* (and *Possessions*)." The Nishmath-Chajim might also account for apparitions of the dead, for Mather considered it probable that upon the body's death "the *Nishmath-Chajim* goes away, as a Vehicle to the *Rational Soul;* and continues unto it an Instrument of many Operations," a ghost thus being a soul inhabiting a Nishmath-Chajim. Similarly he attributed to it cases in which dying persons who strongly desired to visit some distant place had been seen at the place and could describe it. He also speculated that in conjunction with the concept of indestructible animalcules, the Nishmath-Chajim could help explain the ultimate Resurrection of the Dead.

While writing *The Angel of Bethesda* Mather surmised that booksellers would demand a sale of forty or fifty pounds before risking publication. Even before completing the "large Work" he despaired of "my *Angel's* becoming visible" otherwise than in manuscript. Although he determined to "apply myself both to Heaven and Earth, to bring on the Publication" his applications failed, as did those of Samuel, who noted that it had cost his father "many Years study," and in 1739 even advertised for subscribers to bring it into print. The work was not published, however, until the twentieth century.

*

Despite this uncommonly ample late harvest, Mather's health was failing. In the last year of his life, 1727, he suffered three periods of serious illness. In April several ministers met at Joshua Gee's house to pray for his recovery; in June and July he was ill again, *"Chastened sore,* but . . . *not given over to Death";* ill again in October, he characterized himself as *"a Dying Man,* and one that sees himself going out of the World." Although weak, he carried on, preaching, occasionally serving on a committee or at an ordination, holding a church council at his home. He also sat for the well-known portrait of him by Peter Pelham, a 30" x 25" oval painted on canvas. It shows nothing of ill health, and may not be a close likeness, although persons who knew Samuel well when he was older said the portrait much resembled Mather's son. Pelham later prepared and sold a print based on the portrait, the first mezzotint known to have been made in the New World. Mather seems to have been the first American whose portrait others wanted and bought for their homes.

Lacking Mather's diaries, his general mood in the last year or two of his life can only be glimpsed in other sources. His last works and few last letters touch many moods. Some are sombrous, for he no more sentimentalized the dying than he did the elderly:

> They may *Chatter like a Bird* which a violent Hand is pulling out of its Nest; *I shall behold Man no more with the Inhabitants of the World. My Age is departed; My Life is cut off like the Thread of the Weaver. I feel Death like a Lion breaking all my Bonds.* They have no Prospect of any other, but that within a few Days or Hours, they shall have their *Life smitten down to the Ground, and go to dwell in Darkness.* . . .

Yet at other times near the end Mather seems if somber also unsubdued, as in his *Manuductio* and in a letter he wrote one year before his death to Thomas Prince. It concerns the Rev. Nathaniel Clap of Newport, members of whose congregation charged him with neglecting his ministry. Apparently, some Boston ministers asked Mather to write a letter of reproof to Clap, as he did. When he learned that another letter was substituted for it, his old touchy petulance flashed out:

> *I very well understand* the meaning of the indecency and indignity I am treated withal. To order me to draw up letters, and make me lose my time, which grows more and more precious to me . . . and then turn 'em upon me again and substitute instead of them, that which can be of *no other use* but only to render *them useless*—I say, *I very well understand it.* . . .

Assuring Prince that he would remain patient and easy, he added that he would also "look on myself as excused for the time to come from the labors of your clerkship."

Mather's dominant mood, however, seems to have been an agitated exaltation, varying in pitch from lyric joy to hectic merriment. As a Puritan, he believed and often emphasized that the true Christian dies joyously. He had witnessed such victorious deaths many times himself. In 1716, for instance, when "my dear, good, wise, and lovely *Katy"* was told that she was dying, she replied, *"Oh! I could even Sing for Joy, at what you tell me."* So despite his grim imaginings of illness and decay, Mather was moved himself to Whitmanesque carolings of death as liberation and ease:

> In *Death,* what shall we have to be *afraid* of! *Death,* which will be a *Mercy stroke* to finish the uneasy things wherein we *Die daily* and release us from all the Pain, and Grief, and Care, and the Daughters of *Heth,* which made us to say, *What Good shall my Life do unto me!* . . . . The *Angel of Death* coming with a Commission to strike us and kill us, yet says unto us, *I shall do you no hurt. Ben't scared; I won't hurt you!* That which has the Aspect of the *Worst,* as well as the *last Enemy,* becomes a *good Friend* unto us. In the most gloomy *Darkness* of the *Valley,* we may Sing. . . .

Mather's readiness to rejoice at death may account for the heightened lyricism of many of his final works, as expressed in such poetically exotic Hebrew titles as *El-Shaddai* (1725), *Zalmonah* (1725), *Hatzar-Maveth* (1726), and *Hor-Hagidgad* (1727). His late works also cultivate many striking figures of speech (for instance comparing Christ, surprisingly, to the Old Testament brazen serpent) and are pervaded by interacting complex images of trees, birds, and, particularly, singing. When he sat alone during his long illness of 1724–25, unable to read or write, he often composed and sang hymns pertinent to his condition, remarking that a soul in which piety flourishes "can *sing* in the *Valley of the Shadow of Death.* . . . triumphing over the *Fear of Death,* and beginning to *sing the Songs of the Lord,* even in a *strange Land;* the *Songs,* which none but those *chief Musicians,* the *Redeemed from the Earth,* are skilful at." He wrote several poems in his last few years as well. Six of them he included in *Agricola* (1727) as "The *Plain* SONGS OF THE Pious HUSBAND-MAN"; he seems also to have sent his friend Thomas Hollis a poem on spectacles.

At times Mather's lyric joy in the prospect of death was transposed into a feverish levity. Such is the mood of a strange madcap letter he hurriedly wrote to Prince on a cold day in January 1726, dated "Madding Day" and beginning, "If you ask, *What I do?*—Alas, methinks; my name is *Do Little.*" Lopsidedly written, words crowded at the bottom or crosswise in the margin, the letter acknowledges pain ("I want Strength. My Side Aches with This!") and ends by quoting the Protestant martyr Mrs. Askew (whose name also puns on the askew script): "I am, your Brother, *As Merry as one bound for Heaven.*" Still more hectic is the unfinished poem Mather handwrote in 1727 across the title page and inside the covers of a published poem entitled *A Monumental Gratitude* (New London, 1727). The published poem narrates the fate of some Yale students caught in but delivered from a storm on Long Island Sound. Mather wrote across the bottom of its title page:

> Poor Lads! the Storm has whirld your Brains around;
> And all the *Sense* is ship-wrack'd in the SOUND.

There is no knowing whether to take this as literary criticism, a swipe at Yale, self-pity, or all three. Even more bizarre, considering the occasion of the poem (with its overtones of Creasy's drowning), are the mock-heroic verses Mather wrote inside. Suited for no place so much as the *Courant,* they render as a miniature comic apocalypse a rowdy holiday feast of pigeon pie:

> Hark, Stygian Muse; the Noise and discord dire,
> Of Heated Ovens, and of Crackling Fire,
> While Smoke, and Soot, and falling Sticks of Wood,
> And Scattering Coal, and foaming Pidgeons Blood,
> With hideous Riot all deform the Floor,
> Rage, fury, firebrands, bellowing Outrage, roar,
> Reason and Sense avaunt, the py appears,

And charms at once Touch, Eyes, Nose, Mouth, and Ears.
Fall on, Huzza! Break down the Bulwarks Strong
Let Gravy gush and pidgeons Sprawl along.
Salt, pepper, Butter, Marrow, Flesh and Bones,
Mix in the Mouth while Spoons encounter Spoons
Forks rush at Forks, and plates on plates resound,
Knives Knives repel, and crust recrackles round,
War, tumult, Havock, Sputt'ring, Out-cries, Threats. . . .

And so on through about another eight lines. Mather probably wrote the verses when seriously ill, but their unexpected and mysterious death-bound merriment eludes explanation. Perhaps, like some Puritan King Lear, he returned at the worst to laughter.

Having spent much of his life preparing his soul for death, Mather also lived now in a mood of expectancy. A little before dying, he wrote, an old man "Realizes the *Invisible World* more than formerly. *Invisibles* become to him the *greatest Realities.*" When seriously ill in the summer of 1727 he had come close to knowing what would be revealed to the elect at death. He had visited then "the very *Gate* of the *Invisible World,* and had Opportunity to look a little way into the *Paradise* of GOD." What he expected to find in his afterlife he recorded in an unpublished treatise entitled "Tri-Paradisus." Apart from its eschatological interest, this lengthy work is biographically among the most revealing documents that remain from Mather's last years. For although grounded in Scripture, it amounts to an elaborate fantasy of the journey of his own soul after death and for the duration of time.

The three paradises of Mather's title refer respectively to Eden; to the place of departed souls; and to the New Heaven and New Earth to be built after the Second Coming. The first section, drawn largely from "Biblia Americana" and based on writings of Lydia's father, Samuel Lee, is an erudite exercise in scriptural geography, identifying biblical Eden with the whole of Mesopotamia between the Tigris and Euphrates rivers. This part of the work Mather seems to have written in 1712. The descriptions of the other two paradises he seems to have written in 1726, at a time when he believed himself to be hastening to them. His manner through-out the work is tentative and guarded. Praying to be free from error he reckons with what "seems" to be the dark meaning of Scripture, extrapolating the nature of the place of departed souls typologically from the Old Testament depiction of the Jewish Temple of Solomon, and the nature of the New Heaven from the biblical description of Babylon, of which it is the reverse image.

Following Scripture, Mather envisioned the future history of his liberated soul in two epochs, divided by the Second Coming. First, stripped of mortal bodies at death, the *"unsheathed"* souls of the elect shall go to the Heavenly Paradise, seemingly "an *Apartment* of the *Heavenly World,"* distinct from the superior part of Heaven where resides Christ. There the saved soul, *"Escaped as a Bird out of the Snare of the Fowlers,"* perhaps clothed in luminous garments, may see Christ, perhaps at His occasional visits to Paradise, perhaps by the soul's own raised visionary contemplations. In this paradise the departed spirit shall be inconceivably happy, delivered from disease and enemies and sin, transported by its sublimely glad worship of God. There it shall live in joyful hope of its perfected blessedness after the Resurrection, when the elect shall be gathered together and reunited with their bodies.

The second epoch of the soul, Mather believed, shall follow the final Conflagration and the creation of the New Heaven and New Earth darkly shadowed forth in Apocalypse. The wicked having been destroyed, and Satan and his minions imprisoned in places of torment, God shall translate some of the elect souls to the Heavenly City itself, the final dwelling of the Raised Saints, the New Jerusalem. Built by Christ, made of purest matter or perhaps ethereal, peopled with the elect of both sexes and all nations, here the *"Changed Ones"* shall continue as distinct individual beings, even in becoming one with God and penetrated by Him. Receiving the consummate blessedness of which their earthly grace was the token, they shall be able to see Christ and God in Him. Their bodies, material but highly spiritualized, shall be incorruptible, errorless, without deformity, of luminous beauty and brightness, able to move and fly as angels, many of whose former functions they shall assume. Indeed here they shall meet and become intimate with the angels who guarded them in life. To their enormously illuminated understandings, all shall be unriddled; they shall comprehend the obscure places of Scripture, the workings of Providence, the nature of matter. However these elect have been scorned on earth, here Christ shall open His *"Book of Remembrance"* and assign them the *"Degrees of Glory"* to which they are truly entitled.

Personal disasters had often set Mather speculating on the apocalyptic event that divides these two epochs, the Second Coming—the crowning event of human history. In several earlier publications he had projected personal anger into visions of a world consumed, and hopes for personal vindication into sights of Christ returned to punish the wicked and avenge the virtuous. Now, in "Tri-Paradisus," he drew on Isaiah, Ezekiel, and other texts to compose another such disguised malediction, imagining the destruction of a world whose ordeals and traps, at least, he had grown to hate, "a World," he said, "which is not a *Paradise* (nor is Like to afford one) but is an horrid and howling Wilderness; A Land of Pits and of Droughts, and fiery flying Serpents." As Mather envisioned it, Christ's Coming and the attendant conflagration would be heralded by volcanic eruptions and earthquakes. The onset would be sudden: men of business would be busy, the wicked plying their wickedness, the sensuous wallowing. Perhaps first over Italy, seat of the papacy, a sudden light would appear in the heavens.

Then tormenting heat will blast the devils from their high places in the atmosphere. Audible above the thunderclaps reechoing from earth's caverns, the voice of Christ will call the dead to rise from their graves:

> "*COME FORTH, my people, out of the Chambers, where I have hid you. Let my Dead Ones, Live Again.*"

The luminous risen spirits of the Chosen, ascending "as with the Wings of Eagles," will join the flocking squads of angels now visibly accompanying Christ downward to earth. People below, running to and fro, hiding from the fire and falling edifices, will wring their hands, howling one at another in anguish "beyond that of a *Travailing Woman*," as toppling nature turns dark and turns light:

> . . . there will be a *Great Earthquake;* the *Sun* will appear *as black as a Sackcloth of Hair,* by reason of the outshining Lustre in the *Chariots* of God; and the *Moon become as Blood* by reason of the Vapour wherewith our Air will be thickened; the *Stars of Heaven* will appear as if they were *falling to the Earth,* by reason of the Vibrations in the Atmosphere: The *Heaven will depart as a Scrowl when it is rolled together.*

As Christ's voice louder than a million thunderclaps calls "STRIKE!" thunderbolts plentiful as hailstones, "All-Scorching Sheets of Liquid *Fire*" will devour "*His Enemies.*" The veins of sulphur saturating the earth will immediately take fire, "Ten Thousand *Volcano's* will burst out, and throw up Flames and Vapors and Cinders, with a Rage and a Roar, that will reach unto the Heavens." The ground opening up in thousands of places will overturn mountains and swallow cities until the blazing earth itself is consumed.

Mather's vision of the Second Coming represents a drastic change of views in his final years, partly as a result of reading William Burnet's *Essay on Scripture-prophecy* (1724), which he deemed the "most penetrating, Judicious, Decisive Essay, that has ever yet been made upon that noble Subject." First he had become convinced that the conflagration of the earth would be literal, not allegorical as some commentators held, nor limited to the burning of Jerusalem. He had also come to believe that the Second Coming would be personal, an actual return of Christ to earth, a subject on which he had previously had a "thousand hesitations." He also no longer believed that the conversion of the Jews must take place before or during the Second Coming, as many others believed (including his father) and as many passages in Scripture seemed to suggest. With "a most Humble, and even Trembling, Heart and Hand," as he wrote in "Tri-Paradisus," he had come to consider this view both unscriptural and irrational, among other reasons because it seemed to him impossible that anyone could be converted amidst the flames. What the prophecy meant, he now thought, was that the Jews would be converted after Christ's Coming; or, since many Jews had been converted in early Christian times, the prophesied event may have already taken place.

Mather now believed, in fact, that there remained no signs to be looked for, that all the foretold preliminaries of the Second Coming had already occurred. Although he had once accepted the probability of Whiston's date of 1716, he otherwise frowned on commentators who brought prophetical study into disrepute by trying to fix the day and time of Christ's return too precisely. But feeling near the end himself, he was now convinced that the end of time was imminent. He had reached this conclusion by the summer of 1724, but feared publicizing it lest he seem "a vain Dreamer . . . a Man in the Falling Sickness, seized with I know not what kind of Enthusiasm." But reluctance faded in the last year or two of his life, when he at least alluded to the nearness of the Second Coming in the Latin Preface to his *Manuductio,* in such sermons as *Terra Beata* (1726) and *Fasciculus Viventium* (1726), and in a Latin commentary, *Diluvium Ignis* (1726).

Mather does not seem to have fully divulged his view publicly, however, until August 1727, when he preached on the accession of the new king, George II. He may have been encouraged to declare himself by front-page newspaper accounts, early in the year, of earthquakes in Italy. The *Gazette* reported on its front page that in Palermo an earthquake lasting twenty-five minutes had ruined most of the churches and a quarter of the houses, under which were buried more than fifteen-thousand persons; in Sicily people ran from their homes and gathered prostrate on the ground in the squares, "shedding Floods of Tears, smiting their Breasts, and saying over their Rosary with the most fervent Devotion." Whether or not inspired by this news, Mather thundered to his flock stupendous tidings:

. . . it may NOW, most awfully be said, *His Wrath will QUICKLY Flame!*—
we NOW know of nothing that remains to go before the Fulfillment of that
Word, *The Son of Man shall come in the Clouds of Heaven:* At which there
comes a tremendous CONFLAGRATION on a World horribly *Ripened* for
it: and as *Thoughtless* of it!

This was on August 20, 1727, six months before his death.

*

It began, the earthquake, on October 29—a Sabbath, between half-
past ten and ten forty-five at night. The sky, many remembered, had never
been more fair, the air never more serene, the stars never more glittering.
To Mather it became audible as a "horrid rumbling like the Noise of
many Coaches together, driving on the paved Stones with the utmost
Rapidity." Others heard a crashing noise, or violent thunderclap, or a
great fired chimney's bellowing "but inconceivably more fierce and terrible."

Movables clattered as the earth, in the largest quake in New England's
history, began tremblingly reeling. Cups and mugs tumbled off the man-
tel, windows and doors flew open; the kitchen in Judge Sewall's house
"Rocked like a Cradle." Houses cracked as if collapsing. Many wakened
people fled to the streets, fearful they would be buried in rubble. The
booming was not bounded by Boston. The splitting earth upthrew cart-
loads of sulfurous sand and ashes at Newbury, about forty miles northeast.
A bell tolled in Guilford, Connecticut, a hundred and sixty miles away.
Ships along the coast shook. The initial shock lasted only two or three
minutes, but until early morning could be felt the roll of aftershocks and
distant rumbles. Their possible meaning was obvious. Many persons in
Methuen, according to the local minister, feared "that it was the Great
Day of the Son of man's appearing in the clouds of heaven." Bostonians
assembled in the churches throughout the night and day, the *Gazette*
reported, in a state of "great and Just Terror and Dread."

Mather may have been feeble at the time of the quake, for two weeks
earlier he had addressed his congregation as *"One coming to you from
the Dead."* But having also recently warned of an imminent tremendous
conflagration, he felt that if ever he had preached a seasonable word he
must do so now. The Lord had spoken, and he must "render the Voice of
the Glorious GOD in the EARTHQUAKE, while it was yet scarce over,
Articulate and Intelligible unto the Hearers." The morning following the
quake he hurriedly put together what he called a speech rather than a

sermon, on Mic. 6:9—The Voice of the Lord, crieth unto the City. The bells of the North Church rang, and services were held at eleven o'clock in the morning, lasting until two in the afternoon.

Mather spoke now to a full meetinghouse. Nothing is known of his thoughts and his physical condition as he delivered the speech, but he perhaps felt very near death. For although he dealt with the earthquake, his startlingly oral depiction of a vindictive God speaking in fire and convulsion put before his listeners a lifetime of undernourishment and ill reward, its straining vatic energy a personal cry for last-minute retribution. Now no ambidexter tongue-tied jest for some Oldmixon, he commanded his congregation to listen to what he said: "O People *Trembling* before the Lord; *Hear now my SPEECH, and hearken to all my Words. For Indeed, I may declare unto you, The opening of my Lips will be of Right Things.*" They had now heard unmistakably, he said, the voice of the Lord roaring out of Zion: "Who is here of you, among them who felt the *Earth trembling* under them, that said not upon it, *When I heard, my Lips quivered at the Voice.*" They had all heard his copious Voice before but had not attended "the *Sound that went out of His Mouth.*" But now at last they could not ignore the Voice: "I see none *Asleep* at this Time. 'Tis a Congregation of *Hearers,* that I am this Time speaking to. . . . Now, Sirs, you have an *Earthquake* to give you a push." The time called for reformation, "particularly, for the stopping of that *Language of Fiends,* heard so often in our Streets, from the *Tongues that are set on Fire of Hell.*" The rest of what he knew Mather had come to warily, but now, following the quake, it was *"like a Fire in my Bones."* Even so, he divulged it cautiously: "If I should make the Cry, FIRE, FIRE! *The Fire of GOD will sooner than is generally thought for, fall upon a wretched World* . . . I should be as much *mocked,* and as little *minded,* as *Lot* was in the *Morning* of the Day when he went out of *Sodom.*" He might again be mocked, he said, but he believed that the universal conflagration and Christ's "Literal, Personal, Visible *Coming*" were at hand, and that all the promised signs "have been *given;* and are *passed,* and *over.*"

Mather's warning was not easily mocked, for widespread earth tremors continued through November. In December, news also arrived of earthquakes in such improbably remote places as the West Indies, where it was said that mountains shook and that the streets rose and fell like waves of the sea. Coupled with reports of quakes in England, Sicily, and elsewhere in Europe earlier in the year, these unsettling accounts inspired a substantial rise in admissions in many New England churches. Mather's own church admitted seventy-one persons in 1727, the largest number of his entire ministry. (The previous largest number was fifty-five, in 1691, just before the witchcraft crisis.) The converts included, on November 19, his sole surviving daughter, Nancy, for whose conversion he had long prayed.

Hoping to prolong the mood of reformation, Mather sent to Governor Dummer on December 9 a memorial he had prepared, calling for a province-wide Day of Humiliation and Supplication, that "we may be found religiously preparing for the things which may be coming." In further preparation he preached again on the earthquakes on December 14, warning once more that those who denied God would soon be consumed: "I again, and again, declare it unto you; *The Coming of the Son of Man in the Clouds of Heaven,* 'tis what we know of Nothing to Retard it or Protract it."

On December 24, with the shocks continuing, Mather preached for the last time. Speaking to his flock on the death of the Rev. Peter Thacher, he selected the text, Come my People, Enter thou into thy Chambers (Isa. 26:20). He did not threaten or warn. Instead he offered a comforting certainty, that the troubled body which goes to the cold chamber where the sun shines not, shall be reborn at rest in paradise, envisioning God. Beginning in late December, other ministers, including his son Samuel, took his place in his pulpit.

Conclusion: Copp's Hill

A *Post* set out; made the best of his Way; and in a few Hours
Reached the Stage Intended. I'll tell it yet again: A *Ship* Weigh'd, and
under full Sail, right before a Wind, run after the Rate of Twenty
Leagues a Watch, and Anon Bore in with the Harbour . . . once more. An
Eagle Hungry for a Prey, saw it, and with a *Nimble Wing* Seiz'd the *Prey*.
This is the Short and the Long of the *Story*. Sirs, I have told you the
Story of *Life*. This is the *Story*. In the V Chapter of *Genesis,* you have the
Story told, Nine times over, so; *The Man was Born, he had an House,
and he Died*. That's All!

—*A New Year Well-begun* (1719)

COTTON MATHER'S final illness kept him at home for the last five or six
weeks of his life. Certain he was dying, he wished to live only long
enough to force his will into entire resignation to the will of God; after
that, he told his successor Joshua Gee, "*then farewell all friends below; I
shall* have nothing more to do *here*." One other task remained to him,
however. In his last affliction too he wished his own condition to instruct
others, this time in the skill of dying. The many persons who visited him
and recorded his final statements understood his behavior as the final
demonstration of the Christian connoisseurship he had practiced all his
life, a consummate example of meeting the King of Terrors with divine
calm. Throughout his last illness and in his last days and hours, Benjamin
Colman observed, "abundant gracious *Words* . . . flow'd from Him to every one that came about him," making "one of the brightest Accounts we
yet ever had of *Grace and Peace,* and living Comforts in dying Moments."

But to Mather resignation had never come easily. Unlike his father, he
had never been greedy to depart but, however beset, had found much of
his life savory and devoured it, a voluptuary of time. Many comments

ascribed to him at the end (some smacking of deathbed hagiography) suggest a longing to linger. Often, Samuel reported, he quoted the text Thou that hast showed me great and sore Troubles, shalt quicken me again (Ps. 71:20), sometime applying it to the possibility of recovering his strength—but adding that he would be content to have the promise fulfilled at the Resurrection. Or he spoke of wishing to live at least long enough to complete some unfinished writings. And there was Lydia, she who had left him, still a "very valuable fish," he had called her in their courtship. Reminding her of their ardent devotions, he said, *"You and I must never any more retire and pray together, as we used to do."* But he told her to think, when praying by herself, that he at that moment would be singing hallelujahs before the same throne of grace, and he added: *"I'll meet you there as often as you please."*

With a boom "like a great Gun," the earth again shook and rumbled on January 14, a Sabbath, preluding not the vindication Mather predicted but a kind of vindication nevertheless, terrible in form. The next day two brothers, skating at the bottom of Boston Common, fell through the ice and drowned. They were young George and Nathan Howell, the two children of Lydia's daughter, offspring of the "monsters of ingratitude" who Mather believed had designed his ruin. They had been unfortunate sons of a "wretched Father," he wrote when taking on the administration of their father's estate, and he had resolved to extend over them "the Eye of my Care."

At daybreak two Sabbaths later the earth trembled again for a minute. Houses vibrated, rattling glassware and pewter on the shelves. Shocks followed over the next two days—the worst since the first quake in October, again sending people in great consternation into the streets. (Astonishingly, the tremors would continue into September.) The same day, January 28, the brethren of the North Church agreed to call a day of supplication, beseeching God to prolong the life of "Our Reverend and Dear Pastor." God, they said, "has greatly endeared him to us, and threatens his Removal from us by Death, which we would deprecate as a most awful Frown of Heaven."

Saturday, February 10, onlookers judged Mather to be in his worst agonies. In his last illness as before, he prayed to be spared from the torturous stones that had made his father cry for pity. Apparently he was, for Samuel described his condition as "a hard *Cough* and a suffocating *Asthma* with a *Fever*." He even managed to say, with a "sort of triumph in his air and accent," as Gee recorded his words, "And is this dying! This all! is this what I feared when I prayed against a hard death! Is it no more than this! O I can bear this! I can bear it, I can bear it!"

Sunday, as he had done throughout his last days, Mather dispensed blessings and charges to his visitors, according to their character and relation. The surviving accounts do not mention Nancy's presence. But Mather assured Sammy that he knew that his soul was in a state of grace. Instructing his son how to dispose of his private affairs and papers, he also blessed him on bended knee, saying:

> You have been *a dear Son and a pleasant Child* unto me, and I wish you as *many* Blessings as you have done me *Services* which are very many. I wish and Pray the God of ABRAHAM, ISAAC, and JACOB may be yours and His Blessing rest upon you. I wish that, as you have a Prospect of being serviceable in the World, you may be great and considerable, as the Patriarchs were, by introducing a CHRIST into the World.

When Sammy asked him what sentence or word he would have him consider constantly, Mather said, "Remember only that one word *Fructuosus.*" Although he had confided to Gee that his final views of Christ, God, and Heaven had been neither so many nor so lasting as in some former illnesses, when a friend asked what sight he now had of the invisible world he answered, *"All glorious."* Indeed he seems to have felt relief. According to Samuel, when Lydia tried to wipe his eye he said, *"I am going where all* Tears *shall be* wiped *from my Eyes."*

Monday was Cotton Mather's sixty-fifth birthday. Praying as usual with his family in the morning, he told them he had expected to die the day before, but would wait his appointed time patiently. Whether buoyed by his birthday or enacting his exemplary part to the end, he seemed to others in good spirits. A visiting minister was surprised to find him sitting up in bed with his glasses on, reading, and asked whether he was reading his name written in the Book of the Lamb; he replied, *"Yes I have found it,"* and turned down the leaf. When Lydia remarked that he was smiling at her pleasantly while she, at his bedside, was in tears, he said, *"Why should not I smile, when every thing looks smiling upon me."* A few hours before his death, which occurred on Tuesday morning, February 13, between eight and nine o' clock, he called for Gee to pray with him and said to him after the prayer, *"Now I have nothing more to do here. . . . My will is now entirely resigned to the will of* GOD." Someone observed to him that God had heard his prayers for an easy death. He answered, his last word was, *"Grace!"*

✱

By custom, Mather's body lay awaiting burial for nearly a week. Meanwhile, Boston newspapers printed laudatory accounts of his life and death, and Benjamin Colman, Thomas Prince, and other ministers preached eulogistic sermons about him, assessing the human meaning of his life, and its importance to his flock and his colleagues, to Boston, to New England, and to America itself. Many of the sermons have the apologetic air, common to later accounts of Mather, of trying to do justice in limited space to someone gargantuan and perplexing. But all agree that Mather had been an uncommon person, a presence.

It was of course as a minister that Mather's colleagues most extolled him. He had been "the *first Minister in the Town*," as Colman called him, "the first in Age, in Gifts and in Grace. . . . the *first* in the whole *Province* and *Provinces* of *New England,* for universal Literature, and extensive Services." Since his youth he had given an illustrious public example of heaven-minded piety, having lived, said Thomas Prince, "in an eminent manner in the Mount with GOD." His eulogists recalled the untiring earnestness he gave, after much study and writing, to composing and delivering his thousands of sermons. Many recalled how he had zealously awakened the impenitent, heartened the discouraged, pleaded with all to come to Christ. "No more will he here *weep* over perishing Souls in *Prayer;* no more scatter the *thunders and lightnings* of God in flaming *Sermons,*" Colman lamented, "No more is he to *weary* and spend himself, as we have often seen him wearied and *spent* for your Souls; never weary of his work, but often wearied in it." They recalled as well his indefatigable pastoral visits and innumerable consolatory personal calls on the afflicted or bereaved, the tempted and wounded. Nor had his concern been only for the North Church, but for the welfare and the civil and religious liberties of Protestants everywhere.

The ministers who praised Mather recognized themselves also as his beneficiaries. He had been a minister when the eldest of them were children, and before most of them were born, then had supervised their training, performed at their ordinations, obtained jobs for them, presided resourcefully over their councils. Gee recalled Mather's indulgent help in his own youthful ministerial studies, how he "bore with my infirmities; and helped me under difficulties: He quickened me to my work; and showed me an example: He instructed, admonished, and exhorted me as a father; while by his condescending goodness he raised me to the level of a friend and a brother."

Especially Mather's eulogists remembered him as the most learned man and the most voluminous writer New England had ever produced—the 388 works he published, the huge works he left unpublished, his devotion to science, his quick apprehension, tenacious memory, and ready invention. "He was a wonderful *Improver of Time,*" Thomas Prince said, "and 'tis almost amazing how much He had read and studied—How much He has wrote and published—How much He corresponded abroad; not only with the several Provinces in the *British America,* but also with *England, Scotland, Ireland, Holland, Germany,* and even the *Eastern* as well as the *Western Indies.*" Among Mather's works illustrative of his love for the church and its people, Prince singled out *Magnalia Christi Americana* "for the noble Care He has taken to preserve the *Memory* of the great and excellent Fathers of these religious Plantations, that was just a sinking into Oblivion." He also called attention to the ill-fated "Biblia Americana," an "extraordinary Work, that his Heart had been set on from his early Days, and has taken Him up almost *Fifty Years* to compose."

But not even Mather's lively and curious writings, the ministers agreed, conveyed the rich zest of his personality. Only those who had conversed with him knew its tang. Sought and welcome for his instructive and engaging talk, he rewarded all who came to him, the greatest man or meanest child, with some pertinent saying, some agreeable quotation graced with his own improvements, some anecdote fetched from his incomparable knowledge of the New England past, now irrecoverably lost with him. "How easy and natural did his vast Learning appear in every Company," Prince recalled, "How agreeably temper'd with a various mixture of Wit and Cheerfulness? The most knowing cou'd scarce ever leave him without knowing more, the most ungracious without some Impressions of Goodness, or any without a grateful Pleasure."

Among Mather's more general personal qualities his eulogists emphasized his passionate stamina and courteous charity, as well as his parental affection and power of resignation. "He seem'd to have," Prince remarked, "an inexhaustible Source of *divine Flame and Vigour* . . . . . . Tho' fatigued in Body, never tired in Mind." Much of this energy he gave to endless projections to Do Good, abounding in generosity to the poor. Samuel praised his loving qualities as a father:

> . . . how *kind,* how *loving,* nay how *fond:* We went into his *Presence* with *Delight* and never *left* it without *Regret;* His Company was so entertainingly *pleasant* and *profitable;* his *Temper* so free and open, and his *Concern* for us, for our *external,* but much more for our *interior* Welfare, so very great; and, in a Word, *his Carriage* towards us so *all-Christian,* and all Gentlemanly, that in our Opinion, it rendered him *the Delight of Mankind.*

Without mentioning Mather's torments under injury to his reputation and in the deaths of thirteen of his children, several eulogists remembered how as a testimony of faith he had suffered his awesome bereavements in silence. "Scarce any on Earth," Prince said, "have gone thro' such a great Variety and constant Succession of extraordinary *Trials.*"

It was of course not the role of Colman and the others to enlarge on Mather's many and much discussed faults. These his inner fears and historical circumstances make comprehensible but no less disfiguring. His submissiveness that would not grasp that at Salem people were being legally murdered; his meddlesome ambitiousness that stooped or strutted for petty advancement; his guile that wrote self-promoting letters under others' names; his vanity that scented out lurking slurs yet sensed no provocations in himself; his rashness that tendered spite as amity; his envy that sneered at what it could not get. Of this and what else in Mather was odious his eulogists said nothing. "Love to *Christ* and his *Servant* commands me," Colman explained, "to draw a *Veil* over every *Failing:* for *who* is without them?"

Among Mather's eulogists, Samuel probably came closest to identifying the overall achievement on which his father's future reputation might solidly rest. Might solidly: for in the popular panorama of the American past Mather still stands, like some limping Vulcan, in the mists of the country's history, from which only later emerge the more real and substantial figures of Franklin, Jefferson, and Washington. In a country that endorses democratic tolerance, reasonableness, individuality, and downrightness, this nebulous mythological Mather serves to symbolize what American character is not, or should not be—bigoted, superstitious, authoritarian, and devious. In its elements the conception is simplistic and inaccurate, while *in toto* one must look to cultural psychologists and historians of ideas to account for its gross distortion of so complex a man into a national gargoyle. Yet Sammy, in estimating his father's stature, provided part of an explanation: "*he alone* was able to support the Character of *this* Country abroad, and was had in great Esteem thro' many Nations in EUROPE."

Mather looms disfigured but large, that is, in part because he stands alone. Many of the beliefs attached to his name and scorned were after all shared by thousands of other settlers whose names few remember. But no other person born in America between the time of Columbus and of Franklin strove to make himself so conspicuous—strove, more accurately, to become conspicuous as an American. For he looked out eagerly from the New World on major intellectual developments abroad, aspiring to contribute to them by capitalizing on the limitations of provincial life. Unlike his father, who was also born in America and who won lesser (ultimately) fame, he did not hanker to live and die in England. The titles of some of his major works—"Biblia Americana," *Magnalia Christi Americana,* "Curiosa Americana," *Psalterium Americanum*—announce his affection for the place and his hope of putting America on the cultural map.

To speak very generally now, but with no intent of putting Mather in a nutshell: he was the first person to write at length about the New World having never seen the Old. Much of his career illustrates, for the first time, the costs and gains to America's intellectual and artistic life of its divorce from Europe. These costs and gains have been one and the same—a lack of standards or a freedom to create (depending on how it is viewed) which has often inspired works tainted by provincial crabbedness, eccentricity, and overreaching, but also often distinguished by their close kin, pungency, innovation, and grandeur. Some or all of these qualities impart the feel of the New World to work by many later Americans who have accepted or declared, and deeply explored, their isolation from the European mainstream—Herman Melville, Emily Dickinson, Walt Whitman, Charles Ives, Gertrude Stein, Frank Lloyd Wright, Jackson Pollock. The list might be extended (and challenged), and to be sure Mather was far more an artist of sorts than an artist. In his curiousness, epic reach, and quirkily ingenious individualism he was nevertheless the first unmistakably American figure in the nation's history.

*

Mather was buried on February 19, 1728, a cold and cloudy morning. The large number of people who gathered for the event from Boston and other towns made, said one contemporary, a "Vast Concourse Exceeding long Procession and numberless Spectators. Every heart Sad."

Taken from Mather's house on Ship Street near the wharves and harbor, his corpse was borne up Fleet Street past the Old North Church, where it was met by Joshua Gee, in deep mourning, and by the three deacons and the brethren of the church, who as a mark of special respect proceeded to walk before the coffin instead of behind it. Following the identical route that had been taken for the funeral of Increase Mather five years earlier, the procession moved along Hull Street toward the burial ground. On the uphill journey, Colman, Prince, and another Boston minister held down the funeral pall; some brethren took turns at bearing the coffin underneath, behind which walked Mather's family, in mourning, then Lieutenant Governor Dummer, the Council and House of Representatives, followed by a large train of ministers, justices, merchants, scholars, and other principal citizens, both men and women, including Samuel Sewall riding in a coach. "The Streets were crowded with People," the *Weekly Journal* reported, "and the Windows fill'd with Sorrowful Spectators all the way to the Burying Place."

The procession ended on Copp's Hill, the cemetery of the Old North. The level plain atop the hill had been, and probably still was, the site of a windmill. Although only about fifty feet high, Copp's Hill was one of the most commanding spots in Boston, affording a view of Charlestown and of a large part of Boston Harbor. Mather was interred in the large family tomb—the *"Cave of the Treasure,"* he had called it—together with his father and other members of the family. "It look'd very Sad," one observer said, "almost as if it were the funeral of the Country."

Immediately after Mather's death his pulpit was filled by the united ministers of Boston preaching a course of sermons. The North Church voted to continue Mather's salary (presumably to Lydia) as long as these sermons lasted, which was about a week; after that, the church voted £100 to Lydia out of its treasury, at the rate of £5 a month, until the end of 1729—five years before her death. Samuel prepared some of Mather's last works for posthumous publication and also began writing a brief but valuable biography of his father, containing a fresh advertisement to publish "Biblia Americana." Meanwhile his funeral sermon on his father, *The Departure and Character of Elijah* (1728), became the first of his own published works. In January 1732, after a probationary period, he was chosen pastor of the North Church, as the colleague of Joshua Gee; because of contention in the church he stayed only nine years, but remained in the ministry until his death in 1785. In 1762 he learned that his son Increase, also nicknamed Creasy, had fallen mortally ill of a fever in Havannah, only to learn that Creasy was in fact aboard a ship homeward bound . . . only to learn soon after that Creasy had indeed died. After divine services on August 15, 1776, he read to his congregation the Declaration of Independence and urged compliance with it.

Cotton Mather died intestate. The fact is surprising, for he had always been concerned about the plight of orphans and had often called on parents to provide for their children against their deaths: "Make a *Testamentary Provision* for them. Let your *Wills* be made, and in a Good order always Lying by you." Since he left no will, the power of examining and administering his estate fell to Samuel Sewall as probate judge. Sewall called on Lydia to appear in court, but she declined to act as administrator. Samuel petitioned to so act, but for some reason his petition was withdrawn. Sewall then assigned the power of administration to a Boston shopkeeper named Nathaniel Goodwin, who prepared an inventory in July 1728 as Mather's effects were shown to him and others by Lydia and the children. One of Mather's creditors charged that the inventory fraudulently omitted items of great value in order to avoid paying debts. He probably referred to Mather's library, his most valuable property, which does not appear in the inventory and which by some means or other descended to Samuel. Otherwise the only striking item on the inventory is five hundred acres of wasteland in Granville, Massachusetts, valued at only £36, to which Samuel also later laid claim. After some legal wrangling the estate was valued at £245, 5s, 10d of which the judge gave a third to Lydia, a third to Samuel, and divided the other third among the children of Mather's deceased daughter Abigail, and his one other surviving child, Nancy—the hapless daughter who had been burned in childhood, later caught smallpox and was put upon by Lydia, and afterward appears on the surviving records as "Hannah Mather, Spinster." Samuel and Lydia, however, signed over their shares in the estate to Nancy as well, for £30 and for what the quitclaim calls, without explanation, "diverse other good Causes."

But there was little to sign over. However luxuriantly he lived in heaven, Mather had not lived affluently on earth, and had lost much. What he left behind, as set down in the inventory of his estate, was dingy and mean: pie plates, lumber, a crosscut saw, three old rugs, four old bedsteads, two old oval tables, two old chests of drawers, old china curtains, old quilt, old warming pan, old standing candlestick, red curtains motheaten, broken stone table, broken fireplace dogs, broken chairs, broken pewter, broken spoons.

Documentation

IN REPRODUCING printed and manuscript primary sources I have retained the capitals, punctuation, and italics of the originals. But I have modernized spellings, lowered superscript letters, and expanded abbreviations. Legal documents, titles of works, and most quotations of verse, however, appear exactly as in the originals, with a very few deviations mentioned in the notes. In his preaching and writing, Mather apparently used several versions of the Bible, which sometimes makes his citation of texts seem erratic. For the sake of consistency in the text of the book, I have styled biblical citations in the modern fashion (e.g. Phil. 4:20), keyed to the King James version. But in the documentation I have reproduced Mather's own citations. I have reproduced dates according to the modern calendar, although Mather and his contemporaries used the Julian calendar, which began the year on March 25. Thus where Mather dated a letter "12 month 1682" I have used the modern date, February 1683.

I have indicated internal omissions from quoted material by an ellipse. But except for indented quotes, I have not included an ellipse for matter omitted from the end of a quotation. I am keenly aware of the possibilities this affords for misrepresentation, but I believe that in no case in the text does the lack of a final ellipse distort the meaning of the quotation. Where an omission has run over into the following paragraph of the source, I have indicated the gap by a double ellipse (six dots).

In the documentation below, I have used the first three words of each paragraph in the text, printed in bold face, to locate and group references in that paragraph. The references appear serially in the order of their appearance in the text. Individual references are separated by a semicolon. I trust these entries are full and clear, but their large number has made it unwieldy to group them in smaller clusters, or to document every tittle of information. Works specified in the text by date are not further documented in the notes, except in the case of *Magnalia Christi Americana.* Unless otherwise noted, all places of publication are Boston.

In the documentation I have used the following abbreviations:

A: "The Autobiography of Increase Mather," ed. Michael G. Hall, *Proceedings of the American Antiquarian Society,* LXXI (1961), 271–360.

AAS: American Antiquarian Society, Worcester, Mass.

BA: Cotton Mather's manuscript "Biblia Americana," in MAP (below), Reels 10–13; quotations identified by biblical book, chapter, and verse.

BG: *The Boston Gazette.*

BNL: *The Boston News-Letter.*

BPL: Boston Public Library, Boston, Mass.

CM: Cotton Mather.

CMHS: *Collections of the Massachusetts Historical Society.*

DI and DII: *Diary of Cotton Mather,* ed. Worthington Chauncey Ford, *Collections of the Massachusetts Historical Society,* 7th ser., VII–VIII [1912].

DIII: *The Diary of Cotton Mather, D.D., F.R.S. for the Year 1712,* ed. William R. Manierre II (Charlottesville, Va., 1964).

ERB: Extended Record Books, Clerk's Office for Suffolk County of the Supreme Judicial Court, Boston, Mass.

H: *Cotton Mather: A Bibliography of His Works,* ed. Thomas J. Holmes, 3 vols. (1940; rpt. Newton, Mass., 1974).

HCR: *Harvard College Records,* in *Publications of the Colonial Society of Massachusetts,* XV–XVI (I and II; 1925), XXXI (III; 1935), XLIX–L (IV and V: 1975).

HL: Henry E. Huntington Library, San Marino, Calif.

IM: Increase Mather.

IMD: Increase Mather, manuscript diaries, American Antiquarian Society. My deep thanks to Professor Michael G. Hall for allowing me to quote from his painstaking transcript of the diaries.

M: *Collections of the Massachusetts Historical Society,* 4th ser., VIII (1868; "The Mather Papers").

MAP: *The Mather Papers,* Part I (Cambridge, Mass., 1970; microfilm). References are identified in the notes by reel and frame numbers.

MCA: Cotton Mather, *Magnalia Christi Americana* (London, 1702). References are identified in the notes by book and page number.

MHS: Massachusetts Historical Society, Boston, Mass.

NEC: *The New-England Courant.*

NEHGR: *New England Historical and Genealogical Register.*

P: Cotton Mather, *Parentator. Memoirs of . . . Dr. Increase Mather* (1724).

PA: Cotton Mather, *Paterna: The Autobiography of Cotton Mather,* ed. Ronald A. Bosco (Delmar, N.Y., 1976).

PAAS: *Proceedings of the American Antiquarian Society.*

PCSM: *Publications of the Colonial Society of Massachusetts.*

PMHS: *Proceedings of the Massachusetts Historical Society.*

R2C: Manuscript records of the Second Church, Massachusetts Historical Society.

RS: The Royal Society, London.

SF: Suffolk Files, Supreme Judicial Court, Boston, Mass.

SLCM: *Selected Letters of Cotton Mather,* ed. Kenneth Silverman (Baton Rouge, 1971). Citations of this volume give the page number only; full bibliographical information appears on the cited page in the volume itself.

SML: Samuel Mather, *The Life of the Very Reverend and Learned Cotton Mather, D.D. & F.R.S.* (1729).

SPG: Society for the Propagation of the Gospel.

SSD: *The Diary of Samuel Sewall 1674–1729,* ed. M. Halsey Thomas, 2 vols. (New York, 1973).

SVW: *Salem-Village Witchcraft,* ed. Paul Boyer and Stephen Nissenbaum (Belmont, Calif., 1972).

SWP: *The Salem Witchcraft Papers,* ed. Paul Boyer and Stephen Nissenbaum, 3 vols. (New York, 1977).

W: Winthrop Papers, Massachusetts Historical Society (microfilm).

1. *Quantum Nomen! Quanta Nomina!*

Both his grandfathers: quote from MCA, III, 125; other information from B. R. Burg, *Richard Mather of Dorchester* (n.pl., 1976). **Cotton Mather's maternal:** John Cotton, "Gods Promise to His Plantation," in *Literature in America: The Founding of a Nation,* ed. Kenneth Silverman (New York, 1971), p. 36. Other information from A. W. M'Clure, *The Life of John Cotton* (Boston, 1846) and Larzer Ziff, *The Career of John Cotton* (Princeton, 1962). **Except for uncertain:** A, pp. 279, 280. **Increase improved his:** A, pp. 282, 285, 286. **Returned from England:** A, p. 286. **The first eight:** Walter Muir Whitehill, *Boston: A Topographical History* (Cambridge, Mass., 1959), pp. 6–7; Justin Winsor, *et al., The Memorial History of Boston,* II (Boston, 1882–83), 496. **Although settled only:** "Copy of a Curious Paper," CMHS, 1st ser., IV (1795), 217; Whitehill, *Boston,* p. ii; *A Report of the Record Commissioners . . . Containing the Boston Records from 1660 to 1701* (Boston, 1881), pp. 65, 71. **The Mathers' house:** Arthur B. Ellis, *History of the First Church in Boston, 1630–1880* (Boston, 1881), pp. 42–43; Kate M. Cone, "Cotton Mather's Birthplace," *Genealogical Quarterly Magazine,* III (1902), 55–64; Chandler Robbins, *A History of the Second Church, or Old North, in Boston* (Boston, 1852), p. 216; IM, *A Sermon Concerning Obedience & Resignation* (1714), p. 39. **Virtually nothing is:** IMD, 1 Dec 1664, 27 Oct 1664, 28 Jun 1665, 25 Aug 1665. **These and Increase's:** A, p. 314; PA, p. 6; IM, *Pray for the Rising Generation* (Cambridge, Mass., 1678), p. 20. **While such nurture:** IM, *Sermon Concerning Obedience,* sig. A3; A, p. 352; P, p. 182; Benjamin Colman, *The Prophet's Death* (1723), p. 33. **Yet Increase Mather's:** P, p. 40; CM, *Early Religion Urged* (1694), pp. 83–84. **On larger, impersonal:** A, p. 284; M, pp. 96, 156. **But Increase's inwardness:** P, pp. 79, 66; A, pp. 297, 318; Colman, *Prophet's Death,* p. 36. **The years of:** R2C, p. 1; A, p. 287. **The brethren of:** IMD, 10, 11, 16, 19 Apr 1664 and 29 Jul 1664; P, p. 26. **Immediately Increase regretted:** IMD, 14 May 1664, 21–22 Jun 1664, 17 and 29 Feb 1664, 1 Mar 1664, 20 Aug 1664, 8 Sep 1664; P, p. 34; IMD, 2 Jun 1666. **What must have:** A, p. 359; CM, *Maternal Consolations* (1714), *passim.* **But these eulogies:** IMD, 4 May 1663, 28–29 Jun 1663. The speakers in these exchanges appear in IM's diaries as "C" and "M"—undoubtedly "Crescentius" and "Maria." See also IMD, 8 Apr 1664. **In the fall:** A, p. 287; IM, *The Life and Death of . . . Mr. Richard Mather,* in *Collections of the Dorchester Antiquarian Society,* no. 3 (1850), pp. 86, 77; A, pp. 288, 291; P, p. 68. **The possibility of:** A, pp. 291, 293. **During this period:** Annie Haven Thwing, *The Crooked & Narrow Streets of the Town of Boston 1630–1822* (Boston, 1920), p. 52; Robbins, *History of the Second Church,* p. 216. **Cotton later called:** DII, p. 723; Winsor, *Memorial History,* q. I, 548; Peveril Meigs, "Energy in Early Boston," NEHGR, CIV (1950), 83–90; John Bonner, *The Town of Boston in New England* (map, 1722); *Report of the Record Commissioners,* p. 154; *Boston in 1682 and 1699,* ed. George Parker Winship (Providence, 1905), p. 39. Cone, "Cotton Mather's Birthplace," dates the move in 1669, but this seems erroneous. CM remarks that the family lived in the new house for five years, and IM is known to have moved out of it in 1676. **By moving near:** A, pp. 297–98. **Not surprisingly, Cotton's:** PA, pp. 6–7. **In study and:** CM, *Corderius Americanus* (1708), p. 32; PA, p. 7 **By 1674 Cotton:** PA, p. 7; HCR, III, 329; CM, *The Angel of Bethesda,* ed. Gordon W. Jones (Barre, Mass., 1972), p. 231; A, p. 301. **Just when and:** *An Analysis of Stuttering,* ed. L. L. Emerick and C. E. Hamre (Danville, Ill., 1972), p. 12; *Stuttering: A Second Symposium,* ed. Jon Eisenson (New York, 1975), p. 55; SML, p. 26. **In explaining the:** Emerick and Hamre, *Analysis of Stuttering,* p. 128 *et passim;* Eisenson, *Stuttering,* p. 47. **Whether Cotton Mather's:** *Angel of Bethesda,* pp. 230, 226. **Christ was not:** *Angel of Bethesda,* pp. 226, 230–31. **Other**

problems than: Hamilton Vaughan Bail, *Views of Harvard: A Pictorial Record to 1860* (Cambridge, Mass., 1949), pp. 1–25; HCR, I, 1xvii ff. **No ampler facilities:** John Maynard Hoffmann, "Commonwealth College: The Governance of Harvard in the Puritan Period," Diss. Harvard (1972), p. 70; John Langdon Sibley, "Catalogues of Harvard University," PMHS (1864–65), p. 23 (IM's class of 1656 had eight students); *Robert Boyle: The Works,* ed. Thomas Birch (Hildesheim, 1965), VI, 653. **But in the:** SML, p. 4; [fragments of IM's diaries], PMHS, III (1855–58), 317. I see no reason to connect these threats by his fellow students, or general conditions at Harvard during Hoar's administration, with the "onset" of CM's stutter, as David Levin implicitly does in his *Cotton Mather: The Young Life of the Lord's Remembrancer 1663–1703* (Cambridge, Mass., 1978). Very little is known concretely about Hoar's administration, and even far less about CM's years at Harvard. Authorities on stuttering agree that it is extremely unusual for some particular, traumatic event to precipitate the impediment. For other arguments against making the connection see Hoffmann, above, esp. p. 308, n. 62. **President Hoar fared:** *Records of the Governor and Company of the Massachusetts Bay in New England,* ed. Nathaniel B. Shurtleff (Boston, 1853–54), V, 20; [fragments of IM's diaries], pp. 317, 319. **The change in:** [fragments of IM's diaries], p. 318; "Diary of Increase Mather," PMHS, 2nd ser., XIII (1899–1900), 346, 348, 349, 351; [fragments of IM's diaries], p. 319. **The demoralized atmosphere:** A, p. 302; Thomas Hutchinson, *The History of the Colony and Province of Massachusetts-Bay,* ed. Lawrence Shaw Mayo (Cambridge, Mass., 1936), I, 260; John Gorham Palfrey, *History of New England* (Boston, 1875, 1890), III, 215. **While Cotton was:** P, p. 77; Joseph B. Felt, *The Ecclesiastical History of New England* (Boston, 1855), II, 638; MCA, III, 199. **The war hardly:** A, pp. 302-3; MS letter, IM to John Cotton, 13 Dec 1676, AAS. **Increase frequently suffered:** IM to John Cotton, 13 Dec 1676. **Cotton Mather saw:** IM to John Cotton, 13 Dec 1676; A, p. 303. **Increase lost by:** IM to John Cotton, 13 Dec 1676; *Records of the Suffolk County Court 1671–1680,* PCSM, XXIX–XXX (1933), 782; "Diary of John Hull," *Transactions and Collections of the American Antiquarian Society,* III (1857), 242. **After the fire:** A, p. 303; Robbins, *History of the Second Church,* pp. 23, 216. **No record remains:** Josiah Quincy, *The History of Harvard University* (Boston, 1860), I, 591; HCR, III, 333. **Cotton later wrote:** PA, pp. 7–8; M, p. 9; Julius Herbert Tuttle, "The Libraries of the Mathers," PAAS, NS XX (1910), 348–49. **Cotton usually took:** PA, pp. 7–8; I. Bernard Cohen, *Some Early Tools of American Science* (Cambridge, Mass., 1950), p. 27; PA, p. 10. **Cotton came down:** CM, *Angel of Bethesda,* p. 50; PA, p. 8; SLCM, pp. 6–7. CM's 1677 sermon notebooks show him to have been in Boston virtually every week. **For whatever reasons:** PA, p. 10. **During his last:** R2C; PA, p. 10. **At the Commencement:** SML, p. 5

2. The Solemnest Work in the World

The ministry, for: PA, p. 15. **In his sixteenth:** R2C, p. 8; CM, *Religious Societies* (1724); SML, p. 27; R2C, 27 Sep 1680; MS letter, Samuel Bache to CM, 28 Feb 1682, BPL; M, pp. 624, 352, 606; DI, p. 34. **But that Cotton:** PA, pp. 15, 17; IMD, 6 Sep 1680; Chandler Robbins, *A History of the Second Church, or Old North, in Boston* (Boston, 1852), p. 216; A, p. 310; IMD, 11 May 1683. **Cotton feared being:** CM, *Addresses to Old Men, and Young Men, and Little Children* (1690), p. 105; MAP, Reel 3C, fr. 0454; DI, pp. 36, 20. **Increase's grave illnesses:** MAP, Reel 7, fr. 0012; MAP, Reel 3C; DI, p. 22; MS letter, CM to Richard Chiswell, 27 Nov 1683, Bodleian Library; DI, p. 63. **Cotton was correct:** R2C, 23 Feb 1681, 8 Jan 1683. **How intently the:** IMD, 8 Sep 1681; Massachusetts Archives, XI, 15. **Yet Increase did:** IM, *Practical Truths* (1682), Preface; SML, p. 27; A, p. 310. **Cotton also received:** M, pp. 611, 607; DI, p. 53; PA, p. 19. **Yet Increase seems:** PA, p. 19. **Cotton spent much:** DI, p. 9. **To discern whether:** PA, p. 19; CM, *Religious Societies,* p. 11; DI, pp. 79, 32; MAP, Reel 3C, fr. 0537. **Cotton also felt:** DI, p. 15; P, p. 27; DI, pp. 36, 93, 16. As his own son, Samuel, later wrote of CM, "while he was yet young he bid fair to be *great* for he *believed* he should be so: he *expected* it" (SML, p. 6). **The stains on:** DI, pp. 21, 5, 11, 34, 17, 39. **But having identified:** DI, pp. 28, 69. **This certainty that:** DI, pp. 6, 22, 91. **However brokenhearted, Cotton:** DI, p. 8; PA, p. 43. **Cycles of assurance:** DI, p. 35; PA, p. 44. **Such high attainments:** PA, p. 201; MAP, Reel 3D, fr. 0038; PA, p. 38. **Some means of:** CM, *The Retired Christian* (1703), p. 2; DI, p. 58. Until around the fall of 1683, CM apparently kept a diary similar to his father's, telegraphically brief entries on the day's activities, especially his reading. He found this a waste of time, however, and apparently burned the diary. The earlier years of his surviving diaries also are a revised version of some *ur-*Diary, a record of his spiritual struggle intended for profitable reading by his children and others in the future. **As if he:** DI, pp. 41, 37, 72; PA, p. 65; DI, pp. 29, 71; PA, pp. 41, 67; DI, p. 94. **Not even this:** DI, p. 62; PA, p. 50; DI, pp. 81-84; PA, p. 50. **As Cotton noted:** DI, pp. 37, 80, 81. **"Give my Stammering:** CM, *Religious Societies,* p. 18; Carol Gay, "The Fettered Tongue: A Study of the Speech Defect of Cotton Mather," *American Literature,* XLVI (1975), 451-64; IMD, 6 Sep 1680. **During the first:** DI, pp. 2, 49, 50. **Cotton tried as:** DI, p. 49; MAP, Reel 3C, fr. 0426. **In seeking the:** DI, pp. 16, 70; MAP, Reel 3C, fr. 0426; DI, p. 55. **In fact, Cotton:** CM, *The Angel of Bethesda,* ed. Gordon W. Jones (Barre, Mass., 1972), p. 228; MAP, Reel 3C, fr. 0326; DI, p. 67. There seems little doubt that CM's stutter was largely the product of his anger. One authority writes that where anger is inhibited by parental and cultural disapproval, fear and anxiety become attached to it, and to the child's feelings, thoughts, and words at the time he or she feels angry. Among other evidence of the child's distress is stuttering, "the inhibition of speaking for fear of revealing anger and its several associates." *Stuttering: A Second Symposium,* ed. Jon Eisenson (New York, 1975), p. 438. **Cotton seems to:** DI, p. 77; SML, p. 20; DI, p. 93; SLCM, p. 6. **Meanwhile, Cotton had:** PA, p. 54; DI, pp. 92, 132. **Cotton's deliberateness and:** Massachusetts Archives, X, 196. Among CM's adolescent draftings of other public documents see also Massachusetts Archives, XI, 8a and 21a. **And beginning in:** DI, p. 284; CM, *Angel of Bethesda,* p. 228. I do not intend the foregoing discussion as an Ephphatha, magically unlocking the secret of CM's personality and works. Both were obviously the sum of much more than his stutter, whose own origin is anyway obscure. Yet I do believe that his feelings about his stutter and his efforts to control it influenced many of his later non-speaking activities, and help explain many features of his writing—its voluminousness, repetitiousness, frequent long-windedness, and pervasive oral imagery—as well as his acute sensitivity to criticism of his style. Needless to say, these too were not the product of his stutter alone. In his book *Stuttering: A Psychodynamic Approach to its Understanding and Treatment* (New York, 1954), Dominick A. Barbara describes the working in some stutterers of what he calls the "*Demosthenes complex.*" His elaborate discussion defies brief summary, but is virtually a blueprint of CM's adult personality, and applicable to his written work as well. Such stutterers, Barbara explains, are often the children of persons who stress intellectual values and social prominence. Speech begins to dominate their lives, and they feel compelled to excel in something they feel is most lacking in themselves. "Through words," Barbara writes, such a stutterer "feels he can either triumph or succumb in relation to the world about him. Whenever he expresses himself, he should be able to hold the absolute attention of others and to keep his listeners in a constant state of enthusiasm and enlightenment. With words he should be powerful enough 'to build or destroy empires.' His speech becomes filled with feelings of utter perfection, boundless ambition, and rage at the slightest awareness of shortcomings or realistic inconsistencies in himself." In addition to being the wittiest and most intelligent, he must also remain honest, considerate, unselfish, and above all uncomplaining. Yet, understandably, he carries a hidden grudge, in believing he has been humiliated and shamed since childhood because of his affliction. And he uses these early hurts "to feel justified in humiliating, hurting, and vindictively triumphing over others in a compulsively indiscriminate manner" (pp. 103, 110). I believe this goes far in explaining CM's later strong feelings of envy, jealousy, and resentment toward others. **Some connection between:** Thomas Prince, *The Departure of ELIJAH lamented* (1728), p. 24. **Cotton's stutter may:** CM, *Angel of Bethesda,* p. 228; M, p. 379. **Cotton's affections and:** PA, p. 17. **Cotton says virtually:** the volume of John Cotton's sermons is at AAS, among the Cotton Family Papers; MCA, IV, 211; MS letter, Nathanael Mather to John Cotton, [ca. Jul 1685], MHS. **Among his numerous:** Josiah Cotton, MS account of Cotton family, Houghton Library, Harvard University; Josiah Cotton MS journal, MHS; SSD, I, 379, n. 14. **But the many:** Josiah Cotton, MS account; M, p. 251 *et passim;* SLCM, p. 19; M, p. 246; SF #1915 (23 [Jul?]) 1679). **From Boston Cotton:** SLCM, p. 6. **Within his family:** Theodore Hornberger, "Puritanism and Science: The Relationship Revealed in the Writings of John Cotton," *New England Quarterly,* X (1937), q. p. 513; MCA, IV, 211; MS letter, Nathanael Mather to John Cotton; Michael G. Hall, "The Introduction of Modern Science into 17th-Century New England: Increase Mather," *Ithaca 26 VIII 1962-2 IX 1962* (Paris, 1964), pp. 261-64; IM to John Richards, 10 Nov 1682, W, Reel 12. **The Cotton and:** M, p. 63; A, p. 307; Raymond Phineas Stearns, *Science in the British Colonies of America* (Urbana, Ill., 1970), pp. 150 ff.; IMD, 23 Jul 1683. **Cotton later described:** P, p. 86; Massachusetts Archives, LVIII, 133; Stearns, *Science in the British Colonies,* p. 156. **Although far older:** MS letter, Avery to CM, 10 Nov 1683, BPL; on Avery, see notes at Countway Library of Medicine, Harvard Medical School; George L. Kittredge, "Letters of Samuel Lee and Samuel Sewall Relating to New England and the Indians," PCSM, XIV (1913), 164; MS letter, Boyle to Avery, 6 Oct 1685, MHS; MS letter, Avery to Boyle [in CM's hand], [no day] Jul 1683, MHS. **Cotton also took:** M, p. 638; CM, *Elegy on . . . Collins,* p. 5; MAP, Reel 7, fr. 0011. **The beginning of:** R2C, 31 Jul 1684; A, p. 310. **But Increase still:** MAP, Reel 3C, fr. 0596-97; DI, p. 93. **Cotton's ordination was:** DI, p. 97, PA, p. 76. **On the morning:** PA, p. 76; DI, p. 98. **In this state:** DI, p. 98; DII, p. 415. **Cotton began the:** DI, p. 98. **Having spoken three:** MAP, Reel 3D, fr. 0042-48. **Cotton's ordination as:** CM, *Ratio Disciplinae* (1726), pp. 10 ff. **Now Increase and:** DI, p. 99. **The minister chosen:** MCA, III, 186; DI, p. 99. **Elevated into partnership:** MAP, Reel 3D, fr. 0047-48; SSD, I, 63. **Within about a:** DI, pp. 102-3; R2C, Oct and Nov 1685; DI, p. 114; SLCM, p. 17; A, p. 313; Kenneth Ballard Murdock, *Increase Mather: The Foremost American Puritan* (Cambridge, Mass., 1926), pp. 178-79. **Cotton preached extensively:** DI, pp. 109, 122; CM, *The Call of the Gospel (1686),* p. 51; SSD, I, 99; CM, MS sermon notebooks, HL, 11 Mar 1686. **Morgan perhaps sensed:** CM, *Call of the Gospel,* pp. 124 *et passim.* **Cotton's concern for:** DI, pp. 122-23, 132. **While pleased by:** MAP, Reel 3D, fr. 0047; M, p. 514; SSD, I, 94-95. **If Cotton's plush:** MAP, Reel 3D, fr. 0340; MAP, Reel 7, fr. 0477; DI, p. 90; IM, *A Sermon Occasioned by the Execution* (1686), sig. A3. **Especially Cotton feared:** DI, p. 126; Deloraine Pendre Corey, *The History of Malden* (Malden, Mass., 1899), pp. 266 ff.; DI, p. 125. **Cotton completed his:** DI, pp. 104, 107, 124. **Around his birthday:** DI, p. 121; *Genealogies and Estates of Charlestown . . . 1629-1818,* ed. Thomas Wyman (Boston, 1879), II, 740-41; Middlesex County Registry of Deeds, VIII: 501-2, IX:237, X:5; CM, MS sermon notebooks, HL, 30 May 1686. **Despite mounting spiritual:** PA, p. 89; DI,

p. 127. **The wedding, Cotton:** PA, p. 89; DI, pp. 127, 129. **From the first:** DI, pp. 131, 127, 133; MAP, Reel 4A, fr. 0021; DI, p. 131. **Yet as happened:** CM, MS sermon notebooks, HL, 30 May 1686; MAP, Reel 4A, fr. 0044; MS sermon notebooks, HL, 23 May 1686; MAP, Reel 4A, fr. 0049 and 0030. **A year before:** MCA, IV, 206. **It was about:** DI, p. 129.

3. The Glorious Revolution

The mentality of: "Diary of John Hull," *Transactions and Collections of the American Antiquarian Society,* III (1857), 236–37; John Gorham Palfrey, *History of New England* (Boston, 1875, 1890), II, 465 ff. and III, 88 ff. **The elements in:** IM, *Remarkable Providences* (1684; rpt. London, 1890), p. 228; "Diary of Increase Mather," PMHS, 2nd ser., XIII (1899–1900), 407; George J. Lankevich, *Boston: A Chronological & Documentary History* (Dobbs Ferry, N.Y., 1974), p. 11; "Diary of John Hull," *passim;* Peter Gregg Slater, *Children in the New England Mind in Death and in Life* (Hamden, Conn., 1977), p. 16; Lankevich, *Boston,* p. 11; SLCM, p. 7. **The Puritans' habit:** CM, *The Terror of the Lord* (1727), Appendix, p. 4; IM, *Heaven's Alarm to the World* (1682), p. 28; Williston Walker, *The Creeds and Platforms of Congregationalism* (1893; rpt. Philadelphia and Boston, 1969), q. pp. 410–11; M, p. 594. I am aware of the large body of recent scholarship that hears in these groanings a "myth" of decline. It argues that later generations of Puritans felt an exaggerated reverence for their forebears, and demanded more of themselves than did the earlier generations; they perceived a decline, the argument runs, only from the viewpoint of these unrealistic demands. I consider this interpretation wrong, but the question is too complex to discuss here. Generally, it seems to me that most scholars who speak of a myth of decline fail to make clear the standards by which the intensity and authenticity of religious experience may be judged. What the second and third generations of Puritans considered a decline embraced the social as well as the strictly religious; indeed the two were never for the Puritans separable. And the social decline was unmistakably real. **Among the chief:** Walker, *Creeds and Platforms,* p. 264 f. **Christian Israel felt:** "Diary of John Hull," p. 232; Carl Bridenbaugh, *Cities in the Wilderness* (New York, 1938), p. 72; SSD, I, 9, 4, 83; *A Report of the Record Commissioners . . . Containing the Boston Records from 1660 to 1701* (Boston, 1881), p. 139; Hamilton Andrews Hill, *History of the Old South Church* (Boston, 1890), q. p. 193; "Diary of Lawrence Hammond," PMHS, 2nd ser., VII (1891–92), 169. **The courts and:** *Records of the Governor and Company of the Massachusetts Bay in New England,* ed. Nathaniel B. Shurtleff (Boston, 1853–54), V, 59; IM, *A Call from Heaven* (1685), pp. 77, 39; Massachusetts Archives, X, 196. **But however alarming:** *Records of the Governor and Company,* IV, pt. 2, p. 166. **The royal commissioners:** *The Glorious Revolution in America,* ed. Michael G. Hall *et al.* (Chapel Hill, N.C., 1964), p. 10. **In their own:** Palfrey, *History of New England,* III, 39; *Records of the Governor and Company,* IV, pt. 2, p. 216. **Domestic and international:** David S. Lovejoy, *The Glorious Revolution in America* (New York, 1972), ch. 7 *passim; Records of the Governor and Company,* V, 495. **In the public:** MS letter, Nathanael Mather to John Cotton [*ca.* Jul 1685], MHS; IMD, 21 Jan 1684; Lovejoy, *Glorious Revolution,* pp. 154–55. **That New England's:** A, p. 313. **The following Monday:** SSD, I, 113–15. **Until the arrival:** *John Dunton's Letters from New-England* (Boston, 1867), p. 137; SSD, I, 116. **The full meaning:** SSD, I, 128. **Andros's seeming appeasement:** SSD, I, 135; Hill, *History of the Old South,* p. 267; SSD, I, 136. **The new government:** Lovejoy, *Glorious Revolution,* ch. 10; SSD, I, 143; *The Andros Tracts* (Boston, 1868), III, 124; Palfrey, *History of New England,* III, 554. **A possible means:** SSD, I, 140; A, p. 320; *Andros Tracts,* III, 124;

M, pp. 105, 102; A, p. 309; MAP, Reel 4A, fr. 0380. **Increase now openly:** MAP, Reel 4A, fr. 0412; A, p. 322. **About ten o'clock:** this and the next paragraph from A, pp. 322-23. **While Increase was:** this and the next paragraph from DI, pp. xxi-xxii (misdated 1691). **Other fragmentary evidence:** MAP, Reel 3B, fr. 063 [*sic*]; M, p. 388; SLCM, p. 13; DI, pp. 80, 93; MAP, Reel 3D, fr. 0106. Like others, however, CM was at first wary of Andros but not alarmed by his behavior. See SLCM, p. 19. **Exactly how soon:** Thomas Hutchinson, *The History of the Colony and Province of Massachusetts-Bay,* ed. Lawrence Shaw Mayo (Cambridge, Mass., 1936), I, 316n. **Andros had cause:** A, p. 331 (on the lost letters, see IM to John Richards, 17 Oct 1688, W, Reel 13); M, p. 531. **One month into:** *Andros Tracts,* II, 211; *Calendar of State Papers, Colonial Series, America and West Indies* (London, 1896-1937), XIII, 165; *Andros Tracts,* II, 211-12. On the authorship of *Brief Discourse,* see DI, pp. 133-34. **The Mathers' longtime:** *Andros Tracts,* II, 212; PA, p. 96. **The new threat:** Hutchinson, *History,* I, 317; Samuel G. Drake, *The History and Antiquities of Boston* (Boston, 1856), p. 481 f. **What remains of:** MAP, Reel 8, fr. 0069-71. **Four days later:** *Edward Randolph . . . 1678-1700* (1898-1909; rpt. New York, 1967), VI, 313; *Publications of the Prince Society,* XXX (1909), 291. **Whatever Cotton Mather's:** Lovejoy, *Glorious Revolution,* p. 240; Hall *et al., Glorious Revolution,* p. 50. **Cotton Mather spent:** in considering the authorship of the anonymous "Declaration," it should be remembered that the other Boston ministers were also present in the Council chamber. Randolph later said that these ministers, as a group, wrote some of the rebels' "printed papers," suggesting that the "Declaration" was the work of a committee (*Calendar of State Papers,* XIII, 47). Moreover, while no handwritten copy of the "Declaration" has survived, a related "Memoriall to explaine . . . the Declaration" does exist (MHS, Misc. Bound), written as an appendix to the "Declaration," and it is not in CM's hand. For these and other reasons, and lacking any evidence of Mather's authorship, I cannot accept Prof. David Levin's assumption that Mather wrote the "Declaration." See his *Cotton Mather: The Young Life of the Lord's Remembrancer 1663-1703* (Cambridge, Mass., 1978), p. 165. Lovejoy, above, makes no attempt to assign authorship to the document, wisely I believe. On the importance of the "Declaration" as a political document, see Theodore B. Lewis, "A Revolutionary Tradition, 1689-1774," *New England Quarterly,* XLVI (1973), 424-38. **All that can:** CM, *Decennium Luctuosum* (1699), pp. 27-28. **Whether Cotton Mather:** SML, pp. 42-43. **Cotton Mather seems:** *Calendar of State Papers,* XIII, pp. 47, 93; *Edward Randolph . . . 1678-1700,* VI, 313. **By then apparently:** Drake, *History and Antiquities,* p. 484; MCA, II, 45. **Having filled his:** Albert Matthews, "Notes on the Massachusetts Royal Commissions 1681-1775," PCSM, XVII (1915), 17. **Cotton Mather preached:** *The Wall and the Garden: Selected Massachusetts Election Sermons 1670-1775,* ed. A. W. Plumstead (Minneapolis, 1968), p. 135n; CM, *The Way to Prosperity* (1690), p. 30; SML, pp. 43-44; *Calendar of State Papers,* XIII, 95. On the debate over resumption of the charter and CM's position in it, see Richard R. Johnson, *Adjustment to Empire: The New England Colonies, 1675-1715* ([New Brunswick, N.J.,] 1981), pp. 94-106. **Whatever his doubts:** CM, *The Wonderful Works of God Commemorated* (1690), p. 43; Massachusetts Archives, XI, 45a. **Cotton Mather remained:** *Calendar of State Papers,* XIII, 384: M, p. 485; *Calendar of State Papers,* XIII, 165; MS letter, Myles to Board of Trade, 12 Dec. 1690, Phips Papers, MHS. **In July the:** *Calendar of State Papers,* XIII, 120, 111; CM, *The Present State of New-England* (1690), p. 28; SSD, I, 251-52; "Journal of Dr. Benjamin Bullivant," PMHS, 1st ser., XVI (1878), 105. **To eliminate France:** SLCM, p. 27; CM, *Present State of New-England,* p. 38. **The expedition was:** Palfrey, *History of New England,* IV, 51 ff.; SSD, I, 260; *Calendar of State Papers,* XIII, 369; *Publick Occurrences* (1690). **In this edgy:** Victor Hugo

Paltsits, "New Light on 'Publick Occurrences,'" PAAS, NS LIX (1949), 75–88. **Cotton Mather found:** SLCM, pp. 27–28. **Although this contrast:** PA, p. 92; CM, *Right Thoughts in Sad Hours* (London, 1689; text quotes Dunstable edition, 1811), pp. 21–22, 51. **In October 1689:** M, p. 672; MCA, IV, 211, 221–22. **Never able to:** CM, *Little Flocks Guarded* (1691), p. 7; CM bought the new house on 25 Jul 1688 (see Thwing card catalogue at MHS and Suffolk Deeds 17.1); the sermons survive as a bound manuscript of around two hundred very closely written pages in double columns, in MAP, Reel 7, fr. 0895 ff.; MS letter, IM to Richards, 4 Jun 1690 and 4 Jul 1691, W, Reel 13; DI, p. 147. **Much of this:** SLCM, pp. 25–26. **While awaiting his:** A, p. 338; DI, p. 113; Drake, *History and Antiquities,* p. 458n.; SLCM, p. 29. **The rumors came:** SSD, I, 291; DI, pp. 147–48. **Increase's four years:** MS sermon notes 1690–1694/5, AAS (in "Boston, Mass. Church Records"); A, p. 347; MAP, Reel 4B, fr. 0047 ff. **If the Mathers:** MS letter, Josh[ua?] Brodbent to Francis Nicholson, 21 Jun 1692, Phips Papers, II, MHS; DI, p. 148. **Cotton Mather also:** A, pp. 335–36; P, p. 143. **Opposition to the:** MAP, Reel 4B, fr. 0120; CM, *Optanda* (1692), p. 86. **Cotton also wrote:** CM, "Political Fables," in *Cotton Mather: Selections,* ed. Kenneth B. Murdock (New York, 1926), pp. 364, 367. **The charter's full:** MAP, Reel 4B, fr. 0051.

4. Letters of Thanks from Hell

To Cotton Mather: quotations in this and the next six paragraphs are all from CM, *Memorable Providences, Relating to Witchcrafts and Possessions* (1689), in *Narratives of the Witchcraft Cases 1648–1706,* ed. George Lincoln Burr (New York, 1914), pp. 93–143. **Mather's experience with:** CM, *Memorable Providences,* p. 123; R2C, 25 Jan 1691; MS letter, Sir Henry Ashurst to CM, 28 Dec 1691, AAS. The historian Thomas Hutchinson later wrote of the Goodwin case contemptuously, but he also remarked that he knew one of the Goodwin children, probably Martha, when she was an adult, and that she "had the character of a very sober, virtuous woman, and never made any acknowledgment of fraud in this transaction." Samuel G. Drake, *The History and Antiquities of Boston* (Boston, 1856), q. p. 496n. **The book had:** John Hale, *A Modest Enquiry Into the Nature of Witchcraft* (1702), in Burr, *Narratives,* pp. 413–14. **The linking of:** MS letter, Josh[ua?] Brodbent to Francis Nicholson, 21 Jun 1692, Phips Papers, II, MHS; Robert Calef, *More Wonders of the Invisible World* (1700; the text follows the 1861 Salem edition, published as *Salem Witchcraft*), p. 357. **Even ignoring Calef's:** CM, *Little Flocks Guarded* (1691), p. 9; CM, *Addresses to Old Men, and Young Men, and Little Children* (1690), p. 48; CM, *The Present State of New-England* (1690), p. 38; CM, *Fair Weather* (1692), p. 50. **Yet in preaching:** MAP, Reel 4A, fr. 0441; Willard sermons in Edward Bromfield's MS notes of sermons, MHS; MAP, Reels 3C and 3D. IM was widely read in pneumatology and fascinated by the invisible world. In England as a young man he spoke with a jailed witch, who confessed to him that every night for years the devil "had the use of her body." Edward Taylor Commonplace Book, MHS. **More important, if:** *The New York Times,* 23 Mar 1981, p. B6; H. R. Trevor-Roper, *The European Witch-Craze of the Sixteenth and Seventeenth Centuries and Other Essays* (New York, 1969), pp. 156–57; Frederick G. Drake, "Witchcraft in the American Colonies, 1647–62," *American Quarterly,* XX (1968), 697; "Diary of Noahdiah Russell," NEHGR, VII (1853), 59; IM, *Remarkable Providences,* in Burr, *Narratives,* pp. 37–38; CM, *Memorable Providences,* Burr, *Narratives,* pp. 131–34. **It must also:** sociologically, according to Keith Thomas, most witchcraft cases express "an unresolved conflict between the neighbourly conduct required by the ethical code of the old village community, and the increasingly individualistic forms of behaviour which

accompanied the economic changes of the sixteenth and seventeenth centuries."
Thomas, *Religion and the Decline of Magic* (New York, 1971), p. 561. That was true
of Salem, where charges of witchcraft expressed antagonism between the village
and the growingly commercial town. See Paul Boyer and Stephen Nissenbaum, *Salem Possessed: The Social Origins of Witchcraft* (Cambridge, Mass., 1974). **To us,
the:** Gananath Obeyesekere, "The Idiom of Demonic Possession," *Social Science
and Medicine,* IV (1970), 97–111; CM, *Memorable Providences,* Burr, *Narratives,*
p. 121. **When read in:** CM, *Memorable Providences,* Burr, *Narratives,* pp. 109, 125,
119. **Mather and his:** CM, "A Discourse on Witchcraft," in *Memorable Providences
Relating to Witchcrafts and Possessions* (1689), p. 4. CM's definition is close to
perhaps the best-known definition of witchcraft at the time, that in Joseph Glanvill's
Saducismus Triumphatus (3rd ed. 1689; rpt. Gainesville, Fla., 1966). Glanvill calls a
witch one who *"can do or seems to do strange things, beyond the known Power of
Art and ordinary Nature, by vertue of a Confedercy [sic] with Evil Spirits"* (p. 269).
Mather held the: CM, "A Discourse on the Power and Malice of the Devils," in
Memorable Providences (1689), pp. 2, 10, 4; CM, "A Discourse on Witchcraft," p. 6.
In their physical: CM, "Discourse on . . . Devils," p. 2; Wallace Notestein, *A History of Witchcraft in England* (1911; rpt. New York, 1968), p. 286. **Mather's view of:**
Moody E. Prior, "Joseph Glanvill, Witchcraft, and Seventeenth-Century Science,"
Modern Philology, XXI (1932–33), q. pp. 178–79; CM, "Discourse on Witchcraft,"
p. 16; CM, *Memorable Providences,* Burr, *Narratives,* p. 98. **Mather also longed:**
CM, *Memorable Providences,* Burr, *Narratives,* p. 98; DI, p. 23; MS sermon notebooks, HL, 23 May 1686; CM, *Memorable Providences,* Burr, *Narratives,* p. 120.
Mather's determined defense: Prior, "Joseph Glanvill," pp. 170–93; Glanvill,
Saducismus, Introduction. Glanvill and IM corresponded. **In the style:** CM, *Brontologia Sacra* (London, 1695), in MCA, VI, 16–17, 20; CM, "Another Brand Pluckt
out of the Burning," in Burr, *Narratives,* p. 313; CM, *The Wonders of the Invisible
World* (1693; London, 1862), p. 52. **Cotton Mather's concern:** CM, "Discourse on
Witchcraft," p. 25; "Mather-Calef Paper on Witchcraft," PMHS, XLVII (1913–14),
258; CM, *Memorable Providences,* Burr, *Narratives,* p. 102. Like other ministers, CM
often denounced the widespread dabbling in amulets, fortune-telling, astrology,
and other magical practices, inveighing against them not only as a form of non-
institutional popular religion, but also because he believed in magic and feared its
potency. In BA, he transcribed a magical practice in Latin and Hebrew so that "Ordinary Readers" would not be tempted to test it "and give the *Devil* a command over
themselves" (section headed "Psalms Psalms"). CM often flirted with magic himself, especially sortilege. In the "Mather-Calef Paper" he claims to have personal
knowledge of someone who could find missing objects by muttering a charm. See
also Jon Butler, "Magic, Astrology, and the Early American Religious Heritage,
1600–1760," *American Historical Review,* LXXXIV (1979), 317–46. **The Goodwin
case:** CM, "Discourse on Witchcraft," p. 29. **The surest test:** CM, *Wonders of the
Invisible World,* q. p. 32; CM, "Discourse on Witchcraft," p. 9. **Pretrial examinations were:** SVW, pp. 5, 8, 10, 9. **A jury found:** SVW, pp. 10, 16; "Sundry Documents Relating to Witchcraft in Massachusetts," NEHGR, LXX (1916), 65–66; Deodat Lawson, *A Brief and True Narrative* (1692), in Burr, *Narratives,* p. 159; SVW,
p. 16. **By April 11:** SVW, pp. 99, 120. **As these events:** DI, pp. 147, 152; SLCM,
p. 35. Judging by the unusual gaps, brief entries, and messy script of CM's sermon
notebooks in this period, he seems to have been ill much of March, April, and May
1692. See MAP, Reel 4B. **However ill, Cotton:** SLCM, pp. 35–40. **Much as he:** SWP,
III, 749; George Lyman Kittredge, "Notes on Witchcraft," PAAS, NS XVIII (1906–7),
197–98; SLCM, p. 36. CM believed that devils could produce whatever shapes they
pleased. In BA (I Sam. 27, 28) he argues that such biblical apparitions as the specter

of Samuel that appeared to Saul were probably "*Cacodaemons,* which feigned themselves to be the *Spirits* of men departed." While the devil cannot use a departed soul for his purpose, CM explains, he can feign its likeness, having power to assume an innocent shape. By witches, it might be added, CM understood both men and women. See BA, Exod. 22. **Such further evidence:** SLCM, pp. 39, 37–38. **On the ultimate:** DI, p. 149; SLCM, p. 40. **By the standards:** SVW, pp. 45, 47, 51. **Bishop's execution alarmed:** italics reversed in quotations in this and the next paragraph. **Had this document:** Robert Calef, *More Wonders* (Salem ed.), p. 362. **Calef's very astute:** on Richards's close ties to the Mathers, see "Richards, John" Thwing card catalogue, MHS; MS document, "Cotton Mather, subscribers to salary," Curwen Papers, AAS; M, p. 494; John Richards Treasurer's Accounts 1669–1693, Pusey Library, Harvard University; SLCM, pp. 46–50. On CM's ties to the others see, *inter alia,* CM, *Memorable Providences,* Burr, *Narratives,* p. 94; SLCM, M, SSD, DI and DII. **And, in particular:** John L. Sibley, *Biographical Sketches of Graduates of Harvard University* (Cambridge, Mass., 1873–1975), I, q. 200; *Records of the First Church in Dorchester* (Boston, 1891), pp. 41, 93; inscribed copy at MHS; SLCM, p. 43. CM may have composed the very lengthy, adulatory epitaph on Stoughton's tombstone. See *History of the Town of Dorchester, Massachusetts* (Boston, 1859), p. 277. **Cotton Mather's relation:** DI, p. 148; CM, *Optanda* (1692), pp. 86, 14, 68. **The "ambidexterity" of:** DI, p. 151; SLCM, pp. 40, 37. Stoughton aside, the judges' behavior should not be too quickly dismissed as irrational. Some judges tried to square their legal principles with the facts of the case viewed in light of recent scientific knowledge. See for instance Burr, *Narratives,* pp. 171–72. **Indeed, Cotton Mather:** SLCM, p. 37; DI, p. 150 (the revision appears in the MS diary, MAP, Reel 1); SLCM, p. 37. **The court turned:** Brodbent to Nicholson; SVW, pp. 13 ff. **Despite the cautions:** SVW, p. 121; SWP, I, pp. 376, 375, 374; Calef, *More Wonders,* Burr, *Narratives,* p. 358. **Considering Cotton Mather's:** SLCM, p. 40. **The confession of:** "Letter of Thomas Brattle," in Burr, *Narratives,* pp. 180–81; Calef, *More Wonders,* Burr, *Narratives,* p. 375; SWP, II, 689. **Cotton Mather may:** CM, *Wonders of the Invisible World,* pp. 102–3; SWP, III, 882. **Virtually all the:** SWP, II, 527–28 *et passim.* **But the most:** SWP, II, 522; SWP, I, 66; SWP, II, 647–48; SWP, III, 769. **To Cotton Mather:** see Norman Cohn, *Europe's Inner Demons* (New York, 1975), esp. p. 262. **On August 4:** SLCM, p. 40; "Diary of Lawrence Hammond," PMHS, 2nd ser., VII (1891–92), 163; CM, *Wonders of the Invisible World,* p. 38. **Like other Puritan:** quotations in this and the next two paragraphs are from the sermon as printed in CM, *Wonders of the Invisible World,* pp. 38–107. **Knowing his time:** *The Works of the Pious and Profoundly-Learned Joseph Mede, B.D.* (3rd ed., London, 1672), p. 800. Mede seems to apply his theory to Mexico and South America, but it became extended, perhaps by the Puritans, to North America as well. Many in England saw America as uniquely prone to pneumatological wonders. Richard Baxter, for instance, reported the view "That in *America,* it is a common thing to see Spirits appear to Men in various Shapes day and night." *The Certainty of the Worlds of Spirits* (London, 1691), p. 107. For CM's other versions of Mede's views see his *Souldiers Counselled and Comforted* (1689) and his French Preface to Ezekiel Carré's *Enchantillon* (1690). **Mather's sermon indicates:** CM's bafflement also appears in his letter to the witchcraft judge John Foster on August 17, in which he offers the judges, in about equal measure, encouragement, caution, and perplexity, and rightly concludes, "Sir, you see the incoherence of my thoughts" (SLCM, p. 43). **For the first:** DI, pp. 151–52. **The two surviving:** SSD, I, 294; Calef, *More Wonders,* Burr, *Narratives,* pp. 360–61. **Both these accounts:** SWP, I, 132, and II, 617; SLCM, p. 43; SVW, p. 75; CM, *Wonders of the Invisible World,* p. 159; SLCM, p. 40. **With apparently hundreds:** H, III, 1261, n. 12; *Calendar of State Papers, Colonial*

Series, America and West Indies (London, 1896-1937), XIV, 63; Hamilton Andrews Hill, *History of the Old South Church* (Boston, 1890), pp. 286 ff.; P, p. 167. **Accustomed to putting:** SLCM, pp. 43-44. **While Cotton Mather:** Calef, *More Wonders,* Burr, *Narratives,* p. 367. **The next day:** "Letters of Cotton Mather," NEHGR, XXIV (1870), 107-8. **The same day:** "Diary of Lawrence Hammond," p. 164; SVW, p. 121. **Advice came to:** I have followed the text of *Cases* included in the London 1862 edition of CM's *Wonders of the Invisible World.* **The one was:** SLCM, pp. 45-46. **Around mid-October, just:** all quotations from *Wonders of the Invisible World* in this and the following four paragraphs are from the London 1862 edition. **Although the book:** on English notices, see George H. Moore, "Notes on the Bibliography of Witchcraft in Massachusetts," PAAS, NS V (1887-88), 259 ff. **These insistent disclosures:** on Baxter, see Drake, *History and Antiquities,* p. 496n.; DI, pp. 153-54. **Cotton Mather's book:** DI, p. 153. **But Cotton Mather:** PA, p. 131. **Cotton Mather did:** DI, p. 154. **About ten days:** SSD, I, 299; SVW, p. 121. **Despite the suspension:** DI, p. 156; SLCM, p. 47. **Because of Increase's:** SLCM, pp. 46-47; R2C; DI, p. 162. **About three years:** R2C; on the significance of CM's *Companion,* see E. Brooks Holifield, "The Renaissance of Sacramental Piety in Colonial New England," *William and Mary Quarterly,* 3rd ser., XXIX (1972), 33-48. **The crux of:** "The Commonplace Book of Joseph Green (1675-1715)," ed. Samuel E. Morison, PCSM, XXXIV (1943), 240. **The acceptance of:** SVW, pp. 121-22. **On November 29:** the account of Mercy Short's case in this and the following paragraphs is drawn from CM, "A Brand Pluck'd out of the Burning," Burr, *Narratives,* pp. 259-87. **These and many:** CM, *Wonders of the Invisible World,* p. 161. **The notion of:** William B. Hunter, Jr., "The Seventeenth Century Doctrine of Plastic Nature," *Harvard Theological Review,* XLIII (1950), 197-213. **Just as important:** DI, pp. 156, 152; SLCM, p. 42. **On March 28:** DI, pp. 163-64. In a footnote, the editor of CM's *Diary* incorrectly identifies this infant as "Joseph." His error represents a misreading of CM's handwriting. In the list of his children that CM drew up on the back of one of his notebooks in late 1713 or early 1714 (MAP, Reel 2, fr. 0061), the infant is plainly listed as "Increase." The editor also wrongly attributed to CM a child named William, based on a like misreading of the handwritten name "Katharin" in this list. **Mather may have:** DI, p. 164. **Mercy's "Wonderful Spirit":** for Mercy's admission, see R2C, 21 Jan 1694. **Such good angels:** Calef, *More Wonders,* Burr, *Narratives,* p. 346. **Mather began longing:** PA, p. 110; DI, p. 163. **Mather's prayers for:** CM, *The Way to Excel* (1697), p. 6; CM, *Meat Out of the Eater* (1703), p. 88; MAP, Reel 7, fr. 0297. **While Mather's views:** IM, *Angelographia* (1696), p. 65; *The Practical Works of Richard Baxter* (London, 1845), I, 625; Jacques Guillet *et al., Discernment of Spirits* (Collegeville, Minn., 1970; my thanks to Mr. Jeff Donnelly for introducing me to the subject of spiritual discernment); Richard Baxter, *The Certainty of the Worlds of Spirits,* p. 222. **However it risked:** DI, pp. 166-67; PA, p. 111. **Mather made another:** DI, pp. 171-72; **As if in:** DI, pp. 172-73; CM, "Another Brand Pluckt out of the Burning," Burr, *Narratives,* pp. 308-23 (from which also the quotes in the next paragraph). **In its other:** DI, p. 175. **It was probably:** this and the next four paragraphs from DI, pp. 86-87. On the question of dating this visitation see my "Note on the Date of Cotton Mather's Visitation by an Angel," *Early American Literature,* XV (1980), 82-86, and compare David Levin, "When Did Cotton Mather See the Angel?" *ibid.,* pp. 271-75. Some further supporting evidence for dating the visitation around September 1693 is the sermon CM preached on 3 Sep 1693, in which he remarked suggestively that "Of the beings of spirits there is manifest demonstration as Good Angels appearing to some" (MS sermon notes, 1690-94/5, AAS, identified as "Boston, Mass. Church Records"). For the translation of CM's Latin here I have followed that given in DI, with some revisions by Professor Robert Raymo. Here and elsewhere I have also reproduced the Latin entries in CM's diaries as transcribed by their editor, although the transcriptions would seem in a few places to be inaccurate. **However extraordinary, Cotton:** *Hallucinations: Behaviour, Experience, and Theory,* ed. R. K. Siegel and L. J. West (New York, 1975), *passim;* BA Cor. I. 10. **As a Puritan:** A, p. 345; MAP, Reel 4B, fr. 0362 ff. Hallucinatory experiences occurred often enough among Puritans to create notice but not wonderment. Several are recorded in the diary of the Harvard tutor Noahdiah Russell, NEHGR, VII (1853), 53-59. **Like the demons:** one authority remarks that the voices in the auditory hallucinations of schizophrenic persons are "fused with the patient's image of self" and "speak the patient's own thoughts." *Hallucinations,* ed. Louis Jolyon West (New York and London, 1962), p. 169; DI, p. 16. **Mather's need at:** CM, "Another Brand," Burr, *Narratives,* p. 321. **As Mather usually:** CM, *The Day, & the Work of the Day* (1693), p. 65; CM, *The Short History of New-England* (1694), p. 32; DI, p. 175; CM, "Another Brand," Burr, *Narratives,* p. 320; CM, *Meat Out of the Eater,* p. 35. For CM's further references to good and evil angels at this time see his *Warnings from the Dead* (1693) and the MS sermon notes, 1690-94/5, at AAS. **Mather's most vigorous:** a "Robert Calef of Boston Dyer" appears in an anonymous MS account book, 1702-1715, MHS (Ms-L); Calef, *More Wonders,* Salem ed., pp. 359, 113; Burr, *Narratives,* p. 326. **On September 13:** Calef, *More Wonders,* Burr, *Narratives,* pp. 324-26. **This "lying Libel":** DI, pp. 172-73; Calef, *More Wonders,* Burr, *Narratives,* p. 329. **Instead Mather indignantly:** this and the next paragraph from Calef, *More Wonders,* Burr, *Narratives,* pp. 333-39. **Mather and Calef:** Calef, *More Wonders,* Salem ed., pp. 116-17, 90. **Calef kept needling:** quotations in this and the next two paragraphs from the "Mather-Calef Paper." **The good angels:** "Records of the Cambridge Association," PMHS, XVII (1879-80), 271. **The counterdescent of:** R2C; MAP, Reel 4B, fr. 0249; P, p. 194. CM's nephew, Mather Byles, later recalled this rise in admissions as "a great Revival of the Work of God . . . at the Old No. Church." *Savage Papers,* PMHS, XLIV (1910-11), 685. **Both Mathers regarded:** *Savage Papers,* pp. 685-86. This episode and the one recounted in the next paragraph cannot be dated certainly, but both seem to have occurred in the fall of 1694. **A second young:** "Mather-Calef Paper," pp. 266-67. **However cautious about:** this and the last two paragraphs from PA, pp. 120-26.

5. The Parter's Portion

Six months into: MCA, II, 67; oath of Joseph Short and John Hams, 25 Mar 1693, Phips Papers, III, MHS; deposition of William Hill and Henry Francklyn, 17 Jul 1694, Phips Papers, V, MHS. **The governor treated:** unsigned, unaddressed "Letter from New England," 1 Nov 1694, Phips Papers, IV, MHS; SSD, I, 323 and n. **The unreliability of:** MS diary of Thomas Marshall, 1689-1711, MHS; CM, *To His Excellency Richard, Earl of Bellomont* (1699); DI, p. 302. **Cotton Mather's hope:** "Earl of Bellomont," NEHGR, XIX (1865), 236. **The succession of:** CM, *A Pillar of Gratitude* (1700), pp. 32-33; on the adaptation of New England to English political standards after the loss of the charter see Richard R. Johnson, *Adjustment to Empire: The New England Colonies 1675-1715* ([New Brunswick, N.J.], 1981), ch. V. **In this spirit:** the *Heads of Agreement* is reprinted in Williston Walker, *The Creeds and Platforms of Congregationalism* (1893; rpt. Philadelphia, 1960), pp. 455-62; CM, *A Letter of Advice to the . . . Non-conformists* (London, 1700), pp. 1-2. In England the union was short-lived, for the United Brethren fell apart within a few years in theological controversy. **Mather moved even:** DI, p. 149. On the growth of toleration, see G. R. Cragg, *From Puritanism to the Age of Reason* (Cambridge, England, 1950), ch. IX. **To show himself:** MS "Ratio Disciplinae," MAP, Reel 5, fr. 0130; CM, *Blessed Unions* (1692), pp. 76, 75. Becoming something of a spiritual statesman, CM also wrote at this time many works calling attention to distant religious persecution and assaying the current conditions of global Protestantism. See for instance *A Pastoral Letter to the English Captives, in Africa* (1698), *A Letter Concerning . . . Our Protestant Brethren, on Board the French Kings Galleyes* (1701), and *American Tears upon the Ruines of the Greek Churches* (1701). **While opening Christian:** on IM's opposition, see Niel Caplan, "Some Unpublished Letters of Benjamin Colman, 1717–1725," PMHS, LXXVII (1965), 116. **Yet in an:** MAP, Reel 8, fr. 0488–89; MS letter, CM to brethren of Marlborough church, 28 May 1702, Marlborough Public Library; SVW, p. 308. **In the same:** Walker, *Creeds and Platforms,* p. 469; "Records of the Cambridge Association," PMHS, XVII (1879–80), 254–81. **Mather also wished:** on May see also DI, pp. 313–15, 318, 323–24. **A more dolorous:** SSD, I, 378 and n. (the same shipbuilder called the charge "a Base piece of villainy that the man was no more Guilty of . . . than you or I was," *ibid.*); DI, p. 236 (on CM's agreement with the condemnation, see SSD, I, 379, where "Mr. Mather" probably refers to CM, as opposed to his father, "Dr." Mather); MS letter, John Cotton to Rowland Cotton, 1 Feb 1698, MHS; MS letter, John Cotton to Joanna Cotton, 6 Jul 1698, MHS; DI, p. 277. **In or out:** of CM's many writings on reform in this period (which make a valuable digest of his social views), see for instance *A Good Master Well Served* (1696), *A Family Well-Ordered* (1699), *The Young Man's Preservative* (1701), *A Christian at his Calling* (1701), *A Cloud of Witnesses* (1701?), *Methods and Motives for Societies to Suppress Disorders* (1703), and *The Day Which the LORD hath made* (1707). **Mather did not:** Richard F. Lovelace, *The American Pietism of Cotton Mather* (Grand Rapids, 1979), pp. 258–59; Robert Middlekauff, *The Mathers* (New York, 1971), p. 215. **It is more:** Henry Latimer Seaver, "Hair and Holiness," PMHS, LXVIII (1944–47), q. p. 16; SSD, I, 276. **In another dozen:** "Letter of Reverend Benjamin Colman," PCSM, VIII (1906), 247, 249. **This genial advice:** John L. Sibley, *Biographical Sketches of Graduates of Harvard University* (Cambridge, Mass., 1873–1975), IV, 122–23; Ebenezer Turell, *The Life and Character of the Reverend Benjamin Colman, D.D.* (1749; rpt. Delmar, N.Y., 1972), pp. 231, 5. **A Presbyterian Board:** "Memoirs of Rev. Benjamin Colman," NEHGR, III (1849), 112n. *et passim.* On ministerial identity, see David D. Hall, *The Faithful Shepherd* (Chapel Hill, 1972), pp. 223, 272. **The organizers of:** Henry Wilder Foote, *Annals of King's Chapel* (Boston, 1882), I, 89–93; Marian Card Donnelly, "New England Meetinghouses in the Seventeenth Century," *Old-Time New England,* XLVII (1957), 91. **In December, shortly:** on the change in psalmody, see *Records of the Church in Brattle Square* (Boston, 1902), p. 5; typed transcript of MS letter, Henry Newman to the Bishop of London, 26 Feb 1726, MHS. **In fact the:** DI, pp. 325–26. **As a first:** DI, p. 326; "Memoir of Rev. Benjamin Colman," p. 117; SSD, I, 419; MS letter, IM and James Allen to Benjamin Colman (but in CM's hand), 28 Dec 1699, MHS; DI, pp. 329–30. **With Sewall and:** SSD, I, 421; DI, p. 332; R2C; SSD, I, 422. **But the darkness:** DI, p. 333. **By coincidence, Increase's:** M, pp. 83–84; IM, *A Call from Heaven* (1685), p. 119. **Now, atop the:** DI, pp. 364, 358, 384–88. **Caught in the:** Bartholomew Green, *The Printer's Advertisement* (1700). **The publication of:** DI, p. 378. **All of the:** *The Letter-Book of Samuel Sewall,* CMHS, 6th ser., I (1886), 255. **Indeed Colman and:** Caplan, "Some Unpublished Letters," q. p. 104; on IM's opposition to the proposal, see Middlekauff, *The Mathers,* p. 225. **Mather proposed the:** "Records of the Cambridge Association," p. 270; IM, MS sermon (partly in CM's hand), 10 Jul 1679, Dreer Collection, Historical Society of Pennsylvania; MS "proposals Concerning the Recording of Illustrious providences," 12 May 1681, BPL; MCA, VI, 2. **Mather having begun:** Chester N.

Greenough, "A Letter Relating to the Publication of Cotton Mather's Magnalia," PCSM, XXVI (1927), 297–312; DI, pp. 400, 427 *et passim.* **As published in:** Samuel Stone to Wait Winthrop, 9 Jun 1696, W, Reel 14. CM's friend Nicholas Noyes of Salem also apparently donated much material. **What unifies this:** MCA, III, 13; Sacvan Bercovitch, "Cotton Mather," in *Major Writers of Early American Literature,* ed. Everett Emerson (Madison, 1972), p. 138, and see also Bercovitch's analysis of CM's life of Winthrop in *The Puritan Origins of the American Self* (New Haven and London, 1975); MCA, III, 11. **Typical of Mather's:** MCA, III, 176, 179, 180. **Virtually the whole:** MCA, "General Introduction"; MCA, III, 11–12, 74. See also the important article by Peter H. Smith, "Politics and Sainthood: Biography by Cotton Mather," *William and Mary Quarterly,* 3rd ser., XX (1963), 186–206. **Indeed Mather recreates:** MCA, III, 12, and "General Introduction." **Although Mather set:** MCA, "General Introduction." **Perhaps no feature:** Cyrus H. Karraker, "The Treasure Expedition of Captain William Phips to the Bahama Banks," *New England Quarterly,* V (1932), q. pp. 736, 740. **Yet Mather gave:** MCA, II, 66. **Mather had a:** MCA, II, 39–40. **Although Magnalia places:** MCA, II, 38, 68, 39, 42. **Like John Eliot:** MCA, II, 38–39, 41; Robert H. George, "The Treasure Trove of William Phips," *New England Quarterly,* VI (1933), 294–318. **The disparate voices:** MCA, III, 180. **For all its:** CM speaks of "Massy" writing in his *Manuductio ad Ministerium* (1726), p. 45; MCA, I, 31. **For all its:** DI, pp. 230, 169. **In several ways:** SML, "Preface," p. 3, italics reversed; DI, pp. 230–31. **Mather began the:** BA, Ps. CIV; the index appears in MAP, Reel 2; DI, pp. 170, 231. **Later chapters will:** Theodore Hornberger, "Cotton Mather's Annotations on the First Chapter of Genesis," *University of Texas Publications,* no. 3826 (1938), pp. 112–22. **"Let it not:** on Boyle and the corpuscular theory, see E. J. Dijksterhuis, *The Mechanization of the World Picture* (Oxford, 1961), pp. 40 ff. As early as 1689 CM declared corpuscularianism the "only right" philosophy. See *Early Piety, Exemplified* (1689), in MCA, IV, 211. **In many sermons:** CM, MS sermon on Eph. I. 2. (17? May 1702), Yale University Library; *Winter-Meditations* (1693), pp. 19–20.

6. Particular Faiths

Until May, 1702: DI, pp. 430, 449. **Cotton Mather's bodings:** DI, pp. 222, 264. **Such revelations would:** DI, pp. 198, 191; CM, *The Retired Christian* (1703), p. 32; CM, *The Faith of the Fathers* (1699), p. 3; DI, pp. 261–62. **Like many others:** Robert Middlekauff, *The Mathers* (New York, 1971), ch. 18; CM, *Things to be Look'd for* (1691), p. 46. **At this time:** "Problema Theologicum," MAP, Reel 7, fr. 0492–0539; IM's eschatological sermons are preserved in CM's sermon notebooks, MAP, Reel 4B, esp. fr. 0246–49; *Tulley's Almanack* (1699), n.p.; CM, *Things for a Distress'd People to think upon* (1696), p. 34. **Together with hints:** DI, pp. 316, 195; PA, p. 143; DI, p. 368. **If the caliber:** DI, pp. 204, 422. **With these many:** DI, pp. 188, 193, 206, 311. In 1701 CM published a now lost work entitled *The Good Linguist, or, Directions to avoid the Sins of the Tongue.* In part he wrote the work, he explained, in gratitude for "the wonderful Work of God, in restoring, and enlarging of my once-fettered *Speech*" (DI, p. 348). **One sort of:** *Retired Christian,* p. 27; PA, p. 102; CM, *Christianus per Ignem* (1702), p. 47. **Most of Mather's:** DI, pp. 185, 217, 282–83, 376. **Only two months:** DI, pp. 380, 382. **Mather's longing for:** DI, p. 307; PA, pp. 157–58. **The Christ-like birth:** DI, p. 336; R2C; MS letter, IM to [probably his brother Nathaniel], 4 Sep 1699, MHS; CM, *Parental Wishes and Charges* (1705); PA, *passim.* **Increase, Jr., became:** DI, pp. 336, 340, 345, 348. **Under the Phips:** HCR, IV, 174. **For years after:** DI, p. 305; Massachusetts Archives, LVIII, 187; DI, p. 308. **This time Mather's:** DI, pp. 308–9, 327–28. **The test

of: DI, pp. 354-55. **But it, Mather:** DI, p. 356. **But by next:** HCR, IV, 173; John Maynard Hoffmann, "Commonwealth College: The Governance of Harvard in the Puritan Period," Diss. Harvard (1972), pp. 418 ff.; *The Acts and Resolves, Public and Private, of the Province of the Massachusetts Bay* (Boston, 1869-1922), VII, 255. **Perhaps because there:** DI, p. 360; HCR, IV, 146; *Acts and Resolves,* VII, 271-72; DI, p. 400; P, p. 175. **Both Mathers felt:** A, p. 352. **Abigail Mather had:** DI, p. 437; R2C, 25 Aug 1689; DI, pp. 405, 452. **A week after:** with the exception noted in the next entry, the account in this and the following five paragraphs is based on DI, pp. 405, 430-49. **By October, after:** CM's later remark about Abigail's prophetic dream appears in SLCM, p. 116. **Pleased with seeing:** DI, p. 445; *A Report of the Record Commissioners of the City of Boston . . . 1701 to 1715* (Boston, 1884), pp. 23 ff.; Ernest Caulfield, "Some Common Diseases of Colonial Children," PCSM, XXXV (1951), 24-25. **Within a month:** DI, pp. 449, 447. **Always busy, Mather:** DI, p. 446; CM, MS sermon on Eph. I. 14., 1 Nov 1702, Houghton Library, Harvard University; DI, p. 447; CM, *Wholesome Words* (1702?; rpt. 1713), pp. 4, 23. **Whatever Mather's fears:** DI, pp. 447, 452, 448. **Abigail lingered in:** DI, pp. 448-49. **Mather took pride:** DI, pp. 449-50; MAP, Reel 8, fr. 0218. **While stressing such:** MAP, Reel 8, fr. 0221; CM, *Meat out of the Eater* (1703), Preface to final sermon. **As the year:** quotations in this and the next two paragraphs from DI, pp. 448-57. **To the extent:** DI, p. 451; MAP, Reel 8, fr. 0219. **Or, Mather speculated:** DI, pp. 453-54. **Yet Mather's puzzling:** DI, p. 454. **Only two months:** DI, p. 457. **Mather never names:** DI, pp. 457-58. On the Maccartys see "Cotton Mather and Miss Maccarty," PMHS, XLVIII (1914-15), 135-38; Middlesex County Registry of Deeds, 19: 397; "The King's Arms Tavern in Boston," NEHGR, XXXIV (1880), 44. **As Mather pondered:** this and the next two paragraphs based on DI, pp. 457-59, 466-83. **Mather's heavenly messages:** DI, p. 457; MS letter, [Elizabeth Maccarty] to CM, 3 Jun 1703, transcribed in CM's hand on *verso* of her letter to him on 7 Jun 1703, MHS. **Susceptible to flattery:** Elizabeth Maccarty to CM, 7 Jun 1703. **Mather felt that:** this and the next four paragraphs based on DI, pp. 488-95.

7. Joseph Dudley

As the new: IMD, 1704 *passim;* on the gloves, see the MS letter, IM to unaddressed, 4 Dec 1704, MHS; IMD, 1 Jan 1704. **Increase conspired in:** IM, *Soul-Saving Gospel Truths* (1703), pp. 3, 6; IM, *Meditations on the Glory of the Lord Jesus Christ* (1705), p. viii; IM, *An Earnest Exhortation to the Children* (1711), "To the Reader"; A, p. 353. **The congregation Mather:** R2C, *passim.* IM speaks in 1714 of preaching to two thousand persons. See the typescript of his letter to William Ashurst, 22 Jun 1714, MHS. CM noted on one occasion that of the persons recommended by the congregation that day for particular prayers, some ninety were then abroad at sea. See CM, *The Bostonian Ebenezer* (1698), p. 77; on the widows, see *ibid.,* p. 9. The Mathers' salaries and the distribution of church donations are recorded in the MS Treasurer's Account Book in vol. 1A of R2C. Gifts of money to the Mathers appear in many different sources, for instance the will of John Richards (Suffolk Probate #2140) and SSD, II, 676. Richards left CM and IM £20 each. **Mather approached his:** DI, p. 319; on the number of sermons CM preached each year, see his annual lists in DI and DII; DI, p. 100; PA, p. 219. **Differing considerations dictated:** DII, p. 241; CM, *Brontologia Sacra* (London, 1695), Preface; CM, *Man Eating the Food of Angels* (1710), Preface. **Mather devoted equally:** on the length of CM's sermons, see for instance DII, p. 237, and CM, *Ratio Disciplinae* (1726), pp. 57 ff.; M, p. 34; CM's views on delivering sermons appear in his *Manuductio ad Ministerium* (1726), pp. 103-7, and PA, p. 77; DI, p. 531. **However demanding, preaching:**

CM, MS list of marriages, 1709, Dartmouth College Library; on CM's connection to religious societies, see PA, p. 224; on his deathbed witness, see his *Thoughts of a Dying Man* (1697), p. 4; on his nearly four hundred prayers, see DIII, p. 85. **Some at least:** MS letter, Elizabeth Atwood to CM, 2 Jul 1720, AAS; MS letter, Edward Goddard to CM, 19 Feb 1727[8?], AAS; DII, pp. 98–99. **But no aspect:** I here accept the number of CM's publications as thoughtfully computed in George Selement, "Publication and the Puritan Minister," *William and Mary Quarterly,* 3rd ser., XXXVII (1980), 219–41. Selement omits from his count reprints under new titles, fragmentary pieces, postscripts to other works, etc., and notes that if such materials were included, the number of CM's publications would reach 468. On CM's plan to bring forth one title a month, see DII, p. 162. In 1713, CM also published an *A,B,C. of Religion.* **One reason Mather:** DI, pp. 539, 518, 548; CM, *The Nets of Salvation* (1704), p. 48; DI, p. 520; DII, pp. 14, 28; DI, p. 568. **The sheer number:** CM, MS sermon on Eph. I. 3., 23 Mar 1702, New York Public Library. CM's other MS sermons on Ephesians in this series are deposited at the Historical Society of Pennsylvania, and at the libraries of Yale University, the University of Virginia, Brown University, and Harvard University. CM's "Quotidiana" appears in MAP, Reel 7. **Mather also maintained:** DIII, p. 124; DII, pp. 74, 227, 212. **Mather alternately gloried:** DIII, p. 108; DI, p. 228; CM, *Winter-Meditations* (1693), Introduction; DI, p. 340; IM, *An Earnest Exhortation,* "To the Reader"; CM, *Utilia* (1716), Preface. IM often made public his dislike for elaborately learned prose. See, for instance, his *Practical Truths* (1704) and especially his Preface to Joseph Capen's funeral sermon on Joseph Green, published in Boston in 1717. That CM took his father's stylistic criticisms personally is suggested by his having declined contributing a preface to a funeral sermon in 1717, in part because he was "warned . . . in a very odd preface to a funeral sermon on Mr. Green, by a javelin thrown, as it was thought, with a particular aim at me" (SLCM, p. 250). IM in his Preface had attacked the preacher *"whose design is to set forth himself, to show his Wit and Learning, that would lace his Discourse with fine florid Phrases,"* etc. **In a variant:** MCA, II, 63; DI, p. 335. **Whatever his misgivings:** CM mentions the bishop in his *Grace Triumphant* (1700), "To the Reader"; DI, pp. 593, 545–47; DII, p. 162. **Unlike his father:** Benjamin Colman, *The Holy Walk and Glorious Translation of Blessed Enoch* (1728), p. 24; Thomas Prince, *The Departure of Elijah Lamented* (1728), p. 20. **Both Mathers had:** M, p. 482; Everett Kimball, *The Public Life of Joseph Dudley* (London, 1911), ch. I, *passim;* IM to Joseph Dudley, 20 Jan 1708, CMHS, 1st ser., III (1794), p. 128. **With the appointment:** John Gorham Palfrey, *History of New England* (Boston, 1875, 1890), III, q. 526n.; Kimball, *Public Life,* q. p. 14. **Particularly because of:** Kimball, *Public Life,* q. p. 52; Dudley to CM, 5 Jun 1689, CMHS, 6th ser., III (1899), 503; *Calendar of State Papers, Colonial Series, America and West Indies* (London, 1896–1937), XIII, 111, 120; Kimball, *Public Life,* p. 53. **Dudley's political career:** Kimball, *Public Life,* p. 67; on the scientific activities of Dudley and his son Paul, see Raymond Phineas Stearns, *Science in the British Colonies of America* (Urbana, Ill., 1970), pp. 455–72; on Dudley's activities in London, see the correspondence in CMHS, 6th ser, III (1899), 513 ff., where the quoted phrases appear on pp. 529 and 514. **Dudley began determinedly:** MS letter, Joseph Dudley to William Blathwayt, 29 Jul 1701, MHS; Sir Henry Ashurst to Wait Winthrop, 10 Jul 1701, CMHS, 6th ser., V (1892), 91; MS letter, Joseph Dudley to William Blathwayt, 22 Jul 1701, MHS; MS letter, John Quick and other London Presbyterian ministers to IM, 28 Jul 1701, HL. **Dudley also sought:** MS letter, Jacob Melyen to Abraham Gouvernour, 25 Jun 1692, Melyen Letterbook, AAS; Ashurst q. in Richard R. Johnson, *Adjustment to Empire: The New England Colonies 1675-1715* ([New Brunswick, N.J.], 1981), p. 336; MS letter, Joseph Dudley to CM, 10 May 1701, AAS.

Mather of course: SLCM, p. 65. **Like his defense:** Thomas Hutchinson, *The History of the Colony and Province of Massachusetts-Bay,* ed. Lawrence Shaw Mayo (Cambridge, Mass., 1936), II, q. 92n.; MS extract of unaddressed letter from John Leverett, 28 Oct 1701, in MS "Extract of Severall Letters from New England," HL. **However recent or:** Palfrey, *History of New England,* IV, 246n.; SSD, I, 469–70. **Five days later:** DI, pp. 464–65. **From the beginning:** William Pencak, *War, Politics & Revolution in Provincial Massachusetts* (Boston, 1981), pp. 45–46; Kimball, *Public Life,* p. 90; Philip S. Haffenden, *New England in the English Nation 1689–1713* (Oxford, 1974), pp. 123, 184; Hutchinson, *History of the Colony and Province,* II, q. p. 101; Palfrey, *History of New England,* IV, q. 253. **Dudley offended others:** George Keith, *The Doctrine of the Holy Apostles & Prophets* (1702); petition to the Archbishop of Canterbury, 23 Dec 1702, *The American Papers of the Society for the Propagation of the Gospel* (World Microfilms, 1974), Reel 12; Henry Wilder Foote, *Annals of King's Chapel* (Boston, 1882), I, 226. **Dudley's patronage encouraged:** Christopher Bridge to SPG, 19 Nov 1702, *American Papers,* Reel 12; John Chamberlayne to Joseph Dudley, *ca.* 1705, *American Papers,* Reel 12; Foote, *Annals,* I, 176. ***Quid pro quo:*** John Chamberlayne to Joseph Dudley, 10 Apr 1703, CMHS, 6th ser., III (1899), 537; SSD, I, 502, 475. Dudley's large bills for silver, wigs, and other such items survive at the Massachusetts State House, Boston. **At first the:** IMD, 1 Jul 1702; IM to William Blathwayt, 6 Mar 1705, HCR, IV, 209. Christopher Bridge, one of the ministers at King's Chapel, wrote home: "you cannot think how very industrious both the Mathers have been in opposing this design [of opening chapels outside Boston]. They have preached and prayed against it, and have treated [severely?] with many of them that come to hear me" (to SPG, 19 Nov 1702). **By contrast, Cotton:** CM, *The Pourtraiture of a Good Man* (1702), pp. 21–22; Palfrey, *History of New England,* IV, 248. **Mather and Dudley:** MS letter, Joseph Dudley to CM, 25 Dec 1706, AAS; MS letter, Joseph Dudley [unaddressed but certainly to CM], 16 Jan 1706, MHS. **While playing now-you-see-it-now-you-don't:** SLCM, p. 70; on the rumored plot, see MS deposition of Joshua Gee, 21 Sep 1702, BPL; Ashurst letters in CMHS, 6th ser., III (1899), 324 ff. **Mather's main choice:** DIII, p. 72; SLCM, pp. 68, 70, 71. **This hint of:** on the Deerfield massacre, see SSD, I, 498 and n.; on costs of the war, see *Commonwealth History of Massachusetts,* ed. Albert Bushnell Hart *et al.* (1928; rpt. New York, 1966), II, 75 ff. **That Dudley's handling:** on Dudley's wartime efforts see the correspondence in CMHS, 6th ser., III (1899), *passim;* on the new fortifications see Massachusetts Archives, 244. **Nevertheless, in the:** DI, p. 565; Palfrey, *History of New England,* IV, q. 302. **Mather and Sir:** SLCM, p. 73; John Winthrop to Fitz-John Winthrop, [no day] Jul 1707, CMHS, 6th ser., III (1899), 388. **The new accusations:** SSD, I, 576; Palfrey, *History of New England,* IV, q. 303. **Dudley's remarkable comeback:** SLCM, pp. 75–76. **The justness of:** Kimball, *Public Life,* p. 187; SSD, I, 578, 587; John Chamberlayne to Joseph Dudley, 16 Dec 1702, CMHS, 6th ser., III (1899), 534. **In the added:** SLCM, p. 105; SSD, I, 573. CM himself had been nominated for college president by the House in 1703, but the Overseers replied that they could not accept a president "Named by that House." See *Calendar of State Papers,* XXI, 256. Most writers on CM have assumed that at the time Leverett was chosen he wished the presidency for himself. But no evidence exists that at this time he, any more than his father, desired to trade Boston for Cambridge. **But the man:** MS letter, CM to unaddressed, 7 Oct 1707, Pusey Library, Harvard University. **In behalf of:** Hoffmann, "Commonwealth College," q. p. 461. Leverett in fact is viewed as a rather conservative man concerned with reviving disused academic traditions, in Arthur D. Kaledin, "The Mind of John Leverett," Diss. Harvard (1965). **Yet Mather's view:** MS letter (typed transcript), Henry Newman to _____ Taylor, 29 Mar 1714, MHS; on Leverett's connection to the SPG see

American Papers, Reel 12; Henry Ashurst to Gurdon Saltonstall, 27 Jun 1709, CMHS, 6th ser., V (1892), 196; Henry Ashurst to IM, 10 Oct 1709, CMHS, 6th ser., V (1892), 199. **In one of:** *The Acts and Resolves, Public and Private, of the Province of the Massachusetts Bay* (Boston, 1869-1922), VIII, 796; photostated MS letter, CM to unaddressed, 7 Oct 1707, MHS. **However Dudley obtained:** Leo M. Kaiser, "'We Are All Filled with the Greatest Hope . . .' An Installation Speech of Governor Joseph Dudley," *Harvard Library Bulletin,* XXVII (1979), 443-44. **For Mather, who:** the account of CM's letter in this and the next two paragraphs is drawn from SLCM, pp. 77-82. **Taken aback by:** Joseph Dudley to CM, 3 Feb 1708, CMHS, 1st ser., III (1794), 135-37; SSD, I, 586-87. **Dudley's stiff personal:** I have followed the text of Dudley's *Modest Inquiry* in CMHS, 5th ser., VI (1879), 65-95. **Later generations can:** CM's superb bibliographer, Thomas J. Holmes, accepted the whole of the *Deplorable State* as his, but large portions of it seem to me both not high-toned enough and overly factual to be by him; DII, p. 15; SSD, II, 627, 663. IM may have been among the North End ministers who dined with Dudley, for he wrote later in the year that he had no personal quarrel with the governor. "He treats me with all Respect, calling me his Spiritual Father" (HCR, IV, 229). IM seems to have remained amicable with Leverett as well. **For Mather, the:** DII, p. 146. **Pranks had often:** PA, p. 183; DII, p. 139; DIII, p. 59; DII, pp. 216-17. **Abuse issued from:** John Winthrop to CM, *ca.* 1725, CMHS, 6th ser., V (1892), 428; SLCM, p. 32. **Mather of course:** SLCM, p. 72; DII, p. 105; Register of Diplomas and MS Faculty Minutes (GUA 21320, 26632), University of Glasgow (for this information I am indebted to my fine graduate student Patricia Thompson; the degree was sent to CM together with letters from the Principal of the school and the Dean of Faculty); HCR, IV, 244; MS letter, CM to Principal John Stirling, *ca.* 1712 (beginning "Most Reverend Sir. Every opportunity of addressing you"), National Library of Scotland; for one such letter of congratulations see the MS letter, Thomas Reynolds to CM, 19 Jun 1711, MHS. **Inwardly Mather always:** DII, pp. 63-64, 77. **But however guilty:** CM, *To the . . . Professors, of the Renowned University of Glasgow* (1710); MS letter, CM to Principal John Stirling, 21 Aug 1713, National Library of Scotland; *The Correspondence of the Rev. Robert Wodrow,* ed. Thomas M'Crie (Edinburgh, 1843), II, 504. **However honored abroad:** *Letter-Book of Samuel Sewall,* CMHS, 6th ser., I (1886), 407; SSD, II, 645-46; the jury message was apparently printed in BNL, 18 Dec 1710, but unfortunately no copy of this issue has survived. See Sewall's *Letter-Book,* p. 408. Unfortunately also, I am unable to identify "Facetious George" in the verses, although the name may refer to John George, the husband of the woman who later became CM's third wife. **The question of:** CM's letter appears in HCR, IV, 244; MS diary of John Leverett, 16 May 1712 and Jun 1712, Pusey Library, Harvard University. **The addition did:** DIII, pp. 44, 32. **Within a year:** A, p. 359; DII, pp. 195, 213. **Publicly forbearing, Mather:** DII, p. 194; "Autobiography of the Rev. John Barnard," CMHS, 3rd ser., V (1836), 214-15. IM's instincts may have been sound, for Barnard later donated money to the new Anglican chapel in Marblehead. See Thomas C. Barrow, "Church Politics in Marblehead, 1715," *Essex Institute Historical Collections,* XCVIII (1962), 121-27. **At Webb's ordination:** SSD, II, 772.

8. Bonifacius

"The Minister's *Tongue"*: BA, James III.1; SSD, I, 455. **With unrelenting, sometimes:** DIII, p. 39; DII, p. 204; DI, p. 333; CM, *Golden Curb for the Mouth* (1707; rpt. 1709, which text I have followed); CM, *The Sad Effects of Sin* (1713), pp. 49-50; CM, *Faithful Warnings* (1704). p. 33. **In whole works:** CM, *The Right Way to Shake off a Viper* (London, 1711; rpt. Boston, 1720, which text I have followed), pp. 48, 15;

SML, p. 65; DIII, p. 67. **In his mighty:** for CM's notes in 1684 on one sermon by IM concerning Doing Good, see MAP, Reel 3C, fr. 0533; CM, undated MS sermon on Col. IV. 5., *ca.* 1685, Brown University Library; PA, p. 217. **Yet Mather's acts:** DII, pp. 26, 126, CM, *Desiderius* (1719), p. 7; MAP, Reel 8, fr. 0146. **How fully Mather:** CM, *The Minister* (1722), p. 14; DII, pp. 41–42, 263. **Mather's numberless acts:** DI, p. 518; DII for 1711, pp. 93, 148, 151 *et passim; A Report of the Record Commissioners of the City of Boston . . . 1701 to 1715* (Boston, 1884), p. 102; PA, p. 229. **Mather's program for:** DII, p. 23. The discussion of Pietism which follows is indebted to Dale W. Brown, *Understanding Pietism* (Grand Rapids, Mich., 1978); F. Ernest Stoeffler, *German Pietism During the Eighteenth Century* (Leiden, 1973); F. Ernest Stoeffler, *The Rise of Evangelical Pietism* (Leiden, 1971). **Some more personal:** CM, *The Echo's of Devotion* (1716), p. 11; John Arndt, *True Christianity,* trans. William Boehm (Boston, 1809), pp. xiii, 462, 247. When CM first read Arndt is uncertain. Anthony Boehm sent him an English translation of *True Christianity* in 1716. See MS letter, Boehm to CM, 28 May 1716, AAS. But CM mentions the work as early as *Nuncia Bona,* below. **One other side:** CM, *Man Eating the Food of Angels* (1710), p. 63; Kuno Francke, "The Beginning of Cotton Mather's Correspondence with August Hermann Francke," *Philological Quarterly,* V (1926), 193–95. **Mather publicized Francke's:** I have followed the text of *Nuncia Bona* in Kuno Francke, "Further Documents Concerning Cotton Mather and August Hermann Francke," *Americana Germanica,* I (New York, 1897), 54–66. **The impact of:** on Pietist references to *Bonifacius,* see the MS letter, Anthony Boehm to CM, 19 Mar 1717, AAS, wherein Boehm notes that to make CM's work known in Germany he has inserted a passage from *Bonifacius* in some historical collections printed at Halle in High Dutch. In discussing *Bonifacius* I have followed the edition by David Levin (Cambridge, Mass., 1966). **In recognizing the:** on CM's place in the history of American philanthropy, see Robert H. Bremner, *American Philanthropy* (Chicago, 1960), pp. 12–14; *The Complete Works of Benjamin Franklin,* ed. John Bigelow, VIII (New York, 1888), 484. **Besides its value:** for other works of the period in which CM explains the propriety of flaunting one's authorship, see the prefaces to *Christianity Demonstrated* (1710) and *Memorials of Early Piety* (1711). **Brazened by Doing:** DI, pp. 563–64, 570. **After advertising "Biblia:** DII, p. 162; SLCM, p. 176. ***Namma* [etc.]. Christianizing the:** MCA, III, 193; CM, *Another Tongue brought in* (1707), p. 2; CM, *The Nets of Salvation* (1704), p. 35. **In converting the:** CM, *Souldiers Counselled and Comforted* (1689), p. 28; MCA, III, 191–92; CM, *Decennium Luctuosum* (1699), p. 154; CM, *The Way to Prosperity* (1690), in *The Wall and the Garden: Selected Massachusetts Election Sermons 1670–1775,* ed. A.W. Plumstead (Minneapolis, 1968), p. 133. **More than that:** CM, *Memorable Providences* (1689), in *Narratives of the Witchcraft Cases 1648–1706,* ed. George Lincoln Burr (New York, 1914), p. 99; CM, *Souldiers Counselled and Comforted,* p. 31; BA, II Kings 1; *The Works of The Pious and Profoundly-Learned Joseph Mede, B.D.* (3rd ed. London, 1672), p. 800; Higginson quoted in CM, *Wonders of the Invisible World* (1693; London, 1862), p. 160; CM, *Decennium Luctuosum,* p. 103. **In hopes of:** on the New England Company, see William Kellaway, *The New England Company 1649–1776* (New York, 1962), and Frederick L. Weis, "The New England Company of 1649 and its Missionary Enterprises," PCSM, XXXVIII (1959), 134–218; on the choice of CM as a commissioner, see *Letterbook, 1688–1761, of the Company for the Propagation of the Gospel in New England,* ed. Vesta Lee Gordon, University of Virginia Library Microfilm Publications #8 (Charlottesville, 1969), p. 25; on the Indian youth, see MS letter, CM to William Ashurst, 7 Sep 1714, HL. **Mather's involvement in:** SSD, II, 621–22; *Letter-Book of Samuel Sewall,* CMHS, 6th ser., I (1886), 400–3 (Sewall's note to this letter seems to identify these views as CM's);

SLCM, p. 27; on the difficulties of the London printers, see *Letterbook . . . of the Company,* p. 126. **Mather also personally:** SLCM, p. 127; DIII, p. 54; MS letter, CM to William Ashurst, 7 Apr 1713; HL; SLCM, p. 152; CM, *Just Commemorations* (1715), p. 56. **Mather and the:** *Letterbook . . . of the Company,* pp. 71–72; *SPG Minute Books,* Lambeth Palace Library (microfilm edition, 1974), 19 Oct 1705; John Chamberlayne to William Ashurst, 23 Jan 1706, in *The American Papers of the Society for the Propagation of the Gospel* (World Microfilms, 1974), Reel 12. **Mather generally approved:** MS letter, Thomas Reynolds to CM, 9 Jun 1711 (but containing CM's letter of 1706), MHS; DII, p. 416. **Mather received no:** William Ashurst to Samuel Sewall, 3 May 1709, *American Papers,* Reel 12. **Writing from a:** CM speaks of his design for the work in DI, p. 271. **A final, outstandingly:** DII, p. 85–86. **Founded around 1660:** on the Royal Society, see Dorothy Stimson, *Scientists and Amateurs: A History of the Royal Society* (New York, 1948), and Raymond Phineas Stearns, "Colonial Fellows of the Royal Society of London, 1661–1788," *William and Mary Quarterly,* 3rd ser., III (1946), 208–68; SLCM, p. 175. **In addition to:** DII, p. 266; the drawings appear in CM's MS communication to Richard Waller, 25 Nov 1712, RS; MS communication ("Uncommon Dentition"), CM to Dr. John Woodward (but not in CM's hand), 30 Sep [1724], RS; SLCM, pp. 119–20. On dates and other bibliographical issues concerning "Curiosa Americana" I have followed George Lyman Kittredge, "Cotton Mather's Communications to the Royal Society," PAAS, NS XXVI (1916), 18–57. **The weakness was:** SLCM, p. 135; CM to Waller, 25 Nov 1712. **In terms of:** MS draft communication ("A Triton"), CM to Dr. John Woodward, 5 Jul 1716, MHS: Kittredge, "Cotton Mather's Communications," *passim.* **Mather collected his:** Kittredge, "Cotton Mather's Communications," *passim.* **Mather's favorite source:** M, pp. 442, 421; CM, *Hades Look'd into* (1717), p. 40; on rubila, see IM to John Winthrop, 23 Jun 1718, W, Reel 19, and Winthrop Commonplace Book, W, Reel 39. A large part of the second John Winthrop's library survives at the New York Academy of Medicine. See Ronald Sterne Wilkinson, "The Alchemical Library of John Winthrop, Jr., (1606–1676), and his Descendants in Colonial America," *Ambix,* II (1963), 33–51. **Mather frequently praised:** John Winthrop to Fitz-John Winthrop, CMHS, 6th ser., III (1899), 333–34; M, pp. 427, 417; SLCM, pp. 245–48; MS letter, John Winthrop to CM, 29 Dec 1719, MHS. **Mather's letters to:** on the plants, see CM's letters to the naturalist James Petiver, SLCM, pp. 216–19, and Raymond Phineas Stearns, "James Petiver Promoter of Natural Science, c. 1663–1718," PAAS, NS LXII (1952), 243–365; on the piece-of-eight, see MS draft communication ("A Singular Lime-stone"), CM to Dr. John Woodward, 24 Sep 1716, RS. **The first series:** in the account of the first series I have followed the MS versions at RS; on the reported merman, see NEC, 16–23 Apr 1726; on the bass, see BG, 17–24 Feb 1724; on the waterspout, see *The New York Times,* 11 July 1979, p. A18. **But the very:** on the tendency of natural religion to displace Christianity, see John Dillenberger, "The Apologetic Defence of Christianity," in *Science and Religious Belief,* ed. C.A. Russell (London, 1973), pp. 170–94, and John Redwood, *Reason, Ridicule and Religion* (London, 1976). **Mather shrank, however:** the final quotation is from CM, *Utilia* (1716), p. 272. **Mather also considered:** MS draft communication ("Monstrous Impregnations"), CM to Dr. John Woodward, 2 Jul 1716, MHS; MAP, Reel 7, fr. 0564. See also Lester S. King, "Basic Concepts of Early 18th-Century Animism," *American Journal of Psychiatry,* CXXIV (1967), 797–802. **In conceiving of:** on the New Science and the experimental method, see Richard S. Westfall, *The Construction of Modern Science* (Cambridge, England, 1977), esp. pp. 115 ff. **Leaving aside Mather's:** on CM's Copernican views, see SSD, II, 779; on spontaneous generation, see *Christian Philosopher,* p. 145; on scrofula, see MS letter, CM to Jos[eph] Web [undated, but beginning "Sir, At your desire"], AAS; on hybridization, see SLCM, p. 218; on dominance, see I. Bernard Cohen, "Ethan Allen Hitchcock," PAAS, NS LXI (1951), 30; for a thoughtful assessment of CM's achievements, see Raymond Phineas Stearns, *Science in the British Colonies of America* (Urbana, Ill., 1970), pp. 403–26. **The Royal Society:** Stearns, *Science in the British Colonies,* q.p. 407; MS "Notes from Dr. Woodward," 1714, W, Reel 18; CM's hint appears at the close of his MS communication to Richard Waller, 25 Nov 1712, RS. **Seeking recognition even:** DIII, p. 93; Stearns, *Science in the British Colonies,* q. pp. 405–6; DII, p. 246; MS communication (identified as "Separate Letter"), CM to [probably Richard Waller], [*ca.* Nov 1713], MHS. **In the "F.R.S.":** DII, p. 246. **The defining moods:** DII, p. 423–24. **Squire was not:** MS letter, Benjamin Colman to CM, 25 Dec 1711, AAS: DII, p. 235. **When not surfacing:** CM, *Man Eating the Food of Angels* (1710), p. 41; CM, *The Wayes and Joyes of Early Piety* (1712), p. 43; CM, *Perswasions from the Terror of the Lord* (1711), pp. 34, 35. **Mather's tantrums and:** DIII, p. 39. **Some of this:** SLCM, p. 231; Niel Caplan, "Some Unpublished Letters of Benjamin Colman, 1717–1725," PMHS, LXXVII (1965), 106–7. **Mather's stepped-up promotion:** on the size of "Biblia Americana," see DII, p. 416. **Yet English readers:** SLCM, pp. 170, 190; MS draft letter, CM to Anthony Boehm, 6 Aug 1716, AAS; DII, p. 312. **The New Offer:** *The Correspondence of the Rev. Robert Wodrow,* ed. Thomas M'Crie (Edinburgh, 1842), I, 628; DII, p. 332; MS letter, Anthony Boehm to CM, 19 Mar 1717, AAS. Boehm indicates that CM had at this point deposited the manuscript at Harvard. **Mather was wholly:** MS draft letter, CM to Thomas Reinolds, [*ca.* 1715, beginning "Reverend and very dear, Sr. The Generous Friendship"], AAS; MS letter, CM to William Ashurst, 18 Oct 1715, HL; DII, p. 376. **Mather's service to:** SLCM, p. 146; on Leverett, see MS letter, IM to William Ashurst, 22 Dec 1712, HL; on the commissioners' sluggishness, see DIII, p. 65; on the award, see *Some Correspondence between . . . the New England Company and . . . America,* ed. John W. Ford (London, 1896), p. 89; MS letter, CM to William Ashurst, 10 Dec 1712, HL; DII, p. 252. **New frustrations came:** *Correspondence of . . . Wodrow,* II, 361; *Philosophical Transactions of the Royal Society,* #339 (Apr–Jun 1714), p. 64; SLCM, p. 129. **Mather also discovered:** SLCM, p. 219.

9. Of 15, Dead, 9

At the time: Isaac J. Greenwood, "A Review of William Clarke's Genealogical Statement," NEHGR, XXXIII (1879), 226–29; James Savage, *A Genealogical Dictionary of the First Settlers of New England* (Boston, 1860–62), II, 485; SML, p. 13. **Elizabeth may have:** Henry Wilder Foote, *Annals of King's Chapel* (Boston, 1882), I, 46–48; CM, *The Religion of the Cross* (1714), pp. 44–45; R2C, 24 Feb 1706; DII, pp. 185–86, 132. 210; DIII, pp. 7, 81. **Mather and Elizabeth:** on CM's house, see Suffolk Deeds 33. 131, quoted in Thwing Card Catalogue, MHS. See also DII, pp. 239, 54; DI, p. 428; DIII, p. 72; CM, *Christianus per Ignem* (1702), p. 195; SML, pp. 98, 22. CM seems also to have owned a farm at this time, which he leased out. See the appendix to the MS lease of 26 Jul 1705, Williams College Library. **The center of:** CM describes his library in PA, p. 42, and DI, p. 447; on the volumes CM owned, see Julius Herbert Tuttle, "The Libraries of the Mathers," PAAS, NS XX (1909–10), 268–356; on the large accessions, see Clarence S. Brigham, "Harvard College Library Duplicates, 1682," PCSM, XVIII (1917), 407–17, and DII, p. 2; DI, p. 548; PA, p. 42. **How many books:** *John Dunton's Letters from New-England* (Boston, 1867), p. 75 and n. **Entering middle age:** IMD, 1710 *passim;* DII, pp. 204, 51. On the birth dates of CM's children, see Horace E. Mather, *Lineage of Rev. Richard Mather* (Hartford, 1890); MS list of marriages (in CM's hand), 1704, University of Virginia Library (Elizabeth); *A Report of the Record Commissioners . . .*

Containing Boston births from A.D. 1700 to A.D. 1800 (Boston, 1894), p. 46 (Samuel); DII, pp. 8, 20 (Nathanael); DII, p. 57 (Jerusha). **Mather's household also:** DII, p. 687; CM, *The Negro Christianized* (1706), p. 26; DI, p. 570; CM, *Grata Brevitas* (1712), p. 8; PA, p. 221; DII, p. 364. In his lifetime CM owned at least three and probably more black slaves. His church records suggest that his congregation contained thirty or forty blacks, whom he often addressed in sermons. The subject of CM and slavery deserves book-length treatment, but for a useful brief study, see Daniel K. Richter, "'It Is God Who Has Caused Them To Be Servants': Cotton Mather and Afro-American Slavery in New England," *Bulletin of the Congregational Library,* XXX (1979), 4-13. **In 1706 some:** DI, p. 579; DII, pp. 222, 271, 282; DIII, p. 83; DII, p. 139. **Amidst his multitudinous:** CM, *Orphanotrophium* (1711), p. 20; CM, *The Man of God Furnished* (1708), pp. 138-39; DI, p. 536. **To induce children:** DI, p. 536. **Mather conscientiously applied:** DII, p. 21; DIII, p. 14; DII, p. 149; DIII, p. 91; DII, p. 53. **True to his:** DIII, p. 105; DI, p. 535; DII, pp. 113, 144, 198; DIII, p. 85. **As Mather proposed:** DI, p. 536; DII, pp. 127, 44. **In attending to:** DII, p. 140; DIII, p. 33; DII, pp. 245, 4, 134. **In preparing his:** DII, pp. 51, 153, 111-12; CM, *Victorina* (1717), sig. A2 *et passim;* DII, p. 78. **Mather's two sons:** DIII, p. 89; DI, p. 583; DIII, pp. 41, 72; DII, p. 106; DIII, p. 45; DII, pp. 161, 151; DIII, p. 9. **But Creasy somehow:** DIII, p. 110; DII, p. 203; DII, pp. 76, 92, 212. **When Creasy reached:** DII, p. 204; samples of Creasy's handwriting survive in the Mellen Chamberlain Autograph Collection, MHS; DII, pp. 278, 239, 225. **The winter of:** Ernest Caulfield, "Some Common Diseases of Colonial Children," PCSM, XXXV (1951), 5-6; CM, *A perfect Recovery* (1714), p. 47; DII, p. 248. **In about two:** DII, pp. 249-52. **As such threats:** DII, pp. 252, 272. **One historian of:** Caulfield, "Some Common Diseases," p. 8. **Elizabeth was the:** DII, pp. 254, 250-51. **Three days after:** DII, pp. 252-53; DI, p. 568; DII, p. 255. **On November 8:** CM, *The Will of a Father submitted to* (1713), pp. 28, 31; DII, p. 254. **Whatever Mather's own:** CM, *The Religion of the Cross* (1714), *passim;* DII, pp. 254-55. **The next to:** DII, pp. 257-58. **The twins Eleazer:** DII, pp. 258, 260. **The need to:** CM, *Orphanotrophium,* p. 12; on the older Jerusha, see CM, *Memorials of Early Piety* (1711), and DII, p. 38; DII, pp. 258, 256, 261. **Next day, with:** CM, *The Best Way of Living* (1713), p. 23; DII, pp. 263, 259, 261; CM, *The Best Way,* sig. A3 *et passim;* SLCM, p. 145; CM, *Hezekiah* (1713), pp. 1, 35. **In December, with:** DII, pp. 266, 270, 273. **As Mather digested:** DII, p. 266; MAP, Reel 2, fr. 0061; DII, p. 283. **Mather's fifty-second year:** IM, *A Sermon Concerning Obedience & Resignation* (1714), sig. A2; A, p. 359; CM, *Maternal Consolations* (1714), pp. 5-6, 40.

10. Lydia Lee George

To be sure: The description of Boston in this and the six following paragraphs draws on a very wide variety of sources, of which only the more substantial can be cited. On the quake, see BNL, 18-25 Jun 1705; many accounts of the 1711 fire survive, but see esp. BNL, 1-8 Oct 1711, and CM, *Advice from Taberah* (1711); on the new First Church building and the new Town House, see esp. Walter Muir Whitehill, *Boston: A Topographical History* (Cambridge, Mass., 1959), pp. 26-27. **Indeed a half:** Carl Bridenbaugh, *Cities in the Wilderness* (New York, 1938), pp. 146, 155-65; on the fire department, see *A Report of the Record Commissioners . . . 1716 to 1736* (Boston, 1885), p. 279. **Despite the restraining:** the quotation and most of the details are drawn from Daniel Neal, *The History of New-England* (London, 1720), II, 587 *et passim.* **To walk that:** details gleaned from advertisements in various Boston newspapers, esp. BG, 4-11 Apr 1720 ("choice Pictures"); NEC, 31 Dec-7 Jan 1723 (Boyer); BG, 8-15 Feb 1720 (Faneuil); BG, 12-19 Jul 1725 (Hedman); BG 29 May–5 Jun 1727 ("Black Boy"). **Social life kept:** Neal, *History of New-England,* II, 587, 591; Bridenbaugh, *Cities in the Wilderness,* pp. 291–92; on Harvard enrollment, see Niel Caplan, "Some Unpublished Letters of Benjamin Colman, 1717–1725," PMHS, LXXVII (1965), 111; BNL, 2–9 Mar 1713 (Brownell); BNL, 7–14 Mar 1715 (moving pictures); BNL, 22–29 Aug 1715 (horse race); BG, 23–30 May 1726 (bear). **Urban pleasures also:** on the growth of crime, see CM, *A Flying Roll* (1713); on the 1711 statute, see *The Acts and Resolves, Public and Private, of the Province of the Massachusetts Bay* (Boston, 1869–1922), I, 673–74; on the report of slaves, see Caplan, "Some Unpublished Letters," p. 131, and Robert C. Twombly and Robert H. Moore, "Black Puritan: The Negro in Seventeenth-Century Massachusetts," *William and Mary Quarterly,* 3rd ser., XXIV (1967), 224–42; BNL, 17–24 Dec 1711, 26 Nov–3 Dec 1711, 20–27 Apr 1713; Caplan, "Some Unpublished Letters," p. 131; SLCM, p. 368. **Here a John:** Neal, *History of New-England,* II, 590. **In some ways:** MCA, III, 223; PCSM, XXXIII (1940), xiii; Wilfred H. Munro, *The History of Bristol, R.I.* (Providence, 1880), pp. 131–33. **Although Lee returned:** "Letters of Samuel Lee and Samuel Sewall Relating to New England and the Indians," PCSM, XIV (1913), 142–86; Samuel A. Green, "An Early Book-catalogue printed in Boston," PMHS, 2nd ser., X (1895–96), 540–45; "Dr. Stiles's account of Rev. Samuel Lee," PMHS (1864–65), pp. 219–20; Samuel Lee to IM, 25 Aug 1687, in M, pp. 540–42; CM's sermon notebooks, MAP, Reel 4A, Jul 1686–May 1687. **This heritage of:** "The Story of Boston Light," *Bostonian Society Publications,* VII (1910), 64–65 and n.; Long Wharf Corporation Documents 1713–1729, BPL; advertisements for John George, BNL, 18–25 Aug 1707 and 16–23 Mar 1713; on George's sloops, see Massachusetts Archives, VII: 370, 396, 482. **Well-to-do and socially:** Henry Wilder Foote, *Annals of King's Chapel* (Boston, 1882), I, 137; "A List of all the Stated Communicants," in *Records of the Church in Brattle Square, Boston,* (Boston, 1902), n.p.; "Letter of Reverend Benjamin Colman," PCSM, VIII (1906), pp. 248–49; Suffolk Probate #3629 (27 Nov 1714). **Mather waited scarcely:** SLCM, pp. 166–67; DI, pp. 581–82. **Even more than:** SLCM, pp. 166–68. **But actually Mather:** SLCM, pp. 173–74. **In the same:** SLCM, pp. 171–73. **Lydia did grant:** this and the next three paragraphs from DII, pp. 305–8. **In the spring:** SLCM, p. 131; *Boston Marriages 1700–1751* (Boston, 1898), 26 May 1715; Kenneth Ballard Murdock, *Increase Mather* (Cambridge, Mass., 1926), p. 385; MAP, Reel 6, fr. 0112, 0114; SLCM, p. 174. **On June 24:** "Will of Increase Mather," NEHGR, V (1851), 445–47; Suffolk Deeds 35. 34 (24 June 1715). **Ten days later:** CM, MS "Extract of passages in my Diaries," Houghton Library, Harvard University; SLCM, p. 183. CM's wedding sermon was printed as "Shemajah" in his *Utilia* (1716). For identification of the connection of the sermon with his marriage, see MS letter, CM to Elizabeth Clark, 13 Oct 1718, AAS. **It seemed that:** CM, MS "Extract of passages"; CM, *The Sacrificer* (1714), p. 45; DII, pp. 325, 392; MS "Extract of passages." **No portrait of:** CM, MS "Extract of passages." **Whatever subtle sensuality:** DII, pp. 481, 335–36, 340; MAP, Reel 16, fr. 0658; DII, p. 346. **Mather's removal to:** MS Second Church Treasurer's Accounts, MHS; Chandler Robbins, *A History of the Second Church* (Boston, 1852), p. 298. Surviving evidence about the house conflicts. Samuel Sewall described it as "the house that was Mr. Kellond's" (SSD, II, 794), but the Second Church account says that it belonged to Thomas Hutchinson. It seems probable that Kellond owned the house but conveyed it to Hutchinson, and that it was known locally by the names of both former owners. See also Thwing Catalogue of Suffolk Deeds, MHS (14 May 1713). The house and land CM had bought in 1688 he put up for sale around 1717. See SLCM, p. 249. **Mather now lived:** Abbott Lowell Cummings, "The Foster-Hutchinson House," *Old-Time New England,* LIV (1964), pp. 61 ff.; DII, pp. 770, 577, 619, 458, 363 and n., 384, 477, 549. **Altogether, in his:** DII, p. 360. **To**

Mather's great: CM, MS "Extract of passages"; SLCM, p. 184; *Boston Marriages,* 28 Aug 1716; CM, *The Tribe of Asher* (1717), title page. **Samuel, about eight:** DII, pp. 459, 353, 565, 499, 554; Samuel's "Quotidiana" are preserved at AAS; MS draft letter, CM to Jeremiah Dummer, 13 Jul 1720, AAS. **Sammy's admission forced:** SLCM, p. 294; "A Mather Manuscript in the Congregational Library," *Bulletin of the American Congregational Association,* III (1952), 16-17. **One dark intrusion:** CM, *Bethiah* (1722), p. 4; SML, p. 14; CM, *Victorina* (1717), sig. A2, pp. 66, 80. **But about a:** DII, p. 370; on Culver's Root, see SLCM, pp. 220, 224, and Winthrop Commonplace Book, W, Reel 39; CM, *Victorina,* p. 79; DII, p. 388; SSD, II, 840. **Katharine's death did:** SLCM, pp. 179, 169. **The visit turned:** Thomas J. Holmes, "Samuel Mather of Witney, 1674-1733," PCSM, XXVI (1926), 312-22; A, p. 360; DII, pp. 322-23. **But curing Creasy:** DII, pp. 322-23. **Mather's disappointment in:** DII, p. 347. **For once, Mather:** DII, p. 352; SLCM, p. 207; DII, p. 354. **By the time:** Sir Henry Ashurst to Wait Winthrop, 24 Aug 1708, CMHS, 6th ser., V (1892), 173; DIII, p.81; Alan Simpson, "A Candle in a Corner: How Harvard College Got the Hopkins Legacy," PCSM, XLIII (1966), 304-24. **Dudley also gave:** Foote, *Annals of King's Chapel,* p. 224; on Dudley's alleged Congregationalism, see CMHS, 1st ser., VII (1801), 216-17; SSD, II, 792. **Nothing so nearly:** DII, pp. 292-93; Albert Matthews, "Colonel Elizeus Burges," PCSM, XIV (1913), 360-72. **Mather was glad:** SLCM, p. 168; on Shute, see DNB. **Shute no sooner:** DII, p. 375; MS draft letter, CM to [Samuel Shute], [undated, beginning "Sr, The God of Heaven"], AAS; on Shute's membership in a Congregational church, see HCR, IV, 265 (the pronouns are confused, but "He" seems to refer to Shute); on Shute and King's Chapel, see Foote, *Annals of King's Chapel,* pp. 267-68; CM, *A Speech Made unto His Excellency* (1717), p. 2; SLCM, p. 244. **For his efforts:** DIII, p. 380; MS draft letter, CM to Samuel Shute, [16?] Oct 1719, AAS; MS draft letter, CM to John Shute Barrington, [undated but *ca.* Oct 1716, beginning "Sr, An *American* Composure"], AAS; MS draft letter, CM to Thomas Bradbury, 13 Oct 1718, AAS. **The change of:** on Dummer generally, see Charles L. Sanford, "The Days of Jeremy Dummer, Colonial Agent," Diss. Harvard, 1952; on the "female beauties," see MS Memoranda of Jeremy Dummer, 1709-11, MHS; on Dummer as prime minister, see "A Sketch of Eminent Men in New-England," CMHS, 1st ser., X (1809), 155. **Dummer greatly admired:** MS Memoranda; on the pigs, see Sanford, "The Days of Jeremy Dummer," q. p. 90; on Waller, see MS letter, Jeremiah Dummer to Stephen Sewall, 23 Jan 1712, AAS; on "Religio Generosi," see MS draft letter, CM to "J.[eremiah] D.[ummer] Esq.," 7 Sep 1719, AAS; CM's attack on Dummer appears in *The Day which the Lord hath made* (1703); DII, p. 414. **Dummer's value to:** mention of CM for rector appears in a letter from Rev. James Noyes (a Yale trustee) in 1717, cited in Sanford, "The Days of Jeremy Dummer," p. 239; DII, p. 474; HCR, II, 424. **Yale College began:** Franklin B. Dexter, "The Founding of Yale College," *New Haven Historical Society Papers,* III (1882), 1-31; Franklin B. Dexter, "Governor Elihu Yale," *ibid.,* pp. 227-48; Sanford, "The Days of Jeremy Dummer," p. 237. **Mather wrote to:** Yale's comment q. in Dexter, "Governor Elihu Yale," p. 244; MS draft letter, CM to Elihu Yale, 14 Jan 1718, AAS; Dexter, "Governor Elihu Yale," pp. 242-43. **Mather was greatly:** MS draft letter, CM to Gurdon Saltonstall, 25 Jun 1718, AAS; MS letter, Yale trustees to CM, *ca.* Sep 1718, Yale University Library. **A simultaneous and:** on the development of CM's ecumenism, see Richard F. Lovelace, *The American Pietism of Cotton Mather* (Grand Rapids, Mich., 1979), pp. 251-81. **Around 1715 Mather:** CM, *Malachi* (1717), p. 36; DII, p. 416; the list of places to which CM intended sending the work is compiled from various mentions of *Lapis* in DII, SLCM, and *India Christiana* (1721); SLCM, p. 205; MS fragmentary draft letter, CM to Anthony Boehm, [undated but *ca.* 1716, beginning "there is none that has more"], AAS. **In *Lapis,***

Mather: all quotations from *Malachi,* except the last, which appears in SLCM, p. 205. How far CM had drifted from the older Congregational view of church government appears in his blasts at the publication in Boston of an edition of *The Churches Quarrel Espoused,* by the Ipswich minister John Wise. Here and in his later *Vindication of the Government of New-England Churches* (1717) Wise attacked as a departure from Congregationalism the movement to develop formal clerical associations. For CM's furious response, see SLCM, p. 185. **Mather's Universal Religion:** all quotes from *Malachi.* **Mather's ecumenism increasingly:** *Malachi,* p. 69; CM, "To my much Honoured Mr. *Francis De la Pillonniere,*" in *The Occasional Paper* (London), III (1718), 25–29; CM, *Brethren dwelling together in Unity* (1718), p. 37. **Many different features:** on the Pietists' praise, see MS letter, Anthony Boehm to CM, [undated but *ca.* 1716, beginning "Reverend Sir. It was in the Month"], AAS. Boehm added that some persons to whom he gave copies of *Lapis* called it "a Compendium of Mystical and Universal Divinity." CM entitled one of his own works *Pia Desideria* (1722), after a famous work of Spener's. **Mather's career in:** CM, *Zelotes* (1717), pp. 41–42. **At various times:** on Whiston, see Margaret C. Jacob, *The Newtonians and the English Revolution 1689–1720,* (Ithaca, N.Y., 1976), pp. 130–34; on Louis XIV, see CM, *Shaking Dispensations* (1715), pp. 42, 45; on the "greatest Sign," see MS draft letter, CM to Henry Walrond, 11 Jan 1718, AAS. **One other ambitious:** DII, p. 786; H, III, 1008. Both of CM's grandfathers had been involved in the production of *The Bay Psalm Book* (1640), and his grandfather John Cotton had written a treatise on psalmody, *Singing of Psalmes A Gospel-Ordinance* (London, 1650). **In 1718 Mather:** CM, *Proposals for Printing by Subscription* (1718); SLCM, pp. 311, 188; CM, *The Accomplished Singer* (1721), p. 15. For an expanded study of CM's *Psalterium,* see my article "Cotton Mather and the Reform of Puritan Psalmody," *Seventeenth-Century News,* XXXIV (1976), 53–57. **Mather had a:** Richard Baxter, *Paraphrase on the Psalms of David in Metre* (London, 1692); DII, p. 437. **To improve public:** SLCM, pp. 376, 388; Ebenezer Parkman, MS singing book, dated Jul 1721, MHS. **Often sympathetic to:** DII, p. 608; SSD, II, 976. David P. McKay has published a sermon on psalm singing allegedly preached by CM on 18 Apr 1721, as "Cotton Mather's Unpublished Singing Sermon," *New England Quarterly,* XLVIII (1975), 410–22. The manuscript does contain CM's name at the end, but seemingly not his signature. I cannot accept the sermon as his, first because the manuscript is not in his hand, second because the sermon emphasizes the musical and aesthetic side of singing whereas CM paid these lip service while emphasizing the exegetical and devotional aspects. Most important, CM's sermon list for 1721 (DII, pp. 677–81) shows that he preached on April 16 and 20, but not on April 18.

11. *Tria Carcinomata*

Mather's newfound happiness: DII, p. 480; CM, *Help for Distressed Parents* (1695), p. 13. **"Suppose," Mather asked:** DII, pp. 465–66. **But by November:** DII, p. 484. **However shaken, Mather:** MS Book of Sessions, 1712–1719, Suffolk County Supreme Court, Boston (17 Jan 1718 and p. 201); DII, p. 485. **But despite Mather's:** DII, p. 489; PA, p. xvii. **Powerless to reclaim:** DII, p. 583. **Whatever her other:** on Lee's daughters, see "Dr. Stiles's account of Rev. Samuel Lee," PMHS (1864–65), 219–20, and "Genealogical Gleanings in England," NEHGR, XLIV (1890), 393–94; on Augustus, see MAP, Reel 4C, fr. 0299. **Early in their:** DII, pp. 583–86. **Among the objects:** DII, p. 584; CM, MS "Extract of passages in my Diaries," Houghton Library, Harvard University. **Fear of what:** DII, pp. 584–85.

Lydia turned her: DII, pp. 338, 590–91; on the possibility of revolution, see CM, *Concio ad Populum* (1719), p. 25; SLCM, p. 317; HCR, IV, 302–3. **Increase himself added:** IMD for 1717, *passim;* R2C, 13 Oct 1717; "Earliest Wills on Record in Suffolk County, Ms.," NEHGR, V (1851), 445–47; DII, p. 512. IM showed CM the provisions of his will more than a year before drawing it up. See DII, p. 505. **Mather dealt with:** DII, pp. 523, 533, 557, 514. **Mather's distress also:** DII, pp. 589, 571, 578, 521, 579. **On March 9:** SF #13120 (24 Mar 1719). The following account of CM's legal difficulties appeared previously as my article "Cotton Mather and the Howell Estate," *Boston Bar Journal,* XXVI (1982), 5–13. **This ominous summons:** Samuel Sewall, MS Probate Records, MHS (the administration appears as "Nota" written in the margin of a grant of administration to Ebenezer Withrington on 29 Mar 1716); SF #15183 (25 May 1721). **In taking on:** DII, p. 410; SSD, II, 817n.; DII, p. 349. **Mather undertook this:** CM, "The Answer of the Administrator of the Estate of Nathan Howel deceased, unto the Citation served upon him," MS document reproduced in sale catalogue of Charles Hamilton Galleries Inc., New York, XC (4 Sep 1975), 46; DII, pp. 386, 444, 136; CM, *Fair Dealing* (1716), p. 12. **Mather explained later:** CM, "The Answer"; BNL, 31 Dec–7 Jan 1716/17. **Forever bent on:** SF #11222 (14 Dec 1716); Mather v. Oliver &c., ERB (1 Jan 1717); SF #11386 (19 Feb 1717). Packanet was apparently released when he promised to pay off the debt to CM at the rate of forty shillings a month. **For Mather this:** SF #11588 [*sic*] (5 Mar 1717); SF #11453 (5 Mar 1717); SF #11454 (18 Mar 1717); Mather v. Dunham and Mather v. James, ERB (2 Apr 1717); Mather v. Davison, ERB (2 Jul 1717). **These cases can:** Mather v. Morrell, ERB (1 Apr 1718); *York Deeds* (Portland, Maine, 1894), X, fol. 22; *Province and Court Records of Maine* (Portland, Maine, 1964), V, 106; Mather v. Marshall, ERB (2 Apr 1717). **Other of Mather's:** DII, p. 494; MS draft letter, CM to Pelatiah Whittemore, 11 Dec 1717, AAS; BNL, 9–16 Dec 1717; CM, "The Answer." **The sheriff who:** SF #13120 (24 Mar 1719). **The manuscript probably:** MAP, Reel 8, fr. 0135, 0138. Several of CM's published sermons in this period also refer to his marital and financial difficulties. See for instance *Febrifugium. An Essay for the Cure of Ungoverned Anger* (1717) and *A Glorious Espousal* (1719). In the latter, CM speaks of "the *Curse,* which every *Marriage* in *this World,* is likely to be more or less Encumbered and Embittered withal!" **Aside from venting:** see "The Answer"; Mico v. Mather, ERB (7 Jul 1719). **Mather began trying:** "Supposed Letter from Rev. Cotton Mather, D.D.," CMHS, 4th ser., II (1854), 122–29. **Judge Sewall did:** *Letter-Book of Samuel Sewall,* CMHS, 6th ser. (1886–88), II, 111. **With his passion:** this and the next paragraph drawn from the "Supposed Letter." **The seriousness of:** [John Colman], *The Distressed State of the Town of Boston* (1720), p. 2 *et passim.* **Mather depicted his:** M, pp. 460–62. The editors assigned this undated document the date 1725, but its content makes a date of 1720 far more probable. **Certain that Sewall's:** DII, p. 630; SLCM, pp. 326–27. **Apparently despairing of:** MAP, Reel 6, fr. 642-43 [*sic*]. **Auspiciously, this time:** MS "Petition of Dr. Cotton Mather," 8 Nov 1720, Council Records, Massachusetts State House, Boston. **But no proper:** SLCM, pp. 333, 336. **Mather needed no:** DII, pp. 611–12; IMD, 14 Apr 1721. CM does not say what happened during this "Night-Riot." But documents do survive of a riotous episode apparently two weeks later, which may by some confusion of dates be the same episode. On the streets of Boston on the evening of April 20, three young male servants cursed, swore, broke windows, threatened to break down doors, and offered "affronts and abuses" to women, for which the court offered them the choice of a fine or a public whipping. See MS Sessions Minutes (1719–1728), Suffolk County Supreme Judicial Court, Boston, pp. 85 ff. That Creasy may have been involved with this group is suggested by the fact that one of the young men was a servant to Foxley Sanderson, to whom Creasy owed money. See documents related to Creasy in Mellen Chamberlain Auto-graph Collection, MHS. **As always, Mather's:** SLCM, p. 337; DII, pp. 614–15. **Seeking some help:** SLCM, p. 337. **Opposition to Shute:** SLCM, p. 156. **The change of:** SLCM, p. 223. **Amid this plethora:** CM, *Concio ad Populum,* p. 25. **Mather had been:** H, II, 537–40; "Dr. Mather's Letter to Lord Barrington," CMHS, I (1792), 105–6; SLCM, pp. 291, 292; for Cooke's alleged drunkenness and the retraction, see SLCM, pp. 295–96, and the undated draft memorandum in CM's hand beginning "Desirous forever to preserve the most unspotted care," AAS; for the "party of Tip-plers," see MS draft letter, CM to William Ashurst, 10 Sep 1719, AAS. **Opposition to Shute:** John L. Sibley, *Biographical Sketches of Graduates of Harvard University* (Cambridge, Mass., 1873–1975), IV, 351–52. **Apprehensive that such:** Thomas Hutchinson, *The History of the Colony and Province of Massachusetts-Bay,* ed. Law-rence Shaw Mayo (Cambridge, Mass., 1936), II, 218. **Although the House:** Hutch-inson, *History of the Colony,* II, 185; text of *Reflections upon Reflections* in *Colonial Currency Reprints,* ed. Andrew McFarland Davis (1911; rpt. New York, 1971), II, 118. **Mather, probably hoping:** CM, undated MS draft document, beginning "An Extract of a passage in *Eachards,"* AAS. **Mather was also:** SLCM, pp. 319, 304–5. **A new session:** CM, undated MS draft document, beginning "In case the Representa-tives," AAS; Hutchinson, *History of the Colony,* II, q. 179. **At this point:** SLCM, pp. 334–35; MS draft letter, CM to Samuel Penhallow, 21 Nov 1720, AAS; SLCM, p. 335. **In this Mather:** Perry Miller, *The New England Mind: From Colony to Prov-ince* (Cambridge, Mass., 1953), p. 310. **Neither upbringing nor:** SLCM, p. 229; MS draft letter, CM to Samuel Penhallow, 8 Sep 1718, AAS; SLCM, pp. 327–28. **The other case:** SLCM, p. 312; Daniel Neal, *The History of New-England* (London, 1720), II, viii. **The day before:** SLCM, pp. 313–15, 269. **In the past:** CM, *A Voice from Heaven* (1719), p. 13; DII, p. 607. **Mather's ministry dealt:** CM, MS sermon on Eph I. 13. (20 Sep 1702), University of Virginia Library. **That Arianism might:** I. Bernard Cohen, "Introduction" to William Whiston, *Astronomical Lectures* (1728; rpt. New York, 1972), p. v ff.; DII, p. 106; DIII, p. 48. On Arianism in general, see Ronald N. Stromberg, *Religious Liberalism in Eighteenth-Century England* (Oxford, 1954). **Mather wrote several:** on the advance of Arianism, see MS letter, CM to John Stirling, 10 Dec 1717, National Library of Scotland; on Salters' Hall, see Henry W. Clark, *History of English Nonconformity* (1911–13; rpt. New York, 1965), II, 193–95. **Mather learned of:** SLCM, p. 289; MS draft letter, CM to Isaac Watts, 7 Sep 1719, AAS; MS letter, Isaac Watts to CM, 11 Feb 1720, MHS. **Mather regarded the:** Richard F. Lovelace, *The American Pietism of Cotton Mather* (Grand Rapids, Mich., 1979), p. 273. **Mather also set:** SLCM, p. 273; *Some American Sentiments* in *Three Letters from New-England* (London, 1721), pp. 7–27. **Mather's professions of:** SLCM, p. 303; HCR, IV, 349; Niel Caplan, "Some Unpublished Letters of Benjamin Colman, 1717–1725," PMHS, LXXVII (1965), 128. **At the same:** Caplan, "Some Unpublished Letters," p. 119. **Almost all the:** Hamilton Andrews Hill, *History of the Old South Church* (Boston, 1890), I, 400. **Shaken by the:** Thomas Lechmere to John Winthrop, Jr., 18 Jan 1720 and 14 Mar 1720, W, Reel 19; CM *et al., An Account of the Reasons* (1720). **Despite this resistance:** SSD, II, 940n.; Sibley, *Biographical Sketches,* IV, 306; Lechmere to Winthrop, 14 Mar 1720. **The end result:** DII, p. 615; Samuel G. Drake, *The History and Antiquities of Boston* (Boston, 1856), p. 558n.; DII, p. 615; CM, MS draft document, undated but beginning "Considering the crazy condition of the Old N.M.," AAS; DII, p. 617. **How many left:** DII, p. 616; CM, *A Vision in the Temple* (1721), pp. 37, 42–43; DII, p. 617. **Suddenly, just two:** DII, pp. 620–21.

12. The Paths of the Destroyer

Mather himself observed: SLCM, p. 213; P, p. 198; DII, p. 487. **Civic authorities seem:** *The Acts and Resolves, Public and Private, of the Province of the Massachusetts Bay* (Boston, 1869–1922), II, 91; *A Report of the Record Commissioners of the City of Boston . . . 1716 to 1736* (Boston, 1885), p. 76; *Acts and Resolves,* X, 28. **It was the:** SSD, II, 979; *Report of the Record Commissioners . . . 1716 to 1736,* p. 81; *A Report of the Record Commissioners of the City of Boston . . . from 1700 to 1728* (Boston, 1883), p. 154. **The next week:** BNL, 15–22 May 1721; *Report of the Record Commissioners . . . 1716 to 1736,* p. 82. **Mather feared for:** Zabdiel Boylston, *Historical Account of the Small-pox Inoculated* (1726; rpt. Boston, 1730), p. 38; DII, pp. 622, 621, 623, 628. **Mather's charitable and:** *Robert Boyle: The Works,* ed. Thomas Birch (1722; rpt. Hildesheim, 1965), VI, 610–11; DII, p. 388; SLCM, p. 214. **Mather now did:** on the June 6 address and CM's other unpublished writings during the smallpox epidemic, I have followed the exhaustive and dependable account of their dates and content in George Lyman Kittredge, "Some Lost Works of Cotton Mather," PMHS, 2nd ser., XLV (1911–12), 418–79; Otho T. Beall, Jr., and Richard H. Shryock, "Cotton Mather: First Significant Figure in American Medicine," PAAS, LXIII (1953), 137–38; John B. Blake, "The Inoculation Controversy in Boston: 1721–1722," *New England Quarterly,* XXV (1952), 489. **Mather based the:** on discussion of inoculation in Boston, see Niel Caplan, "Some Unpublished Letters of Benjamin Colman, 1717–1725," PMHS, LXXVII (1965), 124; SLCM, p. 214. **In his letter:** accepting the history of the June 6 address given in Kittredge, "Some Lost Works," I have followed the text in CM, *The Angel of Bethesda,* ed. Gordon W. Jones (Barre, Mass., 1972), pp. 107–12. **How many physicians:** BNL, 23–30 Mar 1713, 5–12 Mar 1711, 3–10 Mar 1707, 28 Nov–5 Dec 1720; BG, 21–28 Nov 1720; Raymond Phineas Stearns, *Science in the British Colonies of America* (Urbana, Ill., 1970), pp. 435–42. **Boylston approved of:** *Massachusetts Magazine,* I (1789), 778; Boylston, *Historical Account,* p. 2. **The news of:** Boylston, *Historical Account,* p. 53; Thomas Robie, MS Smallpox Journal, 1721–22, MHS. **Mather found himself:** DII, pp. 631–32; BG, 10–17 Jul 1721. **With Mather certain:** CM's characterization of Dalhonde appears in his MS "Case of the Small-pox Inoculated, further cleared," 21 May 1723, RS; Dalhonde's testimony appears in the appendix to Boylston's "Historical Account." **Three days after:** BNL, 17–24 Jul 1721. **These charges of:** MS letter, Benjamin Colman to unaddressed, 25 Jul 1721, Francis A. Countway Library, Harvard Medical School; BG, 27–31 Jul 1721; NEC, 7 Aug 1721. **This flurry opened:** BNL, 24–31 Jul 1721; NEC, 7–14 Aug 1721; BNL, 7–14 Aug 1721. **Despite the thickening:** Boylston, "Historical Account." Again following Kittredge, I have quoted the text of this essay in *The Angel of Bethesda,* p. 94. **Opposition to Mather's:** NEC, 14–21 Aug 1721; on Douglass, see Stearns, *Science in the British Colonies;* for Douglass's remark on CM, see "Letters from Dr. William Douglass to Cadwallader Colden of New York," CMHS, 4th ser., II (1854), 169. **Douglass first sprang:** NEC, 7–14 Aug 1721, 14–21 Aug 1721. **What made Douglass:** "Letters from Dr. William Douglass," pp. 166, 170; William Douglass, *Inoculation of the Small Pox as Practised in Boston* (1722), p. 20; Caplan, "Some Unpublished Letters," p. 124; "Letters from Dr. William Douglass," p. 171. **The tense, charnal:** DII, pp. 641, 635, 634, 636–37. **Very tryingly, Mather:** DII, p. 634; Creasy had signed a promissory note for £3 15s on 9 Sep 1721 to the dancing master Increase Gatchell (see SF #16999, 17 Jun 1723); DII, pp. 647, 669, 674. **Smallpox or no:** Faneuil v. Mather, ERB (4 Apr 1721); SF #15183 (25 May 1721) and documents attached to SF #15308 (17 Apr 1721); the allowance of CM's petition appears in the MS records and Minute Books of the Superior Court of Judicature, 1702–27, Supreme Judicial

Court, Boston (25 May 1721); DII, p. 630; SLCM, p. 345. **But having borne:** DII, pp. 626, 632, 628, 635, 638. **A few days:** DII, pp. 639–43. **Unexpectedly, however, two:** DII, pp. 643–44, 648–49. **A canvass of:** NEC and BNL, 2–9 Oct 1721; Thomas Lechmere to John Winthrop, Jr., 2 Oct 1721, W, Reel 19; *Report of the Record Commissioners . . . 1716 to 1736,* p. 89; *Report of the Record Commissioners . . . 1700 to 1728,* p. 159. **Mather and Boylston:** Boylston, *Historical Account,* p. 50; DI, pp. 683, 650, 654; BG, 23–30 Oct 1721 (for the identification of this as CM's, see H, I, 357). **Someone tried to:** NEC, 14–21 Aug 1721; DII, pp. 657–58. This episode was much talked of and distorted, so that to prevent misrepresentation, CM gave the NEC his own account, which the newspaper published. It closely resembles the account in DII, except that in NEC the message fixed to the shell reads: "*Cotton Mather*—I was once of your Meeting; But the cursed Lye you told of—you know who, made me leave you, you Dog. And Damn you, I'll Inoculate you with this, with a Pox to you" (NEC, 13–20 Nov 1721). **The attempted assassination:** SLCM, pp. 345–46; DII, p. 659; General Court Records, Massachusetts State House (15 Nov 1721), and BNL, 13–20 Nov 1721. **Not everyone, Mather:** DII, pp. 659–60, 663. **Insidiously the smallpox:** on inoculations outside Boston, see Stearns, *Science in the British Colonies,* p. 444; DII, pp. 662, 670. **Mather also addressed:** that CM was unaware of the April inoculation in London is suggested by his remark on August 17 that he hoped the method "may be introduced into the English nation" (DII, p. 638); CM [but published as "*Communicated by* Henry Newman"], "*The way of proceeding in the* Small Pox inoculated," *Philosophical Transactions of the Royal Society,* XXXII (1722), 33–35; CM, MS communication headed "Dr Mather of New-England" (but not in CM's hand), 10 Mar 1722, The British Library, identified by Kittredge, "Some Lost Works," as "Curiosa Variolarum." **Whether the accounts:** on the debate, see Genevieve Miller, "Smallpox Inoculation in England and America: A Reappraisal," *William and Mary Quarterly,* 3rd ser., XIII (1956), 476–92. **By about mid-December:** for works by other ministers, see for instance Benjamin Colman, *Some Observations on the New Method of . . . Inoculating* (1721); IMD, 22 Jun 1721; MS letter, Samuel Sewall to Benjamin Colman, 12 Sep 1721, MHS. **The number of:** NEC, 30 Oct–6 Nov 1721; John Williams, *Several Arguments, Proving, That Inoculating the Small Pox Is not contained in the Law of Physick* (1721), p. 14. In this and the following paragraphs I have tried to convey the main themes of the debate, especially as they concerned CM, rather than to capture its escalating effect of attack and rejoinder. As a result the summaries of various arguments are not chronological, and some later works may in the accounting precede earlier ones. **While some anti-inoculators:** NEC, 1–8 Jan 1722; on Williams, see Kittredge, "Some Lost Works," pp. 471–72; John Williams, *An Answer To a Late Pamphlet* (1722), pp. 9, 4; Douglass, *Inoculation of the Small Pox,* sig. A2. **Pro-inoculation allies of:** on CM's part in writing this pamphlet, see Kittredge, "Some Lost Works," pp. 428, 467, and DII, p. 672. **Mather needed vindicating:** NEC, 30 Oct–6 Nov 1721; Douglass, *Inoculation of the Small Pox,* and *Postscript to Abuses, &c. Obviated* (1722), p. 4. **Mather's detractors often:** on the itch, see Douglass, *Postscript to Abuses,* p. 6; on CM's grammar and his opinion of his works, see Williams, *Several Arguments,* pp. 14, 15; on quoting CM against himself, see NEC, 15–22 Jan 1722; on Oldmixon and on CM's posturing, see [Anon.], *A Friendly Debate; or, A Dialogue between Rusticus and Academicus* (1722), pp. 6, 1; on "Curiosa," see Douglass, *Inoculation of the Small Pox,* p. 20, and Introduction, and his *The Abuses and Scandals of some late Pamphlets* (1722), p. 6; on the D.D., see Douglass, *The Abuses and Scandals,* Introduction, and NEC, 15–22 Jan 1722. **Mather's membership in:** on Checkley, see George L. Kittredge, "Further Notes on Cotton Mather and the Royal Society," PCSM, XIV (1913), 281–92; MS letter, John

Checkley to Edmund Halley, 26 Apr 1721, BPL. **Amidst the winter:** NEC, 15–22 Jan 1722; Douglass, *The Abuses and Scandals,* Introduction; on CM's membership in the Royal Society, see Kittredge, "Further Notes," and Stearns, *Science in the British Colonies,* pp. 110–11 and 111, n. 65. **Mather wrote to:** SLCM, p. 360; Raymond Phineas Stearns, "Colonial Fellows of the Royal Society, 1661–1788," *William and Mary Quarterly,* 3rd ser., III (1946), 228–29. **This onslaught of:** DII, p. 664; BG, 8–15 Jan 1722; NEC, 15–22 Jan 1722; MCA, VII, 86. **Although well practiced:** DII, p. 622; NEC, 27 Nov–4 Dec 1721; DII, p. 667. **In this defeated:** DII, pp. 670–71. **Mather's announcement of:** NEC, 15–22 Jan 1722 and 5–12 Feb 1722. **By the time:** selectmen's figures in NEC, 19–26 Feb 1722; the quotations from Silence Dogood appear in NEC, 26 Mar–2 Apr 1722 and 9–16 Apr 1722. **The selectmen found:** BG, 14–21 May 1722; *Report of the Record Commissioners . . . 1716 to 1736,* p. 96; NEC, 16–23 Apr 1722 and 28 May–4 Jun 1722. **Ironically for Mather:** DII, p. 669; Writ of Execution, 23 Oct 172[1?], with note by Edward Winslow dated 1 Jan 1722, State Records Center, Grafton, Mass. (the exact dates and details of this transaction are obscure: the date on the writ is torn, and the date on the note could represent 1722/3); CM's petition appears in SF #16015 (May 1722), which also contains Sewall's reply from Spectacle Island, dated 11 Jun 1722; on the selectmen, see *Report of the Record Commissioners . . . 1716 to 1736,* p. 97; on the "mobbish Crew," see MS letter, Thomas Robie [to John Higginson], 18 May 1722, AAS; on the condition of the Sewalls, see Robie, Smallpox Journal. **These final inoculations:** NEC and BG, 14–21 May 1722. **Impaled by the:** "Letters from Dr. William Douglass," p. 170. **To say that:** for a judicious assessment of CM's part in the inoculation controversy, see Beall and Shryock, "Cotton Mather." **Of course Mather:** DII, pp. 664–65; SLCM, p. 402. **A year after:** NEC, 14–21 May 1722; Stearns, *Science in the British Colonies,* p. 411; NEC, 13–20 Apr 1724; CM, MS communication ("The Case of the Small-pox Inoculated, further cleared"), 21 May 1723, RS (not in CM's hand, but signed by him).

13. Crackling of Thorns Under a Pot

The two years: Hamilton Andrews Hill, *History of the Old South Church* (Boston, 1890), I, 409. **Together with its:** IM, *A Dying Legacy of a Minister* (1722), p. 2; SSD, II, 996; P, p. 201. **Other losses beset:** SSD, II, 1001; SLCM, pp. 356, 375; William Pencak, *War, Politics & Revolution in Provincial Massachusetts* (Boston, 1981), p. 71. **Mather quickly gained:** SSD, II, 992; on CM's claims of foresight, see SLCM, pp. 375–76; NEC, 7–14 Jan 1723; BNL, 15–21 Mar 1723; SLCM, p. 384. **Losing money also:** Appleton v. Mather, ERB (3 Jul 1722); Baxter v. Dr. Mather, ERB (2 Oct 1722); on the irregularities, see Appleton v. Mather, ERB (2 Oct 1722), and Dr. Mather v. Baxter, ERB (1 Oct 1723); on CM's countersuit, see SF #17269 (10 Sep 1723); on Creasy and Sanderson, see SF #16702 (18 Mar 1723) and Writ of Execution, 9 May 1723, State Records Center, Grafton, Mass.; on Creasy's suits in June, see SF #16980 (17 Jun 1723) and SF #16999 (17 Jun 1723); on Gatchel, see NEC, 25 May–1 Jun 1724 and 4–11 Mar 1723. **In these circumstances:** Kenneth B. Murdock, "Cotton Mather and the Rectorship of Yale College," PCSM, XXVI (1927), 397; P, p. 201; "Original Paper Respecting the Episcopal Controversy in Connecticut, MDCCXXII," CMHS, 2nd ser., IV (1816), 298. **Mather was aghast:** SLCM, p. 356; SSD, II, 996; BG, 8–15 Oct 1722; "Original Paper," p. 299; on the "glorious revolution," see Carl Bridenbaugh, *Mitre and Sceptre: Transatlantic Faiths, Ideas, Personalities, and Politics 1689–1775* (New York, 1962), q. p. 68; Henry Wilder Foote, *Annals of King's Chapel* (Boston, 1882), I, 316. **The tumult brought:** Murdock, "Cotton Mather and the Rectorship," q. p. 395; "Original Paper," p. 297;

"Some Original Papers Respecting the Episcopal Controversy in Connecticut, MDCCXXII," CMHS, 2nd ser., II (1814), 130. **Mather and the:** Bridenbaugh, *Mitre and Sceptre,* q. p. 70; [CM], undated MS document, *ca.* Nov 1722, entitled "A Faithful Relation, of a Late Occurence in the Churches of *New England,*" MHS; "Some Original Papers," pp. 133–36; CM, *Some Seasonable Enquiries* (1723), p. 12. The MS "Faithful Relation" appears to be in the hand of Samuel Mather, but contains interpolations in CM's hand, thus my attribution of it to him. Many key words and phrases in the essay also appear in "The sentiments of several ministers" (in "Some Original Papers"), which is known to be by CM. **Increase reacted to:** P, pp. 201, 207, 66; SSD, II, 1007. **Helpless to pluck:** P, p. 207; DII, p. 686; P, p. 13; *Letter-Book of Samuel Sewall,* CMHS, 6th ser. (1886–88), II, 151. **Appropriately, Increase's final:** P, p. 210; Edward Taylor, "A funerall Teare . . . upon . . . Dr. Increase Mather," *Edward Taylor's Minor Poetry,* ed. Thomas M. and Virginia L. Davis (Boston, 1981), p. 247; P, p. 210; MS letter, William Waldron to Richard Waldron, 26 Aug 1723, MHS. **Mather had always:** P, p. 211; SSD, II, 1008; "Diary of Jeremiah Bumstead of Boston, 1722–1727," NEHGR, XV (1861), 199. **Increase had drawn:** this and the next paragraph from "Earliest Wills on Record in Suffolk County, Ms.," NEHGR, V (1851), 445–47. **Two days after:** CM, *A Father Departing* (1723), pp. 23–24, 28–29. **Mather may have:** CM, MS sermon on Phil. IV. 20., 15 Sep 1723, New York Public Library. **What few other:** on neighborhood visitations and Nathanael, see MAP, Reel 7, fr. 0557–58, 0583; on the "Courts," see CM, *A Father Departing,* p. 31. **Whatever else Increase's:** Chandler Robbins, *A History of the Second Church* (Boston, 1852), pp. 115, 312–13. **On January 19:** R2C, 19 Jan 1724. **Other vexations and:** SLCM, p. 390; Abraham English Brown, "The Builder of the Old South Meeting House," *New England Magazine,* NS XIII (1895), 397. **Shortly after arriving:** MS letter, William Waldron to Richard Waldron, 9 Oct 1723, MHS; Suzanne Foley, "Christ Church, Boston," *Old-Time New England,* LI (1961), 67–85. **Mather usually shrugged:** SLCM, p. 387; on McSparran, see Wilfred H. Munro, *The History of Bristol, R.I.* (Providence, 1880), pp. 135–40; for CM's inquiry, see *Letter-Book of Samuel Sewall,* II, 118–20; Rena Vassar, "Testimony of Frances Davis," *William and Mary Quarterly,* XXXIV (1977), 475; SLCM, pp. 344, 375. **The mediocre success:** Foote, *Annals of King's Chapel,* I, 325; DII, p. 806n.; Murdock, "Cotton Mather and the Rectorship," p. 395n.; MS letter, Timothy Cutler to unaddressed, 2 Apr 1725, BPL. **But Mather soon:** Cutler to unaddressed, 2 Apr 1725; Bridenbaugh, *Mitre and Sceptre,* p. 73; BG, 26 Jul–2 Aug 1725. **Mather later felt:** *The Acts and Resolves, Public and Private, of the Province of the Massachusetts Bay* (Boston, 1869–1922), X, 628; MS letter, John Checkley to "Doctor Bennet," 15 Jun 1725, BPL. **The Council approved:** MS "Memorial of Dr. Timothy Cutler and Mr. Samuel Myles," 23 Jun 1725, MHS; John Gorham Palfrey, *History of New England* (Boston, 1875, 1890), IV, 454–55. **Mather professed to:** CM, *Ratio Disciplinae* (1726), p. 174; Foley, "Christ Church," p.75. **While looking for:** MS letter, Jeremiah Dummer to Timothy Woodbridge, 10 Sep 1723, MHS. Apparently CM and Colman were able to get an address signed by ministers in Essex County, however. See MS letter, William Waldron to Richard Waldron, 2 Dec 1723, MHS. **In Boston Mather's:** SLCM, p. 376; NEC, 7–14 Jan 1723; SLCM, pp. 354, 378. **Mather's fidelity to:** SLCM, p.385. **Mather denied this:** DII, p. 794; MS letter, Jeremiah Dummer to CM, 22 Aug 1726, AAS; MS draft letter, CM to unaddressed, undated [*ca.* 1725, and beginning "I had for many years, the Happiness of a Correspondence"], AAS. **Mather may well:** SLCM, p. 385; MS letter, Jeremiah Dummer to CM, 15 Mar 1726, MHS; for the explanatory charter, see *Acts and Resolves,* I, 21–23. **As he had:** DII, pp. 800, 792–94. **The load now:** DII, pp. 703–4. **Worst of all:** this and the next paragraph from DII, pp. 705–8. CM may well have sold off at this time some of his beloved books. Thomas Prince recorded that in 1724 he bought the six-volume *Biblia Polyglotta* (London, 1657) from a Boston bookseller, who had bought them from CM (who had a second copy). "Harvard Text-Books and Reference Books of the Seventeenth Century," PCSM, XXVIII (1935), 393. **About two weeks:** DII, p.713; SLCM, p. 383; DII, p.712. **The same evening:** DII, pp. 713–14. **But there was:** DII, p. 715. **Exactly what set:** SLCM, pp. 379, 384; DII, pp. 709, 712; Checkley v. Dr. Mather and Willard, ERB (7 Apr 1724). Lydia's reasons for particularly abusing "Nancy" (Hannah) are unclear. Of all CM's children she makes the most puzzling figure in his diary. He often speaks of her as a child particularly afflicted, but without specifying what her afflictions were. Intriguingly, within days or weeks after he mentions sending her to board elsewhere, a "Hannah Mather" at nearby Roxbury (where CM had some close relatives, the Walter family) gave birth to an illegitimate child. She was ordered to pay a fine of three pounds or to suffer ten stripes at the public whipping post. See MS Sessions Minutes, 1719–1728, Suffolk County Supreme Court, Boston. Whether this was CM's daughter I have been unable to determine. **Lydia's new paroxysms:** DII, pp. 715, 717. **Virtually week by:** DII, p. 719. **Whatever the case:** DII, pp. 719, 723, 725, 727. **A historically fascinating:** *The Complete Works of Benjamin Franklin,* ed. John Bigelow, VIII (New York, 1888), 484–85; DII, p. 731. **But with July:** DII, pp. 739, 745; CM, *The True Riches* (1724); DII, p. 745. CM mentions the first debt in his diary on 6 Jul 1724, the second on 31 Jul. The language he uses in describing them is so similar that it is possible, but I believe unlikely, that the two entries describe a single demand against the estate. **Inundated with new:** DII, pp. 735, 744–45. **The next five:** Leverett's death is noted in"Diary of Jeremiah Bumstead," p. 201; for CM's conflicting characterizations of Leverett, see SLCM, p. 294, and HCR, V, 566; for the "unhappy Man," see DII, p.723; for CM's report on Harvard, see Josiah Quincy, *The History of Harvard University* (Boston, 1860), I, 558–60; for the Overseers' investigation, see John Maynard Hoffmann, "Commonwealth College: The Governance of Harvard in the Puritan Period," Diss. Harvard, 1972, p. 588. **With Leverett's death:** DII, p. 723; Niel Caplan, "Some Unpublished Letters of Benjamin Colman, 1717–1725," PMHS, LXXVII (1965), 133–34; DII, p. 736. **But Mather learned:** this and the next four paragraphs from DII, pp. 748–53. **At the time:** DII, p. 701; Sammy's admission appears in R2C, 22 Dec 1722; SML, p. 14. Like his father, Creasy had a fine handwriting, good enough for him to make something of a living as a "writer," as he is designated in SF #16702 (18 Mar 1723)—presumably a scribe or amanuensis. **Creasy, Mather was:** DII, p. 753; CM, *Things that Young People should Think upon* (1700), pp. 8, 6; DII, pp. 736, 744. **But no afflations:** DII, p. 753; Creasy's "Instrument" appears in CM, *The Words of Understanding* (1724), pp. 98–105; PA, p. 158. **Three days after:** with one exception, this and the next five paragraphs are drawn from DII, pp. 755–68. The sermon on August 30, however, appears in *The Words of Understanding,* pp. 9, 33. **On November 6:** SLCM, p. 401. Writing to Robert Wodrow, Colman mentioned CM's "hard Letter" to him and remarked that the choice of Mather "could not be obtained of the Electo[rs]." Caplan, "Some Unpublished Letters," p. 136. **On November 18:** DII, pp. 774–75; on Colman's disrelish for the presidency, see Caplan, "Some Letters"; HCR, II, cxv. **For all the:** CM, attestation in Azariah Mather, *Sabbath-Day's Rest* (1725), p. 3; DII, pp. 764, 776; CM, *Light in Darkness* (1724), p. 3. **As the event:** DII, p. 776. **Late in December:** DII, pp. 777–78. This passage in CM's diary contains the inexplicable comment, "If this Child [Samuel], must after his two Brothers, be Buried in the *Atlantic Ocean.*" As far as is known, Creasy was the only one of CM's children to have drowned. The entry seems a slip. **As had not:** DII, p. 779.

14. As Merry as One Bound for Heaven

A cough, a: DII, p. 775; SLCM, p. 404; *Letter-Book of Samuel Sewall,* CMHS, 6th ser. (1886–88), II, 223. **Seemingly drained by:** MS letter, Jeremiah Dummer to CM, 22 Aug 1726, AAS; SML, p. 139; Tallcott v. Dr. Mather, ERB (5 Oct 1724). **Sixty-two years old:** SLCM, p. 413. **Despite Mather's filiopietism:** SLCM, p. 413; BA, Eccl. XII. 2.; CM, *A Good Old Age* (1726), p. 28. **Some of these:** DII, p. 696; MS letter, Thomas Hollis to Samuel Mather, 27 Jul 1727, MHS; CM, *A Good Old Age,* p. 21; CM's first public sermon appears in his *Religious Societies* (1724); "Presentation Copy of the Rev. Cotton Mather's Ratio Disciplinae," NEHGR, XXXI (1877), 222. **But above all:** DII, p. 778; SML, p. 139. **Except his withdrawal:** on "Biblia Americana," see SLCM, p. 414; on Arianism, see SLCM, p. 408; on Pietist missionaries, see Henry Newman to Benjamin Colman, 30 Jul 1726, MHS (typed transcript); on Winthrop, see Winthrop to CM, undated [*ca.* 1726], CMHS, 6th ser., V (1892), 423 ff. **Mather also continued:** DII, p. 803; SLCM, p. 381. **In his final:** for the petitions, addresses, and decisions of church councils, see for instance CM *et al., A Serious Address To those Who unnecessarily frequent The Tavern* (1726), and MS letter, CM to brethren of the church at Lynn, 25 Feb 1727, Essex Institute; on the pirates, see DII, p. 729, and CM, *The Vial poured out upon the Sea* (1726). **On one grimly:** on Elizabeth's marriage, see Thwing Card Catalogue, MHS, and H, II, 809; CM, *Pietas Matutina* (1726), p. 39, and "The Occasion" (italics reversed). **Mather earnestly wished:** for Cutler's petition, see MS records of King's Chapel, vol. 8, MHS; on the *"Excellent Young Men,"* see CM, *The Minister* (1722), p. 45; on Prince, see SSD, II, 858, and DII, p. 812, as well as DII and SLCM, *passim.* **Mather's successors also:** SLCM, p. 391; DII, pp. 762–63, 769–70. **Mather viewed Sammy:** CM, *Hor-Hagid-gad* (1727), p. 1. **Mather did not:** I have followed the translation of CM's Latin Preface to *Manuductio* in *Dr. Cotton Mather's Student and Preacher* (London, 1789), pp. 2–59. **To the churches:** SLCM, p. 411. The 1701 version appears in MAP, Reel 5. On *Ratio* as a substitute for a new church platform, see this version, p. 174. **Age did not:** BNL, 18 Feb–7 Mar 1723 (CM probably contributed the article on a fever cure in the issue of 22–29 Aug 1723); on Feveryear, see Raymond Phineas Stearns, *Science in the British Colonies of America* (Urbana, Ill., 1970), p. 448; on Greenwood, see DII, p. 741, and Stearns, *Science in the British Colonies,* pp. 446–55, also SLCM, pp. 388–89, and I. Bernard Cohen, *Some Early Tools of American Science* (Cambridge, Mass., 1977), pp. 31–33. **Mather was disappointed:** some of CM's complaints appear in his MS letter to John Winthrop, 10 Jan 1723, MHS; on the "Curiosa Americana" of 1720, 1723, and 1724, see George Lyman Kittredge, "Cotton Mather's Communications to the Royal Society," PAAS, NS XXVI (1916), 45–57. **In sending his:** SLCM, p. 400. In quoting from *The Angel of Bethesda* here and in the next paragraphs, I follow the edition of Gordon W. Jones (Barre, Mass., 1972), and draw some points of interpretation from his excellent introduction, pp. xi–xl. *The Angel of:* on the historical significance of "Ephphatha," see Ernest G. Bormann, "Ephphatha, or, Some Advice to Stammerers," *Journal of Speech and Hearing Research,"* XII (1969), 453–61. **In the most:** on CM's early interest in van Helmont, see M, p. 673. CM thought highly enough of the concept of the "Nishmath-Chajim" to print this Capsula separately as a short work also entitled *The Angel of Bethesda* (New London, 1722), and to have included it again in his unpublished "Tri-Para-disus." **Mather saw this:** for CM's remark on *Ratio,* see SLCM, p. 411. **While writing The:** SLCM, p. 336; DII, p. 699; SLCM, p. 72; H, II, 739. **Despite this uncommonly:** SSD, II, 1052; CM, *Restitutus* (1727), pp. 22–23; CM, *The Balance of the Sanctuary* (1727), p. 24; on CM's occasional committee work and the like during his last year, see for instance Hamilton Andrews Hill, *History of the Old South*

Church (Boston, 1890), I, 421; *Boston Prints and Printmakers 1670–1775,* PCSM, XLVI (1973), 134 ff.; Frederick L. Weis, "Checklist of Portraits in the Library of the American Antiquarian Society," PAAS, NS LVI (1946), 89–90. **Lacking Mather's diaries:** CM, *Restitutus,* pp. 8–9; SLCM, p. 415. **Mather's dominant mood:** DII, p. 373; Katy's deathbed remark appears in CM's unpublished "Tri-Paradisus," MAP, Reel 7, fr. 0579; CM, *Hatzar-Maveth* (1726), pp. 13–14; the brazen serpent comparison appears in *Zalmonah* (1725); DII, pp. 785–86; MS letter, Thomas Hollis to Samuel Mather, 27 Jul 1727, MHS. **At times Mather's:** MS letter, CM to Thomas Prince, 31 Jan 1726, MHS; CM's verses appear in a privately owned copy of *Monumental Gratitude,* reproduced in facsimile in *Photostat Americana.* **Having spent much:** CM, *A Year and a Life Well Concluded* (1720), pp. 7–8; CM, *Restitutus,* p. 23. **The three paradises:** on the dates of composition, see DIII, p. 91, and DII, p. 811; the text of "Tri-Paradisus" appears in MAP, Reel 7. **Mather's vision of:** DII, p. 805n.; SLCM, p. 377; CM's earlier views on the Second Coming appear in his unpublished "Problema Theologicum," MAP, Reel 7. **Mather now believed:** translation of CM's Latin Preface to *Manuductio,* in *Dr. Cotton Mather's Student,* p. 9. **Mather does not:** BG, 26 Dec–2 Jan 1726/7 and 5–12 Jun 1727; CM, *Christian Loyalty* (1727), pp. 21–22. **It began, the:** CM, *The Terror of the Lord* (1727), p. 1; Arthur B. Ellis, *History of the First Church in Boston, 1630–1880* (Boston, 1881), q. p. 198. **Movables clattered as:** William T. Youngs, Jr., *God's Messengers: Religious Leadership in Colonial New England, 1700–1750* (Baltimore, 1976), p. 111 (cups and mugs, "the Great Day"); SSD, II, 1055; CM, *The Terror of the Lord,* p. 2 (ships); *Philosophical Transactions of the Royal Society,* #409 (1729), p. 125 (Newbury); BG, 6–13 Nov 1727 (Guilford); BG, 30 Oct–6 Nov 1727. **Mather may have:** CM, *Juga Jucunda* (1727), p. 1; on the length of the services and the size of the gathering, see BNL, 26 Oct–3 Nov 1727, and CM, *The Terror of the Lord,* pp. 1–2. **Mather spoke now:** CM, *The Terror of the Lord,* pp. 14, 6, 13, 19, 25, 27–28. **Mather's warning was:** Samuel G. Drake, *The History and Antiquities of Boston* (Boston, 1856), p. 577; on the rise in admissions, see Youngs, *God's Messengers,* p. 111, and R2C. **Hoping to prolong:** SLCM, p. 418; CM, *Boanerges* (1727), p. 43. **On December 24:** CM, *The Comfortable Chambers* (1728); MS Treasurer's Accounts of the Second Church, MHS.

Conclusion: Copp's Hill

Cotton Mather's final: SML, p. 153; Joshua Gee, *Israel's Mourning for Aaron's Death* (1728), p. 27; Benjamin Colman, *The Holy Walk and Glorious Translation of Blessed Enoch* (1728), p. 27. **But to Mather:** Samuel Mather, *The Departure and Character of Elijah Considered and Improved* (1728), p. 14; Gee, *Israel's Mourning,* p. 29. **With a boom:** *New-England Weekly Journal,* 12 Feb 1728 and 15 Jan 1728; DII, p. 444. **At daybreak two:** *New-England Weekly Journal,* 12 Feb 1728; on the ultimate duration of the quakes, see *Philosophical Transactions of the Royal Society,* #409 (1729), p. 127; R2C. **Saturday, February 10:** SML, p. 159; Gee, *Israel's Mourning,* p. 30. **Sunday, as he:** SML, pp. 154, 156; Gee, *Israel's Mourning,* p. 25; Samuel Mather, *Departure and Character,* pp. 14–15. **Monday was Cotton:** Samuel Mather, *Departure and Character,* pp. 15–16; Gee, *Israel's Mourning,* pp. 29, 27. **It was of:** all quotations in this and the following six paragraphs drawn from Thomas Prince, *The Departure of Elijah lamented* (1728), and from the above sermons by Gee, Colman, and Samuel Mather. **Mather was buried:** MS diary of Benjamin Walker, 1726–42, MHS; "The Diary of Ebenezer Parkman 1719–1728," PAAS, LXXI (1961), 211. **Taken from Mather's:** MS diary of Benjamin Walker; SSD, II, 1959–60; *New-England Weekly Journal,* 26 Feb 1728. **The procession ended:** Nathaniel B.

Index

UPROOTING POVERTY
The South African Challenge

Francis Wilson &
Mamphela Ramphele

Report for the Second Carnegie Inquiry into Poverty and
Development in Southern Africa

W. W. Norton & Company
New York · London

First published 1989 in southern Africa by David Philip, Publisher (Pty) Ltd,
208 Werdmuller Centre, Claremont 7700, South Africa

First American edition, 1989

© 1989 Francis Wilson and Mamphela Ramphele

ISBN 0-393-02610-8

W. W. Norton & Company, Inc., 500 Fifth Avenue, New York, NY 10110
W. W. Norton & Company, Ltd., 37 Great Russell Street, London WC1B 3NU

Printed in the Republic of South Africa

1 2 3 4 5 6 7 8 9 0

Contents

Photographs

Preface

The Second Carnegie Inquiry into Poverty and Development in Southern Africa came at a period of great upheaval in the sub-continent, a time of truth when, finally, the illusions were stripped away and the rulers and the rich had to face what the prophets and the poets had long been saying. This process of uncovering the truth took many forms and was accompanied by much wilful refusal to face facts and to understand. The Yiddish phrase, *Sie mach sig nicht wissen dich* (You make yourself not to know), much used in Europe in the 1930s, conveys this state of mind most accurately. The television service, a state monopoly, refused to run footage showing unrest in the townships, and the state declared a two-stage (and, after June 1986, seemingly endless) State of Emergency with dictatorial rules about what might or might not be reported (even by overseas journalists), thus drawing a veil over much of what was happening in the country and plunging white South Africans, in particular, into even greater darkness and misunderstanding.

But this censorship, though powerfully distorting, could not sustain the illusion. Although the system was enormously powerful and although those working for change often overestimated their own strength relative to those forces maintaining the existing power structure, there is no doubt that during the 1980s a sea-change took place in South African politics – a change which future historians may date back to 1976 – whereby the certainties and seeming permanence of the Verwoerdian apartheid era gave way to a recognition that South Africa had a future beyond apartheid. The monster was still alive and kicking all too hard, but virtually everybody recognised that it could not go on for ever. The major African political organisations, banned in 1960 and virtually unmentionable for two decades, resurfaced in the public conscious-ness. People began to talk and think about a post-apartheid society. This Inquiry is part of that broader historical process.

The origins of this book go back more than fifty years to the Great Depression, when the rulers of South Africa were troubled by the fact that large numbers of whites, uprooted from the land during the previous generation by war, drought, pestilence, population growth, and the capitalisa-tion of agriculture, were pouring into the cities to live, ill-equipped for modern industrial society, in dire poverty. Faced with this problem, but unwilling to consider the wider ramifications of poverty in general and the no less dire straits of the black population in particular, a team of university and church people set up the Carnegie Commission on the Poor White Problem in South Africa with help from a non-profit philanthropic trust, the Carnegie Corporation of New York. Within the limits of its terms of reference the Commission performed its task well and emerged at the end of several years with a number of reports that spelled out the dimensions of poverty amongst white (particularly Afrikaans-speaking) South Africans, drew attention to 'the process of impoverishment', and made recommendations for action. The failure of the Commission lay in the extent to which the limitation of its concern to whites only meant that its findings were used to promote strategies for improving the position of poor whites, often at the expense of poor blacks. For these findings were eventually incorporated into the thinking of the National Party in its drive for power, and in the implementation of some of its subsequent policies.

Although the first Commission did note that the problems of black poverty were no less acute than those of poor whites and that they would require study on their own, the focus remained primarily on whites, and, as the economy grew with the expansion of gold mining in the 1930s and the industrial developments of the Second World War and post-war years, poverty amongst whites receded almost to nothing. Blacks too were drawn into the economy in increasing numbers but poverty remained acute, although largely unexamined. The idea of another major study was suggested from time to time, including in the mid-1930s by one of the first Carnegie Commissioners and in the late 1940s by the historian C. W. de Kiewiet. But it lay dormant until the beginning of 1980 when finally it was decided to begin work on a second major inquiry into poverty and development.

In January 1980, a feasibility study was commissioned. Thus began more than two years of preparatory work and a great deal of travelling by a number of different people in order to discuss the idea throughout the length and breadth of the country, across a wide political spectrum, and particularly amongst black South Africans, to see whether such a study made sense in terms of priorities and, if it did, on what basis it should be organised. This period included time spent assessing other research around the world. The rash of poverty studies during the 1970s in Britain, Ireland, the European Common Market, Australia, and the United States were compared and contrasted not only with each other but with numerous studies, often sponsored by the World Bank or the International Labour Organisation (ILO), in Kenya, Sri Lanka, Brazil, India, and elsewhere.

During the preliminary phase when soundings were being taken three important aspects of the Inquiry became abundantly clear. Firstly, that any study of poverty can only be truly meaningful if there is real inside understanding and participation of those communities that have to endure poverty. In the South African context where the vast majority of those who are poor are black, this meant that, as far as possible, the centre of gravity of the Inquiry had to be black rather than white. Secondly, it became clear that the Inquiry should be designed as an open-ended, ongoing process rather than as a once-off affair. The original idea of appointing a Commission of Wise Persons that would travel around the country in the steps of the first Carnegie Commission taking evidence and then writing a report, was rejected for a number of reasons, including a belated realisation that such a procedure would not involve many people in wrestling with the issues over any length of time. What was needed was a structure that would draw in a large number of people, across a wide political spectrum and from diverse disciplines. Thirdly, whilst the study gradually took shape in discussions around the country, a striking contrast in views became apparent. White South Africans were generally enthusiastic about the need for research to gather facts on poverty. Black South Africans were unimpressed by data-gathering. 'Why spend money finding out what we already know?', they asked. 'What we need is action against poverty.' That view was crucial in guiding the subsequent work of the Carnegie Inquiry.

How then was the Inquiry conducted? From its base at the University of Cape Town the Inquiry sought to involve all those interested in thinking and writing about the problem. In the first instance the organisers visited some 22 universities around southern Africa inviting people to participate; looking for research already under way that could fit into the Inquiry; and suggesting areas that needed to be researched. In addition a number of working groups were set up to focus particularly on strategies for action against poverty. These met over a period of two years to discuss strategies, and in the process themselves generated a range of papers. The groups, led by their chairpersons and secretaries, focused on: law (Fikile Bam and Wallace Mgoqi); education (John Samuel and Bill Nasson); the role of the church (Allan Boesak and Margaret Nash); public allocation of resources (Pieter le Roux and Delia Hendrie); food and nutrition (J. V. O. Reid and Peter Moll). In addition a number of photographers, led by Omar Badsha, worked on finding ways of complementing the work of writers by means of documentary photography. Other less formal groups focused on a number of other areas including health, housing, energy, labour, and rural development.

Into these various groupings were drawn not only university people but also lawyers, teachers, pastors, social workers, farmers, journalists, and doctors. Emphasis was placed on involving people whose own experience gave them insight into what it means to be poor.

The Inquiry was not publicly launched until more than two years after work on it first began. Then followed another two years of active research before all those working on the subject were drawn together in a conference held at the University of Cape Town in April 1984. Just over 300 papers (see list in Appendix 1) were delivered at the conference, in which some 450 people participated. Although it was by no means the main object of the Inquiry, the conference itself was a happening of some significance. Those who came, all in their individual capacities, had thought deeply about poverty and represented a wide spectrum of all South African society. In addition to the papers there was a photographic exhibition; an art display; music and drama; and documentary films made in South Africa. There was also a festival ('Signs of Hope') – drawn from around the world – of films showing development projects that have been successful, ranging from the Self-Employed Women's Association of Ahmedabad, India, through the Mondragón industrial co-operative in Spain, to adult literacy training in Peru; from bio-gas digesters in China to the achievements of the New Deal's Tennessee Valley Authority (see Appendix 2). But the most important part of the whole conference was the informal discussion between people as they met each other in an atmosphere that encouraged the exchange of ideas. The conference was, as was said at the time, an exhilarating experience with its diversity and its sense of energy focused on a common problem. There was a sense in which it was itself, for six brief but hectic days, a small model of what South Africa could be.

The Inquiry did not end there. Once all the papers had been gathered together it was possible to identify a number of gaps where further work needed to be done. Thus, for example, the population issue was seen at the conference as having been inadequately tackled, and a subsequent workshop made it possible to analyse the matter in more depth. Other workshops looked also at the role of co-operatives, at macro-economic policy, and at public works programmes. A series of post-conference papers was initiated (see Appendix 1) to clarify understanding of issues raised at the conference and to provide a forum to generate recommendations by individuals and working groups for strategies and action. A series of books was planned. To disseminate basic information as widely as possible, a book of the best photographs exhibited at the conference together with an introductory essay was published, entitled *South Africa: The Cordoned Heart*, edited by Omar Badsha (1986). This book captures the insights of some of the country's best photographers, who were asked simply to share their interpretation of the meaning of poverty. Most striking of all is their unanimous concentration on the dignity of all those enduring poverty. Subsequently a report on children in South Africa, drawing on the work of the Carnegie Inquiry, was prepared for the United Nations Children's Fund (Unicef) and published as *Children on the Frontline* (1987).

Several other books analysing specific issues in some depth have been prepared. One focuses on education; another two are geographic in their focus, looking at poverty in the cities and on the farms and smaller towns of the 'platteland'. One or two other volumes may follow.

This book is an overview. Drawing primarily on all the conference and post-conference papers, we have tried to provide a coherent analysis of the nature and causes of poverty in South Africa, and have then drawn together the main ideas regarding strategies for action that have emerged during the course of inquiry. Although the book is by two people, it is important to stress that this is not exclusively our work. Whilst others must not be held responsible for analyses or strategies, nuances or ideas, which they do not share, it is nevertheless true that this book belongs to all those who have participated, by writing and discussion, in the Carnegie Inquiry. This book is not a consensus document. Its substance has been quarried from the mine of information and ideas contained in the hundreds of research papers written during the eight years since the Inquiry was first mooted in Cape Town in

January 1980. At one level this book should be used merely as a guide to the wealth of material that is there. Readers are urged to go back to the original papers (Appendix 1), all of which have been published and which may be found in a number of libraries around the world.

The second Carnegie Inquiry did not take place in a vacuum. It was built firmly on the foundations laid by earlier generations (Wentzel, 1983). We are only too conscious of its own shortcomings which will require further work in later years. At the same time it was designed as part of an ongoing process which we trust will continue – from gathering basic data, through analysis, to strategies for action. Whilst there may be readers who disagree with our political analyses we invite them to accompany us through the argument of this book in order to put poverty firmly at the centre of the national agenda. The Inquiry may be judged to have been a failure if, finally, it has no impact on the lives of those who are poor. It is our hope that this book, and its companion volumes, will prove useful to all those struggling for a just, non-racial, non-sexist, and democratic South Africa.

Acknowledgements

It is not possible to name all the people who have contributed, in one way or another, to the work that has gone into this book. In the long list of papers delivered at the Carnegie conference in 1984 (including those that preceded the conference) and of the subsequent post-conference papers (see Appendix 1) there are the names of about 450 researchers whose writing provided the primary source of information and ideas for this book. We have tried to ensure that all quotations and the main facts derived from these papers are acknowledged in the text but we are mindful that we have often drawn from our reading of these papers without specific reference. We wish simply to acknowledge our debt to all our colleagues and express the hope that this book will encourage readers to go back to the wealth of material contained in the original papers. In addition to these writers we also wish to thank all the photographers, film-makers, artists, musicians, and participants in working groups and workshops whose involvement in the Second Carnegie Inquiry enriched all our understanding.

The writers of research papers could not have got anywhere without the willingness of people to answer questions and to provide information as they went about their own lives, often in circumstances of great difficulty. On behalf of these research workers we wish to acknowledge our gratitude for the patient help provided to probing outsiders.

Academics from some 22 universities around southern Africa were involved, at one time or another, in the work of the Inquiry. Supported by these institutions people gave freely of their time, thus enabling the Inquiry to generate far more research than it could possibly have commissioned. We are grateful to all these universities. We would add a special word of thanks to the University of Cape Town and its Vice-Chancellor, Stuart Saunders. The Inquiry was based at UCT, which provided administrative and institutional backing so necessary in a venture of this kind. The Vice-Chancellor chaired the finance committee and was supportive of the Inquiry in a host of ways. So too were all our colleagues in the university but especially those in the Southern Africa Labour and Development Research Unit (Saldru) which organised the Inquiry, and in the teaching departments of Anthropology and Economics which bore the brunt of our prolonged absence from other duties. Dudley Horner (Deputy Director of Saldru) and Martin West (Professor of Anthropology) carried heavy loads on our behalf. Wilfred Wentzel and Helen

Zille, working full-time for the Inquiry, played key roles in mobilising research around the country.

During the long process of the Inquiry and whilst writing this book, seminars and discussions have been held and lectures given in many places around southern Africa and in different parts of the world. The encouragement, criticism, and suggestions that flowed from these have been invaluable.

Long before the Inquiry began, one of us spent seven weeks as a guest of the Indian Council for Cultural Relations lecturing at Jawaharlal Nehru University in New Delhi. The opportunity to travel through much of India visiting development projects and listening to what was happening was enriching and thought-provoking. So too was the opportunity to spend a year at the beginning of the Inquiry in Oxford (at Balliol College and in the Institute for Economics and Statistics) reading about studies of poverty in different parts of the world. Both experiences have left their mark on this book.

At the other end of the Inquiry, the opportunity to spend five months as a Visiting Research Fellow writing in a stimulating international environment at the Center for Health and Human Resources Policy in the Kennedy School of Government, Harvard University, was invaluable, as was the invitation to deliver the Commonwealth Lectures in Cambridge, England, early in 1988. Based on a draft of the book, they provided the opportunity to test and clarify the main arguments.

A host of friends and colleagues have read and commented on parts or all of various drafts. We shall not name them here but we are deeply grateful for their generous help. In addition there were two seminars, one in Amsterdam (December 1986) organised under the auspices of the South Africa Economic Research and Training Project, the other at Yale (November 1987) organised by the Southern African Research Program. The criticisms and comments received were particularly helpful in reshaping the book.

We wish also to acknowledge our thanks to the Carnegie Corporation of New York, its trustees, two successive presidents, and the staff including David Hood, Director of the International Program when the project was launched. Funding for the Second Inquiry into Poverty and Development in Southern Africa was generous and came entirely without strings. Conceived in South Africa and run by South Africans, this Inquiry has been rooted in the area of study. At the same time, the sensitive involvement of the Carnegie Corporation, led first by Alan Pifer and subsequently by David Hamburg, provided invaluable encouragement, experience and perspective. The Inquiry has benefited from the opportunity to test ideas in the international arena. The Ford Foundation provided substantial help for a programme which enabled a number of young black South Africans to be trained as research workers during the course of the Inquiry so that not only did they learn but they also produced useful papers. In this way it was possible to use the Inquiry itself as a pilot project for the sort of organisation of training and research discussed in the strategy section of this book (see Chapter 14).

Readers will agree that visual material can add a great deal to the written word, not least when the latter contains a lot of statistics. We are grateful to

Tina Coombes for the diagrams; to Ralene van Staden of the Institute for Cartographic Analysis at the University of Stellenbosch who drew the maps; and to Omar Badsha who, as photographic editor, found the remarkable pictures used to introduce each chapter. As far as the text itself is concerned, Michael King supported the writing down the years in a host of practical ways including making the index. Liz King went through the penultimate draft inserting many corrections. Russell Martin, as publisher's editor, worked long hours at great speed with his special combination of gentleness and firmness both to edit the text and to design the book.

Finally a word of appreciation, inadequate as it is, to the various members of our families, especially Lindy Wilson, who have lived with, participated in, encouraged, supported, criticised, and generally made possible the Carnegie Inquiry and the writing of this book for many more years than they had bargained.

Authors' note

References, adapted from the Harvard style, are included in the text and kept as simple as possible. The book draws primarily from the Carnegie research papers which are listed in Appendix 1. References in the book identify simply the number of the paper and the page number. Thus *33: 23* refers to the Carnegie conference paper by Mary-Jane Morifi, 'Life among the poor in Philipstown', page 23. Where reference is to a paper from the post-conference series (PCS), or to a policy paper (PP), the number is preceded by the appropriate initials. All other references are identified by the author's surname, date of publication, and page number. The full details can then be traced in the Bibliography.

Acronyms and abbreviations are identified in full the first time they are used, thus: Southern Africa Labour and Development Research Unit (Saldru). Where, as easily happens, readers forgets an acronym they may refer to the list on p. *xix*. Other terms (e.g. *platteland*) with which some readers may be unfamiliar are explained the first time they are used.

Exchange rates for different currencies are troublesome. The value of the rand against most other currencies has changed sharply during the 1980s. In terms of the US dollar it has fallen, as shown in the accompanying diagram, from $1.30 in January 1980 to 43 US cents in January 1988.

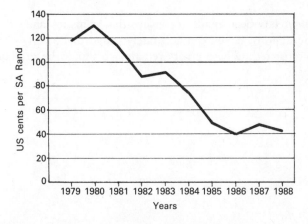

Fig. A.01: Exchange rate, 1979–88

In general, monetary values in the text are given in rands. Where conversions to other currencies are made there is a note indicating the rate, appropriate to the date, for which the conversion is made.

Due to inflation the purchasing power of the rand has itself changed markedly over time. If we take 1985 as the base year (=100), the consumer price index rose from 59 in June 1980 to 154 in June 1988. The following diagram shows how the value of the rand, in terms of the goods that it could buy, has fallen over the decade.

Fig. A.02: Purchasing power of the rand, 1981-88

If we take 1985 = 1.00, the value of the rand fell from 1.70 in 1981 to 0.65 in 1988. Given these changes it is important that where comparisons are made due note is taken of the year to which such figures as wages or minimum living levels refer.

Every effort has been made to ensure that statistics and all other facts, including quotations, have been accurately transcribed, fairly presented, and correctly interpreted. Where errors remain we should be grateful if readers would tell us.

Abbreviations

BLS	Botswana, Lesotho and Swaziland
BMR	Bureau of Market Research, University of South Africa
Cosatu	Congress of South African Trade Unions
CPI	consumer price index
CPS	Current Population Survey
DET	Department of Education and Training
EGS	employment guarantee scheme
Escom	Electricity Supply Commission
GDP	gross domestic product
GNP	gross national product
HEL	household effective level
HSL	household subsistence level
ILO	International Labour Organisation
IMF	International Monetary Fund
IMR	infant mortality rate
Iscor	Iron and Steel Corporation
MAG	Montagu en Ashton Gemeenskapsdiens
MLL	minimum living level
MNR	Movement for National Resistance (Renamo)
NAMDA	National Medical and Dental Association
NCHS	National Center for Health Statistics
NECC	National Education Crisis Committee
NGO	non-governmental organisation
PCS	post-Carnegie conference series
PDL	poverty datum line
PEM	protein-energy malnutrition
PWV	Pretoria–Witwatersrand–Vereeniging
Sached	South African Committee for Higher Education
SADCC	Southern African Development Co-ordination Conference
SATS	South African Transport Services
SLL	supplementary living level
SPP	Surplus People Project
SWP	Saldru working paper
TBVC	Transkei, Bophuthatswana, Venda and Ciskei
Teba	The Employment Bureau of Africa
UIF	unemployment insurance fund
Unicef	United Nations Children's Fund
WHO	World Health Organisation

Introduction:
The challenge

Poverty is a profoundly political issue. Thousands of South African babies are dying of malnutrition and associated diseases; two million children are growing up stunted for lack of sufficient calories in one of the few countries in the world that exports food; tens of thousands of men are spending their entire working years as lonely 'labour units' in single-sex hostels whilst their wives and children live generally in great poverty in the overcrowded reserves. This structural violence assaults the majority of people living in South Africa as harshly as any physical confrontation.

There are four reasons why poverty is significant. The first is because of the damage it inflicts upon individuals who must endure it; the second is its sheer inefficiency in economic terms. Hungry children cannot study properly; malnourished adults cannot be fully productive as workers; and an economy where a large proportion of the population is very poor has a structure of demand that does not encourage the production and marketing of the goods that are most needed. The third reason relates to the consequences for any society where poverty is also the manifestation of great inequality. As Raymond Aron has reminded us, the existence of too great a degree of inequality makes human community impossible. Finally there is the fact that poverty in many societies is itself symptomatic of a deeper malaise. For it is often the consequence of a process which simultaneously produces wealth for some whilst impoverishing others. 'Poverty', writes C. T. Kurien, 'is the carcass left over from wealth acquisition.'

Nowhere is this more true than in South Africa where poverty is deep and widespread and where the degree of inequality is as great as in any other country in the world. Indeed, in terms of the Gini coefficient, South Africa has the highest measure of inequality of the 57 countries for which data are available (PCS 16: 23). It is clear that any attempt to understand the nature of poverty and the process of impoverishment here must take one to the heart of the society and its contradictions. Indeed we would argue that the development of effective strategies to deal with poverty in South Africa constitutes the central, fundamental challenge to our society.

But poverty is not confined to South Africa nor indeed will the country's Gini coefficient necessarily remain at the top of the world table. Grinding poverty is to be found in many different parts of the world; gaping inequality between rich and poor is visible virtually everywhere. Why then should one focus on poverty in South Africa as being a special case ? There are, as we have argued elsewhere (Badsha, 1985: 9), three interlocking factors which, taken together, justify the assertion that poverty in South Africa is unique. First is the width of the gulf between rich and poor, the degree of inequality. Second, as we shall see in the second part of this book, is the extent to which the poverty that exists is a consequence of deliberate policy. The third aspect has to do with the way in which material poverty in South Africa is reinforced by racist policies that are an assault on people's humanity. As David Hamburg, president of both the American Association for the Advancement of Science, and the Carnegie Corporation of New York, argued at the University of Cape Town in 1984:

Poverty is partly a matter of income and partly a matter of human dignity. It is one thing to have a very low income but to be treated with respect by your compatriots; it is quite another matter to have a very low income and to be harshly depreciated by more powerful compatriots. Let us speak then of human impoverishment: low income plus harsh disrespect ... To speak of impoverishment in this sense is to speak of human degradation so profound as to undermine any reasonable and decent standard of human life. (309: 7)

In South Africa that harsh disrespect is embedded in the very structure of the society in many different ways, including the migrant labour system and a set of laws that both classifies and discriminates against people according to racist criteria that are unacceptable anywhere in the world.

In using the metaphor of uprooting poverty we wish to emphasise the need for radical action. The roots of impoverishment in southern Africa lie deep, as we shall see in Chapter 10, in the history of the region's political economy which includes not only apartheid as it evolved after 1948 but also the pattern of racial capitalism that grew during the centuries before that. We use the metaphor also because it suggests a paradigm of growth rather than of engineering. Whilst it is helpful and encouraging to think of rebuilding or reconstructing a new South Africa we believe it is important not to lose sight of the extent to which society is an organism that grows rather than a structure that can be dismantled and reassembled like a motorcar engine. Strategies against poverty involve not only pulling up the roots of processes that impoverish people but also planting (and nurturing) those seeds that will produce good fruit.

Uprooting poverty implies not only a transformation of agriculture including redistribution of land, but also a restructuring of relations between capital and labour. Questions of power and ownership are crucial. So too is ideology. Renewal of South African society is not possible without the defeat of the racist ideology which sustains the current ruling elite. Apartheid cannot be reformed. It is a way of thinking about human beings and their social relationships which, like Nazism, has to be rooted out of both individual and collective consciousness so that the society can grow along entirely different lines. Underlying all strategies against poverty must be clear recognition of the necessity for a fundamental redistribution of power.

The confrontation between rich and poor is very real. War rages in the country although it is often hidden. During 1985 and 1986 the street battles between township teenagers and the police and military forces of the Botha government were a visible manifestation of a civil war that was first declared in 1960 with the banning of the major African Congress organisations which forced the democratic movements to establish underground military units. Whilst the upheavals of 1985 and 1986 were apparently succeeded by a quiet period it would be a mistake to assume that the war no longer exists. The army has moved in to control the townships. Systematic raids by police and soldiers on all centres of protest and resistance – whether in Worcester, Beaufort West, Cradock or in the townships or the trade-union offices of the major metropolitan centres – are part of an ongoing civil war. So too is the continued wave of bannings of organisations and detentions of people dedicated to peaceful political activity against apartheid. The superficial calm of Casspirs and censorship is not a sign of peace as many whites in the protected suburbs listening to the propaganda of the state broadcasting and television system wish to believe. It is the enforced silence of people under occupation.

By many criteria South Africa, in the latter half of the 1980s, has reached a classic pre-revolutionary situation. But it is just such times in history whose signs are notoriously difficult to read. It is thus not surprising that the feelings of those working for a new order in South Africa tend to vacillate between moods of wild optimism when the system is believed to be tottering on its last legs, and moods of deep depression when everything seems stuck, the status quo is firmly entrenched, and the transformation of the society into a real democracy unlikely in the extreme. It would be foolish for anyone to claim certainty in predicting the future, particularly when the history of the region is littered with unfulfilled predictions, ranging from expectations amongst South African progressive forces in the late 1950s that by the mid-1960s, at the latest, majority rule would be firmly established, to confident assertions by conservative voices in the early 1970s that Portuguese rule of Mozambique and Angola would surely last for another century. It is all too easy to become swayed by wishful thinking or alternatively to fail to see the significance of some critical shift.

No matter how cool the analysis, predictions about the future will continue to differ. Nevertheless, we believe it is possible to sketch out strategies of action against poverty that allow for a range of future possibilities that lies somewhere between the two extremes of revolution-around-the-corner and the-system-is-here-for-ever. Our starting point is that the structure of power currently in place in South Africa is such that there is virtually no likelihood of the present government (or some revised version of it) either voluntarily handing over power to democratic rulers or finding itself coerced by guerilla activity, economic sanctions and other pressures into negotiating away its entrenched position, in the immediate future. The struggle for liberation in South Africa has gone on for many years and our assessment, alas, is that it still has long years to run. We do not believe that the euphoria of imminent salvation in the mid-1980s was based upon a convincing analysis, nor that it is politically helpful (not least because of the gigantic hangover it can leave behind when the mood subsides). Nor do we believe however that despair is an appropriate response to the situation. Times are very tough and it is easy to be paralysed by a feeling of hopelessness or to join the system so that one survives without challenging it in any way. But that response too is based upon an unconvincing analysis. For, underneath all the smoke and trauma, South Africa is changing. Urbanisation, education, unionisation, population growth and the emerging culture of liberation to name only five processes, are altering the very framework within which the political debate takes place. Such change does not inevitably lead towards liberation of the society but it can do so. The crucial point is that the status quo itself is not static.

Furthermore we know that society does not change in its entirety overnight. Whilst sharp breaks may happen, history teaches that many of the underlying structures in society continue to evolve out of their past. Thus it is surely true that the shape of South African society in future, 'after the revolution', will depend critically on the foundations that are laid now. It is helpful to see today's present as tomorrow's past; that is, as a period when work is done that will help to shape the future.

But what sort of work can do this? It is useful to start by considering the time-frame and to make a distinction between short-run and long-run action. Long-run strategies against poverty in South Africa may be defined as those which may be considered in a frame where there is sufficient time to assume political flexibility. The absence of those current political constraints that hamper or prevent the immediate adoption of particular policies which would benefit the poor does not of course imply that there will be no constraints in the long run. But it shifts the focus from concentration on current political policies to consideration of other parameters. No matter how much political flexibility there might be in the long run, certain hard facts have to be taken into account in the formulation of any policy. These include such matters as the harshness of the agricultural climate throughout much of the country; demographic patterns; the bias, both racial and geographic, in the pattern of capital accumulation particularly during the past hundred years; the central role played by gold mining in the generation of wealth in the economy; and the fact that provision of formal education, technical training, and experience in management has generally been of far better quality for, and gone to a much larger proportion of, whites than blacks. However much one might wish it to be otherwise, history cannot be changed. But to deal effectively with its legacy and to change the future it is necessary to face squarely the realities which would constrain any policy proposals. Thus, one of the major tasks facing all those concerned about the future of the country is tough thinking about the policies that should be pursued by a democratic government wishing to develop effective strategies against poverty. In a later chapter (15) we focus on these questions.

In the short run we consider those strategies which are viable in the current (1988) political context. People are sometimes tempted to reject all such strategies against poverty on the grounds that they serve merely to legitimise, prop up, or otherwise reinforce an unjust status quo. Thus rural development projects, for example, are questioned on the grounds that if they are located in the reserves – where the need is greatest – they will be used by the 'homeland' governments to bolster their own credibility and so reinforce the Bantustan structure of the apartheid system. There may well be projects which do strengthen the system in this way, but it is not inevitable that they do so. Our analysis suggests that independent, generally non-governmental,* organisa-

---

* We note that there are some bodies which, though largely funded by the state, can contribute meaningfully to the process of change. A good example is the University of the Western Cape which, together with some of the other, older, open universities, has won an important measure of freedom that places it in a very different position from such places as Turfloop (the University of

tions (NGOs) have a vital role to play in the wider liberation struggle provided that their goals are carefully thought through so as to be consistent with the long-run goals of a truly free society and that the methods they use are consistent with, and help towards achieving, the ends they seek.

The distinction between short run and long run helps to clarify the need for two types of thinking: one relating to what can be done within present political constraints, and the other focusing on policies that should be pursued in the entirely different political circumstances of a fully democratic, non-racial government being in power in South Africa. The distinction also helps draw attention to the need for consistency and interaction between these two modes of thought so that strategies conceived in the two paradigms should be mutually reinforcing. Whilst time is a significant component of this distinction it seems more helpful to distinguish between the potential of independent organisations, particularly in the short run, on one hand, and the role of the state, considering mainly the long run, on the other (see Chapters 14 and 15).

It is necessary to be clear as to what such an approach does not do. It does not address itself to the specific political questions about what strategies should be pursued in order to bring about the fundamental redistribution of power from the present pattern to one that would be appropriate in a democratic non-racial society. Whilst such a redistribution is a prerequisite of any fundamental attack on poverty in South Africa we have deliberately excluded any direct consideration as to how this might be brought about, in order to focus attention on what we believe to be important (and complementary) strategies outlined here.

If we are to develop strategies against poverty we ought to know in some detail the nature of the problem with which we are dealing. This implies not only a factual description of what exists but also an analysis that illuminates as clearly as possible why it exists. Facts are essential for two reasons. Firstly, they are politically powerful on their own account. The scandalous particularity of the detail of what it means to be poor can jolt people into an awareness that something must be done. Secondly, and most important, facts are necessary as a foundation on which to build strategies for action. Without knowing some details about the nature of poverty in a particular situation, it is not possible to work out specific proposals or even general lines of action about it. To be told, for example, that one-half of all households in South Africa are poor is important but, from a strategic point of view, not especially helpful. To find out, on the other hand, that two-thirds of all black households do not have access to electricity in a country that generates 60 per cent of the electrical energy on the African continent stimulates all sorts of ideas about what could be done, as well as questions about the forces shaping the existing political economy of fuel.

The first part of this book, then, consists of an examination of the pattern of poverty in South Africa. It is essentially an exploration into the shadow side

the North), where the campus is under military occupation and there is no room for independent thought and action. For an important debate about the limits of state-funded institutions, see Jakes Gerwel and Neville Alexander in *Die Suid-Afrikaan* (June/July 1988).

of an apparently gleaming economy, and we invite readers to keep going through the nine chapters that spell out, as succinctly as we can, the main features of the problem. The information contained there is, we believe, the minimum necessary for the purpose of thinking through both the possibilities and the limits of strategies for action.

The second part of the book seeks to deepen understanding of why the pattern of poverty uncovered in the previous part should be shaped as it is. We try to move beyond a simplistic analysis which tends to blame poverty on some single, vague, but fashionable reason such as 'population explosion', 'drought', 'incompetence', 'capitalism', 'socialism', or even 'apartheid'. We would certainly not exclude any of these factors from serious consideration but we would insist that each one be carefully defined and analysed. Any connections between these factors also need to be explored.

Facts and analysis are, as we have argued, necessary pre-conditions for the major goal of the Carnegie Inquiry, which has been to encourage tough realistic thinking about strategies. Facts may be startling; analysis may be correct; but unless an Inquiry such as this generates effective strategies against poverty one may legitimately ask what value it has. It is the attempt to meet this goal that forms the third part of the book, where a framework for thinking about the problems is proposed and a set of concrete suggestions put forward for consideration by all those concerned with the future of the country.

PART ONE
The many faces of poverty

1
A matter of definition

> Poverty is not knowing where your next meal is going to come from, and always wondering when the council is going to put your furniture out and always praying that your husband must not lose his job. To me that is poverty.
> – Mrs. Witbooi, Philipstown, Karoo
> (33: 23)

Poverty is like illness. It shows itself in different ways in different historical situations, and it has diverse causes. Treatment generally requires careful diagnosis. In this book we are concerned with discovering the nature of poverty as it exists in South Africa today, and with understanding its root causes in order that we may think through as systematically as possible what action must be taken both to 'cure', or remove, existing poverty as well as to prevent further outbreaks of this scourge. We shall find that it is not always easy to make a clear distinction between the facts or symptoms of poverty and its origins. Not only are there several different dimensions of material and non-material poverty but there is also a complex interaction between cause and effect, which makes it difficult to describe a state of poverty without considering those factors, themselves aspects of poverty, that cause further misery (4: 1–18). For example, is it best to think of illiteracy in modern society as a manifestation, even a consequence, of poverty or as one of its causes? There is no clear answer to this question, but we have wrestled with it as we have sought to bring some sort of order to the mass of material quarried for this book by hundreds of different research workers all over the sub-continent.

Danger of statistics

In his classic study on *The Mismeasure of Man* (1981), Stephen Jay Gould has shown the great dangers facing all scientists who seek to reduce complex phenomena (such as intelligence) to single numbers. Lest we fall into the same trap of those white, middle-class, male natural scientists of Europe and North America who for years and years persuaded themselves (by careful statistical measurement of cranium size, skull capacity, or whatever) that somehow the owners of white, middle-class, male skulls were naturally more intelligent than those unfortunate beings who were black, poor, and/or female, it is important that we begin with an explicit recognition of the complexity of poverty.

In seeking to define the phenomenon we must be careful not to confine our thinking to those characteristics that appear important to people living within the sheltered walls of an urban university. For this reason when the Carnegie Inquiry began, research workers were not provided with a nice clean definition of poverty that they could measure (and compare with other places and other times), but were told instead to go out into the highways and byways of the country to meet people who endured poverty and those who lived or worked with them and to listen to what they, from their own experience, understood poverty to mean. And then to describe and try to measure that.

This is an untidy process and was scathingly condemned by an economist of the World Bank, at a seminar in Washington on the Inquiry, as one that produced mere 'anecdotal evidence'. What he failed to note was that until one has a real feel for the situation in which one is working, the most sophisticated statistical sampling techniques in the world can serve, like Gould's biologists, to obscure rather than to illuminate the truth. Polly Hill has written with telling effect about the devastating consequences of the failure of economists to understand crucial aspects (such as the economic role of women) in societies for which they were presuming to advocate development policies (1986).

We do not wish to be misunderstood: statistical analysis is essential, and the effort to toughen up the soft social sciences by improving the quality of statistics is one of the most significant intellectual advances of our time. But precisely because the numbers are so important it is vital to pause at the beginning to consider what we are measuring and, perhaps even more significant, what we are not measuring. In the social sciences there has to be a constant tension between the case-study methodology as practised by anthropologists, and the representative statistical sample derived from questionnaires beloved by sociologists and economists. Each is periodically driven to distraction by the other. But each badly needs the other in order to avoid the Scylla of assuming that a particular case study is typical of a whole population and the Charybdis of asserting that what has been enumerated (and statistically analysed) is necessarily the whole (or even the most important part) of the truth.

For this reason the various field reports from many different parts of the country that were amongst the papers presented at the Carnegie conference are invaluable, for whilst they are not always comparable they draw attention to aspects of poverty that might otherwise fall through the grid of the university-based statistician and be neither noticed nor measured, let alone assessed. It is from these papers that we learn that no adequate description of poverty can satisfactorily reduce it to a single number. Poverty is not one-dimensional; it has many faces as we shall see in the chapters that follow.

At the same time we recognise that an overall statistic, however simplified, can furnish invaluable information, provided its limitations are clearly recognised. To return to our medical analogy for a moment, we know that a simple statistical indicator such as body temperature is useful in the early stages of examination to indicate whether the patient is unwell or not, but it is of little help in diagnosing whether the disease is measles, chicken-pox, polio, or the common cold. Similarly, in seeking to deal with poverty it is helpful to 'take the temperature' of the society, as it were, before delving deeper to discover precisely what is wrong, and why.

In his magisterial history of *The African Poor* John Iliffe, wrestling to carve out a usable definition of poverty, has drawn attention to the fact that

two levels of want have existed in Africa for several centuries. On one level have been the very large numbers – perhaps most Africans at most times – obliged to struggle continuously to preserve themselves and their dependants from physical want. These will be called the poor. On another level have been smaller numbers who have permanently or temporarily failed in that struggle and have fallen into physical want. These will be called the very poor or destitute. Of course there was no sharp dividing line between them. Yet the distinction has cross-cultural validity. It existed in ancient Greece. It was identified by Charles Booth's pioneer study of London during the 1880s, which defined the poor as those 'living under a struggle to obtain the necessaries of life and make both ends meet' and the very poor as those who 'live in a state of chronic want'. The distinction between *pauvre* and *indigent* was drawn in early modern France, where 'both *pauvre* and *indigent* knew hunger, but the *indigent* were never free from it'. In Africa the distinction existed in some, but not all, pre-colonial languages and has appeared frequently since, most recently in accounts of South African resettlement sites during the early 1980s. (1987: 2)

Some basic statistics

The distinction is useful not least in focusing attention upon the vulnerability of those enduring poverty. Sudden changes can throw people, who are just managing to make ends meet, into a situation of utter destitution. We shall begin by trying to measure the wider numbers of those who are poor in the sense of 'living under a struggle to obtain the necessaries of life'. We use for our calibrations the various poverty lines that have been developed in the country.

The poverty datum line (PDL) was introduced to South Africa by Batson at the University of Cape Town during the Second World War in order to help measure the extent of poverty in the rapidly growing slums and townships of the western Cape. It was subsequently refined and modified, at the beginning of the 1970s, as the trade unions re-emerged as a force for change and guidelines were needed in the debate with management about minimum wages. The minimum living level (MLL) and the supplementary living level (SLL) developed by Nel are used by the Bureau of Market Research at the University of South Africa. The household subsistence level (HSL) and the household effective level (HEL) have been monitored by Potgieter at the University of Port Elizabeth. The following table summarises the basic information about these various levels of poverty.

All the measures have been severely criticised, not least for the degree of subjectivity involved in estimating theoretical minima (Budlender 1985: 2). Indeed there is considerable dispute in the learned international journals as to whether it is even theoretically possible to determine a minimum level of calorie intake to ensure subsistence of the human body, for it has been shown that, depending on food intake, the human body can sustain itself for long periods of time at different weight equilibria (Timmer, 1987: 689). Besides, as Beckerman has cryptically observed (3: 10), it does not really make sense to define poverty at some minimum living level when people continue to survive below it. Measurement of the extent of poverty can be extremely sensitive both to tiny variations in its definition as well as to ways of adjusting for inflation. In some Third World countries, for example, economists have found that a 10 per cent change in the number of calories assumed necessary for subsistence can shift the proportion of households living in poverty by 50 per cent or more. And in Britain, Beckerman has shown how in measuring the impact of social security on poverty over the period 1961 to 1976, 'alternative methods of adjusting the estimates for demographic changes or for inflation meant that the estimates of poverty, over this period, doubled, fell by 30%, or remained more or less the same, depending on which method one adopted!' (3: 5) Such cautionary tales serve as a salutary warning against the misuse, whether conscious or unconscious, of poverty statistics to prove what one is wanting to prove and of the need to interpret them with a due sense of their fragility.

Table 1.01: Levels of poverty: definitions and statistics, 1980–5

Initials	Value (R/month)		Coverage	Poverty level as % of average white mining earnings in 1980
	1980	1985		
PDL	195	345	Food, clothing, fuel/lighting, washing/cleansing, rent, transport	19%
MLL*	189	350	As above + tax, medical expenses, education, household equipment replacement	18%
SLL*	240	446	MLL + more for each item + + recreation/entertainment, personal care, pension, UIF, medical, burial contributions. Approx. MLL + 30%	23%
HSL†	195	345	As for PDL	19%
HEL†	293	518	HSL + 50%	28%

Sources: Potgieter, 1974, 1978 and 1985; Budlender, 1985: 1; Bureau of Market Research (BMR) cited in Saldru Handbook, 1986: 407 and 17: 5
* These figures are for an average-sized African household of 5.45 persons and are the weighted average (in August) for 25 urban areas covered by the BMR. Particular figures will vary according to size of household, colour-caste, and area.
† Average costs for African households of 6 persons in the 5 major urban areas.
Note: In the rural areas cash required for subsistence is not much less despite lower costs for such items as housing and transport, and despite some food production by the household. For example in the Transkei, 1983/4, when the urban HSL (for a family of 5) was R296, that for a household (of 6 persons) in the rural areas was R246 (44: 4).

In South Africa as a whole, including the reserves, the proportion of the total population living, in 1980, below subsistence (measured as the urban MLL) was estimated to be 50 per cent. For Africans throughout the country the proportion was estimated to be nearly two-thirds (60.5 per cent), whilst for those living in the reserves no less than 81 per cent of the households were in dire poverty (Simkins, 1984: 181).

However, the most striking feature of poverty in South Africa is the degree of inequality that exists. The statistics, rough as they are, show the width of the gulf between grinding poverty and massive wealth. In 1970, the richest 20 per cent of the population in South Africa owned 75 per cent of the wealth, compared with 62 per cent in Brazil and 39 per cent in the United States. In 1978, according to a careful statistical analysis by De Lange and Van Seventer at the University of Stellenbosch, South Africa's Gini coefficient (which measures inequality) was the highest of any of the 57 countries in the world for which data are available (PCS 16: 23). In South Africa its value is 0.66.*

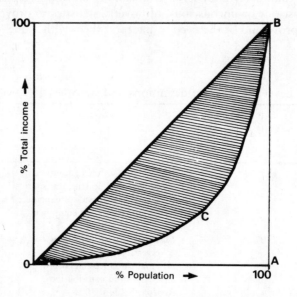

Fig. 1.01: Gini coefficient

In the diagram, the Gini coefficient measures the ratio of the area OCB to the triangle OAB. Where there was no inequality (and the bottom 10 per cent of the population earned 10 per cent of the total income) the shaded area would vanish and the Gini coefficient would be zero.

And income is closely correlated with 'race' or colour-caste, as may be seen from the following tables, the first of which shows the distribution of households by colour-caste and income. Whilst almost one-third of all African households, for example, earned less than R500 per year in 1975, only one in fifty (2 per cent) of whites were so poor. Similarly, whilst 95 per cent of African households had an annual income of less than R3 000, only 11 per cent of whites were in the same position.

* An earlier study (Devereux, 1983: 35) found that between 1976 and 1980 the Gini coefficient in South Africa fell 'quite dramatically' from 0.65 to 0.57. There is certainly evidence to suggest that over the decade 1970 and 1980 the share of total income going to blacks rose whilst that going to whites fell substantially. However our assessment is that the 1978 figure (0.66) for the Gini coefficient, calculated from the detailed information in the Social Accounting Matrix now available for that year, is the most accurate to date.

Table 1.02: Household annual income distribution, 1975 *(as a percentage of households in each group)*

	<R500	<R1 500	<R3 000	<R8 000
White	2	4	11	50
Asian	12	35	69	96
Coloured	25	54	78	98
African	31	74	95	99.6
Total	24	56	74	88

Source: (269: 3)

Fig. 1.02: Household annual income distribution, 1975

Whilst poverty is not confined to any one racial-caste in South Africa it is concentrated mostly amongst blacks, particularly Africans. The following table shows the estimated real disposable income per person, in 1983, according to group.

Table 1.03: Annual disposable income per capita, 1983

	Rands
White	6 242
Asian	2 289
Coloured	1 630
African – metropolitan areas*	1 366
– non-growth areas†	388

Source: Van Wyk, 1984 cited in Eberstadt, 1988: 23
* As defined by the BMR
† Also defined by the BMR. Areas relate primarily to the reserves.

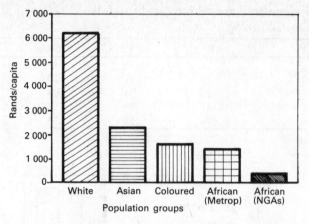

Fig. 1.03: Annual disposable income, 1983

But have things changed in recent years? And if so how? The following table shows the changing pattern of income distribution over the period 1960–80.

Table 1.04: Income distribution in South Africa, 1960–1980 *(as a percentage of 'census income' going to each racial-caste)*

	1960*	1970	1980	% 1980 population
White	72.9	71.2	64.9	15
Asian	1.9	2.4	3.0	3
Coloured	5.5	6.7	7.2	9
African	19.7	19.8	24.9	73
Total	100	100	100	100

Source: McGrath as cited in Saldru Handbook, 1986: 536
* Census data for 1960 was adjusted.

Fig. 1.04: Income and population distribution, by colour-caste, 1980

In 1980 (whites who constituted less than one-sixth of the population) earned almost two-thirds of the income, whilst Africans (who made up nearly three-quarters of the people) earned only one-quarter. But in 1970 the situation had been even worse The above statistics and other indicators show that during the 1970s there was a marked shift in the distribution of income away from whites to blacks, particularly Africans. In the reserves, for example, between 1960 and 1980 the proportion of households living in poverty (below the minimum living level) seems to have fallen from 99 per cent to 81 per cent whilst in the country as a whole, considering households of all races, the proportion enduring poverty fell from 75 to 50 per cent (Simkins, 1984: 181). Another indication of the shift in income distribution during the 1970s is the fact that the income share of the richest 20 per cent fell from 75 to 61 per cent.

But these hopeful signs have to be set against a number of other considerations. First, given the increase in total population over the same period, the absolute number of those living in poverty in South Africa has probably risen from 13 million to 15 million persons (Simkins, 1984: 181). Second, the numbers of those who are very poor, if not utterly destitute, have risen dramatically. In the reserves, for example, the number of destitute persons − defined as those living in households with no visible means of support from remittances, local jobs, land, cattle, pensions or other transfer payments − rose six-fold over the period 1960–80 from 250 000 to 1 430 000 (7: 12 and 311: 5). It has been estimated, moreover, that in 1980 the bottom 40 per cent of the population earned only 8 per cent of the income (Devereux, 1984: 37). Amongst the very poor the indicators suggest strongly that the position has been getting worse. Third, these figures take no account of what has been happening to levels of poverty and to income distribution in limitrophe countries such as Lesotho and Mozambique as a result of changes in the structure and policies (particularly with regard to labour recruitment) of the South African political economy. It is also important to note that these statistics refer only to income streams and not to the stock of assets (such as land, housing, or industrial shares) whose distribution between racial-castes is likely to be even more skewed.

What seems to have happened is that, as in the United States over much the same period, inequalities between blacks widened as wealth trickled down to a small but growing middle class, whilst the majority were left far behind (Harrington, 1984: 125–6). This conclusion is reinforced by the significant finding that within the African population, taken separately, the most recent calculation (for 1978) of the Gini coefficient (=0.55) indicates a relatively high degree of inequality. Amongst whites alone, on the other hand, income is distributed fairly evenly and the Gini coefficient of 0.39 is similar to that of Western democratic countries (PCS 16: 23). The fact that the wealth of the country is more equitably distributed amongst whites, at the top end of the economic spectrum, serves to reinforce the high degree of inequality within the society as a whole.

One consequence of the link between inequality and poverty in South

Africa may be seen in the following table drawn up by Amartya Sen from the 1986 World Development Report, showing life-expectancy at birth compared with average resources (measured in terms of gross national product) in various countries. South Africa, with a per capita gross national product six or seven times higher than that of China or Sri Lanka, has a life-expectancy at birth less than four-fifths that of the two much poorer countries.

Table 1.05: Opulence and life-expectancy, 1984

Country	GNP per head ($)	Life-expectancy at birth (years)
China	310	69
Sri Lanka	360	70
Brazil	1 720	64
Mexico	2 040	66
South Africa	2 340	54

Source: Sen, 1987: 17

Fig. 1.05: Opulence and life-expectancy, 1984

Who's who

For those unfamiliar with the finer details of South African definitions of racial categories it is perhaps helpful to know who's who and to recognise there is more to colour than meets the eye. Not even the architects of apartheid have been able to develop a clear, let alone scientific, basis for dividing the population. In terms of the Population Registration Act (1950) the people of South Africa are divided into a number of so-called 'racial' or 'ethnic' groups. Quite apart from the unscientific basis of such divisions, and the breathtaking oversimplification of the country's history which they assert, the very words used to identify each group are contentious. The divisions are essentially political and, at this stage, are perhaps best seen as 'colour-castes'. For our purposes we follow the official terminology for those who are classified as 'white', 'coloured', and 'Asian'. For the remaining three-quarters of the population we shall use the term 'African' without generally breaking them down into the various ethnic components used by Pretoria. The term 'black' will be used in the inclusive sense to refer to all those who are not classified as 'white'. At the time of the 1985 census, the total population of South Africa (including the independent homelands) was 33.7 million of whom 25.0 million (74 per cent) were African; 4.9 million (15 per cent) were white; 2.9 million (8 per cent) were coloured; and 0.9 million (3 per cent) were Asian (Eberstadt, 1988: 22).

Cutting across, but also partly reinforcing, these colour-castes are the boundaries of language. Four major languages are spoken in the country whilst a host of others, from Africa, Europe, and India, are each the mother tongue of anything up to one million people. Two out of every five (43 per cent) South Africans speaks one of the Nguni dialects (Zulu, Xhosa, Swazi and Ndebele) whilst one in four (24 per cent) speaks a form of Sotho (North Sotho or Pedi, South Sotho, and Tswana). One in six (16 per cent) speaks Afrikaans as a first language, whilst English is the mother tongue of only one in twelve (8 per cent) although it is rapidly becoming the common means of communication, as a second (or third) language for the majority of South Africans.

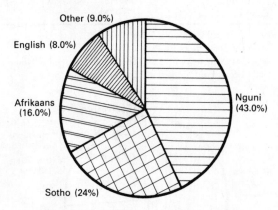

Fig. 1.06: Home languages, 1980

Geography of poverty

In South Africa the inequalities of colour-caste are reinforced by those of geographic administration, particularly amongst Africans. Indicators such as income per head or infant mortality rates all suggest that poverty (and the form it takes) varies widely according to certain geographic, or rather geo-administrative, categories. South Africa, like Gaul, can be divided broadly into three parts: the metropolitan areas of the major cities; the platteland comprising the towns and the white-owned commercial farms together with the smaller dorps or villages of the country; and the reserves (sometimes called homelands, or Bantustans, or even Black National States) originally set aside in terms of the 1913 Natives Land Act for occupation by Africans. Further land was allocated in 1936 to make a total, scattered in hundreds of fragments across the country, of 13.7 per cent of the whole. It is these reserves (now partly consolidated), the residue of nearly three centuries of conquest by white invaders, that form the ten 'Black states' which are the centrepiece of government policy with regard to Africans. The following table shows the breakdown of the African population at the time of the 1980 census, by the geo-administrative divisions of the political economy.

Table 1.06: Geographic distribution of African population, 1980

	Number (× 1 000)	Proportion (%)
Metropolitan areas	3 916	18.7
Platteland: urban	1 691	8.1
rural	4 310	20.6
total	6 001	28.7
Reserves: urban	1 521	7.3
rural	9 738	46.4
total	11 056*	53.7
Total: urban	7 128	34.0
rural	14 048	67.0
Grand total	20 972†	

Source: Saldru Handbook, 1986: 9–14
* Another estimate is 11 245.
† Another estimate is 21 367. (The numbers do not all add up exactly because different statistical sources were used.)

Fig. 1.07: Geographic distribution of African population, 1980

The importance of where people live in determining the degree of poverty they must endure is shown in the following table.

Table 1.07: The geography of poverty (Africans only), 1975

	Percentage households in each income category			Mean annual income (rands)
	<R500	<R1500	<R3000	
Reserves*	40	84	98	925
Platteland rural	45	95	99,6	670
Platteland urban	6	49	90	1 709
Metropolitan†	4	38	84	2 017
Total	31	74	95	1 152

Source: 269: 5
* Excluding overlapping segments of the metropolitan regions.
† Including overlapping segments of the metropolitan regions in the reserves.

Fig. 1.08: Geography of poverty, Africans only, 1975

Several important points emerge. Poverty in the rural platteland (that is, on white-owned farms and the small dorps or villages) seems to be worse than anywhere else, with average income in 1975 being approximately half that of all African households in the country as a whole. The really poor households (with annual incomes of <R500) are concentrated on the rural platteland and in the reserves, rather than in the towns and cities. It is also surprising to note that in 1975 poverty in the towns and dorps of South Africa (excluding the eleven major metropolitan centres) seemed to be less pervasive than either in the rural areas of the platteland or the reserves.

For the South African population as a whole the primary geographic division is between those who are urbanised and those still living in the rural areas. The following table shows the pattern of urbanisation and the dramatic changes under way, particularly for Africans, during the last two decades of the twentieth century.

Table 1.08: Proportion of population estimated in urban areas

	1904 (%)	1936 (%)	1960 (%)	1980 (%)	2000 (%)
African	10	17	32	33	47
Coloured	51	54	68	77	85
Asian	37	66	83	91	91
White	53	65	84	88	90
Total	23	31	47	47	58

Source: RSA, Department of Statistics, 1974: 1.12 and Simkins, 1983: 143ff

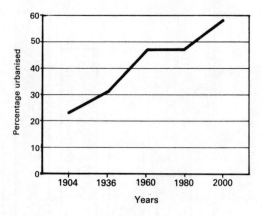

Fig. 1.09: Urbanisation, 1904–2000

South Africa in southern Africa

It is important that this study of poverty should be made with a clear recognition of the wider regional context in which it occurs. Southern Africa is a region in which a century of industrial revolution centred on the gold-mining industry and based on a system of oscillating labour migration has forged a single economy whose boundaries are far wider than those of the political nation-state in which the gold mines are located.

In the light of the region's economic history it is clear than any attempt to localise poverty by focusing on one small area (for example the Ciskei) in isolation from the wider economy would be profoundly misleading. Even more seriously, too narrow a geographic focus could easily result in strategies being developed to reduce poverty in one area (such as the Transkei) but which did so primarily at the expense of poor people somewhere else (such as in Lesotho or Mozambique).

Southern Africa: labour migrancy and the South African gold mines

The precise nature of the economic linkages (including labour migration, transport infrastructure, investment, or trade) between South Africa and the different countries in the region varies considerably and is the subject of a good deal of current analysis and writing (see, for example, Minter, 1986 and Lewis, forthcoming). For our purposes it is sufficient, at this stage, simply to place South Africa within the wider context of southern Africa, defined in this study to include also Namibia and the nine countries of the Southern African Development Co-ordination Conference (SADCC). In 1980 the area, population, and gross domestic product of these ten countries were as follows:

Table 1.09: Southern Africa, 1984: area, population, and GDP per capita

	Area (x1000 sq. km)	Population (millions)	Pop. density (persons/km)	GDP ($bn)	GDP/capita ($)
Angola	1 247	9.9	8	4.7	470
Botswana	600	1.0	2	1.0	990
Lesotho	30	1.5	50	0.4*	240*
Malawi	118	6.8	58	1.1	160
Mozambique	802	13.4	17	2.8	210
Swaziland	17	0.7	41	0.6	770
Tanzania	945	21.5	23	4.4	200
Zambia	753	6.4	8	2.6	410
Zimbabwe	391	8.1	21	4.6	570
Namibia	824	1.1	1	1.2	1 100
The Ten	5 727	69.3	12	23.4	330
South Africa	1 221	31.6	26	73.4*	2300*†
Southern Africa	6 948	102.0	15	96.8	950

Source: Lewis, 1987

* Figures are for 1983.

† See table 1.03 for a disaggregation of this average. Using a 1983 exchange rate of R1.20 = $1.00 white income averaged $5202 per annum whilst Africans in the 'non-growth areas' (i.e. the reserves) had a disposable income of $323 which was no better than the average in the ten SADCC countries of southern Africa, including Namibia.

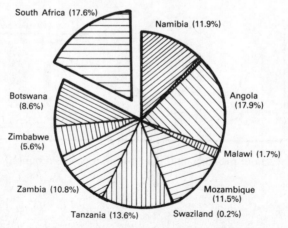

Fig. 1.10a: Southern Africa land area

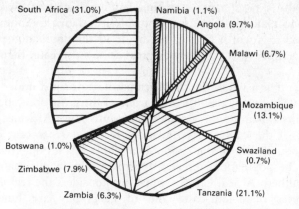

Fig. 1.10b: Southern Africa population, 1984

Fig. 1.10c: Southern Africa GDP, 1984

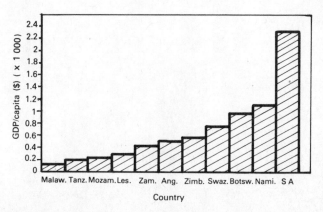

Fig. 1.10d: Southern Africa GDP per capita, 1984

Four of the six countries touching South Africa (Botswana, Lesotho, Swaziland and Namibia) have tiny populations relative to South Africa as a whole. Indeed it is worth noting that by 1980 the population of Soweto in Johannesburg alone was probably as great as, if not greater than, any one of them.*

In the region as a whole South Africa accounts for just under one-third of the population but more than three-quarters of the gross domestic product. If, as a first approximation, one assumes that white South Africans, constituting 15 per cent of the country's population, receive 60 per cent of the gross domestic product, then in the region as a whole this group, constituting 4.7 per cent of the population, receives approximately 45 per cent of the total wealth in southern Africa. Clearly, when one considers the region as a whole the boundaries of colour-caste and of geography are fundamental in determining the distribution of income and the incidence of poverty.

In this book we shall focus primarily on South Africa, but always within the wider context of the region as a whole. For an understanding of the dynamics of the economic, political, and military interaction between South Africa and these SADCC/Frontline states will do much to illuminate the nature of poverty and the twin processes of accumulation and impoverishment in what is simultaneously the richest and the poorest region in Africa.

* We are indebted to the late Charles Bloomberg for this observation.

2

Earth, fire,
and water

The great red hills stand desolate, and the earth has torn away like flesh. The lightning flashes over them, and the clouds pour down upon them, the dead streams come to life, full of the red blood of the earth. Down in the valleys women scratch the soil that is left, and the maize hardly reaches the height of a man. They are valleys of old men and old women, of mothers and children. The men are away, the young men and the girls are away. The soil cannot keep them anymore.

— Alan Paton, *Cry, the Beloved Country*, 1948

Earth

In South Africa one must never lose sight of the land. For it is in struggle with the soil in a harsh and dry climate that men and women have for thousands of years learnt to survive, changing from hunter and gatherer, to herder and cultivator (and to underground miner) in the process. It is conflict over land, particularly between black and white, that has run like a seismic fault, through the body of South Africa, dividing people along a line that even today, three centuries after the first permanent settlement by well-armed white invaders, threatens to engulf the country in the flames of civil war. And it is the destruction of the land through modern human foolishness and greed that may yet remove the foundations of existence in the very place where humanity first evolved.*

At first glance there is little wrong with South African farming. The country is self-sufficient in basic foodstuffs, including wheat, and regularly exports substantial quantities of maize, deciduous fruit, citrus and sugar as well as other agricultural products, wool, hides and skins, all of which earn valuable foreign exchange.

But such production has been won at considerable cost; for the country has neither the climate nor the soil to make it a natural grain-basket. Much of the country is arid, and even where, as on the eastern seaboard, the rain does fall it is erratic, and the country is subject to frequent droughts. In general, despite notable exceptions, it has not been well farmed, as Drought Commissions down the years have testified (144: 1–4). Bad land-management including the ploughing of marginal land, combined with overstocking, has led to heavy erosion by wind and water. Even today, on the white-owned farms of the Cape Midlands and the eastern Karoo, overstocking is calculated to vary between 27 and 36 per cent (144: 1). From the dry sands of the south-west the desert is advancing into the heart of the country at an estimated rate of 2.6 km every year (Downing, 1978: 422). In 1400, before white conquest and settlement, the vegetation around Cradock and Queenstown in the eastern Cape, seems likely to have been sweet grassveld. By 1950, after a century of overgrazing on white-owned farms the sweet grassveld had been replaced by scrub vegetation. By the year 2050 it is predicted that the area will be dominated by desert and

* This paragraph owes its existence to Manning Clarke's observation that whilst all history is about conflict, there is not one but three conflicts: conflict between people and the land; class conflict; and conflict within the human heart (1976).

South Africa:
rainfall and
population
density

Reserves
Isohyets (mm)
Metropoles
678 Population in thousands

VENDA 345
GAZANKULU 514
KANGWANE 161
KWAZULU 3422
NATAL 2676
TRANSKEI 2623
CISKEI 678
QWAQWA 158
KWANDEBELE 156
LEBOWA 1747
TRANSVAAL 8351
ORANGE FREE STATE 1932
BOPHUTHATSWANA 1511
CAPE PROVINCE 5091
LESOTHO

Pretoria
Johannesburg
Vaal Triangle
Welkom
Bloemfontein
Kimberley
Durban
Pietermaritzburg
East London
Port Elizabeth
Cape Town

300 km
200
100
0
100

the succulents that can grow under such conditions (144: 2–3, based on Acocks, 1975 and Roux, 1981). The combination of soil erosion and deteriorating vegetation is held, by some who have thought deeply on these matters, to be far and away the most serious of the many problems facing South Africa. For land is not, as some economists have maintained, indestructible. And when it is destroyed those who have nowhere else to live have nothing to sustain them.

The number of people who live on the land varies greatly, depending of course partly on the amount of regular rainfall and on the quality of the soil. Thus in the dry, bleak magisterial district of Kenhardt in the north-west Cape, for example, rural population density in 1960 was only 0.14 persons per sq. km, whilst on the well-watered, intensively cultivated soils of Paarl near Cape Town population density on the commercial farms was 22 persons per sq. km, 154 times greater (Urban and Rural Population of South Africa 1904–1960, report no. 02–02–01).

But in South Africa, rural population density is not simply a matter of climate and soil. Consider the accompanying table. The figures cannot, as we have seen, always be used for comparative purposes because of wide climatic differences around the country, but they can certainly be used to examine similar areas. What they show is astonishing. We find that in 1980 in the rural Transvaal, excluding the reserves, the population density is 11 persons per sq. km, yet in those reserves that are scattered in many different bits and pieces through that same Transvaal the rural population densities (in persons per sq. km) are Bophuthatswana 29; Lebowa 65; Gazankulu 74; Kangwane 63; and KwaNdebele 193. For Transvaal reserves as a whole the average rural density is 47.

Fig. 2.01: Rural population density, 1980

Table 2.01: Rural population density by area in South Africa, 1980

	Area (×1000 sq. km)	Population (×1000)			Proportion urbanised (%)	Pop. density (persons/sq. km)	
		Total	Urban*	Rural		Total	Rural†
Transkei	45.0	2 623	129	2 494	5	58	55
Ciskei	5.3	678	243	435	36	128	82
Bop.	44.1	1 511	239	1 272	16	34	29
Venda	6.5	345	7	338	2	53	52
KwaNdebele	0.7	156	15	141	10	214	193
KwaZulu	35.0	3 422	755	2 667	22	98	76
Lebowa	25.0	1 747	111	1 636	6	70	65
Gazankulu	6.8	514	15	500	3	76	74
Kangwane	2.4	161	9	152	6	67	63
Qwa Qwa	0.5	158	14	143	9	329	298
All reserves	171.2	11 315	1 537	9 778	14	66	57
Transvaal	227.6	8 351	5 926	2 425	71	37	11
Cape	656.7	5 091	3 801	1 291	75	8	2
Natal	52.0	2 676	1 516	1 161	57	51	22
OFS	127.5	1 932	824	1 108	43	15	9
All white areas	1 063.7	18 050	12 066	5 984	67	17	6
Total SA	1 235.0	29 365	13 603	15 762	46	24	13

Sources: Saldru Handbook, 1986: 10–15
* Urban, 1980 census, areas are defined as those having some form of local authority. Non-urban, or rural, areas include some mines and other places where there is no proclaimed local authority.
† Rural population density is an underestimate for two reasons: (a) in calculating area available for rural population we have assumed urban dwellers occupy no space at all; (b) official figures for the 1980 census are known to be well below the actual numbers, e.g. for Nkandla (53a: 9) and Qwa Qwa (282: 2).

In Natal population density on the white farms is 22; in the rural areas of KwaZulu it averages 76. In the Cape Province the contrast is even greater (only partly because the reserves lie in the better-watered eastern seaboard) whilst a substantial part of the white area (which also includes the intensely cultivated western Cape) stretches into the arid north-west. But in the province as a whole, rural population density outside the reserves is only 2 persons per sq. km whilst in the Transkei it is 55 and in the rural Ciskei 82. In the Orange Free State where climatically there is no difference between the reserves and the farms the contrast is, if anything, more marked. In the province, rural population density is 9 persons per sq. km, yet in Qwa Qwa the official figures for *rural* population yield a density of 298 persons. In actual fact the density is probably at least three times this high, making it overall ten times higher than on the surrounding white farms. In the country as a whole population density on the white farms is 6 persons per sq. km. In the rural parts of the reserves it is 57, almost ten times greater.

Some idea of the degree to which the actual density exceeds the carrying capacity of the land for agricultural purposes may be gained from the following calculation. Population density on the white-owned farms of the Orange Free State is 9 persons per sq. km. Assume that the Ciskei could support a similar population, but not more. The area of the Ciskei is 5 300 sq.

km which means that it could support 47 700 people living permanently on the land. Rural population in 1980 was 435 000, which means that the land has a human population density (to say nothing of the animal population) at least nine times higher than its agricultural carrying capacity.

No less striking than the sheer density of population in the rural (that is, non-urban) parts of the reserves is the speed with which it has increased in many of these areas in recent years. In 1954 a government commission (Tomlinson, UG 61/1955) calculated that the reserves could support only about 60 per cent of the 1951 reserve population in full-time farming, albeit at relatively low income levels, and recommended that the remaining 40 per cent would have to be drawn off the land into non-agricultural jobs created by massive capital expenditure in and near the reserves. In the event not only was the government's response to the call for development woefully inadequate (De Wet, 1988) but policy was directed at increasing, rather than decreasing, the number of people in the reserves.

Between 1960 and 1980, according to official statistics, the population of the reserves increased from approximately 4.5 million to 11 million people (Simkins, 1983: 54–6). Part of this increase was due to natural population growth; part of it was the result of redrawing boundaries so as to include some urban areas, notably KwaMashu and Umlazi outside Durban, within a homeland; part of it was caused by insisting that new suburbs for blacks moving to cities be sited within a homeland, notably Mdantsane (Ciskei) outside East London and Winterveld (Bophuthatswana) outside Pretoria. But much of it was due to people being compelled to move (for reasons that will be analysed later) from both urban and rural South Africa into the reserves.

In the Ciskei, for example, not one of the major mining or manufacturing areas of the country, population doubled over the 12 years from 1970 to 1982. This implied an annual increase of 5.9 per cent per annum compared with a natural population growth rate of approximately 3.3 per cent over the same period. In Qwa Qwa, the smallest of the reserves, population, according to official statistics, grew from 23 000 in 1970 to 158 000 in 1980. Unofficial, but more reliable, estimates put the actual population in 1982 at between two or three times that number (282: 2). The demographic history of Qwa Qwa is instructive. According to a government commission at the time of the First World War, the reserve had a population of 6 000, which was considered then to be more than the area could support on the land. Over the next 55 years population grew at an annual rate of 2.5 per cent to a total of 23 000 persons in 1970. Over the next decade, according to official statistics, the annual growth rate was 21 per cent. Yet unofficial estimates suggest that these figures are seriously under-enumerated. Similar evidence of official undercounting comes from the district of Nkandla in KwaZulu where in a careful survey it was found that the population density was double that of the 1980 census (53a: 9).

At the grassroots level population growth in different villages varies widely depending on whether it is a natural growth or immigrants have come in from white farms or other homelands or, indeed, been sent back from the towns

(66: 2). In the Mhala district of Gazankulu population almost doubled in ten years from 66 300 in 1970 to 128 500 in 1980. In central Gazankulu the populations in three different areas grew at annual rates of 8, 12 and 25 per cent over the six years 1970–6 (67: 7), which implies a doubling of population every nine, six and three years respectively.

The reasons for the astronomical increases in rural population density in the reserves, particularly during the 1970s, are explored elsewhere in this book (Chapter 11). At this point we examine simply the consequences of the existing demographic pattern of settlement in the rural areas of the country. Throughout the reserves the picture is much the same. Almost everywhere the land is breaking under the burden that has been laid upon it.

Msinga, for example, on the banks of the Tugela River in KwaZulu contains seven times as many people and seven times as many large stock units as could, according to a government commission, be sustained agriculturally on its land. 'The results of this almost savage overstocking', writes David Robbins, 'are everywhere plain to see.' One landscape in the south-west of the district sums it up: 'Dongas have become small valleys which split the hillsides; soil has given way to a crumbling grey shale, stone-built huts squat in a scene which is almost lunar in its desolation' (55: 5). 'The hills', writes Creina Bond Alcock,

are not what they seem, fixed in position. They were lifted from lava pools, or dropped from old tides. All rock was flowing once. Sometimes the ripple lines emerge, swirls of sandstone in an eroding field. A man can ignore history until his plough scrapes a ripple. Other rocks can be rolled aside. There is usually room for manoeuvre, there are options to juggle. Sandstone is different however. You can't budge the ripple of a sandstone sea. Old fields have vanished completely in some parts of Msinga, opening up extraordinary expanses of stone. Bedrock is beautiful although there is strangeness walking on solid currents. The rigid lagoons are hot in the sun, the grey eddies unmoving. In 100 years a centimetre of dust will have grown from the rock. In 10 000 years there could be soil to plough. Rock is not motionless.

For a man in a hurry, however, bedrock is the end of time. When he hits bedrock he is face to face with nothing. (1986: 4)

Face to face with nothing. For without soil nothing grows: not trees, nor grass, nor other indigenous plants, nor seeds for harvest. Such pressure on the land creates a downward spiral into deeper and deeper impoverishment for all those without jobs elsewhere.

Consequences of population pressure

The pressure makes itself felt in a variety of ways. First, growth in population for whatever reason reduces the amount of land of those who have, and increases the numbers of those who have not (45: 2). Thus in the Chata Valley near Keiskammahoek in the Ciskei, over the generation 1946–81 the average size of land-holding fell by 75 per cent from 1.72 ha to 0.43 ha and landlessness increased from 10 to 43 per cent of all families (De Wet and McAllister, 1983, cited in PCS 8: 7). In the Transkei, according to a 61-year-old man living at Etoleni:

During the olden days things were better. One could get a plot of a satisfying size. This is not the case now at Etoleni. . . . Our arable plots have been reduced. My arable plot was eight morgens [6.9 ha], but now it is two-and-a-half morgens. Just compare two-and-a-half morgens with eight morgens. (45: 2)

But many are without any land at all. Throughout the Transkei the degree of landlessness falls generally within the range of 20 to 30 per cent. But a survey in the south-west Transkei found that 42 per cent of the households had no arable plots. In this sample, 29 per cent had vegetable plots only; 19 had arable land only; 40 had both arable land and vegetable plots; 13 had neither (45: 3). In another part of the Transkei 41 per cent had no arable fields; and 25 had neither fields nor cattle. Further north, in Polela (KwaZulu), 37 per cent had no fields and 37 had no cattle (51: 50). But in a different part of KwaZulu, Nkandla in the north, only one household, in a large sample, was found to be without access to land (53b: 69).

In Venda, a reserve slightly bigger in area than Ciskei and with a rural population density only two-thirds as great, approximately 36 per cent of the rural households had no land rights. In calculating what proportion of the existing rural population could make a full-time living as farmers, Moody and Golino found that if they assumed optimal cash crops and modern farming methods and a relatively low family-farm income (in 1979) of R200 per month, then in all of Venda there was room to support nearly 14 000 farmers, approximately 60 000 people. But if this were to happen then the existing 45 000 rural families without land rights plus another 10 000 families with land rights, a total of approximately 300 000 people, would have to move from the land to live permanently in town (251: 10). But the movement has been all the other way. As in other reserves rural population has increased dramatically in recent years. In one mountain community the number of households nearly trebled over eight years from 1975 to 1983 and the proportion of families with access to land fell from 100 to 33 per cent (64: 14).

In Gazankulu the situation is even worse. As in Venda the overwhelming majority of the people live in the rural areas but in Gazankulu, whose size is only 8 per cent larger than Venda there are 49 per cent more people. Thus we find that, depending on which population estimates we use, whilst there are 31 000 families with agricultural rights there are another 31 000 (or 49 000) families living in the rural areas without land. If we use the conservative, and probably less accurate, estimate, at least 50 per cent of the rural households are landless (252: 8). And here, too, rural population has increased rather than decreased in recent years (67: 7).

But there is an apparent paradox that needs to be explained. Despite the very high degree of landlessness throughout the rural parts of the reserves, the evidence also shows that much arable land lies untilled each year. In Libode in the Transkei, for example, whilst 28 per cent of the homesteads do not have any arable lands, Hendricks reported that a substantial proportion of the arable land that is available is, in fact, unused (294: 17 and personal communication). An earlier study of three villages in another, also overcrowded, part of the Transkei found 10 per cent of the land to be unused (Westcott, 1977 cited in PCS 8: 13). Various other studies, including departmental reports, found the proportion of arable land unused to vary between 16 and 30 per cent, although in Nkandla it rose as high as 55 (53b: 71).

Surveying the evidence for reserves in the area of the eastern seaboard, Peter Moll concludes that overall the degree of underutilisation of land is of the order of one-fifth (PCS 8: 12). Although this might seem surprising at first sight there are reasons for the situation. First, of course, is that it is sound agricultural practice to leave land fallow. We should bear in mind that on the white-owned farms of South Africa it is officially estimated that almost exactly the same proportion (21 per cent) of land was left temporarily fallow in 1976 (PCS 8: 15). But (as may well be the case on white farms) there are other reasons why arable land in the reserves is not fully cultivated every year. The most important of these seem to be insufficient labour, insufficient capital, and the high risk of much toil yielding little fruit as a result of drought, theft, or damage to crops by both wild and domestic animals. The risk of crop loss is very real. In many places the government policy of 'betterment' (see Chapter 11) has, in the process of gathering scattered homesteads into villages, created a situation where fields are far from home and householders could no longer keep a watchful eye out for straying cattle, wild pigs, or thieves. In many instances people are too poor to farm; they cannot afford protective fencing or even to buy seed and fertiliser. Tractors may be too expensive to hire and oxen too weak to plough (53b: 73; 261: 16; PCS 8:13ff, and see 296: 4 re West Africa).

The shortage of labour arises not from a lack of people who, as we have seen, overcrowd the rural reserves but from the peculiar (and quite unnatural) household structure that has emerged in these areas as a result of the migrant labour system – a system (see Chapter 10) which has been part and parcel of the South African economy for the full century of its industrial revolution. In Nkandla, a relatively stable area in KwaZulu with almost no immigrants in recent years and where virtually all households had access to at least some land, a detailed survey of three wards found that, if the migrants who were away from home were excluded from the statistics, then of the people between the ages of 20 and 50 who lived in the area no less than 81 per cent were women. Of people in their late twenties and late forties (age groups 25–9 and 45–9) more than 90 in every 100 were women. Furthermore if all the men currently at home (because they were unemployed) managed to get the jobs they sought in town, then in the entire age group 15–60, 85 per cent of the males would be out of the area and the male–female ratio in that working-age range would be nearly 7:1. At the same time it was found that one in every four household heads was a pensioner (53a: 17). In other areas where population pressure on the land is greater than Nkandla the situation is considerably worse, although as the younger women may also have fled to town, leaving their children in the care of grannies, the male–female ratio may, paradoxically, be not quite so lop-sided.

Ciskei: Amatola basin

Source (208)

Gazankulu: Mahatlani village

Source (277:13)

Fig. 2.02: African population structure in rural reserves

One measure of pressure is the labour participation rate. This indicates the number of people working out of every 100 living permanently in the area. In the Amatola Basin, for example, in the Ciskei the rate is only 11 (277: 7). The large number of dependants consists of children (many of them sent back from the harsh urban environment to the care of grandparents and other relatives), women blocked by laws and other obstacles from moving to town, men unable to find jobs, and old people. In the resettlement area of Tsweletswele near East London (subsequently knocked out of existence by government authorities) two-thirds of the population were under 20 and most of the adult residents were women. Perhaps it is not surprising that here, two out of five young children were found to be wasting and underweight whilst one in ten suffered from the protein-deficiency disease, kwashiorkor (277: 9–10). In the Transkei village of Ntshiqo 70 per cent or more of the adults between the ages of 20 and 49 were away from home. Of those in their early thirties and early forties, 85 per cent were away and the male–female ratio among those left behind was 17:100 (46: 24). The accompanying diagrams, one from the Amatola Basin in the Ciskei (277: 13) and the other from Mahatlani village, Gazankulu in the northern Transvaal (208: 33), show clearly the ravages to normal population structure, and to the households which reflect this, that have been wrought by South Africa's political economic system. They show too the absence of able-bodied men and younger women who would perform agricultural work.

In the light of these factors, of the overwhelming pressure on the land and of the flight of anybody who can get out to go and earn money for their families, it is hardly necessary to draw attention to the impossibility of people who have to remain there, surviving on the agricultural land of the reserves. We have already seen how, more than thirty years ago, a government commission recommended that at least 40 per cent of the population then (1951) living in the reserves would have to move from the land to leave space for those who remained to farm full-time. We have seen too how today in Venda approximately 300 000 (that is, 83 per cent) of the 360 000 currently living in the rural areas would have to move off the land to make agricultural space for the remaining 60 000 people. Even in areas where population pressure is not quite so great and rainfall better, the basic conclusion holds. People do not have enough land to make a living. In Nkandla, for example, it is estimated that the minimum land necessary for a family to meet its maize requirements would be 4 ha but the average holding is only 1.5 ha (53b: 76). In the Transkei, a study of three villages showed that the average Transkei farmer is a consumer of agricultural produce, not a producer (261: 15). In another part of the Transkei:

It is significant that even the most productive villagers cannot meet their subsistence requirements through farming alone and have to supplement their diets with purchases of consumer goods. This points to the fact that the size of fields, even in the fertile area, is not sufficiently large to support economically viable farming activities. With growing population pressure in Ramohlakoana it is unlikely that the size of fields will do anything other than decrease, making the need for cash and therefore wage employment more and more urgent. (49: 22)

Without food people perish. But there are other elements, no less necessary to sustain life, which vanish under such pressure. They too can no longer be taken for granted (145: 1–24).

Fire

Since the beginning of time, women and men have needed fire to cook food, to warm themselves, and to ward off danger. Legends in many cultures are focused on the discovery or the bringing of fire. It is so much part of human existence that one takes it for granted, seldom thinking what life would be like without it. Thus it is with something of a shock that one discovers that fire, or the fuel that feeds it, can no longer be guaranteed; that for millions of people around the world poverty means increasing difficulty in obtaining the basic energy necessary for cooking, heating, and lighting. As an Indian official put it in a famous question, 'Even if we somehow grow enough food for our people in the year 2000, how in the world will they cook it?' (cited in Eckholm, 1975: 12).

In South Africa the question is particularly poignant. One of the clearest images of the nature of poverty in the country is the sight of a group of elderly black women, each carrying home on her head a load of firewood weighing up to 50 kg,* passing underneath the high-tension cables that carry the electric energy between the towns (and farmsteads) of the Republic. South Africa produces 60 per cent of the electricity in the entire continent yet almost two-thirds of the total population (and approximately 80 per cent of all Africans) within the country do not have access to that energy for their household requirements. Even within major cities whole townships are still erected without provision for electricity being made. In identifying the key basic needs of South Africa in 1980 the National Health Policy Board failed even to mention fuel (166: 27). But, as various research workers reported to the Carnegie conference, millions of South Africans face enormous difficulties in obtaining the fuel they need for cooking, warmth, and light.

In the high grassland areas of KwaZulu, for example, the average distance walked in collecting one headload was a little over 5 miles (8.3 km) and the average time taken in collecting the one load was 4.5 hours. In one extreme case Gandar found a woman who had to walk 19 km and spend 9.5 hours collecting each load. In the valley lowveld the distance and time were 3.6 km. and 2.5 hours. Households required between two and three headloads per week (156: 3). In a later study which covered six widely separated rural areas in four different reserves (Ciskei, Transkei, Lebowa, and Gazankulu) Eberhard found the situation to be even worse. Average distances walked, on the round trip, varied from 5.6 to 9.4 km and the average times to collect each load took anything from two and a half to a little over six hours (Eberhard, 1986: 34). Small wonder that, as Gandar writes, 'If wood gathering is counted as part of food preparation, more effort is put into the preparation of food than the growing of it' (156: 5).

Nor is the prodigious amount of time that has to be spent in gathering fuel the only problem. It is becoming more dangerous as well. For women 'the risk of being molested by strangers in the woodlands' was reported in KwaZulu and elsewhere. In Qwa Qwa women have to walk far into the mountains to gather fuel and the danger of rape is ever present (297: 13ff).

Not only is the collecting of firewood exhausting, time-consuming, and dangerous but it has serious ecological consequences. Each household uses between three and four tons of wood a year; a per capita consumption of between 500 and 800 kg annually (Eberhard, 1986: 29). In KwaZulu Gandar notes that in recent years the people have moved from gathering dead wood to cutting off green branches or felling trees. Over the relatively brief span of the past fifty years, 200 of the 250 forests in KwaZulu have disappeared (156:

* The highest recorded is 67 kg, but few more than 50 kg. The most representative survey of the rural reserve areas of the country found women collecting an average headload of 30 kg (Eberhard, 1986).

11). This fact is dramatically illustrated by Elisabeth Ardington's observation that Cetshwayo was buried 100 years ago deep inside the Nkandla forest yet, today, his grave lies a kilometre or two outside the edge of the trees (53b: 133).

Rapid and artificial increase in rural population in the reserves over the past decade has put huge additional pressure on already overburdened natural resources with consequences that have been vividly described by Daniel in his account of the district of Hewu in the northern Ciskei, near Queenstown.

The Thornhill resettlement provides an example of vegetation annihilation. In 1976/1977 about 40 000 people moved from the Herschel district and were settled on the flanks of Ntabathemba, the hill of hope. The area, suited to extensive stock farming, was dramatically changed into an area of dense human settlement with disastrous results on the physical environment. From the air this area stands out as a reddish patch of bare soil, virtually devoid of vegetation. In 1976 Ntabathemba had a good cover of thorn trees and bush. By 1981 hardly a tree was to be seen on the slopes of the hill. These slopes are now subject to greater run-off and erosion by water and wind. What has happened here is happening in all areas of denser settlement, unless located near plantations. The influx of large numbers of people has upset any balance that may have existed before between man and his environment. The change is readily observed but there is no hard data as a result of measuring it. . . . The energy crisis in the underdeveloped rural areas of South Africa has been recognised . . . the public [needs to be made] aware of the mutilation of the environment that is taking place as a consequence of the extensive use of wood for fuel, even to the extent of the roots of trees being completely removed. Man is playing a direct role in the destruction of the vegetation cover. (144: 6–7)

Evidence from many different parts of the country, particularly in the reserves, strongly supports this conclusion. In Lebowa, for example, the slopes of the Leolo Mountains near Maandagshoek were completely covered by trees as recently as the 1960s. Twenty years later a large amount of rock is visible because people come up from the plain to cut down the trees for firewood. On the other side of the country, in the resettlement area of Bendell in Bophuthatswana north of Kuruman, the shortage of fuel is a major problem (77: 26). And we have already seen how in Qwa Qwa the possibility of gathering firewood for oneself has almost completely gone. In our own experience growing up in rural South Africa, one in the northern Transvaal and the other in the eastern Cape, we have seen how during our own lifetimes women in the reserves have had to walk further and further as the vegetation has been remorselessly eaten away in the unending search, by more and more people, for fuel.

In the more densely settled parts of the reserves the pressure of population on the land has become so severe that whilst people still try to collect wood they use very little and rely heavily instead on coal. Thus in the resettlement area of Atamalang in Bophuthatswana where people are so poor that families cannot afford to cook every day and frequently run out of fuel, the annual per capita consumption of wood is only 26 kg, about one-twentieth as much as the average used in the reserves generally. And in Qwa Qwa where, as we shall see, pressure on existing natural resources has become intolerable, wood is generally bought only to light the coal which is trucked in (Eberhard, 1986: 86). The seriousness of the situation is highlighted in Qwa Qwa where the combination of the distance women have to go to collect fuel, the dangers inherent in going, and the further possibility that they may be fined by the chief for gathering fuel, may lead those who have no money to buy coal or paraffin sometimes to cut off branches from their fruit trees (297: 15).

Where wood is hard to come by the alternatives are expensive. In a study of three villages in the Transkei, Bembridge found that the average household spent 10 per cent of its income on fuel (mainly paraffin) which it could ill afford (261: 14).

But it is not only in the underdeveloped reserves that fuel is such a problem. Both on the platteland and in the cities evidence of severe hardship due to lack of fuel was found. For example, in Hanover in the Karoo, Archer and Meyer reported:

Wood is so scarce that people chop out the wooden window frames and doors of old deserted houses in the white 'dorp' for firewood. This happens especially during winter when coal is in short supply, as it is delivered to Hanover only twice in that season. Some families cannot afford to buy coal. . . . They are forced to collect papers which litter the area, partly from the open garbage carts; paper cartons of aloe beer (the cheapest liquor around town) are used for the same purpose. It is not unusual for people to scratch in dirtbins for paper to burn. Often the ashes of one household are collected by another for the bits of coal left over. A few years ago people could go into the veld to collect what wood there was; now farmers have fenced their properties making access difficult. (34: 19)

On the farms themselves the great majority of black households are without electricity and have to rely mainly on wood, the availability of which varies widely (41: 15 and Eberhard, 1986: 104).

In the big cities the problem is often no less acute as was illustrated with the discovery in East London in 1976 of severe brain damage in six black children from a cause originally identified in Baltimore, USA as lead encephalopathy and christened the 'depression disease'. Three of the children were visited at home and all three families were found to have burnt discarded storage-battery casings in open braziers for fuel (Harris, 1976 cited in 180: 2).

In Crossroads, Cape Town, where there is no electricity, paraffin is the standard fuel used by everybody but more than a third of the households also burn wood, most of which they collect themselves. Indeed these city dwellers consume five times as much wood per person as do the 'rural' inhabitants of Qwa Qwa (Eberhard, 1986: 85–7).

Another dimension of the problem of fuel was shown by a study of energy and poverty in Cape Town, where Eberhard found that fuel for cooking, heating and lighting often costs more per unit of energy for the poor than it does for those who are better off. In Valhalla Park, a coloured township, for example, those households wealthy enough to afford the connection fee (or who were not so poor that they had defaulted on their electricity bills and been disconnected as a result) spent an average of R25 per month on energy. Poorer households that had to use paraffin and candles, incurred running costs nearly three times as high – R65 per month. Households without electricity in the poorer suburbs of Lotus River, Grassy Park, and Bellville South all spent more absolutely on energy each month than did those living in the white, middle-class electrified homes in Pinelands (155: 9). Rivett-Carnac (1979, cited in 156: 13) had found the same thing in Umlazi outside Durban, where households without electricity spent more than twice as much (R42 per month) on fuel as did those better-off households in the same township who spent only R18. This conclusion was confirmed by even starker findings in a later survey. Poor households in five different areas where wood could not easily be collected spent between 10 (in Vulindlela outside Pietermaritzburg) to 20 per cent (in Crossroads outside Cape Town) of their income on fuel alone, compared with 3 per cent in the white middle-class suburbs of Cape Town or even 5–7 per cent in poorer, but electrified, coloured areas (Eberhard, 1986: 9).

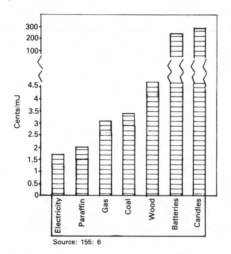

Fig. 2.03: Comparative costs of energy, Cape Town, 1983

It is worth noting that as a source of light, candles are 173 times more expensive per unit of energy (mJ) than electricity. Even wood, a major source of fuel used by more than half (57 per cent) the households living in the non-electrified areas around Cape Town, costs nearly three times as much. The question about fuel, as Gandar has pointed out (156: 13), is not whether the poor can afford electricity in South Africa but whether they can afford not to have it. Indeed, given the ecological consequences of the 'relentless search for fuel' by people without electricity, the real question surely is whether the country as a whole can possibly afford not to ensure that everybody has access to it.

For, when the trees and bushes go (as fuel), the springs of water tend to dry up. The sponge effect of forests enables them to act as regulators of our water supply. When they are removed, rivers that once flowed perennially now alternate between drying up completely and flooding. 'The flooding is physically destructive and [the] desiccation disastrous for man and beast' (156: 12). When the soil is laid bare, floods can remove a hundred years of precious topsoil in a day. This leads to silting of river bottoms, thus preventing the rocky bed from aerating the water. This, in turn, harms the bacteria which would otherwise purify the water (156: 12). In these ways the disappearance of natural vegetation, whether as food for hungry cattle and goats or as fuel for cooking and warmth, has led in turn to the disappearance of clean drinking water from much of the country.

Water

Without clean drinking water, life can be very precarious. In one Venda village in the northern Transvaal it was reported that in the twelve months preceding a survey in 1982, ten of the thirty babies born to 86 households had died (64: 12). From comparison with another village which had access to uncontaminated water piped from sealed fountains and where no babies died, it seems reasonable to conclude, even from so small a sample, that the purity of the water significantly affected the children's health. In KwaZulu, a dietician who travelled the length and breadth of the reserves in order to describe conditions and health status in different parts, commented again and again on how muddy and dirty the water was. 'One lady', writes Nomusa Ndaba,

whose house I went to at Esikhawini near Empangeni, showed me pure mud in a glass jar. She was waiting for all the dirt to form a sediment so that she could use the top part. The alternative was walking over a kilometre to fetch water from one of the location houses. She was at the time highly pregnant and to have to carry a heavy bucket of water for that distance in the scorching February sun must be absolutely terrible. She showed me some of the places where they fetched water, fountains in the middle of their banana plantation. It was plain mud; the situation is made even worse by the fact that people have cattle and that is where they drink. (206: 38)

In the Mhala district of Gazankulu in the eastern Transvaal there was found to be an average of one water tap for every 760 people. This contrasts somewhat starkly with the statistic of two or three taps per inhabitant in the middle-class metropolitan homes in which most white South Africans live. In Mhala South, half of the 25 villages had no access to clean water (192: 3). Several hundred miles further south, in the Chalumna area of the Ciskei, between Grahamstown and East London, a detailed study of 19 villages showed that 90 per cent of the households drew their water from sources unprotected from cattle and other stock. The problem of contaminated drinking water is widespread throughout the country, and, at the same time, infant mortality rates in the rural areas are high. Indeed, for Africans in the country as a whole, they are considerably higher than in various other parts of Africa.

One of the most striking features of poverty in South Africa is the cost, to the poor, of water (which is by no means always clean) in terms of time, effort, and money. In the Transkei, for example, a study of three widely separated villages showed that the average household spent 187 minutes – more than three hours – every day fetching and carrying water (261: 13). The effort too is considerable. In the 19 villages of Chalumna in the Ciskei research showed that the energy expended in the average walk to the homestead carrying a container of water (weighing 21 kg) was equivalent to that used by miners wielding a pick, rather more than the energy needed in mixing cement. For one village, the hill up from the water was so steep that the energy expended (for the duration of the journey) was equivalent to that needed in cross-country running. The average one-way journey from homestead to the water supply was 15 minutes, ranging from a low of 5 minutes to a high of 40 minutes. In other parts of the country the time spent was mainly in waiting. In Lebowa during the height of a drought in the winter of 1983 people were found queuing in the middle of the night at the village pump as the only way of ensuring that they obtained water from a borehole that filled slowly.

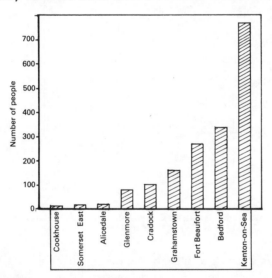

Fig. 2.04: Number of persons per water tap in eastern Cape African townships, 1983 (147: 4)

Even more striking than the time or energy spent in collecting water is the amount of money that poor people in some parts of the country have to spend to obtain it. In one small eastern Cape town, not far from Port Elizabeth, it was found that although there was water laid on to the black township it was brak and undrinkable. Buying fresh water from a distant source cost R1.70 for a 44-gallon drum, equivalent to R8.40 for 1 000 litres (Roberts, 1984). This was exactly 28 times as much as it cost middle-class householders in Cape Town for the fresh water flowing out of their kitchen taps. In rural KwaZulu, close to the largest fresh-water lake in Africa, in the area of Mseleni where three out of every five women over the age of 30 suffer from a crippling and painful form of progressive arthritis, nearly two-thirds (60 per cent) of the households were more than a one-hour round trip from water. For those too disabled to fetch their own, the cost of buying water was also 28 times that for urban healthy and wealthy families (191 and 288). But the worst area of all was found in Gazankulu in the northern Transvaal where, in some areas, water cost 50 cents for a 25-litre drum; that is, 67 times as much as the tap water in Cape Town suburbs at the time (67: 17). This means that if well-to-do people were using 200 litres of water a day and very poor people in Gazankulu were using 20 litres each for drinking, cooking, and washing, then the amount of hard cash spent by each person on water every day would be 6 cents for the rich and 40 cents for the poor: seven times as much for using only one-tenth of the water. Poverty, as Mary-Jane Morifi remarked in another context, can indeed be expensive (33: 3).

Source: 147: 4-5

Fig. 2.05: Daily water consumption per person in the eastern Cape, by colour-caste and area, 1983

It would be misleading to suggest that the supply of clean drinking water is a problem in all black communities. In Soweto and many other townships the formal, state-built houses all have at least a cold-water tap inside. And in the rural areas both on farms and in the reserves there are many homesteads with reasonably adequate supplies. In the peri-urban areas the situation varies a good deal but here too are places where supplies are considered reasonable. Indeed one study found that in the area between Sundumbili township and the Isithebe factories north of Mandini in Natal the access to clean piped water is seen as a great benefit of living in the area. Nevertheless it is fair to say that the overwhelming mass of evidence points to the lack of adequate supplies of clean drinking water as a major problem facing black communities throughout the rural areas of South Africa, particularly but not only in the reserves. From Bendell north of Kuruman to KwaZulu in the east, the story was the same: 'We need water.'

Yet, as with energy, the fundamental problem is not so much an absolute lack of water for all the people but rather a question of its distribution. In the Transkei, for instance where, during the drought, women were reported to be walking anything from 4 to 12 kilometres to fetch water (149: 11), Muller notes that only 7 per cent of usable water, from the rivers, was currently being consumed (or only 1 per cent if one includes extractable underground water).

Once again access and distribution seem to depend on a combination of geography and colour-caste. This fact was highlighted by a study in the eastern Cape which showed that the daily per capita consumption of water within one part of the Ciskei averaged 9 litres, which compares unfavourably with the World Health Organisation's goal of 50 litres per person per day. In the smaller towns of the eastern Cape platteland, Stone reported the per capita consumption in the black townships was 19 litres – double that in the reserves, but still only a fraction of the white per capita consumption of 314 litres. In the metropolitan area of Port Elizabeth black consumption rose to 80 litres but was still well below the white daily average of 200 litres (147: 5–6).

It so happened that the second Carnegie Inquiry, like the first one, fifty years earlier, collected most of its evidence during a period when the country was held in the grip of a fearful drought. As in the 1930s, so in the 1980s, one consequence of drought is to make visible the accumulated vulnerabilities and weaknesses of life in rural areas, which otherwise lie hidden from view. For those living on the land in South Africa the drought of the early 1980s was a frightening thing. The consequence of decades of pressure, due to bad farming, overgrazing and (in the reserves) intolerable population density on the rural areas of the country, became even more apparent. Agricultural labourers lost their jobs and were pushed from the land as farms wilted under the harsh sun; rivers which had never failed dried up and the army had to be called in to transport water to parched communities, both urban and rural. Cattle into which poor men put their life's savings died in their thousands; the subsistence crops and indigenous plants which for many people were the only buffer against starvation shrivelled. The drought of the early 1980s may be the last warning South Africa receives about the urgent necessity of undoing the long chain of events outlined in this chapter. In that drought inhabitants of one of the few countries in the world that exports food, lived in fear of famine, which hovered over parts of the land (67: 9). Next time it may descend.

3
Work, wages and other sources of income

Poverty is just people not paid enough for what we done.
— May Alice Jeffers, Rustdene,
Beaufort West (35: 17)

For most people work is the primary source of income. In South Africa, as elsewhere, the proximate cause of much poverty lies in the fact that the wages earned by men and women for the work they do are insufficient to cover basic needs for themselves and their dependants. Thus it is helpful to begin this chapter with a general examination of employment and earnings in the economy as a whole.

According to official statistics there were, out of a total population of 28.8 million persons in 1980, some 9.6 million (33 per cent) who were economically active. The figure is approximate for it includes estimates not only of those who are unemployed but also of those working in subsistence agriculture in the reserves as well as in the informal sector, both urban and rural. Of these nearly 10 million people economically active in 1980, approximately 2 million people (20 per cent) worked in each of the three major sectors: services (including government); agriculture (including the reserves); and manufacturing (including construction). The two other major sectors, commerce and mining, each employed roughly 1 million or 10 per cent of the total (Saldru Handbook, 1986: 59).

The following table shows the structure of earnings in 1980, broken down by racial category, in various specific sectors.

Table 3.01: Average monthly earnings, by racial category, 1980 (*measured in rands*)

	African	Coloured	Asian	White
Agriculture (regular farm workers)	38	63	157	529
Mining and quarrying	172	318	439	1 040
Central government	204	276	547	629
Manufacturing	224	261	302	956

Source: Saldru Handbook, 1986: 295–318

Fig. 3.01: Average monthly earnings, by racial category, 1980

There are three particularly striking features of this table. First is the consistent racial bias. In all sectors African earnings are lower than those of any other group whilst white earnings are always the highest. Second is the wide variation between sectors. Third is the fact that given a monthly minimum living level in 1980 of approximately R180 and a supplementary living level of roughly R240, most African earnings were below the SLL. Furthermore, in agriculture, even allowing for wages in kind, virtually all blacks (including those classified coloured or Asian) were living in dire poverty with earnings below the MLL.

Table 3.02: Average African monthly real earnings, 1970–85 *(measured in constant (1980) rands)*

	1970	1985	% change
Mining and quarrying	50	170	+240
Manufacturing	143	243	+70
Construction	135	200	+48
Trade and accommodation:			
wholesale	149	178	+19
retail	120	159	+33
SA Transport Services	134	219	+63
Banking institutions	167	340	+104
Services:			
central government	124	249	+101
govt of non-indep. homelands	126*	277	n.a.
provincial admins	95	186	+96
local authorities	117	190	+62
universities	148	245	+66
laundries and drycleaning	132	118	−11

Source: Saldru Handbook, 1986: 62–88 and 296–320
* Figure is for 1972.

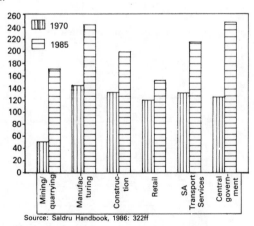

Source: Saldru Handbook, 1986: 322ff

Fig. 3.02: Changes in African real earnings, 1970–85

There have been some improvements in recent years. Over the period 1970–85 real earnings (after allowing for inflation) of African workers in major sectors of the economy increased markedly as the accompanying table shows. Despite the increase in real earnings for Africans that took place in most parts of mining, manufacturing, construction, and government services over the fifteen years since 1970, poverty – even for those employed in formal, urban jobs – remains acute.

The following table shows figures, for 1985, of the number of Africans employed and their average cash earnings in major sectors of the South African economy but excluding agriculture.

Table 3.03: African employment and earnings, 1985

Sector	African employment (×1 000)	Average earnings (current rands per month)	
		African	White
Banking institutions	11	655	1 432
Homeland governments*	117	534	–
Central government	142	480	1 307†
Universities	9	472	1 833
Manufacturing	704	468	1 848
Supplementary Living Level (August 1985)		445	
SA Transport Services	106	421	1 600
Construction	204	384	1 807
Local authorities‡	138	367	1 823
Provincial administration	96	357	1 341
Minimum Living Level (August 1985)		350	
Wholesale trade	97	343	1 750
Mining and quarrying	637	327	1 675
Retail trade	176	307	864
Drycleaning	10	227	672

Source: Saldru Handbook, 1986: 62–88 and 296–320
* Figures exclude independent homelands.
† Includes white civil servants seconded to homeland governments.
‡ Excludes Divisional Councils.

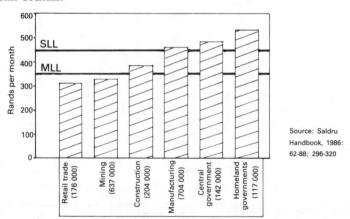

Source: Saldru Handbook, 1986: 62-88; 296-320

Fig. 3.03: African employment and earnings by sector, 1985

From this table, which excludes workers employed in agriculture and domestic service where wages are generally much lower, we see that in 1985 for approximately one million African workers, in manufacturing, government service, universities and banking, average earnings were above the SLL. For the rest earnings were lower, and for many workers, assuming that they are the sole bread-winners in an average-sized family, average wages were below the minimum living level.

Manufacturing sector

Moreover, even in the relatively better-paid sectors the picture is not all rosy. Whilst in 1985 average monthly earnings of the 704 000 Africans employed in the manufacturing sector (excluding construction) were R468, which was just above the SLL, and whilst there were 235 000 African workers earning at least 25 per cent more than the SLL, nevertheless, as the following table shows, there were more than 200 000 African workers employed by manufacturing industries whose average earnings were below the SLL, and a further 74 000 whose average earnings, assuming that they were the sole bread-winner in an average-sized household, were below the MLL. What is more, even in those industries where average African wages are higher than the SLL there may be substantial numbers of workers, particularly those classified as labourers, whose earnings are very low.

Evidence for this may be found in the Industrial Council agreements which cover 1.27 million workers, most of them in the manufacturing sector.

Labourers, who constitute 22 per cent of all economically active workers, form the biggest single job category; yet of the 182 Industrial Council wage rates set for labourers only one exceeds the SLL. It is true that these are minimum rates but in practice wages are unlikely to be substantially higher than this and most of the Industrial Council rates set for labourers are less than two-thirds (in some cases less than one-quarter) of the SLL and thus below the MLL as well.

Although wages for those classified coloured or Asian are generally somewhat higher than for Africans there are nevertheless some industries, even in urban, formal-sector jobs, where average earnings are below the supplementary living level. In the clothing industry, for example, average earnings for the 49 000 coloured workers in 1985 were R343 per month, well below the estimated SLL of R400 for coloured workers who were the only bread-winners in average-sized households. Indian workers in the same industry averaged R399 per month.

The overall picture, then, is that in the modern industrial, urban sector of the economy African wages, despite some real gains over the period 1970–85, remain low. For the vast majority of African workers (plus some who are coloured or Indian) earnings are below the SLL and tens of thousands are paid less than the MLL. Elsewhere in the economy, whether in commercial agriculture, domestic service, subsistence agriculture or other informal-sector jobs both urban and rural, wages are generally even lower.

Table 3.04: African employment and earnings in manufacturing, 1985

Branch	Employment (×1 000)	Average earnings (rands/month)
Rubber	11	698
Chemicals	49	636
Printing	12	599
Paper	18	588
Basic metal	62	584
Beverages	23	577
Machinery	30	572
Electrical machinery	30	565
Transport equipment	47	530
Plastics	13	529
Metal products	76	524
Professional equipment	3	502
Tobacco	2	485
Supplementary Living Level (August)		445
Nonmetallic minerals	58	434
Furniture	13	410
Footwear	6	396
Construction	204	384
Food	108	380
Other manufacturing	9	377
Textiles	62	370
Minimum Living Level (August)		350
Leather	5	294
Clothing	31	217*
Wood and cork	38	199
Total manufacturing	704	468

Source: Saldru Handbook, 1986: 65–76; 299–310
* In this sector average monthly earnings for coloured persons (R343) are also below the MLL.

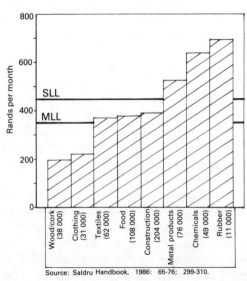

Source: Saldru Handbook, 1986: 65-76; 299-310.

Fig. 3.04: African employment and earnings in manufacturing, 1985

Agriculture

In agriculture, the official statistics of employment and earnings fluctuate from year to year in such a way that they may not be altogether reliable. The general picture which emerges however is of cash incomes that have, as in manufacturing, risen somewhat in real terms during recent years, but which, in absolute terms, are well below earnings in town, even when due allowance is made for wages-in-kind provided on farms and the absence of transport costs which eat into urban budgets.

In real terms, taking 1975 as the base year, cash wages of farm labourers in four different areas of the country were as follows:

Table 3.05: Changes in African annual real wages in agriculture *(measured in 1975 rands)*

	1976/7	1980/1	% change
Transvaal highveld	254	290	+14
North-west OFS	221	333	+51
Swartland (W. Cape)	332	337	+2
Western Transvaal	186	250	+34

Source: Fenyes, 1983 cited in 134: 39

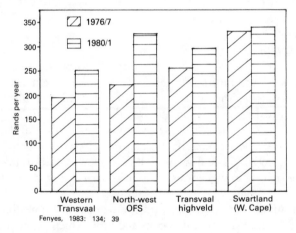

Fenyes, 1983: 134; 39

Fig. 3.05: African annual wages in agriculture, 1976/7–1980/1 (measured in 1975 rands)

Wages on farms vary widely, not only between individual farms but also from area to area. In 1979, the latest year for which national data is available, the average value of monthly wages – in cash and kind – for African regular workers was R46 for the country as a whole, varying from R95 in the Cape Peninsula to R35 in the northern Transvaal. For coloured workers the monthly average was R69, ranging from R1 363 in the magisterial districts of Johannesburg and Randburg to R28 in the north-eastern Orange Free State. In both these areas coloured farm workers form a small proportion of the total and cannot be taken as representative although they are certainly illuminating.

For those classified as Asian (or Indian), farm wages for regular workers averaged R158, ranging from R452 on the east Rand to R47 a month in northern Natal around Babanango and Vryheid, an area long notorious for its farm labour conditions.

The map opposite shows the topography of farm wages paid to Africans, regular farm workers only, in 1979. Those areas where wages are particularly low, notably the north-eastern Cape (Barkly East), north-western Natal (Vryheid), and the northern Transvaal (Waterberg–Pietersburg), have long been at the bottom of the list (25: 17). But even in the relatively high-wage districts average earnings for African farm labourers are abysmally low, even though earnings on some individual farms compare favourably with those in town.

A generation ago, the proportion of farm wages received as cash varied from less than one-third to three-quarters and more. The trend since then has been for a greater and greater proportion of remuneration on farms to be paid directly in cash, although housing, rations and, in some parts of the country, arable and grazing rights, remain important. There is evidence of acute poverty in many farming areas, with conditions of virtual serfdom prevailing in some parts (Wilson, Kooy, and Hendrie, 1976; 306: 1; and Saldru Handbook, 1986: 355).

Domestic service

Another major sector on which it is difficult to obtain full information is domestic service. But one striking table shows that in the major metropolitan areas of the country, the wages, in cash and kind, of full-time domestic servants fell in real terms (taking 1975 as the base year) by 16 per cent over the period 1973–80 (134: 40). If we examine the position of African women employed as domestic workers in the major metropolitan areas we find that over the period 1970–81 real wages (allowing for inflation), taking cash and kind together, fell in some centres, rose in other centres, and remained static elsewhere.

Bearing in mind that wages in kind for women in domestic service come mainly in the form of meals and accommodation which is generally of no use to their families, we need to focus on the cash component. This, as can be seen from the above table, is very low, ranging from R74 a month in Cape Town to R48 a month in Bloemfontein and East London in 1981 when the minimum living level for urban African families was approximately R180 per month. Small wonder that in those households headed by African women poverty is particularly acute.

In the urban areas of the country, wages and salaries (paid mainly in cash) are the primary source of income for most households. For example, surveys by the University of South Africa's Bureau of Market Research showed that on the Witwatersrand and in Durban in 1980 wages and salaries constituted between 86 and 92 per cent of incomes received by African households (134: 35).

South Africa:
topography of
farm wages paid
to Africans

Table 3.06: Monthly earnings of African women in domestic service, 1970–81

| | Constant (1981) rands, cash and kind | | | Current rands, cash only: |
	1970	1981	% change	1981
Cape Town	139	108	−22	74
Witwatersrand	107	107	0	67
Pretoria	102	99	− 3	62
Durban	95	100	+ 5	58
Port Elizabeth	102	92	−10	58
Pietermaritzburg	92	90	− 2	55
OFS gold fields	84	86	+ 2	52
Kimberley	86	86	0	53
Vaal Triangle	94	82	−13	52
Bloemfontein	87	88	+ 1	48
East London	89	86	− 3	48

Source: Saldru Handbook, 1986: 373–7

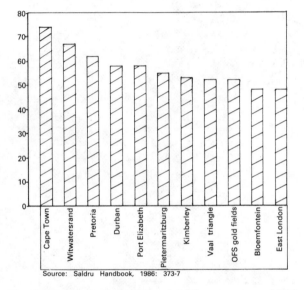

Source: Saldru Handbook, 1986: 373-7

Fig. 3.06: Domestic wages of African women, 1981

Remittances

However, in the rural areas, particularly in the reserves, the lack of jobs and the even lower level of wages mean that other sources of income assume much greater importance. Of these sources, remittances sent by migrants working away from home and old-age pensions emerged, from micro-study after micro-study, as critical.

Indeed, from these studies, we know that for households in most parts of the reserves access to regular cash income is the single most important determinant of their well-being. In a striking table on sources of income for Transkei rural households in 1982, it is shown that for those households with an annual income of less than R1 500 (that is, less than R125 per month), two-thirds (66–71 per cent) of it came from remittances sent by migrants working away from home; 14–19 of it came from pensions; 11–15 from wages in local jobs; and only 2–3 per cent from home production (134: 41 and 149: 5). Expenditure on food was found to be five-and-a-half times that of net farming income (261: 14).

As far as remittances are concerned, there is some useful information available regarding mineworkers, but for migrants in other sectors of the economy there is little systematic data available on either the regularity or the amount sent back home by workers out of their wages. The following table shows average remittances per migrant (on mines affiliated to the Chamber of Mines) sent to different parts of southern Africa in 1985.

Table 3.07: African mineworkers' remittances, by area, 1985

Area of origin	Annual	Monthly average	No. migrants
	(rands)		(×1 000)
South Africa			
Transkei	461	38	144
Bophuthatswana	399	33	39
Venda	226	19	3
Ciskei	186	15	15
Other reserves	384	32	51
SA excl. reserves	–	–	64*
Lesotho	1 921	160	109
Malawi	1 503	125	20
Mozambique	1 439	120	58
Botswana	1 089	91	20
Swaziland	846	70	14
Total	–	–	536

Source: Saldru Handbook, 1986: 253–5 and The Employment Bureau of Africa (Teba), Annual Report, 1986: 11
* Whilst a substantial proportion of these men may be migrants, they sign up at the mine rather than at a rural recruiting office.

These figures reflect remittances sent through recruiting organisations by miners to their families, and exclude anything miners may take home or send in other ways. Official remittances to foreign countries are considerably greater than those within South Africa itself because of government agreements by these countries with the Chamber of Mines specifying what wages are to be remitted.

Pensions

But pensions are sometimes even more important. In the Transkei, for example, for households whose annual income in 1982 was R500 (or R42 per month) or less, pensions constituted one-fifth of income. In the Ciskei, in three resettlement camps, the primary source of income for half the households was the pension (189: 4). In KwaZulu, in the remote rural district of Nkandla, the sources of cash income, excluding the value of agricultural produce, were remittances (46 per cent); pensions including disability and maintenance grants (29); and local employment plus small business activity in the area, including traditional healing (25). The importance of pensions can be seen, for example, in the fact that the average male contribution to the household quadruples from R265 to R920 per annum as men reach the pensionable age of 65 (53a: 48).

Old-age pensions became payable to white people in 1928 and disability grants in 1946. The position of the state's responsibility for African pensioners was that they had their own 'Native custom which makes provision for maintaining dependant persons'. Only in 1943 did urban Africans start receiving pensions. The rationale was that rural Africans should not be provided with benefits which would 'conflict with or break down their tribal food-sharing habits'. This practice was only abolished in 1965 when official policy claimed that because 70 per cent of African pensioners were living in rural areas, there was then a need 'to avoid providing an incentive to Africans to move to the cities' (138: 1–2).

The current position is that the state is responsible for more than 35 per cent of the total number of pensions paid in South Africa. The number reached just under 700 000 people in 1982, of whom just less than 300 000 were Africans representing 1.5 per cent of that population. By contrast 6 per cent of whites received state pensions. These state pensions apply only to people who have no private pensions and can no longer work (138: 8).

Average old-age pensions paid to Africans by the state rose in real (1975) terms from R67 per annum in 1970 to R162 in 1981, an increase of 142 per cent. Over the same period pensions for Asians, coloured and whites also rose in real terms, although not so fast. The value of white pensions rose only 4 per cent over the eleven years (134: 42).

Other calculations show that maximum old-age pensions paid to Africans by the state rose in real (1980) terms from R14 per month in 1970 to R45 in 1983, an increase of 221 per cent. White pensions increased by 40 per cent in real terms, from R97 to R136, over the same period (Saldru Handbook, 1986: 478). Despite the relatively rapid rise (from a tiny base) of African pensions, we find that in 1985 white pensioners, badly off as they were (particularly in view of the exploding rents of flats in areas they had occupied in the past), were still earning over twice as much as their black counterparts. White pensioners, receiving R180 per month and living alone, could only just (and not always) keep their heads above water. Black pensions, averaging R79 per month, were below the poverty datum line.

Given the low level of wages for the majority of black workers and given the importance of remittances (which are paid from these same wages) and of pensions (which are very low), it is not surprising to find an acute racial bias in the overall distribution of income in South Africa. Whilst real wages for those employed in most sectors, with the notable exception of laundries and domestic service, rose between 1970 and 1985, poverty remains acute and widespread. Moreover the number of households that have to endure poverty seems to have increased. This conclusion is certainly strengthened when one considers conditions in Mozambique, Lesotho, Namibia, Swaziland, and

Botswana, where not only are there no state pensions for the vast majority, but access to jobs in the industrial heart of the economy is made more and more difficult by the South African authorities.

Interesting though the overall picture may be, and necessary as it is to understand the geographic and racial framework of poverty in southern Africa, it only becomes meaningful if one gets down to the grassroots to examine the nature of poverty in a particular geographic context as it affects specific people.

It is not possible, nor even desirable, in a book such as this, to tour every dorp and city, every farming district or every village in the reserves in order to describe in detail the nature and extent of poverty in these different places. But a brief visit to no more than half a dozen of them should prove instructive.

On the platteland

Let us begin in the middle of South Africa, in the dry Karoo. Beaufort West is a railway town, one-third of the way up the long haul from Cape Town to the country's industrial heart on the Witwatersrand. Population in 1980 was 25 000 of whom 14 000 were coloured, 6 000 white and 5 000 African. Three-quarters of the coloured population live in Rustdene, a township of 'subeconomic' houses built over thirty years ago after the Second World War. 'Very few houses have incomes above the minimum living level' (35: 33). In Rustdene itself, over 50 per cent of the households live below the minimum living level. One-quarter of the households are headed by a woman. Of these female-headed households, nearly three-quarters (72 per cent) were below the MLL in 1983, and nine out of every ten of them were below the supplementary living level.

The only employment for unskilled 'coloured' women in Beaufort West is domestic work, apart from a handful of petrol attendant and shop counter jobs. Wages are relatively low and jobs are scarce. The usual wage for full-time domestic work is around R30 per month. (35: 21)

But not everyone can get jobs; 41 per cent of economically active coloured women were unemployed according to a municipal census in 1982. For many coloured women, maintenance grants provided by the state for single mothers (whether widowed, divorced or unmarried) have been a more realistic way of ensuring a regular income than trying to find a job. Over 20 per cent of all adults over the age of 16 in Rustdene receive an old-age pension, or a maintenance grant, or a disability grant (35: 23). For Africans, employment opportunities are even worse and the state does not provide anything like the support which it makes available to the coloured poor in Rustdene. Monthly pensions, for example, in 1985 were R117 for coloureds and for Africans R79 (paid in a lump sum of R158 every second month).

Calitzdorp is a small agricultural town in the Little Karoo. Total population is only 6 500, of whom 5 000 are coloured, 1 300 are white, and less than 200 are African. Whites are mainly farmers; coloured persons work mainly as labourers on the farms in the district. In Calitzdorp the mean income of regular farm workers was R69 a month compared with a civil pension of R83.

Household conditions vary dramatically. Despite the generally depressed conditions in Calitzdorp, there are some households where at least two members have regular jobs and the household size is small. Such families, especially where at least one member received a state pension, are in the most fortunate position. Such households are able to rise above the seasonal slump in the local economy without too much difficulty. There are however many large households dependent on the income of a single breadwinner fortunate to have secured a regular job, or on a pensioner whose monthly income of R83 has to be spread among 8 or more members. The most unfortunate are those households where nobody has a regular job and where there is almost complete dependence on casual labour during the fruit season. Such households are in a desperate situation and are haunted by the spectre of starvation during the months outside the fruit season. (36: 54)

For one-third of the households in Bergsig, the coloured township, pensions provide the main source of income (36: 59). Some 40 per cent of the regular workers of Calitzdorp are migrants who live and work outside the district. Of these less than one-fifth send regular remittances to their families, and another one-tenth or less send irregular remittances. In Calitzdorp, therefore, the major sources of income are wages from farm labour and state grants and pensions. In Bergsig it was found that pensions and state grants represented 39 per cent of cash income, and in 18 per cent of households these were the principal source, and in 8 per cent of households the only source (36: 59).

Within the cities

Moving from the platteland into the metropolitan centres, we go to the heart of industrial South Africa. At first glance, living standards seem to have improved dramatically. In Soweto for example, between 1962 and 1980, the proportion of African households with an income (measured in constant 1980 prices) less than R2 000 a year halved from 42 per cent to 21 per cent. And at the other end of the spectrum, the proportion of households with over R4 500 more than quadrupled from 7 per cent to 33 per cent (18: 17). These figures

A *widow's mite*

Mrs Cornelius, aged 65, is head of a nine-member household. She is a widow receiving an old age-pension of R83 per month. She is the sole breadwinner. Her only son works away from Calitzdorp. He makes no contribution to the household. There are six grandchildren, all attending school. Her daughter aged 29 years, . . . is at home waiting for the start of the fruit season so that she can obtain some casual work. A total of R17,83 is set aside for rent, electricity, water, and sanitation each month. Only R65,17 is left to pay for fuel, food, and other household expenses for the month (36: 61). With a little more than R7 per person to buy food, fuel and other household expenses, how does a household survive when the minimum food required for each person costs at least four times as much?

The woodseller of Bergsig

Mr J. J., aged 57 years, sells wood to households in Bergsig. He is unable to find regular employment. He receives an average monthly income of R35. His wife is a domestic worker earning R65 a month. They have two daughters aged 26 and 18 who can only find casual work during the fruit season. At the time the survey was conducted [1983] they were unemployed. The total household income at the time came to R100 per month. There are 9 members in the household including three scholars attending school and two children aged 2 and 4 years. They live in a two-bedroomed house with a separate lounge, kitchen and bathroom. Their expenditure for rent, water, electricity and sanitation amounted to R29,14 in September 1983, leaving them with a balance of R70,86 to feed a family of nine for the month (36: 60). At this time the MLL for a coloured family of 5 in the nearest city, Port Elizabeth, was R257, of which approximately 55 per cent, i.e. R141, was for food. In other words, when the cost per person of buying the bare minimum of food necessary was R28 per month, the woodseller of Bergsig had less than R8 to spend on food for each member of his household.

exaggerate, to some extent, the changes that have taken place; over the same period African households became much bigger as a result of the lack of housing, which compelled many families to 'double-up' as one household. Nevertheless the figures do reflect significant improvements that took place over the two decades, but particularly during the first half of the 1970s. Despite this, however, poverty remains endemic in the area. After a careful survey of nearly twenty studies undertaken on the Witwatersrand between 1966 and 1982, Pillay concluded in 1984:

The quality of life in Soweto and other PWV [Pretoria–Witwatersrand–Vereeniging] townships can be ascribed to the meagre amounts of disposable income available per household. Although a range of incomes is found across the different townships the broad pattern is one of a universe of poverty. . . . The average household income in Soweto for example was estimated at a quarter of that recorded in white Johannesburg. . . . [The surveys] show a substantial portion (anything between 20 and 40 per cent) of the population living below the PDL. The PDL used here, however, is a highly conservative index and if items such as costs of education, recreation, necessary savings, medical expenses, household utensils and other family essentials are considered it is likely that as many as 80% of Soweto households, for example, receive less than this adjusted income level. (18: 16)

Moving off the Witwatersrand to other major metropolitan areas, we find a similar pattern. From a detailed survey of sub-standard housing areas and squatter communities of Africans in both Cape Town and Durban, and also of coloured communities in Cape Town, a comprehensive picture was built up of the income and expenditure patterns of the urban poor in these two cities. Prinsloo found that the proportion of households existing below the minimum living level ranged from 9 per cent in Guguletu and Bonteheuwel (African and coloured townships in Cape Town) through 30 per cent in Cape Town's squatter communities, and 40 in parts of Durban to 67 in Lamontville, an African township outside Durban. The following table shows something of the different levels of poverty facing people living in various townships and squatter communities in Cape Town and Durban at the time of the Carnegie survey in 1982–3.

Table 3.08: Poverty in Cape Town and Durban townships, 1982–3

Place	City	Township or squatter camp	Percentage households below MLL	Monthly per capita income (rands)
Gugulethu	CT	Tn	9	96
Bonteheuwel	CT	Tn	9	101
Clermont	Dbn	Sq	43	62
Lamontville	Dbn	Tn	67	48

Source: 16: 14

Further insight into the distribution of poverty was provided for the Carnegie Inquiry by three communities and their organisations, working through the Community Research Unit, an independent body based in Durban. The three communities were chosen to present a synoptic view of communities in the Durban metropolitan area (17: 2–3). The information is summarised in the following table:

Table 3.09: Poverty in three Natal townships, 1983–4

	Chatsworth	Orient Hills	Hambanati
Average monthly household income	R789	R410	R270
Mean per capita income	R139	R 84	R 44
Percentage households below HSL	23%	58%	68%
Percentage households below HEL	43%	85%	89%

Source: 17: 10–13

Chatsworth, with a population of more than one-quarter of a million people, is regarded as the largest Indian public housing scheme outside of India. There are some 21 000 housing units built by the Durban City Council (on which Indian residents have no representation) with funds from the National Housing Commission, and a further 3 000 houses built privately. A majority of the houses are occupied by people who were forced to move there in terms of the Group Areas Act. The study, conducted by an umbrella residents' association, the Chatsworth Housing Action Committee (CHAC), through its affiliates, found that the average household monthly income was R789 and the mean monthly per capita income was R139. Some 23 per cent of the households had income below the HSL and 43 below the HEL.

In Orient Hills, a relatively small and recently established Indian township some 25 km south of Durban, the mean monthly income of the head of the households ranged from R130 for a one-person household to R550 for an eleven-person household. The mean total household income ranged from

R130 to R1 394. The average household income was R410; the mean monthly per capita income was R84. In terms of poverty 58 per cent of the households had incomes that fell below the HSL and 85 per cent below the HEL.

Hambanati is a more established African township, built just after the Second World War. Economically it is part of the Tongaat sugar estate some 40 km north of Durban whilst politically it has been excised from the town pending possible incorporation into KwaZulu. The Joint Rent Action Committee (JORAC) which conducted the survey is a community-based organisation with extensive support in the township (17: 3). Here the average household income was R270 and mean per capita income was R44. Two-thirds (68 per cent) of the households were below the HSL and no less than nine out of ten (89 per cent) were below the HEL.

Inside the reserves

From the cities we move to consider those rural areas, the reserves, which provide much of the labour without which South Africa's industrial economy would grind to a rapid halt. We go first to a place lying roughly half-way between Durban and East London, Lower Roza, an administrative area comprising six dispersed settlements outside the small town of Qumbu in the Transkei. In a study of 200 households it was found that average monthly income was R152 (November–December 1983). Some three-quarters (76 per cent) of the households were estimated to have incomes below the HSL and 88 per cent were below the HEL (47: 33).

In addition to the extent of poverty documented in the study, the degree of inequality that emerged in this remote rural area was remarkable. The richest 10 per cent of households received one-third of all the income whilst the poorest 10 per cent got only one-fiftieth. Thus average monthly household income of the top 10 per cent was R410 compared with R27 per household for the poorest 10 per cent: a ratio of 15:1. Even allowing for the fact that richer households had more members than poorer households, the per capita income differences were startling. Moreover, unlike many gaps between rich and poor this chasm in Lower Roza was due not so much to the wealth of the rich as to the depth of poverty of the very poor.

The poorest quarter of the community had a mean annual per capita income of R93, ranging from R7 to R147. In monthly terms that works out at a mean of less than R8, ranging from 50 cents to R12 per person. At these income levels, remarks the researcher, 'it becomes difficult to afford food apart from simple mielie-meal, samp and porridge, clothing is a luxury, and schooling cost impossible – thus ensuring that the legacy of abject poverty will be passed on to the next generation' (47: 38). Yet Lower Roza is probably one of the more prosperous peri-urban areas in Transkei. In 1979 Qumbu district was found to have the third-highest average household income in Transkei.

Furthermore, Lower Roza is a prosperous, monetised area in the district, with ten good primary schools and access to the secondary school in Qumbu. In a way, Lower Roza as a minute sub-section of the Transkei economy exhibits the classic signs of under-

70

development. Massive internal income differences are present (especially if migrants are allowed for), with a few people earning high wages while the bulk of the population has no access to lucrative income sources. (47: 40)

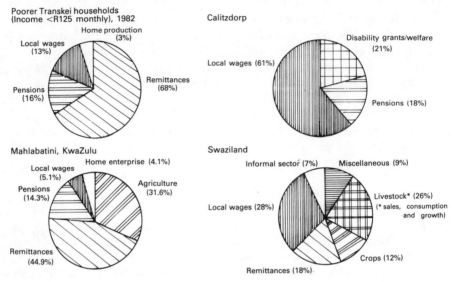

Fig. 3.07: Sources of household income in four rural areas

In the sample as a whole the major sources of income were remittances 33 per cent; local jobs 26; pensions and disability grants 17; casual work in the informal sector 16; and income from subsistence farming only 8 per cent (47: 35). The worst-off households in the sample were those without pensions and with small and erratic remittances, if at all. Some of these were involved in the informal sector, and were marginally better off than the very poorest group – the handful surviving only on agriculture (47: 37).

It is worth noting that migrants from Lower Roza remit only 20 per cent of salaries, keeping approximately R196 per month: this is substantially higher than the average monthly income of R152 for all rural families, which has to be divided among an average of 5.7 people. At least a quarter of the migrants work on the mines, which provide free food and accommodation. Even allowing for higher urban living costs, migrants live, relatively speaking, rather better than their families at home.

The Mahlabatini district in KwaZulu is 'genuinely rural', perhaps even more so than Lower Roza. It lies about 60 km north-west of Melmoth and 90 km south-east of Vryheid. Local towns such as Mahlabatini and Ulundi are, like Qumbu, small-scale. The most striking difference from Lower Roza is the role played by subsistence agriculture. The value of the produce, both consumed and sold, constitutes roughly 30 per cent on average of income from all sources (56: 3–11).

The most striking feature of the agricultural situation in Mahlabatini in 1981 was the central role of cattle despite the low sales turn-over. Their importance as a store of wealth is underlined by the fact that the value of the average cattle-holding was roughly equivalent to the average household cash income over a period of 2.5 years (over R2 300). We found that milk production was higher (in terms of cash equivalent) than all major agricultural production put together. Draught power was another major contribution. (56: 21)

Income from agricultural sources was even more important for poorer families, as may be seen in the following table.

Table 3.10: Sources of income to households in Mahlabatini, 1981

Non-agric. income range (R/annum)	No. of households	Mean non-agric. income	Mean agric. income*	Mean agric. income as % of total income
		(R/annum)		
0–499	27	259	351	58
500–999	19	789	291	27
1 000–1 499	11	1 282	474	27
1500–	8	2 700	886	25

Source: 56: 20

* Agricultural income includes the value of all crops, milk, eggs and meat produced and consumed or sold.

For households with non-agricultural incomes of R500 or more per year agriculture accounted for roughly one-quarter of total income. But for the poorest families, with non-agricultural incomes of less than R500 a year, agriculture constituted well over half of their livelihood.

Significant though agriculture was in Mahlabatini it was considerably less important for the average household than the flow of cash coming from outside the district in the form of remittances (44 per cent) and pensions (16 per cent), which together accounted for 60 per cent of household income. Agriculture accounted for 31 per cent, wages from local employment 5, and income from home enterprises 4. With remittances alone making up nearly half of household income in rural Mahlabatini, the study highlighted the fact that 'the income level of rural households is dramatically affected by the wage-remittance behaviour of absent members of their households' (56: 22).

Poverty in Mahlabatini is deep and widespread. The average monthly household income of R114 in the district was well below the estimated household subsistence level of R184 for the area and only 41 per cent of the household effective level. More than half the households studied had incomes below the HSL (56: 24).

In another remote rural part of KwaZulu, close to the Nkandla forest 50 km west of Eshowe, the inequalities of Lower Roza are echoed but not quite as starkly. Nevertheless poverty is acute. The bottom 10 per cent of households in the Nkandla survey received 2.4 per cent of total income and the top 10 per cent received 24.3, a ratio of 10:1. (The figures for Lower Roza were 1.9 and 32.9 per cent, making a ratio or gap of 17:1 (53a: 37 and 47: 32).) The poor are very poor. Half of all households receive a monthly income of only R94. This means that half of the household had per capita incomes of less than R12 a month and 30 per cent had only R8. The poorest group comprises households without a migrant worker or pensioner. There were seven such households and half of them had per capita incomes of less than R6 per month. The second poorest group were the ten households headed by women, with half the households receiving just over R6 per person per month. The third poorest group were the households containing an unemployed migrant. The median income was R8 per month (53a: 39). These figures, it should not be forgotten, already include the value of all agricultural production available to the household concerned.

Another measure of inequality in the reserves is the distribution of ownership of cattle. In the Libode district of the Transkei, for example, in the period 1980–3, a wide variation was reported.

Table 3.11: Distribution of cattle ownership in Libode, 1980–3

Herd size	No. of families	%
0	6 968	54
1–2	1 045	8
3–5	1 675	13
6–10	1 885	15
11–20	1 016	8
21–49	258	2
50+	7	0.1

Source: 294: 7

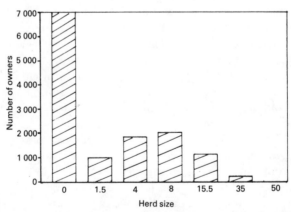

Fig. 3.08: Distribution of cattle ownership in Libode, 1980–3

More than half the households in Libode had no cattle at all, and one in five had between one and five beasts. One household in ten had eleven or more. No figures are available which correlate land-holdings, cattle and sheep ownership, and remittances from town but there is some evidence that those who are rich in cattle are rich in other ways as well.

From South Africa we move to consider, briefly, those countries which though politically independent of South Africa are nevertheless economically locked into the single economy of the region by virtue of the extensive migrant labour links, going back over a century of mineral development.

Botswana

Mosolotshane is a small village of approximately a thousand people on the eastern edge of the Kalahari sandveld in the central district of Botswana. The inhabitants are predominantly BaKgalagadi ex-*malata* ('serfs'), who lived as herders (*badisa*) looking after the cattle of the BaNgwato royalty (*dikgosana*). The people of this village appear to be relatively well-off with 95 per cent of households engaged in arable farming, 70 per cent owning cattle and 34 per cent having herds sufficiently large to provide independent draft power. But these statistics tell us nothing about the enormous variations in the size of harvests and herds. Moreover, many poor people who live as dependants of wealthy households and – using the conventional definition of 'households' – would be seen as part of these households, have no legal right to any of their resources. These dependants may be poor relatives or they may be unrelated, as in the case of the 30–40 Basarwa (San) families who have remained with their former 'masters' after legal emancipation (284: 1). In this study poorer households are defined as those 'that do not have – or have very limited – access to the major economic resources, i.e. arable land, draft power, ploughs and seed, cattle, labour and/or regular transfer from wage earners' (284: 3).

Some 30 per cent of households owned no cattle at all; 34 per cent owned herds sufficiently large (12 cattle or more) to provide the household with draft power; and 37 per cent had herds smaller than this. There is also wide variation in the actual size of the land cultivated by the different households (284: 11, 16).

'Poorer households do not have separate fields for their adult women. This is not because there is insufficient arable land in the area, but rather because these households lack the necessary resources to plough larger areas, viz draft power and/or labour.' (284: 16) The evidence also suggests that harvest size is correlated with having the necessary draft power so as to be able to plough with the early rains (284: 17).

One-third (31 per cent) of the households in the village had wage-earners. Of those earning wages only one-sixth (16 per cent) worked in Botswana; the vast majority (84 per cent) were all migrants working on the South African mines. The precise importance of remittances to the village has not been established but it would seem that one-third (36 per cent or even more) of the herds were built up, at least in part, through wages mainly from the South African mines. The magnitude of the remittance seems to depend on a number of factors including the relationship of the worker to the household and the economic status of the household itself. There is evidence to suggest, interestingly, that 'sons and daughters in extremely poor households are more likely to cut their ties completely during their period of employment . . . while those from more fortunate households retain their rural links.' (284: 23)

The evidence suggests too that, in addition to providing resources for building up herds, the earnings of migrants help to increase the returns to

Profile of households in Mosolotshane

- 6%   of households were completely destitute, living off begging and 'piece-jobs'.

- 22% were very poor having no cattle, no wage-earners, and harvesting 4 or fewer bags of sorghum in 1978.

- 30% were less poor, pooling resources with other households in order to obtain draft power and obtaining harvest of 5–7 bags. Some of these households had a few cattle of their own while others had *mafisa* [loan] cattle or both. Some also had wage-earners but remittances were insufficient to enable independent ploughing.

- 27% were relatively wealthy, owning sufficient cattle to supply their own draft power and obtaining harvests in excess of 6 bags. Most of this group employed outside labour on their arable lands or at their cattle posts and some had wage-earners.

- 15% were very wealthy, having large herds which were watered at privately owned or syndicate boreholes. Some also engaged in large-scale arable production, harvesting 50–150 bags of sorghum which they sold in Mahalapye. Some of these households also had wage-earners.

agriculture. This, of course, may be partly due to the availability of draft power in the larger herds. But Polly Hill's observation from West Africa that people, despite the availability of land, may be too poor to farm (296: 8) seems to apply in this Botswana village where there is a correlation between those households with wage-earners and the returns in arable income.

Other sources of income derive from small local industries or 'penny-capitalist self-employment'. 'In Mosolotshane this includes a whole range of activities, the most important of which are beer brewing (30%); collection and sale of firewood and water (18%); leatherwork (8%); carpentry, collection and sale of building timbers (8%); sale of agricultural produce on a regular basis (milk, eggs) (9%); dress-making, knitting, brick-making, building, grinding and selling snuff together with more lucrative businesses which include hawking and Setswana medicine' (284: 26). As in agriculture those with resources get a better return than those without. 'The poorest members of the community lack capital and are generally unable to deal in credit. Living from hand to mouth they are unable to delay payment for their produce. While they may possess the ability to organise, low social status makes it difficult for them to deal with village institutions . . . which control (or interfere with) a large number of productive activities.' (Kjaer-Olsen cited in 284: 28)

For most poor people 'piece-jobs' constitute their most important source of food. There is very little straightforward charity in the village and most of the wealthier households who help poorer people with food do this primarily in exchange for the performance of domestic chores . . . men and women destump agricultural fields; whole families may

Abandoned in Mosolotshane

In Mosolotshane there were a number of elderly people despairing that their children who had gone to the towns to work had 'forgotten' them. One frail old woman dressed in tatters said that the last time she had heard from her son was six years ago when he had given her the clothes that she was wearing. Since then she had heard nothing from him even though 'he knows how to write'. . . . Perhaps he had indeed died but what had happened to her other children and those in the other cases? Some had probably never managed to get regular employment while others probably earned too little to share. (284: 23)

be involved in constructing thorn-bush fences around arable lands; men may help with the watering of livestock in exchange for free water for their own animals or food; women usually stamp corn in exchange for the husk which is eaten; they collect the manure and mud for repairing or building houses and assist in this; fetch water, wash clothes, sweep the *lolwapa*'s – in short, all the more laborious household chores are done as 'piece-jobs' in exchange for food or a few *thebe*. (284: 28)

The *majako* system provides a highly precarious source of livelihood for those who participate in it. It enables wealthier households to employ women and their children to work on their fields in exchange for food during the season and an unspecified part of the crop. The risky element for those who do *majako* occurs in times of crop failure when the employer is not obligated to pay the labourer anything at all although in most cases they will be given a small amount of cash (5–10 pula) or perhaps a bucket of sorghum – scant reward for four months' labour. (284: 19)

Swaziland

In Swaziland a large survey in 1978–9 of over 1 100 households living on Swazi National Land, under communal tenure, provides detailed information on the sources of income received by rural households. Wages earned locally by consumers were the single most important source (28 per cent), followed by the return – in the form of sales, consumption, and growth – on livestock (26 per cent). Remittances in cash and kind accounted for just under one-fifth (18 per cent), whilst crops (12 per cent), the informal sector (7 per cent), and miscellaneous sources (9 per cent), accounted for the rest. What is interesting about this is the extent to which agriculture, totalling (38 per cent), and local wage-paying jobs (28 per cent), provide the average household's income.

Remittances are certainly needed from workers going to the gold mines and elsewhere but rural households in Swaziland have far more local resources – in terms both of subsistence agriculture and of wage-paying jobs – to draw on than do their counterparts in the Transkei or, indeed, the other reserves of South Africa. In absolute terms, moreover, the average Swazi rural household in 1978–9 received an annual income of E915.* In Lower Roza, by comparison, the average family income at the end of 1983 was R1 825 or

* The exchange rate is fixed at one elangeni to the rand.

R324 per resident. However, both poverty and inequality are acute. In terms of wealth (measured by a system of points which takes into consideration livestock-holding, vehicles owned, and a selection of other household assets as well as cash income) the poorest 10 per cent of households received only 1 per cent of the wealth points whilst the richest 10 per cent received 33 per cent – a gap between rich and poor far greater than that measured in Lower Roza or Nkandla. In terms of cash income alone the chasm was even greater: the poorest 10 per cent of households had no cash income at all, and the bottom 20 per cent only 0.4 per cent of all cash income, whilst the top 10 per cent received nearly half (47 per cent) and the top 20 per cent received two-thirds (65 per cent) of the cash.

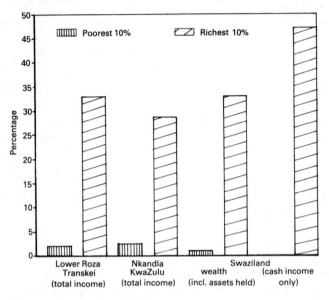

Fig. 3.09: Rural inequality

Despite the extent of inequality amongst rural households and despite the low average level of income, the evidence seems to suggest that rural poverty is not as pervasive as in most countries of the sub-continent. For example, in terms of malnutrition, measured as a proportion of rural under-5-year-olds being below 80 per cent of the international weight-for-age standards, it is estimated that 10–15 per cent of small children in Swaziland are malnourished compared with 20 per cent in Botswana, 20–5 per cent in Lesotho, and 30–3 per cent in Zimbabwe (285: 17).

Figures are not always consistent nor is it possible to measure rural incomes, coming from such diverse sources, with quite the accuracy that the precise percentages suggest. Nevertheless the overall picture is clear. Average incomes in urban centres are considerably higher than in rural areas but the wide distribution of income, around very low average figures, means that both in town and in the country there is acute poverty in southern Africa. Poverty is deep (with a not insignificant number of households having no assets or income of any kind) and widespread. Large proportions (ranging up to 90 per cent in some rural areas) of the population have to survive on incomes that are below the poverty datum line, which itself makes no provision for education, for medicine, for tobacco, sweets, saving, or the replacement of blankets, furniture or crockery (17: 6).

Working conditions

Almost as important as the income that people receive for their labour are the conditions under which they must work. These too vary widely and it is difficult to generalise. Nevertheless some attempt must be made for, like housing, the conditions under which people work determine the quality of much of their lives. Moreover, for those whose incomes are low, conditions of work are often abysmal and there is a tendency for these different aspects of poverty to reinforce each other. Even if it is impossible to generalise, nevertheless some useful insights can be gained from consideration of a few case studies which illustrate some of the many different environments.

We start inside one of the reserves, KwaZulu, near Empangeni, with a bustling peri-urban scene, reminiscent of *The Threepenny Opera*, as described by Ruth Buthelezi.

Every day of the week as early as 04h00, one can see men and women in buses, lorries (trucks or pick-up vans) and bicycles, in their work clothes, getting to work, be it at Richards Bay, Empangeni town or Esikhawini Township or the University campus – where they work as labourers, cleaners, builders, drivers, farm labourers in sugar cane fields, etc. Women are seen also in the busy roads, at bus stops, at gates of schools or on building contractor sites, trading [all through the week]. They deal in small fresh produce, cooked food and fruit and crafts, sometimes alcoholic drinks. They sometimes carry small children on their backs. They are at these roadside or gate markets and stalls every day of the week whatever the weather. Young children of school-going age or teenage girls are normally at school, but some herd cattle, and of course some are at home doing home chores, fulfilling the housewife role, where parents are away all day and there are small children left behind. These chores are: fetching firewood some 5 to 8 km away from their homes and carrying as much as possible on one's head; fetching water from the streams and carrying the tins on the head; it means doing laundry by hand at the river and hanging the clothes in the sun to dry; doing the ironing by hand, fixing a coal iron; scrubbing the house or tending the vegetable/mealie plots around the home; cooking large quantities for large families in an open fire in a small kitchen and so on. The home chores take up the entire day – which day is short because of poor lighting. . . . The people of this community, like other similar communities, do lead very 'full' lives. They are busy surviving in a relatively impoverished environment. But their efforts have not made it possible for their community to develop and to negotiate for proper services such as roads and adequate transport, adequate telecommunications, proper housing and water resources – nor have their efforts sustained them as full participants in the country's mainstream economy. (239: 9)

From this brief glimpse into one of the less remote, less economically depressed parts of the reserves, we move on to the platteland, first on a farm, then into one or two of the small dorps.

The farm is near Middelburg in the eastern Transvaal. The following account by one worker was recorded for the Carnegie Inquiry at the end of 1982, by Mandla Seleoane.

I am approximately 48 years of age and was born on this farm. I am chief S's brother [S is an 'Ndebele' petty chief who seems to have worked himself to a favourable position on the farm. He acts as a tribunal wherever there are disputes between families on this and neighbouring farms and imposes fines. Gossip has it that the fines are shared between him and the farmer.] . . . My main duty is to scout for workers on behalf of the farmer. Most of these are orphans. They stay and work on the farm for six months and are then discharged, whereupon I must obtain others. They live in a kind of compound, and no salary, cash or in kind, is paid to them. They have two meals per day, one boiled egg for breakfast and potatoes for lunch. If they complain about the food, he either beats them up or sends them to the chief for punishment.

Four families live on the farm permanently. I do not know if they receive any salary for the work they do but I have my doubts. You see, the farmer's house was built by me from start to end, and he did not pay me a penny. People do not stay long on this farm. Two families . . . left two years ago because of the treatment we get from the farmer. When people report late for work, when they complain or when animals get into the fields, he beats them up. Working day starts at 5 am and ends at 6 pm. On Saturdays and Sundays people milk only and therefore they work shorter hours. I do not know what would happen to old people who can no longer work. People don't stay so long here. We do not get help whatsoever from the farmer, not even in the case of death in the family. I tried to leave the farm once but he confiscated my reference book and keeps it in his house. (29: 43)

It is perhaps misleading to leave readers with only this one vivid impression of life as experienced by one labourer on one farm in the whole of South Africa, and we are mindful of the fact that he cannot be considered typical. Most farm workers are paid cash wages and many who are seasonal migrant workers on the sugar estates of Natal or the fruit farms of the western Cape, for example, have considerable mobility not only across the country but also between sectors. And some have excellent relations with their employers. But the man from the farm near Middelburg does exist and the conditions described are not unique. Life as a labourer on many farms in South Africa is extremely harsh. And workers are subject to the most stringent control.

Eight hundred miles or more south-west of Middelburg in the Transvaal is the town of Oudtshoorn on the dry edge of the Little Karoo. World-famous as the centre of the ostrich boom in the generation before the First World War, Oudtshoorn remains an agricultural centre, one of the larger platteland towns. It boasts a tobacco factory to cure and roll what has long been one of the leading products of the district.

The factory employing 150 labourers, 50 of whom commute to work daily from Dysselsdorp, some 30 km away, is the only remainder of an industry that in the 1920s and early 1930s dominated the local labour market, employing between 1 300 and 1 600 people. . . . Roll tobacco used chiefly for chewing and aimed mainly at black consumers, continues nevertheless to be produced in much the same unhealthy way as in the early years of this century. The dry tobacco leaves are steeped in water to which

is added a quantity of ash – this mixture of ash and water is called *loog* and the persons who steep the leaves therein are called the *loogers*. The process is wet and dirty. After being removed from the *loog*, the wet leaves are packed in large bins to dry, where they remain for some time. This is known as sweating. The leaves are then ready for twisting into roll tobacco – but because at this stage they are in a crumpled state, the leaves have first to be opened by leaf openers and sorters. The leaves are then twisted on wooden spindles into long ropes of varying thickness. The ropes are finally made into rolls by the rollmakers. The entire process of manufacturing roll tobacco evidently injures the hands ... when Piet Jager, a seventy-five-year-old rollmaker was asked about the health conditions in the factory, his response was to show me his badly blistered hands.
...

To the casual observer, however, the most unpleasant and pronounced effect of roll tobacco production is the extremely strong smell of nicotine fumes released by the tobacco. The production room is permeated by a suffocating, semi-sweet, thick and pungent smell of tobacco. One of the twisters, Mina Lewis, stated that so strong are the fumes that workers cough and spit as soon as they get out of the factory, and that this lasts throughout the night. These were precisely the symptoms noted by the Wage Board in 1926, where in addition to loss of appetite, workers complained of nausea, lack of sleep, raw and burning feelings in the chest, and smarting of eyes, nose and throat as a result of the fumes, adding that the feelings of suffocation were experienced by all new entrants to the work. (37: 27–9)

From farm work and the processing of agricultural produce let us go briefly down one of the huge gold mines, where over half-a-million men burrow down as far as two miles beneath the surface of the earth, digging out the mineral wealth that has been the foundation of South Africa's spectacular economic transformation over the past century.

It is easy to describe the process of mining gold without conveying adequately the immense difficulties which those involved have had to overcome. The sorts of problems encountered by managers and engineers are perhaps best summarised in the following passage from the Public Relations Department of the Chamber of Mines. 'Imagine a solid mass of rock tilted ... like a fat 1 200-page dictionary lying at an angle. The gold-bearing reef would be thinner than a single page, and the amount of gold contained therein would hardly cover a couple of commas in the entire book. It is the miner's job to bring out that single page – but his job is made harder because the "page" has been twisted and torn by nature's forces, and pieces of it may have been thrust between other leaves of the book.'

And the analogy says nothing about the dangers and difficulties added to the extraction of this single page by the existence, in some mines, of highly dangerous explosive methane gas; of the ever-present possibility of a stope face, two miles below the surface, bursting under pressure; or of unexpected flooding where, as in the case of West Driefontein mine in 1969, 85 million gallons of water can rush into a mine in a single day. For someone who has never been down a mine to get some idea of the working conditions with which those actually mining the gold have to cope, it is perhaps easiest to start thinking of a road labourer digging up a pavement with a jack-hammer drill. Now imagine him doing that work thousands of feet underground, in intense heat, where he cannot even begin to stand upright, and where the drill is not going with the aid of gravity into the ground beneath, but where it has to be held horizontal and driven into the wall in front. Add to this picture the noise of a road drill, magnified several times by the confined space; dust which, despite strenuous efforts to control it with water, invades the lungs; and the possibility that the roof of the mine might suddenly cave in under pressure, or that a spark from the drill or a careless cigarette might ignite a pocket of methane gas, and one has some idea of the work of a 'machine-boy'. Echoing Orwell's thoughts about coal miners in Britain, it is impossible to watch such men at work without feeling a pang of envy for their toughness. It is a 'dreadful job . . . an almost superhuman job by the standards of an ordinary person'. And yet, like Orwell's miners they look and work as though they are made of iron. As a mine-manager remarked in 1946 when describing how the 'machine-boy' usually lay on his back or side and provided pressure to the machine with his legs, 'In other lands few men would be able to carry on this arduous operation for many days.' (Wilson, 1972: 20)

The dangers are real. During 1985 over 500 men were killed (a fatality rate of one per thousand people employed) and 13 000 were disabled for at least 14 days by accidents in the gold mines (Saldru Handbook, 1986: 491).

Another dangerous and difficult place to work, no matter where in the world – France or India or wherever it is placed – is in a foundry. South African foundries are no exception but as with mining and much else the South African version seems to turn the screw a notch or two. The following description is drawn from a study of foundries on the Witwatersrand. There cannot be many other countries in the world where one would meet a foundry manager in the second half of the twentieth century who explained: 'We found that the hot metal bounces off people's sweat better so we don't supply them with aprons' (112: 19). Whether other foundry managers believe this arresting rationalisation is not clear but a scientific study of thirty foundries employing 7 000 workers found that half of them spent less than R30 per worker per year on protective clothing and that in over 80 per cent of the foundries, workers have to buy their own boots and overalls (112: 21). The danger of being burnt by flying molten metal, injured in the grinding shop or hit by cranes and falling objects is omnipresent. The noise in many foundries is unbearable and high dust levels are common. As one foundry engineer expressed it, 'To stay alive in this foundry you have to have eyes like a hawk, ears of a bat and the legs of a springbok' (112:3).

George Orwell: Down a mine

In a way it is even humiliating to watch . . . miners working. It raises in you a momentary doubt about your own status as an 'intellectual' and a superior person generally. For it is brought home to you, at least while you are watching, that it is only because miners sweat their guts out that superior persons remain superior. You and I and the Editor of *The Times Literary Supplement* and the poets and the Archbishop of Canterbury and Comrade X, author of *Marxism for Infants* – all of us really owe the comparative decency of our lives to poor drudges underground . . . with their throats full of . . . dust, driving their shovels forward with arms and belly muscles of steel. (Orwell, 1957)

Given these arduous conditions, it is not surprising that foundries find it difficult to persuade local workers to stay on the job. On the Witwatersrand, as in other parts of the world, foundries rely primarily on migrant labour. In the large foundries, nine out of every ten workers were found to be migrant. In the group of thirty foundries as a whole, three-quarters of the 7 000 workers were migrants who are faced with the fact that in many instances, whether it is in a foundry or down a mine, the really hard jobs are likely to fall on their shoulders.

This brief examination of work in four or five specific situations serves to remind us not only of the wide variation of circumstances under which people must earn their daily bread, but also of the fact that in a country without a long tradition of trade unions, for the majority of workers low wages tend to accompany the more arduous and dangerous tasks. Moreover, investigations in recent years, such as that into South African asbestos mines (Myers and Aron, 1987) or into the Kinross gold-mine disaster in 1986 when 177 men lost their lives from toxic fumes after an underground spark ignited a mass of poly-icocyanurate, whose use in mining had long been prohibited in Britain and the United States, emphasise the importance of pressure to improve bad working conditions, which constitute a significant aspect of poverty.

In this chapter we have examined as systematically as we can the major sources of income available to those who are poor. The most important of these, of course, consists of wages paid for work done. We have considered also the role of remittances (which are sent out of wages), of pensions, of self-employment in informal-sector activities, and of agricultural production for home consumption by those households with access to a little land. In all of these we have seen how many households simply do not have the income that would enable them to rise above a low level of poverty. But those who do get some income are better off than those with none. We turn now to consider those people who wish to work but who cannot find a job.

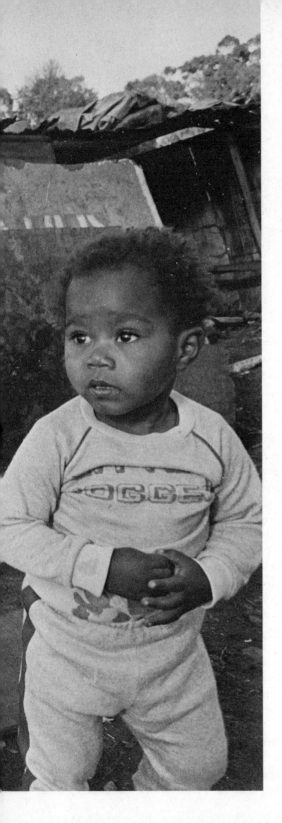

4
Unemployment

I have been staying here for four years now without work but I cannot think of anywhere else where I can go ... I cannot say anything about my future now because my heart is now 'dead' since I am not working. But when I was working, all that I was concerned with was wealth in the form of cattle. Livestock was going to help me in times of starvation and illness because I was going to sell some of my stock. Now, I never achieved that. I am just staying here hopelessly and doing nothing.

— Unemployed man interviewed
in Transkei (46: 17)

Now I am not working it is just like these hands of mine have been cut off and I am useless. Now life for my children will be difficult, they will scarcely eat. Now that I am not working – I do not know what I shall do or what I shall take and put against what.

— Unemployed man interviewed
in Maseru, Lesotho (124: 20)

Theoretical issues

Economists and others have had a lively time in South Africa, over the past ten years, arguing with each about the extent and nature of unemployment. These intellectuals may be divided into basically two camps: the structuralists and the market-clearers, with a few don't-know *ja-nee*s (yes-and-no's) hovering on the edges of the debate. For the structuralists, unemployment is a reality; it exists. The only question is how extensive or pervasive it is. For the market-clearers, the issue is obvious. In the long run the market must clear. Structural unemployment as a permanent feature of the economy is not a theoretical possibility. Therefore it does not exist. What others persist in calling unemployment is in fact a figment of their imagination.

It is perhaps best to start with the somewhat gentlemanly debate amongst the structuralists. Given that unemployment exists, how large a factor is it in South Africa? The pioneering work to measure the level of unemployment amongst all South Africans was done by Charles Simkins and published in June 1976. His finding was not only that the level of unemployment was extremely high – two million people, or 20 per cent of the economically active population of all races – but also that it had risen dramatically since the beginning of the 1960s when the level was just over half a million or approximately 9 per cent of the economically active population. The findings, which were highly controversial, sparked off an unprecedented amount of intellectual activity as academics and others weighed into Simkins's figures, attacked his methodology and tried to find better ways of obtaining reliable statistics.

Perhaps the most important consequence of the furore was the decision by the Central Statistical Service to do something about collecting data on unemployment, particularly amongst Africans. This resulted in the establishment of the Current Population Survey, or CPS, from which has issued a series of statistics, published regularly since October 1977. In the light of this information and of the criticism that had swirled around his earlier paper, Simkins, at the end of 1982, revised his estimates. He conceded that his earlier results needed modifying downward but the broad outline remained unchanged. Unemployment was high and was rising still higher. From a level of 12 per cent in 1970, it had risen to 21 per cent in 1981. These figures were considerably higher than those of the CPS but one important reason for this seems to lie in differences in the definition of unemployment used. The CPS defined unemployment narrowly to include only those who had worked not more than five hours in the last week, who had looked for work in the past month, and who were ready to start a job in the next week, and were between the ages of 15 and 64 if male, and 15 and 59 if female. Simkins, on the other hand, used a concept of 'full-time job equivalents', which included those who were underemployed. Thus if a man or a woman wanted to do a full day's work but could only get a part-time job for ten hours a week, then that person was only counted as one-quarter employed or three-quarters unemployed.

Much of the difficulty in obtaining precise measurements of unemployment in South Africa lies in the area of subsistence agriculture and the informal sector. One interesting paper at the Carnegie conference put the debate between the CPS and the 'twenty percenters' under the microscope by examining employment and unemployment in one small peri-urban area outside Pietermaritzburg in Natal. Bromberger concluded: 'It seems that there is a growing amount of paid or profit-seeking work being done by Africans and that much of this, in addition to casual and temporary work for those with access to labour markets in towns and peri-urban areas, is not reflected in the official employment statistics. However the initial and partial evidence suggests to me that the CPS is failing to register as unemployed many individuals who are doing unpaid work of relatively short duration and low value.' (271: 8) This implies that the level of unemployment is higher than the CPS measure but perhaps a little lower than the Simkins figure of 21 per cent for 1981. But there is general agreement, amongst the structuralists, that the level of unemployment has risen alarmingly over the past two decades and that it is now far too high.

The market-clearers, however, see things differently. For them the problem is not so much a matter of unemployment as one of poverty. People, it is argued, can always find jobs or make money for themselves in some way but sometimes they choose not to work. Where this happens they may be said to be 'voluntarily unemployed'; that is, in a position where they are not working because, under the circumstances, they have chosen not to do so. The market-clearers concede that there will always be a certain amount of frictional unemployment where people are busy finding new jobs in response to changing patterns of demand or the normal expansions and contractions that occur in any economy. But this frictional unemployment, it is argued, is of a temporary nature. What simply does not exist is the possibility of a large proportion of the population being permanently unable to find or create paid work of any sort.

There is certainly evidence that some people choose not to work because of the low level of opportunities available. 'Is it not better', asked an ex-farm worker now living in a relocation area, 'to sit here all day [unemployed] rather than work from sunrise to sunset for a rude farmer and get R1 per day?' (73: 13). And in Beaufort West, 'Many women, who were classed not economically active rather than unemployed because they were not looking for work, said they would work if wages were higher' (35: 22). These people can be said to be 'voluntarily' unemployed although the nature of the alternatives available does not make this a very appropriate word. What is more important to note is the fact that those who do thus 'choose' not to work do not get counted in the statistics as 'unemployed', as their decision means that they are classed rather as 'not economically active.' Moreover, the fact that some people do indeed choose 'to sit in the sun all day' does not for a moment imply that there are not people who wish to work but who cannot find any kind of job.

Reality

One of the most isolated corners of South Africa is a small village north-west of Bendell (which is itself a remote resettlement area) 100 kilometres north of Kuruman into the desert of the northern Cape. This village, technically within the independent 'black national state' of Bophuthatswana, contains a few houses, a school and little else. Some goats graze on scattered tussocks in the dry sand. This is another resettlement area for people who have had to move off land now designated white. In this village in September 1983, one of us (F. W.) met a young man who until 18 months previously had worked on the iron mines at Sishen some 170 kilometres to the south. After losing his job through retrenchment, he could no longer stay on the mine and so he had to leave Sishen and return to his home-village where there was simply no work of any sort. There was no water to grow any crops; there was grazing for very few stock. There were too many people and too little money to provide a market for virtually any informal sector activity. The only hope of a job was to go and look for one in Kuruman or in Sishen but that cost money. First there was a 13 km walk to the nearest bus stop, and from there, a one-way ticket to Kuruman cost R4.50 which he did not possess. Besides, he knew that when he got to Kuruman or even to Sishen, there would be no work available.

We have spent a little time on this story for it serves to illustrate two important truths. First, that involuntary unemployment is a reality. For the man from the village beyond Bendell, unemployment was not a state he had chosen, nor was there any sense in which it could be described as a form of frictional, and therefore temporary, unemployment. And if he existed, then there was no logical reason why there might not be a thousand or a million other people like him: adults wanting work, but unable to find it. (For another specific example see 52: 22–3.) The second truth is that searching for work can be costly, and for some who are unemployed they may simply be too poor to find work. The man from beyond Bendell had no place to stay in Sishen after he had lost his job nor could he have afforded the rent if he had found somewhere. Moreover, once he got back to his resettlement camp he could not afford to leave again in order to go and look for work. As Bell and Padayachee concluded in their analysis of the trends, causes and cures for unemployment in South Africa: 'After more than a decade of secularly rising unemployment, it is beside the point to argue that involuntary unemployment is theoretically inconceivable in the long run' (119: 15).

Let us turn now from the overall picture of unemployment in the country as a whole, to examine its extent in different places. As we do so, one should bear in mind that the definitions of unemployment are not always exactly the same, so whilst the statistics are useful in providing orders of magnitude and, where available, changes over time, they cannot be used for purposes of precise comparison.

In Nkandla, a rural part of KwaZulu some 50 km west of Eshowe:

Unemployment is clearly a significant problem in the area and a lack of employment opportunities was mentioned by 10% of the respondents as the most serious problem they faced. They appeared to accept the fact that employment was not available locally and merely complained at the absence of offers of employment elsewhere. Unemployment statistics are exceedingly difficult to establish. Unemployment for women is virtually a permanent condition – there are almost no employment opportunities for them. However, very few women describe themselves as unemployed as they have never considered paid employment an achievable goal. Similarly, many of the men and women who said they were involved in agriculture or domestic duties were most probably only so involved because they were unemployed. Many others involved in such activities are underemployed. Those persons aged 15 or 16 who were classified as 'not at school' must also be counted among the unemployed. There was no suggestion in their case, as there was in many others, that they were not at school because they were involved in domestic or agricultural duties or herding cattle. (53a: 64)

At a minimum, we can therefore assess that, if we include only those who considered themselves unemployed plus those classified 'not at school', the proportion of people, aged 15–60, who were unemployed was 8 per cent in the case of women and 24 per cent in the case of men. But these statistics, as we have seen, underestimate the true position because, particularly in the case of women, they do not include all those who are below what one might call the unemployment threshold. For them the chances of work are so remote that they do not even consider it a possibility.

In the Ciskei, given the employment figures for the region in 1978, the Quail Commission concluded on the basis of some fairly conservative assumptions that 'massive urban unemployment in the range of 25 to 35 per cent is a central feature of the economy of the Ciskei' (Report of the Ciskei (Quail) Commission, 1980: 68).

A micro-study of employment and poverty in Lower Roza in the Qumbu district of the Transkei threw some interesting light onto who were most likely to be unemployed, and onto the nature of unemployment.

It appears that men and women suffer unemployment for slightly different reasons. Men tend to be unemployed either because they fall beneath minimum secondary school requirements of the labour market (especially the case for novices), or because they are too young – men in their mid-twenties are preferred by the mines and manufacturing firms. Women face a situation in which they are either channelled into very poor jobs, which even then are limited in number (e.g. domestic labour), or are competing hotly for good jobs inside the Transkei, in which case those with Standard 10 and post-matric qualifications are given preference. The unemployed had done relatively little casual work in the past year. Most had done a little agricultural work (62%), but only 18% were currently involved in the informal sector (all women), and were earning an average of R10 per month. Informal sector work involves a certain investment in time and effort which the unemployed (especially men) seemed unprepared to make; they either did nothing or actively looked for formal sector work. They appear to see themselves as firmly aligned towards the capitalist labour market in South Africa and – to a lesser extent – Transkei. [The] figures do not expose the full magnitude of the unemployment problem in Lower Roza. Many more respondents felt that they would work if offered a R50 per month job in Qumbu; some had made rather half-hearted efforts to find work in 1983. Another 63 women said they would like such work but would be unable to accept it as their husbands would not permit it. (47: 29)

It is also worth reporting that at the time of the survey (late 1983) most of those who were classified as unemployed were fairly sanguine about job prospects. Their average age (27) was somewhat younger than that of the average worker, who was 35 years old (47: 29).

But, as one respondent elsewhere in the Transkei remarked:

Our children are staying at home because they are not working. Contracts for labour have been stopped and that is bad. Our children are not working and they have been staying at home for years. When they go to town, they are told that there are no requisitions for labour. (45: 13)

Impact of retrenchment and removals

The impact of recession can be discerned in the remotest corners of the land. In Nkandla, for example, in August 1983, 'the Labour Officer, the magistrate, two storekeepers and two teachers all agreed that the level of unemployment was higher than usual' despite the fact that the registration of workseekers at the Labour Office was half that of the previous August. In one storekeeper's view, 'the people from the area surveyed would always be amongst the first laid off in a recession because they were all unskilled' (53a: 65). And in another, even poorer, part of KwaZulu the recession was biting deeply. 'Unemployment is filling Msinga's valleys with men. Families that lived by selling their labour are now trying to live by selling bones.' (55: 10)

Across the country in another reserve, on the dry fringes of Bophutha-tswana, the severe consequences of retrenchment were exacerbated by the forced removals to which the people were subjected.

Prior to the move from Ga-Tlhose to Bendell the people were involved in subsistence farming and cattle grazing. The economically active men lived within walking distance of the mines at Sishen and found regular employment there. After the move they were much further from the mines and those who did have work found it impossible to return to their families more often than once a year.

Moreover, frustration caused by unemployment seemed to account for an increase in shebeens and excessive drinking amongst able-bodied men. And the women of the village were depressed and bored (77: 22, 27).

In resettlement camps all round the country unemployment emerged as a major problem, notably amongst women. The Surplus People Project found that the average unemployment rate in twelve relocation areas was 17 per cent for men and 36 per cent for women. In Glenmore the figures were 27 per cent and 56 per cent. As one resident reported in 1981: 'We were promised jobs here. I haven't been able to find work here for two years. They lied to us.' (73: 12) In Glenmore at the time, it was found that the labour participation rate (that is, the number of adults employed in the area expressed as a percentage of the total population) was only 7 per cent. Even if the migrants working away from home were included there were only 16 people of Glenmore with jobs for every 100 in the population. Elsewhere in the Ciskei the labour participation rates were: Amatola Basin 11 per cent (28 if migrants were included); Dimbaza 19 (26) and in Mdantsane 29. Such figures, of course, reflect not only high levels of unemployment but also a high proportion of dependants – that is, children and old people in the population (277: 7).

Returning for a moment to the impact of recession in remote corners of the country, we find there was another lethal combination that affected some areas:

White Namaqualanders have not emerged unscathed from recent events. In addition to those who have experienced retrenchment on the mines, many farmers have been hard hit by the recent drought years. Numbers of stock farmers, particularly those in the drought-stricken Bushmanland, have had to abandon their land (leaving their farmworkers to face utter destitution) and try for alternative avenues of employment. (71: 17)

Widespread unemployment in the copper districts, including the fact that many school-leavers could not find local employment, combined with the impact of the drought, produced devastating consequences for those living in the north-western Cape.

In the north-western Transvaal, too, a combination of factors including a steep rise in the price of fuel and drought was reinforcing the pressures pushing white farmers off land in a region where 'economic disintegration became apparent'. Most farms, it seems, had large numbers of unemployed black women and children and old men on them (287: 7 and 12).

Another dry, remote area where jobs were scarce and the climate harsh was Willowmore on the south-eastern corner of the Karoo. A detailed study of the two townships, one coloured, the other primarily for Africans, showed unemployment to be widespread.

In recent times, many men have been made redundant from the mines, particularly early in 1983. There were promises made of employment later in the year but these have not materialised. The people of Gatlhose who were South Africans are now considered 'foreigners' and are only selected for employment when all the local people have been employed.

At present in Bendell there is a 50% unemployment rate amongst the able-bodied male population. This has had serious repercussions on the people of the village. Work is very difficult to find and transport to centres like Kuruman and Sishen where there are recruiting offices, is expensive and infrequent.

Men who were paid off attended meetings at Sishen whilst we were at Bendell. There was general dissatisfaction about redundancy payments and pensions. They received no satisfaction and rioting was reported. There were reports of police brutality and injuries to men. . . . Many seemed to be discharged without the relevant papers which would make it possible for them to find work again. This was an area of great frustration and dissatisfaction. Because there are no organised saving or banking facilities available for the people of Bendell there was a tendency to spend lump sum payments which were received when they left the mines rather than save for the future.

Unemployment is therefore one of the most serious problems affecting the people of Bendell at the present moment. (77: 17)

Table 4.01: Unemployment and age in the Karoo

	Age range (years)					Total
	16–20 %	21–30 %	31–40 %	41–50 %	51–60 %	16–65 %
Willowmore: (Coloured)	44	21	19	11	4	23
(Down: African)	31	12	8	17	12	16
Steytlerville: (Coloured)	39	33	21	16	28	30
(Kabah: African)	43	32	34	19	18	32

Source: 38: 43, 119, 132, 135

The high level of persons classed as not economically active in their late-teens suggests that the level of unemployment shown in these statistics is in fact an understatement of the true position. But whatever the precise figure, the general picture is quite clear. Unemployment is extremely high, particularly amongst younger people under 30. There is an interesting contrast between the two African townships, Down in Willowmore, and Kabah in Steytlerville. Down is poor and the housing is atrocious but a higher proportion of the people have jobs than in the coloured township. In Steytlerville the reverse is true. The figures illustrate the way in which the small platteland dorps can act as unemployment traps. People who live there may find themselves simply too poor to move anywhere else, and so if there are no jobs in the local economy, they are stuck.

Another such small town, but not quite as poor as Willowmore or Steytlerville, is Clarens in the Orange Free State. In the African township,

There are a considerable number unemployed. The problem begins with school-leavers who are normally unable to find work. The men can find a certain amount of work in Clarens and a small number work on the mines. There are opportunities for employment in the factories at Sasolburg and Vanderbijlpark but it is difficult for people from the Clarens area to find money for the bus and train fare to seek employment in the Vaal triangle. There is a recruiting office for the mines in Harrismith but the quota is limited. The women can find some work in Clarens as domestic workers. The lack of opportunity for work other than domestic, gives rise to frustration and a reliance on alcohol. The result is that many of those unemployed become unemployable. (41: 14)

Unemployment in the cities

If we turn now to some of the bigger centres, the picture does not always improve. In the eastern Cape, for example, a study of Grahamstown and Port Elizabeth found that in both centres the level of unemployment was approaching 40 per cent (120: 5). This was in a survey of over 500 adults in 187 households conducted in 1984. Since then the picture has worsened. A subsequent study by Vista University found in mid-1985 that the average level of unemployment in Port Elizabeth was no less than 56 per cent, though by 1987 it was down to 46 per cent (*Monitor*, June 1988: 10). And in Grahamstown, in mid-1988, Professor Davies of the Institute for Social and Economic Research, Rhodes University, responding to the death of Ms Jessie Tamboer (p. 157), said that whilst very few studies had been done, 'Our figures indicate that the unemployment rate among the workforce must be between 60 and 70 per cent' (*Weekend Argus*, 4.6.1988). The combination of recession, rationalisation of the motor industry and political upheaval has caused great economic difficulty in the region.

In Cape Town and Durban detailed studies of African and coloured residential areas, both township and squatter, revealed considerable variation. Three definitions of unemployment were used:

(a) those actively seeking work;

(b) including also those individuals 'who may have worked previously, do intend to work again, and who consider themselves unemployed although they are not currently seeking employment'; and

(c) as for (b), but including a further group of individuals who 'did not think of themselves as unemployed members of the labour pool, but who did mention during the course of their interviews that they would like to work. They had not sought work and were constrained by such problems as pass laws, the need to remain at home to protect possessions or to care for ill or dependent family members, or simply because of prolonged failure to find a job' (16: 47). The results of the studies are shown in the table.

Fig. 4.01: Urban unemployment by area, 1982: three definitions

Table 4.02: Unemployment in Cape Town and Durban, 1982

	Rate (a)	Rate (b)	Rate (c)
Cape Town:			
Crossroads	4	5	8
Gugulethu	6	8	9
Modderdam	7	8	10
Uitsig	8	14	15
Bonteheuwel	4	6	7
Total	6	8	9
Durban squatter:			
Clermont	13	21	26
Folweni	17	29	32
Inanda	12	18	21
Malukazi	17	17	17
Total	14	22	25
Durban township:			
Chesterville	35	52	52
KwaMashu	14	23	23
Lamontville	20	33	33
Umlazi	14	25	30
Total	16	26	29
Grand Total	9	15	17

Source: 16: 51–3

The difference between Cape Town and Durban is striking. Using the most stringent of the three definitions, we find that in Cape Town the level of black unemployment was only 6 per cent whereas in Durban it averaged 15 per cent. Perhaps even more interesting were the variations between different parts of the same town. Using the second definition, which includes all those who consider themselves unemployed even though they are currently not actually looking for a job, we find that within Cape Town, unemployment varies from 5 per cent in Crossroads to 14 per cent in Uitsig, whilst in Durban the level and the range are both much greater, varying from 17 per cent in the squatter settlement of Malukazi to 52 per cent in the township of Chesterville. Given the smallness of the samples and the different sizes of the various settlements, one must not place too much weight on levels obtained in specific settlements, but the overall picture is clear. The level of unemployment depends significantly on the definitions used, and the level is considerably higher in Durban than in Cape Town. And there are considerable variations between different parts of the same town. Overall, unemployment (measured in terms of those who considered themselves unemployed) was 8 per cent in the five African and coloured areas of Cape Town and averaged 24 per cent in the eight African areas of Durban (16: 47ff). One reason for this difference may well be that at the time of the survey (1982–3), pass laws controlling the movement of Africans were still in existence and were being far more stringently applied against people trying to move from rural areas to Cape Town than against those moving to Durban.

On the Witwatersrand, 'the few surveys that have been carried out indicate a high African unemployment rate'. One study, in 1977, estimated that Johannesburg had an African unemployment rate of 19.5 per cent (18: 23). 'Of those unemployed or actively seeking work [definition (a)] 51% had been out of work for more than six months. Most of the unemployed had a lower standard of education and about one-third of them fell into the 15–24 age group.' There were other studies which showed African unemployment rates of 24 per cent in Pretoria and 29 per cent in the PWV region.

A pilot survey for the Agency for Industrial Mission on 150 unemployed Sowetans in November 1977 found that more than 30 per cent had lost their jobs in the first half of the year. 10 per cent of the families had no income sources and about 25% had no wage-earners in the household. . . . In a survey of two areas, one urban (Atteridgeville and Mamelodi) and one rural (Saulspoort), Loots (1978) found evidence suggesting a doubling of unemployment between 1970 and 1977. Two-thirds of the unemployment in the urban sample were in the 15–24 age group and was higher amongst women than among men. It was estimated that 15.7 per cent of the men and 34 per cent of the women were unemployed. The relation between education and unemployment indicated that men with a matric certificate and women with a Junior Certificate were somewhat more prone to be unemployed than those with lesser educational qualifications, although in terms of numbers the latter made up the bulk of the unemployed. New entrants to the labour market comprised a quarter of the male unemployed and half of the females. Of the unemployed, 60 per cent were women. (18: 24)

Since those studies were made, it is likely that the situation has worsened. The number of workseekers coming onto the labour market continues to grow each year and the long recession continues to bite. In 1982, for example, it is estimated that there were 10 000 retrenchments in Johannesburg alone.

We have spent time on the statistics of unemployment in order not only to drive home how widespread it is through the length and breadth of the country, but also to find out a little more about who are especially vulnerable to the ravages of unemployment: women; young people leaving school; men with families to support who suddenly find themselves out on the streets as a result of the recession; and those for whom the horror of being laid off work is compounded by resettlement or by drought.

Behind the statistics

But there is a need to go deeper; to get behind the statistics in order to experience through the eyes of those who are unemployed something of what it all means. Our first informant is a woman living in a rural part of the Transkei:

My husband died in 1966. I am now experiencing difficulties in supporting my two children. I haven't got a field although I have a kraal-site. I only depend on my mother's pension which she gets from the government. We share the money because she has her own house and I am staying in my own house. I am not working. If I could get work, the first thing that I would try would be to look for a field, even before building a decent house. Livestock would then follow later. All that would only be achieved when I was working. Now I am in complete darkness. I do not know what can help me. (46: 16)

Even more stark, however, than the position of those who find themselves unemployed in the South African reserves is the lot of those in the surrounding countries, such as Lesotho and Mozambique, 'whose lives and expectations have been determined by labour migrancy' (124: 9), but who are now faced with destitution. For they have been excluded from an economy whose wealth they helped to generate but which now has less and less need of their labour. Until the time of independence (1975), the people of Mozambique had for generations supplied large numbers of migrants to work on the gold mines of the Transvaal and the Orange Free State: 100 000 men a year after the Second World War; 80 000 men annually in the years before that. In the year after independence, when the South African mines were worried about a shortage of labour because of difficulties with Malawi, the number of Mozambicans recruited rose to 118 000. But the following year the mining industry unilaterally cut the number drastically and for the next nine years the number of Mozambicans working in the mines remained at less than 50 000 men. In 1985, in the wake of the Nkomati Accord, the number of Mozambican recruits was increased by 10 000 to 58 000 men, but even then this was 40 per cent lower than the level it had been in the previous generation.

It was unfortunately not possible, at the time of the Carnegie Inquiry, to make any field study of the impact of such a harsh decision on the lives of those who found themselves unemployed in Mozambique as a result. But a study of Lesotho where the doors have started to close, though without the brutal suddenness as in the case of Mozambique, provides a grim picture of what it all means. The following quotations are taken from interviews conducted in Maseru in September 1983 with twenty men who were actively, persistently trying to find work. Their perception of unemployment could be broken down into three distinct categories. Firstly, 'the personal frustration and the sense of having failed others through the inability to obtain contracts' (124: 20).

My children are not living. . . . In order for us to live we should eat. But now I am not working, it is just like these hands of mine have been cut off and I am useless. Now life for my children will be difficult, they will scarcely eat. Now that I am not working, I do not know what I shall do or what I shall take and put against what. . . . They live in a difficult manner, ntate . . . except that I have my brother and he is the one who when I am not working throws something at them so that they can get the means to get food. He is at a mine now. (124: 20)

Secondly, there were those who still have some hope. Maybe they would find a permanent job in Maseru or even, though they hardly dared mention it, a contract to the mines. But others had drifted to despair,

like the man who after twenty years on the mines had been in Maseru for three years 'living a life of suffering'. He was now sleeping in the open and although he had worked through the winter, he had not been paid and was attempting to bring the dispute with his ex-employer to the authorities. He had been unable to make contact with his family. He had come to accept that he could never go back to the mines as he was no longer heavy enough to pass the medical examination. 'When I get there and climb on the scale which people climb onto, I am now old, and I am no longer on that number that could enable me to go and work.' He was now beginning to beg and felt 'like a dead person. Like a person who is not there because you do not know what or whether people at home are still alive.' (124: 22–3)

Finally, there are those 'for whom the links between the work-place and the home have been finally ruptured, those who are beyond being interviewed'.

Those people there are confronted with a huge problem. It is really bad because there are those who have drifted away from being normal people. Even their skin when you look at it, you will find that because of sleeping outside and not eating properly or washing the body they now look frightening. In fact a lot of people are scared of them. . . . Some of them I know, but when I look at them I see that because of the problems of hunger and living in that manner and so on, they have thought too hard and their minds are now not working properly . . . they have just lost hope, they no longer think of anything to do with work or their children. (124: 23–4)

But even for those who are not constrained by political boundaries or by pass laws and who are free to move, the burden of unemployment is heavy. Japie Morrie, his wife, both 24, and their two children of 4 years and 4 months, were sitting on the side of the road between Beaufort West and Graaff-Reinet with a donkey cart, two donkeys and a dog, in September 1983.

I've come from the farm Kammaskraal. We were *losmense*, casual workers, there doing piece-work, I could say. But the work is now finished and I must find another place where I can get work. We've been on the road since yesterday. We're going from farm to farm. I'd make it about a week, about 14 days before we find a place. We are now four men on trek. Yes, four men sitting without work right now. I left the other three back there on the first farm from here. . . . I was born on a farm in the district. We've always been in the district going round the farms. My father also trekked like this. I'm used to it. But if there is a better way out, better work or something, that *meneer* [mister] has, *meneer* must say. People have to struggle here. Even if work is good or bad, if we can just get a place where we can squat, if we can just survive, that's how things work here in the Karoo. It's hard to escape from this life of trek. There's nothing to go to in the town. The problem is the house which you have to get there. And there are also no jobs now. That's the problem. So we have to go from farm to farm to look for work. Maybe you're lucky but it is just for a while. Then we have to go looking again. That's how they treat us in the Karoo. The longest that I've been on a farm is four years eight months. In March I had to leave that farm. We had to because the veld was so dry. We were then nine men on the farm. Then the farmer says there are too many of us and he has to pay out too much money. He only wants four men. Five must leave. He gives you nothing except the money you earned. Not even food for the road. Then you must be off his property as fast as possible. Work is hard to find, very hard. (35: 43)

In the small towns of the platteland, unemployment, as we have seen, is severe. One woman, living in Oudtshoorn, explained what it was like. She was a 50-year-old grandmother who told a Carnegie Inquiry researcher the story of how her husband, having worked for thirty years in a local laundry, was unemployed since the laundry had closed down the previous year. Since then neither he nor she has been able to find any regular employment. He receives unemployment insurance of about R65 per month, but as the sole income-earner in a household of 18 (there is a shortage of some 2 000 houses in the township) this is not enough to support the home.

Daai tyd het dit goed gegaan – nou gaan dit bitter. Daai tyd het ek nooit met my kinders sonder kos gaan slaap nie, maar hier's nou al baie aande wat ek moet kinders op koffie en brood gaan lê, of party maal is daar net 'n bietjie koffie. (37: 30) [Things went well then – but now it is bitter. At that time I never went with my children to bed without food, but now many is the evening when they must go to sleep on coffee and bread; sometimes even with only a little coffee.]

In the big cities, the plight of the unemployed is no easier. Sometimes, in truth, it is even more difficult. In Durban an analysis of interviews with over 200 unemployed people found that many of them 'are men distraught with anxiety at being quite unable to meet any of the expectations which their family places on them as breadwinners'. (125: 15) And in Soweto, interviews in the same year, 1983, with 45 women revealed similar levels of despair and frustration.

I've been without a job since from October last year until the present day. Yes, I want a job. If it could be anywhere. Even if it could be far from home – as long as I can get something like money to help my husband with all the needies. I always go looking for a job and only go for places where there are advertisements concerning jobs. It is hard because whenever you get to a place where jobs are advertised you would find by the time you come in someone else has already taken it. At other places they want to see an unemployment card. I don't have it. All employers are looking for experienced people with unemployment cards. (82: 24)

Another woman who was only 42 at the time, reported: 'I once went to Baragwanath [the big hospital on the edge of Soweto] looking for a job as a cleaner, and was told by the superintendent that I was too old. Since then I have not looked for work.' (82: 25)

'Unemployment', reported another woman, 'has brought me loneliness and frustration, because what happens is that the whole day when my family members are away at work, I stay alone and there isn't enough money. So sometimes I stay without money for the whole month until my daughter comes in to give me something.' (82: 26) As one woman put it succinctly: 'Unemployment brings three difficulties: sickness, starvation, and staying without clothes' (82: 26). But it is from Cape Town, the city where statistically the level of unemployment has been lowest, that the most harrowing evidence comes of what it actually means to be unemployed. 'You feel really sick when you haven't got a job. It's there in the bottom of your stomach. You think that something's eating you. They have to change sometime. The days are so long. I don't know what to do with myself anymore.' (126: 24) 'I used to be a good fitter . . . people think you're worthless. Any real man can support his family. . . .' (126: 25)

Unemployment is a fearful scourge in any society. In South Africa it is a

Unemployed in Cape Town

My husband lost his job about five months ago. It was a big shock but we thought we could cope. I was earning a reasonably good wage. We had to cut a few corners though. We had to eat less meat. We had to save on all kinds of things. I had to now catch the train to work, 'cause it was cheaper than the bus even though it took a lot longer. I also took in other people's washing. There are a few people here who pay you a little bit to wash their clothes. I used to wash clothes every Sunday. Then two months ago I lost my job. We were desperate. There was no money coming in now. We had to spend everything we had in the time my husband was without a job. Now they've cut off the electricity and we're two months in arrears with rent. They're going to evict us I'm sure, we just can't pay though. My husband decided to go to Jo'burg. He went a month ago. He said he would get a job there. He sent some money the first week. But I haven't had any more money since. I don't know where he is. I haven't been able to get hold of him. I would like to go to Jo'burg to look for him but what can I do with the children? Before he left we used to take turns to look for work because the children can't go to crèche because there's no money. Sometimes they lie awake at night crying. I know they are crying because they are hungry. I feel like feeding them Rattex. When your children cry hunger-crying, your heart wants to break. It will be better if they were dead. When I think things like that I feel worse. It's terrible when a mother wants to kill her own children. But what can I do, I'm not a mother worth having.

I worry about my husband. I think he might have run away with someone else. Maybe he's got a job and just doesn't want to come home. But why isn't he sending any money? I'm sick. I'm sick because of the cold. I can't take my children to the doctor when they're sick because there's no money. My mother and father said that they would try and help. But they've got very little money and my brother and sister to support. It's a hard time for all of us. We're just not cared to find jobs. What can one do? You must start looking. You can also pray to God that he will keep you from killing your children. (126: 16)

spectre that is huge and growing. And there is no doubt that the political economy of apartheid has exacerbated both its magnitude and its consequences. As one African migrant worker expressed it:

When you are out of job, you realise that the boss and the government have the power to condemn you to death. If they send you back home (and back home now there's a drought) and you realise you can't get any new job, it's a death sentence. The countryside is pushing you into the cities to survive, the cities are pushing you into the countryside to die. (281: 50)

5
Hunger and sickness

We just sleep in the wilderness. You sleep without having eaten and you get up without having eaten. Tomorrow you go and look for a job, you don't get it, you come back. When you come back you go about uncovering rubbish bins thinking: 'Could it not be there is something that has been thrown in here, *banna*, just a little something that I can chew?'

— Unemployed worker in Lesotho
(124: 20)

The synergism between enteritis and malnutrition has been well documented in South Africa and is the reason why gastroenteritis is one of the biggest killers of black children.

— Caroline Ntoane, 1987

South Africa is one of the few countries in the world which normally exports food in considerable quantities. Yet it is also a country in which there is widespread hunger and malnutrition; and where diseases associated with poor nutrition take a heavy toll in deaths, particularly amongst children. However, for nearly twenty years malnutrition, even in its most acute form, has not been a notifiable disease in South Africa, so there are no precise national figures to provide a clear picture of the pattern of malnutrition through space and time. However, there is a good deal of material available about the situation in specific areas on certain dates, and for some places over a period of years, and from this it is possible to piece together a reasonably comprehensive picture, although some glaring gaps, requiring further research, still remain.

There is no single measurement of PEM [protein–energy–malnutrition] which is universally accepted. Therefore some degree of controversy prevails on methods of estimating prevalence or incidence of malnutrition. Most workers would agree that kwashiorkor, marasmus, and marasmic–kwashiorkor represent the extreme end of the spectrum and form the visible tip of the iceberg of malnutrition in the community. (165: 59)

But it is a very jagged tip. There are few more harrowing experiences than walking into the kwashiorkor ward of one of the state-run, formerly mission-led, hospitals in the rural areas of South Africa and finding 60 emaciated children in a forty-bed ward, many of them on the drip, starving. And all this within little more than a hundred miles of the richest city in Africa. In 1968 when it was last a notifiable disease in South Africa, there were nearly 11 000 cases of kwashiorkor reported. Of these 9 800 were African; 1 000 were coloured; 12 were Asian; and 7 were white. At this time Africans formed 70 per cent of the total population and accounted for 89 per cent of all notified cases, whilst whites who formed 17 per cent of the population made up less than 0.1 per cent of those with kwashiorkor, an insignificant number.

How big then is the iceberg? The extent of malnutrition is generally assessed by what is called 'anthropometric' data, which can take several forms: weight-for-age; height-for-age; and weight-for-height. Without getting bogged down in the detail of the respective merits of these different indicators we note simply that they all serve to measure the extent to which individuals have grown, or failed to grow, when compared with some international norm. The norm most frequently used in the past was one established by a group of medical scientists in Boston, but this has now been superseded by a very similar one determined at the National Center for Health Statistics (NCHS) in Washington. There has been some dispute in South Africa as to whether or not such norms are truly valid in all societies. But the argument that 'the Japanese' or 'Bushmen' or 'blacks' are naturally smaller has worn increasingly thin as more evidence has been collected. And it is now generally accepted that the NCHS norms are valid in South Africa as well.

It has been estimated, conservatively, that in 1975 somewhere between 15 000 and 27 000 children under 5 years died from malnutrition in South Africa, including the reserves (Fehrsen cited in 223: 2). By the beginning of the 1980s it was estimated that, not counting children in the reserves, some 136 000 children under 15 were less than 65 per cent of expected weight for age and thus in grave danger of infection and death (Kotze cited in 223: 2). Allowing for the fact that more than half of all African children live in the reserves where nutritional status is worse than elsewhere in the country, Moll concludes, 'it is clear that several hundred thousand children are seriously at risk' (223: 4).

In a careful study of the literature in South Africa, John Hansen, one of the country's leading paediatricians, found:

From all these sources it can be said that approximately a third of black [African], coloured and Asian children below the age of 14 years are underweight and stunted for their age. In some areas, e.g. parts of the Ciskei and Chatsworth in Durban, the situation is worse (rising to 60–70% or more). In other areas, particularly in Cape Town and Soweto, the figures for underweight, mortality rate and hospital admissions have shown great improvement in recent years. (205: 7)

An iceberg which freezes no less than one-third (and in some areas two-thirds) of all black children in the grip of malnutrition in a society where blacks constitute over 80 per cent of the population is vast by any standards.

In summarising the findings not only of Hansen's review of the earlier literature but also of the numerous studies done for the Carnegie Inquiry itself, Fincham concludes that location is a vital factor in the level of nutrition one can expect to enjoy. Homeland areas appear to be the worst environments in which to raise children. Community surveys of ambulant pre-school children in the Elim Hospital area of Gazankulu and the Driefontein Tribal Trust area near Piet Retief showed one-third to be underweight. Buch, Nyathi and Ntlemo emphasise the high incidence of malnutrition in the Mhala area of Gazankulu. They reveal that even within the area variations in the level of malnutrition occur. Villages in the central district had on average a 9 per cent rate of malnutrition compared with 27 in the southern district and 33 in the eastern district. However, once a community has more than 15 per cent of its children at risk from malnutrition (that is, below the third percentile of weight-for-age on the Harvard norm) that community has a serious nutritional problem; all the above areas mentioned have levels of malnutrition or undernourishment well above 15 per cent. Similar high figures of undernutrition were reported from Esikhawini township and Mpukunyoni in KwaZulu and from the Ciskei.

The resettlement camps within the homelands appear to be particularly hazardous areas in which to raise children. Severe malnutrition in the form of kwashiorkor and marasmus is clearly a major problem in these poverty pockets. In Tsweletswele, a closer settlement in the Ciskei, for example, as many as 10% of the pre-school children surveyed had clinically definable signs of kwashiorkor, well above the 3% national average. (PCS 1: 4)

This conclusion was reinforced by a study undertaken for Operation Hunger in mid-1987 of some 400 children in 28 villages in the northern Transvaal, northern Cape, and eastern Cape (mainly Ciskei). Although the villages were not randomly selected and cannot be taken as representative of the rural areas as a whole, and although the methodology used means that infant mortality rates may not be comparable with other studies, nevertheless the results tell us much about the seriousness of the problem of hunger in the reserves. Stunting, which provides evidence of chronic or long-term malnutrition, was found to characterise an average of 49 per cent of the children in the fifteen Transvaal villages, 58 per cent in eleven eastern Cape villages, and no less than 80 per cent in the two villages studied in the northern Cape. In 5 villages more than one in ten of the children were reported to be wasted, and thus victims of acute malnutrition (D' Souza, Mashanini, Pongoma, and Mashanini, 1987).

But the problem is not only in the homelands. In the Stellenbosch district of the western Cape, an area noted for its wealthy farms, a survey of nearly 2 000 Sub. A children in 21 coloured schools found that no less that 21 per cent of them suffered from what is clinically defined as both stunting and malnutrition. This reflects 'acute and chronic malnutrition in the area' (184: 9).

Moreover, the nutritional status of young children seems to have got worse, not better, in the recession of recent years as may be seen from the following table drawn from studies in the rural western Transvaal and Bophuthatswana and in urban Johannesburg.

In Namibia, a study for Oxfam of some 700 pre-school children south of the war zone in 1986, reported evidence of widespread malnutrition. One quarter (26 per cent) of the children surveyed were found to be underweight, one in ten (11 per cent) were acutely malnourished and thus wasted, and one in seven (15 per cent) were stunted and so gave evidence of chronic or long-term malnutrition.

In general, the children had very monotonous diets with only 19% of children eating four or more different foods in one day. Most children did not eat any fruit or vegetables at all at the time of the survey. Some (1%) children were given nothing to eat on the day surveyed and others (21%) were given only maize. However, the high proportion of four- and five-year-olds (about 90%) observed to have dental caries suggests that many children frequently eat sweet sugary snacks and drinks. (Hughson, 1986: 17)

Table 5.01: Nutritional status of children (1–5 years), South Africa (*expressed as percentages*)

	1981/3			1985		
	Stunting*	Under-weight†	Wasting‡	Stunting*	Under-weight†	Wasting‡
Rural African	16	31	7	41	43	3
Urban African	4	7	2	12	28	7
Urban coloured	2	17	8	20	49	11
Urban Asian	2	22	1	6	35	15
Urban white	0.3	3	4	4	16	8

Source: Richardson, 1986 cited in Yach, 1988: table 21
* <90% height-for-age.
† <80% weight-for-age.
‡ <80% weight-for-height.

An examination of diets of people in various parts of the country tells a sad tale of deprivation. Consider that of a 3½-year-old child, from a farm in Stellenbosch. The daily diet was as follows:

Breakfast: slice of brown bread and margarine; coffee with half-teaspoon of sugar and Cremora.

Lunch: coffee with half-teaspoon of sugar and Cremora.

Supper: coffee with half-teaspoon of sugar and Cremora.

Between meals: dry bread. (184: 13)

Old people in rural Ciskei

These old people are past fending and fighting for their rights. They may be found in dark rooms, on ragged beds. Mostly hungry, often filthy. Their hunger makes them confused and even less able to manage, and if you visit their homes you may find:

• An emaciated old woman, dignified and uncomplaining, until she becomes confused from her hunger and cries out again and again, 'I am hungry, I am hungry.'

• A thorough search of the room and cupboards reveals only some salt, and her primus and pot are shining bright as if waiting for food to cook.

• Or a paralysed old woman, persistently scraping the bottom of an empty pot and putting her claw-like hand to her mouth in despairing imitation of eating.

• This week, I saw an old man bludgeoned by poverty into . . . vacant apathy, alive only because he was not dead; who only said when asked what was wrong, 'I am hungry.' (Trudi Thomas, cited in 138: 75)

Children, however, are not the only people facing the problem of malnutrition as Nomusa Ndaba's survey in Willowmore showed. She found that 25 per cent of the female adult population and 63 per cent of the males in this area were underweight (209: 1). O'Keefe's study, on the other hand, demonstrates the co-existence of undernutrition in adults and obesity, especially in women. His findings were that 26 per cent of rural males (in KwaZulu) were more than 20 per cent underweight, with signs of stunting among rural, as compared with urban, black people. The problem of obesity was found in 33 per cent of urban black females who were 40 per cent overweight, compared with 18 per cent of rural women (266: 6). Amongst men, however, obesity is not a problem. Its prevalence among women who are poor is related to the high intake of carbohydrates. O'Keefe notes in his studies that massive amounts of *putu* (up to 24 cups of dry mealie-meal porridge) or sugar would be required for those who get insufficient protein in order to meet additional demands of stress, sickness, or pregnancy (266: 5).

In the same communities as one finds stunted children there are adults in whom malnutrition manifests itself in many forms, including wasting and pellagra (PCS 1: 6).

Over a thousand kilometres to the east, in the rural Transkei, a survey of three widely separated villages found that 50–60 per cent of respondents did not consume any meat, milk, eggs, or fish. One-third (33 per cent) of the families had diets which were deficient not only in quality protein but also in calories, certain minerals, and vitamins (261: 10–11). In another survey, of a resettlement camp in the Ciskei, it was found that 'the most striking feature, in the face of all other problems, is the perceived problem of lack of food at Oxton', where 'out of 189 respondents . . . who answered about meals eaten the previous day, 174 (92%) had eaten *pap* [mealie-meal porridge], 53 (28%) samp, 28 (15%) bread, 80 (42%) tea. Only 5 (3%) had had mealies, 12 (6%) cabbage, 3 spinach, 1 beans, 1 chicken, 1 potatoes, 1 fruit, 6 milk. None had had eggs or meat.' (189: 7–8)

In KwaZulu and in Natal there is also widespread evidence of bleak diets. In her study of the nutritional status of adults, Ndaba found:

Most people in KwaZulu eat maize on average twice per day in the form of mealie-meal, samp and mealie rice. Brown bread enjoys second place in popularity, thanks to the subsidy, because it provides a valuable source of protein. People tend to eat foods they can afford. . . . There is a positive correlation between income and the consumption of commodities like meat, *maas* [sour milk], eggs, etc. Unfortunately the consumption of these protein-rich foods is largely culturally determined as well. A young wife, living with her husband and parents-in-law, is not allowed to eat *maas*, milk produced by family cows, fish, eggs and chicken, until certain family rituals have been performed. She may remain on a low protein diet throughout her child-bearing period. (306: 19)

In Willowmore in the Karoo, 'where people were asked about diet, the inventory suggested a very low intake of nutritionally important foods. Meat and vegetables are eaten only once a week on Sundays. Indeed most of the pensioners said that they bought meat only on pension days.' It is striking to observe that in Willowmore today, the diet of the poor, who are black, is 'even more lacking in variety than that of the poor whites in the 1920s, nearly sixty years ago' (209: 7).

Summarising the evidence from surveys by the Surplus People Project (SPP) in 21 relocation (or threatened) areas, Laurine Platsky concluded that while the general standard of nutrition was poor in all the areas, the degree of malnutrition varied quite considerably (73:15). Everywhere the staple diet of starch (in the form of maize, bread, rice, and potatoes plus tea, coffee, and sugar) was deficient in protein and greens. The consumption of meat, eggs, milk and greens all followed a similar pattern: ranging from poor in those townships where there was some money coming in, to 'totally inadequate' in the more isolated and economically depressed closer settlements. Thus, taking meat consumption as an index of nutrition levels, the SPP survey reported that near Cape Town 50 per cent of the people questioned in Atlantis ate meat daily, and near Durban 40 per cent of those in Phoenix ate meat at least twice a week. In some of the resettlement camps in the reserves, on the other hand, two-thirds and more of the people ate meat less than once a week. In Sahlumbe in KwaZulu, the vast majority (92 per cent) reported that they ate meat less than once a month (73: 15). At the same time it is significant to note that in those rural areas where households had access to agricultural land, food consumption was considerably better than elsewhere. Thus, although agricultural activity in these areas is not the main source of household income it is nevertheless important in supplementing the average standard of living (73: 16).

The evidence suggests that for many people diet today is considerably worse than it was for their grandparents. As Liz Clarke has pointed out in this context: 'The Zulu diet included meat from periodic feasts, quantities of *amasi* [sour milk], and a wide range of vegetables including sorghum, millet, pumpkins, gourds, yams, various tubers akin to the potato, various nuts and indigenous beans and a wide variety of green herbs and plants' (295: 4). It should be noted that the natural vegetation still provides an important food supplement for the poor in some areas, but this base is being rapidly eroded. Even in more recent years, Ndaba is convinced, from her observations, that 'nutritional status in the whole of Zululand has undoubtedly worsened in most of the areas' (206: 42).

As one might expect, an inverse relationship between income and hunger or malnutrition emerges from several studies. Ndlovu's comparison between Mpukunyoni, a rural area with migrant workers, and Esikhawini, a semi-urban area with better employment opportunities (especially for women) and higher incomes, revealed that 40 per cent of the under-fives in Mpukunyoni were underweight for age compared to 24 per cent in Esikaweni (278: 4). In metropolitan Cape Town, Ann Glyn Thomas found an inverse relationship between income and undernutrition (210: 12). One study compared Indian children in Chatsworth, Durban, and in Laudium, Pretoria: 'There is a striking difference in weights and heights reflecting the better-off Indian community at Laudium' (205: 6).

The problem of low income is further exacerbated by high prices of foodstuffs in rural areas compared with those in urban centres. Ndaba's comparative figures of prices in Willowmore and Cape Town clearly illustrate the point (209: 6). Buch and De Beer uncovered a similar trend in Mhala, Gazankulu. Even for foodstuffs with price control like brown bread, the difference was as much as 21 per cent (192: 2). Moreover, 'there is little doubt, on the basis of the Conference papers, that lack of income whether in cash or kind is the single most important determinant of nutritional status' (PCS 1: 13).

Lack of income is all the more serious because of the large dependency burdens placed on the limited numbers of money-earners. In many cases migration on the part of the breadwinner, while the rest of the family remains in the rural homeland environment, is the only answer to boosting household income. Migrancy, in turn, creates a whole new set of problems. . . . What is crucial from the nutritional point of view is that family cohesion and organisation is often impaired as the family unit is broken up in the effort to solicit more income. A causal relationship appears to exist between family disorganisation and increased incidence of malnutrition in the household. Invariably it is the young and aged who are most seriously affected by malnutrition. . . . The break-up of the family unit also spawns other social maladies, including the breakdown of family discipline and promiscuity among young adults which invariably leads to illegitimate pregnancies: the resulting illegitimate, and often unwanted, children are the ones who become the malnourished in a community. (PCS 1: 13)

Ndaba also draws attention to an important psychological aspect of hunger. In Willowmore,

where the household income was more than R200 a month, and people were healthy and well nourished, the house was much cleaner and pleasanter. Where they had very little income, looked unhealthy and had nothing, the house was often very dirty and neglected. People did not even bother to line their shelves with patterned old newspaper, which they did in 'higher' income houses. This can be attributed to mental fatigue. People who get hungry have no energy for cleaning or tidying up a house which gives them nothing more than just shelter. (209: 9)

Mortality rates

Perhaps the most devastating consequence of hunger and malnutrition in any society is the high death rate of young children, although the causal connection is often hidden.

Malnutrition is often in combination with other conditions like tuberculosis, which in Zululand is also on the increase. Among protein-energy-malnutrition cases, the death rate is high but usually the cause of death is . . . officially attributed to some infection or parasitic disease which in most cases only dealt the final blow. Diseases that are usually only minor ailments in well-nourished individuals are devastating to the malnourished. Even if they do not kill them they tend to intensify the malnourishment by draining the individual's reserves. Extremely poor sanitary conditions further complicate the picture, gastro-enteritis and infestation of various kinds of worms are commonplace. (206: 42–3)

As the Food and Nutrition Report (PCS 1: 2) points out: 'The major causes of post-neonatal death are gastro-enteritis and pneumonia. As with other infectious and parasitic diseases such as measles and tuberculosis, poor nutrition is an important factor in disease mortality.'

There are various measures of the death rate amongst the very young. Following the lead of Unicef, we shall focus on two of these: the infant mortality rate and the child mortality rate.

The Infant Mortality Rate (IMR) measures the number of children who die before their first birthday out of every thousand children born alive. Besides being an 'excellent indicator of the level of health' it is increasingly being seen and used as one of the best measures available of the general economic conditions under which people are living. Child mortality, which is generally measured as a rate per thousand of children dying before their fifth birthday (U5MR), reflects the main environment: factors affecting the health of a child such as nutrition, sanitation, communicable diseases of childhood, and accidents occurring in and around the home. Overall figures for mortality rates in South Africa do exist, but they are averages which not only cover wide variations between one area and another but are also based (particularly as far as the black population is concerned) on very incomplete sampling. The following tables summarise the evidence.

Table 5.02a: Infant and under-five mortality rate in South Africa, 1960–85

	Overall average	
Mortality rate	1960	1985
Infant (IMR)	135	78
Under-five (U5MR)	192	104

Source: Unicef, 1987

Table 5.02b: Infant mortality in South Africa, 1981–5

	Overall average			
	White	Asian	Coloured	African
IMR 1981–85*				
National	12	18	52	94–124
Ten major urban areas†	12	17	26	39
Rural and peri-urban	12	20	66	100–135

Sources: Bradshaw *et al.*, 1987: table 6; Yach, 1988: table 2
* Figures averaged over these five years exclude Bophuthatswana, Ciskei, Transkei, and Venda where the IMR for Africans is probably higher than elsewhere in South Africa.
† Excludes peri-urban areas.

The above tables, read together, show how aggregated figures mask racial differences, but they do not show the extent of geographical differences: 'Five rural surveys over the period 1982–87 have obtained IMRs for rural Africans ranging from 130 (for Transkei) to 36 (for Bophuthatswana). The lowest rates were found in areas where health services were well developed and were therefore not representative of rural conditions.' (Bradshaw *et al.*, 1987: 34) In general it would seem that infant mortality rates for Africans in rural areas are

Infant mortality rate

From the naked helplessness at his birth to the milestone of his first birthday the human infant is particularly exposed and vulnerable to the hazards of a hostile environment. At few other times of his life is he so insecure and utterly dependent on the benevolence of his family and the generosity of his society. It is generally recognised that the infant mortality rate in any country is an excellent indicator of the level of health of its population and reflects on the quality of its paediatric services. (H. M. Coovadia, cited in Community Health Research Project, 1983: 30)

far higher than in the cities although we cannot be certain, as estimates of the urban IMRs 'generally exclude informal settlements, while analysis of secular trends is precluded by the variability in the quality of information being collected' (Bradshaw *et al.*, 1987: 34). Amongst the coloured population between 1981 and 1985 the IMR in non-urban areas was 2.6 times higher than in ten major urban areas. Amongst whites and Indians there was far less variation (165: 64). From the figures it emerges that there is an urban–rural differential as well as a racial one, which reflects relative privilege in socio-economic terms. For Africans it is clearly far preferable to raise children in Cape Town than in an area like the Transkei, which should be avoided at all costs. Furthermore, we see that African children are eight to ten times more likely to die before their first birthday than are white children in South Africa. For coloured children, the risk is four time greater.

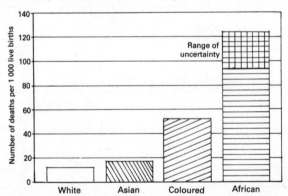

Fig. 5.01: Infant mortality in South Africa, by colour-caste, 1981–5

The following diagram, based on a table drawn up by Caroline Ntoane, shows the wide range by geographic location of African infant mortality rates in a number of studies done between 1980 and 1986.

For Africans in South Africa as a whole the infant mortality rate, averaging somewhere between 94 and 124 over the period 1981–5, was considerably worse than the national average (for 1985) in Botswana (72), Zimbabwe and Kenya (76), Congo (77), Tunisia (78), Algeria (81) and Zambia (84). It was of the same order of magnitude as that in another dozen African countries ranging from Morocco (90) to Burundi (119) (Unicef, 1987: 90).

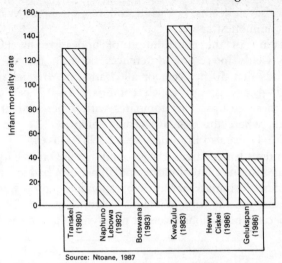

Source: Ntoane, 1987

Fig. 5.02: African infant mortality rates in different rural areas, 1980–6

It is illuminating to look at the three most common causes of infant deaths in the different South African categories. Amongst those classified African and coloured they are pneumonia, gastroenteritis and immaturity. For whites, on the other hand, the killers are peri-natal problems (difficulties with breathing at birth), congenital anomalies (such as Down's syndrome), and pneumonia.

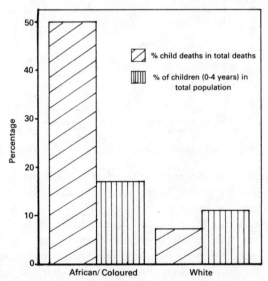

Fig. 5.03: Child mortality as a percentage of all deaths

For children between the ages of 1 to 5, causes of death also vary between the different groups. For Africans gastroenteritis remains predominant but, in addition to pneumonia, inadequate nutrition is a major cause, accounting for one out of every seven deaths. For white children, on the other hand, injuries are by far the commonest cause.

An examination of the contribution of under-five mortality to total mortality also yields interesting differences between the various groups. Herman contends that 50 per cent of all deaths in Africans and coloureds occur in the 0–4 age group, which comprises 16–17 per cent of total population of these groups. This compares with 7 per cent of total deaths amongst whites, where the 0–4 age group comprises 11 per cent of that population (171: 1; see also Bradshaw *et al.*, 1987: 35–6).

In the Ciskei resettlement areas it was found that in Oxton 61 per cent of all respondents had lost one child or more, and 30 per cent had lost three children or more. In Peddie (Kammaskraal) the corresponding figures were 32 and 14, while at Ndevana, outside King William's Town, they were 22 and 4. These differences reflected the various levels of poverty in these areas (189: 9).

Fig. 5.04: Infant mortality in Cape Town, 1941–81

It is also important to examine the trend of infant mortality rates over the years to see what is happening in the society. In the urban areas the picture seems to be clearer. In Soweto, for example, between 1950 and 1979 the infant mortality rate (per thousand) fell from 232 to 35. In Cape Town there was a similar dramatic decline in infant mortality as may be seen in the accompanying graph. Nor were these improvements confined to the metropolitan centres. In the smaller towns too, much has changed for the better. In Worcester in the western Cape, for example, the changes since the end of the Second World War are detailed in the next table.

The decline in infant mortality is notable. So too, however, are the differences that remain between the groups. In Cape Town for example, in 1981 the infant mortality rate for Africans was double that of the coloured population and four times that of whites. In Worcester the differences are even more marked. Although there were notable improvements for all groups, the infant mortality for the coloured population in 1981 was still worse than that for whites at the end of the Second World War. For Africans, the rate in 1981 was over 40 per cent higher than that for whites 35 years previously, and no less than fifteen times greater than that for whites in 1981.

Table 5.03: Infant mortality rates in Worcester, 1944/5–81

	White	Coloured	African	Total	Index
1944/5	43	281	338	225	100
1960	24	133	210	138	61
1981	4	49	61	44	20

Source: 32: 79

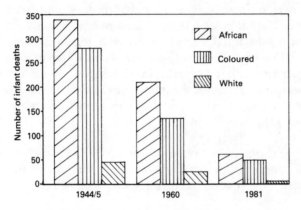

Fig. 5.05: Infant mortality in Worcester, 1944/5–81

Moreover, the story that despite these racial differences, the general situation with regard to infant mortality has been one of consistent and substantial improvement, does not hold true throughout the country. There is some evidence that in several places the infant mortality rate, after falling, appears to have risen significantly in the decade after 1972 (Olver, personal communication). This period coincided with greatly increased pressure on the urban infrastructure because the rise in the population in these towns, through natural growth and through urbanisation as people moved off the land, was not matched by adequate investment in housing and other infrastructure necessary to sustain urban living. For in 1972 the central government, through the establishment of Bantu Affairs Administration Boards, took over from local authorities the running of the black townships. This switch in control was accompanied by a decrease in financial provision for the black urban areas, as the local authorities no longer made any contribution and the central government used its funds to develop housing and infrastructure in far-away homelands and, in most cases, not for black suburbs in what were seen to be 'white' cities.

There is some debate as to the reliability of the various infant mortality figures reported by the various medical officers of health, and they must clearly be used with caution. Indeed, the Medical Research Council review of mortality concludes that even in the major urban areas analysis of secular trends is not really possible because of the variability in the quality of data collected and because the data generally exclude informal settlements. But if they are used, then one must draw both sets of conclusions to which they point. The first is that in a number of places, notably Soweto, Cape Town, and some of the smaller towns, the infant mortality rate has improved dramatically since the Second World War. The second is that in some towns, notably on the east Rand and in the eastern Cape, the decline seems to have been checked, if not actually reversed, during the past decade. Both conclusions are inherently plausible.

As far as the rural areas are concerned, there is even less evidence, particularly over time, so it is not possible to draw any conclusions about overall trends. What does seem to be clear, however, is firstly that, as we have seen, there are substantial variations between regions. Secondly, it would appear that there have been different trends in different places. In some, marked improvement has occured. In Gelukspan, south of Mafikeng in Bophuthatswana, for example, the intervention led by Dr Martin Bac and his colleagues at the hospital has resulted in a measured fall in the child (under-five) mortality rate from 95 in 1979 to 18 in 1982 (268: 18). But in some other areas it seems likely that infant mortality has increased, especially in such resettlement places as Oxton in the Ciskei (189: 1–12) or the Venda village in the northern Transvaal where no less than ten of the thirty babies born alive during the year preceding the survey died before their first birthday (64: 12).

With regard to the situation on the farms we know very little; the fragmentary evidence suggests wide variations. Finally, notwithstanding these differences both by area and in trends, it seems accurate to conclude that the infant mortality rate in most rural areas remains well above that in the towns and cities.

Gastroenteritis

The incidence, prevalence, and severity of gastroenteritis in a given community provide a fair reflection of its socio-economic status, especially regarding children, whose vulnerability is increased by poor nutrition, sanitation, water supply, and organisation of the household. Adults, however, are also exposed to the hazards of enteric diseases such as typhoid, cholera, and dysentery. Gastroenteritis is the most common cause of death in the coloured community (176 per 100 000) and the second most common amongst Africans (86 per 100 000). The corresponding figure for whites is 4 per 100 000 (165: 79). The latest (1984) figures available show that amongst African children between the age of 1 month and 5 years gastroenteritis accounts for well over one-third (39 per cent) of all deaths. If we include children who die in their first month, then gastroenteritis accounts for more than one-quarter (28 per cent) of the deaths of all infants under the age of 1 year (Bradshaw *et al.*, 1987: 35).

These national figures are consistent with findings of local studies carried out by various researchers throughout the country. In Naphuno (south of Tzaneen in the north-eastern Transvaal) Ntoane and colleagues in their study of infant mortality reported that gastroenteritis was the commonest cause of death in those under 12 months (188: 6). In Philipstown in the Karoo, Morifi found that the commonest diseases were gastroenteritis and tuberculosis in adults, and malnutrition in children (33: 15). The Ciskei study by Schweitzer shows not only a high prevalence of gastroenteritis in the sample drawn from Cecilia Makiwane Hospital (18 per cent of all paediatric admissions in 1981/2) but also indicates important differences between those with gastroen-teritis and the control group in relation to access to clean water supplies. The significance lay not so much in whether or not people had access to water but in whether or not the water to which they had access was piped into the house (190: 1, 6). The Orange Free State study by Walwyn reports that gastroenteritis is a major health problem in the black township of Bethlehem (41: 19). In Cape Town, André Botha demonstrated that not only is there a relationship between the incidence of gastroenteritis and poverty but also that the duration of the disease is longer amongst the poor than amongst the privileged. This was related to the concomitant problems that complicated the disease in the former group (290: 6–11).

Cholera, typhoid and dysentery

The outbreak of cholera in the eastern Transvaal in 1980, more than any other epidemic, brought into public focus the unsatisfactory water and sewerage facilities of the deprived communities in those areas. More than a hundred thousand people were treated for this disease over the next two years. Given the epidemiology of this disease, the above figure, which represents merely the tip of the iceberg, indicates that there were 2–3 million infections over the same period. Cases were reported from areas as widely scattered as Natal coastal district, Johannesburg single men's hostels, and the eastern Transvaal. These are all areas characterised by large concentrations of people with poor water supplies and sanitation (295: 45).

Other diseases like typhoid and dysentery follow the same geographic distribution and have a similar epidemiology. Conditions conducive to their persistence as endemic problems in these areas are also similar. The only difference lies in the less publicity attached to them as opposed to cholera, which was forcefully brought to the public notice by a sustained media campaign, mainly motivated by the threat of spread to the privileged groups through contact with carriers of the disease.

Virchow's conclusions made in Europe in 1848 when he was studying typhoid remain valid for South Africa today. As he remarked, political powerlessness and economic insecurity lead, through a complex web of interactions, to a preponderance of illness and early death (cited in 290: 1).

Measles

Measles is generally regarded as a mild childhood illness in industrialised societies and amongst the elite in developing communities. Amongst the poor, however, measles represents the most serious and severe disease encountered by children. It is a highly infectious viral disease characterised by fever, mucosal inflammation, and a typical skin rash. The resultant depression of the immune system of the body during the infection brings about secondary bacterial infection. The complications of measles which may lead to death are pneumonia, gastroenteritis, and encephalitis, but blindness also results from eye infections in the presence of vitamin deficiencies.

The official statistics of the incidence of and mortality from measles are a gross underestimate of the true picture in South Africa. Their accuracy is a function of access to proper health facilities, which are known to be inversely related to need. The following table, however, gives an indication of the position with respect to the different race groups, which closely parallel social class.

Table 5.04: Incidence (per 100 000) in measles, 1979/80*–1987

	White	Asian	Coloured	African
Range of rate, 1980–87†	8–27	2–35	25–57	53–105
Incidence 1979/80*	30	27	44	67
1987†	14	7	39	105
Case fatality rate, 1979/80 (%)	0.2	0.5	2.8	1.8

Source: 165: 79 and Yach, 1988: table 14
* Twelve months from August–July.
† These figures exclude the TBVC areas.

It has been estimated that 15.5 per cent of African child mortality (under fives) is due to measles (172: 1), yet the official statistics (excluding the TBVC regions) are considerably lower. Amongst African children between 1 and 4 years of age, 8 per cent of all deaths reported are caused by measles (Bradshaw et al., 1987: 36). In Bophuthatswana, Bac and his health team found that measles was the second commonest cause of the high child mortality of 95 per 1 000 in the Gelukspan district, south of Mafikeng, over the period 1975–9 (268: 5). But the most dramatic pointer to the problem was the outbreak of measles in Port Elizabeth between December 1982 and July 1983 which affected 2 000 children and resulted in 295 deaths, a case fatality rate of 15 per cent. In this epidemic 88 per cent of all notifications and 91 per cent of all deaths were in the African groups, with the coloured figures being 11 and 8 per cent respectively. There were only eighteen cases amongst whites, one of whom died (172: 3). The evidence for the country as a whole in the above table suggests that whilst measles seems to be becoming less prevalent amongst whites, coloureds, and Asians, the incidence amongst Africans is high and increasing. The differences in the population distribution of cases and fatalities are a clear reflection of the relative socio-economic position of the groups. A close examination of these conditions in Port Elizabeth revealed three significant variables that were correlated with the disease.

Overcrowding encourages a more rapid spread of measles with the possibility of larger doses of the virus per individual child (personal communication from Dr Dilima, Livingstone Hospital, Port Elizabeth). There is also an increased risk of infection of younger children who are known to have a higher age-specific fatality rate. Aaby, in Guinea-Bissau, found that family size was a greater risk factor than malnutrition, but a combination of the two factors is mutually reinforcing (cited in 172: 2). Fisher discovered that the squatter area of Little Soweto (Veeplaas) was the hardest hit in the 1982–3 epidemic in Port Elizabeth. The measles epidemic clearly indicated the correlation between inadequate housing and disease. 'The highest attack rate was found in the area with the lowest standard of housing, hygiene, and sanitation' (21: 15).

Age. More than half of all African and coloured cases of measles were aged 1 year or less (54 and 62 per cent respectively). The vulnerability of the very young is seen even more clearly in the fact that 84 per cent of all African (and 79 per cent of all coloured) deaths from measles were under 2 years. The highest age-specific fatality rate was 44 per cent for Africans under 6 months.

Nutritional status. There is a strong correlation between weight-for-age and prognosis. Some 36 per cent of those who died were below the third centile on the NCHS.

Measles is a preventable disease par excellence and has been eradicated from many countries in the world, by extensive immunisation campaigns. In the United States, for example, there were more than 500 000 cases every year before the measles vaccine became available in the 1960s but by 1981 the incidence had been reduced to little more than 3 000 cases – a reduction of over 99 per cent (295: 67). The power of immunisation has been demonstrated in South Africa itself where 15 000 children every year get measles and see a doctor whilst a far great number get the disease but no medical attention. In a study in Cape Town, Bruce Dick calculated the relative costs of hospitalisation and a vaccination programme against measles. The simple cost-benefit analysis strongly favoured vaccination (1975).

Some years later in the Mhala district of Gazankulu, the Health Services Department Unit of the University of the Witwatersrand ran three mass immunisation campaigns inoculating more than 30 000 children each time against poliomyelitis. In the second and third campaigns most of the children were also inoculated against diphtheria, tetanus and measles, and some against whooping cough and tuberculosis as well. The impact was dramatic. Although heavily at risk from a poliomyelitis epidemic which had started six weeks previously, not one child in the district caught the disease. Moreover, 'the total cost of the first immunisation campaign was much less than the cost of ensuring the long-term treatment for a single case of paralytic polio' (200: 9). As far as measles was concerned, the impact of immunisation was even more apparent. In the three years 1980–2, the average annual number of people admitted to the hospital with measles was 143. In 1983, the year after immunisation, the number of admissions dropped to 19. And as Eric Buch and his co-workers at the Tintswalo Hospital point out, 'The cost of all three campaigns is covered if we have prevented a single child going blind as a result of a vitamin A deficiency following measles' (200: 9). Further north in Gazankulu, around the Elim Hospital, health workers found the prevalence of blindness in all age groups over the period 1976–9 to be 15 to 20 per 1 000 inhabitants, which is far beyond the World Health Organisation norm of 1 to 3 persons per 1 000 of the population of children of 0–6 years of age.

The prevalence of corneal scarring, mostly due to vitamin A deficiency with or without concomitant measles infection, was five times higher than the level at which the WHO considered the problem to be a public health priority. 'Blindness presented in children seen at Elim hospital over the period 1967–1972 was in 41% of the cases associated with measles and malnutrition and in 15% with malnutrition alone' (208: 16). By March 1983 effective immunisation in the district had eliminated measles among the under-fives, and the widespread distribution of vitamin A via the under-five clinics had done much to prevent these cases of blindness.

Clearly there is a need for these individual campaigns, waged often against great odds, to be multiplied through the country as part of a national health service. It is simply not acceptable for an easily preventable disease such as measles to become an epidemic, claiming hundreds of young lives and causing untold suffering from life-long blindness as it still does in South Africa.

Tuberculosis

More prevalent and more disturbing even than measles is tuberculosis. This disease, perhaps more than any other, reflects not only the poor socio-economic conditions of its victims but also the historical factors that led to its taking root in those vulnerable groups.

Until the 1890s tuberculosis was almost unknown in the Transkei and equally rare in Basutoland (SAMJ, 1944 and De Beer, 1980: 3–7). The evidence indicates that, more than any other historical process, it was the development of the mining industry which, by increasing the inflow of Europeans infected with tuberculosis who then worked together with black miners under dusty, damp, and poorly ventilated conditions, set the scene for infection of these black workers, who had no resistance and were poorly fed and housed.

Surveys done in the Transkei, Ciskei and Basutoland around 1930 show that between 69 and 88 per cent of men aged approximately 20 were infected with tuberculosis and that 72 per cent of those applying for jobs were similarly affected. Migratory labour had obviously completed the cycle of infection, which came to include women and children. Although we have no direct evidence, it is likely that a similar cycle of infection was introduced into other major labour-supplying areas such as Mozambique.

Tuberculosis is acknowledged by all, including the South African health authorities, to be a major health problem. It constitutes 61 per cent of all notifiable diseases (Bradshaw et al., 1987: 46). A total of 61 980 notifications in 1982 is broken down as follows:

Table 5.05: Tuberculosis notifications in South Africa,* 1982

		Number	Percentage
White		626	1
Coloured		10 422	17
Asian		556	1
Africans: RSA	40 578⎫	50 256	81
Indep. homelands	9 678⎭		
Total		61 980	100

Source: 173a: 22
* Including TBVC areas.

These figures should be multiplied by two or three to approach the true incidence of the disease, because the official figures are nowhere near an adequate reflection of the actual situation, particularly in the reserves where high proportions of the population have open pulmonary, that is infectious, tuberculosis.

In Lebowa, in 1981, the total number of tuberculosis cases officially notified was 766, yet in one hospital alone, which we visited, there were estimated to be between 300 and 400 new cases. Given that there are four hospitals in Lebowa and that by no means all those suffering from tuberculosis reach hospital and are registered, the incidence of the disease is clearly far higher than the statistics allow. Indeed the Medical Research Council estimates that 'only a third to a half of all tuberculosis cases that really occur each year are notified to the authorities' (Bradshaw *et al.*, 1987: 46). Nevertheless, if we assume that the degree of under-enumeration has been consistent down the years, it is possible to obtain some idea of the trend. There does seem to have been a decline in the rate of infection, for all groups, over the last 20 years as may be seen in the following graph.

The gap between Africans and others has, however, widened. Twenty years ago the risk of infection for Africans was 3.3 times greater than that for whites. By the early 1980s the risk was 22 times greater in South Africa (excluding the independent homelands) and 50 times greater in the Transkei (173a: 2).

Tuberculosis meningitis has been used as an indicator of the extent of the control of tuberculosis in the population. It has an incidence of 7.5 per 100 000 in the western Cape according to a survey done of notifications (over the period 1979–81), which was three times higher than the recent national figures. Some rural areas were found to have incidence rates as high as 20 per 100 000 (175: 7). Unlike pulmonary tuberculosis, tuberculosis meningitis always causes an illness profound enough to require hospital admission and it carries a high mortality rate, frequently with permanent neurological disabilities in survivors.

From the statistics it is quite apparent that it is the people who are not white who are at risk. This correlates with their vulnerability to poverty with its ramifications of overcrowding, malnutrition and limited access to health facilities. A study amongst 7-year-old children over the period 1977–82 shows that the estimated risk of infection varies significantly according to the South African population group into which the child happens to have been born.

Table 5.06: Estimated risks of infection for tuberculosis in 7-year-olds, South Africa, 1977–82

Racial-caste	Risk of infection (per 1 000 of population)
African	7–22
Coloured	5–10
Asian	3– 4
White	1– 2

Source: Fourie, 1983 cited in Yach, 1988: table 15

During the course of their interviews with people in different parts of the Transvaal, Ntoane and Mokoetle were told that tuberculosis was a major health problem in the farms of the western Transvaal (2: 10). Other rural areas are similarly affected, as was found in surveys from KwaZulu in Natal to Philipstown in the Karoo. But in the urban sample, only Alexandra township residents in Johannesburg isolated tuberculosis as a problem (2: 10).

The effect on the people is not only reflected in the mortality statistics of the disease, which are themselves considerable, estimated at 6 to 10 lives lost daily (295: 28). It is felt also by the survivors, who have problems such as loss of employment, lack of access to medical facilities and disability grants (174: 9).

Experience in Europe and other parts of the world has shown that the best option for tackling tuberculosis is socio-economic advancement because it removes the stresses of poverty which reduce the body's resistance. In the Netherlands, for example, the annual risk of infection declined from 6 per cent in 1920 to 2 per cent in 1950 before the introduction of modern anti-tuberculosis and BCG immunisation (198: 2). The South African experience, however, has been one of total disregard for this logical option and reliance on anti-tuberculotics and immunisation. The national policy with respect to chemotherapy, prophylaxis, contact tracing and immunisation compares favourably with international standards but there are variations with regard to actual practice.

In their study Thompson and Myrdal (173b) reported variations between Cape Town metropolis, Paarl district, and the Ciskei, which were determined mainly by affordability of the ideal treatment regimen by the various local authorities. In the north-eastern Transvaal, it was found (198: 1) that in the Mhala district of Gazankulu nearly half (46 per cent) of a sample of over 2 000 Sub. A and Sub. B pupils had positive reactions to a test for tuberculosis.

There is evidence of a tendency to reduce further the amount allocated by the state for the standard tuberculosis regimen. For example, in a survey done by Judith Cornell in greater Cape Town amongst employers, it was found that only 22 per cent of respondents had regular tuberculosis screening and that

The Sefatse family

Mr Sefatse, his wife and seven children comprised a household living on a closer settlement site. Since 1974 when they arrived in Qwa Qwa from a Free State farm, Sefatse has had intermittent labour contracts. In 1981 he secured a labour contract at Sasol II which he, in common with many others in Qwa Qwa, did not realise was not renewable. He also became ill at this time, which made it difficult to find another job. In mid-1982 he secured work in Bethlehem but after four months was so ill that he returned home. Diagnosed then as having TB, he had not worked since then. During 1982 Sefatse's eldest son secured a contract in Welkom. Since then his son has become seriously ill but has clung to his job because it is the only source of income to the site. The second son was removed from school in mid-1982 because his fees could not be met. He was still too young to be issued with a reference book and has been unable to find a piece job within Qwa Qwa. By 1983 the household was in a deep crisis. Sefatse's wife and oldest daughter had been diagnosed as suffering from pellagra and the wife had suspected TB as well. A younger child had been sent home from school because she was passing out in class as a result of hunger. A combination of drought and illness and hunger in the household had meant that even the small site garden was no longer in use. Sefatse and his wife said that they had exhausted the possibilities for begging or borrowing in the neighbourhood.

Owing to the vagaries of relocation neither Sefatse nor his wife had any kin in Qwa Qwa on whose support they could depend. [They] expressed their anxiety for and guilt about their children and repeatedly said that they had failed as parents. 'I cannot sleep at night any longer,' said Mrs Sefatse, 'because my son was so ill when he last came home [at Easter] but I sent him back to work [in Welkom] because his is the only income we have. I am forced to kill one child in order to feed the others.'

A neighbour to the household noted that she and others were appalled and ashamed of seeing Mrs Sefatse literally starving to death where she lay and of hearing her cries. She was, however, unable to do anything more to help as she also had no food nor money in her house. (52: 15 and 24; 297: 34–5)

others had phased out their screening on the directive of health authorities (289: 20–1).

Yet the situation is explosive and, in some areas at least, is getting worse (93: 8). In Cape Town the medical officer of health has drawn attention to recent increases in the incidence of tuberculosis (198: 3–7). In 1987 the tuberculosis notification rate (per 100 000 population) amongst young children (under 5) in Cape Town was 5 for whites, 289 for coloured persons, and 649 for Africans (Yach, 1988: table 16). This is traceable to the refusal by those in authority to tackle the root cause of the problem: the powerlessness of those most affected to press for changes in that direction. As the Cape Town medical officer of health stated in his 1981 report, tuberculosis 'affects mainly the underprivileged . . . and will remain a problem for as long as sections of

Tuberculosis in one rural district

On the basis of our current data we estimate that there are nearly 8 000 children in Sub. A and Sub. B in Mhala who required tuberculosis care. As we do not have the resources to tackle this massive task, we tried the alternative of arranging supervision of care through school teachers. Unfortunately it was impractical. 138 of the 338 children at one school needed care. The teachers were very willing, but spent more than two hours a day supervising care instead of teaching. The support we had to give to keep this effort going could also not be achieved again. We have therefore had to decide that we will only provide TB care for about 15% of the children needing it. (199: 5)

the Cape Town population remain exposed to the effects of malnutrition, overcrowding, etc.' (13: 15). Indications of further cuts in expenditure even on the less effective form of treatment are a reflection on the lack of public commitment to deal adequately with this national scourge.

The evidence summarised in this chapter shows the extent to which sickness, hunger and malnutrition are connected to each other. Important areas such as mental illness have not been covered although there too the picture is one of inadequate care. These manifestations of acute poverty are not primarily due to a lack of resources in the society as a whole. South Africa has some of the best medical facilities in the world and much work has been done, not least by the medical profession, to reduce infant mortality rates and to curb such diseases as measles and tuberculosis. Yet the situation remains chronic. The country produces enough food to ensure a daily energy availability of well over 6 000 calories per person, more than double the recommended daily allowance of 2 500 to 3 000 calories (223: 29), yet malnutrition continues to ravage thousands of South African children. It is clear that the widespread hunger and disease can only be tackled by strategies that understand the overall pattern of poverty and that deal directly with its causes. But before we focus on either causes or strategies we must first consider other related aspects of poverty as manifested in South Africa. The diseases examined in this chapter are exacerbated by inadequate, over-crowded living conditions; thus it would be instructive if we moved now to consider housing.

124

How can you respect each other when the mother, the father and the children are all sleeping together? If a person gets visitors, he or she cannot receive them properly. You have to sit outside in the open with your visitors because there is no room in the house. You cannot even offer them a place to sleep if they need accommodation, because there is only one room. It is very humiliating.

> – Aunt Bettie, Philipstown,
> in the Karoo (33: 10)

In an autobiographical note describing life when he was interned during the Second World War, Paul Streeten, one of the originators of the 'basic needs' approach to poverty, makes the point that the least disagreeable feature of the voyage from Britain to a camp in Canada was the crammed space. As a result he has never regarded housing as quite so basic a need as food, water or sanitation (1985: 51). In South Africa, this view seems, at first glance, to have been confirmed by a study, for the Carnegie Inquiry, of overcrowding and health issues at Crossroads, the densely populated squatter settlement in Cape Town.

Some tentative enquiries were made at the beginning of the survey to assess how people felt about their crowded conditions. Some complaints were registered about noise, sharing of facilities, etc. On the whole, however, overcrowding was not seen as an issue when faced with the alternative of living as separated families under the migrant labour system. One woman stated, 'Overcrowded, yes, but my children and I have come to live with my husband.' Other typical responses were: 'But what choice is there?' 'Of course it is overcrowded in Crossroads. But if we stayed in the Transkei we would starve.'

It would seem therefore, concluded the researchers, 'that for people struggling under immense pressures of poverty, insecurity and shortage of accommodation, the amount of living space per person is not accorded a high priority' (14: 8).

Clearly if the choice is overcrowding or starvation, people will choose to be overcrowded. And it is important not to impose on the poor priorities which they themselves have not chosen. But it would be equally wrong to ignore the realities of inadequate housing and the destructive social consequences of generally bad living conditions.

One of the most striking features of the Carnegie Inquiry was the extent to which research workers from all over the country wrote about overcrowding and inadequate housing conditions generally, and backed up their objective descriptions with assessments by poor people themselves as to what they thought about it all. For example, there is Aunt Bettie, aged 52, who has been living in the small Karoo dorp of Philipstown all her life. She lives with her bedridden mother and her brother who receives a disability grant because he suffers from tuberculosis. The mother receives a pension. Aunt Bettie does not work because she has to look after her mother. Before the family moved to where they are now living, they were lodgers in a two-roomed house. They moved because the house was overcrowded. There were seven adults and six children staying in the two-roomed house. Because the rondavel where they now stay has only a single room, when Aunt Bettie wants to bath or get dressed she has to go to other people's places or her brother has to move out. The mother, the brother and Aunt Bettie all sleep in one room. The mother, who is old, sleeps on the bed, and Aunt Bettie and her brother sleep on the floor, on the same piece of mat with their heads facing opposite directions. '*Ons moet maar kop-en-punt slaap want daar is nie genoeg plek nie*. [We have to sleep head-to-toe because there is not enough place.] If people are living like this, then they lose respect for each other.' (33: 10)

The absence of privacy for married couples, the need for space for children to play, the impossibility of having visitors, are all part of the pain, quite explicitly felt by those enduring a dimension of poverty that is to be found across the length and breadth of the country. The extent of overcrowding is overwhelming, particularly in the urban areas.

The following table shows the order of magnitude of the housing shortage, and hence the overcrowding, in the country as a whole.

Table 6.01: Housing in South Africa

	Surplus/shortage	No. houses built 1983–5
White	+ 37 000	172 000
Asian	− 44 000	37 000
Coloured	− 52 000	62 000
African	−583 000	41 000

Source: De Vos, 1986 cited in PCS 14:6

Urban housing shortage

On the Witwatersrand, excluding the densely settled homeland area of Winterveld north of Pretoria, there was an estimated housing shortage by the mid-1970s of 90 000 houses (18: 6). In Soweto alone the estimated shortage in 1982 was 35 000 houses and growing at a rate of 4 000 per year, whilst over the previous seven years an average of only 1 100 houses per year had been built (281: 38). Figures like these are difficult to comprehend but, as a doctor who had worked in Soweto for some years put it: 'If senior health officials are correct when they estimate the population of Soweto as being 2 million, then there must be nearly twenty people for each house' (170: 2). Another survey estimates that there are an average of 17 people living in every house in Soweto (Christie, 1987). Even WRAB (the West Rand Administration Board) admitted that the true degree of overcrowding was much worse than their own estimate of seven people per house. Stories of up to thirty people (per four-roomed house) are not uncommon (170: 2).

This, as Tim Wilson points out, is not surprising given that between 1970 and 1980 a total of 5 000 houses were built, enough to accommodate only 3 500 extra people per year at the official 7 people per house, in spite of the fact that in 1981, Baragwanath hospital and its clinics delivered 29 000 babies who, allowing for a death rate of 20 per 1 000 per year, added another 25 000 people to the number of people to be accommodated (170: 2).

On the east Rand, Pillay reports that in Katlehong, there were 17 650 houses and 34 000 shacks, and in Tokoza 10 000 shacks have been put up by residents to house the overflow of people. In Daveyton near Benoni, the population increased from 61 000 in 1967 to 87 000 in 1977 but no new houses were built during that same period, resulting in 3 588 families being forced to live in shacks in that township (18: 8–9). The situation in Alexandra, north of Johannesburg, is one of the worst in the country. The squalor, chronic housing shortage, and overcrowding are both frightening and depressing – the result of systematic neglect of the area by local authorities over many years. The township is situated on 80 ha and supports a population of 50 000–70 000, thus yielding a population density of 625–825 people per hectare, more than ten times the density of the nearest white suburb, Sandton, which stands at 51 persons per hectare. It was found that 81 per cent of households in Alexandra lived in shared accommodation, only 17 per cent had a house to themselves, and the balance had either part of a house or a shack as a home. There was an average of three people in every room in the township (19: 24).

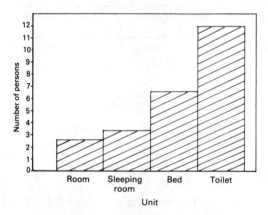

Fig. 6.01: Overcrowding in Crossroads: number of people per unit, 1983

In the coloured areas in Johannesburg, there was evidence of 'up to three families occupying one room in many cases' (18: 9). Sixteen hundred kilometres away, in metropolitan Cape Town, the same claustrophobic conditions prevailed. In 1980 there was an estimated backlog of 48 000 houses, and 59 per cent of all coloured households were overcrowded with more than the desired ratio of 1.5 persons per room (13: 15). In Elsies River, 'the average figure for persons per habitable room . . . is 5.6 per room and in certain neighbourhoods it is much higher' (10c: 11). In Lavender Hill, 'most of the people interviewed had tenants staying with them illegally to help pay the rent, electricity and water accounts. One household had twenty-eight people living in a two-bedroomed flat. Most of the adults were unemployed and the "illegal" tenants were paying the expenses.' (10b: 5) In Crossroads, a careful sample survey measured overcrowding in a number of different ways and found that there was an average of 2.7 persons per room; of 3.3 per sleeping room; of 6.5 per bed; and of 12.0 per toilet (14: 6).

Hundreds of thousands of people manage to live decent lives under such conditions but the strain can and does have devastating consequences:

When we visited this two-roomed house [in Elsies River] at 10.00 a.m., all the occupants of the house were drunk on methylated spirits and therefore it was difficult to assess what was happening there. Living in the house are about six children and nine adults, but it appears that with all the 'booze-gathering' held there almost daily, many more 'overnight' there. Catering for all the occupants are two single beds and one double bed, i.e. approximately five people to a bed. It was possible to discern that the rent and other fixed expenditures are paid by whoever sleeps there and drinks with them. Two of the women indicated that they were on the council waiting list for a house. (10c: 30)

Almost a thousand kilometres due east, in the city of Port Elizabeth, the findings were much the same. In the mid-1980s there was an estimated shortfall of 20 000 houses, and there was need to build over 7 000 a year (instead of the current rate of a few hundred) if there was to be any hope of catching up on the backlog over a ten-year period, and keeping up with the annual increase (21: 5). In the African townships it was found that more than 40 per cent of the households shared accommodation and that in more than 10 per cent of cases three or more families shared the same house (21: 9). Nor is it only black families for whom housing is inadequate. An investigation, early in 1983, into the plight of unemployed whites found 'whole families crowded into barely furnished single rooms and backyard shacks with no electricity, water or sanitary facilities. Rentals of R140 were being charged for single rooms in Sidwell that were accommodating whole families, and R40–R60 for backyard shacks.' (21: 13) Port Elizabeth, like the other metropolitan areas, has seen a mushrooming of squatter shacks over the past ten years. This initiative, taken generally in defiance of the law, has been in response partly to intolerable overcrowding and partly to the fact that a large proportion of black households (in Port Elizabeth an estimated 45 per cent of Africans) are unable to pay an economic rent on any house built either by the state or by the private sector. Without massive support from the wider society, up to half the black population living in the cities can afford to live only in a cheaply built shack or by sharing with one or more other households the space provided by a small four- or five-roomed house (21: 14).

Compounds

Compounds built to house workers only, without their families, have been part of the South African political economy ever since the discovery of diamonds and gold in the nineteenth century led employers to erect these structures as the cheapest way of accommodating their black labour force. A century later huge new 'labour batteries' continue to be built (*Cape Times*, 26.6.1985) whilst the old compounds, even when no longer used by the mines which originally built them, continue to house urban workers unable to find any other accommodation. There are many men in South Africa whose address is not some street number identifying a house, nor even a room number to locate where he might stay in a boarding house, but a bed number to identify where he may be found in a maze of concrete bunks which accommodate perhaps 90 men in a single room. In the early 1970s when these conditions were described in a book, the author was upbraided by a mining official for telling lies; such conditions could not, he knew, possibly be true. Alas, the mining official was wrong.

In Cape Town, Pamela Reynolds found:

there are forty men to a room (or dormitory), no cooking facilities are provided and the noise and crowds, especially at week-ends are, according to the men, difficult to tolerate. At least twenty women and many children share the same space at night and during the week-ends. The dormitory is locked while the men are at work and the women and children roam the streets until the men return in the evenings. (5: 9)

A detailed study, commissioned by migrants themselves, of conditions in the hostels of Nyanga East, Cape Town, in 1984 reported on living conditions which the migrants found 'unbearable'. And they were indeed deplorable. In the eight hostels covered in the survey the provision of toilets was such that if all were in working order there was one toilet for every 22 men. But many toilets were blocked or leaked and were unusable. Some had been out of order for as long as five years, with the responsible authorities simply failing to respond to all requests by the men for action. Showers too were broken and many of these rooms had, for want of an alternative, been turned into latrines (Seleoane, 1985: 24–7). The subsequent emergence of the Western Cape Hostel Dwellers' Association is exerting pressure for the improvement of conditions.

Noise is keenly felt, not only in the hostels but also in the houses built as family accommodation. For example, in Clarke's Estate, Cape Town, 'on Friday night one cannot sleep in this house because of the noise that continues until Sunday evening. It comes from all sides – how can a person take it? It is because of this that my nerves are affected.' (10c: 18)

On the platteland

As we have already seen in the case of Aunt Bettie in Philipstown, overcrowding is not confined to the metropolitan areas. In the dorps of the platteland people find themselves increasingly crowded as they are pushed off the farms into the townships where the supply of new housing has been woefully short of what is required. In Oudtshoorn a Carnegie researcher writes of the 'distress which is most evident in the severe overcrowding that now prevails in the township. . . . I was told of an instance where five families, totalling 27 people, are living in a standard four-room municipal house.' (37: 20) In Worcester another researcher reports that the overcrowded uniform

Life in Beaufort West

Overcrowding. A two-roomed compartment in '*die Treine*'. Nerina Street. The window is boarded up. The walls inside are drab, ageing whitewash. Your eyes take a while to adjust to the darkness. Two beds sit opposite each other against the walls. One is piled high with old blankets. There is just one bed in the other room. A sick-looking middle-aged man sleeps on it. The walls are bare. Not even a painted biscuit tin lid or a religious admonition. There is not a table or a chair. The floor is bare. You write 'very poor!' on the bottom of the questionnaire. The household head is out, I gather from the old lady on the bed opposite me. Six or seven children crowd around. They answer most of the questions. 19 people live in the house. The household head, his wife (common-law), her sister, two aunts, four daughters, eight grandchildren, a boarder. The man on the bed is a son-in-law. Is he regularly employed? 'No, he just rides the blue train,' says the old aunt. 'Blue train' is meths. 'White train' is OMO [detergent] and meths. Bread and brandy makes '*gogga koppe*' [bug heads]. Alcoholism is rampant in '*die Treine*,' the most depressed part of Rustdene. During the warm months ten sleep inside and nine, including the boarder, the son-in-law and daughter and most of the children, sleep outside in the yard. Winter is another story. (35: 18)

structures startle the unsuspecting visitor. 'Fleeting images of Dickensian nineteenth-century London and the Carnegie Commission Inquiry of the 1920s are not out of place in the 106 households of the OVD [*oue van dae*] area and those of Lower Buitenkant street and many parts of Roodewal and Riverview.' (32: 75)

The pain of human degradation and desperation is what characterises the homeless people in Philipstown further north in the Karoo, where

what used to be an animal pound is now inhabited by human beings. The shelter or 'house' consists of pieces of corrugated iron and cardboard. Some use their donkeycarts as shelter. The shelter is no bigger than 1.5 square metres in size, with an average of four people living in the shelter. When asked what happens when it rains, the people said that they have to sleep in garbage bags which they collect from the bins in town. Some said that they cover their blankets to make them waterproof. (33: 7)

In Rustdene, 'the area behind the . . . Junior School is called *die Visblikkies*. The fish-cans. The houses all have cheap steel doors. The grey cement block houses of the later Rustdene developments are *die Ashuise*. The ash houses. And then *die Treine*. The trains. The distinctively long thin rows of slum compartments in the railway brown.' (35: 32)

In the reserves too, following huge increases in population, due primarily to resettlement, houses in some places are overcrowded.

Quality of housing

Dense overcrowding, then, is one of the major aspects of the housing crisis that daily confronts those who are poor in South Africa. But this particular face of poverty has other features as well. Not only are houses overcrowded. All too often they are inadequate in other respects. Returning for a moment to Aunt Bettie's rondavel in Philipstown, we find that it has not been repainted or renovated for more than fifty years, and the roof leaks when it rains. Thus, because it has a dirt floor, the room becomes muddy and the bedding gets wet (33: 9). In Worcester, absence of gutters in many houses meant that in winter tenants were constantly faced with '*water [wat] soos 'n waterval van die dak afstort*' (water that falls off the roof like a waterfall). As many of the houses were below ground level, they were often under water in the winter (32: 74). And Worcester can be very cold.

In Cape Town, one woman who had been resettled under the Group Areas Act was moved to tears by anger and frustration:

My furniture has been spoilt by the rain coming through the hole in my roof. I have no money to replace the roof. I am sick to death of watching my possessions being ruined and not able to prevent it. When it rains, I do not feel like cleaning the house because everything is in a mess, with water dripping and buckets all over the show. *Die mense wat dood is, is beter af as dié wat soos ons lewe.* [The dead are better off than those who live like us.] Sometimes I cry because we are not used to living under such conditions. (10b: 33)

In the extremes of the South African climate, badly designed housing can make life miserable for those too poor to alter things. For example on the Cape Flats, with its high water-table, rising damp is frequently experienced through the thin concrete floor, laid often without damp-proof coursing. And because of the asbestos cement roofs, built without ceilings, the houses are very cold in winter and like ovens in the summer, with mean internal temperatures ranging from 4.2 °C to 43.1 °C; that is, from not far above freezing point to 111 °F (164: 16–18). It is instructive to compare these houses built with all the knowledge and wealth of 'white Western civilisation and technology' with the so-called 'primitive' huts of traditional rural black South Africa where, as was shown in a striking paper to the Carnegie conference, careful design with due regard for the surrounding environment enabled people to build homesteads where 'temperatures within the huts varied only three degrees each side of the 18 degree [Centigrade] stipulated by the [computer] model as the optimum temperature for effective working conditions' (259: 2).

Sewerage and other rubbish disposal

One of the most unpleasant aspects of poor housing in South Africa relates to sewerage and removal of garbage. Evidence was presented to the Carnegie conference from all corners of the country about the chronic failure of local authorities to plan an appropriate infrastructure for the dense concentrations of working-class people, not only in the towns but also in resettlement and peri-urban areas. In Port Elizabeth the outbreak of a measles epidemic which claimed the lives of nearly 300 children in 1982–3 led to the appointment of a special committee to investigate conditions, particularly in Little Soweto, the squatter area on the edge of the city. There the investigation found 'overflow and random dumping of sewerage' from the pit latrines which were still being used. As Caroline White reported: 'Originally sewerage was disposed of by pit latrines, but because of the clay soil they tended to collapse and overflow in wet weather. A bucket system is now provided but, according to residents, they still need pit latrines because the collection is inadequate. . . .' (21: 10) In a much smaller town, Clarens in the Orange Free State, Christine Walwyn discovered appalling conditions with 800 residents of the black township having to use twelve pit toilets, an average of 66 persons to each lavatory. 'Permission has now [1984] been given by the Oranje Vaal Board for residents to dig a pit toilet in each stand' (41: 3)

On the Witwatersrand in Alexandra, a report for the Carnegie Inquiry described 'sewerage flowing in the streets' (2: 9) as a result of the overloading of the existing bucket system. The report also drew attention to the 'uninviting bad odour' in consequence. On the other side of Johannesburg in the Mapetla hostels, there are three toilet pans for a block housing 544 people (2: 9) – one more statistic that the eye slides over without registering anything: an average of 180 people needing to use one toilet in a densely settled city environment. Small wonder that conditions become squalid and people get angry.

In Winterveld, some manage to dig pit latrines very close to homes, resulting in a constant foul odour. In what used to be thought of as a rural part of the northern Transvaal, Harries reports that, 'in order to combat water-borne diseases like cholera and typhoid, aspects of health education such as hygiene and nutrition, the building of toilets and the chlorination of household water are stressed, particularly by the highly successful care groups'. The construction of toilets remains a major problem as it is time-, labour- and capital-consuming. It was estimated in 1980 that, in Gazankulu,

only 50 per cent of schools and 20 per cent of households were equipped with toilets. In 1982 it was admitted in the Giyani legislature of the homeland that only 10 per cent of schools have 'adequate' toilets, 30 per cent have inadequate toilets and 60 per cent have none at all. At Ntlhaveni, the building of a drop pit lavatory system for each stand was enforced. . . . The fine for non-compliance is much resented, particularly as it was raised from R30 to R50 (67: 8).

The dangers of bad lavatories was stressed by Friedman (150: 24) who found a *positive* correlation, in the Valley of a Thousand Hills near Durban, between the existence of toilets and illness. This serves to reinforce the observation of Sikwebu from his study of Nyanga in Cape Town, when he drew attention to the fact that in two schools:

A major complaint was the bucket toilet system still in use. This was said to create an unnecessary health hazard. Apparently this has been the subject of complaint to the bureaucrats for years. Although promises have been made, nothing concrete has been done. In another school . . . the sanitation is even worse. (10a: 10)

Political powerlessness

Sikwebu's observations are important for they draw attention not only to

Inside Windhoek's main township, Katutura

Ill-maintained match-box municipal housing, many with outside latrines and lacking electricity; mainly untarred and unkept roads; inadequate refuse collection with numerous open piles of garbage providing a breeding ground for insects and rodents; poor public facilities; overcrowding; alcoholism, and unemployed people sitting aimlessly around. To residents of Khomasdal and especially Katutura, poverty has *everything* to do with where you live. And where you live is still a function of apartheid geography for 99% of Windhoek's population. (22: 22)

the health issue but also to the underlying problem of political powerlessness. From the mass of evidence presented to the Carnegie conference there is no doubt that the basic infrastructure for sanitation is woefully inadequate in South Africa and also that such systems as have been installed are not properly maintained by the appropriate authorities. And this is primarily because the political structures which make authorities responsible to the broad wishes and needs of the people they have been created to serve, simply do not exist. This fact was dramatically highlighted in the black township near Nigel on the east Rand in February 1985:

Offices of the East Rand Development Board in Duduza were attacked and stoned by hundreds of youths. Police fired rubber bullets and birdshot and used tearsmoke to disperse the rampaging youths. The violence flared after residents started dumping buckets of excrement at the local Council Offices. It was done to protest against the toilet-bucket system in use in the township. (*Cape Times*, 19.2.1985)

From the evidence presented to the Carnegie Inquiry, it is clear that Duduza is by no means the only place in South Africa where people are deeply resentful of having to confront daily this particular face of poverty and powerlessness.

Refuse collection is another indication of the same situation. So too is the lack of adequate drainage; the poor condition of roads; and the absence of basic facilities like post-offices, public telephones and libraries; and recreational amenities such as swimming baths, halls, children's playgrounds and sportsfields.

Clarke's Estate in Cape Town has 1 500 houses, home for 15 000 people. But this community has 'no public telephone, no post-office, no bioscope arena, no sportsfields, parks, swimming pool, community centre, old-age home or bank'. Children play in 'filthy open lots'. Many of them are taking to glue-sniffing, a cheap form of drug addiction (10c: 33–4).

Human beings need time and amenities for recreation and relaxation away from the hassles of daily survival in order to maintain a healthy life-style. This need is even greater amongst the poor, whose daily lives are an endless struggle to make ends meet. There is however an inverse relationship in this country between access to recreational facilities and social need.

The problem is widespread, affecting both rural and urban communities, and impinging on the lives of both young and old. In the Orange Free State, Walwyn found that in Clarens for example, 'recreational facilities are practically non-existent. There is a soccer field which has not even been levelled and otherwise, at present, nothing.' (41: 8) In townships on the east Rand, Nel reported that lack of company ranked third as a problem faced by the aged, surpassed only by lack of money and food (141: 6). Ntoane and Makoetle reported that in the single-sex hostels in Mapetla, Soweto, there was not even a canteen or a telephone (2: 10). In Suurbekom in the western Transvaal platteland, the community complained that alcoholism was rife because alcohol consumption offered the only form of relaxation, even for children (2: 15). As David Dewar has explained:

Children grow up in environments which are totally unscaled in terms of the human activities which they must accommodate. Each area, in terms of its feel and the opportunities it offers, is the same as the others. They are simply uni-functional sleeping areas with little or no sense of place. There is nowhere to escape the privations of the overcrowded private dwellings, save the scaleless streets or windswept 'open spaces' which are, in reality, simply unsightly and dangerous dumping grounds for rubbish. (163: 1–2)

The stark contrast between the above description and the beauty of most suburbs where privileged South Africans live is striking. A walk through the streets of Bonteheuwel in Cape Town on one hand and a walk through the beautiful forests of Newlands give one a completely different feel of space and freshness. In Cape Town, the Sea Point front and the edges of Langa are worlds apart. Privileged children in South Africa play in parks where all the facilities are conducive to relaxation and geared to safety, whereas township children play in the busy streets where the danger of fatal accidents is ever present (179: 4–5). Even in the dorps of the platteland the environment is very different in black and white areas. In Hanover, for example, the white part of town is 'a pretty little place' with furrows of running water down the sides of the tarred streets, and beautiful huge trees offering shade against the scorching sun. The other part of the town, for blacks only,

makes one sweat before entering. There is not a tree to be seen on the roadside. The 'streets' are not tarred . . . the houses are monotonous to look at. . . . The lack of recreational facilities adds to the feeling of frustration about employment, housing, etc. There is no playground. Children play in the sandy 'streets' or veld until sunset. (PCS 9: 55)

The absence of adequate facilities in the townships is compounded by the fact that state planning has decreed that they be sited far from city centres and from the public amenities closer to the wealthier parts of the city. Poor and expensive transport hampers access to public spaces like parks, beaches, and mountains.

For the school-going age group, the time spent away from overcrowded squalid homes should add some richness to the lives of the children of the poor, but unfortunately the same negative physical environment exists in schools. In many cases, school buildings are overcrowded and not only lack adequate fittings (including furniture) but are also in a state of disrepair. Lack of teaching aids and inadequate sporting facilities add to this deprivation.

Work places should provide facilities for social intercourse for workers, but these are, 'themselves uni-functional and sterile : they are simply places where people sell their labour. In most industrial areas, for example, there is nowhere for the worker to shop or browse or kick a ball during his lunch-break: often there is not even a place to buy a sandwich.' (163: 23)

Given the distances between living areas of the poor and their work places, many workers rise at 4–4.30 a.m. and return home not before 8 p.m. 'Life is an endless cycle of sleeping and working' (163: 23).

The general picture of housing in South Africa, then, is that for a variety of reasons, including deliberate policy by the state (see Chapter 11), far fewer houses have been built, either by individuals or by the state, in recent decades than were required both for the growing population and for those needing to move with their families from the countryside to jobs in town. The net result has been heavy overcrowding of existing houses, overloading of the urban infrastructure particularly with regard to sewage removal, and (especially during the 1980s), a rapid increase in the number of self-built shacks erected wherever they could be placed without getting torn down by the authorities. Between 1960 and 1980 the proportion of South Africa's total population living in urban areas remained constant whilst the absolute number grew at the same rate as natural population. But it is estimated that over the following 20 years, 1980–2000, the proportion of South Africa's total population living in the cities will increase from 47 to 58 per cent (see Table 1.08). Signs of what this will mean are already visible in Cape Town where, over the five years 1983–8, anything between 300 000 to 600 000 people have moved, mainly it seems from the reserves of the eastern Cape, to live in flimsy shacks. The need for adequate housing and urban infrastructure is already acute. Without a massive reallocation of political priorities and resources it is likely to become worse.

7
Literacy and learning

Since we are all of us not learned and therefore illiterate, we only depend on this land of our forefathers for a living. We have nowhere to go, we can't read and write, so we can't get employment anywhere. So we can't be assisted in improving our only means of survival, the land, because some of us are unable to pay for the expenses.

> – Unemployed male head of an eight-person household in the Transkei (46: 18)

I remember a time when all the good jobs were reserved for the white people because they were the only people who had education. Now things are different, even Africans and coloureds can work in the banks, the post office, and fill other good paying jobs. But the problem with our people is that they cannot afford to keep their children at school, because if they do, the family will starve and by the time the child has obtained his good paying job there will be no family left to enjoy the benefits.

> – Ouma Anna, Philipstown (33: 19)

Any well-educated urban-dweller who has tried to milk a cow or to track game to shoot it for the pot can testify that the ability to read and write is not necessarily the most useful economic skill in some circumstances. But in a modern industrial economy it is difficult, especially in urban areas, to earn one's living without it, particularly if jobs are scarce and employers make literacy the first criterion for selection.

For a country whose industrial revolution has been under way for a full century and where more than half the population is urbanised, the degree of illiteracy in South Africa is staggering. According to the 1980 census (which excluded Transkei and Bophuthatswana), 33 per cent of those Africans over the age of 15 who filled in the census form, judged themselves to be illiterate, whilst 30 per cent of those older than 20 had not achieved an educational level as high as Standard 4 (six years of schooling) and so were 'functionally illiterate'. Amongst whites, by contrast, less than 1 per cent assessed themselves to be illiterate, and the proportion older than 20 with less than Standard 4 education was only 2 per cent. Those classified as coloured or Asian fell as usual somewhere between Africans and whites (263: 5).

The following diagram shows the picture.

Whilst the general level of education of the population as a whole is improving the number of young illiterates, between the ages of 10 and 24, is highly disturbing. The current estimate, based on very rough calculations, is that there are between two and three million (263: 16). From the detailed studies of the Carnegie Inquiry it is possible to piece together a picture of the extent of illiteracy, particularly in the rural areas.

The diagram opposite (7.02) illustrates the degree of illiteracy, by age, in one rural district, Nkandla in KwaZulu.

Whilst the degree of illiteracy does rise with age – to over 80 per cent for

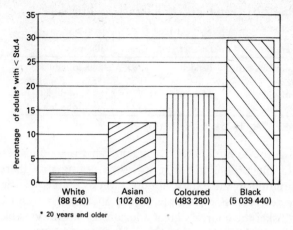

Fig. 7.01: Illiteracy in South Africa, 1980 (263: 5)

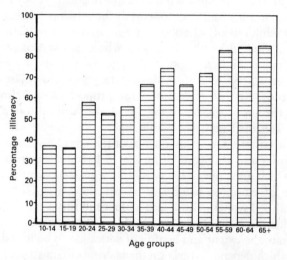

Fig. 7.02: Illiteracy and age, Nkandla, 1983

those who were 55 or older – it is significant to find that more than one-third (35 per cent) of teenagers in the district had never been to school. Ardington notes with regard to Nkandla:

Whereas 68% of the total number of people surveyed had no education at all, this was true of only 48% of the 7–16 age group as opposed to 85% of those over 65 years of age. The speed at which the change is taking place however is quite unsatisfactory and it is unlikely to improve significantly while the system for the provision of education remains unchanged. There can be no justification for providing education in rural areas on a basis different from that in urban areas. (53b: 128)

The story is much the same in other reserves.

Table 7.01: Estimates of illiteracy in different
reserves

Reserve	District	Date	Illiteracy
Bophuthatswana	Bendell	1983	70% of adults
Venda	–	1975	53% of population
KwaZulu	Msinga	1970	80% of population
Transkei	–	1982	66% of adults

Source: 77: 11; 251: 8; 55: 7; 149: 3

The precise figures do not matter too much. What is significant is the order of magnitude of the problem. But it is worth noting that there has been considerable variation in the extent of education available in different areas, even within the reserves. For example, in the Victoria East and Middledrift districts of the Ciskei the church's great educational institutions like Lovedale (Presbyterian), St Matthews (Anglican), and Healdtown (Methodist) took root in the middle of the nineteenth century. An analysis done when the Bantu Education Act of 1953 set up a separate department of education that took over (and, in important instances, destroyed) the mission schools, found that virtually all the children of school-going age in these two districts were at school at a time when in South Africa as a whole it was estimated that only one-third of African children between the ages of 6 and 16 were at school (Wilson and Perrot, 1973: 519). Macquarrie observed: 'The schools in Victoria East and Middledrift, catering for proportionately three times as many pupils as the Union on the average, pass each child through two higher standards than does the Union as a whole' (*ibid*.). The quality of the education was good, albeit austere. One consequence of the mission schools in different parts of the country and of the establishment, in 1916, of the university college of Fort Hare (which grew out of Lovedale) is the existence in the country of a significant elite of educated black South Africans. After all the bible was published in Sotho, Tswana, Xhosa and Zulu a full fifty years before the first Afrikaans (as distinct from High Dutch) bible was published.

The variation in the extent and quality of education to be found in different reserve areas (which depends largely on the historic circumstances as to where churches did or did not plant their schools) is mirrored also on the platteland. Here in some magisterial districts schools up to Standard 4 at least are available for most children, whereas in others, even in the 1980s, there is virtually no provision. In the Hanover district of the Karoo, for example, the only coloured school in a district where 30 per cent of the population was still rural, was in the dorp. There were no coloured farm schools, and only one for Africans. A household survey in the dorp (many of whose inhabitants had of course grown up on farms) revealed that all those over the age of 30 were unlikely to have had more than three years of schooling, whilst those under 30 had an average of five years at school, still not enough for functional literacy. For the sample as a whole, 59 per cent of the adult population living in the town itself had no more than four years of schooling, with more than one-quarter (28 per cent) having had no schooling at all (34: 28–9).

In the magisterial district of Calitzdorp, by contrast, whilst there are no state schools for coloured pupils, there are twelve farm schools plus one big primary school in the town – all owned and administered by the churches, with state assistance. Despite relatively better provision compared with Hanover, the educational status of the population is still low. In a sample survey it was found that 39 per cent of farm workers had received no schooling compared with only 6 per cent in the town itself. The proportions of those who were functionally illiterate (with no more than six years of schooling) were 45 per cent in Bergsig, the coloured township of Calitzdorp, and 80 per cent on the farms (36: 47).

Illiteracy then is a major dimension of poverty all over South Africa, but particularly in the rural areas. It is pervasive throughout the reserves although there are some parts, such as the central Ciskei, where the church's work over a century or more laid a solid educational base. On the platteland the situation varies widely but in general we find that illiteracy is far higher, and educational opportunities much lower, than even in the nearby towns, to say nothing of the more distant cities.

No less striking than the extent of illiteracy is the lack of adequate response to the problem:

State response is most extensively manifested in the Basic Education Programme of the Department of Education and Training (DET), of which several aspects have been criticised. Industrial literacy programmes are on the whole geared to productivity by preparing workers for job-skills training. Three countrywide voluntary organisations and numerous small independent church and community initiatives undertake literacy training according to various methods and with varying degrees of success. While acknowledging the enthusiasm and achievements of many literacy groups, one must not lose sight of the sobering statistic that in 1980, out of an estimated 6 (up to 9) million illiterates in South Africa, all the above efforts taken together assisted no more than 25 000 persons (0.3% of 7.5 million) to attain literacy. (263: 6)

Clearly there is need for a massive literacy campaign. (The degree to which this is possible, let alone probable, in present circumstances will be considered in a later chapter.) The extent of illiteracy and the rate at which it is decreasing (or increasing) is a measure partly of past failures and inadequacies of the educational system and partly of its current capacity. It is to this issue of the current capacity of the formal educational structure that we now turn.

The educational structure

This section draws heavily on the work of Pundy Pillay (95), revised and updated for the book edited for the Carnegie Inquiry by Bill Nasson and John Samuel, *Education: From Poverty to Liberty* (Cape Town, 1989), to which readers are referred for more detail. The basic facts are as follows. Firstly, there is the matter of sheer discrimination in the funding of education by the state, as shown in the accompanying diagram.

African pupils, each with a subsidy of R234 in 1983/4, received only one-seventh (14 per cent) of the subsidy of R1 654 available for white pupils.

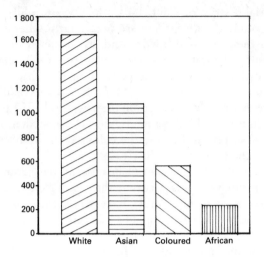

Fig. 7.03: State expenditure per pupil, 1983/4

These statistics understate the actual difference in subsidy to the two groups as virtually all white children of school-going age are at school whilst for black children, particularly in the rural areas, the proportion at school is well below the maximum. If we combine the facts that expenditure per pupil and the proportion of children enrolled at school are lower for blacks than for whites, we find that state expenditure on education per head of population for blacks is one-tenth that for whites.

Bad though these figures are, they mask an even worse inheritance. Only ten years previously, when the country was still in the grip of the Verwoerdian decree that any increase in educational expenditure on blacks had to be paid for by blacks themselves out of funds other than from the central exchequer, the state's contribution to the education of each black pupil was a mere 6.5 per cent (one-fifteenth) that of a white pupil; and the chances, in those days, of a black child actually getting to school was little better than one-half that of the white counterpart.

The absence of resources, not only in the present but also in the past, means that in general the facilities available, and the quality of education provided, for black children of school-going age have always been and remain far below those of white children. As far back as 1920 we discover that whilst four out of every five (78 per cent) white children were at schools, only one in every seven (14 per cent) African children of school-going age was enrolled.

By 1980 virtually all (96 per cent) white children were at school whilst four out of every five (83 per cent) Africans were officially estimated to be at school, although there is strong evidence to suggest that the latter is a considerable overestimate. For example, a detailed study in Nkandla reported that the proportion of children in the 5–14 year age group who were actually in school was less than half (47 per cent) in a district where according to official estimates the proportion was 93 per cent. As there is no apparent reason why the situation should be worse in the area surveyed than in other areas, the question arises 'as to whether possible population undercounts in recent censuses might not have given rise to artificially high national education statistics – there being no reason to question the accuracy of the numbers of children actually at school' (53b: 128). If this is so, then the position is even more serious than that suggested by the official national statistics.

Although the proportion of children at school may be far below the official estimate, the fact remains that the number of black children going to school has risen rapidly over the past decade. Between 1972 and 1982 the total number of African children enrolled at school, from Sub. A to Standard 10, increased by a little more than 7 per cent a year, from 3.1 million to 5.3 million (100: 3). But the failure of government to provide adequate resources to fund this expansion has meant that the quality of education provided has been abysmally low.

Lack of quality

This lack of quality, particularly in comparison with what is available for white pupils, can be measured in a number of different ways. First, there is the provision of teachers. In 1984 the average pupil–teacher ratio (which is somewhat lower than the number of pupils in an average class) was 19:1 for whites and 41:1 for Africans. The following diagram illustrates what has happened to the different racial categories over the period 1970–84.

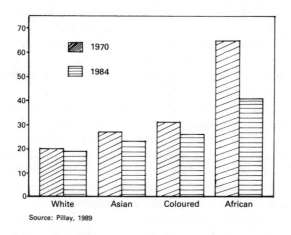

Source: Pillay, 1989

Fig. 7.04: Number of pupils per teacher, 1970–84

There was a considerable improvement from the situation as it was at the beginning of the 1970s, before African schoolchildren started taking direct political action to better their education, but it still remains quite unacceptable. For an average of 41 pupils per teacher (calculated on the assumption that every teacher teaches every available period) often means in practice classes of 90 children or more, which is educationally impossible.

The lack of actual teachers was compounded by the inadequate training which they had received. In KwaZulu, for example, two-thirds of all African teachers in 1982 did not have matric and were teaching, with or without professional qualifications, on the basis of school Junior Certificate or lower. In South Africa as a whole, but excluding the TBVC areas, the proportion of African teachers without matriculation in 1983 was also two-thirds (69 per cent). In the white schools, by contrast, all teachers are matriculated and most of them (97 per cent) have professional teaching qualifications as well (Pillay, 1989).

The lack of proper training is reinforced by a factor that is more difficult to measure yet no less serious – lack of morale. There are, of course, large numbers of dedicated teachers whose lives are devoted to nurturing and enriching the pupils in their charge. But one of the most disturbing insights from the Carnegie Inquiry was the number of reports, seldom committed to paper, that were received of quite appalling breakdown in schools, with teachers often drunk, absent from work, and (in some instances) assaulting – even raping – pupils. This loss of morale in what was long one of the most highly regarded professions amongst South Africans of all races has complex roots that take us to the heart of the South African crisis. For it has much to do with frustration, powerlessness, anger of the unfranchised, combined with the ambivalence and loss of confidence that comes from attacks by schoolchildren who lash out at the teachers as the nearest symbol of an authority they reject. Caught between the government which pays their salaries and militant students intent on overthrowing the whole structure, teachers have little room to manoeuvre and many of them retreat under pressure from all sides into themselves where drink is often the only solace. There can be few more urgent and immediate political tasks in South Africa than rethinking the role of teachers in an oppressive structure so that they may play their full part, with integrity and perseverance in the long march to liberation.

The problems of large classes and poorly qualified teachers, many of them lacking in morale, are compounded by the lack of facilities. Whilst the state has built a number of solid school buildings around the country in recent years the general situation is still chronic. Classrooms are overcrowded, desks insufficient, playing fields inadequate, windows broken, toilets shocking, textbooks unavailable, libraries and laboratories and the various teaching aids, used in modern education, are seldom available.

Consider for example the problems facing an impoverished rural community in Lebowa in the eastern Transvaal, which decided that it simply must have a school for children in the area who had nowhere else to go. The state is willing to subsidise a new school on a rand-for-rand basis, but the money is only paid across after the building is complete and has been passed by the inspector. The community managed to scrape together enough money to build twelve classrooms which enabled 950 children to attend the school. But of the twelve classrooms in existence when one of us visited the school, only five had windowpanes, floors, and blackboards. There were only enough desks for 260 (27 per cent) of the children. One of the classrooms had to be used as the headmaster's study and a staff-room. One day, when they can manage it, the community will finish the school but then, and only then, will the state pay its share.

A further obstacle that faces many black children is one which half a century ago so shocked white South Africa when it was found, by the first Carnegie Commission, to face poor whites. It is the problem of hunger whilst trying to learn. We have already seen the extent to which, in widely differing parts of the country – ranging from the rich farms of Stellenbosch in the western Cape to impoverished Lebowa in the eastern Transvaal – a large proportion of children are reported coming to school hungry. In this context it is worth bearing in mind:

There have been persistent reports from teachers and others, of lessened fatigue and improved powers of concentration with school-feeding and of better school atten-dance. In the study by Reddy (1977) on school failure among coloured children in Cape Town, 90% of the teachers cited absenteeism as the chief cause. As regards malnutrition, 75% emphatically agreed that 'the child who is hungry and ill-fed lacks the energy and enthusiasm to do his school work'. (220: 9)

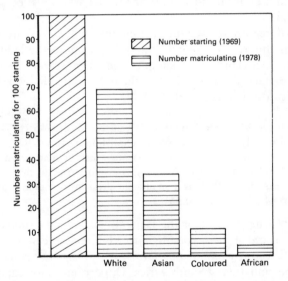

Fig. 7.05: Pupil progress: Standards 1–10, 1969–78

In a country where no less than one-third of black children under 14 are estimated to be malnourished and underweight for their age, it is perhaps small wonder that so many drop out from school. But the rate of attrition is very high. Of every 100 children who started school in 1969 the number who had completed matric by the end of 1978 was only 4. The comparative figure for whites was 69. Moreover, of all those African children who left school in 1982, before the crisis of the mid-1980s erupted, it is estimated that more than half (53 per cent) had got no further than Standard 2. Indeed one-quarter (24 per cent) left school without even obtaining Sub. A. Only 10 per cent of school-leavers in that year had reached Standards 9 or 10 (Pillay, 1989).

Although the number of African pupils passing matriculation increased 14 times between 1970 and 1983, Pillay argues that it is matric exemption (which gives access to university and hence to professional careers) which is more significant than the number of passes. He finds that in 1978, whites (who made up 15 per cent of the population) still constituted three-quarters (74 per cent) of all matric exemptions whilst Africans (who constituted 73 per cent of the population), with only 5 000 pupils qualifying for exemption, made up 16 per cent of the total.

In addition to hunger and the discouraging circumstances of many schools, there are three major reasons for the high drop-out rate. First, there is the sheer cost of education from the family's point of view. Fees and levies are not negligible, especially for those living below the bread-line and costly uniforms are often required as well. In addition, as children get older, there is the opportunity cost of earnings forgone whilst they are studying. Associated with this is a reason which arises from the necessity for many mothers to work. In the absence of crèches or pre-schools, often the only person available to take care of small children is an older sister or brother who must be taken out of school to help at home.

But the third reason is even more fundamental. Places are simply not available for all children who enter school to go on up the ladder. In most districts on the platteland, for example, the farm schools that exist are invariably for primary levels only. Few of them go beyond Standard 6. Thus in a study of Calitzdorp it was found:

There are no high schools for 'coloured' pupils in the whole district. Those who do reach high school usually choose a school in Oudtshoorn. To any Calitzdorp family with a child about to attend high school, it means a drastic increase in the monthly outlay. Boarding fees have to be paid as well as transport costs for the occasional visit home. For these reasons . . . there is a significant drop in the number of those with more than 8 years of schooling. (36: 45)

It is probably true to say that the general educational problems outlined above are experienced at their worst by farm children. One in five of all black South Africans lives on white-owned farms, which together constitute about four-fifths of the land area of South Africa. Opportunities for education there are more constrained than anywhere else in the country. Perhaps the chief difficulty about education on the farms is that the existence of the schools is entirely at the discretion of the farmer. If he decides to build a school for children from his and his neighbours' farms, the state will subsidise the building and pay the salaries of the teachers. If, on the other hand, he decides not to put up a school it will not be built, and if he decides to close an existing school he has the power to do so. Farmers' attitudes vary widely but the prevailing ethos is not hugely in favour of educating the children of their labourers, particularly beyond the first three or four grades. Few children have the opportunity of going to secondary school. Few secondary schools exist in the rural areas outside the reserves, and the few that are available are, by the nature of things, too far away for most farm children to reach, as few farm families can afford boarding fees.

With regard to primary schools, whilst these are more generally available, there is wide variation between areas, with some parts of the country having a fairly comprehensive network of schools and yet in other magisterial districts there are virtually no schools. Even where the lower primary schools do exist, there are several difficulties. First, there is the problem of transport. Most children walk but the distances are often considerable. A second difficulty is that for many children there is not enough food in the family for an adequate breakfast before leaving home. Evidence from the western Cape shows that, on those mornings when schools are able, by means of voluntary contributions and a small levy on pupils, to provide soup for children there is 100 per cent attendance, even through the wettest months; without the soup, attendance would drop to 50 or 60 per cent (97: 24).

A third difficulty concerns the farmers' need for labour. 'School-rooms', reported one research worker for the Carnegie Inquiry, 'are not secure: children are regularly poached at peak harvest periods and also removed to do intermittent work as herd boys, in addition to other agricultural duties' (97: 37). Furthermore, 'earnings, however trifling, are needed as a matter of course, not as an exceptional response to a particular crisis of family poverty. So, at some time between roughly the ages of twelve and fourteen, many farm labourers' children are no longer a costly and burdensome presence at school. For these young people childhood is at an end.' (97: 21)

Fourth, there is a problem difficult to quantify but nonetheless real for all that. Even where children *are* at school there is a social stigma, felt throughout the country but reported particularly in the western Cape, against farm schooling.

In general discussion, teaching staff seemed very aware of urban opinion which persistently devalues and denigrates farm schools. ... [There was] a sharp sense of bitterness, and enormous resentment at the attributional status of educational and social inferiority which defines their position. Headmasters are pretty much unanimously agreed that their schools find it difficult to shake off the derogatory meaning which the term *plaasskool* [farm school] has aquired, with its customary implications of poor status and inferiority. (97: 17)

But the real difficulty facing farm children is that they are growing up in an agricultural world where, because of mechanisation and the changing technology of production, the demand for unskilled labour is steadily shrinking but where they are not getting the education that will enable them to make the transition to urban jobs. In noting the virtual absence of farm schools in the Hanover district of the Karoo and drawing attention to the high proportion (approximately 60 per cent) of both the African and the coloured population who are functionally illiterate, researchers for the Carnegie Inquiry pointed out: 'The average inhabitant of a Hanover township or farm does not have an education base adequate to make the geographic, sectoral, and occupational transition needed to escape poverty' (34: 55).

It is this economic environment in which school-leavers, half of them not even properly literate, find themselves when they leave school that poses the most fundamental educational problem of all. Unemployment in the economy as a whole is rife and getting worse. It is estimated, as we have seen, that between 1970 and 1981 the level of unemployment in South Africa nearly doubled from 11.8 per cent to 21.1 per cent (Simkins, 1982). These statistics give only a general indication of the extent of unemployment. Micro-studies in the Carnegie Inquiry and elsewhere show that the two groups which bear the brunt of unemployment are black women, especially in the rural areas, and black school-leavers.

In a detailed study of unemployment and education in the eastern Cape, it was reported:

A combination of factors operates to nullify the efficacy of education in getting employment. For the majority of Blacks [Africans] destined to work at a semi-skilled and unskilled levels such factors as age, sex, previous experience and, most importantly, access to contacts who are already employed, are better predictors of success than education. The reasons for this are numerous and intertwined. Segmentation, the operation of internal labour markets, deskilling of jobs, the recession and the need to control the labour force all interact to down-grade education as a 'giver of life-chances'. The actual content of education in these circumstances appears almost irrelevant. Similarly it was shown that although on the surface the expectations of school-goers in respect of job opportunities appears unrealistic, given the structure of the racial division of labour in South Africa, attempts to break the 'Standard 8 barrier' offer the only realistic chance of gaining employment on criteria other than happenstance. For the approximately 10 per cent of students who go beyond Standard 8, employment in white-collar jobs is the only realistic alternative facing them. For those who fail the prospects are bleak. (120: 40)

A structural situation where education offers absolutely no guarantee of work except for the few and where one in ten manages to pass 10 years of schooling seems tailor-made to cause huge dissatisfaction. For the vast majority of pupils, there are, as we have seen, all kinds of barriers against reaching the top grades – not least the overcrowded classrooms and the lack of proper library or laboratory facilities. For all those young people the current educational system is clearly worthless.

This view is reinforced by the racist, separatist philosophy underlying the present government's policy of 'Christian National Education' which led, more than 30 years ago, to the imposition of the bitterly resented Bantu education. Government spokesmen at the time made it clear that one goal of the new policy was to ensure that blacks were not educated for jobs beyond their proper station in an apartheid South Africa. Much has changed since those early days, including a vastly increased demand for more highly skilled people of all races, but deep suspicion of the goals of 'Bantu' and 'Coloured' education remains. It is small wonder that, in the light of this philosophy combined with the harsh facts of the country's racist educational system, the crisis in the black schools is so profound. There are few countries of the world at any time in history which have seen children taking to the streets, prepared to make huge sacrifices, even to die, for the sake of better education. And this we have witnessed in South Africa throughout the extraordinary decade which began in 1976 as a peaceful demonstration in Soweto against the language component of the syllabus.

Having to learn Afrikaans instead of English would, the schoolchildren felt, restrict their capacity to find out about the world. In the end the children won that particular battle. But in the process of doing so they brought down upon their heads the armed wrath of the state which, in reacting so violently to the protests, escalated the confrontation to an entirely new level. There is no doubt that the repressive measures by the state led to an increasingly desperate search by schoolchildren to find effective means of changing the structures in which they were trapped. Boycotts, particularly in 1976, 1980 and in the years after 1984, became more frequent and were joined sometimes to general one- or two-day stay-aways by workers. During the harsh months of 1985 the slogan 'Liberation before Education' was increasingly heard; at the same time, voices were raised within the black community warning against too facile an assumption that boycotting of schools would necessarily bring about a speedy end to the existing oppressive political order.

Indeed, although it is hard to see how such boycotts could really challenge the might of the state, the authorities took the most extreme measures in trying to stamp out the protests. In the wake of the Soweto march of 1976 and of subsequent protests against the state's reaction, several hundred children were shot dead. The cycle of violence which starts with peaceful protest (mainly by means of student marches and boycott of classes) followed by the violent reaction of the state (using sjamboks [whips], teargas, rubber bullets, live ammunition, detention and, on occasion, torture) and then by further protest (including stone-throwing), and further state reaction, has grown ever more vicious, especially during 1985 and 1986. After examining the evidence, the New York-based Lawyers' Committee for Human Rights was moved to describe the process as a 'war against children'. The description seems apt. According to official statistics, the police (excluding the Defence Force) killed at least 201 children during 1985. 'A survey of 77 of those deaths . . . revealed that 44 of the children were shot dead, 17 burned to death, three were run over by police vehicles, four were drowned while fleeing from police, two were beaten to death, one was stabbed, and six died of "unknown causes". Nineteen of the [77] victims . . . were under ten years old.' (Lawyers' Committee for Human Rights, 1986: 42)

The report provides detailed and chilling evidence of state violence, largely perpetrated by the police and the army against children. In South Africa education cannot be analysed simply in terms of its contribution to poverty, nor placed in the public arena as a matter only for earnest debate amongst academics. It has become a major battle-ground for the future of the country, requiring special attention from all those wishing to be involved in the search for a more just and humane society.

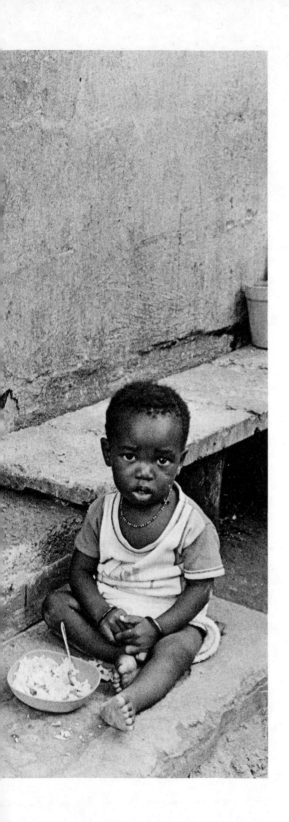

8
Bitter fruit of
powerlessness

I have been looking for work for two years and other people have waited for contracts for longer than six years. This is why there are so many *tsotsis* [gangsters] stealing and kidnapping people.

— Unemployed woman in Kgano,
Qwa Qwa (297: 29)

You can see the cruelty that has befallen those of us who stand here, and what it is. Our small problem is that most people are now drinking liquor because of hunger; because you find sometimes that if you are hungry you must drink to give you support in the stomach. That will be because you have not managed to get a ... job. ... Maybe someone has taken you and made you work and when he was supposed to pay in the evening he was not there, he has disappeared. ... You go and sleep in hunger having worked in hunger. ... Now you will end up seeing a lot of people eating from rubbish bins like this. It is a matter of losing heart because of not having jobs and having to help the stomach through drinking.

— Unemployed man in Maseru,
Lesotho (124: 20).

For those enduring poverty there are two realities that add considerably to the pain caused by the deprivations of hunger and other material want. Both derive from the state of powerlessness in which those who are poor generally have to live. One relates to the harsh circumstances and the sense of despair bred by the economic and social environment in which households and individuals find themselves; the other to the callous impact of state policies and practices. The two aspects are closely interrelated — indeed mutually reinforcing — but for clarity it is helpful to consider them separately, as far as possible.

Economic and social environment

One of the most tangible social consequences of poverty is crime. We shall not explore here the complex roots of criminal behaviour but note simply the observation that where there is acute poverty, where work is difficult to find, and where society is in a process of upheaval for whatever reason (such as urbanisation or resettlement), people are more likely to rob or assault others, sometimes in order to gain a living or to make ends meet; sometimes out of sheer frustration. Crime is both a product and a cause of profound insecurity and despair in which millions of people find themselves trapped.

Cape Town has the reputation of being the most crime-ridden centre in South Africa. Indeed, it is believed to have the highest crime rate of any large city in the Western world (93: 1). More than twice as many people were murdered in the tiny Cape Peninsula as were murdered in the whole of the United Kingdom in 1986. The murder rate in Cape Town (530 murders per 1 million inhabitants in 1985) was nearly three times that of New York (*Cape*

Times, 12.8.1987). The following table highlights the extent to which South Africa as a whole, and the Cape Flats in particular, suffer from a level of violent crime that is staggeringly high.

Table 8.01: International comparisons of crime, 1979 (*rates per 100 000 of population*)

Category	West Germany	United Kingdom	South Africa	Cape Flats
Murder	6	1	27	48
Rape	11	n.a.	63	116
Robbery	379	27	178	481
Assault	278	176	1 047	1 328

Source: 93: 2

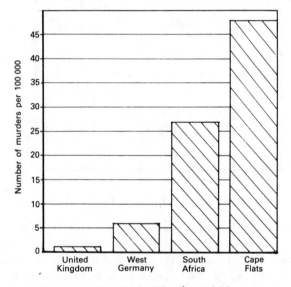

Fig. 8.01: Murder, 1979

Analysis of the situation in Cape Town reveals a clear correlation between levels of crime and the socio-economic environment, as may be seen in the following table showing violent crime rates for two affluent and three poor areas of the city.

The murder rate in the black township of Gugulethu in Cape Town in 1983 was 30–35 times higher than in the economically secure suburbs of Pinelands and Rondebosch in the same city. Reported incidents of rape, robbery, and assault were all far higher in suburbs where poverty is endemic than in the middle-class areas. A similar picture of the level and distribution of crime emerges from examination of other cities in South Africa. In the smaller towns too, such as Worcester, a major source of dissatisfaction expressed by people is 'the poor environment, including gangs' (32: 73).

Table 8.02: Violent crime rates (per 100 000) for affluent and poor areas of Cape Town, 1983

Police district	Murder	Rape	Robbery	Assault
Affluent areas:				
Pinelands	4	0	85	61
Rondebosch	5	34	83	107
Poor areas:				
Gugulethu	150	179	490	1 573
Elsies River	48	71	359	383
Manenberg	63	60	1 072	495

Source: 93: 10

Fig. 8.02: Murder in Cape Town, 1983

One of the more striking features of crime in South Africa is the extent to which it is now to be found in the rural areas, especially in the poorer, more densely populated parts of the reserves such as the resettlement camps. In the tiny homeland of Qwa Qwa, for example (where population increased from an already overcrowded 23 000 in 1970 to approximately 500 000 people by the mid-1980s), one of the closest settlements, Kgano, is notorious for the high rate of crime. Residents recognise that this results from the density of habitation, the high rate of unemployment (and underemployment), and the lack of other income-generating resources.

Migrants returning home with wages know that the walk from the bus-stop home is a risky business; people keep to their own sites after dark to avoid roaming gangs of *tsotsis* (gangsters), and they know that the *tsotsis* are, in fact, their own children and those of their neighbours. Attempts to build networks of neighbourliness are in part a direct response to this menace: people who can be persuaded to address one as 'father' or 'brother' by day are less likely, perhaps, to harass by night. (52: 25)

The *tsotsis* slaughter and kidnap people and ask for their money. They rob people and their things. At night you cannot even walk from here to the church. It is dangerous for a woman because you cannot walk at night. It is therefore better to stay at home and to lock the doors for if you die it is better to die at home. . . . If you have 20 cents in your pocket they will steal it. (297: 28)

Soon after the Mofokeng household arrived in Kgano they experienced great problems with *tsotsis*. 'In the nights when people would sleep, gangs of *tsotsis* would enter into their houses, after breaking open the doors, and demand money from them.' During the course of one night in 1974 Selina and her mother suddenly awoke after hearing a bang on their door. 'Three *tsotsis* were standing in the house. The *tsotsis* told us they were unemployed and demanded money from us, but they did not say how much.' Selina recalled that her mother refused to give them any money. 'The *tsotsis* did not have any money but they fought with my mother.' She and her mother then ran away to sleep in the house of chief Morena as he was the one who had given them their site. When they returned to their homestead the next morning they found that all their dishes, pots and saucepans had been stolen. Selina also heard that the *tsotsis* had broken into the house of their neighbour and forced the lady to give them R20. (297: 29)

In both Pienaar (Kangwane)and Winterveld (Bophuthatswana), 'house-breaking and robbery are very common. People keep their doors locked all the time. In Winterveld people complain that the police give no protection, and are only seen when they come to harass the people for illegal residence and private schools. Alcoholism is a common problem in both areas.' (2: 18)

The vulnerability of a woman living alone, or possibly with her children, in the densely crowded, isolated resettlement areas whilst her husband is away as a migrant worker is one of the hidden realities of life in many parts of the country. In Ekuvukeni in KwaZulu, for example, a graphic description was given to one of us when visiting the area, of how women would lie in fear in their homes whilst outside the *tsotsis* would call, 'Is anybody at home?' If the woman should answer (or indeed not answer at all) then the gang would know that there was no man in the house and that it was thus safe to break down the door and rob the women and children inside. People have not yet, it would seem, learnt the survival technique of the American ghettoes where a woman, caught in a similar situation, will bark like a dog.

Not all resettlement areas are as bad as Qwa Qwa, Ekuvukeni, Pienaar or Winterveld. In Bendell, north of Kuruman: 'There is little crime, a few assaults, and not much theft' (77: 22), but evidence from around the country suggests that Bendell is something of an exception. More and more, in the crowded rural areas crime has become a plague, ravaging the community.

In Vaalkop (KwaZulu), another resettlement camp that looks like an old-style village, quaint and innocuous, one inhabitant describes how:

At night they go from house to house, robbing, raping, threatening to shoot, hacking people up and generally raising Cain. During the day they hang around in local shebeens, get drunk, smoke dagga [marijuana], and generally carry on as if they were in Umlazi [Durban], Jabavu [Johannesburg] or some other township. (78: 17)

'The point is', writes Buntu Mfenyana, 'that knifings, rape, abductions, drunkenness, and all the other aberrations which we tend to associate with urban townships like Soweto, Alexandra, Western Native and many others, have become part of the daily life in the so-called "rural areas" ' (78: 5). In the Msinga district there are 'hut burnings and murder, fence cutting and theft, starvation and ignorance, tribesmen feuding with automatic weapons, tribesmen working in South Africa's towns and cities as migrant labour, women hoeing rocky fields or sitting at the roadside selling produce imported from Natal' (55: 1).

As long ago as 1954 the government-appointed Tomlinson Commission calculated that the Msinga area could only carry 2 100 families adequately, compared to the 1980 estimate of 14 000 extended families of 10–12 individuals each, and cattle numbering 17 400 instead of the estimated 72 600 in 1980 (55: 5). According to the 1970 census, over 80 per cent of Msinga's population was illiterate, which is not surprising given estimates of school attendance as low as 30 per cent of the total number of children of school-going age (55: 7–8). Some Msinga households are surviving on as little as R25 per month. The pressure on the land by man and beast has created an explosive situation where survival depends on an 'underground economy' with theft, poaching, inter-clan fighting, cultivation and sale of dagga. The latter is the best cash crop in the area, for five paces square of land yield up to R200 (55: 11).

The sense of lawlessness and instability in Msinga is frightening. Real power is passing from the chief and his headmen into the hands of young men whose expectations are sharpened by contact with the cities, yet constantly frustrated by the whole apparatus of apartheid: they have learned how to survive by illicit means and how to wield authority through the barrel of a gun. The violence in Msinga left at least 100 people dead in 1983 alone. Although Msinga has been rightly termed a 'community at war with itself' there is evidence that external factors are fuelling the fire of violence in the area in the form of mercenaries like Lieutenant Johann Verster, sentenced to eight years in jail for incidents involving the death of 14 tribesmen in 1979. Guns also find their way into Msinga from national servicemen who exchange them for dagga (55: 13,18).

The effect of crime of such a magnitude in both urban and rural areas has far-reaching implications for the community exposed to it. On one hand there is a sense of fear and insecurity as expressed by residents of Vrygrond in Cape Town, where people live in constant fear of their lives. Youngsters known to residents join the gangs and smash up people's homes and rob them of their possessions (10b: 2). On the other hand there is the effect on the value system of the community, especially the young and their attitude to crime. For example, when asked about her gangster son, a mother answered, 'He had to be a gangster . . . this keeps the family going,' and pointing to a fridge she proudly says, 'Without him I would not have this fridge' (10b: 4).

The most disturbing feature, however, seems to be reflected in the children in some of these areas. For example in Elsies River in Cape Town, because there are no parks or sportsfields in their area, the children are forced to play in filthy open lots and seek their own pastimes. Like all people these children tend to model themselves on the dominant characters in their community, namely the gangsters. And as part of their games they re-enact sensational scenes which they observe. Given the constant contact they have with gang

Jessie Tamboer, Grahamstown, June 1988

Jessie Tamboer loved her children so much that she could not bear to see them suffering. Unable to pay for their education and to buy them food and seeing no alternative, the 36-year-old mother of two decided to kill herself. At the end of last week, after telling her 13-year-old daughter, Grace, to go to sleep, Jessie Tamboer poured 5 litres of paraffin over herself and looked for a match. After searching in vain for a short while, she went to a tin filled with coal standing in front of her little shack and held her paraffin-soaked clothes in the fire. She was immediately engulfed by flames but did not utter a sound as she walked around the yard burning. Mr Gladman Makeba, who lived in a house behind her, was the first to see the horrifying scene. 'I saw a woman burning with big red flames and she was just walking, without even screaming. I quickly fetched some water and threw it at her but there was too much fire. Only after another man also poured water over her did she stop burning. It must have taken about 20 minutes from the time I saw her to the time when there were no flames,' he said. While she was burning somebody called an ambulance which came shortly after the flames had been extinguished. Ms Tamboer was rushed to Settlers Hospital but died later that night. The superintendent of the hospital, Dr Briscoe, said that Ms Tamboer was brought in with 90 percent burns. Jessie's younger sister, who is now looking after the two children, said that Jessie had for some time been depressed. Early last year her husband, Solomon Little, was shot and killed by a policeman in Port Elizabeth. They said at the time that he had been involved in a burglary and had resisted arrest. 'Jessie did not have enough money to bury him and she could not forgive herself for that. At times she would just suddenly start sobbing without any apparent reason,' Julia Tamboer said. Jessie shared two rooms with her sisters and their children and her mother. Because it was so crowded they would take turns at not sleeping at home. Of the 15 people, only one person had a job, while four others received money from old-age pensions and disability grants. 'But Jessie had no money, she could not buy food for her children and could not send them to school. In May she went to the Grahamstown Area's District Relief Association (Gadra) and was given some clothes. Agency workers told her she should get birth certificates for her children. She then went to the Department of Home Affairs to get the birth certificates but was told to wait for three months. 'She could not wait that long,' Julia said. Grace, who in talking about the death of her mother and now having to look after her five-year-old brother, Paul, displays a maturity far beyond her 13 years, says that her mother had tried her best to look after them. 'She was a good mother and cared a lot for us. She wanted to work but could not find anything. . . . After she was taken to the hospital she sent a message to her mother asking for forgiveness and to look after me and my brother,' Grace said. (*Weekend Argus*, 4.6.1988) members hanging around their play area, negative influences on the young are inevitable (10c: 33–4).

Fear and uncertainty

The feelings of insecurity with which those who are poor must live their daily lives are caused not only by the widespread crime detailed above but also by constant economic worries about loss of jobs, income, and homes. Poverty, as Mrs Witbooi of Philipstown has pointed out (p. 14), 'is not knowing where your next meal is going to come from, and always wondering when the council is going to put your furniture out and always praying that your husband must not lose his job.'

The web of insecurity and fear is very real. In Clarke's Estate, Cape Town, explained Mrs Theunis, 'You suffer – you are not certain of your life or anything else. I lost my job because of my nerves. Because there is no crèche to look after my children while I am working, I used to fear for their safety.' (10c: 23) In March 1983 she was evicted for being in arrears with rent and, as a result, her baby was born prematurely at 7 months.

Farm labourers also find themselves under threat of eviction by their employers for failing to satisfy demands, however unreasonable they may be. For example:

The question arises in relation to the practice of a farmer making the continued employment of his employee conditional upon his employee's children or relatives also making themselves available to work. It is common for such a parent to be evicted/ dismissed once one of his children leaves for employment elsewhere. While this condition may be *contra bonos mores* and severable it appears there is nothing to prevent the farmer from terminating his employee's employment on reasonable notice and there is no remedy available to the worker to prevent such termination. (84: 21)

The fear of unemployment and its consequences adds greatly to the burden of poverty. The uncertainty and humiliation experienced by people waiting for UIF benefits, disability grants, workmen's compensation allowances, and old-age pensions, are detailed in the next section but it is important to note the devastating impact that bureaucratic inefficiency has upon the economic environment in which those who are poor must live.

But, when one takes into consideration the risk of family breakdown under the migratory labour system, it is women, in the rural areas, who suffer the heaviest burdens of uncertainty and fear. In Qwa Qwa: 'When the father is gone he forgets about the children.' 'A woman never knows how much her husband earns . . . He may spend his money on drink, or on other women but one can never know' (297: 30). My husband, explained one Transkei mother with three children, 'never sent any money since he went away and he has never come back. I don't know whether he's alive or dead.' (46: 18) And in Gazankulu: 'Men often do not care for their families. When they come back at Christmas or Good Friday, they do not bring anything to their family. The time when the return of the father or the brother was a time of rejoicing and happiness is long past.' (66: 5)

Even when the husband is monogamous, there is the constant problem of reliability of remittances, because of the illiteracy of husbands and wives, the low wages, the poor postal system in the rural areas, and the general inadequate communications between towns and the countryside. The failure of remittances to arrive could signal all sorts of things to the woman in the loneliness of her household. Is he well? Is he injured at work? Has he been assaulted by *tsotsis*? Is he arrested? Or has he lost his job? These agonising questions cause in women serious anxieties that are rarely recognised by health personnel consulted for various ailments. Given the estimate that in Gazankulu in the northern Transvaal, anything between 50 and 75 per cent of households are primarily dependent on incomes from migrant labour and given the assumption that this is likely to be true of other reserves, the problem assumes alarming proportions (67: 6). For those women who, for one reason or another, even before the abolition of the pass laws in 1986, were legally permitted to live with their husbands in urban areas, the disastrous consequences of divorce create a major threat. Because of the highly sexist nature of South African society in general and of the African community in particular, men can hold their wives hostage. Until 1986 the provisions of influx control legislation were such that, if an African woman divorced her husband after acquiring residential rights (in terms of Section 10(c) of the Urban Areas Act), she then lost her right to remain in the city and consequently her job, if she was employed. She had to return to the rural area from which she came (87: 8). The partial relaxation of the pass laws has eased the legal difficulties facing some, though by no means all, women, but the shortage of housing means that the practical problems of finding somewhere to live remain awesome. Moreover the problem of securing maintenance for herself and her children is a nightmare.

Alcohol

The insecurities and fears experienced by those who are poor are further exacerbated by alcohol – the effects of which are wreaking havoc in both urban and, more recently, rural areas of the country. The problems associated with liquor are not, of course, peculiar to the poor but their effects are often considerably more devastating for those involved because of their greater vulnerability coupled with limited access to rehabilitative facilities.

There are no national statistics kept of alcoholism but from reports in the papers, discussions with interested groups, and casual observation in areas where poor people live, one gets a clear impression of the seriousness of the problem. Poor people themselves make plain their concern and their powerlessness to deal adequately with it. On the farms of the western Transvaal, Ntoane and Makoetle were told that alcoholism was a major problem because it was the only available form of relaxation. Children not at school also found pleasure in it (2: 15). In the northern Transvaal widespread alcoholism was also reported (66: 7, 11).

Indeed, from personal experience in the Tzaneen district we know that men and women, young and old, even those breast-feeding their children, sit from morning to evening in beer-gardens with loud music, drinking so-called home-brew which is extensively advertised on the radio. This area has several villages with liquor outlets owned by more powerful members of the local community. However the same villages often lack basic facilities like dairies. Further south too, in the Mhala district of the eastern Transvaal it was reported:

The alcohol trade is flourishing and is supported by extensive radio advertising. Bottlestore owners will not part with the exact sales figures, but say that business is 'very good'. This is confirmed by the number of powerful people getting into the bottle-store business. 8 of the 14 bottle-stores in Mhala are owned by chiefs, headmen, or ex-members of Gazankulu parliament. The Shangaan–Tsonga Development Corporation also owns one. (192: 7)

At the other end of the country, in Stellenbosch – an area well known for its superb wines – it was found that the practice of giving free alcoholic drinks to farm labourers as part of their wages (the tot system) was still very frequent (184: 5–6). The same theme, employer promotion of alcohol abuse, was noted on some Natal sugar-cane farms (278: 11–12).

And, for many, alcohol is also an important means of earning. As Sis Dinah of Nyanga in Cape Town explained:

You know, people do not understand why we sell liquor. They say that we are corrupting the community. They claim that we are evil because we call to other people's husbands and sons to come with their sealed wage packets to our shebeens. They say we are breaking family lives. But I want to tell you the honest truth. I started selling liquor in 1965. This is when my husband left to stay with another woman. He left me with five kids. I had to feed, clothe, and educate them. Mind, these are only the kids. We must still pay rent and do other things. Where are you supposed to get that money, when you know that the money you work for ends up paying the fares to Bellville? If you want to survive you must make a plan. (10a: 16)

Poverty does not always breed boredom, but one of the striking features of the research findings of the Carnegie Inquiry is the extent to which, under the conditions prevailing in the small towns or dorps and in the rural areas (including the resettlement camps), there is virtually nothing to do. There are no fields to till; no cattle to be tended. There is not the rich traditional social structure with the concomitant rituals of kinship and neighbourliness that is to be found in the anthropologists' reports of earlier societies, fifty or even thirty years ago. Boredom hangs like a dark cloud. And, closely associated with it, despair.

In noting the widespread drunkenness amongst the poor in Willowmore in the Karoo, Nomusa Ndaba points out: 'Plain poverty and adverse social circumstances have a lot to do with this high incidence of alcoholism, for alcohol has a numbing and care-diminishing effect which makes life more tolerable for those who have to struggle daily for the bare necessities of living' (209: 9). Behind alcohol and violence lies the despair that eats away at the soul and overwhelms individuals with a sense of utter hopelessness (300: 21).

Burden of the state

As far as those enduring poverty in southern Africa are concerned, there are four main areas where the South African state creates additional burdens for the poor to bear, over and above those already discussed. Firstly, there is a net of legislation and regulations, the most notorious having been the pass laws, in which the poor become entangled because of the fact that virtually all the strategies individuals can adopt against poverty involve breaking the law in some way. Secondly, there is the whole policy of forced removals in both urban and rural environments which impinge primarily upon the poor. Thirdly, there is the burden of taxation, both formal and informal, whereby the state and its officials extract 'surplus' from people who have none to spare, in order to use it for purposes that are seldom of direct, or even indirect, benefit to those who have to pay. Finally, there is the bureaucratic jungle of red tape woven by officials whose actions and inactions can enormously increase human suffering.

As the burden imposed by the South African state is both a manifestation and a cause of poverty, much of the description and analysis of the consequences of state action will be dealt with in a later chapter (11). Here we focus particularly on the web of red tape in which people seeking a way out from poverty have all too frequently become entangled and, because it is closely related, we also focus on the harsh impact of insensitive bureaucrats.

Whilst it is the attempt to move from countryside to town that down the years has probably caused poor people most difficulties in their relations with the South African state, there are other strategies for survival which have also led to direct confrontation with the authorities. Perhaps the most pervasive of these relates to trading. Again and again in research papers prepared for the Carnegie Inquiry, evidence occurs of police harassing people for trying to sell goods. Whether it is hawkers selling food, shebeen-queens providing liquor, or drug-runners peddling their mandrax or (less lethal) dagga, informal trading forms one of the key strategies for survival adopted by poor people (and sometimes by people who are far from poor). It is important to distinguish between different types of trading and to emphasise the harm caused to the poor by making illegal certain kinds of trading that are not damaging to society. Hawking of fruit, vegetables, or even meat may sometimes be a nuisance, occasionally a competitive threat to more established business, possibly an additional health risk, but it is quite different from smuggling hard drugs. Yet time and again hawkers on the edge of survival tell of the additional difficulties caused by police harassment. For example, in Soweto:

I spend my time by selling vegetables, especially spinach. I manage to get this through a friend's transport. He usually collects us – we are about five – from our different places to the farms. For a return trip it is about R5 depending on the distance. Then for the stock R14, and a bundle is about 20 cents, which could make a total of about R22 profit, depending how it sells. One should be stationed at a spot where there are many people passing so that they can see and buy. . . . At times we are harassed by police when conditions are not favourable because they claim the private sector is not hygienic. (82: 27)

In remote rural areas the picture is much the same. For example, in the Nkandla district of KwaZulu, 'a significant number of respondents volunteered the information that they had been harassed by police for selling at pension [pay-out] points without a licence'. Goods had been confiscated and prosecutions threatened. The licence itself seemed to be too expensive or too difficult to obtain (53a: 60). Further south in the small towns of the Transkei the familiar pattern is repeated. After interviews with 137 street traders in 13 of Transkei's 28 small towns, one Carnegie research worker concluded that 'municipal police all over Transkei harass the street traders by confiscating their goods, fining them, and even imprisoning them' (237: 29). In the capital itself, Umtata, new bye-laws have prohibited hawkers from staying in any one place longer than five minutes. At the same time penalties for infringing the regulations have increased, with hawkers being sentenced in 1982 to two months' imprisonment without option of a fine compared with an earlier penalty of a R10 or R20 fine (237: 23). But, as the study confirms, hawkers are themselves amongst the poorest, most marginalised members of the society. The burden of police harassment and magisterial punishment adds a heavy load to shoulders already weighed down by extreme poverty.

Another form of official harassment focuses not on the selling of goods but on the collection of material by people for their own use. In Qwa Qwa, for example, a researcher reported that one chief and his indunas 'often arrested people for collecting firewood and imposed fines' (297: 14). The chief was trying to protect the fuel for other people who had traditionally collected it, but for the people fined there was no other alternative. There were no shops in the area to which they had been forcibly removed and, even when the shops came, not all families had money to buy even basic fuel. They simply had to go out and collect it where they could.

Catch 22 in the bureaucratic jungle

The problems of securing benefits as an unemployed person are exacerbated by structural factors that discriminate against certain sections of the community in South Africa, rendering them more vulnerable to impoverishment. The Act providing for unemployment benefit lays down a minimum period of two weeks' unemployment before one can claim benefits. There is also a penalty clause which raises this period to six weeks for those who have been discharged through their own fault or who have resigned. People who are trying to enter the labour market for the first time do not qualify for benefits at all. ('This is not England,' say the officials to the applicant.) Given the inadequate and limited cover provided by this Act, one would have thought that there would be no major bureaucratic problems in gaining access to the benefits accruing. A study by the Black Sash in Natal provides ample illustration of the major obstacles. These include the failure to pay benefits promptly. The study found that approximately three-quarters of the complaints received in one advice office related to the fact that people had to wait for an average of nearly eight months (125: 2–3). Other difficulties relate to the fact that subsequent payments are often irregular, that cheques get lost

Struggle for survival

Mr Sibisi applied for unemployment benefits in May 1982. He came to the Advice Office in March 1983, ten months later. He had been signing the register every two weeks continuously. In August 1982 he received his card back and was told to expect his money shortly. In October he made enquiries at his UIF office and was given a letter to take to the Department of Manpower. He received no reply to the letter. In November 1982 the clerk at the UIF office suggested that he make another application, which he did. In January he went to see a lawyer who wrote a letter to the Department of Manpower to no effect. When Mr Sibisi came to the Advice Office in March he was desperate. The Legal Resources Centre brought an urgent application to the Supreme Court. Although papers were filed the case was never heard as the Department of Manpower settled immediately and paid Mr Sibisi R794. (125: 5)

especially in rural areas where proper postal services do not exist, and that people get entangled in various bureaucratic regulations such as the requirement to sign the unemployment register every fortnight.

But the most striking difficulty is the catch 22 situation into which South African policy has placed many black South Africans seeking benefits to which they were legally entitled. Mr Luthuli, for example, lived in an urban hostel for migrant workers. He did not have rights to stay permanently in town in terms of Section 10(1)(b) of the Urban Areas Act but he did have a workseeker's permit. When he lost his job and went to apply for unemployment benefits he was told to go back to Harding (in a rural area) because only people with Section 10 qualifications could apply in Durban. When he pointed out that he had a workseeker's permit he was told that if he wanted to look for work in Durban he should forget about his unemployment benefits. There was no way in which he could be in the place where he could look for work whilst receiving unemployment funds to keep himself going in the meantime (125: 13).

Pensioners too have a difficult time. They can run foul of regulations such as those requiring them to prove their date of birth or to apply for grants only on certain days of the year. Once the pensions have been granted there are often long delays of two years, even up to five years, in their payment (65: 10). Even the process of obtaining a pension payment each month is arduous, as the *Sowetan* describes:

About forty pensioners slept in the freezing open veld outside the Soweto council chambers on Monday night in an attempt to beat yesterday's long queue for their bi-monthly pension pay-outs. For the pensioners who started assembling near the chambers at about 9 p.m., it meant queuing in the cold for more than 11 hours before they could start receiving their pensions. Some of them had brought along scraps of cardboard, which they used for making fires to keep themselves warm, while others stayed away from the fire out of fear of losing their positions in the queue. Mrs Elizabeth Morake, who said she believed her age could be 75, said that she had always

Devoid of hope

Their faces were shiny black death masks, asking nothing, expecting nothing, devoid of hope. They spoke of days spent shambling from one district office to another, only to be told their pension records have been 'lost' or 'come again'. From Msinga trading store – the local pension pay-out point – to the Tugela Ferry magistrate, from Tugela Ferry to Zakheni and back to Msinga. Some have been waiting up to six years for pensions. . . . Charlie Dlaladlala showed me a medical report signed by the Johannesburg district surgeon in February 1977. It diagnosed old age, said he was 100% disabled, and recommended an old-age pension. However, he has still [twenty months later] not got one. (138: 17)

been an early bird since she had started receiving her pension ten years earlier. She said she had always suffered from chest problems because of exposure to the freezing weather but insisted that there was no better way of her getting her pay than queuing the night before. (138: 19)

In the rural areas since the handover of pension administration to the various ethnic governments there has been an increase in the delays, irregularities, corruption, and confusion. There is also a problem of prescribed tribalism especially in the huge peri-urban area of Winterveld, Bophuthatswana, where a study of 45 destitute old persons showed that 88 per cent were not in receipt of pensions because they were non-Tswanas (138: 77). Other coercive measures are used to ensure support for ruling parties or to compel people to vote, as evidenced by a case from the Ciskei: 'My mother has joined a cell of Chief Sebe's party. I asked her why she did that and she says it is because she wants the pension and will not get it otherwise.' (138: 51)

Evidence of all the practical difficulties which face black pensioners in trying to get their money reflects the fact that the state has allocated inadequate resources to meet its legal obligations. The problem seems to be especially serious in the rural areas, as summed up by Dr Chuene (then Secretary for Health and Welfare in KwaZulu):

Now we have a terrific backlog. It is a very serious issue because every citizen is entitled to a pension. . . . the situation is exacerbated by the government's policy of moving settled communities to KwaZulu with the result that pensioners arriving in KwaZulu with their families are not transferred with their pensions. The result is that you find many people suddenly flooding the national states and they have to compete for pensions with other applicants. . . . we need an increase of about 50% so that every pensioner can be paid. (143: 2)

Another aspect of the bureaucratic burden in South Africa arises from the fragmentation of services, particularly in the medical field, due in large measure to the ethnic imperatives of apartheid ideology. 'Tintswalo hospital and its neighbour, Masana, were previously responsible for the care of the communities around them.' But with the intensification of the homeland policy in recent years:

Tintswalo now serves the Mhala district of Gazankulu and Masana the Mapulaneng district of Lebowa. The implementation of homeland policy has led to a fragmentation of health services and divisions between people. . . . Each [hospital] is now responsible for community health services on the other's doorstep. This wastes scarce staff-time and transport, and weakens an already inadequate support system. The hospitals no longer co-ordinate policy. For example when we wanted to co-ordinate TB care we were told that 'Gazankulu can do what it wants to, but Masana will follow Lebowa's policy'. During the polio epidemic we again wanted to combine efforts. We were told that 'We must run our own immunisation campaign and they will run theirs'. Even in the face of an epidemic, fragmentation held. Nowadays, Tintswalo and Masana's superintendents and matrons seldom communicate with each other. But it goes deeper than this. The hospitals' nurses are now separated into the Gazankulu and Lebowa Nursing Associations and discuss 'common interests' with nurses of hospitals hundreds of kilometres away, instead of down the road. Even the idea of an informal local discussion group has received little interest.

The health services make no official distinction between the people they treat; nevertheless, as a result of a policy based on ethnic divisions, incidents now occur of staff at one hospital sending some patients to the other hospital, or of ambulance drivers refusing some patients. And nurses of the 'wrong' ethnic group find themselves discriminated against in promotion and in further training opportunities. On the basis of their own day-to-day experience as practising doctors, Buch and de Beer conclude that, 'The pursuit of the homeland policy in our area has created extra problems for the health services because it leads to fragmentation of services and divisions between people.' (192: 19) In urban areas, bureaucratic fragmentation is no less of a problem although the ethnic factor plays a smaller role in government practice. But in Soweto, for example:

The worst aspect of care that was documented at Senaoane was the time wasted by patients on a single visit to the health centre. In this study patients spent an average of over two-and-a-half hours waiting in a succession of four or five queues for a total of 24 minutes of service from the polyclinic staff. The fact that patients all over the world are commonly subjected to such long waits for attention, is no justification for such subjugation. (170: 19)

The reason for the delays was primarily due to the fact that different authorities were responsible for different aspects of health, and maintained separate staffs keeping separate records. 'Concerted action to improve all health services in the whole of Soweto would involve nine different authorities each with their own bureaucracy, and in any one part of Soweto action may have to be sanctioned by any or all of five different authorities' (170: 6). The failure of the state to structure its services in a coherent, unified system undoubtedly reduces the effectiveness of health care and, through gross misallocation and waste of limited resources, ensures that many people, particularly in the rural areas, do not get even the basic services needed. All of which adds considerably to the burden borne by those enduring poverty.

It is easy, and sometimes comforting, for those who have no experience of poverty to blame poor people for the state in which they find themselves.

9
Who are
vulnerable?

My husband died in 1966. I am now experiencing difficulties in supporting my two children. I haven't got a field although I have a kraal-site. I only depend on my mother's pension money which she gets from the government. We share the money because she has her own house and I am staying at my own house. I am not working. If I could get work, the first thing that I would try would be to look for a field even before building a decent house. Livestock would then follow later. All that would only be achieved when I was working. Now I am in complete darkness. I do not know what can help me.

— A widow, in the Transkei (46: 16)

It is a general rule that poor people always receive less per unit of effort than rich people and are far less able to withstand the blows of fate which fall on everyone from time to time.

— Polly Hill (296: 3–4)

The question as to who are vulnerable is best broken into two parts: what are the sudden shifts (such as drought or a rapid rise in food prices) that can plunge people into destitution; and who is most at risk to them? The two parts of the question are, of course, interrelated and cannot always be clearly separated. The essence of vulnerability is the risk of destitution, starvation, and death. A cartoon sums it up at a glance. The person paddling ankle-deep in water risks getting a little wet if she or he should step into a two-foot hole; but the person wading so deep that the water is just below the nose risks drowning if he or she steps into a hole. Strategies against poverty have to identify the holes and find ways of filling them in, as well as enabling people to step onto higher ground.

In seeking to answer the question of vulnerability we shall try first to identify the holes, those sudden shifts, the blows of fate which can destroy those who are poor. Then we shall try to identify who, and where, are the people in South Africa most at risk because they are already so poor as to be 'on the edge of survival'.

For poor people living in rural areas anywhere in the world one of the most frightening events that occurs is drought. In the South African context where drought is frequent, and sometimes very severe, poor people can be affected in three quite different ways. One is the loss of their assets when virtually their entire savings are invested in livestock – generally cattle but also sheep, goats, horses and, in drier parts of the country, two or three donkeys. In the Transkei, for example, between April 1982 and November 1983 one-third of the total herd, over half-a-million cattle, died. In some districts as many as two out of every three of the cattle were lost (149: 9). In the more arid parts of the northern Cape and western Transvaal there were bitter complaints at this time against the Bophuthatswana authorities who had ordered soldiers to shoot donkeys in order to reduce pressure on scarce grass and water.

The second way poor people are affected is the loss of food either in the form of crops which shrivel in the fields or the disappearance – from forests and uncultivated land – of berries, roots, and greens such as *imifino* (spinach). In the Transkei where a prolonged drought began in 1979, production in the homestead gardens of all five vegetables for which figures are available and on which households rely to supplement any cash income, fell markedly between 1980 and 1982. The sorghum harvest was down by 11 per cent; maize by 48; pumkins by 68; cabbages by 76; and potatoes, always the most wildly fluctuating of crops, by 84 per cent. At the same time, in the fields, production of crops needing less water (maize, wheat and peas) increased (149: 7–8). In the following year (1983) 'the almost total absence of rain . . . meant that few crops were sown and even those that did failed' (149: 6). By 1987 the situation in the northern parts of the country was chronic. The report for Operation Hunger, written in 1987, found that all villages studied in the Transvaal had been severely affected by drought in the previous seven lean years.

Rains failed in 1980 and apart from brief respites have substantially failed each year thereafter. Rivers have dried up and the land is parched. In some areas, especially in northern Lebowa and in Venda, the soil consists of inches of sand. In those villages without the benefit of piped water, women may have to travel up to 2 kilometres to fetch water from the nearest river, and the possibility of irrigating fields is non-existent. By far the majority of households interviewed reported that they had not even attempted to plant crops in the last 2–3 years though in a very few cases, farmers had been able to produce perhaps 10–15% of pre-drought harvests. (D'Souza, Mashanini, Pongoma, Mashanini, 1987: 8)

Indigenous plants can provide a major buffer against drought, seasonal famine, and unemployment but they are under increasing pressure not only of population increase in the reserves but also of development projects that upset the ecological balance (145: 1).

The third way poor people are affected is the loss of jobs, when farmers can no longer afford to employ all the labourers who normally work the land. During the long harsh drought of the 1980s, for example, there was considerable evidence, in the eastern Cape, of labourers and their families having to leave farms and trek somewhere else in search of income. And in the even harsher climate of the northern Cape it was not only the labourers but also the farmers themselves who were affected. 'Numbers of stock farmers, particularly those in the drought-stricken Bushmanland, have had to abandon their land (leaving their farm workers to face utter destitution) and try for alternative avenues of employment' (71: 18).

Another primarily rural dimension of vulnerability relates to the seasonality of income available to many poor people working in commercial agriculture. For instance, in his study of maize farming in the western Transvaal, Michael de Klerk shows how most rural families have incomes which fluctuate widely from month to month. Poverty, he concludes, is 'more likely to be a seasonal than a perennial phenomenon in rural areas, and needs to be assessed on this basis' (28: 39).

But the fickleness of weather (whether as drought or, less frequently, in floods) and the seasons is by no means the only source of grief. No less devastating, for the poor, are the blows that come from loss of jobs and income in the urban, non-agricultural sectors of the economy. There seem to be three main reasons why people, despite their best efforts, can suddenly lose their jobs: injury, recession, and age. Against these blows, adequate and reliable insurance by means of workmen's compensation, unemployment funds, and pensions is essential in any large-scale, industrial society. But, as we shall see later in this chapter, there are many people in South Africa who receive no protection from the high risks of destitution which they face. And even those who do receive unemployment insurance or a pension remain acutely vulnerable to bureaucratic mismanagement or corruption, cutting off their only source of income (142: 3).

Closely allied to the vulnerability of low-income workers is that of the network of people, family and others, who rely upon that income (or the remitted part of it) for their entire survival. They run an even greater risk of destitution, for not only are they liable (in the case of migrant families unable to live with their bread-winner) to be poorer but there are additional reasons for their income stream to dry up. Their bread-winner may desert his family, make himself cheap [ukutshipa in Xhosa], and vanish to live his own life in town. Or, like the husband of the woman, quoted at the head of this chapter, he may die.

In Mosolotshane [Botswana] there were a number of elderly people despairing that their children who had gone to the towns to work had 'forgotten' them. One frail old woman dressed in tatters said that the last time she had heard from her son was six years ago when he had given her the clothes she was wearing. Since then she had heard nothing from him even though 'he knows how to write'. (284: 23)

Thus far we have examined vulnerability primarily in terms of events that cause substantial, if not total, loss of income or assets, whether in kind (such as food produced) or in cash. But as Amartya Sen has pointed out, as a result of studying the Bengal famine of 1943, the heart of the matter lies in the loss of what he defines as 'entitlements' (1986: 4); that is, access to or command over resources. In the case of the Bengal famine people starved not so much because of crop failure (in fact, food production was slightly above average) or even because people lost their jobs. They starved primarily because increased war-time demands led to a massive and rapid rise in the price of basic foodstuffs (notably rice) which was not matched by similar wage-rises for the labouring class. Peasants who grew their own food, Sen observed, did not starve. The importance of this analysis is that it compels us to examine the precise cause of the loss of entitlement suffered by the poor who suddenly become destitute. In the case of Bengal in 1943 it was the rapid rise, under boom conditions, of food prices; in the Sahel countries in the early 1970s it was the failure of the crop due to prolonged drought. There are many causes of destitution but underlying them all is the lack of entitlements.

In South Africa, in addition to the factors cited above, ranging from drought to recession, from an absconding migrant bread-winner to rapidly rising prices of basic needs such as cooking fuel, there is also the destitution that can be caused by political decisions. The authorities may, for instance, decide to stop recruiting labour from a particular area, or to resettle a community from a place where it has found a way of making ends meet to another more desolate spot where that is impossible.

In considering the various blows of fate that are liable to fall upon the poor in South Africa, a number of important points become apparent. One is the extent to which manifestations of poverty are also causes. Yet it is the manifestation or identification of poverty, as for example drought-induced destitution, that tells us something about its nature in the region. Another lies in recognition of the fact that the insecurity with which people have to live on the edge of survival is almost more painful than the physical deprivation itself. 'The issue for vulnerable communities', asserts the report for Operation Hunger, 'is not so much the immediate need for material assistance but for some form of insurance for the future' (D'Souza *et al.*, 1987: 33). A third point is the extent to which analysis of these blows drives home the link between poverty and political powerlessness – powerlessness either to prevent blows (such as resettlement) or to mitigate their harsh impact (for example, by adequate unemployment insurance). We turn now to consideration of who is most likely to be vulnerable to the vicissitudes that can lead to destitution. Who and where are the very poor on the edge of survival?

In a society in which it is estimated that 50 per cent of all people live below the minimum living level it may seem somewhat absurd to try to single out those categories of people who are particularly vulnerable to poverty. Approximately two-thirds of all black people in South Africa have to exist below the minimum living level. In the reserves or homelands no less than four-fifths of the people find themselves trapped below this survival line. Thus, in the most general terms, one can say that those who are black are especially vulnerable.

This tells us something although it obscures the fact that not all whites are rich and also that one of the major changes in South Africa in recent years has been a growing class division amongst blacks between those moving into professional, middle-class jobs and everybody else. However, it is important not to lose sight of the basic fact which emerges from the overall survey of incomes and other measures of poverty, namely that poverty is found primarily amongst those who are black.

People residing in rural areas in southern Africa are especially vulnerable because of the interrelatedness of forces that lock them in a cycle of poverty. It is a truism that the wealth of this country has been accumulated at the expense of rural areas, in terms of both human and other resources. And, as in many other parts of the world (Lipton, 1977), there is also discrimination which favours urban areas in the allocation of resources, be they to health, education, social and recreation facilities or manpower. The worst and the smallest slice of the economic cake invariably goes to these areas. Furthermore, there is the complicating factor of rural differentiation referred to by Thabane and Guy: 'Since the mid-1970s there has been an increasing tendency towards rural differentiation – the creation of a social stratum on the southern African periphery with access to wages and, as a result, rural resources and a socially advantageous situation on the one hand, and an increasingly large rural proletariat, on the other, denied access both to wages and to rural resources' (124: 7).

This policy has ensured the perpetuation of the cycle of poverty in these areas through the creation of a rural bourgeoisie, employed largely by the state, which has everything to benefit from the maintenance of the status quo. Masses of people in these areas are marginalised and overwhelmed by the misery of poverty. 'Vulnerable communities, or sectors of communities, in the [rural] South African context', wrote the authors of the report for Operation Hunger in 1987,

are recognised by their reliance on cash income only and, usually, on a single source of income. While some households falling into this category were, apparently, relatively well-off, many others maintained a thinly held balance between coping and, ultimately, catastrophic actions which inevitably create impoverishment. These included increasing credit at local food-stores; selling off assets such as livestock to buy food; making a decision not to send children to school because fees or uniform or both represented too great an inroad on the food budget; abandoning children to old, and even infirm, relatives, in order to migrate to cities or perforce acceptance of low-paid work. The effect of short-term coping strategies is to increase debt to the point of destitution. (D'Souza *et al.*, 1987: 32)

This racial geography of poverty as it is found in southern Africa is a fact fundamental to any understanding of vulnerability and causation, yet there still seem to be many influential urban-dwellers who are unaware of the extent of black poverty or who believe that such poverty as exists is concentrated in the urban, not the rural, areas (83: 29–31).

Against that background, then, what further can be said about categories of people vulnerable to poverty in southern Africa? There are four major groups, each of which can be broken down into sub-categories that need to be considered: children; women; elderly persons; and adults who are disabled or weak in some way.

Consider first the children of our society. In parts of South Africa, as we have seen, particularly in the rural areas, the mortality rate for black children under the age of 12 months is very high. At the same time the evidence shows that this infant mortality rate varies widely between different areas, and also that where it is high intelligent intervention can, at relatively low cost, reduce it substantially and rapidly. A major factor in high infant mortality rates is the practice of feeding children powdered milk (often in insufficient quantities and using contaminated water) rather than breast-feeding. Major responsibility for this malpractice must rest with the manufacturing companies which, by means of advertising, persuade young mothers that somehow the use of the powdered product is more nutritious and more 'modern' than their own breast-milk. Strategies to deal with the high death rates amongst young children will be considered later. We wish here simply to draw attention to their vulnerability.

No less harrowing for parents than the death of their babies is the malnutrition and sickness amongst young pre-school children between weaning and the age of 5. For example, a 1986 study of the nutritional status of children in selected areas of Namibia found that most babies were breast-fed up to six months, and so, despite poverty, were usually better fed and suffered less malnutrition than those who were older. It was also reported that the prevalence of diarrhoea more than doubled in the second six months of life (Hughson, 1986: 16). Indeed, throughout southern Africa there is widespread evidence of the extent of chronic malnutrition amongst young black children. This is especially serious in view of the finding that hunger at this age can damage the growth of the brain in such a way that people become listless, with their energy and intelligence impaired.

There seem to be three underlying causes of this wasting of young children. First is obviously the absence of adequate income amongst the families to which these children belong. Second is the fact that many children are born of young mothers who are unmarried or divorced or whose husbands are away working in town as migrants. The instability of family life, for which the migrant labour system must bear much of the blame, is a major factor in both infant mortality and the malnutrition of children. The third related cause of the problem is the absence, particularly in the urban areas, of adequate child-minding or pre-school facilities for working mothers, whose earnings are vital for the survival of their children but whose hours (including travel over considerable distances) necessitate their being away from home for twelve hours or more each day.

Older children too are vulnerable. For them, the problem of hunger remains, as John Hansen pointed out when he estimated that in South Africa one-third of all black children up to the age of 14 suffer from malnutrition. But it is the famine of the mind and of the spirit which is perhaps even more serious.

One of the more striking findings of recent years comes from the Center for Child and Family Studies at Syracuse University in San Francisco. Here 82 children born into disadvantaged environments that were sparse in terms of money and educational background were provided, for the first five years of their lives, with an enriched, warm and loving environment by means of special day-care. The children

were treated as special creations, each with particular skills and specialities that would be appreciated by and useful to the larger society. . . . The context that was created set a daily tone of freedom of choice and awareness of responsibility; and expectation of success in each child; confidence in the fairness and consistency of the environment; an emphasis on creativity, excitement and exploration in learning; expectation of internal rather than external motivation; and a safe, cheerful place to spend each day. (Lally and Mangione, 1987: 1)

Ten years later, between the ages of 13 and 16, the programme children were compared with a control group from similar background. The results were startling. In terms of social behaviour there was a dramatic difference – which related mainly to the boys – in court, detention, and probation costs. As far as school-work was concerned, teacher ratings of programme girls (but not boys) 'showed them to be rated significantly higher than their controls on school achievement, positive attitude towards self, positive attitude towards others, and impulse control' (*ibid.*). No such study has yet been done in South Africa but there is little doubt that children here are no less vulnerable to the devastating consequences of the impoverished environment in which so many of them have to grow up in both the townships and the rural areas of the country.

One noteworthy feature to emerge from the area studies in the Carnegie Inquiry was the evidence of deprivation caused by absence of adequate facilities for play and recreation. For example in Clarke's Estate, part of Elsies River in Cape Town:

Every day approximately thirty children between the ages of five and sixteen years can be seen playing in sand around each flat, and almost as many older persons will be hanging 'around'. Because there are no parks or sportsfields in their area, the children are forced to play in filthy open lots and seek their own pastimes. Like all people, these children tend to model themselves on the dominant characters in their 'community', viz the gangsters, and as part of their games, they re-enact sensational scenes which they observe. Given the constant contact they have with gang-members hanging around their play area ... negative influences on the young minds are inevitable. ... Glue sniffing is an increasing phenomenon. . . . Just about every resident can give account of an encounter with glue-sniffing children. Given the lack of 'decent' recreation and the pressures on the young children, this phenomenon is not surprising. (10c: 33)

The vulnerability of children in such environments is no less acute than for those to whom poverty means physical hunger. Indeed, one might well argue that the spiritual destruction, though less visible than the bodily wasting or attrition, is even more damaging. Children are the most vulnerable victims of poverty in South African society and they must be the primary target group in any development strategy.

In the light of this awareness it is perhaps trite to point out that children need education. But the most remarkable of all the many features of South African history in recent years, especially during the decade after 1976, has been the extent to which children have been prepared to die in leading a struggle for proper education. Elsewhere in this book we have documented the extent of illiteracy, the high drop-out rates, the absence of schools in rural areas, the inadequacy of teacher training, the demoralisation of teachers themselves. The educational system in South Africa has failed dismally to provide anything like a proper education for all children of school-going age. By the mid-1980s the crisis in the classrooms had reached breaking-point. Boycotts by children, lock-outs by the authorities, lessons in the presence of armed police, saw the schools at the epicentre of the political storm raging in South Africa. In addition to their astonishing courage and their determination to put 'liberation before education,' what also became apparent was the children's vulnerability. In the end stones were no match for whips and bullets; solitary confinement and terror could break practically any courage; student movements could not stand up against military organisation.

Yet despite this vulnerability these young teenagers shook the country. The cost was nevertheless very high, and it throws into sharp relief another aspect of their vulnerability. For if children missed three years of school, or even one year, how would they ever catch up? The problem lies not in the capacity of the child, so much as in the capacity of the educational system. For an individual child who misses a year or more of schooling at some stage of his or her career can always go back and, by working hard, catch up and in due course acquire the necessary qualifications. But for a whole generation that misses a year of school there is no way to catch up the lost time. The school system does not have the capacity of classrooms or teachers to educate in one year, in addition to those whose age is appropriate for that year of schooling, all who should have been educated the previous year but who missed out. The lost years cannot be recovered. This is true for children missing school during time of political crisis, and it is true as well for all those who have dropped out of school at some early stage or who have never even started their formal education. Growing up without school leads to an almost irretrievable loss, which is itself both a manifestation and a cause of poverty. Herein lies the educational vulnerability of children.

After children it is surely women, especially but not only those in the rural areas, whose position in South African society makes them particularly vulnerable. Amongst black women there are four groups that are most likely to find themselves in difficulties: widows; divorcees; wives of migrants; and all women, including those already mentioned, who head their own households.

Widowhood, particularly for a middle-aged woman who is used to receiving a regular remittance from her husband, may come as a severe blow to her sense of personal dignity. Although, in absolute terms, she may be left with more material possessions

Vulnerability of widowhood

Mrs L. K.'s husband had just passed away at the time that I first interviewed her in 1976. At that time she still had a few livestock and other accumulated resources which she managed to eke for her necessities, and to ensure that her one field was worked regularly. Her only son, a migrant labourer whose wife had left him, was a very irregular remitter. But Mrs L. K. was then still able to borrow from neighbours and relatives against the promise of repayment once his remittance arrived. This provided her with a continuing measure of self-perceived independence. During the next five years, however, her son set up housing with the deserted young wife of a migrant from [Lesotho], and his remittances thus became much more undependable for her. In order to be able to purchase her basic necessities, she then sold off her remaining livestock, with the result that her resources were gradually depleted. By 1981, when I interviewed her again, she had finally reached a stage of resourcelessness common to many old people in her environment, particularly widows, but which she herself had never before had to face. For Mrs L. K. this was a traumatic period of her life: she suddenly found herself at the mercy of her relatives' and neighbours' goodwill; and she cried bitter tears as she told me that there were times when she was going without food to cook in her house for up to a week at a time: her domestic independence had finally crumbled. (51: 13) and resources than many others have, her husband's death often signals an increased vulnerability to perceived and real impoverishment. (51: 13)

There are no precise figures of the number of widows in South Africa but demographic analysis together with evidence from local studies suggests that the proportion of women living as widows is high, notably in the rural areas. For example, a detailed and thorough study in two rural districts of the Ciskei in the 1960s found that no less than 30 per cent of the households were headed by widows (De Vos *et al.*, 1970: 46). This figure seemed extraordinarily high but was double-checked (personal communication from Prof. De Vos). The reasons for this state of affairs were believed by those living within the two districts to be, firstly, the high death-rate of men who had contracted pneumoconiosis on the mines and, secondly, the fact that women widowed in town often moved back to the country to live with their fathers' families. These beliefs were not tested but the fact that tuberculosis continues to be a major killer in the rural areas cautions against too quick a rejection of the hypothesis.

Divorcees and deserted wives also often find themselves destitute. For the society has been structured in such a way that women are compelled to be unusually dependent financially on their husbands. In the urban areas, for example, rights to a house or even permission to be in the area at all could until recently be forfeited or withdrawn from a woman who became divorced from her husband. Much grief and hardship was caused by the state's practice of evicting divorcees (and widows) from their homes on the grounds that their right to be in the area, which was based on their husband's right to be there, had now fallen away. In the rural areas, especially those designated independent homelands, African women are trapped by laws which make it illegal for them to move to the cities to look for work. Thus when their husband dies or leaves them, there is no way of replacing the loss of remittances. Moreover, the combination of the migrant system, traditional law, and the sexism of both black and white society can be crippling for widows. For instance if her husband dies on the mines, her money comes through the magistrate who decides how much she should get each month. Furthermore, to wind up the estate there has to be a male relative who becomes the effective custodian. And many widows are impoverished in that process – all in the name of tradition. Moreover if a widow refuses to be the second wife of her husband's brother he can refuse to pass on the assets due to her; thus she is held captive sexually.

For millions of women the reality of this vulnerability makes itself felt even when they are married to husbands still alive who love them. This is because the pattern of migrant labour results again and again in situations where the women left behind in the rural areas find that their husbands' remittances do not always come every month and that the amounts sent imply that the rural family is receiving a far smaller share of their man's income than they would do were he living with them. This is inevitable, for even if the husband is monogamous and does not have a second wife or family in town, the costs of living separately are higher. Moreover, who can live apart from his family year after year without building up a second circle of friends and relationships, which in turn involves the spending of some money upon them?

Like many other societies, the South African economy is biased in such a way as to place most of the paid jobs in the hands of men. For this reason in South Africa, as elsewhere, the degree of poverty is far higher amongst female-headed households than in those homes where a man is at the head. This is to be expected, given the structure of society, which is both sexist and economically exploitative. In South Africa the barriers against women moving freely into the market-place to work where they choose, combined with the educational disadvantages that weigh more heavily on women than on men, place upon them additional burdens which men do not have to carry. For example, women are often considered by male employers to be more 'unreliable' than men in that they may need to be away from work when their children are ill. For this reason there may be a bias against hiring or promoting a woman in a particular job for which she is well qualified.

Women are discriminated against in all aspects of life – in the home as girls being brought up and educated; in the allocation of resources at school and institutions of higher learning; at work; and in society in general. African rural women are at the bottom of the economic pyramid in this country because of the added problem of paucity of resources and more rigid sexist practices in these areas.

In the Vulindlela district in Natal, Bromberger's study of the poorest African households identified the demography of those worst off as female-headed (60 per cent); and elderly, with a lesser dependency ratio, and an average age of 55, 40 per cent of whom were found to be chronically ill, disabled, or physically handicapped (274: 4). In Worcester in the western Cape, Yosslowitz found a similar picture of poverty among the coloured community, where female-headed households were the largest in the poorest category. In the Ciskei more than half (54 per cent) of all households in the two rural districts studied by De Vos (1970: 43) were found to be headed by women.

The exploitation of women in the labour market is all-pervasive, even amongst the relatively well-educated, in the form of differential salary scales, and discriminatory promotional policies. The most exploited categories of workers are, however, domestics and agricultural labourers who work the hardest, for the longest working days and are paid the lowest wages. The lack of legislative protection and of labour organisation is partly to blame for this state of affairs.

Women divorcees trying to secure maintenance of their children from former husbands have to contend with such difficulties that few of them ever succeed. Pat Schwartz had this to say about the problem:

Many women sit in court from 8 a.m. to 4 p.m. without their cases being heard. They are told to come back again and again and in the process lose jobs or have their wages docked. . . . Then again many cases are dismissed on purely technical points – often administrative errors – and some women have to start their matters three or four times. It can take a woman up to 18 months to get an order, cases are postponed for anything up to three months and there is seldom any backdating of orders. (cited in 87: 20)

Poverty under any circumstances is bad enough but the special twist given to it by the sexist laws and practices of the state in South Africa makes the position of black women grindingly hard to endure.

Any study of poverty in southern Africa must focus first on the position of children and women. But there are other categories of people that are also highly vulnerable. Amongst these are older people, of whom two particular groups may be distinguished: the pre-pensioners and a category perhaps best labelled as sans-pensions. For many older people the time of greatest vulnerability is the five-to-ten years before they reach pensionable age. In those years many who have worked as labourers all their lives find it impossible to get work; often they are laid off a job they have been doing for years; or they will simply not be considered as suitable applicants. This problem is found elsewhere in the world but it is a burden which falls harshly on many blacks in southern Africa for whom there are not other forms of effective social security and who have no access to land. In South Africa the opportunity for alternative employment is restricted for those based in the rural areas, whether on the platteland or in the reserves. In Calitzdorp, for example, a young pastor spelt out to us something of the difficulties facing those households whose bread-winner had worked for years on the surrounding farms but who, as he grew older, was unable to get a job. And in Nkandla, KwaZulu, analysis of the cash contributions made to households by their male members showed a startling picture.

Table 9.01: Annual cash contribution by age to households,
Nkandla, 1983 (males only)

Age range	Number	Average contribution (rands/person)
0– 9	119	1
10–14	51	4
15–19	35	18
20–24	27	92
25–29	23	151
30–34	20	184
35–39	20	366
40–44	17	422
45–49	7	531
50–54	9	727
55–59	6	193
60–64	10	264
65+	17	920

Source: 53a: 48

Contributions rise steadily until men reach the age of 54, and then there is a sudden and massive drop until they reach pensionable age at 65 when their contributions to the household rise relatively higher than ever before.

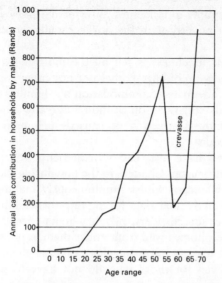

Fig. 9.01: Pre-pension crevasse, Nkandla, 1983

The diagram is striking for two reasons. It illustrates dramatically the depth of the poverty crevasse into which households can fall if their only bread-winner is a man in his mid-fifties whom employers regard as too old to hire but who is too young for a pension. Secondly, the graph illustrates the remarkable fact that, largely because of the migrant labour system and the cost of living in two places at once, a worker can send home less money at the peak of his earning life than he can provide when living at home drawing a tiny pension. The critical importance of pensions becomes even more apparent when the cash contributions of women to the household are considered. In Nkandla the average female pensioner was found to contribute R487 per annum to the household whilst the average woman of 60 or older who did not receive a pension contributed only R26, only 5 per cent of the other (53a: 49). Pensions constituted 54 per cent of the financial contribution of all women to households, double the equivalent percentage for contributions by the whole community, men and women taken together (53a: 50).

The plight of elderly people, especially those without families to support them, is often pitiful. Elsewhere we have noted how low pensions are relative to the cost of living, and have seen something of the hunger amongst people too old and weak to fight for their rights. The vulnerability of old people is seen not only in their inadequate pensions and their hunger, but also in their loneliness and in the particular difficulties they face in coping with such disruptions as forced removals. Elsewhere we examine the harsh impact that state actions – whether in the form of bureaucratic inefficiency or deliberate policy – have upon old people. Loneliness amongst old people, notably in urban environments, is a world-wide phenomenon but is no less of a judgement on society for all that. 'Poverty', says Mother Teresa, 'is not just being without food. It is the absence of love. ... Often in big cities, big countries, people die simply of loneliness, unwanted, unloved, forgotten. This is a much more bitter poverty than the poverty which is not to have food.' (Tower, 1987: 163)

In South Africa this loneliness is felt all the more harshly by blacks for whom there are virtually no old-age homes nor any other social strategies for helping those without adequate accommodation nor families to support them. Moreover, as we shall see, their dislocation is greatly exacerbated by the trauma of forced removals which have caused such pain to black South Africans in recent decades.

Some elderly whites have also had to experience the pain of removal although for a different reason. Changes in the law during the 1970s removed the protection of rent control whilst simultaneously making it possible for developers to sell off individual flats for private ownership under sectional title. As property values soared elderly people who had been living for years in a rented flat found their homes sold from under them at prices they could not possibly afford. They had to move in what was, for them, an exceedingly painful adjustment. Even for those who do not have to move life can be extremely difficult.

Central Johannesburg is probably the most sophisticated financial and business area on the African continent. Behind and above the premises of the prosperous businesses and office blocks the destitute aged are trapped. Here they eke out a living amid squalor and fear of their lives. . . . Dark corridors, doors which provide little or no protection, unserviceable lifts, barely functioning hot-water systems, and drainage in chronic disrepair are common to most of the buildings housing the aged. Poverty is evident everywhere. Small, musty rooms which rarely see the light of day, sufficient only for the bare essentials, are often the only world the aged know. (140: 22)

In addition to children, women, and the elderly there is another, intersecting group of people especially vulnerable to poverty and the conditions which surround it. This group is made up of those who may be defined as disabled in some way. These include not only persons who are physically disabled but also people belonging to what have been defined as 'weak' households.

Analysis of the vulnerability of people who are disabled starts with recognition of the fact that 'the presence of both poverty and disability in the same person will produce a degree of handicap which is far greater than each alone' (186: 5). There is a mutually reinforcing dual problem. Those who are disabled find it difficult to earn a reasonable income, not because they are unable to work but because society assumes that disabled people cannot do as much as others, and does not organise itself in such a way as to make it possible for the disabled to make full use of their potential. Moreover, even if they do have an income, disabled people are often condemned to lead impoverished lives because the structures, both physical and social, of the society are usually designed in such a way as to exclude those who are not 100 per cent physically or mentally fit. Greater awareness of the problems has developed in recent years, often through the work of disabled people themselves. One small sign of this growing awareness is the fact that pavements and buildings are more likely than they were even in the 1970s to be designed with the needs in mind of those who cannot walk and who need to move by means of a wheel-chair.

Then there is the absence of facilities to help such people to lead full lives. In an analysis of facilities available in the Cape Peninsula a number of important points emerged. In the world as a whole, an average of one person in ten is disabled (186: 2). 'One of the major problems in South Africa is the fragmented nature of services both in terms of areas of responsibility and of different racial groups' (186: 11). Lack of sufficient services is a cause for great concern. For example, in the field of mental retardation, a study carried out in 1976 identified the prevalence of mental retardation in one coloured township as 1.24 per 1 000, which was comparable with published data from elsewhere. 'The major deficit appeared to lie in day-care services, nearly three-quarters of the children receiving no adequate therapy. The normal schools were seen to be carrying a disproportionate load of the day care and a particular lack was seen in the care of the most severely handicapped children.' (186: 36) 'It is not easy for any family to accommodate a senile, elderly relative or mentally deficient child. Wealth, however, allows the family members spare time to spend with a disabled person, privacy or the opportunity to delegate responsibility and carry on with their own lives.' (186: 82) Transport is vital if disabled persons are to be able to use an appropriate day-care facility should one be available. Difficult for the poor especially in a society where public transport is bad and expensive.

An important aspect of disability becomes salient in the nuclear family system:

The subsistence provided by each person is vital to survival, the extra burden of a non-contributing member, especially one who has abnormal needs, is all that may be needed to disturb the delicate balance of the budget. The need to redistribute resources perhaps from education and nutrition of 'healthy' members of the family may further cause a cascade of secondary effects, the implications of which are boundless. (186: 83)

This is exacerbated where the disabled person is a child who cannot be left alone, thus necessitating a potentially wage-earning adult staying at home.

There is no general view of the position of disabled people all over southern Africa but it is safe to assume that, in general, the needs of disabled people living in the rural areas are likely to be even less well taken into account than they are for those living in the metropolitan cities.

A striking example of the difficulties facing disabled people in rural areas may be seen in the extreme case of Mseleni in northern KwaZulu. Here no less than three out of every five women are suffering from a crippling form of progressive arthritis which affects above all the hip joints, causing a great deal of pain and making it difficult to walk. Yet although they are not far from the largest natural fresh-water lake in Africa, nearly two-thirds (60 per cent) of the households have a round trip of more than one hour to fetch water. The technology for laying piped water to every household is simple; the cost is relatively small; but the people are poor and the wider society does not regard even such elementary help as a priority (199 and 288).

Turning now to what have been described as 'weak' households, we find that in a study of a peri-urban area of KwaZulu, not far from Durban: 'The risk of poverty for the weak households was just about four times what it was for strong ones' (57: 3). But what makes a 'weak' household? In their study Catherine Cross and Eleanor Preston-Whyte identified several characteristics which, taken together, weaken a household. First is the economic dislocation index, which measures whether or not the household has the personnel to fill its vital economic roles, regardless of how the members are related to each other. 'This meant at least one man and one woman; also at least one person able to move around and work, and at least one capable of staying home and managing the household' (57: 2). Another characteristic is the extent to which the relationships between household members are the expected ones in terms of social norms. The really interesting result of the study was that whilst it was found that the economic dislocation index did indeed correlate with the income level of the family, the social indicator was no guide to a household's well-being as measured by the income coming into the household. But it was correlated with the well-being of the household as perceived by the community. In other words, households that were socially dislocated might (as in the case of single-generation households containing no children) have a high per capita income, but that income tended to be wastefully spent in such a way that members of the household remained essentially very poor, with resources not being effectively pooled. Though results are tentative, and the study needs to be repeated in other areas, they do suggest that economic and social dislocation within a household is a significant proximate cause of poverty. Thus any long-range strategies against poverty have to address the causes of that dislocation. In this context it is worth noting John Iliffe's observation about the importance in Africa for poor people of the family. 'In several African languages the common word for 'poor' – *umphawi* in the Chewa language of modern Malawi, for example – implies lack of kin and friends, while the weak household, bereft of able-bodied male labour, has probably been the most common source of poverty through Africa's recoverable history' (1987: 7).

Finally, in this brief overview of those who are vulnerable, we must mention vagrants. Despite their visibility in the towns and cities of South Africa little is known about them, whether in terms of numbers or of the reasons for their destitution. But an historical survey of vagrancy in Cape Town shows the extent to which it seems to be associated with the socio-economic dislocation brought about by war or by agricultural mechanisation pushing people off the land (11: 1–26). Given the fact that vagrants may perhaps best be defined as urban people who 'sleep rough' (11: 1) they are, by definition, people who do not have adequate housing, either because they are too poor to afford rent or because there is simply no housing available. Clearly the definition (whether in Cape Town or New York) is a loose one but the situation in which vagrants find themselves is tight enough. Essentially it is one of unemployment and homelessness.

Vulnerability is not simply a matter of identifying which groups in a society are likely to be poor. At a deeper level it is recognition of the fact that poverty is 'not merely a problem of special groups or of other people but an atmosphere in which large numbers of people live their lives and which threatens at any time to assume a more concrete presence' (Miliband, 1974 cited in 39: 79).

PART TWO
Many causes of poverty

> By the turn of the century [1900], land companies, mining companies, white farmers and land speculators dominated the land. After the initial breach had been made in traditional African land-holdings and customs using a combination of force, tact and treachery, the law was brought in to consolidate white settler supremacy.
>
> – Fikile Bam (80: 8)
>
> A man cannot go with his wife and children and his goods and chattels on to the labour market. He must have a dumping-ground. Every rabbit has got a warren where he can live and burrow and breed, and every native must have a warren too.
>
> – Sir Godfrey Lagden,
> Transvaal Labour Commission,
> 1903 (cited in 55: 1)

It may seem a little far-fetched to trace the causes of poverty in South Africa at the end of the twentieth century to events that took place in the nineteenth and earlier. There is not much, readers may feel, that can be done about things that happened in the mists of antiquity. This is true. What is past is past. Nevertheless we believe it is important to uncover the roots of a system which continues, despite rapid economic growth during a hundred years of industrial revolution, to impoverish millions of people. For the present has grown out of the past, and so if the future is to be different it is essential to understand the way in which the present has been formed, in order that we may act to overcome the past and, hence, reshape the future.

But this book does not purport to be a full economic history, tracing the growth of the South African political economy out of the capitalist expansion of western Europe in the sixteenth and seventeenth centuries. Nor is it appropriate here to explore even further back to the 'thousand years before Van Riebeeck', which are part and parcel of the whole story. The events that concern us now are confined to those which, although they happened so long ago, continue in a very specific way to affect the ongoing process of impoverishment in South Africa.

Firstly, there is the fact of conquest. When Europeans first came to settle in the southern tip of Africa (originally to provide a staging post for Dutch merchant ships on their way to and from the East Indies) they came with guns. The local Khoisan inhabitants naturally resented the arrival of outsiders moving in permanently to take over valuable grazing land, and attacked the invaders, but they did not have the arms necessary to dislodge them. Within a decade of their arrival the whites raised the first of a long line of apartheid barriers by planting a hedge round the settlement, within which the original inhabitants were not allowed to stay. Subsequent proposals for the digging of a canal to mark a clear boundary between the invaders from Europe and the people of Africa came to nought, not least because the new settlers soon wanted more land and moved out of the Cape Peninsula into the interior.

Thus began the long saga of conquest as whites moved with their guns (and their bibles), trading where it was useful or profitable and taking over land as they required it. In this manner, first the Khoisan, and subsequently Xhosa and other Bantu-speaking people, were either pushed off the land or absorbed onto it as conquered labourers. This process went on for several generations and culminated in a long century of war, fought mainly in the eastern part of the country where African settlement was densest. In the early years indigenous inhabitants were decimated by diseases brought by the whites, notably smallpox. Later in the eighteenth century large numbers of people, particularly Khoisan or 'Bushmen' hunters, were 'systematically exterminated' (Wilson and Thompson, 1969: 184). In the nineteenth century hard wars were fought against the invaders, backed now by the rising British imperial power. But the might of industrial Europe was greater than that of pastoral Africa, and the land was finally conquered, although not without the invaders suffering some spectacular defeats such as that inflicted on the British by a Zulu army at Isandhlwana in 1879.

The long process of conquest may finally be said to have culminated in the notorious Land Act of 1913 whereby the conquerors sought to ensure that the land won by conquest should not be lost through the market in the new industrial society that was emerging. In terms of the Act no African was allowed to purchase land outside the reserves, those 'scheduled' and 'released' areas which eventually added up to a little less than 14 per cent of the total country. Some 75 years later, in 1988, that law remains firmly in place as part of the basic scaffolding of the South African political-economic system.

After conquest, which determined the distribution of land between whites and blacks, the second historical fact most pertinent to this inquiry is slavery. For it too set a pattern, the baleful influence of which continues strongly to this day. The majority of black South Africans were never slaves; but the first white settlers, bringing with themselves the habits of an established colonial power, were soon calling for slaves (or for some 'industrious Chinese') to meet their labour needs. In 1658, only six years after Van Riebeeck's arrival, the first shipment of slaves for private ownership landed at the Cape. Some came from the coast of Guinea; others from Angola. Within sixty years of the establishment of the European colony there were more slaves than free burghers in the western Cape. They were brought from west Africa, from Madagascar, and from south-east Asia. Another half-century later, in 1760, slaves were required, for the first time, to carry passes in moving between rural and urban areas.

By 1775 an indenture system had begun to emerge for the offspring of male slaves and Khoikhoi women. These so-called 'bastaard hottentots' were legally indentured until the age of 25. But there was also raiding of the Khoikhoi and San (together, now called the Khoisan) for children. 'It is clear', writes Worden, that

by the end of the eighteenth century a large number of non-slave labourers were working on the farms of the western Cape. Nevertheless, the fact that the arable economy was still firmly based on slavery meant that those Khoikhoi and *bastaard hottentot* labourers who did live and work on the farms were absorbed into a coercive labour structure and system of living which reduced them to only nominal freedom. This was to have an immense impact on the social structure of the farmsteads and on the formation of racial attitudes within the community. (Worden, 1985: 36)

South Africa's modern capitalist economy thus began in slavery, and it was the final ending of that slavery in the British Empire in 1834 that led directly to the Great Trek, or secondary invasion. Beginning in 1835, whites – who were by now well-settled in the coastal region of the eastern Cape – set off for the northern interior where they hoped to re-establish the old white master–black servant relationships which the new philanthropic spirit blowing from England threatened to disrupt.

But the abolition of slavery, although it was accompanied by an Ordinance (No. 50 of 1828) which effectively freed all coloured people – Khoisan and descendants of intermarriages or affairs between whites and blacks – from pass laws that had previously controlled their mobility, brought about the enactment of a further series of pass and vagrancy laws. These were now directed at controlling the movement into and within the conquered territories of Nguni- and Sotho-speaking Africans. Thus we find, not for the first or last time in South African history, a profound ambiguity. A notable reform became embedded in a wider, contradictory process that did great damage to all those caught up in its meshes. For the thicket of pass and vagrancy laws that grew during the nineteenth century was to develop into the timber of the scaffolding used to build the whole migrant labour system that became one of the distinguishing features of South Africa's industrial revolution. In 1872 the first of the industrial pass laws to control movement of mine labour was enacted in the Cape. And in 1895 a new pass law was drafted by the fledgling Chamber of Mines and enacted by the Transvaal Volksraad (or legislature). Less than thirty years later, in 1921, a Transvaal local government commission, chaired by Colonel Stallard, enunciated the policy that was to cause such pain and damage to black South Africans during the twentieth century.

The native should only be allowed to enter the urban areas, which are essentially the white man's creation, when he is willing to enter and to minister to the needs of the white man and should depart therefrom when he ceases so to minister (Transvaal Province, 1922: para 267).

The third aspect of South African history which has reverberated into the present day has been the systematic assault on the industrial labour movement. In early years the battle lines were clearly drawn between capital and labour, with employers being as ruthlessly opposed to trade unions for white miners as they were to those for black. But gradually white workers, by a combination of strike action with the political and social power which the vote gave them, were able to assert themselves against the cruder attacks of the bosses. In 1883, for example, white workers on the diamond fields (supported by black workers) went on strike against management's practice of strip-searching workers for stolen diamonds. The workers won the strike primarily, it is believed, because employers feared losing all their black labour – which was liable simply to return home to the rural areas – if the strike continued (Turrell, 1987). But the very next year bosses tried to reinstate stripping. In the ensuing confrontation six white workers were shot dead. An emotional and dramatic funeral was held in Kimberley and from then on there was no more stripping for whites.

For black workers, on the other hand, the shooting was a dramatic warning of employer power and determination. In 1885, closed compounds for African workers were instituted. The events of the previous year, concludes Turrell (1987: 145), had 'created the right intimidatory atmosphere for the introduction of closed compounds . . ., the means to control African labour more effectively'. For the entire period they were contracted to the mines, black workers were to be housed in closed compounds where they would stay without opportunity to see family or friends. In this way, it was hoped, illicit diamond buying could be curtailed and the monopoly which kept the price of diamonds high could be held intact. When gold was re-discovered on the Witwatersrand in 1886 the mining magnates from Kimberley moved in to the new Johannesburg to gain control of gold as well. This they did, although gold, which was much more difficult to mine, did not require the cartel arrangements to keep the price artificially high that diamonds needed. In the process of moving from Kimberley to Johannesburg, the mining capitalists brought with them the idea of housing all their black labour in huge compounds. These did not have to be of the closed type, for gold cannot be picked up and sold illicitly like diamonds. But, designed as they were for workers only without their families, compounds were clearly much the cheapest and most profitable way of providing the necessary accommodation for – and controlling – the 100 000 black miners who by the end of the 1890s, little more than a decade after the first outcrop was found, were needed to dig for gold.

In 1897 white miners on the Witwatersrand struck successfully to prevent cuts in white wages. But black wages were reduced. In the process of battling against the bosses, white workers had increasingly distanced themselves from their fellow workers who were black. And in 1907 they struck against competition by them, thus effectively exerting pressure to exclude blacks from better jobs on the mines. Then, in a massive and bloody strike on the eve of the First World War, white miners fought for, and won, recognition of their trade unions from the Chamber of Mines. As soon as this was accomplished there occurred another, larger strike in January 1914 whose purpose was, in C. W. de Kiewiet's words, 'to testify to the common purpose of all white labour to protect its interests' (1941: 168). Another major confrontation took place between capital and white miners in 1922 when workers came out in armed rebellion. The state backed capital, and, led by Smuts, the government moved in decisively to crush the revolt. But it was a Pyrrhic victory: two years later, a coalition of white labour and the Afrikaner National Party defeated the Smuts government in a vigorous election. From then on the white trade unions, with some honourable exceptions, became effectively part of the power structure of

South Africa's unique brand of 'racial capitalism'.

Meanwhile black workers had also been organising, and in 1913, after the successful white strike, they too 'rose in protest against their conditions of employment' (Diamond, 1969: 211). Their fundamental grievance was found by a special commission to be 'the colour bar which blocks practically all opportunities of promotion'. But nothing was done to remove the barrier, and some of their other grievances (such as having to wait at the bottom of the mine-shaft for hours at the end of a shift whilst whites were hauled up first) were still found to be well entrenched half a century later. Then, in 1920, during eleven days in February, some 71 000 men came out on strike for better pay, lower prices in the company stores, and against the colour bar. After a show of force, with police and troops from the South African Mounted Rifles surrounding the compounds, the arrest of strike-leaders, and one violent clash, the miners returned to work having achieved almost nothing. It was not for another quarter of a century that black mineworkers were to strike again.

With the support of the state, and backed by the Native Labour Regulation Act of 1911 which made it a criminal offence for blacks, under contract, to strike, employers were in a powerful position to crush any attempts by black workers at collective bargaining. In response to a great strike in 1946 when 74 000 workers from thirteen different mines came out for better food and higher wages (which were lower in real terms than they had been 35 years earlier), police arrested all strike-leaders, surrounded the compounds and, on one mine where stones were thrown, fired on miners; on another made a baton charge; and on a third, drove the miners underground at bayonet point. Neither the government nor the employers were willing even to discuss the strikers' demands and when, after four days, the strike was broken the Chamber of Mines issued a statement to make clear that

the Gold Mining Industry considers that trade-unionism as practised by Europeans is still beyond the understanding of the tribal Native; nor can he know how to employ it as a means of promoting his advancement. He has no tradition in that respect and has no experience or proper appreciation of the responsibilities arising from collective representation. No proper conduct of a trade union is possible unless the workers have that tradition and such a sense of responsibility. (Wilson, 1972a: 79)

And yet, if the black miners had been able through strike action to shift the balance of power between black and white within the industry, it would have been possible over the period 1936–69 for black wages to have increased in real terms by 40 per cent instead of falling as they in fact did. And this could have been achieved with exactly the same number of workers, both black and white, as were actually employed and with white wages in real terms also rising by 40 per cent (but not more) over the same period (Wilson, 1972: 141–2). It was not for another generation, until the 1970s, that the official view of the mining industry (and of other urban employers) towards unions began to change. Even now, in the latter half of the 1980s, the attitude of some, but by no means all, mining groups to the establishment of the National Union of Mineworkers is scarcely less hostile than 40 years ago.

We turn now to a fourth strand of our history (closely woven with the previous three) which has been used to bind black South Africans. We refer to the colour bar. The use by whites of skin pigmentation as a means of discriminating against potential competitors in the labour market did not originate in the gold mines nor, indeed, on the diamond diggings. Its roots go back, through slavery and conquest, to the different legal categories of people introduced by the Dutch East India Company in 1652 (Giliomee and Elphick, forthcoming). But the mineral discoveries did much to entrench it. In 1893 the Transvaal Volksraad enacted the first legal colour bar in the South African economy. A clause in the first mining law stipulated, in effect, that only whites might perform the actual blasting. The regulations were further tightened with the importation in 1904 of Chinese labourers, who were prohibited from employment in a number of jobs listed to ensure that they did not ever compete with skilled or semi-skilled whites. And in 1907 white miners, as we have seen, struck to prevent blacks performing skilled jobs. Thus in the troubled years between the ending of the Anglo–Boer War and the Act of Union, the white miners of the Witwatersrand were able to entrench themselves firmly in a dominant position by ensuring that black miners, even if they were competent to do so, could carry out no jobs above a certain level of skill.

Almost the first legislation enacted by the new Union of South Africa was the Mines and Works Act of 1911, which empowered the Governor-General to make regulations requiring certificates of competency for the performance of different kinds of work. In the Transvaal and Free State such certificates were granted only to whites, and by 1920 more than 7 000 white men were protected by these regulations and another 4 000 were protected by the force of custom backed up by trade-union action. The Rand Rebellion by white miners in 1922 further entrenched the colour bar both on the mines and, by means of the 'civilised labour policy' adopted by the 1924 coalition government of National and Labour parties, in employment by the state and by parastatal organisations such as the railways. The policy was described, in 1935, by the Secretary for Labour as being one that would ensure that white unskilled workers were

not denied entry into unskilled occupations by virtue of the fact that the lower standard of living to which the Native is accustomed has hitherto kept the rates of pay and their conditions of employment for work of this nature at a level which will not enable such workers to live in accordance with the standard generally observed by civilised persons. The policy is in no way associated with any question of racial segregation. (Wilson, 1972a: 11).

In practice the policy meant employing unskilled whites at higher rates of pay for particular jobs which blacks also needed, even at lower rates of pay. Thus on the railways, for example, between 1924 and 1936 the proportion of whites employed rose from 10 to 29 per cent. In the Depression year of 1933, as had happened even before the First World War, black railway workers were sacked to make room for more highly paid whites, who then constituted 39 per cent of the labour force (Wilson and Perrot, 1973: 330).

There were other barriers, too, to black advancement – indirect but no less effective. One which affected coloured people particularly was the Apprenticeship Act of 1922, which imposed no direct colour bar but set a required education level of entry at Standard 6. As the majority of schools for coloured pupils did not go beyond that level and many not even so far, the effect of the Act was to bar coloured people from the skilled trades which they had traditionally occupied in the Cape. This was reinforced by employers' tacit acceptance that only white youths were to be apprenticed and trained.

With the rapid expansion of the South African economy and the development of the manufacturing sector through the Second World War and in the years that followed, more and more workers of all races were needed to keep the wheels of industry turning. Thus the colour bar was not everywhere so rigid as in mining or the railways, but the combination of law, of custom (backed by white trade-union threats of strikes), and of a discriminatory educational policy effectively ensured that whites were protected and gained preferential access to the more highly skilled, better-paid jobs in the upper levels of the economy; whilst blacks, by and large, were held down in unskilled and semi-skilled occupations.

From the impact of the various colour barriers in the private sector of the economy, we turn briefly to identify, as a fifth interwoven strand of our history, some consequences of the white–black power structure as it manifested itself in the public sector. Our concern here is not so much with the workings of the colour bar (including the 'civilised labour policy') in state or parastatal enterprises such as the post-office, the railways, or the Electricity Supply Commission (Escom), which in large measure followed the pattern set in mining or secondary industry. We focus rather on the cumulative impact of differential power on the allocation of government revenue, specifically on public investment, in the economy as a whole. For just as the distribution of mine earnings could have been very different, so too the pattern (and consequences) of government expenditure down the years could have been radically altered had black South Africans also wielded political power. The topic is one that requires a great deal more research than it has received thus far, but, however briefly, in any analysis of the causes of poverty one cannot ignore the consequences of a systematic and prolonged bias, favouring one particular group, in the allocation of public expenditure. In South Africa this bias has been apparent in many areas, notably education, housing, health, agriculture, job-creation, and energy. In all these areas state expenditure, per capita, on whites has always been far higher than state expenditure on blacks.

In South Africa the evidence reveals clearly how public expenditure in education, agricultural support, job-creation or whatever, has been used down the years to support whites far more than blacks by investing in them as people and by providing them with infrastructural resources, in both rural and urban areas, to boost their economic well-being.

This focus on history arises not because we believe that a mere description of the past should illuminate the present, nor even that the very longevity of certain phenomena should explain anything. No: this process of drawing out some of the pertinent strands of our past has been done in order to demonstrate the extent to which the unfolding of history is shaped by the structure of power, within which events take place. We have been trying in this chapter to identify aspects of South Africa's history which have had a marked, cumulative impact on the shape of income distribution, on the pattern of poverty as it manifests itself in the country towards the end of the twentieth century.

At one level there is nothing particularly unusual about this history. South Africa is not the only country to have been conquered; not the only place where slavery existed; not the only economy whose workers have had a long harsh struggle against militant bosses. Nor indeed is it the only country where one group has used its control over the state to raise barriers against another group, or to capture the lion's share of public resources. But there is one feature of South Africa's industrial history that is unique. Nowhere else in the world has an industrial economy employed for so long such a high proportion of oscillating migrants (coming from both inside and outside the country) in its labour force. The consequences of this migrant labour system have been, as we shall see, profound.

Even before the discovery of gold, employers on the Kimberley diamond fields had fought for and won the power to house their black labourers in all-male closed compounds Then, with the rapid expansion of mining on the Witwatersrand after 1886, employers – in order to obtain an adequate supply of labour at what they regarded as reasonable wages – organised themselves together through the Chamber of Mines into a massive monopsonistic recruiting body which brought in men from all over southern Africa. To ensure that those recruited and sent to Johannesburg did not break their contract either before they started work or whilst they were there, the mine-owners put pressure on the government of the Transvaal Republic to tighten up the pass laws in order better to control the movement of men moving in from the countryside to the mines and back again.

The labour system, with its pattern of oscillating migration, introduced by the mining industry and buttressed by the pass laws, thus became a central feature of the South African political economy from the very beginning of the country's industrial revolution. For the next century virtually all black workers on the diamond mines were housed in closed compounds as migrant labourers until, for a variety of reasons that takes us beyond the scope of this book, the system was phased out of the diamond mines in the early 1970s. In the gold mines, however, which have formed the central dynamo powering South Africa's industrial revolution, the system is still going strong. In 1988 it is estimated that well over 95 per cent of the 500 000 black men at work in the mines are housed, on a single-sex basis, in the massive compounds, each containing several thousand men.

One further aspect of the system is pertinent to the subsequent analysis. That is the extent to which the political boundaries of the region failed to coincide with the economic borders. From the beginning the mines recruited labour from areas of the sub-continent that lay well beyond the region (which, in 1910, was to be forged into the Union of South Africa). As early as 1896, for example, no less than 60 per cent of the black miners digging gold came from Mozambique. By the beginning of the twentieth century many others came from Basutoland, Swaziland, the Bechuanaland Protectorate and even from tropical areas in what was then British Central Africa. With the exception of the northern countries, particularly the Nyasaland Protectorate (Malawi), Tanganyika (Tanzania), and Northern Rhodesia (Zambia) where recruiting was banned largely for health reasons from 1913 until the mid-1930s, the countries neighbouring South Africa continued to supply substantial numbers of men to the mines year after year, throughout the century. The following table traces the geographic origins of black labour working on the mines, mainly gold, affiliated to the Chamber of Mines over the 80 years from 1906 to 1986.

Table 10.01: Geographic origins of African labour on mines affiliated to the Chamber of Mines, 1906–86

Country	Number in thousands (and percentage)			
	1906	1936	1973	1986
South Africa	18 (23)	166 (52)	86 (20)	315 (60)
Lesotho	2 (3)	46 (15)	87 (21)	109 (20)
Botswana	0,3 (0,4)	7 (2)	17 (4)	20 (4)
Swaziland	0,6 (0,7)	7 (2)	17 (4)	14 (3)
Mozambique	53 (65)	88 (28)	99 (24)	58 (10)
Malawi ⎱ Other ⎰	6 (9)	3 (1)	128	20 (4) —
Total	81 (100)	318 (100)	422 (100)	536 (100)

Source: Chamber of Mines, Wenela and Teba annual reports

If we consider for the moment only the period up to the end of the Second World War, the table shows the extent to which, long before the advent of apartheid in 1948, the gold-mining industry and hence the whole South African economy relied on labour from a much wider 'catchment area' than the boundaries of the old Union of South Africa, let alone of the new Republic shorn of its 'independent' homelands of Transkei, Bophuthatswana, Venda, and Ciskei. After the Second World War, as the economy continued to expand, more and more workers were drawn into the manufacturing sector; and the mines, which alone were allowed to recruit black workers from outside the country, held their wages down by bringing in migrants from all over the sub-continent as far north as Zambia, Tanzania, and especially Malawi. By the early 1970s the proportion of South Africans among black mineworkers had fallen to no more than 20 per cent. But in 1974 the suspension by President Banda of recruiting in Malawi and the end of the Portuguese Empire threatening the flow of labour from Mozambique, combined with the dramatic increase in the price of gold, persuaded the Chamber of Mines to raise mine wages. In this way they could compete with the manufacturing sector and draw in more black South Africans, thus reducing the risk of suddenly losing a large proportion of the labour force. The strategy was successful: mine wages were trebled, in real (1980) terms, over the period 1973–83, and the proportion of external migrants (from what are now known as the SADCC countries) was reduced from 80 per cent in 1973 to 40 per cent in 1986.

The migrant system is not confined to the mines. One of the most notable features of the major urban centres of South Africa during the past 25 years has been the building of single-sex barracks to house up to 12 000 black workers at a time. As recently as June 1985, the government announced plans to build more such compounds, making it plain it has no intention of phasing out the system (*Cape Times*, 26.6.1985). It is estimated that over 2 million of the 5 million black workers in the South African economy are migrants; the other 3 million live, with their families, in the urban townships or on the white-owned farms of the country. Approximately one-quarter of them work in the mines. The vast majority of the migrants – over 1.5 million in mid-1984 – come from reserves within the country, while some 350 000 (17 per cent) come from outside South Africa.

Although migrant workers are found in other parts of the world, not least in the United States as seasonal agricultural workers and in western Europe as gastarbeiters, there is no other country where such a system has existed for so long and has trapped so large a proportion of the labour force in a dehumanising structure. The system is all too easy to ignore when one does not have to endure it. One must listen to the voices of those who live in the compounds to understand the grief it causes.

Fathers talk of the pain of seeing their children growing up as strangers. Sons tell of their shock upon going to town. 'We find our fathers with concubines yet our mothers are starving. Besides, the sweethearts are as young as father's children. We get fed up and cannot communicate with our fathers.' (5: 21) And wives point out: 'For our husbands we are just their old-age home or their hospitals. They really come back to us when they are too old to work or when they are sick.' (66: 5) And the men themselves lament: 'We stay a full year without our wives. That makes us go beyond the bounds of the law and become adulterers.' The conclusion, as one of them expressed it, 'is that in the towns we are spilt just like water on the ground' (5: 22).

What have been the broader consequences of this pattern of oscillating migration? How has it affected the rural areas that have for so long sent a large proportion of their economically active males to work in the mines and factories of the South African economy?

According to conventional economic analysis, the matter is relatively straightforward. Men choose to go to the mines because they can earn more money there than they would in whatever alternative work they find at home. Both the sending community and the receiving area benefit. If not, the trade would not take place. The migrant would not be hired, and he would not choose to come.

In the longer run, however, the picture becomes more complicated. One has to look not only at the immediate benefit of profits and wages, but also at the whole process of capital accumulation and the pattern of development in the wider society. As workers are drawn to an area by the jobs offered, money is spent there by workers, by management, and by the various authorities. Gradually, as demand for goods and services increases, whether for clothes, wheelbarrows or lawyers, capital is invested, factories are built, people are trained, organisations are put together. Above the hidden minerals on the bare veld, penetrated by the mine-shafts, a city grows with the capacity to generate large numbers of jobs at a wide range of wage levels. All this is made possible by the work of those who have laboured together, whether as migrant workers two miles below the surface, or as hairdressers – or indeed as such captains of industry as Cecil John Rhodes or Sir Ernest Oppenheimer.

Meanwhile, what of the rural community that has sent most of its able-bodied men away to the cities to work for up to two years at a stretch? As the years have passed, the various sending areas have gradually shifted from producing food within the geographic areas to producing gold and other industrial products elsewhere. As a consequence, local food production has fallen. Seen from the perspective of the economy as a whole, the system makes sense. Men go off to the mines to improve their material position, resources are allocated more efficiently, and output increases. The difficulty comes when one asks what happens to production within the geographic area from which the migrants have come.

Consider, for example, Lesotho. Until the end of the First World War, the country exported maize to the mines. During the 1920s, it remained more or less self-sufficient. However, from the time of the great drought at the beginning of the 1930s, Lesotho had become a net importer of maize (Murray, 1981). There is, of course, nothing intrinsically wrong with a society importing food. Many economies have developed by producing cloth or steel or computers to trade for food. The people of Lesotho did likewise: they produced gold. But the gold they dug was on the Witwatersrand of the southern Transvaal or beneath the maize fields of the Orange Free State. And their work contributed to the transformation of sparsely populated land into job-creating, income-generating cities that were not within the geographic boundaries of the area from which they came. While the miners were paid wages for their work, and they sent or took remittances back to their families, the people bought goods which increasingly were produced in the very cities from which the migrants were sending those remittances.

In other societies, such as those in western Europe, the people who started as migrant workers, or their children, moved permanently to the cities taking their families with them. The rural areas became depopulated until there was some balance between what was produced there and the number of people needed to produce it. But in southern Africa, viewed as a single economy that stretches as far as the recruiting arms of the Chamber of Mines, a bias has been built into the pattern of development.

Many of the rural areas of the region contain far more people than the level of production warrants because the law has prevented them from moving elsewhere. Women and children who should have been living in the cities with the miners and other migrants were not allowed to do so. The accumulation of capital and the capacity to create jobs and generate incomes were biased in the same way. Most of the economic activity was in the cities; some was on the platteland – in the small towns and on white-owned farms; virtually none was in the reserves or in border lands. One important consequence of a century of industrial revolution in southern Africa, combined with a system of migrant labour as described above, is that the black rural areas – the reserves and the neighbouring states (particularly Mozambique and Lesotho) – have become less able to generate, from within their boundaries, a means of livelihood for their inhabitants in 1988 than they were when gold was discovered a full century earlier (see, for example, 252: 8).

A graphic illustration of the consequence of this process may be seen in any of the small commercial centres of Lesotho where practically all the goods for sale, from building materials to groceries, are brought in from South Africa and paid for by the earnings of the migrants working in South Africa. Not only is the entire country dependent upon the access of its citizens to the wider economy, which they themselves have done so much to build, across the political boundary, but also most of the spending by those migrants and their families does almost nothing to generate further jobs and income within Lesotho. To watch, as one of us did in June 1988, an enormous 18-wheeled lorry outside a store in Mohale's Hoek in the south of Lesotho being unloaded of several thousand cartons of long-life milk sent up from Port Elizabeth is to see vividly something of the failure of a century's economic growth in southern Africa to develop the capacity to generate employment and wealth in those very areas that contributed so much to building Africa's most powerful economy.

They said: 'Old man, are you moving ?' And I replied 'I am not moving.' They said: 'It is a pity, father, for you will be crying after a little while. Old man, if you don't take your house down now, and follow the other people now, it will be very bad for you when you have to move.' After they said that, they went away, and I thought this over — what they meant about me crying if I didn't move. I thought the other people, even though they didn't want to move, might go and leave me here. So I took a crowbar, pulled the house down, and called the GG [government] trucks to collect the material. I was afraid maybe they would arrest me if I was left alone.

— Mr Mapapu in Glenmore,
Eastern Cape (76: 10)

The roots of South Africa's current poverty, and of the ongoing process of impoverishment, go deep into the past. But analysis shows that more recent developments, particularly those that have accompanied the emergence of the country's apartheid policies since the National Party came to power in 1948, have also contributed substantially to the problem. We would argue that, seen in its historic perspective, the election of the National Party in 1948 marked not so much a turning-point in South African history as the intensification of a process which had been going on for three hundred years. Thus some of the peculiarities of South Africa's industrial revolution, such as the land laws or the migrant labour system, became even more firmly entrenched as part of the structure of apartheid whilst some of the special features of apartheid, which we shall discuss in this chapter, themselves have roots that can easily be traced to well before 1948. At the same time there is little doubt that it is some of these special policies pursued by the National Party government that have done much to impoverish millions of South Africans.

In what may perhaps best be described as 'apartheid's assault on the poor', waged by the rulers in order to maintain, entrench, and defend white political and economic privilege, we identify six major lines of attack. These are: the shift in policy from incorporation to dispossession; anti-black-urbanisation; forced removals, both rural and urban; Bantu education; crushing of organisation; and destabilisation.

From incorporation to dispossession

There is one especially striking change that has taken place in South Africa's political policy since the Second World War. Though there was a shift to the right after the 1948 election as the Afrikaner nationalist movement took power, the radical change in direction came a decade later, when the National Party government guided by Dr Hendrik Verwoerd renounced a policy that had long been a fundamental plank in the platform of all white political parties.

Ever since the South Africa Act of 1909 had left a door open for other territories to join the four provinces (Cape, Natal, Orange Free State, and

Transvaal) as part of the new Union of South Africa, the policy of successive governments had been to 'incorporate' various parts of southern Africa into the Union. After South West Africa had been brought in as a mandated territory under the Treaty of Versailles in 1919, and the white settlers of Rhodesia had foreclosed their option by voting in 1922 against joining the Union, South Africa set its sights on incorporating the three (British) High Commission Territories of Basutoland, Bechuanaland, and Swaziland. Tshekedi Khama, Regent of the BamaNgwato people of the Bechuanaland Protectorate, spent much of his political life during the 1930s and 1940s seeking to prevent incorporation. In the next decade, Prime Minister J. G. Strijdom, an arch-republican, was willing to forgo turning South Africa into a republic and cutting political ties with Britain if this would help to persuade the British to hand over the High Commission Territories. Minister of foreign affairs Eric Louw and other South African spokesmen were fond of pointing out that, once this incorporation had happened, then half the land in South Africa would be in black hands, and apartheid would be seen by all to be a fair policy!

In 1957, however, the emergence of Ghana as an independent state was the first gust in the winds of change that blew down Africa during the next three decades, as one country after another was freed from political, although not economic, control by one or other of the European colonial powers. There followed the representation in the United Nations of a significant number of highly articulate new governments, each with a vote at the General Assembly. As a result, it was no longer conceivable that Britain would one day allow the incorporation of the High Commission Territories into an enlarged, white-dominated Union. Verwoerd, who had come to power in South Africa the year after Kwame Nkrumah in Ghana, recognised the realities, but even he still tried to persuade the territories to accept incorporation. Faced with their refusal, he countered with a stroke that transformed an apparent defeat into the springboard of a new strategy for the retention of power by whites throughout the sub-continent.

Because of the territories' total economic dependence upon South Africa flowing from the system of migratory labour and the pattern of capital accumulation in South Africa's cities, it was possible for Verwoerd to sell to his electorate the idea that the emergence to independence of the High Commission Territories was in the interest of whites. Far from being a threat to white security or white power, the political independence of areas that had long since been fused into the single wider economy controlled from the Witwatersrand carried with it all sorts of gains for the white Republic. After all, what nation-state can be held responsible for the educational expenditure or the unemployment, old-age, and other welfare benefits needed in another sovereign land? And if that sovereign land should ever try to pursue too independent a political line, then a threatened closure of a border post, a refusal to allow migrant workers to come in (as President P. W. Botha threatened Lesotho in August 1985), or the squeezing of some other less visible economic artery, should persuade that government to rethink its stand.

From there it was but a short step to the revolutionary new policy adopted by the National Party government. If Basutoland could become Lesotho (1966), if the Bechuanaland Protectorate could become Botswana (1966), and if Swaziland could also become independent (1968), then surely the reserves, it was argued, could also be set up as nation-states.

Economically speaking there was little difference between the histories of neighbouring countries like Lesotho and of the areas reserved for Africans under the 1913 Land Act. Both had become recruiting grounds for the mining industry. If the Transkei could be pushed into independence in 1976, then why not other parts of the archipelago of labour reserves? Thus the various bits and pieces of Tswana-speaking reserves scattered across three provinces were declared the independent nation of Bophuthatswana in 1977. Venda, a reserve in the northern Transvaal, acquired its first president in 1979. Ciskei, in the eastern Cape, became the fourth 'black national state' in 1981. There were still six more to go. Some like KwaZulu and Lebowa resisted strongly. Others like KwaNdebele, a fragment of land situated about 130 kilometres north-east of Pretoria in the Transvaal, were in 1988 being relentlessly pushed – despite staunch opposition – towards 'independence' as separate 'national states'.

Ridiculous as these boundaries might appear to outside observers, their consequences are anything but amusing for all the people whom these apartheid borders exclude from the industrial economy, where the jobs and the wealth of the country are generated.

In theoretical terms the pattern of development that has taken place in southern Africa as a consequence of the migrant labour system, decolonisa-tion, and apartheid's shift from incorporation to dispossession may be seen in terms of a series of concentric circles.

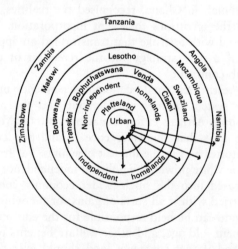

Fig. 11.01: Southern African core and periphery

Urban South Africa, surrounded by its platteland of commercial farms, all under white ownership and control, lies at the centre. Beyond this, in the second circle, are the non-independent reserves such as KwaZulu and Lebowa. Then, in the third circle, lie the independent reserves such as Transkei and Bophuthatswana. Beyond them are the three former High Commission Territories of Botswana, Lesotho and Swaziland; then, yoked together in terms of this analysis, come Mozambique and Malawi. Finally, on the outside edge, lie Zimbabwe, Namibia, Zambia, Tanzania and Angola. The arrows on the accompanying diagram show the flow of workers between these areas and the gold mines (see table 10.01).

Over the decade 1973–83, for a number of reasons, this pattern was to change dramatically as South Africa moved to reduce its dependence on labour from beyond the borders of the old Union. Malawi made the first, unexpected, step in April 1974 when President Banda stopped all recruiting for the South African mines. In the same month the coup in Lisbon heralded the end of the Portuguese Empire and the beginning of Mozambique's difficult years of independence alongside the big neighbour who was extremely hostile to the new Frelimo government. South Africa took the initiative in reducing, virtually overnight, the flow of Mozambican migrant workers to the mines from an annual average of 100 000 down to less than half that number. Subsequently, towards the end of 1986, South Africa threatened to halt the flow entirely. For Lesotho the screws have begun tightening. Already in the mid-1970s the abolition of migrant labour on the diamond mines was accompanied by a refusal to allow Basotho citizens access to the permanent jobs on the mines. Then, in the 1980s, recruiting for the gold mines became more selective. Jobs in South Africa for new entrants to the labour market from Lesotho became much scarcer. It was a far cry from the days when, as recently as three decades earlier, men could simply walk across the river to seek work on the farms or sign up for jobs on the mines which recruited from one area called, in their books, 'Basutoland and OFS'.

As far as the reserves were concerned, the hardening of the boundaries did not as yet adversely affect the flow of migrants. Indeed some areas, such as the Transkei, were used to replace the 50 000 or more recruits no longer being sought in Mozambique. But at the same time the abolition of the pass laws within South Africa specifically excluded migrants and potential migrants from the four independent reserves. For them any move to town was seen by the authorities as movement to a foreign country and required the specific approval of the South African department of foreign affairs. The potential threat of finding themselves shut out, like Mozambique, from the core of the economy of the region increased. There was already some evidence in the 1980s that it was more difficult for those living in the independent reserve of Bophuthatswana to get jobs in Bloemfontein than for those from Qwa Qwa.

Prevention of black urbanisation

For years one of the central thrusts of government policy in South Africa has been to prevent the movement of Africans to the urban areas. As far back as 1921 an official commission argued bluntly that blacks should only be allowed into the towns as temporary workers and should be compelled to leave as soon as their job was done. In 1937 the Native Laws Amendment Act was enacted to control the flow of blacks to the towns. Pass laws were tightened, but with economic expansion thousands of Africans moved, many with their families, to the cities. In 1942 under the liberalising impact of the war (and the threat of Japanese invasion) the Minister of Native Affairs stressed the benefits of abolishing the pass laws and was supported in this by a government commission which reported just before the 1948 election. However, after the change in government in 1948 the stated goal of the intensified anti-urbanisation policy was to slow down the flow to the cities, to halt it, and then (by 1978, it was hoped) to reverse it. 'The native who comes to the white area', proclaimed Dr Verwoerd in 1956, 'does so because he is there to serve, thus no loafing may be permitted. . . . The labour bureau system . . . has been developed for this purpose.' (Wilson 1972b: 167 and 204)

As the pressures for urbanisation mounted, the contradictions within the apartheid policy became more and more difficult to contain. On one hand, the state was pursuing economic growth that led, inevitably, to further urbanisation. On the other hand, it pursued with no less vigour the policy of 'separate development', whose ideological cornerstone from the end of the 1950s was to establish 'national states', or 'homelands', for Africans whose South African citizenship was revoked and converted into that of the appropriate ethnic state as it acquired 'independence'.

This dual policy had the peculiar distinction of requiring African men to be in two places at once: in the cities as 'labour units' to keep the wheels of mining and manufacturing turning; and in the rural labour reserves as husbands, fathers, and citizens. The contradictions of apartheid could only be resolved by a system which kept the workers moving, like shuttlecocks across the looms of the South African economy. But as that economy continued to grow, more and more workers and their wives wished to settle permanently near their places of work in the cities. This was, however, directly contrary to state policy, and so further steps were taken to prevent it from happening.

Of the array of techniques adopted by the state to prevent black urbanisation, there were essentially three kinds: pass laws; the limitations on housing construction; and the outright destruction of black communities. Each of these tactics cruelly disrupted the lives of black South Africans and directly contributed to the process of impoverishment. Under the pass laws, established in the nineteenth century as instruments for the control of blacks after the abolition of slavery, a rapidly increasing number of people, women as well as men, were arrested as the contradiction deepened between labour demands of the growing cities and the imperatives of separate development. An extraordinary number of people have been arrested, as may be seen in the following table.

Over the seventy years from 1916 when the first statistics were recorded until 1986 when the pass laws were formally abolished, the total number of people prosecuted in South Africa for being in some place (generally an urban area) without official permission was well over 17 000 000. All of them were

African. This means that one person was arrested on average once every two minutes, day and night, for the entire period from the year before the Russian Revolution until the time of President Reagan's second term of office. At their peak, during the decade from 1965 to 1975, the number of arrests averaged more than one every minute (281: 9; Wilson, 1972b and 1975; Race Relations Survey, 1976–1986).

Table 11.01: Pass law contraventions, 1921–75

Decade	Average annual no. of contraventions (×1 000)
1921–29	54.7
1930–39	110.8
1940–49	157.7
1950–59	318.7
1960–69	469.1
1970–75	541.5

Source: Wilson, 1984: 304
Note: Until (and including) 1962, figures are for convictions, which are slightly lower than prosecutions.

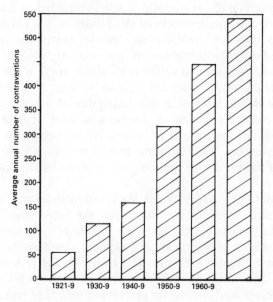

Fig. 11.02: Pass law contraventions, 1921–75

The constant fear of police raids coupled with the indignity of arrest, often from one's bed in the early hours of the morning, makes one of the faces of poverty that is distinctly South African. Whilst considering the overall statistical picture of millions of people entangled in the pass laws down the years, it is important not to lose sight of the way in which they have affected individuals trapped by the laws at a specific time and place. Until 1986, permission to stay in any urban area depended (if one was African) upon whether one had been born in the place, or lived there working continuously for one employer for ten years, or lived there continuously for fifteen years. There were some exceptions to these three criteria as laid down in Section 10 of the Natives (Urban Areas) Act of 1923 as amended in 1952, but these were the basic restrictions. They were themselves further limited, first in 1968 by labour regulations which made it increasingly difficult for workers to acquire residence rights by working continuously for an employer, and then by the thrusting of political independence upon the old reserves, starting in 1976 with the Transkei. Legislation surrounding the creation of these new 'black national states' as the Pretoria government chose to call them, effectively removed the urban birth-right by declaring that all those born (even in a city) of parents who were now (after independence of the relevant homeland) deemed to be citizens of a homeland, were aliens and thus ineligible to acquire urban residence rights in South Africa.

For 25 years, beginning in 1961, the Black Sash – an anti-apartheid women's organisation – has run a number of Advice Offices specifically to assist people caught, in one way or another, in the coils of the pass laws. In their files there are literally thousands of cases, recorded in heart-breaking detail, of the particular circumstances of this person or that family. Each case is different for no individual circumstances are ever exactly the same, but it is impossible to read the records without an overwhelming sense of sadness and of anger; sadness at the pain and suffering involved; anger at the unnecessary cruelty to powerless and vulnerable human beings. It is impossible to summarise all the detail, but just as the description of one day in the life of Ivan Denisovich enabled outsiders to glimpse something of what it meant to be one of the millions imprisoned in Stalin's labour camps, so too can the focus on one person, one 'case' from the files of the Black Sash, help one to feel something of the burden of the state on the shoulders of poor people in South Africa.

The story of Mrs E. N. was recorded nearly two decades ago, in 1971, and is used to illustrate not only the conditions she faced then but also to emphasise that the devastating impact of the pass laws has gone on for years and years. She was born in Nqutu, an area of Natal now designated KwaZulu. In 1961 she married a man who qualified to live in the prescribed area of Johannesburg in terms of the legislation. In 1963 she came to Johannesburg to live with her husband who applied for permission for her to remain with him in his brother's house in Soweto. This was refused, and in May of that year her reference book was stamped that she was not permitted to remain in or to work in Johannesburg. She returned to Nqutu for a short visit where she was told that she could no longer live there and that she should return to her husband. She went back to Johannesburg and lived, unlawfully, with her husband who, in 1968, applied for a house of his own. This was refused because his wife did not have permission to live in Johannesburg. Her reference book was stamped to that effect and she was 'warned to leave the prescribed area of Johannesburg within 72 hours'. But she remained in Johannesburg with her husband, continuing to be daily in danger, as she had been for five years, of arrest. In 1970 her husband went to Nqutu to see the Bantu Affairs Commissioner and was told that his wife and children could not live there. Mrs N. and her children were thus displaced people. There was nowhere for them to go. Although all three children were born in Johannesburg, their father could not put their names down on a house permit nor could he get a house of his own because the presence of his wife in Johannesburg was not legally recognised. Moreover if she had then applied to be resettled somewhere in KwaZulu or any other reserve her children would then have to forfeit their birth-right, in terms of the law, to be in Johannesburg. And even if she did remain in Johannesburg the children would find it difficult to prove that they had resided in the city since their birth as their names did not appear on any housing permit (Wilson, 1972b: 236).

Fifteen years later, in Cape Town, comes this brief glimpse of a young mother, Lydia. Divorced with one child, she went back to look after her 86-year-old mother who lived with her husband in a house tied to a lime-processing plant whose owner forbade anyone else to stay with them. Thus, since Lydia was not allowed to stay there she has been running from the police. She and her 1-year-old baby were amongst those arrested in a police raid. They spent the weekend in jail and were only allowed out because of the baby. She had to reappear in court and, at the time of the interview, did not know what the outcome would be because she did not have money to pay the R20 fine. She did not have anyone to support her. She had divorced her husband about six years previously, but although he was required to support her and the child financially she had not received a cent. 'She has been to court many times for a maintenance grant but is tired of this because nothing ever materialises' (15: 14). Lydia, writes M. M. Gonsalves, is tired of trying to make ends meet as well as running from the police. She states that no matter where one goes, if one does not work and 'live in', and does not have a pass, one has to run, because of the danger of trespassing. She begs for a live-in job as she cannot stand the thought of being caught again and of being constantly on the look-out for the police (15: 5).

Something of the frustration which such legislation has engendered in people may be seen in the statement made from the dock of the Supreme Court in Cape Town in 1987 when Sazi Veldtman, subsequently sentenced to 15 years' imprisonment for participation in the guerilla activities of Umkhonto we Sizwe (military wing of the banned African National Congress), explained to the judge what had driven him to violence:

In my childhood I saw many people arrested for passes and taken to police stations. But my aunt was very careful to keep her pass with her so when she was stopped, she always had it. She taught me that when I was 16 I would need a pass. Unfortunately I was again arrested. That was in 1972. I was in Goodwood [Cape Town] and when I was asked for this pass (which I then already regarded as a badge of slavery) I did not have one. I told the policeman I was only 14 years old but I was not believed and I was locked up. This time I was locked up with drunk people. In the cell they took my money away from me. Fortunately for me after a few hours I was again released. Because of my aunt I continued with my school. ... When I turned 16 years old [August 1973] I went to apply for my reference book. I was refused many times and was told to go back to the Transkei. When I went to the head office of the Bantu Affairs Administration Board, Mr Fourie told me that I do not belong to the western Cape and ordered me to leave. I explained to him the death of my mother and family. He told me he was not interested in my stories. He had heard enough lies from us Bantu. But round about 1981 I saw another official. He told me I must prove how long I have been in Cape Town. I could prove this to him except for one year and that was 1978 when I was at [the University of] Fort Hare. He wanted proof of this and so I went to Alice to go to Fort Hare. There I got a certificate that I was at Fort Hare for 1978. Fortunately this was accepted and I then got my pass.

But, for a decade, from the age of 14 until he was 24, Sazi Veldtman lived in constant fear of arrest despite all attempts to regularise his position. 'I always had to run from the police because I had no pass.'

Some measure of relief from the enforcement and consequences of the pass laws was afforded by their abolition in 1986. Whilst there is no doubt that the removal from the statute book, after a century and a half, of a set of laws which had been such a burden to those enduring poverty represented a significant step, it is important to recognise the limits of what has been done. First of all, the reform did not apply to everybody. Of the estimated 25 million Africans living in South Africa (including the reserves) at the beginning of 1986, some 9 million of them had already been formally deprived of their South African citizenship through the process of declaring Transkei, Bophuthatswana, Venda, and Ciskei independent in the decade since 1976. Of these 9 million, an estimated 2 million were potentially eligible for restoration of South African citizenship under the 1986 legislation (*Weekly Mail*, vol.2, no. 25, 1986). Some 7 million South Africans, more than one-quarter of the African population, were still deemed to be aliens in the land of their birth and subject to 'immigration' laws that gave them no automatic right of entry to most of the mines, factories, and farms of the South African economy. Indeed for Africans in Cape Town, virtually all of whom are Xhosa-speaking and thus deemed to be citizens of either Ciskei or Transkei, the legal or *de jure* position of all those other than the minority which had by 1986 acquired residence rights in the city, has actually worsened. In terms of the alien legislation to which they are now subject, individuals can be administratively expelled to the reserves without recourse to any court of appeal. In practice the government did not immediately resort to mass expulsions but it has the legal authority to do so any time it chooses. Moreover, as we shall see, even for those black South Africans who were no longer constrained by either pass or passport legislation, the government still had other weapons (including trespass laws, the Group Areas Act, and housing policy) to determine whether or not they might be able to live in the cities. One example of the state's continued determination to control African movement is the raid carried out by the army, in March 1988, on the migrant hostels in the African township of Kayamandi in Stellenbosch. The purpose of the raid was, apparently, to evict all women from the hostels even although they had nowhere else to live (Louw, 1988: 15–19).

From about the middle of the 1960s on, the state as a matter of deliberate policy slowed down and, in some cases, actually stopped the building of new houses for Africans in the cities and towns of South Africa. The central government refused to make money available for housing except in the homelands, and in other ways exerted pressure on local authorities not to build such housing (81: 13). Though it seems incredible, officials in 1971 told one of us (F. W.) that the state was seriously considering moving the whole of Soweto, the sprawling black township on the edge of Johannesburg, several hundred kilometres to the KwaZulu reserve in Natal. Workers could then commute, 'like the Japanese', on a monorail system that would whisk them hundreds of miles to work and back every day. Although this mad idea was never implemented for all those already living on the Witwatersrand, it was responsible for the establishment, in the late 1970s, of the new homeland of KwaNdebele situated between 110 and 150 kilometres north-east of Pretoria. Its function was to help stop more black people, squeezed off commercial farms and elsewhere, moving to the industrial core of the South African economy as they would otherwise have done in any normal process of urbanisation. In 1970 the population in the area was approximately 32 000. By the mid-1980s the number of people living in KwaNdebele was anything between 300 000 and half a million. According to the director-general of the South African government department responsible, the people moved to KwaNdebele because they wanted to:

One day the prime minister asked me: 'What motivates these people to trek here like this?' My answer to him was: 'What motivated the Israelis to go to Israel after the Balfour Declaration?' Idealism gripped them and see what happened to Israel. It is the same thing in KwaNdebele. It is all about the magnetism, the pulling power of a spiritual fatherland. They are streaming in and we just can't keep up with services there. They prefer to live there, in their own community. And what is the result? Buses. That is what it is all about. (83: 37)

The director-general's analysis of the causes of the movement of people to KwaNdebele is a supreme example of the self-deception that power can breed; but his assessment of the consequences is entirely accurate. As there are almost no employment opportunities in KwaNdebele the new settlers, if they are not to starve, must immediately move out from the reserve and either get contracts as migrant labourers (staying temporarily, without their families, at their place of work) or else become *pendelaars*. This Afrikaans word was created in the 1970s from the Dutch word for a shuttle service. It is translated in government documents as 'commuters' and is used to describe those who live in parts of reserves that are just close enough to urban areas for them to travel to work on a daily basis. Some may genuinely be called commuters in that the area where they live, such as Umlazi outside Durban or Mdantsane outside East

London, is close enough for a daily bus or train journey to be feasible, although expensive. But for many *pendelaars* the daily journey to work and back is a nightmare.

The shortest bus ride from KwaNdebele to Pretoria takes about one hour and forty-five minutes. The longest journey lasts about three hours. From the terminus at Marabastad, many workers take onward transport, by train, bus or taxi, to get to work. Thus some of those living furthest from Pretoria catch a bus at 2.30 a.m., arrive in Marabastad at 5.30 a.m., and then travel a further hour or more to reach work at 7 a.m. The process is reversed in the evening, and they arrive home at between 9.00 and 10.30 p.m. A study for the Human Sciences Research Council in 1982 found that many of those travelling spent more than sixteen hours away from home (up to eight of them travelling and waiting in queues) five or six days every week (Ehlers, 1982).

The following table shows the increase in the number of daily buses run by a private company, Putco, between Pretoria and the resettlement camps of KwaNdebele, in the five years after the first two buses were introduced in 1979.

Table 11.02: Number of daily buses between KwaNdebele and Pretoria

Year	Number of buses
1979	2
1980	66
1981	105
1982	148
1983	220
1984	263

Source: Lelyveld, 1986: 122

Fig. 11.03: Number of daily buses between KwaNdebele and Pretoria

By 1984 the government paid the bus company a subsidy equivalent to more than R2 000 a year for each *pendelaar* or 'commuter'. This was, writes Lelyveld,

a negative social investment that went up in gas fumes when it might just as easily have gone into new housing for the same black workers nearer the industrial centers if that had not violated the apartheid design. ... The KwaNdebele bus subsidy – the government's largest single expense in the development of this homeland – was higher than the KwaNdebele gross domestic product. (1986: 122)

Quite apart from the wastefulness of the state subsidy is the cost, both in time and in money, to the *pendelaars* themselves. Although no specific study of transport was made for the Carnegie Inquiry it is clear that the cost to poor people of having to live long distances from their places of work as a result of apartheid policies in the form either of anti-urbanisation controls or Group Areas removals is high and, as the pressure on government resources increases – and hence the subsidy the state is able or willing to provide, decreases – is likely to grow higher.

A further consequence of the state's anti-urbanisation policy was, paradoxically, the intensification of extreme overcrowding in the black townships. A doctor who worked in Soweto for several years estimated that by the beginning of the 1980s, approximately twenty people were living in each four-roomed house, 'and stories of thirty people living in a four-roomed house are not uncommon' (170: 2). During the 1970s, only 500 new houses in Soweto were built each year, enough to accommodate just 3 500 extra people at the official rate of seven persons to a house. Yet during this same period the natural population growth annually was of the order of 25 000. There were at least 20 000 extra people each year for whom no houses were built. This figure takes no account of the housing needs of people moving to Johannesburg from rural areas.

Even when the law prohibits it, one way of creating more space is simply to build for oneself. In Soweto and in many other townships throughout South Africa, large numbers of 'backyard shacks' or 'garden huts' have appeared. Most of them are said to be occupied by legal residents who simply cannot fit into the houses any longer (170: 3).

In Soweto as a whole and in Alexandra Township, many houses have more than one family living in them. In Alexandra in particular, the position is particularly bad, with large families cramped into very small single rooms. This situation forces people to build shacks as a relief from overcrowding. If found, the shacks are demolished instantly and all the material taken by WRAB [the West Rand Administration Board]. (2: 8)

In Cape Town all house-building for Africans was halted in 1966 in an attempt by the state to reduce the number of Africans in the western Cape by 5 per cent a year. Even though the city was expanding and more workers were being drawn into it, with the exception of huge barracks for single men no more housing was built. No allowance was made for natural population increase. There was no shelter for the wives and children of migrant workers who crept unauthorised into the city to join their men. Squatter shacks mushroomed, not only in backyards but also on vacant lots: one along Modderdam Road, another close to it at a place called Unibel, and yet another, now very well known, at Crossroads.

Neither the absence of housing and other basic urban infrastructure nor the pass laws were a sufficient deterrent to the flow of Africans into the cities. More force was necessary if the state's policy was to be executed, and so bulldozers were called in to carry out mass demolitions. In the cold, wet winter of 1977, the 10 000 inhabitants of Modderdam Road watched as their shelters were razed to the ground. Six months later, Unibel, home of 20 000 people, was obliterated. Crossroads, declared the officials, was next on the list to be destroyed. But the people there resisted. And the spotlight of the national and international press fell upon them, strengthening their cause.

In the long struggle at Crossroads, bulldozers have been used, batons have been wielded and, in 1985, bullets were fired (at least 18 persons were killed). For now, the people seem to have won the battle; Crossroads is to remain. A new township called Khayelitsha is being built nearby, and the plans to subject three other black townships to forced removals under the Group Areas Act have been shelved. The policy of clearing all Africans from the western Cape at the bottom tip of Africa seems finally to have been abandoned. But the cost has been enormous.

Forced removals

It has been estimated that in the 23 years from 1960 to 1983 a total of 3.5 million people, almost all of them black, have been subject, in terms of government policy, to forced removal from one place to another where they did not choose to go (Platsky and Walker, 1985: 9).

Considerable evidence of the nature and impact of removals was collected during the course of the Carnegie Inquiry. But even more was assembled in the massive Surplus People Project whose five-volume report was published in June 1983 and subsequently condensed, and updated, in a single book published in 1985. It is difficult to summarise this mass of material in a few pages. Perhaps it is most helpful to consider five categories of removals.

First, the removals, largely in terms of the Group Areas Act, from one part of an urban area to another, primarily in order to segregate more clearly one 'ethnic group' from another.

Second, the expulsion, from urban areas, of people who have lived there often for many years, on the grounds that they are not required for the functioning of the particular urban economy and should (for ideological reasons) be sent to one of the reserves or 'black national states'.

Third, are the 'black spot' or Bantustan consolidation removals, whereby people have been moved from one part of rural South Africa to another in an attempt to reduce the number of islands in the archipelagos of 'black national states' dotted across the sea of white-owned land.

Fourth is a type of removal which dates back half a century or more to before the Second World War: the so-called 'betterment' programmes to consolidate people living scattered through the reserves, into villages.

Fifth is the massive movement of those compelled to move off white-owned farms (where they may have lived and worked for generations). Prevented by pass laws and state housing policy from moving to the cities, the majority of these people have found themselves with no option but to move into the already overcrowded reserves.

(1) In the years since it was first introduced in 1950, the Group Areas Act has led directly to the forced removal of well over three-quarters of a million people. It is estimated that 80 000 coloured families, 38 000 Indian, and 2 000 white families have had to move in order to fulfil the apartheid planners' schemes for racially segregated living-areas in the cities, towns, and even villages of South Africa. Residential segregation of Africans was ensured a generation earlier by the urban areas legislation dating from 1923 or before (133: 3 and Walker and Platsky, 1985: 10). There are various levels at which it is possible to analyse the impact of the Group Areas removals. Like the pass laws they are both a manifestation or dimension of poverty as well as a cause of further impoverishment. The burden of the removals has been felt in different ways. One was the sheer pain of moving from well-loved, familiar places:

My father was the last to move [from Simonstown] and before we moved he was standing at this particular window, looking over the bay. We had a very beautiful view; and this was the first time I saw my father cry. I could see that he did not want to leave that place. . . . (10d: 15)

Old people were particularly hard hit by the shock of having to move. 'Among five families who were my immediate neighbours in Harfield Village [Cape Town], two elderly people died after their families received eviction notices and a third had a heart attack within weeks of removal' (258: 1). It was not only the loss of familiar surroundings that mattered to the old people but also the loss of facilities such as a nearby post-office where pensions could be collected. The whole process of uprooting settled communities 'compounded the psychological and social uncertainties associated with aging', not least by increasing the sense of isolation of the elderly (292: 1).

By all acounts, even more burdensome than the more obvious aspects of the Group Areas removals – including increased rents and transport costs, and the overcrowding into shoddy, cheaply built houses – was the destruction of the less visible ties that bound communities together and provided a buffer against the ravages of poverty. It was

like a man with a stick [explained Oscar Wollheim] breaking spiderwebs in a forest. The spider may survive the fall, but he can't survive without his web. When he comes to build it again he finds the anchors are gone, the people are all over and the fabric of generations is lost. Before, there was always something that kept the community ticking over and operating correctly . . . there was the extended family, the granny and grandpa were at home, doing the household chores and looking after the kids. Now, the family is taken out of this environment where everything is safe and known. It is put in a matchbox in a strange place. All social norms have suddenly been abolished. Before, the children who got up to mischief in the streets were reprimanded by neighbours. Now there's nobody and they join gangs because that's the only way to find friends. (258: 14)

As Don Pinnock has pointed out, the extended family was 'the social and economic life-raft of the old ghettoes. Not only were the fragile economic threads broken by the mass removals, but they were prevented from being respun on the hostile sands of the Cape Flats.' Extended families could not reconstitute themselves in houses built to contain only a nuclear family. 'Families were either hopelessly overcrowded or smashed' (258: 1).

One of the most violent and destructive attempts by the state to move people from one part of a city to another had less to do with the ideology of segregation, which lay behind the Group Areas Act, than with the politics of control under pressure of rapid urbanisation. But the net effect was the same. The state moved in to destroy homes with the object of getting people to move to a different part of the city, further away from the major sources of employment.

The appalling events in the Gugulethu–Nyanga–Crossroads complex during May and June 1986 still require detailed investigation and analysis. But the main outlines of the drama are clear (*SA Outlook*, January 1987). During the previous 18 months, after a pitched battle between police and rock-throwing youths when the state had finally conceded the right of the Crossroads squatters to remain in the city (Badsha, 1986: 14), there had been a rapid build-up in various parcels of empty land of self-built accommodation ranging from flimsy plastic shelters to solidly constructed wood-and-iron houses. Some of the residents, it seems, were newly arrived from the countryside; others were old-established city people who had moved out of the intolerably overcrowded houses in nearby townships in order to make more living space for themselves. The new settlements were crowded, lacking in infrastructure, and urgently in need of upgrading. With good government the problem could certainly have been tackled and solved creatively. But the state, whose own anti-urbanisation policies were primarily responsible for the problem in the first place, lacked vision, patience, or any sense of the need to harness the energies and wishes of the people involved. A unilateral decision was made. Everybody must move to a new site (considerably further from the city) selected by the government. When people refused, it is alleged that the state made use of a division (which itself requires further analysis), between different groups of squatters in order to destroy – mainly by fire – all shelters and houses erected in specific areas which it wished to clear. These allegations are the subject of court proceedings, pending before the Cape Supreme Court at the end of 1988.

(2) In addition to moving people from one part of a city to another, the state sought also to remove people from town and send them to the rural reserves. Much of this policy was effected through the pass laws, whereby individuals without rights to be in town were apprehended and railed off. But there were also mass campaigns to expel people using other forms of force, ranging from the destruction of their homes by bulldozers as in the western Cape during the latter half of the 1970s, through batons to bullets, as in the confrontation with the people of Crossroads early in 1985. Some campaigns moved against people, like pensioners, who were acknowledged to have been

long in town but who were now regarded as what one Cabinet Minister referred to as 'surplus appendages'. Thus particularly in the 1960s, large numbers of people were moved (sometimes hundreds of miles) from places like Beaufort West in the Karoo to Dimbaza in the Ciskei (35 and Desmond, 1969); or from towns such as Klerksdorp in the western Transvaal to Itsoseng in Bophuthatswana as part of a long-term plan to reduce and hopefully, one day, to eliminate all African families in these areas (Wilson, 1972b: 86 and 89).

(3) Turning to removals from one rural area to another we find a process that was no less devastating for those compelled to move. In 1983, in a village called Mogopa, in the western Transvaal, one of us saw solidly built churches and schools lying in heaps of rubble. The village had been bulldozed by the government as a prelude to moving people from land they had been able to purchase before the Land Act of 1913 prohibited them as Africans from buying land in most of the country. It was lovely land, well watered and stocked with cattle. The people were moved to a place called Pachsdraai in the independent 'homeland' of Bophuthatswana. Visiting in 1983, one of us saw the stone houses that the people had painstakingly built up over the years; met the village elders gathered anxiously to discuss best how to prevent the great evil that was looming over them – the destruction of their homes and of the community; heard about the water pumps that had been removed and about the buses that were no longer coming. Aninke Claasens, working for the Transvaal Rural Action Committee to help monitor and resist removals, explained what happened next:

What does the state do once [it has] smashed the schools, stopped the transport, cut off the water, threatened force – and people still refuse to move? . . . It waits. There is a limit to how long people can live without schools, without pensions, without migrant labour contracts, and with daily uncertainty about their future. If it is a matter of who can sit it out, the state is the more likely winner. (74: 15)

Still the people refused to move. After the first demolitions they regrouped and set about the reconstruction of Mogopa. They rebuilt the school from rubble. Then, in the early hours of 14 February 1984, Mogopa was surrounded by armed government police. At 4 a.m. the people were informed through loud-hailers that they must load their possessions into trucks and go to Pachsdraai. The government-appointed chief, Jacob More, took the police and the officials first to the houses of the community leaders, who were handcuffed and put into police vans. Their families refused to pack their possessions – a task left to government labourers. Women were carried into lorries and buses. Children were loaded with the furniture and dispatched to Pachsdraai. All of this happened in the presence of scores of armed police with dogs at their disposal. People caught standing together outside their houses were beaten with batons. Parents became desperate to find their children and got onto buses to Pachsdraai to go to look for them there. No outsiders were allowed into Mogopa, excepting the police, of course, and the white farmers who had free access in and out to buy the people's livestock at a tenth of its value (74: 15).

Another example of these rural removals was movingly described in January 1988 on the front page of the *Wall Street Journal* by Roger Thurow reporting from the village of Laxey about 80 kilometres north of Kuruman.

In their old home, in a place called Ga-Tlhose about 40 miles south of the town of Kuruman, jobs could be found. The women could work as domestic servants for white families, and many of the men worked in asbestos or manganese mines or for farmers. Thus, families could stay together. In addition, the land was more fertile and big towns were accessible over adequate roads. But in 1977, government trucks arrived and carried the 40 000 blacks of Ga-Tlhose to the southern edge of the Kalahari Desert. ... Here, in the remote reaches of what has been declared the tribal homeland of Bophuthatswana, jobs are as scarce as rain, and the only commerce consists of a couple of small, overpriced general stores. Raising crops on the parched banks of the Moshaweng River here has proved nearly impossible.

The assessment of the *Wall Street Journal* is entirely consistent with the mountains of evidence that have been collected over many years by individuals and organisations during the course of their work and by studies undertaken specifically for the Surplus People Project, for Operation Hunger, and for the Second Carnegie Inquiry. South Africa, reports Thurow,

is dotted with hundreds of destitute villages like Laxey, a kind of geographic pox spread by a two-decade-long program of herding blacks into self-governing 'tribal homelands'. Their residents are apartheid's dispossessed – people who have been uprooted, dumped in a place far away from home and more or less abandoned. For all its gold, its diamonds and its heart transplants, South Africa has pockets of deprivation worse than the general conditions in some of its much poorer black-ruled neighbours.

(4) The fourth category of resettlement has ostensibly been carried out for the benefit of the poor but seems almost invariably to have impoverished the very poor even further. 'Betterment' schemes to improve farming in the rural reserves have a long history in South Africa. Already in the 1930s attempts were made, within the framework of the reserves, to improve agriculture but it was not until the 1950s and the public discussion of the need to improve the economic viability of the Bantustans which surrounded the publication of the Tomlinson Commission report, that the government embarked on a sustained programme of 'betterment'. Whatever the theory behind the programme, the reality was that for people on the ground the process of betterment was painful, seemed wasteful, and was resisted. Both in Pondoland (Mbeki, 1964) and in the western Transvaal (Hooper, 1960) peasant resistance to the measures flared into revolt. The figure for the total number of people compelled to move from one part of a rural area to another in pursuit of the 'betterment' programme is unknown and is not included within the SPP estimate of 3.5 million persons subject to forced removal since 1960 (Platsky and Walker, 1985: 9). But it is clear that hundreds of thousands of people have had to move, breaking down their old homesteads and building new ones; moved from being scattered around the countryside into the closely settled villages where all houses had to be laid out 'in lines'. The SPP estimates

that in Natal alone more than one million people have had to move since the 1950s in this programme.

One of the main difficulties was that once people had been taken from their fields and collected in villages, the fields, even if they remained in the same hands, were now often a long distance from the homestead. This meant not only that it took a long time to walk there in order to cultivate, but also that it was not possible to keep an eye on the crops. Theft increased and people found it less worthwhile to cultivate. Another difficulty lay in the fact that in the process of rationalisation some people actually lost land. Furthermore, much of the villagisation was enforced on the assumption that plans for ensuring woodlots for fuel and adequate supplies of water to the villages would be carried out. When they failed to materialise the ecological pressure (for water and, especially, fuel) became considerable and led to further deterioration of the environment. The consequence of this process combined with rapid population increase – partly through natural population growth but mainly due to resettlement of people brought in from outside the reserves – was disastrous. Overall, poverty increased (49: 7; 80: 11; 149: 2; 152: for a global perspective see Bruntland report, 1987).

In a careful micro-study of a Transkeian 'betterment' village Julia Segar has examined Joanne Yawitch's general thesis that 'In the process of restructuring the principle was firmly entrenched that those who had access to some resources would end up with less, those who had nothing or minimal resources to begin with, would be plunged into a downward spiral of ever-increasing impoverishment' (49: 17). On the basis of her in-depth study, Segar found that 'betterment' had the effect of increasing inequality. Those who had some resources before the process began, improved their position as a result, whilst those who were very poor to begin with became even poorer as a result. She confirmed Yawitch's main conclusion that 'In terms of the new dispensation created by betterment, it is the poor, or when speaking about the reserves the poorest sections of the population, who fare worst' (Yawitch, cited in 49: 7).

The impact of 'betterment', coupled with other forms of resettlement that brought more people into a particular rural area, was the subject of a special study in Venda, a reserve in the northern Transvaal which had independence thrust upon it in 1979. The study focused on two areas: one in the Nzhelele Valley; the other to the east, on mountains near the source of the river. The people of the valley were resettled into a 'betterment' scheme in 1966 whilst the mountain area remained as it was until early 1972, when it was surveyed with a view to its 'economic' planning. Two plans were proposed for the mountain area: one envisaged that it be divided into 21 economic units (each with 6 ha of arable land) and 37 uneconomic units of 2 ha stands. The alternative plan was for 40 stands of 2 ha each plus another 120 stands of 1 ha each, thus ensuring some land for most of the 180 households. But the master plan for the wider area envisaged further resettlement of households on small plots of 0.2 and 0.1 ha, with those designated as farmers being allocated some land (2–3 ha each) in the vicinity. What happened in fact was that between

1971 and 1983 the population on the mountain area increased more than four-fold from just over 700 persons to approximately 3 000. During this period local employment opportunities in afforestation and at the saw mills improved but the proportion of households with access to arable land fell from 100 to 31 per cent, with only 6 per cent of the households having stands bigger than 1 ha. Nearly half (approximately 45 per cent) of the men were away working, most of them (90 per cent) in the PWV area. Three-quarters of the migrants sent their families an average of R60 per month, but 25 per cent of them sent no money (64).

A similar process of increasing population density and landlessness had happened some years earlier, again following the implementation of 'betterment', in the valley. The social structure of the two communities, reports Schutte, was rapidly transformed. Headmen were willing to encourage newcomers to settle because migrant earnings were the main source of tax revenue in an area where the land was already too crowded to farm. But the increasing population that resulted put great pressure on social relationships.

Traditionally, Venda communities were differentiated into members of the chiefly *singo* clan and commoners. The chief or headman's distribution of resources was controlled by the commoners who could withdraw from his area if he was perceived to be unjust. Nowadays, however, there is nowhere to withdraw to. The headmen of both communities and their classificatory brothers tended to be favoured by the new system. The mountain community provide the clearest example of this. The headman and members of his extended family have the largest economic units of up to 6 ha in size. Some of them are professional people like the headmaster, the chief forestry officer, and minister of religion. In addition to them, there exists another category of favourites such as the shopowner, the chicken farmer, a teacher and the Zionist bishop who received concessions for gardens and orchards. The result was the creation of a wealthy class in distinction to the absolute poor. It is this class also who run the shebeens at weekends, enriching themselves further in the process at the cost of the majority of poverty-stricken households. (64: 16)

As regards the rapid increase of population in the two areas:

the granting of 'independence' to the territory of Venda seems to be the watershed. The Status of Venda Act (107) of 1979, conferred the nationality of this territory on all individuals culturally or socially linked to the area. They were thus deprived of their South African nationality in the process. Any Venda considered to be 'superfluous' in 'white' South Africa could from 1979 onwards be 'repatriated', i.e. removed according to the principles of international law. The South African government could therefore apply urban legislation aimed at control of population growth, unemployment, etc. without opprobrium of the outside world. Under the guise of constitutional development, urban control could be exercised and property excised. This is what happened in the two areas described. The newcomers came as a result of Black Spot removals, unemployment, old age, the tightening of urban influx control, and homeland consolidation. (64: 14)

Thus, concludes Schutte, from a detailed study of two communities in Venda it is possible to see how the interacting process of 'betterment', constitutional development, and urban population control is largely responsible for the increase of misery and poverty in the rural reserves. 'The artificial increase in population was not matched by more and better services and employment opportunities. A certain privileged section in both localities studied managed to derive benefits from the increase in population and its link to migrant labour.'

(5) The fifth major category of removal concerns those caught between agricultural mechanisation on one hand, and the state's policy of preventing all black urbanisation on the other. At the beginning of the 1950s one-third of black South Africans lived on the white-owned farms, which constitute approximately 80 per cent of the area of the country. Changing techniques of agricultural production, particularly the increased use of tractors, combine harvesters, and chemical weed-killers, made it possible for more food to be produced by fewer workers. At first the number of new jobs created each year in agriculture lagged behind the population growth. Then, by the end of the 1960s the absolute number of jobs in agriculture started to fall. More and more people were pushed off the land. There is nothing unusual about the displacement of agricultural workers through mechanisation; many other countries have experienced it. What was unique about South Africa was the response of the state to these changes. Africans evicted from the farms were not allowed to move to the cities. They had to go to the homelands, to the already overcrowded labour reserves. It is estimated that between 1950 and 1980 some 1.4 million people were squeezed off the commercial farms and another 90 000 were pushed off or migrated from towns other than the eleven metropolitan areas in South Africa. Of these 1.4 million ended up in the reserves (Simkins, 1983: 59–61).

The consequences, as we have seen in Chapter 2, were devastating. Population density in the reserves rose dramatically. In Qwa Qwa (an extreme, but by no means unique, example) the population in 1970 was estimated at 24 000, almost five times what it had been during the First World War when a government commission had found it already overcrowded. But by the mid-1980s, through a combination of agricultural mechanisation and the application of an ideological policy to reduce the number of blacks on white-owned farms, the population had risen to approximately 500 000. Whilst there were those who moved voluntarily off the farms in the hopes of obtaining a place of their own on which to build a house in the reserves, the evidence suggests that the vast majority were compelled to move and could not, as in other parts of the world, go directly to live and look for work in the cities. For thousands of individuals and families caught, as it were, in the crossfire, the process was not only impoverishing but also intensely painful.

Mr Mapapu was a farm labourer for many years but now lives in the resettlement camp of Glenmore on the banks of the Fish River, which marks the old eastern Cape frontier as well as the boundary of the Ciskei (whose population doubled in the 12 years prior to independence in 1981). In 1979 he was compelled by government officials to demolish his house and to move to the resettlement camp 100 kilometres away from where he had been working as a casual labourer on chicory farms in the Alexandria district.

Before the move to Glenmore the Mapapus' two small daughters, 18-month-old Nominiki and 5-year-old Ntombiyakhe, had been active, spirited youngsters. Now, however, Mr Mapapu began to notice a difference in their appearance and behaviour.

They were not as active as they had been. They had sunken faces, they got pale, and their bodies were thin. Most of the time they were just lying on the ground, in the daytime too. I was worried about them, more than I can tell. I and my wife talked about them. My wife said if I was a man I would leave this place and go to a farm anywhere and find work. My answer was that I left the farm because I couldn't work there – that was why we went to Klipfontein. She wasn't angry with me. She was mostly worried about the children (76: 14).

The children were not the only ones suffering. 'We were hungry, I and my wife. . . . There is no way you can describe that hunger.' The children became so ill that eventually the baby, Nominiki, was sent from the local clinic to hospital in Grahamstown suffering from malnutrition, gastroenteritis, and primary tuberculosis. There she gained weight and was eventually discharged. Meanwhile the 5-year-old, Ntombiyakhe, became ill with hunger. There was no food in the house and still the promised pension payment did not come. Eventually the shopkeeper would extend credit no longer.

By the end of May the Mapapus had been living for five days on handouts from their neighbours and from Mr Mapapu's brother Bles, who was already having to support his own wife and three children on his pension alone. All that they could show in their kitchen was a cupboard full of empty tins and bottles, and a crumpled bill for R16.28. There was no food whatsoever in the house, and Ntombiyakhe had developed an unpleasant cough that shook her body even when she slept. A few days later she died.

There was no need to dig a grave, as the authorities had already caused a number to be excavated – adults on the east side of the cemetery, and the smaller children's graves on the west. Many of them were already occupied. There was also no need to buy a coffin.

When we arrived at Glenmore, a number of people died, and many people had no money. A number of coffins were sent up to Glenmore from Grahamstown and put in the premises of the superintendent. So when a person or child died you just went to the superintendent and took the size of coffin you wanted, free of charge. (76: 10–18)

From the masses of evidence collected by the Surplus People Project, in the files of the Black Sash and other advice offices, and in the course of the Carnegie Inquiry itself, to say nothing of earlier studies (Desmond, 1969), there is no doubt of the extent to which the practices of the apartheid state in compelling people to move from one place to another increase the burden of poverty for millions of South Africans, already poor, across the length and breadth of the land. During the quarter century that followed the establishment of the white Republic in 1961, under the leadership of Dr Verwoerd, outside the Commonwealth, there were literally dozens if not hundreds of Mogopas, law-abiding, painfully vulnerable communities, uprooted and pushed aside by a ruthless juggernaut that paid scant attention to the wishes

Winter is approaching

Four years ago, Mzolisi Fani had a good job and a secure home on the white-owned farm where he was born. Then ownership of the farm changed hands. That simple transaction set off a chain of personal disasters, turning Mr Fani and his family from comparatively prosperous farm workers into penniless vagrants living in squalor on a patch of scrubland near the Eastern Cape port of East London. . . . It is a problem that has not drawn much sympathy from municipal authorities in East London, whose black townships rank among the most blighted in the country. Last November, the bush hovels of Mr Fani and nine other families living in similar poverty were inexplicably burned down after a police raid. Since then, most of the 81 squatters whose shacks were destroyed have been living in misery in eight small tents loaned by the South African Red Cross. Winter is approaching but they have yet to be offered permanent homes. Mr Fani, 28, says his problems began four years ago when the new owners of Sunsweather Farm, near Beacon's Bay, sacked the previous workforce. The South African employment laws offer no protection to farm workers or domestic servants. When Mr Fani lost his job, he also lost the farm cottage he had lived in all his life. The family travelled to East London; they had relatives living in Cambridge, a tiny township tucked out of sight behind the city's abattoir. Mr Fani joined a small group of other squatters living in rudimentary shacks among the bushes on the edge of the township. They had no water. For toilets they used the bush.

For four years they managed undisturbed. Then, at 3.30 a.m. on 8 November last year, a group of municipal policemen accompanied by South African police *kitskonstabels* (auxiliary special constables) raided the camp. They said they were looking for marijuana. All the men were arrested and charged with illegally squatting. When they were released, they found all their shacks burned down. Mr Fani's wife, Numzi, who had been left at the camp with her baby, said she had seen a blue-uniformed *kitskonstabel* throw something burning into their home. (*The Independent*, London, 20.2.1988)

and needs of powerless human beings. And there were tens of thousands of people, like Mr and Mrs Mapapu and their children, sent, as somebody in the western Transvaal once expressed it, 'to the scrap-yard to rust and to die' (Wilson, 1972b: 86–89).

Bantu education

The radical changes to the country's educational policy made by the National Party after it came to power in 1948 have had a profound impact on the political economy. No analysis of the causes of poverty in South Africa can ignore the consequences of the philosophy and practices of 'Christian National Education' as it has unfolded down the years. The destruction wrought by this government as it moved in either to crush or to straitjacket the famous centres of black education like Lovedale and Fort Hare, Healdtown, St Peter's and Adams College, is one of the most shameful blots on the conscience of white South Africa.

As far as wider educational policy is concerned the essence of the case against apartheid's educational programme has been that it is unfair and racist: that it is one of the fundamental reasons why whites are rich and blacks are poor. This is true. The education process in South Africa is such that, in general, whites have had innumerable advantages over blacks in acquiring the skills necessary to fill jobs at the upper end of the economic pyramid.

But the link between education and poverty is complex, not least because of the difference between the consequences of a particular policy for individuals (or a group of individuals) on one hand and for society as a whole. Does education necessarily increase the capacity of society to produce wealth or does it simply determine who shall have the wealth? Alternatively, does lack of education impoverish a society or does it determine who shall be poor?

The politics are clear enough. There has to be a fair, politically acceptable method of ensuring who gets access to what education. The economics is much more difficult. What kinds of education – and in what combination – does South Africa need to reduce poverty as rapidly as possible ? For example, whilst university education is of economic benefit to those who receive it now, this would cease to be the case if all the country's resources were diverted to ensuring that everybody, on leaving school, went on to obtain a degree. Because of the extent to which education is both a manifestation and a cause of poverty we have found it helpful to consider this together in one place (Chapter 7). Some thinking about strategies is also included in the final part of the book (Chapters 14 and 15). But because of the central importance and complexity of the topic, the Carnegie Inquiry has generated a separate book focused exclusively on education and its potential role in eliminating poverty. (See Nasson and Samuel (eds), *Education: From Poverty to Liberty*, 1989.)

Crushing of organisation

A necessary condition for getting to grips with poverty in any society is that the poor must have political power and be able to participate effectively in the decisions that affect their lives. This is especially true in a country like South Africa, where the majority of people are denied the basic democratic right of voting for or against the government that not only rules their lives but also exercises enormous power over the economy and the decisions that shape its structures. The potential power of blacks in the political economy is immense but it is only by organisation that such potential can be transformed into effective power. This is clearly understood by the ruling party, which acts to tame, or even to break, any organisation that threatens to contribute to this transformation. In South Africa, down the years, political movements, trade unions, and student organisations have been banned, and their leaders harassed, some killed. In 1988 the effective banning, in the midst of a State of Emergency which already gave unbridled powers to the state, of 18 organisations including the United Democratic Front, and an attempt to clip the wings of the trade-union movement, were but one more stage in a long line of action down the years. The repression stretches back from the harsh measures taken by police and army in the townships in the mid-1980s, and the crackdown on the Black Consciousness movement in the 1970s, through the banning and exiling of the major black political movements in the 1960s, to the systematic attack on trade-union leaders during the 1950s. And beyond this, in turn, the breaking of the African Mine Workers' Union in 1946, the removal of Africans from the common voters' roll in 1936, to the wars of conquest in the nineteenth, eighteenth and seventeenth centuries.

Destabilisation

No analysis of the causes of impoverishment in southern Africa can ignore the impact, particularly but not exclusively in Mozambique and Angola, of war, destabilisation, and sheer banditry that have ravaged these countries during the 1980s. It is difficult to disentangle who precisely is responsible for what, and we do not propose to attempt that judgement here. But what does seem incontrovertible is that South Africa's aggressive military presence in Angola and her support, notably through the MNR (Renamo) in the early 1980s, of a policy of destabilisation in Mozambique have been major causes of untold misery for people in those countries. In a report to Unicef, published in March 1987, the situation was summarised as follows:

Since independence, Angola and Mozambique have been beset by internal fighting and external attacks from South Africa. Hardly a week has been passed in peace. . . . Military destabilisation has affected other countries in the region – including direct attacks on Botswana, Lesotho, Zambia and Zimbabwe – and exerts considerable economic pressure on them in various ways. . . .

Economic destabilisation in 1986 alone has included the blockade of Lesotho, and interference with transit shipments to Zambia and Zimbabwe. In addition, the destruction of Malawi's external trade routes to the Mozambican ports of Beira and Nacala has greatly raised [by an estimated 100 per cent] transport costs, delayed crucial imports and rendered two major exports (sugar and maize) uneconomic. The threatened expulsion of Mozambican migrant workers from South Africa will decimate the income of households dependent on remittances, plunging them deeper into destitution and increasing their vulnerability to drought and malnutrition. It will also reduce Mozambique's foreign exchange earning capacity, production and revenue, thereby curtailing programmes to enhance household food security and constricting imports and budgets for education and health.

The use of sabotage units has increased rapidly since 1981. The region's transport and power infrastructures are the main targets, but other targets include major production units, especially those earning foreign exchange such as tea estates, mines and cement plants in Mozambique, and mines and petroleum installations in Angola. The economic costs are evident, but less so at first glance is the reason for the deliberate concentration on destroying regional transport routes. This increases the dependence of land-locked states on routes through South Africa, and forces them to pay additional transport costs amounting to at least US$300 million per year.

The share of national budget that goes to current defence costs in Mozambique is 42 per cent, one of the highest in the world. Angola's defence budget is much larger than Mozambique's in absolute terms and may absorb a comparable percentage of total spending. Tanzania, Zambia, and Zimbabwe also have large armed forces, and Zimbabwe is spending in the order of US$3 million a week to defend its own and the region's trade routes through Mozambique. The effect of such spending on the availability of funds for health, education, water, and food security in such poor countries is self-evident.

One of the deadliest weapons of the war is the mass terrorism carried out by forces which have burned crops and farmhouses, pillaged and destroyed schools, clinics, churches, mosques, stores and villages, poisoned wells by throwing bodies down them, and attacked the transport system, which is a vital part of rural life. Members of religious orders, mainly Catholics, have been murdered and kidnapped. So, too, have foreign aid workers from both the West and the East. In Angola and Mozambique, teachers, nurses, agricultural technicians, engineers and geologists have also been killed and kidnapped, maimed and mutilated.

The carnage has been indiscriminate, with infants and children not exempted. The results are clear and tragic: death for many, and for the survivors fear and flight, destruction and displacement. About 8.5 million Angolans and Mozambicans – roughly half the rural population of the two countries – have been displaced or are internal refugees in their own countries.

The costs of the war are cumulative, have been escalating since 1981 and are likely to continue to do so. (Unicef, 1987: 17)

It is estimated that, over the period 1980–1986, the costs (measured in terms of destruction of assets, enforced military expenditure, higher transport costs, lost output, and the support of large numbers of refugees and displaced persons) of destabilisation and aggression were 'at least of the same order of magnitude as a whole year's production' of the nine states of the SADCC (Unicef, 1987: 18–19).

In Mozambique alone, by the end of 1985, 25 per cent of health facilities had been destroyed and hundreds of medical personnel wounded or maimed; 35–40 per cent of primary schools had been destroyed or abandoned, and 20 per cent of the pupils forced out of school. By late 1987 it was estimated that no less than 600 health facilities were out of operation; 1.6 million persons were displaced within the country and a further 600 000 outside. Another 2.9 million or more people were facing severe food shortages. By the beginning of 1988 international agencies were beginning to warn of an impending disaster even greater than the famines in Ethiopia. Already in 1983–4 some 100 000 persons perished in a famine that 'was not caused primarily by weather nor by agricultural policy. The basic causes were MNR dislocation of rural life and food production in southern Mozambique; the destruction of Mozambique's ability to raise export earnings to purchase food and distribute it; the tardiness of the international community in formulating an effective response; and interference in or outright prevention of food relief distribution.' (Unicef, 1987: 19)

In addition to the deaths from military action and from famine there is also the huge death toll of infants and children under 5. 'Most of these deaths are not caused by bullets or beatings but by malnutrition and diarrhoea, untreated diseases and immunisations not given, lack of access to pure water and to child-care clinics, and inadequate health education' (Unicef, 1987: 20). To calculate the impact of war and destabilisation the Unicef report compared the existing child mortality rates in Angola and Mozambique with what might have been achieved (taking Tanzania as a guideline) in the absence of the destruction. The reasoned estimate is that in 1986: 'Some 140 000 children died in Angola and Mozambique alone from war and destabilization-related causes. This figure represents almost 45 per cent of infant and young child mortality in these two countries.' (Unicef, 1987: 21) But other independent observers with whom we have spoken believe that this estimate is too high.

During the first three months of 1988 the US Department of State's Bureau for Refugee Programs commissioned a careful study of what it perceived as a mounting crisis of Mozambican refugees in southern Africa. Hour-long interviews were conducted with 196 refugees and displaced persons in five countries: Mozambique, Malawi, Zimbabwe, South Africa, and Tanzania. From these eyewitness accounts emerged a consistent story of what can only be described as a reign of terror, waged by Renamo, as brutal as that of the Khmer Rouge in Cambodia. Over half of those who had been compelled to serve as porters for Renamo said that they had actually seen porters beaten to death or executed for not keeping up or refusing to continue on the forced marches. Young girls and women who resisted sexual demands were beaten. In addition to many hundreds of cases of forced portering, beatings, and rape there was also looting, burning of villages, abductions and mutilations. Escape from areas controlled by Renamo is forbidden. When individuals make successful escapes, 'wives and children left behind may be executed in retribution' and to discourage others (US Department of State, 1988: 13). Most of the food produced is appropriated for the Renamo organisation and its combatants. 'The refugees' allegations of food deprivation appear to explain the wasted physical conditions of the men, women and children arriving by the thousands in asylum countries naked and severely malnourished' (1988: 12). There were serious complaints (including murder) against Frelimo and its soldiers (particularly before 1986) but these were a small fraction of the mountain of eyewitness reports of the Renamo terror. It is estimated that there has been a 300 per cent increase in the number of Mozambican refugees in southern Africa over the twelve months from April 1987 to the end of March 1988. In addition to nearly one million (approximately 870 000) refugees it is estimated that a further million or more Mozambicans are internally displaced. Furthermore, if the refugee reports are generally accurate and the sample is reasonably representative, it is conservatively reckoned that 100 000 unarmed civilians may have been murdered by Renamo in rural Mozambique.

In the thirteen years since Mozambique became independent after centuries of colonial rule by distant Portugal the country has suffered a series of reinforcing catastrophes which has turned it into one of the world's major disaster areas; one for which the architects of destabilisation must accept an awful measure of responsibility.

Conclusion

In seeking to understand as clearly as we can the underlying causes of poverty in South Africa and the surrounding countries that are economically so closely linked to it, we have found it necessary to start well beyond the range of more purely economic causes which we shall be considering in the next chapter. The essence of our argument is that the existing distribution of wealth and income has its roots in the way in which the single economy of southern Africa has developed, particularly during the past hundred years of its industrial revolution. This pattern of accumulation and development has been shaped in large measure by the interaction of political and economic forces. In tracing this process of interaction we have found it useful to consider our history in two phases: the period before 1948 and the years of apartheid since then. This division is helpful not least in that it serves to emphasise the important truth that much of the least attractive part of the present South African political economy stems directly from its earlier history as part of the British and, before that, Dutch empires. At the same time, as this chapter makes clear, the political policies of the past 40 years have had a devastating impact on most of the poorer sections of the South African population. Defining apartheid as being what apartheid does, we have examined six policies which the ruling National Party has developed and with which it has clearly identified itself since it came to power in 1948. And we have shown how these policies of separate development, anti-urbanisation, forced removals, Bantu education, the crushing of organisation, and, in more recent years, destabilisation have been directly responsible for increasing poverty amongst millions of people. Indeed it is precisely this dimension of premeditation or deliberate policy in impoverishing people that makes poverty in South Africa different from that in so many other parts of the world. At the same time we recognise that there is much in South African poverty which is similar to that elsewhere. Our analysis would not be complete without some examination of the role of other, more universal forces in bringing into being the sort of poverty described in previous chapters. To this analysis we now turn.

12
Macro-economic
forces

Structural [long-term] poverty resulting from land scarcity appeared only slowly in Africa. ... Extensive landlessness first emerged in South Africa during the eighteenth century ... however, land scarcity was slow to breed extreme poverty because many of the landless could sell their labour at wages which at least ensured subsistence. Only slowly during the twentieth century did Africa – and chiefly southern Africa – see numerous able-bodied men lacking land, work, or wages sufficient to maintain physical efficiency. ... By the 1980s southern Africa had entered a resource crisis as acute as that of thirteenth-century Europe.

– John Iliffe, 1987: 6

Throughout most of history economic well-being has been subject to the vicissitudes of agricultural production. Drought or flood, pestilence and disease, have swooped down on fragile economies precariously tilling the soil. Nowhere has this been more true than in South Africa where, to go no further back than the nineteenth century, droughts were broken by flood, animals were decimated by horse-sickness or rinderpest, and where swarms of locusts, kilometres wide and miles long, blocked out the sun in an almost biblical darkness. Neither drought, floods, nor locusts, alas, are things of the past. During the first seven lean years of the 1980s much of South Africa together with a large proportion of the rest of the continent south of the Sahara has been shrivelled by the worst drought of the century. In the drier western regions one consequence of the long-delayed rain was a visitation in 1985–6 of giant swarms of locusts as bad as any that have ever been recorded. Then, in 1987, floods in the eastern part of the country – particularly Natal – wreaked havoc in the rural areas.

However, as societies become more industrialised and urbanised, many of the plagues which afflict the poor become less visible. As people are squeezed off the land to work in the cities they find themselves subject to other forces, no less arbitrary or dislocating than drought or rinderpest. Once landlessness emerges, then the very poor in society are subjected not so much to the vicissitudes of nature as to the structural weaknesses of the economy. Increasingly they are faced with the twin scourges of unemployment and inflation.

In this chapter we focus on the underlying forces affecting structural poverty in an industrial economy where a large proportion of the population does not have access to land, does not grow its own food, and must rely on the production of non-agricultural goods for its livelihood.

We begin with an examination of the causes of unemployment. We have already seen (in Chapter 4) how widespread it is in southern Africa, how much it is increasing, and what a devastating impact it has on people's lives. This devastation is due not only because it removes the main source of cash income on which people live, but also because of the psychological impact it has in making people feel that 'these hands of mine have been cut off' (124: 20).

Unemployment, measured in full-time job equivalents, rose from 11.8 per cent in 1970 through 15.0 per cent in 1976 to 21.1 per cent in 1981 (Simkins, 1982). Equivalent statistics are not available since that date but all observers are agreed that unemployment has increased even further. Why?

For economists, unemployment is one more of those phenomena which are readily observable, even measurable, but very difficult to explain fully. Indeed if economists fully understood the causes of economic growth, of inflation, and of unemployment, to name but three of the many problems with which we are seeking to grapple in this book, they would long since have melted away. Nevertheless economic analysis does enable us to move, albeit gropingly, towards a clearer understanding. In this process it is important to recognise that, as we have found before in this study, it is as well to eschew the idea of a single cause. Once again we find ourselves enmeshed in a network of interacting strands.

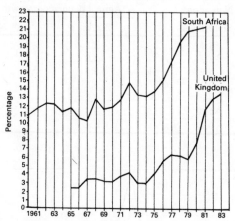

Fig. 12.01: Unemployment trends in South Africa and the United Kingdom

The first of these, advocated forcefully at the Carnegie conference by Bell and Padayachee, is a slow-down in the overall (global) rate of economic growth. By making a comparison between unemployment trends in South Africa and Britain, Bell and Padayachee made the striking finding that 'from 1968 to 1977 the South African and British graphs move up and down together in more or less perfect unison. Both fall in 1968, rise in 1971 and 1972, fall in 1973 and 1974, and rise from 1975 through 1977.' The similarity, they point out, 'is so striking that it must either be dismissed as a rather bizarre coincidence or it must surely lend support to the validity of Simkins' method of estimation, and its sensitivity to cyclical as well as long-term influences.' The significance of Simkins's figures is that whilst they show a sensitivity to fluctuations in the business cycle, they also uncover a steadily rising trend over time since about 1967, which strongly suggests growing structural unemployment, particularly since the late 1960s. This conclusion is reinforced by the behaviour of the statistics on registered unemployment amongst Asians, coloured people and whites (119: 4).

What then is the cause of the growing structural unemployment? Bell and Padayachee argue that it has to do 'primarily with a slowdown in the rate of growth of the demand for labour rather than with any significant shifts in the labour supply'. Analysing the relative annual growth rates of non-agricultural employment and population they demonstrate: there has been a protracted decline in the rate of growth of non-agricultural employment since the early 1960s, checked somewhat, but only temporarily, by the gold boom of 1973–74. Up to the mid-1970s this was accompanied by a declining non-black unemployment rate since, although the unemployment rate was declining, it still exceeded population growth. The situation changed drastically after 1974 when the average employment growth rate fell sharply and an upward trend in the non-black unemployment rate appears to have set in. (119: 8)

Consider the following table.

Table 12.01: Non-agricultural employment and population growth

	Non-agric. employment	Annual population growth-rates (%)	
		Blacks	Non-blacks
1951–55	3.4	2.8	2.4
1955–60	2.3	2.8	2.4
1960–65	4.9	3.5	2.4
1965–70	3.3	3.5	2.4
1970–75	3.6	3.3	2.1
1975–80	1.0	3.3	2.1
1980–85	−0.2	n.a.	n.a.

Source: 119: 9

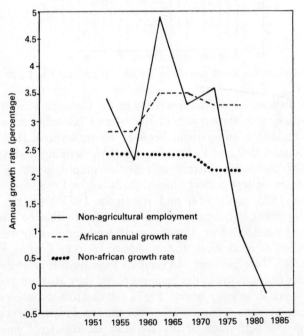

Fig. 12.02: Employment and population growth

Plotting these figures on a graph we can see clearly the significance of the decline in the rate of growth of non-agricultural employment. Apart from the cyclical downturn or recession in the latter half of the 1950s, we notice from the diagram that from 1946 (and possibly earlier) until 1975 the rate of growth of employment in the non-agricultural sectors of the South African economy was either well above or, over the decade 1965–75, roughly equal to the rate of growth of the African population. But from 1975 on, the rate of growth of employment even in all the sectors outside agriculture fell below the population growth-rate of both blacks and non-blacks.

If we include in the analysis the details of what was happening in the agricultural sector, the picture becomes even clearer.

In all countries the proportion of labour in the agricultural sector has declined as a result of industrialisation, and in many of them the stage has been reached where the absolute number of people employed on the land falls as well. South Africa was no exception. The proportion of the total population living in the rural areas (including the reserves) fell from 76 per cent in 1904 to 53 per cent in 1960. In absolute terms the number of whites on the land seems to have reached a peak at the time of the Great Depression and drought in the early 1930s and then fallen: by 20 per cent from 637 000 in 1936 to 507 000 in 1960. For blacks as the following table shows, the numbers rose steadily until 1950. By this time no less than 30 per cent of black South Africans lived on white farms. (Wilson and Thompson, 1971: 168)

Table 12.02: African farm labourers, 1911–52

Date	Numbers employed (× 1 000)	Annual % change
1911	213	–
1918	255	2.8
1925	341	4.8
1930	361	1.2
1937	403	1.7
1946	568	4.5
1950	637	3.0
1952	592	−3.5

Source: Wilson and Thompson, 1971: 168

Whether or not the fall in employment between 1950 and 1952 marked a permanent downturn or was merely the result of weather variations (or statistical error) was not immediately clear. However, subsequent figures do suggest that by the 1960s a turning-point had been reached. Over the five years 1954–8, the average number of people of all races regularly employed on farms was 828 000; for the next five year period, 1959–63, the average annual employment was 826 000. With improved methods of production and increased use of machinery, 'it seemed that South African agriculture would absorb no more labour' (Wilson and Thompson, 1971: 169). Subsequent events have confirmed that analysis. The total number of people (excluding whites and all domestic servants) employed regularly in commercial agriculture (excluding the reserves) over the two decades 1960–80 was as follows:

Table 12.03: Regular farm workers,* 1960–80

Date	Numbers employed (× 1 000)	
	Africans only	All blacks
1960	638	743
1961	731	842
1962	747	857
1963	667	769
1964	635	745
1965	710	820
1969	708	815
1971	636	732
1972	627	725
1973	618	715
1974	602	702
1975	602	703
1976	565	670
1977	n.a.	n.a.
1978	558	665
1979	567	676
1980	548	655

Source: Simkins, 1976: 14–16 and Saldru Handbook, 1986: 60

* Defined as employees normally engaged in farm work including managers, foremen and other farm employees. The number of whites employed in this category remained fairly constant, at between 12 and 14 thousand persons over the period 1961–1980.

Fig. 12.03: Employment of African farm labourers, 1960–80

From these figures it seems clear that by the 1960s a plateau had been reached, which even after 1962 began to fall away, so that after the second half of the 1960s employment in agriculture decreased steadily. Over the five years 1969 to 1974 alone, the number of jobs for African regular employees on the white farms fell by more than 100 000 persons. Between 1970 and 1976 total employment in full-time agriculture fell by the equivalent of 150 000 full-time jobs (Simkins, 1982: 5)

Thus we see that at the very time in which the rate of growth of employment outside agriculture had fallen to the rate at which the black population was growing, the rate of growth of employment in agriculture had actually gone into reverse so that the absolute number of jobs was decreasing. Small wonder then that Simkins, supported by Bell and Padayachee, finds that the long-term rise in the trend of unemployment in South Africa began in the late 1960s.

But the question remains. What caused this slowdown in the demand for labour? Consider first employment in the non-agricultural sectors – in mining, manufacturing, construction, and electricity. One view, widely held, contends that the decline in employment in these sectors has been primarily due to the substitution of capital for labour, which in turn is largely as a result of government policy aiming deliberately to lower the cost of using capital equipment relative to the cost of using labour. Such reduction has been brought about by 'overvalued exchange rates and low real interest rates . . . as well as high rates of inflation resulting from excessive increases in the money supply' (119: 10).

But Bell and Padayachee dismiss this argument on the grounds that the 'scale effect', that is the increase in output as a result of cheaper capital equipment, has outweighed the 'proportions' or 'substitution' effect whereby the shift in the relative prices of capital and labour has encouraged the substitution of capital for labour in production. In other words, whilst the fact that capital has been made relatively cheaper than labour may have persuaded managers to substitute machinery for workers, the fact that capital has been so cheap has enabled these sectors to reduce costs and expand output to such an extent that they have ended up employing even more labour. Examining the evidence, Bell and Padayachee conclude that as far as short-term cyclical movements of the economy are concerned, the scale effect has indeed outweighed the substitution effect. In consequence when interest rates are low employment has soared, and when they have been high employment growth has slowed down (119: 11).

In the longer run interest rates declined sharply after 1968 and, in real terms, were actually negative from 1973 until 1982 (with the exception of 1978). And it is precisely this period that coincides with the steady increase in the level of unemployment. Could this have been caused by the ridiculously cheap price of capital and the consequent substitution of machinery for labour? Bell and Padayachee think not. Their argument rests upon the fact that this period (1968–82) of low interest rates, and hence cheap capital, coincides also with falling rates of growth of production in the economy as a whole. For example, in the manufacturing sector over the years 1960–5 output increased by 9.9 per cent per annum, whilst by 1970–5 this rate had fallen to 5.9 per cent. In the same periods the rate of growth of employment in this sector slowed down from 6.9 per cent to 4.1 per cent per annum (119: 12). The upshot of their argument, then, 'is that the predominant cause of rising Black and Non-Black unemployment rates has been a decline in the rate of growth of the demand for labour and that this has been due primarily to a fall in the rate of economic growth in general rather than to an increase in the capital intensity of production' (119: 13).

But – if we pursue the argument further – what then caused the decline in economic growth-rates at the end of the 1960s and the beginning of the 1970s? In seeking to answer this question, Bell and Padayachee start by noting that the problem of rising unemployment is a world-wide one. Indeed, as they demonstrated earlier, the trend of unemployment in South Africa correlates remarkably closely with that in the United Kingdom.

In the world economy as a whole, it is possible to identify three major forces underlying the long downward movement in output and employment. First, the rise in raw material prices (including oil) from the mid-1960s through the 1970s. Second, the slowing down of the process of diffusion of technology from advanced industrial countries to industrialising Third World countries. Third, the downward pressure on the relative prices of manufactured goods due to the rapidly increasing productivity, and hence international competitiveness, of the 'newly industrialising countries' (such as Taiwan and Hong Kong) and of Japan (119: 14). All this meant a considerable slowing down of growth in the world economy as a whole, but particularly in Western Europe and North America. Moreover, in South Africa, despite the expansionary effect of two major gold booms, the same three forces had the effect of slowing down economic growth and hence increasing unemployment rates. 'In addition to this, political developments in Southern Africa in the past decade have also been unfavourable to private investment by business firms, and though both domestic and foreign capital will, naturally, continue to display cyclical movements, political considerations and the increasingly obvious desire to diversify investment portfolios will doubtless also have a longer-term effect' (119: 15).

From this analysis, which we find to be persuasive, it is clear that a major cause of the rising trend of unemployment in South Africa is due to a long-term slow-down in the world economy, exacerbated in more recent years by an unfavourable political climate for private investment by either local or foreign firms.

But is this the whole story? We think not. What other forces in South Africa may be responsible for the high and increasing levels of unemployment? In doing so we note that the analysis of Bell and Padayachee is focused exclusively on the non-agricultural sectors of the economy – on mining and quarrying, manufacturing, construction, and electricity. But in 1981, these sectors accounted for only just over one-third (36 per cent) of total employment in the South African economy. Consider the following table of employment, measured in terms of full-time job equivalents, in different sectors of the economy from 1970 to 1981.

Throughout the period the combined sectors of mining, manufacturing, electricity and construction (that is, the non-agricultural category) were the largest single employer of labour, and they grew fastest with a total increase of 30 per cent over the eleven years. The second largest category throughout the period was finance and services, which excluded commerce but included all government employees except those in transport. Here too the rate of growth of employment (27 per cent) was slightly less than in 'non-agriculture'. Factors, including of course government policy, affecting employment in finance and services clearly need to be identified. For it is possible that alternative policies by the central government could have a marked impact on overall employment, either by changing the shape of the existing budget so that more people be employed by the state for the given expenditure, or by reducing (or increasing) government expenditure if it could be shown that such a change would increase employment in the private sector (or public sector) more than it would reduce it elsewhere.

Table 12.04: Employment in South Africa, 1970–81

Sector	1970	1976	1981
Mining, manufacturing and constrn.	2 064 562	2 519 700	2 686 406
Agriculture (white-owned farms)	1 074 600	924 200	(924 200)
Agriculture (reserves)	228 400	(228 400)	(228 400)
Commerce	620 268	734 349	764 722
Transport	348 883	396 680	430 728
Finance and services (incl. govt)	1 937 181	2 309 710	2 458 295
Total employment	6 273 894	7 113 039	7 492 751

Source: Simkins, 1982: 5

The third major category in which people in South Africa are employed is in agriculture. And, as we have already noted, employment in this sector decreased substantially, by 150 000 jobs (14 per cent) from 1970 until 1976; and has decreased further since then. For the purposes of this analysis (though not when we come to consider strategies) we shall ignore employment in reserve agriculture partly because we have no knowledge of trends (Simkins assumes employment remained constant through the decade) and partly because employment in reserve agriculture is but a fraction (roughly one-fifth) of employment in South African agriculture as a whole.

What then have been the causes for the dramatic decline in employment on the white-owned farms? The most detailed analysis of the process taking place comes from a study, by Michael de Klerk, of maize farming in the western Transvaal over the period 1968–81 (17: 1–23). 'Maize production almost certainly generates considerably more employment than any other branch of agriculture in South Africa, and the Western Transvaal, in most recent years, produces more maize than any other region' (17:1). An understanding of what happened here will tell us a great deal about commercial agriculture as a whole.

In his study De Klerk collected information about the three processes of weeding, harvesting, and delivery of the harvest, whose technology has changed radically in recent years. Until the end of the 1950s, most reaping of maize in South Africa was done by hand. Reapers walked along the row breaking loose the cobs and putting them into sacks, which were collected for threshing – that is, for separating the grain from the cobs. This process has been performed mechanically for years using either stationary engines (from the time of the First World War) or, from the time of the Second World War, tractors. Combine harvesters which do almost all reaping and threshing in a single operation were virtually non-existent in 1946, with less than 2 000 in the entire country. This increased rapidly to 10 000 by 1960 but it was not until the following two decades that the harvesters spread to include most maize farms in the country. In 1968, although the process of mechanisation was well under way, a considerable amount of harvesting was still done by hand.

Table 12.05: Mechanisation in South African agriculture, 1926–80

Year	Tractors	Combine harvesters (x1 000)	Grain silos
1926	1.3	– 0.5	–
1937	6	0.6	1.7
1946	20	1.7	6
1960	119	10	n.a.
1971	157	16	n.a.
1980	173	24	n.a.

Sources: Union statistics for fifty years I-22 & SA Statistics, 1986

Until the 1950s the delivery of maize to the co-operative depots was also largely a labour-intensive process. 'The filling, weighing, sealing, loading, unloading, sampling, and stacking of 90 kg sacks was back-breaking work, for which many seasonal workers – mainly men from black rural areas – were employed.' However, 'the advent of silos and bulk-transport vehicles completely transformed this: from combine to silo maize is "no longer touched by human hand". Seasonal employment for this operation has almost entirely disappeared.' (27: 2) The technique of weeding also changed markedly during the 1970s with seasonal labourers being largely replaced by chemical weed-killer.

Thus over the period 1968–81 the three most labour-intensive aspects of maize farming were radically changed. Harvesting by combine increased from 25 or 30 per cent of the area planted with maize to 95 per cent of that area. As regards the delivery of maize, the proportion that was sent in bulk to the silos rose from 54 per cent to virtually all of the crop. And the area sprayed with weed-killer rose from 15 to 95 per cent (27: 3–4).

Over the same period, for reasons which are not yet fully understood but which seem largely connected with the fact that only whites may own land – yet it is precisely they who are most likely to find better-paid jobs at the top of the urban economic pyramid, the average size of farm unit in this area increased by no less than 75 per cent from 664 ha in 1968 to 1 155 ha in 1981 (personal communications, Peter Moll and Michael de Klerk). Quite apart from any changes in the technique of production, the increase generally enabled farmers to cut labour. For they were often able to manage the additional farm (or part of a farm) with the workers from their original farm without hiring those living on the new farm (who were consequently told to go).

The cumulative impact on the demand for labour of all these changes was dramatic. Between 1969 and 1978 the number of permanent full-time farming jobs in the six magisterial districts of the western Transvaal fell by 13 per cent from approximately 30 000 to 26 000; whilst the number of seasonal workers fell by over 50 per cent from approximately 105 000 in 1968 to 40 000–45 000 in 1981. In the process of cutting back on the hiring of seasonal workers, farmers shifted from employing people from the reserves (for whom these seasonal jobs were one of the major sources of cash income) to taking on the families (women and sometimes children) of their permanent farm labourers. This combination of reduction of total demand for seasonal labourers with a process of internalisation of the labour market meant that the changing techniques of agricultural production dealt a double blow to the very poor coming from the reserves. De Klerk found that 'whereas in 1968 workers drawn from "external" sources, i.e. Bophuthatswana, Transkei, etc., could count on about 100 workplaces per 1 000 ha of maize harvested, by 1981 the number was less than 20' (27: 9).

What then were the causes of the change? Firstly we see that, unlike in the non-agricultural sectors analysed by Bell and Padayachee, the scale effect was clearly outweighed by the substitution effect, whereby capital (in the form of machinery, silos, and chemical weed-killer) replaced labour. Indeed whilst there was a scale effect in agriculture in that expected yield per hectare rose by more than 6 per cent per annum with a total rise of output of almost 120 per cent in the six magisterial districts, the demand for labour actually fell.

What caused the massive substitution of capital for labour? Although farm wages during the period rose in real terms by 21 per cent for seasonal workers and by 158 per cent for permanent workers (from 39 cents to 47 cents and from 60 cents to R1.55 per day respectively) and although interest rates fell to negative real rates during the decade, De Klerk does not believe that the substitution of capital for labour was primarily due to this shift in the relative prices of the two factors of production. The real reason, he argues (and we agree), lies in the technological advances which led to the development of combine harvesters, bulk-transport vehicles, silos, and chemical weed-killers. All of these new 'best-practice techniques' (to use Salter's term, 1966: 6 and 23) had been introduced by 1968, and although the diffusion of this new technology throughout virtually all the area under maize in the districts covered in the survey may have been further accelerated by changes in the relative prices of capital and labour, the primary reason for the substitution of capital for labour seems to have lain in what economists call autonomous, labour-saving, technological advance.

As with manufacturing and other non-agricultural sectors, the primary reason, although a different one, for the slow-down (in agriculture's case an actual reversal) of the rate of growth of employment since the late 1960s lay beyond southern Africa, in the wider global economy.

But, given these exogenous changes from beyond the local economic system, were the policies pursued in South Africa appropriate for the needs of the poor? Did state policy with regard to agriculture, for example, encourage the introduction of the new technology faster than would otherwise have been the case? It seems likely this was so. At this stage it is sufficient for us to note that the primary cause for the structural unemployment which has increased steadily since the late 1960s is due to the fact that the rate of growth of employment has slowed down. In agriculture the rate slowed down earlier but became negative from the mid-1960s. In the major, private 'non-agricultural' sectors, the rate fell sharply, well below the population growth-rate, after 1975. A similar pattern was found in the finance and service sectors. Thus, so long as the growth of employment in the economy as a whole lies below the rate of growth of population, the level of unemployment must go on rising inexorably.

Population growth

Which leads us to the question of population growth. In South Africa this is a contentious matter because whites have made it so. They have done this in two ways. Firstly, by making it a political issue with crass statements by leading white politicians calling for more white babies to redress what they perceive to be a numerical imbalance in the country. Secondly, by their almost Pavlovian reaction when confronted with the facts of poverty. A common response, sometimes expressed in more (sometimes in less) diplomatic language, is that the poverty to be found in South Africa is primarily caused by the poor themselves, who have 'too many children'. The tendency, often unconscious, to blame the very victims for the poverty they suffer stems from an all too human desire to avoid uncomfortable challenges but it does muddy the waters of the debate by substituting emotive arguments for cool analysis.

Essentially there are three problems to be examined. First is to see if there is any link between past population growth and present poverty in South Africa. Second, at a micro-level, is to ask whether having a large family exacerbates poverty and, if so, whether anything can be done about it? Third is to analyse the likely consequences of the present rate of population growth on future patterns of poverty.

We start with the obvious but valid point that in a country which for the past hundred years has drawn a large proportion of its industrial labour force from beyond its political boundaries, it is difficult to sustain the argument that too rapid a population growth has been the cause of poverty. The South African economy has had a voracious demand for labour, primarily for physically fit men. One of the chief functions of the powerful Chamber of Mines ever since its inception in 1889 has been to recruit labour in Mozambique, Malawi, and other countries lying even beyond the circle that includes South Africa and the three BLS countries – Botswana, Lesotho and Swaziland. Moreover, as far as agriculture is concerned, the signature tune of South African economic history has been composed of the wailing of many, though not all, farmers about the shortage of labour. This is hardly the sound of a labour-surplus economy.

But things have changed. Since the early 1960s it would seem that South Africa has moved increasingly to a situation where far more workseekers are entering the labour market from within the country (particularly if one includes Lesotho) than there are new jobs being created each year. An especially damaging development has been the steady loss of jobs for women in agriculture, both in the reserves because of mounting landlessness and in commercial agriculture. It is they, especially, who have been swelling the ranks of the workseekers unable to find work.

In this context, what is the evidence, at the micro-level, between large families ('too many children') and poverty? The picture is complex. Analysing the data from thirteen different urban settlements around Cape Town and Durban, Jane Prinsloo concludes:

Contrary to often made assertions, demographic issues are not central. An undue preponderance of children does not appear to exist. Demographic data indicates that adults constitute more than 50% of the population in every study area. Even in Durban's settlements of Inanda, Lamontville and KwaMashu, where household sizes are notably large, adults constitute approximately 60% of the population. (16: 55)

Fig. 12.04: Children and poverty, Cape Town and Durban

At the same time we recognise that a substantial number of children from these urban homes may be sent back to the care of grandmothers or aunts in the reserves. However, the link between household size and poverty appears to be extremely weak if it exists at all. For example in Gugulethu, Cape Town, where only 8 per cent of the households were found to have an income below the minimum living level, the average number of children per household was 1.98, whilst in Inanda, Natal, where the average number of children was 2.04, no less than 42 per cent of households lived below the minimum living level. The following graph plots, for each of the thirteen areas, the proportion of households living below the minimum living level against the average number of children in each household in the area. The results suggest that whilst those areas with the higher levels of poverty tend to average slightly more (but never exceeding four) children than other areas, the critical factor affecting the level of poverty in the thirteen townships is their geographic location – whether they were around Cape Town or Durban. The barriers both in terms of distance from the overcrowded reserves and in terms of government policy were far greater against poor people moving to Cape Town than to Durban.

What then of the rural areas? What evidence is there of the link between poverty and family size? From her experience in KwaZulu, Nomusa Ndaba concluded: 'For many mothers, often undernourished, the burden of yet another pregnancy and child outweighs any prospective gain from an additional labourer or security for the family. But many women are powerless to make reproductive decisions. . . .' (278: 13) Here, clearly, the watershed to which Iliffe draws attention has been crossed from a rural situation of land surplus, where large families mean more labour to work the fields, to one of acute deprivation, where large families simply imply too many people relative to the resources available (1987: 277). But if this is so, what are the poor themselves doing to control their family size? In answer to this question, fascinating information was gathered for the Carnegie Inquiry by two doctors in four different environments.

In the settled rural community of Newlands in the Ciskei, 92 per cent of the women practised contraception, using Depo-Provera and breast feeding. In the urban townships of Mdantsane outside East London and of Crossroads, Cape Town, the proportions practising contraception were 89 per cent and 83 per cent respectively. It was only in the impoverished, uprooted resettlement camp of Potsdam that a minority (35 per cent) of women used contraceptives. Potsdam is one of the poorest villages in the eastern Cape where in a later, different study more than half (55 per cent) of the children were found to be stunted (D'Souza et al., 1987: 18). Clearly, poverty in this village was not caused by 'too many babies' but was rather the result of the brutal process of resettlement. The fact that only one-third of the women practised contraception was the result rather than the cause of their poverty. 'Lowering birth rates', writes Nomusa Ndaba,

is not a matter of overcoming ignorance. The poor often know their best interests. Birth rates cannot come down until the poor have overcome their powerlessness, including women's special powerlessness. . . . In the absence of total improvement of living conditions, the birth rate will not come down; and unless the birthrate comes down among the poor, nutritional status will not improve. (278: 13, 20)

In the northern Transvaal it was found that there was a very high birth-rate, with women averaging 6 births but with extremes of up to 18. The reasons for this 'are partly due to the refusal of a lot of men to allow their wives to practise any family planning because of fear of infidelity [whilst they are away as migrants]' or some or other irrational reason (204: 7).

But all would concur with the conclusion drawn by Roberts and Rip from their study of African households in the eastern and western Cape:

The motivation needed to decrease family size probably comes best from the settled family life and job opportunities that normally characterise urban life. It may well be that the best contraceptive is stable family life in conjunction with adequate employment opportunities. (254: 17)

One of the most worrying aspects of family planning in South Africa is the number of unwanted teenage pregnancies. In the rural northern Transvaal, near Tzaneen, the instability of family life combined with poverty and boredom means that teenagers 'escape into alcohol abuse, dagga smoking, premature sexual experimentation with resultant high prevalences of venereal diseases and unplanned pregnancies' (204: 6). In this area it was estimated that, in 1983, no less than 25 per cent of all hospital deliveries were those of mothers of 19 years and less. At the other end of the country, a ten-year study among lower-income groups at hospitals in Paarl in the western Cape found that of the total of 20 590 babies delivered between January 1973 and December 1983, 6 284 of the mothers were 16 or younger. 'It is a demographic disaster as these teenagers are forced to leave school, never to return, and they and their familes don't have the means to support these children.' Moreover, children born to teenage mothers are 'usually about 1 kg underweight, and are physically and mentally deficient' (*Argus*, 27.7.1985).

To summarise the evidence, it would seem that hundreds of thousands of poor couples in South Africa exercise responsible parenthood to space and limit their children to numbers that will not drag them deeper into poverty. At the same time there is evidence (see also SPP cited by Iliffe, 1987: 277) that in particularly impoverished areas and in communities where, for one reason or another, established social structures have been broken, the birth-rate is likely to be higher, with the number of unwanted teenage pregnancies adding a major burden to poor households.

What then are the likely consequences on future patterns of poverty of present population growth? Current projections predict that the gap between this rate and that of employment creation will continue to exist. In a paper prepared for a Carnegie workshop on population growth and poverty, Elizabeth Dostall of the Institute for Futures Research at the University of Stellenbosch forecast that if there was a reasonably favourable rate of economic growth at about 4.5 per cent per annum for the 20 years 1980–2000, there would be a total of just over 12 million jobs available in the formal sector of the economy by the turn of the century. With a less favourable, but more likely, rate of economic growth of 3.1 per cent per annum, the number of jobs available would not be more than 10 million. But by this time population projections suggest that the total number of South Africans on the labour market and needing work will be just under 18 million persons. In other words, even under the most favourable projections of the rate of economic growth within the present structure, not only the absolute number but also the proportion of people unemployed and needing to be absorbed in the peripheral, informal sector of the economy would rise.

If these predictions of a growing labour surplus are correct, then, given the present structures of the political economy of the region, those who are likely to suffer most are people living beyond the political boundaries of the core economy. Indeed they have already begun to do so. In 1973 the Chamber of Mines recruited some 261 000 men from neighbouring countries (excluding Lesotho): this was 62 per cent of the total number of men recruited by the Chamber. By 1986 the total number had fallen to 113 000 and the proportion was only 20 per cent of the total. As far as Lesotho is concerned, the absolute number of recruits to the gold mines has not yet fallen but the political boundaries are far less permeable than they once were. And, within South Africa itself, the new political boundaries created by the apartheid state have played a major role in keeping large numbers of people – the poorest – from entering the labour market of the industrial or even the agricultural core. So long as the economy fails to create jobs as rapidly as population is growing, so long is it likely that political boundaries will be used, in one way or another, to externalise unemployment and poverty. Both will continue to be concentrated in the reserves of South Africa and such countries as Lesotho and Mozambique, which spent a very large proportion of their labour resources over the last century contributing massively to the development of the core economy. In this context it is illuminating to note Cassen's assessment, based largely on his experience in India, of these issues:

Of course population growth is not ... responsible for unemployment in the Third World. That responsibility lies with inadequate access to public services, education and productive assets; with technological choices, fiscal policy and the pattern of demand for goods and services. These in turn depend on power structures, income distribution, the role of multinational corporations, the international economic order – all the much-analysed facets of the employment problem. But the likelihood that these circumstances will change rapidly is itself small, and all paths to speeding up change are fraught with difficulty. ... Such being the case, the only arguments here are that rapid population growth makes the task of creating productive employment harder under any policies, however favourable; and that the abundance of labour may favour the status quo rather than threaten it. (Cassen 1976: 11, cited in Godfrey 1986: 154)

With this assessment we entirely concur.

At the same time it is important not to exaggerate the problem. In terms of the demographic cycle which seems linked to the process of industrialisation, South Africa has already peaked. Fertility is declining and the annual population growth-rate, which averaged 2.7 per cent in the 1970s, is down to 2.5 per cent in the 1980s and expected to be 2.2 per cent in the 1990s. Charles Simkins has assessed three arguments (two produced by the Science Committee of the President's Council) as to why this decline is not rapid enough:

(1) *Natural resource limitations, especially water.* Economists, he writes, 'are inclined to be sceptical of this because supplies of natural resources are rarely perfectly inelastic and even when they are, an outward shifting demand curve leads to a price rise and rationing of the resource.'

(2) *Produce resource limitations, especially in the field of human capital.* 'Here the arguments are more cogent. It is quite possible that the economy will grow at an average of no more than 3% between 1980 and 2000, implying a slow per capita income growth rate of 0.7% per annum. In the short run – i.e.

until children being born reached working age – a fertility reduction would help this figure rise more in line with expectations.'

(3) 'Given historically highly unequal entitlements to government expenditure on personally appropriated items, a high black fertility rate makes it much harder to reach a position of fairness in, for instance, educational spending' (PCS, forthcoming). Under these circumstances, concludes Simkins, additional efforts to reduce fertility appear warranted.

From the preceding analysis we can also see something of the importance of, and the limitations of, economic growth. Where population is increasing it is essential that the economy continue to generate more wealth and more jobs. The crude measure of this process is the annual increase in gross national product. If the society is not to become poorer (measured as an average in terms of GNP per head) then the economy must grow at least as fast as population; or faster if average income is to rise. The importance of pursuing macro-economic policies that encourage the increase of production has been stressed with regard to Africa in the light of the disastrous economic track record of certain economies in the years following their political independence (Sender and Smith, 1986: 110ff). Any analysis of the macro-forces perpetuating poverty has to consider carefully the sources of economic growth. Unfortunately, despite much effort, economists have not really been able to penetrate the mystery of that magic combination of circumstances which enables an economy to grow very rapidly. Most of the key elements in that combination (investment, markets, know-how, etc.) have been minutely investigated and analysed but, in the last resort, the magic as to how they come together in just the right way to make an economy hum eludes us. All we can say is that economic growth is vital and that we have to keep working to improve component parts, finding ways of making them fit together better, and making sure that policies are not pursued which will clearly harm the running of the engine.

Having said this, we have also to recognise the limits of growth. In the preceding analysis, for example, we saw how a projected annual economic growth of 3 per cent would lead, despite projected population growth, to a rising (albeit inadequate) average income over the 20 years from 1980 to 2000. Yet this very economic growth, over the same period, would not generate enough jobs for those seeking work. In consequence, the proportion of population unable to find work in the formal sector of the economy would rise from 30 per cent to approximately 44 per cent and the absolute number would increase from 3.3 to 7.9 million people. In other words, whilst economic growth is a necessary condition for raising the average level of income in a society, the pattern of that growth can, and in South Africa looks set to continue to, be shaped in such a way as to impoverish the poor even further.

Inflation

Inflation is essentially an increase in the general level of prices. For those who are wealthy and have savings on which to draw, or whose income rises at the same rate as (or faster than) prices, inflation may not seem to be too serious; but for those struggling on the breadline a rise in the prices of essential goods may have devastating consequences. For, even should the incomes of the poor rise, if there is a time-lag between the rise in prices and an increase in incomes the period of the lag may be a time of devastation.

The most destructive inflation of this century was the great Bengal famine of 1943 when millions of people died (see Chapter 9 and Sen, 1981). Analysis of famine shows that it can be caused by various factors including, as in Ethiopia in 1973, crop failure due to drought. But Sen demonstrates how vulnerability to the disaster of famine can also be brought about by sudden shifts in relative prices. In South Africa, the worst single year of inflation since statistics were first kept occurred shortly after the First World War in 1920, when prices rose by 24 per cent. The second biggest increase was in 1986 with a price increase of 19 per cent. But after 1920 prices fell back steadily until by 1931 they were back to where they had been in 1917. Indeed, apart from the sudden bubble at the end of the First World War, a rapid and sustained rise in prices is a relatively recent phenomenon in South Africa – at least during this century. It took sixty years from the time of Union in 1910 until 1959 for prices to treble. But the most recent trebling of prices took only nine years, from 1978 to 1986. 'It is clear,' writes Brian Kahn,

that expectations play a central role in the redistributional effects of inflation. It is argued ... that if inflation is anticipated, then inflation effects will be minimal as workers will demand higher wages, which employers will be prepared to pay, and lenders will demand higher nominal interest rates, which borrowers will be prepared to pay. This assumes of course that there is nothing retarding the readjustment of economic contracts, e.g. government rules, long-term contracts, market imperfections and, crucially in the South African context, unequal bargaining power and unequal knowledge. It is extremely important to bear in mind the point often ignored in the literature that the ability to anticipate inflation does not necessarily imply the ability to act upon those expectations to avoid the distributional effects ... the more unequal the bargaining power, the more vulnerable certain groups are to inflation as they are less able to demand higher wages even if we assume that they have perfect information or correct anticipations. (134: 6)

What Kahn is driving home is simply the point that a rise in prices, even if it can be foreseen, cannot always be dealt with, particularly by those who are poor and powerless in society. Moreover, it is worth noting that in a society in which half the people are adjusting to expectations of inflation, some groups may be worse off than they would be in a society in which nobody was anticipating a change, for the very process of anticipation helps, at a macro-level, to fuel inflation. But, of course, many of the worst inflationary shocks are unexpected and their painful effects are often hidden. For example, one result of the oil-price rise in 1973 was a sudden and substantial increase in the cost of paraffin. This was immediately felt by all those households which used paraffin for cooking and lighting. In the Transkei, for example, where paraffin was the most frequently used fuel it was found that the average household spent 10.4 per cent of its total income on fuel (261: 14). Household studies, not least for the Carnegie Inquiry, show that the three major sources of fuel for cooking amongst the poor are electricity, paraffin, and wood. Users of electricity were faced with price increases but they were neither so sudden nor so steep as the behaviour of paraffin prices. Those with access to wood were, at least in the short run, unaffected by the paraffin increase.

Even among paraffin-users there were two groups. On one hand there were households with a bread-winner in the mines whose wages coincidentally rose even faster than the fuel bill of his family in the reserves. But there were others, also using paraffin, whose change in incomes nowhere near matched the increase in the cost of essential fuel. What were rural households, without access to rising urban incomes and too far from any wood, to do as the price of paraffin rose inexorably?

This analysis of the impact of the oil-price rise illustrates a number of important points about inflation and poverty. Firstly, that its most devastating impact can remain hidden. Secondly, changing relative prices (in this case between wood and paraffin), which are themselves a component of inflation, can affect some people worse than others in a way that is difficult to redress in the short run. Expenditure patterns are not always simply a matter of choices but also of what is, or is not, available. Thirdly, the very poor, whose incomes do not rise at the same time as the price increases, do not have savings or other reserves to help cushion the increase. One of the worst aspects of being poor is having to travel the very bumpy road of inflationary times without shock-absorbers. Finally, there is the fact (closely related to the second point) that prices of goods bought by the poor may rise faster than prices of goods bought by the rich. Kahn has shown that in South Africa over the period 1975–82, taking 1975 as the base year, the consumer price index (CPI) for blacks in the lowest-income range rose more rapidly both in Johannesburg and Cape Town than it did for whites in the same cities. In East London, on the other hand, the CPI did not rise quite as fast for blacks as did the overall price index (134: 29).

Which groups, then, have been most vulnerable to inflation in South Africa? From the evidence it would seem that over the ten-year period 1973–82 when the consumer price index (taking 1975 as the base year = 100) rose from 79 to 293, earnings in mining, manufacturing, and in the central government rose even faster, leading to significant gains in real terms. But even in the modern, urban, organised sector of the economy there were areas that did not do well. Amongst workers who were not artisans in the building industry, for example, wages did not rise faster than prices. Indeed, real earnings in 1982 were lower than the peak years of 1975–8. In agriculture the statistics are more scattered, but the evidence there suggests that the real cash wages of labourers did rise during the last half of the 1970s although it is possible they may have declined since then.

But the wage-earners hardest hit by inflation in recent years were domestic workers, who are the most atomised and isolated in the labour market. It is also possible that a large number of them, being women, have been in the cities illegally, without authorised work permits, and so have been particularly powerless and vulnerable to exploitation by employers. In a survey of twelve of the major urban areas over the period 1973–80 it was found that the wages, in both cash and kind, of full-time domestic workers fell in real terms by not less than 16 per cent.

When we turn to those who are without jobs, the following picture emerges. For those who actually receive social welfare benefits, of which state pensions are far and away the most important, we find that over the period 1970–81, real incomes rose, albeit from a very low level. White pensions, for example, increased (in constant 1975 rands) from R618 to R645. African pensioners received far less but their pensions rose, again in real terms, from R67 to R162 per annum. Measured as a ratio, the gap between whites and blacks narrowed from 9.2:1 to 4.0:1; measured in absolute (1975) cash terms the gap also closed from R551 to R483. But either way it remained vast. Nevertheless, as we have seen, the old-age pensions received by blacks, especially in the rural areas, were often the only form of cash income available to households. And in real terms they more than doubled over a period when white pensions grew by only 3 per cent.

But it is those without cash income who are the hardest hit by inflation. Kahn draws attention to the fact that in societies, such as the USA, where there is good, comprehensive social security linked to some index so that it increases automatically as prices rise, 'the very poor are less vulnerable to inflation than the unorganised working poor' (134: 15). But in South Africa, 'social security benefits are minimal for the non-aged unemployed poor, which makes this category far more vulnerable than their counterparts in the UK and US in particular' (134: 16). Likewise for those on a fixed income, such as many who receive private pensions, inflation can be ravaging. If prices are rising at an average of 15 per cent per annum, which they have in South Africa in recent years, then the buying power of a fixed income is halved in only five years; and halved again in another five (134: 17).

Destructive though inflation may be for the poor and the powerless in society, the cure may have side-effects which, like some anti-cancer drugs, are long-lasting and painful (Gordon cited in 134: 21). There is no evidence in South Africa that a higher rate of inflation leads to lower unemployment as predicted by some theorists; indeed the rapid inflation of the 1970s was accompanied in South Africa by rising unemployment rates (134: 20). No case can be argued for allowing inflation to gallop away unchecked, but a real difficulty remains. For anti-inflationary policies can themselves cause real damage to an economy by bringing about significant reductions in output (134: 22).

Macro-economic policies designed to curb inflation have only blunt instruments at their disposal. If one is not to use price control (which itself raises a host of potentially damaging problems), then policy has to be aimed essentially at restricting aggregate demand in the society. This can be done by cutting the budget, by increasing taxes, or by tight monetary policies which raise interest rates, thus making borrowing – and hence investment – more expensive. But, 'as fewer goods and sevices are demanded, producers cut back on production, order fewer raw materials and lay off workers. Alternatively prices are reduced.' (134: 21) If (and the word needs underlining) restrictive demand policies lead to a rapid fall in prices, the effect on aggregate output may not be too severe. But if, as is likely to be the case, businesses respond by keeping prices reasonably firm (as they have costs, including wage bills, to cover), then demand for their product will fall off, production will have to be cut back, and workers will be laid off. Thus we find that, in practice, 'most anti-inflation policies have been accompanied by significant reductions in output' (134: 22), and this leads in turn to unemployment.

The poor are in a no-win situation: they are particularly vulnerable to inflation; but anti-inflationary policies aimed at reducing demand will hit the poor hardest through their effects on employment. Nevertheless it is essential that policy-makers consider in more detail what sort of macro-economic policies should be pursued in an attempt to come to grips with the problem. Precisely because it is the poor who are most vulnerable to the ravages of inflation and of unemployment which can result from trying to curb it, all policies aimed at dealing with the matter need to be examined primarily from the perspective of their impact on the poor, rather than, as is currently the case, from the perspective of big business or the central government.

PART THREE
Towards transformation

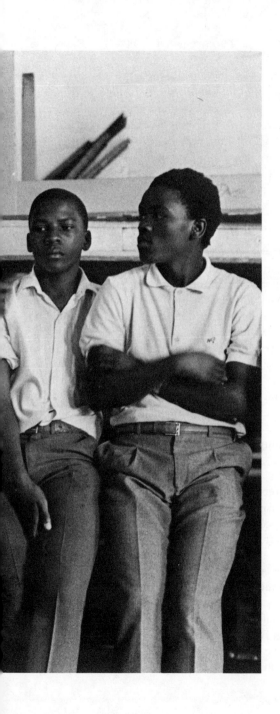

13
Framework for
thinking

Turning the despair and pessimism, which presently affect wide circles of people inside and outside Africa, into hope and optimism for the future will only be possible if all actors involved one way or the other in African development are ready to question the premises on which they have based their outlook, strategies or action to date. Nobody escapes this challenge. . . . There are no shortcuts to progress.

— Goran Hyden (1983: xiv)

Two common motives unite all those in the world who genuinely seek social justice in the form of real human development. On the one hand, a deep serious concern to understand the world as a unity – in its totality; and, on the other hand, a real commitment to transform that world – transformation being understood as the unfolding, or the preservation of structures and processes which can yield and secure the satisfaction of those human needs, be they physical, emotional, or spiritual – for all of the world's citizens under humane and equitable conditions. Only such a transformation merits the word *development*.

— King Moshoeshoe II, 1987

What then is to be done? In this study we have tried, thus far, to identify the main features of poverty in southern Africa and to analyse its major causes. But we cannot leave it at that. Poverty is not some morally neutral phenomenon which needs merely to be understood. It is an evil that must be rooted out. But how? We turn now to examine ways of attacking poverty: strategies for development. No strategy against poverty is ever likely to be wholly effective. The many dimensions of poverty and its interlocking causes require a multiple strategy attack. In the chapters that follow, we identify various measures that could contribute to uprooting the deep causes of poverty in southern Africa and to enabling the growth of a more just society. Before we turn to these measures, however, it seems helpful to consider the conceptual framework, the assumptions and guidelines, within which the proposals are formulated.

Power lies at the heart of the problem of poverty in southern Africa. Without it those who are poor remain vulnerable to an ongoing process of impoverishment. We have emphasised that we will not address directly the question as to how fundamental political change from the present system to a democratic society could most effectively be achieved. We have ruled out discussion of this question for two reasons. Firstly, because we do not wish to distract attention from two other aspects of change which we believe to be vital but which tend to be overlooked because of the urgency of ending the apartheid system. A radical shift of the present political power structure away from a racial oligarchy to a genuine democracy is essential as part of the process of transforming the South African political economy but, in our view, it is unlikely to happen for some years. Secondly, because the history of other countries, not least the United States, serves as ominous reminder of the fact that political democracy, by itself, is not a sufficient condition for ensuring that the poorest – even if they have votes – become full members of a more egalitarian society.

We distinguish, as we have argued in the Introduction, between short-run, or immediate, and long-run action: between what can usefully be done now and what will need to be done, after the political transition, in a more democratic society: the former primarily by independent non-governmental organisations, the latter primarily by the state. Our argument is that much work can be done now, in the present political circumstances, which can also be complementary in important ways to the process of political change itself. It is also necessary to think hard about what can and should be done, by a democratic government, about poverty in South Africa, not only so that ideas are carefully thought through and a consensus developed before political change requires the rapid implementation of new policies, but also because this thinking will itself inform the debate about what can and should be done now. The organic nature of society is such that the actions of independent organisations struggling to make space for themselves and to find ways of operating creatively in what sometimes look like impossible circumstances, will endure. They will have a profound effect on the shape and quality of the future once the fundamental shift in the distribution of political power towards a more democratic society has taken place.

In an important address to the National Education Crisis Committee in March 1986, Zwelakhe Sisulu made a distinction between the transfer of power and a shift in the balance of power in South Africa. The former, he pointed out, is unlikely at this stage. But the latter is a process which has not only been taking place but which is well worth encouraging in the future.

To put it another way, even within a totalitarian system, especially one riddled with so many contradictions as South Africa, it is possible to find a crack in the structure, within which a seed may take root and grow, transforming the landscape in the process. The decade 1973–83 was a period when, particularly after the political desert that prevailed in the aftermath of banning of the African Congress movements in 1960, the germination of a wide range of organisations in many different fields led to the opening up of all sorts of areas for action. The events of the mid-1980s following the introduction of the 1984 constitution, the harsh crackdown of three separate states of emergency, combined with draconian controls on information, have seen the loss of much ground which remains to be won back. This whole process of battling for space within which to operate is complementary to the wider political struggle for a fundamental redistribution of power. It should not be ignored or dismissed as irrelevant. It is a vital component of the new nation struggling to be born.

The most significant illustration of this process in recent years has been the rise of the independent trade-union movement. Before October 1979, Africans were not permitted to be members of registered trade unions. After October 1979 their membership rocketed nine-fold from 57 000 in 1980 to 511 000 in 1985. Total membership (all races) of all registered unions thus rose from

440 000 in 1960, to 614 000 in 1970, to 808 000 in 1980, to 1 391 000 in 1985. These unions (of which the National Union of Mineworkers with 400 000 members is the largest) have limited power (Saldru Directory, 1988: A-50). Trade unions alone, by their very nature, cannot change the minority-controlled government; they cannot create a democratic socialist society out of South Africa's peculiar brand of racial capitalism. But they have made, and continue to make, a substantial contribution to shifting the balance of forces within the existing society in favour of the poor. The independent trade-union movement, growing out of the ashes of the 1960s when the major black political organisations were banned, has altered the political landscape irrevocably, no matter what temporary set-backs the unions may face, including times of recession and harsh police action. Fragile as the unions may be in many respects, it is inconceivable for South Africa's modern industrial economy to go on functioning for long without workers' organisations to articulate workers' rights, their grievances and demands. Unions have become an historical necessity in the ongoing conflict between capital and labour of our industrialising economy.

A detailed analysis of the establishment and consolidation of these unions in the teeth of bitter opposition from employers (with one or two notable exceptions) as well as from the state, lies beyond the scope of this book and is already contained in careful studies by Steven Friedman (1987) and Johann Maree (forthcoming). It is sufficient to note that, in the end, both employers and the state were compelled to concede that, in the light of the determination and courage of workers and the union leaders to establish independent organisations as a basis for industrial bargaining, it would not be possible to keep the economy going unless they were recognised. Once enough workers, with skill and know-how that is not quickly replaceable, are determined to have their own industrial organisations, they have sufficient power, by means of wild-cat strikes and other forms of apparently unorganised resistance, to disrupt production so as to make employers hurt. In these circumstances it becomes in the long-term interest of employers (some but not all of whom recognise the fact) to encourage, or at least to cease actively opposing, union organisation and to find ways of negotiating.

By the beginning of the 1970s, after a century of industrialisation, a sufficient proportion of black workers had moved into skilled and semi-skilled positions throughout the economy to give them enough leverage to organise without either employers or the state confronting them to the point of breaking the economy. One of the triumphs of the early 1970s was the success of the unions in establishing a democratic base. This ensured that workers on the shop floor or at the pit face had a real say in the important decisions made by the unions to which they belonged. The unconditional defeat of black miners which was possible at the time of the First and Second World wars was no longer an option in the 1980s. The rise of the National Union of Mineworkers is both a consequence and a cause of a fundamental shift that is taking place in the balance of power in South Africa.

Given the fact that one measure of all union activity is strike action, it is pertinent to note that the number of working days lost in strikes and other work stoppages by black workers rose from an annual average of 8 000 during the 1960s (most of them in 1961), through 43 200 during the 1970s (most of them in 1973 and 1974), to an annual average of 324 800 working days lost during the 1980s (1980–5), with an all-time high of 678 000 working days lost during 1985 (Saldru Handbook, 1986: 439 and 458). We shall examine the role that can now be played by the unions in more detail in the following chapter.

Empowerment, not co-option

In addition to the trade unions there is, as we shall see in the next chapter, a whole range of independent organisations that can, even within the present political context, not only make a difference to people's lives in existing circumstances but also help, by transforming power relations, to shift the balance of power towards the poor as well as laying foundations which help determine the shape of the society in the long run.

It is important to recognise ill-conceived strategies by independent organisations. These can be used (not least by the state) to further a process of co-option whereby those who are poor are rendered even more dependent and powerless, and must be rejected. An example of this is the philanthropic approach whose destructive consequences have been incisively described by Sally Damana, drawing on her experience as a social worker in the eastern Cape.

What I refer to here as Grahamstown syndrome is merely that whites have for many years been acutely aware of the impoverished black community on the other side of the river. Whites have always been seeing themselves in roles of leaders, guides and philanthropic-givers and blacks were seen developing a habit of dependency and apathy. This is another factor that encouraged a certain portion of the population to sink right down to the bottom of the socio-economic scale and which encourages them even today to go begging. The latter is a problem facing every concerned person today and everybody is trying to think of possible solutions. . . . Welfare organisations have been accused of falling into the same trap than actually practising true social work. This has become a stumbling block in the sense that when we interview our clients one discovers that they always expect the social worker to hand out materially and are not interested in theories like self-help, reconstruction, etc. It is high time that they are re-educated into accepting that hand-outs do more harm than good, and that it is better to equip a poor man with a fishing rod than a fish. These liberal-minded whites and the existing myriad of 'welfare organisations' have gradually led to a hand-out mentality and a hand-out sickness which is now very difficult to cure, both as far as the giver and the receiver are concerned. (40: 5)

There is another kind of respectful support, usually for the destitute and dying. Buntu Mfenyana, after visiting Tin Hut No. 69 in the resettlement camp of Ekuvukeni where he worked, describes this:

Mr Mthethwa was already in bed when we knocked and peered into the dark interior of the shack. We were really looking for MaXaba, but we asked him briefly how things are.

'I became ill some time ago, and the doctors decided to amputate my left leg.'

'Do you receive a disability grant?'

'No, I have to return to Durban to get the doctor's papers. Only then can I claim the D.G.'

'Where is your lamp? It is getting dark now, *Baba*.'

'When it gets dark, I go to sleep. There is no lamp.'

Holy Maria! We gave him one food parcel, and later sent a couple of candles and some matches. Call it what you damn well like: 'my good deed for the day', ambulance work, amelioration or whatever: we could not just stand there and say: Ah, observe now, cadets. Another victim of apartheid. After 214 061 casualties the revolution will occur on 24th September 1984 at 5 a.m.'

That is not how human society works. (78: 37)

Periodic relief measures in times of distress like flood, drought, resettlement, the Crossroads crisis and other social upheavals are necessary. But even this welfare work needs a constant self-critique to make sure that it does not slide into philanthropy, for the dependency thus created cripples the people being 'helped' so that they continue to seek hand-outs rather than finding ways of helping themselves.

Genuine development work is that which empowers people; which enables them to build organisations that, like a hydro-electric dam, pool their resources and generate power where previously there was none. Such organisations are valuable not only for what they can achieve but also as an inspiration to others. At the Carnegie conference held in 1984 the film festival on 'Signs of Hope' showed situations in many parts of the world – ranging from China to Tennessee, from Chile to Nigeria, from the Rajasthan Desert in India to Mondragón in northern Spain, from the Philippines to the northern Transvaal – where people had got together to deal effectively with a range of problems with which they were beset, whether it was lack of water, illiteracy, shortage of energy, absence of credit, or inadequate preventive health care (see Appendix 2 for list of films).

What has been called the 'dense network of grassroots movements and social activist organisations' in political-economic development has been highlighted by various thinkers in recent years. For example, the economist Albert O. Hirschman has described and analysed examples of collective or co-operative action amongst poor people in Latin America. He focused particularly on community self-help projects ranging from the provision of credit, through housing, schooling and co-operative production to job creation. Noting that a similar movement seems to be sweeping India, he concludes, 'perhaps we are in the presence of a world-wide trend' (1984: 100). We believe that this is indeed so; we believe that the collective actions at the grassroots of both rural and urban developments which are now to be found in much of the Third World, particularly in Latin America and Asia, are as profoundly important for the poor as have been the trade-union movements for exploited workers facing powerful employers in industrial countries around the world.

Brief outlines of three such organisations – two from India and one from

Europe – are contained in the accompanying boxes. Details about others in Latin America are contained in Hirschman's book referred to above (see also Unicef, 1987b).

Working Women's Forum

The Working Women's Forum in the city of Madras has about 12 000 members, most of them illiterate, of the untouchable caste, and all very poor. The forum was started in 1977 by Jaya Arunachalam, herself a high-caste Brahmin, but one who married into another, lower caste, lost her status, and began to identify with the poor women of her city. She began simply by talking to the women on the streets – the women who are so common in India that most better-off people hardly see them. She noticed that each of these women actually operated a small business. These one-woman businesses, called in India the 'unstructured sector', did a lot of the work of the city. They did all the laundry, prepared and sold food, made straw mats, butchered chickens, sharpened knives and scissors, sewed simple clothing. When Jaya Arunachalam asked these women what they most needed, their answer was clear. They needed capital – soap for the laundry, materials for the mats – and typically they got it by borrowing money at 30 per cent per month from the street moneylenders. She helped them to group together and apply to the Bank of India for very small loans of $20 to $50 each. These loans allowed them to get out of debt and to use their earnings to feed their families instead of paying exorbitant interest. For most of these very poor women it doubled the family's disposable income from $100 to $200 per year; the difference, for many of them, between starvation and nutrition. Moreover, to the surprise of the Bank of India, these micro-loans were repaid. The forum members banded together in small groups to help and encourage each other to meet payments. The default rate on Working Women's Forum loans is one of the lowest of any of the bank's accounts. The forum is growing quickly in membership and influence. The members themselves are suggesting and starting up projects: crafts co-operatives, literacy training, cleaning up water sources. The movement is spreading out to include rural women in three provinces of southern India.

Its most amazing product is not higher incomes or large numbers of members. Its primary product is empowered women; women who used to regard themselves as the dust of the earth and who now run meetings, make speeches, keep accounts. Wife-beating has just about stopped in the laundry khanas of Madra. Any man who raises his hand to his wife has 40 members of the Working Women's Forum jumping on him before he knows it. (Donella Meadows, 1983)

AMUL

Kaira district comprises some 1 000 villages with three million inhabitants, situated in the middle of the state of Gujarat in India. . . . Some 70 per cent of owner-cultivators are marginal or small with landholdings below one hectare.

Kaira had historically been a major centre of milk production, serving the Bombay market. The first private dairy at Anand was started in 1929, and the Second World War generated a large increase in the demand for milk and milk products. In 1946 a mass rally of farmers was held under the leadership of the Patels to protest the extent to which surplus was appropriated by the private dairy marketing firms; a boycott led to the formation of the Kaira District Cooperative Milk Producers' Union (AMUL).

Verghese Kurien joined in 1950 as an engineer and soon became general manager. Although it took several years to convince producers of the need to organise themselves cooperatively, the movement flourished. The number of milk producers grew from 432 in 1949 to 40 500 in 1961 and 339 000 by 1982; the quantity of milk collected grew at an annual rate of 33.8 per cent over this period.

The AMUL cooperative pattern followed a two-tier system. At village level there were milk-producer cooperative societies – 8 in 1948 and 895 in 1982 – and, at district level, a District Cooperative Milk Producers' Union representing the village cooperatives. The Union aims to develop marketing facilities, to expand cooperative membership and to supply technical assistance and modern inputs.

AMUL has played a large role in facilitating the use of modern inputs. Artificial insemination centres were started in 1950; by 1981 81 per cent of Kaira villages had such centres which performed over 300 000 inseminations. Veterinary services have also expanded rapidly. After 1973 crossbreeding of cows began, but more than 85 per cent of milk supplied by AMUL still comes from buffalo. As a result of improved marketing, feeding and extension, annual output/buffalo is estimated to have risen by 30 per cent over 1946–1961 and by a further 83 per cent over 1961–1976.

It is often stated that landless labourers have been most benefited by AMUL, and indeed, participation in dairying is typically quite widespread. However, landowning or at least some access to land is vital for dairying, as it is not economic to rely entirely on purchased feeds. While considerable participation by the landless in dairy cooperatives is sometimes cited, it would seem that many of these so-called 'landless' do not really lack access to land (for example, they may use the land of relatives) or rely on other occupations (such as teaching) for a primary income source.

Increased regional income appears also to have trickled down quite broadly through improving work opportunities, although the precise magnitude of this effect is hard to estimate. The view that the nutritional status of the poorest might actually have been harmed by the development of the dairy as a consequence of milk by-products becoming less available in the villages is now questioned. The extra income available even to the poorest seems to have ensured that they could buy more food (Reynolds, personal communication).

The extent to which cooperative members participate in and control 'their' milk cooperatives is still a matter for debate. Patel (1983) suggests broad involvement at least at village level, and indeed, relative to the traditional rural economy, some village-level cooperatives seem to provide a forum for joint decision-making along secular, democratic lines. One-third of each nine-member committee retires by rotation each year, and vacant seats are filled by consensus or elections. However, Baviskar (1983) notes the ability of the numerically smaller yet economically dominant Patels to control village-level elections and important society offices through their greater literacy and control of other powerful village institutions. The district-level cooperative unions he considers remote from the average producer, and administrator-controlled rather than run by the farmers. This view concurs with that of Lele (1981). The cooperative nature of the organisation has also had little impact on decisions on major capital expenditures incurred in the phase of replication. It is, however, not clear that participation at this level is a major concern of most existing members, who seem to have little to gain from replication. Indeed, it would not have been possible to involve new members since the decision to replicate AMUL preceded the establishment of the new village-level cooperatives. This is an inevitable dilemma for attempts to accelerate development through cooperative structures. (241: 23–7)

Mondragón

The inspiration for the Mondragón experiment in northern Spain was José Maria Arizmendi, a Jesuit priest who in 1956 inspired the take-over of a small bankrupt factory as a worker-managed experiment. The geographically and culturally isolated yet previously industrial Basque provinces had been devastated by the Spanish Civil War and were suffering the burden of Franco's repression. It is sometimes argued that the consequent Basque solidarity as well as distinctive cultural features were important in Mondragón's success.

Mondragón grew rapidly. Between 1965 and 1975 the number of workers increased by about 2 000 per year; the group now provides some 18 000 jobs, of which 90 per cent represents new employment, as opposed to the absorption of existing firms. As of 1979 it included 70 industrial and three agricultural cooperatives, a cooperative bank with 84 branch offices, research and development, training and social security cooperatives, 43 education cooperatives and 14 housing cooperatives. The manufacturing cooperatives produce a variety of products – machine tools, refrigerators and other kitchen appliances, furniture, bicycles, electrical goods and bus bodies to mention but a few – using a range of technologies.

The present structure of the Mondragón group – several 'second degree' cooperatives providing centralised banking, management, training, research and development and social security services to the cluster of producer cooperatives – evolved as a response to constraints experienced by the isolation of the latter 'primary' cooperatives which individually found it hard to secure loans, provide social security, etc. The ability to learn from experience and adapt structure accordingly has been an important feature of the Mondragón experience. . . . The Mondragón group is considered to have outperformed the capitalist environment in virtually all substantive respects. The statistics on employment growth are especially impressive relative to those for other local firms. So too has been their ability to hold jobs and minimise retrenchment during periods of recession. It is difficult to arrive at any conclusion other than that Mondragón is a most successful group of enterprises when judged by the usual criteria.

Formally, the organisational structure of a typical Mondragón production cooperative does not differ too greatly from that of a capitalist corporation. However, the Junta Rectora (board of directors) is responsible to a General Assembly and is elected by cooperateurs on a one-person one-vote basis. The Social Council is the Mondragón equivalent of the German or French 'works council', representing cooperateurs through a cell-based system to their management and board. In fact the Mondragón production cooperatives are not significantly different in structure and management from democratic employee-owned companies.

Relative to Spanish industry the wage scale is greatly compressed. The ratio of the lowest to highest payment is theoretically 1:3 although special bonuses may extend this to 1:4.5. Further extension follows if account is taken of the method of deducting social security contributions, but compression is still significant. The lowest-paid cooperateurs receive slightly more than their counterparts outside, while managers are estimated to receive less than half their pay in comparable firms.

Net profits (or net revenues minus payroll costs, interest and depreciation) are allocated to individual and to two collective accounts, Collective Reserves and the Social Fund, according to a set formula. This so constrains distribution that Reserves bear a major burden of fluctuations in profitability. When profits are low, only 20 per cent accrues to Reserves but this proportion increases greatly as they rise. Normally the Social Fund receives a flat 10 per cent of profits. Individual accounts receive interest of 6 per cent per annum and are revalued annually to reflect inflation and changed circumstances. The distribution of profit to individuals' accounts is in proportion to their total work and interest incomes so that long-serving and more highly paid worker-members tend to receive larger shares of surplus. The use of non-member hired labour is negligible.

Capital contributions are required from workers joining new or existing cooperatives. On retirement, accumulated profits must, by Spanish law, be paid out within two years. Cooperateurs may not sell their shares, and voluntary departures may involve a penalty of up to 30 per cent of accumulated profits, although this is discretionary and imposed only when capital withdrawal is seen as a threat to the enterprise. Individuals are not 'tied in' to their cooperatives in practice, but circumstances resulting in 'waves' of departures are likely to result in some blocking of funds.

Mondragón provides no formal guarantee of lifetime employment. But it is generally accepted that adjustment to structural or market change will not be through job shedding. Cooperateurs may be reallocated between the coopera-tives which operate a revenue-sharing 'insurance' scheme. They continue to receive 80 per cent of their salary if unavoidably laid off. This, of course, inhibits redundancy since firing costs are so high. (241: 4–9 and Reynolds)

Whilst recognising the potential of these movements, as with trade unions, it is also wise to be realistic, as Alan Gelb is (241), in acknowledging their limits. Stories like these raise almost as many questions as they answer, not least about the special conditions which, in each case, enabled them to succeed. Nevertheless, in addition to their impact on the lives of those working in and around them, they do serve as 'touch-stones of possibility'.

One lesson that can be drawn immediately from the study of such models is their role in changing the low self-image and sense of hopelessness that poor people often have of themselves and their situation. Whilst admiring the extraordinary capacity of poor people to cope with the most difficult circumstances, their primary occupation is actual daily survival. Forward planning is a luxury they can't afford; having the energy to consider getting involved in a communal project is, as we have seen, often too much. Things happen to the poor. They don't decide. They seldom conceive of themselves as makers of history. In so far as this perspective of the poor reflects the values of the wider society, we argue that if the struggle against poverty is to become more than a mere patchwork of hand-outs, if it is to become a process of real development towards freedom in the fullest sense of the word, then others who are not poor need to become involved to inspire and help change the eternal struggle for mere survival. Moreover, the values of society as a whole must be tuned towards eradicating poverty through imaginative thinking so as to enable the poor to participate in organising and controlling their own lives. The goal of the liberation struggle must take explicit cognisance of these needs even now.

Values

It is fundamental that a change in the political power structure in South Africa needs to be infused by a value system which would ensure that the process of transformation and the creation of a new society is of real benefit to all those living in it. This of course is not a new idea. For many years different tendencies within the liberation movement have sought to define more clearly in words the vision of a new society. Thus as early as 1943, the African National Congress published a manifesto on 'African Claims' and the Unity Movement announced its 'Ten-Point Programme'. So too in the 1950s the Congress of the People crystallised thinking at the time in formulating the Freedom Charter, which focused not only on political power and the rule of law, but also on the need for redistribution of wealth (including the land) and the banishment of famine. Woven into this charter was also a specific concern for education and 'the enhancement of our cultural life'.

In the 1970s the emergence of the Black Consciousness movement articulated a whole new wave of thinking which helped to free people from the paralysis that followed the massive state crackdown against the liberation movement at the beginning of the 1960s. This thinking identified blackness in terms of dignity, self-respect, and self-reliance. It rooted itself in cultural values, showing how they affected both the process of change and the nature of the new society. The stimulant for much of this thinking was the work of

Frantz Fanon, with his insistence on an understanding of what happens to national values and culture during the different phases of history of a people. In his book *The Wretched of the Earth*, he reveals, for example, the nature of the impact of French colonialism on the Algerian people: 'Colonialism is not merely satisfied with holding a people in its grip and emptying the native's brain of all form and content. By a kind of perverted logic, it turns to the past of the oppressed people, and distorts, disfigures, and destroys it.' (1963: 169–70)

The colonial analogy has its limitations in the South African context where the struggle is essentially an internal one. Nevertheless the colonial roots of South Africa's problems make Fanon's analysis extraordinarily illuminating. Here too the dominant group has mounted a massive attack on the culture and history of the oppressed. The Black Consciousness movement by its very nature helped to free black South Africans psychologically from the oppressive slave-mentality of apartheid and the claustrophobia of white liberalism in the 1960s. Self-respect and self-reliance replaced attempts to become incorporated into well-meaning, white-dominated institutions. Instead it began to create, for the first time, independent community programmes which sought to live out these ideals in practice. The lessons learnt here were not lost when the state once again moved in to crush resistance, but were transformed into other forms of action and determination during the 1980s.

Liberation movements have therefore to recognise the critical importance of re-rooting people in order to provide them with a sense of identity and dignity, which in turn releases their social energies. This involves participating (both in the short and in the long run) in a process of developing a truly national culture which draws from the rich cultural heritage of all its peoples' past without dehumanising any part of the society. Our rich and varied cultural backgrounds have been seen by the present government as mutually hostile and to be kept segregated. In fact they are an asset that will enrich our future together across class, ethnic, linguistic, and gender lines.

This process involves a number of distinct aspects. Firstly, there is the need to overcome the long-imposed and fragmented view of culture that focuses only on those cultural practices which are specific to a particular area or language, without integrating them with those prevalent in other parts of the country. Secondly, it is necessary to address the contradictions inherent in remaining culturally rooted in a changing society. The system of traditional leadership includes a certain degree of authoritarianism in conflict with the values of a modern democratic society. Women are trapped in the conflict between the demands of a traditional role subservient to men and the requirements of a society free from sexism. For children, there is the contradiction between those attitudes which require discipline and obedience to adults, and the challenges forced upon children to play an active political role. 'The desire to attach oneself to tradition or bring abandoned traditions to life again does not only mean going against the current of history but also opposing one's own people,' wrote Fanon. 'When a people undertakes an armed struggle or even a political struggle against a relentless colonialism, the significance of tradition changes.' (1963: 100)

The main thrust of the Black Consciousness movement was in helping the oppressed to rediscover their sense of worth and human dignity by focusing on the value of their cultural roots and history. This widened the scope of the struggle from being simply a matter of access to power to one where the oppressed were demanding participation in the process of redefining power itself. This process is essential to authentic development.

Our central concern is the importance, the worth, of human beings in any society. This value is best expressed by a fundamental African concept, *ubuntu*. Although not readily translatable into any European language, it shares much common ground with many religious and humanistic movements around the world and has long been a part of political thinking in this country. Indeed many articles of the Freedom Charter affirm this value. A quality of interaction, *ubuntu* is a thread which runs through people's relationships with family members, neighbours, and strangers. The African proverb, *Umntu ungumntu ngabanye abantu* (A person is a person by means of other people), suggests that one's own humanness depends upon recognising the humanity of others and their recognising yours. It is not enough to have a non-racial, non-sexist, and non-exploitative society if the importance of individual human beings within that society is not fully considered. From this perspective it is unacceptable to have decisions over one's life being taken unilaterally either by some multinational corporation in New York or by the politburo in Moscow. *Ubuntu* is a touchstone by which the quality of a society has to be continually tested, no matter what ideology is reigning. It must be incorporated not only in the society of the future but also in the process of the struggle towards that future.

In drawing attention to an important cultural value such as *ubuntu*, it is necessary to distinguish its general meaning from the particular party-political purposes for which it has been used as a basis for Inkatha's syllabus, Ubuntu–Botho, introduced and made compulsory as a non-examinable subject in all KwaZulu schools under its Department of Education and Culture in 1979. In an important analysis of this syllabus, Praisley Mdluli argues:

Inkatha has not created the symbols used in the syllabus, but is in part drawing from traditions and values that are still respected by many people in Natal. However, the appropriation of these symbols by Inkatha has led to their gradual rejection by progressive youth. (Mdluli, 1987: 60)

This is tragic. The value embodied in *ubuntu* is too important to be lost in this fashion. In any consideration of strategies we would stress that means must be consistent with ends. One of the profound lessons of history is that a fundamental difference between means and ends can lead (if the means used lack any moral foundation) to the corruption both of the people involved and of the ends they seek. Moreover, the means used in pursuing short-run ends will themselves determine the nature of society in the long run. Consider the long-run goal of full democratic participation in all aspects of society. In order to achieve this it is essential that short-run strategies strengthen the micro-structures of democracy by creating organisations which are fully democratic and which provide all those within them experience in the democratic process. The struggle for participatory democracy within the independent trade-union movement is one of the most hopeful signs for the future of the country.

At the same time the very concept of 'democracy' which has become popular in the liberation struggle needs to be closely examined in the light of practices within organisations fighting for change. There are two questions. Is it possible to practise democracy even within a relatively small organisation given the overall totalitarian and oppressive atmosphere where the conditions for open debate, consultation, trust, and free flow of information are under sustained attack by the state? Can South Africans, who have never experienced a period of true democracy, develop the capacity to organise and participate in truly democratic processes? Democratic organisations need to face these questions squarely to ensure that they do not fall victim to the historical trap of emulating, in a different form, the very non-democratic practices which they reject. In this context we are forcefully reminded of a haunting insight of Jung's which has been used by Wessel Ebersohn in helping to understand the reasons behind the horror of the 'necklace' (a rubber tyre, doused in petrol, and set alight). 'The aspect of themselves', wrote Jung, 'which human beings sacrifice in the attainment of a given objective in their lives is reborn and returns, knife in hand, to sacrifice that which sacrificed it.' Thus, writes Ebersohn, 'all the aspects of themselves that black South Africans have been forced to sacrifice, their human dignity, their freedom, their very masculinity and femininity, have returned, knife in hand, seeking any possible target for revenge.' (1987: 40) This is a profound insight and a chilling, urgent reminder to all those struggling to build a new South Africa of the need for continual vigilance against the corruption of that process, in unforeseen ways, by the evils of the present system.

One aspect of the present society on which we need to focus particular attention lest it corrupt the future, relates to the much wider debate that goes beyond race and class, to sexism and the interrelationship among all three. The debate is central to any fundamental shift in power relations. Poverty in South Africa can be neither properly understood nor adequately addressed without serious attention to this issue. Freedom is indivisible. The denial of basic human rights to women robs the struggle of the creative energies of half the population. This may well be threatening to some male participants in the liberation struggle because of the immediate implications of taking sexism seriously. It challenges the personal relationships in which people are involved and the structures of the organisations, male-dominated at every level, that are engaged in the struggle.

The political, economic and social powerlessness experienced by a very large proportion of black South African men engenders a frustrated rage that all too often manifests itself in domestic violence, particularly against women. The inferiority complexes of the father- (and mother-) figure engendered by perceptions of powerlessness also lead to loss of respect by children for their parents. It is not easy for young children to understand why their father must accept being called 'boy' by the boss's child who may be their own age. Parents are thus perceived as willing participants, not only in their own oppression, but also in that of their offspring; hence anger against the system spills over into anger against the older generations. The lack of respect for parents also has implications for children in terms of role-modelling. Peer groups become the only point of reference. The wisdom of the older generations becomes discounted by the young, who are not willing to hear their elders.

Because of the constant quarrels and abuses between 'parents', children develop a distorted view of what is a normal relationship between men and women. The view becomes one where one sex (male, naturally) dominates the other, and this is reflected not only in the violence of 'women battering' but also in the allocation of limited resources (with mother only getting a piece of meat after father and then the children) and in the division of labour at home, where women are expected to serve the men.

The liberation of women has to begin in childhood, and in South Africa, as elsewhere, it still has a long, long way to go; not least among black children. And among white children too, who, although cushioned by wealth from much of the drudgery required of girls in poor households, nevertheless still suffer. For South Africa is a very sexist society.

It is important to face squarely one further problem that may loom large in a new South Africa: corruption. We do not agree with those gloomy conservatives who assume that human beings are incapable of altruism, that they pursue always only their own selfish gain, and that bureaucrats can do no good. However it is all too easy for idealists, Marxists no less than democratic socialists and liberals, to be naive about 'the people' or 'the state' or 'the vanguard of the people' or a number of other collections of human beings expected to act for the common good with no thought of their individual self-interest. Corruption can take many forms, including the abuse of power either to manipulate, control, and diminish other people or to enrich oneself and one's family and friends through nepotism and the misappropriation of public funds. What is known further north in Africa as the 'economy of affection' has caused great damage to many of the national economies and harmed the welfare of the poor in the years since independence (Hyden, 1983: 104). To guard against this malpractice it is essential to create a whole system of checks – including structures of accountability – and a free and independent press with access to information and power to publish it. At the same time the values permeating the society must encourage individual integrity, incorrupt-ibility, and a spirit of public service. *Ubuntu* is a vital ingredient of this value system.

A major obstacle to encouraging the growth of these values during the process of transformation in South Africa lies in the high degree of corruption which the apartheid system has bred. Bantustan bureaucrats see that it is illegitimate, and thus feel little moral sanction against 'cheating the system'. They see that it will not last so they should make their pile whilst they can.

Outside the homelands too, corruption is widespread. It ranges from bribery of petty officials endowed with powers affecting people's access to such fundamental needs as housing and jobs, to the huge misuse of public funds as in the Information scandal of the late 1970s involving senior government figures. When the existing structure of apartheid government is destroyed, the old clerks will not necessarily learn .new habits, even in a democratic government.

Common wealth

One important dimension of the framework within which we need to think about strategies against poverty relates to the whole question of boundaries, which we have already considered in some detail. The international implications of this matter are considered in the final chapter. Here we are concerned with South Africa itself, including its Bantustans.

Precisely because political boundaries (no matter how invisible or rejected) within South Africa itself play such an important role in the distribution of wealth, it is necessary for us to shift our thinking away from a powerful popular (and originally illuminating) paradigm. South Africa, it is often argued, is a First World and a Third World existing within one country. This model encourages many of those thinking about poverty as it exists in places such as the Transkei to focus primarily on rural development there, rather than on the more central question of macro-economic policy and the regional pattern of development in the wider economy as a whole. This is *not*, we would hasten to add, an argument against rural development but an assertion that it is vital to see it within its proper context.

The First World–Third World paradigm also encourages a mode of thinking in which a rich 'nation' (governed from Pretoria) generously sends aid to a poor 'country' (governed from, for example, Umtata). But the 'aid' does not of course belong exclusively to the white-controlled government, for it is part of the common wealth belonging to all those living within the boundaries of the old Union of South Africa. This assertion (which is contested by only a small minority of those who call themselves South Africans) is based on the argument, developed by Sir John Hicks and others (Nigeria, 1951), that within a national state of whatever sort (whether it is the 'tightest of tight' states or the 'loosest of loose' federations) the tax revenue derived by the central government is best seen as belonging to all the people who live under its jurisdiction (Wilson, 1980: 13). This means that it is not acceptable for rich people in the society to argue that they should have far better state schools than poor people because they pay higher taxes. Indeed, the criterion by which one judges whether or not people are receiving a 'fair' share of government revenue is not measured by whether they are getting back more or less of the taxes which they paid into the common pool, but whether the quality of public services (such as education) which they are receiving is at least equal to that of others in the society. Indeed, in those circumstances where particular groups have historically received inferior services there is a strong argument for compensatory state expenditure to help catch up on the backlog. To be specific: in South Africa where state expenditure on education for white children in 1985 was seven times higher than expenditure on black children, one cannot begin to assert that blacks are receiving a fair share of government revenue until per capita expenditure is the same; but even then there would be a case for increasing expenditure on black pupils in order to help overcome the legacy of generations of inferior education.

We have tried in this chapter to spell out with some care the reasoned assumptions on which, in the light of all the writing and discussion that have taken place during the long process of the Carnegie Inquiry, it seems to us that thinking about strategies against poverty in South Africa can best be based. We turn now to specific proposals for action.

14
Organisations
for a new
society

Perhaps it needs to be underlined that trade union struggle is not an alternative route to that South Africa of our vision, but rather an indispensable part thereof.

– Cyril Ramaphosa (1987), general secretary, National Union of Mineworkers

One of the most remarkable features of South African society over the past 15 years has been the number of creative initiatives which have been taken in a wide range of fields and which, despite the current political clampdown, doggedly refuse to be obliterated.

In the light of the long debate about strategies that has taken place during the course of the Carnegie Inquiry, we now consider a number of different areas, where organisational initiatives consistent with the goals of a democratic and just society have been, or could be, undertaken. There is no sense in which we attempt a comprehensive or exhaustive survey. We believe however that they point to, and hopefully will stimulate further thinking about, some lines of action which are both useful in the current circumstances and relevant for the future. Our criteria for selection are drawn from the previous chapter, with particular emphasis on the potential capacity of the organisations not only to make a real difference to people's lives now but also to help shift the balance of power towards the poor.

The trade-union movement

Undoubtedly one of the most important shifts in the balance of power between black and white in South Africa since the National Party came to power in 1948 is the rise of the independent trade-union movement since 1972. Indeed it is the most important shift in power since the Act of Union in 1909 entrenched white control of a structure that provided blacks with no peaceful political path to government.

The fundamental importance of trade-union movements, whether in Charles Dickens's England or in Lech Walesa's Poland, is that workers, backed by real power, are able to challenge the economic and political establishment. Trade unions have proved to be the workers' most effective weapon against dehumanisation and exploitation at the work place. The independent trade-union movement in South Africa is no exception. There are a number of different forms of dehumanisation but first and foremost is the low level of real income for most workers.

During the first half of the 1980s we find that of the total of 1.9 million working days lost over the period 1980–5, no less than 60 per cent were related to wages or to wages and another cause; 13 per cent were for disciplinary reasons; 8 per cent due to union matters; 4 per cent due to working conditions and benefits; 3 per cent because of disputes over pensions; and the remainder, 12 per cent, for other or unknown reasons (Saldru Handbook, 1986: 441). Not all disputes, of course, ended in strikes. Some were settled by negotiation and mediation. But clearly, low real wages were perceived to be the single most important problem facing workers.

We do not intend here to enter into a long analysis of the economic impact of unions in raising wages nor of the employment consequences of their doing so. But, in passing, we should like to note two dangers. The first is the possibility, much heralded by opponents of the movement, that unions may in the long run push up wages and create barriers to entry so that the level of employment is restricted, an artificially high level of capital-intensity is encouraged, and large numbers of potential workers are excluded and left unemployed. However, in present circumstances the real barriers are those created by the apartheid policies of Bantustans and others such as education. The unions are fighting to smash these barriers, not to entrench them.

The second danger some perceive is a unionised elite of urban insiders within the South African economy. We would argue simply that the battles for higher wages have to be seen within a context where incomes for the vast majority of black families remain at or below poverty levels.

In recent years there have been circumstances where a substantial increase in wages has taken place without any fall in the level of employment, even in the sector where wages have risen. For example, within the mining industry, the real earnings of black gold miners actually trebled between 1973 and 1983 whilst, over the same period, employment increased by 13 per cent from 400 000 to 451 000 (Saldru Handbook, 1986: 323 and 62). A lot of other things, including the price of gold, changed at the same time but static textbook analysis, based on the economist's security blanket, the assumption of *ceteris paribus* ('other things being equal'), can lead to some very misleading conclusions in the real world.

Wages are by no means the only factor which trade unions influence. In the first instance the trade-union movement has begun to force employers to recognise the power of workers. That power, in turn, generates respect. The 'vulgar capitalism' which has continued to flourish in South Africa in its particular racist form has had no respect for workers as thinking, rational human beings. In the eyes of vulgar capitalists, workers have been mere labour units, used to dig coal, harvest potatoes, or pour steel from blast furnaces, but not people to be consulted about the organisation, the shape and direction of any enterprise in which they often spend most of their lives and certainly not to be endowed with power to make decisions concerning that enterprise. In South Africa in the 1980s some of the conditions of work described earlier are profoundly disquieting.

Publicity is a powerful weapon, but in a society as controlled as South Africa, systematic exposure and campaigning for appropriate legislation is not easy or necessarily successful. Various newspapers and journalists have discovered this to their cost down the years before and since Henry Nxumalo of *Drum* magazine dressed up as a farm labourer in the eastern Transvaal in the 1950s and reported on conditions there. The power of a controlled strike is the ultimate sanction. There is no doubt that the unions (with the help of journalists and lawyers) have a major role to play in continuing to redress those unnecessary and inhuman conditions.

Another target for trade-union action is proper pension provision and insurance against unemployment, which will be considered in more detail in the next chapter, but the unions have a crucial political role to play in ensuring that the state does its duty.

Other targets centre on ensuring compensation for injury or death, on the vulnerability of individual workers or groups and the need to protect them against victimisation of one sort or another. This ranges from the vulnerability of unorganised workers in atomised work places (such as farm labourers or domestic workers) to the ravages of inflation, to discrimination against workers because of their place of birth, their sex, or their leadership role within worker organisations. We have already seen the extent to which domestic workers suffered from inflation during the 1970s when virtually all other workers in the South African economy made real gains in their standard of living. The organisation of a union and the subsequent mobilisation of workers in an effective strike against many small employers scattered widely across the country is difficult. It is particularly difficult in a situation where laws and practices against the mobility of black women are such that one of the few places where the large pool of women trapped in rural areas could find urban jobs, albeit illegally, is in this domestic service sector. But it is precisely because of their vulnerability to inflation, to extremely bad working conditions, including very long hours, as well as sexual harassment by male members of the employing family, that domestic workers need to unionise so as to mobilise some kind of countervailing power against the entrenched might of middle-class families. The establishment, in November 1986, of the South African Domestic Workers' Union on a national basis marked an important step in the labour movement.

Gender discrimination is not only a matter of sexual harassment. It relates to other fundamental matters also, such as differential pay for the same work or non-appointment to senior posts. Gender discrimination (measured by pay differentials) between men and women doing the same job is widespread. Until fairly recently some universities paid women members of the teaching staff on a significantly lower scale than men. Even today housing subsidies are not available to married women. In the public services generally professional women are paid at lower rates than men. Male chauvinism in South Africa amongst both whites and blacks manifests itself not only in differential pay for the same jobs but also in differential access to jobs and in different rates of unemployment (Pillay, 1985). The trade unions have much work to do in this sphere.

Because a large proportion of workers are migrant their place of origin becomes another basis for discrimination. One of the most remarkable stands taken by the union movement in recent years has been its insistence that in times of staff retrenchment due to recession, migrants – whose rights to be in town generally evaporate with their job, even after the modifications to the pass laws in 1986 – be the last to be fired. This is costly solidarity but it measures something of the commitment of the trade-union movement to a wider vision of responsibility than that which exists within the mind of government or most employers.

For years, indeed for more than a century, black South Africans have protested vigorously against the pass laws and the labour system which it entrenched. For years African people have resisted as far as possible, with the result that far more black families live in the cities than were ever planned by the architects of apartheid. Yet still today, 1988, a fundamental component of the economic structure is the existence of migratory labour, whereby workers are housed in single-sex compounds or hostels. Their families are either legally prevented from joining them or in practice unable to acquire accommodation in the cities where their husbands and fathers work, and where the government controls the building of houses. There has been some modification to the laws affecting mobility, making it easier for some, though by no means all, blacks to move to town, but the core of the structure remains intact. So, for hundreds of thousands of workers, oscillating migration is the only way of resolving the impossible contradictions of industrial apartheid. If households are not to starve, somebody must go to town to earn money. In the cities that job – whether down a mine or in a factory – requires the workers to stay nearby, often housed like chickens in a battery, with hundreds, sometimes thousands, of other men.

Whilst the circumstances of some individuals, in the short run, might be such that a spell of work on a migrant contract becomes the preferred option, there is no way in which a modern industrial society can be built in such a way that it divides each individual in half: a husband (or wife) with a family (and citizenship, for what it is worth) in some impoverished rural area; and in town, a labour unit permitted to stay so long as he (or she) is willing and able to work but who must depart therefrom as soon as he (or she) 'ceases so to minister' to the white man (or woman). Although the philosophy is beginning to crumble it has not yet been rooted out of the body politic. Protest by politicians, sermons from clerics, analyses by academics, even pressures from overseas, are all important, but none of them will change the system until workers themselves find an effective way of challenging what is being done to them.

There are signs that the trade-union movement is building its strength to exert pressure precisely on this point. The National Union of Mineworkers, for example, in March 1987, passed strong resolutions urging bosses to begin immediately to negotiate an end to the system of migrant labour and tribally segregated, single-sex hostels (*Cape Times*, 2.3.1987). This was followed a month later by direct action in which the wives and children of some 250 black miners started a 'live-in' at some of the men-only hostels on coal mines owned by the Anglo American Corporation. 'Union officials said that in coal mine hostels one room usually houses four or five men. They said miners without families agreed to move out and sleep elsewhere so that each miner involved in the protest could have a hostel room for his family.' (*Daily Nation*, Nairobi, 4.4.1987)

Another initiative taken by workers in this regard has been the formation, in 1985, of the Western Cape Hostel Dwellers' Association which, under the leadership of trade unionists, was formed specifically to deal with problems facing migrant workers and their families. Whilst pushing for immediate action on such issues as proper toilets and ablution facilities, the Association has the explicit long-term goal of ending the migrant-labour system and making it possible for workers to enjoy a normal life near their place of work.

One of the most vital functions of any trade-union movement is to compel society to find humane ways of adjusting to changing economic circumstances rather than treating workers like obsolete machinery to be discarded when no longer needed. In South Africa there is a clear need, as Maree has argued (122: 1–32), for trade unions to negotiate agreements with management on the introduction of new technology in order to prevent, or at least minimise, any retrenchment which it might otherwise cause. In the Cape Town docks during the 1970s, for example, the introduction of containerisation led to the reduction of the number of stevedores from 2 000 down to 400; whilst on the East Rand changes in the manufacture of telephone equipment, as a result of the new micro-chip technology, led one firm to retrench no less than 92 per cent of its 3 000 employees, 2 750 of whom were sacked (122: 1). Whilst one can see that it is difficult for one small firm to find ways itself of re-employing all those who might otherwise be laid off as a result of some technological breakthrough, one must recognise that it is even more difficult for the workers retrenched in the process. New Technology Agreements which compel firms jointly (possibly in co-operation with the state) to find ways, by retraining younger workers for other jobs or slowing the rate at which new technology is introduced so as to allow older workers time to retire, are an essential part of any civilised political economy.

In the context of the whole global economy, insistence on the centrality of human beings, particularly those who are most vulnerable, in any process of economic and political change is crucial. In southern Africa a singularly divisive strategy, against which the unions are struggling to find an effective response, concerns the playing off of migrant workers, badly in need of jobs, from one area against other migrants, equally badly in need of jobs, from another area – all in the name of economic capitalist efficiency. Thus the deliberate reduction, primarily for military and political reasons, of mineworkers from Mozambique and their replacement by new recruits from the Transkei, has created havoc with the economy of Mozambique. There are no easy short-run solutions to this problem, but the trade-union movement can at least insist that mineworkers are human beings and are not to be switched on and off like so much electricity without a thought for the consequences for families and communities. Indeed, looking slightly further ahead, one of the fundamental tasks facing the trade-union movement will be to ensure that, in the process of shifting from a migrant labour economy to one based on stable urbanised labour, both employers and the state take adequate steps to care for those left behind in rural areas, which have become so largely dependent on remittances from town. For as the process of change takes place, not everybody who shares in some way in the multiplier effect, however small, of the remittance income will be able to move to town with the wage-earner. In the wider world the new thrust in international thinking about the need for 'adjustment with a human face', in times of structural economic change, highlights issues that have to be at the forefront of trade-union concern (see Cornia *et al.*, 1987, 1988). Already the National Union of Mineworkers has initiated a cooperative programme to help create jobs.

Two more issues of concern to workers which are being tackled by the unions relate to housing and to control over resources, such as pension funds, which actually belong to workers but over whose managment they have, thus far, had no say.

Underlying all these issues lies the trade unions' fundamental thrust not only for worker participation in the economy but for political democracy in the wider society. For, as we have argued, without a change in the basic structure of political power the root causes of poverty in South Africa cannot be redressed.

Collective action for job creation

Trade unions are organised primarily by those who have jobs. But what of the increasing army of unemployed? What can be done by way of collective action at the grassroots to stimulate the growth of jobs? There are a number of areas where intelligent organisation has enabled poor people to create jobs and incomes for themselves, despite all the obstacles. We see no reason why such organisations could not be duplicated and a whole network created which materially raises living standards and improves the quality of life of very poor people. In this next section we shall focus particularly on two such areas, namely the provision of credit and co-operative production.

Take credit. Without some resources to start with, it is difficult for even the most energetic person to move. In a Transkei village, for example, 'Only the exceptional few can meet the bulk of their dietary requirements through cultivation and even this accomplishment is usually contingent upon a cash income to meet the costs of ploughing, planting and harvesting' (49: 15). Bembridge found that in the Transkei as a whole it was clear that the only hope for farmers to accumulate the necessary capital to improve their farming output was for them to get jobs in town (261: 15).

Polly Hill has noted that in South India the reason the Harijans ('Untouchables') failed to cultivate was because they were too poor to do so. Land was available but 'they lacked the plough animals, could not afford to hire ploughs, and were obliged to live from hand to mouth, by means of odd jobs . . . ' (296: 8). In South Africa too, although borrowing from relatives or neighbours is often possible (246: 98), it is nevertheless clear that lack of credit can be a major obstacle facing the poor, making any attempt to create jobs difficult.

There are a number of different possible ways of overcoming the problem. First there is the money-lender. In one village in the reserves, we know an enterprising person who established himself as a money-lender, using his railway wages as initial capital. Loans are given to all and sundry, without security. R1.00 has to be repaid at the end of one week plus interest of ten cents. These loans appear to the poor to provide breathing space until pay day, but a rate of interest of 10 per cent per week (or 520 per cent per annum) is exorbitant and has enabled the lender to amass enough money for himself to build a luxury house and still command a lot of cash reserves. The credit, like many other basic needs purchased by the poor, is very expensive compared with that available to the rich who, borrowing from the bank, would be unlikely to pay more than one-twentieth as much. If credit were to be organised on a co-operative basis, not only could it be provided much more cheaply but the interest, after paying basic administrative costs, could be used for productive investment to generate jobs or to develop basic needs (such as growing of fuel-wood) within the community or both.

Then, there are the *umgalelo* (or *stokvel*) savings clubs in the townships, designed chiefly to help save for a big item of expenditure (like a stove) or for times of special need (like Christmas). The difficulty with these clubs – which undoubtedly fulfil a need and which are very popular over a wide range of income levels – is that they tend to work against the very poor, in that the richer members of an *umgalelo* will often draw from the pool early in the round and thus obtain what is, in effect, an interest-free loan at the expense of those (poorer) members whose turn for a draw only comes later.

One recent innovation is a credit scheme which combines ideas from the traditional *stokvel* with those of the well-known Grameen bank of Bangladesh. Money is lent to individual members of recognised *stokvels* by a body called the Get Ahead Foundation. Security for the loan is the good name of the particular *stokvel* combined with peer pressure. It is too early yet to assess the strengths and weaknesses of this movement which seems to be growing rapidly.

A different credit scheme which mobilises the resources within a community in a process of mutual lending and borrowing is the Credit Union. This can not only provide small loans to individual members but, by pooling the resources of a large number of members, can be a source of necessary credit for the launching of a major productive enterprise. The Mondragón producers' co-operative (see Chapter 13) grew out of local savings pooled in this way. In South Africa in recent years, the gradual emergence of the Cape Credit Union League out of very small beginnings could foreshadow the growth of a far wider and more productive credit movement.

From the perspective of sustaining any process whereby people can emerge from poverty, it is clearly better, although not always possible, for credit to be used for investment rather than for consumption. Whilst a boost to the demand for clothing or furniture, say, as a result of the provision of credit may increase employment in those sectors, it is unlikely that jobs will increase as much as they would do, particularly for the very poor, if they used the credit as an investment to buy the tools (a knitting machine for example) needed in order to produce goods for sale. In technical terms, the 'multiplier effect' of expenditure on capital goods is likely to be greater than that of expenditure on consumption goods. Thus the Cape Credit Union League, for example, will only become really effective as it transforms itself from a savings club for the purchase of household goods to a vigorous promoter of self-sustaining economic activity. It is also crucial of course that credit, wherever it is organised, be provided in such a way that people do not drown in debt but can pay back what they owe. There are a number of different credit organisations, especially for women, in various parts of the world (see Chapter 13) which provide models of what can be done.

One of the least attractive aspects of the South African banking system as it currently operates is the extent to which it uses the savings of the poor (from private savings accounts, pension-fund contributions, and the like) for expenditure on schemes conceived by and run for the rich. There is no institutional mechanism whereby a rural community could borrow funds from a commercial bank in order to instal a clean drinking-water system or to help women set up as traders, even if men from that village have, over many years, worked as migrants and kept their savings in a commercial bank. The possibilities of a revolving fund such as that run by Unicef in Colombia to provide micro-credit for poor but enterprising women, or of well-structured relationships between banks and organisations of the poor such as those arising out of the Working Women's Forum in India (see Chapter 13), need urgently to be explored in South Africa.

The second area of focus for collective action relates directly to production. Experience in Canada where the co-operative movement has long been a central component of the political economy, as well as in the history of Danish agriculture, provides solid grounds for belief in the viability of co-operative production. Two of the best examples internationally, one agricultural and one industrial, both developed after the Second World War, were described in the previous chapter.

In southern Africa co-operatives have occasionally emerged but they have been small and generally fairly short-lived. In more recent years, however, the idea has become increasingly popular. Indeed in Zimbabwe during the years since independence in 1980, there has been an explosion of activity in this area as the following comments drawn from a book, published in 1985, on the co-operative movement in Zimbabwe indicate.

The owner of this [shoe] factory wanted to close it because he said he could not make business any more. If he closed the factory we knew we would be unemployed. What could we do, with children to feed and educate? We finally negotiated with him to sell us the machines and the shop so we could start working as a collective co-operative. And, contrary to what he said, we are making a good business despite a few problems that we hope to overcome. (The Zimbabwe Project, 1985: 35)

When we formed our bus co-op, our main objectives were: to curb unemployment among most of us demobilised ex-fighters as well as among the general public; to provide our rural people with good transport; and to promote the spirit of collectivisation in our country. We pooled together our demobilisation money and bought two buses and a garage. We treat our customers with respect because we know we are working for them and they, in turn, are our survival. (*Ibid.* 36)

But we are still islands in the sea. Each and every day is a struggle for us, a struggle to resist and survive. This battle we are waging for survival is part of the war against exploitation and domination. It is a war against poverty, against homelessness, against ignorance, and against suffering. Each small victory we achieve in our own collective production, is another small victory scored in this war, another blow struck for our socialist goals. (*Ibid.* 77)

Our co-operative was formed by a group of comrades from the liberation armies. I was not one of the liberators myself, but I joined the co-op because what they were doing was good. I had not heard of a co-operative before, but when I saw a group of people working together by way of raising chickens and vegetables to sell, I was really impressed and I asked if I could join them. I knew I could not do these things alone. (*Ibid.* 14)

In South Africa too, the idea of co-operatives is starting to spread rapidly. The movement has great potential but the problems should not be underestimated. Indeed, there is a danger that the very excitement about co-operatives betrays a lack of realism which could lead to disillusionment and discouragement when the nitty gritty problems of keeping a co-operative financially viable and running day after day emerge after the first flush of enthusiasm. The current reappraisal of the co-operative movement in Zimbabwe is particularly relevant to South Africa (England, 1987: 122; and Reynolds, personal communication).

Service (including consumer) co-operatives seem likely to prove particularly useful. Producer co-operatives have much to offer but they are no panacea for the host of problems that confronts those who are poor in South Africa, and it is not impossible that their long-term survival, will depend upon their being restructured along the lines of Mondragón, where the producer sections incorporate elements of the limited liability (albeit employee-owned) company. If the movement is to grow and to make a real contribution to the future of the country, then each co-operative will have to be built slowly and carefully, one step at a time.

One such venture which, although still small, has managed to take root and to generate jobs for its members is the Tiakeni Textile Co-operative east of Louis Trichardt in the Transvaal. Beginning in 1980, Tiakeni rapidly became self-sufficient in the sense of paying its running costs, including salaries for 23 worker-members, through the sale of nearly R80 000 worth of hand-printed fabric, well-known for its high quality and original design. Development funds for buildings, facilities, and salaries of resource persons were raised partly from a jumble-sale campaign and partly from grants made by a trust established for the purpose. Working capital needed for running the co-operative on a day-to-day basis was raised from share subscriptions by the members and from long-term and short-term loans. The workers control the affairs of the co-operative democratically in the areas of production, personnel, finance and marketing (240: 4). A more detailed evaluation of the rural co-operative network, including Tiakeni and Twananani, against a number of criteria has been made and further work is being done (240; and Collins, forthcoming) but it seems fair to say that in terms of participation, mutual co-operation, and helping others outside, the co-operatives have done well. Moreover, the workers have managed to maintain their place in the harsh mainstream economy. They have purchased their raw materials and produced goods which have sold competitively all over South Africa.

Nevertheless the going has been extremely difficult. Even in its context in a homeland area, the co-operative has limited connections and access to information. The people with trade links in the area belong to the rural elite: they are unlikely candidates for a workers' co-operative. The co-operative members are not part of that social network in which business and trading connections are made and maintained, even in their region. Because the co-operative is remote and its members have little access to the marketing and supply channels of mainstream business, its competitors have a trading advantage over it. Tiakeni's private enterprise competitors also have the advantage of being part of the class network that links suppliers, producers, distributors and customers (240: 18–19).

Rural development

Despite the extent to which we have focused on employment or job creation we agree with Robert Chambers in his perceptive essay on the crisis of Africa's rural poor:

For most rural people, 'livelihood' can fit their circumstances, wants, and needs better than either 'employment' or 'job'. A livelihood can be defined as a level of wealth, stocks and flows of food and cash, which provide for physical and social well-being and for security against impoverishment. This definition points less towards employment or a job and more towards seeking to assure command over flows of food and cash, over productive assets and over assets which can be buffers against contingencies, enabling poor people to meet sudden or major needs. The significance of buffers deserves stress. Almost everywhere, the poor have become more vulnerable to contingencies through the weakening of traditional social supports which could be relied on in distress and need. (1986: 145)

It is to this broader problem of improving livelihood (which includes creating employment) that we now turn.

In his pioneering paper (1981) on the design of rural development, Norman Reynolds outlined a set of proposals for 'the evolution of a social contract suited to conditions in Southern Africa', stressing that: 'The concept of development used must treat as an integral process a widening of opportunities for individuals, social groups and territorially organised communities at local and intermediate levels, and the mobilisation of human capabilities and resources for common social, economic and political benefit' (1981: 12). He takes as his starting point the astonishing concentration of poverty in the countryside and draws on the basic needs approach, which he sees as being akin to a political movement. It aims to strengthen the poor, the women, and the rural. 'It seeks to define an acceptable social order in which human fulfilment is possible.' (1981: 13) Moreover, as he goes on to point out,

The basic needs approach requires effective decentralisation. The concern with everyday needs suggests that the people rather than central planners, should have the say in setting or defining basic needs, as these are essentially individual or group value judgements. Indeed, the approach advocates decentralisation and de-bureaucratisation; both threats to the status quo.

'There is', he concludes,

strong empirical evidence which suggests that local organisation is a necessary if not sufficient condition for accelerated rural development. Local organisation is especially important if development is to arise from the increased productivity of the majority of poor rural people and lead to their enhanced economic and social welfare. Well-defined individual rights and public interests are vital to institutional functioning. Local institutions require a high degree of autonomy. To be effective, they also require the reinforcement of working links with other institutions above the field which provides more specialist services. These services must reinforce, by way of physical and human investment and of information, local authority, initiative and resource mobilisation.

Thus,

the design of a system of institutions must steer between the paternalistic approach, which treats rural people as passive and fatalistic, necessitating state intervention to improve their lot, and the populist approach which simply asks that politicians and bureaucrats stop blocking local endeavours. The paternalistic model is fatally flawed, for it expects the passive recipients of its attention to become initiators and responsible citizens. The populist model ignores the strength of entrenched local interests, which often only rules and controls imposed from higher levels of administration can move. (1981: 15–16)

Rural development, as outlined in this thinking, is a sensitive balance between the grassroots and the state in an environment, or paradigm, where the state itself is democratic, responsive to an electoral process in which all adult members of the society can participate. And even here, as analysis of rural development around the world makes all too clear, the problem of striking the right balance in such a way that people are really free to grow by combining their energies for the common good, is exceedingly difficult.

What then of an environment where the state itself is part of the problem? Where government does not begin to be democratic? And where the very legitimacy of the structure of authority is widely questioned? In a context where the major political parties have been banned for a quarter of a century, where the state has long held unbridled powers to detain and silence people without trial, and where censorship grievously restricts and distorts the flow of basic information, it is simply not possible to engage in full-scale rural development in the true sense of the word. No matter how clear the motives of individual officials or even, indeed, of particular organisations within the state structure, the overall environment is one which inevitably contaminates all government development work. To pretend otherwise is simply to engage in self-delusion (see also 263: 23–4).

This is very serious, given the symbiotic relationship necessary between government and people in any development process. And for many it has meant that until the present political power structure has been radically transformed, it is simply not possible to support, promote, or engage in any rural development work at all. But is this necessarily so? We recognise that it is vitally important to be fully aware of the potentially corrupting effect of the current political structure on all forms of rural development in South Africa. But we also argue that the ambiguities and contradictions of the society are such that there is, in fact, room for developmental work which can be undertaken by non-governmental organisations within present circumstances in such a way that it is not only consistent with long-run strategies but can actually be part of those strategies.

Before moving to consider particular projects, we must take note of a second fundamental problem about rural development in South Africa over and above the crippling effect of the political structure. This is the economic position in which the rural reserves now find themselves at the end of a century of industrial revolution. Derman and Poultney, who are themselves actively engaged in rural development work, have pointed out:

Rural communities in South Africa have shown a remarkable ability to survive despite limited outside aid. However, rural survival strategies, imaginative as they are, are restricted by the marginality of the rural economy, even in good years. And this is the real issue. Relief programmes must necessarily be coupled with more positive rural development planning. Rural areas should not be regarded as holding areas securing a Black population in subsistence agriculture. If rural areas in South Africa are to be developed, development planning must be redirected. Current development thought in South Africa, caught up as it is in cultural planning, subsistence agriculture and providing for minimum basic needs through appropriate technology, does not address itself to the real issues that concern making a living within the constraints of apartheid society.

[Moreover] state spending in rural areas is grossly inadequate and misdirected. State spending and the way budgets are apportioned do suggest that there is little interest in the transformation of rural society and rural life. The major thrust appears to be towards a holding operation, stemming the tide to urban centres, and this can hardly be construed as development. (226: 12–13)

The question that must now be posed is: can rural areas in South Africa be developed, or has their underdevelopment reached a stage of no return?

It seems clear to us that if development thinking occurs within a dual economy framework, then indeed the rural crisis in South Africa will deepen. As Derman and Poultney have argued (226: 13), any development work within the reserves has to take account of their economic position within South Africa. Current development work, whether by the state or by a number of non-governmental organisations, tends to be focused more on the goal of enabling the reserves to hold or absorb all the people who have been compelled to live there, rather than on enabling those who currently live there to find ways of earning a living somewhere in the South African economy.

Seen in this light, immediate rural development projects would only be consistent with long-run goals if they were designed in such a way that they were enabling the rural areas to be more fully integrated with the wider (urban) economy. This could be done either by training people so they could move permanently to town and get jobs there, or by helping people in the rural areas to compete effectively with commercial agriculture or with the urban areas in the production of goods and services, particularly those that could be sold in the rural areas. We believe this is very important. Population in the rural areas, especially within the reserves, has been dammed up by the pass laws, and artificially increased by resettlement policies, for so long that it is not always easy to visualise what will happen when all the barriers to mobility are removed. South Africa, as Simkins showed some years ago, is heavily under-urbanised for a country at its stage of industrial development. Rural areas, notably the reserves, are heavily overpopulated, and people, especially women, in rural areas (both on the platteland and in the reserves) do not have the education and training necessary to move easily into urban employment. Rural development projects need to focus on this historical reality.

We turn now to look briefly at several rural and small-town development projects in South Africa which have wrestled with these issues. One project, which we know best, is the Ithuseng Community Health Centre which was developed in the northern Transvaal after 1978. We shall consider it in some detail, as the lessons learnt in the process of community development in a particular context over the ten years are not always clear in general textbooks on the topic.

Ithuseng (Help Yourselves), situated 20 km south-east of Tzaneen in the northern Transvaal in the village of Lenyenye, is a community health programme. It serves an impoverished rural population of approximately 100 000 people, a mixture of Tsonga- and North Sotho-speakers who have been living for decades in an area that has in more recent years been arbitrarily divided into parts of Gazankulu and Lebowa. The programme was started after one of us (M. R.) had been banned and restricted to the area the previous year. The major difficulty was to generate a relationship of trust and to affirm people's inherent ability to rise above the degradation of their powerlessness and their sense of despair. In this context it is worth recalling Hirschman's observation, after visiting some 45 grassroots development projects in six Latin American countries: 'As an economist I had expected that the need to mobilize a minimal amount of capital would be at the root of at least some of the cooperative, worker-managed enterprises. But it turned out that a more fundamental need is . . . some experience dispelling isolation and mutual distrust.' (1984: 57) This was precisely the experience at Ithuseng. A health service was set up as the launching pad for a development process that has now become integrated at different levels. This service answered the need of the local people who, until then, depended on the services of three poorly equipped and understaffed rural hospitals. The choice of health as an entry point was made on the basis of the skills of the initiator (who is a medical doctor) and the relevance of the service to all the people, and its consequent unifying potential for the various segments of the community. Also important was the fact that it could logically expand into the various root causes of ill-health, namely poor nutrition, lack of proper housing, water-borne diseases, illiteracy, unemployment, migratory labour, family disorganisation, and so on, which are all traceable to the position of powerlessness of this community in the wider society.

The programme is based on the affirmation of human dignity; and this is done through symbolism in the form of a clean and pleasant environment, encouragement of the use of indigenous names, and respectful relations at all levels of interaction that directly challenge the traditional approach to doctor–patient, nurse–doctor, nurse–patient, and patient–patient relationships. Emphasis is placed on preventive health and demystification of knowledge, through discussion (for instance) of the importance and role of immunisation in health care and the relationship of this to traditional forms of protection against ailments; or the promotion of oral rehydration treatment in the management of diarrhoeal disease for both young and old. The starting point being always the skills base that people already have, and linking that to correct scientific approaches.

The linkage with strategies against poverty was made through programmes that were easy and likely to succeed, thereby promoting a sense of achievement. For example, the co-operative brickyard was started with women who already possessed skills acquired from a local brickyard where they were employed. There was also very little capital required: this minimised the dependence on outsiders and promoted self-reliance amongst the participants. There was also, given the shocking housing situation in the area, a ready market for bricks. Furthermore, the possibility of linking breast-feeding promotion and child care with the project was facilitated by involving those mothers who found it difficult to leave their young children at home. The brick project also had a multiplier effect in that the women produced the bricks which were used in the building of the model day-care centre.

Other aspects of the programme dealt with problems affecting young people of the area, especially in the field of education. Because of the neglect of rural education generally and the poverty of many of the inhabitants of this area, a great number of young people dropped out of school at an early stage, thus boosting the huge number of functional illiterates in the area. The Ipopeng (Build Yourselves) Educational Fund was initiated to provide bursaries for the neediest cases. A resource centre with library facilities, indoor games, and music equipment was started to offer a meeting place for young people, and an environment in which they could study and exchange views creatively. This resource has now been stretched to its limit, and plans are afoot (1988) to build another educational centre in a nearby village.

Adult literacy is also tackled through a programme that not only promotes the acquisition of literacy skills but promotes general organisation of the local people through encouraging critical analysis of their conditions and joint discussion on short-run strategies to deal with some of the problems they face. Out of these efforts have come the promotion of gardening to produce vegetables for home-consumption; the manufacture and use of mud stoves and wonder boxes to conserve energy; the mushrooming of sewing clubs to provide further employment and cheap clothing for the community; and other ventures.

There are, however, a number of problems in this project. First of all, to succeed in making people believe in themselves in an environment where everything negates their very humanity is not easy. And this is reflected in the ease with which people fall back into despair whenever the going gets tough. For example, whenever the brick co-operative faces problems either in the form of poor sales or breakdown of equipment, the participants are quick to blame others than themselves. It therefore requires an enormous amount of time and energy to keep on remotivating people.

The second problem is the lack of local expertise as a result of the cumulative deprivation that people suffer. This lack is felt particularly with regard to the capacity for effective organisation: it creates problems in the field of human relations, co-ordination, and the ability to plan, act, and evaluate.

Thirdly, there is the problem of undue dependence on external funding. Out of the pressures which arise for centralised control in the difficult task of negotiating grants, numerous contradictions develop. These difficulties include the unrealistic demands of some sponsors who load small local communities with heavy administrative requirements; the need to avoid the invisible threads which funders often spin; the minefield laid by the Fund Raising Act; and, underlying all this, the scarcity of fund-raising skills.

The whole matter of dependence on outside funds begs a host of unanswered questions. These relate to the correct balance between self-help and self-reliance on one hand, and realistic appraisal of the inability of those without boots to pull themselves up by the straps. They relate also to the moral question of the extent to which those who are poor are expected to work voluntarily, whereas the very development officers called upon to advise and motivate them are in paid employment. For example, should community health workers be expected to work, even in their own villages, without pay when they actually sacrifice valuable time which they need to survive poverty? Paying them raises the problem of budget limitations, determining the extent to which villagers can be trained to take responsibility for their own health care. There are no final answers to these questions but it is important to keep both perspectives in mind and to promote the values of self-help as well as the responsibilities of the wider society. This might be summarised as *self-help in a global context*.

The Valley Trust socio-medical project in the Valley of a Thousand Hills near Durban has features that are very similar to Ithuseng, and shares many of the problems outlined above. However, it is older and also has linkages with the local university community: this has strengthened its ability to maintain an ongoing research programme that documents the various activities and evaluates them in a scientific way. These activities include health care, both primary and secondary, as well as the training of community health workers, some of whom are illiterate and a significant proportion of whom are *izangoma* (traditional healers). Other activities focus on nutrition education, agriculture, appropriate technology (for water and sanitation), community liaison, an educational resource centre, and the demonstration of ecologically sound organic agriculture.

Appropriate technology

Inadequate water supplies are known to be closely linked with many of the most common and dangerous of human illnesses. The Valley Trust has embarked on a programme, shared by organisations throughout the world, to bring reasonable access to water for all by the end of the decade. Several techniques have been used including the protection of watersheds, conservation dams, the capping and improvement of springs, and the construction of rainwater and storage ferro-cement tanks. In the Valley Trust's spring protection programme, the community participates in the planning, construction, and maintenance of each project. Local committees are established and thereby form the basis for the development of other services to the area. (The Valley Trust, n.d.: 7)

One of the most important new developments in the area is the process whereby local Tribal Authorities are being encouraged to establish development committees. Members are elected by secret ballot and the power is delegated to initiate and manage community projects. One such project has been the building (with funds borrowed specifically for the purpose) of a pipeline to supply clean drinking-water; another has been the building of a much needed road with funds provided by the state, for public works programmes to generate employment. This particular scheme was run by one of the development committees, and employed 200 people for four months. Subsequent evaluation showed that it cost virtually the same as would a far more capital-intensive scheme using heavy machinery and few workers.

The creation of appropriate structures for ensuring that the development process is itself democratic is critically important. What is happening at the Valley Trust could well provide a model for other rural areas, although it is still too early to tell whether the fragile democratic plants growing there will be able to survive the harsh political climate of contemporary South Africa. But the lessons learnt and the experience acquired by the independent trade-union movement as it struggled to build a democratic base for itself during the 1970s, suggest that though the process is difficult it is not impossible. And it is surely one of the most important challenges facing those concerned with rural development.

There are other models of micro-development in the rural areas of South Africa but we do not have space to describe more of them here. Indeed, whilst the country may be lagging behind other parts of the world in this regard, the evidence collected during the course of the Carnegie Inquiry and elsewhere suggests that the same dense network described by Hirschman for Latin America could grow rapidly in South Africa.

Signs of hope, whether in Tiakeni, Ithuseng, the Valley Trust, or elsewhere, are very real but they are at the same time breathtakingly fragile. The fundamental problem facing all who are concerned with real development is how to multiply and then to nurture a whole range or network of small organisations which together can transform the wider environment.

From the field of development, where we have focused primarily on collective action for improving livelihoods, we turn now to consider a number of areas overlapping in many instances with matters already discussed, where not only is much being done but where there is great scope for future work. We shall look briefly at possible action under the general headings of health, children, law, business, and the role of religious organisations and universities.

Health

Health – as we have seen throughout this book, not least in the discussion of Ithuseng and the Valley Trust – is intimately bound up with the wider well-being of the community. Nevertheless it is helpful to consider some of the initiatives centred primarily on health that illustrate what can be done. At a consultative meeting convened by the National Medical and Dental Association (NAMDA) in April 1987 in Cape Town, there were reports on 18 primary health-care projects active in different parts of the country, both urban and rural, (Karim, 1987). In addition to the Valley Trust, these included the Alexandra Health Centre and University Clinic which is particularly interesting because it is the only 'alternative' that runs a full, comprehensive primary health-care service for a large community. It has been the health service for the people of 'Alex' for 60 years and currently serves over 140 000 people. Drawing on the strengths and goodwill of the past there is, writes the director in his report to the NAMDA consultative meeting,

a new vision of what Alexandra Health Centre can and should be. While maintaining its service commitment it is moving away from being purely service-orientated towards becoming a centre for practical research into urban primary and community-based health care. It has four major goals:

1. To provide comprehensive health care to and with the people of Alexandra.
2. To develop services and staff structures that are appropriate for Urban Primary Health Care, both now and in the future in South Africa.
3. To develop ways in which staff and community members can together plan, run and evaluate these services.
4. To train staff, students and community members in pursuit of these other three goals. (T. Wilson, 1987)

The health centre has the flexibility and the potential to serve as a model in which strategies for appropriate primary health care in a poor urban community can be developed and tested in practice (Annual Report, 1988).

Another project is the Health Services Development Unit (HSDU) based at the Tintswalo Hospital, Acornhoek, in the north-eastern Transvaal. Initiated through the Department of Community Health of the University of the Witwatersrand, with which it remains closely linked, the HSDU 'has a broad mandate to initiate and experiment with progressive or alternative health care projects which in the future would be generalisable to other health care organisations and services' (Karim, 1987: 10). Much of its early research and self-assessment is contained in the series of Carnegie conference papers (nos. 192–201) which form the basis for a great deal of our understanding about the interrelationship between medical services, health, and poverty in the harsh conditions of the reserves.

Very early in the unit's history it became evident that the huge inadequacy of appropriate primary health-care workers essentially retarded any meaningful development of any other primary health-care project, e.g. TB services, immunization, sanitation, etc. As a result the unit's major thrust over the past four years (1983–1987) has been in training primary health-care nurses and developing appropriate structures to support this training. A village development programme has also been in operation. (Karim, 1987: 10)

Despite the achievements of these projects and the significant success that many of them have had in moving towards their goals, one must also be aware of the severe difficulties under which many of them have laboured, not least during the political upheavals of the mid-1980s. In Cape Town, one clinic was taken over by the South African Defence Force in June 1986 and has since ceased to function. The staff were evicted from the township (Crossroads) by the leadership of the *witdoek* vigilantes but they subsequently started a more decentralised health project in the wider western Cape region (Toms, 1987: 5–9). In Natal political difficulties have also hampered the work of the Mahatma Gandhi Clinic, whose community development programme has largely collapsed since the time of unrest from August 1985 (1987: 13). Nevertheless the work goes doggedly on, as health workers around the country seek ways of creating and sustaining appropriate structures of health care. They have to wrestle too, like trade unionists and others, with the wider demands of communities under great stress. As Dr Abdool Karim puts it:

In many countries health needs are not a priority issue. Thus a primary health-care programme will have to address both health needs as well as the felt needs of the target community. Hence the line between health and politics becomes blurred, and health professionals may be challenged to be more explicitly against oppression and exploitation and to play a more challenging organisational role rather than a 'professional' role. (1987: 14).

This will not make their lives any easier but the hard-won experience gained in the decade since 1977 suggests that with skill, political sensitivity, and perseverance many kinds of grassroots projects centred on health needs can continue to be initiated and nurtured – all in the context of the longer-term goal of creating a national health service for all South Africans.

Children

By their own actions in recent years the children of South Africa have thrust themselves into a position where they can no longer be ignored. The suffering they have endured and the courage they have displayed are an indictment of the adult world in which they have found themselves. But the price they pay, whether in hunger, in bad education, or in detention, is enormous. No matter how good the visions for a future South Africa may be, if the people who are to inhabit that future are damaged by growing up in the warping pressures of today's society, then that future too will be warped. There is nothing more urgent in South Africa today than to find ways of ensuring that all her children can grow to maturity as human beings who are whole and free.

We believe, too, that there is space for work to be done which would not only make a significant difference to the lives of children now but which would also contribute substantially to the quality of the new society that, underneath all the smoke and trauma, is gradually emerging. This is not the appropriate place for a detailed itemisation of what is being done or for a long shopping list of what is still needed. But it is possible to indicate some of the key areas which research for the Carnegie Inquiry has suggested require immediate attention.

First is the mortality rate amongst very young children. Infant mortality rates vary widely but are at least as high as 130 in some rural areas. But work centred on one hospital in Bophuthatswana has demonstrated that intervention along the lines of the Unicef GOBI-FFF* strategy can have a dramatic impact on the health and survival of young children. In the Gelukspan district over the space of only six years, the child mortality rate was almost halved (Bac 1987: 14; Ntoane, 1987; Setiloane, forthcoming). Clearly there is a need to multiply this programme as rapidly as possible, particularly in rural areas, until the whole country is covered. Similarly there are examples of specific immunisation campaigns, such as those against poliomyelitis and measles in Mhala in 1982–3 (200: 1–11) or the 1986 programme against poliomyelitis by an independent clinic in Alexandra, which need to be nationalised.

Closely associated with this is the need to ensure that children, once weaned, are properly fed. There has been some evidence from other parts of the world that nutritional intervention strategies are more cost-effective if focused on pre-school children rather than on those slightly older, who are already at school. Whilst there is no doubt that pre-school children remain priority, it would be a mistake to ignore the importance of ending hunger in the schools. From Clanwilliam in the south-west Cape where primary schoolchildren were reported to be 'regularly fainting from hunger' (97: 33), to Mhala in the eastern Transvaal where 40 per cent of children in the first two grades were found to come to school without breakfast (192: 3), there was evidence of the urgent need for school-feeding schemes.

During the course of the Carnegie Inquiry a plan has been drawn up to show how such a programme might be introduced. The benefits would be enormous and the costs relatively small, a mere R17 million, or 0.05 per cent of central government annual expenditure in 1985 (PCS 5). But until the state shoulders its proper responsibilities in this area, private initiatives are necessary to minimise the damage. One model is the Peninsula School Feeding Scheme, a voluntary body set up to try to contain some of the damage caused by the Nationalist government which, shortly after it came to power in 1948, ended the national school-feeding programmes which had gradually been extended during the Second World War to children of all races.

But the problem is wider than that facing only schoolchildren. There are, as we have seen, many who never enrol at school or who drop out very young,

* Growth monitoring, Oral rehydration, Breast-feeding, Immunisation, Food supplementation, Family spacing, Female education.

for whom food is perhaps even more needed. Nothing short of a national food-stamp programme (of which school-feeding could be a part) can really deal with the magnitude of the problem. 'Government figures', writes a Carnegie researcher, 'are not given to overstatement, and yet even they suggest that over two million of the country's nine or ten million children are well underweight for age, and that several hundred thousand are at grave risk from malnutrition' (PCS 5: 1).

But it is in the field of learning more than anywhere else that there is both need and scope for imaginative action. There are not many places in the world at any time in history where children have been prepared to die in order to achieve a better education. Despite the intransigence of the state and the harshness of its reaction to protests by children, or to attempts by such bodies as the National Education Crisis Committee (NECC), to organise alternative education, it is nevertheless clear that independent initiative, carefully thought through, can make considerable headway.

One model of such initiative is Sached (the South African Committee for Higher Education) which, over a period of more than 25 years, has enriched the education of thousands of black South Africans by a variety of means. These include the provision of tutorials for those studying by correspondence for degrees, and the production of a teenage magazine, *Upbeat*, which has a wide national circulation. Sached ran educational supplements in the *Weekend World* (until this was banned) and *Post* newspapers. It runs a publishing project which has produced books such as *Read Well*, and *Write Well*, widely used by teachers and pupils throughout the country, and has written a new history of education. The contents of these projects are all of an 'alternative' nature to what is otherwise available. Sached now works closely with trade unions and local communities; it is also trying to help create resources for rural or small-town communities. One of its major tasks has been to establish study-skills courses with content relevant for students struggling out of Bantu education into university degrees. One of its newest projects, Khanya College (with campuses in Cape Town and Johannesburg), provides full-time residential bursaries to students, especially those from outside the large cities. At Khanya students do two first-year university subjects alongside related study-skills courses. The content of these includes the history and literature of Africa, subjects that are not taught in any government school, black or white, in South Africa. The destruction, in January 1988, of its Grahamstown office, and some months earlier of the contents of its East London office, both by arson, is one more reminder of the difficulties which it and other similar organisations face.

Since the 1970s a wide range of private schools, some long established, others very new, have opened their doors to black students. In preparing South Africans for the twenty-first century they face a great challenge in virtually every respect, such as providing a suitable curriculum, recognising language differences, and being prepared to change from the ethos of the white culture to one that is firmly rooted in Africa.

Still in the more formal educational environment, there is a host of immediate needs including proper playing fields, recreational halls, school or community libraries, and teacher resource centres. Ways of sharing resources, even over long distances, have to be found. An example is the use of mobile classrooms and libraries (97: 26ff). In a paper on libraries and poverty, prepared for the Carnegie Inquiry, Mary Nassimbeni reminds us of the fact that the founding of free library services in South Africa was part of the great drive in the 1930s and 1940s to improve conditions for poor whites. The first Carnegie Commission had drawn special attention to the deprivation of children (white, particularly Afrikaans-speaking) in those schools – especially in the rural areas – where libraries were inadequate and suitable reading materials unavailable. Much was done to rectify the situation and facilities improved enormously – for whites. Despite strong efforts, manifest in such developments as the Carnegie Non-European Library, Transvaal, which began in 1931, we find that in the 1980s when the vast majority of those who are poor are black, library facilities are primarily available only to whites. In the Cape Province, for example, according to a 1985 study, three-quarters of all libraries are closed to black South Africans. Clearly there is much work to be done, not only in opening existing libraries to all, but also in building and stocking new ones. Where they are imaginatively run, whether in schools or neighbourhoods, libraries are heavily used even by those who are not considered highly literate. In the process of establishing such libraries, resources centres, or reading rooms, attention will also have to be paid to the training of suitable librarians and the development of appropriate strategies so that each resource centre can better meet the needs (such as illiteracy, unemployment, or simply a desire to know more about the wider world) of those living nearby.

One idea which seems ripe for further development in order to help stimulate and educate children, relates to museums. There are three reasons why museums – also run as resource centres serving individuals, schools and other institutions – could play a particularly important role in enriching the lives of children (and adults) in South Africa at this time. As South Africa moves from white minority rule to a more democratic society, so will the need grow for a deeper understanding and knowledge of the history of Africa. No longer is the perspective of the descendants of conquerors from Europe acceptable, though it is still taught in all South African schools. What is now demanded is also the perspective of those whose ancestors were here long before the arrival of the white settlers; the perspective, too, that South Africa's history is part of the history of the wider continent, with its common experience of slavery, colonial conquest, and the impact of Christian missionaries. And Africa's history, after all, goes back to the origins of the human race! South African archaeologists, among the world's best, are particularly well placed to communicate something of the depth of these roots (Hall, 1987). Museums, like the one in Nairobi, could be in the forefront of an exciting, more realistic, interpretation of history that provides children of the sub-continent not only a sense of their own origins but includes them as heirs also of ancient Egypt, connects them with the art of Benin, reveals the skills of early iron-smelters and gold-smiths, embraces the reality and depth of *ubuntu*, and understands the huge impact of Islam and Christianity.

Not unrelated is the need to forge a truly national culture that is respectful of all, meaningful to all, but not simply a pandering to group interests. This is easier said than done, but it is a challenge that museums cannot evade unless they wish to become slightly ridiculous, completely irrelevant, decorations for the titillation of this or that ethnic ego or sectarian group.

There is also the almost desperate groping by young South Africans for a window on the world, so long denied them, of today and tomorrow. Much of the resistance against the whole concept of 'Bantu' or 'Coloured' education has been due to its quite explicit attempt to cut pupils off from the wider world and to fetter their thinking within the confines of the existing, localised status quo. It is a fundamental weakness of the philosophy of 'Christian National Education' which continues to exert its baleful influence on white children as well, although they have not yet protested against its impact on their minds. South Africa has need for centres modelled on the great science museums of the world to which children from around the country can go, see for themselves, and get a sense of excitement, a vision of what is possible. Smaller centres, modelled on such places as the Children's Museum in Boston or the Anacostia neighbourhood museum in Washington, would likewise transform educational potential in the country: so too would more programmes (through bodies like the Natal Parks Board) for raising national awareness and appropriate action regarding the ecological fragility of southern Africa.

For younger children, too, imaginative action is possible. In Cape Town alone, for example, there are a number of fairly young organisations such as the Early Learning Resource Unit, Grassroots Educare Trust, the Children's Resource Centre, and a delightful magazine called *Molo Songololo*. Similarly, in other parts of the country there has been a mushrooming in recent years of private initiatives (some of them with partial state support) seeking to come to grips with problems facing younger children. Other areas where individual initiative could supplement and strengthen existing efforts until such time as national programmes become possible, include the provision of crèches, recreational parks, adventure play-grounds, and the running of pre-schools and play-groups especially for children of working mothers who cannot afford to hire suitable child-minders at home (115: 5ff).

There is much that is already being done, but has the time not now come for the establishment of a new organisation for the purpose of focusing specific and continuing attention on the problems facing children in southern Africa?* The composition, control and functions of such a body require detailed discussion amongst a wide range of people. However, such an institute could play a very creative role in strengthening the work of existing organisations and in helping to articulate the needs and interests of children.

* This particular proposal was first made publicly in the Unicef report, *Children on the Front Line* (New York, 1986). We repeat it here in the belief that the establishment of such a body has become more, not less, necessary since then.

Amongst the functions with which such a Children's Institute or Centre might be charged are the following:

1. To express publicly a concern for the rights of children in all aspects of society, including the home, school, and in the wider social structures.

2. To focus attention on the law and upon those legal processes that infringe the rights of children. Particular regard would need to be paid to the law affecting the use of child labour and of that relating to the detention of children whether in jails, police cells, or corrective camps.

3. To monitor, expose, and seek to correct anything detrimental to children: ranging from high infant mortality rates to incest; from assaults on children within their homes, to torture in police custody.

4. To stimulate research, thinking and writing about the best ways of mitigating the ill-effects of poverty, racism, sexism and oppression as it affects children.

5. To encourage individual initiative towards and to pressurise local government into the establishment of a stimulating environment within which children can grow. This includes particular attention to the redesign and better use of towns and cities, ranging from the lay-out of streets and recreational spaces to the provision of accessible crèches and pre-schools, libraries and study centres, and imaginative museums.

6. To create centres of concern all over the country to espouse the cause of children and to encourage their growth, through the creation of a loving, caring environment that allows children the space to be children.

Law

In the field of law, as in health care and education, there have been some striking initiatives since the mid-1970s. Many of these have been complementary to the work of the trade-union movement. Indeed, in an interesting way they have risen parallel with it. We are referring to the growth of public interest law and the establishment of a whole network of legal advisory services across a wide range of fields, but particularly in labour. The founding, in 1979, of the independent Legal Resources Centre and its decentralisation to four major cities, together with the setting up, at the University of the Witwatersrand, of the Centre for Applied Legal Studies, have laid the foundations for a remarkable renaissance in the use of law to serve the ends for which it was originally intended – namely, to protect the common person from 'unscrupulous rascals and the tyranny of petty bureaucrats'. Using the law to try and re-establish the rule of law is not always easy, especially in a context where so much law has come into being as the result of administrative fiat. But in a relatively short space of time, some notable successes have been notched up, both for individuals who had been hard done by and in cases which set important precedents. Amongst the more noteworthy of these were the Rikhoto and Komani judgments. Together, despite foot-dragging by the authorities, these breached a major hole in the barrage of laws and regulations whereby the state was trying, particularly after 1968, to ensure that any new black worker who came from country to town did so as a migrant labourer, without his family, on a contract that no matter how often it was renewed, would never allow him to acquire 'rights' to settle permanently in town or to have his wife there with him. Other victories included judgment against a bus company which was trying to use its monopolistic position to increase fares on the basis of arguments which lawyers showed to be spurious.

One notable process in recent years has been the creation (by the state) and use of Industrial Courts, empowered to hear industrial disputes and to pass judgment in the light of what was deemed to be 'fair'. With good legal representation, trade unions and other groups of workers have been able to make significant progress against unfair practices by employers, thus enhancing the possibility of using the law to establish the rule of law. But the possibility is increasingly under threat, and the evidence suggests that the unions will have to struggle to keep and to consolidate the gains made in this field during the early years of the 1980s.

The legal clinics which also spread widely during the 1980s were run by a variety of organisations, including civic associations, trade unions, the Legal Resources Centres, and also the Black Sash. The Sash's advice offices, already established in a number of major cities in the 1960s, had become bywords for their tenacious struggle for the human rights of an endless stream of individuals caught within the web of pass laws and other regulations.

Some judges too, particularly on the Natal Bench, have made a major contribution to justice by questioning the validity of some of the more draconian legislation. But there have been many setbacks, not least in the declaration of the states of emergency, first in 1985 and then, again, in 1986 and 1988, which have provided the state with virtually unlimited powers in a whole range of activities, including widespread detention without trial and rigid control over certain types of information. In a society where the state sees itself as being above the law, there are limits to the extent to which the law can be used to serve and protect the interests of ordinary people.

Business

'The misery of being exploited by capitalists', wrote Joan Robinson in a famous aphorism, 'is nothing compared to the misery of not being exploited at all' (cited by Chambers, 1986: 148). Without here entering into a debate about the pros and cons of nationalising the commanding heights of the South African economy, it is nevertheless necessary to be quite clear that in the struggle against poverty there is a crucial role to be played by private enterprise. There are, as we shall see, plenty of examples in other parts of the world and much room for discussion about how best business organisations, particularly large ones, could be restructured to ensure that they are properly accountable to the wider society and not merely to the narrow interests of shareholders. Some Marxists themselves now argue: 'The emergence of capitalist social relations of production constitutes the central dynamic process in a wide range of African societies' (Sender and Smith, 1986: 128).

During the past quarter of a century a number of African countries have learnt the hard way that progress is not possible unless goods are produced and distributed efficiently. In Tanzania, for example, despite major achievements in primary health care and literacy training, the hostility of the bureaucracy and of the ruling party to private trading had disastrous consequences. Operation Maduka, which sought in 1976 to close down all private retail outlets in rural areas and create communal shops in their place, led immediately to acute shortages of basic goods such as sugar, salt, paraffin, soap, and matches (Chambers, 1986: 147). In Mozambique a similar state hostility to private retail trade exacerbated a situation that was already precarious as a result of the flight of Portuguese traders when the country became independent in 1975. Ten years later at a party congress this was recognised and private trading was restored. In Ghana, too, there was a sharp decrease of production after independence which cannot be blamed simply on deteriorating terms of trade with the world market (Sender and Smith, 1986: 110 ff).

It is in the light of these and other similar experiences that a cross-section of African leaders met in Nairobi, in October 1986, at what was called an Enabling Environment Conference for an Effective Private Sector Contribution in Sub-Saharan Africa. And it was here that the executive secretary of the Economic Commission for Africa, Adebayo Adedeji, summed up the emerging consensus:

Of course, not all private enterprises are efficiently managed just as not all public enterprises are inefficient. Poor management is not reserved for government ministries; it abounds also in boardrooms and other private and public institutions. What is important is that it is the individuals – either as consumers or as producers, working in either the public or private sector – who bear the brunt of this mismanagement. . . . Africa's main dilemma is not one of public sector versus private sector, but finding the most effective means of enhancing growth and development . . . all our governments accept that both have a role to play and that both can and should complement each other. (1987: 7)

The actions of African governments across a wide range of the political spectrum are increasingly consistent with this view, but are, at the same time, directed at ensuring a much deeper sense of social responsibility amongst companies than might otherwise exist. Three examples can quickly illustrate the point. Firstly, the negotiations between the Botswana government and foreign (including South African) mining companies ensured that a far more equitable share of profits was retained within the country for purposes of development than was the case in Zambia under colonial rule or, it seems, in Namibia under South African occupation. Secondly, the protracted negotiations between the government of Zimbabwe and a leading American-based multi-national in the food business led to major new investment on the basis of a 49: 51 percentage shareholding partnership, with mutually agreed responsibilities. These included a major training programme undertaken by the company, and a profit-sharing arrangement whereby 78 per cent of every pre-tax dollar of profit goes to the government. Despite these conditions, hammered out for the maximum benefit of Zimbabwe, the company has gone from strength to strength, and the foreign investor is well pleased with the results. Sales have more than doubled in four years and the investment sustains 1 400 jobs. According to the president* of the multi-national concerned: 'Today, we have a superb, profitable and dynamic partnership in Zimbabwe that has exceeded our mutual expectations and even more importantly, one which has prompted plans for further investment in that country and indeed, in all of the surrounding territories' (Dibb and Heinz, 1987: 36).

The third example relates to the restructuring of business to enable workers to become owners of the companies in which they earn their living, with all the power and sense of participation that ownership confers. In Zimbabwe there is a variety of participatory schemes, but a three-year research project by the Zimbabwe Promotion Council has resulted in the identification of a truly democratic and significant model which is rapidly gaining ground as existing businesses begin to restructure themselves as employee-owned companies (Oakeshott *et al.*, 1987). In South Africa one or two tentative moves have been made in this direction but the idea has not yet been properly thought through and some of the most widely publicised schemes do nothing to restructure production in such a way as to enable employees to acquire real power. South Africa has much to learn from Zimbabwe in this regard, and the process is part of a world-wide movement to find ways of moving beyond political democracy to a democratisation of the economy, which enables workers to have a real sense of participation and power in the decisions that affect their daily lives (see Marshall, 1987).

In South Africa, where private enterprise did much to shape the basic structures of apartheid (such as the migrant labour system) and where, until the recent rise of the trade unions, there has been little democratic pressure compelling it to respond to the needs of the wider society, the business sector has clearly much work to do if it is to win the trust of poor people, who constitute a large majority in the country. Without this trust, political change in South Africa is likely to be accompanied by deep hostility to the very idea of a business sector by new leaders who are likely to be unimpressed with its track record thus far. Deeds speak louder than words, and considerable imagination and some sacrifice will be needed if business people are to find new and acceptable ways of doing business. In addition to employee-ownership, another suggestion, referred to earlier, concerns the creation of banking institutions which can really meet the needs of poor people for credit that will help them to make a living. Other ideas flow from the examples cited from Botswana and Zimbabwe. What is required, above all, is a continuing commitment, backed by adequate resources, to search (including in other parts of the Third World) for new ways to harness the energy, the expertise, and the discipline of business, not simply to make money, but to meet the needs and aspirations of all the people.

---

* Whom South Africans once knew as the teenage Irish (BritishLions) rugby star, Tony O'Reilly.

Religious organisations

In South Africa more than three-quarters (78 per cent) of the total population considers itself to be Christian. Thus, in this section, we concentrate primarily on the role of the church. This in no way detracts from the important work done by all the other religious communities – Hindu, Muslim, Jewish and others – that face the challenge of poverty in South Africa.

Despite its many limitations and failures, the Christian church has a remarkable record down the centuries in creating and nurturing organisations aimed at serving and harnessing the energies of people in need. Indeed many of the finest secular institutions in the world – including many hospitals, schools, and universities – were originally inspired by the church. This restless spirit continues to break out in new forms ranging, in our own day, from Mother Teresa's Order of the Missionaries of Charity in the slums of Calcutta to the politically active base communities of the Brazilian church. In South Africa different denominations have long been active in a host of institutions and other forms of organised compassion or *barmhartigheid*. Although good work continues to be done one has a sense that, whatever may have been true in the past when the church harnessed and poured enormous energy into works (now largely taken over by the state) of healing and teaching, the present reality is that somehow the church has failed to respond adequately to the challenges which surround it. It is easy to criticise, but worthwhile if such criticism is part of an urgent search for new forms of embodying the Christian mission: 'To announce good news to the poor, to proclaim release for prisoners and recovery of sight for the blind; to let the broken victims go free . . .' (Luke 4: 14).

Much of the best work of the church consists, of course, of inspiring and strengthening individuals to work in secular organisations. We believe however that there is still room for church initiatives in setting up new structures appropriate to the needs of the situation. Some of the most urgent of these needs have been spelt out in the first part of this book so that one test for the church, and those who belong to it, is to examine the extent to which it is allocating its resources (including full-time and part-time workers, land and buildings, and prayer for imaginative action) to meeting them. Another no less important test is to examine the extent to which the work of the church has the effect of empowering the poor, of helping to shift the balance of power. It is in Latin America particularly that the church, inspired by the writings of people like Paulo Freire (1972) and the liberation theologians who followed him, has begun to develop new structures that seem appropriate for South Africa today. The emphasis on educating people (especially those who are poor and marginalised) to become critically aware of the reasons for their poverty – 'conscientised' – with a view to their controlling their own destinies by creating alternative centres of power in society, combined with a deeper understanding of the bible as a process of liberation, not least from oppression and poverty, provides a potent vision for the work of the church at the end of the twentieth century (Elliott, 1985: 53ff and 1987). It is a vision which South

Africans, led primarily by their black theologians, are beginning to share.

But in translating that vision into reality there is still a long way to go. The challenge now facing the church is how to use the resources (not least of ideas and people) available from its global network to breathe new life into the old bones of the existing organisation, which, when all is said and done, is better placed than any other institution, religious or secular, to work with poor people.

One of the most impressive examples of what is possible is to be found in two neighbouring platteland towns approximately 200 km north of Cape Town. MAG, literally meaning power, is the Afrikaans acronym for the Montagu en Ashton Gemeenskapsdiens (Montagu and Ashton Community Services). It began in 1976 when a group of concerned people met to plan a programme of action in response to the needs of people both in the local townships and in the surrounding rural areas. Starting as a welfare organisation and registered as a branch of the Diakonal Service of the Dutch Reformed Mission Church, MAG was formed as an ecumenical venture with representation from five denominations. Members meet regularly for lively bible study, reflection, and prayer. In little more than ten years MAG has generated an impressive array of projects and programmes, including some two dozen adult literacy classes, a legal resources office, a school-feeding scheme for 3 000 children at 18 schools, three early learning centres, community gardens, family care, counselling services for teenagers and parents, job creation by means of one farming and two woodwork co-operatives, and an annual carnival to raise funds. Those involved in MAG see that their 'main task lies in community development, and in that sense in political development'. But 'we do not want to do community work with just a political agenda. We want to do good community development with good administration; good management which continues to be critical about the work we do.' MAG is particularly conscious about, and strives towards, an holistic approach. 'Since most problems are interrelated with each other, and since they therefore require interrelated change efforts, the projects attempt to address a number of different problem areas simultaneously.' (Marais, n.d.: 6) Many more such seeds need to be planted. MAG shows how they can grow provided they are properly rooted.

Research and training

One thread that has run through all the discussion in this chapter about different types of organisation in the various areas of concern relates to the need for ongoing training and research. Much of the training has to be done within the organisations themselves although there is much that sensitive outside bodies could do to help. Similarly the research has to be rooted where the action is taking place, lest it be out of touch with the situation. There is always a danger of research, seen as an end in itself, becoming a displacement activity to hide an unwillingness or inability to take effective action to change the conditions being investigated. But there is both opportunity and an obligation for universities and other independent 'think-tanks' to become more involved in digging out facts, wrestling with analysis in order to understand better, and generating ideas for action in the sorts of areas of concern we have been describing in this chapter. Carefully chosen targets such as the monitoring of infant mortality rates, the provision of resources through workshops, books, and films for individuals and organisations, the development of appropriate technology, or long-range thinking about the transformation of South African agriculture, could make a significant difference to the quality and shape of South African society and to the lives of those who are poor within it, both now and in the future.

The Second Carnegie Inquiry into Poverty and Development in Southern Africa was itself structured in a way that attempted to use the process of gathering and analysing data as a means for training students, a number of whom produced important papers for the Inquiry. Interaction between universities and the wider society such as occurs in the medical field at the University of the Witwatersrand, for example, through the primary health-care structures being developed in an urban setting at the Alexandra Clinic or, in an impoverished rural area, by the Health Services Development Unit, need to be expanded and multiplied. Other fields where this could be done include, for example, agriculture for small-scale farming, forestry for fuel and renewal of the environment, engineering for appropriate technology (particularly with regard to the provision of water and the conservation of energy), accounting and management, and architecture to find ways through the housing disaster.

Much good work is already being done by individual departments and research units but, given their resources, the universities, taken as a whole, could be doing considerably more. The major change in the teaching structure of American universities over the past three or four decades is, according to some observers, the shift in emphasis away from the single goal of preparing students for degrees to one which also draws in all sorts of adults (who may or may not have degrees) for short courses (ranging from a few days to several months) in a wide variety of practical topics. Some move in this direction has taken place in South Africa but the universities as a whole have yet to make this major shift in attitude and to find ways of using their considerable resources more fully than they currently do.

Conclusion

The discussion in this long chapter about what sort of independent organisations exist and could expand (or which need to be initiated) to serve poor people in South Africa today makes no attempt to provide a comprehensive shopping list. We have tried instead to consider a cross-section of the sorts of organisations needed in a limited variety of fields in the hope that this will be sufficient to illustrate the sort of action that seems likely to be fruitful. But there are many other areas where work is clearly vitally important. Such work includes support for independent newspapers and journals in order to ensure the free flow of information which is essential for democracy. Democratic political organisations – those in exile as well as internal bodies – have to be thinking not only about what they can do in present circumstances but also about the sorts of strategies that would need to be pursued by a democratic state aiming to deal as effectively as possible with the legacy of poverty that it will inherit. What those policies might be is the subject of the next chapter.

308

Economic regression and impoverishment were universal. . . . In this situation Afrikanerdom needed compassion and help, but above all direction and guidance on the path to rehabilitation and self-reliance. . . . In official circles a sympathetic ear heard the warning signals and the State as a whole became conscious of the problem. Special regulations were introduced to encourage large-scale employment [of poor whites] on the Railways. These were highly successful. . . . A succession of legal measures followed one after the other to ensure, amongst other things, adequate wages, better and safer working conditions, and old-age provision. At the same time the needy farmer was helped by means of state subsidies and other means to counter the blows of nature and of the economic depressions that followed one after the other.
— D. F. Malan, 1950 (translated)

In many African economies, a rapid development of the forces of production was achieved in the post-colonial period. However, in certain economies . . . economic performance has been disastrous, and even in those economies where rapid accumulation has taken place, it is necessary to discuss the macro-economic requirements for sustained accumulation.
— John Sender and Sheila Smith, 1986

People who care about avoidable poverty in Latin America tend to split in two camps, which need not work against each other but often do. One emphasises investment, creation of employment opportunities, and macroeconomic management; the other, such questions as the distribution of land ownership, foreign influence, social barriers to mobility, differential access to education, or use of the political system to stack the cards in favor of special privilege. Both sides are right, except when they disdain the other.
— John Sheahan, 1987: 49

In modern society the state in whatever form, be it American capitalist, European socialist, or Russian communist, plays a central role in the economy. Much debate centres on the structure of ownership of the means of production and on the role that the market should play in allocating productive resources, final goods and services. Part of this debate focuses specifically on the question as to what degree (measured as a percentage of gross national product) of state expenditure is appropriate in a particular society. In South Africa, where one-third (30 per cent) of economically active whites and increasing numbers of blacks work for the government or related public-sector bodies, we would argue that the precise proportion of GNP spent by the state is a less fundamental issue than is the efficiency with which it is spent and the goals to which it is directed.

One of the crucial unanswered questions to which those struggling for a new South Africa must address themselves is what particular form of the state and what degree of nationalisation can best meet the needs of all those living in this society. There are always dangers inherent in strategies that place major emphasis, as we do, on what are and should be the state's responsibilities. The dangers, as Gérard Chaliand has so acutely shown (1977), is that the bourgeoisie can use the state to take over private business in order to serve their own interests, thus entrenching a form of state capitalism rather than empowering or even materially benefiting workers.

It is naive to believe that somehow 'the state' will necessarily embody the 'will of the people' and act automatically for the good of all. One lesson learnt from African independence is the painful truth of the realisation that the state can be taken over by an elite group within society that, although mouthing other truths, manipulates its power to serve its own ends rather than those of all the people, particularly those who are poor. There is urgent need in South Africa for everybody, Marxists, liberals, and conservatives, to engage in hard thinking and debate, as is now beginning to happen in other parts of sub-Saharan Africa (see, for example, Ndegwa, 1985), about the realities of power, the potential for corruption, and the design of appropriate structures together with ongoing political processes, to ensure that programmes created to address the problems of poverty do, in fact, work in such a way as to empower and enrich the lives of the poor.

Our concern, at this stage, is to spell out as clearly as we can some of the vital roles which any democratic state, mindful of the needs of its members who are poor, has to fulfil in South Africa. Essentially, we are looking at some of the longer-run strategies for a democratic society, although it is not impossible that some of the points raised here may be taken up by the present government, unresponsive and unaccountable as it is to the vast majority of the poor.

Another part of the debate about the role of the state in alleviating poverty, as illustrated in the opening quotation about Latin America, tends to be polarised between those who emphasise the more purely economic strategies such as investment or macro-economic management and those who stress more apparently political issues such as the distribution of land or access to education. But this, as Sheahan stresses, is a false dichotomy. No strategies for reducing poverty in South Africa can avoid tackling head on the root causes as uncovered in the analysis of our country's history. Equally, no serious strategy can ignore the issues with which all governments have to wrestle: macro-economic policies with regard to investment, economic growth, inflation, and employment creation.

The first task of any democratic South African government is to stop the juggernaut: to halt the systematic assault by the state on the poor. Some of the major components of this assault include forced removals, anti-urbanisation policies, land laws, colour bars, the migrant labour system, Bantu education, misallocation of public funds, the crushing of organisations, dispossession of citizenship, and (in the surrounding countries) destabilisation.

Some people, pointing to the abolition of the pass laws in 1986, believe that all these changes can be made by the present government. We argue that such belief is naive. Firstly, any action by the government to alter fundamentally the allocation of public resources is constrained by the limits of its whites-only power base. Secondly, attempts to change in response to black political pressure (as in the field of education) are crippled by the white government's inability to let go control, combined with the irreversible loss of its legitimacy in the majority of black eyes. Some important changes in the right direction can be made by a less than monolithic, somewhat contradictory state, but radical transformation is impossible by a government whose power is drawn from only 15 per cent of the population (plus whoever else can be co-opted) at the upper end of the economic pyramid.

The process of dismantling the structures of apartheid is a vitally necessary step in state strategies against poverty, but it is not sufficient. The reason lies in what we call the scaffolding nature of much legislation. Consider, for example, the battery of laws including the Urban Areas Act (1923) and the Group Areas Act (1950), which have shaped the racial geography of the country's towns and cities. Abolition of these laws will enable those black South Africans who can afford it to live in the white, higher-income suburbs, but it will do nothing to alter the fact that those who are poor will continue to live where apartheid dumped them in impoverished ghettoes, miles distant from their work. Policies will have to be developed to overcome the enduring consequences of three centuries of racist laws and practices, in which the roots of South African poverty lie.

Agricultural transformation

One of the major tasks facing any democratic state will be the need for a radical restructuring of the country's land-tenure system. The first change of course, if it has not happened already, must be abolition of those laws, starting with the Land Act of 1913, which, taken together, prevent the vast majority of South Africans from owning or even leasing land throughout most of the country, in both urban and rural areas. Seen from a conservation perspective this legislation has played a major role in the ecological destruction of the reserve areas, where thousands of people, pushed off the white farms by changing techniques of production, have been forced to settle on land that was already overpopulated in terms not only of people but also of stock. The devastating consequences, leading within the space of a few years to dustbowl conditions in what was previously good grazing veld, have been described earlier in this book. Nobody who has flown in a drought year over these areas, which have been growing steadily more overcrowded for two generations now since 1913, can fail to be profoundly alarmed by the extent and depth of the damage. Clearly nothing short of the permanent migration of most of the people to other parts of the country will enable any conservation programme to make a meaningful impact on the environment there.

But there is more to land tenure than simply the abolition of two or three racist laws, no matter how pernicious they have been. One of the most striking features of commercial agriculture in South Africa in recent years has been the growth in the size of farms. Between 1960 and 1975 the average farm size increased from 867 ha to 1 102 ha; that is, by 27 per cent (1 ha=1,16 morgen). But the indications are that the increase has been even more marked since that date, certainly in some areas of the country. For example in the maize-farming region of the western Transvaal, the average size of farm increased, between 1968 and 1981, by almost 75 per cent from 664 ha to 1 155 ha (17: 6). And in the stock, mainly sheep, country of Hanover in the Karoo, between 1952–63 and 1983 the size increased from 4 587 ha to not less than 7 024 ha, a growth of 53 per cent (34: 42).

Research is currently being undertaken (by Peter Moll) to investigate what economies of scale, if any, exist in maize or in wheat (both combined with livestock) production in South Africa. Preliminary results suggest that (taking into account only purchased inputs – excluding any consideration of the farmer's own income) there are few economies of scale once farms reach the size of between 300 and 400 hectares. This means that an economically viable option in any land-reform programme would be to break up the large maize estates into smaller family farms. Then, just as the increase in farm size has led to workers being pushed off the land, so by a reverse process the decrease in farm size could lead to more people being absorbed back onto the land, whose capacity to create and provide jobs would thus have been increased. In passing we note also that labour-intensive agriculture tends also to lead to greater productivity (measured as output per unit of area) of land that is more intensively cultivated by hand than by machinery. Paradoxically, provided the farming is well done, a shift from capital- to labour-intensive agriculture with a concomitant increase of population on the land can have the effect of improving the conservation of that land. Given the fact that significant economies of scale do not appear to exist in maize or wheat farming above the size of 300 ha, then there is a wide range of options facing land-reformers. The main four are: large privately owned estates; large government-owned estates; large communally owned (kibbutz-type) estates; and smaller farms between one-quarter or one-half the size of current ones. And there is a fifth option consisting of some combination of the first four.

One important aspect of agricultural transformation in South Africa is the need to break the rigid boundary between town and country, to open up the possibility of people currently locked into the reserves moving to small-holdings producing food on the outskirts of the cities.

The debate about land reform and agricultural transformation has only just begun in South Africa but in the process it is important that considerations of conservation (or environmental sustainability) and of employment generation remain paramount.

What then of land reform within the reserves where the land-tenure pattern, based originally on communal tenure with land allocated by the chief, has been very different from that in other parts of the country, where individual ownership under Roman–Dutch law has predominated? In an important Carnegie conference paper (260) which itself sparked off consider-able debate (*Reality*, 16 (5), 1984 and subsequent issues), Tapson argued against the (then) commonly held view that the introduction of individual tenure in the reserves would help stimulate agricultural production there. Until then, much of the conventional wisdom suggested that the existing pattern of communal tenure – with no control over the number of cattle put onto the grazing ground or (in the absence of adequate fencing) without any real control against stock destroying maize and other food crops, and with no possibility of good, go-ahead farmers purchasing more land – was the single most important barrier to agricultural development. A necessary first step in the rehabilitation of the reserves, it was argued, was the introduction of individual tenure so that people could own, buy and sell land. Norman Reynolds pointed out the fallacy of this view some years ago in a paper on land reform in Botswana (1977). In it he contended that the disadvantages of the communal tenure system could be best overcome, not by private individual ownership, but by the formation of land companies in which all those with rights to land, under the old system, would have shares. Tapson, in his Carnegie paper, argued forcefully against the 'freehold option' as a 'blind alley' on the grounds that the permanent alienation of land into private ownership would inevitably, in practice, lead to the land being held 'by a wealthy and powerful elite' (260: 9). Far better, he said,

that land be converted to public (community) property with suitable compensation, and made available to land users on the basis of a market-determined rent. This option, he maintained, will deliver all of the advantages claimed for freehold title, plus some additional benefits unique to itself. These are:

1. Land will not be permanently alienated to individuals, but will be made available to all on a regular basis.

2. Those with the resources and expertise to make good use of productive land will be able to do so without the less well-endowed losing all benefit from it.

3. Provided that the principle of distribution of rentals *pro rata* to all families in the tribe is adhered to, it is advantageous to all that land values, and therefore rentals, should rise. In the case of freehold, only land-holders will benefit, and as values rise, the number owning land will shrink.

4. Because land will belong to the tribe as a whole, no landless class will be created.

The leasehold option has the promise of increasing productivity of both grazing and arable land, while at the same time maintaining and improving equity throughout the social and economic strata of the tribe. It will secure some sort of income, even for those lacking resources to work the land themselves, and will permit those better endowed to create opportunities for profitable production. (260: 9)

Drawing on these arguments, together with material from other papers delivered at the Carnegie conference, Moll went on to examine in detail the case for transition to freehold in the reserves. He concluded that more important than the systems of land tenure in affecting productivity in the reserves is lack of government expenditure and price incentives, compared with what the state has done down the years to support the growth of output in white-owned agriculture. Moreover, whilst it could be argued that under communal land tenure women have no access to the land because of the patriarchal system and that some poor (who could afford it) might benefit from private tenure as they could buy land without having to resort to bribes, other poor people, notably women and their children, might become more insecure if their husbands, uncles or brothers, perhaps away for long periods of time as migrant workers, were to sell the land over their heads.

Moll's recommendation, then, is that until such time as the state is willing to invest substantial amounts in agricultural development in these areas – by improving the roads, providing markets, investing in detailed technical and advisory services, supporting agricultural prices and generally helping farmers to take off – it would not be advantageous to introduce freehold tenure. Later, with the migrant labour system gone, with adequate family housing in the cities, and with serious state investment in the rural infrastructure, the case for individual tenure could be re-opened. But even then, as Reynolds and Tapson have both argued, there may be other structures, such as land companies and leasehold tenure, which would encourage agricultural production whilst also protecting the poor from loss of their only asset, the land rights they share as members of rural communities.

In this regard, it is worth noting the intense resistance, particularly by women, to attempts in the so-called coloured reserves in Namaqualand to transform communal rights over access to land into private ownership, with its attendant dangers of enclosures and exclusion. According to the Rural Coloured Areas Act (24 of 1963), 'land which had formerly been commonage could, to facilitate development, be reserved for bona-fide farmers exclusively' (69: 3). The provision in the Act that any (coloured) person could acquire title to land in the reserves 'threatened to do away with all the particularistic features of the individual Reserve communities and to destroy their most important function in the eyes of a considerable section of the Reserve's population: the limited guarantee they had offered, in a situation of insecure wage-employment opportunities, against the danger of total impoverishment' (69: 12 and Boonzaier, 1987). Thus there was staunch resistance to these 'betterment' schemes.

On one notable occasion in the mid-1970s, when a team of bulldozers arrived unannounced in Komaggas (80 km to the south-west of Springbok in the north-western Cape) to begin the task of constructing the planned village, several hundred women from the community marched together to the superintendent's office and barricaded him in it for the day. After several hours in which the women discussed the matter quietly with the police who had been summoned from Nababeep, the superintendent arranged for the workers and their equipment to leave the Reserve and was allowed to go home. (69: 19)

The wrong kind of land 'reform' can be highly regressive and harmful for the poor. Thus any proposals must be examined with great care to analyse 'who benefits'; above all, such proposals must be subject to scrutiny (with a power of veto) by all those most likely to be affected by them. If this simple process had been followed in South Africa, it is unlikely that a single proposal for 'reform' as spelt out in the 'betterment' projects that were undertaken in the reserves would have been accepted, particularly after the Tomlinson Commission report of 1955 with its unhappy mixture of paternalistic good intentions within a totally imposed and unacceptable paradigm of separate (Bantustan) development. For the betterment proposals sounded good on paper, especially when read in a distant city, but in practice what was done (as opposed to what was 'planned' or promised) had the effect, time and again, of worsening the position of the rural poor. In the Chata Valley outside Keiskammahoek in the Ciskei, for example, a careful study by Chris de Wet has compared conditions as they were in 1949–50 (shortly before betterment began), at the time of a major survey of the district (Elton-Mills, 1952), with the situation as he found it in the early 1980s. He concludes:

Betterment planning set out with the explicit goals of combating soil erosion and promoting agricultural development in Chata. With the exception of the 24 fields on the irrigation scheme . . . it has achieved neither. It has in fact left people worse off than before. (De Wet, forthcoming)

The average maize yield per morgen did not increase and may even have fallen whilst, as a result of people losing 60 per cent of their arable land which was deemed unsuitable for cultivation, the average size of land-holding fell from betweeen 1.6 and 2.4 morgen to 0.5 morgen per household. And the number of households with access to arable land actually declined. Analysis of the 'betterment' programme is useful, for it illustrates the necessity not only of assessing any scheme by its results rather than in terms of its stated intentions, but also of ensuring that those who are to benefit from a scheme are part and parcel of the planning process and of the decisions as to what should be done. Where any scheme is designed in such a way that the poor who are supposed to benefit have no power in the design of the scheme or its implementation, then it must be rejected – either because, at best, it is almost certain to fail as a result of unforeseen, unintended consequences or because, at worst, the real aim of the scheme is not so much the benefit of the poor as for their control or for the consolidation of power by those benefiting from maintenance of the status quo. The betterment programme, it seems, failed on both counts.

The lesson from South African experience within the reserves over the past generation is that when the state embarks upon so-called land reform, its motives have to be thoroughly examined (Letsoala, 1988). At the same time the process of drawing up the proposals and subsequently of implementing them has to be done in such a way that officials are accountable to the people who are the object, or rather the subject, of the programme. This is, of course, by no means a simple matter; the appropriate interaction between state and a local community is complex and subject to all sorts of political power-play and potential corruption. There is no cast-iron formula to ensure that the interests of the poor are safeguarded, but it is important when thinking about the long-term structures to guard against the all too alluring temptation of patronising the poor; of deciding what is good for them and planning accordingly. For it is at precisely this point that the worm of bureaucratic self-interest can enter to corrupt the whole revolution.

Macro-economic policy

Researchers on poverty tend to deal with micro-level, grassroots issues in great detail, but often lose sight of the broader context within which ground-level issues are placed. Macro-economists, by contrast, tend to theorise about financial and monetary matters and overlook the implications of macro-economic policy for poorer sections of the population. But the whole question of the impact on the poor of macro-economic policy is coming increasingly under the spotlight, not least because of the debt crisis facing so many countries in the Third World, the harsh consequences of IMF and World Bank prescriptions, and the realisation of the possibility that policies can be devised which in Unicef's words provide for 'adjustment with a human face' by promoting economic growth whilst protecting the vulnerable (Cornia, Jolly and Stewart, 1987). Macro-economic policies include such matters as monetary policy of the central (or Reserve) bank, fiscal (taxation) policy, minimum wage policy, agricultural pricing, exchange rates, and policies relating to tariffs, the control of imports and exports, and other measures to promote economic growth. Also important is the pattern of expenditure by the state whose budget in many countries, including South Africa, is nearly one-third of the gross national product.

In an attempt to bridge the gap between the two types of approach described above, a workshop, held at the University of Cape Town in 1986, brought together a number of economists to think at the macro-economic level about causes of and cures for poverty in South Africa.

A number of papers have been published as a result (PCS 15–19) and the debate has been ably summarised by Terence Moll (PCS 20), thus we do not intend to undertake a detailed analysis of these complex issues here. We simply wish to draw attention to the importance of making quite sure that macro-economic policy is designed and analysed after weighing carefully its impact upon those who are poor. In doing this we would point out that the best measures to promote growth are by no means necessarily those of reducing the role of the state through privatisation, or increasing the scope of market forces in determining exchange rates and the allocation of foreign exchange. Analysis of the role of macro-economic policy in the post-war success of Japan, Korea and Taiwan shows that it has not been modelled on an exclusively free market approach as is frequently asserted, but that the state has played a central role. Indeed, in the light of the Asian experience, Sachs suggests that 'successful development might be helped as much by raising the quality of public sector management as by privatising public enterprises or liberalising markets' (1987: 4). It is also argued that the deliberate policies of these governments to promote relatively equal income distributions on the basis of far-reaching land reforms, which redistributed the land and created a rural sector of small, independent proprietary farmers, were crucial. 'The political and economic importance of these reforms for subsequent growth', concludes Sachs, 'cannot be overstated' (1987: 13). In this context it is salutary to note that in Japan in 1979 the income share of households was 38 per cent for the top 20 per cent whilst in South Africa in 1980 it was 61 per cent. At the other end of the spectrum, 9 per cent of all income in Japan went to the bottom 20 per cent, whereas in South Africa 8 per cent of total income was all that was available for the bottom 40 per cent (Sachs, 1987: 12 and Devereux, 1983: 37).

One important part of any policy of redistribution with growth is the pattern of expenditure by the state. In South Africa Charles Simkins has drawn attention to the fact that in the thirty years after the Second World War expenditure on social security, which had been well above that expected for a country with its per capita income, fell to well below the predicted value from international cross-section data.

Table 15.02: Social security as a proportion of GNP

Date	Per capita SA income in 1966 US dollars	Actual social security expenditure as a % of personal income	Predicted values from international cross-section
1949	362	7.2	3.9
1959	441	6.9	4.6
1969	602	5.1	6.4
1975	658	4.5	7.0

Source: 253: 30

Commenting on these figures, which show a perverse movement since 1949 in the proportion of GNP devoted to social security expenditure by comparison with a norm taken from a cross-sectional study, Simkins grants that they may in part be explained by changing coverage of welfare expenditure in a context of greatly changing entitlements, but that they 'must also be a testimony to a period of rigid political repression' (253: 30). Great damage was done to, for example, black education in the second half of the 1950s and most of the 1960s by Verwoerd's policy with regard to its financing. Are there, asks Simkins,

any indications from the post-1975/6 period to indicate that this percentage decline has been halted or reversed ? One is the rapid expansion of education; another is the rise in old age pensions. No clear indication in respect to agricultural subsidies and health are apparent. Housing policy, on the other hand, is steadily deteriorating under the influence of misguided principles, a circumstance we shall come to regret as surely as we now regret black education policy. (253: 30)

In a later paper, four members of the Carnegie working group on the public allocation of resources examined the consequences of a redistribution with growth policy focused on increasing social-investment expenditure on education, health, social welfare, and housing under different possible growth-rates for the economy over the period 1983–90. The difference in the possibilities are startling. They range from a pessimistic scenario with little movement towards justice and development in the context of declining per capita after-tax incomes. A median scenario suggests a more than 100 per cent increase in African per capita educational expenditures, plus 15 per cent improvements in health expenditure, and more than 50 per cent increase in social-welfare payments to Africans, with the state financing 40 per cent of the serviced housing sites required by the growing urban population. An even more optimistic scenario held out the possibility of a considerably rapid progress towards equal per capita spending by the state on South Africans of all races (PCS 6: 18). In the event, growth-rates have been even slower than the most pessimistic forecast whilst the demands of the state in other areas, notably defence, have escalated. At the end of 1988 the state, warned President Botha at a party congress, was more likely to reduce social-investment expenditure in the future rather than increase it (*Daily Dispatch*, 7.9.1988).

These forecasts of what was seen, even recently, as possible in the 1980s, combined with the apparent failure of the South African economy to meet even the most pessimistic of its targets, serve to underline both the importance of achieving growth and the need to shape state expenditure to the new realities. It is possible that unmeasured developments outside the formal sector of the economy, notably in self-built housing and informal trading, as people have surged to cities in the 1980s when restrictions on mobility were eased, mean that the actual growth of the economy has not been quite as low as the official figures suggest; nevertheless it has certainly not been sufficient. Fundamental to our argument is recognition of the fact that redistribution must be seen as a necessary component of growth rather than a consequence of it.

Job creation

There are some who would argue that the state should play no meaningful role in the provision of jobs. Let the market do the work, they say, otherwise the jobs that are created will not be self-sustaining and will simply increase the burden on the state, and ultimately on the tax-payer, until one day it becomes too heavy to bear and everything collapses. Certainly, there is a danger of the state creating a bloated bureaucracy of people whose jobs are essentially unproductive and whose salary cheques from the government amount to little more than a welfare payment. The argument contains an important truth that should serve as a warning, a salutary reminder, that there are dangers inherent in any state-employment policy. Nevertheless, we would argue that, under the conditions now pertaining in South Africa, with the level of unemployment already high and projected to rise still further, the state has a major role to play in the creation of employment.

This is not a new idea in South Africa. During the early decades of this century, it was widely accepted amongst the ruling class that the state had a responsibility to do what it could to create jobs for the unemployed poor – at least those of them who were white. As Abedian, Schneier and Standish have noted:

The government effort in the reduction of white poverty consisted of three elements: a legislative package in the labour market designed to favour whites at the expense of blacks; a sustained effort at increasing government services to whites, particularly education, health and housing, again partly at the expense of blacks; and finally the government introduced an ambitious public works programme. . . . [This] consisted of three general types of employment creation: employment increases in the railways at the expense of the railways, employment increases in central government at the expense of the fiscus, and employment increases in the railways and, to a limited extent, the private sector, financed by the fiscus. (PCS 10: 16, 18)

In 1932, a year which combined great drought with general economic depression, the number of whites employed in subsidised works increased by 99 per cent whilst those employed in unsubsidised relief schemes trebled. By 1933 a total of 59 000 poor whites were employed by various state relief measures. By 1939, well over half (59 per cent) of central government (white) employment of 98 000 consisted of relief work. The authors conclude that 'it was the introduction of a systematic and elaborate works creation programme which saw the rapid elimination of white poverty and not the extensive legislative assistance given to whites' (PCS 10: 22). In another paper, Abedian and Standish have outlined the sort of projects that the state initiated in order to relieve white unemployment. Irrigation schemes offering piece-work for the unskilled unemployed, and afforestation programmes providing jobs, houses, schools, medical services, and firewood for poor whites and their families, were successfully established. Anti-soil erosion works designed to alleviate rural poverty employed 5 000 men or more at the height of the Depression in the mid-1930s. Industrial jobs were created by the establishment of the parastatal iron and steel corporation, Iscor. The railways too provided work but not so much by the creation of new jobs as by the unedifying process of substituting white labourers for black (1985: 35–48).

It is also worth noting that the programme, highly effective as it seems to have been, was financed more by reallocation of funds within the public budget than by increasing the government's share in the economy as a whole, although during the war years – when virtually the last of the poor whites were absorbed (often as soldiers into the army) – government expenditure as a proportion of the gross domestic product leapt from approximately 15 per cent in the five years before 1939 to approximately 25 per cent during the next five years. In summary, write the researchers:

The poor white phenomenon was caused by a section of the white community being locked out of both the skilled and unskilled market. The introduction of government relief in a number of forms during the 1920s and 1930s plus a period of sustained economic growth, alleviated the poverty by the 1940s and eliminated it in the 1950s. In the short term, the most effective of these government measures was the introduction of an ambitious public works programme. Poor whites were drawn into this programme and physically rehabilitated while being taken into private sector employment or found positions in the public sector. At the same time, this programme generated valuable infrastructure in the form of railways, roads, irrigation schemes, afforestation and other more general public works.

Moreover, the programme 'had little effect on aggregate government expenditure, taxation or debt. The programme was largely funded through reallocation of government expenditure both in the revenue and the loan account.' (PCS 10: 27)

Public works programmes have been implemented in many different forms in various parts of the world (234: 3). One of the most interesting as a model that might be emulated in South Africa and other countries in the region is the

The seven basic rules of an Employment Guarantee Scheme are:

1. People who seek manual labour on public works, register for work at a suitable local office.

2. Government, operating through local government structures, guarantees to provide work within 30 days for a period of at least 40 days if 50 people register in one locality.

3. Labour is contracted to do the work on a piece-rate basis, which eases supervision, encourages group functioning and makes for greater efficiency. Wage rates are determined by piece-rate norms set by government, adjusted against a normative daily wage set below economic wages operative at the time in that locality: i.e. labour is not attracted away from on-going activities.

4. Labour is expected to complete 25 days of continuous work over five weeks, if training is also being provided.

5. When labour has to travel beyond a designated distance for that region to a work site, usually 6 to 8 kilometres, then the scheme must provide transport or a camp-site with latrine, potable water, a store selling necessities of food and fuel.

6. If the government fails to provide work within the 30-day limit, then it must provide applicants with unemployment relief [the dole] until, after another 30 days, they re-register again. And so on, until work is provided.

7. Government deducts 30% at the weekly wage payout. Ten per cent of this is deposited into a savings account in the name of the labourer and cannot be withdrawn for two years except as a loan issued by a Credit Union. The remaining 20% is held against completion of the work or of the 25 days contracted for, whichever occurs first. (Reynolds, 1981: 18–19; see also 234: 30; and personal communication, 1988)

employment guarantee scheme, developed over the past decade in the Indian state of Maharashtra. First proposed for southern Africa in 1981 by Norman Reynolds who had himself been involved in the establishment of the Maharashtra programme, an EGS is defined simply as 'a public works programme that responds to individual demands for work in the countryside within programme rules' (1981: 2). Later, during the course of the Carnegie Inquiry, Reynolds drove home the argument in favour of an employment guarantee scheme by looking first at their capacity to alleviate unemployment and poverty, and then at the relatively easy way of funding them.

The ability of public works programmes to absorb unemployment is significant, though each programme has to be judged in relation to the nature of unemployment in that country and to the resources committed to it. Earlier we referred to China. The Employment Guarantee Scheme started in Maharashtra State in India absorbed 75% of available man-days in the countryside in 1977; that is, three years after it was launched as a reformulation of the conventional relief programmes designed to mobilise rural labour in construction activities on a regular basis.

Maharashtra State finances the Employment Guarantee Scheme in two ways. Half is taken from the normal Capital Budget and half is raised from special taxes aimed at those most likely to benefit from less crowded cities, from thriving rural demand for manufactured goods and from a greater supply of agricultural surpluses. Items taxed include entertainment, professional registration, property and luxury goods. The total cost of the Scheme comes to 9% of the State's Capital Budget. The Scheme represents a socially and politically acceptable additional mobilisation of resources for investment. About one-third of the outlay is recouped in the form of loan repayments and betterment levies from identified beneficiaries of economic investment, such as irrigation and land levelling. A recent paper by the Indian Planning Commission calculates an all-India programme as costing 12%–13% of the combined Central and State Capital Budgets. (234: 7)

By estimating, very roughly of course, the distribution of families and of the income shortfall in urban areas, on white-owned farms and in the reserves, Reynolds and Simkins calculate (16: 17) that to bring families in the reserves (where most of the acute poverty is concentrated) up to the poverty datum line (as measured in 1980), an extra income of R185 million per month would be required. This shortfall, 'if provided through wages on a public works programme with wages at 60% of total cost, would require a programme expenditure of R3.7 billion in 1980. That equals 6% of GDP, or roughly 32% of the Gross Domestic Fixed Investment of public authorities and of public corporations in that year.' (234: 16).

This is not impossible but it puts a heavy strain on the public purse. Thus Reynolds suggests that in addition to providing piece-work, which enables different members of the extended family to earn some money and so increases the possibilities of mutual caring within a reinvigorated social system, other steps are needed which will help to stimulate jobs and income. One of the most cost-effective of these steps is, we believe, the unambiguous adoption of a policy which makes it easier for people to move from impoverished rural areas to the larger cities, where there is more scope for non-state job creation.

But, in terms of the employment guarantee scheme, what work should people do? The basic principle is that the work should be available within reasonable distance of the person's home, and that the beneficiaries of the project involved should also help pay for it. In other words, a project does not have to be a purely public work but can benefit specific households. But these households would then have to take out a loan to pay their share of the costs of this investment. Throughout many of the rural areas there are urgent needs, as we have seen, for clean drinking-water, for the protection of springs, for the building of dams (large and small), construction of rainwater reservoirs, irrigation pipes and ditches for vegetables, and of ventilated improved pit (VIP) toilets. Many areas need better roads, conservation works and woodlots. And bricks can be made for public use or for sale. Rural service centres containing a bank, a post-office, a clinic, a shop, and a market-place, all open at least once or twice a week, need to be built. All this is feasible, but it requires organisation. A wide range of structures is possible.

In Zimbabwe, for example, at least 600 rural service centres have been identified so far, with government commitment to invest in an initial 120. But these centres alone reach relatively few people unless they can be used as bases from which the periodic delivery of services to many different places is organised. The process of developing the most effective use of these centres, including the holding of periodic markets is being organised by a national Rural Market Society. In South Africa these centres could be created by the upgrading of facilities and services at existing business centres on certain days in a cycle to coincide with periodic market days, and should include such features as mobile banks, libraries, bakeries, etc. It is envisaged that these centres would not only provide essential services to the rural periphery, but would stimulate viable economic activities of small entrepreneurs, trades persons and other individuals through the provision of markets for their goods and services, thus stemming the tide of desperate migration to urban areas (65: 15).

In South Africa it might be wise to set up regional structures with links either to an expanded Public Works Department or perhaps to a newly created Rural Works Department, charged specifically with organising projects and contracting (by means of piece-rates) with workers in response to the needs of people for jobs.

In their proposals for public works programmes to combat poverty, Abedian, Schneier and Standish wisely draw attention to the immense political difficulties of the scheme. Whilst it is too much to hope that the present government has the capacity to set up so ambitious a scheme in such a way that it will be 'perceived by the community to be extending democratic rights across a broad frontier [and not as] further oppression' (PCS 10: 29), the proposal to establish some sort of independent PWP body, protected as far as possible from the vagaries of day-to-day party politics, has much to commend it, not least in a democratic society. For in such a society, whether socialist or capitalist, the state itself is responsive to the needs and wishes of people and does not become an oppressive power structure of tyranny and control. Much thought has thus to be given to the structuring of the new society so that even within the state itself there is a decentralisation of power. The existence of independent organisations – such as the British Broadcasting Corporation, universities in many parts of the world, or (at an international level) Unicef, accountable (in their own way) to the wider society – indicates what is possible. A Public Works Authority could be just such a body. If imaginatively led and well run, such a body could cut bureaucratic red-tape to a minimum, it could ensure proper grassroots participation, and maintain civilian control. Despite temptations to the contrary, it would be a grave mistake for such a programme to be run by the military or indeed as simply one more government department, hiring a lot of government employees.

Public investment

Closely linked with any strategy for job creation by means of public works programmes must be consideration of the need for investment in the basic infrastructure. Indeed we would argue that it is precisely by means of massive public investment that the state could simultaneously create large numbers of jobs, whilst undertaking investment that would both substantially improve the quality of life for all people, especially the poor, and also be the necessary engine to power further growth in the economy. We turn in this section to consider some of the infrastructural investment that is required.

Sewerage

Perhaps the most vivid illustration of the necessity for political power in any serious strategy by the poor against their own poverty is to be seen in the somewhat murky area of sewage disposal. As we have seen, there is evidence from all corners of the country about the chronic failure of local authorities to plan an appropriate infrastructure for the dense concentrations of working-class people not only in the towns, but also in the resettlement and peri-urban areas. There is no doubt that the basic infrastructure for sanitation is woefully inadequate in South Africa and also that such systems as have been installed are not properly maintained by the appropriate authorities. And this is primarily because the political structures which make authorities responsible to the broad wishes and needs of the people they have been created to serve simply do not exist. This point is further highlighted by the fact that urban sewage disposal works, which can be exceedingly smelly at certain times of the day, tend to be situated in places where they are far more likely to affect the poor and powerless rather than the rich and powerful in the society. In Cape Town, for example, the smell of sewage disposal afflicts blacks far more than whites, as the inhabitants of Langa and Athlone can testify all too pungently.

Democracy has many disadvantages but it is surely a less messy alternative for bureaucrats and politicians to be subject to the final authority of people at the grassroots than for it to be necessary for residents to start 'dumping buckets of excrement at local council offices', leading police to fire rubber bullets, birdshot, and teargas 'to disperse rampaging youths'. This happened in Duduza township on the east Rand early in 1985 after all attempts to get the authorities to do something about the intolerable sewerage conditions in the township had failed (*Cape Times*, 19.2.1985). Of course, the fact that a society has a democratic government does not necessarily guarantee that appropriate and necessary infrastructure will be laid down for those who most need it, as the appalling slums of many modern democracies testify all too bleakly. To achieve results, poor communities have to mobilise effectively as political pressure groups. Whilst such work can only be really effective in a democratic society, it is nevertheless sometimes possible, even in an authoritarian state such as South Africa, to find ways of organising to pressurise the state into making some move towards fulfilling its obligations. But, of course, it is exceedingly difficult as the massive clampdown since 1985 has made all too plain.

Water-borne sewerage is a minimum requirement in all urban areas and other densely settled areas such as Onverwacht in the Orange Free State or Sada in the Ciskei – which cannot be classified as urban in the sense of having a local economic base, or rural in the sense of being in an agricultural environment with adequate space for pit latrines. One of the most extraordinary sights in recent years has been the vision (which we have seen in many parts of the country) of hundreds of tin lavatories sprouting like mushrooms in an otherwise empty space that has been earmarked for dense resettlement. For the more rural areas, the simple but revolutionary new design, incorporated in the ventilated improved pit (VIP) latrines which are odourless and fly-free, has the potential for local communities to sort out the problem themselves. This has been well demonstrated in the Elim district of the northern Transvaal. We would go a step further and argue that such local initiatives against poverty could be strengthened by carefully structured state support which made them part of a public works programme, thus enabling those building the latrines also to earn some money for their work. For the rest, besides encouraging communities to seek ways and means of organising themselves politically at the local level into pressure groups, we can do no more than highlight three fundamental flaws in local government which the present sewerage mess shows up all too clearly.

First is the fact, already discussed, that people living in these communities have no political power; no say in national planning; no influence in central government decisions regarding the allocation of the budget; no power to create their own appropriate local government structures.

The second flaw is current government policy of trying to ensure that as far as possible each local area pays for its own amenities. Some politicians try to dress this policy in a flimsy tissue of suggestions that it is all part of decentralisation and of empowering local communities. It is nothing of the sort, and its naked selfishness should be seen for what it is. For, it is a fundamental principle of public finance that the money raised through taxation, by the central government, belongs equally to all those who live within that society. At a regional, say city, level that principle is maintained. Thus rates and taxes are levied for the common good, and it is generally accepted that wealthier areas, with higher rates, will help to pay for basic amenities in poorer areas of the same city. In particular the rates and taxes derived from the local economic enterprises in the central business district and elsewhere are part of the common wealth. Thus to carve off the poorer parts of the city (which have been demarcated by the Group Areas Act) and require them to pay for their own services, as is often the case, is simply an expression of calculated selfishness by the rich and powerful (in this case, whites), which is bitterly resented by the poor.

The third flaw arises from the anti-urbanisation policy of recent years. This has resulted not only in deliberate curbing by government of expenditure on housing and other urban infrastructure in an attempt to discourage people moving to the cities, but has also led, possibly as an unintended consequence, to the mushrooming of vast, dense settlements in places such as Winterveld north of Pretoria, or Inanda near Durban, or in remoter areas such as Qwa Qwa, where there simply is no local government structure adequate to undertake all the immediate administrative tasks, let alone the long-term planning, required in areas where population is the size of a small city. Where in Onverwacht, for example, is the equivalent of the Rand Water Board or the

City Engineer's Department of Cape Town, ensuring not only the adequate provision of services now but also wrestling with the implications of the projected population growth rates in their respective areas?

The whole problem of sewage disposal; the need for proper planning and for the allocation of adequate funds by the state; and, underlying all this, the necessity for the poor to obtain effective political power to ensure that such things are not overlooked or skimped – all of this serves as a case study illustrating the basic requirements of a wide range of infrastructure, which is an urgent priority from the point of those enduring poverty in South Africa.

What is true of sewage disposal is true also as regards the provision of clean drinking-water and of basic energy requirements, to say nothing of housing and other general amenities, both in urban and in rural areas. Political power down at the grassroots, proper planning, and the allocation of state funds are three basic requirements to ensure an adequate infrastructure.

Water

We have already seen how acute the problem of clean drinking-water is in many different parts of the country, whether in the Mhala district of the eastern Transvaal with one tap for every 760 persons, or in northern Natal–KwaZulu with disabled people having to walk an hour to fetch water, or in the Ciskei with the average person in the Chalumna district consuming only 9 litres per day, less than one-fifth the minimum recommended by the World Health Organisation for basic cooking, washing, and drinking. Indeed, with each passing drought the country gets closer to that awful edge beyond which there simply is no water for people to drink at all, so they must move (if they can) or die. At the time of the last major drought in the mid-1980s some communities had already gone over that edge, and were saved only by the army bringing in huge tankers of water every day. This happened both in rural areas, as in parts of the Ciskei, and in some of the informal urban settlements, for example in KwaZulu around Durban. The irony of the situation was compounded by the fact that in some places the supply of water actually improved during the drought.

Some indication that the extent of the water crisis has penetrated to the higher councils of state may be seen in the new dams being built, for example on the Keiskamma and Tyhume rivers. But the provision lags far behind the need, and there is no indication of anything like a comprehensive long-term plan for water outside the major metropolitan areas and the towns whose white voters have enough power to ensure that adequate provision is made. But for those areas which have grown more as a result of enforced removals, or because of the anti-urbanisation policies which prevented people from settling nearer to town and where there is little economic rationale for their existence, the inadequacy of water supplies is acute.

The problem of water in South Africa is, in fact, a crisis with two clear but interacting components. First, there is the absence of adequate infrastructure to ensure ready access to clean drinking-water for all. But there is a second, no less important, but more hidden dimension which arises from a combination of drought with the ecological devastation wrought by generations of bad farming and overgrazing (both in the white-owned farming areas and in the communally held reserves) and by the cutting down of trees and other forms of vegetation in order to provide fuel. The impact of drought, when hundreds of thousands of beasts die, is a sharp (but unheeded) reminder of the fragility of the balance between people, animals, and the natural environment.

The history of the country is littered with the reports of carefully conducted commissions of inquiry into drought, with recommendations for appropriate action and, indeed, with actual legislation to promote conservation. Almost all of it to no avail. Ecological devastation continues apace. And with it grows the need for action. Perhaps nowhere is the need for a restructuring of the South African political economy more apparent than in this ongoing massive haemorrhaging of its ecological life-blood. Soil conservation, afforestation, and protection of springs and catchment areas, all require systematic and sustained action. A fundamental component of any programme of reconstruction in South Africa must be to stop the bleeding, to rebuild the soil, and to renew those resources of ground cover and trees, without which springs will run dry and the encroaching desert will engulf us all (see Bruntland report, 1987).

Of course, even in the field of water affairs not everything requires central or local government action. In many situations there is scope for non-governmental initiative. This is particularly true in rural areas, where experience in the Transkei and elsewhere has shown the considerable potential for well-organised but simple initiatives making a great difference to the quantity and quality of water readily available for household and even for the vegetable-growing needs of poor households. But this takes us into the whole field of integrated rural development. In the South African context such development is best located within the paradigm of non-governmental action, well removed from the paralysing contradictions inherent in 'development' undertaken by government departments functioning as executive arms of the policy of 'independent black national states' (which are themselves trapped in the under-developing periphery of the South African political economy). We are not arguing that the state, even in its present undemocratic and apartheid-obsessed form, should not be reminded of its responsibilities or pressurised where possible into providing more infrastructure. The state, whether it is democratic or not, has the obligation to ensure that all those who live within it have clean drinking-water, and it needs constantly to be reminded of its responsibilities. But what we are suggesting is that the real scope for action at this stage in our history lies in the realm of non-governmental initiative. There is much that could be done, not only to improve the water position but also to strengthen the capacity and cohesiveness of impoverished rural communities (PCS 12).

Energy

After water, indeed sometimes even before water, the need expressed most keenly by poor rural families (see PCS 12: 12) is for firewood or some form of energy that is readily available, affordable, and does not involve hours of back-breaking work. The growing shortage of firewood in South Africa has been documented, as has the fact that in the country which produces 60 per cent of the electricity generated in Africa and which has excess capacity in the form of power stations not being used, over two-thirds of the total population do not have access to electricity and use wood (and also paraffin, coal, and gas) to meet their basic energy requirements (PCS 13: 3).

What then is to be done? The strategies proposed here draw heavily on suggestions made by Anton Eberhard of the Energy Research Institute, who with Mark Gandar made the major contributions in this area of the Carnegie Inquiry (see conference papers 154, 155 and 156, together with PCS 13: 8 ff). 'There are', writes Eberhard,

a number of reasons why electrification of urban and peri-urban is the preferred energy supply option for domestic needs:

1. Once the initial extension fee has been paid, electricity is in most cases cheaper than other fuels for cooking, heating and lighting. In a survey by Rivett-Carnac in July 1979 in Umlazi it was determined that households without electricity spent on average R42 a month on fuel, while typical middle-income households with electricity spent on average R18 a month, using energy in a safer and more convenient form. A survey . . . in September 1983 in suburbs around Cape Town revealed that families without electricity could pay up to three times as much on domestic energy than those families which had access to electricity (Eberhard, 1984b). This data clearly dispels the popular myth that most black households cannot afford electricity: the truth is that they can no longer afford not to have electricity.

2. Electrification can substitute for coal and wood usage in urban areas and thus has the potential to substantially reduce the severe air pollution in areas such as the Witwatersrand. More than half-a-million tonnes of coal are used in Soweto each year. South African coal has a high ash content and it is estimated that approximately 10 000 tonnes of ash is released per annum into the atmosphere over Soweto.

3. Electricity may also allow the performance of entirely new tasks, e.g. the use of television, or washing machines. It is difficult to compare the costs of electricity with those of other sources for households, because in many cases the energy service supplied by electricity is of so much higher quality (lighting), convenient (ironing), or unavailable with other energy sources (TV), that the service is essentially a new and different one.

The benefits of grid electrification are not automatic, however, and many electrification schemes in Third World countries have revealed a number of unforeseen problems. Thought should be given as to how the financing of electrification could be structured so as not to unfairly burden the initial consumers. One strategy, in new housing projects, is to build in the cost of reticulation into the lease or purchase cost of the house, so spreading the capital cost of electrification over the longer period of repayment of the mortgage by the householder. Innovative financing schemes could also be developed to ease the initial costs of purchasing a range of electrical appliances. For electrification to be successful, it should be coupled with an integrated package of energy conservation measures, including better house insulation, solar water heating, and awareness programmes of ways to use electricity efficiently in the home.

Unfortunately, it seems that the provision of services such as electricity is still regarded as being of secondary importance in the planning of townships and the upgrading of peri-urban and informal settlements. The massive housing project at Khayelitsha in the Cape is another example of where the electrification of houses has been ignored. There is no doubt that by denying electricity to these areas, communities are further impoverished, by having to meet the higher costs of fuels such as coal, gas, paraffin, candles, and batteries, and quality-of-life expectations are frustrated by being denied the opportunities and benefits of electrification. In addition the pollution caused both within houses and in the wider environment by hundreds of thousands of coal fires and paraffin stoves (often using impure fuel) is a major health hazard. This situation can only exacerbate an already deteriorating social and political climate in these areas.

If all housing in and around the metropolitan areas and towns was to be electrified, an additional 5.5 million people would require less than 8 000 million kWh per annum, or 7% of the total electricity sent out by Escom in 1984. This would require little more than one-third of the capacity of one of the new 3 600MW power stations currently being constructed. (PCS 13: 9–10)

Important though it is, grid electrification is not always the most appropriate option. It is highly capital-intensive, and in less densely populated rural areas the average cost of getting electricity to individual households may be considerably higher than other alternatives available. Such decentralised alternatives as diesel-operated generators or photovoltaics, which use the sun to generate sufficient electric energy to run lighting, television, and radio-hifi sets, do not really require government intervention. However, where the market is patently failing to operate there is certainly scope for action by disinterested bodies to mobilise the funds, the knowledge, and the demonstration models so as to enable poorer households to benefit from the technology that is available. Moreover, a sensitive state could play a role (not least by funding research) in development of these smaller-scale options.

Photovoltaics may be an intermediate solution to electricity demand in underdeveloped areas, but they also have the potential for being a long-term solution to fully meeting household electricity demand. Photovoltaics remain the most elegant and innovative of all the electricity-producing technologies; no working parts, and no high-temperature working fluids mean that the potential for low-cost and relatively maintenance-free electricity production is possible. The constraint, however, as with all solar energy technologies, is the extremely low density of the solar resource, and thus collection areas have to be large, with resultant high equipment costs. (PCS 13: 11)

There have been, and continue to be, rapid developments in photovoltaic technology which aim at minimising material requirements and increasing efficiencies in order to reduce costs. Despite the potential for solar energy in South Africa, virtually no research (and even less funds) have been devoted to this area until very recently. Meanwhile there is considerable scope for universities and other independent bodies to set up structures which will encourage research and application of pilot projects that could serve both as testing laboratories and as models of appropriate energy supply in some future national policy.

328

Afforestation

Other strategies for rural areas must, of course, include programmes to augment the supplies of firewood. Janine Aron has calculated (PCS, forthcoming) that in the reserves the total annual supply of biomass that could possibly be used for fuel in 1990 will be only half (53 per cent) of the total energy requirement for cooking and minimal heating. For the country as a whole, it is estimated that the total fuel-wood requirement (assuming city needs are increasingly met by other forms of fuel such as electricity) is 5.3 million tonnes, more than ten times the current production of less than half-a-million (0.43) tonnes. To provide enough wood would require some 730 000 hectares, which is 28 times more than the total area under woodlots within the reserves (PCS 13: 15). In fact, there is estimated to be only some 180 000 ha available that would be suitable for growing fuel-wood in the reserves, whilst in the rest of the country it is expected that the growing timber shortage will drive up the return on commercial plantations to a level where the growing of fuel-wood will be commercially uncompetitive. Nevertheless, concludes Eberhard,

If the task facing South Africa appears to be daunting, then it is instructive to see what has been achieved elsewhere.

A number of approaches to afforestation could be adopted. State or public wood-lots, which has been the common approach in southern Africa, could be established in those areas in which the community wished the State to assume this responsibility, and large, 'efficiently managed' woodlots would ensure rapid afforestation. At the same time a large number of community woodlots could be initiated in those areas where democratically organised communities were determined to exercise control over new woodlots. The potential of voluntary and non-governmental organisations in this context is something which should not be ignored. Often they can provide a much-needed bridge between local communities and authorities promoting tree-growing programmes. This is particularly the case when it comes to ensuring that the interests of women, and the poor and landless are taken into account.

And then in order to ensure the widest possible spread of tree-planting activity, a number of nursery and demonstration sites could promote the concept of agro-forestry. Village surveys . . . have indicated factors other than fuelwood supply are considered important in the planting of trees; viz shelter, fruit, and building-material supply. It would thus seem to make sense to promote the planting of trees which have multiple uses and benefits. In this regard *Leucaena leucocephala*, the 'wonder tree' from Central America, looks very attractive. It has been planted successfully in trial plots by the ARDRI Forest Farming project at Fort Hare in the Ciskei. For agro-forestry, *Leucaena* is best planted in hedges or rows along roadsides or in fields with intermediate areas cropped for maize, grains, root crops, etc., but it can also be planted in dense stands for pole production and direct grazing, or in mixed woodlots with gum trees. (PCS 13: 16–17)

One idea, practised in the Indian state of Gujerat, might be well worth emulating in this respect. Co-operation between the departments of Forestry and of Roads could lead to substantial tracts of land (the strips that lie on either side from the edge of the road to the barbed-wire fences that keep animals from wandering across) being made available across the length and

Experiment in Korea

The Republic of Korea provides an example of a nationwide tree-growing programme which achieved dramatic results. In 1962, the promotion of reforestation, on a communal basis, was adopted as a major national priority because of the acute wood scarcities and serious environmental consequences. After substantial progress over the next decade, a ten-year National Forest Plan was launched in 1973 with a series of ambitious targets, including the planting of one million hectare of trees. Intensive efforts were made to mobilise village-level support and collaboration. By 1977, the basic targets of the Plan had been reached, five years ahead of schedule. (Foley and Barnard, 1984, cited in PCS 13: 16)

breadth of the country, on which trees could be planted in experimental plots, in woodlots, as a real beginning to a national re-afforestation programme.

Throughout the discussion on water and energy has loomed the question of the environment, of the need to maintain ecological balance, of the urgent necessity of re-establishing the country's renewable resources. In order to hold the country's topsoil on which food is grown, to keep the rain soaking into the underground water reserves rather than rushing headlong for the sea taking the topsoil with it, and to replenish and increase the wood available for fuel, it is clear that one massive task of reconstruction is a coherent programme of conservation. Much good work has been done by individuals and organisations (including some government bodies) but without the political will and without sufficient financial backing from the state, it remains pitifully inadequate. The content and priorities of such a programme still need to be discussed – another major think-tank job requiring attention – but, even at this stage, we would argue that a substantial component of such a programme would have to be a national re-afforestation drive. For trees bind and enrich the soil, making it genuinely 'indestructible'; they attract the rain and hold the water that falls; they remain (and will do so for a long time to come) the major source of fuel for the poor; and, if carefully chosen and tended, they can be harvested for a wide range of products, ranging from food to necessary ingredients in aeroplane glue. The potential for tree-farming, as it has developed in India for example in recent years, has not been fully explored in South Africa (Douglas and Hart, 1976).

As with water and indeed sewerage, particularly in the rural areas, there is much that can be done by non-governmental organisations. But this should not be allowed to obscure the fact that the state itself bears a huge responsibility to redress the balance of public investment that has shaped the basic infrastructure of the past century, in response primarily to the needs of a minority who have held virtually all political and economic power. The provision of this infrastructure will be an urgent priority for the first democratic government. But this responsibility, as we have argued, also provides a major opportunity for employment creation. So too does the shortage of housing.

Housing

In addition to water and sanitation, energy, an improved rural transport network, soil conservation and a carefully thought-through reform of land tenure, there is one other component of infrastructure which must be basic to any serious long-term plan by society to deal properly with poverty. This is housing. There is, as has been argued elsewhere in this report, far more to housing than family shelter. Housing must include ready access to work, to schools, to recreation centres, to shops and service centres such as post-offices, banks, and clinics. Housing or habitat is an overall environment where human beings can live rich lives without fear of murder, rape, armed robbery, or frequent hit-and-run accidents which decimate children who have nowhere else to play but busy streets.

The housing situation in South Africa, whether one is looking simply at units of shelter or whether one is considering the living environment as a whole, is so bad that it is difficult to convey with mere statistical analysis or verbal description. For whites, the situation is generally very good although there are some, notably pensioners and some unemployed persons in the larger cities, for whom the living environment can only be described as stark, lonely, and impoverished. But for the majority of whites, both the shelter available and the environment surrounding it are of a high standard. Indeed the Group Areas Act, which legally forbids all black South Africans from buying or renting property in 'white' areas (although it does occur here and there), has ensured that there is a surplus of no less than 37 000 family units of shelter available in a country where, for the majority of the people, the situation is one of chronic and unrelieved shortage. The figures do not mean much but, for what they are worth, the estimates of housing shortage during the first half of the 1980s range from 300 000 to nearly 700 000 units (PCS 14: 6). In general terms it would be true to say that the existing stock of housing now available for blacks has to be doubled simply to cope with the present shortage.

Table 15.01: Housing in South Africa, 1980s

Racial category	Surplus/shortage	Number houses built 1983–5
White	+ 37 000	172 000
Coloured	− 52 000	62 000
Asian	− 44 000	37 000
African	−583 000	41 000

Source: De Vos, Report of the National Building Research Institute, cited by Kentridge (PCS 14: 6)

Estimates of the number of houses that need to be built over the twenty years 1980–2000 in order to accommodate people who will be moving to the cities, range from 3 to 4 million. 'Taking the backlog of the year 2000 as 4 million units, approximately 600 units would have to be built each working day for the next 20 years. At present the building rate is below 20 units per working day.' (PCS 14: 7) These estimates do not make allowance for the massive rehousing that is needed to do away with the degrading single-sex hostel and compound system, which still accommodates over 95 per cent of half-a-million black miners as well as tens of thousands of the workers in manufacturing industry, the railways, and elsewhere. There are a number of points to note as we start to think about what sort of strategy could or should be developed to deal with the problem.

First is the obvious point, but one necessary to drive home, that the problem is not a new one. It has existed at least since the early days of industrialisation in the country. But whereas the problem which affected those with political power was systematically attacked and solved, the problem as it affects those without political power has got worse, and is projected to deteriorate even further. The problem will really only be properly tackled when those who need the houses wield sufficient political power to affect decisions concerning allocation of resources by the state.

Which brings us to the second point. However much it may have to contribute, and we believe it has a major contribution to make, South Africa's housing crisis cannot be solved by the private sector or indeed by some bootstrap self-help operation. The infrastructure that has to be built, the funds that are required, are too vast for the whole problem simply to be privatised. Moreover, and this is the crucial point, even for those who have full-time jobs the wage level at the bottom of the economic pyramid is such that a large proportion of the working poor simply cannot afford the economic rent on an urban plot serviced with roads, water, refuse removal, water-borne sewerage, to say nothing of electricity.

According to the Urban Foundation, basic costs of housing in 1984 were R7 500 for a fully serviced site, R13 000 for a core house built by the owners themselves ('sweat equity'), and R16 000 for a core house built by contractors. By 1990, conclude members of a Carnegie working group,

the population of South Africa will be growing by about 800 000 per annum. Most of the increase (say 80 per cent) should be taking place in the urban areas because of natural increase and immigration. About 60 per cent of the increase will not be rich enough to be provided for on the market. Sites will need to be provided for at 384 000 persons per annum; at 6 persons per site. This represents 64 000 sites per year at a cost, in 1975 prices, of R153.6 million. (PCS 6: 14)

Glover and Watson have shown that in 1984:

A house costing R15 000 to construct, either sold or rented at market rates of interest, would require a monthly capital and interest repayment of R184. With an additional (estimated) R30 for rates or service charges, total monthly payments would equal R214. This, in effect, would require a tenant or owner to earn at least R856: less than 3 per cent of Coloured household heads in Cape Town fall into this income category. (161: 28)

In line with the Reagan–Thatcher monetarist conservatism that has dominated official thinking in many Western governments during the 1980s in seeking to reduce state expenditure on public services and welfare programmes (excluding, of course, defence) 'so that the market can play its proper role', the South African government decided to restrict the availability of subsidies for completed houses to the very poor earning less than R150 per month. Those earning more than R150 could no longer get subsidies to buy houses, although they were still eligible for help with loans to buy serviced sites and building materials in self-help schemes. But the economics was such that, according to Glover and Watson's calculations, a serviced site, whose average development cost in Cape Town was R4 000 (the figures are for 1983/4), required a monthly repayment of R54.59, excluding rates. This in turn implied a monthly income of R218. But more than half (57 per cent) the coloured population earned under this level so that unless there was more than one wage-earner in a household, more than half the coloured population could not even afford the site on which to build a house. For Africans, whose average income is well below that of the coloured population the situation was even worse.

Changes in housing policy in 1987–8 seem to be aimed at directing more resources at the very poor at the expense of those households earning more than R350 per month. Overall, housing assistance by the state to poor households living in the cities remains inadequate (see Glover and Watson, forthcoming).

As far as the private sector is concerned, the situation has been summed up as follows:

The formation of the Urban Foundation, the granting of 99-year leasehold rights for blacks in 1978, the granting of 99-year leasehold rights to private developers and employers, and the decision to make freehold available to blacks in 1986 have made this option possible. The Urban Foundation, through its self-help schemes and utility companies, as well as its constant appeals to the private sector for greater participation, has played a pivotal role in the privatisation of housing. Between 1977 and 1984, the Urban Foundation launched 82 housing projects, spent over R19 million, and mobilised R170 million in loan capital. Among its most important projects were three formal self-help schemes started at Khutsong near Carletonville in the Transvaal; Katlehong on the East Rand (in conjunction with the United Building Society); and Inanda Newtown in Natal. These schemes were not controlled by the relevant local authorities, but the terms laid down by the Urban Foundation closely matched the government guidelines discussed above. (Urban Foundation, *Ikhaya Lethu Self-Help Housing Project*)

In addition, Foundation utility companies have embarked on projects around the country, the most important of which is the development of 2 500 houses and 800 flats at Protea North in Soweto. (See Steyn, 1985: 40)

Hendler (1986) investigated the extent of private-sector involvement in the provision of black housing and found that all sectors of capital had a stake in the privatisation of housing, although obviously to different degrees. Multinational companies such as Siemens and General Electric were involved in the electrification of Soweto; large national construction companies had large housing developments for upper-income blacks under way; smaller companies undertook smaller projects; small black entrepreneurs emerged in the construction and building-supplies industries; and finally, artisans such as builders, bricklayers and carpenters plied their trade vigorously (Hendler, 1986a: 108).

However, the houses built by the private sector are extremely expensive. Prices of houses built by private housing developers start at R25 000 and then climb steeply (PCS 14: 13–14). And there is also a danger of unscrupulous speculators building shoddy houses and selling them for far more than their cost to people desperate for accommodation (*Cape Times*, 2.4.1987).

Thus although the number of houses built in black areas by the private sector is 'vastly greater than in the past', their cost is such as to put them beyond the range of all but a small proportion of African professionals. For the vast majority, the working class, without support from the state, decent albeit simple housing is impossible. The alternatives are either rudimentary shacks without adequate basic services necessary in an urban area, or intolerable overcrowding to ensure that there are enough bread-winners in the house to pay the rent.

This truth has, in fact, long been recognised in South Africa. Two generations ago, when many whites were still very poor and yet had considerable political power, a government housing commission reported (in 1920) that the poor white had to be treated differently 'as he could not pay an economic rent and it is the duty of the State or the local authority to provide for them with homes at a subsidised rent' (cited in 157: 23). Contrasting this policy with that for Africans, Elias concludes: 'the Housing Act of 1920 was not designed to build homes for those who needed them most. It provided, on the contrary, an excellent vehicle for providing urban accommodation both for the poor white population emigrating to the urban areas and the relief of the housing shortage for whites during the period 1920–1935.' (157: 25). But the policy did make quite clear the responsibility of the state for helping those, albeit only the white minority, who could not afford housing through the market. This principle was subsequently accepted during the 1940s and early 1950s when a crash housing programme, much of it masterminded ironically by Dr H. F. Verwoerd in the years before he had fully evolved a method of implementing the anti-black urbanisation policy, used state funds at heavily subsidised rates of interest to build Soweto and greatly expand other black townships around South Africa.

It is this principle that has been under attack during the 1980s as the state has evolved its new policy of privatisation; but even now a fragment of the old policy remains. It is accepted by the state that urban households with incomes of less than R150 per month will require subsidies for their housing. And those earning between R150 and R750 per month will be eligible for subsidised sites-with-services (that is water, sewerage, and roads) on which they may build their own houses.

The point at issue is not the principle of subsidisation. The argument hinges on the question: how poor should people be before the state should be obliged to provide some help with housing? The answer depends, in practice, largely on how poor those answering the question themselves are. It is not surprising that in a society where a significant proportion of voters are very poor, the state will see the virtues of exercising its responsibility to help provide for the needs of those poor, whilst that same society, at a different time, when the political power of those who are poor has been neutralised in some way, will take a far less generous (but carefully rationalised) view as to its proper function. This has certainly been true in South Africa.

The powerlessness of the poor not only affects the extent to which the state will act to help provide houses but also influences the type of housing that is built. Thus in South Africa most of the housing built for blacks over the past generation has not been of a sort that people would have built for themselves. Housing – whether in the form of huge single-sex hostels for migrant workers, or even the family homes set down like rows and rows of match-boxes in soulless environments miles from work – has been conceived, designed, and built with no consultation whatsoever with those who actually have to live in them.

The arguments in favour of privatisation of housing (and of medicine) have to be seen for what they are: attempts by the privileged to forestall claims by the poor on the common wealth of the society – claims which the privileged themselves, when they were poor, found to be entirely justified. This is not to say there is no merit in those arguments which query the efficiency of state spending or which suggest that the market may be a more appropriate (and efficient) means of allocating some resources than bureaucratic infighting. Part of the whole debate about socialism revolves around the role of the state and the proper place for markets. 'For decades', says a co-editor of the Italian Communist Party's daily newspaper, 'the left pushed for more growth, more public spending, an extended welfare state. Now we have to acknowledge that all these things have created huge problems.' (*Newsweek*, 26.1.1987) In China the unshackling of agriculture from central state control is reported to have doubled rural living standards. Clearly, there is room for discussion amongst those seeking to promote economic justice as to how best this can be done, but it is important to recognise in addition the different historical circumstances of different countries. In South Africa, we are faced with a peculiar combination of a large state sector, which includes centralised control of the distribution of land (along racial lines) and of the movement of (black) labour. This sector has not been developed (as in a Marxist or in a socialist welfare state) with the goal of providing for the needs of the poor. Instead the intervention of the state is directed specifically at ensuring the economic (and political) security of that minority of the population which is white.

These two factors, a critical re-examination of the role of the state by socialists in Europe and elsewhere, and the particular reason behind the expansion of the state in the South African political economy, mean that progressives have to do some especially rigorous thinking in order to sort out what type of housing policies would best serve the interests of the poor in South Africa. Or, to put the matter another way, we know that the inadequacy of housing for the poor, notably in urban areas, is a world-wide problem. The process of transformation towards a democratic society with which South

Africans are now starting all too tentatively to grapple, provides us with an opportunity to consider new ideas from other countries about resolving the problem.

In analysing the issues we find ourselves singularly unimpressed with the arguments of those who would privatise housing policy. Certainly, there is room for a vastly increased role for the private sector; certainly there is considerable scope for creative intervention by big business to help people build (and then expand and improve) their own homes. There is not only an opportunity for the private sector to make a substantial contribution in this area but also, we believe, an obligation for it to do so. This is particularly true in those instances where (as on the gold mines of the Transvaal and the Orange Free State or in the building industry in Cape Town) employers have long benefited from the low costs of housing their workers in hostels. The cumulative deprivation which has resulted from this has to be redressed by a vigorous programme of positive discrimination in favour of those who have been so deprived. There has to be a true restitution process, a form of reparations. The market, by itself, simply cannot meet the need, except for a small proportion of those at the top end of the market. There has to be active intervention by the state to stimulate and support a massive increase of the housing infrastructure.

Precisely what forms such state support should take requires further debate, but a crash programme must surely include both a reformulation and an expansion of a policy whose tentative beginnings have already been made – namely, the preparation and leasing (or selling), at subsidised prices, of sites on which people can erect (or commission) their own houses using materials obtained with heavily subsidised (soft) loans, as well as a rapid programme of building, for purchase or for hire, of state-subsidised houses. Houses that people currently rent, given their value, should be declared by the local authorities to be paid up and ownership should be vested in the occupants.

How then does one formulate a long-term policy for housing in South Africa? Applying his mind to this question and drawing heavily on the divergent views presented and debated at the Carnegie conference, Matthew Kentridge suggests that one should start with the following principles:

There must be sufficient, decent housing for the whole population; the dwelling units themselves must form just one part of an enabling physical environment – the development of the environment must carry as much weight as the construction of the houses themselves; the directing ideology must be one of self-fulfilment, democracy, and creativity; the political function must be one of furthering individual freedom and the development of democratic modes of political action; and finally, housing must be a vehicle of economic redistribution. Through housing, the grotesque economic inequalities which currently characterise the economy can be partially smoothed. (PCS 14: 53)

But how, in the face of scarce resources and competing claims, is a policy which sees housing as a basic right rather than as something available only to those able to pay for accommodation, to be implemented in practice? Firstly, the legitimacy and necessity of state involvement have to be accepted.

Secondly, by contrast, the dangers of such state participation becoming bureaucratically hide-bound or, worse, a means of control have to be zealously guarded against. In this connection, it is worth noting that the Mugabe government specifically refrained from becoming involved in the direct provision of housing after Zimbabwe's independence on the grounds that such involvement would smack too much of the authoritarian practices of the earlier minority governments. The Mugabe government provides loans but does not build houses (Ramphele, 1986: 19).

We do not believe that so massive a crisis as the housing debacle now facing South Africa, which requires an immediate doubling of the entire black-occupied housing stock simply to cope with the current backlog, can be adequately resolved without state intervention. At the same time, the precise form of that intervention, the appropriate structures by which it is mediated, the best way of ensuring real democratic participation and a flexible approach to specific local situations, all require further thought and debate. But one thing is clear: housing, as a basic right for all, will (as it should) have a very high priority next only to the ensuring of jobs, food, water, and energy for all in any democratic reconstruction of South Africa. It will require a massive infusion of funds from the state, not only to ensure that everybody, including the poor, are able to live in conditions that are fit for human habitation, but also as an effective, and feasible, method of starting to redress the vast inequalities, between rich and poor, spawned during this ugly phase of South African history of 'racial capitalism'.

Because of the extent to which 'basic needs' complement each other, such a commitment by the state to housing in the widest, environmental sense of the term would be dovetailed with water and energy and also, of course, with steps towards comprehensive preventive health care. Moreover, if carefully designed, such a housing programme could make a huge contribution to the provision of perhaps the most basic need of all: the provision of jobs.

Health

What we can do here, in the light of the facts and the analysis outlined earlier, is to draw attention to some of the main requirements of any state engaged in the democratic reconstruction of a society's health, education and welfare.

We start with health. There are essentially three aspects with which the state must be concerned. Firstly, there is the allocation of resources. The matter is not simply one of more resources being allocated at present to the health care of the average white than to that of the average black in the country. There are other overlapping and reinforcing differentials such as that between the urban and the rural areas, or between curative and preventive medicine. Also in need of examination is the allocation, at national level, between health and other departments (such as defence), and the allocation as well to departments whose work should be complementary to that of health, such as housing.

Consider, for example, the urban–rural situation. One of the most striking examples of misallocation of resources is the amount of money that has been poured in recent years into massive prestige hospitals in places like Johannesburg and Cape Town. For it was widely agreed that there were already enough big hospitals in those areas and that the real need was for a large number of smaller hospitals or clinics not only on the periphery of the cities but, more especially, in the rural areas. In a country where health workers in one area did not have funds or personnel to treat more than 15 per cent of the young children diagnosed as having chronic tuberculosis, the expenditure of R200 million or more to replace, rather than upgrade, an older building next door with the net addition of few extra beds, as happened in Cape Town at this time, can only be described as culpable.

There is, of course, more to the urban–rural differential than the allocation of state funds. Health workers too, notably doctors, choose (like most academics) to live in the urban areas. But where the state invests huge sums in training each doctor, it would surely not be unreasonable for society to require some repayment, such as a three- or five-year spell after medical school, in some rural area.

The second aspect of health with which the state must be concerned relates to the training of health workers. Medical education is essentially the responsibility of the state, which provides the bulk of the funds for the university medical schools and for the nurses' training colleges. Authority for course content and the nature of the training given rest very properly with the academics employed in those institutions, whilst there is some input as well from the professional bodies such as the Nursing Council. We are not advocating any central state interference with this arrangement, but at the same time it is clear that in any process of transformation, not least within the field of health, the type of medical training being provided will have to be thoroughly re-assessed. Maintenance of international standards is vital; the capacity to exchange, on an equal basis, with colleagues around the world is essential. But these requirements do not imply that medical education in South Africa should produce doctors who are especially well suited to work in, say, Houston, Texas, or some other part of the world, where socio-economic conditions and the pattern of disease are very different from South Africa as a whole. In medicine, as in many other fields, excellence does not necessarily imply practices identical to what is optimal in capital-intensive, wealthy North America. Medical education must excel in its relevance to the needs of the majority of South Africans.

The third area of concern to the state incorporates in a sense the first two. This is the need for a national health service. Again, the idea is not a new one. It was first put forward convincingly in an official government commission, led by Dr Henry Gluckman, whose report, issued in 1944, still stands as a basic document to be read by all those concerned with planning health care for the future in South Africa.

If health care in South Africa is to be judged in terms of heart-transplants or dialysis, then it probably ranks amongst the top five or six in the world. But, if it is to be judged in terms of the health of its children or the incidence of tuberculosis, then it plummets. Indeed, in the Unicef list of 130 countries ranked in terms of the mortality rate of children under 5, South Africa has a higher rate than 60 other countries. Hong Kong and Cuba with mortality rates for under-fives of 11 and 19 respectively certainly make South Africa, with its rate of 104, look backward in terms of health care (Unicef, 1987). Comparable figures for tuberculosis do not exist but South Africa's position there is almost certainly considerably worse.

It is well to start a discussion on a national health service by stressing the word *national*. We do this to distinguish it clearly from the bureaucratic nightmare currently convulsing the body of the medical profession as part of the apartheid dream. In terms of this thinking, forcefully expounded on many occasions by successive National Party leaders, South Africa is a country of many nations, a country of minorities; a multi-national region. In pursuit of the multi-national goal, independent and not so independent black national states have been set up. And each of them has its own national department of health. There were in South Africa, at the last count, 14 Ministers of Health each with responsibility and a budget for people widely scattered through the country. This is not a federal arrangement with rational, clearly defined regional boundaries; this is an arrangement almost tailor-made to encourage the growth of a bureaucratic jungle whilst minimising its efficiency. We have already seen how the creation of separate 'national' health authorities for Gazankulu and Lebowa in the northern and eastern Transvaal not only created conflict over access to scarce resources previously regarded as being available to all those living in a particular area, but also led to ridiculous situations where immunisation campaigns against poliomyelitis in one area near a particular hospital had to be undertaken by another hospital which was miles away, simply because of the new lines drawn across maps in Pretoria. The first task of a national health service will be to re-design a rational administrative structure and to prune heavily the bureaucratic jungle that has expanded so rapidly in the steamy climate of apartheid.

We do not intend in this report to present a blueprint for a national health service but in the light of the papers delivered at the Carnegie conference, and of the subsequent debate, it is quite clear that some form of national health service is an essential component of the process of reconstruction in South Africa. Already a good deal of thinking has been done on this topic in the National Medical and Dental Association (NAMDA), and elsewhere (Owen, 1988). All the same, much systematic work remains to be done in debating, in the light both of South Africa's special historical circumstances as well as of its experience in other parts of the world, how best to structure and finance a service that would effectively do the job.

However, the real difficulty lies not so much in the design of the national health service itself as in ensuring it is part of a wider, integrated approach that can simultaneously ensure clean drinking-water, sufficient food, and adequate living conditions, without which good health is impossible, no matter what the medical profession may do. Proposals regarding water and housing have been discussed above. To the matter of food for all we now turn.

Nutrition

In the light of the evidence presented earlier (Chapter 5), it is clear that one of the most urgent priorities facing any government in South Africa for the foreseeable future is to ensure that every human being gets sufficient food to eat every day. From other parts of the world there is evidence that active measures by the state to guarantee this entitlement can have a major impact on the health and hence the life-expectancy of people even in countries where average income is very low. It is no accident that the citizens of both China and Sri Lanka have life-expectancies at birth that compare with those of the richer countries of Western Europe and North America (Sen, forthcoming; and see table 1.05). Both countries have long-established food policies designed to ensure that, as far as possible, everybody gets enough to eat.

There are various ways of designing such policies, including food fortification (221). We shall not assess them all here, but point simply to one of the more interesting schemes: food stamps. In the United States where, despite great national wealth, hunger is a major problem (Physician Task Force on Hunger in America, 1985), the government has found itself increasingly committed, over the past two decades including the years of the Reagan presidency, to a national Food Stamp Programme (Danziger and Weinberg, 1986; and Patterson, 1986). By 1985 total government expenditure on food stamps for Americans was $11.8 billion; enough money when converted to rands to pay twice over for the not insignificant expenditure by the South African government on defence, police, and education combined. In Sri Lanka the government for years ran a ration scheme offering rice at heavily subsidised prices. This was subsequently transformed into a food-stamp programme targeted at needy families, which received amounts depending on household size, children's age, and income. The stamps could be exchanged for ten major foodstuffs of which rice was the most important. The programme costs the government of Sri Lanka between 11–14 per cent of the national budget (223: 10).

A food-stamp programme in South Africa which was half the size of the Sri Lankan one and which cost 6 per cent, say, of the national budget, would make a significant difference to poorer households. At the same time it would pump a huge demand for food into a sector where increased production could have a substantial multiplier effect in the creation of jobs within the economy. A rough calculation can tell us something about the orders of magnitude involved. If we take estimated state expenditure as R53 billion for 1988/9, 6 per cent of the national budget amounts to a little over R3 billion. Total population in the country (including the TBVC areas) is approximately 34 million persons. Assume that 50 per cent of the population lives in households (with an average size of slightly less than 6 persons) that are below the minimum living level. That makes a total of 3 million households. If each of these households received R1 000 worth of food stamps per year, paid monthly and making no allowance for the cost of administration, each person would get somewhat less than 50 cents' worth of extra food each day. This is not a huge amount but it would nevertheless make a significant difference to households whose income is below, sometimes far below, a minimum living level that works out at approximately R3.30 per person per day in 1988. For a large proportion of these households there seems little doubt that such food stamps, modest though they would be, would double the availability of food.

Education

The debate about black education has raged across the country since 1976 as hundreds of thousands of black schoolchildren have come out in prolonged boycotts during the past decade, often against their parents' express wishes. Whilst the state's heavy counter-measures under cover of two emergencies have appeared, in the short run, to break the boycotts, little has been done to remove the major grievances. A military presence has not dampened the determination of the majority of black South Africans to redesign the goals, the structures, the content and the control of education.

It is crucial also to recognise clearly that education is closely related to jobs. Policy-makers in Zimbabwe are finding a cruel dilemma. It is widely perceived by people that a 'matriculation' certificate will make a substantial difference to the likelihood of getting a job, a better-remunerated job. There are thus enormous pressures on policy-makers to ensure that there are sufficient places in secondary schools to enable everybody, who so wishes, to fill them. However, at a macro-level it may be clear to planners that the rate at which 'matric-level jobs' are likely to be created in the economy is far below the number of matriculants who would come onto the labour market over a foreseeable time-period if the policy of universal secondary school education was implemented. But if universal secondary schooling was not to be implemented immediately, who would decide which students should not go beyond primary school? And what would they do during their teens?

The difficulty is that education performs two distinct, but interrelated, economic functions. The one, on which Marxists tend to focus, is of education as a sorting device; a sophisticated queueing mechanism for jobs. The other, which tends to be considered more seriously by liberals and conservatives, is the recognition that education is also a form of investment ('in human capital'); something which helps to raise the capacity of the society to produce more wealth than it would otherwise be able to do.

In the first instance, education and the 'ideology of merit' helps, so the argument goes, to control people by persuading them that they have equal opportunities ('the schools are open to all') and that if only they have the intelligence and work hard enough, they will get the necessary qualifications for a job. Failure to do so is seen to be their own fault when, in reality, the education system is designed so that only a certain percentage of those who start will ever get through to matric.

Perhaps the most striking illustration of the second function was in Germany after the Second World War when a defeated people who had virtually nothing left except the education and know-how embedded in them, both individually and socially, were able (with the assistance of Marshall Aid) to transform a shattered land into a humming economy within the space of a single decade.

In South Africa at present, educational policy is the subject of intensive debate across the country. Something of that debate is reflected in a special volume on education for the Carnegie Inquiry (Nasson and Samuel, 1989). We shall thus not attempt to say much here except to emphasise two or three points.

Firstly, it is clear that, precisely because education was deliberately used by the Nationalist government as a means of imposing the policy of separate development, there is no possibility of de-politicising the issue. Education is part and parcel of the liberation struggle, and until it reflects people's aspirations it will be rejected. The debate about education is synonymous with the debate about the future shape of South Africa, which is increasingly being seen as a unified, democratic, non-racial, non-exploitative and possibly socialist state. It is clear that there is no possibility whatsoever of an educational policy that embodies these goals being implemented under the present power structure in South Africa.

What, then, is the best way of organising a single, unified (though not necessarily uniform) system of education for all South Africa's children. How should resources be re-allocated? Where could new sources of funds be found in order to overcome the inequities inherent in a century or more of bias in favour of white children? There is much to be learnt from Zimbabwe where, since independence in 1980, there has been a deliberate policy of redistributing national education resources to create greater equity, as evidenced by the change in the composition of school populations in the northern suburbs of Harare where in 1985 the ratio of black to white children was estimated at 35:1. This was achieved by introducing a system of bussing children on a daily basis from the high density areas where there was a shortage of schools, to the middle-class, previously all-white, northern suburbs where there was an oversupply of facilities. Very few incidents of racial friction have been reported and the overall impresssion is that the adjustments have been relatively painless. The same process should be undertaken in South Africa. In the rural areas, white farm schools in small dorps stand empty, while black farm children have few if any facilities (65: 8).

It is important also to face the realities of power and recognise that it is wishful thinking to believe that somehow the present government, or some reformed variation of it, has the capacity to reconstruct an educational system which it has so grievously and wilfully manipulated. The task can only be performed by a genuinely national government as part of a democratic political process. Does this mean that nothing can be done now with regard to education? That South Africa must lurch from one schools' crisis to another until such time as the country can free itself from the shackles of racist, minority control? In one sense that is the reality. Education embodies the contradictions of the apartheid state and it will not change until the society is politically transformed. But at another level, there is much that can be done, as we argued in the previous chapter, through a wide variety of educational institutions to prepare people to live fully and creatively in a non-racial and genuinely participatory society.

Welfare

We turn now to social welfare in general and especially to pensions, unemployment insurance, workmen's compensation and a variety of other transfer payments such as maternity benefits and disability grants.

Given the backlog of unemployment amongst active people, how do social remedies weigh against other forms of expenditure? The indigent, the widowed and other 'social' cases live within communities, however presently weakened. Can they not be incorporated into a renewed network of relationships offering economic security within family kinship and community systems if those networks in turn find the means to realise a modicum of gainful employment in ways which also develop their material, human and institutional basis?

The question is a crucial one, but we do not believe that it is possible to go back to the time when people were knit together in small-scale societies. In one sense history is irreversible and that particular web has been broken for ever. It is too much to expect families that have been systematically impoverished to bear the burden of caring for the indigent. Certainly in South Africa it is the responsibility of society as a whole to provide for those who are, for example, old and destitute in an imaginative way.

However stark and difficult, choices still have to be made. What is a democratic state, no matter how socialist, going to do if there is not enough money to fund both an adequate pension scheme for all the elderly and a public works programme which will guarantee jobs for all the unemployed at a level that, at the very least, is not below the poverty datum line? These are the agonising questions facing any state, especially a state in transition where not everything is possible at once. Calculations have been made to show that if pensions are not financed by compulsory savings throughout people's working lives, then the revenue which the state would have to raise either from taxation or from profits on its own nationalised industries will grow exponentially to a point where pension payments alone would absorb a crippling proportion of the national budget. Even for whites, who form the relatively wealthy class, the figures are startling. Over the eleven years, 1970–80, South Africans (largely white) paid into their pension funds annuities totalling R1.31 billion. Over the same period they withdrew, for reasons other than retirement, an amount of R1.16 billion. In other words, during the entire period the pension funds held onto only 12 per cent of what had actuarially been calculated would be needed to provide pensions for those who made pension payments (but excluding those who were not linked to any pension scheme and who relied on the state) (140: 31ff). Since then, as unemployment has worsened, there has been evidence from the Black Sash advice offices, particularly in the eastern Cape, of people withdrawing their pensions in order simply to make ends meet.

Pringle, who focused solely on the parlous condition of white pensioners, drew attention to the fact that as early as 1943 a parliamentary select committee had recommended that a national contributory pension scheme for all South Africans be set up, with contributions from individuals levied on the basis of income and with equal contributions from the Treasury. However, more than a quarter of a century later the government again, in 1970, firmly rejected the idea. Where the present government is not prepared to introduce such a scheme even for whites, the chances of a genuinely national plan being introduced are virtually non-existent. The state continues to make *ex gratia* payments, but the rates are abysmally low, and costs are further saved by various devious devices, such as making homeland governments responsible and then not transferring enough funds to enable them to pay all pensioners who have a claim.

A major priority for any democratic government will be to find ways of organising adequate provision for all citizens in their old age. In the long run, the only way is through some form of national contributory scheme whereby all people start saving for their old age (with regular, usually equal, contributions from the state) as soon as they enter the labour market, say in their early twenties. The major problem will be the lag between the introduction of the scheme and the time, roughly forty years later, when everybody entering retirement will do so with savings accumulated during their working life. Until then, however, large numbers of people will retire without savings of their own, and the state will be faced with cruel choices in terms of the competing claims for expenditure on a wide range of basic needs, including public works programmes in order to guarantee jobs for all.

There is a strong case for introducing a national contributory scheme as soon as possible, partly in order to ensure that in a largely and increasingly urbanised society there is proper coverage for everybody in their old age and partly to ensure that in so far as possible it is financed out of savings over a long period of time. In this way scarce public resources needed for a wide range of purposes can be used as investment rather than as consumption in the form of *ex gratia* payments (although these will be necessary in some cases such as disability grants).

In the short run, however, where there is no such scheme and where no provision has been made for old age, it is essential that the state maintain pension payments and at the same time increase both the amount paid and the number of pensions made available. Perhaps the most striking aspect of South African poverty uncovered during the course of the Carnegie Inquiry was the extent to which families, often extended families, especially in the rural areas, depended for their sole source of regular income on the pitiful pension paid once every two months to one elderly member of the household. Pensions ranked second only to migrant remittances as a source of cash income without which families throughout the reserves of the country would have starved. Yet, for Africans, they amounted in 1983 to a monthly average of R67. Whilst this was more than treble, in real terms, the 1970 level of R5 per month, the amount was still pitifully small: less than one-third the pensions paid to whites and well under half the minimum living level of a household of two persons (assuming that one of them is not a pensioner). Where a pensioner is *de facto* supporting a family of five, as seems to be frequently the case, the pension payment (1983) is one-fifth of the amount required (1985) for that household to reach the minimum living level.

A situation of desperate poverty prevails. And one that is even more difficult in those households where there are people of pensionable age, but they are unable to obtain a pension because of bureaucratic inefficiency, corruption, or simple lack of funds. In KwaZulu alone it is estimated that there are 100 000 people to whom pensions are due but who are not receiving them, primarily because insufficient funds have been made available to the local authorities (in this case the KwaZulu government) by the central government.

One interim step which would make a substantial and immediate difference to the lives of the poor would be the trebling of all African (and the doubling of coloured and Indian) pensions to bring them onto a par with those paid to whites. At the same time, the number of pensions needs to be increased to cover all those who are of the age to qualify. This would remove the racist structure of the present scheme whilst ensuring an improved source of income to many of the poorest households in the country. Moreover, it is within the capacity of the present economy, if resources were reallocated, to do so.

As regards unemployment insurance, we have already seen something of the state's failure in recent years to build up a proper fund for all workers irrespective of race. The picture is one of steady reduction in contributions by the state, combined with a shabby process of shuffling off responsibility for black unemployment onto the weak shoulders of the 'black national states'. Transformation in this area requires, naturally, a genuinely national plan, based on contributions from employers, employees and the state, to provide for the unemployed. But the matter still requires further debate. Whilst there is a strong case for the state to contribute towards an unemployment fund, which will provide workers laid off by structural change or recession with breathing space whilst they find (or retrain for) a new job, the policy becomes more difficult if there is a situation of substantial structural unemployment, with a large proportion of the economically active population unable to get even their first job for long periods of time. The circumstances under which the state provides funds for employment through public works rather than unemployment benefits are by no means clear. The issue is a political one requiring further debate and clarification.

Similarly with regard to other welfare needs, such as workmen's compensation or disability grants, the present situation is highly unsatisfactory. Inadequate payments, often with a racial bias, reduction of funds made available by the state, bureaucratic inefficiency, unnecessary overlap as well as gaping holes where no welfare services are available – all combine to paint a picture of woeful inadequacy for a modern industrial state. The structures need thorough overhauling and revitalisation. Basically what is required is a national welfare system with proper space for individual agencies. The director of the active and imaginative Catholic Welfare Bureau in Cape Town has put forward a seven-point plan of welfare reform along these lines, which provides an admirable agenda for discussion and clarification of long-run strategies. (PCS 2: 10–11).

Conclusion

To conclude: suppose that South Africa, which is a religious country, were to take the biblical injunction seriously and tithe itself by setting aside 10 per cent of its public funds for work on poverty that is not currently being done. Of the national budget in 1988/9, 10 per cent is estimated to amount to approximately R5.3 billion rand. Suppose that half of this were to be made available as food stamps for all those households (approximately 50 per cent of the total) living below the minimum living level. Suppose that the other half were to be set aside for a guaranteed employment scheme on public works for one member of each of these same households. There would be enough money to guarantee two days' work per week at R7.50 per day. None of this is very startling but it would make a significant difference to the lives of the very poor whilst, at the same time, it would also lead to substantial productive investment in roads, dams, afforestation, etc., as well as generate further employment through the multiplier effect of additional demand being pumped into locally produced basic needs at the bottom of the economy.

But where would the money for all this come from? The 10 per cent tithe could be drawn by cutting back on other public expenditures. In our view defence, which currently absorbs no less than 16 per cent of the national budget, should be the major target. War, including military adventures across international frontiers, is a luxury which South Africa simply cannot afford in current circumstances. Slashing the defence budget in half would impose considerable demands upon the generals and tax their capacity for readjust-ment to the full. But the challenge would not be beyond their ingenuity if it were accompanied by a process of democratisation and a consequent removal of the causes of the very tension which led the defence force to be so rapidly expanded in the first place.

From analysis into the nature and causes of poverty we have argued that the major thrust of any strategy against poverty must be a combination of economic growth (to ensure adequate resources) and redistribution by means of appropriate state policies which we have tried to identify in this chapter. We would also argue that peace and political stability in southern Africa are prerequisites for business confidence, investment, and economic growth in the 1990s. It seems unlikely, despite President Botha's 1988 visits to build links with other African countries, including Mozambique and Malawi, that the peace and political stability which are so badly needed in the sub-continent will come without a process of political democratisation within South Africa combined with active steps, by the state, to reduce inequality. But these steps, some of which have been identified in this chapter, themselves raise a number of difficult questions which must now be faced.

The true lesson of history was this: that the so-called victims, the poor, and downtrodden, the masses, had always struggled with spears and arrows, with their hands and songs of courage and hope, to end their oppression and exploitation: that they would continue struggling until a human kingdom came: a world in which goodness and beauty and strength and courage would be seen not in how cunning one can be, not in how much power to oppress one possessed, but only in one's contribution in creating a more humane world in which the inherited inventive genius of man in culture and science from all ages and climes would not be the monopoly of a few, but for the use of all, so that all flowers in all their different colours would ripen and bear fruits and seeds. And the seeds would be put into the ground and they would once again sprout and flower in rain and sunshine.

— Ngugi wa Thiong'o, *Petals of Blood*

In writing this book we have found it necessary to break down, as far as possible, into its component parts the various faces of poverty as they have manifested themselves in South Africa; as well as a wide range of causes and an array of strategies. But this process of atomisation for the sake of clarity and understanding carries its own dangers, for it risks conveying the impression that somehow the diverse facts and processes are all independent of each other when, in reality, they are closely bound together and must be understood as much in their interaction as in their separation. For not only do many of the different faces of poverty (such as hunger and the lack of adequate fuel) tend to go together but the causes of impoverishment reinforce each other in a web of forces from which it is difficult to escape.

Moreover, as we have argued in earlier chapters, the distinction between cause and symptom or even between diagnosis and prescription is not always so obvious as it may seem at first sight. For example, in South Africa in the 1980s illiteracy amongst farm labourers and the lack of education for their children are important dimensions of their poverty, quite as serious and perhaps even more resented than bad housing conditions. But the illiteracy is more than a symptom or aspect of the poverty of farm labourers. It is also likely to be a major cause of unemployment and hence poverty for the children growing up in a society where mechanisation and industrialisation will have reduced still further the demand for unskilled labourers in agriculture. Or again, the analysis which suggests that the system of oscillating migration in southern Africa has itself been the cause of a major bias in the pattern of accumulation and hence of a process of impoverishment in some rural areas does not necessarily imply that the first step in overcoming this rural poverty is to abolish the migrant system. For in the short run the system itself is a source of remittances, without which rural households would sink even more deeply into poverty. The question then becomes how best to ease the process of transition so that those caught in the coils of a destructive system can move to a situation where their participation in a restructured economy is part of a process of enrichment for all.

In other words, all fact-finding, all analysis and, above everything, all action must continually take place within a wider framework – a framework that is conscious of the interactions from the grassroots- or micro-level through national and regional considerations to the global linkages that affect South Africa's particular place in the international economic system. Poverty is not simply a fact; it is also a process, and thus part of a system. To study this and to put it right requires systems analysis, an understanding of all the linkages. Thus, having spent the best part of this book in isolating the different factors and forces at work in the process of impoverishment, we cannot conclude without emphasising the crucial importance of seeing all facts, each cause, and every strategy as part of the wider, interacting whole. Proposals, no matter how good they may seem in themselves, can all too easily come to grief and cause grave damage to the very people they are designed to assist, if they are made without deep consideration of all the consequences they may have. With this insight the artist is, as so often, way ahead of the social scientist. What one has to do, said E. M. Forster, in *Howards End*, is 'only connect'.

We turn now to a number of tough questions that have been raised by the problems encountered in this book. We consider them explicitly now, albeit briefly, because their answer is not simply technical but rather a matter of political choice and hence of prior political discussion. These are by no means the only questions on the agenda but we would argue that, over and above the strategies proposed in previous chapters, in any process of coming to grips with poverty in South Africa they at least must be faced, debated, and decided by all those involved in the consequences of the answers, not least the poor themselves.

The first question concerns the possible conflict between political change and economic growth. In its most acute form this question is raised by those who, believing that the main impact of sanctions is likely to be increased unemployment, ask how any organisation or individual (such as a trade union or a church leader) genuinely concerned about poverty can possibly campaign for sanctions against South Africa. The question is crucial, for it poses in acute form the central dilemma faced by all those working for economic and political justice in South Africa. In thinking how to think about the issue we start with the fundamental assumption that has underlain all analysis in this book, namely that an essential prerequisite for uprooting poverty in South Africa is a redistribution of political power. Not only does the juggernaut of apartheid that has wrought so much destruction to the lives of poor people have to be halted, but in the long run, as we have argued, the building of a new society sensitive to the needs of the poor requires not only that those who are poor have the political power to bargain for resources but also that they be able to participate actively in the process of shaping the society as it grows. If this assumption is valid, and we believe it is, then a matter of overriding concern – no matter how narrowly one may be focused on the problem of poverty – becomes the question specifically excluded from this book, namely how best to bring about political change that empowers the poor. Further-more, recognition of this fact brings one face to face with the realisation, long understood by the poor, that in South Africa there is no painless way to change; no easy road to freedom.

Seen in this light the question about sanctions becomes not so much a matter of debating whether or not it will cause unemployment (although this is certainly an important consideration), but rather a question as to whether or not it will be effective as one of the pressures towards political change; and a question as to how it compares in both effectiveness and cost with other possible pressures. Not the least harsh of the realities facing the poor in South Africa at the end of the twentieth century is the fact that the process of liberation from the structures that imprison them is itself fraught with uncertainty, danger, and the possibility of further impoverishment. It was not for nothing that the children of Israel complained bitterly to Moses that all his talk about freedom would do nothing but worsen their condition (Exodus 5: 6–18). In focusing, as we have done in this book, on what can be done by building and strengthening independent organisations, by training people for the future, and by thinking through long-term strategies to transform the society, it is important not to lose sight of the central contradiction. The agony of South Africa is due primarily to the fact that those with political power have left no room for those who would change the society to use legitimate democratic political channels to do so. Thus there may be conditions in which actions deemed necessary to redistribute political power in favour of the poor and to improve the growth prospects of the economy in the long run have an immediate, short-term, impact that causes further poverty. We do not intend in this book to analyse or assess any of these actions but we have used the example of sanctions to illustrate the complexity of the dilemma and the need for honesty in avoiding over-simplification.

A second complex set of questions relates to the ownership of land and, of particular importance in South Africa, minerals. With regard to agriculture where more and more land has been locked up in fewer and fewer hands, the fundamental question revolves around the means by which any democratic government should act to redistribute ownership of the soil, and to whom. Enough has been learnt from the chequered history of twentieth-century land reform in different parts of the world, including Eastern Europe, to know how difficult is the process of reaching for equality whilst simultaneously increasing, or even maintaining, production. But the difficulties are not insuperable as the history of Japanese, Korean or Taiwanese agriculture since the Second World War suggests. Indeed it is becoming increasingly clear that land reform in those countries, far from being a constraint on growth, was a vital prerequisite for their subsequent economic dynamism (Sachs, 1987: 12–14). What is needed in South Africa is both a wide-ranging debate about the type of structures that people find desirable as well as detailed technical analysis as to what is possible – in terms of potential crops, techniques of production, etc. – under different patterns of land tenure and various scales of operation.

Elsewhere (P. Moll, forthcoming) there is more detailed discussion about some of the issues involved. Here let it suffice to note that an important debate is already under way. In his account of fieldwork in the Herschel district, south of Lesotho, William Beinart reports on a discussion between two men of the soil (both part-time migrants) as to whether in the future it would be better for land to be excised from the Orange Free State and farmed as small-holdings in denser agricultural settlement or whether the large farms should be taken over as they are and run on some sort of co-operative basis (1988: 134). We believe that there are more than two alternatives, including, as in Zimbabwe, the co-existence of several different forms and scales of tenure. We cannot anticipate the outcome of such a debate, but we would certainly argue that the time is overdue for both an overview, from a South African perspective, of land-reform experience around the world as well as detailed analysis, district by district, of the options for agricultural transformation in terms of crops, scale, land tenure, markets, and supportive structures.

In terms of South African law, mineral rights are vested in the state, which leases them in the first instance to the land-owner, who may then sell, at a considerable premium, to a mining company the option which enables it to apply for the mining lease. It is important to recognise that in South Africa the combination of conquest and law meant that land-owners in almost all the areas where minerals were discovered had to be white. And the mining companies were owned and run by whites. Thus, historically the mineral wealth of the country has been under white control. In effect the state has leased to the highest bidder the right to exploit the minerals in a particular place. But the mines themselves are privately owned and the question arises as to whether so powerful a component of the political economy should be subject to further social control by means of public ownership. Here too the matter is wide open for debate, and there is experience on which to draw from around the world, including nationalisation of copper mines in Zambia, gold mines in Ghana, and oil fields in Algeria. Once again we cannot anticipate the outcome of such a debate, but we would make the observation that in discussing the pros and cons of nationalisation sight should not be lost of the necessity of finding ways of democratising the economy in such a way that those, for example, who daily risk their lives at the stope-face two miles beneath the surface of the earth should have some real say in the running of the mine in which they work, not least with regard to safety. How best such responsiveness to the needs of workers can be structured is one of the central issues of economic life in all parts of the world. It is by no means clear that a change in ownership from private hands to the state will necessarily guarantee it (Marshall, 1987 and Walesa, 1987). The issue is a difficult and complex one requiring rigorous thinking and, as with so much else, the honesty to avoid the over-simplification of half-truths.

A third set of questions which cannot really be answered in advance of the circumstances of a particular time and place relates to public choices regarding the allocation of scarce resources that would have to be made by any newly elected democratic government. Nevertheless it is important to be aware of some of the dilemmas that are likely to emerge, if only to think through some of the options as imaginatively as possible whilst there is yet time to be flexible. The dilemmas relate primarily to the priorities of public expenditure in a situation where there will simply not be sufficient funds to do everything that is deemed essential.

For example, given the crucial importance which state pensions have assumed in the household incomes of the very poor, particularly in the rural areas, a democratic government would be under heavy political pressure to raise pensions to far higher levels than the miserable rates currently being paid. And clearly much could be done. Nevertheless it is quite possible that there would be considerable conflict between the expansion of pension funds, say, and the resources available for a national employment guarantee scheme providing jobs in public works for able-bodied persons unable to find work elsewhere in the economy. How then are the relative needs to be assessed? Choices of this kind will, as everywhere else in the world, be the outcome of all sorts of cross-cutting political pressures but it is important that there be as much thinking and debate as possible about the various alternatives, not least as regards methods of financing, in order to build up an informed public opinion.

There is another question which needs to be answered. Given the way in which the South African economy developed over the century of its industrial revolution, do the people of Lesotho and Mozambique and other parts of southern Africa who have contributed as much as anybody to the growth of the single economy, not also have a claim on the common wealth that is generated and paid to the inland revenue department in Pretoria? Such a question cannot be answered without widespread political debate but it will have to be faced during the process of transformation in South Africa. It would be all too easy to decide, democratically within the nation-state, that the wealth of the country belonged entirely to those living within the boundaries of the nation-state of the old Union of South Africa, thus including all reserves (as well as areas such as Transkei and Bophuthatswana) but excluding Lesotho. Yet we would argue that the claims which different countries surrounding South Africa retain (especially as regards right of access to jobs) on the wealth generated by the single economy have to be considered seriously. For it would be tragic if black South Africans solved their problem of poverty by following a road which caused great suffering to those even more vulnerable than themselves, in the same way that white South Africans dug their way out of poverty by excluding blacks from the wealth which all had generated together. In this connection we would draw attention to the significance of an article in the Freedom Charter, adopted by the Congress of the People in 1955, to the effect that: 'The people of the protectorates – Basutoland, Bechuanaland and Swaziland – shall be free to decide for themselves their own future'. The spirit of that clause was that the people of those three territories should be free to choose whether or not they wished to become part of a larger South Africa. We would argue that that freedom should be maintained until South Africa itself has made the transition to democracy.

Capitalism, socialism, and the future of South Africa

One further question must be considered. Does the struggle against poverty in South Africa require a capitalist framework, or is socialism an essential part of any comprehensive action against poverty? We do not wish to evade this question by simply pushing it forward as a topic for debate in the future; but nor would we be so presumptious as to suggest that we know the full answer. There are, however, a number of points that must be made. Firstly, there is the obvious yet elusive fact that the very definitions of 'capitalism' and 'socialism' are hard to pin down precisely, not least because in particular situations they may be subject to subtle reinterpretations for the benefit of certain interest groups. Moreover, the differences between capitalist societies, such as Britain and Brazil, (or indeed socialist ones) may be greater than those between, say, socialist Hungary and capitalist Sweden. Or is Sweden socialist? In other words, the definitions themselves may obscure more than they illuminate. Nevertheless there is clearly some meaning to the words as currently used by South Africans in an increasingly vigorous debate. Essentially the argument revolves around the role of the market, the function of the state, and the degree of public ownership of such fundamental assets as land and mines. But more deeply, the question is about the distribution of wealth; and about people's participation in economic as well as in political decisions that affect their lives (130; 131; 132).

The strength of the capitalist argument lies in its recognition of the relative efficiency (under some, though by no means all, conditions) of markets in allocating resources, its warning about the dangers of placing economic and political power in the same hands, and its emphasis on the potential energy available to be released through individual initiative freed from the restrictions of rigid, often corrupt, bureaucratic control. These are crucial insights for any society as both the USSR and China have been rediscovering in recent years.

The strength of the socialist argument lies in its insistence that we are all, in St Paul's phrase, members one of another. For socialists human life is not some rat race with honour, comfort, and security going only to the swiftest (sometimes the meanest) rats but a way of being that encourages mutual support and care for the weak. For socialists the state has generally been seen, albeit uncritically at times, as the means whereby the common responsibility which human beings have for each other can best be expressed.

In the historical circumstances in which South Africa finds itself as it approaches the end of the twentieth century, the capitalist argument has a curiously hollow ring when used by those who have themselves benefited from massive interventions by the state. Poor people who for generations have been actively dispossessed or excluded from purchase of land by the racist machinations of the state are unlikely to be that impressed when those who have enjoyed the fruits of such exclusion start talking about the value of the free market in allocating resources. Similarly, discussion about the benefits of 'privatisation' when applied to medical care sound sometimes suspiciously like an attempt to rationalise the abdication of state responsibility, or at least the withdrawal of financial support, for the general health of all. To put it another way, is the abolition of, say, the 1913 Land Act and the subsequent opening up of a free market in agricultural land adequate to deal with the fact that, through conquest and discrimination, virtually all farm land is owned only by white South Africans? Or again, how exactly, in the absence of some kind of national health service would the proponents of privatisation organise even minimal health care for people living in impoverished circumstances such as at Mhala in Gazankulu, eastern Transvaal? There is moreover a curious kind of double-think manifested by some proponents of minimal state interference in the market in their ability to ignore, if not actively support, forceful state action (whether by the police or the army) in support of the status quo.

At the same time the dangers, seen sometimes more clearly by those on the right of the political spectrum than those on the left, of too much economic power in the hands of the state leading to greater inefficiency, corruption, and authoritarianism than would otherwise be the case, need to be taken seriously. The history of many, though by no means all, African countries in the two or three decades since political independence is too serious to be ignored (Chaliand, 1977; Sender and Smith, 1986).

In reflecting upon the relevance for strategies against poverty of the pros and cons of socialism and capitalism, of the tension between the role of the state and the rights of the individual, we can do no better than draw on certain events in China and India used by Amartya Sen to illustrate the heart of the problem. Analysing why India, despite massive crop failures on several occasions since political independence in 1947, has not suffered any major famine, Sen points to the role of a free press in alerting public opinion and, together with opposition parties, in forcing the hands of the government to act. In China on the other hand,

when in 1958–61 there was a disastrous food situation in China [following the failure of the Great Leap Forward], the docility of the controlled Press was particularly striking. . . . The famine raged on in China for more than three years, and the mortality estimates vary between about 16 million and 30 million extra deaths associated with the famine. . . . The instrumental role of freedom in journalism and politics does indeed make it hard for any Indian government to ignore the force of that criticism (and the threat of electoral defeat), if there is open starvation in the country, reported graphically in newspapers and energetically seized by opposition spokesmen. (1987: 27)

However, after pointing out that there is plenty of evidence that even the poorest are not unconcerned with issues of basic political freedom, Sen goes on to show how 'the Chinese system of extensive public distribution of food and health care – when not disrupted by political crisis – has certainly paid rich dividend in reducing the average mortality figures in China'. Furthermore, he argues:

The lives that China lost during the famine years – even in the biggest famine in the world in this century – are far outnumbered by the lives India may be losing gradually over the years. At an extra 3.3 million deaths per year in India, more people lose their lives every nine years through greater normal mortality than the number of people who lost their lives in China through catastrophic famine mortality. The contrasting roles of different types of freedoms in these two contexts are particularly important to study. (1987: 20)

Indeed so.

Which brings us to the fundamental assumption and, simultaneously, the toughest question of this book. Is it really correct to argue that political democracy is a fundamental prerequisite of the long-term struggle against poverty? Will political liberation necessarily be accompanied by a significant improvement in the material conditions and the quality of life of the very poor? The fact that the answer to the latter question could be and has been 'no' for a number of African countries is a measure of the extent of the challenge in South Africa. There is nothing inevitable about the economic consequences of redistributing political power. Everything will depend on the capacity of the new society, not least of its leadership and of the variety of organisational structures available at the time, to move in the right direction within the limits of what is feasible on what has been called 'the terrain of effective reality' (Gramsci cited in Sender and Smith, 1986: 127; see also Nove, 1983). It is not impossible, as the recent history of Latin America makes all too plain and as Charles Elliott warned at the Carnegie conference (137), that the hard-won gains of a long political struggle be lost in a few months or years either by the provocation (for example through unnecessary hyper-inflation) of a revolutionary counter-coup or by the sacrifice of the claims of the poor to the selfishness of a new elite.

It is precisely this latter danger that makes it vital to insist upon the necessity of the democratic process as part and parcel of any long-term struggle against poverty. Quite how this democratic process should be structured in any society is itself a major question that takes us far beyond the limits of this book. It certainly requires further debate but there can be no evasion of the fact that in South Africa one component of that process must be the subjection of those who ultimately control the state (including fiscal policy, the budget, the police, and the army) to the wishes of all the people expressed through regular, free and fair elections (including referenda on some key issues) on the basis of one vote for each adult person. In the last resort nobody is better able to assess the interests of the poor than the poor themselves, and the process of democracy is above all else a means of empowering them to do something about the situation in which they find themselves.

It is in the light of this argument that we would conclude with the thought-provoking contrast between the recent history, during the second half of the twentieth century, of the two countries in Africa where, by 1950, the greatest proportions of inhabitants of European origin were to be found and where the strongest resistance to a fundamental redistribution of political power has been manifest. We refer to South Africa and Algeria. The conventional wisdom in many Western countries and certainly amongst most whites in

South Africa is that the strength and growth of the South African economy has been due not least to the force of the government in withstanding 'majority rule', and that whilst reform would be welcomed, the consequences of a rapid redistribution of political power would probably be harmful to the economy and certainly act as a brake on the growth of gross national product. It is this thinking which underlies much white resistance to political change in South Africa.

The same was also true in Algeria where the white settlers, the *pieds noirs* (who formed 11 per cent of the population), could justifiably point with pride in the 1950s to a well-organised economy. But for the Algerians, the perspective was very different. Average earnings were only one-thirtieth of those paid to the Europeans. In agriculture the average European farm was eleven times greater than that of Muslim land-holdings. Unemployment in the burgeoning urban slums was estimated to be no less than 25 per cent. Albert Camus, himself a *pied noir*, drew attention to the dreadful economic plight of the Algerians both before and after the Second World War (Horne, 1987: 55). The unwillingness of the *pieds noirs* to share political power and hence, in their view, to risk their economic security led directly to the armed uprising of November 1954 and the subsequent savage war. The tragedy of their eventual expulsion, one million strong, from a country that could so easily have been their permanent home is now part of history. But the most striking fact of all is the astonishing growth of the Algerian economy in the quarter century after political independence in 1962. Much had been destroyed, not least by the *pieds noirs* themselves in their rage at leaving, yet despite one of the highest rates of population growth in the world, the gross national product of the country increased so rapidly that by 1984 GNP per capita exceeded that of South Africa; and it continues to do so.

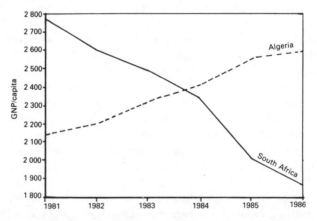

Fig. 16.01: Algeria and South Africa, 1981–6: GNP per capita
(Source: World Development Reports 1983–8)

Although the whites who live in South Africa continue to enjoy the highest standard of living of any comparable proportion of the population anywhere on the continent, the average per capita income (measured as GNP per inhabitant) is no longer – after the peculiar case of Libya with only 4 million inhabitants – the highest in Africa. In Algeria the benefits of political independence boosted by the oil flowing from beneath the Sahara have given the country – despite difficulties, mistakes and setbacks – an economic potential that South Africa by the end of the 1980s can only envy (Ecrement, 1986 and Horne, 1987).

Whilst predictions about the future are hazardous it is nonetheless clear that the greatest single obstacle to economic growth in southern Africa as a whole is the political uncertainty of a region where those with wealth and power refuse to let go and to share with those who are poor. Frantz Fanon, one of the most perceptive observers of the Algerian revolution, expressed the matter succinctly when he wrote: 'The fundamental duel which seemed to be that between colonialism and anti-colonialism, and indeed between capitalism and socialism, is already losing some of its importance. What counts today, the question which is looming on the horizon, is the need for a redistribution of wealth. Humanity must reply to this question, or be shaken to pieces by it.' (1968: 98) That surely is the fundamental question facing South Africa today. Have we the courage to face and answer it?

Appendix 1: Conference and post-conference papers and publications

A. Papers Published as Part of the Inquiry's Activities before the Conference in April 1984

Wentzel, Wilfred, 'Poverty and development in South Africa (1890–1980: a bibliography)', Saldru Working Paper 46 (1982)

Saldru (ed), 'Questionnaires are no short cut', Saldru Working Paper 48 (1982)

Community Health Research Project, 'Access to health services in the greater Cape Town area', Saldru Working Paper 55 (1983)

Ellis, G.F.R. and Erlank, D., 'A quality of life basic needs measurement system with application to Elsies River', Saldru Working Paper 56 (1983)

Mgoqi, Wallace, 'Law, poverty and development in the context of South Africa', Saldru Policy Paper 1 (1983)

Nasson, Bill, 'Education and poverty: some perspectives', Saldru Policy Paper 2 (1983)

Moll, Peter, 'A history and an analysis of the bread subsidy in South Africa', Saldru Policy Paper 3 (1983)

Devereux, Stephen, 'Steffen Schneier's "Occupational Mobility among Blacks in South Africa": A synopsis and evaluation', Saldru Policy Paper 4 (1984)

Community Health Research Project, 'Access to health services in the Paarl area', Saldru Working Paper 60 (1984)

B. Carnegie Conference Papers*

Poverty: Perceptions and Definitions
1. Chabani Manganyi, 'The worst of times: a migrant worker's autobiography'
2. C. Ntoane and K. Mokoetle, 'Major problems as perceived by the community'
3. Wilfred Beckerman, 'Measuring poverty in rich and poor countries'
4. G.F.R. Ellis, 'The dimensions of poverty'
5. Pamela Reynolds, 'Men without children'
6. V. Moller, L. Schlemmer, H.G. Strijdom, and colleagues at the HSRC, 'Poverty and quality of life among blacks in South Africa'

General Overviews
7. Charles Simkins, 'What has been happening to income distribution and poverty in the homelands?'
8. Paul Streeten, 'Basic needs: Some unsettled questions'
9. Steve Tollman, 'Thoughts on planning for basic needs in South Africa'

Area Studies
10a. Dinga Sikwebu, 'Profile of Nyanga'
10b. W. Naidoo and W. Dreyer, 'Vrygrond and Lavender Hill'
10c. Pieter Jansen, Ashley du Plooy, and Faika Esau, 'Elsies River'
10d. D. Maralack and A. Kriel, 'A Streetless wasteland: A preliminary report on Ocean View'
10e. Lucy Edwards, 'Profile on Philippi'
11. B.H. Kinkead-Weekes, 'A history of vagrancy in Cape Town'
12. Di Bishop, 'Poverty experienced by black (African) residents of Cape Town

* There are no papers with numbers marked by an asterisk.

13. N. Riley, C. Schuman, P. Romanovsky, and R. Gentle, 'Spatial variations in the levels of living in the Cape metropolitan area'
14. G. Hewatt, T. Lee, N. Nyakaza, C. Olver, and B. Tyeko, 'An exploratory study of overcrowding and its relationship to health at Old Crossroads'
15. M.M. Gonsalves, 'A community in bondage: A case study'
16. Jane Prinsloo, 'A description of income, expenditure, and earning patterns from households in Cape Town and Durban'
17. Vish Suparsad, 'Socio-economic status of selected communities in the Durban metropolitan area'
18. P.N. Pillay, 'Poverty in the Pretoria-Witwatersrand-Vereeniging area: A survey of research'
19. P.N. Pillay, 'Alexandra: An analysis of socioeconomic conditions in an urban ghetto'
20. David Webster, 'The reproduction of labour power and the struggle for survival in Soweto'
21. Caroline White, 'Poverty in Port Elizabeth'
22. David Simon, 'The end of apartheid? Some dimensions of urban poverty in Windhoek'
23. Debbie Budlender, 'Agriculture and technology: Four case studies'
24. *
25. Charles Simkins, 'African population, employment, and incomes outside the reserves, 1923–69'
26. Debbie Budlender, 'Mechanisation and labour on white farms: A statistical analysis'
27. Michael de Klerk, 'Mechanizing farming: Implications for employment, incomes and population distribution'
28. Michael de Klerk, 'The incomes of farm workers and their families: A study of maize farms in the western Transvaal.'
29. Mandla Seleoane, 'Conditions on eight farms in Middelburg, eastern Transvaal'
30. C.W. Manona, 'Migration from the farms to towns and its implications for urban adaptation'
31. Martin West, 'Vulnerability, isolation and apartheid: A case study of Port Nolloth'
32. Jeff Yosslowitz, 'A study of poverty among the "coloured" community: A general analysis and a case study of Worcester'
33. Mary-Jane Morifi, 'Life among the poor in Philipstown'
34. Sean Archer and Eileen Meyer, 'Hanover: A profile of poverty on the Eiselen line'
35. David Schmidt, 'Beaufort West has many windmills: A look at poverty in the town and district of Beaufort West'
36. Dudley Horner and Graham van Wyk, 'Quiet desperation: The poverty of Calitzdorp'
37. Peter Buirski, 'Poverty in Oudtshoorn: Some impressions'
38. Wilfred Wentzel, 'Hard times in the Karoo: Case studies and statistical profiles from five peri-urban residential areas'
39. Laura Levetan, 'Structural shifts in the George economy: Underemployment and unskilled labour as conditions of impoverishment'
40. Sally Damana, 'Rendering welfare and development services with special reference to Grahamstown'
41. Christine Walwyn, 'Survey of aspects of rural poverty in Clarens and the surrounding areas and of certain aspects in the black townships of Bethlehem and Harrismith'
42. *
43. N.D. Muller, 'The labour market and poverty in the Transkei: Special reference to the implications of the changing spatial division of labour'
44. Carol Cragg, 'Estimated household subsistence levels for the Transkei urban and rural areas 1983'
45. J. Baskin, 'Access to land in the Transkei'
46. N.D. Muller and C.P.G. Tapscott, 'The face of rural poverty in the Transkei: Two village socio-economic profiles'
47. Terence Moll, 'A Mixed and threadbare bag: Employment, incomes and poverty in Lower Roza, Qumbu, Transkei'
48. R.J. Haines, C.P. Tapscott, S.B. Solinjani, and P. Tyali, 'The silence of poverty: Networks of control in rural Transkei'
49. Julia Segar, 'Social inequality in a Transkeian "Betterment" village'
50. Wolfgang Thomas, 'Financing rural development — with particular reference to the Transkei'
51. Andrew Spiegel, ' "Internal" Migration and rural differentiation: A field report from the Matatiele/Qacha's Nek region'
52. John Sharp and Andrew Spiegel, 'Vulnerability to impoverishment in South African rural areas: The erosion of kinship and neighbourhood as social resources'
53a. Elisabeth Ardington, 'Poverty and development in a rural community in KwaZulu' (Part 1:

Chapters I–III)
53b. Elisabeth Ardington, 'Poverty and development in a rural community in KwaZulu' (Part 2: Chapters IV–V)
54. *
55. David Robbins, 'What's the matter with Msinga?'
56. M.V. Gandar and N. Bromberger, 'Economic and demographic functioning of rural households: Mahlabatini District, KwaZulu'
57. Catherine Cross and Eleanor Preston-Whyte, 'Modelling poverty on household dynamics: A data approach through per capita income'
58. Matthew Cobbett, 'Sugarcane farming in KwaZulu: Two communities investigated'
59. Paul Colvin, 'Cattle sales in KwaZulu: Wealth vs Income. Implications for an improved marketing strategy'
60. J.F. deV Graaff, 'Villagers without land: The household subsistence level in a Lehurutshe resettlement village'
61. *
62. Sue Parnell and Alan Mabin, 'Poverty in Mafikeng'
63. E.F.J. van Nieuwenhuizen, 'A socioeconomic survey in Tzikundamalema (Venda): An interim report'
64. A.G. Schutte, 'Poverty and rural deterioration: Two case studies from post-"Independence" Venda'
65. Moses Bopape, 'Social welfare services in Lebowa and poverty related problems'
66. Catherine Schneider, 'Microstudies in Gazankulu: Study of 8 villages in two districts of Gazankulu'
67. Patrick Harries, 'Aspects of poverty in Gazankulu: Three case studies'
68. Emile Boonzaier, 'Economic differentiation and racism in Namaqualand: A case study'
69. John Sharp, 'Rural development schemes and the struggle against impoverishment in the Namaqualand reserves'
70. *
71. John Sharp and Martin West, 'Controls and constraints: Land, labour and mobility in Namaqualand'
72. *

Relocation
73. Laurine Platzky, 'Relocation and poverty'
74. Aninka Claassens, 'The myth of "Voluntary removals" '
75. Ian Donald, 'Removals of a quiet kind: Removals from Indian, "coloured", and white-owned land in Natal'
76. Ben Maclennan, 'Mr Mapapu: A life history'
77. Anne Templeton 'Bendell'
78. Buntu Mfenyana, 'Among the discarded'

Law and Poverty
79. Wallace Mgoqi, 'Law, poverty, and development in the context of South Africa'
80. F.C. Bam, 'Land, law, and poverty'
81. A. Chaskalson and S. Duncan, 'Influx Control: The pass laws'
82. Joanne Yawitch, 'Tightening the noose: African women and Influx Control in South Africa 1950–1980'
83. Helen Zille, 'Political power and poverty: An examination of the role and effect of Influx Control in South Africa'
84. Nicholas Haysom and Clive Thompson, 'Farm labour and the law'
85. The Black Sash, 'Influx Control and poverty: Case studies'
86. Nicholas Haysom and Amanda Armstrong, 'Population relocation and the law: Social engineering on a vast scale'
87. S.B. Burman and J. Barry, 'Divorce and deprivation in South Africa'
88. S.H. Christie, 'Aspects of legal aid in divorces'
89. *
90. Dennis Davis and Hugh Corder, 'Poverty and cooption: The role of the courts'
91. Geoff Budlender, 'Lawyers and poverty: Beyond "access to justice" '
92. Wallace Mgoqi, 'Legal education and the needs of the poor'

93. Roy Gentle, 'Crime and poverty'

Education and Poverty

94. Bill Nasson, 'Education and poverty: Some perspectives'
95. P.N. Pillay, 'The development and underdevelopment of education in South Africa'
96. Linda Chisholm, 'Redefining skills: South African education in the 1980s'
97. Bill Nasson, 'Bitter harvest: Farm schooling for black South Africans'
98. Bob Smith, 'Education: The rural poor: The delusion of basic education'
99. Monty Roodt and Michael Lawrence, 'The effect of socioeconomic locality on student aspirations in three Bophuthatswana schools'
100. D. Vermaak and C.T. Verwey, 'Current statistical profiles of education in the developing states in the South African context'
101. Ian Moll, 'Psychological deprivation theories in South African education'
102. Achmat Davids, 'Preschool education: An interventionist strategy in poverty'
103. Ann Short, 'The role of preschool education in relation to the problems of the poor'
104. K.E.B. von Kleist, 'Aspects of poverty and education in Namibia'
105. Abram L. Mawasha, 'Language, education, and poverty'
106. M.A.S. Corke, 'Business, poverty, and education'

Labour and Unemployment

107. Debbie Budlender, Delia Hendrie, Dudley Horner, and Gordon Young, 'Industrial Council wage rates and poverty'
108. Ari Sitas, John Stanwix, and Cathi Shaw, 'Trade Unions: Monopoly power and poverty in Natal's industries'
109. *
110. Nicholas Haysom and Modise Khoza, 'Trade Unions in the homelands'
111. Eddie Webster, 'A new frontier of control? Case studies in the changing form of job control in South African industrial relations'
112. Freddy Sitas, 'Health and safety conditions in Witwatersrand foundries'
113. Rob Dorrington, 'Where does all the surplus go? A note on the analysis of your employer's profits'
114. Gadija Berhardien, K. Lehulere, and Anita Shaw, 'Domestic workers in poverty'
115. J. Cock, E. Emdon, and B. Klugman, 'Child care and the working mother: A sociological investigation of a sample of urban African women'
116. Virginia van der Vliet, 'Staying single: A strategy against poverty?'
117. Charles Nupen, 'Unfair dismissals'
118. Lieb J. Loots, 'Black unemployment in South Africa: Searching or queueing? An analysis of the current population survey'
119. Trevor Bell and Vishnu Padayachee, 'Unemployment in South Africa: Trends, causes and cures'
120. Dave Gilmour and André Roux, 'Urban black unemployment and education in the eastern Cape'
121. Patrick McCartan, 'Recruitment and wage determination procedures of manufacturing firms in the eastern Cape'
122. Johann Maree, 'Trade unions, redundancies, and New Technology Agreements'
123. Julian Hofmeyr, 'Black unemployment: A case study in a periurban area of Natal'
124. Motlatsi Thabane and Jeff Guy, 'Unemployment and casual labour in Maseru: The impact of changing employment strategies on migrant labourers in Lesotho'
125. Jillian Nicholson, 'Problems with the administration of unemployment insurance to blacks in Natal'
126. Bruce Irvine, 'The psychological effects of unemployment — an exploratory study'

Public Allocation of Resources

127. Iraj Abedian, 'Public sector policies and income distribution in South Africa during the period 1968-1980'
128. Ina Brand, 'Public expenditure in the R.S.A. on health, welfare and education during 1960-1, 1970-1 and 1980-1'
129. Wilmot G. James, 'State, education and income inequality: Quantitative explorations of social inequality'
130. Michael O'Dowd, 'Capitalist approach to the amelioration of poverty'
131. Herbert Vilakazi, 'The Socialist alternative'

132. Pieter le Roux and Jakes Gerwel, 'Combating poverty: Democratic choice in the economic sphere'
133. Sheila van der Horst, 'The relation of industrial legislation and statutory regulations to poverty'
134. Brian Kahn, 'The effects of inflation on the poor in South Africa'
135. Delia Hendrie, 'Ideological background to alternative conceptions of social policy: A case study of housing'
136. *
137. Charles Elliott, 'The economics of transition: Some notes on the supply side'

Old Age and Poverty
138. Human Awareness Programme, 'State pension scheme and private pension funds – how they affect black people in South Africa'
139. Eugenie Gunston, 'The aged and poverty'
140. Anthony Pringle, 'The South African Social Pensioner: A white urban study'
141. Zerilda Nel, 'Poverty and the black aged in the eastern townships of Johannesburg'
142. Jean Ngubane, 'Pensions: The case of Natal'
143. Jillian Nicholson, 'The pension crisis in KwaZulu'

Ecological issues
144. John Daniel, 'Man–Land relationships in the eastern Cape'
145. Tony Cunningham, 'Indigenous plant resources: A buffer against rural poverty'
146. David Rees, 'The economic causes of soil erosion'

Water
147. Andrew Stone, 'A comparison of domestic water use between black and white communities in the eastern Cape'
148. Andrew Stone, 'A case study of water sources and water quality of the Chalumna/Hamburg area of the Ciskei'
149. N.D. Muller, 'Aspects of the political economy of drought and water in the Transkei'
150. Irwin Friedman, 'Basic needs and health in the Valley of a Thousand Hills'
151. Freddy Sitas, 'An investigation of a cholera outbreak at the Umvoti Mission Reserve, Natal: A non-water borne epidemic?'
152. D.G.B. Slade, 'Constraints in local domestic water development in rural KwaZulu: The case of spring protection and rainwater harvesting'
153. *

Fuel
154. A.A. Eberhard and M.V. Gandar, 'Energy, poverty, and development in South Africa'
155. A.A. Eberhard, 'Energy and poverty in urban and periurban areas around Cape Town'
156. M.V. Gandar, 'The poor man's energy crisis: Domestic energy in KwaZulu'

Housing
157. Christiane Elias, 'A housing study: Legislation and the control of the supply of urban African accommodation'
158. June Humphry, 'Lowcost housing in Cape Town: The supply, shortage and possibilities for improvement'
159. Alan Mabin and Sue Parnell, 'The question of workingclass home ownership'
160. Peter Wilkinson, 'The sale of the century? A critical review of recent developments in African housing policy in South Africa'
161. Christine Glover and Vanessa Watson, 'The "affordability" of the new housing policy and its likely impact on the "coloured" housing crisis in Cape Town'
162. D.G.B. Slade, 'Changing patterns of housing and house construction amongst the rural poor in KwaZulu'
163. David Dewar, 'Urban poverty and city development: Some perspectives and guidelines'
164. Myra Lipschitz, 'Housing and health'

Health and Poverty
165. C.C. Jinabhai, H.M. Coovadia, and S.S. Abdool-Karim, 'Sociomedical indicators for monitoring progress towards health for all in southern Africa'
166. Crispian G. Olver, 'Poverty, health, and health care in South Africa'
167. P.N. Pillay, 'The distribution of medical manpower and health care facilities in South Africa'
168. Technical Action Project, 'Medical Aid and benefit schemes'

169. Servaas van den Berg, 'Meeting basic health needs: A cross sectional study of some determinants of mortality and life expectancy among "coloured" South Africans'
170. T.D. Wilson, 'Health services within Soweto'
171. Allen A.B. Herman, 'Trends in perinatal and infant mortality in South Africa'
172. Stewart Fisher, 'Measles and poverty in Port Elizabeth'
173a. Elizabeth Thomson and Susan Myrdal, 'Regional variation in tuberculosis policy in South Africa'
173b. Elizabeth Thomson and Susan Myrdal, 'The implementation of tuberculosis policy in three areas in South Africa'
174. Elizabeth Thomson and Susan Myrdal, 'Tuberculosis: The patients' perspective'
175. J. Deeny, 'Epidemiology of tuberculosis meningitis in the western Cape, 1979-1981'
176. Michael Rip and L. Tibbett, 'The effect of birth weight on infant mortality in a western Cape metropolitan area'
177. Janet Bayley, 'Poverty and Community Mental Health Social Service'
178. Magriet Kemp, 'Poverty and contraception: Family Planning in the western Cape'
179. Marion Jacobs, 'Childhood head injuries and poverty'
180. Yasmin von Schirnding, 'Lead toxicity and poverty: Preliminary case study investigations in Cape Town school children'
181. Derek Yach, 'The impact of smoking in underdeveloped countries'
182. *
183. M.H. Moola, 'Oral health status of different population groups in the Cape Peninsula'
184. Hans Steyn (coordinator), 'Malnutrition in the Stellenbosch area'
185. G.A. Lawrence, 'Epidemiology of stab fatalities in Cape Town, 1981'
186. Peter Disler, 'Poverty and disability'
187. Anthony Zwi, 'Piecing together health in the homelands'
188. C.M. Ntoane, K.E. Mokoetle, and L.D. Saunders, 'Infant mortality in Naphuno 1: Initial results'
189. G. Ellis, D. Muir, and D. Budlender, 'Ciskei health survey'
190. Beverley Schweitzer, 'Gastroenteritis in the Ciskei'
191. David Mann, 'Aspects of the social effects of Mseleni joint disease'
192. Eric Buch and Cedric de Beer, 'Health and health care in Mhala: An overview'
193. Eric Buch, Helen Nyathi, and Ennika Ntlemo, 'The nutritional status of 1-5 year old children in Mhala'
194. Eric Buch, David Stephenson, and Clive Evian, 'How well do our rural clinics function?'
195. Eric Buch and David Stephenson, 'Reviewing the Health Centre policy: The Mhala experience'
196. Eric Buch, 'Mobile clinics — what can they do and achieve?'
197. Eric Buch, Clive Evian, Shirley Maswanganyi, Thoko Maluleke, and Robert Waugh, 'Do the primary health care nurses in Gazankulu provide second-class cheap care to the poor?'
198. Eric Buch, Kathryn Johnson, and Rosemary Mashabane, 'Can good tuberculosis care be provided in the face of poverty?'
199. Eric Buch, 'School health services — problems and prospects'
200. Eric Buch, Ennika Ntlemo, and Helen Nyathi, 'Mass immunisation campaigns — The Tintswalo experience'
201. Merryl Hammond and Eric Buch, 'Community health workers in Mhala, Gazankulu: Perversion of a progressive concept?'
202. *
203. Erika Sutter, 'Effects and limitations of Gazankulu's Care Groups in the prevention of diseases of poverty'
204. M. Ramphele and R. Ramalepe, 'Rural health care — the tears and joy'

Food and Nutrition
205. John Hansen, 'Food and nutrition policy with relation to poverty: The child malnutrition problem in South Africa'
206. Nomusa Ndaba, 'Conditions and health status in KwaZulu: An overview'
207. S.M. Ndlovu, 'The nutritional status of infants and children under the age of five in Esikhawini Township and Mpukunyoni'
208. Karel Ijsselmuiden, 'The nutritional status of inhabitants of northern Gazankulu and the response of the Health services'

245. Alison Todes and Vanessa Watson, 'Growth pole theory and regional development in South Africa: Results of a survey in selected growth areas'
246. Elisabeth Ardington, 'Decentralised industry, poverty, and development in rural KwaZulu'

Historical Perspectives
247. Colin Bundy, 'Vagabond Hollanders and runaway Englishmen: White poverty in the Cape before poor whiteism'
248. Pieter le Roux, 'Poor whites'
249. *
250. Charles Meth and Solveig Piper, 'Social security in historical perspective'

Other Papers
251. Elize Moody and Christina Golino, 'Area study on Venda'
252. Elize Moody and Christina Golino, 'Area study on Gazankulu'
253. Charles Simkins, 'Public expenditure and the poor: Political and economic constraints on policy choices up to the year 2000'
254. Mary Roberts and Michael Rip, 'Black fertility patterns: Cape Town and the Ciskei'
255. Bethuel Setai, 'Constraints to rural development in Lesotho'
256. D.E. Whittaker and F.M. Archer, 'Access to health care in Namaqualand: Klein Nourivier'
257. Paddy Kearney, 'Education for justice'
258. Don Pinnock, 'Breaking the web: Economic consequences of the destruction of extended families by Group Areas relocations in Cape Town'
259. Roy Siegfried, 'Energy conservation in Transkei rural communities'
260. D.R. Tapson, 'Freehold title: Blind alley in the homelands'
261. T.J. Bembridge, 'Aspects of agriculture and rural poverty in the Transkei'
262. T.J. Bembridge, 'Trends and key factors in rural development'
263. Linda Wedepohl, 'Illiteracy and adult basic education in South Africa'
264. Joel Samoff, 'Educational reform in Tanzania: Schools, skills, and social transformation'
265. Martin Carnoy, 'Socialist development and educational reform in Cuba, 1959-1980'
266. Stephen O'Keefe, 'Adult malnutrition in South Africa'
267. Harold Brooks, 'The Children's Care Centre in Vryburg (N. Cape)'
268. Martin Bac, 'A nutrition intervention study in Gelukspan district'
269. Mike McGrath, 'The determinants of poverty: A theoretical analysis'
270. *
271. Norman Bromberger, 'How much work do the African unemployed do?'
272. Norman Bromberger, 'African household incomes in Vulindlela'
273. Norman Bromberger, 'Technical change and the destruction of farm employment'
274. Norman Bromberger, 'A study of relatively poor African households'
275. Francine de Clercq, 'Education and training in the homelands: A separate development'
276. Graham Dyson, 'Lawyers and poverty'
277. Simon Bekker, 'Levels of living in the Ciskei: A quantitative and qualitative analysis'
278. Nomusa Ndaba, 'Malnutrition in children in South Africa'
279. Randall M. Packard, 'The political economy of malaria epidemics in Swaziland'
280. Anne Raynal, 'Post independence health service developments in Zimbabwe: Are there lessons for South Africa?'
281. Michael Savage, 'Pass laws and the disorganisation and reorganisation of the African population in South Africa'
282. Leslie Bank, 'Finding a job in Qwa Qwa: A study of employment opportunity resources'
283. Glenn Turner, 'A critical analysis of the issues of reinstatement, specific performance, and victimisation in the field of labour law'
284. Pia du Pradal, 'Poverty and wealth in a Kalahari village in Botswana'
285. Fion de Vletter, 'The Swazi rural homestead: A case study of subsistence, wage dependency, and misguided rural development'
286. Joanne Martiny and John Sharp, 'An overview of Qwa Qwa: Town and country in a South African Bantustan'
287. Pierre Hugo, 'Afrikaans farmers in the Transvaal: A quality of life profile'
288. Pam McLaren, 'Motor and ocular impairment in rural KwaZulu — a prevalence study'
289. Judith Cornell, 'Workplace health services and employment in manufacturing industry in greater Cape Town'

290. André Botha, 'Poverty and disease: A case study of diarrhoeal disease'
291. *
292. Sedick Isaacs, 'A community health project for the aged in Grassy Park/Lotus River: An assessment and guidelines for the future'
293. Sedick Isaacs, 'A review of some of the sociodemographic variables that affect health'
294. Fred Hendricks, 'Preliminary notes on land and livestock in Libode'
295. Peter Disler and Chippy Olver (eds), 'Some diseases associated with poverty'
296. Polly Hill, 'The study of individual poverty'
297. Izak Niehaus, 'Relocation and deprivation in Qwa Qwa: The experiences, problems and responses of closer settlement residents'
298. *
299. Carole Cooper, 'South Africa's unemployment fund: An inadequate cover for the unemployed'
300. Liz Clarke, 'The effectiveness of a broad-based treatment programme in the treatment of malnutrition'
301. Mary Simons, 'Poverty and powerlessness: The politics of inequality'
302. Ebrahim Patel, 'Cape Town — a statistical summary and analysis of socioeconomic trends for local areas and the 01 economic region'
303. Lionel October and Gordon Young, 'The population of the Cape Peninsula: A statistical summary'
304. Ighsan Schroeder, 'Workmen's compensation in South Africa: A brief overview'
305. Ishmael Mohammed, 'Law and poverty'
306. Nomusa Ndaba, 'The nutritional status of adults in parts of KwaZulu and Natal'
307. Bruce McKenzie, 'Historical, political, and sociological factors affecting land use in the Transkei today: An ecological interpretation'
308. Allan Boesak, 'Poverty: the moral challenge — get up and walk'
309. David A. Hamburg, 'Address from the president of Carnegie Corporation of New York'
310. Noel M. Schwerin, 'Signs of Hope: A review of the Film Festival'
311. Francis Wilson, 'Overview of the Carnegie conference'

C. *Post-Conference Series (PCS)*

1. R.J. Fincham, 'Food and nutrition in South Africa: Report of the Carnegie working group' (1985)
2. P. Templeton, 'Twenty reasons for restructuring the South African social services system' (1985)
3. Charles Simkins, 'What's new in the unemployment debate? A review of nine papers presented at the Carnegie conference.' (1985)
4. M. McGrath, and Reply to Dr McGrath's Criticism by C. Simkins, 'Rejoinder to Simkins on trends in homeland income distribution and poverty' (1985)
5. P. Moll, 'A supplementary children's feeding programme' (1985)
6. C. Simkins, D. Hendrie, I. Abedian and P. le Roux, 'Justice, development, and the national budget' (1985)
7. Laurine Platzky, 'Rural organisations in Latin America: Some lessons for South Africa' (1985)
8. P.G. Moll, 'Transition to freehold in the reserves' (1985)
9. Eileen Meyer, 'Hanover: A forlorn hope?' (1985)
10. I. Abedian, S. Schneier, and B. Standish, 'The role of public works programmes in combating poverty in South Africa' (1985)
11. Anton G. Krone and Timothy T. Dunne, 'An appraisal of domestic water supply in four Transkei villages' (1986)
12. Anton G. Krone, 'Water and development in rural Transkei: Some present needs; current and future strategies' (1986)
13. A. A. Eberhard, 'South African energy crisis: Some suggested strategies' (1986)
14. Matthew Kentridge, 'Housing in South Africa: From political privilege to basic right' (1986)
15. C. M. Jenkins, 'International capital flows and welfare in South Africa' (1986)
16. A. Roukens de Lange and D-E van Seventer, 'Implications and implementation of income redistribution: An investigation based on social accounting matrix' (1986)
17. T. C. Moll, 'Monetary policy, small firms and welfare in South Africa' (1986)

18. T. C. Moll, ' "The art of the possible": Macro-economic policy and income distribution in Latin America and South Africa' (1986)
19. Anthony Black and John Stanwix, 'Crisis and restructuring in South African manufacturing sector' (1987)
20. T. C. Moll, 'Macro-economic policy and poverty: An overview' (forthcoming)
21. Janine Aron, 'Demand and supply of firewood in rural South Africa' (forthcoming)
22. Kelebogile Setiloane, 'Primary health care in Gelukspan Hospital, Bophuthatswana' (forthcoming)
23. Jill Nattrass,Elizabeth Dostal, Mamphela Ramphele and Charles Simkins, 'Population growth and poverty in South Africa: A debate' (forthcoming)

Other post-conference papers

Budlender, Debbie, 'A critique of poverty datum lines', Saldru Working Paper 63 (1985)
Abedian, Iraj, and Standish, Barry, 'An economic inquiry into the poor white saga', Saldru Working Paper 64 (1985)
Ramphele, Mamphela, 'Zimbabwe: Lessons for us in South Africa', Saldru Working Paper 65 (1986)
Ebrahim, M., Roberts, B., Ruyters, A. and Solomons, R., 'Atlantis: A utopian nightmare', Saldru Working Paper 66 (1987)
Lundall, Paul, and Kriel, Paul, 'A socio-economic overview of the Riversdale district with particular reference to the village of Melkhoutfontein', Saldru Working Paper 67 (1987)
Standish, Barry, 'Some statistics on public sector employment in South Africa 1920–80', Saldru Working Paper 69 (1987)
Abedian, Iraj, and Schneier, Steffen, 'An analysis of formal sector employment in South Africa: Its implications for poverty and future economic strategies', Saldru Working Paper 70 (1987)
Wilson, F. and Ramphele, M., 'Children in South Africa', in *Children on the front line*, A report for Unicef (New York, 1987)
Van Heerden, Debbie, 'Friemersheim: A profile', Saldru Working Paper 74 (1988)
Dunne, Janeen, 'Towards a regional development strategy for Namaqualand', Saldru Working Paper 75 (1988)
Collins, Anne, 'Ten years of producer cooperative development in the northern Transvaal, South Africa, 1978–87', Saldru Working Paper (forthcoming)

D. Books

Badsha, Omar (ed), *South Africa: The cordoned heart* (Cape Town and New York, 1986)
Nasson, Bill, and Samuel, John (eds), *Education: From poverty to liberty* (forthcoming, 1989)
White, Caroline, and Pillay, Pundy (eds), *Poor in town* (forthcoming)
Zille, Helen (ed), *Platteland: Roots of resistance* (forthcoming)

Appendix 2: Films and videos

'Signs of Hope' is the name given to the film festival that was screened during the Carnegie conference at the University of Cape Town in April 1984. The films made up a programme which shows, through visual medium, the work done throughout the world in mobilising people in the struggle against poverty. The festival focused primarily on those projects that represent signs of hope. These films draw on experience and work in China, India, the United States, Europe, Latin America and Africa. Brief assessments of most of these films are contained in 310: 1–35 and in the Conference Handbook, pp. 11–20.

'The edge of survival' (Wharton Films)
'Peru, literacy for social change' (Icarus Films)
'The fragile mountain' (Sandra Nichols Film Library)
'That our children will not die' (Documentary Educational Resources)
'Widening the circle: Cameroon' (Decade Media)
'Little by little' (National Film Board of Canada)
'The fight for a shelter' (Habitat)
'Generations of health' (Vanderbilt University)
'The electric valley' (The James Agee Film Project)
'Water means life' (Unicef)
'Energetic Chinese villagers' (Martha Stuart Communications)
'Distant thunder' (International Film Services)
'Seeds of health' (World Council of Churches)
'Mondragón' (BBC)
'Call your centre people for help' (BBC)
'We are so poor, yet we are so many' (BBC)

In addition, a number of videos (including some films) made in South Africa – some of them specially for the Carnegie Inquiry – were shown and discussed in workshops. These included:

'Mayfair' (A. Bensusan)
'Poverty and politics' (Keith Shaw)
'Katberg' (J. Peires, K. Tomaselli and G. Hayman)
'Mgwali' (Paul Crankshaw)
'Out of despair, Ithuseng' (Lindy Wilson)
'Shixini December, responses to poverty in Transkei' (Bob Purdy and Shigs Trautman)
'Loaded dice' (Liz Fish, Community Video Resource Association)
'Woodlots' (made with the Institute of Natural Resources)
'The tot system' (Wilfred Schärf)
'I am Clifford Abrahams, this is Grahamstown' (Graham Hayman and Keyan Tomaselli)
'Last supper in Hortsley Street' (Lindy Wilson)
'Reserve 4' (Gavin Younge)
'The right time' (Kevin Harris)
'Abaphuciwe' (Gavin Younge)
'The San' (John Marshall)
'My country, my hat' (David Bensusan)

Bibliography

Abedian, I. and Standish, B., 'An economic inquiry into the poor white saga', Saldru Working Paper 64 (1985)

Acocks, J. P. H., 'Veld types of South Africa', *Mem. Bot. Surv. South Africa* 40 (1975)

Adedeji, Adebayo, 'An ecology for economic change', *Challenge* (Jan–Feb 1987)

Alcock (Bond), Creina, 'Guts', *South African Outlook* (Jan 1986)

Alexandra Health Centre and University Clinic, *Annual Report* (1988)

Anderson, E., *A history of the Xhosa of the northern Cape 1795–1879* (Cape Town, 1985)

Ardington, E. M., *Nkandla revisited: A longitudinal study of the strategies adopted to alleviate poverty in a rural community* (Durban, 1988)

Arnold, Millard W. (ed), *Steve Biko: No fears expressed* (Johannesburg, 1987)

Aron, J. and Myers, J., 'Asbestos and asbestos related disease in South Africa: An update', Saldru Working Paper 71 (1987)

Bac, M., *Progress towards health for all in the Gelukspan health ward — 1985* (Medical University of Southern Africa, 1987)

Bac, M. (1987). *See* Karim, Abdool S. S. (ed)

Badsha, Omar (ed), *South Africa: The cordoned heart* (Cape Town and New York, 1986)

Baviskar, B. S., 'Some aspects of dairy development in Gujarat and Karnataka', Consultant Report submitted to the World Bank (1983)

Beinart, W., 'Agrarian historiography and agrarian reconstruction', in J. Lonsdale (ed), *South Africa in question* (London, 1988)

Bekker, S. B., De Wet, C. and Manona, C. W., 'A socio-economic survey of the Amatola Basin: An interim report', Institute of Social and Economic Research Working Paper 2 (1981)

Bekker, S. B., Humphries, R. G., and Metelerkamp, D., 'Langkloof farmers' practices and attitudes regarding coloured and black farmworkers', Institute of Social and Economic Research Working Paper 7 (1982)

Berger, Peter L., and Godsell, Bobby, *A future South Africa: Visions, strategies and realities* (Cape Town, 1988)

Boonzaier, E., 'From communal grazing to "economic" units: Changing access to land in a Namaqualand reserve', *Development Southern Africa* 4, 3 (1987)

Boraine, A., 'Wham, sham or scam? Security management, upgrading and resistance in a South African township', Centre for African Studies seminar, University of Cape Town, 1988

Bowles, S. and Gintis, H., *Schooling in capitalist America: Educational reform and the contradictions of economic life* (New York, 1976)

Bradshaw, Debbie (project coordinator), 'Review of South African mortality (1984)', Medical Research Council, Technical Report 1 (1987)

Bruntland, Gro H. (chairperson) (1987). *See* World Commission on Environment and Development

Budlender, Debbie, 'A critique of poverty datum lines', Saldru Working Paper 63 (1985)

Carnegie Commission, Report of the, *The poor white problem in South Africa,* 5 vols. (Stellenbosch, 1932)

Cassen, R., 'Population and development: A survey', *World Development* 4, 10–11 (1976)

Centre for the Study of Health Policy, *A national health service for South Africa. Part 1: The case for change* (Johannesburg, 1988)

Chaliand, Gérard, *Revolution in the Third World: Myths and prospects* (Sussex, 1977)

370

Chambers, R., 'The crisis of Africa's rural poor: Perceptions and priorities', in *The challenge of employment* (Nairobi, 1986)

Christie, R., 'Group Areas and property market economics', SAIRR *Topical Briefing,* 1987

Ciskei Commission, *The Quail Report, 8 February 1980* (Silverton, 1980)

Collins, Anne, 'Ten years of producer cooperative development in the northern Transvaal, South Africa, 1978–87', Saldru Working Paper (forthcoming)

Cornia, G. A., Jolly, R., and Stewart, F., *Adjustment with a human face: Protecting the vulnerable and promoting growth* (Oxford, 1987)

Danziger, S. H., and Weinberg, D. H. (eds), *Fighting poverty: What works and what doesn't* (Cambridge, Mass., 1986)

Dennett, J., James, E., Room, G., and Watson, P., *Europe against poverty: The European poverty programme 1975–80* (London, 1982)

Derman, P. J. and Poultney, C., 'Agricultural reconstruction in a consumer society: The Mboza Village project', *Development Southern Africa* 4, 3 (1987)

Desmond, C., *The discarded people* (Braamfontein, n.d.)

Devereux, S., 'South African income distribution 1900–1980', Saldru Working Paper 51 (1983)

De Vos, P. J. *et al., A socio-economic and educational survey of the Bantu residing in the Victoria East, Middledrift and Zwelitsha areas of the Ciskei* (Fort Hare, 1970)

De Vos, T., *Report of the National Building Research Institute* (Pretoria)

De Wet, C., 'Involuntary relocation as imposed environmental transformation: A South African case study', Paper prepared for the Twelfth International Congress of Anthropological and Ethnological Sciences, Zagreb, 1988

De Wet, C., 'Betterment planning in South Africa: Some thoughts on its history, feasibility and wider policy implications', *Journal of Contemporary African Studies* 6, 1–2 (1988)

De Wet, C., *Betterment planning in a rural village in Keiskammahoek, Ciskei* (forthcoming)

De Wet, C. J. and McAllister, P. A., 'Rural communities in transition: A study of the socio-economic and agricultural implications of agricultural betterment and development', Institute of Social and Economic Research Working Paper 16 (1983)

Diamond, C. R., 'The Native Grievances Inquiry 1913–1914', *South African Journal of Economics* 36 (1968)

Dibb, D. N., 'H. J. Heinz success in Zimbabwe', *Challenge* (Jan–Feb 1987)

Dick, B., 'The provision of measles vaccine for an urban population', *SAMJ* 49, 37 (1975)

Douglas, J. S. and Hart, R. de J., *Forest farming* (London, 1976)

Downing, B. H., 'Environmental consequences of agricultural expansion in South Africa since 1850', *South African Journal of Science* 74 (1978)

Drabek, A. G. (ed), *Development alternatives: The challenge for NGOs* (Oxford, 1987)

D'Souza, F., Mashanini, M., Pongoma, Z., and Mashanini, T., *First report on estimating vulnerability in black rural communities in South Africa* (Operation Hunger, 1987)

Eatwell, J., Milgate, M., and Newman, P., *The new Palgrave: A dictionary of economics,* 4 vols. (London and New York, 1987)

Eberhard, A., *Energy consumption patterns in underdeveloped areas in South Africa* (Cape Town, 1986)

Ebersohn, W., 'Ring of fire', *Leadership* 6, 1 (1987)

Eberstadt, N., 'Poverty in South Africa', *Optima* 36, 1 (1988)

Eckholm, E., 'The other energy crisis: Firewood', *Worldwatch Paper* 1 (1975)

Ecrement, Marc, *Independance politique et liberation economique: Un quart siècle du developpement de l'Algerie 1962–1985* (Alger/Grenoble, 1986)

Ehlers, J. H., *Pendelaars in KwaNdebele* (Pretoria, 1982)

Elliott, C., *Patterns of poverty in the Third World* (New York, 1975)

Elliott, C., *Praying the kingdom: Towards a political spirituality* (London, 1985)

Elliott, C., *Comfortable compassion? Poverty, power and the church* (London, 1987)

Elton-Mills, M. E. and Wilson, M., *Land tenure* (Pietermaritzburg, 1952)

England, R., 'Zimbabwean co-ops and class struggle', *SA Labour Bulletin* 12, 617 (1987)

Fanon, F., *The wretched of the earth* (New York, 1968)

Fenyes, T. I., *Statistiese bylae tot die verslag oor die benutting en vergoeding van plaasarbeid in Suid-Afrikaanse landbou* (1983)

Fields, G. S., *Poverty, inequality and development* (Cambridge, 1980)

Foley, G. and Barnard, G., 'Farm and community forestry', *Technical Report 3, Earthscan* (London, 1984)

Fourie, E. B., 'The prevalence and annual rate of tuberculosis infection in South Africa', *Tubercle* 64 (1983), cited in Yach, D. (1988)

Freire, P., *Pedagogy of the oppressed* (Harmondsworth, 1972)

Friedman, S., *Building tomorrow today: African workers in trade unions 1970–84* (Johannesburg, 1987)

Gelb, S., 'Economic crisis in South Africa, 1974–1986', Seminar paper, University of the Witwatersrand, Aug 1987

George, V. and Lawson, R. (eds), *Poverty and inequality in Common Market countries* (London, 1980)

Gerwel, Jakes and Alexander, Neville, 'Intellectual home of the left? A debate', *Die Suid-Afrikaan* 15 (1988)

Elphick, R. and Giliomee, H. (eds), *The shaping of South African society,* 2nd ed. (forthcoming)

Glover, C., *The interactional dynamics between various groups in Crossroads* (Cape Town, 1987)

Glover, C. and Watson, V., in Caroline White and Pundy Pillay (eds), *Poor in town* (forthcoming)

Godfrey, M., *Global unemployment: The new challenge to economic theory* (Brighton, 1986)

Gordon, R. J., 'Why stopping inflation may be costly: Evidence from 14 historical episodes', in R. E. Hall, *Inflation: Causes and effects* (Chicago, 1982)

Gould, Stephen Jay, *The mismeasure of man* (New York, 1981)

Greenberg, Stanley B., *Legitimating the illegitimate: State, markets and resistance in South Africa* (Berkeley, 1987)

Griesel, R. D., Richter, L. M. and Oberholzer, D., *A bibliography of psycho-social studies of malnutrition in southern Africa* (Koedoespoort, 1988)

Grundy, K. W., *The militarization of South African politics* (Oxford, 1986)

Hall, M., *The changing past: Farmers, kings and traders in southern Africa* (Cape Town, 1987)

Hanlon, J., *Beggar your neighbours: Apartheid power in southern Africa* (London, 1986)

Harrington, Michael, *The new American poverty* (London, 1984)

Harris, J., 'Lead encephalopathy case reports', *South African Medical Journal* (1986)

Haveman, R. H. (ed), *A decade of federal antipoverty programs: Achievements, failures and lessons* (New York, 1977)

Hill, Polly, *Development economics on trial* (Cambridge, 1986)

Hirschman, Albert O., *Getting ahead collectively: Grassroots experiences in Latin America* (New York, 1984)

Hooper, C., *Brief authority* (London, 1960)

Horne, A., *A savage war of peace,* 2nd ed. (London, 1987)

Horner, D. *et al.,* 'Mine wages', *Saldru Labour Research Service Quarterly Bulletin* 4 (1986)

Hughson, H. C., *Survey of nutritional status and related factors in selected areas of Namibia* (Oxfam, 1986)

Hyden, G., *No shortcuts to progress: African development management in perspective* (London, 1983)

Iliffe, John, *The African poor: A history* (Cambridge, 1987)

Jaspa (Jobs and Skills Programme for Africa), *The challenge of employment and basic needs in Africa* (Nairobi, 1986)

Jolly, Richard, 'Adjustment with a human face', The Barbara Ward Lecture (Rome, 1985)

Karim, S. S. Abdool (ed), *Primary health care,* Reports presented at the NAMDA consultative meeting, Cape Town, 1987

Kothari, R., 'NGOs, the state and world capitalism, *Economic and Political Weekly* 21, 50 (1986)

Kruijer, G. J., *Development through liberation: Third World problems and solutions* (London, 1987)

Kurien, C. T., *Poverty, planning and social transformation* (Bombay, 1978)

Lally, J. R. and Mangione, P., 'The impact of intensive intervention (birth to five) on children from low income, multi-risk families: The Syracuse University Children's Center findings 15 years later', Centre for Child and Family Studies. Far West Laboratory for Educational Research and Development: Report (San Francisco, n.d.)

Lawyers' Committee for Human Rights, *The war against children: South Africa's youngest victims* (New York, 1986)

Lelyveld, J., *Move your shadow* (New York, 1985)

Letsoalo, Essy M., *Land reform in South Africa: A black perspective* (Braamfontein, 1987)

Lewis, S. R., 'Economic realities in southern Africa (or, One hundred million futures)', Institute of Development Studies discussion paper 232 (1987)

Lewis, S. R., *Economics and apartheid: The impact of South Africa's economic policies* (forthcoming)

Libby, R. T., *The politics of economic power in southern Africa* (Princeton, 1987)

Lipton, Merle, *Capitalism and apartheid* (Aldershot, 1985)

Lipton, Michael, *Why poor people stay poor: Urban bias in world development* (London, 1977)

Lonsdale, J. (ed), *South Africa in question* (London, 1988)

Louw, Chris, 'Gelaaide gewere moet die boeke laat klop', *Die Suid-Afrikaan* 16 (1988)

McGrath, M. D., 'The distribution of personal income in South Africa in selected years over the period 1945–1980', Ph.D. thesis, University of Natal, 1983

McLean, S. A., *The enabling environment for effective private sector contribution to development in sub-Saharan Africa* (Nairobi, 1986)

Marais, D., 'The role of a local grassroots development project in the present crisis situation in southern Africa' (unpublished)

Maree, J. G. B., 'An analysis of the trade union movement in South Africa in the 1970s', Ph.D. thesis, University of Cape Town, 1986

Marshall, R., *Unheard voices: Labour and economic policy in a competitive world* (New York, 1987)

Marshall, R. and Godwin, L., *Cooperatives and rural poverty in the South* (Baltimore, 1971)

Matlhape, Selebano (ed), 'Beyond apartheid', South Africa Economic Research and Training Project, Working Paper 1 (1988)

Mbeki, G., *The peasants' revolt* (Harmondsworth, 1964)

Mdluli, P., 'Ubuntu-Botho: Inkatha's "People's education",' *Transformation* 5 (1987)

Meadows, Donella, 'The laundry ladies of Madras discover power', *Valley News* (2 July 1983)

Miliband, R., Politics and poverty', in D. Wedderburn (ed), *Poverty, inequality and class structure* (1974)

Minter, W., *King Solomon's Mines revisited: Western interests and the burdened history of southern Africa* (New York, 1986)

Moll, T., 'Mishap or crisis? The apartheid economy's recent record in historical perspective', University of London postgraduate seminar, 1988

Moshoeshoe II, His Majesty the King, 'Alternative strategies for development — a clarion call!', *Development Dialogue* 1 (1987)

Murray, C., *Families divided* (Cambridge, 1981)

Myrdal, G., *An American dilemma: The Negro problem and modern democracy* (New York, 1944)

Nasson, Bill, and Samuel, John (eds), *Education: From poverty to liberty* (forthcoming)

Ndegwa, P., *Africa's development crisis* (Nairobi, 1985)

Ndegwa, P., Mureithi, L. P., and Green, R. H. (eds), *Development options for Africa in the 1980s and beyond* (Nairobi, 1985)

Nigeria, Report of the Commission on Revenue Allocation (Lagos, 1952)

Nove, A., *The economics of feasible socialism* (London, 1983)

Ntoane, C., 'Childhood mortality in Molopo and Gelukspan districts', University of Bophuthatswana paper (n.d.)

Oakeshott, R., Manase, W., and Tsanga, A., 'Employee ownership and profit sharing systems as a development strategy in Zimbabwe', Zimbabwe Promotion Council Report, 1987

O'Malley, P. (ed), 'The search for equitable health', *Energos* 15 (1988)

Owen, C. P. (ed), 'Towards a national health service', *Proceedings of the 1987 NAMDA annual conference* (Cape Town, 1988)

Padron, M., *NGOs and grassroots development: Limits and possibilities* (The Hague, 1982)

Patel, A. S., 'Cooperative dairying and rural development: A case study of Amul', *CRD* (1983)

Patterson, J. T., *America's struggle against poverty 1900–1985* (Cambridge, Mass., 1986)

Phillips, L., 'South Africa's future: No easy walk to freedom', *Working Papers for a New Society* (March–April 1979)

Physician Task Force on Hunger in America, *Hunger in America: The growing epidemic* (Middletown, 1985)

Pillay, P., 'Women in employment in South Africa: Some important trends and issues', *Social*

Dynamics 11, 2 (1985)

Pillay, P., 'Future developments in the South African mining industry' (forthcoming)

Platzky, L. and Walker, C., *The surplus people: Forced removals in South Africa* (Braamfontein, 1985)

Potgieter, J. F., 'Background and interpretation of the household subsistence level', from *Research Report* 14 (1974) and *Fact Paper* 25 (1978)

President's Council, Report of the Committee for Economic Affairs on a Strategy for Employment Creation and Labour-intensive Development (Cape Town, 1987)

Ramphele, Mamphela, 'Zimbabwe: Lessons for us in South Africa', Saldru Working Paper 65 (1986)

Reddy, C. N., *An investigation into the problem of failure among pupils in coloured primary schools* (University of the Western Cape, Bellville, 1977)

Reynolds, N., 'Rural development in Botswana', Saldru Working Paper 13 (1977)

Reynolds, N., 'The design of rural development: Proposals for the evolution of a social contract suited to conditions in southern Africa', Saldru Working Papers 40 and 41 (1981)

Riordan, R., 'The Ukuhleleleka of Port Elizabeth', *Monitor* (June 1988)

Rist, G., Sabelli, F., and Perrot, D., *Il etait une fois le developpement* (Lausanne, 1986)

Roberts, B., 'The cruel Karoo', *Cape Herald*, 2.2.1984

Roux, P. W., 'Interaction between climate, vegetation and run-off in the Karoo', in H. Maaren (ed), *Workshop on the effect of rural land use and catchment management on water resources*, T. R. 113 (Pretoria, 1981)

Rudman, T., *The Third World: South Africa's hidden wealth* (Somerset West, 1988)

Sachs, J. D., 'Trade and exchange rate policies in growth-orientated adjustment programs', National Bureau of Economic Research Working Paper 2226 (1987)

Sachs, J. D., 'External debt and macro-economic performance in Latin America and East Asia', *Brookings Papers on Economic Activity* 2 (1985)

Saldru Handbook of Labour and Social Statistics, compiled by Delia Hendrie, assisted by A. Adams and Y. Ariefdien (Cape Town, 1986)

Saldru Directory of South African Trade Unions, compiled by Najwah Allie, with computerisation by Y. Ariefdien, C. Groenewald and C. Wilhelm

Salter, W. E. G., *Productivity and technical change* (London, 1960)

Seleoane, M., 'Nyanga East men's hostel: The conditions of migrant workers', Saldru Working Paper 62 (1985)

Sen, A., *Poverty and famines: An essay on entitlement and deprivation* (Oxford, 1981)

Sen, A., 'Food, economics and entitlements', *Lloyds Bank Review* (April 1986)

Sen, A., 'Freedom of choice: Concept and content', Harvard Institute of Economic Research discussion paper 1346 (1987)

Sender, J. and Smith, S., *The development of capitalism in Africa* (London, 1986)

Setiloane, Kelebogile, 'Primary health care in Gelukspan Hospital, Bophuthatswana', PCS (forthcoming)

Sheahan, J., *Patterns of development in Latin America: Poverty, repression and economic strategy* (Princeton, 1987)

Simkins, C., 'Structural unemployment revisited', Saldru Fact Sheet 1 (1982)

Simkins, C., *Four essays on the past, present and possible future of the distribution of the black population of South Africa* (Cape Town, 1983)

Simkins, C., 'What has been happening to income distribution and poverty in the homelands?', *Development Southern Africa* 1, 2 (1984)

South Africa, Republic of. Department of Statistics. *Statistical Yearbook*

South Africa, Republic of. *Statistical-economic review in connection with the budget speech 1987/88*

South Africa, Urban and Rural Population of South Africa 1904–1960 (Pretoria, 1960)

South Africa, Union of, Report of the Commission for the Socio-Economic Development of the Bantu Areas Within the Union of South Africa, U. G. 61–1955 (Tomlinson Report)

South Africa, Union of. Bureau of Census and Statistics. *Statistical Yearbook*

South Africa, Union of. Bureau of Census and Statistics. *Union statistics for fifty years* (Pretoria, 1960)

South African Institute of Race Relations. *Annual Survey* (Johannesburg, 1967–)

South African National Scientific Programmes, *Basic needs in rural areas: A report on a seminar held in Cape Town on 19 February 1985,* 116 (Pretoria, 1985)

Streeten, P., *First things first: Meeting basic human needs in developing countries* (Washington, 1981)

Streeten, Paul, 'Autobiographical note', *Balliol Record* (1985)

Surplus People Project, *Forced removals in South Africa,* 5 vols. (Cape Town and Pietermaritzburg, 1983)

Tevoedjre, A., *Poverty: Wealth of mankind* (Oxford, 1978)

Timmer, P., 'Nutrition', in J. Eatwell, M. Milgate and P. Newman (1987)

Tomlinson, F. R. (1955). *See* South Africa, Union of (1955)

Toms, I. (1987). *See* Karim, Abdool S. S.

Tower, C., 'Mother Teresa's work of grace', *Reader's Digest* (December 1987)

Townsend, P., *Poverty in the United Kingdom: A survey of household resources and standards of living* (Harmondsworth, 1979)

Transvaal, Province of, Report of the Local Government Commission (1921), T. P. 1-1922 (Pretoria, 1922)

Turrell, Rob, *Capital and labour on the Kimberley diamond fields* (Cambridge, 1987)

Unicef, *One step for women a mile in development* (Bogota, 1987)

Unicef, *The state of the world's children 1988* (Oxford, 1988)

USA, Department of State, Report to the Bureau for Refugee Programs regarding Mozambican Refugees (Unclassified telex, State 124182/01, 20 April 1988)

Valley Trust, *A socio-medical project for the promotion of health,* Annual Report, 1986

Van Wyk, H. de J., 'The economic importance and growth of selected districts in RSA and TBVC countries 1985', Bureau of Market Research Report 114 (1985)

Walesa Lech, *A path of hope* (London, 1987)

Wentzel, Wilfred, 'Poverty and development in South Africa (1890–1980): A bibliography', Saldru Working Paper 46 (1982)

Wilson, F., 'Farming, 1866-1966', in M. Wilson and L. Thompson (1971)

Wilson, F., *Labour in the South African gold mines 1911-1969* (London, 1972a)

Wilson, F., *Migrant labour in South Africa* (Braamfontein, 1972b)

Wilson, F. and Perrot, D. (eds), *Outlook on a century: South Africa 1870-1970* (Lovedale, 1973)

Wilson, F., *Towards economic and political justice in South Africa: Suggested directions for the future* (Johannesburg, 1980)

Wilson, F., 'Southern Africa', in Michael Crowder (ed), *The Cambridge history of Africa c.1940-c.1975* (Cambridge, 1984)

Wilson, M. and Thompson, L. (eds), *The Oxford history of South Africa,* 2 vols. (Oxford, 1969 and 1971)

Worden, N., *Slavery in Dutch South Africa* (Cambridge, 1986)

World Bank, *Poverty and human development* (Oxford, 1980)

World Bank, *World development report 1987*(New York, 1987)

World Commission on Environment and Development, *Our common future* (Oxford, 1987)

World Health Organisation, *Apartheid and health* (Geneva, 1983)

World Health Organisation, *Intersectoral action for health* (Geneva, 1986)

Wylie, D., 'The changing face of hunger in southern African history', mimeo, 1987

Yach, D., 'Infant mortality rates in urban areas in South Africa, 1981-5, *South African Medical Journal* 73 (1988)

Yach, D., 'Paediatric tables', Centre for Epidemiological Research in Southern Africa, Medical Research Council, mimeo, 1988

Yawitch, J., *Betterment* (Johannesburg, 1981)

Index

Uprooting poverty:
The South African challenge

**DO NOT REMOVE
CARDS FROM POCKET**